Course   ECO 201: Principles of Economics I –
          Macroeconomics

          J Sargeant Reynolds
          Community College

http://create.mheducation.com

ISBN-10: 1308151551   ISBN-13: 9781308151557

Contents

International Economics

Online Supplements

Credits

Online Supplements

1958	1960	1962	1964	1966	1968	1970	1972	1974	1976	1978	1980	1982	1984
482.0	543.3	605.1	685.8	815.0	942.5	1,075.9	1,282.4	1,548.8	1,877.6	2,356.6	2,862.5	3,345.0	4,040.7
296.0	331.6	363.1	411.2	480.6	557.4	647.7	769.4	932.0	1,150.2	1,426.2	1,754.6	2,073.9	2,498.2
70.9	86.5	97.0	112.2	144.2	156.9	170.1	228.1	274.5	323.2	478.4	530.1	581.0	820.1
114.5	121.0	140.9	155.5	186.4	226.8	254.2	288.2	343.1	405.8	477.4	590.8	710.0	825.2
0.5	4.2	4.1	6.9	3.9	1.4	4.0	−3.4	−0.8	−1.6	−25.4	−13.1	−20.0	−102.7
419.6	475.4	531.0	603.4	719.7	829.2	939.1	1,121.5	1,342.6	1,618.4	2,031.5	2,436.5	2,810.7	3,446.4
838.0	953.6	1,062.2	1,206.8	1,429.2	1,652.0	1,867.6	2,228.8	2,670.4	3,195.8	4,016.6	4,785.2	5,607.8	6,815.4
265.1	301.9	332.9	376.8	450.3	532.1	625.1	733.6	890.3	1,051.2	1,320.2	1,626.2	1,894.3	2,217.4
14.8	16.5	18	18.8	19.9	20.1	20.7	22.8	23.3	20.6	16.9	19.7	26.1	27.9
9.6	10.7	14.3	17.5	22.5	27.6	40.5	49.3	73.5	89.9	118.8	186.2	277.5	336.1
43.9	54.7	64	77.7	96.1	101.7	86.2	117.2	125.7	174.3	238.6	223.6	229.9	337.9
50.2	50.6	55.2	59.1	67.9	73.8	77.8	95.1	112.2	131	166	171.6	171.2	228.2
454.4	519.2	577.8	656.9	772.5	896.7	1,017.3	1,210.8	1,445.4	1,728.8	2,156.1	2,557.9	3,008.8	3,667.9
379.5	422.5	469.1	528.4	620.6	730.7	864.6	1,023.6	1,249.3	1,498.1	1,859.5	2,316.8	2,778.8	3,281.3
340.9	376.5	417.5	476.3	554.2	643.8	761.5	899.9	1,098.3	1,325.8	1,630.1	2,018.0	2,424.7	2,903.9
1,958	2,083	2,238	2,482	2,819	3,207	3,713	4,287	5,135	6,079	7,322	8,861	10,442	12,284
11.4	10.0	11.1	11.5	11.1	11.2	12.6	12.1	12.9	11.1	10.2	10.6	11.5	10.7

1958	1960	1962	1964	1966	1968	1970	1972	1974	1976	1978	1980	1982	1984
2,832.6	3,105.8	3,379.9	3,730.5	4,234.9	4,564.7	4,717.7	5,128.8	5,390.2	5,669.3	6,260.4	6,443.4	6,484.3	7,277.2
−0.7	2.6	6.1	5.8	6.6	4.9	0.2	5.2	−0.5	5.4	5.6	−0.2	−1.9	7.3
28.9	29.6	30.2	31.0	32.4	34.8	38.8	41.8	49.3	56.9	65.2	82.4	96.5	103.9
2.8	1.7	1.0	1.3	2.9	4.2	5.7	3.2	11.0	5.8	7.6	13.5	6.2	4.3
134.8	140.7	147.8	160.3	172.0	197.4	214.4	249.2	274.2	306.2	357.3	408.5	474.8	551.6
1.57	3.22	2.71	3.50	5.11	5.66	7.18	4.43	10.50	5.05	7.93	13.36	12.26	10.23
3.83	4.82	4.50	4.50	5.63	6.31	7.91	5.25	10.80	6.84	9.06	15.27	14.86	12.04
174.9	180.7	186.5	191.9	196.6	200.7	205.1	209.9	213.9	218.0	222.6	227.2	231.7	235.8
67.6	69.6	70.6	73.1	75.8	78.7	82.8	87.0	91.9	96.2	102.3	106.9	110.2	113.5
63.0	65.8	66.7	69.3	72.9	75.9	78.7	82.2	86.8	88.8	96.0	99.3	99.5	105.0
4.6	3.9	3.9	3.8	2.9	2.8	4.1	4.9	5.2	7.4	6.2	7.6	10.7	8.5
6.8	5.5	5.5	5.2	3.8	3.6	4.9	5.6	5.6	7.7	6.1	7.1	9.7	7.5
2.9	1.8	4.6	3.4	4.1	3.4	2.0	3.2	−1.7	3.2	1.1	−0.2	−0.8	2.7
4.2	4.4	4.5	5.4	5.6	5.2	4.5	4.4	6.4	5.5	5.3	5.6	4.4	4.8
3.01	2.88	2.90	2.88	2.88	2.94	3.18	3.39	6.87	8.19	9.00	21.59	28.52	25.88
−2.8	0.3	−7.1	−5.9	−3.7	−25.2	−2.8	−23.4	−6.1	−73.7	−59.2	−73.8	−128.0	−185.4
279.7	290.5	302.9	316.1	328.5	368.7	380.9	435.9	483.9	629.0	776.6	909.0	1,137.3	1,564.6
0.8	2.8	3.4	6.8	3.0	0.6	2.3	−5.8	2.0	4.3	−15.1	2.3	−5.5	−94.3

(Continued in back of book)

LEARNSMART ADVANTAGE WORKS

LEARNSMART

A 30.5%	B 33.5%	C 22.6%	D 8.7%	4.7%

A 19.3%	B 38.6%	C 28.0%	D 9.6%	4.5%

Without LearnSmart

More C students earn B's

*Study: 690 students / 6 institutions

Over 20% more students pass the class with LearnSmart

*A&P Research Study

LEARNSMART Pass Rate - 70%

Without LearnSmart Pass Rate - 57%

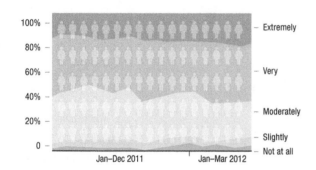

100% — Extremely
80%
60% — Very
40%
20% — Moderately
0 — Slightly
— Not at all

Jan–Dec 2011   Jan–Mar 2012

More than 60% of all students agreed LearnSmart was a very or extremely helpful learning tool

*Based on 750,000 student survey responses

> **AVAILABLE** ON-THE-GO

http://bit.ly/LS4Apple

http://bit.ly/LS4Droid

How do you rank against your peers?

Let's see how confident you are on the questions.

What you know (green) and what you still need to review (yellow), based on your answers.

COMPARE AND CHOOSE WHAT'S RIGHT FOR YOU

	BOOK	LEARNSMART	ASSIGNMENTS	
connect PLUS+	✓	✓	✓	LearnSmart, assignments, and SmartBook—all in one digital product for maximum savings!
connect PLUS+ Looseleaf	✓	✓	✓	Pop the pages into your own binder or carry just the pages you need.
connect PLUS+ Bound Book	✓	✓	✓	The #1 Student Choice!
SMARTBOOK™ Access Code	✓	✓		The first and only book that adapts to you!
LEARNSMART™ ADVANTAGE Access Code		✓		The smartest way to get from a B to an A.
CourseSmart eBook	✓			Save some green and some trees!
create™	✓	✓	✓	Check with your instructor about a custom option for your course.

> Buy directly from the source at www.ShopMcGraw-Hill.com.

Macroeconomics
PRINCIPLES, PROBLEMS, AND POLICIES

THE MCGRAW-HILL SERIES: ECONOMICS

THE SIX VERSIONS OF MCCONNELL, BRUE, FLYNN

Chapter*	Economics	Microeconomics	Microeconomics: Brief Edition	Macroeconomics	Macroeconomics: Brief Edition	Essentials of Economics
1. Limits, Alternatives, and Choices	x	x	x	x	x	x
2. The Market System and the Circular Flow	x	x	x	x	x	x
3. Demand, Supply, and Market Equilibrium	x	x	x	x	x	x
4. Market Failures: Public Goods and Externalities	x	x	x	x	x	x
5. Government's Role and Government Failure	x	x	x	x	x	x
6. Elasticity	x	x	x			x
7. Utility Maximization	x	x				
8. Behavioral Economics	x	x				
9. Businesses and the Costs of Production	x	x	x			x
10. Pure Competition in the Short Run	x	x	x			x
11. Pure Competition in the Long Run	x	x	x			x
12. Pure Monopoly	x	x	x			x
13. Monopolistic Competition and Oligopoly	x	x	x			x
13W. Technology, R&D, and Efficiency (Web Chapter)	x	x				
14. The Demand for Resources	x	x				
15. Wage Determination	x	x	x			x
16. Rent, Interest, and Profit	x	x				
17. Natural Resource and Energy Economics	x	x				
18. Public Finance: Expenditures and Taxes	x	x	x			
19. Antitrust Policy and Regulation	x	x				
20. Agriculture: Economics and Policy	x	x				
21. Income Inequality, Poverty, and Discrimination	x	x	x			x
22. Health Care	x	x				
23. Immigration	x	x				
24. An Introduction to Macroeconomics	x			x		
25. Measuring Domestic Output and National Income	x			x	x	x
26. Economic Growth	x			x	x	x
27. Business Cycles, Unemployment, and Inflation	x			x	x	x
28. Basic Macroeconomic Relationships	x			x		
29. The Aggregate Expenditures Model	x			x		
30. Aggregate Demand and Aggregate Supply	x			x	x	x
31. Fiscal Policy, Deficits, and Debt	x			x	x	x
32. Money, Banking, and Financial Institutions	x			x	x	x
33. Money Creation	x			x		
34. Interest Rates and Monetary Policy	x			x	x	x
35. Financial Economics	x			x		
36. Extending the Analysis of Aggregate Supply	x			x	x	
37. Current Issues in Macro Theory and Policy	x			x		
38. International Trade	x	x	x	x	x	x
39. The Balance of Payments, Exchange Rates, and Trade Deficits	x	x	x	x	x	x
39W. The Economics of Developing Countries (Web Chapter)	x			x		

*Chapter numbers refer to Economics: Principles, Problems, and Policies.
A red "X" indicates chapters that combine or consolidate content from two or more Economics chapters.

Twentieth Edition

Macroeconomics
PRINCIPLES, PROBLEMS, AND POLICIES

Campbell R. McConnell
University of Nebraska

Stanley L. Brue
Pacific Lutheran University

Sean M. Flynn
Scripps College

McGraw Hill Education

MACROECONOMICS: PRINCIPLES, PROBLEMS, AND POLICIES, TWENTIETH EDITION

Published by McGraw-Hill Education, 2 Penn Plaza, New York, NY 10121. Copyright © 2015 by McGraw-Hill Education. All rights reserved. Printed in the United States of America. Previous editions © 2012, 2009, and 2008. No part of this publication may be reproduced or distributed in any form or by any means, or stored in a database or retrieval system, without the prior written consent of McGraw-Hill Education, including, but not limited to, in any network or other electronic storage or transmission, or broadcast for distance learning.

Some ancillaries, including electronic and print components, may not be available to customers outside the United States.

This book is printed on acid-free paper.

1 2 3 4 5 6 7 8 9 0 DOW/DOW 1 0 9 8 7 6 5 4

ISBN   978-0-07-766077-2 (student edition)
MHID   0-07-766077-3 (student edition)
ISBN   978-0-07-766062-8 (instructor's edition)
MHID   0-07-766062-5 (instructor's edition)

Senior Vice President, Products & Markets: *Kurt L. Strand*
Vice President, Content Production & Technology Services: *Kimberly Meriwether David*
Managing Director: *Douglas Reiner*
Brand Manager: *Scott Smith*
Executive Director of Development: *Ann Torbert*
Development Editor: *Casey Rasch*
Director of Digital Content: *Doug Ruby*
Digital Development Editor: *Kevin Shanahan*
Marketing Manager: *Katie Hoenicke*
Director, Content Production: *Terri Schiesl*
Content Project Managers: *Bruce Gin, Lori Koetters*
Senior Buyer: *Michael R. McCormick*
Design: *Debra Kubiak*
Cover Image: *Ingram Publishing*
Lead Content Licensing Specialist: *Keri Johnson*
Typeface: *10/12 Janson Text Lt Std*
Compositor: *Aptara®, Inc.*
Printer: *R. R. Donnelley*

All credits appearing on page or at the end of the book are considered to be an extension of the copyright page.

Library of Congress Cataloging-in-Publication Data

McConnell, Campbell R.
    Macroeconomics : principles, problems, and policies / Campbell R. McConnell, University of Nebraska, Stanley L. Brue, Pacific Lutheran University, Sean M. Flynn, Scripps College.—Twentieth edition.
        pages cm
    Includes index.
    ISBN 978-0-07-766077-2 (student edition : alk. paper)—ISBN 0-07-766077-3 (student edition : alk. paper)—ISBN 978-0-07-766062-8 (instructor's edition : alk. paper)—ISBN 0-07-766062-5 (instructor's edition : alk. paper)
    1. Macroeconomics. I. Brue, Stanley L., 1945- II. Flynn, Sean Masaki. III. Title.
HB172.5.M3743 2015
339—dc23

                                                                    2013043610

The Internet addresses listed in the text were accurate at the time of publication. The inclusion of a website does not indicate an endorsement by the authors or McGraw-Hill Education, and McGraw-Hill Education does not guarantee the accuracy of the information presented at these sites.

www.mhhe.com

To Mem and to Terri and Craig, and to past instructors

CAMPBELL R. MCCONNELL earned his Ph.D. from the University of Iowa after receiving degrees from Cornell College and the University of Illinois. He taught at the University of Nebraska–Lincoln from 1953 until his retirement in 1990. He is also coauthor of *Contemporary Labor Economics*, ninth edition; *Essentials of Economics*, second edition; *Macroeconomics: Brief Edition*; and *Microeconomics: Brief Edition* (all The McGraw-Hill Companies), and has edited readers for the principles and labor economics courses. He is a recipient of both the University of Nebraska Distinguished Teaching Award and the James A. Lake Academic Freedom Award and is past president of the Midwest Economics Association. Professor McConnell was awarded an honorary Doctor of Laws degree from Cornell College in 1973 and received its Distinguished Achievement Award in 1994. His primary areas of interest are labor economics and economic education. He has an extensive collection of jazz recordings and enjoys reading jazz history.

STANLEY L. BRUE did his undergraduate work at Augustana College (South Dakota) and received its Distinguished Achievement Award in 1991. He received his Ph.D. from the University of Nebraska–Lincoln. He is retired from a long career at Pacific Lutheran University, where he was honored as a recipient of the Burlington Northern Faculty Achievement Award. Professor Brue has also received the national Leavey Award for excellence in economic education. He has served as national president and chair of the Board of Trustees of Omicron Delta Epsilon International Economics Honorary. He is coauthor of *Economic Scenes*, fifth edition (Prentice-Hall); *Contemporary Labor Economics*, ninth edition; *Essentials of Economics*, second edition; *Macroeconomics: Brief Edition*; *Microeconomics: Brief Edition* (all The McGraw-Hill Companies); and *The Evolution of Economic Thought*, seventh edition (South-Western). For relaxation, he enjoys international travel, attending sporting events, and skiing with family and friends.

SEAN M. FLYNN did his undergraduate work at the University of Southern California before completing his Ph.D. at U.C. Berkeley, where he served as the Head Graduate Student Instructor for the Department of Economics after receiving the Outstanding Graduate Student Instructor Award. He teaches at Scripps College (of the Claremont Colleges) and is the author of *Economics for Dummies* (Wiley) and coauthor of *Essentials of Economics*, second edition; *Macroeconomics: Brief Edition*; and *Microeconomics: Brief Edition* (all The McGraw-Hill Companies). His research interests include finance, behavioral economics, and health economics. An accomplished martial artist, he has represented the United States in international aikido tournaments and is the author of *Understanding Shodokan Aikido* (Shodokan Press). Other hobbies include running, traveling, and enjoying ethnic food.

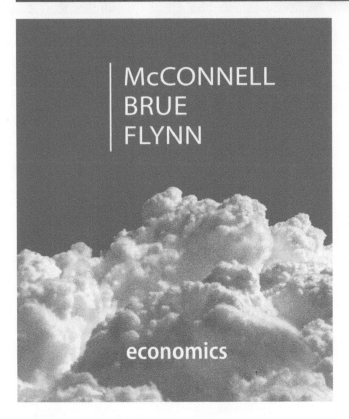

McCONNELL
BRUE
FLYNN

economics

Welcome to the 20th edition of *Economics*, the best-selling economics textbook in the world. An estimated 15 million students have used *Economics* or its companion editions, *Macroeconomics* and *Microeconomics*. *Economics* has been adapted into Australian and Canadian editions and translated into Italian, Russian, Chinese, French, Spanish, Portuguese, and other languages. We are pleased that *Economics* continues to meet the market test: nearly one out of five U.S. students in principles courses used the 19th edition.

Fundamental Objectives

We have three main goals for *Economics*:

- Help the beginning student master the principles essential for understanding the economizing problem, specific economic issues, and policy alternatives.

- Help the student understand and apply the economic perspective and reason accurately and objectively about economic matters.

- Promote a lasting student interest in economics and the economy.

Student Feedback

The twentieth edition has a renewed focus on today's students and their various approaches to learning. How do today's students study? How are they using mobile technology? When are they using the textbook, and how are they using the textbook? To help answer these questions, McGraw-Hill and author Sean Flynn formed a Student Advisory Board consisting of students from Belmont University, the University of Louisiana–Lafayette, Tarrant County College, and West Virginia University Institute of Technology. The Student Advisory Board participated in a wide variety of evaluation and testing activities over six months and provided targeted recommendations to improve the 20th edition and its ancillary learning materials. Their feedback was incredibly valuable, and the authors incorporated their suggestions in this revision.

What's New and Improved?

One of the benefits of writing a successful text is the opportunity to revise—to delete the outdated and install the new, to rewrite misleading or ambiguous statements, to introduce more relevant illustrations, to improve the organizational structure, and to enhance the learning aids.

We trust that you will agree that we have used this opportunity wisely and fully. Some of the more significant changes include the following.

Restructured Introductory Chapters

We have divided the five-chapter grouping of introductory chapters common to *Economics*, *Microeconomics*, and *Macroeconomics* into two parts. Part 1 contains Chapter 1 (Limits, Alternatives, and Choices) and Chapter 2 (The Market System and the Circular Flow). The content in Part 2 has changed and now consists of the following three chapters: Chapter 3 (Demand, Supply, and Market Equilibrium), Chapter 4 (Market Failures: Public Goods and Externalities), and Chapter 5 (Government's Role and Government Failure).

As restructured, the three chapters that now form Part 2 give students a panorama of:

- The efficiency and allocation benefits of competitive markets.

- How and why governments can help when there are cases of market failure.

- An appreciation of government failure so that students do not assume that government intervention is an easy or guaranteed panacea for the misallocations and inefficiencies caused by market failure.

Our new approach responds to suggestions by reviewers to:

- Move the elasticity chapter back into *Microeconomics*.
- Boost the analysis of government failure to help students better understand many of the problems currently besetting the U.S. economy.

Our new approach embraces these suggestions. For microeconomics instructors, the new ordering provides a clear supply-and-demand path to the subsequent chapters on consumer and producer behavior while also giving students a stronger policy background on not only market failures but government interventions in the economy and whether they are likely to improve efficiency. For macroeconomics instructors, the new sequence provides a theoretical grounding that can help students better understand issues such as excessive government deficit spending and why there may be insufficient regulation of the financial sector. And because Chapters 4 and 5 are both optional and modular, instructors can skip them if they wish to move directly from Chapter 3's discussion of supply and demand to the core microeconomics or macroeconomics chapters.

New "Consider This" and "Last Word" Pieces

Our "Consider This" boxes are used to provide analogies, examples, or stories that help drive home central economic ideas in a student-oriented, real-world manner.

CONSIDER THIS ...

Why Do Hospitals Sometimes Charge $25 for an Aspirin?

To save taxpayers money, Medicare and Medicaid set their payment rates for medical services above marginal cost but below average total cost. Doing so gives health care providers an incentive to provide services to Medicare and Medicaid patients because MR > MC. But it also means that government health insurance programs are not reimbursing the full cost of treating Medicare and Medicaid patients. In particular, the programs are not picking up their share of the fixed costs associated with providing health care.

As an example, consider an elderly person who uses Medicare. If he gets into a car accident and is taken to the local emergency room, the hospital will run up a wide variety of marginal costs, including ambulance charges, X-rays, medications, and the time of the nurses and doctors who help him. But the hospital also has a wide variety of fixed costs including rent, utility bills, computer networks, and lots of hideously expensive medical equipment.

These costs have to be borne by somebody. So when Medicare and Medicaid fail to pay their full share of the fixed costs, other patients must pick up the slack. The result has been for hospitals to transfer as much as possible of the fixed costs onto patients with private health insurance. The hospitals overbill private insurance companies so as to make up for the fixed costs that the government refuses to pay.

That is why you will hear stories about hospitals charging

For instance, a "Consider This" box titled "McHits and McMisses" illustrates consumer sovereignty through a listing of successful and unsuccessful products. How businesses exploit price discrimination is driven home in a "Consider This" box that explains why ballparks charge different admission prices for adults and children but only one set of prices at their concession stands. These brief vignettes, each accompanied by a photo, illustrate key points in a lively, colorful, and easy-to-remember way. We have added 14 new "Consider This" boxes in this edition.

Our "Last Word" pieces are lengthier applications or case studies that are placed near the end of each chapter.

For example, the "Last Word" section for Chapter 1 (Limits, Alternatives, and Choices) examines pitfalls to sound economic reasoning, while the "Last Word" section for Chapter 4 (Market Failures: Public Goods and Externalities) examines cap-and-trade versus carbon taxes as policy responses to excessive carbon dioxide emissions. There are 14 new "Last Word" sections in this edition.

If you are unfamiliar with *Economics*, we encourage you to thumb through the chapters to take a quick look at these highly visible features.

New Chapter on Government's Role and Government Failure

We have responded to instructor suggestions by placing this new chapter on Government's Role and Government Failure into the introductory section of the book. Its early placement gives students a taste of political economy and the practical difficulties with government regulation and intervention. Topics covered include the special-interest effect, rent seeking, regulatory capture, political corruption, unfunded liabilities, and unintended consequences.

The chapter begins, however, by reminding students of government's great power to improve equity and efficiency. When read along with Chapter 4 on market failure, this new chapter on government failure should provide students with a balanced perspective. After learning why government intervention is needed to counter market failures, they will also learn that governments often have difficulty in fulfilling their full potential for improving economic outcomes.

An optional appendix incorporates the material on public choice theory and voting paradoxes that was formerly located in Chapter 17 of the 19th edition. Instructors wishing to give their students an even deeper appreciation of government failure may wish to assign this material.

Meanwhile, the material on asymmetric information that was located in Chapter 17 of the 19th edition has been moved into an appendix attached to the current edition's Chapter 4 on market failure. That way, instructors wishing to give their students a deeper look at market failure will have the material on asymmetric information located immediately after that chapter's discussion of public goods and externalities.

New Chapter on Behavioral Economics

By building upon the material on prospect theory that appeared in Chapter 6 of the 19th edition, we have created a new full-length chapter on behavioral economics for the 20th edition. Topics covered include time inconsistency, myopia, decision-making heuristics, framing effects, mental accounting, loss aversion, the endowment effect, and reciprocity. The discussion is couched in terms of consumer decision making and includes numerous concrete examples to bring the material home for students.

We have also striven to make clear to students the ways in which behavioral economics builds upon and augments the insights of traditional neoclassical economics. Thus, the chapter opens with a section comparing and contrasting behavioral economics and neoclassical economics so that students will be able to see how both can be used in tandem to help understand and predict human choice behavior.

The chapter is designed, however, to be modular. So instructors may skip it completely without any fear that its concepts are needed to understand subsequent chapters.

New Discussions of the Financial Crisis and the Recession

Our modernization of the macroeconomics in the 18th edition has met with great success, measured by reviews, instructor feedback, and market response. We recast the entire macro analysis in terms of the modern, dominant paradigm of macroeconomics, using economic growth as the central backdrop and viewing business fluctuations as significant and costly variations in the rate of growth. In this paradigm, business cycles result from demand shocks (or, less often, supply shocks) in conjunction with inflexible short-run product prices and wages. The degree of price and wage stickiness decreases with time. In our models, the *immediate short run* is a period in which both the price level and wages are not only sticky, but stuck; the *short run* is a period in which product prices are flexible but wages are not; and the *long run* is a period in which both product prices and wages are fully flexible. Each of these three periods—and thus each of the models based on them—is relevant to understanding the actual macro economy and its occasional difficulties.

In this edition, we have mainly focused on incorporating into our new macroeconomic schema an analysis of the financial crisis, the recession, and the hesitant recovery. We first introduce the debate over the policy response to the 2007–2009 recession in Chapter 24 (An Introduction to Macroeconomics) via a new "Last Word" that briefly lays out the major opposing viewpoints about the nature and size of the stimulus that was applied during and after the crisis. In Chapter 25 (Measuring Domestic Output and National Income), we point out that the main flows in the National Income and Product Accounts usually expand over time, but not always, as demonstrated by the recession. In Chapter 26 (Economic Growth), we discuss how the recession relates to the growth/production possibilities dynamics of Figure 26.2. In Chapter 27 (Business Cycles, Unemployment, and Inflation), we have a new "Last Word" that discusses the very slow recovery in employment after the Great Recession.

In Chapter 28 (Basic Macroeconomic Relationships), we include two "Consider This" boxes, one on how the paradox of thrift applied to consumer behavior during the recession and the other on the riddle of plunging investment spending at the same time the interest rate dropped to near zero during the recession. In Chapter 29 (The Aggregate Expenditures Model), we use the recession as a timely application of how a decline in aggregate expenditures can produce a recessionary expenditure gap and a highly negative GDP gap. Chapter 30 (Aggregate Demand and Aggregate Supply) features a new "Last Word" on the debate among economists as to why the recovery from the 2007–2009 recession was so slow despite the historically unprecedented amounts of monetary and fiscal stimulus that were applied by policymakers. Chapter 31 (Fiscal Policy, Deficits, and Debt) provided a terrific opportunity to bring each of these timely and relevant subjects up-to-date, and we took full advantage of that opportunity.

In Chapter 32 (Money, Banking, and Financial Institutions), we updated the major section on the financial crisis and added a new "Last Word" on whether the existence of megabanks that are considered "too big to fail" has led prosecutors to hold off on the full enforcement of securities laws and banking regulations. Chapter 33 (Money Creation) includes a new "Last Word" on the potential dangers of excessive leverage in the financial system and whether, consequently, regulators should increase required reserve ratios.

Chapter 34 (Interest Rates and Monetary Policy) features several new discussions relating to Fed policies during the recession and recovery, including quantitative easing, the zero interest rate policy, and Operation Twist. While giving the Fed high marks for dealing with the crisis and its aftermath, we also point out that some economists think the Fed contributed to the financial crisis by keeping interest rates too low for too long during the recovery from the 2001 recession. Chapter 35 (Financial Economics) presented a new opportunity for us to demonstrate how a sharp decline of the "appetite for risk" alters the slope of the Security Market Line (SML) and changes investment patterns between stocks and bonds.

Other mentions of the recession and subsequent recovery are spread throughout the remainder of the macro chapters, including in the discussions of macro debates, trade protectionism, and trade deficits. Although we found these various ways to work the recession and recovery into our macro chapters, we are confident that our basic macroeconomic models will serve equally well in explaining expansion back to the economy's historical growth path. The new inclusions simply help students see the relevance of the models to what they are seeing in the news and perhaps experiencing in their own lives. The overall tone of the book, including the macro, continues to be optimistic with respect to the long-term growth prospects of market economies.

Reorganized and Extended End-of-Chapter Questions and Problems

The 19th edition featured separate sections for end-of-chapter Questions and Problems. Due to strong demand on the part of instructors for an increase in the number of problems that are both autogradable and algorithmic, we have for the 20th edition added about 10 new problems per chapter and have, in addition, revised our organizational scheme for questions and problems.

The questions and problems are now divided into three categories: Discussion Questions, Review Questions, and Problems.

- The Discussion Questions are analytic and often allow for free responses.
- The Review Questions focus on the apprehension of key concepts but are worded so as to always require specific answers, thereby allowing for autograding and algorithmic variation.

- The Problems are quantitative and require specific answers so that they, too, are both autogradable and algorithmic.

All of the questions and problems are assignable through McGraw-Hill's *Connect Economics* and we have additionally aligned all of the questions and problems with the learning objectives presented at the beginning of chapters. The new structure as well as the newly added problems were well received by reviewers, many of them long-time users of the book.

Current Discussions and Examples

The 20th edition of *Economics* refers to and discusses many current topics. Examples include surpluses and shortages of tickets at the Olympics; the myriad impacts of ethanol subsidies; creative destruction; applications of behavioral economics; applications of game theory; the most rapidly expanding and disappearing U.S. jobs; oil and gasoline prices; cap-and-trade systems and carbon taxes; the value-added tax; state lotteries; consumption versus income inequality; the impact of electronic medical records on health care costs; the surprising fall in illegal immigration after the 2007–2009 recession; the massive increase in long-term unemployment; the difficulty of targeting fiscal stimulus; the rapid rise in college tuition; the slow recovery from the Great Recession; ballooning federal budget deficits and public debt; the long-run funding shortfalls in Social Security and Medicare; the effect of rising dependency ratios on economic growth; innovative Federal Reserve policies including quantitative easing, the zero interest rate policy, and explicit inflation targets; the massive excess reserves in the banking system; the jump in the size of the Fed's balance sheet; the effect of the zero interest rate policy on savers; regulation of "too big to fail" banks; trade adjustment assistance; the European Union and the eurozone; changes in exchange rates; and many other current topics.

Chapter-by-Chapter Changes

Each chapter of *Macroeconomics*, 20th edition, contains updated data reflecting the current economy, revised Learning Objectives, and reorganized and expanded end-of-chapter content. Several chapters also contain one or more additional Quick Review boxes to help students review and solidify content as they are reading along.

Chapter-specific updates include:

Chapter 1: Limits Alternatives, and Choices features three refreshed "Consider This" pieces, a more concise definition of macroeconomics, and wording improvements that clarify the main concepts.

Chapter 2: The Market System and the Circular Flow contains a heavily revised introductory section on the different types of economic systems found in the world today as well as a new section on how the market system deals with risk and uncertainty. Reviewers asked for more material on risk and its effects on economic behavior. This short section provides a brief, nontechnical framework for students to understand how the market economy deals with risk and uncertainty. There is also a new "Consider This" box on how insurance encourages investment by transferring risk from those who do not wish to bear it to those who are willing to bear it as a business proposition.

Chapter 3: Demand, Supply, and Market Equilibrium contains a short new section in the appendix that introduces students to markets with vertical supply curves so that the concept of perfectly inelastic supply will come more easily to microeconomics students and the concept of vertical long-run aggregate supply will come more easily to macroeconomics students.

Chapter 4: Market Failures: Public Goods and Externalities includes a new "Consider This" piece on how musicians have reacted to the reality that Internet file sharing has transformed recorded music from a private good into a public good. There is also a new appendix that explains market failures caused by asymmetric information. The appendix gives instructors the option of extending and deepening this chapter's study of market failure. Its content previously appeared in Chapter 17 of the 19th edition.

Chapter 5: Government's Role and Government Failure is a new chapter that offers a balanced treatment of both the great benefits as well as the possible drawbacks of government economic intervention and regulation. The chapter includes topics of interest for both microeconomics and macroeconomics students, such as: regulatory capture, unfunded liabilities, the collective-action problem, bureaucratic inertia, the tendency for politicians to run budget deficits to please voters, and the special-interest effect. So while Chapter 4 makes the case for government regulation to compensate for market failures, this new chapter introduces students to the fact that government interventions are themselves susceptible to both allocative and productive inefficiency. As noted previously, the chapter also includes an appendix that incorporates the voting and public choice material that appeared in Chapter 17 of the 19th edition for instructors who wish to present their students with the most prominent theoretical models dealing with government failure.

Chapter 6: An Introduction to Macroeconomics benefits from extensive revisions to the chapter's header structure, several new Quick Reviews, and a new "Last Word" that covers in a brief and accessible form the major opposing policy viewpoints about the effectiveness and ideal size of government stimulus during and after the 2007–2009 recession.

Chapter 7: Measuring Domestic Output and National Income features two clarifications driven directly by student input. First, the table giving U.S. GDP by both the expenditure method and the income method is more clearly referenced in all instances so as to reduce any possible confusion as to which part of the table is being referred to. Second, there is now a more detailed explanation of the statistical discrepancy that appears when the income method is used to calculate GDP.

Chapter 8: Economic Growth benefits from extensive data updates, a new Quick Review to help solidify comprehension, and a new "Last Word" that discusses the challenges to economic growth posed by falling birth rates and a greying population.

Chapter 9: Business Cycles, Unemployment, and Inflation features a new "Last Word" on the slow recovery of employment after the Great Recession. There are also two new "Consider This" vignettes that discuss, respectively, the relationship between downwardly sticky wages and unemployment and the idea that moderate inflation rates may help to lower unemployment by allowing firms to cut real wages without cutting nominal wages.

Chapter 10: Basic Macroeconomic Relationships features a revised header structure to better guide students through the material, a new Quick Review to help solidify retention, and substantial revisions to several graphs and their captions to further refine and clarify the fundamental concepts introduced in this chapter.

Chapter 11: The Aggregate Expenditures Model has substantial changes to a key figure in order to improve clarity as well as a heavily revised list of Learning Objectives.

Chapter 12: Aggregate Demand and Aggregate Supply features a new "Last Word" on the discussion economists have been having as to why the recovery from the Great Recession has been so slow despite record amounts of monetary and fiscal stimulus.

Chapter 13: Fiscal Policy, Deficits, and Debt features extensive data updates to help students understand the historically unprecedented size of recent federal budget deficits.

Chapter 14: Money, Banking, and Financial Institutions features a new "Last Word" on how some banks are now considered "too big to fail" and how that has affected the prosecution of financial crimes. The chapter also contains four new Quick Reviews to help students better retain the chapter's material.

Chapter 15: Money Creation features a new "Last Word" on the dangers of leverage in the banking system and whether required reserve ratios should consequently be increased.

Chapter 16: Interest Rates and Monetary Policy features a new section on the Fed's monetary policy initiatives after the Great Recession, including quantitative easing (QE), forward guidance, the zero interest rate policy (ZIRP), and Operation Twist. There is also a new "Last Word" discussing the potential unintended consequences of QE and ZIRP.

Chapter 17: Financial Economics features extensive data updates, five new Quick Reviews, and revised section headers to increase clarity.

Chapter 18: Extending the Analysis of Aggregate Supply features data updates, an extended discussion of the Laffer Curve, and a new Quick Review.

Chapter 19: Current Issues in Macro Theory and Policy has a new Quick Review plus a brief discussion of the Fed's recent decisions to (1) have an explicit inflation target and (2) preannounce the likely duration of open-market operations and quantitative easing.

Chapter 20: International Trade features extensive data updates, several revised figure captions, and three new Quick Reviews.

Chapter 21: The Balance of Payments, Exchange Rates, and Trade Deficits features revised problems, extensive data updates, four new Quick Reviews, and a new set of Learning Objectives.

Chapter 21 Web: The Economics of Developing Countries features extensive data revisions and an all-new set of Discussion Questions.

COI1: The United States in the Global Economy features a heavily revised map of the international distribution of income levels, a totally new set of Discussion Questions, and extensive data updates.

COI2: Previous International Exchange Rate Systems remains unchanged for the 20th edition.

Distinguishing Features

Comprehensive Explanations at an Appropriate Level *Economics* is comprehensive, analytical, and challenging yet fully accessible to a wide range of students. The thoroughness and accessibility enable instructors to select topics for special classroom emphasis with confidence that students can read and comprehend other independently assigned material in the book. Where needed, an extra sentence of explanation is provided. Brevity at the expense of clarity is false economy.

Fundamentals of the Market System Many economies throughout the world are still making difficult transitions from planning to markets while a handful of other countries such as Venezuela seem to be trying to reestablish government-controlled, centrally planned economies. Our detailed description of the institutions and operation of the market system in Chapter 2 (The Market System and the Circular Flow) is therefore even more relevant than before. We pay particular attention to property rights, entrepreneurship, freedom of enterprise and choice, competition, and the role of profits because these concepts are often misunderstood by beginning students worldwide.

Extensive Treatment of International Economics We give the principles and institutions of the global economy extensive treatment. The appendix to Chapter 3 (Demand, Supply, and Market Equilibrium) has an application on exchange rates. Chapter 20 (International Trade) examines key facts of international trade, specialization and comparative advantage, arguments for protectionism, impacts of tariffs and subsidies, and various trade agreements. Chapter 21 (The Balance of Payments, Exchange Rates, and Trade Deficits) discusses the balance of payments, fixed and floating exchange rates, and U.S. trade deficits. Web Chapter 21 (The Economics of Developing Countries) takes a look at the special problems faced by developing countries and how the advanced industrial countries try to help them.

As noted previously in this preface, Chapter 20 (International Trade) is constructed such that instructors who want to cover international trade early in the course can assign it immediately after Chapter 3. Chapter 20 requires only a good understanding of production possibilities analysis and supply and demand analysis to comprehend. International competition, trade flows, and financial flows are integrated throughout the micro and macro sections. "Global Perspective" boxes add to the international flavor of the book.

Early and Extensive Treatment of Government The public sector is an integral component of modern capitalism. This book introduces the role of government early. Chapter 4 (Market Failures: Public Goods and Externalities) systematically discusses public goods and government policies toward externalities. Chapter 5 (Government's Role and Government Failure) details the factors that cause government failure. Both the micro and the macro sections of the text include issue- and policy-oriented chapters.

Stress on the Theory of the Firm We have given much attention to microeconomics in general and to the theory of the firm in particular, for two reasons. First, the concepts of microeconomics are difficult for most beginning students; abbreviated expositions usually compound these difficulties by raising more questions than they answer. Second, we wanted to couple analysis of the various market structures with a discussion of the impact of each market arrangement on price, output levels, resource allocation, and the rate of technological advance.

Step-by-Step, Two-Path Macro As in the previous edition, our macro continues to be distinguished by a systematic step-by-step approach to developing ideas and building models. Explicit assumptions about price and wage stickiness are posited and then systematically peeled away, yielding new models and extensions, all in the broader context of growth, expectations, shocks, and degrees of price and wage stickiness over time.

In crafting this step-by-step macro approach, we took care to preserve the "two-path macro" that many instructors appreciated. Instructors who want to bypass the immediate short-run model (Chapter 11: The Aggregate Expenditures Model) can proceed without loss of continuity directly to the short-run AD-AS model (Chapter 12: Aggregate Demand and Aggregate Supply), fiscal policy, money and banking, monetary policy, and the long-run AD-AS analysis.

Emphasis on Technological Change and Economic Growth This edition continues to emphasize economic growth. Chapter 1 (Limits, Alternatives, and Choices) uses the production possibilities curve to show the basic ingredients of growth. Chapter 8 (Economic Growth) explains how growth is measured and presents the facts of growth. It also discusses the causes of growth, looks at productivity growth, and addresses some controversies surrounding economic growth. Chapter 8's "Last Word" examines whether economic growth can survive demographic decline. Web Chapter 21 focuses on developing countries and the growth

obstacles they confront. *Microeconomics* Web Chapter 13 (Technology, R&D, and Efficiency) provides an explicit and cohesive discussion of the microeconomics of technological advance, including topics such as invention, innovation, and diffusion; start-up firms; R&D decision making; market structure and R&D effort; and creative destruction.

Focus on Economic Policy and Issues For many students, the micro chapters on antitrust, agriculture, income inequality, health care, and immigration, along with the macro chapters on fiscal policy and monetary policy, are where the action is centered. We guide that action along logical lines through the application of appropriate analytical tools. In the micro, we favor inclusiveness; instructors can effectively choose two or three chapters from *Microeconomics* Part 6.

Integrated Text and Web Site *Economics* and its Web site are highly integrated through in-text Web buttons, bonus Web chapters, multiple-choice self-tests at the Web site, math notes, and other features. Our Web site is part and parcel of our student learning package, customized to the book.

The in-text Web buttons (or indicators) merit special mention. Two differently colored rectangular indicators appear throughout the book, informing readers that complementary content on a subject can be found at our Web site, **www.mcconnell20e.com.** The indicator types are:

Worked Problems Written by Norris Peterson of Pacific Lutheran University (WA), these pieces consist of side-by-side computational questions and computational procedures used to derive the answers. In essence, they extend the textbook's explanations of various computations—for example, of real GDP, real GDP per capita, the unemployment rate, the inflation rate, per-unit production costs, economic profit, and more. From a student's perspective, they provide "cookbook" help for solving numerical problems.

WORKED PROBLEMS

W1.1
Budget lines

Origin of the Ideas These pieces, written by Randy Grant of Linfield College (OR), are brief histories of 70 major ideas discussed in the book. They identify the particular economists who developed ideas such as opportunity cost, equilibrium price, the multiplier, comparative advantage, and elasticity.

ORIGIN OF THE IDEA

O1.1
Origin of the term "economics"

Organizational Alternatives

Although instructors generally agree on the content of principles of economics courses, they sometimes differ on how to arrange the material. *Economics* includes 11 parts, and thus provides considerable organizational flexibility. We place microeconomics before macroeconomics because this ordering is consistent with how contemporary economists view the direction of linkage between the two components. The introductory material of Parts 1 and 2, however, can be followed immediately by the macroanalysis of Parts 7 and 8. Similarly, the two-path macro enables covering the full aggregate expenditures model or advancing directly from the basic macro relationships chapter to the AD-AS model.

Some instructors will prefer to intersperse the microeconomics of Parts 4 and 5 with the problems chapters of Part 6. Chapter 20 on agriculture may follow Chapters 10 and 11 on pure competition; Chapter 19 on antitrust and regulation may follow Chapters 12, 13, and 13 Web on imperfect competition models and technological advance. Chapter 23 on immigration may follow Chapter 15 on wages; and Chapter 21 on income inequality may follow Chapters 15 and 16 on distributive shares of national income.

Instructors who teach the typical two-semester course and feel comfortable with the book's organization will find that, by putting Parts 1 to 6 in the first semester and Parts 7 to 11 in the second, the material is divided logically between the two semesters.

Finally, Chapter 38 on international trade can easily be moved up to immediately after Chapter 3 on supply and demand for instructors who want an early discussion of international trade.

Pedagogical Aids

Economics is highly student-oriented. The "To the Student" statement at the beginning of Part 1 details the book's many pedagogical aids. The 20th edition is also accompanied by a variety of high-quality supplements that help students master the subject and help instructors implement customized courses.

Supplements for Students and Instructors

Study Guide One of the world's leading experts on economic education, William Walstad of the University of Nebraska–Lincoln, prepared the *Study Guide*. Many students find either the printed or digital version indispensable. Each chapter contains an introductory statement, a checklist of behavioral objectives, an outline, a list of important terms, fill-in questions, problems and projects, objective questions, and discussion questions.

The *Guide* comprises a superb "portable tutor" for the principles student. Separate *Study Guides* are available for the macro and micro paperback editions of the text.

Instructor's Manual Shawn Knabb of Western Washington University revised and updated the *Instructor's Manuals* to accompany the 20th edition of the text. The revised *Instructor's Manual* includes:

- Chapter summaries.
- Listings of "what's new" in each chapter.
- Teaching tips and suggestions.
- Learning objectives.
- Chapter outlines.
- Extra questions and problems.
- Answers to the end-of-chapter questions and problems, plus correlation guides mapping content to the learning objectives.

The *Instructor's Manual* is available on the instructor's side of the Online Learning Center.

Three Test Banks Test Bank I contains about 6,500 multiple-choice and true-false questions, most of which were written by the text authors. Randy Grant revised Test Bank I for the 20th edition. Test Bank II contains around 6,000 multiple-choice and true-false questions, updated by Felix Kwan of Maryville University. All Test Bank I and II questions are organized by learning objective, topic, AACSB Assurance of Learning, and Bloom's Taxonomy guidelines. Test Bank III, written by William Walstad, contains more than 600 pages of short-answer questions and problems created in the style of the book's end-of-chapter questions. Test Bank III can be used to construct student assignments or design essay and problem exams. Suggested answers to the essay and problem questions are included. In all, more than 14,000 questions give instructors maximum testing flexibility while ensuring the fullest possible text correlation.

Test Banks I and II are available in *Connect Economics*, through EZ Test Online, and in MS Word. EZ Test allows professors to create customized tests that contain both questions that they select from the test banks as well as questions that they craft themselves. Test Bank III is available in MS Word on the password-protected instructor's side of the Online Learning Center, and on the Instructor Resource CD.

PowerPoint Presentations The PowerPoint Presentations for the 20th edition were updated by a dedicated team of instructors: Stephanie Campbell of Mineral Area College, Amy Chataginer of Mississippi Gulf Coast Community College, and Shannon Aucoin of the University of Louisiana at Lafayette. Each chapter is accompanied by a concise yet thorough tour of the key concepts.

Instructors can use these Web site presentations in the classroom, and students can use them on their computers.

Digital Image Library Every graph and table in the text is available on the instructor's side of the Web site and on the Instructor's Resource CD-ROM.

Scanning Barcodes For students using smartphones and tablets, scanning barcodes (or QR codes) located within the chapter guide students to additional chapter resources, including:

Try It Now!

- Web buttons
- Student PowerPoints
- Worked problems

Students not using smartphones or tablets can access the same resources by clicking the barcodes when viewing the eBook or by going to **www.mcconnell20e.com**.

Online Learning Center (www.mcconnell20e.com) The Web site accompanying this book is a central resource for students and instructors alike. The optional Web Chapters (Technology, R&D, and Efficiency and The Economics of Developing Countries) plus the two Content Options for Instructors (The United States in the Global Economy and Previous International Exchange-Rate Systems), are posted as full-color PDF files. The in-text Web buttons alert the students to points in the book where they can springboard to the Web site to get more information. Students can also review PowerPoint presentations and test their knowledge of a chapter's concepts with a self-graded multiple-choice quiz. The password-protected Instructor Center houses the Instructor's Manual, all three Test Banks, and links to EZ Test Online, PowerPoint presentations, and the Digital Image Library.

Computerized Test Bank Online A comprehensive bank of test questions is provided within McGraw-Hill's flexible electronic testing program EZ Test Online (**www. eztestonline.com**). EZ Test Online allows instructors to simply and quickly create tests or quizzes for their students. Instructors can select questions from multiple McGraw-Hill test banks or author their own, and then either print the finalized test or quiz for paper distribution or publish it online for access via the Internet.

This user-friendly program allows instructors to sort questions by format; select questions by learning objectives or Bloom's taxonomy tags; edit existing questions or add new ones; and scramble questions for multiple versions of the same test. Instructors can export their tests for use in WebCT, Blackboard, and PageOut, making it easy to share assessment materials with colleagues, adjuncts,

and TAs. Instant scoring and feedback are provided, and EZ Test Online's record book is designed to easily export to instructor gradebooks.

Assurance-of-Learning Ready Many educational institutions are focused on the notion of assurance of learning, an important element of some accreditation standards. *Economics* is designed to support your assurance-of-learning initiatives with a simple yet powerful solution. Each chapter in the book begins with a list of numbered learning objectives to which each end-of-chapter question and problem is then mapped. In this way, student responses to those questions and problems can be used to assess how well students are mastering each particular learning objective. Each test bank question for *Economics* also maps to a specific learning objective.

You can use our test bank software, EZ Test Online, or *Connect Economics* to easily query for learning outcomes and objectives that directly relate to the learning objectives for your course. You can then use the reporting features to aggregate student results in a similar fashion, making the collection and presentation of assurance-of-learning data simple and easy.

AACSB Statement The McGraw-Hill Companies is a proud corporate member of AACSB International. Understanding the importance and value of AACSB accreditation, *Economics*, 20th edition, has sought to recognize the curricula guidelines detailed in the AACSB standards for business accreditation by connecting end-of-chapter questions in *Economics*, 20th edition, and the accompanying test banks to the general knowledge and skill guidelines found in the AACSB standards.

This AACSB Statement for *Economics*, 20th edition, is provided only as a guide for the users of this text. The AACSB leaves content coverage and assessment within the purview of individual schools, their respective missions, and their respective faculty. While *Economics*, 20th edition, and the teaching package make no claim of any specific AACSB qualification or evaluation, we have, within *Economics*, 20th edition, labeled selected questions according to the six general knowledge and skills areas.

Digital Solutions
McGraw-Hill *Connect*® *Economics*

connect | ECONOMICS **Less Managing. More Teaching. Greater Learning.** *Connect Economics* is an online assignment and assessment solution that offers a number of powerful tools and features that make managing assignments easier so faculty can spend more time teaching. With *Connect Economics*, students can engage with their coursework anytime and anywhere, making the learning process more accessible and efficient.

Simple Assignment Management With *Connect Economics*, creating assignments is easier than ever, so you can spend more time teaching and less time managing. The assignment management function enables you to:

- Create and deliver assignments easily with selectable end-of-chapter questions and test bank items.
- Streamline lesson planning, student progress reporting, and assignment grading to make classroom management more efficient than ever.
- Go paperless with online submission and grading of student assignments.

Smart Grading *Connect Economics* helps students learn more efficiently by providing feedback and practice material when they need it, where they need it. The grading function enables instructors to:

- Score assignments automatically, giving students immediate feedback on their work and side-by-side comparisons with correct answers.
- Access and review each response; manually change grades or leave comments for students to review.
- Reinforce classroom concepts with practice tests and instant quizzes.

Instructor Library The *Connect Economics* Instructor Library is your repository for additional resources to improve student engagement in and out of class. You can select and use any asset that enhances your lecture.

Student Study Center The *Connect Economics* Student Study Center is the place for students to access additional resources. The Student Study Center offers students quick access to lectures, practice materials, eBooks, study questions, and more.

Student Progress Tracking *Connect Economics* keeps instructors informed about how each student, section, and class is performing, allowing for more productive use of lecture and office hours. The progress-tracking function enables instructors to:

- View scored work immediately and track individual or group performance with assignment and grade reports.
- Access a real-time view of student or class performance relative to learning objectives.
- Collect data and generate reports required by many accreditation organizations like AACSB.

McGraw-Hill *Connect® Plus Economics*

McGraw-Hill reinvents the textbook learning experience for the modern student with *Connect Plus Economics*. A seamless integration of an eBook and *Connect Economics*, *Connect Plus Economics* provides all of the *Connect Economics* features plus the following:

- An integrated eBook, allowing for anytime, anywhere access to the textbook.
- Dynamic links between the problems or questions you assign to your students and the location in the eBook where that problem or question is covered.
- A powerful search function to pinpoint and connect key concepts in a snap.

In short, *Connect Plus Economics* offers you and your students powerful tools and features that optimize your time and energies, enabling you to focus on course content, teaching, and student learning. *Connect Plus Economics* also offers a wealth of content resources for both instructors and students. This state-of-the-art, thoroughly tested system supports you in preparing students for the world that awaits.

For more information about *Connect*, go to **www.mcgrawhillconnect.com**, or contact your local McGraw-Hill sales representative.

LearnSmart Advantage

LEARNSMART ADVANTAGE New from McGraw-Hill Education, LearnSmart Advantage is a series of adaptive learning products fueled by LearnSmart, the most widely used and intelligent adaptive learning resource on the market. Developed to deliver demonstrable results in boosting grades, increasing course retention, and strengthening memory recall, LearnSmart Advantage spans the entire learning process, from course preparation to the first adaptive reading experience. A smarter learning experience for students coupled with valuable reporting tools for instructors, LearnSmart Advantage is advancing learning like no other product in higher education today. Products in McConnell's LearnSmart Advantage Suite include:

LearnSmart LearnSmart is one of the most effective and successful adaptive learning resources in the market today, proven to strengthen memory recall, keep students in class, and boost grades. Distinguishing what students know from what they don't, and honing in on the concepts they are most likely to forget, LearnSmart continuously adapts to each student's needs to build an individual learning path so students study smarter and retain more knowledge. Reports provide valuable insight to instructors, so precious class time can be spent on higher-level concepts and discussion.

LearnSmart Achieve LearnSmart Achieve is a revolutionary new learning system that combines a continually adaptive learning experience with necessary course resources to focus students on mastering concepts they don't already know. The program adjusts to each student individually as he or she progresses, creating just-in-time learning experiences by presenting interactive content that is tailored to each student's needs. A convenient time-management feature and reports for instructors also ensure students stay on track.

SmartBook SmartBook is the first and only adaptive reading experience available today. SmartBook changes reading from a passive and linear experience to an engaging and dynamic one in which students are more likely to master and retain important concepts, coming to class better prepared. Valuable reports provide instructors insight as to how students are progressing through textbook content, and are useful for shaping in-class time or assessment.

This revolutionary technology suite is available only from McGraw-Hill Education. To learn more, go to **http://learnsmartadvantage.com** or contact your representative for a demo.

Tegrity Campus: Lectures 24/7

 Tegrity Campus is a service that makes class time available 24/7 by automatically capturing every lecture in a searchable format for students to review when they study and complete assignments. With a simple one-click start-and-stop process, you capture all computer screens and corresponding audio. Students can replay any part of any class with easy-to-use browser-based viewing on a PC or Mac.

Educators know that the more students can see, hear, and experience class resources, the better they learn. In fact, studies prove it. With Tegrity Campus, students quickly recall key moments by using Tegrity Campus's unique search feature. This search function helps students efficiently find what they need, when they need it, across an entire semester of class recordings. Help turn all your students' study time into learning moments immediately supported by your lecture.

To learn more about Tegrity, you can watch a two-minute Flash demo at **tegritycampus.mhhe.com.**

CourseSmart

 CourseSmart is a new way for faculty to find and review eTextbooks. It's also a great option for students who are interested in accessing their course materials digitally. CourseSmart offers thousands of the most commonly adopted textbooks across hundreds of courses from a wide variety of higher education publishers. It is the only place for faculty to review and compare the full text of a textbook online. At CourseSmart, students can save up to 50% off the cost of a print book, reduce their impact on the environment, and gain access to powerful Web tools for learning, including full text search, notes and highlighting, and e-mail tools for sharing notes between classmates. Complete tech support is also included with each title. Finding your eBook is easy. Visit **www.CourseSmart.com** and search by title, author, or ISBN.

McGraw-Hill Customer Care Contact Information

Getting the most from new technology can be challenging. So McGraw-Hill offers a large suite of complementary support services for faculty using *Economics*. You can contact our Product Specialists 24 hours a day to set up online technology instruction. Or you can contact customer support at any time by either calling **800-331-5094** or by visiting the Customer Experience Group (CXG) Support Center at **www.mhhe.com/support.** They will put you in touch with a Technical Support Analyst familiar with *Economics* and its technology offerings. And, of course, our online knowledge bank of Frequently Asked Questions is always available at the just-mentioned Web site for instant answers to the most common technology questions.

Acknowledgments

We give special thanks to Norris Peterson and Randy Grant, who created the "button" content on our Web site. We again thank James Reese of the University of South Carolina at Spartanburg, who wrote the original Internet exercises. Although many of those questions were replaced or modified in the typical course of revision, several remain virtually unchanged. Ryan Umbeck, Peter Staples, and Heather Schumacker deserve considerable credit for their hard work on the questions and problems in *Connect*. Thanks to the many dedicated instructors who accuracy-checked the end-of-chapter content, test banks, and Instructor's Manuals: Jennifer Pate, Charles Harrington,

Rick Hirschi, Melissa Rueterbusch, Gregory McGiffney, and Mike Winterhalter. Finally, we thank William Walstad and Tom Barbiero (the coauthor of our Canadian edition) for their helpful ideas and insights.

We are greatly indebted to an all-star group of professionals at McGraw-Hill—in particular Douglas Reiner, Lori Koetters, Casey Rasch, Scott Smith, Bruce Gin, and Katie Hoenicke—for their publishing and marketing expertise. We thank Keri Johnson for her selection of the "Consider This" and "Last Word" photos and Debra Kubiak for the design.

The 20th edition has benefited from a number of perceptive formal reviews. The reviewers, listed at the end of the preface, were a rich source of suggestions for this revision. To each of you, and others we may have inadvertently overlooked, thank you for your considerable help in improving *Economics*.

Sean M. Flynn
Stanley L. Brue
Campbell R. McConnell

Lowell Glenn, *Utah Valley University*
Terri Gonzales, *Delgado Community College*
Moonsu Han, *North Shore Community College*
Virden Harrison, *Modesto Junior College*
Richard R. Hawkins, *University of West Florida*
Kim Hawtrey, *Hope College*
Glenn Haynes, *Western Illinois University*
Michael Heslop, *Northern Virginia Community College, Annandale*
Jesse Hoyt Hill, *Tarrant County College*
Calvin Hoy, *County College of Morris*
Jim Hubert, *Seattle Central Community College*
Greg W. Hunter, *California State Polytechnic University, Pomona*
Christos Ioannou, *University of Minnesota–Minneapolis*
Faridul Islam, *Utah Valley University*
Mahshid Jalilvand, *University of Wisconsin–Stout*
Ricot Jean, *Valencia Community College–Osceola*
Jonatan Jelen, *City College of New York*
Brad Kamp, *University of South Florida, Sarasota-Manatee*
Kevin Kelley, *Northwest Vista College*
Chris Klein, *Middle Tennessee State University*
Barry Kotlove, *Edmonds Community College*
Richard Kramer, *New England College*
Felix Kwan, *Maryville University*
Ted Labay, *Bishop State Community College*
Tina Lance, *Germanna Community College–Fredericksburg*
Yu-Feng Lee, *New Mexico State University–Las Cruces*
Adam Y.C. Lei, *Midwestern State University*
Phillip Letting, *Harrisburg Area Community College*
Brian Lynch, *Lake Land College*
Zagros Madjd-Sadjadi, *Winston-Salem State University*
Laura Maghoney, *Solano Community College*
Vincent Mangum, *Grambling State University*
Benjamin Matta, *New Mexico State University–Las Cruces*
Pete Mavrokordatos, *Tarrant County College–Northeast Campus*
Frederick May, *Trident Technical College*
Katherine McClain, *University of Georgia*
Michael McIntyre, *Copiah-Lincoln Community College*
Robert McKizzie, *Tarrant County College–Southeast Campus*
Kevin McWoodson, *Moraine Valley Community College*
Edwin Mensah, *University of North Carolina at Pembroke*
Randy Methenitis, *Richland College*
Ida Mirzaie, *The Ohio State University*
David Mitch, *University of Maryland–Baltimore County*
Ramesh Mohan, *Bryant University*
Daniel Morvey, *Piedmont Technical College*

Shahriar Mostashari, *Campbell University*
Ted Muzio, *St. John's University*
Cliff Nowell, *Weber State University*
Albert Okunade, *University of Memphis*
Mary Ellen Overbay, *Seton Hall University*
Tammy Parker, *University of Louisiana at Monroe*
Alberto Alexander Perez, *Harford Community College*
David Petersen, *American River College*
Mary Anne Pettit, *Southern Illinois University–Edwardsville*
Jeff Phillips, *Morrisville State College*
Robert Poulton, *Graceland University*
Dezzie Prewitt, *Rio Hondo College*
Joe Prinzinger, *Lynchburg College*
Jaishankar Raman, *Valparaiso University*
Natalie Reaves, *Rowan University*
Virginia Reilly, *Ocean County College*
Tim Reynolds, *Alvin Community College*
John Romps, *Saint Anselm College*
Tom Scheiding, *Elizabethtown College*
Amy Schmidt, *Saint Anselm College*
Ron Schuelke, *Santa Rosa Junior College*
Alexandra Shiu, *McLennan Community College*
Dorothy Siden, *Salem State University*
Timothy Simpson, *Central New Mexico Community College*
Jonathan Sleeper, *Indian River State College*
Jose Rodriguez Solis, *Northern Virginia Community College*
Camille Soltau-Nelson, *Oregon State University*
Robert Sonora, *Fort Lewis College*
Nick Spangenberg, *Ozarks Technical Community College*
Dennis Spector, *Naugatuck Valley Community College*
Thomas Stevens, *University of Massachusetts, Amherst*
Tamika Steward, *Tarrant County College, Southeast*
Robin Sturik, *Cuyahoga Community College Western–Parma*
Travis Taylor, *Christopher Newport University*
Ross Thomas, *Central New Mexico Community College*
Mark Thompson, *Augusta State University*
Deborah Thorsen, *Palm Beach State College*
Michael Toma, *Armstrong Atlantic State University*
Dosse Toulaboe, *Fort Hays State University*
Jeff Vance, *Sinclair Community College*
Cheryl Wachenheim, *North Dakota State University–Fargo*
Christine Wathen, *Middlesex County College*
Wendy Wysocki, *Monroe County Community College*
Edward Zajicek, *Winston-Salem State University*

BRIEF CONTENTS

CONTENTS

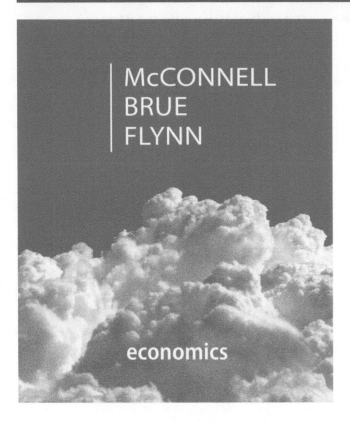

Introduction to Economics and the Economy

INTRODUCTION TO ECONOMICS AND THE ECONOMY

TO THE STUDENT

Economics students learn more, understand more, and make better choices for themselves and others. This book and its interactive learning materials like LearnSmart will speed you on your way to mastering the principles of economics and making a better life for yourself and those around you.

This book and its ancillaries contain several features designed to help you learn economics:

- **Web buttons (indicators)** A glance through the book reveals many pages with rectangular icons set into the text. These "buttons" alert you to helpful learning aids available with the book. The orange button symbolizes "Worked Problems." Numeric problems are presented and then solved, side-by-side, step-by-step. Seeing how the problems are worked will help you solve similar problems on quizzes and exams. The green button stands for "Origin of the Idea." Each of these pieces traces a particular economic idea to the people who first developed it.

After reading a chapter, look back at the chapter's Web buttons and their associated numbers. On the home page of our Internet site, **www.mcconnell20e.com**, select Student Edition and use the pull-down list under "Choose one" to find the Web button content for each chapter. You can also scan the accompanying QR code with your smartphone or tablet. Need a bar-code reader? Try ScanLife, available in your app store.

- **Other Internet aids** Our Web site contains many other aids. In the Student Edition you will find self-testing multiple-choice quizzes, PowerPoint presentations, and much more. For those of you with a very strong mathematics background, be sure to note the "See the Math" section on the Web site. There you will find nearly 50 notes that develop the algebra and, in a few cases, the calculus that underlie the economic concepts.
- **Appendix on graphs** Be assured, however, that you will need only basic math skills to do well in your introductory economics course. In particular, you will need to be comfortable with basic graphical analysis and a few quantitative concepts. The appendix at the end of Chapter 1 reviews graphs and slopes of curves. You may want to read it before starting Chapter 1.
- **Reviews** Each chapter contains several Quick Reviews as well as an end-of-chapter summary. These review sections will help you focus on essential ideas and study for exams.
- **Key terms and Key Graphs** Key terms are set in boldface type within the chapters, listed at the end of each chapter, and again defined in the glossary at the end of the book. Graphs with special importance are labeled Key Graphs, and each includes a multiple-choice Quick Quiz. Your instructor may or may not emphasize all of these figures, but you should pay special attention to those that

are discussed in class; you can be certain there will be exam questions on them.
- **Consider This and Last Word boxes** Many chapters include a "Consider This" box. These brief pieces provide commonplace analogies, examples, and stories that help you understand and remember central economic ideas. Each chapter concludes with a "Last Word" box. Some of them are revealing applications of economic ideas; others are short case studies. While it is tempting to ignore in-text boxes, don't. Most are fun to read, and all will improve your grasp of economics.
- **Questions and Problems** The end of each chapter features separate sections of Discussion Questions, Review Questions, and Problems. The Discussion Questions are analytic and often ask for free responses, and the Review Questions require either specific answers to short computations or brief definitions about important concepts. The Problems involve longer computations for which a series of specific answers must be given. Each is keyed to a particular learning objective (LO) in the list of LOs at the beginning of the chapter. At the Web site is a multiple-choice quiz for each chapter.
- **Study Guide** We enthusiastically recommend the *Study Guide* accompanying this text. This "portable tutor" contains not only a broad sampling of various kinds of questions but a host of useful learning aids. Software-driven tutorials, including the Self Quiz and Study in *Connect Economics*, are also available with the text.

Our two main goals are to help you understand and apply economics and help you improve your analytical skills. An understanding of economics will enable you to comprehend a whole range of economic, social, and political problems that otherwise would seem puzzling and perplexing. Also, your study will enhance reasoning skills that are highly prized in the workplace.

Good luck with your study. We think it will be well worth your time and effort.

CHAPTER 1

Limits, Alternatives, and Choices

Learning Objectives

LO1.1 Define economics and the features of the economic perspective.

LO1.2 Describe the role of economic theory in economics.

LO1.3 Distinguish microeconomics from macroeconomics and positive economics from normative economics.

LO1.4 Explain the individual's economizing problem and how trade-offs, opportunity costs, and attainable combinations can be illustrated with budget lines.

LO1.5 List the categories of scarce resources and delineate the nature of society's economizing problem.

LO1.6 Apply production possibilities analysis, increasing opportunity costs, and economic growth.

LO1.7 Explain how economic growth and international trade increase consumption possibilities.

LO1.8 (Appendix) Understand graphs, curves, and slopes as they relate to economics.

(An appendix on understanding graphs follows this chapter. If you need a quick review of this mathematical tool, you might benefit by reading the appendix first.) People's wants are numerous and varied. Biologically, people need only air, water, food, clothing, and shelter. But in modern societies people also desire goods and services that provide a more comfortable or affluent standard of living. We want bottled water, soft drinks, and fruit juices, not just water from the creek. We want salads, burgers, and pizzas, not just berries and nuts. We want jeans, suits, and coats, not just woven reeds. We want apartments, condominiums, or houses, not just mud huts. And, as the saying goes, "That is not

the half of it." We also want flat-panel TVs, Internet service, education, national defense, cell phones, health care, and much more.

Fortunately, society possesses productive resources, such as labor and managerial talent, tools and machinery, and land and mineral deposits. These resources, employed in the economic system (or simply the economy), help us produce goods and services that satisfy many of our economic wants. But the blunt reality is that our economic wants far exceed the productive capacity of our scarce (limited) resources. We are forced to make choices. This unyielding truth underlies the definition of **economics,** which is the social science concerned with how individuals, institutions, and society make optimal (best) choices under conditions of scarcity.

The Economic Perspective

LO1.1 Define economics and the features of the economic perspective.

Economists view things from a unique perspective. This **economic perspective,** or economic way of thinking, has several critical and closely interrelated features.

Scarcity and Choice

The economic resources needed to make goods and services are in limited supply. This **scarcity** restricts options and demands choices. Because we "can't have it all," we must decide what we will have and what we must forgo.

At the core of economics is the idea that "there is no free lunch." You may be treated to lunch, making it "free" from your perspective, but someone bears a cost. Because all resources are either privately or collectively owned by members of society, ultimately society bears the cost. Scarce inputs of land, equipment, farm labor, the labor of cooks and waiters, and managerial talent are required. Because society could have used these resources to produce something else, it sacrifices those other goods and services in making the lunch available. Economists call such sacrifices **opportunity costs:** To obtain more of one thing, society forgoes the opportunity of getting the next best thing. That sacrifice is the opportunity cost of the choice.

Purposeful Behavior

Economics assumes that human behavior reflects "rational self-interest." Individuals look for and pursue opportunities to increase their **utility**—the pleasure, happiness, or satisfaction obtained from consuming a good or service. They allocate their time, energy, and money to maximize their

ORIGIN OF THE IDEA

01.2
Utility

satisfaction. Because they weigh costs and benefits, their economic decisions are "purposeful" or "rational," not "random" or "chaotic."

Consumers are purposeful in deciding what goods and services to buy. Business firms are purposeful in deciding what products to produce and how to produce them. Government entities are purposeful in deciding what public services to provide and how to finance them.

"Purposeful behavior" does not assume that people and institutions are immune from faulty logic and therefore are perfect decision makers. They sometimes make mistakes. Nor does it mean that people's decisions are unaffected by emotion or the decisions of those around them. Indeed, economists acknowledge that people are sometimes impulsive or emulative. "Purposeful behavior" simply means that people make decisions with some desired outcome in mind.

Rational self-interest is not the same as selfishness. In the economy, increasing one's own wage, rent, interest, or profit normally requires identifying and satisfying *somebody else's* wants! Also, people make personal sacrifices for others. They contribute time and money to charities because they derive pleasure from doing so. Parents help pay for their children's education for the same reason. These self-interested, but unselfish, acts help maximize the givers' satisfaction as much as any personal purchase of goods or services. Self-interested behavior is simply behavior designed to increase personal satisfaction, however it may be derived.

Marginal Analysis: Comparing Benefits and Costs

The economic perspective focuses largely on **marginal analysis**—comparisons of marginal benefits and marginal costs, usually for decision making. To economists, "marginal" means "extra," "additional," or "a change in." Most choices or decisions involve changes in the status quo, meaning the existing state of affairs.

Should you attend school for another year? Should you study an extra hour for an exam? Should you supersize your fries? Similarly, should a business expand or reduce its output? Should government increase or decrease its funding for a missile defense system?

Each option involves marginal benefits and, because of scarce resources, marginal costs. In making choices rationally, the deci-

ORIGIN OF THE IDEA

01.3
Marginal analysis

Fast-Food Lines

The economic perspective is useful in analyzing all sorts of behaviors. Consider an everyday example: the behavior of fast-food customers. When customers enter the restaurant, they go to the shortest line, believing that line will minimize their time cost of obtaining food. They are acting purposefully; time is limited, and people prefer using it in some way other than standing in line.

If one fast-food line is temporarily shorter than other lines, some people will move to that line. These movers apparently view the time saving from the shorter line (marginal benefit) as exceeding the cost of moving from their present line (marginal cost). The line switching tends to equalize line lengths. No further movement of customers between lines occurs once all lines are about equal.

Fast-food customers face another cost-benefit decision when a clerk opens a new station at the counter. Should they move to the new station or stay put? Those who shift to the new line decide that the time saving from the move exceeds the extra cost of physically moving. In so deciding, customers must also consider just how quickly they can get to the new station compared with others who may be contemplating the same move. (Those who hesitate in this situation are lost!)

Customers at the fast-food establishment do not have perfect information when they select lines. Thus, not all decisions turn out as expected. For example, you might enter a short line only to find that someone in front of you is ordering hamburgers and fries for 40 people in the Greyhound bus parked out back (and also that the guy taking orders in your new line is a trainee)! Nevertheless, at the time you made your decision, you thought it was optimal.

Finally, customers must decide what food to order when they arrive at the counter. In making their choices, they again compare marginal costs and marginal benefits in attempting to obtain the greatest personal satisfaction for their expenditure.

Economists believe that what is true for the behavior of customers at fast-food restaurants is true for economic behavior in general. Faced with an array of choices, consumers, workers, and businesses rationally compare marginal costs and marginal benefits when making decisions.

sion maker must compare those two amounts. Example: You and your fiancée are shopping for an engagement ring. Should you buy a $\frac{1}{2}$-carat diamond, a $\frac{3}{4}$-carat diamond, a 1-carat diamond, or something even larger? The marginal cost of a larger-size diamond is the added expense beyond the cost of the smaller-size diamond. The marginal benefit is the perceived lifetime pleasure (utility) from the larger-size stone. If the marginal benefit of the larger diamond exceeds its marginal cost (and you can afford it), buy the larger stone. But if the marginal cost is more than the marginal benefit, you should buy the smaller diamond instead—even if you can afford the larger stone!

In a world of scarcity, the decision to obtain the marginal benefit associated with some specific option always includes the marginal cost of forgoing something else. The money spent on the larger-size diamond means forgoing some other product. An opportunity cost—the value of the next best thing forgone—is always present whenever a choice is made.

Theories, Principles, and Models

LO1.2 Describe the role of economic theory in economics. Like the physical and life sciences, as well as other social sciences, economics relies on the **scientific method.** That procedure consists of several elements:

- Observing real-world behavior and outcomes.

- Based on those observations, formulating a possible explanation of cause and effect (hypothesis).

- Testing this explanation by comparing the outcomes of specific events to the outcome predicted by the hypothesis.

- Accepting, rejecting, and modifying the hypothesis, based on these comparisons.

- Continuing to test the hypothesis against the facts. If favorable results accumulate, the hypothesis evolves into a theory. A very well-tested and widely accepted theory is referred to as an economic law or an **economic principle**—a statement about economic behavior or the economy that enables prediction of the probable effects of certain actions. Combinations of such laws or principles are incorporated into models, which are simplified representations of how something works, such as a market or segment of the economy.

Economists develop theories of the behavior of individuals (consumers, workers) and institutions (businesses, governments) engaged in the production, exchange, and consumption of goods and services. Theories, principles, and models are "purposeful simplifications." The full scope of economic reality itself is too complex and bewildering to be understood as a whole. In developing theories, principles, and models economists remove the clutter and simplify.

Economic principles and models are highly useful in analyzing economic behavior and understanding how the economy operates. They are the tools for ascertaining cause and effect (or action and outcome) within the economic system. Good theories do a good job of explaining and predicting. They are supported by facts concerning how individuals and institutions actually behave in producing, exchanging, and consuming goods and services.

There are some other things you should know about economic principles.

- **Generalizations** Economic principles are generalizations relating to economic behavior or to the economy itself. Economic principles are expressed as the tendencies of typical or average consumers, workers, or business firms. For example, economists say that consumers buy more of a particular product when its price falls. Economists recognize that some consumers may increase their purchases by a large amount, others by a small amount, and a few not at all. This "price-quantity" principle, however, holds for the typical consumer and for consumers as a group.

- **Other-things-equal assumption** In constructing their theories, economists use the *ceteris paribus* or **other-things-equal assumption**—the assumption that factors other than those being considered do not change. They assume that all variables except those under immediate consideration are held constant for a particular analysis. For example, consider the relationship between the price of Pepsi and the amount of it purchased. Assume that of all the factors that might influence the amount of Pepsi purchased (for example, the price of Pepsi, the price of Coca-Cola, and consumer incomes and preferences), only the price of Pepsi varies. This is helpful because the economist can then focus on the relationship between the price of Pepsi and purchases of Pepsi in isolation without being confused by changes in other variables.

ORIGIN OF THE IDEA

01.4

Ceteris paribus

- **Graphical expression** Many economic models are expressed graphically. Be sure to read the special appendix at the end of this chapter as a review of graphs.

Microeconomics and Macroeconomics

LO1.3 Distinguish microeconomics from macroeconomics and positive economics from normative economics. Economists develop economic principles and models at two levels.

Microeconomics

Microeconomics is the part of economics concerned with decision making by individual customers, workers, households, and business firms. At this level of analysis, we observe the details of their behavior under a figurative microscope. We measure the price of a specific product, the number of workers employed by a single firm, the revenue or income of a particular firm or household, or the expenditures of a specific firm, government entity, or family. In microeconomics, we examine the sand, rocks, and shells, not the beach.

Macroeconomics

Macroeconomics examines the performance and behavior of the economy as a whole. It focuses its attention on economic growth, the business cycle, interest rates, inflation, and the behavior of major economic aggregates such as the government, household, and business sectors. An **aggregate** is a collection of specific economic units treated as if they were one unit. Therefore, we might lump together the millions of consumers in the U.S. economy and treat them as if they were one huge unit called "consumers."

In using aggregates, macroeconomics seeks to obtain an overview, or general outline, of the structure of the economy and the relationships of its major aggregates. Macroeconomics speaks of such economic measures as total output, total employment, total income, aggregate expenditures, and the general level of prices in analyzing various economic problems. Very little attention is given to the specific units making up the various aggregates.

Figuratively, macroeconomics looks at the beach, not the pieces of sand, the rocks, and the shells.

The micro–macro distinction does not mean that economics is so highly compartmentalized that every topic can be readily labeled as either micro or macro; many topics and subdivisions of economics are rooted in both. Example: While the problem of unemployment is usually treated as a macroeconomic topic (because unemployment relates to aggregate production), economists recognize that the decisions made by *individual* workers on how long to search for jobs and the way *specific* labor markets encourage or impede hiring are also critical in determining the unemployment rate.

Positive and Normative Economics

Both microeconomics and macroeconomics contain elements of positive economics and normative economics.

Positive economics focuses on facts and cause-and-effect relationships. It includes description, theory development, and theory testing. Positive economics avoids value judgments. It tries to establish scientific statements about economic behavior and deals with what the economy is actually like. Such scientific-based analysis is critical to good policy analysis.

Economic policy, on the other hand, involves **normative economics,** which incorporates value judgments about what the economy should be like or what particular policy actions should be recommended to achieve a desirable goal. Normative economics looks at the desirability of certain aspects of the economy. It underlies expressions of support for particular economic policies.

Positive economics concerns *what is,* whereas normative economics embodies subjective feelings about *what ought to be.* Examples: Positive statement: "The unemployment rate in France is higher than that in the United States." Normative statement: "France ought to undertake policies to make its labor market more flexible to reduce unemployment rates." Whenever words such as "ought" or "should" appear in a sentence, you are very likely encountering a normative statement.

Most of the disagreement among economists involves normative, value-based policy questions. Of course, economists sometime disagree about which theories or models best represent the economy and its parts, but they agree on a full range of economic principles. Most economic controversy thus reflects differing opinions or value judgments about what society should be like.

QUICK REVIEW 1.1

- Economics examines how individuals, institutions, and society make choices under conditions of scarcity.
- The economic perspective stresses (a) resource scarcity and the necessity of making choices, (b) the assumption of purposeful (or rational) behavior, and (c) comparisons of marginal benefit and marginal cost.
- In choosing the best option, people incur an opportunity cost—the value of the next-best option.
- Economists use the scientific method to establish economic theories—cause-effect generalizations about the economic behavior of individuals and institutions.
- Microeconomics focuses on specific decision-making units within the economy. Macroeconomics examines the economy as a whole.
- Positive economics deals with factual statements ("what is"); normative economics involves value judgments ("what ought to be").

Individual's Economizing Problem

LO1.4 Explain the individual's economizing problem and how trade-offs, opportunity costs, and attainable combinations can be illustrated with budget lines.

A close examination of the **economizing problem**—the need to make choices because economic wants exceed economic means—will enhance your understanding of economic models and the difference between microeconomic and macroeconomic analysis. Let's first build a microeconomic model of the economizing problem faced by an individual.

Limited Income

We all have a finite amount of income, even the wealthiest among us. Even Donald Trump must decide how to spend his money! And the majority of us have much more limited means. Our income comes to us in the form of wages, interest, rent, and profit, although we may also receive money from government programs or family members. As Global Perspective 1.1 shows, the average income of Americans in 2011 was $48,450. In the poorest nations, it was less than $500.

Unlimited Wants

For better or worse, most people have virtually unlimited wants. We desire various goods and services that provide utility. Our wants extend over a wide range of products, from *necessities* (for example, food, shelter, and clothing) to *luxuries* (for example, perfumes, yachts, and sports cars). Some wants such as basic food, clothing, and shelter have biological roots. Other wants, for example, specific kinds of food, clothing, and shelter, arise from the conventions and customs of society.

Over time, as new and improved products are introduced, economic wants tend to change and multiply. Only recently have people wanted iPods, Internet service, or camera phones because those products did not exist a few decades ago. Also, the satisfaction of certain wants may trigger others: the acquisition of a Ford Focus or a Honda Civic has been known to whet the appetite for a Lexus or a Mercedes.

Services, as well as goods, satisfy our wants. Car repair work, the removal of an inflamed appendix, legal and accounting advice, and haircuts all satisfy human wants. Actually, we buy many goods, such as automobiles and washing machines, for the services they render. The differences between goods and services are often smaller than they appear to be.

For most people, the desires for goods and services cannot be fully satisfied. Bill Gates may have all that he

GLOBAL PERSPECTIVE 1.1

Average Income, Selected Nations

Average income (total income/population) and therefore typical individual budget constraints vary greatly among nations.

Country	Per Capita Income, 2011 (U.S. dollars, based on exchange rates)
Norway	$88,890
Switzerland	76,380
United States	48,450
Singapore	42,930
France	42,420
South Korea	20,870
Mexico	9240
China	4940
Iraq	2640
India	1410
Madagascar	430
Congo	190

Source: World Bank, **www.worldbank.org**.

wants for himself, but his massive charitable giving suggests that he keenly wants better health care for the world's poor. Our desires for a particular good or service can be satisfied; over a short period of time we can surely get enough toothpaste or pasta. And one appendectomy is plenty. But our broader desire for more goods and services and higher-quality goods and services seems to be another story.

Because we have only limited income (usually through our work) but seemingly insatiable wants, it is in our self-interest to economize: to pick and choose goods and services that maximize our satisfaction given the limitations we face.

A Budget Line

We can clarify the economizing problem facing consumers by visualizing a **budget line** (or, more technically, a *budget constraint*). It is a schedule or curve that shows various combinations of two products a consumer can purchase with a specific money income. Although we assume two products, the analysis generalizes to the full range of products available to consumers.

FIGURE 1.1 A consumer's budget line. The budget line (or budget constraint) shows all the combinations of any two products that can be purchased, given the prices of the products and the consumer's money income.

The Budget Line: Whole-Unit Combinations of DVDs and Paperback Books Attainable with an Income of $120		
Units of DVDs (Price = $20)	Units of Books (Price = $10)	Total Expenditure
6	0	$120 (= $120 + $0)
5	2	$120 (= $100 + $20)
4	4	$120 (= $80 + $40)
3	6	$120 (= $60 + $60)
2	8	$120 (= $40 + $80)
1	10	$120 (= $20 + $100)
0	12	$120 (= $0 + $120)

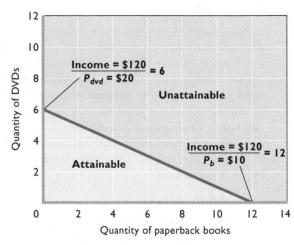

To understand the idea of a budget line, suppose that you received a Barnes & Noble gift card as a birthday present. The $120 card is soon to expire. You take the card to the store and confine your purchase decisions to two alternatives: DVDs and paperback books. DVDs are $20 each and paperback books are $10 each. Your purchase options are shown in the table in Figure 1.1.

At one extreme, you might spend all of your $120 "income" on 6 DVDs at $20 each and have nothing left to spend on books. Or, by giving up 2 DVDs and thereby gaining $40, you can have 4 DVDs at $20 each and 4 books at $10 each. And so on to the other extreme, at which you could buy 12 books at $10 each, spending your entire gift card on books with nothing left to spend on DVDs.

The graph in Figure 1.1 shows the budget line. Note that the graph is not restricted to whole units of DVDs and books as is the table. Every point on the graph represents a possible combination of DVDs and books, including fractional quantities. The slope of the graphed budget line measures the ratio of the price of books (P_b) to the price of DVDs (P_{dvd}); more precisely, the slope is $P_b/P_{dvd} = \$-10/\$+20 = -\frac{1}{2}$. So you must forgo 1 DVD (measured on the vertical axis) to buy 2 books (measured on the horizontal axis). This yields a slope of $-\frac{1}{2}$ or $-.5$.

The budget line illustrates several ideas.

Attainable and Unattainable Combinations All the combinations of DVDs and books on or inside the budget line are *attainable* from the $120 of money income. You can afford to buy, for example, 3 DVDs at $20 each and 6 books at $10 each. You also can obviously afford to buy 2 DVDs and 5 books, thereby using up only $90 of the $120 available on your gift card. But to achieve maximum

utility you will want to spend the full $120. The budget line shows all combinations that cost exactly the full $120.

In contrast, all combinations beyond the budget line are *unattainable*. The $120 limit simply does not allow you to purchase, for example, 5 DVDs at $20 each and 5 books at $10 each. That $150 expenditure would clearly exceed the $120 limit. In Figure 1.1 the attainable combinations are on and within the budget line; the unattainable combinations are beyond the budget line.

Trade-Offs and Opportunity Costs The budget line in Figure 1.1 illustrates the idea of trade-offs arising from limited income. To obtain more DVDs, you have to give up some books. For example, to obtain the first DVD, you trade off 2 books. So the opportunity cost of the first DVD is 2 books. To obtain the second DVD the opportunity cost is also 2 books. The straight-line budget constraint, with its constant slope, indicates constant opportunity cost. That is, the opportunity cost of 1 extra DVD remains the same (= 2 books) as more DVDs are purchased. And, in reverse, the opportunity cost of 1 extra book does not change (= $\frac{1}{2}$ DVD) as more books are bought.

ORIGIN OF THE IDEA

01.5
Opportunity costs

Choice Limited income forces people to choose what to buy and what to forgo to fulfill wants. You will select the combination of DVDs and paperback books that you think is "best." That is, you will evaluate your marginal benefits and marginal costs (here, product price) to make choices that maximize your satisfaction. Other people, with the same $120 gift card, would undoubtedly make different choices.

Income Changes The location of the budget line varies with money income. An increase in money income shifts the budget line to the right; a decrease in money income shifts it to the left. To verify this, recalculate the table in Figure 1.1, assuming the card value (income) is (a) $240 and (b) $60, and plot the new budget lines in the graph. No wonder people like to have more income: That shifts their budget lines outward and enables them to buy more goods and services. But even with more income, people will still face spending trade-offs, choices, and opportunity costs.

WORKED PROBLEMS

W1.1
Budget lines

CONSIDER THIS . . .

Did Zuckerberg, Winfrey, and James Make Bad Choices?

Opportunity costs come into play in decisions well beyond simple buying decisions. Consider the different choices people make with respect to college. The average salaries earned by college graduates are nearly twice as high as those earned by persons with just high school diplomas. For most capable students, "Go to college, stay in college, and earn a degree" is very sound advice.

Yet Facebook founder Mark Zuckerberg and talk show host Oprah Winfrey* both dropped out of college, and basketball star LeBron James never even bothered to start classes. What were they thinking? Unlike most students, Zukerberg faced enormous opportunity costs for staying in college. He had a vision for his company, and dropping out helped to ensure Facebook's success. Similarly, Winfrey landed a spot in local television news when she was a teenager, eventually producing and starring in the Oprah Winfrey Show when she was 32 years old. Getting a degree in her twenties might have interrupted the string of successes that made her famous talk show possible. And James knew that professional athletes have short careers. Therefore, going to college directly after high school would have taken away four years of his peak earning potential.

So Zuckerberg, Winfrey, and James understood opportunity costs and made their choices accordingly. The size of opportunity costs matters greatly in making individual decisions.

---

*Winfrey eventually went back to school and earned a degree from Tennessee State University when she was in her thirties.

Society's Economizing Problem

LO1.5 List the categories of scarce resources and delineate the nature of society's economizing problem.

Society must also make choices under conditions of scarcity. It, too, faces an economizing problem. Should it devote more of its limited resources to the criminal justice system (police, courts, and prisons) or to education (teachers, books, and schools)? If it decides to devote more resources to both, what other goods and services does it forgo? Health care? Energy development?

Scarce Resources

Society has limited or scarce **economic resources,** meaning all natural, human, and manufactured resources that go into the production of goods and services. This includes the entire set of factory and farm buildings and all the equipment, tools, and machinery used to produce manufactured goods and agricultural products; all transportation and communication facilities; all types of labor; and land and mineral resources.

Resource Categories

Economists classify economic resources into four general categories.

Land Land means much more to the economist than it does to most people. To the economist **land** includes all natural resources ("gifts of nature") used in the production process. These include forests, mineral and oil deposits, water resources, wind power, sunlight, and arable land.

Labor The resource **labor** consists of the physical actions and mental activities that people contribute to the production of goods and services. The work-related activities of a logger, retail clerk, machinist, teacher, professional football player, and nuclear physicist all fall under the general heading "labor."

Capital For economists, **capital** (or capital goods) includes all manufactured aids used in producing consumer goods and services. Included are all factory, storage, transportation, and distribution facilities, as well as tools and machinery. Economists use the term **investment** to describe spending that pays for the production and accumulation of capital goods.

Capital goods differ from consumer goods because consumer goods satisfy wants directly, whereas capital goods do so indirectly by aiding the production of consumer goods. For example, large commercial baking ovens (capital goods) help make loaves of bread (consumer goods). Note that the term "capital" as used by economists refers not to money but to tools, machinery, and other productive equipment. Because money produces nothing, economists do not include it as an economic resource. Money (or money capital or financial capital) is simply a means for purchasing goods and services, including capital goods.

Entrepreneurial Ability Finally, there is the special human resource, distinct from labor, called **entrepreneurial ability**. It is supplied by **entrepreneurs**, who perform several critically important economic functions:

- The entrepreneur takes the initiative in combining the resources of land, labor, and capital to produce a good or a service. Both a sparkplug and a catalyst, the entrepreneur is the driving force behind production and the agent who combines the other resources in what is hoped will be a successful business venture.

- The entrepreneur makes the strategic business decisions that set the course of an enterprise.

- The entrepreneur innovates. He or she commercializes new products, new production techniques, or even new forms of business organization.

- The entrepreneur bears risk. Innovation is risky, as nearly all new products and ideas are subject to the possibility of failure as well as success. Progress would cease without entrepreneurs who are willing to take on risk by devoting their time, effort, and ability—as well as their own money and the money of others—to commercializing new products and ideas that may enhance society's standard of living.

Because land, labor, capital, and entrepreneurial ability are combined to produce goods and services, they are called the **factors of production**, or simply "inputs."

Production Possibilities Model

LO1.6 Apply production possibilities analysis, increasing opportunity costs, and economic growth.

Society uses its scarce resources to produce goods and services. The alternatives and choices it faces can best be understood through a macroeconomic model of production possibilities. To keep things simple, let's initially assume

- *Full employment* The economy is employing all of its available resources.

- *Fixed resources* The quantity and quality of the factors of production are fixed.

- *Fixed technology* The state of technology (the methods used to produce output) is constant.

- *Two goods* The economy is producing only two goods: pizzas and industrial robots. Pizzas symbolize **consumer goods**, products that satisfy our wants directly; industrial robots (for example, the kind used to weld automobile frames) symbolize **capital goods**, products that satisfy our wants indirectly by making possible more efficient production of consumer goods.

Production Possibilities Table

A production possibilities table lists the different combinations of two products that can be produced with a specific set of resources, assuming full employment. Table 1.1 presents a simple, hypothetical economy that is producing pizzas and industrial robots; the data are, of course, hypothetical. At alternative A, this economy would be devoting all its available resources to the production of industrial robots (capital goods); at alternative E, all resources would go to pizza production (consumer goods). Those alternatives are unrealistic extremes; an economy typically produces both capital goods and consumer goods, as in B, C, and D. As we move from alternative A to E, we increase the production of pizzas at the expense of the production of industrial robots.

Because consumer goods satisfy our wants directly, any movement toward E looks tempting. In producing more pizzas, society increases the satisfaction of its current wants. But there is a cost: More pizzas mean fewer industrial robots. This shift of resources to consumer goods catches up with society over time because the stock of capital goods expands more slowly, thereby reducing potential future production. By moving toward alternative E, society chooses "more now" at the expense of "much more later."

By moving toward A, society chooses to forgo current consumption, thereby freeing up resources that can be used to increase the production of capital goods. By building up

TABLE 1.1 Production Possibilities of Pizzas and Industrial Robots

Type of Product	Production Alternatives				
	A	**B**	**C**	**D**	**E**
Pizzas (in hundred thousands)	0	1	2	3	4
Robots (in thousands)	10	9	7	4	0

FIGURE 1.2 **The production possibilities curve.** Each point on the production possibilities curve represents some maximum combination of two products that can be produced if resources are fully employed. When an economy is operating on the curve, more industrial robots means fewer pizzas, and vice versa. Limited resources and a fixed technology make any combination of industrial robots and pizzas lying outside the curve (such as at W) unattainable. Points inside the curve are attainable, but they indicate that full employment is not being realized.

QUICK QUIZ FOR FIGURE 1.2

1. Production possibilities curve *ABCDE* is bowed out from the origin because:
   a. the marginal benefit of pizzas declines as more pizzas are consumed.
   b. the curve gets steeper as we move from *E* to *A*.
   c. it reflects the law of increasing opportunity costs.
   d. resources are scarce.

2. The marginal opportunity cost of the second unit of pizza is:
   a. 2 units of robots.
   b. 3 units of robots.
   c. 7 units of robots.
   d. 9 units of robots.

3. The total opportunity cost of 7 units of robots is:
   a. 1 unit of pizza.
   b. 2 units of pizza.
   c. 3 units of pizza.
   d. 4 units of pizza.

4. All points on this production possibilities curve necessarily represent:
   a. society's optimal choice.
   b. less than full use of resources.
   c. unattainable levels of output.
   d. full employment.

Answers: 1. c; 2. a; 3. b; 4. d

its stock of capital this way, society will have greater future production and, therefore, greater future consumption. By moving toward A, society is choosing "more later" at the cost of "less now."

Generalization: At any point in time, a fully employed economy must sacrifice some of one good to obtain more of another good. Scarce resources prohibit a fully employed economy from having more of both goods. Society must choose among alternatives. There is no such thing as a free pizza, or a free industrial robot. Having more of one thing means having less of something else.

Production Possibilities Curve

The data presented in a production possibilities table are shown graphically as a **production possibilities curve.** Such a curve displays the different combinations of goods and services that society can produce in a fully employed economy, assuming a fixed availability of supplies of resources and fixed technology. We arbitrarily represent the economy's output of capital goods (here, industrial robots) on the vertical axis and the output of consumer goods (here, pizzas) on the horizontal axis, as shown in **Figure 1.2 (Key Graph).**

Each point on the production possibilities curve represents some maximum output of the two products. The curve is a "constraint" because it shows the limit of attainable outputs. Points on the curve are attainable as long as the economy uses all its available resources. Points lying inside the curve are also attainable, but they reflect less total output and therefore are not as desirable as points on the curve. Points inside the curve imply that the economy could have more of both industrial robots and pizzas if it achieved full employment of its resources. Points lying beyond the production possibilities curve, like *W*, would represent a greater output than the output at any point on the curve. Such points, however, are unattainable with the current availability of resources and technology.

Law of Increasing Opportunity Costs

Figure 1.2 clearly shows that more pizzas mean fewer industrial robots. The number of units of industrial robots that must be given up to obtain another unit of pizzas, of course, is the opportunity cost of that unit of pizzas.

In moving from alternative A to alternative B in Table 1.1, the cost of 1 additional unit of pizzas is 1 fewer unit of industrial robots. But when additional units are considered—B to C, C to D, and D to E—an important economic principle is revealed: For society, the opportunity cost of each additional unit of pizzas is greater than the opportunity cost of the preceding one. When we move from A to B, just 1 unit of industrial robots is sacrificed for 1 more unit of pizzas; but in going from B to C we sacrifice 2 additional units of industrial robots for 1 more unit of pizzas; then 3 more of industrial robots for 1 more of pizzas; and finally 4 for 1. Conversely, confirm that as we move from E to A, the cost of an additional unit of industrial robots (on average) is $\frac{1}{4}$, $\frac{1}{3}$, $\frac{1}{2}$, and 1 unit of pizzas, respectively, for the four successive moves.

Our example illustrates the **law of increasing opportunity costs.** As the production of a particular good increases, the opportunity cost of producing an additional unit rises.

Shape of the Curve The law of increasing opportunity costs is reflected in the shape of the production possibilities curve: The curve is bowed out from the origin of the graph. Figure 1.2 shows that when the economy moves from *A* to *E*, it must give up successively larger amounts of industrial robots (1, 2, 3, and 4) to acquire equal increments of pizzas (1, 1, 1, and 1). This is shown in the slope of the production possibilities curve, which becomes steeper as we move from *A* to *E*.

Economic Rationale The law of increasing opportunity costs is driven by the fact that economic resources are not completely adaptable to alternative uses. Many resources are better at producing one type of good than at producing others. Consider land. Some land is highly suited to growing the ingredients necessary for pizza production. But as pizza production expands, society has to start using land that is less bountiful for farming. Other land is rich in mineral deposits and therefore well-suited to producing the materials needed to make industrial robots. That land will be the first land devoted to the production of industrial robots. But as society steps up the production of robots, it must use land that is less and less suited to making their components.

If we start at *A* and move to *B* in Figure 1.2, we can shift resources whose productivity is relatively high in pizza production and low in industrial robots. But as we move from *B* to *C*, *C* to *D*, and so on, resources highly productive in pizzas become increasingly scarce. To get more pizzas, resources whose productivity in industrial robots is relatively great will be needed. Increasingly more of such resources, and hence greater sacrifices of industrial robots, will be needed to achieve each 1-unit increase in pizzas. This lack of perfect flexibility, or interchangeability, on the part of resources is the cause of increasing opportunity costs for society.

WORKED PROBLEMS

W1.2 Production possibilities

Optimal Allocation

Of all the attainable combinations of pizzas and industrial robots on the curve in Figure 1.2, which is optimal (best)? That is, what specific quantities of resources should be allocated to pizzas and what specific quantities should be allocated to industrial robots in order to maximize satisfaction?

Recall that economic decisions center on comparisons of marginal benefit (MB) and marginal cost (MC). Any economic activity should be expanded as long as marginal benefit exceeds marginal cost and should be reduced if marginal cost exceeds marginal benefit. The optimal amount of the activity occurs where MB = MC. Society needs to make a similar assessment about its production decision.

Consider pizzas. We already know from the law of increasing opportunity costs that the marginal cost of additional units of pizza will rise as more units are produced. At the same time, we need to recognize that the extra or marginal benefits that come from producing and consuming pizza decline with each successive unit of pizza. Consequently, each successive unit of pizza brings with it both increasing marginal costs and decreasing marginal benefits.

The optimal quantity of pizza production is indicated by point *e* at the intersection of the MB and MC curves: 200,000 units in Figure 1.3. Why is this amount the optimal quantity? If only 100,000 units of pizzas were produced, the marginal benefit of an extra unit of pizza (point *a*) would exceed its marginal cost (point *b*). In money terms, MB is $15, while MC is only $5. When society gains something worth $15 at a marginal cost of only $5, it is better off. In Figure 1.3, net gains can continue to be realized until pizza-product production has been increased to 200,000.

FIGURE 1.3 Optimal output: MB = MC. Achieving the optimal output requires the expansion of a good's output until its marginal benefit (MB) and marginal cost (MC) are equal. No resources beyond that point should be allocated to the product. Here, optimal output occurs at point *e,* where 200,000 units of pizzas are produced.

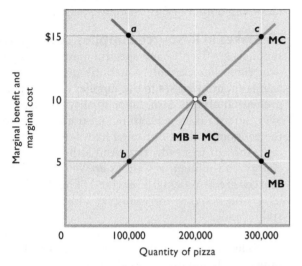

In contrast, the production of 300,000 units of pizzas is excessive. There the MC of an added unit is $15 (point *c*) and its MB is only $5 (point *d*). This means that 1 unit of pizza is worth only $5 to society but costs it $15 to obtain. This is a losing proposition for society!

So resources are being efficiently allocated to any product when the marginal benefit and marginal cost of its output are equal (MB = MC). Suppose that by applying the same analysis to industrial robots, we find that the optimal (MB = MC) quantity of robots is 7,000. This would mean that alternative *C* (200,000 units of pizzas and 7,000 units of industrial robots) on the production possibilities curve in Figure 1.2 would be optimal for this economy.

QUICK REVIEW 1.3

- Economists categorize economic resources as land, labor, capital, and entrepreneurial ability.
- The production possibilities curve illustrates several ideas: (a) scarcity of resources is implied by the area of unattainable combinations of output lying outside the production possibilities curve; (b) choice among outputs is reflected in the variety of attainable combinations of goods lying along the curve; (c) opportunity cost is illustrated by the downward slope of the curve; (d) the law of increasing opportunity costs is reflected in the bowed-outward shape of the curve.
- A comparison of marginal benefits and marginal costs is needed to determine the best or optimal output mix on a production possibilities curve.

CONSIDER THIS . . .

The Economics of War

Production possibilities analysis is helpful in assessing the costs and benefits of waging the broad war on terrorism, including the wars in Afghanistan and Iraq. At the end of 2011, the estimated cost of these efforts exceeded $1.4 trillion.

If we categorize all U.S. production as either "defense goods" or "civilian goods," we can measure them on the axes of a production possibilities diagram such as that shown in Figure 1.2. The opportunity cost of using more resources for defense goods is the civilian goods sacrificed. In a fully employed economy, more defense goods are achieved at the opportunity cost of fewer civilian goods—health care, education, pollution control, personal computers, houses, and so on. The cost of war and defense is the other goods forgone. The benefits of these activities are numerous and diverse but clearly include the gains from protecting against future loss of American lives, assets, income, and well-being.

Society must assess the marginal benefit (MB) and marginal cost (MC) of additional defense goods to determine their optimal amounts—where to locate on the defense goods–civilian goods production possibilities curve. Although estimating marginal benefits and marginal costs is an imprecise art, the MB-MC framework is a useful way of approaching choices. An optimal allocation of resources requires that society expand production of defense goods until MB = MC.

The events of September 11, 2001, and the future threats they foreshadowed increased the marginal benefits of defense goods, as perceived by Americans. If we label the horizontal axis in Figure 1.3 "defense goods" and draw in a rightward shift of the MB curve, you will see that the optimal quantity of defense goods rises. In view of the concerns relating to September 11, the United States allocated more of its resources to defense. But the MB-MC analysis also reminds us we can spend too much on defense, as well as too little. The United States should not expand defense goods beyond the point where MB = MC. If it does, it will be sacrificing civilian goods of greater value than the defense goods obtained.

Unemployment, Growth, and the Future

LO1.7 Explain how economic growth and international trade increase consumption possibilities.

In the depths of the Great Depression of the 1930s, one-quarter of U.S. workers were unemployed and one-third of

U.S. production capacity was idle. Subsequent downturns have been much less severe. During the deep 2007–2009 recession, for instance, production fell by a comparably smaller 3.7 percent and 1-in-10 workers was without a job.

Almost all nations have experienced widespread unemployment and unused production capacity from business downturns at one time or another. Since 2000, for example, many nations—including Argentina, Japan, Mexico, Germany, and South Korea—have had economic downturns and unemployment.

How do these realities relate to the production possibilities model? Our analysis and conclusions change if we relax the assumption that all available resources are fully employed. The five alternatives in Table 1.1 represent maximum outputs; they illustrate the combinations of pizzas and industrial robots that can be produced when the economy is operating at full employment. With unemployment, this economy would produce less than each alternative shown in the table.

Graphically, we represent situations of unemployment by points inside the original production possibilities curve (reproduced here in Figure 1.4). Point *U* is one such point. Here the economy is falling short of the various maximum combinations of pizzas and industrial robots represented by the points on the production possibilities curve. The arrows in Figure 1.4 indicate three possible paths back to full employment. A move toward full employment would yield a greater output of one or both products.

FIGURE 1.4 Unemployment and the production possibilities curve. Any point inside the production possibilities curve, such as *U*, represents unemployment or a failure to achieve full employment. The arrows indicate that by realizing full employment, the economy could operate on the curve. This means it could produce more of one or both products than it is producing at point *U*.

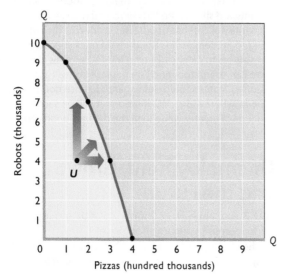

A Growing Economy

When we drop the assumptions that the quantity and quality of resources and technology are fixed, the production possibilities curve shifts positions and the potential maximum output of the economy changes.

Increases in Resource Supplies Although resource supplies are fixed at any specific moment, they change over time. For example, a nation's growing population brings about increases in the supplies of labor and entrepreneurial ability. Also, labor quality usually improves over time via more education and training. Historically, the economy's stock of capital has increased at a significant, though unsteady, rate. And although some of our energy and mineral resources are being depleted, new sources are also being discovered. The development of irrigation systems, for example, adds to the supply of arable land.

The net result of these increased supplies of the factors of production is the ability to produce more of both consumer goods and capital goods. Thus, 20 years from now, the production possibilities may supersede those shown in Table 1.1. The new production possibilities might look like those in the table in Figure 1.5. The greater abundance of resources will result in a greater potential output of one or both products at each alternative. The economy will have achieved economic growth in the form of expanded potential output. Thus, when an increase in the quantity or quality of resources occurs, the production possibilities curve shifts outward and to the right, as illustrated by the move from the inner curve to curve *A′B′C′D′E′* in Figure 1.5. This sort of shift represents growth of economic capacity, which, when used, means **economic growth:** a larger total output.

Advances in Technology An advancing technology brings both new and better goods and improved ways of producing them. For now, let's think of technological advance as being only improvements in the methods of production, for example, the introduction of computerized systems to manage inventories and schedule production. These advances alter our previous discussion of the economizing problem by allowing society to produce more goods with available resources. As with increases in resource supplies, technological advances make possible the production of more industrial robots *and* more pizzas.

A real-world example of improved technology is the recent surge of new technologies relating to computers, communications, and biotechnology. Technological advances have dropped the prices of computers and greatly

FIGURE 1.5 Economic growth and the production possibilities curve. The increase in supplies of resources, improvements in resource quality, and technological advances that occur in a dynamic economy move the production possibilities curve outward and to the right, allowing the economy to have larger quantities of both types of goods.

Type of Product	Production Alternatives				
	A′	B′	C′	D′	E′
Pizzas (in hundred thousands)	0	2	4	6	8
Robots (in thousands)	14	12	9	5	0

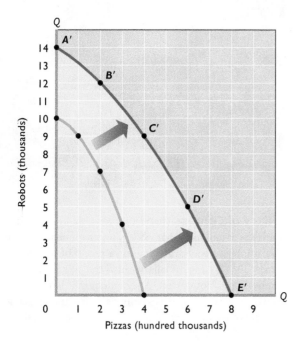

Present Choices and Future Possibilities

An economy's current choice of positions on its production possibilities curve helps determine the future location of that curve. Let's designate the two axes of the production possibilities curve as "goods for the future" and "goods for the present," as in Figure 1.6. Goods for the future are such

FIGURE 1.6 Present choices and future locations of production possibilities curves. (a) Presentville's current choice to produce more "present goods" and fewer "future goods," as represented by point *P*, will result in a modest outward shift of the production possibilities curve in the future. (b) Futureville's current choice of producing fewer "present goods" and more "future goods," as depicted by point *F*, will lead to a greater outward shift of the production possibilities curve in the future.

(a)
Presentville

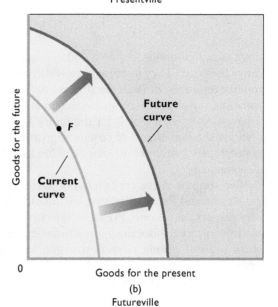

(b)
Futureville

increased their speed. Improved software has greatly increased the everyday usefulness of computers. Cellular phones and the Internet have increased communications capacity, enhancing production and improving the efficiency of markets. Advances in biotechnology have resulted in important agricultural and medical discoveries. These and other new and improved technologies have contributed to U.S. economic growth (outward shifts of the nation's production possibilities curve).

Conclusion: Economic growth is the result of (1) increases in supplies of resources, (2) improvements in resource quality, and (3) technological advances. The consequence of growth is that a full-employment economy can enjoy a greater output of both consumption goods and capital goods. Whereas static, no-growth economies must sacrifice some of one good to obtain more of another, dynamic, growing economies can have larger quantities of both goods.

Pitfalls to Sound Economic Reasoning

Because They Affect Us So Personally, We Often Have Difficulty Thinking Accurately and Objectively About Economic Issues.

Here are some common pitfalls to avoid in successfully applying the economic perspective.

Biases Most people bring a bundle of biases and preconceptions to the field of economics. For example, some might think that corporate profits are excessive or that lending money is always superior to borrowing money. Others might believe that government is necessarily less efficient than businesses or that more government regulation is always better than less. Biases cloud thinking and interfere with objective analysis. All of us must be willing to shed biases and preconceptions that are not supported by facts.

Loaded Terminology The economic terminology used in newspapers and broadcast media is sometimes emotionally biased, or loaded. The writer or spokesperson may have a cause to promote or an ax to grind and may slant comments accordingly. High profits may be labeled "obscene," low wages may be called "exploitative," or self-interested behavior may be "greed." Government workers may be referred to as "mindless bureaucrats" and those favoring stronger government regulations may be called "socialists." To objectively analyze economic issues, you must be prepared to reject or discount such terminology.

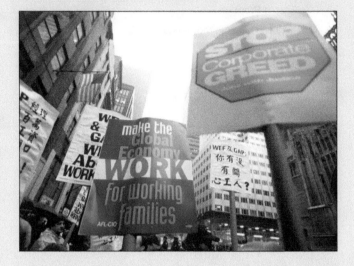

Fallacy of Composition Another pitfall in economic thinking is the assumption that what is true for one individual or part of a whole is necessarily true for a group of individuals or the whole. This is a logical fallacy called the *fallacy of composition;* the assumption is not correct. A statement that is valid for an individual or part is not necessarily valid for the larger group or whole. Noneconomic example: You may see the action better if

things as capital goods, research and education, and preventive medicine. They increase the quantity and quality of property resources, enlarge the stock of technological information, and improve the quality of human resources. As we have already seen, goods for the future such as capital goods are the ingredients of economic growth. Goods for the present are consumer goods such as food, clothing, and entertainment.

Now suppose there are two hypothetical economies, Presentville and Futureville, that are initially identical in every respect except one: Presentville's current choice of positions on its production possibilities curve strongly favors present goods over future goods. Point *P* in Figure 1.6a indicates that choice. It is located quite far down the curve to the right, indicating a high priority

for goods for the present, at the expense of less goods for the future. Futureville, in contrast, makes a current choice that stresses larger amounts of future goods and smaller amounts of present goods, as shown by point *F* in Figure 1.6b.

Now, other things equal, we can expect Futureville's future production possibilities curve to be farther to the right than Presentville's future production possibilities curve. By currently choosing an output more favorable to technological advances and to increases in the quantity and quality of resources, Futureville will achieve greater economic growth than Presentville. In terms of capital goods, Futureville is choosing to make larger current additions to its "national factory" by devoting more of its current output to capital than does Presentville. The you leap to your feet to see an outstanding play at a football game. But if all the spectators leap to their feet at the same time, nobody—including you—will have a better view than when all remained seated.

Here are two economic examples: An individual stockholder can sell shares of, say, Google stock without affecting the price of the stock. The individual's sale will not noticeably reduce the share price because the sale is a negligible fraction of the total shares of Google being bought and sold. But if all the Google shareholders decide to sell their shares the same day, the market will be flooded with shares and the stock price will fall precipitously. Similarly, a single cattle ranch can increase its revenue by expanding the size of its livestock herd. The extra cattle will not affect the price of cattle when they are brought to market. But if all ranchers as a group expand their herds, the total output of cattle will increase so much that the price of cattle will decline when the cattle are sold. If the price reduction is relatively large, ranchers as a group might find that their income has fallen despite their having sold a greater number of cattle because the fall in price overwhelms the increase in quantity.

Post Hoc Fallacy You must think very carefully before concluding that because event A precedes event B, A is the cause of B. This kind of faulty reasoning is known as the *post hoc, ergo propter hoc,* or "after this, therefore because of this," fallacy. Noneconomic example: A professional football team hires a new coach and the team's record improves. Is the new coach the cause? Maybe. Perhaps the presence of more experienced and talented players or an easier schedule is the true cause. The rooster crows before dawn but does not cause the sunrise.

Economic example: Many people blamed the Great Depression of the 1930s on the stock market crash of 1929. But the crash did not cause the Great Depression. The same severe weaknesses in the economy that caused the crash caused the Great Depression. The depression would have occurred even without the preceding stock market crash.

Correlation but Not Causation Do not confuse correlation, or connection, with causation. Correlation between two events or two sets of data indicates only that they are associated in some systematic and dependable way. For example, we may find that when variable X increases, Y also increases. But this correlation does not necessarily mean that there is causation—that increases in X cause increases in Y. The relationship could be purely coincidental or dependent on some other factor, Z, not included in the analysis.

Here is an example: Economists have found a positive correlation between education and income. In general, people with more education earn higher incomes than those with less education. Common sense suggests education is the cause and higher incomes are the effect; more education implies a more knowledgeable and productive worker, and such workers receive larger salaries.

But might the relationship be explainable in other ways? Are education and income correlated because the characteristics required for succeeding in education—ability and motivation—are the same ones required to be a productive and highly paid worker? If so, then people with those traits will probably both obtain more education and earn higher incomes. But greater education will not be the sole cause of the higher income.

payoff from this choice for Futureville is greater future production capacity and economic growth. The opportunity cost is fewer consumer goods in the present for Futureville to enjoy.

Is Futureville's choice thus necessarily "better" than Presentville's? That, we cannot say. The different outcomes simply reflect different preferences and priorities in the two countries. But each country will have to live with the economic consequences of its choice.

A Qualification: International Trade

Production possibilities analysis implies that an individual nation is limited to the combinations of output indicated by its production possibilities curve. But we must modify this principle when international specialization and trade exist.

You will see in later chapters that an economy can circumvent, through international specialization and trade, the output limits imposed by its domestic production possibilities curve. Under international specialization and trade, each nation first specializes in the production of those items for which it has the lowest opportunity costs (due to an abundance of the necessary resources). Countries then engage in international trade, with each country exchanging the items that it can produce at the lowest opportunity costs for the items that other countries can produce at the lowest opportunity costs.

International specialization and trade allow a nation to get more of a desired good at less sacrifice of some other good. Rather than sacrifice three units of domestically produced robots to get a third unit of domestically produced pizza, as in Table 1.1, a nation that engages in international specialization and trade might be able to do much better. If it specializes in robots while another country specializes in pizza, then it may be able to obtain the third unit of pizza by trading only two units of domestically produced robots for one unit of foreign-produced pizza. Specialization and trade have the same effect as having more and better resources or discovering improved production techniques; both increase the quantities of capital and consumer goods available to society. Expansion of domestic production possibilities and international trade are two separate routes for obtaining greater output.

QUICK REVIEW 1.4

- Unemployment causes an economy to operate at a point inside its production possibilities curve.
- Increases in resource supplies, improvements in resource quality, and technological advance cause economic growth, which is depicted as an outward shift of the production possibilities curve.
- An economy's present choice of capital and consumer goods helps determine the future location of its production possibilities curve.
- International specialization and trade enable a nation to obtain more goods than its production possibilities curve indicates.

SUMMARY

LO1.1 Define economics and the features of the economic perspective.

Economics is the social science that examines how individuals, institutions, and society make optimal choices under conditions of scarcity. Central to economics is the idea of opportunity cost: the value of the next-best good or service forgone to obtain something.

The economic perspective includes three elements: scarcity and choice, purposeful behavior, and marginal analysis. It sees individuals and institutions making rational decisions based on comparisons of marginal costs and marginal benefits.

LO1.2 Describe the role of economic theory in economics.

Economists employ the scientific method, in which they form and test hypotheses of cause-and-effect relationships to generate theories, laws, and principles. Economists often combine theories into representations called models.

LO1.3 Distinguish microeconomics from macroeconomics and positive economics from normative economics.

Microeconomics examines the decision making of specific economic units or institutions. Macroeconomics looks at the economy as a whole or its major aggregates.

Positive economic analysis deals with facts; normative economics reflects value judgments.

LO1.4 Explain the individual's economizing problem and how trade-offs, opportunity costs, and attainable combinations can be illustrated with budget lines.

Individuals face an economizing problem. Because their wants exceed their incomes, they must decide what to purchase and what to forgo. Society also faces an economizing problem. Societal wants exceed the available resources necessary to fulfill them. Society therefore must decide what to produce and what to forgo.

Graphically, a budget line (or budget constraint) illustrates the economizing problem for individuals. The line shows the various combinations of two products that a consumer can purchase with a specific money income, given the prices of the two products.

LO1.5 List the categories of scarce resources and delineate the nature of society's economizing problem.

Economic resources are inputs into the production process and can be classified as land, labor, capital, or entrepreneurial ability. Economic resources are also known as factors of production or inputs.

Economists illustrate society's economizing problem through production possibilities analysis. Production possibilities tables and curves show the different combinations of goods and services that can be produced in a fully employed economy, assuming that resource quantity, resource quality, and technology are fixed.

LO1.6 Apply production possibilities analysis, increasing opportunity costs, and economic growth.

An economy that is fully employed and thus operating on its production possibilities curve must sacrifice the output of some types of goods and services to increase the production of others. The gain of one type of good or service is always accompanied by an opportunity cost in the form of the loss of some of the other type of good or service.

Because resources are not equally productive in all possible uses, shifting resources from one use to another creates increasing opportunity costs. The production of additional units of one product requires the sacrifice of increasing amounts of the other product.

The optimal (best) point on the production possibilities curve represents the most desirable mix of goods and is determined by expanding the production of each good until its marginal benefit (MB) equals its marginal cost (MC).

LO1.7 Explain how economic growth and international trade increase consumption possibilities.

Over time, technological advances and increases in the quantity and quality of resources enable the economy to produce more of all goods and services, that is, to experience economic growth. Society's choice as to the mix of consumer goods and capital goods in current output is a major determinant of the future location of the production possibilities curve and thus of the extent of economic growth.

International trade enables a nation to obtain more goods from its limited resources than its production possibilities curve indicates.

TERMS AND CONCEPTS

economics	macroeconomics	investment
economic perspective	aggregate	entrepreneurial ability
scarcity	positive economics	entrepreneurs
opportunity cost	normative economics	factors of production
utility	economizing problem	consumer goods
marginal analysis	budget line	capital goods
scientific method	economic resources	production possibilities curve
economic principle	land	law of increasing
other-things-equal assumption	labor	opportunity costs
microeconomics	capital	economic growth

The following and additional problems can be found in **connect**
ECONOMICS

DISCUSSION QUESTIONS

1. What is an opportunity cost? How does the idea relate to the definition of economics? Which of the following decisions would entail the greater opportunity cost: Allocating a square block in the heart of New York City for a surface parking lot or allocating a square block at the edge of a typical suburb for such a lot? Explain. **LO1.1**

2. Cite three examples of recent decisions that you made in which you, at least implicitly, weighed marginal cost and marginal benefit. **LO1.1**

3. What is meant by the term "utility" and how does the idea relate to purposeful behavior? **LO1.1**

4. What are the key elements of the scientific method and how does this method relate to economic principles and laws? **LO1.2**

5. State (a) a positive economic statement of your choice, and then (b) a normative economic statement relating to your first statement. **LO1.3**

6. How does the slope of a budget line illustrate opportunity costs and trade-offs? How does a budget line illustrate scarcity and the effect of limited incomes? **LO1.4**

7. What are economic resources? What categories do economists use to classify them? Why are resources also called factors of production? Why are they called inputs? **LO1.5**

8. Why is money not considered to be a capital resource in economics? Why is entrepreneurial ability considered a category of economic resource, distinct from labor? What are the major functions of the entrepreneur? **LO1.5**

9. Specify and explain the typical shapes of marginal-benefit and marginal-cost curves. How are these curves used to determine the optimal allocation of resources to a particular product? If current output is such that marginal cost exceeds marginal benefit, should more or fewer resources be allocated to this product? Explain. **LO1.6**

10. Suppose that, on the basis of a nation's production possibilities curve, an economy must sacrifice 10,000 pizzas domestically to get the 1 additional industrial robot it desires but that it can get the robot from another country in exchange for 9,000 pizzas. Relate this information to the following statement: "Through international specialization and trade, a nation can reduce its opportunity cost of obtaining goods and thus 'move outside its production possibilities curve.'" **LO1.7**

11. **LAST WORD** Studies indicate that married men on average earn more income than unmarried men of the same age and education level. Why must we be cautious in concluding that marriage is the cause and higher income is the effect?

REVIEW QUESTIONS

1. Match each term with the correct definition. **LO1.1**
   economics
   opportunity cost
   marginal analysis
   utility
   a. The next-best thing that must be forgone in order to produce one more unit of a given product.
   b. The pleasure, happiness, or satisfaction obtained from consuming a good or service.
   c. The social science concerned with how individuals, institutions, and society make optimal (best) choices under conditions of scarcity.
   d. Making choices based on comparing marginal benefits with marginal costs.

2. Indicate whether each of the following statements applies to microeconomics or macroeconomics: **LO1.3**
   a. The unemployment rate in the United States was 8.1 percent in August 2012.
   b. A U.S. software firm discharged 15 workers last month and transferred the work to India.
   c. An unexpected freeze in central Florida reduced the citrus crop and caused the price of oranges to rise.
   d. U.S. output, adjusted for inflation, decreased by 2.4 percent in 2009.
   e. Last week Wells Fargo Bank lowered its interest rate on business loans by one-half of 1 percentage point.
   f. The consumer price index rose by 3.8 percent from August 2011 to August 2012.

3. Suppose that you initially have $100 to spend on books or movie tickets. The books start off costing $25 each and the movie tickets start off costing $10 each. For each of the following situations, would the attainable set of combinations that you can afford increase or decrease? **LO1.4**
   a. Your budget increases from $100 to $150 while the prices stay the same.

   b. Your budget remains $100, the price of books remains $25, but the price of movie tickets rises to $20.
   c. Your budget remains $100, the price of movie tickets remains $10, but the price of a book falls to $15.

4. Suppose that you are given a $100 budget at work that can be spent only on two items: staplers and pens. If staplers cost $10 each and pens cost $2.50 each, then the opportunity cost of purchasing one stapler is: **LO1.4**
   a. 10 pens.
   b. 5 pens.
   c. zero pens.
   d. 4 pens.

5. For each of the following situations involving marginal cost (MC) and marginal benefit (MB), indicate whether it would be best to produce more, fewer, or the current number of units. **LO1.4**
   a. 3,000 units at which MC = $10 and MB = $13.
   b. 11 units at which MC = $4 and MB = $3.
   c. 43,277 units at which MC = $99 and MB = $99.
   d. 82 units at which MC < MB.
   e. 5 units at which MB < MC.

6. Explain how (if at all) each of the following events affects the location of a country's production possibilities curve: **LO1.6**
   a. The quality of education increases.
   b. The number of unemployed workers increases.
   c. A new technique improves the efficiency of extracting copper from ore.
   d. A devastating earthquake destroys numerous production facilities.

7. What are the two major ways in which an economy can grow and push out its production possibilities curve? **LO1.7**
   a. Better weather and nicer cars.
   b. Higher taxes and lower spending.
   c. Increases in resource supplies and advances in technology.
   d. Decreases in scarcity and advances in auditing.

PROBLEMS

1. Potatoes cost Janice $1 per pound, and she has $5.00 that she could possibly spend on potatoes or other items. If she feels that the first pound of potatoes is worth $1.50, the second pound is worth $1.14, the third pound is worth $1.05, and all subsequent pounds are worth $0.30, how many pounds of potatoes will she purchase? What if she only had $2 to spend? **LO1.1**

2. Pham can work as many or as few hours as she wants at the college bookstore for $9 per hour. But due to her hectic schedule, she has just 15 hours per week that she can spend working at either the bookstore or other potential jobs. One potential job, at a café, will pay her $12 per hour for up to 6 hours per week. She has another job offer at a garage that will pay her $10 an hour for up to 5 hours per

week. And she has a potential job at a daycare center that will pay her $8.50 per hour for as many hours as she can work. If her goal is to maximize the amount of money she can make each week, how many hours will she work at the bookstore? **LO1.1**

3. Suppose you won $15 on a lotto ticket at the local 7-Eleven and decided to spend all the winnings on candy bars and bags of peanuts. Candy bars cost $0.75 each while bags of peanuts cost $1.50 each. **LO1.5**
   a. Construct a table showing the alternative combinations of the two products that are available.
   b. Plot the data in your table as a budget line in a graph. What is the slope of the budget line? What is the opportunity cost of one more candy bar? Of one more bag of

peanuts? Do these opportunity costs rise, fall, or remain constant as additional units are purchased?

c. Does the budget line tell you which of the available combinations of candy bars and bags of peanuts to buy?

d. Suppose that you had won $30 on your ticket, not $15. Show the $30 budget line in your diagram. Has the number of available combinations increased or decreased?

4. Suppose that you are on a desert island and possess exactly 20 coconuts. Your neighbor, Friday, is a fisherman, and he is willing to trade 2 fish for every 1 coconut that you are willing to give him. Another neighbor, Kwame, is also a fisherman, and he is willing to trade 3 fish for every 1 coconut. **LO1.5**

a. On a single figure, draw budget lines for trading with Friday and for trading with Kwame. (Put coconuts on the vertical axis.)

b. What is the slope of the budget line from trading with Friday?

c. What is the slope of the budget line from trading with Kwame?

d. Which budget line features a larger set of attainable combinations of coconuts and fish?

e. If you are going to trade coconuts for fish, would you rather trade with Friday or Kwame?

5. To the right is a production possibilities table for consumer goods (automobiles) and capital goods (forklifts): **LO1.6**

a. Show these data graphically. Upon what specific assumptions is this production possibilities curve based?

b. If the economy is at point C, what is the cost of one more automobile? Of one more forklift? Which characteristic of the production possibilities curve reflects the law of increasing opportunity costs: its shape or its length?

c. If the economy characterized by this production possibilities table and curve were producing 3 automobiles and 20 forklifts, what could you conclude about its use of its available resources?

d. Is production at a point outside the production possibilities curve currently possible? Could a future advance in technology allow production beyond the current production possibilities curve? Could international trade allow a country to consume beyond its current production possibilities curve?

Type of Production	Production Alternatives				
	A	**B**	**C**	**D**	**E**
Automobiles	0	2	4	6	8
Forklifts	30	27	21	12	0

6. Look at Figure 1.3. Suppose that the cost of cheese falls, so that the marginal cost of producing pizza decreases. Will the MC curve shift up or down? Will the optimal amount of pizza increase or decrease? **LO1.6**

7. Referring to the table in problem 5, suppose improvement occurs in the technology of producing forklifts but not in the technology of producing automobiles. Draw the new production possibilities curve. Now assume that a technological advance occurs in producing automobiles but not in producing forklifts. Draw the new production possibilities curve. Now draw a production possibilities curve that reflects technological improvement in the production of both goods. **LO1.7**

8. Because investment and capital goods are paid for with savings, higher savings rates reflect a decision to consume fewer goods for the present in order to be able to invest in more goods for the future. Households in China save 40 percent of their annual incomes each year, whereas U.S. households save less than 5 percent. At the same time, production possibilities are growing at roughly 9 percent per year in China but only about 3.5 percent per year in the United States. Use graphical analysis of "present goods" versus "future goods" to explain the difference between China's growth rate and the U.S. growth rate. **LO1.7**

Graphs and Their Meaning

LO1.8 Understand graphs, curves, and slopes as they relate to economics.

If you glance quickly through this text, you will find many graphs. Some seem simple, while others seem more formidable. All are included to help you visualize and understand economic relationships. Physicists and chemists sometimes illustrate their theories by building arrangements of multicolored wooden balls, representing protons, neutrons, and electrons, that are held in proper relation to one another by wires or sticks. Economists most often use graphs to illustrate their models. By understanding these "pictures," you can more readily comprehend economic relationships.

Construction of a Graph

A *graph* is a visual representation of the relationship between two economic quantities, or variables. The table in Figure 1 is a hypothetical illustration showing the relationship between income and consumption for the economy as a whole. Without even studying economics, we would logically expect that people would buy more goods and services when their incomes go up. Thus, it is not surprising to find in the table that total consumption in the economy increases as total income increases.

The information in the table is expressed graphically in Figure 1. Here is how it is done: We want to show visually how consumption changes as income changes. We therefore represent income on the **horizontal axis** of the graph and consumption on the **vertical axis.**

Now we arrange the vertical and horizontal scales of the graph to reflect the ranges of values of consumption and

income and mark the scales in convenient increments. As you can see, the values marked on the scales cover all the values in the table. The increments on both scales are $100.

Because the graph has two dimensions, each point within it represents an income value and its associated consumption value. To find a point that represents one of the five income-consumption combinations in the table in Figure 1, we draw straight lines from the appropriate values on the vertical and horizontal axes. For example, to plot point *c* (the $200 income–$150 consumption point), we draw straight lines up from the horizontal (income) axis at $200 and across from the vertical (consumption) axis at $150. These lines intersect at point *c*, which represents this particular income-consumption combination. You should verify that the other income-consumption combinations shown in the table are properly located in the graph in Figure 1. Finally, by assuming that the same general relationship between income and consumption prevails for all other incomes, we draw a line or smooth curve to connect these points. That line or curve represents the income-consumption relationship.

If the curve is a straight line, as in Figure 1, we say the relationship is *linear.* (It is permissible, and even customary, to refer to straight lines in graphs as "curves.")

Direct and Inverse Relationships

The line in Figure 1 slopes upward to the right, so it depicts a direct relationship between income and consumption. By a **direct relationship** (or positive relationship) we mean that two variables—in this case, consumption and

FIGURE 1 **Graphing the direct relationship between consumption and income.** Two sets of data that are positively or directly related, such as consumption and income, graph as an upsloping line.

Income per Week	Consumption per Week	Point
$ 0	$ 50	a
100	100	b
200	150	c
300	200	d
400	250	e

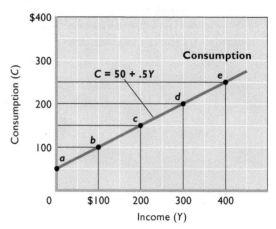

income—change in the *same* direction. An increase in consumption is associated with an increase in income; a decrease in consumption accompanies a decrease in income. When two sets of data are positively or directly related, they always graph as an *upsloping* line, as in Figure 1.

In contrast, two sets of data may be inversely related. Consider the table in Figure 2, which shows the relationship between the price of basketball tickets and game attendance at Gigantic State University (GSU). Here we have an **inverse relationship** (or negative relationship) because the two variables change in *opposite* directions. When ticket prices decrease, attendance increases. When ticket prices increase, attendance decreases. The six data points in the table in Figure 2 are plotted in the graph. Observe that an inverse relationship always graphs as a *downsloping* line.

Dependent and Independent Variables

Although it is not always easy, economists seek to determine which variable is the "cause" and which is the "effect." Or, more formally, they seek the independent variable and the dependent variable. The **independent variable** is the cause or source; it is the variable that changes first. The **dependent variable** is the effect or outcome; it is the variable that changes because of the change in the independent variable. As in our income-consumption example, income generally is the independent variable and consumption the dependent variable. Income causes consumption to be what it is rather than the other way around. Similarly, ticket prices (set in advance of the season and printed on the ticket) determine attendance at GSU basketball games; attendance at games

does not determine the printed ticket prices for those games. Ticket price is the independent variable and the quantity of tickets purchased is the dependent variable.

You may recall from your high school courses that mathematicians put the independent variable (cause) on the horizontal axis and the dependent variable (effect) on the vertical axis. Economists are less tidy; their graphing of independent and dependent variables is more arbitrary. Their conventional graphing of the income-consumption relationship is consistent with mathematical convention, but economists put price and cost data on the vertical axis. Hence, economists' graphing of GSU's ticket price–attendance data differs from normal mathematical procedure. This does not present a problem, but we want you to be aware of this fact to avoid any possible confusion.

Other Things Equal

Our simple two-variable graphs purposely ignore many other factors that might affect the amount of consumption occurring at each income level or the number of people who attend GSU basketball games at each possible ticket price. When economists plot the relationship between any two variables, they employ the *ceteris paribus* (other-things-equal) assumption. Thus, in Figure 1 all factors other than income that might affect the amount of consumption are presumed to be constant or unchanged. Similarly, in Figure 2 all factors other than ticket price that might influence attendance at GSU basketball games are assumed constant. In reality, "other things" are not equal; they often change, and when they do, the relationship represented in our two tables and graphs will change. Specifically, the lines we have plotted would *shift* to new locations.

FIGURE 2 Graphing the inverse relationship between ticket prices and game attendance. Two sets of data that are negatively or inversely related, such as ticket price and the attendance at basketball games, graph as a downsloping line.

Ticket Price	Attendance, Thousands	Point
$50	0	a
40	4	b
30	8	c
20	12	d
10	16	e
0	20	f

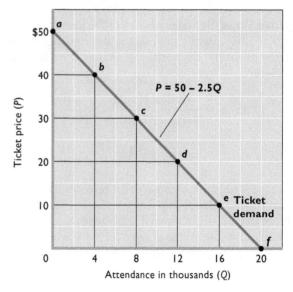

Consider a stock market "crash." The dramatic drop in the value of stocks might cause people to feel less wealthy and therefore less willing to consume at each level of income. The result might be a downward shift of the consumption line. To see this, you should plot a new consumption line in Figure 1, assuming that consumption is, say, $20 less at each income level. Note that the relationship remains direct; the line merely shifts downward to reflect less consumption spending at each income level.

Similarly, factors other than ticket prices might affect GSU game attendance. If GSU loses most of its games, attendance at GSU games might be less at each ticket price. To see this, redraw Figure 2 assuming that 2,000 fewer fans attend GSU games at each ticket price.

Slope of a Line

Lines can be described in terms of their slopes. The **slope of a straight line** is the ratio of the vertical change (the rise or drop) to the horizontal change (the run) between any two points of the line.

Positive Slope Between point b and point c in Figure 1, the rise or vertical change (the change in consumption) is +$50 and the run or horizontal change (the change in income) is +$100. Therefore:

$$\text{Slope} = \frac{\text{vertical change}}{\text{horizontal change}} = \frac{+50}{+100} = \frac{1}{2} = .5$$

Note that our slope of $\frac{1}{2}$ or .5 is positive because consumption and income change in the same direction; that is, consumption and income are directly or positively related.

The slope of .5 tells us there will be a $0.50 increase in consumption for every $1 increase in income. Similarly, there will be a $0.50 decrease in consumption for every $1 decrease in income.

Negative Slope Between any two of the identified points in Figure 2, say, point c and point d, the vertical change is −10 (the drop) and the horizontal change is +4 (the run). Therefore:

$$\text{Slope} = \frac{\text{vertical change}}{\text{horizontal change}} = \frac{-10}{+4}$$

$$= -2\frac{1}{2} = -2.5$$

This slope is negative because ticket price and attendance have an inverse relationship.

Note that on the horizontal axis attendance is stated in thousands of people. So the slope of −10/+4 or −2.5 means that lowering the price by $10 will increase attendance by 4,000 people. That ratio also implies that a $2.50 price reduction will increase attendance by 1,000 persons.

Slopes and Measurement Units The slope of a line will be affected by the choice of units for either variable. If, in our ticket price illustration, we had chosen to measure attendance in individual people, our horizontal change would have been 4,000 and the slope would have been

$$\text{Slope} = \frac{-10}{+4,000} = \frac{-1}{+400} = -.0025$$

The slope depends on the way the relevant variables are measured.

Slopes and Marginal Analysis Recall that economics is largely concerned with changes from the status quo. The concept of slope is important in economics because it reflects marginal changes—those involving 1 more (or 1 fewer) unit. For example, in Figure 1 the .5 slope shows that $0.50 of extra or marginal consumption is associated with each $1 change in income. In this example, people collectively will consume $0.50 of any $1 increase in their incomes and reduce their consumption by $0.50 for each $1 decline in income.

Infinite and Zero Slopes Many variables are unrelated or independent of one another. For example, the quantity of wristwatches purchased is not related to the price of bananas. In Figure 3a we represent the price of bananas on the vertical axis and the quantity of watches demanded on the horizontal axis. The graph of their relationship is the line parallel to the vertical axis. The line's vertical slope indicates that the same quantity of watches is purchased no matter what the price of bananas. The slope of vertical lines is *infinite*.

Similarly, aggregate consumption is completely unrelated to the nation's divorce rate. In Figure 3b we put consumption on the vertical axis and the divorce rate on the horizontal axis. The line parallel to the horizontal axis represents this lack of relatedness because the amount of consumption remains the same no matter what happens to the divorce rate. The slope of horizontal lines is *zero*.

Vertical Intercept

A line can be positioned on a graph (without plotting points) if we know just two things: its slope and its vertical intercept. We have already discussed slope. The **vertical intercept** of a line is the point where the line meets the vertical axis. In Figure 1 the intercept is $50. This intercept means that if current income were zero, consumers would still spend $50. They might do this through borrowing or by selling some of their assets. Similarly, the $50 vertical intercept in Figure 2 shows that at a $50 ticket price, GSU's basketball team would be playing in an empty arena.

FIGURE 3 **Infinite and zero slopes.** (a) A line parallel to the vertical axis has an infinite slope. Here, purchases of watches remain the same no matter what happens to the price of bananas. (b) A line parallel to the horizontal axis has a slope of zero. In this case, consumption remains the same no matter what happens to the divorce rate. In both (a) and (b), the two variables are totally unrelated to one another.

Equation of a Linear Relationship

If we know the vertical intercept and slope, we can describe a line succinctly in equation form. In its general form, the equation of a straight line is

$$y = a + bx$$

where y = dependent variable
a = vertical intercept
b = slope of line
x = independent variable

For our income-consumption example, if C represents consumption (the dependent variable) and Y represents income (the independent variable), we can write $C = a + bY$. By substituting the known values of the intercept and the slope, we get

$$C = 50 + .5Y$$

This equation also allows us to determine the amount of consumption C at any specific level of income. You should use it to confirm that at the $250 income level, consumption is $175.

When economists reverse mathematical convention by putting the independent variable on the vertical axis and the dependent variable on the horizontal axis, then y stands for the independent variable, rather than the dependent variable in the general form. We noted previously that this case is relevant for our GSU ticket price–attendance data. If P represents the ticket price (independent variable) and Q represents attendance (dependent variable), their relationship is given by

$$P = 50 - 2.5Q$$

where the vertical intercept is 50 and the negative slope is $-2\frac{1}{2}$, or -2.5. Knowing the value of P lets us solve for Q, our dependent variable. You should use this equation to predict GSU ticket sales when the ticket price is $15.

Slope of a Nonlinear Curve

We now move from the simple world of linear relationships (straight lines) to the more complex world of nonlinear relationships (curvy lines). The slope of a straight line is the same at all its points. The slope of a line representing a nonlinear relationship changes from one point to another. Such lines are always referred to as *curves*.

Consider the downsloping curve in Figure 4. Its slope is negative throughout, but the curve flattens as we move down along it. Thus, its slope constantly changes; the curve has a different slope at each point.

To measure the slope at a specific point, we draw a straight line tangent to the curve at that point. A straight line is *tangent* at a point if it touches, but does not intersect, the curve at that point. Thus line *aa* is tangent to the curve in Figure 4 at point A. The slope of the curve at that point is equal to the slope of the tangent line. Specifically, the total vertical change (drop) in the tangent line *aa* is -20 and the total horizontal change (run) is $+5$. Because the slope of the tangent line *aa* is $-20/+5$, or -4, the slope of the curve at point A is also -4.

Line *bb* in Figure 4 is tangent to the curve at point B. Following the same procedure, we find the slope at B to be $-5/+15$, or $-\frac{1}{3}$. Thus, in this flatter part of the curve, the slope is less negative.

FIGURE 4 **Determining the slopes of curves.** The slope of a nonlinear curve changes from point to point on the curve. The slope at any point (say, B) can be determined by drawing a straight line that is tangent to that point (line *bb*) and calculating the slope of that line.

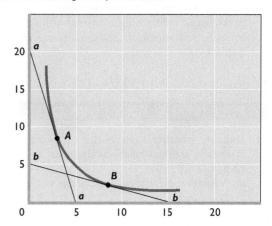

APPENDIX SUMMARY

LO1.8 Understand graphs, curves, and slopes as they relate to economics.

Graphs are a convenient and revealing way to represent economic relationships.

Two variables are positively or directly related when their values change in the same direction. The line (curve) representing two directly related variables slopes upward.

Two variables are negatively or inversely related when their values change in opposite directions. The line (curve) representing two inversely related variables slopes downward.

The value of the dependent variable (the "effect") is determined by the value of the independent variable (the "cause").

When the "other factors" that might affect a two-variable relationship are allowed to change, the graph of the relationship will likely shift to a new location.

The slope of a straight line is the ratio of the vertical change to the horizontal change between any two points. The slope of an upsloping line is positive; the slope of a downsloping line is negative.

The slope of a line or curve depends on the units used in measuring the variables. The slope is especially relevant for economics because it measures marginal changes.

The slope of a horizontal line is zero; the slope of a vertical line is infinite.

Together, the vertical intercept and slope of a line determine its location; they are used in expressing the line—and the relationship between the two variables—as an equation.

The slope of a curve at any point is determined by calculating the slope of a straight line tangent to the curve at that point.

APPENDIX TERMS AND CONCEPTS

horizontal axis

vertical axis

direct relationship

inverse relationship

independent variable

dependent variable

slope of a straight line

vertical intercept

The following and additional problems can be found in **connect** | ECONOMICS

APPENDIX DISCUSSION QUESTIONS

1. Briefly explain the use of graphs as a way to represent economic relationships. What is an inverse relationship? How does it graph? What is a direct relationship? How does it graph? **LO1.8**
2. Describe the graphical relationship between ticket prices and the number of people choosing to visit amusement parks. Is that relationship consistent with the fact that, historically, park attendance and ticket prices have both risen? Explain. **LO1.8**
3. Look back at Figure 2, which shows the inverse relationship between ticket prices and game attendance at Gigantic State University. (a) Interpret the meaning of both the slope and the intercept. (b) If the slope of the line were steeper, what would that say about the amount by which ticket sales respond to increases in ticket prices? (c) If the slope of the line stayed the same but the intercept increased, what can you say about the amount by which ticket sales respond to increases in ticket prices? **LO1.8**

APPENDIX REVIEW QUESTIONS

1. Indicate whether each of the following relationships is usually a direct relationship or an inverse relationship. **LO1.8**
    a. A sports team's winning percentage and attendance at its home games.
    b. Higher temperatures and sweater sales.
    c. A person's income and how often he or she shops at discount stores.
    d. Higher gasoline prices and miles driven in automobiles.

2. Erin grows pecans. The number of bushels (B) that she can produce depends on the number of inches of rainfall (R) that her orchards get. The relationship is given algebraically as follows: $B = 3,000 + 800R$. Match each part of this equation with the correct term. **LO1.8**

B	slope
3,000	dependent variable
800	vertical intercept
R	independent variable

APPENDIX PROBLEMS

1. Graph and label as either direct or indirect the relationships you would expect to find between (a) the number of inches of rainfall per month and the sale of umbrellas, (b) the amount of tuition and the level of enrollment at a university, and (c) the popularity of an entertainer and the price of her concert tickets. **LO1.8**

2. Indicate how each of the following might affect the data shown in the table and graph in Figure 2 of this appendix: **LO1.8**
   a. GSU's athletic director schedules higher-quality opponents.
   b. An NBA team locates in the city where GSU plays.
   c. GSU contracts to have all its home games televised.

3. The following table contains data on the relationship between saving and income. Rearrange these data into a meaningful order and graph them on the accompanying grid. What is the slope of the line? The vertical intercept? Write the equation that represents this line. What would you predict saving to be at the $12,500 level of income? **LO1.8**

Income per Year	Saving per Year
$15,000	$1,000
0	−500
10,000	500
5,000	0
20,000	1,500

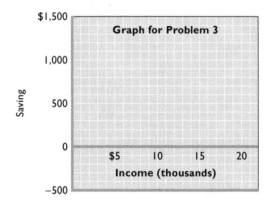

4. Construct a table from the data shown in the accompanying graph. Which is the dependent variable and which is the independent variable? Summarize the data in equation form. **LO1.8**

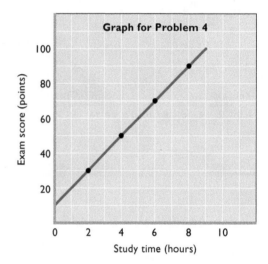

5. Suppose that when the interest rate on loans is 16 percent, businesses find it unprofitable to invest in machinery and equipment. However, when the interest rate is 14 percent, $5 billion worth of investment is profitable. At 12 percent interest, a total of $10 billion of investment is profitable. Similarly, total investment increases by $5 billion for each successive 2-percentage-point decline in the interest rate. Describe the relevant relationship between the interest rate and investment in a table, on a graph, and as an equation. Put the interest rate on the vertical axis and investment on the horizontal axis. In your equation use the form $i = a + bI$, where i is the interest rate, a is the vertical intercept, b is the slope of the line (which is negative), and I is the level of investment. **LO1.8**

6. Suppose that $C = a + bY$, where C = consumption, a = consumption at zero income, b = slope, and Y = income. **LO1.8**
   a. Are C and Y positively related or are they negatively related?
   b. If graphed, would the curve for this equation slope upward or slope downward?
   c. Are the variables C and Y inversely related or directly related?
   d. What is the value of C if $a = 10$, $b = 0.50$, and $Y = 200$?
   e. What is the value of Y if $C = 100$, $a = 10$, and $b = 0.25$?

7. The accompanying graph shows curve *XX'* and tangents at points *A*, *B*, and *C*. Calculate the slope of the curve at these three points. **LO1.8**

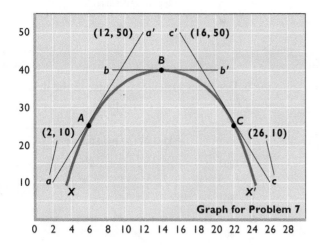

Graph for Problem 7

8. In the accompanying graph, is the slope of curve *AA'* positive or negative? Does the slope increase or decrease as we move along the curve from *A* to *A'*? Answer the same two questions for curve *BB'*. **LO1.8**

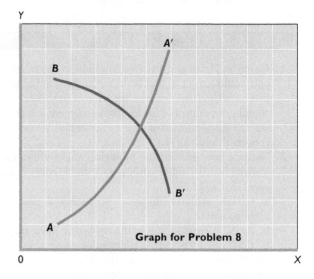

Graph for Problem 8

The Market System and the Circular Flow

Learning Objectives

LO2.1 Differentiate between laissez-faire capitalism, the command system, and the market system.

LO2.2 List the main characteristics of the market system.

LO2.3 Explain how the market system answers the five fundamental questions of what to produce, how to produce, who obtains the output, how to adjust to change, and how to promote progress.

LO2.4 Explain the operation of the "invisible hand" and why market economies usually do a better job than command economies at efficiently transforming economic resources into desirable output.

LO2.5 Describe the mechanics of the circular flow model.

LO2.6 Explain how the market system deals with risk.

You are at the mall. Suppose you were assigned to compile a list of all the individual goods and services there, including the different brands and variations of each type of product. That task would be daunting and the list would be long! And even though a single shopping mall contains a remarkable quantity and variety of goods, it is only a tiny part of the national economy.

Who decided that the particular goods and services available at the mall and in the broader economy should be produced? How did the producers determine which technology and types of resources to use in producing these particular goods? Who will obtain these products? What accounts for the new and improved products among

these goods? This chapter will answer these and related questions.

Economic Systems

LO2.1 Differentiate between laissez-faire capitalism, the command system, and the market system.

Every society needs to develop an **economic system**—a particular set of institutional arrangements and a coordinating mechanism—to respond to the economizing problem. The economic system has to determine what goods are produced, how they are produced, who gets them, how to accommodate change, and how to promote technological progress.

Economic systems differ as to (1) who owns the factors of production and (2) the method used to motivate, coordinate, and direct economic activity.

Economics systems can be classified by the degree to which they rely upon decentralized decision making based upon markets and prices or centralized government control based upon orders and mandates. At one extreme lies *laissez-faire capitalism*, in which government intervention is at a very minimum and markets and prices are allowed to direct nearly all economic activity. At the other extreme lie *command systems*, in which governments have total control over all economic activity. The vast majority of national economies lie somewhere in the middle, utilizing some mixture of centralized government regulation and decentralized markets and prices. These economies are said to have *market systems* or *mixed economies*.

Laissez-Faire Capitalism

In **laissez-faire capitalism**—or "pure capitalism"—the government's role would be limited to protecting private property from theft and aggression and establishing a legal environment in which contracts would be enforced and people could interact in markets to buy and sell goods, services, and resources.

The term "laissez-faire" is the French for "let it be," that is, keep the government from interfering with the economy. Proponents of laissez-faire believe that such interference reduces human welfare. They maintain that any government that intervenes widely in the economy will end up being corrupted by special interests that will use the government's economic influence to benefit themselves rather than society at large.

To prevent that from happening, the proponents of laissez-faire argue that government should restrict itself to preventing individuals and firms from coercing each other.

By doing so, it will ensure that only mutually beneficial economic transactions get negotiated and completed. That should lead to the highest possible level of human satisfaction because, after all, who knows better what people want than the people themselves?

It is important to note, however, that no society has ever employed a laissez-faire system. In fact, no government has *ever* limited its economic actions to the short list of functions that would be allowed under laissez-faire. Instead, every government known to history has undertaken a wider range of economic activities, many of which are widely popular and which include industrial safety regulations, various taxes and subsidies, occupational licensing requirements, and income redistribution.

ORIGIN OF THE IDEA

O2.1
Laissez-faire

Thus, you should think of laissez-faire capitalism as a hypothetical system that is viewed by proponents as the ideal to which all economic systems should strive—but which is opposed by those who welcome greater government intervention in the economy.

The Command System

The polar opposite of laissez-faire capitalism is the **command system,** in which government owns most property resources and economic decision making is set by a central economic plan created and enforced by the government. The command system is also known as *socialism* or *communism*.

Under the command system, a central planning board appointed by the government makes all the major decisions concerning the use of resources, the composition and distribution of output, and the organization of production. The government owns most of the business firms, which produce according to government directives. The central planning board determines production goals for each enterprise and specifies the amount of resources to be allocated to each enterprise so that it can reach its production goals. The division of output between capital and consumer goods is centrally decided, and capital goods are allocated among industries on the basis of the central planning board's long-term priorities.

A pure command economy would rely exclusively on a central plan to allocate the government-owned property resources. But, in reality, even the preeminent command economy—the Soviet Union—tolerated some private ownership and incorporated some markets before its collapse in 1992. Recent reforms in Russia and most of the eastern European nations have, to one degree or another, transformed their command economies to capitalistic, market-oriented systems. China's reforms have not gone as far, but they have greatly reduced the reliance on central planning. Although government ownership of resources and capital in China is still extensive, the nation has increasingly relied on free markets to organize and coordinate its economy. North Korea and Cuba are the last prominent remaining examples of largely centrally planned economies. Other countries using mainly the command system include Turkmenistan, Laos, Belarus, Myanmar, and Iran. Later in this chapter, we will explore the main reasons for the general demise of command systems.

The Market System

The vast majority of the world's economies utilize the **market system,** which is also known as *capitalism* or the *mixed economy.*

The market system is characterized by a mixture of centralized government economic initiatives and decentralized actions taken by individuals and firms. The precise mixture varies from country to country, but in each case the system features the private ownership of resources and the use of markets and prices to coordinate and direct economic activity.

In the market system, individuals and businesses seek to achieve their economic goals through their own decisions regarding work, consumption, or production. The system allows for the private ownership of capital, communicates through prices, and coordinates economic activity through markets—places where buyers and sellers come together to buy and sell goods, services, and resources.

Participants act in their own self-interest and goods and services are produced and resources are supplied by whoever is willing and able to do so. The result is competition among independently acting buyers and sellers of each product and resource and an economic system in which decision making is widely dispersed.

The market system also offers high potential monetary rewards that create powerful incentives for existing firms to innovate and for entrepreneurs to pioneer new products and processes despite the financial risks involved and despite most innovations failing to catch on with consumers.

It is the case, however, that in the capitalism practiced in the United States and most other countries, the government plays a substantial role in the economy. It not only provides the rules for economic activity but also promotes economic stability and growth, provides certain goods and services that would otherwise be underproduced or not produced at all, and modifies the distribution of income. The government, however, is not the dominant economic force in deciding what to produce, how to produce it, and who will get it. That force is the market.

Characteristics of the Market System

LO2.2 List the main characteristics of the market system.
An examination of some of the key features of the market system in detail will be very instructive.

Private Property

In a market system, private individuals and firms, not the government, own most of the property resources (land and capital). It is this extensive private ownership of capital that gives capitalism its name. This right of **private property,** coupled with the freedom to negotiate binding legal contracts, enables individuals and businesses to obtain, use, and dispose of property resources as they see fit. The right of property owners to designate who will receive their property when they die helps sustain the institution of private property.

The most important consequence of property rights is that they encourage people to cooperate by helping to ensure that only *mutually agreeable* economic transactions take place. To consider why this is true, imagine a world without legally enforceable property rights. In such a world, the strong could simply take whatever they wanted from the weak without giving them any compensation. But in a world of legally enforceable property rights, any person wanting something from you has to get you to agree to give it to them. And you can say no. The result is that if they really want what you have, they must offer you something that you value more highly in return. That is, they must offer you a mutually agreeable economic transaction—one that benefits you as well as them.

Property rights also encourage investment, innovation, exchange, maintenance of property, and economic growth. Nobody would stock a store, build a factory, or clear land for farming if someone else, or the government itself, could take that property for his or her own benefit.

Property rights also extend to intellectual property through patents, copyrights, and trademarks. Such long-term protection encourages people to write books, music, and computer programs and to invent new products and production processes without fear that others will steal them and the rewards they may bring.

Moreover, property rights facilitate exchange. The title to an automobile or the deed to a cattle ranch assures the buyer that the seller is the legitimate owner. Also, property rights encourage owners to maintain or improve their property so as to preserve or increase its value. Finally, property rights enable people to use their time and resources to produce more goods and services, rather than using them to protect and retain the property they have already produced or acquired.

Freedom of Enterprise and Choice

Closely related to private ownership of property is freedom of enterprise and choice. The market system requires that various economic units make certain choices, which are expressed and implemented in the economy's markets:

- **Freedom of enterprise** ensures that entrepreneurs and private businesses are free to obtain and use economic resources to produce their choice of goods and services and to sell them in their chosen markets.

- **Freedom of choice** enables owners to employ or dispose of their property and money as they see fit. It also allows workers to try to enter any line of work for which they are qualified. Finally, it ensures that consumers are free to buy the goods and services that best satisfy their wants and that their budgets allow.

These choices are free only within broad legal limitations, of course. Illegal choices such as selling human organs or buying illicit drugs are punished through fines and imprisonment. (Global Perspective 2.1 reveals that the degree of economic freedom varies greatly from economy to economy.)

Self-Interest

In the market system, **self-interest** is the motivating force of the various economic units as they express their free choices. Self-interest simply means that each economic unit tries to achieve its own particular goal, which usually requires delivering something of value to others. Entrepreneurs try to maximize profit or minimize loss. Property owners try to get the highest price for the sale or rent of their resources. Workers try to maximize their utility (satisfaction) by finding jobs that offer the best combination of wages, hours,

ORIGIN OF THE IDEA

O2.2 Self-interest

GLOBAL PERSPECTIVE 2.1

Index of Economic Freedom, Selected Economies

The Index of Economic Freedom measures economic freedom using 10 major groupings such as trade policy, property rights, and government intervention, with each category containing more than 50 specific criteria. The index then ranks 179 economies according to their degree of economic freedom. A few selected rankings for 2012 are listed below.

FREE
1 Hong Kong
3 Australia
5 Switzerland

MOSTLY FREE
10 United States
18 Taiwan
26 Germany

MOSTLY UNFREE
99 Brazil
123 India
144 Russia

REPRESSED
158 Argentina
171 Iran
179 North Korea

Source: Used by permission of The Heritage Foundation, **www.heritage.org**.

fringe benefits, and working conditions. Consumers try to obtain the products they want at the lowest possible price and apportion their expenditures to maximize their utility. The motive of self-interest gives direction and consistency to what might otherwise be a chaotic economy.

Competition

The market system depends on **competition** among economic units. The basis of this competition is freedom of choice exercised in pursuit of a monetary return. Very broadly defined, competition requires

- Two or more buyers and two or more sellers acting independently in a particular product or resource market. (Usually there are many more than two buyers or sellers.)

- Freedom of sellers and buyers to enter or leave markets, on the basis of their economic self-interest.

Competition among buyers and sellers diffuses economic power within the businesses and households that make up the economy. When there are many buyers and sellers acting independently in a market, no single buyer or seller can dictate the price of the product or resource because others can undercut that price.

Competition also implies that producers can enter or leave an industry; no insurmountable barriers prevent an industry's expanding or contracting. This freedom of an industry to expand or contract provides the economy with the flexibility needed to remain efficient over time. Freedom of entry and exit enables the economy to adjust to changes in consumer tastes, technology, and resource availability.

The diffusion of economic power inherent in competition limits the potential abuse of that power. A producer that charges more than the competitive market price will lose sales to other producers. An employer who pays less than the competitive market wage rate will lose workers to other employers. A firm that fails to exploit new technology will lose profits to firms that do. A firm that produces shoddy products will be punished as customers switch to higher-quality items made by rival firms. Competition is the basic regulatory force in the market system.

Markets and Prices

We may wonder why an economy based on self-interest does not collapse in chaos. If consumers want breakfast cereal, but businesses choose to produce running shoes and resource suppliers decide to make computer software, production would seem to be deadlocked by the apparent inconsistencies of free choices.

In reality, the millions of decisions made by households and businesses are highly coordinated with one another by markets and prices, which are key components of the market system. They give the system its ability to coordinate millions of daily economic decisions. A **market** is an institution or mechanism that brings buyers ("demanders") and sellers ("suppliers") into contact. A market system conveys the decisions made by buyers and sellers of products and resources. The decisions made on each side of the market determine a set of product and resource prices that guide resource owners, entrepreneurs, and consumers as they make and revise their choices and pursue their self-interest.

Just as competition is the regulatory mechanism of the market system, the market system itself is the organizing and coordinating mechanism. It is an elaborate communication network through which innumerable individual free choices are recorded, summarized, and balanced.

Those who respond to market signals and heed market dictates are rewarded with greater profit and income; those who do not respond to those signals and choose to ignore market dictates are penalized. Through this mechanism society decides what the economy should produce, how production can be organized efficiently, and how the fruits of production are to be distributed among the various units that make up the economy.

> ## QUICK REVIEW 2.1
>
> - The market system rests on the private ownership of property and on freedom of enterprise and freedom of choice.
> - Property rights encourage people to cooperate and make mutually agreeable economic transactions.
> - The market system permits consumers, resource suppliers, and businesses to pursue and further their self-interest.
> - Competition diffuses economic power and limits the actions of any single seller or buyer.
> - The coordinating mechanism of capitalism is a system of markets and prices.

Technology and Capital Goods

In the market system, competition, freedom of choice, self-interest, and personal reward provide the opportunity and motivation for technological advance. The monetary rewards for new products or production techniques accrue directly to the innovator. The market system therefore encourages extensive use and rapid development of complex capital goods: tools, machinery, large-scale factories, and facilities for storage, communication, transportation, and marketing.

Advanced technology and capital goods are important because the most direct methods of production are often the least efficient. The only way to avoid that inefficiency is to rely on capital goods. It would be ridiculous for a farmer to go at production with bare hands. There are huge benefits to be derived from creating and using such capital equipment as plows, tractors, and storage bins. More efficient production means much more abundant output.

Specialization

The extent to which market economies rely on **specialization** is extraordinary. Specialization means using the resources of an individual, firm, region, or nation to produce one or a few goods or services rather than the entire range of goods and services. Those goods and services are then exchanged for a full range of desired products. The majority of consumers produce virtually none of the goods and services they consume, and they consume little or nothing of the items they produce. The person working nine to five installing windows in commercial aircraft may rarely fly. Many farmers sell their milk to the local dairy and then buy margarine at the local grocery store. Society learned long ago that self-sufficiency breeds inefficiency. The jack-of-all-trades may be a very colorful individual but is certainly not an efficient producer.

Division of Labor   Human specialization—called the **division of labor**—contributes to a society's output in several ways:

- *Specialization makes use of differences in ability.* Specialization enables individuals to take advantage of existing differences in their abilities and skills. If Peyton is strong, athletic, and good at throwing a football and Beyoncé is beautiful, is agile, and can sing, their distribution of talents can be most efficiently used if Peyton plays professional football and Beyoncé records songs and gives concerts.

ORIGIN OF THE IDEA

02.3
Specialization: division of labor

- *Specialization fosters learning by doing.* Even if the abilities of two people are identical, specialization may still be advantageous. By devoting time to a single task, a person is more likely to develop the skills required and to improve techniques than by working at a number of different tasks. You learn to be a good lawyer by studying and practicing law.
- *Specialization saves time.* By devoting time to a single task, a person avoids the loss of time incurred in shifting from one job to another. Also, time is saved by not "fumbling around" with tasks that one is not trained to do.

For all these reasons, specialization increases the total output society derives from limited resources.

Geographic Specialization   Specialization also works on a regional and international basis. It is conceivable that oranges could be grown in Nebraska, but because of the unsuitability of the land, rainfall, and temperature, the costs would be very high. And it is conceivable that wheat could be grown in Florida, but such production would be costly for similar geographical reasons. So Nebraskans produce products—wheat in particular—for which their resources are best suited, and Floridians do the same,

producing oranges and other citrus fruits. By specializing, both economies produce more than is needed locally. Then, very sensibly, Nebraskans and Floridians swap some of their surpluses—wheat for oranges, oranges for wheat.

Similarly, on an international scale, the United States specializes in producing such items as commercial aircraft and software, which it sells abroad in exchange for video cameras from Japan, bananas from Honduras, and woven baskets from Thailand. Both human specialization and geographic specialization are needed to achieve efficiency in the use of limited resources.

Use of Money

A rather obvious characteristic of any economic system is the extensive use of money. Money performs several functions, but first and foremost it is a **medium of exchange.** It makes trade easier.

Specialization requires exchange. Exchange can, and sometimes does, occur through **barter**—swapping goods for goods, say, wheat for oranges. But barter poses serious problems because it requires a *coincidence of wants* between the buyer and the seller. In our example, we assumed that Nebraskans had excess wheat to trade and wanted oranges. And we assumed that Floridians had excess oranges to trade and wanted wheat. So an exchange occurred. But if such a coincidence of wants is missing, trade is stymied.

Suppose that Nebraska has no interest in Florida's oranges but wants potatoes from Idaho. And suppose that Idaho wants Florida's oranges but not Nebraska's wheat. And, to complicate matters, suppose that Florida wants some of Nebraska's wheat but none of Idaho's potatoes. We summarize the situation in Figure 2.1.

In none of the cases shown in the figure is there a coincidence of wants. Trade by barter clearly would be difficult. Instead, people in each state use **money,** which is simply a convenient social invention to facilitate exchanges of goods and services. Historically, people have used cattle, cigarettes, shells, stones, pieces of metal, and many other commodities, with varying degrees of success, as money. To serve as money, an item needs to pass only one test: It must be generally acceptable to sellers in exchange for their goods and services. Money is socially defined; whatever society accepts as a medium of exchange *is* money.

Today, most economies use pieces of paper as money. The use of paper dollars (currency) as a medium of exchange is what enables Nebraska, Florida, and Idaho to overcome their trade stalemate, as demonstrated in Figure 2.1.

On a global basis, specialization and exchange are complicated by the fact that different nations have different currencies. But markets in which currencies are bought

FIGURE 2.1 Money facilitates trade when wants do not coincide. The use of money as a medium of exchange permits trade to be accomplished despite a noncoincidence of wants. (1) Nebraska trades the wheat that Florida wants for money from Floridians; (2) Nebraska trades the money it receives from Florida for the potatoes it wants from Idaho; (3) Idaho trades the money it receives from Nebraska for the oranges it wants from Florida.

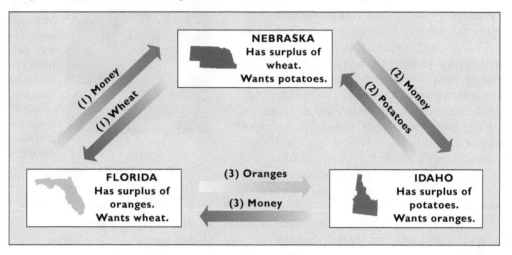

and sold make it possible for people living in different countries to exchange goods and services without resorting to barter.

Active, but Limited, Government

An active, but limited, government is the final characteristic of market systems in modern advanced industrial economies. Although a market system promotes a high degree of efficiency in the use of its resources, it has certain inherent shortcomings, called "market failures." We will discover in subsequent chapters that governments can often increase the overall effectiveness of a market system in several ways. That being said, governments have their own set of shortcomings that can themselves cause substantial misallocations of resources. Consequently, we will also investigate several types of "government failure."

QUICK REVIEW 2.2

- The market systems of modern industrial economies are characterized by extensive use of technologically advanced capital goods. Such goods help these economies achieve greater efficiency in production.

- Specialization is extensive in market systems; it enhances efficiency and output by enabling individuals, regions, and nations to produce the goods and services for which their resources are best suited.

- The use of money in market systems facilitates the exchange of goods and services that specialization requires.

Five Fundamental Questions

LO2.3 Explain how the market system answers the five fundamental questions of what to produce, how to produce, who obtains the output, how to adjust to change, and how to promote progress.

The key features of the market system help explain how market economies respond to five fundamental questions:

- What goods and services will be produced?
- How will the goods and services be produced?
- Who will get the goods and services?
- How will the system accommodate change?
- How will the system promote progress?

These five questions highlight the economic choices underlying the production possibilities curve discussed in Chapter 1. They reflect the reality of scarce resources in a world of unlimited wants. All economies, whether market or command, must address these five questions.

What Will Be Produced?

How will a market system decide on the specific types and quantities of goods to be produced? The simple answer is this: The goods and services that can be produced at a continuing profit will be produced, while those whose production generates a continuing loss will be discontinued. Profits and losses are the difference between the total revenue (TR) a firm receives from the sale of its products and the total cost (TC) of producing those products. (For economists, total costs include not only wage and salary payments to labor, and interest and rental payments for capital and land, but also payments to the entrepreneur for organizing and combining the other resources to produce a product.)

Continuing economic profit (TR > TC) in an industry results in expanded production and the movement of resources toward that industry. Existing firms grow and new firms enter. The industry expands. Continuing losses (TC > TR) in an industry lead to reduced production and the exit of resources from that industry. Some existing firms shrink in size; others go out of business. The industry contracts. In the market system, consumers are sovereign (in command). **Consumer sovereignty** is crucial in determining the types and quantities of goods produced. Consumers spend their income on the goods they are most willing and able to buy. Through these **"dollar votes"** they register their wants in the market. If the dollar votes for a certain product are great enough to create a profit, businesses will produce that product and offer it for sale. In contrast, if the dollar votes do not create sufficient revenues to cover costs, businesses will not produce the product. So the consumers are sovereign. They collectively direct resources to industries that are meeting consumer wants and away from industries that are not meeting consumer wants.

The dollar votes of consumers determine not only which industries will continue to exist but also which products will survive or fail. Only profitable industries, firms, and products survive. So firms are not as free to produce whatever products they wish as one might otherwise think. Consumers' buying decisions make the production of some products profitable and the production of other products unprofitable, thus restricting the choice of businesses in deciding what to produce. Businesses must match their production choices with consumer choices or else face losses and eventual bankruptcy.

The same holds true for resource suppliers. The employment of resources derives from the sale of the goods and services that the resources help produce. Autoworkers are employed because automobiles are sold. There are few remaining professors of early Latin because there are few people desiring to learn the Latin language. Resource suppliers, desiring to earn income, are not truly free to allocate their resources to the production of goods that consumers do not value highly. Consumers register their preferences in the market; producers and resource suppliers, prompted by their own self-interest, respond appropriately.

How Will the Goods and Services Be Produced?

What combinations of resources and technologies will be used to produce goods and services? How will the

McHits and McMisses

McDonald's has introduced several new menu items over the decades. Some have been profitable "hits," while others have been "misses." In a market system, consumers ultimately decide whether a menu item is profitable and therefore whether it stays on the McDonald's menu.

- Hulaburger (1962)—McMiss
- Filet-O-Fish (1963)—McHit
- Strawberry shortcake (1966)—McMiss
- Big Mac (1968)—McHit
- Hot apple pie (1968)—McHit
- Egg McMuffin (1975)—McHit
- Drive-thru (1975)—McHit
- Chicken McNuggets (1983)—McHit
- Extra Value Meal (1991)—McHit
- McLean Deluxe (1991)—McMiss
- Arch Deluxe (1996)—McMiss
- 55-cent special (1997)—McMiss
- Big Xtra (1999)—McHit
- McSalad Shaker (2000)—McMiss
- McGriddle (2003)—McHit
- Snack Wrap (2006)—McHit

Source: "Polishing the Golden Arches," *Forbes,* June 15, 1998, pp. 42–43, updated. Reprinted by permission of Forbes Media LLC © 2010.

production be organized? The answer: In combinations and ways that minimize the cost per unit of output. This is true because inefficiency drives up costs and lowers profits. As a result, any firm wishing to maximize its profits will make great efforts to minimize production costs. These efforts will include using the right mix of labor and capital, given the prices and productivity of those resources. They also mean locating production facilities optimally to hold down production and transportation expenses.

Those efforts will be intensified if the firm faces competition, as consumers strongly prefer low prices and will shift their purchases over to the firms that can produce a quality product at the lowest possible price. Any firm foolish enough to use higher-cost production methods will go bankrupt as it is undersold by its more efficient competitors who can still make a profit when

TABLE 2.1 Three Techniques for Producing $15 Worth of Bar Soap

| Resource | Price per Unit of Resource | Units of Resource | | | | | |
| | | Technique 1 | | Technique 2 | | Technique 3 | |
		Units	Cost	Units	Cost	Units	Cost
Labor	$2	4	$ 8	2	$ 4	1	$ 2
Land	1	1	1	3	3	4	4
Capital	3	1	3	1	3	2	6
Entrepreneurial ability	3	1	3	1	3	1	3
Total cost of $15 worth of bar soap			$15		$13		$15

selling at a lower price. Simply stated: Competition eliminates high-cost producers.

Least-cost production means that firms must employ the most economically efficient technique of production in producing their output. The most efficient production technique depends on

- The available technology, that is, the available body of knowledge and techniques that can be used to combine economic resources to produce the desired results.
- The prices of the needed resources.

A technique that requires just a few inputs of resources to produce a specific output may be highly inefficient economically if those resources are valued very highly in the market. Economic efficiency requires obtaining a particular output of product with the least input of scarce resources, when both output and resource inputs are measured in dollars and cents. The combination of resources that will produce, say, $15 worth of bathroom soap at the lowest possible cost is the most efficient.

Suppose there are three possible techniques for producing the desired $15 worth of bars of soap. Suppose also that the quantity of each resource required by each production technique and the prices of the required resources are as shown in Table 2.1. By multiplying the required quantities of each resource by its price in each of the three techniques, we can determine the total cost of producing $15 worth of soap by means of each technique.

Technique 2 is economically the most efficient because it is the least costly. It enables society to obtain $15 worth of output by using a smaller amount of resources—$13 worth—than the $15 worth required by the two other techniques. Competition will dictate that producers use technique 2. Thus, the question of how goods

WORKED PROBLEMS

W2.1
Least-cost production

will be produced is answered. They will be produced in a least-cost way.

A change in either technology or resource prices, however, may cause a firm to shift from the technology it is using. If the price of labor falls to $0.50, technique 1 becomes more desirable than technique 2. Firms will find they can lower their costs by shifting to a technology that uses more of the resource whose price has fallen. Exercise: Would a new technique involving 1 unit of labor, 4 of land, 1 of capital, and 1 of entrepreneurial ability be preferable to the techniques listed in Table 2.1, assuming the resource prices shown there?

Who Will Get the Output?

The market system enters the picture in two ways when determining the distribution of total output. Generally, any product will be distributed to consumers on the basis of their ability and willingness to pay its existing market price. If the price of some product, say, a small sailboat, is $3,000, then buyers who are willing and able to pay that price will "sail, sail away." Consumers who are unwilling or unable to pay the price will be "sitting on the dock of the bay."

The ability to pay the prices for sailboats and other products depends on the amount of income that consumers have, along with the prices of, and preferences for, various goods. If consumers have sufficient income and want to spend their money on a particular good, they can have it. The amount of income they have depends on (1) the quantities of the property and human resources they supply and (2) the prices those resources command in the resource market. Resource prices (wages, interest, rent, profit) are crucial in determining the size of each person's income and therefore each person's ability to buy part of the economy's output. If a lawyer earning $200 an hour and a janitor earning $10 an hour both work the same number of hours each year, then each year the lawyer will be able to purchase 20 times more of society's output than the janitor.

How Will the System Accommodate Change?

Market systems are dynamic: Consumer preferences, technologies, and resource supplies all change. This means that the particular allocation of resources that is now the most efficient for a specific pattern of consumer tastes, range of technological alternatives, and amount of available resources will become obsolete and inefficient as consumer preferences change, new techniques of production are discovered, and resource supplies change over time. Can the market economy adjust to such changes?

Suppose consumer tastes change. For instance, assume that consumers decide they want more fruit juice and less milk than the economy currently provides. Those changes in consumer tastes will be communicated to producers through an increase in spending on fruit and a decline in spending on milk. Other things equal, prices and profits in the fruit juice industry will rise and those in the milk industry will fall. Self-interest will induce existing competitors to expand output and entice new competitors to enter the prosperous fruit industry and will in time force firms to scale down—or even exit—the depressed milk industry.

The higher prices and greater economic profit in the fruit-juice industry will not only induce that industry to expand but will also give it the revenue needed to obtain the resources essential to its growth. Higher prices and profits will permit fruit producers to attract more resources from less urgent alternative uses. The reverse occurs in the milk industry, where fewer workers and other resources are employed. These adjustments in the economy are appropriate responses to the changes in consumer tastes. This is consumer sovereignty at work.

The market system is a gigantic communications system. Through changes in prices and profits, it communicates changes in such basic matters as consumer tastes and elicits appropriate responses from businesses and resource suppliers. By affecting price and profits, changes in consumer tastes direct the expansion of some industries and the contraction of others. Those adjustments are conveyed to the resource market. As expanding industries employ more resources and contracting industries employ fewer, the resulting changes in resource prices (wages and salaries, for example) and income flows guide resources from the contracting industries to the expanding industries.

This directing or guiding function of prices and profits is a core element of the market system. Without such a system, a government planning board or some other administrative agency would have to direct businesses and resources into the appropriate industries. A similar analysis shows that the system can and does adjust to other fundamental changes—for example, to changes in technology and in the prices of various resources.

How Will the System Promote Progress?

Society desires economic growth (greater output) and higher standards of living (greater output *per person*). How does the market system promote technological improvements and capital accumulation, both of which contribute to a higher standard of living for society?

Technological Advance The market system provides a strong incentive for technological advance and enables better products and processes to supplant inferior ones. An entrepreneur or firm that introduces a popular new product will gain revenue and economic profit at the expense of rivals. Firms that are highly profitable one year may find they are in financial trouble just a few years later. Technological advance also includes new and improved methods that reduce production or distribution costs. By passing part of its cost reduction on to the consumer through a lower product price, a firm can increase sales and obtain economic profit at the expense of rival firms.

Moreover, the market system promotes the *rapid spread* of technological advance throughout an industry. Rival firms must follow the lead of the most innovative firm or else suffer immediate losses and eventual failure. In some cases, the result is **creative destruction:** The creation of new products and production methods completely destroys the market positions of firms that are wedded to existing products and older ways of doing business. Example: The advent of compact discs largely demolished long-play vinyl records, and iPods and other digital technologies subsequently supplanted CDs.

Capital Accumulation Most technological advances require additional capital goods. The market system provides the resources necessary to produce additional capital goods through increased dollar votes for those goods. That is, the market system acknowledges dollar voting for capital goods as well as for consumer goods.

But who counts the dollar votes for capital goods? Answer: Entrepreneurs and business owners. As receivers of profit income, they often use part of that income to purchase capital goods. Doing so yields even greater profit income in the future if the technological innovation that required the additional capital goods is successful. Also, by paying interest or selling ownership shares, the entrepreneur and firm can attract some of the income of households as saving to increase their dollar votes for the production of more capital goods.

The "Invisible Hand"

LO2.4 Explain the operation of the "invisible hand" and why market economies usually do a better job than command economies at efficiently transforming economic resources into desirable output.

In his 1776 book *The Wealth of Nations*, Adam Smith first noted that the operation of a market system creates a curious unity between private interests and social interests. Firms and resource suppliers, seeking to further their own self-interest and operating within the framework of a highly competitive market system, will simultaneously, as though guided by an **"invisible hand,"** promote the public or social interest. For example, we have seen that in a competitive environment, businesses seek to build new and improved products to increase profits. Those enhanced products increase society's well-being. Businesses also use the least costly combination of resources to produce a specific output because doing so is in their self-interest. To act otherwise would be to forgo profit or even to risk business failure. But, at the same time, to use scarce resources in the least costly way is clearly in the social interest as well. It "frees up" resources to produce other things that society desires.

Self-interest, awakened and guided by the competitive market system, is what induces responses appropriate to the changes in society's wants. Businesses seeking to make higher profits and to avoid losses, and resource suppliers pursuing greater monetary rewards, negotiate changes in the allocation of resources and end up with the output that society wants. Competition controls or guides self-interest such that self-interest automatically and quite unintentionally furthers the best interest of society. The invisible hand ensures that when firms maximize their profits and resource suppliers maximize their incomes, these groups also help maximize society's output and income.

Of the various virtues of the market system, three merit reemphasis:

- *Efficiency* The market system promotes the efficient use of resources by guiding them into the production of the goods and services most wanted by society. It forces the use of the most efficient techniques in organizing resources for production, and it encourages the development and adoption of new and more efficient production techniques.

- *Incentives* The market system encourages skill acquisition, hard work, and innovation. Greater work skills and effort mean greater production and higher incomes, which usually translate into a higher standard of living. Similarly, the assuming of risks by entrepreneurs can result in substantial profit incomes. Successful innovations generate economic rewards.

- *Freedom* The major noneconomic argument for the market system is its emphasis on personal freedom. In contrast to central planning, the market system coordinates economic activity without coercion. The market system permits—indeed, it thrives on—freedom of enterprise and choice. Entrepreneurs and workers are free to further their own self-interest, subject to the rewards and penalties imposed by the market system itself.

Of course, no economic system, including the market system, is flawless. In Chapter 4 we will explain two well-known shortcomings of the market system and examine the government policies that try to remedy them.

The Demise of the Command Systems

Our discussion of how a market system answers the five fundamental questions provides insights on why the command systems of the Soviet Union, eastern Europe, and China (prior to its market reforms) failed. Those systems encountered two insurmountable problems.

The Coordination Problem The first difficulty was the coordination problem. The central planners had to coordinate the millions of individual decisions by consumers, resource suppliers, and businesses. Consider the setting up of a factory to produce tractors. The central planners had to establish a realistic annual production target, for example, 1,000 tractors. They then had to make available all the necessary inputs—labor, machinery, electric power, steel, tires, glass, paint, transportation—for the production and delivery of those 1,000 tractors.

Because the outputs of many industries serve as inputs to other industries, the failure of any single industry to achieve its output target caused a chain reaction of repercussions. For example, if iron mines, for want of machinery or labor or transportation, did not supply the steel industry with the required inputs of iron ore, the steel mills were unable to fulfill the input needs of the many industries that depended on steel. Those steel-using industries (such as tractor, automobile, and transportation) were unable to fulfill their planned production goals. Eventually the chain reaction spread to all firms that used steel as an input and from there to other input buyers or final consumers.

The coordination problem became more difficult as the economies expanded. Products and production processes grew more sophisticated and the number of industries requiring planning increased. Planning techniques that worked for the simpler economy proved highly inadequate and inefficient for the larger economy. Bottlenecks and production stoppages became the norm, not the exception. In trying to cope, planners further suppressed product variety, focusing on one or two products in each product category.

A lack of a reliable success indicator added to the coordination problem in the Soviet Union and China prior to its market reforms. We have seen that market economies rely on profit as a success indicator. Profit depends on consumer demand, production efficiency, and product quality. In contrast, the major success indicator for the command economies usually was a quantitative production target that the central planners assigned. Production costs, product quality, and product mix were secondary considerations. Managers and workers often sacrificed product quality and variety because they were being awarded bonuses for meeting quantitative, not qualitative, targets. If meeting production goals meant sloppy assembly work and little product variety, so be it.

It was difficult at best for planners to assign quantitative production targets without unintentionally producing distortions in output. If the plan specified a production target for producing nails in terms of *weight* (tons of nails), the enterprise made only large nails. But if it specified the target as a *quantity* (thousands of nails), the firm made all small nails, and lots of them! That is precisely what happened in the centrally planned economies.

The Incentive Problem

The command economies also faced an incentive problem. Central planners determined the output mix. When

they misjudged how many automobiles, shoes, shirts, and chickens were wanted at the government-determined prices, persistent shortages and surpluses of those products arose. But as long as the managers who oversaw the production of those goods were rewarded for meeting their assigned production goals, they had no incentive to adjust production in response to the shortages and surpluses. And there were no fluctuations in prices and profitability to signal that more or less of certain products was desired. Thus, many products were unavailable or in short supply, while other products were overproduced and sat for months or years in warehouses.

The command systems of the former Soviet Union and China before its market reforms also lacked entrepreneurship. Central planning did not trigger the profit motive, nor did it reward innovation and enterprise. The route for getting ahead was through participation in the political hierarchy of the Communist Party. Moving up the hierarchy meant better housing, better

FIGURE 2.2   The circular flow diagram.
Resources flow from households to businesses through the resource market, and products flow from businesses to households through the product market. Opposite these real flows are monetary flows. Households receive income from businesses (their costs) through the resource market, and businesses receive revenue from households (their expenditures) through the product market.

QUICK QUIZ FOR FIGURE 2.2

1. The resource market is the place where:
   a. households sell products and businesses buy products.
   b. businesses sell resources and households sell products.
   c. households sell resources and businesses buy resources (or the services of resources).
   d. businesses sell resources and households buy resources (or the services of resources).

2. Which of the following would be determined in the product market?
   a. a manager's salary.
   b. the price of equipment used in a bottling plant.
   c. the price of 80 acres of farmland.
   d. the price of a new pair of athletic shoes.

3. In this circular flow diagram:
   a. money flows counterclockwise.
   b. resources flow counterclockwise.
   c. goods and services flow clockwise.
   d. households are on the selling side of the product market.

4. In this circular flow diagram:
   a. households spend income in the product market.
   b. firms sell resources to households.
   c. households receive income through the product market.
   d. households produce goods.

Answers: 1.c; 2.d; 3.b; 4.a

---

access to health care, and the right to shop in special stores. Meeting production targets and maneuvering through the minefields of party politics were measures of success in "business." But a definition of business success based solely on political savvy was not conducive to technological advance, which is often disruptive to existing products, production methods, and organizational structures.

The Circular Flow Model

LO2.5 Describe the mechanics of the circular flow model.
The dynamic market economy creates continuous, repetitive flows of goods and services, resources, and money. The **circular flow diagram,** shown in **Figure 2.2 (Key Graph),** illustrates those flows for a simplified economy in which there is no government. Observe that in the

ORIGIN OF THE IDEA

O2.4
Circular flow
diagram

diagram we group this economy's decision makers into *businesses* and *households*. Additionally, we divide this economy's markets into the *resource market* and the *product market*.

Households

The blue rectangle on the right side of the circular flow diagram in Figure 2.2 represents **households,** which are defined as one or more persons occupying a housing unit. There are currently about 118 million households in the U.S. economy. Households buy the goods and services that businesses make available in the product market. Households obtain the income needed to buy those products by selling resources in the resource market.

All the resources in our no-government economy are ultimately owned or provided by households. For instance, the members of one household or another directly provide all of the labor and entrepreneurial ability in the economy. Households also own all of the land and all of the capital in the economy either directly, as personal property, or indirectly, as a consequence of owning all of the businesses in the economy (and thereby controlling all of the land and capital owned by businesses). Thus, all of the income in the economy—all wages, rents, interest, and profits—flows to households because they provide the economy's labor, land, capital, and entrepreneurial ability.

Businesses

The blue rectangle on the left side of the circular flow diagram represents **businesses,** which are commercial establishments that attempt to earn profits for their owners by offering goods and services for sale. Businesses fall into three main categories.

- A **sole proprietorship** is a business owned and managed by a single person. The proprietor (the owner) may work alone or have employees. Examples include a woman who runs her own tree-cutting business and an independent accountant who, with two assistants, helps his clients with their taxes.
- The **partnership** form of business organization is a natural outgrowth of the sole proprietorship. In a partnership, two or more individuals (the partners) agree to own and operate a business together. They pool their financial resources and business skills to operate the business, and they share any profits or

losses that the business may generate. Many law firms and dental practices are organized as partnerships, as are a wide variety of firms in many other industries.
- A **corporation** is an independent legal entity that can—on its own behalf—acquire resources, own assets, produce and sell products, incur debts, extend credit, sue and be sued, and otherwise engage in any legal business activity.

The fact that a corporation is an independent legal entity means that its owners bear no personal financial responsibility for the fulfillment of the corporation's debts and obligations. For instance, if a corporation has failed to repay a loan to a bank, the bank can sue the corporation but not its owners. Professional managers run most corporations. They are hired and supervised by a board of directors that is elected annually by the corporation's owners. Google, Ford, and American Airlines are examples of large corporations, but corporations come in all sizes and operate in every type of industry.

There currently are about 30 million businesses in the United States, ranging from enormous corporations like Walmart, with 2012 sales of $444 billion and 2.2 million employees, to single-person sole proprietorships with sales of less than $100 per day.

Businesses sell goods and services in the product market in order to obtain revenue, and they incur costs in the resource market when they purchase the labor, land, capital, and entrepreneurial ability that they need to produce their respective goods and services.

Product Market

The red rectangle at the bottom of the diagram represents the **product market,** the place where the goods and services produced by businesses are bought and sold. Households use the income they receive from the sale of resources to buy goods and services. The money that they spend on goods and services flows to businesses as revenue.

Resource Market

Finally, the red rectangle at the top of the circular flow diagram represents the **resource market** in which households sell resources to businesses. The households sell resources to generate income, and the businesses buy resources to produce goods and services. Productive resources flow from households to businesses, while money flows from businesses to households in the form of wages, rents, interest, and profits.

To summarize, the circular flow model depicts a complex web of economic activity in which businesses and households are both buyers and sellers. Businesses buy resources and sell products. Households buy products and sell resources. The counterclockwise flow of economic resources and finished products that is illustrated by the red arrows in Figure 2.2 is paid for by the clockwise flow of money income and consumption expenditures illustrated by the blue arrows.

QUICK REVIEW 2.4

- Competition directs individuals and firms to unwittingly promote the social interest, as if guided by a benevolent "invisible hand."
- The command systems of the Soviet Union and pre-reform China failed as a result of the coordination problem and the incentive problem.
- The circular flow model illustrates how resources flow from households to businesses and how payments for those resources flow from businesses to households.

How the Market System Deals with Risk

LO2.6 Explain how the market system deals with risk.
Producing goods and services is risky. Input shortages can suddenly arise. Consumer preferences can quickly change. Natural disasters can destroy factories and cripple supply chains.

For an economic system to maximize its potential, it must develop methods for assessing and managing risk. The market system does so by confronting business owners with the financial consequences of their decisions. If they manage risks well, they may prosper. If they manage risks poorly, they may lose everything.

The Profit System

As explained in Chapter 1, entrepreneurial ability is the economic resource that organizes and directs the other three resources of land, labor, and capital toward productive uses. The owners of a firm may attempt to supply the entrepreneurial ability themselves. Or they can hire professional managers to supply the necessary leadership and decision making. Either way, it falls to those acting as the firm's entrepreneurs to deal with risk.

They are guided toward sensible decisions by the so-called *profit system*. This system is actually a *profit and loss*

system because the entrepreneurs who must deal with risk and uncertainty gain profits if they choose wisely but suffer losses if they choose poorly. That provides them with a large financial incentive to avoid unnecessary risks and make prudent decisions.

By contrast, risk management tends to be done very poorly in command economies because the central planners who must allocate resources and deal with risk do not themselves face the possibility of losing money if they make bad decisions. As government employees, they tend to receive the same salaries whether things go well or poorly.

Shielding Employees and Suppliers from Business Risk

Under the market system, only a firm's owners are subject to business risk and the possibility of losing money. By contrast, the firm's employees and suppliers are shielded from business risk because they are legally entitled to receive their contracted wages and payments on time and in full regardless of whether the firm is earning a profit or generating a loss.

To see how this works, consider a pizza parlor that is being started in a small town. Its investors put up $50,000 to get it going. They rent a storefront, lease ovens, purchase computers, and leave some money set aside as a reserve.

The firm then has to attract employees. To do so, it will offer wage contracts that promise to pay employees every two weeks without regard to whether the firm is making a profit or generating a loss. This guarantee shields the firm's employees from the risks of owning and operating the business. They will get paid even if the pizza parlor is losing money.

In the same way, the contracts that the firm signs with its suppliers and with anyone who loans the firm money (for instance, the local bank) will also specify that they will be paid on time and in full no matter how the firm is doing in terms of profitability.

Dealing with Losses So what happens if the firm starts losing money? In that case, the owners will take the financial hit. To be concrete, suppose that the pizza parlor loses $1,500 during the month of October because it runs up $11,500 in costs but generates only $10,000 in revenue. In that situation, the investors' wealth will shrink by $1,500 as the firm is forced to dip into its reserve to cover the loss. If the firm continues to lose money in subsequent months and exhausts the reserve, the owners will then have to decide whether they want to close the shop or put in additional money in the hope that things will turn around.

CONSIDER THIS . . .

Insurance

Insurance promotes economic growth and investment by transferring risk from those who have a low tolerance for risk to those who have a high tolerance for risk.

Consider fire insurance. Homeowners pay a monthly premium in exchange for which their insurance company guarantees to reimburse them if their house burns down. That guarantee transfers the risk of fire damage from the homeowners (who do not want to bear the risk) to the insurance company's owners (who are happy to bear the risk as a business proposition).

The insurance company will save the premiums that it receives from homeowners to help cover the rebuilding costs of any homes that do end up burning down. But it is quite possible that there will be so many fires that the insurance company will spend more money repairing fire damage than it received in premiums.

If that happens, the insurance company will suffer a loss that will fall upon the insurance company's owners. Their personal wealth will decline in order to make up for the unexpectedly high number of fires. Thus, the insurance company's owners ultimately bear the fire risk; it is to them that the insurance contract transfers risk.

But if the number of fires is unexpectedly small, the insurance company will turn a nice profit and the insurance company's owners will benefit from having been willing to bear the fire risk that the homeowners did not wish to bear.

More importantly, the economy's overall level of investment rises because the availability of insurance means that those who dislike risk are much more willing to invest their savings into the construction and purchase of capital goods like houses, cars, and factories.

But throughout all those months of losses, the suppliers and employees are safeguarded. Because they are paid on time and in full, they are shielded from the firm's business risks and whether it is generating a profit or a loss.

As a result, however, they are not legally entitled to share in the profits if the firm does end up being profitable. That privilege is reserved under the market system for the firm's owners as their reward for bearing business risk. In exchange for making sure that everyone else is shielded if things go badly, the owners are legally entitled to take all of the profits if things go well.

Benefits of Restricting Business Risk to Owners

There are two major benefits that arise from the market system's restriction of business risk to owners and investors.

Attracting Inputs Many people deeply dislike risk and would not be willing to participate in a business venture if they were exposed to the possibility of losing money. That is the case with many workers, who just want to do their jobs and get paid twice a month without having to worry about whether their employer is doing well or not. The same is true for most suppliers, who just want to get paid on time and in full for the inputs they supply to the firm.

For both groups, the concentration of business risk on owners and investors is very welcome because they can supply their resources to a firm without having to worry about the firm's profitability. That sense of security makes it much easier for firms to attract labor and other inputs, which in turn helps the economy innovate and grow.

Focusing Attention The profit system helps to achieve prudent risk management by focusing both the responsibility and the rewards for successfully managing risk onto a firm's owners. They can provide the risk-managing input of entrepreneurial ability themselves or hire it by paying a skilled manager. But either way, some individual's full-time job includes the specialized task of managing risk and making prudent decisions about the allocation of resources. By contrast, in a command system, the responsibility for managing risk tends to be spread out over several layers of government and many different committees so that nobody is personally responsible for bad outcomes.

QUICK REVIEW 2.5

- The market system incentivizes the prudent management of business risk by concentrating any profit or loss upon a firm's owners and investors.
- The market system shields employees, suppliers, and lenders from business risks, but in exchange for that protection, they are excluded from any profit that may be earned.
- By focusing risk on owners and investors, the market system (a) creates an incentive for owners and investors to hire managerial and entrepreneurial specialists to prudently manage business risks and (b) encourages the participation of workers, suppliers, and lenders who dislike risk.

LAST WORD

Shuffling the Deck

Economist Donald Boudreaux Marvels at the Way the Market System Systematically and Purposefully Arranges the World's Tens of Billions of Individual Resources.

In *The Future and Its Enemies*, Virginia Postrel notes the astonishing fact that if you thoroughly shuffle an ordinary deck of 52 playing cards, chances are practically 100 percent that the resulting arrangement of cards has never before existed. *Never.* Every time you shuffle a deck, you produce an arrangement of cards that exists for the first time in history.

The arithmetic works out that way. For a very small number of items, the number of possible arrangements is small. Three items, for example, can be arranged only six different ways. But the number of possible arrangements grows very large very quickly. The number of different ways to arrange five items is 120 . . . for ten items it's 3,628,800 . . . for fifteen items it's 1,307,674,368,000.

The number of different ways to arrange 52 items is 8.066×10^{67}. This is a *big* number. No human can comprehend its enormousness. By way of comparison, the number of possible ways to arrange a mere 20 items is 2,432,902,008,176,640,000—a number larger than the total number of seconds that have elapsed since the beginning of time ten billion years ago—and this number is Lilliputian compared to 8.066×10^{67}.

What's the significance of these facts about numbers? Consider the number of different resources available in the world—my labor, your labor, your land, oil, tungsten, cedar, coffee beans, chickens, rivers, the Empire State Building, [Microsoft] Windows, the wharves at Houston, the classrooms at Oxford, the airport at Miami, and on and on and on. No one can possibly count all of the different productive resources available for our use. But we can be sure that this number is at least in the tens of billions.

When you reflect on how incomprehensibly large is the number of ways to arrange a deck containing a mere 52 cards, the mind boggles at the number of different ways to arrange all the world's resources.

If our world were random—if resources combined together haphazardly, as if a giant took them all into his hands and tossed them down like so many [cards]—it's a virtual certainty that the resulting combination of resources would be useless. Unless this chance arrangement were quickly rearranged according to some productive logic, nothing worthwhile would be produced. We would all starve to death. Because only a tiny fraction of

possible arrangements serves human ends, any arrangement will be useless if it is chosen randomly or with inadequate knowledge of how each and every resource might be productively combined with each other.

And yet, we witness all around us an arrangement of resources that's productive and serves human goals. Today's arrangement of resources might not be perfect, but it is vastly superior to most of the trillions upon trillions of other possible arrangements.

How have we managed to get one of the minuscule number of arrangements that works? The answer is private property—a social institution that encourages mutual accommodation.

Private property eliminates the possibility that resource arrangements will be random, for each resource owner chooses a course of action only if it promises rewards to the owner that exceed the rewards promised by all other available courses.

[The result] is a breathtakingly complex and productive arrangement of countless resources. This arrangement emerged over time (and is still emerging) as the result of billions upon billions of individual, daily, small decisions made by people seeking to better employ their resources and labor in ways that other people find helpful.

Source: Abridged from Donald J. Boudreaux, "Mutual Accommodation," *Ideas on Liberty*, May 2000, pp. 4–5. Used by permission of *The Freeman*.

47

SUMMARY

LO2.1 Differentiate between laissez-faire capitalism, the command system, and the market system.

Laissez-faire capitalism is a hypothetical economic system in which government's role would be restricted to protecting private property and enforcing contracts. All real-world economic systems have featured a more extensive role for government. Governments in command systems own nearly all property and resources and make nearly all decisions about what to produce, how to produce it, and who gets the output. Most countries today, including the United States, have market systems in which the government does play a large role, but in which most property and resources are privately owned and markets are the major force in determining what to produce, how to produce it, and who gets it.

LO2.2 List the main characteristics of the market system.

The market system is characterized by the private ownership of resources, including capital, and the freedom of individuals to engage in economic activities of their choice to advance their material well-being. Self-interest is the driving force of such an economy and competition functions as a regulatory or control mechanism.

In the market system, markets, prices, and profits organize and make effective the many millions of individual economic decisions that occur daily.

Specialization, use of advanced technology, and the extensive use of capital goods are common features of market systems. Functioning as a medium of exchange, money eliminates the problems of bartering and permits easy trade and greater specialization, both domestically and internationally.

LO2.3 Explain how the market system answers the five fundamental questions of what to produce, how to produce, who obtains the output, how to adjust to change, and how to promote progress.

Every economy faces five fundamental questions: (a) What goods and services will be produced? (b) How will the goods and services be produced? (c) Who will get the goods and services? (d) How will the system accommodate change? (e) How will the system promote progress?

The market system produces products whose production and sale yield total revenue sufficient to cover total cost. It does not produce products for which total revenue continuously falls short of total cost. Competition forces firms to use the lowest-cost production techniques.

Economic profit (total revenue minus total cost) indicates that an industry is prosperous and promotes its expansion. Losses signify that an industry is not prosperous and hasten its contraction.

Consumer sovereignty means that both businesses and resource suppliers are subject to the wants of consumers. Through their dollar votes, consumers decide on the composition of output.

The prices that a household receives for the resources it supplies to the economy determine that household's income. This income determines the household's claim on the economy's output. Those who have income to spend get the products produced in the market system.

By communicating changes in consumer tastes to entrepreneurs and resource suppliers, the market system prompts appropriate adjustments in the allocation of the economy's resources. The market system also encourages technological advance and capital accumulation, both of which raise a nation's standard of living.

LO2.4 Explain the operation of the "invisible hand" and why market economies usually do a better job than command economies at efficiently transforming economic resources into desirable output.

Competition, the primary mechanism of control in the market economy, promotes a unity of self-interest and social interests. As if directed by an invisible hand, competition harnesses the self-interested motives of businesses and resource suppliers to further the social interest.

The command systems of the Soviet Union and prereform China met their demise because of coordination difficulties caused by central planning and the lack of a profit incentive. The coordination problem resulted in bottlenecks, inefficiencies, and a focus on a limited number of products. The incentive problem discouraged product improvement, new product development, and entrepreneurship.

LO2.5 Describe the mechanics of the circular flow model.

The circular flow model illustrates the flows of resources and products from households to businesses and from businesses to households, along with the corresponding monetary flows. Businesses are on the buying side of the resource market and the selling side of the product market. Households are on the selling side of the resource market and the buying side of the product market.

LO2.6 Explain how the market system deals with risk.

By focusing business risks onto owners, the market system encourages the participation of workers and suppliers who dislike risk while at the same time creating a strong incentive for owners to manage business risks prudently.

TERMS AND CONCEPTS

economic system	market	"invisible hand"
laissez-faire capitalism	specialization	circular flow diagram
command system	division of labor	households
market system	medium of exchange	businesses
private property	barter	sole proprietorship
freedom of enterprise	money	partnership
freedom of choice	consumer sovereignty	corporation
self-interest	dollar votes	product market
competition	creative destruction	resource market

The following and additional problems can be found in **connect** | ECONOMICS

DISCUSSION QUESTIONS

1. Contrast how a market system and a command economy try to cope with economic scarcity. **LO2.1**
2. How does self-interest help achieve society's economic goals? Why is there such a wide variety of desired goods and services in a market system? In what way are entrepreneurs and businesses at the helm of the economy but commanded by consumers? **LO2.2**
3. Why is private property, and the protection of property rights, so critical to the success of the market system? How do property rights encourage cooperation? **LO2.2**
4. What are the advantages of using capital in the production process? What is meant by the term "division of labor"? What are the advantages of specialization in the use of human and material resources? Explain why exchange is the necessary consequence of specialization. **LO2.2**
5. What problem does barter entail? Indicate the economic significance of money as a medium of exchange. What is meant by the statement "We want money only to part with it"? **LO2.2**
6. Evaluate and explain the following statements: **LO2.2**
   a. The market system is a profit-and-loss system.
   b. Competition is the disciplinarian of the market economy.
7. Some large hardware stores, such as Home Depot, boast of carrying as many as 20,000 different products in each store. What motivated the producers of those individual products

to make them and offer them for sale? How did the producers decide on the best combinations of resources to use? Who made those resources available, and why? Who decides whether these particular hardware products should continue to be produced and offered for sale? **LO2.3**
8. What is meant by the term "creative destruction"? How does the emergence of MP3 (or iPod) technology relate to this idea? **LO2.3**
9. In a sentence, describe the meaning of the phrase "invisible hand." **LO2.4**
10. In market economies, firms rarely worry about the availability of inputs to produce their products, whereas in command economies input availability is a constant concern. Why the difference? **LO2.4**
11. Distinguish between the resource market and the product market in the circular flow model. In what way are businesses and households both sellers and buyers in this model? What are the flows in the circular flow model? **LO2.5**
12. How does shielding employees and suppliers from business risk help to improve economic outcomes? Who is responsible for managing business risks in the market system? **LO2.6**
13. **LAST WORD** What explains why millions of economic resources tend to get arranged logically and productively rather than haphazardly and unproductively?

REVIEW QUESTIONS

1. Decide whether each of the following descriptions most closely corresponds to being part of a command system, a market system, or a laissez-faire system. **LO2.1**
   a. A woman who wants to start a flower shop finds she cannot do so unless the central government has already decided to allow a flower shop in her area.
   b. Shops stock and sell the goods their customers want but the government levies a sales tax on each transaction in

order to fund elementary schools, public libraries, and welfare programs for the poor.
   c. The only taxes levied by the government are to pay for national defense, law enforcement, and a legal system designed to enforce contracts between private citizens.

2. Match each term with the correct definition. **LO2.2**

private property
freedom of enterprise
mutually agreeable
freedom of choice
self-interest
competition
market

a. An institution that brings buyers and sellers together.

b. The right of private persons and firms to obtain, control, employ, dispose of, and bequeath land, capital, and other property.

c. The presence in a market of independent buyers and sellers who compete with one another and who are free to enter and exit the market as they each see fit.

d. The freedom of firms to obtain economic resources, decide what products to produce with those resources, and sell those products in markets of their choice.

e. What each individual or firm believes is best for itself and seeks to obtain.

f. Economic transactions willingly undertaken by both the buyer and the seller because each feels that the transaction will make him or her better off.

g. The freedom of resource owners to dispose of their resources as they think best; of workers to enter any line of work for which they are qualified; and of consumers to spend their incomes in whatever way they feel is most appropriate.

3. True or False: Money must be issued by a government for people to accept it. **LO2.2**

4. Assume that a business firm finds that its profit is greatest when it produces $40 worth of product A. Suppose also that each of the three techniques shown in the table to the right will produce the desired output. **LO2.3**

a. With the resource prices shown, which technique will the firm choose? Why? Will production using that technique entail profit or loss? What will be the amount of that profit or loss? Will the industry expand or contract? When will that expansion or contraction end?

b. Assume now that a new technique, technique 4, is developed. It combines 2 units of labor, 2 of land, 6 of capital, and 3 of entrepreneurial ability. In view of the resource prices in the table, will the firm adopt the new technique? Explain your answer.

c. Suppose that an increase in the labor supply causes the price of labor to fall to $1.50 per unit, all other resource prices remaining unchanged. Which technique will the producer now choose? Explain.

d. "The market system causes the economy to conserve most in the use of resources that are particularly scarce in supply. Resources that are scarcest relative to the demand for them have the highest prices. As a result, producers use these resources as sparingly as is possible." Evaluate this statement. Does your answer to part *c*, above, bear out this contention? Explain.

Resource	Price per Unit of Resource	Resource Units Required		
		Technique 1	Technique 2	Technique 3
Labor	$3	5	2	3
Land	4	2	4	2
Capital	2	2	4	5
Entrepreneurial ability	2	4	2	4

5. Identify each of the following quotes as being an example of either: the coordination problem, the invisible hand, creative destruction, or the incentive problem. **LO2.4**

a. "If you compare a list of today's most powerful and profitable companies with a similar list from 30 years ago, you will see lots of new entries."

b. "Managers in the old Soviet Union often sacrificed product quality and variety because they were being awarded bonuses for quantitative, not qualitative, targets."

c. "Each day, central planners in the old Soviet Union were tasked with setting 27 million prices—correctly."

d. "It is not from the benevolence of the butcher, the brewer, or the baker that we expect our dinner, but from their regard to their own interest."

6. True or False: Households sell finished products to businesses. **LO2.6**

7. Franklin, John, Henry, and Harry have decided to pool their financial resources and business skills in order to open up and run a coffee shop. They will share any profits or losses that the business generates and will be personally responsible for making good on any debt that their business undertakes. Their business should be classified as a: **LO2.6**

a. Corporation.

b. Sole proprietorship.

c. Partnership.

d. None of the above.

8. Ted and Fred are the owners of a gas station. They invested $150,000 each and pay an employee named Lawrence $35,000 per year. This year revenues are $900,000, while costs are $940,000. Who is legally responsible for bearing the $40,000 loss? **LO2.6**

a. Lawrence.

b. Ted.

c. Fred.

d. Ted and Fred.

e. Lawrence, Ted, and Fred.

PROBLEMS

1. Table 2.1 contains information on three techniques for producing $15 worth of bar soap. Assume that we said "$15 worth of bar soap" because soap cost $3 per bar and all three techniques produce 5 bars of soap ($15 = $3 per bar × 5 bars). So you know each technique produces 5 bars of soap. **LO2.3**
   a. What technique will you want to use if the price of a bar of soap falls to $2.75? What if the price of a bar of soap rises to $4? To $5?
   b. How many bars of soap will you want to produce if the price of a bar of soap falls to $2.00?
   c. Suppose that the price of soap is again $3 per bar but that the prices of all four resources are now $1 per unit. Which is now the least-profitable technique?
   d. If the resource prices return to their original levels (the ones shown in the table), but a new technique is invented that can produce 3 bars of soap (yes, 3 bars, not 5 bars!), using 1 unit of each of the four resources, will firms prefer the new technique?
2. Suppose Natasha currently makes $50,000 per year working as a manager at a cable TV company. She then develops two possible entrepreneurial business opportunities. In one, she will quit her job to start an organic soap company. In the other, she will try to develop an Internet-based competitor to the local cable company. For the soap-making opportunity, she anticipates annual revenue of $465,000 and costs for the necessary land, labor, and capital of $395,000 per year. For the Internet opportunity, she anticipates costs for land, labor, and capital of $3,250,000 per year as compared to revenues of $3,275,000 per year. (a) Should she quit her current job to become an entrepreneur? (b) If she does quit her current job, which opportunity would she pursue? **LO2.3**
3. With current technology, suppose a firm is producing 400 loaves of banana bread daily. Also assume that the least-cost combination of resources in producing those loaves is 5 units of labor, 7 units of land, 2 units of capital, and 1 unit of entrepreneurial ability, selling at prices of $40, $60, $60, and $20, respectively. If the firm can sell these 400 loaves at $2 per unit, what is its total revenue? Its total cost? Its profit or loss? Will it continue to produce banana bread? If this firm's situation is typical for the other makers of banana bread, will resources flow toward or away from this bakery good? **LO2.3**
4. Let's put dollar amounts on the flows in the circular flow diagram of Figure 2.2. **LO2.5**
   a. Suppose that businesses buy a total of $100 billion of the four resources (labor, land, capital, and entrepreneurial ability) from households. If households receive $60 billion in wages, $10 billion in rent, and $20 billion in interest, how much are households paid for providing entrepreneurial ability?
   b. If households spend $55 billion on goods and $45 billion on services, how much in revenues do businesses receive in the product market?

FURTHER TEST YOUR KNOWLEDGE AT www.mcconnell20e.com

Practice quizzes, student PowerPoints, worked problems, Web-based questions, and additional materials are available at the text's Online Learning Center (OLC), **www.mcconnell20e.com**, or scan here. Need a barcode reader? Try ScanLife, available in your app store.

Price, Quantity, and Efficiency

PRICE, QUANTITY, AND EFFICIENCY

Demand, Supply, and Market Equilibrium

Learning Objectives

LO3.1 Characterize and give examples of markets.

LO3.2 Describe *demand* and explain how it can change.

LO3.3 Describe *supply* and explain how it can change.

LO3.4 Relate how supply and demand interact to determine market equilibrium.

LO3.5 Explain how changes in supply and demand affect equilibrium prices and quantities.

LO3.6 Identify what government-set prices are and how they can cause product surpluses and shortages.

LO3.7 (Appendix) Illustrate how supply and demand analysis can provide insights on actual-economy situations.

The model of supply and demand is the economics profession's greatest contribution to human understanding

ORIGIN OF THE IDEA

O3.1
Demand and supply

because it explains the operation of the markets on which we depend for nearly everything that we eat, drink, or consume. The model is so powerful and so widely used that to many people it *is* economics.

This chapter explains how the model works and how it can explain both the *quantities* that are bought and sold in markets as well as the *prices* at which they trade.

Marks

LO3.1 Characterize and give examples of markets.

Markets bring together buyers ("demanders") and sellers ("suppliers"). The corner gas station, an e-commerce site, the local music store, a farmer's roadside stand—all are familiar markets. The New York Stock Exchange and the Chicago Board of Trade are markets in which buyers and sellers from all over the world communicate with one another to buy and sell bonds, stocks, and commodities. Auctioneers bring together potential buyers and sellers of art, livestock, used farm equipment, and, sometimes, real estate. In labor markets, new college graduates "sell" and employers "buy" specific labor services.

Some markets are local; others are national or international. Some are highly personal, involving face-to-face contact between demander and supplier; others are faceless, with buyer and seller never seeing or knowing each other.

To keep things simple, we will focus in this chapter on markets in which large numbers of independently acting buyers and sellers come together to buy and sell standardized products. Markets with these characteristics are the economy's most highly competitive. They include the wheat market, the stock market, and the market for foreign currencies. All such markets involve demand, supply, price, and quantity. As you will soon see, the price is "discovered" through the interacting decisions of buyers and sellers.

Demand

LO3.2 Describe *demand* and explain how it can change.

Demand is a schedule or a curve that shows the various amounts of a product that consumers are willing and able to purchase at each of a series of possible prices during a specified period of time.[1] Demand shows the quantities of a product that will be purchased at various possible prices, *other things equal*. Demand can easily be shown in table form. The table in Figure 3.1 is a hypothetical **demand schedule** for a *single consumer* purchasing bushels of corn.

The table reveals the relationship between the various prices of corn and the quantity of corn a particular consumer would be willing and able to purchase at each of these prices. We say "willing and able" because willingness alone is not effective in the market. You may be willing to buy a plasma television set, but if that willingness is not backed by the necessary dollars, it will not be effective and, therefore, will not be reflected in the market. In the table in Figure 3.1, if the price of corn were $5 per bushel, our consumer would be willing and able to buy 10 bushels per week; if it were $4, the consumer would be willing and able to buy 20 bushels per week; and so forth.

---

[1]This definition obviously is worded to apply to product markets. To adjust it to apply to resource markets, substitute the word "resource" for "product" and the word "businesses" for "consumers."

FIGURE 3.1   An individual buyer's demand for corn.   Because price and quantity demanded are inversely related, an individual's demand schedule graphs as a downsloping curve such as *D*. Other things equal, consumers will buy more of a product as its price declines and less of the product as its price rises. (Here and in later figures, *P* stands for price and *Q* stands for quantity demanded or supplied.)

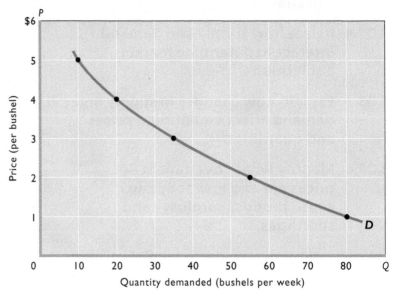

Demand for Corn	
Price per Bushel	Quantity Demanded per Week
$5	10
4	20
3	35
2	55
1	80

The table does not tell us which of the five possible prices will actually exist in the corn market. That depends on the interaction between demand and supply. Demand is simply a statement of a buyer's plans, or intentions, with respect to the purchase of a product.

To be meaningful, the quantities demanded at each price must relate to a specific period—a day, a week, a month. Saying "A consumer will buy 10 bushels of corn at $5 per bushel" is meaningless. Saying "A consumer will buy 10 bushels of corn *per week* at $5 per bushel" is meaningful. Unless a specific time period is stated, we do not know whether the demand for a product is large or small.

Law of Demand

A fundamental characteristic of demand is this: Other things equal, as price falls, the quantity demanded rises, and

ORIGIN OF THE IDEA

O3.2
Law of demand

as price rises, the quantity demanded falls. In short, there is a negative or *inverse* relationship between price and quantity demanded. Economists call this inverse relationship the **law of demand.**

The other-things-equal assumption is critical here. Many factors other than the price of the product being considered affect the amount purchased. For example, the quantity of Nikes purchased will depend not only on the price of Nikes but also on the prices of such substitutes as Reeboks, Adidas, and New Balances. The law of demand in this case says that fewer Nikes will be purchased if the price of Nikes rises and if the prices of Reeboks, Adidas, and New Balances all remain constant. In short, if the *relative price* of Nikes rises, fewer Nikes will be bought. However, if the price of Nikes and the prices of all other competing shoes increase by some amount—say, $5—consumers might buy more, fewer, or the same number of Nikes.

Why the inverse relationship between price and quantity demanded? Let's look at three explanations, beginning with the simplest one:

- The law of demand is consistent with common sense. People ordinarily *do* buy more of a product at a low price than at a high price. Price is an obstacle that deters consumers from buying. The higher that obstacle, the less of a product they will buy; the lower the price obstacle, the more they will buy. The fact that businesses have "sales" to clear out unsold items is evidence of their belief in the law of demand.

- In any specific time period, each buyer of a product will derive less satisfaction (or benefit, or utility) from

each successive unit of the product consumed. The second Big Mac will yield less satisfaction to the consumer than the first, and the third still less than the second.

ORIGIN OF THE IDEA

O3.3
Diminishing marginal utility

That is, consumption is subject to **diminishing marginal utility.** And because successive units of a particular product yield less and less marginal utility, consumers will buy additional units only if the price of those units is progressively reduced.

- We can also explain the law of demand in terms of income and substitution effects. The **income effect** indicates that a lower price increases the purchasing power of a buyer's money income, enabling the buyer to purchase more of the product than before. A higher price has the opposite effect. The **substitution effect** suggests that at a lower price buyers have the incentive to substitute what is now a less expensive product for other products that are now *relatively* more expensive. The product whose price has fallen is now "a better deal" relative to the other products.

For example, a decline in the price of chicken will increase the purchasing power of consumer incomes, enabling people to buy more chicken (the income effect). At a lower price, chicken is relatively more attractive and consumers tend to substitute it for pork, lamb, beef, and fish (the substitution effect). The income and substitution effects com-

ORIGIN OF THE IDEA

O3.4
Income and substitution effects

bine to make consumers able and willing to buy more of a product at a low price than at a high price.

The Demand Curve

The inverse relationship between price and quantity demanded for any product can be represented on a simple graph, in which, by convention, we measure *quantity demanded* on the horizontal axis and *price* on the vertical axis. In the graph in Figure 3.1 we have plotted the five price-quantity data points listed in the accompanying table and connected the points with a smooth curve, labeled *D*. Such a curve is called a **demand curve.** Its downward slope reflects the law of demand—people buy more of a product, service, or resource as its price falls. The relationship between price and quantity demanded is inverse (or negative).

The table and graph in Figure 3.1 contain exactly the same data and reflect the same relationship between price and quantity demanded. But the graph shows that relationship much more simply and clearly than a table or a description in words.

Market Demand

So far, we have concentrated on just one consumer. But competition requires that more than one buyer be present in each market. By adding the quantities demanded by all consumers at each of the various possible prices, we can get from *individual* demand to *market* demand. If there are just three buyers in the market, as represented in the table in Figure 3.2, it is relatively easy to determine the total quantity demanded at each price. Figure 3.2 shows the graphical summing procedure: At each price we sum horizontally the quantities demanded by Joe, Jen, and Jay to obtain the total quantity demanded at that price; we then plot the price and the total quantity demanded as one point on the market demand curve. At the price of $3, for example, the three individual curves yield a total quantity demanded of 100 bushels (= 35 + 39 + 26).

Competition, of course, ordinarily entails many more than three buyers of a product. To avoid hundreds or thousands or millions of additions, we suppose that all the buyers in a market are willing and able to buy the same amounts at each of the possible prices. Then we just multiply those amounts by the number of buyers to obtain the market demand. That is how we arrived at the demand schedule and demand curve D_1 in Figure 3.3 for a market of 200 corn buyers, each with a demand as shown in the table in Figure 3.1.

In constructing a demand curve such as D_1 in Figure 3.3, economists assume that price is the most important influence on the amount of any product purchased. But economists know that other factors can and do affect purchases. These factors, called **determinants of demand,** are assumed to be constant when a demand curve like D_1 is drawn. They are the "other things equal" in the relationship between price and quantity demanded. When any of these determinants changes, the demand curve will shift to the right or left. For this reason, determinants of demand are sometimes referred to as *demand shifters*.

The basic determinants of demand are (1) consumers' tastes (preferences), (2) the number of buyers in the market, (3) consumers' incomes, (4) the prices of related goods, and (5) consumer expectations.

Changes in Demand

A change in one or more of the determinants of demand will change the demand data (the demand schedule) in the table accompanying Figure 3.3 and therefore the location of the demand curve there. A change in the

FIGURE 3.2 Market demand for corn, three buyers. The market demand curve *D* is the horizontal summation of the individual demand curves (D_1, D_2, and D_3) of all the consumers in the market. At the price of $3, for example, the three individual curves yield a total quantity demanded of 100 bushels (= 35 + 39 + 26).

Market Demand for Corn, Three Buyers					
Price per Bushel	Joe	Quantity Demanded Jen		Jay	Total Quantity Demanded per Week
$5	10	+ 12	+	8 =	30
4	20	+ 23	+	17 =	60
3	35	+ 39	+	26 =	100
2	55	+ 60	+	39 =	154
1	80	+ 87	+	54 =	221

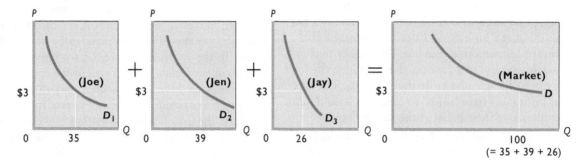

FIGURE 3.3 **Changes in the demand for corn.** A change in one or more of the determinants of demand causes a change in demand. An increase in demand is shown as a shift of the demand curve to the right, as from D_1 to D_2. A decrease in demand is shown as a shift of the demand curve to the left, as from D_1 to D_3. These changes in demand are to be distinguished from a change in quantity demanded, which is caused by a change in the price of the product, as shown by a movement from, say, point a to point b on fixed demand curve D_1.

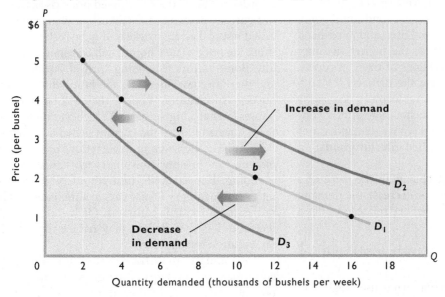

Market Demand for Corn, 200 Buyers, (D_1)	
(1) Price per Bushel	(2) Total Quantity Demanded per Week
$5	2,000
4	4,000
3	7,000
2	11,000
1	16,000

demand schedule or, graphically, a shift in the demand curve is called a *change in demand*.

If consumers desire to buy more corn at each possible price than is reflected in column 2 in the table in Figure 3.3, that *increase in demand* is shown as a shift of the demand curve to the right, say, from D_1 to D_2. Conversely, a *decrease in demand* occurs when consumers buy less corn at each possible price than is indicated in column 2. The leftward shift of the demand curve from D_1 to D_3 in Figure 3.3 shows that situation.

Now let's see how changes in each determinant affect demand.

Tastes A favorable change in consumer tastes (preferences) for a product—a change that makes the product more desirable—means that more of it will be demanded at each price. Demand will increase; the demand curve will shift rightward. An unfavorable change in consumer preferences will decrease demand, shifting the demand curve to the left.

New products may affect consumer tastes; for example, the introduction of digital cameras greatly decreased the demand for film cameras. Consumers' concern over the health hazards of cholesterol and obesity have increased the demand for broccoli, low-calorie beverages, and fresh fruit while decreasing the demand for beef, veal, eggs, and whole milk. Over the past several years, the demand for coffee drinks and table wine has greatly increased, driven by a change in tastes. So, too, has the

demand for touch-screen mobile phones and fuel-efficient hybrid vehicles.

Number of Buyers An increase in the number of buyers in a market is likely to increase demand; a decrease in the number of buyers will probably decrease demand. For example, the rising number of older persons in the United States in recent years has increased the demand for motor homes, medical care, and retirement communities. Large-scale immigration from Mexico has greatly increased the demand for a range of goods and services in the Southwest, including Mexican food products in local grocery stores. Improvements in communications have given financial markets international range and have thus increased the demand for stocks and bonds. International trade agreements have reduced foreign trade barriers to American farm commodities, increasing the number of buyers and therefore the demand for those products.

In contrast, emigration (out-migration) from many small rural communities has reduced the population and thus the demand for housing, home appliances, and auto repair in those towns.

Income How changes in income affect demand is a more complex matter. For most products, a rise in income causes an increase in demand. Consumers typically buy more steaks, furniture, and electronic equipment as their incomes increase. Conversely, the demand for such products declines as their incomes fall. Products whose demand varies *directly* with money income are called *superior goods*, or **normal goods.**

Although most products are normal goods, there are some exceptions. As incomes increase beyond some point, the demand for used clothing, retread tires, and third-hand automobiles may decrease because the higher incomes enable consumers to buy new versions of those products. Rising incomes may also decrease the demand for soy-enhanced hamburger. Similarly, rising incomes may cause the demand for charcoal grills to decline as wealthier consumers switch to gas grills. Goods whose demand varies *inversely* with money income are called **inferior goods.**

Prices of Related Goods

A change in the price of a related good may either increase or decrease the demand for a product, depending on whether the related good is a substitute or a complement:

- A **substitute good** is one that can be used in place of another good.
- A **complementary good** is one that is used together with another good.

Substitutes Häagen-Dazs ice cream and Ben & Jerry's ice cream are substitute goods or, simply, *substitutes*. When two products are substitutes, an increase in the price of one will increase the demand for the other. Conversely, a decrease in the price of one will decrease the demand for the other. For example, when the price of Häagen-Dazs ice cream rises, consumers will buy less of it and increase their demand for Ben & Jerry's ice cream. When the price of Colgate toothpaste declines, the demand for Crest decreases. So it is with other product pairs such as Nikes and Reeboks, Budweiser and Miller beer, or Chevrolets and Fords. They are *substitutes in consumption*.

Complements Because complementary goods (or, simply, *complements*) are used together, they are typically demanded jointly. Examples include computers and software, cell phones and cellular service, and snowboards and lift tickets. If the price of a complement (for example, lettuce) goes up, the demand for the related good (salad dressing) will decline. Conversely, if the price of a complement (for example, tuition) falls, the demand for a related good (textbooks) will increase.

Unrelated Goods The vast majority of goods are not related to one another and are called *independent goods*. Examples are butter and golf balls, potatoes and automobiles, and bananas and wristwatches. A change in the price of one has little or no effect on the demand for the other.

Consumer Expectations

Changes in consumer expectations may shift demand. A newly formed expectation of higher future prices may cause consumers to buy now in order to "beat" the anticipated price rises, thus increasing current demand. That is often what happens in so-called hot real estate markets. Buyers rush in because they think the price of new homes will continue to escalate rapidly. Some buyers fear being "priced out of the market" and therefore not obtaining the home they desire. Other buyers—speculators—believe they will be able to sell the houses later at a higher price. Whichever their motivation, these buyers increase the current demand for houses.

Similarly, a change in expectations concerning future income may prompt consumers to change their current spending. For example, first-round NFL draft choices may splurge on new luxury cars in anticipation of lucrative professional football contracts. Or workers who become fearful of losing their jobs may reduce their demand for, say, vacation travel.

In summary, an *increase* in demand—the decision by consumers to buy larger quantities of a product at each possible price—may be caused by:

- A favorable change in consumer tastes.
- An increase in the number of buyers.
- Rising incomes if the product is a normal good.
- Falling incomes if the product is an inferior good.
- An increase in the price of a substitute good.
- A decrease in the price of a complementary good.
- A new consumer expectation that either prices or income will be higher in the future.

You should "reverse" these generalizations to explain a *decrease* in demand. Table 3.1 provides additional illustrations of the determinants of demand.

Changes in Quantity Demanded

A *change in demand* must not be confused with a *change in quantity demanded*. A **change in demand** is a shift of the demand curve to the right (an increase in demand) or to the left (a decrease in demand). It occurs because the consumer's state of mind about purchasing the product has been altered in response to a change in one or more of the determinants of demand. Recall that "demand" is a schedule or a curve; therefore, a "change in demand" means a change in the schedule and a shift of the curve.

In contrast, a **change in quantity demanded** is a movement from one point to another point—from one price-quantity combination to another—on a fixed demand curve. The cause of such a change is an increase or

TABLE 3.1 Determinants of Demand: Factors That Shift the Demand Curve

Determinant	Examples
Change in buyer tastes	Physical fitness rises in popularity, increasing the demand for jogging shoes and bicycles; cell phone popularity rises, reducing the demand for landline phones.
Change in number of buyers	A decline in the birthrate reduces the demand for children's toys.
Change in income	A rise in incomes increases the demand for normal goods such as restaurant meals, sports tickets, and necklaces while reducing the demand for inferior goods such as cabbage, turnips, and inexpensive wine.
Change in the prices of related goods	A reduction in airfares reduces the demand for bus transportation (substitute goods); a decline in the price of DVD players increases the demand for DVD movies (complementary goods).
Change in consumer expectations	Inclement weather in South America creates an expectation of higher future coffee bean prices, thereby increasing today's demand for coffee beans.

decrease in the price of the product under consideration. In the table in Figure 3.3, for example, a decline in the price of corn from $5 to $4 will increase the quantity demanded of corn from 2,000 to 4,000 bushels.

In Figure 3.3 the shift of the demand curve D_1 to either D_2 or D_3 is a change in demand. But the movement from point *a* to point *b* on curve D_1 represents a change in quantity demanded: Demand has not changed; it is the entire curve, and it remains fixed in place.

QUICK REVIEW 3.1

- Demand is a schedule or a curve showing the amount of a product that buyers are willing and able to purchase, in a particular time period, at each possible price in a series of prices.
- The law of demand states that, other things equal, the quantity of a good purchased varies inversely with its price.
- The demand curve shifts because of changes in (a) consumer tastes, (b) the number of buyers in the market, (c) consumer income, (d) the prices of substitute or complementary goods, and (e) consumer expectations.
- A change in demand is a shift of the demand curve; a change in quantity demanded is a movement from one point to another on a fixed demand curve.

Supply

LO3.3 Describe *supply* and explain how it can change.

Supply is a schedule or curve showing the various amounts of a product that producers are willing and able to make available for sale at each of a series of possible prices during a specific period.[2] The table in Figure 3.4 is a hypothetical **supply schedule** for a single producer of corn. It shows the quantities of corn that will be supplied at various prices, other things equal.

Law of Supply

The table in Figure 3.4 shows that a positive or direct relationship prevails between price and quantity supplied. As price rises, the quantity supplied rises; as price falls, the quantity supplied falls. This relationship is called the **law of supply.** A supply schedule tells us that, other things equal, firms will produce and offer for sale more of their product at a high price than at a low price. This, again, is basically common sense.

Price is an obstacle from the standpoint of the consumer, who is on the paying end. The higher the price, the less the consumer will buy. But the supplier is on the receiving end of the product's price. To a supplier, price represents *revenue*, which serves as an incentive to produce and sell a product. The higher the price, the greater this incentive and the greater the quantity supplied.

Consider a farmer who is deciding on how much corn to plant. As corn prices rise, as shown in the table in Figure 3.4, the farmer finds it profitable to plant more corn. And the higher corn prices enable the farmer to cover the increased costs associated with more intensive cultivation and the use of more seed, fertilizer, and pesticides. The overall result is more corn.

Now consider a manufacturer. Beyond some quantity of production, manufacturers usually encounter increases in *marginal cost*—the added cost of producing one more unit of output. Certain productive resources—in particular, the firm's plant and machinery—cannot be expanded quickly, so the firm uses more of other resources such as labor to produce more output. But as labor becomes more abundant relative to the fixed plant and equipment, the additional workers have relatively less space and access to equipment. For example, the added workers may have to wait to gain access to machines. As a result, each added worker produces less added output, and the marginal cost of successive units of output rises accordingly. The firm will not produce the

---

[2]This definition is worded to apply to product markets. To adjust it to apply to resource markets, substitute "resource" for "product" and "owners" for "producers."

FIGURE 3.4   An individual producer's supply of corn. Because price and quantity supplied are directly related, the supply curve for an individual producer graphs as an upsloping curve. Other things equal, producers will offer more of a product for sale as its price rises and less of the product for sale as its price falls.

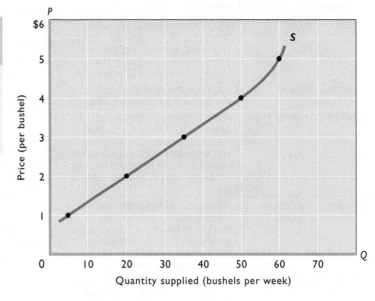

Supply of Corn	
Price per Bushel	Quantity Supplied per Week
$5	60
4	50
3	35
2	20
1	5

more costly units unless it receives a higher price for them. Again, price and quantity supplied are directly related.

The Supply Curve

As with demand, it is convenient to represent individual supply graphically. In Figure 3.4, curve S is the **supply curve** that corresponds with the price–quantity supplied data in the accompanying table. The upward slope of the curve reflects the law of supply—producers offer more of a good, service, or resource for sale as its price rises. The relationship between price and quantity supplied is positive, or direct.

Market Supply

Market supply is derived from individual supply in exactly the same way that market demand is derived from individual demand. We sum the quantities supplied by each producer at each price. That is, we obtain the market supply curve by "horizontally adding" the supply curves of the individual producers. The price–quantity supplied data in the table accompanying Figure 3.5 are for an assumed 200 identical producers in the market, each willing to supply corn according to the supply schedule shown in Figure 3.4. Curve S_1 in Figure 3.5 is a graph of the market supply data. Note that the values of the axes in Figure 3.5 are the same as those used in our graph of market demand (Figure 3.3). The only difference is that we change the label on the horizontal axis from "quantity demanded" to "quantity supplied."

Determinants of Supply

In constructing a supply curve, we assume that price is the most significant influence on the quantity supplied of any product. But other factors (the "other things equal") can and do affect supply. The supply curve is drawn on the assumption that these other things are fixed and do not change. If one of them does change, a *change in supply* will occur, meaning that the entire supply curve will shift.

The basic **determinants of supply** are (1) resource prices, (2) technology, (3) taxes and subsidies, (4) prices of other goods, (5) producer expectations, and (6) the number of sellers in the market. A change in any one or more of these determinants of supply, or *supply shifters*, will move the supply curve for a product either right or left. A shift to the *right*, as from S_1 to S_2 in Figure 3.5, signifies an *increase* in supply: Producers supply larger quantities of the product at each possible price. A shift to the *left*, as from S_1 to S_3, indicates a *decrease* in supply: Producers offer less output at each price.

Changes in Supply

Let's consider how changes in each of the determinants affect supply. The key idea is that costs are a major factor underlying supply curves; anything that affects costs (other than changes in output itself) usually shifts the supply curve.

Resource Prices   The prices of the resources used in the production process help determine the costs of production incurred by firms. Higher *resource* prices raise

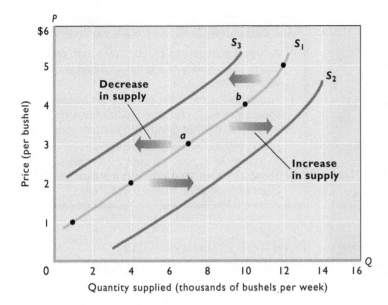

FIGURE 3.5 Changes in the supply of corn. A change in one or more of the determinants of supply causes a change in supply. An increase in supply is shown as a rightward shift of the supply curve, as from S_1 to S_2. A decrease in supply is depicted as a leftward shift of the curve, as from S_1 to S_3. In contrast, a change in the *quantity supplied* is caused by a change in the product's price and is shown by a movement from one point to another, as from *b* to *a* on fixed supply curve S_1.

Market Supply of Corn, 200 Producers, (S_1)	
(1) Price per Bushel	(2) Total Quantity Supplied per Week
$5	12,000
4	10,000
3	7,000
2	4,000
1	1,000

production costs and, assuming a particular *product* price, squeeze profits. That reduction in profits reduces the incentive for firms to supply output at each product price. For example, an increase in the price of sand, crushed rock, or Portland cement will increase the cost of producing concrete and reduce its supply.

In contrast, lower *resource* prices reduce production costs and increase profits. So when resource prices fall, firms supply greater output at each product price. For example, a decrease in the price of iron ore will decrease the price of steel.

Technology Improvements in technology (techniques of production) enable firms to produce units of output with fewer resources. Because resources are costly, using fewer of them lowers production costs and increases supply. Example: Technological advances in producing flat-panel computer monitors have greatly reduced their cost. Thus, manufacturers will now offer more such monitors than previously at the various prices; the supply of flat-panel monitors has increased.

Taxes and Subsidies Businesses treat most taxes as costs. An increase in sales or property taxes will increase production costs and reduce supply. In contrast, subsidies are "taxes in reverse." If the government subsidizes the production of a good, it in effect lowers the producers' costs and increases supply.

Prices of Other Goods Firms that produce a particular product, say, soccer balls, can sometimes use their plant and equipment to produce alternative goods, say, basketballs and volleyballs. The higher prices of these "other

goods" may entice soccer ball producers to switch production to those other goods in order to increase profits. This *substitution in production* results in a decline in the supply of soccer balls. Alternatively, when the prices of basketballs and volleyballs decline relative to the price of soccer balls, producers of those goods may decide to produce more soccer balls instead, increasing their supply.

Producer Expectations Changes in expectations about the future price of a product may affect the producer's current willingness to supply that product. It is difficult, however, to generalize about how a new expectation of higher prices affects the present supply of a product. Farmers anticipating a higher wheat price in the future might withhold some of their current wheat harvest from the market, thereby causing a decrease in the current supply of wheat. In contrast, in many types of manufacturing industries, newly formed expectations that price will increase may induce firms to add another shift of workers or to expand their production facilities, causing current supply to increase.

Number of Sellers Other things equal, the larger the number of suppliers, the greater the market supply. As more firms enter an industry, the supply curve shifts to the right. Conversely, the smaller the number of firms in the industry, the less the market supply. This means that as firms leave an industry, the supply curve shifts to the left. Example: The United States and Canada have imposed restrictions on haddock fishing to replenish dwindling stocks. As part of that policy, the federal government has bought the boats of some of the haddock fishers as a way of putting

TABLE 3.2 Determinants of Supply: Factors That Shift the Supply Curve

Determinant	Examples
Change in resource prices	A decrease in the price of microchips increases the supply of computers; an increase in the price of crude oil reduces the supply of gasoline.
Change in technology	The development of more effective wireless technology increases the supply of cell phones.
Changes in taxes and subsidies	An increase in the excise tax on cigarettes reduces the supply of cigarettes; a decline in subsidies to state universities reduces the supply of higher education.
Change in prices of other goods	An increase in the price of cucumbers decreases the supply of watermelons.
Change in producer expectations	An expectation of a substantial rise in future log prices decreases the supply of logs today.
Change in number of suppliers	An increase in the number of tattoo parlors increases the supply of tattoos; the formation of women's professional basketball leagues increases the supply of women's professional basketball games.

them out of business and decreasing the catch. The result has been a decline in the market supply of haddock.

Table 3.2 is a checklist of the determinants of supply, along with further illustrations.

Changes in Quantity Supplied

The distinction between a *change in supply* and a *change in quantity supplied* parallels the distinction between a change in demand and a change in quantity demanded. Because supply is a schedule or curve, a **change in supply** means a change in the schedule and a shift of the curve. An increase in supply shifts the curve to the right; a decrease in supply shifts it to the left. The cause of a change in supply is a change in one or more of the determinants of supply.

In contrast, a **change in quantity supplied** is a movement from one point to another on a fixed supply curve. The cause of such a movement is a change in the price of the specific product being considered.

Consider supply curve S_1 in Figure 3.5. A decline in the price of corn from $4 to $3 decreases the quantity of corn supplied per week from 10,000 to 7,000 bushels. This movement from point *b* to point *a* along S_1 is a change in quantity supplied, not a change in supply. Supply is the full schedule of prices and quantities shown, and this schedule does not change when the price of corn changes.

Market Equilibrium

LO3.4 Relate how supply and demand interact to determine market equilibrium.

With our understanding of demand and supply, we can now show how the decisions of buyers of corn and sellers of corn interact to determine the equilibrium price and quantity of corn. In the table in Figure 3.6, columns 1 and 2 repeat the market supply of corn (from the table in Figure 3.5), and columns 2 and 3 repeat the market demand for corn (from the table in Figure 3.3). We assume this is a competitive market so that neither buyers nor sellers can set the price.

Equilibrium Price and Quantity

We are looking for the equilibrium price and equilibrium quantity. The **equilibrium price** (or *market-clearing price*) is the price where the intentions of buyers and sellers match. It is the price where quantity demanded equals quantity supplied. The table in Figure 3.6 reveals that at $3, *and only at that price*, the number of bushels of corn that sellers wish to sell (7,000) is identical to the number consumers want to buy (also 7,000). At $3 and 7,000 bushels of corn, there is neither a shortage nor a surplus of corn. So 7,000 bushels of corn is the **equilibrium quantity**: the quantity at which the intentions of buyers and sellers match, so that the quantity demanded and the quantity supplied are equal.

Graphically, the equilibrium price is indicated by the intersection of the supply curve and the demand curve in **Figure 3.6 (Key Graph).** (The horizontal axis now measures both quantity demanded and quantity supplied.) With neither a shortage nor a surplus at $3, the market is *in equilibrium*, meaning "in balance" or "at rest."

Competition among buyers and among sellers drives the price to the equilibrium price; once there, it will remain there unless it is subsequently disturbed by changes in demand or supply (shifts of the curves). To better understand the uniqueness of the equilibrium price, let's consider other

FIGURE 3.6 Equilibrium price and quantity. The intersection of the downsloping demand curve *D* and the upsloping supply curve *S* indicates the equilibrium price and quantity, here $3 and 7,000 bushels of corn. The shortages of corn at below-equilibrium prices (for example, 7,000 bushels at $2) drive up price. The higher prices increase the quantity supplied and reduce the quantity demanded until equilibrium is achieved. The surpluses caused by above-equilibrium prices (for example, 6,000 bushels at $4) push price down. As price drops, the quantity demanded rises and the quantity supplied falls until equilibrium is established. At the equilibrium price and quantity, there are neither shortages nor surpluses of corn.

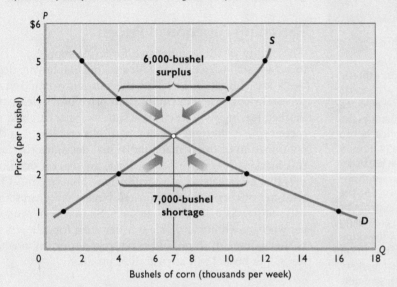

Market Supply of and Demand for Corn			
(1) Total Quantity Supplied per Week	(2) Price per Bushel	(3) Total Quantity Demanded per Week	(4) Surplus (+) or Shortage (−)*
12,000	$5	2,000	+10,000 ↓
10,000	4	4,000	+6,000 ↓
7,000	3	7,000	0
4,000	2	11,000	−7,000 ↑
1,000	1	16,000	−15,000 ↑

*Arrows indicate the effect on price.

QUICK QUIZ FOR FIGURE 3.6

1. Demand curve *D* is downsloping because:
   a. producers offer less of a product for sale as the price of the product falls.
   b. lower prices of a product create income and substitution effects that lead consumers to purchase more of it.
   c. the larger the number of buyers in a market, the lower the product price.
   d. price and quantity demanded are directly (positively) related.

2. Supply curve *S*:
   a. reflects an inverse (negative) relationship between price and quantity supplied.
   b. reflects a direct (positive) relationship between price and quantity supplied.
   c. depicts the collective behavior of buyers in this market.

   d. shows that producers will offer more of a product for sale at a low product price than at a high product price.

3. At the $3 price:
   a. quantity supplied exceeds quantity demanded.
   b. quantity demanded exceeds quantity supplied.
   c. the product is abundant and a surplus exists.
   d. there is no pressure on price to rise or fall.

4. At price $5 in this market:
   a. there will be a shortage of 10,000 units.
   b. there will be a surplus of 10,000 units.
   c. quantity demanded will be 12,000 units.
   d. quantity demanded will equal quantity supplied.

Answers: 1. b; 2. b; 3. d; 4. b

prices. At any above-equilibrium price, quantity supplied exceeds quantity demanded. For example, at the $4 price, sellers will offer 10,000 bushels of corn, but buyers will purchase only 4,000. The $4 price encourages sellers to offer lots of corn but discourages many consumers from buying it. The result is a **surplus** (or *excess supply*) of 6,000 bushels. If corn sellers produced them all, they would find themselves with 6,000 unsold bushels of corn.

Surpluses drive prices down. Even if the $4 price existed temporarily, it could not persist. The large surplus would

prompt competing sellers to lower the price to encourage buyers to take the surplus off their hands. As the price fell, the incentive to produce corn would decline and the incentive for consumers to buy corn would increase. As shown in Figure 3.6, the market would move to its equilibrium at $3.

Any price below the $3 equilibrium price would create a shortage; quantity demanded would exceed quantity supplied. Consider a $2 price, for example. We see both from column 2 of the table and from the demand curve in Figure 3.6 that quantity demanded exceeds quantity supplied at

63

that price. The result is a **shortage** (or *excess demand*) of 7,000 bushels of corn. The $2 price discourages sellers from devoting resources to corn and encourages consumers to desire more bushels than are available. The $2 price cannot

---

CONSIDER THIS . . .

Ticket Scalping: A Bum Rap!

Ticket prices for athletic events and musical concerts are usually set far in advance of the events. Sometimes the original ticket price is too low to be the equilibrium price. Lines form at the ticket window and a severe shortage of tickets occurs at the printed price. What happens next? Buyers who are willing to pay more than the original price bid up the ticket price in resale ticket markets.

Tickets sometimes get resold for much greater amounts than the original price—market transactions known as "scalping." For example, an original buyer may resell a $75 ticket to a concert for $200. Reporters sometimes denounce scalpers for "ripping off" buyers by charging "exorbitant" prices.

But is scalping really a rip-off? We must first recognize that such ticket resales are voluntary transactions. If both buyer and seller did not expect to gain from the exchange, it would not occur! The seller must value the $200 more than seeing the event, and the buyer must value seeing the event at $200 or more. So there are no losers or victims here: Both buyer and seller benefit from the transaction. The scalping market simply redistributes assets (game or concert tickets) from those who would rather have the money (and the other things that the money can buy) to those who would rather have the tickets.

Does scalping impose losses or injury on the sponsors of the event? If the sponsors are injured, it is because they initially priced tickets below the equilibrium level. Perhaps they did this to create a long waiting line and the attendant news media publicity. Alternatively, they may have had a genuine desire to keep tickets affordable for lower-income, ardent fans. In either case, the event sponsors suffer an opportunity cost in the form of less ticket revenue than they might have otherwise received. But such losses are self-inflicted and separate and distinct from the fact that some tickets are later resold at a higher price.

So is ticket scalping undesirable? Not on economic grounds! It is an entirely voluntary activity that benefits both sellers and buyers.

---

persist as the equilibrium price. Many consumers who want to buy corn at this price will not obtain it. They will express a willingness to pay more than $2 to get corn. Competition among these buyers will drive up the price, eventually to the $3 equilibrium level. Unless disrupted by changes of supply or demand, this $3 price of corn will continue to prevail.

Rationing Function of Prices

The ability of the competitive forces of supply and demand to establish a price at which selling and buying decisions are consistent is called the rationing function of prices. In our case, the equilibrium price of $3 clears the market, leaving no burdensome surplus for sellers and no inconvenient shortage for potential buyers. And it is the combination of freely made individual decisions that sets this market-clearing price. In effect, the market outcome says that all buyers who are willing and able to pay $3 for a bushel of corn will obtain it; all buyers who cannot or will not pay $3 will go without corn. Similarly, all producers who are willing and able to offer corn for sale at $3 a bushel will sell it; all producers who cannot or will not sell for $3 per bushel will not sell their product.

Efficient Allocation

A competitive market such as that we have described not only rations goods to consumers but also allocates society's resources efficiently to the particular product. Competition among corn producers forces them to use the best technology and right mix of productive resources. If they didn't, their costs would be too high relative to the market price, and they would be unprofitable. The result is **productive efficiency:** the production of any particular good in the least costly way. When society produces corn at the lowest achievable per-unit cost, it is expending the least-valued combination of resources to produce that product and therefore is making available more-valued resources to produce other desired goods. Suppose society has only $100 worth of resources available. If it can produce a bushel of corn using $3 of those resources, then it will have available $97 of resources remaining to produce other goods. This is clearly better than producing the corn for $5 and having only $95 of resources available for the alternative uses.

Competitive markets also produce **allocative efficiency:** the *particular mix* of goods and services most highly valued by society (minimum-cost production assumed). For example, society wants land suitable for growing corn used for that purpose, not to grow dandelions. It wants diamonds to be used for jewelry, not crushed up and used as an additive to give concrete more sparkle. It wants iPods and MP4 players, not cassette players and tapes. Moreover, society does not want to devote all its resources to corn, diamonds, and portable digital media players. It wants to assign some resources to wheat, gasoline, and cell phones. Competitive markets make those allocatively efficient assignments.

The equilibrium price and quantity in competitive markets usually produce an assignment of resources that is "right" from an economic perspective. Demand essentially reflects the marginal benefit (MB) of the good, based on the utility received. Supply reflects the marginal cost (MC) of producing the good. The market ensures that firms produce all units of goods for which MB exceeds MC and no units for which MC exceeds MB. At the intersection of the demand and supply curves, MB equals MC and allocative efficiency results. As economists say, there is neither an "underallocaton of resources" nor an "overallocation of resources" to the product.

Changes in Supply, Demand, and Equilibrium

LO3.5 Explain how changes in supply and demand affect equilibrium prices and quantities.

We know that demand might change because of fluctuations in consumer tastes or incomes, changes in consumer expectations, or variations in the prices of related goods. Supply might change in response to changes in resource prices, technology, or taxes. What effects will such changes in supply and demand have on equilibrium price and quantity?

Changes in Demand

Suppose that the supply of some good (for example, health care) is constant and demand increases, as shown in Figure 3.7a. As a result, the new intersection of the supply and demand curves is at higher values on both the price and the quantity axes. Clearly, an increase in demand raises both equilibrium price and equilibrium quantity. Conversely, a decrease in demand such as that shown in Figure 3.7b reduces both equilibrium price and equilibrium quantity. (The value of graphical analysis is now apparent: We need not fumble with columns of figures to determine the outcomes; we need only compare the new and the old points of intersection on the graph.)

Changes in Supply

What happens if the demand for some good (for example, flash drives) is constant but supply increases, as in Figure 3.7c? The new intersection of supply and demand is located at a lower equilibrium price but at a higher equilibrium quantity. An increase in supply reduces equilibrium price but increases equilibrium quantity. In con-

trast, if supply decreases, as in Figure 3.7d, equilibrium price rises while equilibrium quantity declines.

Complex Cases

When both supply and demand change, the effect is a combination of the individual effects.

Supply Increase; Demand Decrease What effect will a supply increase and a demand decrease for some good (for example, apples) have on equilibrium price? Both changes decrease price, so the net result is a price drop greater than that resulting from either change alone.

What about equilibrium quantity? Here the effects of the changes in supply and demand are opposed: the increase

CONSIDER THIS . . .

Salsa and Coffee Beans

If you forget the other-things-equal assumption, you can encounter situations that *seem* to be in conflict with the laws of demand and supply. For example, suppose salsa manufacturers sell 1 million bottles of salsa at $4 a bottle in one year; 2 million bottles at $5 in the next year; and 3 million at $6 in the year thereafter. Price and quantity purchased vary directly, and these data seem to be at odds with the law of demand.

But there is no conflict here; the data do not refute the law of demand. The catch is that the law of demand's other-things-equal assumption has been violated over the three years in the example. Specifically, because of changing tastes and rising incomes, the demand for salsa has increased sharply, as in Figure 3.7a. The result is higher prices *and* larger quantities purchased.

Another example: The price of coffee beans occasionally shoots upward at the same time that the quantity of coffee beans harvested declines. These events seemingly contradict the direct relationship between price and quantity denoted by supply. The catch again is that the other-things-equal assumption underlying the upsloping supply curve is violated. Poor coffee harvests decrease supply, as in Figure 3.7d, increasing the equilibrium price of coffee and reducing the equilibrium quantity.

The laws of demand and supply are not refuted by observations of price and quantity made over periods of time in which either demand or supply curves shift.

FIGURE 3.7   Changes in demand and supply and the effects on price and quantity. The increase in demand from D_1 to D_2 in (a) increases both equilibrium price and equilibrium quantity. The decrease in demand from D_3 to D_4 in (b) decreases both equilibrium price and equilibrium quantity. The increase in supply from S_1 to S_2 in (c) decreases equilibrium price and increases equilibrium quantity. The decline in supply from S_3 to S_4 in (d) increases equilibrium price and decreases equilibrium quantity. The boxes in the top right corners summarize the respective changes and outcomes. The upward arrows in the boxes signify increases in equilibrium price (P) and equilibrium quantity (Q); the downward arrows signify decreases in these items.

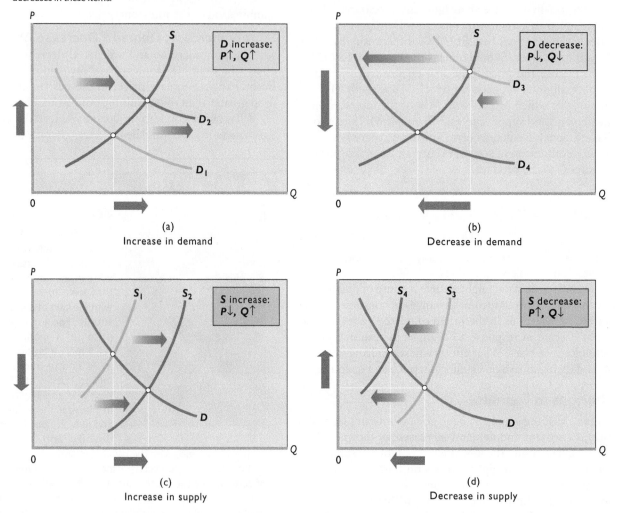

in supply increases equilibrium quantity, but the decrease in demand reduces it. The direction of the change in equilibrium quantity depends on the relative sizes of the changes in supply and demand. If the increase in supply is larger than the decrease in demand, the equilibrium quantity will increase. But if the decrease in demand is greater than the increase in supply, the equilibrium quantity will decrease.

Supply Decrease; Demand Increase A decrease in supply and an increase in demand for some good (for example, gasoline) both increase price. Their combined effect is an increase in equilibrium price greater than that caused by either change separately. But their effect on the equilibrium quantity is again indeterminate, depending on

the relative sizes of the changes in supply and demand. If the decrease in supply is larger than the increase in demand, the equilibrium quantity will decrease. In contrast, if the increase in demand is greater than the decrease in supply, the equilibrium quantity will increase.

Supply Increase; Demand Increase What if supply and demand both increase for some good (for example, cell phones)? A supply increase drops equilibrium price, while a demand increase boosts it. If the increase in supply is greater than the increase in demand, the equilibrium price will fall. If the opposite holds, the equilibrium price will rise.

The effect on equilibrium quantity is certain: The increases in supply and demand both raise the equilibrium

TABLE 3.3 Effects of Changes in Both Supply and Demand

Change in Supply	Change in Demand	Effect on Equilibrium Price	Effect on Equilibrium Quantity
1. Increase	Decrease	Decrease	Indeterminate
2. Decrease	Increase	Increase	Indeterminate
3. Increase	Increase	Indeterminate	Increase
4. Decrease	Decrease	Indeterminate	Decrease

quantity. Therefore, the equilibrium quantity will increase by an amount greater than that caused by either change alone.

Supply Decrease; Demand Decrease What about decreases in both supply and demand for some good (for example, new homes)? If the decrease in supply is greater than the decrease in demand, equilibrium price will rise. If the reverse is true, equilibrium price will fall. Because the decreases in supply and demand each reduce equilibrium quantity, we can be sure that equilibrium quantity will fall.

Table 3.3 summarizes these four cases. To understand them fully, you should draw supply and demand diagrams for each case to confirm the effects listed in this table.

Special cases arise when a decrease in demand and a decrease in supply, or an increase in demand and an increase in supply, exactly cancel out. In both cases, the net effect on equilibrium price will be zero; price will not change.

The optional appendix accompanying this chapter provides additional examples of situations in which both supply and demand change at the same time.

Application: Government-Set Prices

LO3.6 Identify what government-set prices are and how they can cause product surpluses and shortages.

Prices in most markets are free to rise or fall to their equilibrium levels, no matter how high or low those levels might be. However, government sometimes concludes that supply and demand will produce prices that are unfairly high for buyers or unfairly low for sellers. So government may place legal limits on how high or low a price or prices may go. Is that a good idea?

Price Ceilings on Gasoline

A **price ceiling** sets the maximum legal price a seller may charge for a product or service. A price at or below the ceiling is legal; a price above it is not. The rationale for establishing price ceilings (or ceiling prices) on specific products is that they purportedly enable consumers to obtain some

FIGURE 3.8 A price ceiling. A price ceiling is a maximum legal price such as P_c. When the ceiling price is below the equilibrium price, a persistent product shortage results. Here that shortage is shown by the horizontal distance between Q_d and Q_s.

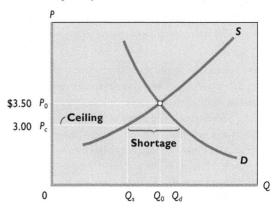

"essential" good or service that they could not afford at the equilibrium price. Examples are rent controls and usury laws, which specify maximum "prices" in the forms of rent and interest that can be charged to borrowers.

Graphical Analysis We can easily show the effects of price ceilings graphically. Suppose that rapidly rising world income boosts the purchase of automobiles and shifts the demand for gasoline to the right so that the market equilibrium price reaches $3.50 per gallon, shown as P_0 in Figure 3.8. The rapidly rising price of gasoline greatly burdens low- and moderate-income households, which pressure government to "do something." To keep gasoline prices down, the government imposes a ceiling price P_c of $3 per gallon. To impact the market, a price ceiling must be below the equilibrium price. A ceiling price of $4, for example, would have had no effect on the price of gasoline in the current situation.

What are the effects of this $3 ceiling price? The rationing ability of the free market is rendered ineffective. Because the ceiling price P_c is below the market-clearing price P_0, there is a lasting shortage of gasoline. The quantity of gasoline demanded at P_c is Q_d and the quantity supplied is only Q_s; a persistent excess demand or shortage of amount $Q_d - Q_s$ occurs.

The price ceiling P_c prevents the usual market adjustment in which competition among buyers bids up price, inducing more production and rationing some buyers out of the market. That process would normally continue until the shortage disappeared at the equilibrium price and quantity, P_0 and Q_0.

By preventing these market adjustments from occurring, the price ceiling poses two related problems.

Rationing Problem How will the available supply Q_s be apportioned among buyers who want the greater

A Legal Market for Human Organs?

A Legal Market Might Eliminate the Present Shortage of Human Organs for Transplant. But There Are Many Serious Objections to "Turning Human Body Parts into Commodities" for Purchase and Sale.

It has become increasingly commonplace in medicine to transplant kidneys, lungs, livers, corneas, pancreases, and hearts from deceased individuals to those whose organs have failed or are failing. But surgeons and many of their patients face a growing problem: There are shortages of donated organs available for transplant. Not everyone who needs a transplant can get one. In 2012, there were 116,000 Americans on the waiting list for transplants. Indeed, an inadequate supply of donated organs causes an estimated 6,900 deaths in the United States each year.

Why Shortages? Seldom do we hear of shortages of desired goods in market economies. What is different about organs for transplant? One difference is that no legal market exists for human organs. To understand this situation, observe the demand curve D_1 and supply curve S_1 in the accompanying figure. The downward slope of the demand curve tells us that if there

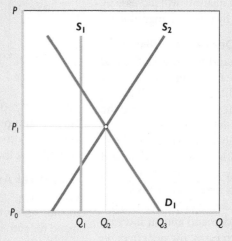

were a market for human organs, the quantity of organs demanded would be greater at lower prices than at higher prices. Vertical supply curve S_1 represents the fixed quantity of human organs now donated via consent before death. Because the price of these donated organs is in effect zero, quantity demanded Q_3 exceeds quantity supplied Q_1. The shortage of $Q_3 - Q_1$ is rationed through a waiting list of those in medical need of transplants. Many people die while still on the waiting list.

Use of a Market A market for human organs would increase the incentive to donate organs. Such a market might work like this: An individual might specify in a legal document that he or she is willing to sell one or more usable human organs upon death or near-death. The person could specify where the money from the sale would go, for example, to family, a church, an educational institution, or a charity. Firms would then emerge to purchase

amount Q_d? Should gasoline be distributed on a first-come, first-served basis, that is, to those willing and able to get in line the soonest or stay in line the longest? Or should gas stations distribute it on the basis of favoritism? Since an unregulated shortage does not lead to an equitable distribution of gasoline, the government must establish some formal system for rationing it to consumers. One option is to issue ration coupons, which authorize bearers to purchase a fixed amount of gasoline per month. The rationing system might entail first the printing of coupons for Q_s gallons of gasoline and then the equal distribution of the coupons among consumers so that the wealthy family of four and the poor family of four both receive the same number of coupons.

Black Markets But ration coupons would not prevent a second problem from arising. The demand curve in Figure 3.8 reveals that many buyers are willing to pay more than the ceiling price P_c. And, of course, it is more profit-

able for gasoline stations to sell at prices above the ceiling. Thus, despite a sizable enforcement bureaucracy that would have to accompany the price controls, *black markets* in which gasoline is illegally bought and sold at prices above the legal limits will flourish. Counterfeiting of ration coupons will also be a problem. And since the price of gasoline is now "set by government," government might face political pressure to set the price even lower.

Rent Controls

About 200 cities in the United States, including New York City, Boston, and San Francisco, have at one time or another enacted rent controls: maximum rents established by law (or, more recently, maximum rent increases for existing tenants). Such laws are well intended. Their goals are to protect low-income families from escalating rents caused by perceived housing shortages and to make housing more affordable to the poor.

organs and resell them where needed for profit. Under such a system, the supply curve of usable organs would take on the normal upward slope of typical supply curves. The higher the expected price of an organ, the greater the number of people who would be willing to have their organs sold at death. Suppose that the supply curve is S_2 in the figure. At the equilibrium price P_1, the number of organs made available for transplant (Q_2) would equal the number purchased for transplant (also Q_2). In this generalized case, the shortage of organs would be eliminated and, of particular importance, the number of organs available for transplanting would rise from Q_1 to Q_2. This means more lives would be saved and enhanced than under the present donor system.

Objections In view of this positive outcome, why is there no such market for human organs? Critics of market-based solutions have two main objections. The first is a moral objection: Critics feel that turning human organs into commodities commercializes human beings and diminishes the special nature of human life. They say there is something unseemly about selling and buying body organs as if they were bushels of wheat or ounces of gold. (There is, however, a market for blood!) Moreover, critics note that the market would ration the available organs (as represented by Q_2 in the figure) to people who either can afford them (at P_1) or have health insurance for transplants. The poor and uninsured would be left out.

Second, a health-cost objection suggests that a market for body organs would greatly increase the cost of health care. Rather than obtaining freely donated (although "too few") body organs, patients or their insurance companies would have to pay market prices for them, further increasing the cost of medical care.

Rebuttal Supporters of market-based solutions to organ shortages point out that the laws against selling organs are simply driving the market underground. Worldwide, an estimated $1 billion-per-year illegal market in human organs has emerged. As in other illegal markets, the unscrupulous tend to thrive. This fact is dramatized by the accompanying photo, in which four Pakistani villagers show off their scars after they each sold a kidney to pay off debts. Supporters say that legalization of the market for human organs would increase organ supply from legal sources, drive down the price of organs, and reduce the abuses such as those now taking place in illegal markets.

What have been the actual economic effects? On the demand side, the below-equilibrium rents attract a larger number of renters. Some are locals seeking to move into their own places after sharing housing with friends or family. Others are outsiders attracted into the area by the artificially lower rents. But a large problem occurs on the supply side. Price controls make it less attractive for landlords to offer housing on the rental market. In the short run, owners may sell their rental units or convert them to condominiums. In the long run, low rents make it unprofitable for owners to repair or renovate their rental units. (Rent controls are one cause of the many abandoned apartment buildings found in larger cities.) Also, insurance companies, pension funds, and other potential new investors in housing will find it more profitable to invest in office buildings, shopping malls, or motels, where rents are not controlled.

In brief, rent controls distort market signals and thus resources are misallocated: Too few resources are allocated to rental housing and too many to alternative uses. Ironically, although rent controls are often legislated to lessen the effects of perceived housing shortages, controls in fact are a primary cause of such shortages. For that reason, most American cities either have abandoned or are in the process of dismantling rent controls.

Price Floors on Wheat

A **price floor** is a minimum price fixed by the government. A price at or above the price floor is legal; a price below it is not. Price floors above equilibrium prices are usually invoked when society feels that the free functioning of the market system has not provided a sufficient income for certain groups of resource suppliers or producers. Supported prices for agricultural products and current minimum wages are two examples of price (or wage) floors. Let's look at the former.

Suppose that many farmers have extremely low incomes when the price of wheat is at its equilibrium value of $2 per bushel. The government decides to help out by establishing a legal price floor or price support of $3 per bushel.

What will be the effects? At any price above the equilibrium price, quantity supplied will exceed quantity demanded—that is, there will be a persistent excess supply or surplus of the product. Farmers will be willing to produce and offer for sale more than private buyers are willing to purchase at the price floor. As we saw with a price ceiling, an imposed legal price disrupts the rationing ability of the free market.

Graphical Analysis   Figure 3.9 illustrates the effect of a price floor graphically. Suppose that S and D are the supply and demand curves for wheat. Equilibrium price and quantity are P_0 and Q_0, respectively. If the government imposes a price floor of P_f, farmers will produce Q_s but private buyers will purchase only Q_d. The surplus is the excess of Q_s over Q_d.

The government may cope with the surplus resulting from a price floor in two ways:

- It can restrict supply (for example, by instituting acreage allotments by which farmers agree to take a certain amount of land out of production) or increase demand (for example, by researching new uses for the product involved). These actions may reduce the difference between the equilibrium price and the price floor and that way reduce the size of the resulting surplus.

- If these efforts are not wholly successful, then the government must purchase the surplus output at the $3 price (thereby subsidizing farmers) and store or otherwise dispose of it.

Additional Consequences   Price floors such as P_f in Figure 3.9 not only disrupt the rationing ability of prices

but distort resource allocation. Without the price floor, the $2 equilibrium price of wheat would cause financial losses and force high-cost wheat producers to plant other crops or abandon farming altogether. But the $3 price floor allows them to continue to grow wheat and remain farmers. So society devotes too many of its scarce resources to wheat production and too few to producing other, more valuable, goods and services. It fails to achieve allocative efficiency.

That's not all. Consumers of wheat-based products pay higher prices because of the price floor. Taxpayers pay higher taxes to finance the government's purchase of the surplus. Also, the price floor causes potential environmental damage by encouraging wheat farmers to bring hilly, erosion-prone "marginal land" into production. The higher price also prompts imports of wheat. But, since such imports would increase the quantity of wheat supplied and thus undermine the price floor, the government needs to erect tariffs (taxes on imports) to keep the foreign wheat out. Such tariffs usually prompt other countries to retaliate with their own tariffs against U.S. agricultural or manufacturing exports.

So it is easy to see why economists "sound the alarm" when politicians advocate imposing price ceilings or price floors such as price controls, rent controls, interest-rate lids, or agricultural price supports. In all these cases, good intentions lead to bad economic outcomes. Government-controlled prices cause shortages or surpluses, distort resource allocation, and produce negative side effects.

FIGURE 3.9   A price floor.   A price floor is a minimum legal price such as P_f. When the price floor is above the equilibrium price, a persistent product surplus results. Here that surplus is shown by the horizontal distance between Q_s and Q_d.

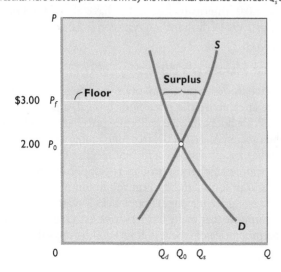

QUICK REVIEW 3.3

- In competitive markets, prices adjust to the equilibrium level at which quantity demanded equals quantity supplied.
- The equilibrium price and quantity are those indicated by the intersection of the supply and demand curves for any product or resource.
- An increase in demand increases equilibrium price and quantity; a decrease in demand decreases equilibrium price and quantity.
- An increase in supply reduces equilibrium price but increases equilibrium quantity; a decrease in supply increases equilibrium price but reduces equilibrium quantity.
- Over time, equilibrium price and quantity may change in directions that seem at odds with the laws of demand and supply because the other-things-equal assumption is violated.
- Government-controlled prices in the form of ceilings and floors stifle the rationing function of prices, distort resource allocations, and cause negative side effects.

SUMMARY

LO3.1 Characterize and give examples of markets.

Markets bring buyers and sellers together. Some markets are local, others international. Some have physical locations while others are online. For simplicity, this chapter focuses on highly competitive markets in which large numbers of buyers and sellers come together to buy and sell standardized products. All such markets involve demand, supply, price, and quantity, with price being "discovered" through the interacting decisions of buyers and sellers.

LO3.2 Describe *demand* and explain how it can change.

Demand is a schedule or curve representing the willingness of buyers in a specific period to purchase a particular product at each of various prices. The law of demand implies that consumers will buy more of a product at a low price than at a high price. So, other things equal, the relationship between price and quantity demanded is negative or inverse and is graphed as a downsloping curve.

Market demand curves are found by adding horizontally the demand curves of the many individual consumers in the market.

Changes in one or more of the determinants of demand (consumer tastes, the number of buyers in the market, the money incomes of consumers, the prices of related goods, and consumer expectations) shift the market demand curve. A shift to the right is an increase in demand; a shift to the left is a decrease in demand. A change in demand is different from a change in the quantity demanded, the latter being a movement from one point to another point on a fixed demand curve because of a change in the product's price.

LO3.3 Describe *supply* and explain how it can change.

Supply is a schedule or curve showing the amounts of a product that producers are willing to offer in the market at each possible price during a specific period. The law of supply states that, other things equal, producers will offer more of a product at a high price than at a low price. Thus, the relationship between price and quantity supplied is positive or direct, and supply is graphed as an upsloping curve.

The market supply curve is the horizontal summation of the supply curves of the individual producers of the product.

Changes in one or more of the determinants of supply (resource prices, production techniques, taxes or subsidies, the prices of other goods, producer expectations, or the number of sellers in the market) shift the supply curve of a product. A shift to the right is an increase in supply; a shift to the left is a decrease in supply. In contrast, a change in the price of the product being considered causes a change in the quantity supplied, which is shown as a movement from one point to another point on a fixed supply curve.

LO3.4 Relate how supply and demand interact to determine market equilibrium.

The equilibrium price and quantity are established at the intersection of the supply and demand curves. The interaction of market demand and market supply adjusts the price to the point at which the quantities demanded and supplied are equal. This is the equilibrium price. The corresponding quantity is the equilibrium quantity.

The ability of market forces to synchronize selling and buying decisions to eliminate potential surpluses and shortages is known as the rationing function of prices. The equilibrium quantity in competitive markets reflects both productive efficiency (least-cost production) and allocative efficiency (producing the right amount of the product relative to other products).

LO3.5 Explain how changes in supply and demand affect equilibrium prices and quantities.

A change in either demand or supply changes the equilibrium price and quantity. Increases in demand raise both equilibrium price and equilibrium quantity; decreases in demand lower both equilibrium price and equilibrium quantity. Increases in supply lower equilibrium price and raise equilibrium quantity; decreases in supply raise equilibrium price and lower equilibrium quantity.

Simultaneous changes in demand and supply affect equilibrium price and quantity in various ways, depending on their direction and relative magnitudes (see Table 3.3).

LO3.6 Identify what government-set prices are and how they can cause product surpluses and shortages.

A price ceiling is a maximum price set by government and is designed to help consumers. Effective price ceilings produce persistent product shortages, and if an equitable distribution of the product is sought, government must ration the product to consumers.

A price floor is a minimum price set by government and is designed to aid producers. Effective price floors lead to persistent product surpluses; the government must either purchase the product or eliminate the surplus by imposing restrictions on production or increasing private demand.

Legally fixed prices stifle the rationing function of prices and distort the allocation of resources.

TERMS AND CONCEPTS

demand	income effect	normal goods
demand schedule	substitution effect	inferior goods
law of demand	demand curve	substitute good
diminishing marginal utility	determinants of demand	complementary good

change in demand	determinants of supply	shortage
change in quantity demanded	change in supply	productive efficiency
supply	change in quantity supplied	allocative efficiency
supply schedule	equilibrium price	price ceiling
law of supply	equilibrium quantity	price floor
supply curve	surplus	

The following and additional problems can be found in connect ECONOMICS

DISCUSSION QUESTIONS

1. Explain the law of demand. Why does a demand curve slope downward? How is a market demand curve derived from individual demand curves? **LO3.2**

2. What are the determinants of demand? What happens to the demand curve when any of these determinants change? Distinguish between a change in demand and a movement along a fixed demand curve, noting the cause(s) of each. **LO3.2**

3. Explain the law of supply. Why does the supply curve slope upward? How is the market supply curve derived from the supply curves of individual producers? **LO3.3**

4. What are the determinants of supply? What happens to the supply curve when any of these determinants changes? Distinguish between a change in supply and a change in the quantity supplied, noting the cause(s) of each. **LO3.3**

5. In 2001 an outbreak of hoof-and-mouth disease in Europe led to the burning of millions of cattle carcasses. What impact do you think this had on the supply of cattle hides, hide prices, the supply of leather goods, and the price of leather goods? **LO3.5**

6. For each stock in the stock market, the number of shares sold daily equals the number of shares purchased. That is, the quantity of each firm's shares demanded equals the quantity supplied. So, if this equality always occurs, why do the prices of stock shares ever change? **LO3.5**

7. What do economists mean when they say "price floors and ceilings stifle the rationing function of prices and distort resource allocation"? **LO3.6**

8. **LAST WORD** In some countries, such as France, every corpse is available for doctors to "harvest" for organs unless the deceased, while still alive, signed a form forbidding the organs to be harvested. In the United States, it is the opposite: No harvesting is allowed unless the deceased had signed, while still alive, an organ donor form authorizing doctors to harvest any needed organs. Use supply and demand figures to show in which country organ shortages are likely to be less severe.

REVIEW QUESTIONS

1. What effect will each of the following have on the demand for small automobiles such as the Mini-Cooper and Fiat 500? **LO3.2**
   a. Small automobiles become more fashionable.
   b. The price of large automobiles rises (with the price of small autos remaining the same).
   c. Income declines and small autos are an inferior good.
   d. Consumers anticipate that the price of small autos will greatly come down in the near future.
   e. The price of gasoline substantially drops.

2. True or False: A "change in quantity demanded" is a shift of the entire demand curve to the right or to the left. **LO3.2**

3. What effect will each of the following have on the supply of auto tires? **LO3.3**
   a. A technological advance in the methods of producing tires.
   b. A decline in the number of firms in the tire industry.
   c. An increase in the prices of rubber used in the production of tires.
   d. The expectation that the equilibrium price of auto tires will be lower in the future than currently.

   e. A decline in the price of the large tires used for semi trucks and earth-hauling rigs (with no change in the price of auto tires).
   f. The levying of a per-unit tax on each auto tire sold.
   g. The granting of a 50-cent-per-unit subsidy for each auto tire produced.

4. "In the corn market, demand often exceeds supply and supply sometimes exceeds demand." "The price of corn rises and falls in response to changes in supply and demand." In which of these two statements are the terms "supply" and "demand" used correctly? Explain. **LO3.3**

5. Suppose that in the market for computer memory chips, the equilibrium price is $50 per chip. If the current price is $55 per chip, then there will be _____ of memory chips. **LO3.4**
   a. A shortage.
   b. A surplus.
   c. An equilibrium quantity.
   d None of the above.

6. Critically evaluate: "In comparing the two equilibrium positions in Figure 3.7b, I note that a smaller amount is actually demanded at a lower price. This refutes the law of demand." **LO3.5**

7. Label each of the following scenarios with the set of symbols that best indicates the price change and quantity change that occur in the scenario. In some scenarios, it may not be possible from the information given to determine the direction of a particular price change or a particular quantity change. We will symbolize those cases as, respectively, "P?" and "Q?" The four possible combinations of price and quantity changes are:. **LO3.5**

P↓ Q?   P? Q↓
P↑ Q?   P? Q↑

a. On a hot day, both the demand for lemonade and the supply of lemonade increase.
b. On a cold day, both the demand for ice cream and the supply of ice cream decrease.
c. When Hawaii's Mt. Kilauea erupts violently, the demand on the part of tourists for sightseeing flights increases but the supply of pilots willing to provide these dangerous flights decreases.
d. In a hot area of Arizona where they generate a lot of their electricity with wind turbines, the demand for electricity falls on windy days as people switch off their air conditioners and enjoy the breeze. But at the same time, the amount of electricity supplied increases as the wind turbines spin faster.

8. Suppose the total demand for wheat and the total supply of wheat per month in the Kansas City grain market are as shown in the table below. Suppose that the government establishes a price ceiling of $3.70 for wheat. What might prompt the government to establish this price ceiling? Explain carefully the main effects. Demonstrate your answer graphically. Next, suppose that the government establishes a price floor of $4.60 for wheat. What will be the main effects of this price floor? Demonstrate your answer graphically. **LO3.6**

Thousands of Bushels Demanded	Price per Bushel	Thousands of Bushels Supplied
85	$3.40	72
80	3.70	73
75	4.00	75
70	4.30	77
65	4.60	79
60	4.90	81

9. A price ceiling will result in a shortage only if the ceiling price is _____ the equilibrium price. **LO3.6**
a. Less than.
b. Equal to.
c. Greater than.
d. Louder than.

PROBLEMS

1. Suppose there are three buyers of candy in a market: Tex, Dex, and Rex. The market demand and the individual demands of Tex, Dex, and Rex are shown on the next page. **LO3.2**
a. Fill in the table for the missing values.
b. Which buyer demands the least at a price of $5? The most at a price of $7?
c. Which buyer's quantity demanded increases the most when the price is lowered from $7 to $6?
d. Which direction would the market demand curve shift if Tex withdrew from the market? What if Dex doubled his purchases at each possible price?
e. Suppose that at a price of $6, the total quantity demanded increases from 19 to 38. Is this a "change in the quantity demanded" or a "change in demand"?

Price per Candy	Individual Quantities Demanded						Total Quantity Demanded
	Tex		Dex		Rex		
$8	3	+	1	+	0	=	___
7	8	+	2	+	___	=	12
6	___	+	3	+	4	=	19
5	17	+	___	+	6	=	27
4	23	+	5	+	8	=	___

2. The figure on the right shows the supply curve for tennis balls, S_1, for Drop Volley Tennis, a producer of tennis equipment.

Use the figure and the table below to give your answers to the following questions. **LO3.3**

a. Use the figure to fill in the quantity supplied on supply curve S_1 for each price in the table below.

Price	S_1 Quantity Supplied	S_2 Quantity Supplied	Change in Quantity Supplied
$3	_____	4	_____
2	_____	2	_____
1	_____	0	_____

b. If production costs were to increase, the quantities supplied at each price would be as shown by the third column of the table ("S_2 Quantity Supplied"). Use those data to draw supply curve S_2 on the same graph as supply curve S_1.

c. In the fourth column of the table, enter the amount by which the quantity supplied at each price changes due to the increase in product costs. (Use positive numbers for increases and negative numbers for decreases.)

d. Did the increase in production costs cause a "decrease in supply" or a "decrease in quantity supplied"?

3. Refer to the expanded table below from review question 8. **LO3.4**

   a. What is the equilibrium price? At what price is there neither a shortage nor a surplus? Fill in the surplus-shortage column and use it to confirm your answers.

   b. Graph the demand for wheat and the supply of wheat. Be sure to label the axes of your graph correctly. Label equilibrium price P and equilibrium quantity Q.

   c. How big is the surplus or shortage at $3.40? At $4.90? How big a surplus or shortage results if the price is 60 cents higher than the equilibrium price? 30 cents lower than the equilibrium price?

Thousands of Bushels Demanded	Price per Bushel	Thousands of Bushels Supplied	Surplus (+) or Shortage (−)
85	$3.40	72	_____
80	3.70	73	_____
75	4.00	75	_____
70	4.30	77	_____
65	4.60	79	_____
60	4.90	81	_____

4. How will each of the following changes in demand and/or supply affect equilibrium price and equilibrium quantity in a competitive market; that is, do price and quantity rise, fall, or remain unchanged, or are the answers indeterminate because they depend on the magnitudes of the shifts? Use supply and demand to verify your answers. **LO3.5**

   a. Supply decreases and demand is constant.

   b. Demand decreases and supply is constant.

   c. Supply increases and demand is constant.

   d. Demand increases and supply increases.

   e. Demand increases and supply is constant.

   f. Supply increases and demand decreases.

   g. Demand increases and supply decreases.

   h. Demand decreases and supply decreases.

5. Use two market diagrams to explain how an increase in state subsidies to public colleges might affect tuition and enrollments in both public and private colleges. **LO3.5**

6. **ADVANCED ANALYSIS** Assume that demand for a commodity is represented by the equation $P = 10 - .2Q_d$ and supply by the equation $P = 2 + .2Q_s$, where Q_d and Q_s are quantity demanded and quantity supplied, respectively, and P is price. Using the equilibrium condition $Q_s = Q_d$, solve the equations to determine equilibrium price. Now determine equilibrium quantity. **LO3.5**

7. Suppose that the demand and supply schedules for rental apartments in the city of Gotham are as given in the table below. **LO3.6**

Monthly Rent	Apartments Demanded	Apartments Supplied
$2,500	10,000	15,000
2,000	12,500	12,500
1,500	15,000	10,000
1,000	17,500	7,500
500	20,000	5,000

   a. What is the market equilibrium rental price per month and the market equilibrium number of apartments demanded and supplied?

   b. If the local government can enforce a rent-control law that sets the maximum monthly rent at $1,500, will there be a surplus or a shortage? Of how many units? And how many units will actually be rented each month?

   c. Suppose that a new government is elected that wants to keep out the poor. It declares that the minimum rent that can be charged is $2,500 per month. If the government can enforce that price floor, will there be a surplus or a shortage? Of how many units? And how many units will actually be rented each month?

   d. Suppose that the government wishes to decrease the market equilibrium monthly rent by increasing the supply of housing. Assuming that demand remains unchanged, by how many units of housing would the government have to increase the supply of housing in order to get the market equilibrium rental price to fall to $1,500 per month? To $1,000 per month? To $500 per month?

FURTHER TEST YOUR KNOWLEDGE AT www.mcconnell20e.com

Practice quizzes, student PowerPoints, worked problems, Web-based questions, and additional materials are available at the text's Online Learning Center (OLC), **www.mcconnell20e.com**, or scan here. Need a barcode reader? Try ScanLife, available in your app store.

Additional Examples of Supply and Demand

LO3.7 Illustrate how supply and demand analysis can provide insights on actual-economy situations.

Our discussion has clearly demonstrated that supply and demand analysis is a powerful tool for understanding equilibrium prices and quantities. The information provided in the main body of this chapter is fully sufficient for moving forward in the book, but you may find that additional examples of supply and demand are helpful. This optional appendix provides several concrete illustrations of changes in supply and demand.

Your instructor may assign all, some, or none of this appendix, depending on time availability and personal preference.

Changes in Supply and Demand

As Figure 3.7 of this chapter demonstrates, changes in supply and demand cause changes in price, quantity, or both. The following applications illustrate this fact in several real-world markets. The simplest situations are those in which either supply changes while demand remains constant or demand changes while supply remains constant. Let's consider two such simple cases first, before looking at more complex applications.

Lettuce

Every now and then we hear on the news that extreme weather has severely reduced the size of some crop. Suppose, for example, that a severe freeze destroys a sizable portion of the lettuce crop. This unfortunate situation implies a significant decline in supply, which we represent as a leftward shift of the supply curve from S_1 to S_2 in Figure 1. At each price, consumers desire as much lettuce as before, so the freeze does not affect the demand for lettuce. That is, demand curve D_1 does not shift.

What are the consequences of the reduced supply of lettuce for equilibrium price and quantity? As shown in Figure 1, the leftward shift of the supply curve disrupts the previous equilibrium in the market for lettuce and drives the equilibrium price upward from P_1 to P_2. Consumers respond to that price hike by reducing the quantity of lettuce demanded from Q_1 to Q_2. Equilibrium is restored at P_2 and Q_2.

FIGURE 1 The market for lettuce. The decrease in the supply of lettuce, shown here by the shift from S_1 to S_2, increases the equilibrium price of lettuce from P_1 to P_2 and reduces the equilibrium quantity from Q_1 to Q_2.

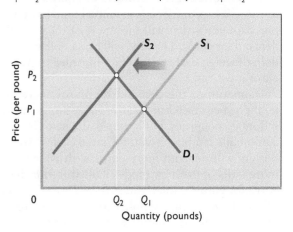

Consumers who are willing and able to pay price P_2 obtain lettuce; consumers unwilling or unable to pay that price do not. Some consumers continue to buy as much lettuce as before, even at the higher price. Others buy some lettuce but not as much as before, and still others opt out of the market completely. The latter two groups use the money they would have spent on lettuce to obtain other products, say, carrots. (Because of our other-things-equal assumption, the prices of other products have not changed.)

Exchange Rates

Exchange rates are the prices at which one currency can be traded (exchanged) for another. Exchange rates are normally determined in foreign exchange markets. One of the largest foreign exchange markets is the euro-dollar market in which the currency used in most of Europe, the *euro*, is exchanged for U.S. dollars. In the United States, this market is set up so that euros are priced in dollars—that is, the "product" being traded is euros and the "price" to buy that product is quoted in dollars. Thus, the market equilibrium price one day might be $1.25 to buy 1 euro, while on another day it might be $1.50 to buy 1 euro.

Foreign exchange markets are used by individuals and companies that need to make purchases or payments in a different currency. U.S. companies exporting goods to Germany, for instance, wish to be paid in U.S. dollars. Thus, their German customers will need to convert euros into dollars. The euros that they bring to the euro-dollar market will become part of the overall market supply of euros. Conversely, an American mutual fund may wish to purchase some French real estate outside of Paris. But to purchase that real estate, it will need to pay in euros because the current French owners will only accept payment in euros. Thus, the American mutual fund has a demand to purchase euros that will form part of the overall market demand for euros. The fund will bring dollars to the euro-dollar foreign exchange market in order to purchase the euros it desires.

Sometimes, the demand for euros increases. This might be because a European product surges in popularity in foreign countries. For example, if a new German-made automobile is a big hit in the United States, American car dealers will demand more euros with which to pay for more units of that new model. This will shift the demand curve for euros to the right, as from D_1 to D_2 in Figure 2. Given the fixed euro supply curve S_1, the increase in demand raises the equilibrium exchange rate (the equilibrium number of dollars needed to purchase 1 euro) from \$1.25 to \$1.50. The equilibrium quantity of euros purchased increases from Q_1 to Q_2. Because a higher dollar amount is now needed to purchase one euro, economists say that the dollar has *depreciated*—gone down in value—relative to the euro. Alternatively, the euro has *appreciated*—gone up in

value—relative to the dollar, because one euro now buys \$1.50 rather than \$1.25.

Pink Salmon

Now let's see what happens when both supply and demand change at the same time. Several decades ago, people who caught salmon earned as much as \$1 for each pound of pink salmon—the type of salmon most commonly used for canning. In Figure 3 that price is represented as P_1, at the intersection of supply curve S_1 and demand curve D_1. The corresponding quantity of pink salmon is shown as Q_1 pounds.

As time passed, supply and demand changed in the market for pink salmon. On the supply side, improved technology in the form of larger, more efficient fishing boats greatly increased the catch and lowered the cost of obtaining it. Also, high profits at price P_1 encouraged many new fishers to enter the industry. As a result of these changes, the supply of pink salmon greatly increased and the supply curve shifted to the right, as from S_1 to S_2 in Figure 3.

Over the same years, the demand for pink salmon declined, as represented by the leftward shift from D_1 to D_2 in Figure 3. That decrease was caused by increases in consumer income and reductions of the price of substitute products. As buyers' incomes rose, consumers shifted demand away from canned fish and toward higher-quality fresh or frozen fish, including more-valued Atlantic, chinook, sockeye, and coho salmon. Moreover, the emergence of fish farming, in which salmon are raised in ocean

FIGURE 2 **The market for euros.** The increase in the demand for euros, shown here by the shift from D_1 to D_2, increases the equilibrium price of one euro from \$1.25 to \$1.50 and increases the equilibrium quantity of euros that are exchanged from Q_1 to Q_2. The dollar has depreciated.

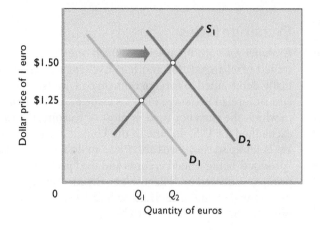

FIGURE 3 **The market for pink salmon.** In the last several decades, the supply of pink salmon has increased and the demand for pink salmon has decreased. As a result, the price of pink salmon has declined, as from P_1 to P_2. Because supply has increased by more than demand has decreased, the equilibrium quantity of pink salmon has increased, as from Q_1 to Q_2.

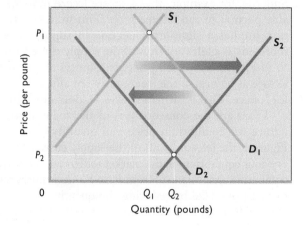

net pens, lowered the prices of these substitute species. That, too, reduced the demand for pink salmon.

The altered supply and demand reduced the price of pink salmon to as low as $0.10 per pound, as represented by the drop in price from P_1 to P_2 in Figure 3. Both the supply increase and the demand decrease helped reduce the equilibrium price. However, in this particular case the equilibrium quantity of pink salmon increased, as represented by the move from Q_1 to Q_2. Both shifts reduced the equilibrium price, but equilibrium quantity increased because the increase in supply exceeded the decrease in demand.

Gasoline

The price of gasoline in the United States has increased rapidly several times during the past several years. For example, the average price of a gallon of gasoline rose from around $2.60 in October 2010 to about $3.90 in May 2011. What caused this 50 percent rise in the price of gasoline? How would we diagram this increase?

We begin in Figure 4 with the price of a gallon of gasoline at P_1, representing the $2.60 price. Simultaneous supply and demand factors disturbed this equilibrium. Supply uncertainties relating to Middle East politics and warfare and expanded demand for oil by fast-growing countries such as China pushed up the price of a barrel of oil from under $80 per barrel in October 2010 to well over $100 per barrel in May 2011. Oil is the main input for producing gasoline, so any sustained rise in its price boosts the per-unit cost of producing gasoline. Such cost rises decrease the supply of gasoline, as represented by the

leftward shift of the supply curve from S_1 to S_2 in Figure 4. At times refinery breakdowns in the United States also contributed to this reduced supply.

While the supply of gasoline declined between October 2010 and May 2011, the demand for gasoline increased, as depicted by the rightward shift of the demand curve from D_1 to D_2. Incomes in general were rising over this period because the U.S. economy was expanding. Rising incomes raise demand for all normal goods, including gasoline. An increased number of low-gas-mileage SUVs and light trucks on the road also contributed to growing gas demand.

The combined decline in gasoline supply and increase in gasoline demand boosted the price of gasoline from $2.60 to $3.90, as represented by the rise from P_1 to P_2 in Figure 4. Because the demand increase outweighed the supply decrease, the equilibrium quantity expanded, here from Q_1 to Q_2.

In other periods the price of gasoline has *declined* as the demand for gasoline has increased. Test your understanding of the analysis by explaining how such a price decrease could occur.

Sushi

Sushi bars are springing up like Starbucks in American cities (well, maybe not that fast!). Consumption of sushi, the raw-fish delicacy from Japan, has soared in the United States in recent years. Nevertheless, the price of sushi has remained relatively constant.

Supply and demand analysis helps explain this circumstance of increased quantity and constant price. A change in tastes has increased the U.S. demand for sushi. Many consumers of sushi find it highly tasty when they try it. And, as implied by the growing number of sushi bars in the United States, the supply of sushi has also expanded.

We represent these supply and demand changes in Figure 5 as the rightward shift of the demand curve from D_1 to D_2 and the rightward shift of the supply curve from S_1 to S_2. Observe that the equilibrium quantity of sushi increases from Q_1 to Q_2 and equilibrium price remains constant at P_1. The increase in supply, which taken alone would reduce price, has perfectly offset the increase in demand, which taken alone would raise price. The price of sushi does not change, but the equilibrium quantity greatly increases because both the increase in demand and the increase in supply expand purchases and sales.

Simultaneous increases in demand and supply can cause price to either rise, fall, or remain constant, depending on the relative magnitudes of the supply and demand increases. In this case, price remained constant.

FIGURE 4 **The market for gasoline.** An increase in the demand for gasoline, as shown by the shift from D_1 to D_2, coupled with a decrease in supply, as shown by the shift from S_1 to S_2, boosts equilibrium price (here from P_1 to P_2). In this case, equilibrium quantity increases from Q_1 to Q_2 because the increase in demand outweighs the decrease in supply.

FIGURE 5 **The market for sushi.** Equal increases in the demand for sushi, as from D_1 to D_2, and in the supply of sushi, as from S_1 to S_2, expand the equilibrium quantity of sushi (here from Q_1 to Q_2) while leaving the price of sushi unchanged at P_1.

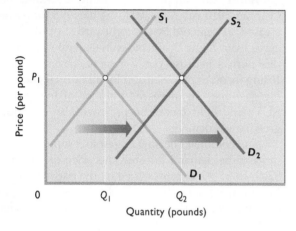

FIGURE 6 **The market for land in San Francisco.** Because the quantity of land in San Francisco is fixed at Q_0, the supply curve is vertical above Q_0 in order to indicate that the same quantity of land will be supplied no matter what the price is. As demand increases from D_1 to D_2, the equilibrium price rises from P_1 to P_2. Because the quantity of land is fixed at Q_0, the movement from equilibrium a to equilibrium b involves only a change in the equilibrium price; the equilibrium quantity remains at Q_0 due to land being in fixed supply.

Upsloping versus Vertical Supply Curves

As you already know, the typical good or service possesses an upsloping supply curve because a higher market price will cause producers to increase the quantity supplied. There are, however, some goods and services whose quantities supplied are fixed and totally unresponsive to changes in price. Examples include the amount of land in a given area, the number of seats in a stadium, and the limited part of the electromagnetic spectrum that is reserved for cellular telephone transmissions. These sorts of goods and services have vertical supply curves because the same fixed amount is available no matter what price is offered to suppliers.

Reactions to Demand Shifts

Markets react very differently to a shift in demand depending upon whether they have upsloping or vertical supply curves.

Upsloping Supply Curves When a market has an upsloping supply curve, any shift in demand will cause both the equilibrium price *and* the equilibrium quantity to adjust. Consider Figure 2. When the demand for euros increases, the movement from the initial equilibrium to the final equilibrium involves the equilibrium price rising from $1.25 to $1.50 while the equilibrium quantity increases from Q_1 to Q_2. Price and quantity *both* change.

Vertical Supply Curves When a market has a vertical supply curve, any shift in demand will cause only the

equilibrium price to change; the equilibrium quantity remains the same because the quantity supplied is fixed and cannot adjust.

Consider Figure 6, in which the supply of land in San Francisco is fixed at quantity Q_0. If demand increases from D_1 to D_2, the movement from the initial equilibrium at point a to the final equilibrium at point b is accomplished solely by a rise in the equilibrium price from P_1 to P_2. Because the quantity of land is fixed, the increase in demand cannot cause any change in the equilibrium quantity supplied. The entire adjustment from the initial equilibrium to the final equilibrium has to come in the form of a higher equilibrium price.

This fact explains why real estate prices are so high in San Francisco and other major cities. Any increase in demand cannot be met by a combination of increases in price and increases in quantity. With the quantity of land in fixed supply, any increase in demand results solely in higher equilibrium land prices.

Preset Prices

In the body of this chapter, we saw that an effective government-imposed price ceiling (legal maximum price) causes quantity demanded to exceed quantity supplied—a shortage. An effective government-imposed price floor (legal minimum price) causes quantity supplied to exceed quantity demanded—a surplus. Put simply: Shortages result when prices are set below, and surpluses result when prices are set above, equilibrium prices.

We now want to establish that shortages and surpluses can occur in markets other than those in which government imposes price floors and ceilings. Such market imbalances happen when the seller or sellers set prices in advance of sales and the prices selected turn out to be below or above equilibrium prices. Consider the following two examples.

Olympic Figure Skating Finals

Tickets for the women's figure skating championship at the Olympics are among the world's "hottest tickets." The popularity of this event and the high incomes of buyers translate into tremendous ticket demand. The Olympic officials set the price for the tickets in advance. Invariably, the price, although high, is considerably below the equilibrium price that would equate quantity demanded and quantity supplied. A severe shortage of tickets therefore occurs in this *primary market*—the market involving the official ticket office.

The shortage, in turn, creates a *secondary market* in which buyers bid for tickets held by initial purchasers rather than the original seller. Scalping tickets—selling them above the original ticket price—may be legal or illegal, depending on local laws.

Figure 7 shows how the shortage in the primary ticket market looks in terms of supply and demand analysis. Demand curve D represents the strong demand for tickets

and supply curve S represents the supply of tickets. The supply curve is vertical because a fixed number of tickets are printed to match the capacity of the arena. At the printed ticket price of P_1, the quantity of tickets demanded, Q_2, exceeds the quantity supplied, Q_1. The result is a shortage of ab—the horizontal distance between Q_2 and Q_1 in the primary market.

If the printed ticket price had been the higher equilibrium price P_2, no shortage of tickets would have occurred. But at the lower price P_1, a shortage and secondary ticket market will emerge among those buyers willing to pay more than the printed ticket price and those sellers willing to sell their purchased tickets for more than the original price. Wherever there are shortages and secondary markets, it is safe to assume the original price was set below the equilibrium price.

Olympic Curling Preliminaries

Contrast the shortage of tickets for the women's figure skating finals at the Olympics to the surplus of tickets for one of the preliminary curling matches. For the uninitiated, curling is a sport in which participants slide a heavy round object called a "stone" down the ice toward a target while teammates called "sweepers" use brooms to alter the course of the stone when desired.

Curling is a popular spectator sport in a few nations such as Canada, but it does not draw many fans in most countries. So the demand for tickets to most of the preliminary curling events is not very strong. We demonstrate this weak demand as D in Figure 8. As in our previous

FIGURE 7 **The market for tickets to the Olympic women's figure skating finals.** The demand curve D and supply curve S for the Olympic women's figure skating finals produce an equilibrium price that is above the P_1 price printed on the ticket. At price P_1 the quantity of tickets demanded, Q_2, greatly exceeds the quantity of tickets available, Q_1. The resulting shortage of ab $(= Q_2 - Q_1)$ gives rise to a legal or illegal secondary market.

FIGURE 8 **The market for tickets to the Olympic curling preliminaries.** The demand curve D and supply curve S for the Olympic curling preliminaries produce an equilibrium price below the P_1 price printed on the ticket. At price P_1 the quantity of tickets demanded is less than the quantity of tickets available. The resulting surplus of ba $(= Q_1 - Q_2)$ means the event is not sold out.

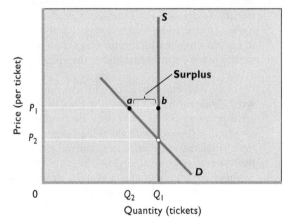

example, the supply of tickets is fixed by the size of the arena and is shown as vertical line S.

We represent the printed ticket price as P_1 in Figure 8. In this case the printed price is much higher than the equilibrium price of P_2. At the printed ticket price, quantity supplied is Q_1 and quantity demanded is Q_2. So a surplus of tickets of ba ($= Q_1 - Q_2$) occurs. No ticket scalping occurs and there are numerous empty seats. Only if the

Olympic officials had priced the tickets at the lower price P_2 would the event have been a sellout. (Actually, the Olympic officials try to adjust to demand realities for curling contests by holding them in smaller arenas and by charging less for tickets. Nevertheless, the stands are rarely full for the preliminary contests, which compete against final events in other winter Olympic sports.)

APPENDIX SUMMARY

LO3.7 Illustrate how supply and demand analysis can provide insights on actual-economy situations.

A decrease in the supply of a product increases its equilibrium price and reduces its equilibrium quantity. In contrast, an increase in the demand for a product boosts both its equilibrium price and its equilibrium quantity.

Simultaneous changes in supply and demand affect equilibrium price and quantity in various ways, depending on the relative magnitudes of the changes in supply and demand. Equal increases in supply and demand, for example, leave equilibrium price unchanged.

Products (such as land) whose quantities supplied do not vary with price have vertical supply curves. For these products, any shift in demand will lead to a change in the equilibrium price but no change in the equilibrium quantity.

Sellers set prices of some items such as tickets in advance of the event. These items are sold in the primary market that involves the original sellers and buyers. If preset prices turn out to be below the equilibrium prices, shortages occur and scalping in legal or illegal secondary markets arises. The prices in the secondary market then rise above the preset prices. In contrast, surpluses occur when the preset prices happen to exceed the equilibrium prices.

The following and additional problems can be found in **connect**
ECONOMICS

APPENDIX DISCUSSION QUESTIONS

1. Why are shortages or surpluses more likely with preset prices, such as those on tickets, than flexible prices, such as those on gasoline? **LO3.7**

2. Most scalping laws make it illegal to sell—but not to buy—tickets at prices above those printed on the tickets. Assuming that is the case, use supply and demand analysis to explain why the equilibrium ticket price in an illegal secondary market tends to be higher than in a legal secondary market. **LO3.7**

3. Go to the Web site of the Energy Information Administration, **www.eia.doe.gov**, and follow the links to find the current retail price of gasoline. How does the current price of regular gasoline compare with the price a year ago? What must have happened to either supply, demand, or both to explain the observed price change? **LO3.7**

4. Suppose the supply of apples sharply increases because of perfect weather conditions throughout the growing season. Assuming no change in demand, explain the effect on the

equilibrium price and quantity of apples. Explain why quantity demanded increases even though demand does not change. **LO3.7**

5. Assume the demand for lumber suddenly rises because of a rapid growth of demand for new housing. Assume no change in supply. Why does the equilibrium price of lumber rise? What would happen if the price did not rise under the demand and supply circumstances described? **LO3.7**

6. Assume that both the supply of bottled water and the demand for bottled water rise during the summer but that supply increases more rapidly than demand. What can you conclude about the directions of the impacts on equilibrium price and equilibrium quantity? **LO3.7**

7. When asked for investment advice, humorist Will Rogers joked that people should "[b]uy land. They ain't making any more of the stuff." Explain his advice in terms of the supply and demand model. **LO3.7**

APPENDIX REVIEW QUESTIONS

1. Will the equilibrium price of orange juice increase or decrease in each of the following situations? **LO3.7**
   a. A medical study reporting that orange juice reduces cancer is released at the same time that a freak storm destroys half of the orange crop in Florida.
   b. The prices of all beverages except orange juice fall by half while unexpectedly perfect weather in Florida results in an orange crop that is 20 percent larger than normal.
2. Consider the market for coffee beans. Suppose that the prices of all other caffeinated beverages go up 30 percent while at the same time a new fertilizer boosts production at coffee plantations dramatically. Which of the following best describes what is likely to happen to the equilibrium price and quantity of coffee beans? **LO3.7**
   a. Both the equilibrium price and the quantity will rise.
   b. The equilibrium price will rise but the equilibrium quantity will fall.
   c. The equilibrium price may rise or fall but the equilibrium quantity will rise for certain.
   d. Neither the price change nor the quantity change can be determined for certain.
   e. None of the above.
3. A price ceiling will result in a shortage only if the ceiling price is _____ the equilibrium price. **LO3.7**
   a. Less than.
   b. Equal to.
   c. Greater than.
   d. Faster than.

4. Suppose that you are the economic advisor to a local government that has to deal with a politically embarrassing surplus that was caused by a price floor that the government recently imposed. Your first suggestion is to get rid of the price floor, but the politicians don't want to do that. Instead, they present you with the following list of options that they hope will get rid of the surplus while keeping the price floor. Identify each one as either *could work* or *can't work.* **LO3.7**
   a. Restricting supply.
   b. Decreasing demand.
   c. Purchasing the surplus at the floor price.
5. Suppose both the demand for olives and the supply of olives decline by equal amounts over some time period. Use graphical analysis to show the effect on equilibrium price and quantity. **LO3.7**
6. Governments can use subsidies to increase demand. For instance, a government can pay farmers to use organic fertilizers rather than traditional fertilizers. That subsidy increases the demand for organic fertilizer. Consider two industries, one in which supply is nearly vertical and the other in which supply is nearly horizontal. Assume that firms in both industries would prefer a higher market equilibrium price because a higher market equilibrium price would mean higher profits. Which industry would probably spend more resources lobbying the government to increase the demand for its output? (Assume that both industries have similarly sloped demand curves.) **LO3.7**
   a. The industry with a nearly flat supply curve.
   b. The industry with a nearly vertical supply curve.

APPENDIX PROBLEMS

1. Demand and supply often shift in the retail market for gasoline. Here are two demand curves and two supply curves for gallons of gasoline in the month of May in a small town in Maine. Some of the data are missing. **LO3.7**

Price	Quantities Demanded		Quantities Supplied	
	D_1	D_2	S_1	S_2
$4.00	5,000	7,500	9,000	9,500
____	6,000	8,000	8,000	9,000
2.00	____	8,500	____	8,500
____	____	9,000	5,000	____

   a. Use the following facts to fill in the missing data in the table. If demand is D_1 and supply is S_1, the equilibrium quantity is 7,000 gallons per month. When demand is D_2 and supply is S_1, the equilibrium price is $3.00 per gallon. When demand is D_2 and supply is S_1, there is an excess

demand of 4,000 gallons per month at a price of $1.00 per gallon. If demand is D_1 and supply is S_2, the equilibrium quantity is 8,000 gallons per month.
   b. Compare two equilibriums. In the first, demand is D_1 and supply is S_1. In the second, demand is D_1 and supply is S_2. By how much does the equilibrium quantity change? By how much does the equilibrium price change?
   c. If supply falls from S_2 to S_1 while demand declines from D_2 to D_1, does the equilibrium price rise, fall, or stay the same? What if only supply falls? What if only demand falls?
   d. Suppose that supply is fixed at S_1 and that demand starts at D_1. By how many gallons per month would demand have to increase at each price level such that the equilibrium price per gallon would be $3.00? $4.00?
2. The table at the top of the next page shows two demand schedules for a given style of men's shoe—that is, how many pairs per month will be demanded at various prices at a men's clothing store in Seattle called Stromnord.

Price	D_1 Quantity Demanded	D_2 Quantity Demanded
$75	53	13
70	60	15
65	68	18
60	77	22
55	87	27

Suppose that Stromnord has exactly 65 pairs of this style of shoe in inventory at the start of the month of July and will not receive any more pairs of this style until at least August 1. LO3.7

a. If demand is D_1, what is the lowest price that Stromnord can charge so that it will not run out of this model of shoe in the month of July? What if demand is D_2?

b. If the price of shoes is set at $75 for both July and August and demand will be D_2 in July and D_1 in August, how many pairs of shoes should Stromnord order if it wants to end the month of August with exactly zero pairs of shoes in its inventory? What if the price is set at $55 for both months?

3. Use the table below to answer the questions that follow: LO3.7

a. If this table reflects the supply of and demand for tickets to a particular World Cup soccer game, what is the stadium capacity?

b. If the preset ticket price is $45, would we expect to see a secondary market for tickets? Would the price of a ticket in the secondary market be higher than, the same as, or lower than the price in the primary (original) market?

c. Suppose for some other World Cup game the quantity of tickets demanded is 20,000 lower at each ticket price than shown in the table. If the ticket price remains $45, would the event be a sellout?

Quantity Demanded, Thousands	Price	Quantity Supplied, Thousands
80	$25	60
75	35	60
70	45	60
65	55	60
60	65	60
55	75	60
50	85	60

Market Failures: Public Goods and Externalities

Learning Objectives

LO4.1 Differentiate between demand-side market failures and supply-side market failures.

LO4.2 Explain the origin of both consumer surplus and producer surplus, and explain how properly functioning markets maximize their sum, total surplus, while optimally allocating resources.

LO4.3 Describe free riding and public goods, and illustrate why private firms cannot normally produce public goods.

LO4.4 Explain how positive and negative externalities cause under- and overallocations of resources.

LO4.5 Show why we normally won't want to pay what it would cost to

eliminate every last bit of a negative externality such as air pollution.

LO4.6 (Appendix) Describe how information failures may justify government intervention in some markets.

Competitive markets usually do a remarkably effective job of allocating society's scarce resources to their most highly valued uses. Thus, we begin this chapter by demonstrating how properly functioning markets efficiently allocate resources. We then explore what happens when markets don't function properly. In some circumstances, economically desirable goods are not produced at all. In other situations, they are either overproduced or underproduced. This chapter focuses on these situations, which economists refer to as **market failures.**

In such situations, an economic role for government may arise. We will examine that role as it relates to public goods and so-called externalities—situations where market failures lead to suboptimal outcomes that the government may be able to improve upon by using its powers to tax, spend, and regulate. The government may, for instance, pay for the production of goods that the private sector fails to produce. It may also act to reduce the production of those goods and services that the private sector overproduces. Implementing such policies can, however, be both costly and complicated. Thus, we conclude the chapter by noting the government inefficiencies that can hinder government efforts to improve economic outcomes.

Market Failures in Competitive Markets[1]

LO4.1 Differentiate between demand-side market failures and supply-side market failures.

In Chapter 3 we asserted that "competitive markets usually produce an assignment of resources that is 'right' from an economic perspective." We now want to focus on the word "usually" and discuss exceptions. We must do this because it is unfortunately the case that the presence of robust competition involving many buyers and many sellers may not, by itself, be enough to guarantee that a market will allocate resources correctly. Market failures sometimes happen in competitive markets. The focus of this chapter is to explain how and why such market failures can arise.

Fortunately, the broad picture is simple. Market failures in competitive markets fall into just two categories:

- **Demand-side market failures** happen when demand curves do not reflect consumers' full willingness to pay for a good or service.
- **Supply-side market failures** occur when supply curves do not reflect the full cost of producing a good or service.

Demand-Side Market Failures

Demand-side market failures arise because it is impossible in certain cases to charge consumers what they are willing to pay for a product. Consider outdoor fireworks displays. People enjoy fireworks and would therefore be *willing* to pay to see a fireworks display if the only way to see it was to have to pay for the right to do so. But because such displays are outdoors and in public, people don't actually *have* to pay to see the display because there is no way to exclude those who haven't paid from also enjoying the show. Private firms will therefore be unwilling to produce outdoor fireworks displays, as it will be nearly impossible for them to raise enough revenue to cover production costs.

Supply-Side Market Failures

Supply-side market failures arise in situations in which a firm does not have to pay the full cost of producing its output. Consider a coal-burning power plant. The firm running the plant will have to pay for all of the land, labor, capital, and entrepreneurship that it uses to generate electricity by burning coal. But if the firm is not charged for the smoke that it releases into the atmosphere, it will fail to pay another set of costs— the costs that its pollution imposes on other people. These include future harm from global warming, toxins that affect wildlife, and possible damage to agricultural crops downwind.

A market failure arises because it is not possible for the market to correctly weigh costs and benefits in a situation in which some of the costs are completely unaccounted for. The coal-burning power plant produces more electricity and generates more pollution than it would if it had to pay for each ton of smoke that it released into the atmosphere. The extra units that are produced are units of output for which the costs are *greater than* the benefits. Obviously, these units should not be produced.

---

[1]Other market failures arise when there are not enough buyers or sellers to ensure competition. In those situations, the lack of competition allows either buyers or sellers to restrict purchases or sales below optimal levels for their own benefit. As an example, a monopoly—a firm that is the only producer in its industry—can restrict the amount of output that it supplies in order to drive up the market price and thereby increase its own profit.

Efficiently Functioning Markets

LO4.2 Explain the origin of both consumer surplus and producer surplus, and explain how properly functioning markets maximize their sum, total surplus, while optimally allocating resources.

The best way to understand market failure is to first understand how properly functioning competitive markets achieve economic efficiency. We touched on this subject in Chapter 3, but we now want to expand and deepen that analysis, both for its own sake and to set up our discussion of public goods and externalities. Two conditions must hold if a competitive market is to produce efficient outcomes: The demand curve in the market must reflect consumers' full willingness to pay, and the supply curve in the market must reflect all the costs of production. If these conditions hold, then the market will produce only units for which benefits are at least equal to costs. It will also maximize the amount of "benefit surpluses" that are shared between consumers and producers.

Consumer Surplus

The benefit surplus received by a consumer or consumers in a market is called **consumer surplus.** It is defined as the difference between the maximum price a consumer is (or consumers are) willing to pay for a product and the actual price that they do pay.

The maximum price that a person is willing to pay for a unit of a product depends on the opportunity cost of that person's consumption alternatives. Suppose that Ted is offered the chance to purchase an apple. He would of course like to have it for free, but the maximum amount he would be willing to pay depends on the alternative uses to which he can put his money. If his maximum willingness to pay for that particular apple is $1.25, then we know that he is willing to forgo up to—but not more than—$1.25 of other goods and services. Paying even one cent more would entail having to give up too much of other goods and services.

It also means that if Ted is charged any market price less than $1.25, he will receive a consumer surplus equal to the difference between the $1.25 maximum price that he would have been willing to pay and the lower market price. For instance, if the market price is $0.50 per apple, Ted will receive a consumer surplus of $0.75 per apple (= $1.25 − $0.50). In nearly all markets, consumers individually and collectively gain greater total utility or satisfaction in dollar terms from their purchases than the amount of their expenditures (= product price × quantity). This utility surplus arises because each consumer who buys the product only has to pay the market equilibrium price

TABLE 4.1 Consumer Surplus

(1) Person	(2) Maximum Price Willing to Pay	(3) Actual Price (Equilibrium Price)	(4) Consumer Surplus
Bob	$13	$8	$5 (= $13 − $8)
Barb	12	8	4 (= $12 − $8)
Bill	11	8	3 (= $11 − $8)
Bart	10	8	2 (= $10 − $8)
Brent	9	8	1 (= $9 − $8)
Betty	8	8	0 (= $8 − $8)

even though many of them would have been willing to pay more than the equilibrium price to obtain the product.

The concept of maximum willingness to pay also gives us another way to understand demand curves. Consider Table 4.1, where the first two columns show the maximum amounts that six consumers would each be willing to pay for a bag of oranges. Bob, for instance, would be willing to pay a maximum of $13 for a bag of oranges. Betty, by contrast, would only be willing to pay a maximum of $8 for a bag of oranges.

Notice that the maximum prices that these individuals are willing to pay represent points on a demand curve because the lower the market price, the more bags of oranges will be demanded. At a price of $12.50, for instance, Bob will be the only person listed in the table who will purchase a bag. But at a price of $11.50, both Bob and Barb will want to purchase a bag. And at a price of $10.50, Bob, Barb, and Bill will each want to purchase a bag. The lower the price, the greater the total quantity demanded as the market price falls below the maximum prices of more and more consumers.

Lower prices also imply larger consumer surpluses. When the price is $12.50, Bob only gets $0.50 in consumer surplus because his maximum willingness to pay of $13 is only $0.50 higher than the market price of $12.50. But if the market price were to fall to $8, then his consumer surplus would be $5 (= $13 − $8). The third and fourth columns of Table 4.1 show how much consumer surplus each of our six consumers will receive if the market price of a bag of oranges is $8. Only Betty receives no consumer surplus because her maximum willingness to pay exactly matches the $8 equilibrium price.

It is easy to show on a graph both the individual consumer surplus received by each particular buyer in a market as well as the collective consumer surplus received by all buyers. Consider Figure 4.1, which shows the market equilibrium price P_1 = $8 as well as the downsloping

FIGURE 4.1 **Consumer surplus.** Consumer surplus—shown as the green triangle—is the difference between the maximum prices consumers are willing to pay for a product and the lower equilibrium price, here assumed to be $8. For quantity Q_1, consumers are willing to pay the sum of the amounts represented by the green triangle and the yellow rectangle. Because they need to pay only the amount shown as the yellow rectangle, the green triangle shows consumer surplus.

demand curve *D* for bags of oranges. Demand curve *D* includes not only the six consumers named in Table 4.1 but also every other consumer of oranges in the market. The individual consumer surplus of each particular person who is willing to buy at the $8 market price is simply the vertical distance from the horizontal line that marks the $8 market price up to that particular buyer's maximum willingness to pay. The collective consumer surplus obtained by all of our named and unnamed buyers is found by adding together each of their individual consumer surpluses. To obtain the Q_1 bags of oranges represented, consumers collectively are willing to pay the total amount shown by the sum of the green triangle and yellow rectangle under the demand curve and to the left of Q_1. But consumers need pay only the amount represented by the yellow rectangle ($= P_1 \times Q_1$). So the green triangle is the consumer surplus in this market. It is the sum of the vertical distances between the demand curve and the $8 equilibrium price at each quantity up to Q_1. Alternatively, it is the sum of the gaps between maximum willingness to pay and actual price, such as those we calculated in Table 4.1. Thus, consumer surplus can also be defined as the area that lies below the demand curve and above the price line that extends horizontally from P_1.

Consumer surplus and price are inversely (negatively) related. Given the demand curve, higher prices reduce consumer surplus; lower prices increase it. To test this generalization, draw in an equilibrium price above $8 in Figure 4.1 and observe the reduced size of the triangle representing

consumer surplus. When price goes up, the gap narrows between the maximum willingness to pay and the actual price. Next, draw in an equilibrium price below $8 and see that consumer surplus increases. When price declines, the gap widens between maximum willingness to pay and actual price.

Producer Surplus

Like consumers, producers also receive a benefit surplus in markets. This **producer surplus** is the difference between the actual price a producer receives (or producers receive) and the minimum acceptable price that a consumer would have to pay the producer to make a particular unit of output available.

A producer's minimum acceptable price for a particular unit will equal the producer's marginal cost of producing that particular unit. That marginal cost will be the sum of the rent, wages, interest, and profit that the producer will need to pay in order to obtain the land, labor, capital, and entrepreneurship required to produce that particular unit. In this section, we are assuming that the marginal cost of producing a unit will include *all* of the costs of production. Unlike the coal-burning power plant mentioned previously, the producer must pay for all of its costs, including the cost of pollution. In later sections, we will explore the market failures that arise in situations where firms do not have to pay all their costs.

In addition to equaling marginal cost, a producer's minimum acceptable price can also be interpreted as the opportunity cost of bidding resources away from the production of other products. To see why this is true, suppose that Leah is an apple grower. The resources necessary for her to produce one apple could be used to produce other things. To get them directed toward producing an apple, it is necessary to pay Leah what it will cost her to bid the necessary resources away from other entrepreneurs who would like to use them to produce other products. Leah would, naturally, like to get paid as much as possible to produce the apple for you. But her minimum acceptable price is the lowest price you could pay her such that she can just break even after bidding away from other uses the land, labor, capital, and entrepreneurship necessary to produce the apple.

The size of the producer surplus earned on any particular unit will be the difference between the market price that the producer actually receives and the producer's

TABLE 4.2 Producer Surplus

(1) Person	(2) Minimum Acceptable Price	(3) Actual Price (Equilibrium Price)	(4) Producer Surplus
Carlos	$3	$8	$5 (= $8 − $3)
Courtney	4	8	4 (= $8 − $4)
Chuck	5	8	3 (= $8 − $5)
Cindy	6	8	2 (= $8 − $6)
Craig	7	8	1 (= $8 − $7)
Chad	8	8	0 (= $8 − $8)

FIGURE 4.2 Producer surplus. Producer surplus—shown as the blue triangle—is the difference between the actual price producers receive for a product (here $8) and the lower minimum payments they are willing to accept. For quantity Q_1, producers receive the sum of the amounts represented by the blue triangle plus the yellow area. Because they need to receive only the amount shown by the yellow area to produce Q_1, the blue triangle represents producer surplus.

minimum acceptable price. Consider Table 4.2, which shows the minimum acceptable prices of six different orange growers. With a market price of $8, Carlos, for instance, has a producer surplus of $5, which is equal to the market price of $8 minus his minimum acceptable price of $3. Chad, by contrast, receives no producer surplus because his minimum acceptable price of $8 just equals the market equilibrium price of $8.

Carlos's minimum acceptable price is lower than Chad's minimum acceptable price because Carlos is a more efficient producer than Chad, by which we mean that Carlos produces oranges using a less-costly combination of resources than Chad uses. The differences in efficiency between Carlos and Chad are likely due to differences in the type and quality of resources available to them. Carlos, for instance, may own land perfectly suited to growing oranges, while Chad has land in the desert that requires costly irrigation if it is to be used to grow oranges. Thus, Chad has a higher marginal cost of producing oranges.

The minimum acceptable prices that producers are willing to accept form points on a supply curve because the higher the price, the more bags of oranges will be supplied. At a price of $3.50, for instance, only Carlos would be willing to supply a bag of oranges. But at a price of $5.50, Carlos, Courtney, and Chuck would all be willing to supply a bag of oranges. The higher the market price, the more oranges will be supplied, as the market price surpasses the marginal costs and minimum acceptable prices of more and more producers. Thus, supply curves shown in this competitive market are both marginal-cost curves and minimum-acceptable-price curves.

The supply curve in Figure 4.2 includes not only the six producers named in Table 4.2 but also every other producer of oranges in the market. At the market price of $8 per bag, Q_1 bags are produced because only those producers whose minimum acceptable prices are less than $8 per bag will choose to produce oranges with their

resources. Those lower acceptable prices for each of the units up to Q_1 are shown by the portion of the supply curve lying to the left of and below the assumed $8 market price.

The individual producer surplus of each of these sellers is thus the vertical distance from each seller's respective minimum acceptable price on the supply curve up to the $8 market price. Their collective producer surplus is shown by the blue triangle in Figure 4.2. In that figure, producers collect revenues of $P_1 \times Q_1$, which is the sum of the blue triangle and the yellow area. As shown by the supply curve, however, revenues of only those illustrated by the yellow area would be required to entice producers to offer Q_1 bags of oranges for sale. The sellers therefore receive a producer surplus shown by the blue triangle. That surplus is the sum of the vertical distances between the supply curve and the $8 equilibrium price at each of the quantities to the left of Q_1.

There is a direct (positive) relationship between equilibrium price and the amount of producer surplus. Given the supply curve, lower prices reduce producer surplus; higher prices increase it. If you pencil in a lower equilibrium price than $8, you will see that the producer surplus triangle gets smaller. The gaps between the minimum acceptable payments and the actual prices narrow when the price falls. If you pencil in an equilibrium price

WORKED PROBLEMS

W4.1

Consumer and producer surplus

above $8, the size of the producer surplus triangle increases. The gaps between minimum acceptable payments and actual prices widen when the price increases.

Efficiency Revisited

In Figure 4.3 we bring together the demand and supply curves of Figures 4.1 and 4.2 to show the equilibrium price and quantity and the previously described regions of consumer and producer surplus. All markets that have downsloping demand curves and upsloping supply curves yield consumer and producer surplus.

Because we are assuming in Figure 4.3 that the demand curve reflects buyers' full willingness to pay and the supply curve reflects all of the costs facing sellers, the equilibrium quantity in Figure 4.3 reflects economic efficiency, which consists of productive efficiency and allocative efficiency.

- *Productive efficiency* is achieved because competition forces orange growers to use the best technologies and combinations of resources available. Doing so minimizes the per-unit cost of the output produced.
- *Allocative efficiency* is achieved because the correct quantity of oranges—Q_1—is produced relative to other goods and services.

There are two ways to understand why Q_1 is the correct quantity of oranges. Both involve realizing that any resources directed toward the production of oranges are

resources that could have been used to produce other products. Thus, the only way to justify taking any amount of any resource (land, labor, capital, entrepreneurship) away from the production of other products is if it brings more utility or satisfaction when devoted to the production of oranges than it would if it were used to produce other products.

The first way to see why Q_1 is the allocatively efficient quantity of oranges is to note that demand and supply curves can be interpreted as measuring marginal benefit (MB) and marginal cost (MC). Recall from the discussion relating to Figure 1.3 that optimal allocation is achieved at the output level where MB = MC. We have already seen that supply curves are marginal cost curves. As it turns out, demand curves are marginal benefit curves. This is true because the maximum price that a consumer would be willing to pay for any particular unit is equal to the benefit that she would get if she were to consume that unit. Thus, each point on a demand curve represents both some consumer's maximum willingness to pay as well as the marginal benefit that he or she would get from consuming the particular unit in question.

Combining the fact that supply curves are MC curves with the fact that demand curves are MB curves, we see that points on the demand curve in Figure 4.3 measure the marginal benefit of oranges at each level of output, while points on the supply curve measure the marginal cost of oranges at each level of output. As a result, MB = MC where the demand and supply curves intersect—which means that the equilibrium quantity Q_1 must be allocatively efficient.

To gain a deeper understanding of why Q_1 is allocatively efficient, notice that for every unit up to Q_1 marginal benefit exceeds marginal cost (MB > MC). And because marginal cost includes the opportunity cost of not making other things with the resources needed to make these units, we know that people are made better off when the resources necessary to make these units are allocated to producing oranges rather than to producing anything else.

The second way to see why Q_1 is the correct quantity of oranges is based on our analysis of consumer and producer surplus and the fact that we can interpret demand and supply curves in terms of maximum willingness to pay and minimum acceptable price. In Figure 4.3, the maximum willingness to pay on the demand curve for each bag of oranges up to Q_1 exceeds the corresponding minimum acceptable price on the supply curve. Thus, each of these bags adds a positive amount (= maximum willingness to pay *minus* minimum acceptable price) to the *total* of consumer and producer surplus.

FIGURE 4.3 Efficiency: maximum combined consumer and producer surplus. At quantity Q_1 the combined amount of consumer surplus, shown as the green triangle, and producer surplus, shown as the blue triangle, is maximized. Efficiency occurs because, at Q_1, maximum willingness to pay, indicated by the points on the demand curve, equals minimum acceptable price, shown by the points on the supply curve.

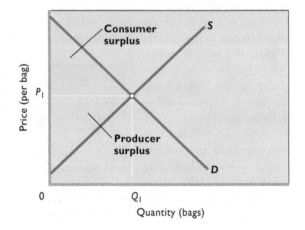

The fact that maximum willingness to pay exceeds minimum acceptable price for every unit up to Q_1 means that people gain more utility from producing and consuming those units than they would if they produced and consumed anything else that could be made with the resources that went into making those units. This is true because both the maximum willingness to pay and the minimum acceptable price take opportunity costs into account. As long as the maximum willingness to pay exceeds the minimum acceptable price, people are willing to pay more to consume a unit of the good in question (here, bags of oranges) than they would pay to consume anything else that could be made with the same resources. Only at the equilibrium quantity Q_1—where the maximum willingness to pay exactly equals the minimum acceptable price—does society exhaust all opportunities to produce units for which benefits exceed costs (including opportunity costs). Producing Q_1 units therefore achieves allocative efficiency because the market is producing and distributing only those units that make people happier with bags of oranges than they would be with anything else that could be produced with the same resources.

Geometrically, producing Q_1 units maximizes the combined area of consumer and producer surplus in Figure 4.3. In this context, the combined area is referred to as *total surplus*. Thus, when Q_1 units are produced, total surplus is equal to the large triangle formed by the green consumer-surplus triangle and the blue producer-surplus triangle.

When demand curves reflect buyers' full willingness to pay and when supply curves reflect all the costs facing sellers, competitive markets produce equilibrium quantities that maximize the sum of consumer and producer surplus. Allocative efficiency occurs at the market equilibrium quantity where three conditions exist simultaneously:

- MB = MC (Figure 1.3).
- Maximum willingness to pay = minimum acceptable price.
- Total surplus (= sum of consumer and producer surplus) is at a maximum.

Economists are enamored of markets because properly functioning markets automatically achieve allocative efficiency. Other methods of allocating resources—such as government central planning—do exist. But because other methods cannot do any better than properly functioning markets—and may, in many cases, do much worse—economists usually prefer that resources be allocated through markets whenever properly functioning markets are available.

Efficiency Losses (or Deadweight Losses)

Figures 4.4a and 4.4b demonstrate that **efficiency losses**—reductions of combined consumer and producer surplus—result from both underproduction and overproduction. First, consider Figure 4.4a, which analyzes the case of underproduction by considering what happens if output falls from the efficient level Q_1 to the smaller amount Q_2. When that happens, the sum of consumer and producer surplus, previously *abc*, falls to *adec*. So the combined consumer and producer surplus declines by the amount of the gray triangle to the left of Q_1. That triangle represents an efficiency loss to buyers and sellers. And because buyers

FIGURE 4.4 Efficiency losses (or deadweight losses). Quantity levels either less than or greater than the efficient quantity Q_1 create efficiency losses. (a) Triangle *dbe* shows the efficiency loss associated with underproduction at output Q_2. (b) Triangle *bfg* illustrates the efficiency loss associated with overproduction at output level Q_3.

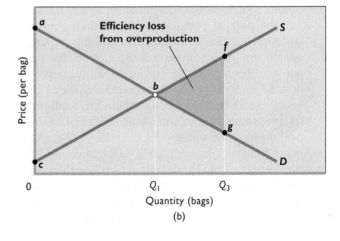

and sellers are members of society, it represents an efficiency loss (or a so-called **deadweight loss**) to society.

For output levels from Q_2 to Q_1, consumers' maximum willingness to pay (as reflected by points on the demand curve) exceeds producers' minimum acceptable price (as reflected by points on the supply curve). By failing to produce units of this product for which a consumer is willing to pay more than a producer is willing to accept, society suffers a loss of net benefits. As a concrete example, consider a particular unit for which a consumer is willing to pay $10 and a producer is willing to accept $6. The $4 difference between those values is a net benefit that will not be realized if this unit is not produced. In addition, the resources that should have gone to producing this unit will go instead to producing other products that will not generate as much utility as if those resources had been used here to produce this unit of this product. The triangle *dbe* in Figure 4.4a shows the total loss of net benefits that results from failing to produce the units from Q_2 to Q_1.

In contrast, consider the case of overproduction shown in Figure 4.4b, in which the number of oranges produced is Q_3 rather than the efficient level Q_1. In Figure 4.4b the combined consumer and producer surplus therefore declines by *bfg*—the gray triangle to the right of Q_1. This triangle subtracts from the total consumer and producer surplus of *abc* that would occur if the quantity had been Q_1. That is, for all units from 0 to Q_1, benefits exceed costs, so that those units generate the economic surplus shown by triangle *abc*. But the units from Q_1 to Q_3 are such that costs exceed benefits. Thus, they generate an economic loss shown by triangle *bfg*. The total economic surplus for all units from 0 to Q_3 is therefore the economic surplus given by *abc* for the units from 0 to Q_1 *minus* the economic loss given by *bfg* for the units from Q_1 to Q_3.

Producing any unit beyond Q_1 generates an economic loss because the willingness to pay for such units on the part of consumers is less than the minimum acceptable price to produce such units on the part of producers. As a concrete example, note that producing an item for which the maximum willingness to pay is, say, $7 and the minimum acceptable price is, say, $10 subtracts $3 from society's net benefits. Such production is uneconomical and creates an efficiency loss (or deadweight loss) for society. Because the net benefit of each bag of oranges from Q_1 to Q_3 is negative, we know that the benefits from these units are smaller than the opportunity costs of the other products that could have been produced with the resources that were used to produce these bags of oranges. The resources used to produce

the bags from Q_1 to Q_3 could have generated net benefits instead of net losses if they had been directed toward producing other products. The gray triangle *bfg* to the right of Q_1 in Figure 4.4b shows the total efficiency loss from overproduction at Q_3.

The magic of markets is that when demand reflects consumers' full willingness to pay and when supply reflects all costs, the market equilibrium quantity will automatically equal the allocatively efficient output level. Under these conditions, the market equilibrium quantity will ensure that there are neither efficiency losses from underproduction nor efficiency losses from overproduction. As we are about to see, however, such losses do happen when either demand does not reflect consumers' full willingness to pay or supply does not reflect all costs.

QUICK REVIEW 4.1

- Market failures in competitive markets have two possible causes: demand curves that do not reflect consumers' full willingness to pay and supply curves that do not reflect producers' full cost of production.

- Consumer surplus is the difference between the maximum price that a consumer is willing to pay for a product and the lower price actually paid.

- Producer surplus is the difference between the minimum price that a producer is willing to accept for a product and the higher price actually received.

- At the equilibrium price and quantity in competitive markets, marginal benefit equals marginal cost, maximum willingness to pay equals minimum acceptable price, and the total of consumer surplus and producer surplus is maximized. Each of these conditions defines allocative efficiency.

- Quantities less than or greater than the allocatively efficient level of output create efficiency losses, often called deadweight losses.

Public Goods

LO4.3 Describe free riding and public goods, and illustrate why private firms cannot normally produce public goods.

Demand-side market failures arise in competitive markets when demand curves fail to reflect consumers' full willingness to pay for a good or service. In such situations, markets fail to produce all of the units for which there are net benefits because demand curves underreport how much consumers are willing and able to pay. This underreporting problem reaches its most extreme form in the case of a public good: Markets may fail to produce *any* of the public good because its demand curve may reflect *none* of its consumers' willingness to pay.

To understand public goods, we first need to understand the characteristics that define private goods.

Private Goods Characteristics

We have seen that the market system produces a wide range of **private goods.** These are the goods offered for sale in stores, in shops, and on the Internet. Examples include automobiles, clothing, personal computers, household appliances, and sporting goods. Private goods are distinguished by rivalry and excludability.

- **Rivalry** (in consumption) means that when one person buys and consumes a product, it is not available for another person to buy and consume. When Adams purchases and drinks a bottle of mineral water, it is not available for Benson to purchase and consume.

- **Excludability** means that sellers can keep people who do not pay for a product from obtaining its benefits. Only people who are willing and able to pay the market price for bottles of water can obtain these drinks and the benefits they confer.

Consumers fully express their personal demands for private goods in the market. If Adams likes bottled mineral water, that fact will be known by her desire to purchase the product. Other things equal, the higher the price of bottled water, the fewer bottles she will buy. So Adams's demand for bottled water will reflect an inverse relationship between the price of bottled water and the quantity of it demanded. This is simply *individual* demand, as described in Chapter 3.

The *market* demand for a private good is the horizontal summation of the individual demand schedules (review Figure 3.2). Suppose just two consumers comprise the market for bottled water and the price is $1 per bottle. If Adams will purchase 3 bottles and Benson will buy 2, the market demand will reflect consumers' demand for 5 bottles at the $1 price. Similar summations of quantities demanded at other prices will generate the market demand schedule and curve.

Suppose the equilibrium price of bottled water is $1. Adams and Benson will buy a total of 5 bottles, and the sellers will obtain total revenue of $5 (= $1 × 5). If the sellers' cost per bottle is $0.80, their total cost will be $4 (= $0.80 × 5). So sellers charging $1 per bottle will obtain $5 of total revenue, incur $4 of total cost, and earn $1 of profit on the 5 bottles sold.

Because firms can profitably "tap market demand" for private goods, they will produce and offer them for sale. Consumers demand private goods, and profit-seeking suppliers produce goods that satisfy the demand. Consumers willing to pay the market price obtain the goods; nonpayers go without. A competitive market not only makes private goods available to consumers but also allocates society's resources efficiently to the particular product. There is neither underproduction nor overproduction of the product.

Public Goods Characteristics

Public goods have the opposite characteristics of private goods. Public goods are distinguished by nonrivalry and nonexcludability.

- **Nonrivalry** (in consumption) means that one person's consumption of a good does not preclude consumption of the good by others. Everyone can simultaneously obtain the benefit from a public good such as national defense, street lighting, a global positioning system, or environmental protection.

- **Nonexcludability** means there is no effective way of excluding individuals from the benefit of the good once it comes into existence. Once in place, you cannot exclude someone from benefiting from national defense, street lighting, a global positioning system, or environmental protection.

These two characteristics create a **free-rider problem.** Once a producer has provided a public good, everyone, including nonpayers, can obtain the benefit.

Because most people do not voluntarily pay for something that they can obtain for free, most people become free riders. These free riders like the public good and would be willing to pay for it if producers could somehow force them to pay—but nonexcludability means that there is no way for producers to withhold the good from the free riders without also denying it to the few who do pay. As a result, free riding means that the willingness to pay of the free riders is not expressed in the market. From the viewpoint of producers, free riding reduces demand. The more free riding, the less demand. And if all consumers free ride, demand will collapse all the way to zero.

The low or even zero demand caused by free riding makes it virtually impossible for private firms to profitably provide public goods. With little or no demand, firms cannot effectively "tap market demand" for revenues and profits. As a result, they will not produce public goods. Society will therefore suffer efficiency losses because

CONSIDER THIS . . .

Street Entertainers

Street entertainers are often found in tourist areas of major cities. These entertainers illuminate the concepts of free riders and public goods.

Most street entertainers have a hard time earning a living from their activities (unless event organizers pay them) because they have no way of excluding nonpayers from the benefits of their entertainment. They essentially are providing public, not private, goods and must rely on voluntary payments.

The result is a significant free-rider problem. Only a few in the audience put money in the container or instrument case, and many who do so contribute only token amounts. The rest are free riders who obtain the benefits of the street entertainment and retain their money for purchases that they initiate.

Street entertainers are acutely aware of the free-rider problem, and some have found creative ways to lessen it. For example, some entertainers involve the audience directly in the act. This usually creates a greater sense of audience willingness (or obligation) to contribute money at the end of the performance.

"Pay for performance" is another creative approach to lessening the free-rider problem. A good example is the street entertainer painted up to look like a statue. When people drop coins into the container, the "statue" makes a slight movement. The greater the contributions, the greater the movement. But these human "statues" still face a free-rider problem: Nonpayers also get to enjoy the acts.

goods for which marginal benefits exceed marginal costs are not produced. Thus, if society wants a public good to be produced, it will have to direct government to provide it. Because the public good will still feature nonexcludability, the government won't have any better luck preventing free riding or charging people for it. But because the government can finance the provision of the public good through the taxation of other things, the government does not have to worry about profitability. It can therefore provide the public good even when private firms can't.

Examples of public goods include national defense, outdoor fireworks displays, the light beams thrown out by lighthouses, public art displays, public music concerts, MP3 music files posted to file-sharing Web sites, and ideas and inventions that are not protected by patents or copyrights. Each of these goods or services shows both nonrivalry and nonexcludability.

In a few special cases, private firms can provide public goods because the production costs of these public goods can be covered by the profits generated by closely related private goods. For instance, private companies can make a profit providing broadcast TV—which is a nonrival, nonexcludable public good—because they control who gets to air TV commercials, which are rival and excludable private goods. The money that broadcasters make from selling airtime for ads allows them to turn a profit despite having to give their main product, broadcast TV, away for free.

Unfortunately, only a few public goods can be subsidized in this way by closely related private goods. For the large majority of public goods, private provision is unprofitable. As a result, there are only two remaining ways for a public good to be provided: private philanthropy or government provision. For many less expensive or less important public goods like fireworks displays or public art, society may feel comfortable relying on private philanthropy. But when it comes to public goods like national defense, people normally look to the government.

This leads to an important question: Once a government decides to produce a particular public good, how can it determine the optimal amount that it should produce? How can it avoid either underallocating or overallocating society's scarce resources to the production of the public good?

Optimal Quantity of a Public Good

If consumers need not reveal their true demand for a public good in the marketplace, how can society determine the optimal amount of that good? The answer is that the government has to try to estimate the demand for a public good through surveys or public votes. It can then compare the marginal benefit (MB) of an added unit of the good against the government's marginal cost (MC) of providing it. Adhering to the MB = MC rule, government can provide the "right," meaning "efficient," amount of the public good.

Demand for Public Goods

The demand for a public good is somewhat unusual. Suppose Adams and Benson are the only two people in the society, and their marginal willingness to pay for a public good, national defense, is as shown in columns 1 and 2 and columns 1 and 3 in Table 4.3. Economists might have

TABLE 4.3 Demand for a Public Good, Two Individuals

(1) Quantity of Public Good	(2) Adams's Willingness to Pay (Price)		(3) Benson's Willingness to Pay (Price)		(4) Collective Willingness to Pay (Price)
1	$4	+	$5	=	$9
2	3	+	4	=	7
3	2	+	3	=	5
4	1	+	2	=	3
5	0	+	1	=	1

discovered these schedules through a survey asking hypothetical questions about how much each citizen was willing to pay for various types and amounts of public goods rather than go without them.

CONSIDER THIS . . .

Responding to Digital Free Riding

Four teenage friends start a rock band. They practice hard, master their instruments, write their own songs, and do gig after gig for nearly nothing at local bars to gain experience and perfect their music.

After nearly five years of effort, they get signed to a major record label. But the year is 2005 and record sales are collapsing due to digital piracy. The rise of Internet file sharing has turned music into a public good and sales of recorded music have collapsed as hundreds of millions of music lovers have become digital free riders.

At first, the band struggles with the new reality. If they can't make a living selling music, they might have to quit music and get regular jobs. But then they realize that while recorded music is now free for anyone who wants it to be free, live music isn't. And neither are T-shirts or memorabilia.

So the band promotes itself online and allows free downloads to help propel its popularity. But then it charges steep prices at live concerts and makes sure that its T-shirts and memorabilia also generate substantial revenues. By doing so, the band adjusts to the new reality in which music has become a public good, but live concerts and T-shirts have not. They charge for the items that are still private goods.

Notice that the schedules in Table 4.3 are price-quantity schedules, implying that they are demand schedules. Rather than depicting demand in the usual way—the quantity of a product someone is willing to buy at each possible price—these schedules show the price someone is willing to pay for an extra unit at each possible quantity. That is, Adams is willing to pay $4 for the first unit of the public good, $3 for the second, $2 for the third, and so on.

Suppose the government produces 1 unit of this public good. Because of nonrivalry, Adams's consumption of the good does not preclude Benson from also consuming it, and vice versa. So both consume the good, and neither volunteers to pay for it. But from Table 4.3 we can find the amount these two people would be willing to pay, together, rather than do without this 1 unit of the good. Columns 1 and 2 show that Adams would be willing to pay $4 for the first unit of the public good; columns 1 and 3 show that Benson would be willing to pay $5 for it. So the two people are jointly willing to pay $9 (= $4 + $5) for this first unit.

For the second unit of the public good, the collective price they are willing to pay is $7 (= $3 from Adams + $4 from Benson); for the third unit they would pay $5 (= $2 + $3); and so on. By finding the collective willingness to pay for each additional unit (column 4), we can construct a collective demand schedule (a willingness-to-pay schedule) for the public good. Here we are *not* adding the quantities demanded at each possible price, as we do when we determine the market demand for a private good. Instead, we are adding the prices that people are willing to pay for the last unit of the public good at each possible quantity demanded.

Figure 4.5 shows the same adding procedure graphically, using the data from Table 4.3. Note that we sum Adams's and Benson's willingness-to-pay curves *vertically* to derive the collective willingness-to-pay curve (demand curve). The summing procedure is downward from the top graph to the middle graph to the bottom (total) graph. For example, the height of the collective demand curve D_c at 2 units of output in the bottom graph is $7, the sum of the amounts that Adams and Benson are each willing to pay for the second unit (= $3 + $4). Likewise, the height of the collective demand curve at 4 units of the public good is $3 (= $1 + $2).

What does it mean in Figure 4.5a that, for example, Adams is willing to pay $3 for the second unit of the public good? It means that Adams expects to receive $3 of extra benefit or utility from that unit. And we know from our discussion of diminishing marginal utility in Chapter 3 that successive units of any good yield less and less added

FIGURE 4.5 The optimal amount of a public good. Two people—Adams and Benson—are the only members of a hypothetical economy. (a) D_1 shows Adams's willingness to pay for various quantities of a particular public good. (b) D_2 shows Benson's willingness to pay pay for these same quantities of this public good. (c) The collective demand for this public good is shown by D_c and is found by summing vertically Adams's and Benson's individual willingness-to-pay curves. The supply (S) of the public good is upsloping, reflecting rising marginal costs. The optimal amount of the public good is 3 units, determined by the intersection of D_c and S. At that output, marginal benefit (reflected in the collective demand curve D_c) equals marginal cost (reflected in the supply curve S).

(a)
Adams

(b)
Benson

(c)
Collective demand and supply

benefit. This is also true for public goods, explaining the downward slope of the willingness-to-pay curves of Adams, Benson, and society. These curves, in essence, are marginal-benefit (MB) curves.

Comparing MB and MC

We can now determine the optimal quantity of the public good. The collective demand curve D_c in Figure 4.5c measures society's marginal benefit of each unit of this particular good. The supply curve S in that figure measures society's marginal cost of each unit. The optimal quantity of this public good occurs where marginal benefit equals marginal cost, or where the two curves intersect. In Figure 4.5c that point is 3 units of the public good, where the collective willingness to pay for the last (third) unit—the marginal benefit—just matches that unit's marginal cost ($5 = $5). As we saw in Chapter 1, equating marginal benefit and marginal cost efficiently allocates society's scarce resources.

WORKED PROBLEMS

W4.2

Optimal amount of a public good

Cost-Benefit Analysis

The above example suggests a practical means, called **cost-benefit analysis,** for deciding whether to provide a particular public good and how much of it to provide. Like our example, cost-benefit analysis (or marginal-benefit–marginal-cost analysis) involves a comparison of marginal costs and marginal benefits.

Concept Suppose the federal government is contemplating a highway construction plan. Because the economy's resources are limited, any decision to use more resources in the public sector will mean fewer resources for the private sector. There will be an opportunity cost, as well as a benefit. The cost is the loss of satisfaction resulting from the accompanying decline in the production of private goods; the benefit is the extra satisfaction resulting from the output of more public goods. Should the needed resources be shifted from the private to the public sector? The answer is yes if the benefit from the extra public goods exceeds the cost that results from having fewer private goods. The answer is no if the cost of the forgone private goods is greater than the benefit associated with the extra public goods.

Cost-benefit analysis, however, can indicate more than whether a public program is worth doing. It can also help the government decide on the *extent* to which a project should be pursued. Real economic questions cannot usually be answered simply by "yes" or "no" but, rather, involve questions such as "how much" or "how little."

Illustration Roads and highways can be run privately, as excludability is possible with toll gates. However, the federal highway system is almost entirely nonexclusive

TABLE 4.4 Cost-Benefit Analysis for a National Highway Construction Project (in Billions)

(1) Plan	(2) Total Cost of Project	(3) Marginal Cost	(4) Total Benefit	(5) Marginal Benefit	(6) Net Benefit (4) − (2)
No new construction	$ 0		$ 0		$ 0
A: Widen existing highways	4	$ 4	5	$ 5	1
B: New 2-lane highways	10	6	13	8	3
C: New 4-lane highways	**18**	**8**	**23**	**10**	**5**
D: New 6-lane highways	28	10	26	3	−2

because anyone with a car can get on and off most federal highways without restriction anytime they want. Federal highways therefore satisfy one characteristic of a public good, nonexcludability. The other characteristic, nonrivalry, is also satisfied by the fact that unless a highway is already extremely crowded, one person's driving on the highway does not preclude another person's driving on the highway. Thus, the federal highway system is effectively a public good. This leads us to ask: Should the federal government expand the federal highway system? If so, what is the proper size or scope for the overall project?

Table 4.4 lists a series of increasingly ambitious and increasingly costly highway projects: widening existing two-lane highways; building new two-lane highways; building new four-lane highways; building new six-lane highways. The extent to which government should undertake highway construction depends on the costs and benefits. The costs are largely the costs of constructing and maintaining the highways; the benefits are improved flows of people and goods throughout the country.[2]

The table shows that total annual benefit (column 4) exceeds total annual cost (column 2) for plans A, B, and C, indicating that some highway construction is economically justifiable. We see this directly in column 6, where total costs (column 2) are subtracted from total annual benefits (column 4). Net benefits are positive for plans A, B, and C. Plan D is not economically justifiable because net benefits are negative.

But the question of optimal size or scope for this project remains. Comparing the marginal cost (the change in total cost) and the marginal benefit (the change in total benefit) relating to each plan determines the answer. The guideline is well known to you from previous discussions: Increase an activity, project, or output as long as the marginal benefit (column 5) exceeds the marginal cost (column 3). Stop the

activity at, or as close as possible to, the point at which the marginal benefit equals the marginal cost. Do not undertake a project for which marginal cost exceeds marginal benefit.

In this case plan C (building new four-lane highways) is the best plan. Plans A and B are too modest; the marginal benefits exceed the marginal costs, and there is a better option. Plan D's marginal cost ($10 billion) exceeds the marginal benefit ($3 billion) and therefore cannot be justified; it overallocates resources to the project. Plan C is closest to the theoretical optimum because its marginal benefit ($10 billion) still exceeds marginal cost ($8 billion) but approaches the MB = MC (or MC = MB) ideal.

This **marginal-cost–marginal-benefit rule** actually tells us which plan provides the maximum excess of total benefits over total costs or, in other words, the plan that provides society with the maximum net benefit. You can confirm directly in column 6 that the maximum net benefit (= $5 billion) is associated with plan C.

Cost-benefit analysis shatters the myth that "economy in government" and "reduced government spending" are synonymous. "Economy" is concerned with using scarce resources efficiently. If the marginal cost of a proposed government program exceeds its marginal benefit, then the proposed public program should not be undertaken. But if the marginal benefit exceeds the marginal cost, then it would be uneconomical or "wasteful" not to spend on that government program. Economy in government does not mean minimization of public spending. It means allocating resources between the private and public sectors and among public goods to achieve maximum net benefit.

Quasi-Public Goods

Government provides many goods that fit the economist's definition of a public good. However, it also provides other goods and services that could be produced and delivered in such a way that exclusion would be possible. Such goods, called **quasi-public goods,** include education, streets and highways, police and fire protection, libraries and museums, preventive medicine, and sewage disposal. They could all be

[2]Because the costs of public goods typically are immediate while the benefits often accrue over longer time periods, economists convert both costs and benefits to present values for comparison. Doing so properly accounts for the time-value of money, discussed at length in later chapters.

priced and provided by private firms through the market system. But, because the benefits of these goods flow well beyond the benefit to individual buyers, these goods would be underproduced by the market system. Therefore, government often provides them to avoid the underallocation of resources that would otherwise occur.

The Reallocation Process

How are resources reallocated from the production of private goods to the production of public and quasi-public goods? If the resources of the economy are fully employed, government must free up resources from the production of private goods and make them available for producing public and quasi-public goods. It does so by reducing private demand for them. And it does that by levying taxes on households and businesses, taking some of their income out of the circular flow. With lower incomes and hence less purchasing power, households and businesses must curtail their consumption and investment spending. As a result, the private demand for goods and services declines, as does the private demand for resources. So by diverting purchasing power from private spenders to government, taxes remove resources from private use.

Government then spends the tax proceeds to provide public and quasi-public goods and services. Taxation releases resources from the production of private consumer goods (food, clothing, television sets) and private investment goods (printing presses, boxcars, warehouses). Government shifts those resources to the production of public and quasi-public goods (post offices, submarines, parks), changing the composition of the economy's total output.

QUICK REVIEW 4.2

- Public goods are characterized by nonrivalry and nonexcludability.
- The demand (marginal-benefit) curve for a public good is found by vertically adding the prices that all the members of society are willing to pay for the last unit of output at various output levels.
- The socially optimal amount of a public good is the amount at which the marginal cost and marginal benefit of the good are equal.
- Cost-benefit analysis is the method of evaluating alternative projects or sizes of projects by comparing the marginal cost and marginal benefit and applying the MC = MB rule.
- The government uses taxes to reallocate resources from the production of private goods to the production of public and quasi-public goods.

Externalities

LO4.4 Explain how positive and negative externalities cause under- and overallocations of resources.

In addition to providing public goods, governments can also improve the allocation of resources in the economy by correcting for market failures caused by externalities. An **externality** occurs when some of the costs or the benefits of a good or service are passed onto or "spill over to" someone other than the immediate buyer or seller. Such spillovers are called externalities because they are benefits or costs that accrue to some third party that is external to the market transaction.

There are both positive and negative externalities. An example of a negative externality is the cost of breathing polluted air; an example of a positive externality is the benefit of having everyone else inoculated against some disease. When there are negative externalities, an overproduction of the related product occurs and there is an overallocation of resources to this product. Conversely, underproduction and underallocation of resources result when positive externalities are present.

Negative Externalities

Negative externalities cause supply-side market failures. These failures happen because producers do not take into account the costs that their negative externalities impose on others. This failure to account for all production costs causes firms' supply curves to shift to the right of (or below) where they would be if firms properly accounted for all costs. Consider the costs of breathing polluted air that are imposed on third parties living downwind of smoke-spewing factories. Because polluting firms do not take account of such costs, they oversupply the products they make, producing units for which total costs (including those that fall on third parties) exceed total benefits. The same is true when airlines fail to account for the costs that noisy jet engines impose on people living near airports and when biodiesel factories that convert dead animal parts into fuel release foul smelling gases that disgust those living nearby.

Figure 4.6a illustrates how negative externalities affect the allocation of resources. When producers shift some of their costs onto the community as external costs, producers' marginal costs are lower than they would be if they had to pay for those costs. So their supply curves do not include or "capture" all the costs legitimately associated with the production of their goods. A polluting producer's supply curve such as S in Figure 4.6a therefore understates the total cost of production. The firm's supply curve lies to the right of (or below) the total-cost supply curve S_t, which

(a)
Negative externalities

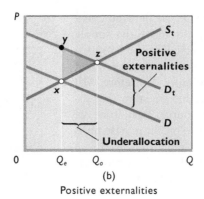

(b)
Positive externalities

FIGURE 4.6 **Negative externalities and positive externalities.** (a) With negative externalities borne by society, the producers' supply curve S is to the right of (below) the total-cost supply curve S_t. Consequently, the equilibrium output Q_e is greater than the optimal output Q_o, and the efficiency loss is *abc*. (b) When positive externalities accrue to society, the market demand curve D is to the left of (below) the total-benefit demand curve D_t. As a result, the equilibrium output Q_e is less than the optimal output Q_o, and the efficiency loss is *xyz*.

would include the spillover cost. Through polluting and thus transferring costs to society, the firm enjoys lower production costs and has the supply curve S.

The outcome is shown in Figure 4.6a, where equilibrium output Q_e is larger than the optimal output Q_o. This means that resources are overallocated to the production of this commodity; too many units of it are produced. In fact, there is a net loss to society for every unit from Q_o to Q_e because, for those units, the supply curve that accounts for all costs, S_t, lies above the demand curve. Therefore, MC exceeds MB for those units. The resources that went into producing those units should have been used elsewhere in the economy to produce other things.

In terms of our previous analysis, the negative externality results in an efficiency loss represented by triangle *abc*.

Positive Externalities

Positive externalities cause demand-side market failures. These failures happen because market demand curves in such cases fail to include the willingness to pay of the third parties who receive the external benefits caused by the positive externality. This failure to account for all benefits shifts market demand curves to the left of (or below) where they would be if they included all benefits and the willingness to pay of both the third parties as well as the primary beneficiaries. Because demand curves fail to take into account all benefits when there are positive externalities, markets in such cases fail to produce all units for which benefits (including those that are received by third parties) exceed costs. As a result, products featuring positive externalities are underproduced.

Vaccinations are a good example of how positive externalities reduce demand and shift demand curves down and to the left. When John gets vaccinated against a disease, he benefits not only himself (because he can no

longer contract the disease) but also everyone else around him (because they know that in the future he will never be able to infect them). These other people would presumably be willing to pay some positive amount of money for the benefits they receive when John is vaccinated. But because his vaccination is a public good, there is no way to make them pay.

To see why his vaccination is a public good, note that the vaccination benefits that John provides to others feature nonrivalry and nonexcludability. There is nonrivalry because the protection his vaccination provides to one person does not lessen the protection that it provides to other people. There is nonexcludability because once he is vaccinated, there is no way to exclude anyone in particular from benefiting from his vaccination. Thus, the market demand for vaccinations will only include John's personal willingness to pay for the benefits that he personally receives from the vaccination. The market demand will fail to include the benefits that others receive. As a result, demand will be too low and vaccinations will be underproduced.

ORIGIN OF THE IDEA

O4.2
Externalities

Figure 4.6b shows the impact of positive externalities on resource allocation. When external benefits occur, the market demand curve D lies to the left of (or below) the total-benefits demand curve, D_t. That is, D does not include the external benefits of the product, whereas D_t does.

The outcome is that the equilibrium output Q_e is less than the optimal output Q_o. The market fails to produce enough vaccinations, and resources are underallocated to this product. The underproduction implies that society is missing out on a significant amount of potential net benefits. For every unit from Q_e to Q_o, the demand curve that accounts for all benefits, D_t, lies above the supply curve that accounts for all costs—including the opportunity cost of producing other items with the resources that would be needed to produce these units. Therefore, MB exceeds MC for each of these units, and we know that society should redeploy some of its resources away from the production of other things in order to produce these units that generate net benefits.

In terms of our previous analysis, the positive externality results in an efficiency loss represented by triangle *xyz*.

Government Intervention

Government intervention may be called upon to achieve economic efficiency when externalities affect large numbers of people or when community interests are at stake. Government can use direct controls and taxes to counter negative externalities; it may provide subsidies or public goods to deal with positive externalities.

Direct Controls   The direct way to reduce negative externalities from a certain activity is to pass legislation limiting that activity. Such direct controls force the offending firms to incur the actual costs of the offending activity. Historically, direct controls in the form of uniform emission standards—limits on allowable pollution—have dominated American air pollution policy. For example, the Clean Air Act of 1990 (1) forced factories and businesses to install "maximum achievable control technology" to reduce emissions of 189 toxic chemicals by 90 percent between 1990 and 2000; (2) required a 30 to 60 percent reduction in tailpipe emissions from automobiles by 2000; (3) mandated a 50 percent reduction in the use of chlorofluorocarbons (CFCs), which deplete the ozone layer (CFCs were used widely as a coolant in refrigeration, a blowing agent for foam, and a solvent in the electronics industry); and (4) forced coal-burning utilities to cut their emissions of sulfur dioxide by about 50 percent to reduce the acid-rain destruction of lakes and forests. Clean-water legislation limits the amount of heavy metals, detergents, and other pollutants firms can discharge into rivers and bays. Toxic-waste laws dictate special procedures and dump sites for disposing of contaminated soil and solvents. Violating these laws means fines and, in some cases, imprisonment.

Direct controls raise the marginal cost of production because the firms must operate and maintain pollution-control equipment. The supply curve S in Figure 4.7b, which does not reflect the external costs, shifts leftward to

CONSIDER THIS . . .

The Fable of the Bees

Economist Ronald Coase received the Nobel Prize for his so-called **Coase theorem**, which pointed out that under the right conditions, private individuals could often negotiate their own mutually agreeable solutions to externality problems through *private bargaining* without the need for government interventions like pollution taxes.

This is a very important insight because it means that we shouldn't automatically call for government intervention every time we see a potential externality problem. Consider the positive externalities that bees provide by pollinating farmers' crops. Should we assume that beekeeping will be underprovided unless the government intervenes with, for instance, subsidies to encourage more hives and hence more pollination?

As it turns out, no. Research has shown that farmers and beekeepers long ago used private bargaining to develop customs and payment systems that avoid free riding by farmers and encourage beekeepers to keep the optimal number of hives. Free riding is avoided by the custom that all farmers in an area simultaneously hire beekeepers to provide bees

ORIGIN OF THE IDEA

O4.3
Coase theorem

to pollinate their crops. And farmers always pay the beekeepers for their pollination services because if they didn't, then no beekeeper would ever work with them in the future—a situation that would lead to massively reduced crop yields due to a lack of pollination.

The "Fable of the Bees" is a good reminder that it is a fallacy to assume that the government must always get involved to remedy externalities. In many cases, the private sector can solve both positive and negative externality problems on its own.

the total-cost supply curve, S_t. Product price increases, equilibrium output falls from Q_e to Q_o, and the initial overallocation of resources shown in Figure 4.7a is corrected. Observe that the efficiency loss shown by triangle *abc* in Figure 4.7a disappears after the overallocation is corrected in Figure 4.7b.

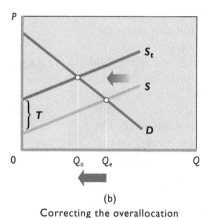

FIGURE 4.7 Correcting for negative externalities. (a) Negative externalities result in an overallocation of resources. (b) Government can correct this overallocation in two ways: (1) using direct controls, which would shift the supply curve from S to S_t and reduce output from Q_e to Q_o, or (2) imposing a specific tax T, which would also shift the supply curve from S to S_t, eliminating the overallocation of resources and thus the efficiency loss.

(a)
Negative externalities

(b)
Correcting the overallocation
of resources via direct controls
or via a tax

Specific Taxes A second policy approach to negative externalities is for government to levy taxes or charges specifically on the related good. For example, the government has placed a manufacturing excise tax on CFCs, which deplete the stratospheric ozone layer protecting the earth from excessive solar ultraviolet radiation. Facing such an excise tax, manufacturers must decide whether to pay the tax or expend additional funds to purchase or develop substitute products. In either case, the tax raises the marginal cost of producing CFCs, shifting the private supply curve for this product leftward (or upward).

In Figure 4.7b, a tax equal to T per unit increases the firm's marginal cost, shifting the supply curve from S to S_t.

The equilibrium price rises, and the equilibrium output declines from Q_e to the economically efficient level Q_o. The tax thus eliminates the initial overallocation of resources and therefore the efficiency loss.

Subsidies and Government Provision Where spillover benefits are large and diffuse, as in our earlier example of inoculations, government has three options for correcting the underallocation of resources:

- *Subsidies to buyers* Figure 4.8a again shows the supply-demand situation for positive externalities. Government could correct the underallocation of

FIGURE 4.8 Correcting for positive externalities. (a) Positive externalities result in an underallocation of resources. (b) This underallocation can be corrected through a subsidy to consumers, which shifts market demand from D to D_t and increases output from Q_e to Q_o. (c) Alternatively, the underallocation can be eliminated by providing producers with a subsidy of U, which shifts their supply curve from S_t to S_t', increasing output from Q_e to Q_o and eliminating the underallocation, and thus the efficiency loss, shown in graph a.

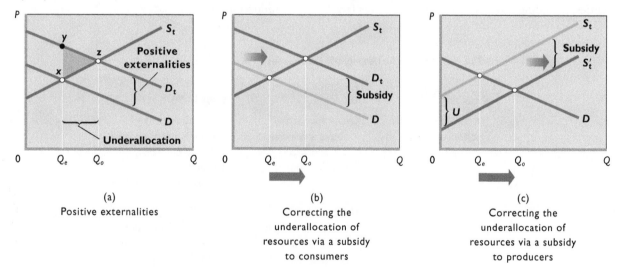

(a)
Positive externalities

(b)
Correcting the
underallocation of
resources via a subsidy
to consumers

(c)
Correcting the
underallocation of
resources via a subsidy
to producers

resources, for example, to inoculations, by subsidizing consumers of the product. It could give each new mother in the United States a discount coupon to be used to obtain a series of inoculations for her child. The coupon would reduce the "price" to the mother by, say, 50 percent. As shown in Figure 4.8b, this program would shift the demand curve for inoculations from too-low D to the appropriate D_t. The number of inoculations would rise from Q_e to the economically optimal Q_0, eliminating the underallocation of resources and efficiency loss shown in Figure 4.8a.

- *Subsidies to producers* A subsidy to producers is a tax in reverse. Taxes are payments *to* the government that increase producers' costs. Subsidies are payments *from* the government that decrease producers' costs. As shown in Figure 4.8c, a subsidy of U per inoculation to physicians and medical clinics would reduce their marginal costs and shift their supply curve rightward from S_t to S_t'. The output of inoculations would increase from Q_e to the optimal level Q_0, correcting the underallocation of resources and efficiency loss shown in Figure 4.8a.

- *Government provision* Finally, where positive externalities are extremely large, the government may decide to provide the product for free to everyone. The U.S. government largely eradicated the crippling disease polio by administering free vaccines to all children. India ended smallpox by paying people in rural areas to come to public clinics to have their children vaccinated.

Table 4.5 lists several methods for correcting externalities, including those we have discussed thus far.

Society's Optimal Amount of Externality Reduction

LO4.5 Show why we normally won't want to pay what it would cost to eliminate every last bit of a negative externality such as air pollution.

Negative externalities such as pollution reduce the utility of those affected, rather than increase it. These spillovers are not economic goods but economic "bads." If something is bad, shouldn't society eliminate it? Why should society allow firms or municipalities to discharge *any* impure waste into public waterways or to emit *any* pollution into the air?

Economists answer these questions by pointing out that reducing pollution and negative externalities is not free. There are costs as well as benefits to reducing pollution. As a result, the correct question to ask when it comes to cleaning up negative externalities is not, "Do we pollute a lot or pollute zero?" That is an all-or-nothing question that ignores marginal costs and marginal benefits. Instead, the correct question is, "What is the optimal amount to clean up—the amount that equalizes the marginal cost of cleaning up with the marginal benefit of a cleaner environment?"

If we ask that question, we see that reducing a negative externality has a "price." Society must decide how much of a reduction it wants to "buy." High costs may mean that totally eliminating pollution might not be desirable, even if it is technologically feasible. Because of the law of diminishing returns, cleaning up the second 10 percent of pollutants from an industrial smokestack normally is more costly than cleaning up the first 10 percent. Eliminating the third 10 percent is more costly than cleaning up the second 10 percent, and so on. Therefore, cleaning up the last 10 percent of pollutants is the most costly reduction of all.

TABLE 4.5 Methods for Dealing with Externalities

Problem	Resource Allocation Outcome	Ways to Correct
Negative externalities (spillover costs)	Overproduction of output and therefore overallocation of resources	1. Private bargaining 2. Liability rules and lawsuits 3. Tax on producers 4. Direct controls 5. Market for externality rights
Positive externalities (spillover benefits)	Underproduction of output and therefore underallocation of resources	1. Private bargaining 2. Subsidy to consumers 3. Subsidy to producers 4. Government provision

The marginal cost (MC) to the firm and hence to society—the opportunity cost of the extra resources used—rises as pollution is reduced more and more. At some point MC may rise so high that it exceeds society's marginal benefit (MB) of further pollution abatement (reduction). Additional actions to reduce pollution will therefore lower society's well-being; total cost will rise more than total benefit.

MC, MB, and Equilibrium Quantity

Figure 4.9 shows both the rising marginal-cost curve, MC, for pollution reduction and the downsloping marginal-benefit curve, MB, for pollution reduction. MB slopes downward because of the law of diminishing marginal utility: The more pollution reduction society accomplishes, the lower the utility (and benefit) of the next unit of pollution reduction.

The **optimal reduction of an externality** occurs when society's marginal cost and marginal benefit of reducing that externality are equal (MC = MB). In Figure 4.9 this optimal amount of pollution abatement is Q_1 units. When MB exceeds MC, additional abatement moves society toward economic efficiency; the added benefit of cleaner air or water exceeds the benefit of any alternative use of the required resources. When MC exceeds MB, additional abatement reduces economic efficiency;

there would be greater benefits from using resources in some other way than to further reduce pollution.

In reality, it is difficult to measure the marginal costs and benefits of pollution control. Nevertheless, Figure 4.9 demonstrates that some pollution may be economically efficient. This is so not because pollution is desirable but because beyond some level of control, further abatement may reduce society's net well-being. As an example, it would cost the government billions of dollars to clean up every last piece of litter in America. Thus, it would be better to tolerate some trash blowing around if the money saved by picking up less trash would yield larger net benefits when spent on other things.

Shifts in Locations of the Curves

The locations of the marginal-cost and marginal-benefit curves in Figure 4.9 are not forever fixed. They can, and probably do, shift over time. For example, suppose that the technology of pollution-control equipment improved noticeably. We would expect the cost of pollution abatement to fall, society's MC curve to shift rightward, and the optimal level of abatement to rise. Or suppose that society were to decide that it wanted cleaner air and water because of new information about the adverse health effects of pollution. The MB curve in Figure 4.9 would shift rightward, and the optimal level of pollution control would increase beyond Q_1. Test your understanding of these statements by drawing the new MC and MB curves in Figure 4.9.

Government's Role in the Economy

Market failures can be used to justify government interventions in the economy. The inability of private-sector firms to break even when attempting to provide public goods and the over- and underproduction problems caused by positive and negative externalities mean that government can have an important role to play if society's resources are to be efficiently allocated to the goods and services that people most highly desire.

Correcting for market failures is not, however, an easy task. To begin with, government officials must correctly identify the existence and the cause of any given market failure. That by itself may be difficult, time-consuming, and costly. But even if a market failure is correctly identified and diagnosed, government may still fail to take appropriate corrective action due to the fact that government undertakes its economic role in the context of politics.

To serve the public, politicians need to get elected. To stay elected, officials (presidents, senators, representatives, mayors, council members, school board members) need to satisfy their particular constituencies. At best, the political

FIGURE 4.9 Society's optimal amount of pollution abatement. The optimal amount of externality reduction—in this case, pollution abatement—occurs at Q_1, where society's marginal cost MC and marginal benefit MB of reducing the spillover are equal.

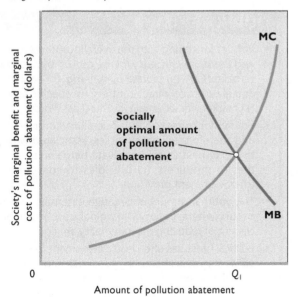

LAST WORD

Carbon Dioxide Emissions, Cap and Trade, and Carbon Taxes

Cap-and-trade systems and carbon taxes are two approaches to reducing carbon dioxide (CO_2) emissions.

Externality problems are property rights problems. Consider a landfill. Because the owner of the landfill has full rights to his land, people wishing to dump their trash into the landfill have to pay him. This payment implies that there is no externality: He happily accepts their trash in exchange for a dumping fee. By contrast, because nobody owns the atmosphere, all air pollution is an externality, since there is no way for those doing the polluting to work out a payment to compensate those affected by the pollution or for those threatened with pollution to simply refuse to be polluted on.

Conventional property rights therefore cannot fix the externalities associated with air pollution. But that does not mean property rights can't help fight pollution. The trick to making them work is to assign property rights not to the atmosphere itself, but to *polluting* the atmosphere. This is done in "cap-and-trade" systems, under which the government sets an annual limit, or cap, to the number of tons of a pollutant that firms can emit into the atmosphere.

Consider carbon dioxide, or CO_2. It is a colorless, odorless gas that many scientists consider to be a contributing cause of climate change, specifically global warming. To reduce CO_2 emissions, the U.S. government might set a cap of 5 billion tons of CO_2 emissions per year in the United States (which would be about 25 percent below 2010 emissions levels for that molecule). The government then prints out emissions permits that sum to the limit set in the cap and distributes them to polluting firms. Once they are distributed, the only way a firm can legally emit a ton of CO_2 is if it owns a permit to do so.

Under this policy, the government can obviously adjust the total amount of air pollution by adjusting the cap. This by itself improves efficiency because the cap imposes scarcity. Because each firm has only a limited number of permits, each firm has a strong incentive to maximize the net benefit that it produces from every ton of pollution that it emits. But the *cap-and-trade* scheme leads to even greater improvements in efficiency because firms are free to trade (sell) them to each other in what are referred to as *markets for externality rights*.

For instance, suppose Smokestack Toys owns permits for 100 tons of CO_2 emissions and that it could use them to produce toy cars that would generate profits of $100,000. There is a power plant, however, that could make up to $1 million of profits by using those 100 tons of emissions permits to generate electricity. Because firms can trade their permits, Smokestack Toys will sell its permits to the power plant for more than the $100,000 in profits that it could make if it kept them and

realities complicate government's role in the economy; at worst, they produce undesirable economic outcomes.

In the political context, overregulation can occur in some cases; underregulation, in others. Some public goods and quasi-public goods can be produced not because their benefits exceed their costs but because their benefits accrue to firms located in states served by powerful elected officials. Inefficiency can easily creep into government activities because of the lack of a profit incentive to hold down costs. Policies to correct negative externalities can be politically blocked by the very parties that are producing the spillovers. In short, the economic role of government, although critical to a well-functioning economy, is not always perfectly carried out.

Economists use the term "government failure" to describe economically inefficient outcomes caused by shortcomings in the public sector.

QUICK REVIEW 4.3

- Policies for coping with the overallocation of resources, and therefore efficiency losses, caused by negative externalities are (a) private bargaining, (b) liability rules and lawsuits, (c) direct controls, (d) specific taxes, and (e) markets for externality rights (Last Word).

- Policies for correcting the underallocation of resources, and therefore efficiency losses, associated with positive externalities are (a) private bargaining, (b) subsidies to producers, (c) subsidies to consumers, and (d) government provision.

- The optimal amount of negative-externality reduction occurs where society's marginal cost and marginal benefit of reducing the externality are equal.

- Political pressures often lead government to respond inefficiently when attempting to correct for market failures.

produced toy cars. And the power plant will gladly pay more than $100,000 for those permits because it can turn around and use them to make up to $1 million of profits by using them to generate electricity.

Society will benefit hugely from this transaction because while 100 tons of CO_2 will be emitted no matter which firm uses the permits, society will receive much greater net benefits when they are used by the power plant, as indicated by the fact that the power plant can produce much larger profits than the toy company when using the same amount of this scarce resource.

Several words of caution, however! Cap-and-trade systems have proven very difficult to implement in cases where it is difficult for regulators to effectively check whether firms are obeying the system. This has been a major problem with the European Union's cap-and-trade system for CO_2 emissions. Because nearly every type of industrial activity releases CO_2 into the atmosphere, enforcement involves monitoring many thousands of factories of all sizes. That is very difficult and cheating has resulted. In addition, politically connected industries got politicians to give them exemptions or free permits.

By contrast, a cap-and-trade system on sulfur dioxide emissions from coal-burning public utilities has worked well in the United States since the 1980s. But in that case, there were only a few hundred polluting utilities, and they were already being monitored for emissions. So there was little ability to cheat. In addition, all of the firms were treated equally, with no firms allowed exemptions or free permits.

Due to the mixed results, many economists have concluded that a cap-and-trade system would not be the best way to curb CO_2 emissions in the United States. They believe that there are simply too many sources of pollution to make monitoring either possible or cost-effective. And it seems likely that politically connected industries will be granted exemptions. So, instead, many economists favor a carbon tax, which would involve taxing each ton of coal, each gallon of gasoline, and each barrel of oil on the basis of how much carbon it contains (and thus how much CO_2 will eventually be released into the atmosphere when it is used). By raising the cost of polluting, the tax would reduce consumption and lessen the externalities associated with CO_2 emissions. It would also be nearly impossible to evade, so that we would not have to worry about cheating.

SUMMARY

LO4.1 Differentiate between demand-side market failures and supply-side market failures.

A market failure happens in a particular market when the market produces an equilibrium level of output that either overallocates or underallocates resources to the product being traded in the market. In competitive markets that feature many buyers and many sellers, market failures can be divided into two types: Demand-side market failures occur when demand curves do not reflect consumers' full willingness to pay; supply-side market failures occur when supply curves do not reflect all production costs, including those that may be borne by third parties.

LO4.2 Explain the origin of both consumer surplus and producer surplus, and explain how properly functioning markets maximize their sum, total surplus, while optimally allocating resources.

Consumer surplus is the difference between the maximum price that a consumer is willing to pay for a product and the lower price actually paid; producer surplus is the difference between the minimum price that a producer is willing to accept for a product and the higher price actually received. Collectively, consumer surplus is represented by the triangle under the demand curve and above the actual price, whereas producer surplus is shown by the triangle above the supply curve and below the actual price.

Graphically, the combined amount of producer and consumer surplus is represented by the triangle to the left of the intersection of the supply and demand curves that is below the demand curve and above the supply curve. At the equilibrium price and quantity in competitive markets, marginal benefit equals marginal cost, maximum willingness to pay equals minimum acceptable price, and the combined amount of consumer surplus and producer surplus is maximized.

Output levels that are either less than or greater than the equilibrium output create efficiency losses, also called deadweight losses. These losses are reductions in the combined amount of consumer surplus and producer surplus. Underproduction creates efficiency losses because output is not being produced for which maximum willingness to pay exceeds minimum acceptable price. Overproduction creates efficiency losses because output is being produced for which minimum acceptable price exceeds maximum willingness to pay.

LO4.3 Describe free riding and public goods, and illustrate why private firms cannot normally produce public goods.

Public goods are distinguished from private goods. Private goods are characterized by rivalry (in consumption) and excludability. One person's purchase and consumption of a private good precludes others from also buying and consuming it. Producers can exclude nonpayers (free riders) from receiving the benefits. In contrast, public goods are characterized by nonrivalry (in consumption) and nonexcludability. Public goods are not profitable to private firms because nonpayers (free riders) can obtain and consume those goods without paying. Government can, however, provide desirable public goods, financing them through taxation.

The collective demand schedule for a particular public good is found by summing the prices that each individual is willing to pay for an additional unit. Graphically, that demand curve is found by summing vertically the individual demand curves for that good. The resulting total demand curve indicates the collective willingness to pay for (or marginal benefit of) any given amount of the public good.

The optimal quantity of a public good occurs where the society's willingness to pay for the last unit—the marginal benefit of the good—equals the marginal cost of the good.

LO4.4 Explain how positive and negative externalities cause under- and overallocations of resources.

Externalities, or spillovers, are costs or benefits that accrue to someone other than the immediate buyer or seller. Such costs or benefits are not captured in market demand or supply curves and therefore cause the output of certain goods to vary from society's optimal output. Negative externalities (or spillover costs or external costs) result in an overallocation of resources to a particular product. Positive externalities (or spillover benefits or external benefits) are accompanied by an underallocaton of resources to a particular product.

Direct controls and specific taxes can improve resource allocation in situations where negative externalities affect many people and community resources. Both direct controls (for example, smokestack emission standards) and specific taxes (for example, taxes on firms producing toxic chemicals) increase production costs and hence product price. As product price rises, the externality, overallocation of resources, and efficiency loss are reduced since less of the output is produced.

Government can correct the underallocation of resources and therefore the efficiency losses that result from positive externalities in a particular market either by subsidizing consumers (which increases market demand) or by subsidizing producers (which increases market supply). Such subsidies increase the equilibrium output, reducing or eliminating the positive externality and consequent underallocation of resources and efficiency loss.

The Coase theorem suggests that under the right circumstances private bargaining can solve externality problems. Thus, government intervention is not always needed to deal with externality problems.

LO4.5 Show why we normally won't want to pay what it would cost to eliminate every last bit of a negative externality such as air pollution.

The socially optimal amount of externality abatement occurs where society's marginal cost and marginal benefit of reducing the externality are equal. With pollution, for example, this optimal amount of pollution abatement is likely to be less than a 100 percent reduction. Changes in technology or changes in society's attitudes toward pollution can affect the optimal amount of pollution abatement.

Market failures present government with opportunities to improve the allocation of society's resources and thereby enhance society's total well-being. But even when government correctly identifies the existence and cause of a market failure, political pressures may make it difficult or impossible for government officials to implement a proper solution.

TERMS AND CONCEPTS

market failures	producer surplus	excludability
demand-side market failures	efficiency losses (or deadweight losses)	public goods
supply-side market failures	private goods	nonrivalry
consumer surplus	rivalry	nonexcludability

free-rider problem

cost-benefit analysis

marginal-cost–marginal-benefit rule

quasi-public goods

externality

Coase theorem

optimal reduction of an externality

The following and additional problems can be found in **connect** ECONOMICS

DISCUSSION QUESTIONS

1. Explain the two causes of market failures. Given their definitions, could a market be affected by both types of market failures simultaneously? **LO4.1**
2. Use the ideas of consumer surplus and producer surplus to explain why economists say competitive markets are efficient. Why are below- or above-equilibrium levels of output inefficient, according to these two sets of ideas? **LO4.2**
3. What are the two characteristics of public goods? Explain the significance of each for public provision as opposed to private provision. What is the free-rider problem as it relates to public goods? Is U.S. border patrol a public good or a private good? Why? How about satellite TV? Explain. **LO4.3**
4. What divergences arise between equilibrium output and efficient output when (a) negative externalities and (b) positive externalities are present? How might government correct these divergences? Cite an example (other than the text examples) of an external cost and an external benefit. **LO4.4**
5. Why are spillover costs and spillover benefits also called negative and positive externalities? Show graphically how a tax can correct for a negative externality and how a subsidy to producers can correct for a positive externality. How does a subsidy to consumers differ from a subsidy to producers in correcting for a positive externality? **LO4.4**
6. An apple grower's orchard provides nectar to a neighbor's bees, while the beekeeper's bees help the apple grower by pollinating his apple blossoms. Use Figure 4.6b to explain

why this situation of dual positive externalities might lead to an underallocation of resources to both apple growing and beekeeping. How might this underallocation get resolved via the means suggested by the Coase theorem? **LO4.4**
7. The LoJack car recovery system allows the police to track stolen cars. As a result, they not only recover 90 percent of LoJack-equipped cars that are stolen but also arrest many auto thieves and shut down many "chop shops" that take apart stolen vehicles to get at their used parts. Thus, LoJack provides both private benefits and positive externalities. Should the government consider subsidizing LoJack purchases? **LO4.4**
8. Explain why zoning laws, which allow certain land uses only in specific locations, might be justified in dealing with a problem of negative externalities. Explain why in areas where buildings sit close together tax breaks to property owners for installing extra fire prevention equipment might be justified in view of positive externalities. Explain why excise taxes on beer might be justified in dealing with a problem of external costs. **LO4.5**
9. **LAST WORD** Distinguish between a carbon-tax and a cap-and-trade strategy for reducing carbon dioxide and other so-called greenhouse gases (that are believed by many scientists to be causing global warming). Which of the two strategies do you think would have the most political support in an election in your home state? Explain your thinking.

REVIEW QUESTIONS

1. Draw a supply and demand graph and identify the areas of consumer surplus and producer surplus. Given the demand curve, what impact will an increase in supply have on the amount of consumer surplus shown in your diagram? Explain why. **LO4.2**
2. Assume that candle wax is traded in a perfectly competitive market in which the demand curve captures buyers' full willingness to pay while the supply curve reflects all production costs. For each of the following situations, indicate whether the total output should be increased, decreased, or kept the same in order to achieve allocative and productive efficiency. **LO4.2**
   a. Maximum willingness to pay exceeds minimum acceptable price.
   b. MC > MB.

   c. Total surplus is at a maximum.
   d. The current quantity produced exceeds the market equilibrium quantity.
3. Efficiency losses _____. **LO4.2**
   a. Are not possible if suppliers are willing to produce and sell a product.
   b. Can only result from underproduction.
   c. Can only result from overproduction.
   d. None of the above.
4. Draw a production possibilities curve with public goods on the vertical axis and private goods on the horizontal axis. Assuming the economy is initially operating on the curve, indicate how the production of public goods might be increased. How might the output of public goods be increased

if the economy is initially operating at a point inside the curve? **LO4.3**

5. Use the distinction between the characteristics of private and public goods to determine whether the following should be produced through the market system or provided by government: (a) French fries, (b) airport screening, (c) court systems, (d) mail delivery, and (e) medical care. State why you answered as you did in each case. **LO4.3**

6. Match each of the following characteristics or scenarios with either the term *negative externality* or the term *positive externality*. **LO4.4**

   a. Overallocation of resources.

   b. Tammy installs a very nice front garden, raising the property values of all the other houses on her block.

   c. Market demand curves are too far to the left (too low).

   d. Underallocation of resources.

   e. Water pollution from a factory forces neighbors to buy water purifiers.

7. Use marginal cost/marginal benefit analysis to determine if the following statement is true or false: "The optimal amount of pollution abatement for some substances, say, dirty water from storm drains, is very low; the optimal amount of abatement for other substances, say, cyanide poison, is close to 100 percent." **LO4.5**

PROBLEMS

1. Refer to Table 4.1. If the six people listed in the table are the only consumers in the market and the equilibrium price is $11 (not the $8 shown), how much consumer surplus will the market generate? **LO4.2**

2. Refer to Table 4.2. If the six people listed in the table are the only producers in the market and the equilibrium price is $6 (not the $8 shown), how much producer surplus will the market generate? **LO4.2**

3. Look at Tables 4.1 and 4.2 together. What is the total surplus if Bob buys a unit from Carlos? If Barb buys a unit from Courtney? If Bob buys a unit from Chad? If you match up pairs of buyers and sellers so as to maximize the total surplus of all transactions, what is the largest total surplus that can be achieved? **LO4.2**

4. **ADVANCED ANALYSIS**   Assume the following values for Figures 4.4a and 4.4b. $Q_1 = 20$ bags. $Q_2 = 15$ bags. $Q_3 = 27$ bags. The market equilibrium price is $45 per bag. The price at a is $85 per bag. The price at c is $5 per bag. The price at f is $59 per bag. The price at g is $31 per bag. Apply the formula for the area of a triangle (Area = ½ × Base × Height) to answer the following questions. **LO4.2**

   a. What is the dollar value of the total surplus (producer surplus plus consumer surplus) when the allocatively efficient output level is being produced? How large is the dollar value of the consumer surplus at that output level?

   b. What is the dollar value of the deadweight loss when output level Q_2 is being produced? What is the total surplus when output level Q_2 is being produced?

   c. What is the dollar value of the deadweight loss when output level Q_3 is produced? What is the dollar value of the total surplus when output level Q_3 is produced?

5. On the basis of the three individual demand schedules in the following table, and assuming these three people are the only ones in the society, determine (a) the market demand schedule on the assumption that the good is a private good

and (b) the collective demand schedule on the assumption that the good is a public good. **LO4.3**

P	$Q_d (D_1)$	$Q_d (D_2)$	$Q_d (D_3)$
$8	0	1	0
7	0	2	0
6	0	3	1
5	1	4	2
4	2	5	3
3	3	6	4
2	4	7	5
1	5	8	6

6. Use your demand schedule for a public good, determined in problem 5, and the following supply schedule to ascertain the optimal quantity of this public good. **LO4.3**

P	Q_s
$19	10
16	8
13	6
10	4
7	2
4	1

7. Look at Tables 4.1 and 4.2, which show, respectively, the willingness to pay and willingness to accept of buyers and sellers of bags of oranges. For the following questions, assume that the equilibrium price and quantity will depend on the indicated changes in supply and demand. Assume that the only market participants are those listed by name in the two tables. **LO4.4**

   a. What are the equilibrium price and quantity for the data displayed in the two tables?

b. What if, instead of bags of oranges, the data in the two tables dealt with a public good like fireworks displays? If all the buyers free ride, what will be the quantity supplied by private sellers?

c. Assume that we are back to talking about bags of oranges (a private good), but that the government has decided that tossed orange peels impose a negative externality on the public that must be rectified by imposing a $2-per-bag tax on sellers. What is the new equilibrium price and quantity? If the new equilibrium quantity is the optimal quantity, by how many bags were oranges being overproduced before?

Information Failures

LO4.6 Describe how information failures may justify government intervention in some markets.

This chapter discussed the two most common types of market failure, public goods and externalities. But there is also another, subtler, type of market failure. This one results when either buyers or sellers have incomplete or inaccurate information and their cost of obtaining better information is prohibitive. Technically stated, this market failure occurs because of **asymmetric information**—unequal knowledge possessed by the parties to a market transaction. Buyers and sellers do not have identical information about price, quality, or some other aspect of the good or service.

Sufficient market information is normally available to ensure that goods and services are produced and purchased efficiently. But in some cases inadequate information makes it difficult to distinguish trustworthy from untrustworthy sellers or trustworthy from untrustworthy buyers. In these markets, society's scarce resources may not be used efficiently, thus implying that the government should intervene by increasing the information available to the market participants. Under rare circumstances the government may itself supply a good for which information problems have prohibited efficient production.

ORIGIN OF THE IDEA

O4.4
Information failures

Inadequate Buyer Information about Sellers

Inadequate information among buyers about sellers and their products can cause market failure in the form of underallocation of resources. Two examples will help you understand this point.

Example: Gasoline Market

Assume an absurd situation: Suppose there is no system of weights and measures established by law, no government inspection of gasoline pumps, and no law against false advertising. Each gas station can use whatever measure it chooses; it can define a gallon of gas as it pleases. A station can advertise that its gas is 87 octane when in fact it is only

75. It can rig its pumps to indicate that it is providing more gas than the amount being delivered.

Obviously, the consumer's cost of obtaining reliable information under such chaotic conditions is exceptionally high, if not prohibitive. Customers or their representatives would have to buy samples of gas from various gas stations, have them tested for octane level, and test the accuracy of calibrations at the pump. And these activities would have to be repeated regularly, since a station owner could alter the product quality and the accuracy of the pump at will.

Because of the high cost of obtaining information about the seller, many consumers would opt out of this chaotic market. One tankful of a 50 percent mixture of gasoline and water would be enough to discourage most motorists from further driving. More realistically, the conditions in this market would encourage consumers to vote for political candidates who promise to provide a government solution. The oil companies and honest gasoline stations would most likely welcome government intervention. They would realize that accurate information, by enabling this market to work, would expand their total sales and profits.

The government has in fact intervened in the market for gasoline and other markets with similar potential information difficulties. It has established a system of weights and measures, employed inspectors to check the accuracy of gasoline pumps, and passed laws against fraudulent claims and misleading advertising. Clearly, these government activities have produced net benefits for society.

Example: Licensing of Surgeons

Suppose now that anyone could hang out a shingle and claim to be a surgeon, much as anyone can become a house painter. The market would eventually sort out the true surgeons from those who are "learning by doing" or are fly-by-night operators who move into and out of an area. As people died from unsuccessful surgeries, lawsuits for malpractice eventually would identify and eliminate most of the medical impostors. People needing surgery for themselves or their loved ones could obtain information from newspaper reports, Internet sites, or people who have undergone similar operations.

But this process of obtaining information for those needing surgery would take considerable time and would impose unacceptably high human and economic costs.

There is a fundamental difference between getting an amateurish paint job on one's house and being on the receiving end of heart surgery by a bogus physician. The marginal cost of obtaining information about sellers in the surgery market would be excessively high. The risk of proceeding without good information would result in much less surgery than desirable—an underallocation of resources to surgery.

The government has remedied this market failure through a system of qualifying tests and licensing. The licensing provides consumers with inexpensive information about a service they only infrequently buy. The government has taken a similar role in several other areas of the economy. For example, it approves new medicines, regulates the securities industry, and requires warnings on containers of potentially hazardous substances. It also requires warning labels on cigarette packages and disseminates information about communicable diseases. And it issues warnings about unsafe toys and inspects restaurants for health-related violations.

Inadequate Seller Information about Buyers

Just as inadequate information about sellers can keep markets from achieving economic efficiency, so can inadequate information about buyers. The buyers may be consumers who buy products or firms that buy resources.

Moral Hazard Problem

Private markets may underallocate resources to a particular good or service for which there is a severe **moral hazard problem.** The moral hazard problem is the tendency of one party to a contract or agreement to alter her or his behavior, after the contract is signed, in ways that could be costly to the other party.

Suppose a firm offers an insurance policy that pays a set amount of money per month to people who suffer divorces. The attractiveness of such insurance is that it would pool the economic risk of divorce among thousands of people and, in particular, would protect spouses and children from the economic hardship that divorce often brings. Unfortunately, the moral hazard problem reduces the likelihood that insurance companies can profitably provide this type of insurance.

After taking out such insurance, some people would alter their behavior in ways that impose heavy costs on the insurer. For example, married couples would have less of an incentive to get along and to iron out marital difficulties. At the extreme, some people might be motivated to obtain a divorce, collect the insurance, and then continue to live together. Such insurance could even promote divorce, the very outcome that it is intended to protect against. The moral hazard problem would force the insurer to charge such high premiums for this insurance that few policies would be bought. If the insurer could identify in advance those people most prone to alter their behavior, the firm could exclude them from buying it. But the firm's marginal cost of getting such information is too high compared with the marginal benefit. Thus, this market would fail.

Although divorce insurance is not available in the marketplace, society recognizes the benefits of insuring against the hardships of divorce. It has corrected for this underallocation of "hardship insurance" through child-support laws that dictate payments to the spouse who retains the children, when the economic circumstances warrant them. Alimony laws also play a role.

The government also supplies "divorce insurance" of a sort through the Temporary Assistance for Needy Families (TANF) program. Though aimed at helping poor children in general rather than children of divorce specifically, parents with children can receive TANF payments if they are left destitute by divorce. Because government does not have to earn a profit when supplying services, it can offer this type of "divorce insurance" despite the fact that it, too, may be susceptible to the moral hazard problem.

The moral hazard problem is also illustrated in the following statements:

- Drivers may be less cautious because they have car insurance.
- Medical malpractice insurance may increase the amount of malpractice.
- Guaranteed contracts for professional athletes may reduce the quality of their performance.
- Unemployment compensation insurance may lead some workers to shirk.
- Government insurance on bank deposits may encourage banks to make risky loans.

Adverse Selection Problem

Another information problem resulting from inadequate information about buyers is the **adverse selection problem.** This problem arises when information known by the first party to a contract or agreement is not known by the second and, as a result, the second party incurs major costs. Unlike the moral hazard problem, which arises after a person signs a contract, the adverse selection problem arises at the time a person signs a contract.

In insurance, the adverse selection problem is that people who are most likely to need insurance payouts are those who buy insurance. For example, those in poorest health will seek to buy the most generous health insurance policies. Or, at the extreme, a person planning to hire an arsonist to "torch" his failing business has an incentive to buy fire insurance.

Our hypothetical divorce insurance sheds further light on the adverse selection problem. If the insurance firm sets the premiums on the basis of the average divorce rate, many married couples who are about to obtain a divorce will buy insurance. An insurance premium based on average probabilities will make a great buy for those about to get divorced. Meanwhile, those in highly stable marriages will not buy it.

The adverse selection problem thus tends to eliminate the pooling of low and high risks, which is the basis of profitable insurance. Insurance rates then must be so high that few people would want to (or be able to) buy such insurance.

Where private firms underprovide insurance because of information problems, the government often establishes some type of social insurance. It can require that everyone in a particular group take the insurance and thereby can overcome the adverse selection problem. Example: Although the Social Security system in the United States is partly insurance and partly an income transfer program, in its broadest sense it is insurance against poverty during old age. The Social Security program requires nearly universal participation: People who are most likely to need the minimum benefits that Social Security provides are automatically participants in the program. So, too, are those not likely to need the benefits. Consequently, no adverse selection problem emerges.

Qualification

Households and businesses have found many ingenious ways to overcome information difficulties without government intervention. For example, many firms offer product warranties to overcome the lack of information about themselves and their products. Franchising also helps overcome this problem. When you visit a Wendy's or a Marriott, you know what you are going to get, as opposed to stopping at Slim's Hamburger Shop or the Triple Six Motel.

Also, some private firms and organizations specialize in providing information to buyers and sellers. *Consumer Reports, Mobil Travel Guide*, and numerous Internet sites provide product information; labor unions collect and disseminate information about job safety; and credit bureaus provide information about credit histories and past bankruptcies to lending institutions and insurance companies. Brokers, bonding agencies, and intermediaries also provide information to clients.

Economists agree, however, that the private sector cannot remedy all information problems. In some situations, government intervention is desirable to promote an efficient allocation of society's scarce resources.

APPENDIX SUMMARY

LO4.6 Describe how information failures may justify government intervention in some markets.

Asymmetric information occurs when buyers and sellers do not have the same information about a product. It is a source of potential market failure, causing society's scarce resources to be allocated inefficiently.

Asymmetric information can cause a market to fail if the party that has less information decides to withdraw from the market because it fears that its lack of knowledge may be exploited by the party that has more information.

If the party that has less information reduces its participation in a market, the reduction in the size of the market may cause an underallocation of resources to the product produced for the market.

The moral hazard problem is the tendency of one party to a contract or agreement to alter its behavior in ways that are costly to the other party; for example, a person who buys insurance may willingly incur added risk.

The adverse selection problem arises when one party to a contract or agreement has less information than the other party and incurs a cost because of that asymmetrical information. For example, an insurance company offering "no medical-exam-required" life insurance policies may attract customers who have life-threatening diseases.

APPENDIX TERMS AND CONCEPTS

asymmetric information

moral hazard problem

adverse selection problem

The following and additional problems can be found in **connect** ECONOMICS

APPENDIX DISCUSSION QUESTIONS

1. Because medical records are private, an individual applying for health insurance will know more about his own health conditions than will the insurance companies to which he is applying for coverage. Is this likely to increase or decrease the insurance premium that he will be offered? Why? **LO4.6**

2. Why is it in the interest of new homebuyers and builders of new homes to have government building codes and building inspectors? **LO4.6**

3. Place an "M" beside the items in the following list that describe a moral hazard problem and an "A" beside those that describe an adverse selection problem. **LO4.6**

   a. A person with a terminal illness buys several life insurance policies through the mail.

   b. A person drives carelessly because she has automobile insurance.

   c. A person who intends to torch his warehouse takes out a large fire insurance policy.

   d. A professional athlete who has a guaranteed contract fails to stay in shape during the off season.

   e. A woman who anticipates having a large family takes a job with a firm that offers exceptional childcare benefits.

APPENDIX REVIEW QUESTIONS

1. People drive faster when they have auto insurance. This is an example of: **LO4.6**
   a. Adverse selection.
   b. Asymmetric information.
   c. Moral hazard.

2. Government inspectors who check on the quality of services provided by retailers as well as government requirements for licensing in various professions are both attempts to resolve: **LO4.6**
   a. The moral hazard problem.
   b. The asymmetric information problem.

3. True or False: A market may collapse and have relatively few transactions between buyers and sellers if buyers have more information than sellers. **LO4.6**

APPENDIX PROBLEMS

1. Consider a used car market with asymmetric information. The owners of used cars know what their vehicles are worth but have no way of credibly demonstrating those values to potential buyers. Thus, potential buyers must always worry that the used car they are being offered may be a low quality "lemon." **LO4.6**

   a. Suppose that there are equal numbers of good and bad used cars in the market and that good used cars are worth $13,000 while bad used cars are worth $5,000. What is the average value of a used car?

   b. By how much does the average value exceed the value of a bad used car? By how much does the value of a good used car exceed the average value?

   c. Would a potential seller of a good used car be willing to accept the average value as payment for her vehicle?

   d. If a buyer negotiates with a seller to purchase the seller's used car for a price equal to the average value, is the car more likely to be good or bad?

   e. Will the used-car market come to feature mostly—if not exclusively—lemons? How much will used cars end up costing if all the good cars are withdrawn?

CHAPTER 5

Government's Role and Government Failure

Learning Objectives

LO5.1 Describe how government's power to coerce can be economically beneficial and list some of the difficulties associated with managing and directing the government.

LO5.2 Discuss "government failure" and explain why it happens.

LO5.3 (Appendix) Explain the difficulties of conveying economic preferences through majority voting.

Governments in market economies perform several economic tasks. As discussed in various places in the book, these include promoting production and trade by defining property rights, enforcing contracts, and settling disputes; enforcing laws designed to maintain competition; redistributing income via taxes and transfers; reallocating resources by producing public goods and intervening to correct negative and positive externalities; and promoting economic growth and full employment.

In this chapter, we deepen our understanding of government's role in the market economy by examining some of the difficulties that democratic governments face when making specific laws related to the economy. We will find that governments sometimes pursue policies for which costs outweigh benefits. These inefficient outcomes happen often enough that we need to be just as vigilant in looking for instances of *government failure* as we are in looking for instances of *market failure*.

Government's Economic Role

LO5.1 Describe how government's power to coerce can be economically beneficial and list some of the difficulties associated with managing and directing the government.

As discussed in Chapter 2, the U.S. economy is a *market system* that uses mostly markets and prices to coordinate and direct economic activity. But the government also has a prominent role in how the economy functions. Among other things, the government sets the laws governing economic activity, provides goods and services that would otherwise be underproduced by private firms, and modifies the distribution of income. The government also promotes both economic stability and economic growth.

Government's Right to Coerce

One key difference between the economic activities of government and those of private firms and individuals is that government possesses the legal right to force people to do things. Whereas private-sector economic activities consist primarily of voluntary transactions, government has the legal right to enforce involuntary transactions. Among other things, the government can put you in jail if you do not pay your taxes, fine you if you violate pollution laws, jail you if you commit fraud, and remove your business license if you violate health and safety regulations.

Force and Economic Efficiency   From an economic perspective, the government's ability to force people to do things can be quite beneficial because it can be used to increase economic efficiency.

Correcting for Market Failures   Consider public goods and externalities. As discussed in Chapter 4, these market failures cause resource misallocations. When it comes to both public goods and products offering positive externalities, private producers fail to produce enough output because it is impossible to charge many of the beneficiaries for the benefits that they receive from the producers' products. In such cases, the government can improve economic efficiency by using involuntarily collected tax money to subsidize production.

By contrast, products that generate negative externalities are overproduced by the private sector because many of their costs are borne by third parties rather than by their producers. The government can reduce that overproduction and improve economic efficiency by using involuntary policies such as direct controls, pollution taxes, and cap-and-trade schemes to force producers to bear higher costs.

Reducing Private-Sector Economic Risks   Government's ability to force people to do things is also crucial in reducing private-sector economic risks. To begin with, the government helps to ensure that only mutually agreeable transactions take place by making blackmail, extortion, and other forms of private coercion illegal. The government also uses its legal powers to outlaw various forms of theft, deception, and discrimination as well as restraints on trade, price-fixing, and refusal to honor a contract.

These limitations encourage economic activity by giving greater security to both individuals and firms. Because they know that the government will use its massive resources to arrest and punish those who break the law, they know that other individuals and firms are less likely to try to take advantage of them. That reduction in risk encourages higher levels of investment, the formation of more new businesses, and the introduction of more new goods and services. In economic terminology, both allocative and productive efficiency increase.

The Problem of Directing and Managing Government

As just discussed, the government can substantially improve allocative and productive efficiency if it directs its awesome coercive powers toward rectifying market failures and providing a low-risk economic environment for the private sector. However, it has only been in recent centuries that democratic political institutions have been able to tame government and direct it toward those goals. Until that happened, most governments were tyrannical, with their powers almost always directed toward enriching the small minority that controlled each government.

Because modern democratic governments serve much broader constituencies, they are much more likely to pursue economic policies with widespread social benefits. Their ability to deliver economically optimal outcomes is hindered, however, by the wide variety of government failures that this chapter will discuss in detail.

But before discussing them, it will be useful to first point out that governing a nation is not easy. In particular, governments face the daunting challenge of organizing millions of employees to carry out thousands of tasks—everything from cleaning sewers to researching cures for cancer to delivering the mail. An understanding

Does Big Government Equal Bad Government?

You will sometimes hear politicians (and maybe your grumpy uncle) complaining about Big Government. Their implication is that large government initiatives are inherently inefficient or incompetent.

Since economics is focused on efficiency, you might wonder where economists stand on the subject.

The answer is that economists focus not on bigness or smallness *per se*, but on marginal benefit (MB) and marginal cost (MC). Spending should be increased up to the point where MB = MC. For some programs, that will be a small dollar amount. For other programs, that will be a large dollar amount.

Thus, economists don't see much point in having an abstract debate over "big government" versus "small government." What matters is allocative and productive efficiency and directing government's limited resources toward the programs that generate the largest net benefits for society.

From that vantage point, we should not condemn large government programs just for being large. We must first compare MB with MC. Only if MB < MC should large programs be reduced or eliminated.

of those challenges and complexities will give you a better sense of how well most governments manage to do *despite* all of the problems associated with government failure.

No Invisible Hand
Government economic polices are not self-correcting. Unlike the private sector—where competitive forces and Adam Smith's "invisible hand" help to automatically direct resources to their best uses—poorly designed government policies can misallocate resources indefinitely unless active steps are taken by legislators or administrators.

Massive Size and Scope
Identifying and correcting inefficient government policies is hampered by government's massive size and scope. Consider the U.S. federal government. In 2010, it had 4.4 million employees spread over 500 agencies that were collectively charged with enforcing hundreds of thousands of pages

of laws and regulations while attempting to wisely spend $3.4 trillion.

The Need for Bureaucracy
By law, those 4.4 million federal employees are ultimately supervised and directed by just 536 elected officials: one president, 435 representatives, and 100 senators. Since 536 elected officials could never hope to directly supervise 4.4 million people, governments rely on many layers of supervisors and supervisors-of-supervisors to manage the government's affairs. They collectively form a massive, hierarchical, many-layered bureaucracy.

The Need for Paperwork and Inflexibility
To make sure that laws are uniformly enforced and do not vary at the whim of individual bureaucrats, the bureaucracy is regulated by detailed rules and regulations governing nearly every possible action that any individual bureaucrat might be called upon to make. These rules and regulations ensure that laws and regulations are uniformly applied. But they do so at the cost of massive amounts of paperwork and an inability to expeditiously process non-routine situations and requests.

The Information Aggregation Problem
Because of their massive size and scope, bureaucracies have difficulty with effectively aggregating and conveying information from their bottom layers to their top layers. As a result, top officials will tend to make many inefficient choices because they do not have enough information to sensibly compare the marginal benefits and marginal costs of individual programs and because they are unable to comprehensively assess opportunity costs and where to best spend funds across the wide variety of programs run by the government.

Lack of Accountability
Governments also struggle with accountability. Democratic elections do take place for the elected officials at the top, but because the government undertakes so many activities simultaneously, it is difficult for the electorate to know the details of even a small fraction of what the government is up to at any particular time. As a result, hundreds or even thousands of individual programs may be poorly run without affecting the reelection chances of the incumbent politicians who are supposed to be supervising everything.

Within the bureaucracy itself, individual accountability is also hard to enforce because most bureaucrats have civil service protections that effectively guarantee them a job for life. Those protections reduce corruption by shielding bureaucrats from political pressures. But they also severely constrain the ability of elected officials to hold individual bureaucrats personally responsible for bad decisions.

QUICK REVIEW 5.1

- Government's ability to enforce nonvoluntary transactions can improve economic outcomes by compensating for resource misallocations and by providing a low-risk economic environment for individuals and firms.
- Government economic actions are not automatically self-correcting (as with the "invisible hand" in competitive markets.)
- Democratic governments face several challenges in directing and supervising government's actions, including inflexibility, information aggregation, comparing marginal costs with marginal benefits, assessment of opportunity costs, and accountability.

Government Failure

LO5.2 Discuss "government failure" and explain why it happens.

The term **government failure** refers to economically inefficient outcomes caused by shortcomings in the public sector. One cause of government failure is the voting problems that we discuss at length in this chapter's appendix. But government failures caused by voting problems are somewhat unique in that they are driven by a lack of information about voter preferences. By contrast, most instances of government failure happen *despite* government officials knowing what voters prefer.

In these situations, government failures occur because the incentive structures facing government officials lead them to either put their own interests ahead of voter interests or to put the interests of a minority of voters ahead of those of the majority of voters. Let's examine what economic theory has to say about these situations.

Representative Democracy and the Principal-Agent Problem

Our system of representative democracy has the advantage of allowing us to elect full-time representatives who can specialize in understanding the pros and cons of different potential laws and who have more time to digest their details than the average citizen. But the system also suffers from principal-agent problems.

Principal-agent problems are conflicts that arise when tasks are delegated by one group of people (principals) to another group of people (agents). The conflicts arise because the interests of the agents may not be the same as the interests of the principals, so that the agents may end up taking actions that are opposed by the principals whom they are supposed to be representing.

In the business world, principal-agent problems often arise when the company's managers (the agents) take actions that are not in the best interests of the company's shareholders (the principals). Examples include the managers spending huge amounts of company money on executive jets and lavish offices or holding meetings at expensive resorts. These luxuries are obviously enjoyable to managers but are, of course, not in the best interest of shareholders because the money spent on them could either be reinvested back into the firm to increase future profits or paid out to shareholders immediately as dividends. But to the extent that managers are free to follow their own interests rather than those of their shareholders, they may indeed take these and other actions that are not in the better interests of their shareholders. Hence the conflicts.

In a representative democracy, principal-agent problems often arise because politicians have goals such as reelection that may be inconsistent with pursuing the best interests of their constituents. Indeed, casual reflection suggests that "sound economics" and "good politics" often differ. Sound economics calls for the public sector to pursue various programs as long as marginal benefits exceed marginal costs. Good politics, however, suggests that politicians support programs and policies that will maximize their chances of getting reelected. The result may be that the government will promote the goals of groups of voters that have special interests to the detriment of the larger public. Economic inefficiency is the likely outcome.

Special-Interest Effect Efficient public decision making is often impaired by the **special-interest effect.** This is any outcome of the political process whereby a small number of people obtain a government program or policy that gives them large gains at the expense of a much greater number of persons who individually suffer small losses.

The small group of potential beneficiaries is well informed and highly vocal on the issue in question, and they press politicians for approval. The large number of people facing the very small individual losses, however, are generally uninformed on the issue. Politicians feel they will lose the campaign contributions and votes of the small special-interest group that backs the issue if they legislate against it but will lose very little support from the large group of

CONSIDER THIS . . .

Mohair and the Collective-Action Problem

Smaller groups can sometimes achieve political victories against larger groups by taking advantage of the **collective-action problem**—the fact that larger groups are more difficult to organize and motivate than smaller groups.

Larger groups are harder to organize and motivate for two main reasons. First, the larger the group, the smaller each member's share of the benefits if the group gets its way. Second, the larger the group, the higher its organizing costs, as it will have to contact and recruit large numbers of strangers via e-mails, telephone calls, and mass mailings.

Smaller groups can take advantage of these difficulties and generally get their way against larger groups as long as they are pressing for policies that only cause small amounts of harm to the members of the larger groups.

Consider the infamous subsidy for mohair, the wool produced by Angora goats. Each year the federal government provides millions of dollars in subsidized loans to Angora goat farmers in Texas, Arizona, and New Mexico. The federal government began the subsidy in the late 1940s to ensure a large supply of insulation for the jackets needed to keep pilots and other crew members warm in the unheated airplanes used during that period.

The mohair subsidy should have ended in the 1950s when heated cabins were developed, but it survives because it costs taxpayers only a few cents each. This means that it would cost them more to organize and defeat the mohair subsidy than they would save by having the subsidy terminated.

More generally, the collective-action problem explains why nearly every example of the special-interest effect is characterized by "concentrated benefits and diffuse costs." Concentrated benefits make proponents easy to organize, while diffuse costs make opponents difficult to organize.

uninformed voters, who are likely to evaluate the politicians on other issues of greater importance to them.

The special-interest effect is also evident in so-called *pork-barrel politics*, a means of securing a government project that yields benefits mainly to a single political district and its political representative. In this case, the special-interest group comprises local constituents, while the larger group consists of relatively uninformed taxpayers scattered across a much larger geographic area. Politicians clearly have a strong incentive to secure government projects ("pork") for their local constituents. Such projects win political favor because they are highly valued by constituents and the costs are borne mainly by taxpayers located elsewhere.

At the federal level, pork-barrel politics often consist of congressional members inserting specific provisions that authorize spending for local projects (that will benefit only local constituents) into comprehensive legislation (that is supposed to be about making laws for the entire country). Such narrow, specifically designated authorizations of expenditure are called **earmarks.** In 2012, legislation contained 152 such earmarks, totaling $3.3 billion. These earmarks enable senators and representatives to provide benefits to in-state firms and organizations without subjecting the proposals to the usual evaluation and competitive bidding. Although some of the earmarked projects deliver benefits that exceed costs, many others are questionable, at best. These latter expenditures very likely reallocate some of society's scarce resources from higher-valued uses to lower-valued uses. Moreover, logrolling, discussed in the chapter appendix, typically enters the picture. "Vote for my special local project and I will vote for yours" becomes part of the overall strategy for securing "pork" and remaining elected.

Finally, a politician's inclination to support the smaller group of special beneficiaries is enhanced because special-interest groups are often quite willing to help finance the campaigns of "right-minded" politicians and politicians who "bring home the pork." The result is that politicians may support special-interest programs and projects that cannot be justified on economic grounds.

Rent-Seeking Behavior The appeal to government for special benefits at taxpayers' or someone else's expense is called **rent seeking.** The term "rent" in "rent seeking" is used loosely to refer to any payment in excess of the minimum amount that would be needed to keep a resource employed in its current use. Those engaged in "rent seeking" are attempting to use government influence to get themselves into a situation in which they will get paid more for providing a good or service than the minimum amount you would actually have to pay them to provide that good or service. (These excess, or surplus, payments are akin to *land rent*, which is also a surplus payment.)

Rent seeking goes beyond the usual profit seeking through which firms try to increase their profits by adjusting their output levels, improving their products, and incorporating cost-saving technologies. Rent seeking looks to obtain extra profit or income by influencing government policies. Corporations, trade associations, labor unions, and professional organizations employ vast resources to secure favorable government policies that result in rent—higher profit or income than would otherwise occur. The government is able to dispense such rent directly or indirectly through laws, rules, hiring, and purchases. Elected officials are willing to provide such rent because they want to be responsive to the key constituents who can help them remain in office.

Here are some examples of "rent-providing" legislation or policies: tariffs on foreign products that limit competition and raise prices to consumers; tax breaks that benefit specific corporations; government construction projects that create union jobs but cost more than the benefits they yield; occupational licensing that goes beyond what is needed to protect consumers; and large subsidies to farmers by taxpayers. None of these is justified by economic efficiency.

Clear Benefits, Hidden Costs

Some critics say that vote-seeking politicians will ignore economic rationality by failing to objectively weigh costs and benefits when deciding which programs to support. Because political officeholders must seek voter support every few years, they favor programs that have immediate and clear-cut benefits and vague or deferred costs. Conversely, politicians will reject programs with immediate and easily identifiable costs but with less measurable but very high long-term benefits.

Such biases may lead politicians to reject economically justifiable programs and to accept programs that are economically irrational. Example: A proposal to construct or expand mass-transit systems in large metropolitan areas may be economically rational on the basis of cost-benefit analysis. But if (1) the program is to be financed by immediate increases in highly visible income or sales taxes and (2) benefits will occur only years from now when the project is completed, then the vote-seeking politician may oppose the program.

Assume, on the other hand, that a program of federal aid to municipal police forces is not justifiable on the basis of cost-benefit analysis. But if the cost is paid for from budget surpluses, the program's modest benefits may seem so large that it will gain approval.

Unfunded Liabilities

The political tendency to favor spending priorities that have immediate payouts but deferred costs also leads to many government programs having unfunded liabilities. A government creates an **unfunded liability** when it commits to making a series of future expenditures without simultaneously committing to collect enough tax revenues to pay for those expenditures.

The most famous example of an unfunded liability belongs to the Social Security program, under which the U.S. federal government supplements the incomes of the elderly and the disabled. The government does collect Social Security taxes to help defray the expected future costs of the program, but the current tax rates will not generate nearly enough revenue to pay for all of the expected outlays. In fact, it is estimated that Social Security has an unfunded liability (= total value of spending commitments minus expected value of tax revenues) of $20.5 trillion.

Social Security is not the only major unfunded government liability. Medicare, which provides healthcare to the elderly and disabled in the United States, has an unfunded liability of $4.8 trillion, while state and local governments are estimated to have $4.6 trillion in unfunded retirement and healthcare commitments.

Chronic Budget Deficits

A government runs an annual **budget deficit** whenever its tax revenues are less than its spending during a particular year. To make up for the shortfall, the government must borrow money, usually by issuing bonds. Whatever it borrows in a given year gets added to its overall pile of debt, which is the accumulation of all past budget deficits and budget surpluses.

Many governments run budget deficits year after year. These chronic deficits can be attributed to a pair of conflicting incentives that confront politicians. On the one hand, many government programs are highly popular with voters, so that there is almost always political pressure to either maintain or increase spending. On the other hand, hardly anyone likes paying taxes, so there is almost always political pressure to reduce taxes. Faced with those two conflicting pressures, politicians tend to opt for spending levels that exceed tax revenues.

That may be problematic because chronic deficits can pose several economic challenges, including

- *Economic Inefficiency* Deficits may allow the government to control and direct an inefficiently large fraction of the economy's resources. To the extent that deficit spending facilitates an underallocation of resources to the private sector and an overallocation of resources to the government sector, there will be a tendency to underproduce private goods and overproduce public goods. If that occurs, the economy will experience a decrease in both allocative and productive efficiency.

- *Debt Crises* A government's accumulated debt level may rise so high that investors lose faith in the government's ability or willingness to repay its debts.

If that happens, the government will find itself in the middle of a **debt crisis,** unable to borrow any more money. Cut off from borrowing, the government will be forced to undertake some combination of drastic spending cuts or massive tax increases. Either of those actions will tend to plunge the economy into a recessionary period in which unemployment rises and output falls.

To prevent politicians from succumbing to voter preferences for deficits, many state and local governments have balanced-budget laws that make deficits illegal. No such law exists at the national level, however. As a result, federal politicians were able to run budget deficits in 47 of the 52 years between 1960 and 2012.

Misdirection of Stabilization Policy

Economies go through alternating periods of expansion and recession. Multiyear periods during which output expands, employment increases, and living standards rise alternate with periods during which output contracts, employment decreases, and living standards fall.

Governments often attempt to smooth out these so-called *business cycles* by using two types of macroeconomic stabilization policy:

- **Fiscal policy** attempts to use changes in tax rates and spending levels to offset the business cycle. For example, if the economy is going into a recessionary period with falling output and rising unemployment, the government may attempt to stimulate the economy by lowering tax rates or increasing government spending. Either action should increase spending on goods and services and consequently induce business to produce more output and hire more workers.

- **Monetary policy** attempts to use changes in interest rates to regulate the economy. In particular, the government can use its control over the money supply to lower interest rates during a recession. The lower interest rates stimulate spending by making it cheaper for individuals and businesses to borrow money to pay for capital goods such as houses, cars, and machinery. As spending on those items increases, firms are induced to produce more output and hire more workers.

Politicization of Fiscal and Monetary Policy   Fiscal and monetary policy are both subject to politicization. In the case of fiscal policy, if the economy goes into recession

and there are calls to stimulate the economy through lower taxes or increased spending, politicians often spend more time attempting to target any tax cuts or spending increases toward special interests than they do making sure that their fiscal policy actions will actually stimulate the overall economy. The recession also provides political cover for increasing the size of the deficit.

Monetary policy can be similarly politicized, with the biggest problem being that incumbent politicians will want to cut interest rates to boost the economy right before they are up for reelection. That is problematic because monetary stimulus is only helpful if the economy is in recession. If the economy is doing well, monetary stimulus can actually make things worse because it can raise the rate of inflation and drive up prices all over the economy.

To prevent that, most countries have put politically independent central banks in charge of monetary policy. In the United States, the Federal Reserve serves this function. Other top central banks include the Bank of Japan, the Bank of England, and the European Central Bank. Each is run by professional economists who are insulated from political pressures so that they may use their independent expertise and judgment to decide if and when monetary stimulus should be used.

> **QUICK REVIEW 5.2**
>
> - Principal-agent problems are conflicts that occur when the agents who are supposed to be acting in the best interests of their principals instead take actions that help themselves but hurt their principals.
> - Because larger groups are more difficult to organize and motivate than smaller groups, special interests can often obtain what they want politically even when what they want is opposed by a majority of voters.
> - Rent seeking involves influencing government policies so that one can get paid more for providing a good or service than it costs to produce.
> - Political pressures cause politicians to favor policies such as unfunded liabilities and budget deficits that have immediate benefits and delayed costs.

Limited and Bundled Choice

Economic theory points out that the political process forces citizens and their elected representatives to be less selective in choosing public goods and services than they are in choosing private goods and services.

In the marketplace, the citizen as a consumer can exactly satisfy personal preferences by buying certain goods and not buying others. However, in the public sector the citizen as a voter is confronted with, say, only two or three candidates for an office, each representing a different "bundle" of programs (public goods and services). None of these bundles of public goods is likely to fit exactly the preferences of any particular voter. Yet the voter must choose one of them. The candidate who comes closest to voter Smith's preference may endorse national health insurance, increases in Social Security benefits, subsidies to tobacco farmers, and tariffs on imported goods. Smith is likely to vote for that candidate even though Smith strongly opposes tobacco subsidies.

In other words, the voter must take the bad with the good. In the public sector, people are forced to "buy" goods and services they do not want. It is as if, in going to a sporting-goods store, you were forced to buy an unwanted pool cue to get a wanted pair of running shoes. This is a situation where resources are not being used efficiently to satisfy consumer wants. In this sense, the provision of public goods and services is inherently inefficient.

Congress is confronted with a similar limited-choice, bundled-goods problem. Appropriations legislation combines hundreds, even thousands, of spending items into a single bill. Many of these spending items may be completely unrelated to the main purpose of the legislation. Yet congressional representatives must vote on the entire package—yea or nay. Unlike consumers in the marketplace, they cannot be selective.

Bureaucracy and Inefficiency

Some economists contend that public agencies are generally less efficient than private businesses. The reason is not that lazy and incompetent workers somehow end up in the public sector while ambitious and capable people gravitate to the private sector. Rather, it is that the market system creates incentives for internal efficiency that are absent from the public sector. Private enterprises have a clear goal—profit. Whether a private firm is in a competitive or monopolistic market, efficient management means lower costs and higher profit. The higher profit not only benefits the firm's owners but enhances the promotion prospects of the firm's managers. Moreover, part of the managers' pay may be tied to profit via profit-sharing plans, bonuses, and stock options. There is no similar gain to government agencies and their managers—no counterpart to profit—to create a strong incentive to achieve efficiency.

CONSIDER THIS . . .

Unintended Consequences

As explained in Chapters 2 and 4, the "invisible hand" of a properly functioning market will allocate resources to their best uses without anyone being in charge or intentionally aiming for efficiency. By contrast, governments are willful and intentional. They deliberately create and enforce laws to try to make improvements in society. In some cases, however, government actions can have **unintended consequences** that offset some or all of the intended benefits.

- Government fuel-efficiency requirements for automobiles have forced automakers to produce smaller, lighter vehicles. But when smaller, lighter vehicles get into accidents, their occupants are more likely to be killed or severely injured. Some estimates put the death toll at over 120,000 additional deaths in the United States since 1970.

- San Francisco banned plastic grocery bags in 2007. This led to about 5 additional deaths per year from foodborne illnesses because reusable grocery bags almost never get washed out. Drippings from one trip often fester and contaminate whatever they touch on subsequent trips.

- The main point of the 2010 healthcare reform law (commonly known as Obamacare) was to get health insurance coverage for all Americans. To that end, the law required larger companies to either pay for extremely costly health insurance policies for their full-time workers or face massive fines. But since that requirement only applied to full-time workers, many firms responded by cutting a lot of their employees' work hours down from full time to part time. Thus, millions of workers went from lacking health insurance but having a full-time job to still lacking health insurance but only having a part-time job.

The market system imposes a very obvious test of performance on private firms: the test of profit and loss. An efficient firm is profitable and therefore successful; it survives, prospers, and grows. An inefficient firm is unprofitable and unsuccessful; it declines and in time goes out of business. But there is no similar, clear-cut test with which to assess the efficiency or inefficiency of public agencies. How can anyone determine whether a public hydroelectricity provider, a state university, a local fire department, the Department of Agriculture, or the Bureau of Indian Affairs is operating efficiently?

Cynics even argue that a public agency that inefficiently uses its resources is likely to survive and grow! In the private sector, inefficiency and monetary loss lead to the abandonment of certain activities or products or even firms. But the government, they say, does not like to abandon activities in which it has failed. Some suggest that the typical response of the government to a program's failure is to increase its budget and staff. This means that public sector inefficiency just continues on a larger scale.

Furthermore, economists assert that government employees, together with the special-interest groups they serve, often gain sufficient political clout to block attempts to pare down or eliminate their agencies. Politicians who attempt to reduce the size of huge federal bureaucracies such as those relating to agriculture, education, health and welfare, and national defense incur sizable political risk because bureaucrats and special-interest groups will team up to defeat them.

Finally, critics point out that government bureaucrats tend to justify their continued employment by looking for and eventually finding new problems to solve. It is not surprising that social "problems," as defined by government, persist or even expand.

The Last Word at the end of this chapter highlights several recent media-reported examples of the special-interest effect (including earmarks), the problem of limited and bundled choices, and problems of government bureaucracy.

Inefficient Regulation and Intervention

Governments regulate many aspects of the market economy. Examples include health and safety regulations, environmental laws, banking supervision, restrictions on monopoly power, and the imposition of wage and price controls.

These interventions are designed to improve economic outcomes, but several forms of regulation and intervention have been known to generate outcomes that are less beneficial than intended.

Regulatory Capture A government agency that is supposed to supervise a particular industry is said to have suffered from **regulatory capture** if its regulations and enforcement activities come to be heavily influenced by the industry that it is supposed to be regulating.

Regulatory capture is often facilitated by the fact that nearly everyone who knows anything about the details of a regulated industry works in the industry. So when it comes time for the regulatory agency to find qualified people to help write intelligent regulations, it ends up hiring a lot of people from regulated firms. Those individuals bring their old opinions and sympathies with them when they become bureaucrats. As a result, many regulations end up favoring the interests of the regulated firms.

Regulatory Capture in the Railroad Industry The classic example of regulatory capture is that of railroad regulation during the nineteenth and twentieth centuries. In response to public complaints that the nation's railroads were often charging exorbitant rates, the federal government established the Interstate Commerce Commission (ICC) in 1887 as the government agency charged with regulating competition and prices within the railroad industry.

Within a generation, railroad executives had achieved regulatory capture by manipulating the ICC into a policy that simultaneously fixed rates at profitable levels while also eliminating competition between different railroad companies. The public justification for these policies was that competition had to be restricted in order to prevent larger railroads from bankrupting smaller railroads and thereby becoming monopolies that could easily exploit the public. But the railroad industry's true motive was to establish a regulatory regime in which both larger and small railroads were guaranteed steady, competition-free profits.

These days, activists often complain that various government bureaucracies are subject to regulatory capture. At the federal level, complaints are voiced about the Food and Drug Administration's supervision of the pharmaceutical industry, the Securities and Exchange Commission's supervision of Wall Street financial firms, and the Bureau of Land Management's policies with respect to leasing federal lands for oil drilling, mining, and forestry.

Deregulation as an Alternative Economists are divided about the intensity and inefficiency of regulatory capture as well as what to do about it. One potential solution is for the government to engage in **deregulation** and intentionally remove most or even all of the regulations governing an industry.

Deregulation solves the problem of regulatory capture because there is no regulatory agency left to capture. But it only works well in terms of economic efficiency if the deregulated industry becomes competitive and is automatically guided toward allocative and productive efficiency by competitive forces and the invisible hand. If the deregulated industry instead tends toward monopoly or ends up generating substantial negative externalities, continued regulation might be the better option.

Proponents of deregulation often cite the deregulation of interstate trucking, railroads, and airlines in the 1970s and 1980s as examples of competition successfully replacing regulation. They do so because after regulation was removed, robust competition led to lower prices, increased output, and higher levels of productivity and efficiency.

But for government agencies tasked with environmental protection, human safety, and financial regulation, there is less confidence as to whether competitive pressures might be able to replace regulation. For those industries, regulation may always be necessary. If so, then some amount of regulatory capture may always be likely due to the fact that regulated firms will always want to capture their regulators.

Government's Poor Investment Track Record

Governments are often asked to use taxpayer money to directly invest in private businesses that have been unable to secure funding from private sources such as banks. Unfortunately, researchers have found that low and negative rates of return are the norm for government investments. In addition, government funding often allows inefficient firms to persist in operation long after competitive forces would have put them out of operation and freed up their resources for higher-valued projects elsewhere in the economy.

Critics also note that many government investments look like prime examples of rent seeking and the special-interest effect, especially when the firms receiving government investments are found to have made substantial financial contributions to influential politicians. In too many cases, the government's investment decisions appear to be based on political connections rather than on whether specific investments can produce substantial net benefits for society.

Loan Guarantees The government also tends to earn low or negative returns when it subsidizes private-sector investments with **loan guarantees.** The startup company named Solyndra provides a good example of what can go wrong.

The Solyndra Subsidy In 2009, Solyndra was unable to convince private investors to lend it enough money to start producing solar panels with its new technology. The private investors sensibly feared that the company's new technology was too expensive and that its solar panels would not be able to compete with those made by the industry's more established firms.

At that point, Solyndra turned to a federal loan-guarantee program under which the Department of Energy told potential investors that it would cosign any loan taken out by Solyndra and thereby guarantee that if Solyndra went bankrupt, the federal government would use taxpayer money to repay the loan.

With that loan guarantee in place, the otherwise-reluctant private investors were willing to put in $535 million. After all, they had nothing to lose and everything to gain. If Solyndra went bankrupt, they would get their money back from the government. But if Solyndra somehow did well, they would collect substantial returns.

Unfortunately, the investors' original doubts proved to be well founded. Solyndra was unable to compete effectively with incumbent firms and went bankrupt in 2011, leaving taxpayers on the hook for the full $535 million.

Socializing Losses, Privatizing Gains Government loan guarantees can be socially beneficial if they help to increase the production of beneficial products that are being underproduced by the private sector—as would be the case for products that generated positive externalities. But the loan guarantees also provide an inducement toward reckless investing because they remove from private investors any consideration of losses. Indeed, loan guarantees are often criticized for "socializing losses and privatizing gains" because if things go wrong, any losses go to the taxpayer, while if things go well, any profits go to private investors.

In addition, the process by which loan guarantees are awarded is often criticized for being highly politicized and likely to award loan guarantees not to the firms whose projects are the most likely to increase economic efficiency but to those with the best political connections.

On the other hand, there may be legitimate cases where a new technology that would generate net benefits cannot be developed without government loan guarantees, so proponents of loan-guarantee programs argue that the programs should remain in place, but with tight controls against rent seeking and the special-interest effect.

Corruption

Political corruption is the unlawful misdirection of governmental resources or actions that occurs when government officials abuse their entrusted powers for personal gain. For instance, a police supervisor engages in political corruption if she accepts a bribe in exchange for illegally freeing a thief who had been lawfully arrested by another

GLOBAL PERSPECTIVE 5.1

Percentage of Households Paying a Bribe in the Past Year

The Global Corruption Barometer is an international survey that asks individuals about their personal experiences with government corruption. The 2010–2011 survey of 105,507 people in 100 countries included a question that asked participants whether they or anyone in their respective households had paid a bribe in any form during the previous 12 months. Here are the results for 10 selected countries.

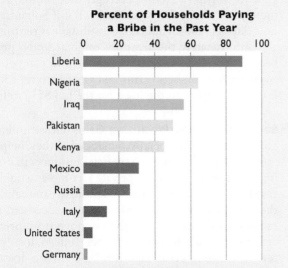

Percent of Households Paying a Bribe in the Past Year

Source: Adapted from *Global Corruption Barometer.* Copyright 2011 Transparency International: the global coalition against corruption. Used with permission. For more information, visit **www.transparency.org**.

officer. Similarly, a government bureaucrat engages in political corruption if he refuses to issue a building permit to a homebuilder who is in full compliance with the law unless the homebuilder makes a "voluntary contribution" to the bureaucrat's favorite charity.

While relatively uncommon in the United States, political corruption is a daily reality in many parts of the world, as can be seen in Global Perspective 5.1, which gives the percentages of survey respondents in 15 countries who reported that they or someone else in their respective households paid a bribe during the previous 12 months.

Political corruption comes in two basic forms. In the first, a government official must be bribed to do what he should be doing as part of his job—as with the bureaucrat in our earlier example who demands a bribe to issue a permit to a homebuilder who is in full compliance with the law. In the second, a government official demands a bribe to do something that she is not legally entitled to do—as

with the police supervisor in our earlier example who illegally freed a thief.

If a candidate accepts campaign contributions from a special-interest group and then shows subsequent support for that group's legislative goals, has a subtle form of political corruption taken place? While there are strong opinions on both sides of the issue, it is often hard to tell in any particular case whether a special interest's campaign contribution amounts to a bribe. On the one hand, the special interest may indeed be trying to influence the politician's vote. On the other hand, the special interest may simply be trying to support and get elected a person who already sees things their way and who would vote the way they wanted no matter what.

That being said, the impression of impropriety lingers, and so laws have been passed in the United States limiting the amount of money that individuals can donate to specific candidates and making it illegal for certain groups such as companies to donate money directly to individual politicians (as distinct from directing funds toward supporting specific issues or advocacy groups—which is both legal and unrestricted). Proponents of these laws hope that the limitations strike a good balance—allowing contributions to be large enough that individuals and groups can meaningfully support candidates they agree with but keeping contributions small enough that no one individual or group can singlehandedly donate enough money to sway a politician's vote.

Imperfect Institutions

It is possible to argue that the wide variety of criticisms of public sector inefficiency that we have discussed in this chapter are exaggerated and cynical. Perhaps they are. Nevertheless, they do tend to shatter the concept of a benevolent government that responds with precision and efficiency to the wants of its citizens. The market system of the private sector is far from perfectly efficient, and government's economic function is mainly to correct that system's shortcomings. But the public sector is also subject to deficiencies in fulfilling its economic function. "The relevant comparison is not between perfect markets and imperfect governments, nor between faulty markets and all-knowing, rational, benevolent governments, but between inevitably imperfect institutions."[1]

Because markets and governments are both imperfect, it is sometimes difficult to determine whether a particular activity can be performed with greater success in the private

---

[1]Otto Eckstein, *Public Finance*, 3d ed. (Englewood Cliffs, N.J.: Prentice-Hall, 1973), p. 17.

"Government Failure" in the News

The Media Continually Report Government Actions That Illustrate Pork-Barrel Politics, Limited and Bundled Choices, or Bureaucratic Inefficiency.

Examples:

- A 2004 spending bill set aside $1 million for the Norwegian American Foundation; $443,000 to develop salmon-fortified baby food; $350,000 for music education programs at the Rock and Roll Hall of Fame in Cleveland; and $250,000 for sidewalks, street furniture, and façade improvements in Boca Raton, Florida. (Associated Press)

- The corporate tax relief bill of 2004 contained 633 pages, with 276 special provisions. Included were provisions that benefited "restaurant owners and Hollywood producers; makers of bows, arrows, tackle boxes, and sonar fish finders; NASCAR track owners; native Alaska whalers; and even importers of Chinese fans." (*The Washington Post*)

- Government investigations determined that millions of dollars of disaster relief for victims of Hurricane Katrina were squandered. For example, investigators discovered that the Federal Emergency Management Agency (FEMA) made payouts on as many as 900,000 claims for disaster relief that contained invalid Social Security numbers or false names and addresses. (*The Seattle Times*)

- The $878 billion American Recovery and Reinvestment Act of 2009 was laden with many dubious spending projects, including $10 million to renovate a train station in Elizabethtown, Pennsylvania, that hadn't been used in 30 years; $1.15 million to build a guardrail for an artificial lake in Woodward, Oklahoma, that had never been filled with water; and an unrequested $587,661 grant that was given to the upscale town of Union, New York, to fight a homeless problem that it didn't have. (*Lancaster Newspapers*, **newson6.com**, *Binghamton Press & Sun Union*)

- The year 2009 also saw Congress approve a $2.5 billion earmark to purchase ten C-17 aircraft despite the Department of Defense adamantly stating that its existing fleet of 205 C-17s was "sufficient to meet the Department's future airlift needs—even under the most stressing situations." (**investinganswers.com**)

- In 2011, Congress funded a sanctuary for white squirrels, an antique bicycle museum, and a giant roadside coffee pot as part of 2011 federal highway spending. It also spent $765,828 to subsidize the construction of an IHOP restaurant and $113,277 to aid in the historical preservation of video games. (*Human Events, Washington Examiner, Gamasutra*)

- A 2011 audit revealed that the federal government had paid $600 million in retirement benefits to deceased federal retirees over the previous five years. Checks had been illegally cashed by living relatives. One son received cumulative payments of $515,000 over the 37 years after his father died in 1971. The fraud was only discovered after the son died in 2008. (Associated Press)

sector or in the public sector. It is easy to reach agreement on opposite extremes: National defense must lie with the public sector, while automobile production can best be accomplished by the private sector. But what about health insurance? Parks and recreation areas? Fire protection? Garbage collection? Housing? Education? It is hard to assess every good or service and to say absolutely that it should be assigned to either the public sector or the private sector. Evidence: All the goods and services just mentioned are provided in part by *both* private enterprises and public agencies.

SUMMARY

LO5.1 Describe how government's power to coerce can be economically beneficial and list some of the difficulties associated with managing and directing the government.

Government's legal right to use coercion and force can help to improve economic efficiency by correcting for market failures and by enforcing laws and regulations that reduce the risk that individuals and firms will be taken advantage of.

LO5.2 Discuss "government failure" and explain why it happens.

Special interests can succeed in perpetuating policies that are opposed by the majority of voters because the costs of organizing and motivating groups to take political action increase with group size. This collective-action problem implies that special interests can perpetuate unpopular policies as long as the costs of organizing an opposition exceed the costs that the general public is currently suffering as a result of those policies.

There are powerful incentives for politicians to accommodate rent seeking and support special-interest legislation.

Because voters like receiving the benefits of government programs but do not like having to pay the taxes necessary to finance them, politicians tend to favor programs that offer easily identified immediate benefits but vague or deferred costs. This tendency helps to explain the unfunded liabilities of programs including Social Security as well as the federal government's tendency to run budget deficits.

When the economy goes into recession, politicians often use the need for fiscal policy stimulus as political cover to direct lower taxes or increased spending toward politically powerful special-interest groups. To prevent politicians from using lower interest rates and monetary stimulus as a way of increasing their reelection chances, most governments have put politically independent central banks in charge of monetary policy.

Economic theorists cite several reasons why government might be inefficient in providing public goods. (a) Citizens as voters and congressional representatives face limited and bundled choices as to public goods, whereas consumers in the private sector can be highly selective in their choices. (b) Government bureaucracies have less incentive to operate efficiently than do private businesses. (c) Regulated industries may sometimes capture their government regulatory agencies and mold government polices toward their own best interests.

Government's track record as an investor in private-sector firms is very poor, with most government investments into private sector businesses generating low or negative returns for taxpayers.

Government attempts to increase private investment by offering loan guarantees often cause resources to be misdirected toward high-risk projects that have an extremely low likelihood of success. These arrangements "socialize losses and privatize gains" because if the businesses go bankrupt, the government bears the losses, but if they do well, private individuals receive the profits.

Political corruption may cause governmental resources or actions to be misdirected.

Neither governments nor markets are perfect economic institutions. Each has its own set of shortcomings and citizens should be aware of where each is likely to fail and where each is likely to succeed.

TERMS AND CONCEPTS

government failure

principal-agent problems

collective-action problem

special-interest effect

earmarks

rent seeking

unfunded liability

budget deficit

debt crisis

fiscal policy

monetary policy

unintended consequences

regulatory capture

deregulation

loan guarantees

political corruption

The following and additional problems can be found in **connect**
ECONOMICS

DISCUSSION QUESTIONS

1. Why might citizens interested in maximizing economic efficiency be happy to invest their government with the right to coerce them in at least some situations? **LO5.1**

2. Jean-Baptiste Colbert was the Minister of Finance under King Louis XIV of France. He famously observed, "The art of taxation consists in so plucking the goose as to obtain the

largest possible amount of feathers with the smallest possible amount of hissing." How does his comment relate to special interests and the collective-action problem? **LO5.2**

3. What is rent seeking and how does it differ from the kinds of profit maximization and profit seeking that we discussed in previous chapters? Provide an actual or hypothetical example of rent seeking by firms in an industry. By a union. By a professional association (for example, physicians, school teachers, or lawyers). Why do elected officials often accommodate rent-seeking behavior, particularly by firms, unions, and professional groups located in their home states? **LO5.2**

4. How does the problem of limited and bundled choice in the public sector relate to economic efficiency? Why are public bureaucracies possibly less efficient than business firms? **LO5.2**

5. Discuss the political incentives that helped motivate federal politicians to approve budget deficits in all but four years between 1960 and 2012. **LO5.2**

6. Explain: "Politicians would make more rational economic decisions if they weren't running for reelection every few years." **LO5.2**

7. Critique: "Thank goodness we have so many government regulatory agencies. They keep Big Business in check." **LO5.2**

8. **LAST WORD** How do the concepts of pork-barrel politics and the special-interest effect relate to the items listed in the Last Word?

REVIEW QUESTIONS

1. Select all of the following that are true. To an economist, a coercive government can be useful in order to: **LO5.1**
   a. Reallocate resources in order to improve efficiency.
   b. Fight negative externalities.
   c. Ensure low gasoline prices.
   d. Provide a low-risk economic environment for individuals and firms.

2. To an economist, a government program is too big if an analysis of that program finds that MB _____ MC. **LO5.1**
   a. Is greater than.
   b. Is less than.
   c. Is equal to.
   d. Is less than twice as large as.
   e. Is more than twice as large as.

3. Tammy Hall is the mayor of a large U.S. city. She has just established the Office of Window Safety. Because windows sometimes break and spray glass shards, every window in the city will now have to pass an annual safety inspection. Property owners must pay the $5-per-window cost—and by the way, Tammy has made her nephew the new head of the Office of Window Safety. This new policy is an example of: **LO5.2**
   a. Political corruption.
   b. Earmarks.
   c. Rent seeking.
   d. Adverse selection.

4. A few hundred U.S. sugar makers lobby the U.S. government each year to make sure that the government taxes imported sugar at a high rate. They do so because the policy drives up the domestic price of sugar and increases their profits. It is estimated that the policy benefits U.S. sugar producers by about $1 billion per year while costing U.S. consumers upwards of $2 billion per year. Which of the following concepts apply to the U.S. sugar tax? **LO5.2**
   Select one or more of the choices shown.
   a. Political corruption.
   b. Rent-seeking behavior.
   c. The collective-action problem.
   d. The special-interest effect.

5. _____ occur when politicians commit to making a series of future expenditures without simultaneously committing to collect enough tax revenues to pay for those expenditures. **LO5.2**
   a. Budget deficits.
   b. Debt crises.
   c. Loan guarantees.
   d. Unfunded liabilities.

PROBLEMS

1. Suppose that there are 1 million federal workers at the lowest level of the federal bureaucracy and that above them there are multiple layers of supervisors and supervisors-of-supervisors. Assume that each higher level is one-tenth the size of the one below it because the government is using a 10:1 ratio of supervisees to supervisors. That is, for every 10 workers at the bottom, there is 1 supervisor; for every 10 of those supervisors, there is 1 supervisor-of-supervisors; for every one of those supervisors-of-supervisors, there is a supervisor-of-supervisors-of-supervisors; and so on, all the way up the bureaucratic pyramid to the president. **LO5.1**
   a. How many supervisors will there be in each supervisory layer of the federal bureaucracy? Start with the layer of supervisors directly above the 1 million workers at the bottom.
   b. How many supervisors are there in total at all levels of the federal bureaucratic pyramid, including the president?

c. If you count the 1 million workers at the bottom as the first layer of the federal bureaucracy, how many total layers are there, including the president?

d. How many federal employees are there in total at all layers, including the president?

e. What fraction of all federal employees are supervisory, including the president?

2. Consider a specific example of the special-interest effect and the collective-action problem. In 2009, it was estimated that the total value of all corn production subsidies in the United States was about $4 billion. The population of the United States was approximately 300 million people that year. **LO5.2**

a. On average, how much did corn subsidies cost per person in the United States in 2009? (Hint: A billion is a 1 followed by nine zeros. A million is a 1 followed by six zeros.)

b. If each person in the United States is only willing to spend $0.50 to support efforts to overturn the corn subsidy, and if antisubsidy advocates can only raise funds from 10 percent of the population, how much money will they be able to raise for their lobbying efforts?

c. If the recipients of corn subsidies donate just one percent of the total amount that they receive in subsidies, how much could they raise to support lobbying efforts to continue the corn subsidy?

d. By how many dollars does the amount raised by the recipients of the corn subsidy exceed the amount raised by the opponents of the corn subsidy?

3. Consider a corrupt provincial government in which each housing inspector examines two newly built structures each week. All the builders in the province are unethical and want to increase their profits by using substandard construction materials, but they can't do that unless they can bribe a housing inspector into approving a substandard building. **LO5.2**

a. If bribes cost $1,000 each, how much will a housing inspector make each year in bribes? (Assume that each inspector works 52 weeks a year and gets bribed for every house he inspects.)

b. There is a provincial construction supervisor who gets to hire all of the housing inspectors. He himself is corrupt and expects his housing inspectors to share their bribes with him. Suppose that 20 inspectors work for him and that each passes along half the bribes collected from builders. How much will the construction supervisor collect each year?

c. Corrupt officials may have an incentive to reduce the provision of government services to help line their own pockets. Suppose that the provincial construction supervisor decides to cut the total number of housing inspectors from 20 to 10 in order to decrease the supply of new housing permits. This decrease in the supply of permits raises the equilibrium bribe from $1,000 to $2,500. How much per year will the construction supervisor now receive if he is still getting half of all the bribes collected by the 10 inspectors? How much more is the construction supervisor getting now than when he had 20 inspectors working in part *b*? Will he personally be happy with the reduction in government services?

d. What if reducing the number of inspectors from 20 to 10 only increased the equilibrium bribe from $1,000 to $1,500? In this case, how much per year would the construction supervisor collect from his 10 inspectors? How much *less* is the construction supervisor getting than when he had 20 inspectors working in part *b*? In this case, will the construction supervisor be happy with the reduction in government services? Will he want to go back to using 20 inspectors?

FURTHER TEST YOUR KNOWLEDGE AT www.mcconnell20e.com

Practice quizzes, student PowerPoints, worked problems, Web-based questions, and additional materials are available at the text's Online Learning Center (OLC), **www.mcconnell20e.com**, or scan here. Need a barcode reader? Try ScanLife, available in your app store.

Public Choice Theory and Voting Paradoxes

LO5.3 Explain the difficulties of conveying economic preferences through majority voting.

Public Choice Theory

Market failures, such as public goods and externalities, impede economic efficiency and justify government intervention in the economy.

But the government's response to market failures is not without its own problems and pitfalls. In fact, government can sometimes fail as badly or even worse than markets in terms of delivering economic efficiency and directing resources to the uses where they will bring the largest net benefits.

That is why it is important to study **public choice theory**—the economic analysis of government decision making, politics, and elections. Just as the study of *market failure* helps us to understand how regulating markets may help to improve the allocation of resources, the study of *government failure* can help us to understand how changes in the way government functions might help it to operate more efficiently.

ORIGIN OF THE IDEA

O5.1
Public choice theory

As we will discuss shortly, many instances of government failure can be traced to incentive structures that lead political representatives to pursue policies that go against the preferences of the people that they are representing. But an even more fundamental problem exists. The majority voting systems that we rely upon may make it difficult or even impossible to correctly discern voter preferences. In such cases, it is not surprising that government fails to deliver what the voters actually want.

Revealing Preferences through Majority Voting

Through some process, society must decide which public goods it wants and in what amounts. It also must determine the extent to which it wants government to intervene in private markets to correct externalities. Decisions need to be made about the extent and type of regulation of business that is necessary, the amount of income redistribution that is desirable, what policies the government might enact to mitigate asymmetric information problems, and other such choices. Furthermore, society must determine the set of taxes it thinks is best for financing government. How should government apportion (divide) the total tax burden among the public?

Decisions such as these are made collectively in the United States through a democratic process that relies heavily on majority voting. Candidates for office offer alternative policy packages, and citizens elect people who they think will make the best decisions on their collective behalf. Voters "retire" officials who do not adequately represent their collective wishes and elect persons they think do. Also, citizens periodically have opportunities at the state and local levels to vote directly on public expenditures or new legislation.

Although the democratic process does a reasonably good job of revealing society's preferences, it is imperfect. Public choice theory demonstrates that majority voting can produce inefficiencies and inconsistencies.

Inefficient Voting Outcomes

Society's well-being is enhanced when government provides a public good whose total benefit exceeds its total cost. Unfortunately, majority voting does not always deliver that outcome.

Illustration: Inefficient "No" Vote Assume that the government can provide a public good, say, national defense, at a total expense of $900. Also assume that there are only three individuals—Adams, Benson, and Conrad—in the society and that they will share the $900 tax expense equally, each being taxed $300 if the proposed public good is provided. And assume, as Figure 1a illustrates, that Adams would receive $700 worth of benefits from having this public good; Benson, $250; and Conrad, $200.

What will be the result if a majority vote determines whether or not this public good is provided? Although people do not always vote strictly according to their own economic interest, it is likely Benson and Conrad will vote "no"

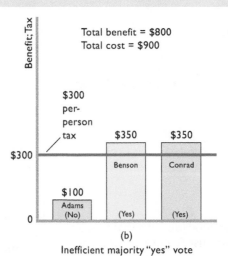

FIGURE 1 Inefficient voting outcomes. Majority voting can produce inefficient decisions. (a) Majority voting leads to rejection of a public good that would entail a greater total benefit than total cost. (b) Majority voting results in acceptance of a public good that has a higher total cost than total benefit.

because they will incur tax costs of $300 each while gaining benefits of only $250 and $200, respectively. Adams will vote "yes." So the majority vote will defeat the proposal even though the total benefit of $1,150 (= $700 for Adams + $250 for Benson + $200 for Conrad) exceeds the total cost of $900. Resources should be devoted to this good, but they will not be. Too little of this public good will be produced.

Illustration: Inefficient "Yes" Vote Now consider a situation in which the majority favors a public good even though its total cost exceeds its total benefit. Figure 1b shows the details. Again, Adams, Benson, and Conrad will equally share the $900 cost of the public good; each will be taxed $300. But since Adams' benefit now is only $100 from the public good, she will vote against it. Meanwhile, Benson and Conrad will benefit by $350 each. They will vote for the public good because that benefit ($350) exceeds their tax payments ($300). The majority vote will provide a public good costing $900 that produces total benefits of only $800 (= $100 for Adams + $350 for Benson + $350 for Conrad). Society's resources will be inefficiently allocated to this public good. Too much of it will be produced.

Implications The point is that an inefficient outcome may occur as either an overproduction or an underproduction of a specific public good, and therefore as an overallocation or underallocation of resources for that particular use. In Chapter 4 we saw that government can improve economic efficiency by providing public goods that the market system will not make available. Now we have extended that analysis to reveal that government may not provide some of those public goods or may provide them in the wrong amounts. In other cases, it may provide public goods that are not economically warranted.

In our examples, each person has only a single vote, no matter how much he or she might gain or lose from a public good. In the first example (inefficient "no" vote), Adams

would be willing to purchase a vote from either Benson or Conrad if buying votes were legal. That way Adams could be assured of obtaining the national defense she so highly values. But since buying votes is illegal, many people with strong preferences for certain public goods may have to go without them.

When individual consumers have a strong preference for a specific *private good*, they usually can find that good in the marketplace even though it may be unpopular with the majority of consumers. A consumer can buy beef tongue, liver, and squid in some supermarkets, although it is doubtful that any of these products would be available if majority voting stocked the shelves. But a person cannot easily "buy" a *public good* such as national defense once the majority has decided against it.

Conversely, a consumer in the marketplace can decide against buying a particular product, even a popular one. But although you may not want national defense, you must "buy" it through your tax payments when the majority have decided they want it.

Conclusion: Because majority voting fails to incorporate the *strength* of the preferences of the individual voter, it may produce economically inefficient outcomes.

Interest Groups and Logrolling Some, but not all, of the inefficiencies of majority voting get resolved through the political process. Two examples follow.

Interest Groups People who share strong preferences for a public good may band together into interest groups and use advertisements, mailings, and direct persuasion to convince others of the merits of that public good. Adams might try to persuade Benson and Conrad that it is in their best interest to vote for national defense—that national defense is much more valuable to them than their $250 and $200 valuations. Such appeals are common in democratic politics. Sometimes they are successful; sometimes they are not.

Political Logrolling Perhaps surprisingly, **logrolling**—the trading of votes to secure desired outcomes—can also turn an inefficient outcome into an efficient one. In our first example (Figure 1a), suppose that Benson has a strong preference for a different public good, for example, a new road, which Adams and Conrad do not think is worth the tax expense. That would provide an opportunity for Adams and Benson to trade votes to ensure provision of both national defense and the new road. That is, Adams and Benson would each vote "yes" on both measures. Adams would get the national defense and Benson would get the road. Without the logrolling, both public goods would have been rejected. This logrolling will add to society's well-being if, as was true for national defense, the road creates a greater overall benefit than cost.

But logrolling need not increase economic efficiency. Even if national defense and the road each cost more than the total benefit each produces, both might still be provided if there is vote trading. Adams and Benson might still engage in logrolling if each expects to secure a sufficient net gain from her or his favored public good, even though the gains would come at the clear expense of Conrad.

Logrolling is very common in state legislatures and Congress. It can either increase or diminish economic efficiency, depending on the circumstances.

Paradox of Voting

Another difficulty with majority voting is the **paradox of voting**, a situation in which society may not be able to rank its preferences consistently through paired-choice majority voting.

Preferences Consider Table 1, in which we again assume a community of three voters: Adams, Benson, and Conrad. Suppose the community has three alternative public goods from which to choose: national defense, a road, and a weather warning system. We expect that each member of the community prefers the three alternatives in a certain order. For example, one person might prefer national defense to a road and a road to a weather warning system. We can attempt to determine the preferences of the community through paired-choice majority voting. Specifically, a vote can be held between any two of the public goods, and the winner of that vote can then be matched against the third public good in another vote.

The three goods and the assumed individual preferences of the three voters are listed in the top part of Table 1.

TABLE 1 Paradox of Voting

Public Good	Preferences		
	Adams	Benson	Conrad
National defense	1st choice	3d choice	2d choice
Road	2d choice	1st choice	3d choice
Weather warning system	3d choice	2d choice	1st choice
Election	**Voting Outcomes: Winner**		
1. National defense vs. road	National defense (preferred by Adams and Conrad)		
2. Road vs. weather warning system	Road (preferred by Adams and Benson)		
3. National defense vs. weather warning system	Weather warning system (preferred by Benson and Conrad)		

The data indicate that Adams prefers national defense to the road and the road to the weather warning system. This implies also that Adams prefers national defense to the weather warning system. Benson values the road more than the weather warning system and the warning system more than national defense. Conrad's order of preference is weather warning system, national defense, and road.

Voting Outcomes The lower part of Table 1 shows the outcomes of three hypothetical elections decided through majority vote. In the first, national defense wins against the road because a majority of voters (Adams and Conrad) prefer national defense to the road. In the second election, to see whether this community wants a road or a weather warning system, a majority of voters (Adams and Benson) prefer the road.

We have determined that the majority of people in this community prefer national defense to a road and prefer a road to a weather warning system. It seems logical to conclude that the community prefers national defense to a weather warning system. But it does not!

To demonstrate this conclusion, we hold a direct election between national defense and the weather warning system. Row 3 shows that a majority of voters (Benson and Conrad) prefer the weather warning system to national defense. As listed in Table 1, then, the three paired-choice majority votes imply that this community is irrational: It seems to prefer national defense to a road and a road to a weather warning system, but would rather have a weather warning system than national defense.

The problem is not irrational community preferences but rather a flawed procedure for determining those preferences. We see that the outcome from paired-choice majority voting may depend on the order in which the votes are taken. Different sequences of majority votes can lead to different outcomes, many of which may fail to reflect the electorate's underlying preferences. As a consequence, government may find it difficult to provide the "correct" public goods by acting in accordance with majority voting. Important note: This critique is not meant to suggest that some better procedure exists. Majority voting is much more likely to reflect community preferences than decisions by, say, a dictator or a group of self-appointed leaders.

Median-Voter Model

One other aspect of majority voting reveals further insights into real-world phenomena. The **median-voter model** suggests that, under majority rule and consistent voting preferences, the median voter will in a sense determine the outcomes of elections. The median voter is the person holding the middle position on an issue: Half the other voters have stronger preferences for a public good,

---

CONSIDER THIS . . .

Voter Failure

Inefficient voting outcomes and the paradox of voting imply that governments may sometimes fail to deliver the best combination of public goods because it may be very difficult for politicians to discern what voters actually want. In other cases, though, economists worry that governments may end up failing to deliver allocative and productive efficiency not because politicians can't tell what people want—but because they *can*.

The problem is that voters sometimes support policies that reduce rather than enhance allocative and productive efficiency. Examples include several types of wage and price controls, punitive tariffs on foreign products, and various industrial and agricultural subsidies.

These policies almost always reduce economic efficiency, but they are also extremely popular with voters in many countries. Faced with that reality, a politician may well end up supporting such policies even if he personally understands that they will create more economic harm than benefit.

That behavior makes some observers wish for braver politicians who might be willing to oppose these instances of "voter failure." But others argue that it is too much to hope for braver politicians. Instead, efforts should be directed toward educating the public and convincing them to support government policies that are economically efficient.

---

amount of taxation, or degree of government regulation, while half have weaker or negative preferences. The extreme voters on each side of an issue prefer the median choice rather than the other extreme position, so the median voter's choice predominates.

Example Suppose a society composed of Adams, Benson, and Conrad has reached agreement that as a society it needs a weather warning system. Each person independently is to submit a total dollar amount he or she thinks should be spent on the warning system, assuming each will be taxed one-third of that amount. An election will determine the size of the system. Because each person can be expected to vote for his or her own proposal, no majority will occur if all the proposals are placed on the ballot at the same time. Thus, the group decides on a paired-choice vote: They will first vote between two of the proposals and then match the winner of that vote against the remaining proposal.

The three proposals are as follows: Adams desires a $400 system; Benson wants an $800 system; Conrad opts for a $300 system. Which proposal will win? The median-voter model suggests it will be the $400 proposal submitted by the median voter, Adams. Half the other voters favor a more costly system; half favor a less costly system. To understand why the $400 system will be the outcome, let's conduct the two elections.

First, suppose that the $400 proposal is matched against the $800 proposal. Adams naturally votes for her $400 proposal, and Benson votes for his own $800 proposal. Conrad, who proposed the $300 expenditure for the warning system, votes for the $400 proposal because it is closer to his own. So Adams' $400 proposal is selected by a 2-to-1 majority vote.

Next, we match the $400 proposal against the $300 proposal. Again the $400 proposal wins. It gets a vote from Adams and one from Benson, who proposed the $800 expenditure and for that reason prefers a $400 expenditure to a $300 one. Adams, the median voter in this case, is in a sense the person who has decided the level of expenditure on a weather warning system for this society.

Real-World Applicability Although our illustration is simple, it explains a great deal. We do note a tendency for public choices to match most closely the median view. Political candidates, for example, take one set of positions to win the nomination of their political parties; in so doing, they tend to appeal to the median voter within the party to get the nomination. They then shift their views more closely to the political center when they square off against opponents from the opposite political party. In effect, they redirect their appeal toward the median voter within the total population. They also try to label their opponents as being too liberal, or too conservative, and out of touch with "mainstream America." And they conduct polls and adjust their positions on issues accordingly.

Implications The median-voter model has two important implications:

- At any point in time, many people will be dissatisfied by the extent of government involvement in the economy. The size of government will largely be determined by the median preference, leaving many people desiring a much larger, or a much smaller, public sector. In the marketplace you can buy no zucchinis, 2 zucchinis, or 200 zucchinis, depending on how much you enjoy them. In the public sector you will tend to get the number of Stealth bombers

and new highway projects that the median voter prefers.

- Some people may "vote with their feet" by moving into political jurisdictions where the median voter's preferences are closer to their own. They may move from the city to a suburb where the level of government services, and therefore taxes, is lower. Or they may move into an area known for its excellent, but expensive, school system. Some may move to other states; a few may even move to other countries.

For these reasons, and because our personal preferences for publicly provided goods and services are not static, the median preference shifts over time. Moreover, information about people's preferences is imperfect, leaving much room for politicians to misjudge the true median position. When they do, they may have a difficult time getting elected or reelected.

APPENDIX SUMMARY

LO5.3 Explain the difficulties of conveying economic preferences through majority voting.

Public choice theory suggests that governments may sometimes suffer from government failures because majority voting fails to correctly indicate voter preferences.

Majority voting creates the possibility of (a) underallocations or overallocations of resources to particular public goods

and (b) inconsistent voting outcomes that make it impossible for a democratic political system to definitively determine the will of the people.

The median-voter model predicts that, under majority rule, the person holding the middle position on an issue will determine the outcome of an election involving that issue.

APPENDIX TERMS AND CONCEPTS

public choice theory

logrolling

paradox of voting

median-voter model

The following and additional problems can be found in **connect**
ECONOMICS

APPENDIX DISCUSSION QUESTIONS

1. Explain how affirmative and negative majority votes can sometimes lead to inefficient allocations of resources to public goods. Is this problem likely to be greater under a benefits-received or an ability-to-pay tax system? Use the information in Figures 1a and 1b to show how society might be better off if Adams were allowed to buy votes. **LO5.3**

2. "Majority voting ensures that government will produce only those public goods for which benefits exceed costs." Discuss. **LO5.3**

3. "The problem with our democratic institutions is that they don't correctly reflect the will of the people! If the people—rather than self-interested politicians or lobbyists—had control, we wouldn't have to worry about government taking actions that don't maximize allocative and productive efficiency." Critique. **LO5.3**

APPENDIX REVIEW QUESTIONS

1. Explain the paradox of voting through reference to the accompanying table, which shows the ranking of three public goods by voters Jay, Dave, and Conan: **LO5.3**

Public Good	Rankings		
	Jay	Dave	Conan
Courthouse	2nd choice	1st choice	3d choice
School	3d choice	2d choice	1st choice
Park	1st choice	3d choice	2d choice

2. We can apply voting paradoxes to the highway construction example of Chapter 4. Suppose there are only five people in a society and each favors one of the five highway construction options listed in Table 4.4 ("No new construction" is one of the five options). Explain which of these highway options will be selected using a majority paired-choice vote. Will this option be the optimal size of the project from an economic perspective? **LO5.3**

3. True or False: The median-voter model explains why politicians so often stake out fringe positions that appeal only to a small segment of the electorate. **LO5.3**

APPENDIX PROBLEMS

1. Look back at Figures 1a and 1b, which show the costs and benefits to voters Adams, Benson, and Conrad of two different public goods that the government will produce if a majority of Adams, Benson, and Conrad support them. Suppose that Adams, Benson, and Conrad have decided to have one single vote at which the funding for both of those public goods will be decided simultaneously. **LO5.3**
   a. Given the $300 cost per person of each public good, what are Adams' net benefits for each public good individually and for the two combined? Will he want to vote yes or no on the proposal to fund both projects simultaneously?
   b. What are Conrad's net benefits for each public good individually and for the two combined? Will he want to vote yes or no on the proposal to fund both projects simultaneously?
   c. What are Benson's net benefits for each public good individually and for the two combined? Will he want to vote yes or no on the proposal to fund both projects simultaneously—or will he be indifferent?
   d. Who is the median voter here? Who will the two other voters be attempting to persuade?

2. Political advertising is often directed at winning over so-called swing voters, whose votes might go either way. Suppose that two political parties—the Freedom Party and the Liberty Party—disagree on whether to build a new road. Polling shows that of 1,000 total voters, 450 are firmly for the new road and 450 are firmly against the new road. Thus, each party will try to win over a majority of the 100 remaining swing voters. **LO5.3**
   a. Suppose that each party spends $5,000 on untargeted TV, radio, and newspaper ads that are equally likely to reach any and all voters. How much per voter will be spent by both parties combined?
   b. Suppose that, instead, each party could direct all of its spending toward just the swing voters by using targeted ads that exploit Internet social media. If all of the two parties' combined spending was targeted at just swing voters, how much would be spent per swing voter?
   c. Suppose that only the Freedom Party knows how to target voters using social media. How much per swing voter will it be spending? If at the same time the Liberty Party is still using only untargeted TV, radio, and newspaper ads, what portion of its total spending is likely to be reaching the 100 swing voters? How much per swing voter does that portion amount to?
   d. Looking at your answers to part *c*, how much more per swing voter will the Freedom Party be spending than the Liberty Party? If spending per swing voter influences elections, which party is more likely to win?

GDP, Growth, and Instability

GDP, GROWTH, AND INSTABILITY

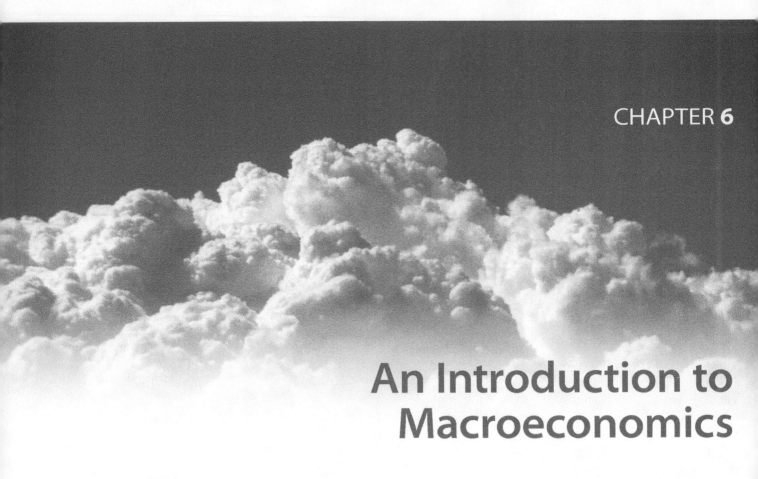

An Introduction to Macroeconomics

Learning Objectives

LO6.1 Explain why economists focus on GDP, inflation, and unemployment when assessing the health of an entire economy.

LO6.2 Discuss why sustained increases in living standards are a historically recent phenomenon.

LO6.3 Identify why saving and investment are key factors in promoting rising living standards.

LO6.4 Describe why economists believe that "shocks" and "sticky prices" are responsible for short-run fluctuations in output and employment.

LO6.5 Characterize the degree to which various prices in the economy are sticky.

LO6.6 Explain why the greater flexibility of prices as time passes causes economists to utilize different macroeconomic models for different time horizons.

Macroeonomics focuses its attention on national economies while seeking answers to the largest of economic questions. For instance: Why are some countries really rich while others are really poor? Why do some countries enjoy sustained, long-run increases in living standards, while other countries simply stagnate? Why do all countries—even the richest—go through alternating boom and bust periods? And is there anything that governments can do to improve living standards or fight recessions?

This chapter provides an overview of the data that macroeconomists use to measure the status and growth of an entire economy as well as a preview of the models that they use to help explain both long-run growth and short-run fluctuations.

Because it is an overview chapter, it raises many unanswered questions. Subsequent chapters will explain these topics in much greater detail.

Performance and Policy

LO6.1 Explain why economists focus on GDP, inflation, and unemployment when assessing the health of an entire economy.

As you know from Chapter 1, macroeconomics studies the behavior of the economy as a whole. It is primarily concerned with two topics: long-run economic growth and the short-run fluctuations in output and employment that are often referred to as the **business cycle.** These phenomena are closely related because they happen simultaneously. Economies show a distinct growth trend that leads to higher output and higher standards of living in the long run, but in the short run there is considerable variability. Sometimes growth proceeds more rapidly and sometimes it proceeds more slowly. It may even turn negative for a while so that output and living standards actually decline, a situation referred to as a **recession.** That is precisely what happened in late 2007 and continued through 2008 and into 2009. The economy experienced what has come to be called the Great Recession.

To understand how economies operate and how their performance might be improved, economists collect and analyze economic data. An almost infinite number of data items can be looked at, including the amount of new construction taking place each month, how many ships laden with cargo are arriving at our ports each year, and how many new inventions have been patented in the last few weeks. That being said, macroeconomists tend to focus on just a few statistics when trying to assess the health and development of an economy. Chief among these are real GDP, unemployment, and inflation.

- **Real GDP,** or **real gross domestic product,** measures the value of final goods and services produced within the borders of a country during a specific period of time, typically a year. This statistic is very useful because it can tell us whether an economy's output is growing. For instance, if U.S. real GDP in one year is larger than in the previous year, we know that U.S. output increased from the first year to the next. To determine real GDP, government statisticians first calculate **nominal GDP,** which totals the dollar value of all goods and services produced within the borders of a country using *their current prices during the year that they were produced.* But because nominal GDP uses the prices in place in the year the output was produced, it suffers from a major problem: It can increase from one year to the next even if there is no increase in output. To see how, consider a commercial blacksmith who produced 10 iron spiral staircases last year and 10 identical staircases this year. Clearly, the blacksmith's output did not change. But if the price of each staircase rose from $10,000 last year to $20,000 this year, nominal GDP increased from $100,000 (= 10 × $10,000) to $200,000 (= 10 × $20,000). Without knowing about the price increase, we might unwisely conclude that the output of staircases increased from 10 to 20. Real GDP statistically eliminates these kinds of price changes. As a result, we can compare real GDP numbers from one year to the next and really know if there is a change in output (rather than prices). Because more output means greater consumption possibilities—including not only the chance to consume more fun things such as movies, vacations, and video games, but also more serious things like better health care and safer roads—economists and policymakers are deeply committed to encouraging a large and growing real GDP.

- **Unemployment** is the state a person is in if he or she cannot get a job despite being willing to work and actively seeking work. High rates of unemployment are undesirable because they indicate that a nation is not using a large portion of its most important resource—the talents and skills of its people. Unemployment is a waste because we must count as a loss all the goods and services that unemployed workers could have produced if they had been working. Researchers have also drawn links between higher rates of unemployment and major social problems like higher crime rates and greater political unrest as well as higher rates of depression, heart disease, and other illnesses among unemployed individuals.

- **Inflation** is an increase in the overall level of prices. As an example, consider all the goods and services bought by a typical family over the course of one year. If the economy is experiencing inflation, it will cost the family more money to buy those goods and services this year than it cost to buy them last year. This can be troublesome for several reasons. First, if the family's income does not rise as fast as the prices of the goods and services that it consumes, it won't be able to purchase as much as it used to and its standard of living will fall. Along the same lines, a surprise jump in inflation reduces the purchasing power of people's savings. Savings that they believed would be able to buy them a specific amount of goods and services will turn out to buy them less than they expected due to the higher-than-expected prices.

Because these statistics are the standards by which economists keep track of long-run growth and short-run fluctuations, we will spend a substantial amount of time in the next few chapters examining how these statistics are computed, how well they are able to capture the well-being of actual people, and how they vary both across countries and over time. Once they are understood, we will build on them in subsequent chapters by developing macroeconomic models of both long-run growth and short-run fluctuations. These will help us understand how policymakers attempt to maximize growth while minimizing unemployment and inflation.

Macroeconomic models also clarify many important questions about the powers and limits of government economic policy. These include:

- Can governments promote long-run economic growth?
- Can they reduce the severity of recessions by smoothing out short-run fluctuations?
- Are certain government policy tools such as manipulating interest rates (monetary policy) more effective at mitigating short-run fluctuations than other government policy tools such as changes in tax rates or levels of government spending (fiscal policy)?
- Is there a trade-off between lower rates of unemployment and higher rates of inflation?
- Does government policy work best when it is announced in advance or when it is a surprise?

The answers to these questions are of crucial importance because of the vast differences in economic performance experienced by national economies at different times. For instance, the amount of output generated by the U.S. economy grew at an average rate of 2.7 percent per year between 1995 and the start of the recession of 2007–2009, while the amount of output generated by the Japanese economy grew at an average rate of only 1.0 percent per year over the same time period. In 2008 and 2009, however, the U.S. economy lost 8 million jobs, and the

unemployment rate rose from 4.6 percent to as high as 10.1 percent. A couple of years later, in 2011, the unemployment rate was 9.1 percent in the United States, 17.9 percent in Greece, 3.5 percent in South Korea, 9.3 percent in France, and 40.6 percent in Haiti. At the same time, the inflation rate was 3.0 percent in the United States, 1.3 percent in Norway, 14.0 percent in Kenya, 21.0 percent in Argentina, and 3.4 percent in Mexico.

Our models will help us understand why such large differences in rates of growth, unemployment, and inflation exist among countries and why those rates can change so substantially from one period to another. These models also will provide significant insights on how government policies can influence rates of growth, unemployment, and inflation.

> ### QUICK REVIEW 6.1
>
> - Macroeconomics studies long-run economic growth and short-run economic fluctuations.
> - Macroeconomists focus their attention on three key economic statistics: real GDP, unemployment, and inflation.
> - Macroeconomic models help to clarify many important questions about government economic policy.

The Miracle of Modern Economic Growth

LO6.2 Discuss why sustained increases in living standards are a historically recent phenomenon.

Rapid and sustained economic growth is a modern phenomenon. Before the Industrial Revolution began in the late 1700s in England, standards of living showed virtually no growth over hundreds or even thousands of years. For instance, the standard of living of the average Roman peasant was virtually the same at the start of the Roman Empire around the year 500 B.C. as it was at the end of the Roman Empire 1,000 years later. Similarly, historians and archaeologists have estimated that the standard of living enjoyed by the average Chinese peasant was essentially the same in the year A.D. 1800 as it was in the year A.D. 100.

That is not to say that the Roman and Chinese economies did not expand over time. They did. In fact, their total outputs of goods and services increased many times over. The problem was that as they did, their populations went up by similar proportions so that the amount of output *per person* remained virtually unchanged.

This historical pattern continued until the start of the Industrial Revolution, which ushered in not only factory production and automation but also massive increases in research and development so that new and better technologies were constantly being invented. The result was that output began to grow faster than the population. This meant that living standards began to rise as the amount of output *per person* increased.

Not all countries experienced this phenomenon, but those that did were said to be experiencing **modern economic growth** (in which output per person rises) as compared with earlier times in which output (but not output per person) increased. Under modern economic growth, the annual increase in output per person is often not large, perhaps 2 percent per year in countries such as England that were the first to industrialize. But when compounded over time, an annual growth rate of 2 percent adds up very rapidly. Indeed, it implies that the standard of living will double every 35 years. So if the average citizen of a country enjoying 2 percent growth begins this year with an income of $10,000, in 35 years that person will have an income of $20,000. And 35 years after that there will be another doubling so that her income in 70 years will be $40,000. And 35 years after that, the average citizen's income will double again to $80,000. Such high rates of growth are amazing when compared to the period before modern economic growth when standards of living remained unchanged century after century.

The vast differences in living standards seen today between rich and poor countries are almost entirely the result of the fact that only some countries have experienced modern economic growth. Indeed, before the start of the Industrial Revolution in the late 1700s, living standards around the world were very similar, so much so that the average standard of living in the richest parts of the world was at most only two or three times higher than the standard of living in the poorest parts of the world. By contrast, the citizens of the richest nations today have material standards of living that are on average more than 50 times higher than those experienced by citizens of the poorest nations, as can be seen by the GDP per person data for the year 2011 given in Global Perspective 6.1.

Global Perspective 6.1 facilitates international comparisons of living standards by making three adjustments to each country's GDP. First, it converts each country's GDP from its own currency into U.S. dollars so that there is no confusion about the values of different currencies. Second, it divides each country's GDP measured in dollars by the size of its population. The resulting number, *GDP per person*, is the average amount of output each person in each country could have if each country's total output were divided equally among its citizens. It is a measure of each country's average standard of living. Third, the table uses a method called *purchasing power*

GLOBAL PERSPECTIVE 6.1

GDP per Person, Selected Countries

Country	GDP per Person, 2011 (U.S. dollars based on purchasing power parity)
Canada	$50,496
United States	48,328
Japan	45,870
France	44,007
United Kingdom	38,811
South Korea	31,700
Saudi Arabia	21,196
Russia	12,993
Mexico	10,146
China	5,417
North Korea	1,800
India	1,514
Zimbabwe	752
Tanzania	566
Burundi	275

Source: International Monetary Fund, **www.imf.org**, for all countries except for North Korea, the estimate for which is from the *CIA World Factbook*, **www.cia.gov**.

parity to adjust for the fact that prices are much lower in some countries than others. By making this adjustment, we can trust that $1 of GDP per person in the United States represents about the same quantity of goods and services as $1 of GDP per person in any of the other countries. The resulting numbers—GDP per person adjusted for purchasing power parity—are presented in Global Perspective 6.1.

QUICK REVIEW 6.2

- Before the Industrial Revolution, living standards did not show any sustained increases over time because any increase in output tended to be offset by an equally large increase in population.
- Since the Industrial Revolution, many nations have experienced *modern economic growth* in which output grows faster than population—so that living standards rise over time.

Saving, Investment, and Choosing between Present and Future Consumption

LO6.3 Identify why saving and investment are key factors in promoting rising living standards.

At the heart of economic growth is the principle that to raise living standards over time, an economy must devote at least some fraction of its current output to increasing future output. As implied in Chapter 1, this process requires flows of both saving and investment, which we will define and discuss before returning to why they are so important for economic growth.

- **Saving** occurs when current consumption is less than current output (or when current spending is less than current income).
- **Investment** happens when resources are devoted to increasing future output—for instance by building a new research facility in which scientists invent the next generation of fuel-efficient automobiles or by constructing a modern, super-efficient factory. (A caution: In economics, the term "investment" differs from common usage. To understand why, be sure to read the Consider This box.)

When thinking about why saving and investment are so important for economic growth, the key point is that the amount of investment is ultimately limited by the amount of saving. The only way that more output can be directed at investment activities is if saving increases. But that, in turn, implies that individuals and society as a whole must make trade-offs between current and future consumption. This is true because the only way to pay for more investment—and the higher levels of future consumption that more investment can generate—is to increase present saving. But increased saving can only come at the price of reduced current consumption. Individuals and society as a whole must therefore wrestle with a choice between present consumption and future consumption. They must decide how to balance the reductions in current consumption required to fund current investment against the increases in future consumption that the added current investment will make possible.

Banks and Other Financial Institutions

Households are the principal source of savings. But businesses are the main economic investors. So how does the pool of savings generated by households when they spend less than they consume get transferred to businesses so that they can purchase newly created capital goods? The answer is through banks and other financial institutions

CONSIDER THIS . . .

Economic versus Financial Investment

Economics students often are confused by how the word "investment" is used in economics. This is understandable, because economists draw a distinction between "financial investment" and "economic investment."

Financial investment captures what ordinary people mean when they say investment, namely, the purchase of assets like stocks, bonds, and real estate in the hope of reaping a financial gain. Anything of monetary value is an asset and, in everyday usage, people purchase—or "invest" in—assets hoping to receive a financial gain, either by eventually selling them at higher prices than they paid for them or by receiving a stream of payments from others who are allowed to use the asset. By contrast, when economists say "investment," they are referring to **economic investment,** which relates to the creation and expansion of business enterprises. Specifically, economic investment only includes spending on the production and accumulation of newly created capital goods such as machinery, tools, factories, and warehouses. For example, economic investment will occur when the airplane shown in the accompanying photo is purchased by a commercial airline.

For economists, purely financial transactions, such as swapping cash for a stock or a bond, are not "investment." Neither are the purchases of factories or apartment buildings built in previous years. These transactions simply transfer the ownership of financial assets or existing real assets from one party to another. They do not purchase newly created capital goods. As such, they are great examples of financial investment, but not of economic investment. So now that you know the difference, remember that purely financial transactions, like buying Google stock or a five-year-old factory, are indeed referred to as "investment"—except in economics!

such as mutual funds, pension plans, and insurance companies. These institutions collect the savings of households, rewarding savers with interest and dividends and sometimes capital gains (increases in asset values). The banks and other financial institutions then lend the funds to businesses, which invest in equipment, factories, and other capital goods.

Macroeconomics devotes considerable attention to money, banking, and financial institutions because a well-functioning financial system helps to promote economic growth and stability by encouraging saving and by properly directing that saving into the most productive possible investments. In contrast, a poorly functioning financial system can create serious problems for an economy.

QUICK REVIEW 6.3

- An economy can only grow if it invests, and it can only invest if it saves some of its current output. Thus, saving is crucial to increasing investment and, consequently, future output.
- Banks and other financial institutions channel household savings toward businesses, which invest in equipment, factories, and other capital goods.

Uncertainty, Expectations, and Shocks

LO6.4 Describe why economists believe that "shocks" and "sticky prices" are responsible for short-run fluctuations in output and employment.

Decisions about savings and investment are complicated by the fact that the future is uncertain. Investment projects sometimes produce disappointing results or even fail totally. As a result, firms spend considerable time trying to predict future trends so that they can, hopefully, invest only in projects that are likely to succeed. This implies that macroeconomics has to take into account **expectations** about the future.

The Importance of Expectations and Shocks

Expectations are hugely important for two reasons. The more obvious reason involves the effect that changing expectations have on current behavior. If firms grow more pessimistic about the future returns that are likely to come from current investments, they are going to invest less today than they would if they were more optimistic. Expectations therefore have a large effect on economic growth since increased pessimism will lead to less current investment and, subsequently, less future consumption.

The less-obvious reason that expectations are so important has to do with what happens when expectations are unmet. Firms are often forced to cope with **shocks**—situations in which they were expecting one thing to happen but then something else happened. For instance, consider a situation in which a firm decides to build a high-speed railroad that will shuttle passengers between Los Angeles and Las Vegas. The firm expects it to be very popular and make a handsome profit. But if it unexpectedly turns out to be unpopular and loses money, the railroad

must figure out how to respond. Should the railroad go out of business completely? Should it attempt to see if it can turn a profit by hauling cargo instead of passengers? Is there a possibility that the venture might succeed if the firm borrows $30 million from a bank to pay for a massive advertising campaign? These sorts of decisions are necessitated by the shock and surprise of having to deal with an unexpected situation.

Economies are exposed to both demand shocks and supply shocks. **Demand shocks** are unexpected changes in the demand for goods and services. **Supply shocks** are unexpected changes in the supply of goods and services. Note that the word *shock* only reveals that something unexpected has happened. It does not tell us whether what has happened is unexpectedly good or unexpectedly bad. To clarify this, economists use more specific terms. For instance, a *positive demand shock* refers to a situation in which demand turns out to be higher than expected, while a *negative demand shock* refers to a situation in which demand turns out to be lower than expected.

Demand Shocks and Sticky Prices

Economists believe that most short-run fluctuations in GDP and the business cycle are the result of demand shocks. Supply shocks do happen in some cases and are very important when they do occur. But we will focus most of our attention in this chapter and subsequent chapters on demand shocks, how they affect the economy, and how government policy may be able to help the economy adjust to them.

But why are demand shocks such a big problem? Why would we have to consider calling in the government to help deal with them? And why can't firms deal with demand shocks on their own?

The answer to these questions is that the prices of many goods and services are inflexible (slow to change, or "sticky") in the short run. As we will explain, this implies that price changes do not quickly equalize the quantities demanded of such goods and services with their respective quantities supplied. Instead, because prices are inflexible, the economy is forced to respond in the short run to demand shocks primarily through changes in output and employment rather than through changes in prices.

Example: A Single Firm Dealing with Demand Shocks and Sticky Prices

Although an economy as a whole is vastly more complex than a single firm, an analogy that uses a single car factory will be helpful in explaining why demand shocks and inflexible prices are so important to understanding most of the short-run fluctuations that affect the entire economy. Consider a car manufacturing company named Buzzer Auto. Like most companies, Buzzer Auto is in business to try to make a profit. Part of turning a profit involves trying to develop accurate expectations about future market conditions. Consequently, Buzzer constantly does market research to estimate future demand conditions so that it will, hopefully, only build cars that people are going to want to buy.

Setting Expectations After extensive market research, Buzzer concludes that it could earn a modest profit if it builds and staffs an appropriately sized factory to build an environmentally friendly SUV, which it decides to call the Prion. Buzzer's marketing economists collaborate with Buzzer's engineers and conclude that expected profits will be maximized if the firm builds a factory that has an optimal output rate of 900 cars per week. If the factory operates at this rate, it can produce Prions for only $36,500 per vehicle. This is terrific because the firm's estimates for demand indicate that a supply of 900 vehicles per week can be sold at a price of $37,000 per vehicle—meaning that if everything goes according to plan, Buzzer Auto should make an accounting profit of $500 on each Prion that it produces and sells. Expecting these future conditions, Buzzer decides to build the factory, staff it with workers, and begin making the Prion.

Look at Figure 6.1a, which shows the market for Prions when the vertical supply curve for Prions is fixed at the factory's optimal output rate of 900 cars per week. Notice that we have drawn in three possible demand curves. D_L corresponds to low demand for the Prion; D_M corresponds to the medium level of demand that Buzzer's marketing economists are expecting to materialize; and D_H corresponds to high demand for the Prion. Figure 6.1a is consistent with the marketing economists' expectations: if all goes according to plan and the actual demand that materializes is D_M, the equilibrium price will in fact be $37,000 per Prion and the equilibrium quantity demanded will be 900 cars per week. Thus, if all goes according to expectations, the factory will have exactly the right capacity to meet the expected quantity demanded at the sales price of $37,000 per vehicle. In addition, the firm's books will show a profit of $500 per vehicle on each of the 900 vehicles that it builds and expects to sell each week at that price.

Full Employment If There Are No Shocks Here is the key point. If expectations are always fulfilled, Buzzer Auto will never contribute to any of the short-run fluctuations in output and unemployment that affect real-world economies. First, if everything always goes according to plan and Buzzer Auto's expectations always come true, then the factory will always produce and sell at its optimal

FIGURE 6.1 **The effect of unexpected changes in demand under flexible and fixed prices.** (a) If prices are flexible, then no matter what demand turns out to be, Buzzer Auto can continue to sell its optimal output of 900 cars per week since the equilibrium price will adjust to equalize the quantity demanded with the quantity supplied. (b) By contrast, if Buzzer Auto sticks with a fixed-price policy, then the quantity demanded will vary with the level of demand. At the fixed price of $37,000 per vehicle, the quantity demanded will be 700 cars per week if demand is D_L, 900 cars per week if demand is D_M, and 1,150 cars per week if demand is D_H.

output rate of 900 cars per week. This would mean that it would never experience any fluctuations in output—either in the short run or in the long run. At the same time, since producing a constant output of 900 cars each week will always require the same number of workers, the factory's labor demand and employment should never vary. So if everything always goes according to plan, Buzzer Auto will never have any effect on unemployment because it will always hire a constant number of workers.

These facts imply that the short-run fluctuations in output and unemployment that we do see in the real world must be the result of shocks and things *not* going according to plan. In particular, business cycle fluctuations typically arise because the actual demand that materializes ends up being either lower or higher than what people were expecting. When this occurs, some adjustments will be necessary to bring quantity demanded and quantity supplied back into alignment. As we are about to explain, the nature of these adjustments varies hugely depending on whether prices are flexible or inflexible.

Price Changes If There Are Demand Shocks and Flexible Prices

Figure 6.1a illustrates the case of adjusting to unexpected changes in demand *when prices are flexible.* Here, if demand is unexpectedly low at D_L, the market price can adjust downward to $35,000 per vehicle so that the quantity demanded at that price will still be equal to the factory's optimal output rate of 900 cars per week. On the other hand, if demand is unexpectedly high at D_H, the market price can adjust upward to $40,000 per vehicle so that the quantity demanded will still be equal to the factory's optimal output rate of 900 cars per week. These adjustments imply that *if* the price of Prions is free to quickly adjust to new equilibrium levels in response to unexpected changes in demand, the factory could always operate at its optimal output rate of 900 cars per week. Only the amount of profit or loss will vary with demand.

Applying this logic to the economy as a whole, *if* the prices of goods and services could always adjust quickly to unexpected changes in demand, then the economy could always produce at its optimal capacity since prices would adjust to ensure that the quantity demanded of each good and service would always equal the quantity supplied. Simply put, if prices were fully flexible, there would be no short-run fluctuations in output. Production levels would remain constant and unemployment levels would not change because firms would always need the same number of workers to produce the same amount of output.

Output Changes If There Are Demand Shocks and Sticky Prices

In reality, many prices in the economy are inflexible and are not able to change rapidly when demand changes unexpectedly. Consider the extreme case shown in Figure 6.1b, in which the price of Prions is totally inflexible, fixed at $37,000 per Prion. Here, if demand unexpectedly falls from D_M to D_L, the quantity demanded at the fixed price of $37,000 will only be 700 cars per week, which is 200 cars fewer than the factory's optimal output of 900 cars per week. On the other hand, if demand is unexpectedly high at D_H, the quantity demanded at the fixed price of $37,000 will be 1,150 cars per week, which is 250 cars more than the factory's optimal output of 900 cars per week.

One way for companies to deal with these unexpected shifts in quantity demanded would be to try to adjust the factory's output to match them. That is, during weeks of low demand, Buzzer Auto could attempt to produce only 700 Prions, while during weeks of high demand it could try to produce 1,150 Prions. But this sort of flexible output strategy is very expensive because factories operate at their lowest costs when they are producing constantly at their optimal output levels; operating at either a higher or a lower production rate results in higher per-unit production costs.[1]

Knowing this, manufacturing firms typically attempt to deal with unexpected changes in demand by maintaining an inventory. An **inventory** is a store of output that has been produced but not yet sold. Inventories are useful because they can be allowed to grow or decline in periods when demand is unexpectedly low or high—thereby allowing production to proceed smoothly even when demand is variable. In our example, Buzzer Auto would maintain an inventory of unsold Prions. In weeks when demand is unexpectedly low, the inventory will increase by 200 Prions as the quantity demanded falls 200 vehicles short of the factory's optimal output. By contrast, during weeks when demand is unexpectedly high, the inventory will decrease as the quantity demanded exceeds the factory's optimal output by 250 cars. By allowing inventory levels to fluctuate with these unexpected shifts in demand, Buzzer Auto can respond by adjusting inventory levels rather than output levels. In addition, with any luck, the overall inventory level will stay roughly constant over time as unexpected increases and decreases in demand cancel each other out.

But consider what will happen if the firm experiences many successive weeks of unexpectedly low demand. For each such week, the firm's inventory of unsold Prions will increase by 200 cars. The firm's managers will not mind if

---

[1]If you have studied microeconomics, you will recognize that the firm's optimal output level of 900 cars per week is the level that minimizes the factory's average total cost (ATC) per vehicle of producing the Prion. Producing either more or fewer Prions will result in higher per-vehicle production costs.

this happens for a few weeks, but if it continues for many weeks, then the managers will be forced to cut production because, among other things, there will simply be no place to park so many unsold vehicles. More importantly, holding large numbers of unsold cars in inventory is unprofitable because while costs must be incurred to build an unsold car, an unsold car obviously brings in no revenue. Constantly rising inventories hurt firm profits and the management will want to reduce output if it sees inventories rising week after week due to unexpectedly low demand.

Generalizing from a Single Firm to the Entire Economy

This simplified story about a single car company explains why economists believe that a combination of unexpected changes in demand and inflexible prices are the key to understanding the short-run fluctuations that affect real-world economies. If prices were flexible, then the firm could always operate at the factory's optimal output level because prices would always adjust to ensure that it could sell its optimal output of 900 cars per week no matter what happens to demand. But if prices are inflexible, then an unexpected decline in demand that persists for any length of time will result in increasing inventories that will eventually force the firm's management to cut production to less than the optimal output level of 900 cars per week. When this happens, not only will output fall, but unemployment will also rise. The firm will lay off workers because fewer employees will be needed to produce fewer cars.

Generalizing this story to the economy as a whole, if demand falls off for many goods and services across the entire economy for an extended period of time, then the firms that make those goods and services will be forced to cut production. Manufacturing firms that maintain inventories will do so as they find inventories piling up due to sluggish sales. And services firms will do so as they encounter slow sales for their services. As both manufacturing and service output declines, the economy will recede, with GDP falling and unemployment rising.

On the other hand, if demand is unexpectedly high for a prolonged period of time, the economy will boom and unemployment will fall. In the case of our Prion example, for each week that demand is unexpectedly high, inventories will fall by 250 cars. If this keeps happening week after week, inventories will start to run out and the firm will have to react by increasing production to more than the optimal output rate of 900 cars per week so that orders do not go unfilled. When this happens, GDP will increase as more cars per week are produced and unemployment will fall because the factory will need to hire more workers to produce the larger number of cars.

QUICK REVIEW 6.4

- Economic shocks occur when events unfold in ways that people were not expecting.
- Demand and supply shocks take place when demand or supply ends up being either higher or lower than expected.
- Real-world prices are often inflexible or "sticky" in the short run.
- When prices are sticky, the economy adjusts to demand shocks mostly through changes in output and employment (rather than through changes in prices).

Debating the Great Recession

Economists Disagreed Vigorously about Both the Causes of the Great Recession and the Best Ways to Speed a Recovery.

The Great Recession of 2007–2009 was the worst economic downturn since the Great Depression of the 1930s. The government intervened massively to help promote recovery, but the recession was long-lasting and the subsequent recovery was the weakest since the Great Depression.

Explanations about what caused the Great Recession differ sharply among economists. Here are two of the more popular hypotheses.

The Minksy Explanation: Euphoric Bubbles Economist Hyman Minksy believed that severe recessions are often preceded by *asset-price bubbles*—periods during which euphoria and debt-fueled speculation cause the price of one or more financial assets to irrationally skyrocket before collapsing down to more realistic levels. Those who apply his ideas to the Great Recession note that easily obtained home-mortgage loans drove a massive bubble in housing prices.

When the bubble eventually collapsed, investors lost trillions of dollars in wealth. As a result, the demand for goods and services fell dramatically and unexpectedly. When combined with sticky prices, that leftward shift in demand forced many companies to reduce output and lay off workers (as in our Buzzer Auto

example in this chapter). The weakest firms went bankrupt and had to permanently fire all of their workers.

The Austrian Explanation: Excessively Low Interest Rates Economists of the so-called Austrian School also blame bubbles for severe recessions, but they put the blame for bubbles not on euphoria but on government actions that they say keep interest rates too low. Their contention is that excessively low interest rates induce firms and individuals to borrow excessively. Individuals borrow excessively to fund consumption. Firms borrow excessively for construction and investment. When the bubble pops, society has too many factories (as a result of the massive increase in construction and investment on the part of firms) combined with too little demand (as consumers struggle to repay all the money they borrowed to fund their consumption).

In terms of this chapter's Buzzer Auto example, it would be as though Buzzer borrowed lots of money to build several factories only to discover that demand was much lower than expected because consumers were cutting back on spending in order to repay debt. With demand shifting left and prices sticky, Buzzer and other companies are forced to reduce output and lay off workers. Thus begins the recession.

How Sticky Are Prices?

LO6.5 Characterize the degree to which various prices in the economy are sticky.

We have just shown that **inflexible prices**—or **"sticky prices"** as economists are fond of saying—help to explain how unexpected changes in demand lead to the fluctuations in GDP and employment that occur over the course of the business cycle. Of course, not all prices are sticky. Indeed, the markets for many commodities and raw materials such as corn, oil, and natural gas feature extremely **flexible prices** that react within seconds to changes in supply and demand. By contrast, the prices of most of the final goods and services that people consume are quite sticky, with the average good or service going 4.3 months between price changes. To get a better appreciation for the fact that price stickiness varies greatly by product or service, look at Table 6.1, which gives the average number of months between price

TABLE 6.1 Average Number of Months between Price Changes for Selected Goods and Services

Item	Months
Coin-operated laundry machines	46.4
Newspapers	29.9
Haircuts	25.5
Taxi fare	19.7
Veterinary services	14.9
Magazines	11.2
Computer software	5.5
Beer	4.3
Microwave ovens	3.0
Milk	2.4
Electricity	1.8
Airline tickets	1.0
Gasoline	0.6

Source: Mark Bils and Peter J. Klenow, "Some Evidence on the Importance of Sticky Prices." *Journal of Political Economy,* October 2004, pp. 947–985. Used with permission of The University of Chicago Press via Copyright Clearance Center.

Because economists did not have a consensus about what caused the Great Recession, it should not be surprising that they were also divided over the best policies for fighting the recession and improving upon the sluggish recovery that began in 2009. For simplicity, the wide variety of opinions can be grouped into two broad camps promoting two very different solutions.

The Stimulus Solution The majority of economists argued that the solution to the collapse in demand was to have the government take actions to shift demand curves rightward. For instance, the government could lower interest rates so that consumers and businesses would borrow and spend more. The government could also massively increase its purchases of goods and services so that a rightward shift in the government's demand for output could help to make up for the leftward shift in the private-sector demand for output.

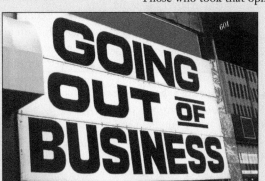

This opinion in favor of *government stimulus* was the most commonly held view among economists and the government did in fact push interest rates very low while also massively increasing government spending.

The Structural Solution A vocal minority of economists rejected the stimulus policies. They argued that the economy required a *structural adjustment*. In their opinion, the bubble period before the recession had seen a major misallocation of resources toward inefficient firms that generated net losses for society (MB < MC). The only way to redirect the resources that those firms were using back toward productive activities would be to let the inefficient firms go bankrupt. The resources would then flow toward efficient firms whose output generated net benefits for society (MB > MC).

Under this way of thinking, government stimulus efforts delayed recovery by keeping many wasteful firms on life support. Those who took that opinion wanted the government to mostly hang back, let inefficient firms go bankrupt, and allow the invisible hand to reallocate resources.

This debate over government stimulus was ongoing and continual during the sluggish recovery from the Great Recession. Those in favor of stimulus argued that the sluggish recovery was the result of too little stimulus. Those against stimulus argued that the sluggish recovery was the result of too much stimulus.

One of your tasks as you work your way through the subsequent chapters will be to understand the nature of this debate and the arguments and evidence on both sides. But don't look for a definitive answer. The complexities of giant national economies are only partly understood and the best policy may turn out to be something unseen by either of the two camps.

changes for various common goods and services. The prices of some products like gasoline and airline tickets change very rapidly—about once a month or even less than once a month. By contrast, haircuts and newspapers average more than two years between price changes. And coin-operated laundry machines average nearly four years between price changes!

An important recent study has found that product prices are particularly sticky in response to widespread macroeconomic and monetary disturbances.[2] In later chapters, we will identify and discuss several factors that cause short-run price stickiness. But to keep the current discussion brief, let's focus on just two factors here. One factor is that companies selling final goods and services know that consumers prefer stable, predictable prices that do not fluctuate rapidly with changes in demand. Consumers would be annoyed if the same bottle of soda or shampoo cost one price one day, a different price the next day, and yet another price a week later. Volatile prices make planning more difficult, and, in addition, consumers who come in to buy the product on a day when the price happens to be high will likely feel that they are being taken advantage of. To avoid this, most firms try to maintain stable prices that do not change very often. Firms do have occasional sales where they lower prices, but on the whole they tend to try to keep prices stable and predictable—the result being price inflexibility.

Another factor that causes sticky prices has to do with the fact that in certain situations, a firm may be afraid that cutting its price may be counterproductive because its rivals might simply match the price cut—a situation often referred to as a "price war." This possibility is common among firms that only have one or two

---

[2]Jean Boivin, Marc P. Giannoni, and Illian Mihov, "Sticky Prices and Monetary Policy: Evidence from Disaggregated US Data," *American Economic Review*, March 2009, pp. 350–384.

major rivals. Consider Coca-Cola and Pepsi. If Coca-Cola faces unexpectedly low demand for its product, it might be tempted to reduce its price in the hope that it can steal business away from Pepsi. But such a strategy would only work if Pepsi left its price alone when Coca-Cola cut its price. That, of course, is not likely. If Coca-Cola cuts its price, Pepsi will very likely cut its price in retaliation, doing its best to make sure that Coca-Cola doesn't steal away any of its customers. Thus, if Pepsi retaliates, Coca-Cola will only be made worse off by its decision to cut its price: It will not pick up much more business (because Pepsi also cut its price) and it will also be receiving less money for each bottle of Coke that it sells (because it lowered its own price.) Thus, firms that have to deal with the possibility of price wars often have sticky prices.

Categorizing Macroeconomic Models Using Price Stickiness

LO6.6 Explain why the greater flexibility of prices as time passes causes economists to utilize different macroeconomic models for different time horizons.

We have now demonstrated why price stickiness is believed to have such a large role in short-run economic fluctuations. It should be noted, however, that price stickiness moderates over time. This is true because firms that choose to use a fixed-price policy in the short run do not have to stick with that policy permanently. In particular, if unexpected changes in demand begin to look permanent, many firms will allow their prices to change so that price changes (in addition to quantity changes) can help to equalize quantities supplied with quantities demanded.

For this reason, economists speak of "sticky prices" rather than "stuck prices." Only in the very short run are prices totally inflexible. As time passes and prices are revised, the world looks much more like Figure 6.1a, in which prices are fully flexible, rather than Figure 6.1b, in which prices are totally inflexible. Indeed, the totally inflexible case shown in Figure 6.1b can be thought of as the extremely short-run response to an unexpected change in demand, while the fully flexible case shown in Figure 6.1a can be thought of as a longer-run response to an unexpected change in demand. In terms of time durations, the extreme short run can be thought of as the first few weeks and months after a demand shock, while the long run can be thought of as extending from many months to several years after a demand shock happens.

This realization is very useful in categorizing and understanding the differences between the various macroeconomic models that we will be presenting in subsequent chapters. For instance, the aggregate expenditures model presented in Chapter 11 assumes perfectly inflexible prices (and wages) and thus is a model in which prices are not just sticky but completely stuck. By contrast, the aggregate demand–aggregate supply model presented in Chapter 12 allows for flexible prices (with or without flexible wages) and is therefore useful for understanding how the economy behaves over longer periods of time.

As you study these various models, keep in mind that we need different models precisely because the economy behaves so differently depending on how much time has passed after a demand shock. The differences in behavior result from the fact that prices go from stuck in the extreme short run to fully flexible in the long run. Using different models for different stages in this process gives us much better insights into not only how economies actually behave but also how various government and central bank policies may have different effects in the short run when prices are fixed versus the long run when prices are flexible.

Where will we go from here? In the remainder of Part 3, we examine how economists measure GDP and why GDP has expanded over time. Then, we discuss the terminology of business cycles and explore the measurement and types of unemployment and inflation. At that point you will be well-prepared to examine the economic models, monetary considerations, and stabilization policies that lie at the heart of macroeconomics.

> ## QUICK REVIEW 6.5
>
> - Many commodity prices are extremely flexible and change constantly, but other prices in the economy change only very infrequently.
> - Some prices are inflexible in order to please retail customers, others because rival firms are afraid that price changes may trigger a price war.
> - Prices tend to become more flexible over time, so that as time passes, the economy can react to demand shocks with price changes as well as with output and employment changes.
> - Different macroeconomics models are required for the short run, during which prices are inflexible (so that demand shocks lead almost exclusively to output and employment changes), and for longer periods, during which prices become increasingly flexible (so that demand shocks lead more to price changes rather than output and employment changes).

SUMMARY

LO6.1 Explain why economists focus on GDP, inflation, and unemployment when assessing the health of an entire economy.

Macroeconomics studies long-run economic growth and short-run economic fluctuations.

Macroeconomists focus their attention on three key economic statistics: real GDP, unemployment, and inflation. Real GDP measures the value of all final goods and services produced in a country during a specific period of time. The unemployment rate measures the percentage of all workers who are not able to find paid employment despite being willing and able to work at currently available wages. The inflation rate measures the extent to which the overall level of prices is rising in the economy.

LO6.2 Discuss why sustained increases in living standards are a historically recent phenomenon.

Before the Industrial Revolution, living standards did not show any sustained increases over time. Economies grew, but any increase in output tended to be offset by an equally large increase in the population, so that the amount of output per person did not rise. By contrast, since the Industrial Revolution began in the late 1700s, many nations have experienced modern economic growth in which output grows faster than population—so that standards of living rise over time.

LO6.3 Identify why saving and investment are key factors in promoting rising living standards.

Macroeconomists believe that one of the keys to modern economic growth is the promotion of saving and investment (for economists, the purchase of capital goods). Investment activities increase the economy's future potential output level. But investment must be funded by saving, which is only possible if people are willing to reduce current consumption. Consequently, individuals and society face a trade-off between current consumption and future consumption since the only way to fund the investment necessary to increase future consumption is by reducing current consumption in order to gather the savings necessary to fund that investment. Banks and other financial institutions help to convert saving into investment by taking the savings generated by households and lending it to businesses that wish to make investments.

LO6.4 Describe why economists believe that "shocks" and "sticky prices" are responsible for short-run fluctuations in output and employment.

Expectations have an important effect on the economy for two reasons. First, if people and businesses are more positive about the future, they will save and invest more. Second, individuals and firms must make adjustments to shocks—situations in which expectations are unmet and the future does not turn out the way people were expecting. In particular, shocks often imply situations where the quantity supplied of a given good or service does not equal the quantity demanded of that good or service.

If prices were always flexible and capable of rapid adjustment, then dealing with situations in which quantities demanded did not equal quantities supplied would always be easy since prices could simply adjust to the market equilibrium price at which quantities demanded equal quantities supplied. Unfortunately, real-world prices are often inflexible (or "sticky") in the short run so that the only way for the economy to adjust to such situations is through changes in output levels.

Sticky prices combine with shocks to drive short-run fluctuations in output and employment. Consider a negative demand shock in which demand is unexpectedly low. Because prices are fixed, the lower-than-expected demand will result in unexpectedly slow sales. This will cause inventories to increase. If demand remains low for an extended period of time, inventory levels will become too high and firms will have to cut output and lay off workers. Thus, when prices are inflexible, the economy adjusts to unexpectedly low demand through changes in output and employment rather than through changes in prices (which are not possible when prices are inflexible).

LO6.5 Characterize the degree to which various prices in the economy are sticky.

Prices are inflexible in the short run for various reasons, two of which are discussed in this chapter. First, firms often attempt to set and maintain stable prices to please customers who like predictable prices because they make for easy planning (and who might become upset if prices were volatile). Second, a firm with just a few competitors may be reluctant to cut its price due to the fear of starting a price war, a situation in which its competitors retaliate by cutting their prices as well—thereby leaving the firm worse off than it was to begin with.

LO6.6 Explain why the greater flexibility of prices as time passes causes economists to utilize different macroeconomic models for different time horizons.

Price stickiness moderates over time. As a result, economists have found it sensible to build separate economic models for different time horizons. For instance, some models are designed to reflect the high degree of price inflexibility that occurs in the immediate short run, while other models reflect the high degree of price flexibility that occurs in the long run. The different models allow economists to have a better sense for how various government policies will affect the economy in the short run when prices are inflexible versus the long run when prices are flexible.

TERMS AND CONCEPTS

business cycle	modern economic growth	shocks
recession	saving	demand shocks
real GDP (gross domestic product)	investment	supply shocks
nominal GDP	financial investment	inventory
unemployment	economic investment	inflexible prices ("sticky prices")
inflation	expectations	flexible prices

The following and additional problems can be found in connect™
ECONOMICS

DISCUSSION QUESTIONS

1. Why do you think macroeconomists focus on just a few key statistics when trying to understand the health and trajectory of an economy? Would it be better to try to examine all possible data? **LO6.1**

2. Consider a nation in which the volume of goods and services is growing by 5 percent per year. What is the likely impact of this high rate of growth on the power and influence of its government relative to other countries experiencing slower rates of growth? What about the effect of this 5 percent growth on the nation's living standards? Will these also necessarily grow by 5 percent per year, given population growth? Why or why not? **LO6.2**

3. Did economic output start growing faster than population from the beginning of the human inhabitation of the earth? When did modern economic growth begin? Have all of the world's nations experienced the same extent of modern economic growth? **LO6.2**

4. Why is there a trade-off between the amount of consumption that people can enjoy today and the amount of consumption that they can enjoy in the future? Why can't people enjoy more of both? How does saving relate to investment and thus to economic growth? What role do banks and other financial institutions play in aiding the growth process? **LO6.3**

5. How does investment as defined by economists differ from investment as defined by the general public? What would happen to the amount of economic investment made today if firms expected the future returns to such investment to be very low? What if firms expected future returns to be very high? **LO6.3**

6. Why, in general, do shocks force people to make changes? Give at least two examples from your own experience. **LO6.4**

7. Catalog companies are committed to selling at the prices printed in their catalogs. If a catalog company finds its inventory of sweaters rising, what does that tell you about the demand for sweaters? Was it unexpectedly high, unexpectedly low, or as expected? If the company could change the price of sweaters, would it raise the price, lower the price, or keep the price the same? Given that the company cannot change the price of sweaters, consider the number of sweaters it orders each month from the company that makes its sweaters. If inventories become very high, will the catalog company increase, decrease, or keep orders the same? Given what the catalog company does with its orders, what is likely to happen to employment and output at the sweater manufacturer? **LO6.4**

8. Are all prices in the economy equally inflexible? Which ones show large amounts of short-run flexibility? Which ones show a great deal of inflexibility even over months and years? **LO6.5**

9. Why do many firms strive to maintain stable prices? **LO6.5**

10. Do prices tend to become more or less flexible as time passes? If there is a trend, how does it affect macroeconomists' choice of models? **LO6.6**

11. **LAST WORD** How do the Minsky and Austrian explanations for the causes of the Great Recession differ? Explain how the proponents of government stimulus believe that it will affect aggregate demand and employment (be specific!). How might government stimulus possibly slow rather than accelerate a recovery?

REVIEW QUESTIONS

1. An increase in _____ GDP guarantees that more goods and services are being produced by an economy. **LO6.1**
   a. Nominal.
   b. Real.

2. True or False. The term *economic investment* includes purchasing stocks, bonds, and real estate. **LO6.3**

3. If an economy has sticky prices and demand unexpectedly increases, you would expect the economy's real GDP to: **LO6.4**
   a. Increase.
   b. Decrease.
   c. Remain the same.

4. If an economy has fully flexible prices and demand unexpectedly increases, you would expect that the economy's real GDP would tend to: **LO6.4**

   a. Increase.

   b. Decrease.

   c. Remain the same.

5. If the demand for a firm's output unexpectedly decreases, you would expect that its inventory would: **LO6.4**

   a. Increase.

   b. Decrease.

   c. Remain the same.

   d. Increase or remain the same, depending on whether prices are sticky.

6. True or False. Because price stickiness only matters in the short run, economists are comfortable using just one macroeconomic model for all situations. **LO6.6**

PROBLEMS

1. Suppose that the annual rates of growth of real GDP of Econoland over a five-year period were sequentially as follows: 3 percent, 1 percent, –2 percent, 4 percent, and 5 percent. What was the average of these growth rates in Econoland over these 5 years? What term would economists use to describe what happened in year 3? If the growth rate in year 3 had been a positive 2 percent rather than a negative 2 percent, what would have been the average growth rate? **LO6.1**

2. Suppose that Glitter Gulch, a gold mining firm, increased its sales revenues on newly mined gold from $100 million to $200 million between one year and the next. Assuming that the price of gold increased by 100 percent over the same period, by what numerical amount did Glitter Gulch's real output change? If the price of gold had not changed, what would have been the change in Glitter Gulch's real output? **LO6.1**

3. A mathematical approximation called the rule of 70 tells us that the number of years that it will take something that is growing to double in size is approximately equal to the number 70 divided by its percentage rate of growth. Thus, if Mexico's real GDP per person is growing at 7 percent per year, it will take about 10 years (= 70/7) to double. Apply the rule of 70 to solve the following problem. Real GDP per person in Mexico in 2005 was about $11,000 per person, while it was about $44,000 per person in the United States. If real GDP per person in Mexico grows at the rate of 5 percent per year, about how long will it take Mexico's real GDP per person to reach the level that the United States was at in 2005? (Hint: How many times would Mexico's 2005 real GDP per person have to double to reach the United States' 2005 real GDP per person?) **LO6.2**

4. Assume that a national restaurant firm called BBQ builds 10 new restaurants at a cost of $1 million per restaurant. It outfits each restaurant with an additional $200,000 of equipment and furnishings. To help partially defray the cost of this expansion, BBQ issues and sells 200,000 shares of stock at $30 per share. What is the amount of economic investment that has resulted from BBQ's actions? How much purely financial investment took place? **LO6.3**

5. Refer to Figure 6.1b and assume that price is fixed at $37,000 and that Buzzer Auto needs 5 workers for every 1 automobile produced. If demand is D_M and Buzzer wants to perfectly match its output and sales, how many cars will Buzzer produce and how many workers will it hire? If instead, demand unexpectedly falls from D_M to D_L, how many fewer cars will Buzzer sell? How many fewer workers will it need if it decides to match production to these lower sales? **LO6.4**

Measuring Domestic Output and National Income

Learning Objectives:

LO7.1 Explain how gross domestic product (GDP) is defined and measured.

LO7.2 Describe how expenditures on goods and services can be summed to determine GDP.

LO7.3 Explain how GDP can be determined by summing up all of the incomes that were derived from producing the economy's output of goods and services.

LO7.4 Describe the relationships among GDP, net domestic product, national income, personal income, and disposable income.

LO7.5 Discuss the nature and function of a GDP price index, and describe

the difference between nominal GDP and real GDP.

LO7.6 List and explain some limitations of the GDP measure.

"Disposable Income Flat." "Personal Consumption Surges." "Investment Spending Stagnates." "GDP Up 4 Percent." These headlines, typical of those found on Yahoo! Finance or in *The Wall Street Journal*, give knowledgeable readers valuable information on the state of the economy. This chapter will help you interpret such headlines and understand the stories reported under them. Specifically, it will help you become familiar with the vocabulary and methods of national income accounting. Such accounting enables economists to measure the long-run rate of economic growth and identify the recessions and expansions associated with the economic ups and downs known as the business cycle. In addition, the terms and ideas that you encounter in this chapter will provide a needed foundation for the macroeconomic models found in subsequent chapters.

Assessing the Economy's Performance

LO7.1 Explain how gross domestic product (GDP) is defined and measured.

National income accounting measures the economy's overall performance. It does for the economy as a whole what private accounting does for the individual firm or for the individual household.

A business firm measures its flows of income and expenditures regularly—usually every 3 months or once a year. With that information in hand, the firm can gauge its economic health. If things are going well and profits are good, the accounting data can be used to explain that success. Were costs down? Was output up? Have market prices risen? If things are going badly and profits are poor, the firm may be able to identify the reason by studying the record over several accounting periods. All this information helps the firm's managers plot their future strategy.

National income accounting operates in much the same way for the economy as a whole. The Bureau of Economic Analysis (BEA), an agency of the Commerce Department, compiles the National Income and Product Accounts (NIPA) for the U.S. economy. This accounting enables economists and policymakers to:

- Assess the health of the economy by comparing levels of production at regular intervals.
- Track the long-run course of the economy to see whether it has grown, been constant, or declined.
- Formulate policies that will safeguard and improve the economy's health.

Gross Domestic Product

The primary measure of the economy's performance is its annual total output of goods and services or, as it is called, its *aggregate output.* There are several ways to measure aggregate output depending upon how one wishes to define "an economy." For instance, should the value of the cars produced at a Toyota plant in Ohio count as part of the output of the U.S. economy because they are made within the United States or as part of the Japanese economy

TABLE 7.1 Comparing Heterogeneous Output by Using Money Prices

Year	Annual Output	Market Value
1	3 sofas and 2 computers	3 at $500 + 2 at $2,000 = $5,500
2	2 sofas and 3 computers	2 at $500 + 3 at $2,000 = $7,000

because Toyota is a Japanese company? As mentioned in Chapter 6, **gross domestic product (GDP)** defines aggregate output as the dollar value of all final goods and services produced within the borders of a country during a specific period of time, typically a year. Under this definition, the value of the cars produced at the Toyota factory in Ohio clearly count as part of U.S. aggregate output rather than Japanese aggregate output because the cars are made within the borders of the United States.[1]

A Monetary Measure

By necessity, GDP is a *monetary measure.* To see why, suppose that the economy produces three sofas and two computers in year 1 and two sofas and three computers in year 2. In which year is output greater? We can't answer that question until we attach a price tag to each of the two products to indicate how society evaluates their relative worth.

That's what GDP does. It measures the value of output in monetary terms. Without such a measure we would have no way of comparing the relative values of the vast number of goods and services produced in different years. In Table 7.1 the price of sofas is $500 and the price of computers is $2,000. GDP would gauge the output of year 2 ($7,000) as greater than the output of year 1 ($5,500) because society places a higher monetary value on the output of year 2. Society is willing to pay $1,500 more for the combination of goods produced in year 2 than for the combination of goods produced in year 1.

---

[1]In contrast to GDP, U.S. gross *national* product (GNP) consists of the total value of all the final goods and services produced by American-supplied resources, whether those goods and services are produced within the borders of the United States or abroad. The U.S. switched from GNP to GDP accounting in 1992 to match the type of accounting used by other countries worldwide.

Avoiding Multiple Counting

To measure aggregate output accurately, all goods and services produced in a particular year must be counted once and only once. Because most products go through a series of production stages before they reach the market, some of their components are bought and sold many times. To avoid counting those components each time, GDP includes only the market value of *final goods* and ignores *intermediate goods* altogether.

Intermediate goods are products that are purchased for resale or further processing or manufacturing. **Final goods** are products that are purchased by their end users. Crude oil is an intermediate good; gasoline used for personal transportation is a final good. Steel beams are intermediate goods; completed high-rise apartments are final goods. Lettuce, carrots, and vinegar in restaurant salads are intermediate goods; restaurant salads are final goods. Other examples of final goods are sunglasses bought by consumers, assembly machinery purchased by businesses, surveillance satellites bought by government, and smart phones purchased by foreign buyers.

Why is the value of final goods included in GDP but the value of intermediate goods excluded? Because the value of final goods already includes the value of all the intermediate goods that were used in producing them. Including the value of intermediate goods would amount to **multiple counting**, and that would distort the value of GDP.

To see why, suppose that five stages are needed to manufacture a wool coat and get it to the consumer—the final user. Table 7.2 shows that firm A, a sheep ranch, sells $120 worth of wool to firm B, a wool processor. Firm A pays out the $120 in wages, rent, interest, and profit. Firm B processes the wool and sells it to firm C, a coat manufacturer, for $180. What does firm B do with the $180 it receives? It pays $120 to firm A for the wool and uses the remaining $60 to pay wages, rent,

interest, and profit for the resources used in processing the wool. Firm C, the manufacturer, sells the coat to firm D, a wholesaler, which sells it to firm E, a retailer. Then at last a consumer, the final user, comes in and buys the coat for $350.

How much of these amounts should we include in GDP to account for the production of the coat? Just $350, the value of the final product. The $350 includes all the intermediate transactions leading up to the product's final sale. Including the sum of all the intermediate sales, $1,140, in GDP would amount to multiple counting. The production and sale of the final coat generated just $350 of output, not $1,140.

Alternatively, we could avoid multiple counting by measuring and cumulating only the *value added* at each stage. **Value added** is the market value of a firm's output *less* the value of the inputs the firm has bought from others. At each stage, the difference between what a firm pays for inputs and what it receives from selling the product made from those inputs is paid out as wages, rent, interest, and profit. Column 3 of Table 7.2 shows that the value added by firm B is $60, the difference between the $180 value of its output and the $120 it paid for the input from firm A. We find the total value of the coat by adding together all the values added by the five firms. Similarly, by calculating and summing the values added to all the goods and services produced by all firms in the economy, we can find the market value of the economy's total output—its GDP.

GDP Excludes Nonproduction Transactions

Although many monetary transactions in the economy involve final goods and services, many others do not. These nonproduction transactions must be excluded from GDP because they have nothing to do with the generation of final goods. *Nonproduction transactions* are

TABLE 7.2 Value Added in a Five-Stage Production Process

(1) Stage of Production	(2) Sales Value of Materials or Product	(3) Value Added
	$ 0	
Firm A, sheep ranch	120	$120 (= $120 − $ 0)
Firm B, wool processor	180	60 (= 180 − 120)
Firm C, coat manufacturer	220	40 (= 220 − 180)
Firm D, clothing wholesaler	270	50 (= 270 − 220)
Firm E, retail clothier	**350**	80 (= 350 − 270)
Total sales values	$1,140	
Value added (total income)		**$350**

of two types: purely financial transactions and second-hand sales.

Financial Transactions Purely financial transactions include the following:

- *Public transfer payments* These are the social security payments, welfare payments, and veterans' payments that the government makes directly to households. Since the recipients contribute nothing to *current production* in return, to include such payments in GDP would be to overstate the year's output.

- *Private transfer payments* Such payments include, for example, the money that parents give children or the cash gifts given during the holidays. They produce no output. They simply transfer funds from one private individual to another and consequently do not enter into GDP.

- *Stock market transactions* The buying and selling of stocks (and bonds) is just a matter of swapping bits of paper. Stock market transactions create nothing in the way of current production and are not included in GDP. Payments for the services provided by a stockbroker *are* included, however, because their services are currently provided and are thus a part of the economy's current output of goods and services.

Secondhand Sales Secondhand sales contribute nothing to current production and for that reason are excluded from GDP. Suppose you sell your 2005 Ford Mustang to a friend; that transaction would be ignored in reckoning this year's GDP because it generates no current production. The same would be true if you sold a brand-new Mustang to a neighbor a week after you purchased it.

Two Ways of Looking at GDP: Spending and Income

Let's look again at how the market value of total output—or of any single unit of total output—is measured. Given the data listed in Table 7.2, how can we measure the market value of a coat?

One way is to see how much the final user paid for it. That will tell us the market value of the final product. Or we can add up the entire wage, rental, interest, and profit incomes that were created in producing the coat. The second approach is the value-added technique used in Table 7.2.

The final-product approach and the value-added approach are two ways of looking at the same thing. What is spent on making a product is income to those who helped make it. If $350 is spent on manufacturing a coat, then $350 is the total income derived from its production.

We can look at GDP in the same two ways. We can view GDP as the sum of all the money spent in buying it. That is the *output approach*, or **expenditures approach.** Or we can view GDP in terms of the income derived or created from producing it. That is the *earnings* or *allocations approach*, or the **income approach.**

As illustrated in Figure 7.1, we can determine GDP for a particular year either by adding up all that was spent to buy total output or by adding up all the money that was derived as income from its production. Buying (spending money) and selling (receiving income) are two aspects of the same transaction. On the expenditures side of GDP, all final goods produced by the economy are bought either by three domestic sectors (households, businesses, and government) or by foreign buyers. On the income side (once certain statistical adjustments are made), the

FIGURE 7.1 The expenditures and income approaches to GDP. There are two general approaches to measuring gross domestic product. We can determine GDP as the value of output by summing all expenditures on that output. Alternatively, with some modifications, we can determine GDP by adding up all the components of income arising from the production of that output.

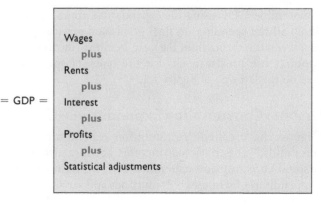

Expenditures, or output, approach

Income, or allocations, approach

TABLE 7.3 Accounting Statement for the U.S. Economy, 2012 (in Billions)*

Receipts: Expenditures Approach		Allocations: Income Approach	
Sum of:		Sum of:	
Personal consumption expenditures (C)	$11,150	Compensation of employees	$8,612
Gross private domestic investment (I_g)	2,475	Rents	541
Government purchases (G)	3,167	Interest	440
Net exports (X_n)	−547	Proprietors' income	1,225
		Corporate profits	2,031
		Taxes on production and imports	1,123
		Equals:	
		National income	**$13,972**
		National income	$13,972
		Less: Net foreign factor income	253
		Plus: Consumption of fixed capital	2,543
		Plus: Statistical discrepancy	−17
Equals:		*Equals:*	
Gross domestic product	**$16,245**	**Gross domestic product**	**$16,245**

*Some of the items in the Allocations column combine related categories that appear in the more detailed accounts. All data are subject to government revision.

Source: Bureau of Economic Analysis, **www.bea.gov**.

total receipts acquired from the sale of that total output are allocated to the suppliers of resources as wage, rent, interest, and profit.

Table 7.3 shows U.S. GDP for the year 2012 totaled up using both the expenditures approach (on the left side) and the income approach (on the right side). As you would expect, both methods reach the same conclusion: U.S. GDP in 2012 was $16,245 billion.

We will now go through both approaches in detail. Doing so will help you better understand both methods and, in particular, why the income side of Table 7.3 looks substantially more complicated than the income side of Figure 7.1.

The Expenditures Approach

LO7.2 Describe how expenditures on goods and services can be summed to determine GDP.

To determine GDP using the expenditures approach, we add up all the spending on final goods and services that has taken place throughout the year. National-income accountants use precise terms for the types of spending listed on the left side of Figure 7.1.

Personal Consumption Expenditures (C)

What we have called "consumption expenditures by households," the national income accountants call **personal consumption expenditures.** This term covers all expenditures by households on goods and services.

In a typical year, roughly 10 percent of these personal consumption expenditures are on **durable goods**—products that have expected lives of three years or more. Such goods include new automobiles, furniture, and refrigerators. Another 30 percent are on **nondurable goods**—products with less than three years of expected life. Included are goods like food, clothing, and gasoline. About 60 percent of personal consumption expenditures are on **services**—the work done by lawyers, hair stylists, doctors, mechanics, and other service providers. Because of this high percentage, economists sometimes refer to the U.S. economy as a *service economy*. National income accountants combine the household spending on durable goods, nondurable goods, and services and use the symbol C to designate the personal consumption expenditures component of GDP.

Gross Private Domestic Investment (I_g)

Under the heading **gross private domestic investment,** the accountants include the following items:

- All final purchases of machinery, equipment, and tools by business enterprises.
- All construction.
- Changes in inventories.
- Money spent on research and development (R&D) or for the creation of new works of art, music, writing, film, and so on.

Notice that this list, except for the first item, includes more than we have meant by "investment" so far. The second item includes residential construction as well as the construction of new factories, warehouses, and stores. Why do the accountants regard residential construction as investment rather than consumption? Because apartment buildings and houses, like factories and stores, earn income when they are rented or leased. Owner-occupied houses are treated as investment goods because they *could be* rented to bring in an income return. So the national income accountants treat all residential construction as investment.

Increases in inventories (unsold goods) are considered to be investment because they represent, in effect, "unconsumed output." For economists, all new output that is not consumed is, by definition, capital. An increase in inventories is an addition (although perhaps temporary) to the stock of capital goods, and such additions are precisely how we define investment.

Starting in 2013, the NIPA accountants who compile U.S. GDP statistics began to include expenditures on R&D as well as money spent to develop new works of writing, art, music, and software as a form of investment. They did so because a country's stock of "capital goods" useful in producing output can be thought of as including not only tangible pieces of physical capital like fiber optic networks and factories but also useful ideas that increase the economy's ability to produce goods and services.

Software is a great example, as it is merely sets of instructions for telling computers what to do. But without those instructions, computers would be useless. So spending on software as well as on R&D and other intellectual activities that improve the economy's stock of "know-how" are now counted as investment.

To make it possible to compare GDP numbers across time, the accountants have gone back and applied the new, more comprehensive definition of investment all the way back to 1929. The numbers for U.S. GDP for the year 2012 that are used in this chapter incorporate the revised definition of investment.

Positive and Negative Changes in Inventories

We need to look at changes in inventories more closely. Inventories can either increase or decrease over some period. Suppose they increased by $10 billion between December 31, 2012, and December 31, 2013. Therefore, in 2013 the economy produced $10 billion more output than people purchased. We need to count all output produced in 2013 as part of that year's GDP, even though some of it remained unsold at the end of the year. This is accomplished by including the $10 billion increase in inventories as investment in 2013. That way the expenditures in 2013 will correctly measure the output produced that year.

Alternatively, suppose that inventories decreased by $10 billion in 2013. This "drawing down of inventories" means that the economy sold $10 billion more of output in 2013 than it produced that year. It did this by selling goods produced in prior years—goods already counted as GDP in those years. Unless corrected, expenditures in 2013 will overstate GDP for 2013. So in 2013 we consider the $10 billion decline in inventories as "negative investment" and subtract it from total investment that year. Thus, expenditures in 2013 will correctly measure the output produced in 2013.

Noninvestment Transactions So much for what investment *is*. You also need to know what it *isn't*. For economists and NIPA accountants, investment does *not* include noninvestment transactions such as the transfer of paper assets (stocks, bonds) or the resale of tangible assets (houses, jewelry, boats). Such financial transactions merely transfer the ownership of existing assets. The investment in the GDP accounts is economic investment—the creation of *new* capital assets. The mere transfer (sale) of claims to existing capital goods does not produce new capital goods. Therefore such transactions (so-called financial investments) are not included as investment in the GDP accounts.

Gross Investment versus Net Investment As we have seen, the category gross private domestic investment includes (1) all final purchases of machinery, equipment, and tools; (2) all construction; (3) changes in inventories; and (4) spending on R&D and other activities that expand the economy's stock of technology and know-how. The words "private" and "domestic" mean that we are speaking of spending by private businesses, not by government (public) agencies, and that the investment is taking place inside the country, not abroad.

The word "gross" means that we are referring to *all* investment goods—both those that replace machinery, equipment, and buildings that were used up (worn out or made obsolete) in producing the current year's output and any net additions to the economy's stock of capital. Gross investment includes investment in replacement capital *and* in added capital.

In contrast, **net private domestic investment** includes *only* investment in the form of added capital. The amount of capital that is used up over the course of a year is called *depreciation*. So

Net investment = gross investment − depreciation

FIGURE 7.2 Gross investment, depreciation, net investment, and the stock of capital. When gross investment exceeds depreciation during a year, net investment occurs. This net investment expands the stock of private capital from the beginning of the year to the end of the year by the amount of the net investment. Other things equal, the economy's production capacity expands.

In typical years, gross investment exceeds depreciation. Thus net investment is positive and the nation's stock of capital rises by the amount of net investment. As illustrated in Figure 7.2, the stock of capital at the end of the year exceeds the stock of capital at the beginning of the year by the amount of net investment.

Gross investment need not always exceed depreciation, however. When gross investment and depreciation *are equal*, net investment is zero and there is no change in the size of the capital stock. When gross investment *is less than* depreciation, net investment is negative. The economy then is *disinvesting*—using up more capital than it is producing—and the nation's stock of capital shrinks. That happened in the Great Depression of the 1930s.

National income accountants use the symbol I for private domestic investment spending. To differentiate between gross investment and net investment, they add either the subscript g or the subscript n. But it is gross investment, I_g, that they use when tallying up GDP.

Government Purchases (G)

The third category of expenditures in the national income accounts is **government purchases,** officially labeled "government consumption expenditures and gross investment." These expenditures have three components: (1) expenditures for goods and services that government consumes in providing public services; (2) expenditures for *publicly owned capital* such as schools and highways, which have long lifetimes; and (3) government expenditures on R&D and other activities that increase the economy's stock of know-how. Government purchases (federal, state, and local) include all government expenditures on final goods and all direct purchases of resources, including labor. It does *not* include government transfer payments because, as we have seen, they merely transfer government receipts to certain households and generate no production of any sort. National income accountants use the symbol G to signify government purchases.

Net Exports (X_n)

International trade transactions are a significant item in national income accounting. But when calculating U.S. GDP, we must keep in mind that we want to total up only those expenditures that are used to purchase goods and services produced *within the borders of the United States*. Thus, we must add in the value of exports, X, since exports are by definition goods and services produced within the borders of the United States. Don't be confused by the fact that the expenditures made to buy our exports are made by foreigners. The definition of GDP does not care about *who* is making expenditures on U.S.-made goods and services—only that the goods and services that they buy are made within the borders of the United States. Thus, foreign spending on our exports *must* be included in GDP.

At this point, you might incorrectly think that GDP should be equal to the sum of $C + I_g + G + X$. But this sum overstates GDP. The problem is that, once again, we must consider only expenditures made on *domestically produced* goods and services. As it stands, C, I_g, and G count expenditures on consumption, investment, and government purchases *regardless* of where those goods and services are made. Crucially, not all of the C, I_g, or G expenditures are for domestically produced goods and services. Some of the expenditures are for imports— goods and services produced outside of the United States. Because we wish to count *only* the part of C, I_g, and G that goes to purchasing domestically produced goods and services, we must subtract the spending that goes to imports, M. That subtraction yields the correct formula for calculating gross domestic product: GDP = $C + I_g + G + X - M$.

Accountants simplify this formula for GDP by defining **net exports,** X_n, to be equal to exports minus imports:

$$\text{Net exports } (X_n) = \text{exports } (X) - \text{imports } (M)$$

CONSIDER THIS . . .

Stocks versus Flows

An analogy of a reservoir is helpful in thinking about a nation's capital stock, investment, and depreciation. Picture a reservoir that has water flow-ing in from a river and flowing out from an outlet after it passes through turbines. The volume of water in the reservoir *at any particular point in time* is a "stock." In contrast, the inflow from the river and outflow from the outlet are "flows."

The volume or stock of water in the reservoir will rise if the weekly inflow exceeds the weekly outflow. It will fall if the inflow is less than the outflow. And it will remain constant if the two flows are equal.

Now let's apply this analogy to the stock of capital, gross investment, and depreciation. The stock of capital is the total capital in place at any point in time and is analogous to the level of water in the reservoir. Changes in this capital stock over some period, for example, one year, depend on *gross investment* and *depreciation*. Gross investment (analogous to the reservoir inflow) is an addition of capital goods and therefore adds to the stock of capital, while depreciation (analogous to the reservoir outflow) is the using up of capital and thus sub-tracts from the capital stock. The capital stock increases when gross investment exceeds depreciation, declines when gross investment is less than depreciation, and remains the same when gross investment and depreciation are equal.

Alternatively, the stock of capital increases when *net investment* (gross investment *minus* depreciation) is positive. When net investment is negative, the stock of capital de-clines, and when net investment is zero, the stock of capital remains constant.

Using this definition of net exports, the formula for gross domestic product simplifies to,

$$\text{GDP} = C + I_g + G + X_n$$

The left side of Table 7.3 shows that in 2012 Americans spent $560 billion more on imports than foreigners spent on U.S. exports. That is, net exports in 2012 were a *minus* $560 billion.

Putting It All Together: GDP = C + I_g + G + X_n

Taken together, the four categories of expenditures pro-vide a measure of the market value of a specific year's total

GLOBAL PERSPECTIVE 7.1

Comparative GDPs in Trillions of U.S. Dollars, Selected Nations, 2011

The United States, China, and Japan have the world's highest GDPs. The GDP data charted below have been converted to U.S. dollars via international exchange rates.

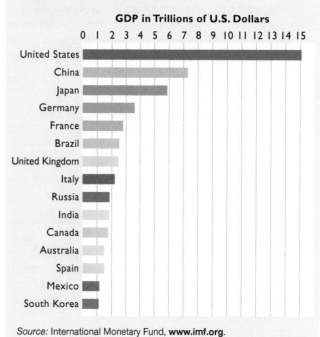

Source: International Monetary Fund, **www.imf.org**.

output—its GDP. For the United States in 2012, the left side of Table 7.3 indicates that

$$\text{GDP} = \$11,150 + \$2,475 + \$3,167 - 547 \text{ billion}$$

Global Perspective 7.1 lists the GDPs of several countries. The values of GDP are converted to dollars using international exchange rates.

The Income Approach

LO7.3 Explain how GDP can be determined by summing up all of the incomes that were derived from producing the economy's output of goods and services.

The right side of Table 7.3 shows how 2012's expenditures of $16,245 billion were allocated as income to those re-sponsible for producing the output. It would be simple if we could say that the entire amount of expenditures flowed back to them in the form of wages, rent, interest, and profit. But some expenditures flow to other recipients (such as the government) or to other uses (such as paying to replace the capital goods that have worn out while producing this year's

GDP). These must be accounted for to balance the expenditures and income sides of the overall account. We will begin by looking at the items that make up *national income*.

Compensation of Employees

By far the largest share of national income—$8,612 billion in 2012—was paid as wages and salaries by business and government to their employees. That figure also includes wage and salary supplements, in particular, payments by employers into social insurance and into a variety of private pension, health, and welfare funds for workers.

Rents

Rents consist of the income received by the households and businesses that supply property resources. They include the monthly payments tenants make to landlords and the lease payments corporations pay for the use of office space. The figure used in the national accounts is *net* rent—gross rental income minus depreciation of the rental property.

Interest

Interest consists of the money paid by private businesses to the suppliers of loans used to purchase capital. It also includes such items as the interest households receive on savings deposits, certificates of deposit (CDs), and corporate bonds.

Proprietors' Income

What we have loosely termed "profits" is broken down by the national income accountants into two accounts: proprietors' income, which consists of the net income of sole proprietorships, partnerships, and other unincorporated businesses; and corporate profits. Proprietors' income flows to the proprietors.

Corporate Profits

Corporate profits are the earnings of corporations. National income accountants subdivide corporate profits into three categories:

- *Corporate income taxes* These taxes are levied on corporations' profits. They flow to the government.
- *Dividends* These are the part of after-tax profits that corporations choose to pay out, or distribute, to their stockholders. They thus flow to households—the ultimate owners of all corporations.
- *Undistributed corporate profits* Any after-tax profits that are not distributed to shareholders are saved, or

retained, by corporations to be invested later in new plants and equipment. Undistributed corporate profits are also called *retained earnings*.

Taxes on Production and Imports

The account called **taxes on production and imports** includes general sales taxes, excise taxes, business property taxes, license fees, and customs duties. Why do national income accountants add these indirect business taxes to wages, rent, interest, and profits in determining national income? The answer is, "to account for expenditures that are diverted to the government." Consider an item that would otherwise sell for $1 but costs $1.05 because the government has imposed a 5 percent sales tax. When this item is purchased, consumers will expend $1.05 to buy it. But only $1 will go to the seller (who will then distribute it as income in the form of wages, rent, interest, and profit in order to compensate resource providers). The remaining 5 cents will flow as revenue to the government. The GDP accountants handle the extra 5 cents by placing it into the category called "Taxes on Production and Imports" and loosely consider it to be "income" to government.

From National Income to GDP

We have just shown that expenditures on final goods and services flow either as income to private citizens or as "income" to government. As a result, **national income** is the total of all sources of private income (employee compensation, rents, interest, proprietors' income, and corporate profits) plus government revenue from taxes on production and imports. National income is all the income that flows to American-supplied resources, whether here or abroad, plus taxes on production and imports. But notice that the figure for national income shown in Table 7.3—$13,972 billion—is less than GDP as reckoned by the expenditures approach shown on the left side of the table. The two sides of the accounting statement are brought into balance by subtracting one item from national income and adding two others.

Net Foreign Factor Income First, we need to make a slight adjustment in "national" income versus "domestic" income. National income includes the total income of Americans, whether it was earned in the United States or abroad. But GDP is a measure of *domestic* output—total output produced within the United States regardless of the nationality of those who provide the resources. So in moving from national income to GDP, we must take out the income Americans gain from supplying resources abroad and add in the income that foreigners gain by supplying resources in the United States. That process provides *net foreign factor income*. In 2012, net foreign factor income was $253 billion, meaning that American-owned resources earned $253 billion more in other countries than foreign-owned resources earned in the United States. Because this $253 billion is earnings of Americans, it is included in U.S. national income. But this income is not part of U.S. domestic income because it reflects earnings from output produced in other nations. It is part of those nations' domestic income, derived from production of their domestic output. Thus, we subtract net foreign factor income from U.S. national income to stay on the correct path to use the income approach to determine the value of *U.S. domestic output* (output produced within U.S. borders).

Consumption of Fixed Capital Next, we must recognize that the useful lives of private capital equipment (such as bakery ovens or automobile assembly lines) extend far beyond the year in which they were produced. To avoid understating profit and income in the year of purchase and to avoid overstating profit and income in succeeding years, the cost of such capital must be allocated over its lifetime. The amount allocated is an estimate of how much of the capital is being used up each year. It is called *depreciation*. Accounting for depreciation results in a more accurate statement of profit and income for the economy each year. Publicly owned capital, such as courthouses and bridges, also requires a depreciation allowance in the national income accounts.

The huge depreciation charge made against private and publicly owned capital each year is called **consumption of fixed capital** because it is the allowance for capital that has been "consumed" in producing the year's GDP. It is the portion of GDP that is set aside to pay for the ultimate replacement of those capital goods.

The money allocated to consumption of fixed capital (the depreciation allowance) is a cost of production and thus included in the gross value of output. But this money is not available for other purposes, and, unlike other costs of production, it does not add to anyone's income. So it is not included in national income. We must therefore add it to national income to achieve balance with the economy's expenditures.

Statistical Discrepancy As you know, it should be possible to calculate GDP either by totaling up expenditures or by summing up incomes. Either method should give the same result.

In practice, however, it is not possible for NIPA accountants to measure every input into either set of calculations with total precision. Difficulties arise due to a wide range of factors including people misreporting their in-

comes on tax returns and the difficulty involved with accurately estimating depreciation. As a result, the GDP number produced by the income method always differs by a small percentage from the GDP number produced by the expenditures method.

To account for this difference, NIPA accountants add a statistical discrepancy to national income. The addition of that number equalizes the GDP totals produced by the two methods. In 2012 the discrepancy value was negative $17 billion, or less than one-half of one percent of GDP.

Table 7.3 summarizes both the expenditures approach and the income approach to GDP. The left side shows how much the U.S. economy produced in 2012 by showing how much was spent to purchase that year's output of goods and services. The right side shows how those expenditures were allocated either as income to individuals, as revenue to the government, or to other uses such as paying for the replacement of depreciated capital.

QUICK REVIEW 7.1

- Gross domestic product (GDP) is a measure of the total market value of all final goods and services produced by the economy in a specific year.
- The expenditures approach to GDP sums the total spending on final goods and services: GDP = $C + I_g + G + X_n$.
- The economy's stock of private capital expands when net investment is positive; stays constant when net investment is zero; and declines when net investment is negative.
- The income approach to GDP sums compensation to employees, rent, interest, proprietors' income, corporate profits, and taxes on production and imports to obtain national income, and then subtracts net foreign factor income and adds consumption of fixed capital and a statistical discrepancy to obtain GDP.

Other National Accounts

LO7.4 Describe the relationships among GDP, net domestic product, national income, personal income, and disposable income.

Several other national accounts provide additional useful information about the economy's performance. We can derive these accounts by making various adjustments to GDP.

Net Domestic Product

As a measure of total output, GDP does not make allowances for replacing the capital goods used up in each year's production. As a result, it does not tell us how much new output was available for consumption and for additions to the stock of capital. To determine that, we must subtract from GDP the capital that was consumed in producing the GDP and that had to be replaced. That is, we need to subtract consumption of fixed capital (depreciation) from GDP. The result is a measure of **net domestic product (NDP):**

$$\text{NDP} = \text{GDP} - \text{consumption of fixed capital (depreciation)}$$

For the United States in 2012:

	Billions
Gross domestic product	$16,245
Less: Consumption of fixed capital	2,543
Equals: Net domestic product	$13,702

NDP is simply GDP adjusted for depreciation. It measures the total annual output that the entire economy—households, businesses, government, and foreigners—can consume without impairing its capacity to produce in ensuing years.

National Income

Sometimes it is useful to know how much Americans earned for their contributions of land, labor, capital, and entrepreneurial talent. Recall that U.S. national income (NI) includes all income earned through the use of American-owned resources, whether they are located at home or abroad. It also includes taxes on production and imports. To derive NI from NDP, we must subtract the aforementioned statistical discrepancy from NDP and add net foreign factor income, since the latter is income earned by Americans overseas minus income earned by foreigners in the United States.

For the United States in 2012:

	Billions
Net domestic product	$13,702
Less: Statistical discrepancy	−17
Plus: Net foreign factor income	253
Equals: National income	$13,972

We know, too, that we can calculate national income through the income approach by simply adding up employee compensation, rent, interest, proprietors' income, corporate profit, and taxes on production and imports.

Personal Income

Personal income (PI) includes all income received, whether earned or unearned. It is likely to differ from national income (income earned) because some income earned—taxes on production and imports, Social Security taxes (payroll taxes), corporate income taxes, and undistributed corporate profits—is not received by households. Conversely, some income received—such as Social Security payments, unemployment compensation payments, welfare payments, disability and education payments to veterans, and private pension payments—is not earned. These transfer payments must be added to obtain PI.

In moving from national income to personal income, we must subtract the income that is earned but not received and add the income that is received but not earned. For the United States in 2012:

	Billions
National income	$13,972
Less: Taxes on production and imports	1,066
Less: Social Security contributions	951
Less: Corporate income taxes	435
Less: Undistributed corporate profits	542
Plus: Transfer payments	2,766*
Equals: Personal income	$13,744

*Includes statistical discrepancy and rounding error.

Disposable Income

Disposable income (DI) is personal income less personal taxes. Personal taxes include personal income taxes, personal property taxes, and inheritance taxes. Disposable income is the amount of income that households have left over after paying their personal taxes. They are free to divide that income between consumption (*C*) and saving (*S*):

WORKED PROBLEMS

W7.1

Measuring output and income

$$\text{DI} = C + S$$

For the United States in 2012:

	Billions
Personal income	$13,744
Less: Personal taxes	1,498
Equals: Disposable income	$12,246

Table 7.4 summarizes the relationships among GDP, NDP, NI, PI, and DI.

TABLE 7.4 The Relationship between GDP, NDP, NI, PI, and DI in the United States, 2012*

	Billions
Gross domestic product (GDP)	$16,245
Less: Consumption of fixed capital	2,543
Equals: Net domestic product	$13,702
Net domestic product (NDP)	$13,702
Less: Statistical discrepancy	−17
Plus: Net foreign factor income	253
Equals: National income (NI)	$13,972
National income (NI)	$13,972
Less: Taxes on production and imports	1,066
Less: Social Security contributions	951
Less: Corporate income taxes	435
Less: Undistributed corporate profits	542
Plus: Transfer payments	2,766
Equals: Personal income (PI)	$13,744
Personal income (PI)	$13,744
Less: Personal taxes	1,498
Equals: Disposable income (DI)	$12,246

*Some of the items combine categories that appear in the more detailed accounts.
Source: Bureau of Economic Analysis, **www.bea.gov**.

The Circular Flow Revisited

Figure 7.3 is an elaborate flow diagram that shows the economy's four main sectors along with the flows of expenditures and allocations that determine GDP, NDP, NI, and PI. The orange arrows represent the spending flows— $C + I_g + G + X_n$—that together measure gross domestic product. To the right of the GDP rectangle are green arrows that show first the allocations of GDP and then the adjustments needed to derive NDP, NI, PI, and DI.

The diagram illustrates the adjustments necessary to determine each of the national income accounts. For example, net domestic product is smaller than GDP because consumption of fixed capital flows away from GDP in determining NDP. Also, disposable income is smaller than personal income because personal taxes flow away from PI (to government) in deriving DI.

Note the three domestic sectors of the economy: households, government, and businesses. The household sector has an inflow of disposable income and outflows of consumption spending and savings. The government sector has an inflow of revenue in the form of types of taxes and an outflow of government disbursements in the form of purchases and transfers. The business sector has inflows from three major sources of funds for business investment and an outflow of investment expenditures.

Also, take a look at the foreign sector (all other countries) in the flow diagram. Spending by foreigners on U.S. exports adds to U.S. GDP, but some of U.S. consumption, government, and investment expenditures buy imported products. The flow from foreign markets shows that we handle this complication by calculating net exports (U.S. exports minus U.S. imports). The net export flow may be a positive or negative amount, adding to or subtracting from U.S. GDP.

Finally, you need to be aware that the flows shown in Figure 7.3 are dynamic entities and generally expand in size over time as the economy grows. But not always! Case in point: The Great Recession of 2007–2009—first discussed in the Consider This box on page 143—produced a pronounced slowing of the main spending and income flows. Specifically, U.S. businesses greatly reduced investment expenditures and households initially reduced personal consumption expenditures. Consequently, GDP, NDP, NI, and PI all significantly declined.

QUICK REVIEW 7.2

- Net domestic product (NDP) is the market value of GDP minus consumption of fixed capital (depreciation).
- National income (NI) is all income earned through the use of American-owned resources, whether located at home or abroad. NI also includes taxes on production and imports.
- Personal income (PI) is all income received by households, whether earned or not.
- Disposable income (DI) is all income received by households minus personal taxes.

Nominal GDP versus Real GDP

LO7.5 Discuss the nature and function of a GDP price index, and describe the difference between nominal GDP and real GDP.

Recall that GDP is a measure of the market or money value of all final goods and services produced by the economy in a given year. We use money or nominal values as a common denominator to sum that heterogeneous output into a meaningful total. But, as alluded to in Chapter 6, that creates a problem: How can we compare the market values of GDP from year to year if the value of money itself changes in response to inflation (rising prices) or deflation (falling prices)? After all, we determine the value of GDP by multiplying total output by market prices.

Whether there is a 5 percent increase in output with no change in prices or a 5 percent increase in prices with no change in output, the change in the value of GDP will

FIGURE 7.3 **U.S. domestic output and the flows of expenditure and income.** This figure is an elaborate circular flow diagram that fits the expenditures and allocations sides of GDP to one another. The expenditures flows are shown in orange; the allocations or income flows are shown in green. You should trace through the income and expenditures flows, relating them to the five basic national income accounting measures.

be the same. And yet it is the *quantity* of goods and services that get produced and distributed to households that affects our standard of living, not the price of those goods and services. For instance, the McDonald's hamburger that sold for 95 cents in 2013 yields the same satisfaction as a nearly identical McDonald's hamburger that sold for 18 cents in 1967.

The way around this problem is to *deflate* GDP when prices rise and to *inflate* GDP when prices fall. These adjustments give us a measure of GDP for various years as if the value of the dollar had always been the same as it was in some reference year. A GDP based on the prices that prevailed when the output was produced is called unadjusted GDP, or **nominal GDP**. A GDP that has been deflated or inflated to reflect changes in the price level is called adjusted GDP, or **real GDP**.

Adjustment Process in a One-Product Economy

There are two ways we can adjust nominal GDP to reflect price changes. For simplicity, let's assume that the economy produces only one good, pizza, in the amounts indicated in Table 7.5 for years 1, 2, and 3. Suppose that we gather revenue data directly from the financial reports of the economy's pizza businesses to measure nominal GDP in various years. After completing our effort, we will have determined nominal GDP for each year, as shown in column 4 of Table 7.5. We will have no way of knowing to what extent changes in price and/or changes in quantity of output have accounted for the increases or decreases in nominal GDP that we observe.

GDP Price Index How can we determine real GDP in our pizza economy? One way is to assemble data on the price changes that occurred over various years (column 2) and use them to establish an overall price index for the entire period. Then we can use the index in each year to adjust nominal GDP to real GDP for that year.

In the actual economy, a **price index** is a measure of the price of a specified collection of goods and services, called a "market basket," in a given year as compared to the price of an identical (or highly similar) collection of goods and services in a reference year. That point of reference, or benchmark, is known as the base period, **base year**, or, simply, the reference year. More formally,

$$\begin{array}{c} \text{Price} \\ \text{index} \\ \text{in given} \\ \text{year} \end{array} = \dfrac{\begin{array}{c}\text{price of market basket} \\ \text{in specific year}\end{array}}{\begin{array}{c}\text{price of same market} \\ \text{basket in base year}\end{array}} \times 100 \quad (1)$$

By convention, the price ratio between a given year and the base year is multiplied by 100 to facilitate computation. For example, a price ratio of 2/1 (= 2) is expressed as a price index of 200. A price ratio of 1/3 (= 0.33) is expressed as a price index of 33.

In our pizza-only example, of course, our market basket consists of only one product. Column 2 of Table 7.5 reveals that the price of pizza was $10 in year 1, $20 in year 2, $25 in year 3, and so on. Let's select year 1 as our base year. Now we can express the successive prices of the contents of our market basket in, say, years 2 and 3 as compared to the price of the market basket in year 1:

$$\text{Price index, year 2} = \frac{\$20}{\$10} \times 100 = 200$$

$$\text{Price index, year 3} = \frac{\$25}{\$10} \times 100 = 250$$

For year 1 the index has to be 100, since that year and the base year are identical.

The index numbers tell us that the price of pizza rose from year 1 to year 2 by 100 percent {= [(200 − 100)/100] × 100} and from year 1 to year 3 by 150 percent {= [(250 − 100)/100] × 100}.

Dividing Nominal GDP by the Price Index We can now use the index numbers shown in column 3 to deflate

TABLE 7.5 Calculating Real GDP (Base Year = Year 1)

Year	(1) Units of Output	(2) Price of Pizza per Unit	(3) Price Index (Year 1 = 100)	(4) Unadjusted, or Nominal, GDP, (1) × (2)	(5) Adjusted, or Real, GDP
1	5	$10	100	$ 50	$50
2	7	20	200	140	70
3	8	25	250	200	80
4	10	30	—	—	—
5	11	28	—	—	—

the nominal GDP figures in column 4. The simplest and most direct method of deflating is to express the index numbers as hundredths—in decimal form—and then to divide them into corresponding nominal GDP. That gives us real GDP:

$$\text{Real GDP} = \frac{\text{nominal GDP}}{\text{price index (in hundredths)}} \qquad (2)$$

WORKED PROBLEMS

W7.2

Real GDP and price indexes

Column 5 shows the results. These figures for real GDP measure the market value of the output of pizza in years 1, 2, and 3 as if the price of pizza had been a constant $10 throughout the 3-year period. In short, real GDP reveals the market value of each year's output measured in terms of dollars that have the same purchasing power as dollars had in the base year.

To test your understanding, extend Table 7.5 to years 4 and 5, using equations 1 and 2. Then run through the entire deflating procedure, using year 3 as the base period. This time you will have to inflate some of the nominal GDP data, using the same procedure as we used in the examples.

ORIGIN OF THE IDEA

O7.1

GDP price index

An Alternative Method

Another way to calculate real GDP is to gather separate data on physical outputs (as in column 1) and their prices (as in column 2) of Table 7.5. We could then determine the market value of outputs in successive years *if the base-year price ($10) had prevailed*. In year 2, the 7 units of pizza would have a value of $70 (= 7 units × $10). As column 5 confirms, that $70 worth of output is year 2's real GDP. Similarly, we could determine the real GDP for year 3 by multiplying the 8 units of output that year by the $10 price in the base year.

Once we have determined real GDP through this method, we can identify the price index for a given year simply by dividing the nominal GDP by the real GDP for that year:

$$\begin{array}{c}\text{Price index}\\\text{(in hundredths)}\end{array} = \frac{\text{nominal GDP}}{\text{real GDP}} \qquad (3)$$

Example: In year 2 we get a price index of 200—or, in hundredths, 2.00—which equals the nominal GDP of

TABLE 7.6 Steps for Deriving Real GDP from Nominal GDP

Method 1

1. Find nominal GDP for each year.
2. Compute a GDP price index.
3. Divide each year's nominal GDP by that year's price index (in hundredths) to determine real GDP.

Method 2

1. Break down nominal GDP into physical quantities of output and prices for each year.
2. Find real GDP for each year by determining the dollar amount that each year's physical output would have sold for if base-year prices had prevailed. (The GDP price index can then be found by dividing nominal GDP by real GDP.)

$140 divided by the real GDP of $70. Note that equation 3 is simply a rearrangement of equation 2. Table 7.6 summarizes the two methods of determining real GDP in our single-good economy.

Real-World Considerations and Data

In the real world of many goods and services, of course, determining GDP and constructing a reliable price index are far more complex matters than in our pizza-only economy. The government accountants must assign a "weight" to each of several categories of goods and services based on the relative proportion of each category in total output. They update the weights annually as expenditure patterns change and roll the base year forward year by year using a moving average of expenditure patterns. The GDP price index used in the United States is called the *chain-type annual-weights price index*—which hints at its complexity. We spare you the details.

Table 7.7 shows some of the relationships between nominal GDP, real GDP, and the GDP price index for the

TABLE 7.7 Nominal GDP, Real GDP, and GDP Price Index for the United States, Selected Years

(1) Year	(2) Nominal GDP, Billions	(3) Real GDP, Billions	(4) GDP Price Index (2009 = 100)
1995	$ 7,664.0	$10,167.3	——
2000	10,289.7	————	81.9
2005	13,095.4	14,235.6	92.0
2009	14,417.9	————	100.0
2010	14,958.3	14,779.4	101.2
2012	16,244.6	15,547.0	104.5

Source: Bureau of Economic Analysis, **www.bea.gov**. All data are subject to government revision.

U.S. economy. Here the base year is 2009, where the value of the index is set at 100. Because the U.S. price level has been rising over the long run, the pre-2009 values of real GDP (column 3) are higher than the nominal values of GDP for those years (column 2). This upward adjustment acknowledges that prices were lower in the years before 2009, and thus nominal GDP understated the real output of those years in 2009 prices and must be inflated to show the correct relationship to other years.

Conversely, the rising price level of the post-2009 years caused nominal GDP figures for those years to over-state real output. So the statisticians deflate those figures to determine what real GDP would have been in other years if 2009 prices had prevailed. Doing so reveals that real GDP has been less than nominal GDP since 2009.

By inflating the nominal pre-2009 GDP data and de-flating the post-2009 data, government accountants deter-mine annual real GDP, which can then be compared with the real GDP of any other year in the series of years. So the real GDP values in column 3 are directly comparable with one another.

Once we have determined nominal GDP and real GDP, we can compute the price index. And once we have determined nominal GDP and the price index, we can cal-culate real GDP. Example: Nominal GDP in 2012 was $16,244.6 billion and real GDP was $15,547.0 billion. So the price level in 2012 was 104.5 (= $16,244.6/$15,547.0 × 100), or 4.5 percent higher than in 2009. If we knew the nominal GDP and the price level only, we could find the real GDP for 2012 by dividing the nominal GDP of $15,684.8 by the 2012 price index, expressed in hun-dredths (1.045).

To test your understanding of the relationships be-tween nominal GDP, real GDP, and the price level, deter-mine the values of the price index for 1995 in Table 7.7 and determine real GDP for 2000 and 2009. We have left those figures out on purpose.

QUICK REVIEW 7.3

- Nominal GDP is output valued at current prices. Real GDP is output valued at constant base-year prices.

- The GDP price index compares the price (market value) of all the goods and services included in GDP in a given year to the price of the same market basket in a refer-ence year.

- Nominal GDP can be transformed into real GDP by dividing the nominal GDP by the GDP price index expressed in hundredths.

Shortcomings of GDP

LO7.6 List and explain some limitations of the GDP measure.

GDP is a reasonably accurate and highly useful measure of how well or how poorly the economy is performing. But it has several shortcomings as a measure of both total output and well-being (total utility).

Nonmarket Activities

Certain productive activities do not take place in any market—the services of stay-at-home parents, for exam-ple, and the labor of carpenters who repair their own homes. Such activities never show up in GDP because the accountants who tally up GDP only get data on economic transactions involving *market activities*—that is, transac-tions in which output or resources are traded for money. Consequently, GDP understates a nation's total output be-cause it does not count *unpaid work*. There is one excep-tion: The portion of farmers' output that farmers consume themselves *is* estimated and included in GDP.

Leisure

The average workweek (excluding overtime) in the United States has declined since the beginning of the 1900s—from about 53 hours to about 35 hours. Moreover, the greater frequency of paid vacations, holidays, and leave time has shortened the work year itself. This increase in leisure time has clearly had a positive effect on overall well-being. But our system of national income accounting understates well-being by ignoring leisure's value. Nor does the system accommodate the satisfaction—the "psy-chic income"—that many people derive from their work.

Improved Product Quality

Because GDP is a quantitative measure rather than a qual-itative measure, it fails to capture the full value of im-provements in product quality. A $200 cell phone purchased today is of very different quality than a cell phone that cost $200 just a decade ago. Today's cell phone is digital and has greater memory capacity, a viewing screen, and quite likely a camera and a music player.

Obviously quality improvement has a great effect on economic well-being, as does the quantity of goods pro-duced. Although the BEA adjusts GDP for quality im-provement for selected items, the vast majority of such improvement for the entire range of goods and services does not get reflected in GDP.

Magical Mystery Tour

The Bureau of Economic Analysis (BEA), an Agency of the Department of Commerce, Compiles the NIPA Tables. Where Does It Get the Actual Data?

Discussions of national income accounting often leave the impression that the data for the National Income and Product Accounts magically appear from some mysterious place. Let's take a tour to see where economists get their data.

Consumption The BEA derives the data for the consumption component of the GDP accounts from four main sources:

- The Census Bureau's *Retail Trade Survey*, which gains sales information from a sample of 22,000 firms.
- The Census Bureau's *Survey of Manufacturers*, which gathers information on shipments of consumer goods from 50,000 establishments.
- The Census Bureau's *Service Survey*, which collects sales data from 30,000 service businesses.
- Industry trade sources. For example, data on auto sales and aircraft are collected directly from auto and aircraft manufacturers.

Investment The sources of the data for the investment component of GDP include:

- All the sources above used to determine consumption. Purchases of capital goods are separated from purchases of consumer goods. For example, estimates of investment in equipment and software are based on manufacturers' shipments reported in the *Survey of Manufacturers*, the *Service Survey*, and industry sources.
- Census construction surveys. The Census Bureau's *Housing Starts Survey* and *Housing Sales Survey* produce the data used to measure the amount of housing construction, and the *Construction Progress Reporting Survey* is the source of data on nonresidential construction. The BEA determines

changes in business inventories through the *Retail Trade Survey*, the *Wholesale Trade Survey* (of 7,100 wholesale firms), and the *Survey of Manufacturing*.

Government Purchases The data for government purchases (officially "government consumption and investment expenditures") are obtained through the following sources:

- The U.S. Office of Personnel Management, which collects data on wages and benefits, broken out by the private and public sector. Wages and benefits of government employees are the single largest "purchase" by federal, state, and local government.
- The previously mentioned Census Bureau's construction surveys, which break out private and public sector construction expenditures.
- The Census Bureau's *Survey of Government Finance*, which provides data on government consumption and investment expenditures.

Net Exports The BEA determines net exports through two main sources:

- The U.S. Customs Service, which collects data on exports and imports of goods.
- BEA surveys of potential domestic exporters and importers of services, which collect data on exports and imports of services.

So there you have it. Not so magical after all!

Source: Based on Joseph A. Ritter, "Feeding the National Accounts," Federal Reserve Bank of St. Louis *Review*, March–April 2000, pp. 11–20. For those interested, this article also provides information on the sources of data for the income side of the national accounts.

The Underground Economy

Embedded in our economy is a flourishing, productive underground sector. Some of the people who conduct business there are gamblers, smugglers, prostitutes, "fences" of stolen goods, drug growers, and drug dealers. They have good reason to conceal their incomes.

Most participants in the underground economy, however, engage in perfectly legal activities but choose illegally not to report their full incomes to the Internal Revenue Service (IRS). A barista at a coffee shop may report just a portion of the tips received from customers. Storekeepers may report only a portion of their sales receipts. Workers who want to hold on to their unemployment compensation benefits may take an "off-the-books" or "cash-only" job. A brick mason may agree to rebuild a neighbor's fireplace in exchange for the neighbor's repairing his boat engine. The value of none of these transactions shows up in GDP.

The value of underground transactions is estimated to be about 8 percent of the recorded GDP in the United States. That would mean that GDP in 2012 was understated by about $1.3 trillion. Global Perspective 7.2 shows estimates of the relative sizes of underground economies in selected nations.

GDP and the Environment

The growth of GDP is inevitably accompanied by "gross domestic by-products," including dirty air and polluted water, toxic waste, congestion, and noise. The social costs of the negative by-products reduce our economic well-being. And since those costs are not deducted from total output, GDP overstates our national well-being. Ironically, when money is spent to clean up pollution and reduce congestion, those expenses are added to GDP!

Composition and Distribution of Output

The composition of output is undoubtedly important for well-being. But GDP does not tell us whether the currently produced mix of goods and services is enriching or potentially detrimental to society. GDP assigns equal weight to an assault rifle and a set of encyclopedias, as long as both sell for the same price. Moreover, GDP reveals nothing about the way output is distributed. Does 90 percent of the output go to 10 percent of the households, for example, or is the output more evenly distributed? The distribution of output may make a big difference for society's overall well-being.

Noneconomic Sources of Well-Being

Finally, the connection between GDP and well-being is problematic for another reason. Just as a household's

GLOBAL PERSPECTIVE 7.2

The Underground Economy as a Percentage of GDP, Selected Nations

Underground economies vary in size worldwide. Three factors that help explain the variation are (1) the extent and complexity of regulation, (2) the type and degree of taxation, and (3) the effectiveness of law enforcement.

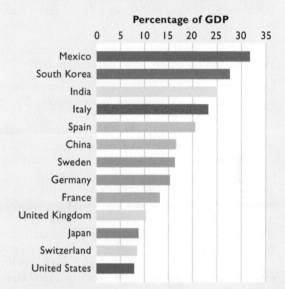

Source: Friedrich Schneider, "Shadow Economies and Corruption All Over the World: New Estimates for 145 Countries," *Economics: The Open-Access, Open-Assessment E-Journal,* vol. 1, no. 2007-9 (July 24, 2007). Used with permission of Friedrich Schneider.

income does not measure its total happiness, a nation's GDP does not measure its total well-being. Many things could make a society better off without necessarily raising GDP: a reduction of crime and violence, peaceful relations with other countries, people's greater civility toward one another, better understanding between parents and children, and a reduction of drug and alcohol abuse.

QUICK REVIEW 7.4

- GDP is a reasonably accurate and very useful indicator of a nation's economic performance but should not be interpreted as a comprehensive measure of well-being.
- The major limitations of GDP as an indicator of well-being are that it fails to account for nonmarket and illegal transactions, changes in leisure and in product quality, the composition and distribution of output, and the environmental effects of production.

SUMMARY

LO7.1 Explain how gross domestic product (GDP) is defined and measured.

Gross domestic product (GDP), a basic measure of an economy's economic performance, is the market value of all final goods and services produced within the borders of a nation in a year.

Final goods are those purchased by end users, whereas intermediate goods are those purchased for resale or for further processing or manufacturing. Intermediate goods, nonproduction transactions, and secondhand sales are purposely excluded in calculating GDP.

LO7.2 Describe how expenditures on goods and services can be summed to determine GDP.

GDP may be calculated by summing total expenditures on all final output or by summing the income derived from the production of that output.

By the expenditures approach, GDP is determined by adding consumer purchases of goods and services, gross investment spending by businesses, government purchases, and net exports: $GDP = C + I_g + G + X_n$.

Personal consumption expenditures consist of expenditures on goods (durable goods and nondurable goods) and services. About 60 percent of consumer expenditures in the United States are on services, leading economists to refer to the U.S. economy as a *service economy*.

Gross investment is divided into (*a*) replacement investment (required to maintain the nation's stock of capital at its existing level) and (*b*) net investment (the net increase in the stock of capital). In most years, net investment is positive and therefore the economy's stock of capital and production capacity increase.

LO7.3 Explain how GDP can be determined by summing up all of the incomes that were derived from producing the economy's output of goods and services.

By the income or allocations approach, GDP is calculated as the sum of compensation to employees, rents, interest, proprietors' income, corporate profits, taxes on production and imports *minus* net foreign factor income, *plus* consumption of fixed capital and a statistical discrepancy.

LO7.4 Describe the relationships among GDP, net domestic product, national income, personal income, and disposable income.

Other national accounts are derived from GDP. Net domestic product (NDP) is GDP less the consumption of fixed capital. National income (NI) is total income earned by a nation's resource suppliers plus taxes on production and imports; it is found by subtracting a statistical discrepancy from NDP and adding net foreign factor income to NDP. Personal income (PI) is the total income paid to households prior to any allowance for personal taxes. Disposable income (DI) is personal income after personal taxes have been paid. DI measures the amount of income available to households to consume or save.

LO7.5 Discuss the nature and function of a GDP price index, and describe the difference between nominal GDP and real GDP.

Price indexes are computed by dividing the price of a specific collection or market basket of output in a particular period by the price of the same market basket in a base period and multiplying the result (the quotient) by 100. The GDP price index is used to adjust nominal GDP for inflation or deflation and thereby obtain real GDP.

Nominal (current-dollar) GDP measures each year's output valued in terms of the prices prevailing in that year. Real (constant-dollar) GDP measures each year's output in terms of the prices that prevailed in a selected base year. Because real GDP is adjusted for price-level changes, differences in real GDP are due only to differences in production activity.

LO7.6 List and explain some limitations of the GDP measure.

GDP is a reasonably accurate and very useful indicator of a nation's economic performance, but it has its limitations. It fails to account for nonmarket and illegal transactions, changes in leisure and in product quality, the composition and distribution of output, and the environmental effects of production. GDP should not be interpreted as a complete measure of well-being.

TERMS AND CONCEPTS

national income accounting	durable goods	consumption of fixed capital
gross domestic product (GDP)	nondurable goods	net domestic product (NDP)
intermediate goods	services	personal income (PI)
final goods	gross private domestic investment (I_g)	disposable income (DI)
multiple counting	net private domestic investment	nominal GDP
value added	government purchases (G)	real GDP
expenditures approach	net exports (X_n)	price index
income approach	taxes on production and imports	base year
personal consumption expenditures (C)	national income	

DISCUSSION QUESTIONS

1. In what ways are national income statistics useful? LO7.1
2. Why do national income accountants compare the market value of the total outputs in various years rather than actual physical volumes of production? What problem is posed by any comparison over time of the market values of various total outputs? How is this problem resolved? LO7.1
3. Which of the following goods are usually intermediate goods and which are usually final goods: running shoes, cotton fibers, watches, textbooks, coal, sunscreen lotion, lumber? LO7.1
4. Why do economists include only final goods and services when measuring GDP for a particular year? Why don't they include the value of the stocks and bonds bought and sold? Why don't they include the value of the used furniture bought and sold? LO7.1
5. Explain why an economy's output, in essence, is also its income. LO7.1
6. Provide three examples of each: consumer durable goods, consumer nondurable goods, and services. LO7.2
7. Why are changes in inventories included as part of investment spending? Suppose inventories declined by $1 billion during 2014. How would this affect the size of gross private domestic investment and gross domestic product in 2014? Explain. LO7.2
8. What is the difference between gross private domestic investment and net private domestic investment? If you were to determine net domestic product (NDP) through the expenditures approach, which of these two measures of investment spending would be appropriate? Explain. LO7.2
9. Use the concepts of gross investment and net investment to distinguish between an economy that has a rising stock of capital and one that has a falling stock of capital. Explain: "Though net investment can be positive, negative, or zero, it is impossible for gross investment to be less than zero." LO7.2

10. Define net exports. Explain how U.S. exports and imports each affects domestic production. How are net exports determined? Explain how net exports might be a negative amount. LO7.2
11. Contrast the ideas of nominal GDP and real GDP. Why is one more reliable than the other for comparing changes in the standard of living over a series of years? What is the GDP price index and what is its role in differentiating nominal GDP and real GDP? LO7.5
12. Which of the following are included or excluded in this year's GDP? Explain your answer in each case. LO7.6
    a. Interest received on an AT&T corporate bond.
    b. Social Security payments received by a retired factory worker.
    c. Unpaid services of a family member in painting the family home.
    d. Income of a dentist from the dental services provided.
    e. A monthly allowance a college student receives from home.
    f. Money received by Josh when he resells his nearly brand-new Honda automobile to Kim.
    g. The publication and sale of a new college textbook.
    h. An increase in leisure resulting from a 2-hour decrease in the length of the workweek, with no reduction in pay.
    i. A $2 billion increase in business inventories.
    j. The purchase of 100 shares of Google stock.
13. **LAST WORD** What government agency compiles the U.S. NIPA tables? In what U.S. department is it located? Of the several specific sources of information, name one source for each of the four components of GDP: consumption, investment, government purchases, and net exports.

REVIEW QUESTIONS

1. Tina walks into Ted's sporting goods store and buys a punching bag for $100. That $100 payment counts as _____ for Tina and _____ for Ted. LO7.1
   a. Income; expenditure.
   b. Value added; multiple counting.
   c. Expenditure; income.
   d. Rents; profits.
2. Which of the following transactions would count in GDP? LO7.1
   *Select **one or more** answers from the choices shown.*
   a, Kerry buys a new sweater to wear this winter.
   b. Patricia receives a Social Security check.
   c. Roberto gives his daughter $50 for her birthday.
   d. Latika sells $1,000 of General Electric stock.
   e. Karen buys a new car.
   f. Amy buys a used car.

3. A small economy starts the year with $1 million in capital. During the course of the year, gross investment is $150,000 and depreciation is $50,000. How big is the economy's stock of capital at the end of the year? LO7.2
   a. $1,150,000.
   b. $1,100,000.
   c. $1,000,000.
   d. $850,000.
   e. $800,000.
4. Suppose that this year a small country has a GDP of $100 billion. Also assume that I_g = $30 billion, C = $60 billion, and X_n = − $10 billion. How big is G? LO7.3
   a. $0.
   b. $10 billion.
   c. $20 billion.
   d. $30 billion.

5. Suppose that California imposes a sales tax of 10 percent on all goods and services. A Californian named Ralph then goes into a home improvement store in the state capital of Sacramento and buys a leaf blower that is priced at $200. With the 10 percent sales tax, his total comes to $220. How much of the $220 paid by Ralph will be counted in the national income and product accounts as private income (employee compensation, rents, interest, proprietor's income, and corporate profits)? **LO7.3**
   a. $220.
   b. $200.
   c. $180.
   d. None of the above.

6. Suppose GDP is $16 trillion, with $10 trillion coming from consumption, $2 trillion coming from gross investment, $3.5 trillion coming from government expenditures, and $500 billion coming from net exports. Also suppose that across the whole economy, depreciation (consumption of fixed capital) totals $1 trillion. From these figures, we see that net domestic product equals: **LO7.4**
   a. $17.0 trillion.
   b. $16.0 trillion.
   c. $15.5 trillion.
   d. None of the above.

7. Suppose GDP is $15 trillion, with $8 trillion coming from consumption, $2.5 trillion coming from gross investment, $3.5 trillion coming from government expenditures, and $1 trillion coming from net exports. Also suppose that across the whole economy, personal income is $12 trillion. If the government collects $1.5 trillion in personal taxes, then disposable income will be: **LO7.4**
   a. $13.5 trillion.
   b. $12.0 trillion.
   c. $10.5 trillion.
   d. None of the above.

8. Suppose that this year's nominal GDP is $16 trillion. To account for the effects of inflation, we construct a price-level index in which an index value of 100 represents the price level five years ago. Using that index, we find that this year's real GDP is $15 trillion. Given those numbers, we can conclude that the current value of the index is: **LO7.5**
   a. Higher than 100.
   b. Lower than 100.
   c. Still 100.

9. Which of the following items will be included in official U.S. GDP statistics? **LO7.6**
   *Select **one or more** answers from the choices shown.*
   a. Revenue generated by illegal marijuana growers in Oregon.
   b. Money spent to clean up a local toxic waste site in Ohio.
   c. Revenue generated by legal medical marijuana sales in California.
   d. The dollar value of the annoyance felt by local citizens living near a noisy airport in Georgia.
   e. Robert paying Ted for a haircut in Chicago.
   f. Emily and Rhonda trading an hour of dance lessons for a haircut in Dallas.

PROBLEMS

1. Suppose that annual output in year 1 in a 3-good economy is 3 quarts of ice cream, 1 bottle of shampoo, and 3 jars of peanut butter. In year 2, the output mix changes to 5 quarts of ice cream, 2 bottles of shampoo, and 2 jars of peanut butter. If the prices in both years are $4 per quart for ice cream, $3 per bottle of shampoo, and $2 per jar of peanut butter, what was the economy's GDP in year 1? What was its GDP in year 2? **LO7.1**

2. Assume that a grower of flower bulbs sells its annual output of bulbs to an Internet retailer for $70,000. The retailer, in turn, brings in $160,000 from selling the bulbs directly to final customers. What amount would these two transactions add to personal consumption expenditures and thus to GDP during the year? **LO7.1**

3. If in some country personal consumption expenditures in a specific year are $50 billion, purchases of stocks and bonds are $30 billion, net exports are −$10 billion, government purchases are $20 billion, sales of secondhand items are $8 billion, and gross investment is $25 billion, what is the country's GDP for the year? **LO7.2**

4. To the right is a list of domestic output and national income figures for a certain year. All figures are in billions. The questions that follow ask you to determine the major national

Personal consumption expenditures	$245
Net foreign factor income	4
Transfer payments	12
Rents	14
Consumption of fixed capital (depreciation)	27
Statistical discrepancy	8
Social Security contributions	20
Interest	13
Proprietors' income	33
Net exports	11
Dividends	16
Compensation of employees	223
Taxes on production and imports	18
Undistributed corporate profits	21
Personal taxes	26
Corporate income taxes	19
Corporate profits	56
Government purchases	72
Net private domestic investment	33
Personal saving	20

income measures by both the expenditures and the income approaches. The results you obtain with the different methods should be the same. **LO7.4**

  a. Using the above data, determine GDP by both the expenditures and the income approaches. Then determine NDP.

  b. Now determine NI in two ways: first, by making the required additions or subtractions from NDP; and second, by adding up the types of income and taxes that make up NI.

  c. Adjust NI (from part *b*) as required to obtain PI.

  d. Adjust PI (from part *c*) as required to obtain DI.

5. Using the following national income accounting data, compute (*a*) GDP, (*b*) NDP, and (*c*) NI. All figures are in billions. **LO7.4**

Compensation of employees	$194.2
U.S. exports of goods and services	17.8
Consumption of fixed capital	11.8
Government purchases	59.4
Taxes on production and imports	14.4
Net private domestic investment	52.1
Transfer payments	13.9
U.S. imports of goods and services	16.5
Personal taxes	40.5
Net foreign factor income	2.2
Personal consumption expenditures	219.1
Statistical discrepancy	0

6. Suppose that in 1984 the total output in a single-good economy was 7,000 buckets of chicken. Also suppose that in 1984 each bucket of chicken was priced at $10. Finally, assume that in 2005 the price per bucket of chicken was $16 and that 22,000 buckets were produced. Determine the GDP price index for 1984, using 2005 as the base year. By what percentage did the price level, as measured by this index, rise between 1984 and 2005? What were the amounts of real GDP in 1984 and 2005? **LO7.5**

7. The following table shows nominal GDP and an appropriate price index for a group of selected years. Compute real GDP. Indicate in each calculation whether you are inflating or deflating the nominal GDP data. **LO7.5**

Year	Nominal GDP, Billions	Price Index (2005 = 100)	Real GDP, Billions
1968	$ 909.8	22.01	$_____
1978	2,293.8	40.40	$_____
1988	5,100.4	66.98	$_____
1998	8,793.5	85.51	$_____
2008	14,441.4	108.48	$_____

8. Assume that the total value of the following items is $600 billion in a specific year for Upper Mongoose: net exports = $50 billion; value of new goods and services produced in the underground economy = $75 billion; personal consumption expenditures = $300 billion; value of the services of stay-at-home parents = $25 billion; gross domestic investment = $100 billion; government purchases = $50 billion. What is Upper Mongoose's GDP for the year? What is the size of the underground economy as a percentage of GDP? By what percentage would GDP be boosted if the value of the services of stay-at-home spouses were included in GDP? **LO7.6**

Economic Growth

Learning Objectives

LO8.1 List two ways that economic growth is measured.

LO8.2 Define "modern economic growth" and explain the institutional structures needed for an economy to experience it.

LO8.3 Identify the general supply, demand, and efficiency forces that give rise to economic growth.

LO8.4 Describe "growth accounting" and the specific factors accounting for economic growth in the United States.

LO8.5 Explain why the trend rate of U.S. productivity growth has increased since the earlier 1973–1995 period.

LO8.6 Discuss differing perspectives as to whether growth is desirable and sustainable.

People living in rich countries tend to take economic growth and rising standards of living for granted. Recessions—periods during which output declines—are normally infrequent and temporary, usually lasting less than a year. Once they pass, modern capitalistic economies return to growing, and living standards continue their seemingly inexorable rise.

But a look back at history or a look around the world today quickly dispels any confidence that economic growth and rising standards of living are automatic or routine. Historically, continually rising living standards are a recent phenomenon, seen only during the last century or two. Before that time, living standards barely rose—if at all—from one generation to the next. And a look around the world today reveals huge differences in standards of living resulting from the disturbing fact that, although some countries have enjoyed decades or even centuries of steadily rising per capita income levels, other countries have experienced hardly any economic growth at all.

This chapter investigates the causes of economic growth, what institutional structures appear to promote economic growth, and the controversies surrounding the benefits and costs of economic growth. As you will see, economic growth has been perhaps the most revolutionary and powerful force in history. Consequently, no study of economics is complete without a thorough understanding of the causes and consequences of economic growth.

Economic Growth

LO8.1 List two ways that economic growth is measured. Economists define and measure **economic growth** as either:

- An increase in real GDP occurring over some time period.
- An increase in real GDP per capita occurring over some time period.

With either definition, economic growth is calculated as a percentage rate of growth per quarter (3-month period) or per year. For the first definition, for example, real GDP in the United States was $15,052.4 billion in 2011 and $15,470.0 in 2012. So the U.S. economic growth rate for 2007 was 2.8 percent {= [(15,470.0 billion − $15,052.4 billion)/$15,052.4 billion] × 100}. Growth rates normally are positive, but not always. In recession year 2009, for instance, the U.S. rate of economic growth was a *minus* 2.4 percent.

The second definition of economic growth in the bulleted list takes into consideration the size of the population. **Real GDP per capita** (or per capita output) is the amount of real output per person in a country. It is calculated, as follows.

$$\text{Real GDP per capita} = \frac{\text{Real GDP}}{\text{Population}}$$

For example, in 2011 the real GDP in the United States was $15,052.4 billion and population was 311.6 million. Therefore, real GDP per capita in that year was $48,307. In 2012 real GDP per capita increased to $49,283. So the growth rate of real GDP per capita in 2012 was 2.0 percent {= [($49,283 − $48,307)/$48,307] × 100}. In contrast, real GDP per capita fell by 3.3 percent in recession year 2009.

For measuring expansion of military potential or political preeminence, the growth of real GDP is more useful. Unless specified otherwise, growth rates reported in the news and by international agencies use this definition of economic growth. For comparing living standards, however, the second definition is superior. While China's GDP in 2012 was $12,380 billion compared with Denmark's $332 billion, Denmark's real GDP per capita was $37,700 compared with China's hugely lower $9,100. And in some cases growth of real GDP can be misleading. The African nation of Eritrea had real GDP growth of 1.3 percent per year from 2000–2008. But over the same period its annual growth of population was 3.8 percent, resulting in a decline in real GDP per capita of roughly 2.5 percent per year.

Growth as a Goal

Growth is a widely held economic goal. The expansion of total output relative to population results in rising real wages and incomes and thus higher standards of living. An economy that is experiencing economic growth is better able to meet people's wants and resolve socioeconomic problems. Rising real wages and income provide richer opportunities to individuals and families—a vacation trip, a personal computer, a higher education—without sacrificing other opportunities and pleasures. A growing economy can undertake new programs to alleviate poverty, embrace diversity, cultivate the arts, and protect the environment without impairing existing levels of consumption, investment, and public goods production.

In short, *growth lessens the burden of scarcity*. A growing economy, unlike a static economy, can consume more today while increasing its capacity to produce more in the future. By easing the burden of scarcity—by relaxing society's constraints on production—economic growth enables a nation to attain its economic goals more readily and to undertake new endeavors that require the use of goods and services to be accomplished.

Arithmetic of Growth

Why do economists pay so much attention to small changes in the rate of economic growth? Because those changes really matter! For the United States, with a current nominal GDP of about $16.2 trillion, the difference between a 3 percent and a 4 percent rate of growth is about $162 billion of output each year. For a poor country, a difference of one-half of a percentage point in the rate of growth may mean the difference between starvation and mere hunger.

The mathematical approximation called the **rule of 70** provides a quantitative grasp of the effect of economic growth. The rule of 70 tells us that we can find the number of years it will take for some measure to double, given its annual percentage increase, by dividing that percentage increase into the number 70. So

$$\begin{matrix} \text{Approximate} \\ \text{number of years} \\ \text{required to double} \\ \text{real GDP} \end{matrix} = \frac{70}{\begin{matrix}\text{annual percentage rate}\\\text{of growth}\end{matrix}}$$

Examples: A 3 percent annual rate of growth will double real GDP in about 23 (= 70 ÷ 3) years. Growth of 8 percent per year will double real GDP in about 9 (= 70 ÷ 8) years. The rule of 70 is applicable generally. For example, it works for estimating how long it will take the price level or a savings account to double at various percentage rates of inflation or interest. When compounded over many years, an apparently small difference in the rate of growth thus becomes highly significant. Suppose China and Italy start with identical GDPs, but then China grows at an 8 percent yearly rate, while Italy grows at 2 percent. China's GDP would double in about 9 years, while Italy's GDP would double in 35 years.

WORKED PROBLEMS

W8.1
GDP growth

Growth in the United States

Table 8.1 gives an overview of economic growth in the United States since 1950. Column 2 reveals strong growth as measured by increases in real GDP. Note that between 1950 and 2012 real GDP increased more than sevenfold. But the U.S. population also increased. Nevertheless, in column 4 we find that real GDP per capita rose more than threefold over these years.

What has been the *rate* of U.S. growth? Real GDP grew at an annual rate of about 3.2 percent between 1950 and 2012. Real GDP per capita increased at roughly 2 percent per year over that time. But we must qualify these raw numbers in several ways:

- **Improved products and services** Since the numbers in Table 8.1 do not fully account for improvements

TABLE 8.1 Real GDP and Real GDP per Capita, Selected Years, 1950–2012

(1) Year	(2) Real GDP, Billions of 2009 $	(3) Population, Millions	(4) Real GDP Per Capita, 2009 $ (2) ÷ (3)
1950	$ 2,182	152	$14,355
1960	3,106	181	17,160
1970	4,718	205	23,015
1980	6,443	228	28,259
1990	8,945	250	35,780
2000	12,565	282	44,557
2012	15,471	313	49,428

Source: Data are from the Bureau of Economic Analysis, **www.bea.gov**, and the U.S. Census Bureau, **www.census.gov**. All data are subject to government revision.

in products and services, they understate the growth of economic well-being. Such purely quantitative data do not fully compare an era of vacuum tube computers and low-efficiency V8 hot rods with an era of digital cell phone networks and fuel-sipping, hybrid-drive vehicles.

- **Added leisure** The increases in real GDP and per capita GDP identified in Table 8.1 were accomplished despite increases in leisure. The average workweek, once 50 hours, is now about 35 hours (excluding overtime hours). Again the raw growth numbers understate the gain in economic well-being.

- **Other impacts** These measures of growth do not account for any effects growth may have had on the environment and the quality of life. If growth debases the physical environment, excessively warms the planet, and creates a stressful work environment, the bare growth numbers will overstate the gains in well-being that result from growth. On the other hand, if growth leads to stronger environmental protections or a more secure and stress-free lifestyle, these numbers will understate the gains in well-being.

In Chapter 6, we made two other key points about U.S. growth rates. First, they are not constant or smooth over time. Like those of other countries, U.S. growth rates vary quarterly and annually depending on a variety of factors such as the introduction of major new inventions and the economy's current position in the business cycle. Second, many countries share the U.S. experience of positive and ongoing economic growth. But sustained growth is both a historically new occurrence and also one that is not shared equally by all countries.

Modern Economic Growth

LO8.2 Define "modern economic growth" and explain the institutional structures needed for an economy to experience it.

We now live in an era of wireless high-speed Internet connections, genetic engineering, and space exploration. New inventions and new technologies drive continual economic growth and ongoing increases in living standards. But it wasn't always like this. Economic growth and sustained increases in living standards are a historically recent phenomenon that started with the Industrial Revolution of the late 1700s. Before the Industrial Revolution, living standards were basically flat over long periods of time so that, for instance, Greek peasants living in the year 300 B.C. had about the same material standard of living as Greek peasants living in the year A.D. 1500. By contrast, our current era of **modern economic growth** is characterized by sustained and ongoing increases in living standards that can cause dramatic increases in the standard of living within less than a single human lifetime.

Economic historians informally date the start of the Industrial Revolution to the year 1776, when the Scottish inventor James Watt perfected a powerful and efficient steam engine. This steam engine inaugurated the modern era since the device could be used to drive industrial factory equipment, steamships, and steam locomotives.

The new industrial factories mass-produced goods for the first time. This meant that nearly all manufacturing shifted from items produced by hand by local craftsmen to items mass-produced in distant factories. The new steamships and steam locomotives meant that resources could easily flow to factories and that the products of factories could be shipped to distant consumers at low cost. The result was a huge increase in long-distance trade and a major population shift as people left farms to go work in the towns and cities where the new industrial factories were concentrated.

Steam power would later be largely replaced by electric power, and many more inventions would follow the steam engine that started the Industrial Revolution. These included railroads, motorized vehicles, telephones, airplanes, container ships, computers, the Internet, and many more. But the key point is that the last 200 or so years of history have been fundamentally different from anything that went before.

The biggest change has been change itself. Whereas in earlier times material standards of living and the goods and services that people produced and consumed changed very little even over the course of an entire human life span, today people living in countries experiencing modern economic growth are constantly exposed to new technologies, new products, and new services.

What is more, modern economic growth has vastly affected cultural, social, and political arrangements.

- Culturally, the vast increases in wealth and living standards have allowed ordinary people for the first time in history to have significant time for leisure activities and the arts.

- Socially, countries experiencing modern economic growth have abolished feudalism, instituted universal public education, and largely eliminated ancient social norms and legal restrictions against women and minorities doing certain jobs or holding certain positions.

- Politically, countries experiencing modern economic growth have tended to move toward democracy, a form of government that was extremely rare before the start of the Industrial Revolution.

In addition, the average human lifespan has more than doubled, from an average of less than 30 years before modern economic growth began in the late 1700s to a worldwide average of over 67 years today. Thus, for the first time in world history, the average person can expect to live into old age. These and other changes speak to the truly revolutionary power of economic growth and naturally lead economists to consider the causes of economic growth and what policies could be pursued to sustain and promote it. Their desire is intensified by the reality that economic growth is distributed so unevenly around the world.

The Uneven Distribution of Growth

Modern economic growth has spread only slowly from its British birthplace. It first advanced to France, Germany, and other parts of western Europe in the early 1800s before spreading to the United States, Canada, and Australia by the mid 1800s. Japan began to industrialize in the 1870s, but the rest of Asia did not follow until the early to mid 1900s, at which time large parts of Central and South America as well

FIGURE 8.1 **The great divergence in standards of living.** Income levels around the world were very similar in 1820. But they are now very different because certain areas, including the United States and western Europe, began experiencing modern economic growth much earlier than other areas.

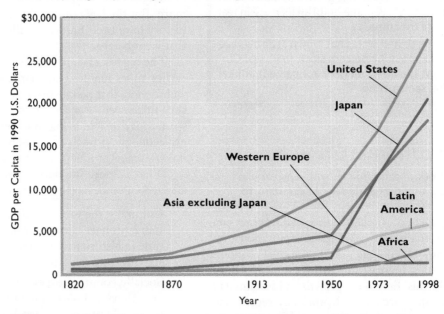

Source: Angus Maddison, *The World Economy: A Millennial Perspective* (Paris: OECD, 2001), p. 264.

as the Middle East also began to experience modern economic growth. Most recent has been Africa, which for the most part did not experience modern economic growth until the last few decades. Notably, some parts of the world have yet to experience modern economic growth at all.

The different starting dates for modern economic growth in various parts of the world are the main cause of the vast differences in per capita GDP levels seen today. The current huge gaps between rich countries like the United States and Japan and poor countries like North Korea and Burundi were shown previously in Global Perspective 6.1. But the huge divergence in living standards caused by the fact that different countries started modern economic growth at different times is best seen in Figure 8.1, which shows how GDP per capita has evolved since 1820 in the United States, western Europe, Latin America, Asia, and Africa.

To make the comparison of living standards easier, income levels in all places and at all times have been converted into 1990 U.S. dollars. Using this convention, it is clear that in 1820 per capita incomes in all areas were quite similar, with the richest area in the world in 1820, western Europe, having an average per capita income of $1,232, while the poorest area of the world at that time, Africa, had an average per capita income of $418. Thus, in 1820, average incomes in the richest area were only about three times larger than those in the poorest area.

But because western Europe and the United States started experiencing modern economic growth earlier than other areas, they have now ended up vastly richer than other areas, despite the fact that per capita incomes in nearly all places have increased at least a bit. For instance, per capita GDP in the United States in 1998 was $27,331 while it was only $1,368 in Africa. Thus, because modern economic growth has occurred for nearly two centuries in the United States compared to a few decades in Africa, average living standards in the United States in 1998 were nearly 20 times higher than those in Africa.

Catching Up Is Possible

Do not get the wrong impression looking at Figure 8.1. Countries that began modern economic growth more recently are *not* doomed to be permanently poorer than the countries that began modern economic growth at an earlier date. This is true because people can adopt technology more quickly than they can invent it. Broadly speaking, the richest countries today have achieved that status because they have the most advanced technology. But because they already have the most advanced technology, they must invent new technology to get even richer. Because inventing and implementing new technology is slow and costly, real GDP per capita in the richest **leader countries** typically grows by an average annual rate of just 2 or 3 percent per year.

By contrast, poorer **follower countries** can grow much faster because they can simply adopt existing technologies from rich leader countries. For instance, in many places in Africa today, the first telephones most people have ever been able to use are cell phones. That is, these countries have not even bothered to install the copper wires necessary for land-line telephones, which are basically a nineteenth-century technology. Instead, they have gone directly for Internet-capable mobile phone networks, a twenty-first-century technology. By doing so, they skip past many stages of technology and development that the United States and other currently rich countries had to pass through. In effect, they jump directly to the most modern, most highly productive technology. The result is that, under the right circumstances, it is possible for poorer countries to experience extremely rapid increases in living standards. This can continue until they have caught up with the leader countries and become leader countries themselves. Once that happens, their growth rates fall down to the 2 or 3 percent rate typical of leader countries. This happens because once they are also rich and using the latest technology, their growth rates are limited by the rate at which new technology can be invented and applied.

Table 8.2 shows both how the growth rates of leader countries are constrained by the rate of technological progress as well as how certain follower countries have been able to catch up by adopting more advanced technologies and growing rapidly. Table 8.2 shows real GDP per capita in 1960 and 2010 as well as the average annual growth rate of real GDP per capita between 1960 and 2010 for three countries—the United States, the United Kingdom, and France—that were already rich leader countries in 1960 as well as for five other nations that were relatively poor follower countries at that time. To make comparisons easy, the GDPs and GDPs per capita for all countries are expressed in terms of 2005 U.S. dollars. The countries are ordered by their respective GDPs per capita in 1960, so that the richest country in the world at the time, the United States, is listed first while the poorest of the eight selected countries at the time, South Korea, is listed last.

First, notice that the average annual growth rates of the three leader countries—the United States, the United Kingdom, and France—have all been between 2.1 and 2.5 percent per year because their growth rates are limited by the rate at which new technologies can be invented and applied. By contrast, the five countries that were follower countries in 1960 have been able to grow much faster, between 3.3 percent per year and 5.4 percent per year. This has had remarkable effects on their standards of living relative to the leader countries. For instance, Ireland's

TABLE 8.2 Real GDP per Capita in 1960 and 2010 Plus Average Annual Growth Rates of Real GDP per Capita from 1960–2010 for Selected Countries. (Figures are in 2005 dollars.)

Country	Real GDP per Capita, 1960	Real GDP per Capita, 2010	Average Annual Growth Rate, 1960–2010
United States	$14,766	$41,365	2.1
United Kingdom	11,257	34,268	2.2
France	9,347	31,299	2.4
Ireland	6,666	34,877	3.3
Japan	5,472	31,477	3.5
Singapore	4,149	55,862	5.2
Hong Kong	3,849	38,865	4.6
South Korea	1,765	26,609	5.4

Note: GDP figures for all countries are measured in "international dollars" of equal value to U.S. dollars in 2005.

Source: Penn World Table version 6.3, **pwt.econ.upenn.edu**. Used by permission of the Center for International Comparisons at the University of Pennsylvania.

CONSIDER THIS...

Economic Growth Rates Matter!

When compounded over many decades, small absolute differences in rates of economic growth add up to substantial differences in real GDP and standards of living. Consider three hypothetical countries—Slogo, Sumgo, and Speedo. Suppose that in 2014 these countries have identical levels of real GDP ($6 trillion), population (200 million), and real GDP per capita ($30,000). Also, assume that annual real GDP growth is 2 percent in Slogo, 3 percent in Sumgo, and 4 percent in Speedo.

How will these alternative growth rates affect real GDP and real GDP per capita over a long period, say, a 70-year lifespan? By 2084 the 2, 3, and 4 percent growth rates would boost real GDP from $6 trillion to:

- $24 trillion in Slogo.
- $47 trillion in Sumgo.
- $93 trillion in Speedo.

For illustration, let's assume that each country experienced an average annual population growth of 1 percent over the 70 years. Then, in 2084 real GDP per capita would be about:

- $60,000 in Slogo.
- $118,000 in Sumgo.
- $233,000 in Speedo.

Even small differences in growth rates matter!

GDP per capita was only 60 percent that of its neighbor, the United Kingdom, in 1960. But because Ireland grew at a 3.3 percent rate for the next 50 years while the United Kingdom grew at only a 2.2 percent rate over that time period, by 2010 Ireland's GDP per capita was actually higher than the United Kingdom's GDP per capita. Ireland had become a leader country, too.

The growth experiences of the other four nations that were poor in 1960 have been even more dramatic. Hong Kong, for instance, moved from a GDP per capita that was less than one-third of that enjoyed by the United Kingdom in 1960 to a GDP per capita 13 percent higher than that of the United Kingdom in 2010. The Consider This box on the previous page emphasizes both how quickly small differences in growth rates can change the level of real GDP per capita and how countries stand in relation to each other in terms of real GDP per capita.

Finally, you may be puzzled as to why the GDP per capita of the United States in 2011 in Table 8.2 is so much higher than that of other rich leader countries. Why, for instance, is U.S. GDP per capita 32 percent higher than French GDP per capita? One important reason is that U.S. citizens put in substantially more labor time than do the citizens of most other leader countries. First, a much larger fraction of the U.S. population is employed than in other rich leader countries. Second, U.S. employees work many more hours per year than do employees in other rich leader countries. For example, 58 percent of the working-age population of the United States was employed in 2010 compared to 51 percent in France. That's a difference of about 14 percent. And American employees worked an average of 1,778 total hours during 2010, compared to an average of 1,478 total hours for French workers. That's a difference of about 20 percent. Added together, these two differences between U.S. and French labor supply imply about a 34 percent difference in the total number of hours worked in the French and American economies. Thus, differences in labor supply help explain differences between rich leader countries in terms of their differing levels of GDP per person.

Buy why do Americans supply so much more labor than workers in France and some of the other rich leader countries? Explanations put forth by economists include cultural differences regarding the proper balance between work and leisure, stronger unions in France and other rich leader countries, and more generous unemployment and welfare programs in France and other rich leader countries. France and other rich leader countries also tend to have higher tax rates than the United States—something that may significantly discourage employment. And, finally, the legal workweek is shorter in some countries than it is in the United States.

QUICK REVIEW 8.2

- Before the advent of modern economic growth starting in England in the late 1700s, living standards showed no sustained increases over time.
- Large differences in standards of living exist today because certain areas like the United States have experienced nearly 200 years of modern economic growth while other areas have had only a few decades of economic growth.
- Poor follower countries can catch up with and even surpass the living standards of rich leader countries by adopting the cutting-edge technologies and institutions already developed by rich leader countries.
- Substantial differences in GDP per capita among technologically advanced leader countries are often caused by differences in the amount of labor supplied.

Institutional Structures That Promote Modern Economic Growth

Table 8.2 demonstrates that poor follower countries can catch up and become rich leader countries by growing rapidly. But how does a country start that process and enter into modern economic growth? And once it has started modern economic growth, how does it keep the process going?

Economic historians have identified several institutional structures that promote and sustain modern economic growth. Some structures increase the savings and investment that are needed to fund the construction and maintenance of the huge amounts of infrastructure required to run modern economies. Other institutional structures promote the development of new technologies. And still others act to ensure that resources flow efficiently to their most productive uses. These growth-promoting institutional structures include:

- *Strong property rights* These appear to be absolutely necessary for rapid and sustained economic growth. People will not invest if they believe that thieves, bandits, or a rapacious and tyrannical government will steal their investments or their expected returns.

- *Patents and copyrights* Before patents and copyrights were first issued and enforced, inventors and authors usually saw their ideas stolen before they could profit from them. By giving inventors and authors the exclusive right to market and sell their creations, patents and copyrights give a strong financial incentive to invent and create.

- *Efficient financial institutions* These are needed to channel the savings generated by households toward the businesses, entrepreneurs, and inventors that do most of society's investing and inventing. Banks as well as stock and bond markets appear to be institutions crucial to modern economic growth.

- *Literacy and widespread education* Without highly educated inventors, new technologies do not get developed. And without a highly educated workforce, it is impossible to implement those technologies and put them to productive use.

- *Free trade* Free trade promotes economic growth by allowing countries to specialize so that different types of output can be produced in the countries where they can be made at the lowest opportunity cost. In addition, free trade promotes the rapid spread of new ideas so that innovations made in one country quickly spread to other countries.

- *A competitive market system* Under a market system, prices and profits serve as the signals that tell firms what to make and how much of it to make. Rich leader countries vary substantially in terms of how much government regulation they impose on markets, but in all cases, firms have substantial autonomy to follow market signals in deciding on current production and in making investments to produce what they believe consumers will demand in the future.

Several other difficult-to-measure factors also influence a nation's capacity for economic growth. The overall social-cultural-political environment of the United States, for example, has encouraged economic growth. Beyond the market system that has prevailed in the United States, the United States also has had a stable political system characterized by democratic principles, internal order, the right of property ownership, the legal status of enterprise, and the enforcement of contracts. Economic freedom and political freedom have been "growth-friendly."

In addition, and unlike some nations, there are virtually no social or moral taboos on production and material progress in the United States. The nation's social philosophy has embraced wealth creation as an attainable and desirable goal and the inventor, the innovator, and the businessperson are accorded high degrees of prestige and respect in American society. Finally, Americans have a positive attitude toward work and risk taking, resulting in an ample supply of willing workers and innovative entrepreneurs. A flow of energetic immigrants has greatly augmented that supply.

The nearby Consider This box deals with how fast-growing follower countries such as India sometimes alter their growth-related institutional structures as they grow richer. Web Chapter 21 looks at the special problems of economic growth in developing nations.

CONSIDER THIS . . .

Patents and Innovation

It costs U.S. and European drug companies about $1 billion to research, patent, and safety-test a new drug because literally thousands of candidate drugs fail for each drug that succeeds. The only way to cover these costs is by relying on patent protections that give a drug's developer the exclusive monopoly right to market and sell the new drug for 20 years following the patent application. The revenues over that time period will hopefully be enough to cover the drug's development costs and—if the drug is popular—generate a profit for the drug company.

Leader and follower countries have gotten into heated disputes over patented drugs, however, because the follower countries have often refused to recognize the patents granted to pharmaceutical companies in rich countries. India, for instance, has allowed local drug companies to copy and sell drugs that were developed by U.S. companies and are still under patent protection in the United States.

That policy benefits Indian consumers because competition among the local drug companies drives down the price to below the monopoly price that would be charged by the patent owner. But the weak patent protections in India have a side effect. They make it completely unprofitable for local drug producers to try to develop innovative new drugs. Local rivals would simply copy the new drugs and sell them at very low prices. So India has recently moved to strengthen its patent protections to try to provide financial incentives to transform its local drug companies from copycats into innovators. But note that the innovative new drugs that may result from the increased patent protections are not without a cost. As patent protections in India are improved, inexpensive local drugs copied from the leader countries will no longer be available to Indian consumers.

Determinants of Growth

LO8.3 Identify the general supply, demand, and efficiency forces that give rise to economic growth.

Our discussion of modern economic growth and the institutional structures that promote it has purposely been general. We now want to focus our discussion on six factors that directly affect the *rate* and quality of economic growth. These determinants of economic growth can be grouped into four supply factors, one demand factor, and one efficiency factor.

Supply Factors

The first four determinants of economic growth relate to the physical ability of the economy to expand. They are:

- Increases in the quantity and quality of natural resources.
- Increases in the quantity and quality of human resources.
- Increases in the supply (or stock) of capital goods.
- Improvements in technology.

Any increases or improvements in these **supply factors** will increase the *potential* size of an economy's GDP. The remaining two factors are necessary for that potential to be fulfilled not just in terms of the overall quantity of output but also in terms of the quality of that output and whether it is properly directed toward producing the items most highly valued by society.

Demand Factor

The fifth determinant of economic growth is the **demand factor:**

- To actually achieve the higher production potential created when the supply factors increase or improve, households, businesses, and the government must also expand their purchases of goods and services so as to provide a market for all the new output that can potentially be produced.

If that occurs, there will be no unplanned increases in inventories and resources will remain fully employed. The demand factor acknowledges that economic growth requires that increases in total spending must occur if we are to actually realize the output gains made available by increased production capacity.

Efficiency Factor

The sixth determinant of economic growth is the **efficiency factor:**

- To reach its full production potential, an economy must achieve economic efficiency as well as full employment.

The economy must use its resources in the least costly way (productive efficiency) to produce the specific mix of goods and services that maximizes people's well-being (allocative efficiency). The ability to expand production, together with the full use of available resources, is not sufficient for achieving maximum possible growth. Also required is the efficient use of those resources.

The supply, demand, and efficiency factors in economic growth are related. Unemployment caused by insufficient total spending (the demand factor) may lower the rate of new capital accumulation (a supply factor) and delay expenditures on research (also a supply factor). Conversely, low spending on investment (a supply factor) may cause insufficient spending (the demand factor) and unemployment. Widespread inefficiency in the use of resources (the efficiency factor) may translate into higher costs of goods and services and thus lower profits, which in turn may slow innovation and reduce the accumulation of capital (supply factors). Economic growth is a dynamic process in which the supply, demand, and efficiency factors all interact.

ORIGIN OF THE IDEA

O8.1
Growth theory

Production Possibilities Analysis

To put the six factors affecting the rate of economic growth into better perspective, let's use the production possibilities analysis introduced in Chapter 1.

Growth and Production Possibilities Recall that a curve like *AB* in Figure 8.2 is a production possibilities

FIGURE 8.2 Economic growth and the production possibilities curve. Economic growth is made possible by the four supply factors that shift the production possibilities curve outward, as from *AB* to *CD*. Economic growth is realized when the demand factor and the efficiency factor move the economy from points such as *a* and *c* that are inside *CD* to the optimal output point, which is assumed to be point *b* in this figure.

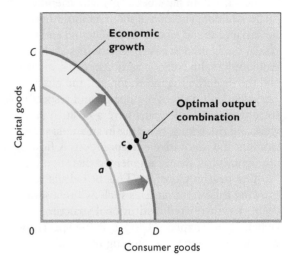

curve. It indicates the various *maximum* combinations of products an economy can produce with its fixed quantity and quality of natural, human, and capital resources and its stock of technological knowledge. An improvement in any of the supply factors will push the production possibilities curve outward, as from *AB* to *CD*.

But the demand factor reminds us that an increase in total spending is needed to move the economy from a point like *a* on curve *AB* to any of the points on the higher curve *CD*. And the efficiency factor reminds us that we need least-cost production and an optimal location on *CD* for the resources to make their maximum possible dollar contribution to total output. You will recall from Chapter 1 that this "best allocation" is determined by expanding the production of each good until its marginal benefit equals its marginal cost. Here, we assume that this optimal combination of capital and consumer goods occurs at point *b*. If the efficiency factor is in full effect, then the economy will produce at point *b* rather than at any other point along curve *CD*.

Example: The net increase in the size of the labor force in the United States in recent years has been 1.5 to 2 million workers per year. That increment raises the economy's production capacity. But obtaining the extra output that these added workers could produce depends on their success in finding jobs. It also depends on whether or not the jobs are in firms and industries where the workers' talents are fully and optimally used. Society does not want new labor-force entrants to be unemployed. Nor does it want pediatricians working as plumbers or pediatricians producing pediatric services for which marginal costs exceed marginal benefits.

Normally, increases in total spending match increases in production capacity, and the economy moves from a point on the previous production possibilities curve to a point on the expanded curve. Moreover, the competitive market system tends to drive the economy toward productive and allocative efficiency. Occasionally, however, the economy may end up at some point such as *c* in Figure 8.2. That kind of outcome occurred in the United States during the severe recession of 2007–2009. Real output fell far below the amount of output that the economy could have produced if it had achieved full employment and operated on its production possibilities curve.

Labor and Productivity Although the demand and efficiency factors are important, discussions of economic growth focus primarily on supply factors. Society can increase its real output and income in two fundamental ways: (1) by increasing its inputs of resources and (2) by raising the productivity of those inputs. Figure 8.3 concentrates

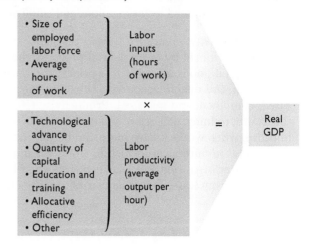

FIGURE 8.3 The supply determinants of real output. Real GDP is usefully viewed as the product of the quantity of labor inputs (hours of work) multiplied by labor productivity.

on the input of *labor* and provides a useful framework for discussing the role of supply factors in growth. A nation's real GDP in any year depends on the input of labor (measured in hours of work) multiplied by **labor productivity** (measured as real output per hour of work):

Real GDP = hours of work × labor productivity

Thought of this way, a nation's economic growth from one year to the next depends on its *increase* in labor inputs (if any) and its *increase* in labor productivity (if any).

Illustration: Assume that the hypothetical economy of Ziam has 10 workers in year 1, each working 2,000 hours per year (50 weeks at 40 hours per week). The total input of labor therefore is 20,000 hours. If productivity (average real output per hour of work) is $10, then real GDP in Ziam will be $200,000 (= 20,000 × $10). If work hours rise to

WORKED PROBLEMS

W8.2

Productivity and economic growth

20,200 and labor productivity rises to $10.40, Ziam's real GDP will increase to $210,080 in year 2. Ziam's rate of economic growth will be about 5 percent [= ($210,080 − $200,000)/$200,000] for the year.

Hours of Work What determines the number of hours worked each year? As shown in Figure 8.3, the hours of labor input depend on the size of the employed labor force and the length of the average workweek. Labor-force size depends on the size of the working-age population and the **labor-force participation rate**—the percentage of the working-age population actually in the labor force. The length of the average workweek is governed by legal and institutional considerations and by collective bargaining agreements negotiated between unions and employers.

Labor Productivity Figure 8.3 tells us that labor productivity is determined by technological progress, the quantity of capital goods available to workers, the quality of labor itself, and the efficiency with which inputs are allocated, combined, and managed. Productivity rises when the health, training, education, and motivation of workers improve; when workers have more and better machinery and natural resources with which to work; when production is better organized and managed; and when labor is reallocated from less-efficient industries to more-efficient industries.

Accounting for Growth

LO8.4 Describe "growth accounting" and the specific factors accounting for economic growth in the United States.

The president's Council of Economic Advisers uses a system called **growth accounting** to assess the relative importance of the supply-side elements that contribute to changes in real GDP. This system groups these elements into two main categories:

- Increases in hours of work.
- Increases in labor productivity.

Labor Inputs versus Labor Productivity

Table 8.3 provides the relevant data for the United States for five periods. The symbol "Q" in the table stands for "quarter" of the year. The beginning points for the first four periods are business-cycle peaks, and the last period includes future projections by the Council of Economic Advisers. It is clear from the table that both increases in the quantity of labor and increases in labor productivity are important sources of economic growth. Between 1953

and 2012, the labor force increased from 63 million to 155 million workers. Over that period the average length of the workweek remained relatively stable. Falling birthrates slowed the growth of the native population, but increased immigration partly offset that slowdown. As indicated in the Consider This box on the next page, of particular significance was a surge of women's participation in the labor force. Partly as a result, U.S. labor-force growth averaged 1.6 million workers per year over those 56 years.

The growth of labor productivity also has been important to economic growth. In fact, productivity growth has usually been the more significant factor, with the exception of 1973–1995 when productivity growth greatly slowed. For example, between 2001 and 2011, productivity growth was responsible for all of the 1.7 percent average annual economic rate because labor inputs were shrinking over that time period. The size of the labor force did increase over that decade, but fewer total hours were worked due to many workers shifting from full-time to part-time work and because of the high rates of unemployment experienced during and after that decade's two recessions (in 2001 and 2007–2009). As shown in the far right column of Table 8.3, productivity growth is projected to account for 92 percent of the growth of real GDP between 2011 and 2021.

Because increases in labor productivity are so important to economic growth, economists go to the trouble of investigating and assessing the relative importance of the factors that contribute to productivity growth. There are five factors that, together, appear to explain changes in productivity growth rates: technological advance, the amount of capital each worker has to work with, education and training, economies of scale, and resource allocation. We will examine each factor in turn, noting how much each factor contributes to productivity growth.

Technological Advance

The largest contributor to productivity growth is technological advance, which is thought to account for about

TABLE 8.3 Accounting for the Growth of U.S. Real GDP, 1953–2011 Plus Projection from 2011 to 2022 (Average Annual Percentage Changes)

Item	Actual				Projected
	1953 Q2 to 1973 Q4	1973 Q4 to 1995 Q2	1995 Q2 to 2001 Q1	2001 Q1 to 2011 Q1	2011 Q1 to 2021 Q4
Increase in real GDP	3.6	2.8	3.8	1.7	2.5
Increase in quantity of labor	1.1	1.3	1.4	−0.7	0.2
Increase in labor productivity	2.5	1.5	2.4	2.4	2.3

Source: Derived from *Economic Report of the President, 2008,* p. 45; *Economic Report of the President, 2010,* p. 76; *Economic Report of the President 2011,* p. 52; Bureau of Economic Analysis; and Bureau of Labor Statistics.

40 percent of productivity growth. As economist Paul Romer stated, "Human history teaches us that economic growth springs from better recipes, not just from more cooking."

Technological advance includes not only innovative production techniques but new managerial methods and new forms of business organization that improve the process of production. Generally, technological advance is generated by the discovery of new knowledge, which allows resources to be combined in improved ways that increase output. Once discovered and implemented, new knowledge soon becomes available to entrepreneurs and firms at relatively low cost. Technological advance therefore eventually spreads through the entire economy, boosting productivity and economic growth.

Technological advance and capital formation (investment) are closely related, since technological advance usually promotes investment in new machinery and equipment. In fact, technological advance is often *embodied* within new capital. For example, the purchase of new computers brings into industry speedier, more powerful computers that incorporate new technology.

Technological advance has been both rapid and profound. Gas and diesel engines, conveyor belts, and assembly lines are significant developments of the past. So, too, are fuel-efficient commercial aircraft, integrated microcircuits, personal computers, digital photography, and containerized shipping. More recently, technological advance has exploded, particularly in the areas of computers, photography, wireless communications, and the Internet. Other fertile areas of recent innovation are medicine and biotechnology.

Quantity of Capital

A second major contributor to productivity growth is increased capital, which explains roughly 30 percent of productivity growth. More and better plant and equipment make workers more productive. And a nation acquires more capital by saving some of its income and using that savings to invest in plant and equipment.

Although some capital substitutes for labor, most capital is complementary to labor—it makes labor more productive. A key determinant of labor productivity is the amount of capital goods available *per worker*. If both the aggregate stock of capital goods and the size of the labor force increase over a given period, the individual worker is not necessarily better equipped and productivity will not necessarily rise. But the quantity of capital equipment available per U.S. worker has increased greatly over time. (In 2011 it was about $126,062 per worker.)

Women, the Labor Force, and Economic Growth

The substantial rise in the number of women working in the paid workforce in the United States has been one of the major labor market trends of the last 50 years. In 1960, about 40 percent of women worked full-time or part-time in paid jobs. Today, that number is about 60 percent.

Women have greatly increased their productivity in the workplace, mostly by becoming better educated and professionally trained. Rising productivity has increased women's wage rates. Those higher wages have raised the opportunity costs—the forgone wage earnings—of staying at home. Women have therefore substituted employment in the labor market for traditional home activities. This substitution has been particularly pronounced among married women. (Single women have always had high labor-force participation rates.)

Furthermore, changing lifestyles and the widespread availability of birth control have freed up time for greater labor-force participation by women. Women not only have fewer children, but those children are spaced closer together in age. Thus women who leave their jobs during their children's early years return to the labor force sooner.

Greater access to jobs by women also has raised the labor-force participation of women. Service industries—teaching, nursing, and office work, for instance—that traditionally have employed many women have expanded rapidly in the past several decades. Also, the population in general has shifted from farms and rural regions to urban areas, where jobs for women are more abundant and more geographically accessible. Additionally, occupational barriers to professions have greatly eroded, resulting in many more women becoming business managers, lawyers, professors, and physicians.

In summary, women in the United States are better educated, more productive, and more efficiently employed than ever before. Their greater presence in the labor force has contributed greatly to U.S. economic growth.

Public investment in the U.S. **infrastructure** (highways and bridges, public transit systems, wastewater treatment facilities, water systems, airports, educational facilities, and so on) has also grown over the years. This publicly owned capital complements private capital. Investments in new highways promote private investment in new factories and retail stores along their routes.

Industrial parks developed by local governments attract manufacturing and distribution firms.

Private investment in infrastructure also plays a large role in economic growth. One example is the tremendous growth of private capital relating to communications systems over the years.

Education and Training

Ben Franklin once said, "He that hath a trade hath an estate," meaning that education and training contribute to a worker's stock of **human capital**—the knowledge and skills that make a worker productive. Investment in human capital includes not only formal education but also on-the-job training. Like investment in physical capital, investment in human capital is an important means of increasing labor productivity and earnings. An estimated 15 percent of productivity growth derives from investments in people's education and skills.

One measure of a nation's quality of labor is its level of educational attainment. Figure 8.4 shows large gains in education attainment over the past several decades. In 1960 only 41 percent of the U.S. population age 25 or older had at least a high school education; and only 8 percent had a college or postcollege education. By 2012, those numbers had increased to 88 and 31 percent, respectively. Clearly, more people are receiving more education than ever before.

But all is not upbeat with education in the United States. Many observers think that the quality of education in the United States has declined. For example, U.S. students perform poorly on science and math tests relative to students in many other nations (see Global

FIGURE 8.4 Changes in the educational attainment of the U.S. adult population. The percentage of the U.S. adult population, age 25 or older, completing high school and college has been rising over recent decades.

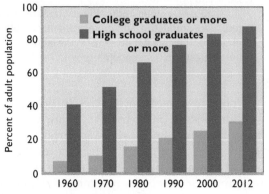

Source: U.S. Census Bureau, **www.census.gov**.

GLOBAL PERSPECTIVE 8.1

Average Test Scores of Eighth-Grade Students in Math and Science, Top 10 Test-Taking Countries

The test performance of U.S. eighth-grade students did not compare favorably with that of eighth-graders in several other nations in the Fifth International Math and Science Study (2011).

Mathematics

Rank		Score
1	South Korea	613
2	Singapore	611
3	Taiwan	609
4	Hong Kong	586
5	Japan	570
6	Russia	539
7	Israel	516
8	Finland	514
9	United States	509
10	Great Britain	507

Science

Rank		Score
1	Singapore	590
2	Taiwan	564
3	South Korea	560
4	Japan	558
5	Finland	552
6	Slovenia	543
7	Russia	542
8	Hong Kong	535
9	Great Britain	533
10	United States	525

Perspective 8.1). And the United States has been producing fewer engineers and scientists, a problem that may trace back to inadequate training in math and science in elementary and high schools. For these reasons, much recent public policy discussion and legislation have been directed toward improving the quality of the U.S. education and training system.

Economies of Scale and Resource Allocation

Economies of scale and improved resource allocation are a fourth and fifth source of productivity growth, and together they explain about 15 percent of productivity growth.

Economies of Scale Reductions in per-unit production costs that result from increases in output levels are called **economies of scale.** Markets have increased in size over time, allowing firms to increase output levels and thereby achieve production advantages associated with greater size. As firms expand their size and output, they are able to use larger, more productive equipment and employ methods of manufacturing and delivery that increase productivity. They also are better able to recoup substantial investments in developing new products and production methods. Examples: A large manufacturer of autos can use elaborate assembly lines with computerization and robotics, while smaller producers must settle for less-advanced technologies using more labor inputs. Large pharmaceutical firms greatly reduce the average amount of labor (researchers, production workers) needed to produce each pill as they increase the number of pills produced. Accordingly, economies of scale result in greater real GDP and thus contribute to economic growth.

Improved Resource Allocation Improved resource allocation means that workers over time have moved from low-productivity employment to high-productivity employment. Historically, many workers have shifted from agriculture, where labor productivity is low, to manufacturing, where it is quite high. More recently, labor has shifted away from some manufacturing industries to even higher-productivity industries such as computer software, business consulting, and pharmaceuticals. As a result of such shifts, the average productivity of U.S. workers has increased.

Also, discrimination in education and the labor market has historically deterred some women and minorities from entering high-productivity jobs. With the decline of such discrimination over time, many members of those groups have shifted from lower-productivity jobs to higher-productivity jobs. The result has been higher overall labor productivity and real GDP.

Finally, things such as tariffs, import quotas, and other barriers to international trade tend to relegate resources to relatively unproductive pursuits. The long-run movement toward liberalized international trade through international agreements has improved the allocation of resources, increased labor productivity, and expanded real output, both here and abroad.

> **QUICK REVIEW 8.3**
>
> - Institutional structures that promote growth include strong property rights, patents, efficient financial institutions, education, and a competitive market system.
> - The determinants of economic growth include four supply factors (increases in the quantity and quality of natural resources, increases in the quantity and quality of human resources, increases in the stock of capital goods, and improvements in technology); one demand factor (increases in total spending); and one efficiency factor (achieving allocative and productive efficiency).
> - Improvements in labor productivity accounted for about two-thirds of the increase in U.S. real GDP between 1990 and 2012; the use of more labor inputs accounted for the remainder.
> - Improved technology, more capital, greater education and training, economies of scale, and better resource allocation have been the main contributors to U.S. productivity growth and thus to U.S. economic growth.

The Rise in the Average Rate of Productivity Growth

LO8.5 Explain why the trend rate of U.S. productivity growth has increased since the earlier 1973–1995 period.

Figure 8.5 shows the growth of labor productivity (as measured by changes in the index of labor productivity) in the United States from 1973 to 2012, along with separate trend lines for 1973–1995 and 1995–2012. Labor productivity in the business sector grew by an average of only 1.5 percent yearly over the 1973–1995 period. But productivity growth averaged 2.4 percent between 1995 and 2012. Many economists believe that this higher productivity growth resulted from a significant new wave of technological advance, coupled with global competition. Some economists think there is a good chance that the higher trend rates of productivity growth could continue for many years to come.

This increase in productivity growth is important because real output, real income, and real wages are linked to labor productivity. To see why, suppose you are alone on an uninhabited island. The number of fish you can catch or coconuts you can pick per hour—your productivity—is your real wage (or real income) per hour. By *increasing* your productivity, you can improve your standard of living because you can gather more fish and more coconuts (goods) for each hour of work.

So it is for the economy as a whole: Over long periods, the economy's labor productivity determines its average real hourly wage, which includes fringe benefits such as health

FIGURE 8.5 Growth of labor productivity in the United States, 1973–2012. U.S. labor productivity (here, for the business sector) increased at an average annual rate of only 1.5 percent from 1973 to 1995. But between 1995 and 2012, it rose at an annual rate of 2.4 percent.

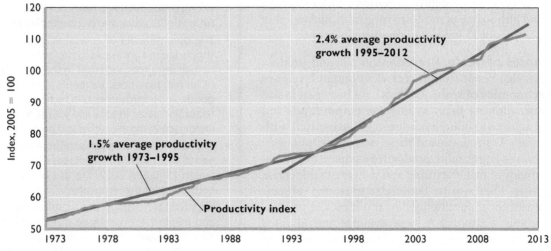

Source: U.S. Bureau of Labor Statistics, **www.bls.gov**.

care insurance and contributions to pensions. The economy's income per hour is equal to its output per hour. So productivity growth is the economy's main route for improving the living standards for its workers. It allows firms to pay higher wages without lowering their business profits.

Reasons for the Rise in the Average Rate of Productivity Growth

Why has productivity growth increased relative to earlier periods?

The Microchip and Information Technology The core element of the productivity speedup is an explosion of entrepreneurship and innovation based on the microprocessor, or *microchip*, which bundles transistors on a piece of silicon. Some observers liken the invention of the microchip to that of electricity, the automobile, air travel, the telephone, and television in importance and scope.

The microchip has found its way into thousands of applications. It has helped create a wide array of new products and services and new ways of doing business. Its immediate results were the pocket calculator, the bar-code scanner, the personal computer, the laptop computer, and more powerful business computers. But the miniaturization of electronic circuits also advanced the development of many other products such as cell phones and pagers, computer-guided lasers, global positioning equipment, energy conservation systems, Doppler radar, digital cameras, and machines to decipher the human genome.

Perhaps of greatest significance, the widespread availability of personal and laptop computers stimulated the desire to tie them together. That desire promoted rapid development of the Internet and all its many manifestations, such as business-to-household and business-to-business electronic commerce (e-commerce). The combination of the computer, fiber-optic cable, wireless technology, and the Internet constitutes a spectacular advance in **information technology,** which has been used to connect all parts of the world.

New Firms and Increasing Returns Hundreds of new **start-up firms** advanced various aspects of the new information technology. Many of these firms created more "hype" than goods and services and quickly fell by the wayside. But a number of firms flourished, eventually to take their places among the nation's largest firms. Examples of those firms include Intel (microchips); Apple and Dell (personal computers); Microsoft and Oracle (computer software); Cisco Systems (Internet switching systems); America Online (Internet service provision); Yahoo and Google (Internet search engines); and eBay, PayPal, and Amazon.com (electronic commerce). There are scores more! Most of these firms were either "not on the radar" or "a small blip on the radar" 30 years ago. Today each of them has large annual revenue and employs thousands of workers.

Successful new firms often experience **increasing returns,** a situation in which a given percentage increase in the amount of inputs a firm uses leads to an even larger percentage increase in the amount of output the firm produces. For example, suppose that a company called Techco decides to double the size of its operations to meet the growing demand for its services. After doubling its plant and equipment and doubling its workforce, say, from

100 workers to 200 workers, it finds that its total output has tripled from 8,000 units to 24,000 units. Techco has experienced increasing returns; its output has increased by 200 percent, while its inputs have increased by only 100 percent. That is, its labor productivity has gone up from 80 units per worker (= 8,000 units/100 workers) to 120 units per worker (= 24,000 units/200 workers). Increasing returns boost labor productivity and reduce per-unit production costs. Since these cost reductions result from increases in output levels, they are examples of *economies of scale.*

Both emerging firms as well as established firms can exploit several different sources of increasing returns and economies of scale:

- *More specialized inputs* Firms can use more specialized and thus more productive capital and workers as they expand their operations. A growing new e-commerce business, for example, can purchase highly specialized inventory management systems and hire specialized personnel such as accountants, marketing managers, and system maintenance experts.

- *Spreading of development costs* Firms can spread high product development costs over greater output. For example, suppose that a new software product costs $100,000 to develop and only $2 per unit to manufacture and sell. If the firm sells 1,000 units of the software, its per-unit cost will be $102 [= ($100,000 + $2,000)/1,000], but if it sells 500,000 units, that cost will drop to only $2.20 [= ($100,000 + $1 million)/500,000].

- *Simultaneous consumption* Many recently developed products and services can satisfy large numbers of customers at the same time. Unlike a gallon of gas that needs to be produced for each buyer, a software program needs to be produced only once. It then becomes available at very low expense to thousands or even millions of buyers. The same is true of books delivered to electronic reading devices, movies distributed on DVDs, and information disseminated through the Internet.

- *Network effects* Software and Internet service become more beneficial to a buyer the greater the number of households and businesses that also buy them. When others have Internet service, you can send e-mail messages to them. And when they also have software that allows display of documents and photos, you can attach those items to your e-mail messages. These interconnectivity advantages are called **network effects,** which are increases in the value of a product to each user, including existing users, as the total number of users rises. The domestic and global expansion of the Internet in particular has produced network effects, as have cell phones, pagers, tablet computers, and other aspects of wireless communication. Network effects magnify the value of output well beyond the costs of inputs.

- *Learning by doing* Finally, firms that produce new products or pioneer new ways of doing business experience increasing returns through **learning by doing.** Tasks that initially may have taken firms hours may take them only minutes once the methods are perfected.

Whatever the particular source of increasing returns, the result is higher productivity, which tends to reduce the per-unit cost of producing and delivering products.

Global Competition The recent economy is characterized not only by information technology and increasing returns but also by heightened global competition. The collapse of the socialist economies in the late 1980s and early 1990s, together with the success of market systems, has led to a reawakening of capitalism throughout the world. The new information technologies have "shrunk the globe" and made it imperative for all firms to lower their costs and prices and to innovate in order to remain competitive. Free-trade zones such as NAFTA and the European Union (EU), along with trade liberalization through the World Trade Organization (WTO), have also heightened competition internationally by removing trade protection from domestic firms. The larger geographic markets, in turn, have enabled firms to expand beyond their national borders.

Implications for Economic Growth

Other things equal, stronger productivity growth and heightened global competition allow the economy to achieve a higher rate of economic growth. A glance back at Figure 8.2 will help make this point. Suppose that the shift of the production possibilities curve from *AB* to *CD* reflects annual changes in potential output levels before the recent increase in growth rates. Then the higher growth rates of the more recent period of accelerated productivity growth would be depicted by a *larger* outward shift of the economy's production possibilities from *AB* to a curve beyond *CD*. When coupled with economic efficiency and increased total spending, the economy's real GDP would rise by even more than what is shown.

Two cautions: Although the trend line of productivity growth seems to be steeper than in the past and bodes well for long-term economic growth, fluctuations of the rate of economic growth will still occur. Because of demand factors, real output periodically deviates below and above the growth trend—as it certainly did during the recession of 2007–2009. Also, you need to know that the growth of the U.S. labor force may be declining. That slowing may offset some or all of the extra potential for economic growth that would arise from greater productivity growth.

Skepticism about Longevity

Although most macroeconomists have revised their forecasts for long-term productivity growth upward, at least slightly, others are still skeptical and urge a "wait-and-see" approach. These macroeconomists acknowledge that the economy has experienced a rapid advance of new technology, some new firms have experienced increasing returns, and global competition has increased. But they wonder if these factors are sufficiently profound to produce a long-lasting new era of substantially higher rates of productivity growth and real GDP growth.

They also point out that productivity surged between 1975 and 1978 and between 1983 and 1986 but in each case soon reverted to its lower long-run trend. The higher trend line of productivity inferred from the short-run spurt of productivity could prove to be transient. Only by looking backward over long periods can economists distinguish the start of a new long-run trend from a shorter-term boost in productivity related to the business cycle and temporary factors.

What Can We Conclude?

Given the different views on the recent productivity acceleration, what should we conclude? Perhaps the safest conclusions are these:

- The prospects for a lasting increase in productivity growth are good (see Global Perspective 8.2). Studies indicate that productivity increases related to information technology have spread to a wide range of industries, including services. Even during the severe 2007–2009 recession, when real GDP fell by nearly 5 percent, productivity growth continued. Specifically, it ran at a 2.1 percent rate in 2007 just as the recession was starting, fell to 0.9 percent in 2008 when the recession was at its worst, and then jumped up to a very brisk 4.9 percent as the economy began to recover in 2009.

- Time will tell. After the rapid productivity growth of 2009, the growth rate fell to just 0.5 percent in 2010, 0.9 percent in 2011, and 1.0 percent in 2012. Consequently, the average growth rate over those four years is lower than the 2.4 percent rate shown by the trend line in Figure 8.5—but it is higher than the 1.5 percent rate for the 1973–1995 period. Clearly, many more years must elapse before economists will be ready to declare the post-1995 productivity acceleration a long-run, sustainable trend.

GLOBAL PERSPECTIVE 8.2

Global Competitiveness Index

The Global Competitiveness Index, published annually by the World Economic Forum, measures each country's potential for economic growth. The index uses various factors—such as innovativeness, the capability to transfer technology among sectors, the efficiency of the financial system, rates of investment, and the degree of integration with the rest of the world—to measure a country's ability to achieve economic growth over time. Here is the top 10 list for 2012–2013.

Country	Global Competitiveness Ranking, 2012–2013
Switzerland	1
Singapore	2
Finland	3
Sweden	4
Netherlands	5
Germany	6
United States	7
United Kingdom	8
Hong Kong	9
Japan	10

Source: Copyright World Economic Forum, **www.weforum.org**.

QUICK REVIEW 8.4

- Over long time periods, labor productivity growth determines an economy's growth of real wages and its standard of living.

- Many economists believe that the United States has entered a period of faster productivity growth and possibly higher rates of economic growth.

- The rise in the average rate of productivity growth is based on rapid technological change in the form of the microchip and information technology, increasing returns and lower per-unit costs, and heightened global competition that helps hold down prices.

- More-rapid U.S. productivity growth means that, other things equal, the U.S. economy can grow at higher annual rates than it could with less-rapid productivity growth. Nonetheless, many economists caution that it is still too early to determine whether the higher rates of productivity growth since 1995 are a lasting long-run trend or a fortunate short-lived occurrence.

Is Growth Desirable and Sustainable?

LO8.6 Discuss differing perspectives as to whether growth is desirable and sustainable.

Economists usually take for granted that economic growth is desirable and sustainable. But not everyone agrees.

The Antigrowth View

Critics of growth say industrialization and growth result in pollution, climate change, ozone depletion, and other environmental problems. These adverse negative externalities occur because inputs in the production process reenter the environment as some form of waste. The more rapid our growth and the higher our standard of living, the more waste the environment must absorb—or attempt to absorb. In an already wealthy society, further growth usually means satisfying increasingly trivial wants at the cost of mounting threats to the ecological system.

Critics of growth also argue that there is little compelling evidence that economic growth has solved sociological problems such as poverty, homelessness, and discrimination. Consider poverty: In the antigrowth view, American poverty is a problem of distribution, not production. The requisite for solving the problem is a firm commitment to redistribute wealth and income, not further increases in output.

Antigrowth sentiment also says that while growth may permit us to "make a better living," it does not give us "the good life." We may be producing more and enjoying it less. Growth means frantic paces on jobs, worker burnout, and alienated employees who have little or no control over decisions affecting their lives. The changing technology at the core of growth poses new anxieties and new sources of insecurity for workers. Both high-level and low-level workers face the prospect of having their hard-earned skills and experience rendered obsolete by onrushing technology. High-growth economies are high-stress economies, which may impair our physical and mental health.

Finally, critics of high rates of growth doubt that they are sustainable. The planet Earth has finite amounts of natural resources available, and they are being consumed at alarming rates. Higher rates of economic growth simply speed up the degradation and exhaustion of the earth's resources. In this view, slower economic growth that is environmentally sustainable is preferable to faster growth.

In Defense of Economic Growth

The primary defense of growth is that it is the path to the greater material abundance and higher living standards desired by the vast majority of people. Rising output and incomes allow people to buy

> more education, recreation, and travel, more medical care, closer communications, more skilled personal and professional services, and better-designed as well as more numerous products. It also means more art, music, and poetry, theater, and drama. It can even mean more time and resources devoted to spiritual growth and human development.[1]

Growth also enables society to improve the nation's infrastructure, enhance the care of the sick and elderly, provide greater access for the disabled, and provide more police and fire protection. Economic growth may be the only realistic way to reduce poverty, since there is only limited political support for greater redistribution of income. The way to improve the economic position of the poor is to increase household incomes through higher productivity and economic growth. Also, a no-growth policy among industrial nations might severely limit growth in poor nations. Foreign investment and development assistance in those nations would fall, keeping the world's poor in poverty longer.

Economic growth has not made labor more unpleasant or hazardous, as critics suggest. New machinery is usually less taxing and less dangerous than the machinery it replaces. Air-conditioned workplaces are more pleasant than steamy workshops. Furthermore, why would an end to economic growth reduce materialism or alienation? The loudest protests against materialism are heard in those nations and groups that now enjoy the highest levels of material abundance! The high standard of living that growth provides has increased our leisure and given us more time for reflection and self-fulfillment.

Does growth threaten the environment? The connection between growth and environment is tenuous, say growth proponents. Increases in economic growth need not mean increases in pollution. Pollution is not so much a by-product of growth as it is a "problem of the commons." Much of the environment—streams, lakes, oceans, and the air—is treated as common property, with insufficient or no restrictions on its use. The commons have become our dumping grounds; we have overused

---

[1] Alice M. Rivlin, *Reviving the American Dream* (Washington, D.C.: Brookings Institution, 1992), p. 36.

Can Economic Growth Survive Population Decline?

The Demographic Transition Is Causing Greying Populations, Shrinking Labor Forces, and Overall Population Decreases in Many Nations. Can Economic Growth Survive?

As you know from this chapter, Real GDP = hours of work × labor productivity. The number of *hours of work* depends heavily, however, on the size of the working-age population. If it begins to shrink, the number of *hours of work* almost always falls. In such cases, the only way real GDP can rise is if *labor productivity* increases faster than *hours of work* decreases. The world is about to see if that can happen in countries that have populations that are greying and shrinking.

The historical background has to do with the fact that as nations industrialize, their economies shift from agriculture to industry. As that happens, fertility levels plummet because the shift to modern technology transforms children from being economically essential farm hands that can contribute to their families' incomes from a young age to expensive investment goods that require many years of costly schooling before they can support themselves.

As people react to this change, birthrates tend to fall quite dramatically. The key statistic is the *total fertility rate* that keeps track of the average number of births that women have during their lifetimes. To keep the population stable in modern societies, the total fertility rate must be about 2.1 births per woman per lifetime (= 1 child to replace mom, 1 child to replace dad, and 0.1 child to compensate for those people who never end up reproducing as adults).

Every rich industrial nation has now seen its total fertility rate drop below the replacement level of 2.1 births per woman per lifetime. In Japan and many Eastern European countries, the number has been so low for so long that

and debased them. Environmental pollution is a case of negative externalities, and correcting this problem involves regulatory legislation, specific taxes ("effluent charges"), or market-based incentives to remedy misuse of the environment.

Those who support growth admit there are serious environmental problems. But they say that limiting growth is the wrong solution. Growth has allowed economies to reduce pollution, be more sensitive to environmental considerations, set aside wilderness, create national parks and monuments, and clean up hazardous waste, while still enabling rising household incomes.

Is growth sustainable? Yes, say the proponents of growth. If we were depleting natural resources faster than their discovery, we would see the prices of those resources rise. That has not been the case for most natural resources; in fact, the prices of most of them have declined. And if one natural resource becomes too expensive, another resource will be substituted for it. Moreover, say economists, economic growth has to do

with the expansion and application of human knowledge and information, not of extractable natural resources. In this view, economic growth is limited only by human imagination.

QUICK REVIEW 8.5

- Critics of growth argue that it adds to environmental degradation, increases human stress, and exhausts the earth's finite supply of natural resources.
- Defenders of growth say that it is the primary path to the rising living standards, that it need not debase the environment, and that there are no indications that we are running out of resources.
- Defenders of growth argue that it is sustainable because growth is based on the expansion and application of human knowledge, which is limited only by human imagination.

there are no longer enough children being born each year to re-place the old folks who are dying. As a result, their overall popu-lations are shrinking.

Economists only expect that pattern to become more com-mon and more rapid, so that by the year 2050 the majority of na-tions will have decreasing populations. But decades before a nation's overall population begins to decrease, it faces a situation in which the labor force shrinks while the elderly population swells.

That pattern is the result of each generation being smaller than the one before. As an example, the Baby Boom generation born between 1946 and 1964 is much larger than the Baby Bust generation that followed it. So as the Boomers retire over the next two decades, there will be a lot of retirees as compared to working-age adults.

This trend can be quantified by the *inverse dependency ratio*, which is defined as the number of people of working age (ages 20 to 64) divided by the number of dependents (seniors over age 65 plus youths under age 20). In the United States, the inverse de-pendency ratio is set to fall from 1.5 people of working age per dependent in 2010 to just 1.16 people of working age per depen-dent in 2050. That is extremely problematic because it implies that worker productivity will have to rise dramatically just to make up for the relative decline in the number of workers as compared to dependents. If productivity doesn't keep up with the fall in the inverse dependency ratio, living standards will have to decline because there will simply be too many nonworking consumers relative to working-age producers.

The place where this problem is likely to show up first is Social Security. There are currently 2.9 workers paying into the Social Security system for each retiree receiving Social Security benefits. But that number is set to fall to just 2.0 workers per retiree in 2030. So worker productivity would have to increase by almost a third in under 20 years just to keep up with the decline in the number of workers relative to retirees.

Economists are uncertain about whether such large produc-tivity increases will be forthcoming. The problem is that con-sumption competes with investment. A society with a larger fraction of dependents is a society that is likely to devote an in-creasingly high fraction of total output toward consumption rather than investment. If so, productivity growth may slow considerably.

Another possible problem is that, historically, most transfor-mative new technologies and businesses have been created by energetic young people under the age of 40. With each genera-tion getting smaller, there will be fewer people in that age range and thus, possibly, less innovation and slower productivity growth.

Other economists are more hopeful, however. They view old people as consumers and demanders. As their numbers swell, in-ventors may simply switch from inventing products for young people to inventing products for old people. If so, productivity growth and living standards could keep on rising at the rates we have come to expect.

SUMMARY

LO8.1 List two ways that economic growth is measured.

A nation's economic growth can be measured either as an in-crease in real GDP over time or as an increase in real GDP per capita over time. Real GDP in the United States has grown at an average annual rate of about 3.2 percent since 1950; real GDP per capita has grown at roughly a 2 percent annual rate over that same period.

LO8.2 Define "modern economic growth" and explain the institutional structures needed for an economy to experience it.

Sustained increases in real GDP per capita did not happen until the past two centuries, when England and then other countries began to experience modern economic growth, which is char-acterized by institutional structures that encourage savings,

investment, and the development of new technologies. Institutional structures that promote growth include strong property rights, patents, efficient financial institutions, educa-tion, and a competitive market system.

Because some nations have experienced nearly two centuries of modern economic growth while others have only recently be-gun to experience modern economic growth, some countries to-day are much richer than other countries.

It is possible, however, for countries that are currently poor to grow faster than countries that are currently rich because the growth of real GDP per capita for rich countries is limited to about 2 percent per year. To continue growing, rich countries must invent and apply new technologies. By contrast, poor coun-tries can grow much faster because they can simply adopt the institutions and cutting-edge technologies already developed by the rich countries.

LO8.3 Identify the general supply, demand, and efficiency forces that give rise to economic growth.

The determinants of economic growth to which we can attribute changes in growth rates include four supply factors (changes in the quantity and quality of natural resources, changes in the quantity and quality of human resources, changes in the stock of capital goods, and improvements in technology); one demand factor (changes in total spending); and one efficiency factor (changes in how well an economy achieves allocative and productive efficiency).

The growth of a nation's capacity to produce output can be illustrated graphically by an outward shift of its production possibilities curve.

LO8.4 Describe "growth accounting" and the specific factors accounting for economic growth in the United States.

Growth accounting attributes increases in real GDP either to increases in the amount of labor being employed or to increases in the productivity of the labor being employed. Increases in U.S. real GDP are mostly the result of increases in labor productivity. The increases in labor productivity can be attributed to technological progress, increases in the quantity of capital per worker, improvements in the education and training of workers, the exploitation of economies of scale, and improvements in the allocation of labor across different industries.

LO8.5 Explain why the trend rate of U.S. productivity growth has increased since the earlier 1973–1995 period.

Over long time periods, the growth of labor productivity underlies an economy's growth of real wages and its standard of living. U.S. productivity rose by 2.4 percent annually between 1995 and 2012, compared to 1.5 percent annually between 1973 and 1995.

This post-1995 increase in the average rate of productivity growth is based on (a) rapid technological change in the form of the microchip and information technology, (b) increasing returns and lower per-unit costs, and (c) heightened global competition that holds down prices.

The main sources of increasing returns in recent years are (a) the use of more specialized inputs as firms grow, (b) the spreading of development costs, (c) simultaneous consumption by consumers, (d) network effects, and (e) learning by doing. Increasing returns mean higher productivity and lower per-unit production costs.

LO8.6 Discuss differing perspectives as to whether growth is desirable and sustainable.

Skeptics wonder if the recent rise in the average rate of productivity growth is permanent, and suggest a wait-and-see approach. They point out that surges in productivity and real GDP growth have previously occurred but do not necessarily represent long-lived trends.

Critics of rapid growth say that it adds to environmental degradation, increases human stress, and exhausts the earth's finite supply of natural resources. Defenders of rapid growth say that it is the primary path to the rising living standards nearly universally desired by people, that it need not debase the environment, and that there are no indications that we are running out of resources. Growth is based on the expansion and application of human knowledge, which is limited only by human imagination.

TERMS AND CONCEPTS

economic growth	demand factor	economies of scale
real GDP per capita	efficiency factor	information technology
rule of 70	labor productivity	start-up firms
modern economic growth	labor-force participation rate	increasing returns
leader countries	growth accounting	network effects
follower countries	infrastructure	learning by doing
supply factors	human capital	

The following and additional problems can be found in **connect** | ECONOMICS

DISCUSSION QUESTIONS

1. How is economic growth measured? Why is economic growth important? Why could the difference between a 2.5 percent and a 3 percent annual growth rate be of great significance over several decades? **LO8.1**

2. When and where did modern economic growth first happen? What are the major institutional factors that form the foundation for modern economic growth? What do they have in common? **LO8.2**

3. Why are some countries today much poorer than other countries? Are today's poor countries destined to always be poorer than today's rich countries? If so, explain why. If not, explain how today's poor countries can catch or even pass today's rich countries. **LO8.2**

4. What are the four supply factors of economic growth? What is the demand factor? What is the efficiency factor? Illustrate these factors in terms of the production possibilities curve. **LO8.3**

5. Suppose that Alpha and Omega have identically sized working-age populations but that total annual hours of work are much greater in Alpha than in Omega. Provide two possible reasons for this difference. **LO8.3**

6. What is growth accounting? To what extent have increases in U.S. real GDP resulted from more labor inputs? From greater labor productivity? Rearrange the following contributors to the growth of productivity in order of their quantitative importance: economies of scale, quantity of capital, improved resource allocation, education and training, and technological advance. **LO8.4**

7. True or False: If false, explain why. **LO8.4**
   a. Technological advance, which to date has played a relatively small role in U.S. economic growth, is destined to play a more important role in the future.

b. Many public capital goods are complementary to private capital goods.

c. Immigration has slowed economic growth in the United States.

8. Explain why there is such a close relationship between changes in a nation's rate of productivity growth and changes in its average real hourly wage. **LO8.5**

9. Relate each of the following to the recent increase in the trend rate of productivity growth: **LO8.5**
   a. Information technology.
   b. Increasing returns.
   c. Network effects.
   d. Global competition.

10. What, if any, are the benefits and costs of economic growth, particularly as measured by real GDP per capita? **LO8.6**

11. **LAST WORD** Would you expect a country with a total fertility rate of 2.7 to have a growing or a shrinking population over the long run? What about a country with a total fertility rate of 1.2? In 20 years, will America have more or fewer workers per retiree than it does today? Why does a falling inverse dependency ratio make it harder for real GDP to continue growing?

REVIEW QUESTIONS

1. If real GDP grows at 7 percent per year, then real GDP will double in approximately _____ years. **LO8.1**
   a. 70.
   b. 14.
   c. 10.
   d. 7.

2. In 1820 living standards in various places around the globe were _____ they are today. **LO8.2**
   a. More widely varying than.
   b. Just as widely varying as.
   c. Less widely varying than.

3. True or False: Countries that currently have low real GDPs per capita are destined to always have lower living standards than countries that currently have high real GDPs per capita. **LO8.2**

4. Identify each of the following situations as something that either promotes growth or retards growth. **LO8.2**
   a. Increasing corruption allows government officials to steal people's homes.
   b. A nation introduces patent laws for the first time.
   c. A court order shuts down all banks permanently.
   d. A poor country extends free public schooling from 8 years to 12 years.
   e. A nation adopts a free-trade policy.
   f. A formerly communist country adopts free markets.

5. Real GDP equals _____ times _____. **LO8.4**
   a. Average hours of work; quantity of capital.

b. Average hours of work; allocative efficiency.
   c. Labor input; labor productivity.
   d. Natural resources; improvements in technology.

6. Suppose that just by doubling the amount of output that it produces each year, a firm's per-unit production costs fall by 30 percent. This is an example of: **LO8.4**
   a. Economies of scale.
   b. Improved resource allocation.
   c. Technological advance.
   d. The demand factor.

7. True or False: Computers and increased global competition have retarded economic growth in recent decades. **LO8.5**

8. Identify following arguments about economic growth as being either anti-growth or pro-growth. **LO8.6**
   a. Growth means worker burnout and frantic schedules.
   b. Rising incomes allow people to buy more education, medical care, and recreation.
   c. The Earth has only finite amounts of natural resources.
   d. We still have poverty, homelessness, and discrimination even in the richest countries.
   e. Richer countries spend more money protecting the environment.
   f. Natural resource prices have fallen rather than increased over time.

PROBLEMS

1. Suppose an economy's real GDP is $30,000 in year 1 and $31,200 in year 2. What is the growth rate of its real GDP? Assume that population is 100 in year 1 and 102 in year 2. What is the growth rate of real GDP per capita? **LO8.1**

2. What annual growth rate is needed for a country to double its output in 7 years? In 35 years? In 70 years? In 140 years? **LO8.1**

3. Assume that a "leader country" has real GDP per capita of $40,000, whereas a "follower country" has real GDP per capita of $20,000. Next suppose that the growth of real GDP per capita falls to zero percent in the leader country and rises to 7 percent in the follower country. If these rates continue for long periods of time, how many years will it take for the follower country to catch up to the living standard of the leader country? **LO8.2**

4. Refer to Figure 8.2 and assume that the values for points *a*, *b*, and *c* are $10 billion, $20 billion, and $18 billion respec-

tively. If the economy moves from point *a* to point *b* over a 10-year period, what must have been its annual rate of economic growth? If, instead, the economy was at point *c* at the end of the 10-year period, by what percentage did it fall short of its production capacity? **LO8.3**

5. Suppose that work hours in New Zombie are 200 in year 1 and productivity is $8 per hour worked. What is New Zombie's real GDP? If work hours increase to 210 in year 2 and productivity rises to $10 per hour, what is New Zombie's rate of economic growth? **LO8.4**

6. The per-unit cost of an item is its average total cost (= total cost/quantity). Suppose that a new cell phone application costs $100,000 to develop and only $0.50 per unit to deliver to each cell phone customer. What will be the per-unit cost of the application if it sells 100 units? 1,000 units? 1 million units? **LO8.5**

FURTHER TEST YOUR KNOWLEDGE AT www.mcconnell20e.com

Practice quizzes, student PowerPoints, worked problems, Web-based questions, and additional materials are available at the text's Online Learning Center (OLC), **www.mcconnell20e.com**, or scan here. Need a barcode reader? Try ScanLife, available in your app store.

CHAPTER 9

Business Cycles, Unemployment, and Inflation

Learning Objectives

LO9.1 Describe the business cycle and its primary phases.

LO9.2 Illustrate how unemployment is measured and explain the different types of unemployment.

LO9.3 Explain how inflation is measured and distinguish between cost-push inflation and demand-pull inflation.

LO9.4 Relate how unanticipated inflation can redistribute real income.

LO9.5 Discuss how inflation may affect the economy's level of real output.

As indicated in Chapter 8, the United States has experienced remarkable economic growth over time. But this growth has not been smooth, steady, and predictable from year to year. At various times the United States has experienced recessions, high unemployment rates, or high inflation rates. For example, U.S. unemployment rose by 8 million workers and the unemployment rate increased from 4.7 percent to 10.1 percent during the 2007–2009 recession. Other nations have also suffered high unemployment rates at times. As just one example, Spain's unemployment rate exceeded 26 percent in 2012. Also, inflation has occasionally plagued the United States and other nations. For instance, the U.S. inflation rate in 1980 was 13.5 percent. Zimbabwe's inflation soared to 26,000 percent in 2007!

Our goal in this chapter is to examine the concepts, terminology, and facts relating to macroeconomic instability. Specifically, we want to discuss the business cycle, unemployment, and inflation. The concepts discussed are extremely important for understanding subsequent chapters on economic theory and economic policy.

The Business Cycle

LO9.1 Describe the business cycle and its primary phases.

The long-run trend of the U.S. economy is one of economic growth, as stylized by the upsloping line labeled "Growth Trend" in Figure 9.1. But growth has been interrupted by periods of economic instability usually associated with **business cycles.** Business cycles are alternating rises and declines in the level of economic activity, sometimes over several years. Individual cycles (one "up" followed by one "down") vary substantially in duration and intensity.

ORIGIN OF THE IDEA

O9.1
Business cycles

Phases of the Business Cycle

Figure 9.1 shows the four phases of a generalized business cycle:

- At a **peak,** such as the middle peak shown in Figure 9.1, business activity has reached a temporary maximum. Here the economy is near or at full employment and the level of real output is at or very close to the economy's capacity. The price level is likely to rise during this phase.

- A **recession** is a period of decline in total output, income, and employment. This downturn, which lasts 6 months or more, is marked by the widespread contraction of business activity in many sectors of the economy. Along with declines in real GDP, significant increases in unemployment occur. Table 9.1

TABLE 9.1 U.S. Recessions since 1950

Period	Duration, Months	Depth (Decline in Real Output)
1953–54	10	−2.6%
1957–58	8	−3.7
1960–61	10	−1.1
1969–70	11	−0.2
1973–75	16	−3.2
1980	6	−2.2
1981–82	16	−2.9
1990–91	8	−1.4
2001	8	−0.4
2007–09	18	−4.3

Source: National Bureau of Economic Research, **www.nber.org**, Bureau of Economic Analysis, **www.bea.gov**, and Minneapolis Federal Reserve Bank, "The Recession and Recovery in Perspective," **www.minneapolisfed.gov**. Output data are in 2000 dollars.

documents the 10 recessions in the United States since 1950.

- In the **trough** of the recession or depression, output and employment "bottom out" at their lowest levels. The trough phase may be either short-lived or quite long.

- A recession is usually followed by a recovery and **expansion,** a period in which real GDP, income, and employment rise. At some point, the economy again approaches full employment. If spending then expands more rapidly than does production capacity, prices of nearly all goods and services will rise. In other words, inflation will occur.

Although business cycles all pass through the same phases, they vary greatly in duration and intensity. Many economists prefer to talk of business "fluctuations" rather than cycles because cycles imply regularity while fluctuations do not. The Great Depression of the 1930s resulted in a 27 percent decline in real GDP over a 3-year period in the United States and seriously impaired business activity for a decade. By comparison, the U.S. recessions detailed in Table 9.1 were less severe in both intensity and duration.

The Business Cycle Dating Committee of the National Bureau of Economic Research (NBER), a nonprofit economic research organization, declares the start and end of recessions in the United States. Citing evidence of declining real output and falling employment, the NBER officially declared that the latest recession began in December 2007. The NBER subsequently declared that the Great Recession ended in June 2009, 18 months after it began. In making this announcement, the NBER pointed out

FIGURE 9.1 The business cycle. Economists distinguish four phases of the business cycle; the duration and strength of each phase may vary.

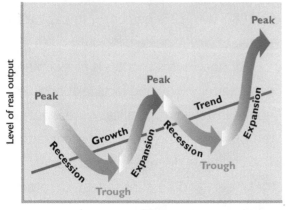

that its declaration was not a forecast for the future path of the economy.

Recessions, of course, occur in other countries, too. For example, nearly all industrial nations and many developing nations have suffered recessions in the past several years.

Causation: A First Glance

The long-run trend of the U.S. economy is expansion and growth. That is why the business cycles in Figure 9.1 are drawn against a trend of economic growth. A key issue in macroeconomics is why the economy sees business cycle fluctuations rather than slow, smooth growth. In terms of Figure 9.1, why does output move up and down rather than just staying on the smooth growth trend line?

Economists have developed several possible explanations. But before turning to them, recall that in Chapter 6 we explained that these theories are founded on the idea that fluctuations are driven by shocks—unexpected events that individuals and firms may have trouble adjusting to. Also recall that short-run price stickiness is widely believed to be a major factor preventing the economy from rapidly adjusting to shocks. With prices sticky in the short run, price changes cannot quickly equalize the quantities demanded of goods and services with their respective quantities supplied after a shock has happened. Instead, the economy is forced to respond to shocks in the short run primarily through changes in output and employment rather than through changes in prices.

Economists cite several possible general sources of shocks that can cause business cycles.

- *Irregular innovation* Significant new products or production methods, such as those associated with the railroad, automobile, computer, and Internet, can rapidly spread through the economy, sparking sizable increases in investment, consumption, output, and employment. After the economy has largely absorbed the new innovation, the economy may for a time slow down or possibly decline. Because such innovations occur irregularly and unexpectedly, they may contribute to the variability of economic activity.

- *Productivity changes* When productivity—output per unit of input—unexpectedly increases, the economy booms; when productivity unexpectedly decreases, the economy recedes. Such changes in productivity can result from unexpected changes in resource availability (of, say, oil or agricultural commodities) or from unexpected changes in the general rate of technological advance.

- *Monetary factors* Some economists see business cycles as purely monetary phenomena. When a nation's central bank shocks the economy by creating more money than people were expecting, an inflationary boom in output occurs. By contrast, printing less money than people were expecting triggers an output decline and, eventually, a price-level fall.

- *Political events* Unexpected political events, such as peace treaties, new wars, or the 9/11 terrorist attacks, can create economic opportunities or strains. In adjusting to these shocks, the economy may experience upswings or downswings.

- *Financial instability* Unexpected financial bubbles (rapid asset price increases) or bursts (abrupt asset price decreases) can spill over to the general economy by expanding or contracting lending, and boosting or eroding the confidence of consumers and businesses. Booms and busts in the rest of the economy may follow.

The severe recession of 2007–2009 was precipitated by a combination of excessive money and a financial frenzy that led to overvalued real estate and unsustainable mortgage debt. Institutions bundled this debt into new securities ("derivatives") that were sold to financial investors. Some of the investors, in turn, bought insurance against losses that might arise from the securities. As real estate prices plummeted and mortgage defaults unexpectedly rocketed, the securitization and insurance structure buckled and nearly collapsed. Credit markets froze, pessimism prevailed, and spending by businesses and households declined.

Whatever the source of economic shocks, most economists agree that the *immediate* cause of the large majority of cyclical changes in the levels of real output and employment is unexpected changes in the level of total spending. If total spending unexpectedly sinks and firms cannot lower prices, firms will find themselves selling fewer units of output (since with prices fixed, a decreased amount of spending implies fewer items purchased). Slower sales will cause firms to cut back on production. As they do, GDP will fall. And because fewer workers will be needed to produce less output, employment also will fall. The economy will contract and enter a recession.

By contrast, if the level of spending unexpectedly rises, output, employment, and incomes will rise. This is true because, with prices sticky, the increased spending will mean that consumers will be buying a larger volume of goods and services (since, with prices fixed, more spending means more items purchased). Firms will respond by increasing output. This will increase GDP. And because firms will need to hire more workers to produce the larger volume of output, employment also will increase. The economy will boom and enjoy an expansion. Eventually, as time passes and prices become more flexible, prices are also likely to rise as a result of the increased spending.

Cyclical Impact: Durables and Nondurables

Although the business cycle is felt everywhere in the economy, it affects different segments in different ways and to different degrees.

Firms and industries producing *capital goods* (for example, housing, commercial buildings, heavy equipment, and farm implements) and *consumer durables* (for example, automobiles, personal computers, and refrigerators) are affected most by the business cycle. Within limits, firms can postpone the purchase of capital goods. For instance, when the economy goes into recession, producers frequently delay the purchase of new equipment and the construction of new plants. The business outlook simply does not warrant increases in the stock of capital goods. In good times, capital goods are usually replaced before they depreciate completely. But when recession strikes, firms patch up their old equipment and make do. As a result, investment in capital goods declines sharply. Firms that have excess plant capacity may not even bother to replace all the capital that is depreciating. For them, net investment may be negative. The pattern is much the same for consumer durables such as automobiles and major appliances. When recession occurs and households must trim their budgets, purchases of these goods are often deferred. Families repair their old cars and appliances rather than buy new ones, and the firms producing these products suffer. (Of course, producers of capital goods and consumer durables also benefit most from expansions.)

In contrast, *service* industries and industries that produce *nondurable consumer goods* are somewhat insulated from the most severe effects of recession. People find it difficult to cut back on needed medical and legal services, for example. And a recession actually helps some service firms, such as pawnbrokers and law firms that specialize in bankruptcies. Nor are the purchases of many nondurable goods such as food and clothing easy to postpone. The quantity and quality of purchases of nondurables will decline, but not so much as will purchases of capital goods and consumer durables.

> ### QUICK REVIEW 9.1
>
> - The typical business cycle goes through four phases: peak, recession, trough, and expansion.
> - Fluctuations in output and employment are caused by economic shocks combining with sticky prices.
> - Sources of shocks that cause recessions include irregular innovation, productivity changes, monetary factors, political events, and financial instability.
> - During a recession, industries that produce capital goods and consumer durables normally suffer greater output and employment declines than do service and nondurable consumer goods industries.

Unemployment

LO9.2 Illustrate how unemployment is measured and explain the different types of unemployment.

Two problems that arise over the course of the business cycle are unemployment and inflation. Let's look at unemployment first.

Measurement of Unemployment

The U.S. Bureau of Labor Statistics (BLS) conducts a nationwide random survey of some 60,000 households each month to determine who is employed and who is not employed. In a series of questions, it asks which members of the household are working, unemployed and looking for work, not looking for work, and so on. From the answers, it determines an unemployment rate for the entire nation.

Figure 9.2 helps explain the mathematics. The BLS divides the total U.S. population into three groups. One group is made up of people under 16 years of age and people who are institutionalized, for example, in mental hospitals or correctional institutions. Such people are not considered potential members of the labor force.

A second group, labeled "Not in labor force," is composed of adults who are potential workers but are not employed and are not seeking work. For example, they are stay-at-home parents, full-time students, or retirees.

The third group is the **labor force**, which constituted slightly more than 50 percent of the total population in 2009. The labor force consists of people who are able and willing to work. Both those who are employed and those who are unemployed but actively seeking work are counted as being in the labor force. The **unemployment rate** is the percentage of the labor force unemployed:

$$\text{Unemployment rate} = \frac{\text{unemployed}}{\text{labor force}} \times 100$$

FIGURE 9.2 The U.S. labor force, employment, and unemployment, 2012.* The labor force consists of persons 16 years of age or older who are not in institutions and who are (1) employed or (2) unemployed but seeking employment.

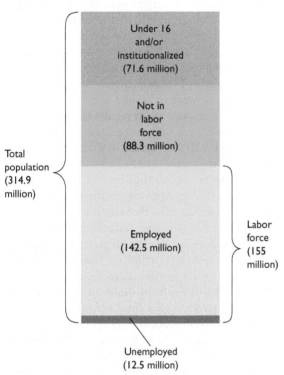

*Civilian labor-force data, which excludes military employment.
Source: Bureau of Labor Statistics, **www.bls.gov**.

The statistics underlying the rounded numbers in Figure 9.2 show that in 2012 the unemployment rate averaged

$$\frac{12{,}506{,}000}{154{,}975{,}000} \times 100 = 8.1\%$$

WORKED PROBLEMS

W9.1 Unemployment rate

Unemployment rates for selected years appear on the inside covers of this book.

Despite the use of scientific sampling and interviewing techniques, the data collected in this survey are subject to criticism:

- *Part-time employment* The BLS lists all part-time workers as fully employed. In 2012 about 26 million people worked part-time as a result of personal choice. But another 8 million part-time workers either wanted to work full-time and could not find suitable full-time work or worked fewer hours because of a temporary slack in consumer demand. These last two groups were, in effect, partially employed and partially unemployed. By counting them as fully employed, say critics, the official BLS data understate the unemployment rate.

- *Discouraged workers* You must be actively seeking work in order to be counted as unemployed. An unemployed individual who is not actively seeking employment is classified as "not in the labor force." The problem is that many workers, after unsuccessfully seeking employment for a time, become discouraged and drop out of the labor force. The number of such **discouraged workers** was roughly 909,000 in 2012, up from 396,000 in 2007. By not counting discouraged workers as unemployed, say critics, the official BLS data understate the unemployment problem.

Types of Unemployment

There are three *types* of unemployment: frictional, structural, and cyclical.

Frictional Unemployment At any given time some workers are "between jobs." Some of them will be moving voluntarily from one job to another. Others will have been fired and will be seeking reemployment. Still others will have been laid off temporarily because of seasonal demand. In addition to those between jobs, many young workers will be searching for their first jobs.

As these unemployed people find jobs or are called back from temporary layoffs, other job seekers and laid-off workers will replace them in the "unemployment pool." It is important to keep in mind that while the pool itself persists because there are always newly unemployed workers flowing into it, most workers do *not* stay in the unemployment pool for very long. Indeed, when the economy is strong, the majority of unemployed workers find new jobs within a couple of months. One should be careful not to make the mistake of confusing the permanence of the pool itself with the false idea that the pool's membership is permanent, too. On the other hand, there are workers who do remain unemployed and in the pool for very long periods of time—sometimes for many years. As we discuss the different types of unemployment below, notice that certain types tend to be transitory while others are associated with much longer spells of unemployment.

Economists use the term **frictional unemployment**—consisting of *search unemployment* and *wait unemployment*—for workers who are either searching for jobs or waiting to take jobs in the near future. The word "frictional" implies

CONSIDER THIS . . .

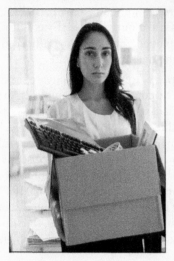

Downwardly Sticky Wages and Unemployment

Labor markets have an important quirk that helps to explain why unemployment goes up so much during a recession.

The quirk is that wages are flexible upward but sticky downward.

On the one hand, workers are perfectly happy to accept wage increases. So when the economy is booming and firms start bidding for the limited supply of labor, wages rise—often quite rapidly.

On the other hand, workers deeply resent pay cuts. So if the economy goes into a recession and firms need to reduce labor costs, managers almost never cut wages because doing so would only lead to disgruntled employees, low productivity, and—in extreme cases—workers stealing supplies or actively sabotaging their own firms.

Instead, managers usually opt for layoffs. The workers who are let go obviously don't like being unemployed. But those who remain get to keep their old wages and, consequently, keep on being as productive and cooperative as they were before.

This preference that firms show for layoffs over wage cuts results in downwardly sticky wages and an informal price floor that helps to explain why unemployment goes up so much during a recession. The problem is that when the demand for labor falls during a recession, the informal price floor prevents wages from falling. As a result, there is no way for falling wages to help entice at least some firms to hire a few more workers. Thus, when a recession hits, employment falls more precipitously than it would if wages were downwardly flexible and falling wages could help to increase hiring.

that the labor market does not operate perfectly and instantaneously (without friction) in matching workers and jobs.

Frictional unemployment is inevitable and, at least in part, desirable. Many workers who are voluntarily between jobs are moving from low-paying, low-productivity jobs to higher-paying, higher-productivity positions. That means greater income for the workers, a better allocation of labor resources, and a larger real GDP for the economy.

Structural Unemployment Frictional unemployment blurs into a category called **structural unemployment**. Here, economists use "structural" in the sense of "compositional." Changes over time in consumer demand and in technology alter the "structure" of the total demand for labor, both occupationally and geographically.

Occupationally, the demand for certain skills (for example, sewing clothes or working on farms) may decline or even vanish. The demand for other skills (for example, designing software or maintaining computer systems) will intensify. Unemployment results because the composition of the labor force does not respond immediately or completely to the new structure of job opportunities. Workers who find that their skills and experience have become obsolete or unneeded thus find that they have no marketable talents. They are structurally unemployed until they adapt or develop skills that employers want.

Geographically, the demand for labor also changes over time. An example: the migration of industry and thus of employment opportunities from the Snowbelt to the Sunbelt over the past few decades. Another example is the movement of jobs from inner-city factories to suburban industrial parks. And a final example is the so-called *off-shoring* of jobs that occurs when the demand for a particular type of labor shifts from domestic firms to foreign firms. As job opportunities shift from one place to another, some workers become structurally unemployed.

The distinction between frictional and structural unemployment is hazy at best. The key difference is that *frictionally* unemployed workers have marketable skills and either live in areas where jobs exist or are able to move to areas where they do. *Structurally* unemployed workers find it hard to obtain new jobs without retraining, gaining additional education, or relocating. Frictional unemployment is short-term; structural unemployment is more likely to be long-term and consequently more serious.

Cyclical Unemployment Unemployment that is caused by a decline in total spending is called **cyclical unemployment** and typically begins in the recession phase of the business cycle. As the demand for goods and services decreases, employment falls and unemployment rises. Cyclical unemployment results from insufficient demand for goods and services. The 25 percent unemployment rate in the depth of the Great Depression in 1933 reflected mainly cyclical unemployment, as did significant parts of the 9.7 percent unemployment rate in 1982, the 7.5 percent rate in 1992, the 5.8 percent rate in 2002, and the 9.3 percent rate in 2009.

Cyclical unemployment is a very serious problem when it occurs. We will say more about its high costs later, but first we need to define "full employment."

Definition of Full Employment

Because frictional and structural unemployment are largely unavoidable in a dynamic economy, *full employment* is something less than 100 percent employment of the labor force. Economists say that the economy is "fully employed" when it is experiencing only frictional and structural unemployment. That is, full employment occurs when there is no cyclical unemployment.

Economists describe the unemployment rate that is consistent with full employment as the **full-employment rate of unemployment,** or the **natural rate of unemployment (NRU).** At the NRU, the economy is said to be producing its **potential output.** This is the real GDP that occurs when the economy is "fully employed."

Note that a fully employed economy does not mean zero unemployment. Even when the economy is fully employed, the NRU is some positive percentage because it takes time for frictionally unemployed job seekers to find open jobs they can fill. Also, it takes time for the structurally unemployed to achieve the skills and geographic relocation needed for reemployment.

"Natural" does not mean, however, that the economy will always operate at this rate and thus realize its potential output. When cyclical unemployment occurs, the economy has much more unemployment than that which would occur at the NRU. Moreover, the economy can operate for a while at an unemployment rate *below* the NRU. At times, the demand for labor may be so great that firms take a stronger initiative to hire and train the structurally unemployed. Also, some parents, teenagers, college students, and retirees who were casually looking for just the right part-time or full-time jobs may quickly find them. Thus the unemployment rate temporarily falls below the natural rate.

Also, the NRU can vary over time as demographic factors, job-search methods, and public policies change. In the 1980s, the NRU was about 6 percent. Today, it is 5 to 6 percent.

Economic Cost of Unemployment

Unemployment that is excessive involves great economic and social costs.

GDP Gap and Okun's Law The basic economic cost of unemployment is forgone output. When the economy fails to create enough jobs for all who are able and willing to work, potential production of goods and services is irretrievably lost. In terms of Chapter 1's analysis, unemployment above the natural rate means that society is operating at some point inside its production possibilities curve. Economists call this sacrifice of output a **GDP gap**—the difference between actual and potential GDP. That is:

$$\text{GDP gap} = \text{actual GDP} - \text{potential GDP}$$

The GDP gap can be either negative (actual GDP < potential GDP) or positive (actual GDP > potential GDP). In the case of unemployment above the natural rate, it is negative because actual GDP falls short of potential GDP.

Potential GDP is determined by assuming that the natural rate of unemployment prevails. The growth of potential GDP is simply projected forward on the basis of the economy's "normal" growth rate of real GDP. Figure 9.3 shows the GDP gap for recent years in the United States. It also indicates the close correlation between the actual unemployment rate (Figure 9.3b) and the GDP gap (Figure 9.3a). The higher the unemployment rate, the larger is the GDP gap.

Macroeconomist Arthur Okun was the first to quantify the relationship between the unemployment rate and the GDP gap. **Okun's law** indicates that for every 1 percentage point by which the actual unemployment rate exceeds the natural rate, a negative GDP gap of about 2 percent occurs. With this information, we can calculate the absolute loss of output associated with any above-natural unemployment rate. For example, in 2009 the unemployment rate was

WORKED PROBLEMS

W9.2
Okun's law

9.3 percent, or 4.3 percentage points above that period's 5.0 percent natural rate of unemployment. Multiplying this 4.3 percent by Okun's 2 indicates that 2009's GDP gap was 8.6 percent of potential GDP (in real terms). By applying this 8.6 percent loss to 2009's potential GDP of $13,894 billion, we find that the economy sacrificed $1,195 billion of real output because the natural rate of unemployment was not achieved.

As you can see in Figure 9.3, sometimes the economy's actual output will exceed its potential or full-employment output. Figure 9.3 reveals that an economic expansion in 1999 and 2000, for example, caused actual GDP to exceed potential GDP in those years. There was a positive GDP gap in 1999 and 2000. Actual GDP for a time can exceed potential GDP, but positive GDP gaps create inflationary pressures and cannot be sustained indefinitely.

Unequal Burdens An increase in the unemployment rate from 5 to, say, 9 or 10 percent might be more tolerable to society if every worker's hours of work and wage

FIGURE 9.3 Actual and potential real GDP and the unemployment rate. (a) The difference between actual and potential GDP is the GDP gap. A negative GDP gap measures the output the economy sacrifices when actual GDP falls short of potential GDP. A positive GDP gap indicates that actual GDP is above potential GDP. (b) A high unemployment rate means a large GDP gap (negative), and a low unemployment rate means a small or even positive GDP gap.

(a)
The GDP gap

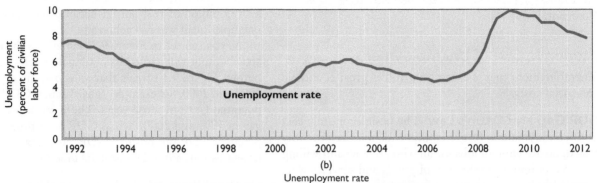

(b)
Unemployment rate

Source: Congressional Budget Office, **www.cbo.gov**; Bureau of Economic Analysis, **www.bea.gov**; and the Bureau of Labor Statistics, **www.bls.gov**. Note that the data for actual real GDP and potential real GDP above differ from the real GDP data in the previous two chapters. The data above are in 2005 dollars, not 2009 dollars, and do not reflect the 2013 redefinition of investment expenditures in the National Income and Product Accounts to include research and development spending.

TABLE 9.2 Unemployment Rates by Demographic Group: Full Employment Year (2007) and Recession Year (2009)*

Demographic Group	Unemployment Rate 2007	2009
Overall	4.6%	9.3%
Occupation:		
Managerial and professional	2.1	4.6
Construction and extraction	7.6	19.7
Age:		
16–19	15.7	24.3
African American, 16–19	29.4	39.5
White, 16–19	13.9	21.8
Male, 20+	4.1	9.6
Female, 20+	4.0	7.5
Race and ethnicity:		
African American	8.3	14.8
Hispanic	5.6	12.1
White	4.1	8.5
Gender:		
Women	4.5	8.1
Men	4.7	10.3
Education:†		
Less than high school diploma	7.1	14.6
High school diploma only	4.4	9.7
College degree or more	2.0	4.6
Duration:		
15 or more weeks	1.5	4.7

*Civilian labor-force data.

†People age 25 or over.

*Source: Economic Report of the President; Bureau of Labor Statistics, **www.bls.gov**; Census Bureau, **www.census.gov**.*

income were reduced proportionally. But this is not the case. Part of the burden of unemployment is that its cost is unequally distributed.

Table 9.2 examines unemployment rates for various labor market groups for 2 periods. In 2007, the economy achieved full employment, with a 4.6 percent unemployment rate. The economy receded in December 2007 and two years later was feeling the full unemployment impact of the Great Recession. By observing the large variance in unemployment rates for the different groups within each period and comparing the rates between the 2 periods, we can generalize as follows:

- *Occupation* Workers in lower-skilled occupations (for example, laborers) have higher unemployment rates than workers in higher-skilled occupations (for example, professionals). Lower-skilled workers have more and longer spells of structural unemployment than higher-skilled workers. They also are less likely to be self-employed than are higher-skilled workers. Moreover, lower-skilled workers usually bear the brunt of recessions. Manufacturing, construction, and mining tend to be particularly hard-hit, and businesses generally retain most of their higher-skilled workers, in whom they have invested the expense of training.

- *Age* Teenagers have much higher unemployment rates than adults. Teenagers have lower skill levels, quit their jobs more frequently, are more frequently fired, and have less geographic mobility than adults. Many unemployed teenagers are new in the labor market, searching for their first jobs. Male African-American teenagers, in particular, have very high unemployment rates. The unemployment rate for all teenagers rises during recessions.

- *Race and ethnicity* The unemployment rates for African Americans and Hispanics are higher than that for whites. The causes of the higher rates include lower rates of educational attainment, greater concentration in lower-skilled occupations, and discrimination in the labor market. In general, the unemployment rate for African Americans is twice that of whites and rises by more percentage points than for whites during recessions.

- *Gender* The unemployment rates for men and women normally are very similar. But in the recent recession, the unemployment rate for men significantly exceeded that for women.

- *Education* Less-educated workers, on average, have higher unemployment rates than workers with more education. Less education is usually associated with lower-skilled, less-permanent jobs; more time between jobs; and jobs that are more vulnerable to cyclical layoff.

- *Duration* The number of persons unemployed for long periods—15 weeks or more—as a percentage of the labor force is much lower than the overall unemployment rate. But that percentage rises significantly during recessions. Notice from Table 9.2 that it rose from 1.5 percent of the labor force in 2007 to 4.7 percent in 2009.

Noneconomic Costs

Severe cyclical unemployment is more than an economic malady; it is a social catastrophe. Unemployment means idleness. And idleness means loss of skills, loss of self-respect, plummeting morale, family disintegration, and sociopolitical unrest. Widespread joblessness increases poverty, heightens racial and ethnic tensions, and reduces hope for material advancement.

History demonstrates that severe unemployment can lead to rapid and sometimes violent social and political change. Witness Hitler's ascent to power against a background of unemployment in Germany. Furthermore, relatively high unemployment among some racial and ethnic minorities has contributed to the unrest and violence that has periodically plagued some cities in the United States and abroad. At the individual level, research links increases in suicide, homicide, fatal heart attacks and strokes, and mental illness to high unemployment.

International Comparisons

Unemployment rates differ greatly among nations at any given time. One reason is that nations have different natural rates of unemployment. Another is that nations may be in different phases of their business cycles. Global Perspective 9.1 shows unemployment rates for five industrialized nations for the years 2002 through 2012. Between 2002 and 2008, the U.S. unemployment rate was considerably lower than the rates in Italy, France, and Germany. But during the Great Recession, U.S. unemployment spiked to the highest level among the five countries.

GLOBAL PERSPECTIVE 9.1

Unemployment Rates in Five Industrial Nations, 2002–2012

Compared with Italy, France, and Germany, the United States had a relatively low unemployment rate until the start of the 2007–2009 Great Recession, when the U.S. rate shot up to become the highest among the five nations.

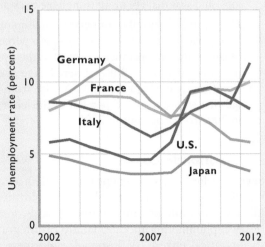

Source: Bureau of Labor Statistics, **www.bls.gov**. Based on U.S. unemployment concepts.

Inflation

LO9.3 Explain how inflation is measured and distinguish between cost-push inflation and demand-pull inflation.

We now turn to inflation, another aspect of macroeconomic instability. The problems inflation poses are subtler than those posed by unemployment.

Meaning of Inflation

Inflation is a rise in the general level of prices. When inflation occurs, each dollar of income will buy fewer goods and services than before. Inflation reduces the "purchasing power" of money. But inflation does not mean that *all* prices are rising. Even during periods of rapid inflation, some prices may be relatively constant and others may even fall. For example, although the United States experienced high rates of inflation in the 1970s and early 1980s, the prices of video recorders, digital watches, and personal computers declined.

Measurement of Inflation

The main measure of inflation in the United States is the **Consumer Price Index (CPI)**, compiled by the BLS. The government uses this index to report inflation rates each month and each year. It also uses the CPI to adjust Social Security benefits and income tax brackets for inflation. The CPI reports the price of a "market basket" of some 300 consumer goods and services that are purchased by a typical urban consumer. (The GDP price index of Chapter 7 is a much broader measure of inflation since it includes not only consumer goods and services but also capital goods, goods and services purchased by government, and goods and services that enter world trade.)

The composition of the market basket for the CPI is based on spending patterns of urban consumers in a specific period, presently 2009–2010. The BLS updates the composition of the market basket every 2 years so that it reflects the most recent patterns of consumer purchases and captures the inflation that consumers are currently experiencing. The BLS arbitrarily sets the CPI equal to 100 for 1982–1984. So the CPI for any particular year is found as follows:

$$\text{CPI} = \frac{\begin{array}{c}\text{price of the most recent market} \\ \text{basket in the particular year}\end{array}}{\begin{array}{c}\text{price estimate of the market} \\ \text{basket in 1982–1984}\end{array}} \times 100$$

The rate of inflation is equal to the percentage growth of CPI from one year to the next. For example, the CPI was 207.3 in 2007, up from 201.6 in 2006. So the rate of inflation for 2007 is calculated as follows:

$$\text{Rate of inflation} = \frac{207.3 - 201.6}{201.6} \times 100 = 2.8\%$$

In rare cases, the CPI declines from one year to the next. For example, the CPI fell from 215.3 in 2008 to 214.5 in 2009. The rate of inflation for 2009 therefore was −0.4 percent. Such price level declines are called **deflation.**

In Chapter 8, we discussed the mathematical approximation called *the rule of 70*, which tells us that we can find the number of years it will take for some measure to double, given its annual percentage increase, by dividing that percentage increase into the number 70. So a 3 percent annual rate of inflation will double the price level in about 23 (= 70 ÷ 3) years. Inflation of 8 percent per year will double the price level in about 9 (= 70 ÷ 8) years.

Facts of Inflation

Figure 9.4 shows December-to-December rates of annual inflation in the United States between 1960 and 2011. Observe that inflation reached double-digit rates in the 1970s and early 1980s but has since declined and has been relatively mild recently.

In recent years U.S. inflation has been neither unusually high nor low relative to inflation in several other industrial countries (see Global Perspective 9.2). Some nations (not shown) have had double-digit or even higher annual rates of inflation in recent years. In 2009, for example, the annual inflation rate in the Democratic Republic of Congo was 46 percent; Eritrea, 35 percent; Afghanistan, 31 percent; and Venezuela, 27 percent. Zimbabwe's inflation rate was 14.9 billion percent in 2008 before Zimbabwe did away with its existing currency.

Types of Inflation

Nearly all prices in the economy are set by supply and demand. Consequently, if the economy is experiencing inflation and the overall level of prices is rising, we need to look for an explanation in terms of supply and demand.

FIGURE 9.4 Annual inflation rates in the United States, 1960–2011 (December-to-December changes in the CPI). The major periods of inflation in the United States in the past 51 years were in the 1970s and 1980s.

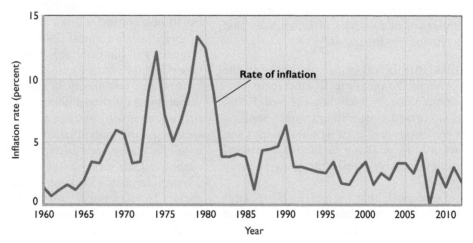

Source: Bureau of Labor Statistics, **www.bls.gov**.

GLOBAL PERSPECTIVE 9.2

Inflation Rates in Five Industrial Nations, 2002–2012

Inflation rates in the United States in recent years were neither extraordinarily high nor extraordinarily low relative to rates in other industrial nations.

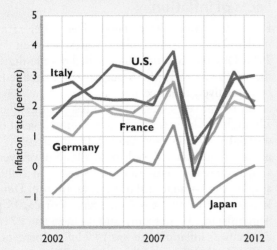

Source: World Economic Outlook Database, April 2013, International Monetary Fund, **www.imf.org**.

Demand-Pull Inflation Usually, increases in the price level are caused by an excess of total spending beyond the economy's capacity to produce. Where inflation is rapid and sustained, the cause invariably is an overissuance of money by the central bank (the Federal Reserve in the United States). When resources are already fully employed, the business sector cannot respond to excess demand by expanding output. So the excess demand bids up the prices of the limited output, producing **demand-pull inflation.** The essence of this type of inflation is "too much spending chasing too few goods."

Cost-Push Inflation Inflation also may arise on the supply, or cost, side of the economy. During some periods in U.S. economic history, including the mid-1970s, the price level increased even though total spending was not excessive. These were periods when output and employment were both *declining* (evidence that total spending was not excessive) while the general price level was *rising.*

The theory of **cost-push inflation** explains rising prices in terms of factors that raise **per-unit production costs** at each level of spending. A per-unit production cost is the average cost of a particular level of output. This average cost is found by dividing the total cost of all resource inputs by the amount of output produced. That is,

$$\text{Per-unit production cost} = \frac{\text{total input cost}}{\text{units of output}}$$

Rising per-unit production costs squeeze profits and reduce the amount of output firms are willing to supply at the existing price level. As a result, the economy's supply of goods and services declines and the price level rises. In this scenario, costs are *pushing* the price level upward, whereas in demand-pull inflation demand is *pulling* it upward.

The major source of cost-push inflation has been so-called *supply shocks.* Specifically, abrupt increases in the costs of raw materials or energy inputs have on occasion driven up per-unit production costs and thus product prices. The rocketing prices of imported oil in 1973–1974 and again in 1979–1980 are good illustrations. As energy prices surged upward during these periods, the costs of producing and transporting virtually every product in the economy rose. Cost-push inflation ensued.

Complexities

The real world is more complex than the distinction between demand-pull and cost-push inflation suggests. It is difficult to distinguish between demand-pull inflation and cost-push inflation unless the original source of inflation is known. For example, suppose a significant increase in total spending occurs in a fully employed economy, causing demand-pull inflation. But as the demand-pull stimulus works its way through various product and resource markets, individual firms find their wage costs, material costs, and fuel prices rising. From their perspective they must raise their prices because production costs (someone else's prices) have risen. Although this inflation is clearly demand-pull in origin, it may mistakenly appear to be cost-push inflation to business firms and to government. Without proper identification of the source of the inflation, government and the Federal Reserve may be slow to undertake policies to reduce excessive total spending.

Another complexity is that cost-push inflation and demand-pull inflation differ in their sustainability. Demand-pull inflation will continue as long as there is excess total spending. Cost-push inflation is automatically self-limiting; it will die out by itself. Increased per-unit costs will reduce supply, and this means lower real output and employment. Those decreases will constrain further per-unit cost increases. In other words, cost-push inflation generates a recession. And in a recession, households and businesses concentrate on keeping their resources employed, not on pushing up the prices of those resources.

Core Inflation

Another complication relating to inflation (regardless of type) is noteworthy. Some price-flexible items within the consumer price index—particularly, food and energy—experience rapid changes in supply and demand and therefore considerable price volatility from month to month and year to year. For example, the prices of grain, fruit, vegetables, and livestock sometimes move rapidly in one direction or the other, leading to sizable changes in the prices of food items such as bread, oranges, lettuce, and beef. Also, energy items such as gasoline and natural gas

can rise or fall rapidly from period to period. These ups and downs of food and energy prices usually are temporary and often cancel each other out over longer periods.

In tracking inflation, policymakers want to avoid being misled by rapid but temporary price changes that may distort the inflation picture. They mainly are interested in how rapidly the prices of the typically more stable components of the CPI are rising. By stripping volatile food and energy prices from the CPI, policymakers isolate so-called **core inflation,** the underlying increases in the CPI after volatile food and energy prices are removed.

If core inflation is low and stable, policymakers may be satisfied with current policy even though changes in the overall CPI index may be suggesting a rising rate of inflation. But policymakers become greatly concerned when core inflation is high and rising and take deliberate measures to try to halt it. We discuss these policies in later chapters.

CONSIDER THIS . . .

Clipping Coins

Some interesting early episodes of demand-pull inflation occurred in Europe from the ninth century to the fifteenth century under feudalism. In that economic system, *lords* (or *princes*) ruled individual fiefdoms and their *vassals* (or *peasants*) worked the fields. The peasants initially paid parts of their harvest as taxes to the princes. Later, when the princes began issuing "coins of the realm," peasants began paying their taxes with gold coins.

Some princes soon discovered a way to transfer purchasing power from their vassals to themselves without explicitly increasing taxes. As coins came into the treasury, princes clipped off parts of the gold coins, making them slightly smaller. From the clippings they minted new coins and used them to buy more goods for themselves.

This practice of clipping coins was a subtle form of taxation. The quantity of goods being produced in the fiefdom remained the same, but the number of gold coins increased. With "too much money chasing too few goods," inflation occurred. Each gold coin earned by the peasants therefore had less purchasing power than previously because prices were higher. The increase of the money supply shifted purchasing power away from the peasants and toward the princes just as surely as if the princes had increased taxation of the peasants.

In more recent eras some dictators have simply printed money to buy more goods for themselves, their relatives, and their key loyalists. These dictators, too, have levied hidden taxes on their population by creating inflation.

The moral of the story is quite simple: A society that values price-level stability should not entrust the control of its money supply to people who benefit from inflation.

QUICK REVIEW 9.3

- Inflation is a rising general level of prices and is measured as a percentage change in a price index such as the CPI; deflation is a decline in the general level of prices.
- For the past several years, the U.S. inflation rate has been within the general range of the rates of other advanced industrial nations and far below the rates experienced by some nations.
- Demand-pull inflation occurs when total spending exceeds the economy's ability to provide goods and services at the existing price level; total spending *pulls* the price level upward.
- Cost-push inflation occurs when factors such as rapid increases in the prices of imported raw materials drive up per-unit production costs at each level of output; higher costs *push* the price level upward.
- Core inflation is the underlying inflation rate after volatile food and energy prices have been removed.

Redistribution Effects of Inflation

LO9.4 Relate how unanticipated inflation can redistribute real income.

Inflation redistributes real income. This redistribution helps some people and hurts some others while leaving many people largely unaffected. Who gets hurt? Who benefits? Before we can answer, we need some terminology.

Nominal and Real Income There is a difference between money (or nominal) income and real income.

Nominal income is the number of dollars received as wages, rent, interest, or profit. **Real income** is a measure of the amount of goods and services nominal income can buy; it is the purchasing power of nominal income, or income adjusted for inflation. That is,

$$\text{Real income} = \frac{\text{nominal income}}{\text{price index (in hundredths)}}$$

Inflation need not alter an economy's overall real income—its total purchasing power. It is evident from the above equation that real income will remain the same when nominal income rises at the same percentage rate as does the price index.

But when inflation occurs, not everyone's nominal income rises at the same pace as the price level. Therein lies the potential for redistribution of real income from some to others. If the change in the price level differs from the change in a person's nominal income, his or her real income will be affected. The following approximation (shown by the ≅ sign) tells us roughly how much real income will change:

Percentage change in real income	≅	percentage change in nominal income	−	percentage change in price level

For example, suppose that the price level rises by 6 percent in some period. If Bob's nominal income rises by 6 percent, his real income will *remain unchanged*. But if his nominal income instead rises by 10 percent, his real income will *increase* by about 4 percent. And if Bob's nominal income rises by only 2 percent, his real income will *decline* by about 4 percent.[1]

WORKED PROBLEMS

W9.3
Nominal and real income

Anticipations The redistribution effects of inflation depend upon whether or not it is expected. We will first discuss situations involving **unanticipated inflation**. As you will see, these cause real income and wealth to be redistributed, harming some and benefiting others. We will then discuss situations involving **anticipated inflation**. These are situations in which people see an inflation coming in advance. With the ability to plan ahead, people are able to avoid or lessen the redistribution effects associated with inflation.

Who Is Hurt by Inflation?

Unanticipated inflation hurts fixed-income recipients, savers, and creditors. It redistributes real income away from them and toward others.

Fixed-Income Receivers People whose incomes are fixed see their real incomes fall when inflation occurs. The classic case is the elderly couple living on a private pension or annuity that provides a fixed amount of nominal income each month. They may have retired in, say, 1993 on what

CONSIDER THIS . . .

Could a Little Inflation Help Reduce Unemployment?

Economists have debated whether a little inflation—say two or three percent per year—might help to reduce the unemployment rate during recessions.

Proponents argue that a little inflation might have this beneficial effect by boosting firms' profits and their demand for labor. Their argument goes like this. If wages and other costs were to remained fixed while inflation increased the prices at which firms could sell their output, firms would see their profitability increase. That in turn would cause firms to want to hire more workers.

The economists who disagree argue that it is implausible to assume that wages and other costs would remain fixed while inflation drives up the price of output. They point out that wages and other costs may well rise as fast or possibly even faster than output prices rise. If so, firms would not see any increase in their profitability—and thus they would not see any reason to hire more workers.

In addition, the economists who disagree also point out that even if inflation did lower unemployment, it would do so at the cost of lowering real wages. That's because if wages stay fixed while output prices rise, workers' fixed paychecks would only be able to purchase a smaller amount of goods and services. So while more workers might have jobs, those with jobs would have a lower standard of living.

---

[1] A more precise calculation uses our equation for real income. In our first illustration above, if nominal income rises by 10 percent from $100 to $110 and the price level (index) rises by 6 percent from 100 to 106, then real income has increased as follows:

$$\frac{\$110}{1.06} = \$103.77$$

The 4 percent increase in real income shown by the simple formula in the text is a reasonable approximation of the 3.77 percent yielded by our more precise formula.

appeared to be an adequate pension. However, by 2009 they would have discovered that inflation had cut the annual purchasing power of that pension—their real income—by one-third.

Similarly, landlords who receive lease payments of fixed dollar amounts will be hurt by inflation as they receive dollars of declining value over time. Likewise, public sector workers whose incomes are dictated by fixed pay schedules may suffer from inflation. The fixed "steps" (the upward yearly increases) in their pay schedules may not keep up with inflation. Minimum-wage workers and families living on fixed welfare incomes also will be hurt by inflation.

Savers Unanticipated inflation hurts savers. As prices rise, the real value, or purchasing power, of an accumulation of savings deteriorates. Paper assets such as savings accounts, insurance policies, and annuities that were once adequate to meet rainy-day contingencies or provide for a comfortable retirement decline in real value during inflation. The simplest case is the person who hoards money as a cash balance. A $1,000 cash balance would have lost one-half its real value between 1985 and 2009. Of course, most forms of savings earn interest. But the value of savings will still decline if the rate of inflation exceeds the rate of interest.

Example: A household may save $1,000 in a certificate of deposit (CD) in a commercial bank or savings and loan association at 6 percent annual interest. But if inflation is 13 percent (as it was in 1980), the real value or purchasing power of that $1,000 will be cut to about $938 by the end of the year. Although the saver will receive $1,060 (equal to $1,000 plus $60 of interest), deflating that $1,060 for 13 percent inflation means that its real value is only about $938 (= $1,060 ÷ 1.13).

Creditors Unanticipated inflation harms creditors (lenders). Suppose Chase Bank lends Bob $1,000, to be repaid in 2 years. If in that time the price level doubles, the $1,000 that Bob repays will have only half the purchasing power of the $1,000 he borrowed. True, if we ignore interest charges, the same number of dollars will be repaid as was borrowed. But because of inflation, each of those dollars will buy only half as much as it did when the loan was negotiated. As prices go up, the purchasing power of the dollar goes down. So the borrower pays back less-valuable dollars than those received from the lender. The owners of Chase Bank suffer a loss of real income.

Who Is Unaffected or Helped by Inflation?

Some people are unaffected by inflation and others are actually helped by it. For the second group, inflation redistributes real income toward them and away from others.

Flexible-Income Receivers People who have flexible incomes may escape inflation's harm or even benefit from it. For example, individuals who derive their incomes solely from Social Security are largely unaffected by inflation because Social Security payments are *indexed* to the CPI. Benefits automatically increase when the CPI increases, preventing erosion of benefits from inflation. Some union workers also get automatic **cost-of-living adjustments (COLAs)** in their pay when the CPI rises, although such increases rarely equal the full percentage rise in inflation.

Some flexible-income receivers and all borrowers are helped by unanticipated inflation. The strong product demand and labor shortages implied by rapid demand-pull inflation may cause some nominal incomes to spurt ahead of the price level, thereby enhancing real incomes. For some, the 3 percent increase in nominal income that occurs when inflation is 2 percent may become a 7 percent increase when inflation is 5 percent. As an example, property owners faced with an inflation-induced real estate boom may be able to boost rents more rapidly than the rate of inflation. Also, some business owners may benefit from inflation. If product prices rise faster than resource prices, business revenues will increase more rapidly than costs. In those cases, the growth rate of profit incomes will outpace the rate of inflation.

Debtors Unanticipated inflation benefits debtors (borrowers). In our earlier example, Chase Bank's loss of real income from inflation is Bob's gain of real income. Debtor Bob borrows "dear" dollars but, because of inflation, pays back the principal and interest with "cheap" dollars whose purchasing power has been eroded by inflation. Real income is redistributed away from the owners of Chase Bank toward borrowers such as Bob.

The federal government, which had amassed $16.1 trillion of public debt through 2012, has also benefited from inflation. Historically, the federal government regularly paid off its loans by taking out new ones. Inflation permitted the Treasury to pay off its loans with dollars of less purchasing power than the dollars originally borrowed. Nominal national income and therefore tax collections rise with inflation; the amount of public debt owed does not. Thus, inflation reduces the real burden of the public debt to the federal government.

Anticipated Inflation

The redistribution effects of inflation are less severe or are eliminated altogether if people anticipate inflation and can adjust their nominal incomes to reflect the expected price-level rises. The prolonged inflation that began in the late 1960s prompted many labor unions in the 1970s to insist on labor contracts with cost-of-living adjustment clauses.

Similarly, if inflation is anticipated, the redistribution of income from lender to borrower may be altered. Suppose a lender (perhaps a commercial bank or a savings and loan institution) and a borrower (a household) both agree that 5 percent is a fair rate of interest on a 1-year loan provided the price level is stable. But assume that inflation has been occurring and is expected to be 6 percent over the next year. If the bank lends the household $100 at 5 percent interest, the bank will be paid back $105 at the end of the year. But if 6 percent inflation does occur during that year, the purchasing power of the $105 will have been reduced to about $99. The lender will, in effect, have paid the borrower $1 for the use of the lender's money for a year.

The lender can avoid this subsidy by charging an *inflation premium*—that is, by raising the interest rate by 6 percent, the amount of the anticipated inflation. By charging 11 percent, the lender will receive back $111 at the end of the year. Adjusted for the 6 percent inflation, that amount will have roughly the purchasing power of $105 worth of today's money. The result then will be a mutually agreeable transfer of purchasing power from borrower to lender of $5, or 5 percent, for the use of $100 for 1 year. Financial institutions have also developed variable-interest-rate mortgages to protect themselves from the adverse effects of inflation. (Incidentally, this example points out that, rather than being a *cause* of inflation, high nominal interest rates are a *consequence* of inflation.)

Our example reveals the difference between the real rate of interest and the nominal rate of interest. The **real interest rate** is the percentage increase in *purchasing power* that the borrower pays the lender. In our example the real interest rate is 5 percent. The **nominal interest rate** is the percentage increase in *money* that the borrower pays the lender, including that resulting from the built-in expectation of inflation, if any. In equation form:

ORIGIN OF THE IDEA

O9.2
Real interest rates

Nominal interest rate = real interest rate +
inflation premium
(the expected rate of
inflation)

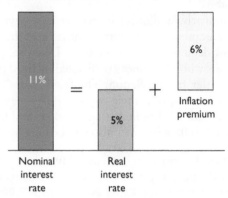

FIGURE 9.5 The inflation premium and nominal and real interest rates. The inflation premium—the expected rate of inflation—gets built into the nominal interest rate. Here, the nominal interest rate of 11 percent comprises the real interest rate of 5 percent plus the inflation premium of 6 percent.

As illustrated in Figure 9.5, the nominal interest rate in our example is 11 percent.

Other Redistribution Issues

We end our discussion of the redistribution effects of inflation by making three final points:

- *Deflation* The effects of unanticipated deflation—declines in the price level—are the reverse of those of inflation. People with fixed nominal incomes will find their real incomes enhanced. Creditors will benefit at the expense of debtors. And savers will discover that the purchasing power of their savings has grown because of the falling prices.

- *Mixed effects* A person who is simultaneously an income earner, a holder of financial assets, and a debtor will probably find that the redistribution impact of unanticipated inflation is cushioned. If the person owns fixed-value monetary assets (savings accounts, bonds, and insurance policies), inflation will lessen their real value. But that same inflation may produce an increase in the person's nominal wage. Also, if the person holds a fixed-interest-rate mortgage, the real burden of that debt will decline. In short, many individuals are simultaneously hurt and helped by inflation. All these effects must be considered before we can conclude that any particular person's net position is better or worse because of inflation.

- *Arbitrariness* The redistribution effects of inflation occur regardless of society's goals and values. Inflation lacks a social conscience and takes from some and gives to others, whether they are rich, poor, young, old, healthy, or infirm.

QUICK REVIEW 9.4

- Inflation harms those who receive relatively fixed nominal incomes and either leaves unaffected or helps those who receive flexible nominal incomes.
- Unanticipated inflation hurts savers and creditors while benefiting debtors.
- The nominal interest rate equals the real interest rate plus the inflation premium (the expected rate of inflation).

Does Inflation Affect Output?

LO9.5 Discuss how inflation may affect the economy's level of real output.

Thus far, our discussion has focused on how inflation redistributes a specific level of total real income. But inflation also may affect an economy's level of real output (and thus its level of real income). The direction and significance of this effect on output depend on the type of inflation and its severity.

Cost-Push Inflation and Real Output

Recall that abrupt and unexpected rises in key resource prices such as oil can sufficiently drive up overall production costs to cause cost-push inflation. As prices rise, the quantity demanded of goods and services falls. So firms respond by producing less output, and unemployment goes up.

Economic events of the 1970s provide an example of how inflation can reduce real output. In late 1973 the Organization of Petroleum Exporting Countries (OPEC), by exerting its market power, managed to quadruple the price of oil. The cost-push inflationary effects generated rapid price-level increases in the 1973–1975 period. At the same time, the U.S. unemployment rate rose from slightly less than 5 percent in 1973 to 8.5 percent in 1975. Similar outcomes occurred in 1979–1980 in response to a second OPEC oil supply shock.

In short, cost-push inflation reduces real output. It redistributes a decreased level of real income.

Demand-Pull Inflation and Real Output

Economists do not fully agree on the effects of mild inflation (less than 3 percent) on real output. One perspective is that even low levels of inflation reduce real output because inflation diverts time and effort toward activities designed to hedge against inflation. Here are some examples of this:

- Businesses must incur the cost of changing thousands of prices on their shelves and in their computers simply to reflect inflation.
- Households and businesses must spend considerable time and effort obtaining the information they need to distinguish between real and nominal values such as prices, wages, and interest rates.
- To limit the loss of purchasing power from inflation, people try to limit the amount of money they hold in their billfolds and checking accounts at any one time and instead put more money into interest-bearing accounts and stock and bond funds. But cash and checks are needed in even greater amounts to buy the higher-priced goods and services. So more frequent trips, phone calls, or Internet visits to financial institutions are required to transfer funds to checking accounts and billfolds, when needed.

Without inflation, these uses of resources, time, and effort would not be needed, and they could be diverted toward producing more valuable goods and services. Proponents of "zero inflation" bolster their case by pointing to cross-country studies that indicate that lower rates of inflation are associated with higher rates of economic growth. Even mild inflation, say these economists, is detrimental to economic growth.

In contrast, other economists point out that full employment and economic growth depend on strong levels of total spending. Such spending creates high profits, strong demand for labor, and a powerful incentive for firms to expand their plants and equipment. In this view, the mild inflation that is a by-product of strong spending is a small price to pay for full employment and continued economic growth.

Moreover, a little inflation may have positive effects because it makes it easier for firms to adjust real wages downward when the demands for their products fall. With mild inflation, firms can reduce real wages by holding nominal wages steady. With zero inflation firms would need to cut nominal wages to reduce real wages. Such cuts in nominal wages are highly visible and may cause considerable worker resistance and labor strife.

Finally, defenders of mild inflation say that it is much better for an economy to err on the side of strong spending, full employment, economic growth, and mild inflation than on the side of weak spending, unemployment, recession, and deflation.

Unemployment after the Great Recession

Economists Have Been Vigorously Debating Why Employment Recovered So Slowly after the Great Recession of 2007–2009.

The Great Recession began in December 2007 and ended in June 2009. The downturn was the most severe since the Great Depression of the 1930s, with real GDP falling 4.3 percent from peak to trough. After growth returned in mid-2009, real GDP increased slowly, taking until July 2011 to pass its prerecession peak.

Employment showed a similar pattern of rapid decline followed by slow recovery: 8.7 million people lost their jobs after employment peaked in January 2008. Employment began to expand again in early 2010, but job growth was so slow that in December 2012—more than three years after the recession ended and more than a year after real GDP had passed its prerecession high—employment was still 3.4 million less than it had been at the start of the recession.

The recession also dramatically increased the average length of time that workers spent unemployed before finding a new job. The typical (median) spell of unemployment went from lasting 7.7 weeks in June 2007 to a peak of 24.8 weeks in June 2010. By way of comparison, the highest previous measurement for this statistic had been 12.3 weeks during the 1981–1982 recession. Thus, the Great Recession saw not only the loss of 8.7 million jobs, but unprecedentedly long wait times for unemployed workers to find new jobs.

When real GDP initially fell by 4.3 percent, it was easy to understand why employers might have shed 8.7 million jobs: Fewer workers were needed to produce less output. But after real GDP recovered fully and passed its prerecession peak, economists began to debate why employment was still millions of jobs lower than it had been before the recession began.

Here are a few of the possible culprits.

Hyperinflation

All economists agree that **hyperinflation,** which is extraordinarily rapid inflation, can have a devastating impact on real output and employment.

As prices shoot up sharply and unevenly during hyperinflation, people begin to anticipate even more rapid inflation and normal economic relationships are disrupted. Business owners do not know what to charge for their products. Consumers do not know what to pay. Resource suppliers want to be paid with actual output, rather than with rapidly depreciating money. Money eventually becomes almost worthless and ceases to do its job as a medium of exchange. Businesses, anticipating further price increases, may find that hoarding both materials and finished products is profitable. Individual savers may decide to buy nonproductive wealth—jewels,

gold and other precious metals, real estate, and so forth—rather than providing funds that can be borrowed to purchase capital equipment. The economy may be thrown into a state of barter, and production and exchange drop further. The net result is economic collapse and, often, political chaos.

Examples of hyperinflation are Germany after the First World War and Japan after the Second World War. In Germany, "prices increased so rapidly that waiters changed the prices on the menu several times during the course of a lunch. Sometimes customers had to pay double the price listed on the menu when they ordered."[2] In postwar Japan in 1947, "fisherman and farmers . . . used

---

[2]Theodore Morgan, *Income and Employment,* 2nd ed. (Englewood Cliffs, N.J.: Prentice Hall, 1952), p. 361.

Higher Federal Minimum Wage It is widely acknowledged that raising the minimum wage may increase unemployment by pricing low-productivity workers out of the labor market. Thus, one potential culprit for the slow recovery in employment was the July 2009 increase in the federal minimum wage from $6.55 to $7.25. But, at any given time, fewer than 3 percent of workers are employed at minimum-wage jobs. So it would be hard to blame the increase in the minimum wage for more than a very small fraction of the slow post-recession recovery in employment.

Longer Unemployment Benefits In November 2009, Congress decided to extend the maximum period of time that unemployed workers could draw unemployment benefits from 26 weeks to 99 weeks. That decision is believed by many economists to have affected a large enough fraction of unemployed workers to have contributed to the slow recovery in employment.

Congress had two intents when it extended the maximum draw period for unemployment benefits. The first was to help unemployed workers financially. The second was to help keep the economy moving by giving unemployed workers money to spend on goods and services.

One unintended consequence, however, was "inefficiently long search," meaning that many unemployed workers used the extended period during which they could survive on unemployment benefits to keep searching for perfect jobs even after they had been offered several so-so jobs. As a result, the unemployment rate stayed higher than it would have if benefits had continued to end after just 26 weeks and workers had felt financial pressure at an earlier date to accept so-so jobs rather than to keep on searching for perfect jobs.

Structural Adjustments Another explanation for the slow recovery in employment was that the economy required *structural adjustments*—changes in the basic structure of what was being produced and thus which industries needed workers. Consider the housing bubble that preceded the Great Recession. After the housing bubble collapsed, the economy needed to transition several million unemployed construction workers into other lines of work. Creating that many new jobs in other industries was going to take time. Thus, it was to be expected that employment was slow to recover after the recession ended.

Higher Labor Costs Other economists argued that worries about higher labor costs also contributed to the slow recovery in employment. In particular, they argued that several provisions of the 2010 health care reform law commonly known as Obamacare discouraged firms from hiring workers. One provision was an increase in the Medicare payroll tax. Another was the requirement that by 2014 any firm with more than 50 employees would have to provide health insurance coverage for all of its full-time workers.

That insurance provision was problematic because health insurance is very costly. In 2012, for example, the average cost for family coverage was $15,745 per worker. So, as the economy was making its way out of recession, it was the case that forward-looking employers may have reduced their hiring so as to have fewer full-time workers on the payroll when that provision of the law was scheduled to go into effect in 2014.

scales to weigh currency and change, rather than bothering to count it."[3]

There are also more recent examples: Between June 1986 and March 1991 the cumulative inflation in Nicaragua was 11,895,866,143 percent. From November 1993 to December 1994 the cumulative inflation rate in the Democratic Republic of Congo was 69,502 percent. From February 1993 to January 1994 the cumulative inflation rate in Serbia was 156,312,790 percent.[4]

Such dramatic hyperinflations are always the consequence of highly imprudent expansions of the money supply by government. The rocketing money supply produces frenzied total spending and severe demand-pull inflation. Zimbabwe's 14.9 billion percent inflation in 2008 is just the latest example.

[3]Raburn M. Williams, *Inflation! Money, Jobs, and Politicians* (Arlington Heights, Ill.: AHM Publishing, 1980), p. 2.
[4]Stanley Fischer, Ratna Sahay, and Carlos Végh, "Modern Hyper- and High Inflations," *Journal of Economic Literature*, September 2002, p. 840.

QUICK REVIEW 9.5

- Cost-push inflation reduces real output and employment.
- Economists argue about the effects of demand-pull inflation. Some argue that even mild demand-pull inflation (1 to 3 percent) reduces the economy's real output. Other say that mild inflation may be a necessary by-product of the high and growing spending that produces high levels of output, full employment, and economic growth.
- Hyperinflation, caused by highly imprudent expansions of the money supply, may undermine the monetary system and cause severe declines in real output.

SUMMARY

LO9.1 Describe the business cycle and its primary phases.

The United States and other industrial economies have gone through periods of fluctuations in real GDP, employment, and the price level. Although they have certain phases in common—peak, recession, trough, expansion—business cycles vary greatly in duration and intensity.

Although economists explain the business cycle in terms of underlying causal factors such as major innovations, productivity shocks, money creation, and financial crises, they generally agree that changes in the level of total spending are the immediate causes of fluctuating real output and employment.

The business cycle affects all sectors of the economy, though in varying ways and degrees. The cycle has greater effects on output and employment in the capital goods and durable consumer goods industries than in the services and nondurable goods industries.

LO9.2 Illustrate how unemployment is measured and explain the different types of unemployment.

Economists distinguish between frictional, structural, and cyclical unemployment. The full-employment or natural rate of unemployment, which is made up of frictional and structural unemployment, is currently between 5 and 6 percent. The presence of part-time and discouraged workers makes it difficult to measure unemployment accurately.

The GDP gap, which can be either a positive or a negative value, is found by subtracting potential GDP from actual GDP. The economic cost of unemployment, as measured by the GDP gap, consists of the goods and services forgone by society when its resources are involuntarily idle. Okun's law suggests that every 1-percentage-point increase in unemployment above the natural rate causes an additional 2 percent negative GDP gap.

LO9.3 Explain how inflation is measured and distinguish between cost-push inflation and demand-pull inflation.

Inflation is a rise in the general price level and is measured in the United States by the Consumer Price Index (CPI). When

inflation occurs, each dollar of income will buy fewer goods and services than before. That is, inflation reduces the purchasing power of money. Deflation is a decline in the general price level.

Unemployment rates and inflation rates vary widely globally. Unemployment rates differ because nations have different natural rates of unemployment and often are in different phases of their business cycles. Inflation and unemployment rates in the United States recently have been in the middle to low range compared with rates in other industrial nations.

Economists discern both demand-pull and cost-push (supply-side) inflation. Demand-pull inflation results from an excess of total spending relative to the economy's capacity to produce. The main source of cost-push inflation is abrupt and rapid increases in the prices of key resources. These supply shocks push up per-unit production costs and ultimately raise the prices of consumer goods.

LO9.4 Relate how unanticipated inflation can redistribute real income.

Unanticipated inflation arbitrarily redistributes real income at the expense of fixed-income receivers, creditors, and savers. If inflation is anticipated, individuals and businesses may be able to take steps to lessen or eliminate adverse redistribution effects.

When inflation is anticipated, lenders add an inflation premium to the interest rate charged on loans. The nominal interest rate thus reflects the real interest rate plus the inflation premium (the expected rate of inflation).

LO9.5 Discuss how inflation may affect the economy's level of real output.

Cost-push inflation reduces real output and employment. Proponents of zero inflation argue that even mild demand-pull inflation (1 to 3 percent) reduces the economy's real output. Other economists say that mild inflation may be a necessary by-product of the high and growing spending that produces high levels of output, full employment, and economic growth.

Hyperinflation, caused by highly imprudent expansions of the money supply, may undermine the monetary system and cause severe declines in real output.

TERMS AND CONCEPTS

business cycles	frictional unemployment	inflation
peak	structural unemployment	Consumer Price Index (CPI)
recession	cyclical unemployment	deflation
trough	full-employment rate of unemployment	demand-pull inflation
expansion	natural rate of unemployment (NRU)	cost-push inflation
labor force	potential output	per-unit production costs
unemployment rate	GDP gap	core inflation
discouraged workers	Okun's law	nominal income

real income

unanticipated inflation

anticipated inflation

cost-of-living adjustments (COLAs)

real interest rate

nominal interest rate

hyperinflation

The following and additional problems can be found in connect
ECONOMICS

DISCUSSION QUESTIONS

1. What are the four phases of the business cycle? How long do business cycles last? Why does the business cycle affect output and employment in capital goods industries and consumer durable goods industries more severely than in industries producing consumer nondurables? **LO9.1**

2. How, in general, can a financial crisis lead to a recession? How, in general, can a major new invention lead to an expansion? **LO9.1**

3. How is the labor force defined and who measures it? How is the unemployment rate calculated? Does an increase in the unemployment rate necessarily mean a decline in the size of the labor force? Why is a positive unemployment rate—one more than zero percent—fully compatible with full employment? **LO9.2**

4. How, in general, do unemployment rates vary by race and ethnicity, gender, occupation, and education? Why does the average length of time people are unemployed rise during a recession? **LO9.2**

5. Why is it difficult to distinguish between frictional, structural, and cyclical unemployment? Why is unemployment an economic problem? What are the consequences of a negative GDP gap? What are the noneconomic effects of unemployment? **LO9.2**

6. Because the United States has an unemployment compensation program that provides income for those out

of work, why should we worry about unemployment? **LO9.2**

7. What is the Consumer Price Index (CPI) and how is it determined each month? How does the Bureau of Labor Statistics calculate the rate of inflation from one year to the next? What effect does inflation have on the purchasing power of a dollar? How does it explain differences between nominal and real interest rates? How does deflation differ from inflation? **LO9.3**

8. Distinguish between demand-pull inflation and cost-push inflation. Which of the two types is most likely to be associated with a negative GDP gap? Which with a positive GDP gap, in which actual GDP exceeds potential GDP? What is core inflation? Why is it calculated? **LO9.3**

9. Explain how an increase in your nominal income and a decrease in your real income might occur simultaneously. Who loses from inflation? Who gains? **LO9.4**

10. Explain how hyperinflation might lead to a severe decline in total output. **LO9.5**

11. **LAST WORD** Why was the 2009 hike in the minimum wage probably not responsible for much of the slow growth in employment after the Great Recession? What is inefficiently long search and how is it affected by the duration of unemployment benefits? How might Obamacare have discouraged hiring?

REVIEW QUESTIONS

1. Place the phases of the business cycle in order. **LO9.1**
   Recession
   Trough
   Peak
   Expansion

2. Most economists agree that the immediate cause of the large majority of cyclical changes in the levels of real output and employment is unexpected changes in _____. **LO9.1**
   a. The level of total spending.
   b. The level of the stock market.
   c. The level of the trade deficit.
   d. The level of unemployment.

3. Suppose that an economy has 9 million people working full-time. It also has 1 million people who are actively seeking work but currently unemployed as well as 2 million discouraged workers who have given up looking for work and are

currently unemployed. What is this economy's unemployment rate? **LO9.2**
   a. 10 percent.
   b. 15 percent.
   c. 20 percent.
   d. 25 percent.

4. Label each of the following scenarios as either frictional unemployment, structural unemployment, or cyclical unemployment. **LO9.2**
   a. Tim just graduated and is looking for a job.
   b. A recession causes a local factory to lay off 30 workers.
   c. Thousands of bus and truck drivers permanently lose their jobs when driverless, computer-driven vehicles make human drivers redundant.
   d. Hundreds of New York legal jobs permanently disappear when a lot of legal work gets outsourced to lawyers in India.

5. The unemployment rate that is consistent with full employment is known as _____. **LO9.2**
   a. The natural rate of unemployment.
   b. The unnatural rate of unemployment.
   c. The status quo rate of unemployment.
   d. Cyclical unemployment.
   e. Okun's rate of unemployment.

6. A country's current unemployment rate is 11 percent. Economists estimate that its natural rate of unemployment is 6 percent. About how large is this economy's negative GDP gap? **LO9.2**
   a. 1 percent.
   b. 3 percent.
   c. 6 percent.
   d. 10 percent.

7. Cost-push inflation occurs when there is _____. **LO9.3**
   a. Excess inventory.
   b. A trade deficit.
   c. Rising per-unit production costs.
   d. Excess demand for goods and services.

8. Jimmer's nominal income will go up by 10 percent next year. Inflation is expected to be −2 percent next year. By approximately how much will Jimmer's real income change next year? **LO9.3**
   a. −2 percent.
   b. 8 percent.
   c. 10 percent.
   d. 12 percent.

9. Kaitlin has $10,000 of savings that she may deposit with her local bank. Kaitlin wants to earn a real rate of return of at least 4 percent and she is expecting inflation to be exactly 3 percent. What is the lowest nominal interest rate that Kaitlin would be willing to accept from her local bank? **LO9.4**
   a. 4 percent.
   b. 5 percent.
   c. 6 percent.
   d. 7 percent.

10. True or False: Lenders are helped by unanticipated inflation. **LO9.4**

11. Economists agree that _____ inflation reduces real output. **LO9.5**
   a. Cost-push.
   b. Demand-pull.
   c. Push-pull.

PROBLEMS

1. Suppose that a country's annual growth rates were 5, 3, 4, −1, −2, 2, 3, 4, 6, and 3 in yearly sequence over a 10-year period. What was the country's trend rate of growth over this period? Which set of years most clearly demonstrates an expansionary phase of the business cycle? Which set of years best illustrates a recessionary phase of the business cycle? **LO9.1**

2. Assume the following data for a country: total population, 500; population under 16 years of age or institutionalized, 120; not in labor force, 150; unemployed, 23; part-time workers looking for full-time jobs, 10. What is the size of the labor force? What is the official unemployment rate? **LO9.2**

3. Suppose that the natural rate of unemployment in a particular year is 5 percent and the actual rate of unemployment is 9 percent. Use Okun's law to determine the size of the GDP gap in percentage-point terms. If the potential GDP is $500 billion in that year, how much output is being forgone because of cyclical unemployment? **LO9.2**

4. If the CPI was 110 last year and is 121 this year, what is this year's rate of inflation? In contrast, suppose that the CPI was 110 last year and is 108 this year. What is this year's rate of inflation? What term do economists use to describe this second outcome? **LO9.3**

5. How long would it take for the price level to double if inflation persisted at (a) 2 percent per year, (b) 5 percent per year, and (c) 10 percent per year? **LO9.3**

6. If your nominal income rose by 5.3 percent and the price level rose by 3.8 percent in some year, by what percentage would your real income (approximately) increase? If your nominal income rose by 2.8 percent and your real income rose by 1.1 percent in some year, what must have been the (approximate) rate of inflation? **LO9.4**

7. Suppose that the nominal rate of inflation is 4 percent and the inflation premium is 2 percent. What is the real interest rate? Alternatively, assume that the real interest rate is 1 percent and the nominal interest rate is 6 percent. What is the inflation premium? **LO9.4**

FURTHER TEST YOUR KNOWLEDGE AT www.mcconnell20e.com

Macroeconomic Models and Fiscal Policy

MACROECONOMIC MODELS AND FISCAL POLICY

Basic Macroeconomic Relationships*

Learning Objectives

LO10.1 Describe how changes in income affect consumption (and saving).

LO10.2 List and explain factors other than income that can affect consumption.

LO10.3 Explain how changes in real interest rates affect investment.

LO10.4 Identify and explain factors other than the real interest rate that can affect investment.

LO10.5 Illustrate how changes in investment (or one of the other components of total spending) can increase or decrease real GDP by a multiple amount.

In Chapter 9 we discussed the business cycle, unemployment, and inflation. Our eventual goal is to build economic models that can explain these phenomena. This chapter begins that process by examining the basic relationships that exist between three different pairs of economic aggregates. (Recall that to economists "aggregate" means "total" or "combined.") Specifically, this chapter looks at the relationships between:

- income and consumption (and income and saving).

- the interest rate and investment.

- changes in spending and changes in output.

---

*Note to the Instructor: If you wish to bypass the aggregate expenditures model (Keynesian cross model) covered in full in Chapter 11, assigning the present chapter will provide a seamless transition to the AD-AS model of Chapter 12 and the chapters beyond. If you want to cover the aggregate expenditures model, this present chapter provides the necessary building blocks.

What explains the trends in consumption (consumer spending) and saving reported in the news? How do changes in interest rates affect investment? How can initial changes in spending ultimately produce multiplied changes in GDP? The basic macroeconomic relationships discussed in this chapter answer these questions.

The Income-Consumption and Income-Saving Relationships

LO10.1 Describe how changes in income affect consumption (and saving).

The other-things-equal relationship between income and consumption is one of the best-established relationships in macroeconomics. In examining that relationship, we are also exploring the relationship between income and saving. Recall that economists define *personal saving* as "not spending" or as "that part of disposable (after-tax) income not consumed." Saving (S) equals disposable income (DI) *minus* consumption (C).

Many factors determine a nation's levels of consumption and saving, but the most significant is disposable income. Consider some recent historical data for the United States. In Figure 10.1 each dot represents consumption and disposable income for 1 year since 1987. The line C that is loosely fitted to these points shows that consumption is directly (positively) related to disposable income; moreover, households spend most of their income.

But we can say more. The **45°(degree) line** is a reference line. Because it bisects the 90° angle formed by the two axes of the graph, each point on it is equidistant from the two axes. At each point on the 45° line, consumption would equal disposable income, or $C = DI$. Therefore, the vertical

FIGURE 10.1 Consumption and disposable income, 1990–2012. Each dot in this figure shows consumption and disposable income in a specific year. The line C, which generalizes the relationship between consumption and disposable income, indicates a direct relationship and shows that households consume most of their after-tax incomes.

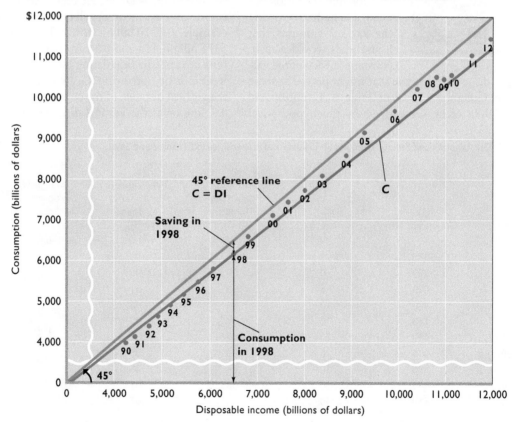

Source: Bureau of Economic Analysis, **www.bea.gov.**

distance between the 45° line and any point on the horizontal axis measures either consumption *or* disposable income. If we let it measure disposable income, the vertical distance between it and the consumption line labeled *C* represents the amount of saving (*S*) in that year. Saving is the amount by which actual consumption in any year falls short of the 45° line—(*S* = DI − *C*). For example, in 1998 disposable income was $6,498.9 billion and consumption was $6,157.5 billion, so saving was $341.4 billion. Observe that the vertical distance between the 45° line and line *C* increases as we move rightward along the horizontal axis and decreases as we move leftward. Like consumption, saving typically varies directly with the level of disposable income. However, that historical pattern broke down somewhat in several years preceding the recession of 2007–2009.

The Consumption Schedule

The dots in Figure 10.1 represent historical data—the actual amounts of DI, *C*, and *S* in the United States over a period of years. But, because we want to understand how the economy would behave under different possible scenarios, we need a schedule showing the various amounts that households would *plan* to consume at each of the various levels of disposable income that might prevail at some specific time. Columns 1 and 2 of Table 10.1, represented in **Figure 10.2a (Key Graph)**, show the hypothetical

ORIGIN OF THE IDEA
O10.1
Income-consumption relationship

consumption schedule that we require. This **consumption schedule** (or "consumption function") reflects the direct consumption–disposable income relationship suggested by the data in Figure 10.1, and it is consistent with many household budget studies. In the aggregate, households increase their spending as their disposable income rises and spend a larger proportion of a small disposable income than of a large disposable income.

The Saving Schedule

It is relatively easy to derive a **saving schedule** (or "saving function"). Because saving equals disposable income less consumption (*S* = DI − *C*), we need only subtract consumption (Table 10.1, column 2) from disposable income (column 1) to find the amount saved (column 3) at each DI. Thus, columns 1 and 3 in Table 10.1 are the saving schedule, represented in Figure 10.2b. The graph shows that there is a direct relationship between saving and DI but that saving is a smaller proportion of a small DI than of a large DI. If households consume a smaller and smaller proportion of DI as DI increases, then they must be saving a larger and larger proportion.

Remembering that at each point on the 45° line consumption equals DI, we see that *dissaving* (consuming in excess of after-tax income) will occur at relatively low DIs. For example, at $370 billion (row 1, Table 10.1), consumption is $375 billion. Households can consume more than their current incomes by liquidating (selling for cash) accumulated wealth or by borrowing. Graphically, dissaving is shown as the vertical distance of the consumption schedule above the 45° line or as the vertical distance of the saving schedule

TABLE 10.1 Consumption and Saving Schedules (in Billions) and Propensities to Consume and Save

(1) Level of Output and Income (GDP = D1)	(2) Consumption (C)	(3) Saving (S), (1) − (2)	(4) Average Propensity to Consume (APC), (2)/(1)	(5) Average Propensity to Save (APS), (3)/(1)	(6) Marginal Propensity to Consume (MPC), Δ(2)/Δ(1)*	(7) Marginal Propensity to Save (MPS), Δ(3)/Δ(1)*
(1) $370	$375	$−5	1.01	−.01		
					.75	.25
(2) 390	390	0	1.00	.00		
					.75	.25
(3) 410	405	5	.99	.01		
					.75	.25
(4) 430	420	10	.98	.02		
					.75	.25
(5) 450	435	15	.97	.03		
					.75	.25
(6) 470	450	20	.96	.04		
					.75	.25
(7) 490	465	25	.95	.05		
					.75	.25
(8) 510	480	30	.94	.06		
					.75	.25
(9) 530	495	35	.93	.07		
					.75	.25
(10) 550	510	40	.93	.07		

*The Greek letter Δ, delta, means "the change in."

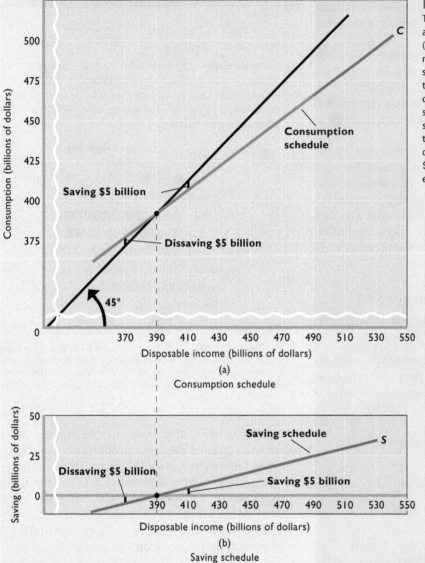

FIGURE 10.2 Consumption and saving schedules.
The two parts of this figure show the income-consumption and income-saving relationships in Table 10.1 graphically. (a) Consumption rises as income increases. Saving is negative (dissaving occurs) when the consumption schedule is above the 45° line, and saving is positive when the consumption schedule is below the 45° line. (b) Like consumption, saving increases as income goes up. The saving schedule is found by subtracting the consumption schedule in the top graph vertically from the 45° line. For these hypothetical data, saving is −$5 billion at $370 billion of income, zero at $390 billion of income, and $5 billion at $410 billion of income. Saving is zero where consumption equals disposable income.

QUICK QUIZ FOR FIGURE 10.2

1. The slope of the consumption schedule in this figure is 0.75. Thus, the:
   a. slope of the saving schedule is 1.33.
   b. marginal propensity to consume is 0.75.
   c. average propensity to consume is 0.25.
   d. slope of the saving schedule is also 0.75.

2. In this figure, when consumption is a positive amount, saving:
   a. must be a negative amount.
   b. must also be a positive amount.
   c. can be either a positive or a negative amount.
   d. is zero.

3. In this figure:
   a. the marginal propensity to consume is constant at all levels of income.
   b. the marginal propensity to save rises as disposable income rises.
   c. consumption is inversely (negatively) related to disposable income.
   d. saving is inversely (negatively) related to disposable income.

4. When consumption equals disposable income:
   a. the marginal propensity to consume is zero.
   b. the average propensity to consume is zero.
   c. consumption and saving must be equal.
   d. saving must be zero.

Answers: 1. b; 2. c; 3. a; 4. d

below the horizontal axis. We have marked the dissaving at the $370 billion level of income in Figure 10.2a and 10.2b. Both vertical distances measure the $5 billion of dissaving that occurs at $370 billion of income.

In our example, the **break-even income** is $390 billion (row 2, Table 10.1). This is the income level at which households plan to consume their entire incomes ($C = DI$). Graphically, the consumption schedule cuts the 45° line, and the saving schedule cuts the horizontal axis (saving is zero) at the break-even income level.

At all higher incomes, households plan to save part of their incomes. Graphically, the vertical distance between the consumption schedule and the 45° line measures this saving (see Figure 10.2a), as does the vertical distance between the saving schedule and the horizontal axis (see Figure 10.2b). For example, at the $410 billion level of income (row 3, Table 10.1), both these distances indicate $5 billion of saving.

Average and Marginal Propensities

Columns 4 to 7 in Table 10.1 show additional characteristics of the consumption and saving schedules.

APC and APS The fraction, or percentage, of total income that is consumed is the **average propensity to consume (APC)**. The fraction of total income that is saved is the **average propensity to save (APS)**. That is,

$$APC = \frac{consumption}{income}$$

and

$$APS = \frac{saving}{income}$$

For example, at $470 billion of income (row 6, Table 10.1), the APC is $\frac{450}{470} = \frac{45}{47}$, or about 0.96 (= 96 percent), while the APS is $\frac{20}{470} = \frac{2}{47}$, or about 0.04 (= 4 percent). Columns 4 and 5 in Table 10.1 show the APC and APS at each of the 10 levels of DI. As implied by our previous discussion, the APC falls as DI increases, while the APS rises as DI goes up.

Because disposable income is either consumed or saved, the fraction of any DI consumed plus the fraction saved (not consumed) must exhaust that income. Mathematically, APC + APS = 1 at any level of disposable income, as columns 4 and 5 in Table 10.1 illustrate. So if 0.96 of the $470 billion of income in row 6 in consumed, 0.04 must be saved. That is why APC + APS = 1.

Global Perspective 10.1 shows APCs for several countries.

MPC and MPS The fact that households consume a certain proportion of a particular total income, for example,

GLOBAL PERSPECTIVE 10.1

Average Propensities to Consume, Selected Nations

There are surprisingly large differences in average propensities to consume (APCs) among nations. In 2011, Italy, the United States, Canada, and the Netherlands in particular had substantially higher APCs, and thus lower APSs, than several other advanced economies.

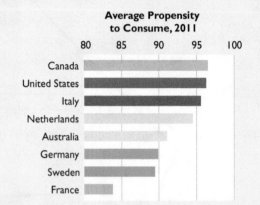

Average Propensity to Consume, 2011

Source: Organization for Economic Cooperation and Development, OECD, **www.oecd.org**. Derived from OECD household saving rates as percentages of disposable income. Econ Outlook 86, Annex Table 23, extracted March 2013.

$\frac{45}{47}$ of a $470 billion disposable income, does not guarantee they will consume the same proportion of any *change* in income they might receive. The proportion, or fraction, of any change in income consumed is called the **marginal propensity to consume (MPC)**, "marginal" meaning "extra" or "a change in." Equivalently, the MPC is the ratio of a change in consumption to a change in the income that caused the consumption change:

$$MPC = \frac{change\ in\ consumption}{change\ in\ income}$$

Similarly, the fraction of any change in income saved is the **marginal propensity to save (MPS)**. The MPS is the ratio of a change in saving to the change in income that brought it about:

$$MPS = \frac{change\ in\ saving}{change\ in\ income}$$

If disposable income is $470 billion (row 6 horizontally in Table 10.1) and household income rises by $20 billion to $490 billion (row 7), households will consume $\frac{15}{20}$, or $\frac{3}{4}$, and save $\frac{5}{20}$, or $\frac{1}{4}$, of that increase in income. In other words, the MPC is $\frac{3}{4}$ or 0.75, and the MPS is $\frac{1}{4}$ or 0.25, as shown in columns 6 and 7.

The sum of the MPC and the MPS for any change in disposable income must always be 1. Consuming or saving out of extra income is an either-or proposition; the fraction of any change in income not consumed is, by definition, saved. If 0.75 of extra disposable income is consumed, 0.25 must be saved. The fraction consumed (MPC) plus the fraction saved (MPS) must exhaust the whole change in income:

$$MPC + MPS = 1$$

In our example, 0.75 plus 0.25 equals 1.

MPC and MPS as Slopes The MPC is the numerical value of the slope of the consumption schedule, and the MPS is the numerical value of the slope of the saving

schedule. We know from the appendix to Chapter 1 that the slope of any line is the ratio of the vertical change to the horizontal change occasioned in moving from one point to another on that line.

Figure 10.3 measures the slopes of the consumption and saving lines, using enlarged portions of Figure 10.2a

FIGURE 10.3 The marginal propensity to consume and the marginal propensity to save. In the two parts of this figure, the Greek letter delta (Δ) means "the change in." (a) The MPC is the slope (ΔC/ΔDI) of the consumption schedule. (b) The MPS is the slope (ΔS/ΔDI) of the saving schedule.

and 10.2b. Observe that consumption changes by $15 billion (the vertical change) for each $20 billion change in disposable income (the horizontal change). The slope of the consumption line is thus 0.75 (= $15/$20), which is the value of the MPC. Saving changes by $5 billion (shown as the vertical change) for every $20 billion change in disposable income (shown as the horizontal change). The slope of the saving line therefore is 0.25 (= $5/$20), which is the value of the MPS.

Nonincome Determinants of Consumption and Saving

LO10.2 List and explain factors other than income that can affect consumption.

The amount of disposable income is the basic determinant of the amounts households will consume and save. But certain determinants other than income might prompt households to consume more or less at each possible level of income and thereby change the locations of the consumption and saving schedules. Those other determinants are wealth, borrowing, expectations, and interest rates.

- *Wealth* A household's wealth is the dollar amount of all the assets that it owns minus the dollar amount of its liabilities (all the debt that it owes). Households build wealth by saving money out of current income. The point of building wealth is to increase consumption possibilities. The larger the stock of wealth that a household can build up, the larger will be its present and future consumption possibilities.

  Events sometimes suddenly boost the value of existing wealth. When this happens, households tend to increase their spending and reduce their saving. This so-called **wealth effect** shifts the consumption schedule upward and the saving schedule downward. They move in response to households taking advantage of the increased consumption possibilities afforded by the sudden increase in wealth. Examples: In the late 1990s, skyrocketing U.S. stock values expanded the value of household wealth by increasing the value of household assets. Predictably, households spent more and saved less. In contrast, a strong "reverse wealth effect" occurred in 2008. Plunging real estate and stock market prices joined together to erase $11.2 trillion (yes, trillion) of household wealth. Consumers quickly reacted by reducing their consumption spending. The consumption schedule shifted downward.

- *Borrowing* Household borrowing also affects consumption. When a household borrows, it can increase current consumption beyond what would be possible if its spending were limited to its disposable income. By allowing households to spend more, borrowing shifts the current consumption schedule upward.

But note that there is no "free lunch." While borrowing in the present allows for higher consumption in the present, it necessitates lower consumption in the future when the debts that are incurred due to the borrowing must be repaid. Stated a bit differently, increased borrowing increases debt (liabilities), which in turn reduces household wealth (since *wealth = assets − liabilities*). This reduction in wealth reduces future consumption possibilities in much the same way that a decline in asset values would. But note that the term "reverse wealth effect" is reserved for situations in which wealth unexpectedly changes because asset values unexpectedly change. It is not used to refer to situations such as the one being discussed here where wealth is intentionally reduced by households through borrowing and piling up debt to increase current consumption.

- *Expectations* Household expectations about future prices and income may affect current spending and saving. For example, the expectation of higher prices tomorrow may cause households to buy more today while prices are still low. Thus, the current consumption schedule shifts up and the current saving schedule shifts down. Or expectations of a recession and thus lower income in the future may lead households to reduce consumption and save more today. Their greater present saving will help build wealth that will help them ride out the expected bad times. The consumption schedule therefore will shift down and the saving schedule will shift up.

- *Real interest rates* When real interest rates (those adjusted for inflation) fall, households tend to borrow more, consume more, and save less. A lower interest rate, for example, decreases monthly loan payments and induces consumers to purchase automobiles and other goods bought on credit. A lower interest rate also diminishes the incentive to save because of the reduced interest "payment" to the saver. These effects on consumption and saving, however, are very modest. They mainly shift consumption toward some products (those bought on credit) and away from others. At best, lower interest rates shift the consumption schedule slightly

upward and the saving schedule slightly downward. Higher interest rates do the opposite.

Other Important Considerations

There are several additional important points regarding the consumption and saving schedules:

- *Switching to real GDP* When developing macroeconomic models, economists change their focus from the relationship between consumption (and saving) and *disposable income* to the relationship between consumption (and saving) and *real domestic output (real GDP)*. This modification is reflected in Figure 10.4a and 10.4b, where the horizontal axes measure real GDP.

FIGURE 10.4 Shifts of the (a) consumption and (b) saving schedules. Normally, if households consume more at each level of real GDP, they are necessarily saving less. Graphically this means that an upward shift of the consumption schedule (C_0 to C_1) entails a downward shift of the saving schedule (S_0 to S_1). If households consume less at each level of real GDP, they are saving more. A downward shift of the consumption schedule (C_0 to C_2) is reflected in an upward shift of the saving schedule (S_0 to S_2). This pattern breaks down, however, when taxes change; then the consumption and saving schedules move in the *same* direction—opposite to the direction of the tax change.

(a)
Consumption schedule

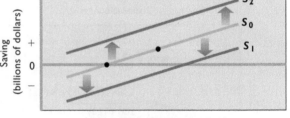

(b)
Saving schedule

CONSIDER THIS ...

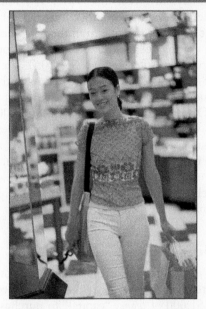

The Great Recession and the Paradox of Thrift

The Great Recession of 2007–2009 altered the prior consumption and saving behavior in the economy. Concerned about reduced wealth, high debt, and potential job losses, households increased their saving and reduced their consumption at each level of after-tax income (or each level of GDP). In Figure 10.4, this outcome is illustrated as the downward *shift* of the consumption schedule in the top graph and the upward *shift* of the saving schedule in the lower graph.

This change of behavior illustrates the so-called **paradox of thrift,** which refers to the possibility that a recession can be made worse when households become more thrifty and save in response to the downturn. The paradox of thrift rests on two major ironies. One irony is that saving more is *good* for the economy in the long run, as noted in Chapter 1 and Chapter 6. It finances investment and therefore fuels subsequent economic growth. But saving more can be *bad* for the economy during a recession. Because firms are pessimistic about future sales, the increased saving is not likely to be matched by an equal amount of added investment. The extra saving simply reduces spending on currently produced goods and services. That means that even more businesses suffer, more layoffs occur, and people's incomes decline even more.

The paradox of thrift has a second irony related to the *fallacy of composition* (Chapter 1, Last Word): Households as a group may inadvertently end up saving less when each individual household tries to save more during a recession. This is because each household's attempt to save more implies that it is also attempting to spend less. Across all households, that collective reduction in total spending in the economy creates additional job losses and further drives down total income. The decline in total income reduces the ability of households as a group to save as much as they did before their spending reduction and subsequent income decline.

- **Changes along schedules** The movement from one point to another on a consumption schedule (for example, from *a* to *b* on C_0 in Figure 10.4a) is a *change in the amount consumed* and is solely caused by a change in real GDP. On the other hand, an upward or downward shift of the entire schedule, for example, a shift from C_0 to C_1 or C_2 in Figure 10.4a, is a *shift of the consumption schedule* and is caused by changes in any one or more of the *nonincome* determinants of consumption just discussed.

  A similar distinction in terminology applies to the saving schedule in Figure 10.4b.

- **Simultaneous shifts** Changes in wealth, expectations, interest rates, and household debt will shift the consumption schedule in one direction and the saving schedule in the opposite direction. If households decide to consume more at each possible level of real GDP, they must save less, and vice versa. (Even when they spend more by borrowing, they are, in effect, reducing their current saving by the amount borrowed since borrowing is, effectively, "negative saving.") Graphically, if the consumption schedule shifts upward from C_0 to C_1 in Figure 10.4a, the saving schedule shifts downward, from S_0 to S_1 in Figure 10.4b. Similarly, a downward shift of the consumption schedule from C_0 to C_2 means an upward shift of the saving schedule from S_0 to S_2.

- **Taxation** In contrast, a change in taxes shifts the consumption and saving schedules in the same direction. Taxes are paid partly at the expense of consumption and partly at the expense of saving. So an increase in taxes will reduce both consumption and saving, shifting the consumption schedule in Figure 10.4a and the saving schedule in Figure 10.4b downward. Conversely, households will partly consume and partly save any decrease in taxes. Both the consumption schedule and saving schedule will shift upward.

- **Stability** The consumption and saving schedules usually are relatively stable unless altered by major tax increases or decreases. Their stability may be because consumption-saving decisions are strongly influenced by long-term considerations such as saving to meet emergencies or saving for retirement. It may also be because changes in the nonincome determinants frequently work in opposite directions and therefore may be self-canceling.

QUICK REVIEW 10.1

- Both consumption spending and saving rise when disposable income increases; both fall when disposable income decreases.
- The average propensity to consume (APC) is the fraction of any specific level of disposable income that is spent on consumer goods; the average propensity to save (APS) is the fraction of any specific level of disposable income that is saved. The APC falls and the APS rises as disposable income increases.
- The marginal propensity to consume (MPC) is the fraction of a change in disposable income that is consumed and it is the slope of the consumption schedule; the marginal propensity to save (MPS) is the fraction of a change in disposable income that is saved and it is the slope of the saving schedule.
- Changes in consumer wealth, consumer expectations, interest rates, household debt, and taxes can shift the consumption and saving schedules (as they relate to real GDP).

The Interest-Rate–Investment Relationship

LO10.3 Explain how changes in real interest rates affect investment.

In our consideration of major macro relationships, we next turn to the relationship between the real interest rate and investment. Recall that investment consists of expenditures on new plants, capital equipment, machinery, inventories, and so on. The investment decision is a marginal-benefit–marginal-cost decision: The marginal benefit from investment is the expected rate of return businesses hope to realize. The marginal cost is the interest rate that must be paid for borrowed funds. Businesses will invest in all projects for which the expected rate of return exceeds the interest rate. Expected returns (profits) and the interest rate therefore are the two basic determinants of investment spending.

Expected Rate of Return

Investment spending is guided by the profit motive; businesses buy capital goods only when they think such purchases will be profitable. Suppose the owner of a small cabinetmaking shop is considering whether to invest in a new sanding machine that costs $1,000 and has a useful life of only 1 year. (Extending the life of the machine beyond 1 year complicates the economic decision but does

not change the fundamental analysis. We discuss the valuation of returns beyond 1 year in Chapter 17.) The new machine will increase the firm's output and sales revenue. Suppose the net expected revenue from the machine (that is, after such operating costs as power, lumber, labor, and certain taxes have been subtracted) is $1,100. Then, after the $1,000 cost of the machine is subtracted from the net expected revenue of $1,100, the firm will have an expected profit of $100. Dividing this $100 profit by the $1,000 cost of the machine, we find that the **expected rate of return**, r, on the machine is 10 percent (= $100/$1,000). It is important to note that this is an *expected* rate of return, not a *guaranteed* rate of return. The investment may or may not generate as much revenue or as much profit as anticipated. Investment involves risk.

The Real Interest Rate

One important cost associated with investing that our example has ignored is interest, which is the financial cost of borrowing the $1,000 of *money* "capital" to purchase the $1,000 of *real* capital (the sanding machine).

The interest cost of the investment is computed by multiplying the interest rate, i, by the $1,000 borrowed to buy the machine. If the interest rate is, say, 7 percent, the total interest cost will be $70. This compares favorably with the net expected return of $100, which produced the 10 percent expected rate of return. If the investment works out as expected, it will add $30 to the firm's profit.

We can generalize as follows: If the expected rate of return (10 percent) exceeds the interest rate (here, 7 percent), the investment should be undertaken. The firm expects the investment to be profitable. But if the interest rate (say, 12 percent) exceeds the expected rate of return (10 percent), the investment should not be undertaken. The firm expects the investment to be unprofitable. The firm should undertake all investment projects it thinks will be profitable. This means that the firm should array its prospective investment projects from the highest expected rate of return, r, downward and then invest in all projects for which r exceeds i. The firm therefore should invest to the point where $r = i$ because then it will have undertaken all investments for which r is greater than i.

This guideline applies even if a firm finances the investment internally out of funds saved from past profit rather than borrowing the funds. The role of the interest rate in the investment decision does not change. When the firm uses money from savings to invest in the sander, it incurs an opportunity cost because it forgoes the interest income it could have earned by lending the funds to someone else. That interest cost, converted to percentage terms, needs to be weighed against the expected rate of return.

The *real* rate of interest, rather than the *nominal* rate, is crucial in making investment decisions. Recall from Chapter 9 that the nominal interest rate is expressed in dollars of current value, while the real interest rate is stated in dollars of constant or inflation-adjusted value. Recall that the real interest rate is the nominal rate less the rate of inflation. In our sanding machine illustration, our implicit assumption of a constant price level ensures that all our data, including the interest rate, are in real terms.

But what if inflation *is* occurring? Suppose a $1,000 investment is expected to yield a real (inflation-adjusted) rate of return of 10 percent and the nominal interest rate is 15 percent. At first, we would say the investment would be unprofitable. But assume there is ongoing inflation of 10 percent per year. This means the investing firm will pay back dollars with approximately 10 percent less in purchasing power. While the nominal interest rate is 15 percent, the real rate is only 5 percent (= 15 percent − 10 percent). By comparing this 5 percent real interest rate with the 10 percent expected real rate of return, we find that the investment is potentially profitable and should be undertaken.

Investment Demand Curve

We now move from a single firm's investment decision to total demand for investment goods by the entire business sector. Assume that every firm has estimated the expected rates of return from all investment projects and has recorded those data. We can cumulate (successively sum) these data by asking: How many dollars' worth of investment projects have an expected rate of return of, say, 16 percent or more? How many have 14 percent or more? How many have 12 percent or more? And so on.

Suppose no prospective investments yield an expected return of 16 percent or more. But suppose there are $5 billion of investment opportunities with expected rates of return between 14 and 16 percent; an additional $5 billion yielding between 12 and 14 percent; still an additional $5 billion yielding between 10 and 12 percent; and an additional $5 billion in each successive 2 percent range of yield down to and including the 0 to 2 percent range.

To cumulate these figures for each rate of return, *r*, we add the amounts of investment that will yield each particular rate of return *r* or higher. This provides the data in the table in Figure 10.5. The data are shown graphically in **Figure 10.5 (Key Graph).** In the table, the number opposite 12 percent, for example, means there are $10 billion of investment opportunities that will yield an expected rate of return of 12 percent or more. The $10 billion includes the $5 billion of investment expected to yield a return of 14 percent or more plus the $5 billion expected to yield between 12 and 14 percent.

We know from our example of the sanding machine that an investment project will be undertaken if its expected rate of return, *r*, exceeds the real interest rate, *i*. Let's first suppose *i* is 12 percent. Businesses will undertake all investments for which *r* exceeds 12 percent. That is, they will invest until the 12 percent rate of return equals the 12 percent interest rate. Figure 10.5 reveals that $10 billion of investment spending will be undertaken at a 12 percent interest rate; that means $10 billion of investment projects have an expected rate of return of 12 percent or more.

Put another way: At a financial "price" of 12 percent, $10 billion of investment goods will be demanded. If the interest rate is lower, say, 8 percent, the amount of investment for which *r* equals or exceeds *i* is $20 billion. Thus, firms will demand $20 billion of investment goods at an 8 percent real interest rate. At 6 percent, they will demand $25 billion of investment goods.

By applying the marginal-benefit–marginal-cost rule that investment projects should be undertaken up to the point where *r* = *i*, we see that we can add the real interest rate to the vertical axis in Figure 10.5. The curve in Figure 10.5 not only shows rates of return; it shows the quantity of investment demanded at each "price" *i* (interest rate) of investment. The vertical axis in Figure 10.5 shows the various possible real interest rates, and the horizontal axis shows the corresponding quantities of investment demanded. The inverse (downsloping) relationship between the interest rate (price) and dollar quantity of investment demanded conforms to the law of demand discussed in Chapter 3. The curve *ID* in Figure 10.5 is the economy's **investment demand curve.** It shows the amount of investment forthcoming at each real interest rate. The level of investment depends on the expected rate of return and the real interest rate.

ORIGIN OF THE IDEA

O10.2

Interest-rate–investment relationship

Shifts of the Investment Demand Curve

LO10.4 Identify and explain factors other than the real interest rate that can affect investment.

Figure 10.5 shows the relationship between the interest rate and the amount of investment demanded, other things equal. When other things change, the investment

KEY GRAPH

FIGURE 10.5 The investment demand curve. The investment demand curve is constructed by arraying all potential investment projects in descending order of their expected rates of return. The curve slopes downward, reflecting an inverse relationship between the real interest rate (the financial "price" of each dollar of investing) and the quantity of investment demanded.

Real Interest Rate (*i*) and Expected Rate of Return (*r*)	Cumulative Amount of Investment Having This Rate of Return or Higher, Billions per Year
16%	$ 0
14	5
12	10
10	15
8	20
6	25
4	30
2	35
0	40

QUICK QUIZ FOR FIGURE 10.5

1. The investment demand curve:
   a. reflects a direct (positive) relationship between the real interest rate and investment.
   b. reflects an inverse (negative) relationship between the real interest rate and investment.
   c. shifts to the right when the real interest rate rises.
   d. shifts to the left when the real interest rate rises.

2. In this figure:
   a. greater cumulative amounts of investment are associated with lower real interest rates.
   b. lesser cumulative amounts of investment are associated with lower expected rates of return on investment.
   c. higher interest rates are associated with higher expected rates of return on investment, and therefore greater amounts of investment.
   d. interest rates and investment move in the same direction.

3. In this figure, if the real interest rate falls from 6 to 4 percent:
   a. investment will increase from 0 to $30 billion.
   b. investment will decrease by $5 billion.
   c. the expected rate of return will rise by $5 billion.
   d. investment will increase from $25 billion to $30 billion.

4. In this figure, investment will be:
   a. zero if the real interest rate is zero.
   b. $40 billion if the real interest rate is 16 percent.
   c. $30 billion if the real interest rate is 4 percent.
   d. $20 billion if the real interest rate is 12 percent.

demand curve shifts. In general, any factor that leads businesses collectively to expect greater rates of return on their investments increases investment demand. That factor shifts the investment demand curve to the right, as from ID_0 to ID_1 in Figure 10.6. Any factor that leads businesses collectively to expect lower rates of return on their investments shifts the curve to the left, as from ID_0 to ID_2. What are those non-interest-rate determinants of investment demand?

- *Acquisition, maintenance, and operating costs* The initial costs of capital goods, and the estimated costs of operating and maintaining those goods, affect the expected rate of return on investment. When these costs rise, the expected rate of return from prospective investment projects falls and the investment demand curve shifts to the left. Example: Higher electricity costs associated with operating tools and machinery shifts the investment

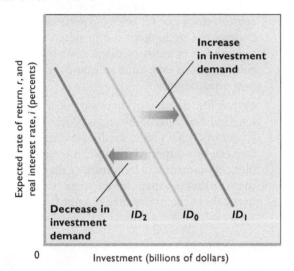

FIGURE 10.6 Shifts of the investment demand curve. Increases in investment demand are shown as rightward shifts of the investment demand curve; decreases in investment demand are shown as leftward shifts of the investment demand curve.

demand curve to the left. Lower costs, in contrast, shift it to the right.

- **Business taxes** When government is considered, firms look to expected returns *after taxes* in making their investment decisions. An increase in business taxes lowers the expected profitability of investments and shifts the investment demand curve to the left; a reduction of business taxes shifts it to the right.

- **Technological change** Technological progress—the development of new products, improvements in existing products, and the creation of new machinery and production processes—stimulates investment. The development of a more efficient machine, for example, lowers production costs or improves product quality and increases the expected rate of return from investing in the machine. Profitable new products (cholesterol medications, Internet services, high-definition televisions, cellular phones, and so on) induce a flurry of investment as businesses tool up for expanded production. A rapid rate of technological progress shifts the investment demand curve to the right.

- **Stock of capital goods on hand** The stock of capital goods on hand, relative to output and sales, influences investment decisions by firms. When the economy is overstocked with production facilities and when firms have excessive inventories of finished goods, the expected rate of return on new investment declines. Firms with excess production

capacity have little incentive to invest in new capital. Therefore, less investment is forthcoming at each real interest rate; the investment demand curve shifts leftward.

When the economy is understocked with production facilities and when firms are selling their output as fast as they can produce it, the expected rate of return on new investment increases and the investment demand curve shifts rightward.

- **Planned inventory changes** Recall from Chapter 7 that the definition of investment includes changes in inventories of unsold goods. An increase in inventories is counted as positive investment while a decrease in inventories is counted as negative investment. It is important to remember that some inventory changes are planned, while others are unplanned. Since the investment demand curve deals only with *planned* investment, it is only affected by *planned* changes that firms desire to make to their inventory levels. If firms are planning to increase their inventories, the investment demand curve shifts to the right. If firms are planning on decreasing their inventories, the investment demand curve shifts to the left.

Firms make planned changes to their inventory levels mostly because they are expecting either faster or slower sales. A firm that expects its sales to double in the next year will want to keep more inventory in stock, thereby increasing its investment demand. By contrast, a firm that is expecting slower sales will plan on reducing its inventory, thereby reducing its overall investment demand. But because life often does not turn out as expected, firms often find that the actual amount of inventory investment that they end up making is either more or less than what they had planned. The size of the gap is, naturally, the dollar amount of their *unplanned* inventory changes. These unplanned inventory adjustments will play a large role in the aggregate expenditures model studied in Chapter 11.

- **Expectations** We noted that business investment is based on expected returns (expected additions to profit). Most capital goods are durable, with a life expectancy of 10 or 20 years. Thus, the expected rate of return on capital investment depends on the firm's expectations of future sales, future operating costs, and future profitability of the product that the capital helps produce. These expectations are based on forecasts of future business conditions as well as on such elusive and difficult-to-predict factors as changes in

Gross Investment Expenditures as a Percentage of GDP, Selected Nations

As a percentage of GDP, investment varies widely by nation. These differences, of course, can change from year to year.

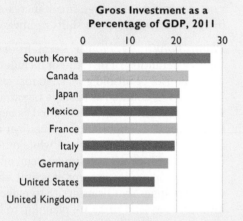

Gross Investment as a Percentage of GDP, 2011

Source: Gross fixed capital formation data from International Financial Statistics, International Monetary Fund, **www.imf.org**.

the domestic political climate, international relations, population growth, and consumer tastes. If executives become more optimistic about future sales, costs, and profits, the investment demand curve will shift to the right; a pessimistic outlook will shift the curve to the left.

Global Perspective 10.2 compares investment spending relative to GDP for several nations in a recent year. Domestic real interest rates and investment demand determine the levels of investment relative to GDP.

Instability of Investment

In contrast to consumption, investment is unstable; it rises and falls quite often. Investment, in fact, is the most volatile component of total spending—so much so that most of the fluctuations in output and employment that happen over the course of the business cycle can be attributed to demand shocks relating to unexpected increases and decreases in investment. Figure 10.7 shows just how volatile investment in the United States has been. Notice that the percentage swings in investment in real terms are greater than the percentage swings in real GDP. Several interrelated factors drawn from our previous discussion explain the variability of investment.

- *Variability of expectations* Business expectations can change quickly when some event suggests a significant possible change in future business conditions. Changes in exchange rates, trade barriers, legislative actions, stock market prices, government economic policies, the outlook for war or peace, court decisions in key labor or antitrust cases, and a host of similar considerations may cause substantial shifts in business expectations.

- *Durability* Because of their durability, capital goods have indefinite useful lifespans. Within limits, purchases of capital goods are discretionary and therefore can be postponed. Firms can scrap or replace older equipment and buildings, or they can patch them up and use them for a few more years. Optimism about the future may prompt firms to replace

CONSIDER THIS . . .

The Great Recession and the Investment Riddle

During the severe recession of 2007–2009, real interest rates essentially declined to zero. Figure 10.5 suggests that this drop in interest rates should have boosted investment spending. But investment declined substantially during this period. On an annual basis, it declined by 9 percent in 2008 and 26 percent in 2009. Does this combination of lower real interest rates and reduced investment make Figure 10.5 irrelevant?

Definitely not! The key to the investment riddle is that during the recession, the investment demand curve shifted inward, as from ID_0 to ID_2 in Figure 10.6. This inward shift overwhelmed any investment-increasing effects of the decline of real interest rates. The net result turned out to be less investment, not more.

The leftward shift of the investment demand reflected a decline in the expected returns from investment. Firms envisioned zero or negative returns on investment in new capital because they were facing an overstock of existing capital relative to their current sales. Understandably, they therefore were not inclined to invest. Also, firms were extremely pessimistic about when the economy would regain its strength. This pessimism also contributed to low expected rates of return on investment and thus to exceptionally weak investment demand. Further, even though the interest rate was so low, firms that wanted to borrow and invest found that lenders were reluctant to lend them money for fear that they would not be able to pay back the loans.

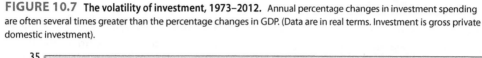

FIGURE 10.7 **The volatility of investment, 1973–2012.** Annual percentage changes in investment spending are often several times greater than the percentage changes in GDP. (Data are in real terms. Investment is gross private domestic investment).

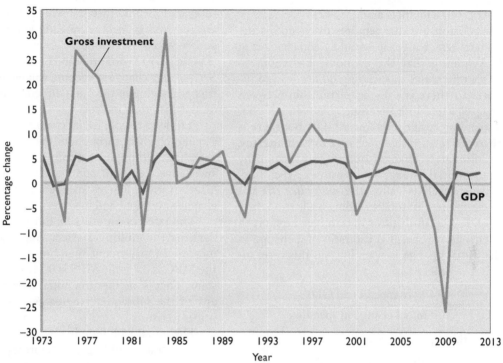

Source: Bureau of Economic Analysis, **www.bea.gov**.

their older facilities and such modernizing will call for a high level of investment. A less optimistic view, however, may lead to smaller amounts of investment as firms repair older facilities and keep them in use.

- *Irregularity of innovation* New products and processes stimulate investment. Major innovations such as railroads, electricity, airplanes, automobiles, computers, the Internet, and cell phones induce vast upsurges or "waves" of investment spending that in time recede. But such innovations occur quite irregularly, adding to the volatility of investment.

- *Variability of profits* High current profits often generate optimism about the future profitability of new investments, whereas low current profits or losses spawn considerable doubt about the wisdom of new investments. Additionally, firms often save a portion of current profits as retained earnings and use these funds (as well as borrowed funds) to finance new investments. So current profits affect both the incentive and ability to invest. But profits themselves

are highly variable from year to year, contributing to the volatility of investment.

In terms of our previous analysis, we would represent volatility of investment as occasional and substantial unexpected shifts of the investment demand curve (as in Figure 10.6), which cause significant changes in investment spending (as in Figure 10.7). These demand shocks can contribute to cyclical instability.

QUICK REVIEW 10.2

- A specific investment will be undertaken if the expected rate of return, *r*, equals or exceeds the real interest rate, *i*.

- The investment demand curve shows the total monetary amounts that will be invested by an economy at various possible real interest rates.

- The investment demand curve shifts when changes occur in (a) the costs of acquiring, operating, and maintaining capital goods, (b) business taxes, (c) technology, (d) the stock of capital goods on hand, and (e) business expectations.

The Multiplier Effect*

LO10.5 Illustrate how changes in investment (or one of the other components of total spending) can increase or decrease real GDP by a multiple amount.

A final basic relationship that requires discussion is the relationship between changes in spending and changes in real GDP. Assuming that the economy has room to expand—so that increases in spending do not lead to increases in prices—there is a direct relationship between these two aggregates. More spending results in a higher GDP; less spending results in a lower GDP. But there is much more to this relationship. A change in spending, say, investment, ultimately changes output and income by more than the initial change in investment spending. That surprising result is called the *multiplier effect*: a change in a component of total spending leads to a larger change in GDP. The **multiplier** determines how much larger that change will be; it is the ratio of a change in GDP to the initial change in spending (in this case, investment). Stated generally,

$$\text{Multiplier} = \frac{\text{change in real GDP}}{\text{initial change in spending}}$$

By rearranging this equation, we can also say that

Change in GDP = multiplier × initial change in spending

So if investment in an economy rises by $30 billion and GDP increases by $90 billion as a result, we then know from our first equation that the multiplier is 3 (= $90/$30).

Note these three points about the multiplier:

- The "initial change in spending" is usually associated with investment spending because of investment's volatility. But changes in consumption (unrelated to changes in income), net exports, and government purchases also lead to the multiplier effect.

- The "initial change in spending" associated with investment spending results from a change in the real interest rate and/or a shift of the investment demand curve.

- Implicit in the preceding point is that the multiplier works in both directions. An increase in initial spending will create a multiple increase in GDP, while a decrease in spending will create a multiple decrease in GDP.

---

*Instructors who cover the full aggregate expenditures (AE) model (Chapter 11) rather than moving directly to aggregate demand and aggregate supply (Chapter 12) may choose to defer this discussion until after the analysis of equilibrium real GDP.

Rationale

The multiplier effect follows from two facts. First, the economy supports repetitive, continuous flows of expenditures and income through which dollars spent by Smith are received as income by Chin and then spent by Chin and received as income by Gonzales, and so on. (This chapter's Last Word presents this idea in a humorous way.) Second, any change in income will change both consumption and saving in the same direction as, and by a fraction of, the change in income.

It follows that an initial change in spending will set off a spending chain throughout the economy. That chain of spending, although of diminishing importance at each successive step, will cumulate to a multiple change in GDP. Initial changes in spending produce magnified changes in output and income.

The table in Figure 10.8 illustrates the rationale underlying the multiplier effect. Suppose that a $5 billion increase in investment spending occurs. We assume that the MPC is 0.75, the MPS is 0.25, and prices remain constant. That is, neither the initial increase in spending nor any of the subsequent increases in spending will cause prices to rise.

The initial $5 billion increase in investment generates an equal amount of wage, rent, interest, and profit income because spending and receiving income are two sides of the same transaction. How much consumption will be induced by this $5 billion increase in the incomes of households? We find the answer by applying the marginal propensity to consume of 0.75 to this change in income. Thus, the $5 billion increase in income initially raises consumption by $3.75 (= 0.75 × $5) billion and saving by $1.25 (= 0.25 × $5) billion, as shown in columns 2 and 3 in the table.

Other households receive as income (second round) the $3.75 billion of consumption spending. Those households consume 0.75 of this $3.75 billion, or $2.81 billion, and save 0.25 of it, or $0.94 billion. The $2.81 billion that is consumed flows to still other households as income to be spent or saved (third round). And the process continues, with the added consumption and income becoming less in each round. The process ends when there is no more additional income to spend.

The bar chart in Figure 10.8 shows several rounds of the multiplier process of the table graphically. As shown by rounds 1 to 5, each round adds a smaller and smaller blue block to national income and GDP. The process, of course, continues beyond the five rounds shown (for convenience we have simply cumulated the subsequent declining blocks into a single block labeled "All other"). The

FIGURE 10.8   The multiplier process (MPC = 0.75). An initial change in investment spending of $5 billion creates an equal $5 billion of new income in round 1. Households spend $3.75 (= 0.75 × $5) billion of this new income, creating $3.75 billion of added income in round 2. Of this $3.75 billion of new income, households spend $2.81 (= 0.75 × $3.75) billion, and income rises by that amount in round 3. Such income increments over the entire process get successively smaller but eventually produce a total change of income and GDP of $20 billion. The multiplier therefore is 4 (= $20 billion/$5 billion).

	(1) Change in Income	(2) Change in Consumption (MPC = 0.75)	(3) Change in Saving (MPS = 0.25)
Increase in investment of **$5.00**	$5.00	$ 3.75	$1.25
Second round	3.75	2.81	0.94
Third round	2.81	2.11	0.70
Fourth round	2.11	1.58	0.53
Fifth round	1.58	1.19	0.39
All other rounds	4.75	3.56	1.19
Total	**$20.00**	$15.00	$5.00

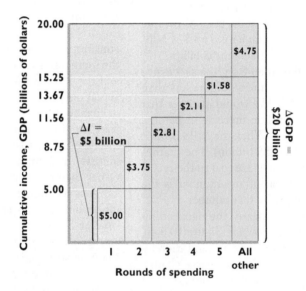

accumulation of the additional income in each round—the sum of the blue blocks—is the total change in income or GDP resulting from the initial $5 billion change in spending. Because the spending and respending effects of the increase in investment diminish with each successive round of spending, the cumulative increase in output and income eventually ends. In this case, the ending occurs when $20 billion of additional income accumulates. Thus, the multiplier is 4 (= $20 billion/$5 billion).

The Multiplier and the Marginal Propensities

You may have sensed from the table in Figure 10.8 that the fractions of an increase in income consumed (MPC)

and saved (MPS) determine the cumulative respending effects of any initial change in spending and therefore determine the size of the multiplier. The MPC and the multiplier are directly related and the MPS and the multiplier are inversely related. The precise formulas are as shown in the next two equations:

$$\text{Multiplier} = \frac{1}{1 - \text{MPC}}$$

Recall, too, that MPC + MPS = 1. Therefore MPS = 1 − MPC, which means we can also write the multiplier formula as

$$\text{Multiplier} = \frac{1}{\text{MPS}}$$

This latter formula is a quick way to determine the multiplier. All you need to know is the MPS.

The smaller the fraction of any change in income saved, the greater the respending at each round and, therefore, the greater the multiplier. When the MPS is 0.25, as in our example, the multiplier is 4. If the MPS were 0.2, the multiplier would be 5. If the MPS were 0.33, the multiplier would be 3. Let's see why.

Suppose the MPS is 0.2 and businesses increase investment by $5 billion. In the first round of the table in Figure 10.8, consumption will rise by $4 billion (= MPC of 0.8 × $5 billion) rather than by $3.75 billion because saving will increase by $1 billion (= MPS of 0.2 × $5 billion) rather than $1.25 billion. The greater rise in consumption in round 1 will produce a greater increase in income in round 2. The same will be true for all successive rounds. If we worked through all rounds of the multiplier, we would find that the process ends when income has cumulatively increased by $25 billion, not the $20 billion shown in the table. When the MPS is 0.2 rather than 0.25, the multiplier is 5 (= $25 billion/$5 billion) as opposed to 4 (= $20 billion/$5 billion.)

If the MPS were 0.33 rather than 0.25, the successive increases in consumption and income would be less than those in the table in Figure 10.8. We would discover that the process ended with a $15 billion increase in income rather than the $20 billion shown. When the MPS is 0.33, the multiplier is 3 (= $15 billion/$5 billion). The mathematics works such that the multiplier is equal to the reciprocal of the MPS. The reciprocal of any number is the quotient you obtain by dividing 1 by that number.

A large MPC (small MPS) means the succeeding rounds of consumption spending shown in Figure 10.8 diminish slowly and thereby cumulate to a large change in income. Conversely, a small MPC (a large MPS) causes the increases in consumption to decline quickly, so the cumulative change in income is small. The relationship between the MPC (and thus the MPS) and the multiplier is summarized in Figure 10.9.

WORKED PROBLEMS

W10.2
Multiplier effect

How Large Is the Actual Multiplier Effect?

The multiplier we have just described is based on simplifying assumptions. Consumption of domestic output rises by the increases in income minus the increases in saving. But in reality, consumption of domestic output increases in each round by a lesser amount than implied by the MPS alone. In addition to saving, households use some of the

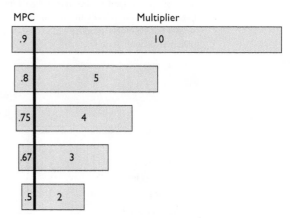

FIGURE 10.9 The MPC and the multiplier. The larger the MPC (the smaller the MPS), the greater the size of the multiplier.

extra income in each round to purchase additional goods from abroad (imports) and pay additional taxes. Buying imports and paying taxes drains off some of the additional consumption spending (on domestic output) created by the increases in income. So the multiplier effect is reduced and the 1/MPS formula for the multiplier overstates the actual outcome. To correct that problem, we would need to change the multiplier equation to read "1 divided by the fraction of the change in income that is not spent on domestic output." Also, we will find in later chapters that an increase in spending may be partly dissipated as inflation rather than realized fully as an increase in real GDP. This happens when increases in spending drive up prices. The multiplier process still happens, but it induces a much smaller change in real output because, at higher prices, any given amount of spending buys less real output. Economists disagree on the size of the actual multiplier in the United States. Estimates range from as high as 2.5 to as low as zero. So keep in mind throughout later discussions that the actual multiplier is much lower than the multipliers in our simple explanatory examples.

QUICK REVIEW 10.3

- The multiplier effect reveals that an initial change in spending can cause a larger change in domestic income and output. The multiplier is the factor by which the initial change is magnified: multiplier = change in real GDP/initial change in spending.

- The higher the marginal propensity to consume (the lower the marginal propensity to save), the larger the multiplier: multiplier = 1/(1 − MPC) or 1/MPS.

- Economists disagree on the size of the actual multiplier in the U.S. economy; estimates range all the way from zero to 2.5.

Squaring the Economic Circle

Humorist Art Buchwald Examines the Multiplier

WASHINGTON—The recession hit so fast that nobody knows exactly how it happened. One day we were the land of milk and honey and the next day we were the land of sour cream and food stamps.

This is one explanation.

Hofberger, the Ford salesman in Tomcat, Va., a suburb of Washington, called up Littleton, of Littleton Menswear & Haberdashery, and said, "Good news, the new Fords have just come in and I've put one aside for you and your wife."

Littleton said, "I can't, Hofberger, my wife and I are getting a divorce."

"I'm sorry," Littleton said, "but I can't afford a new car this year. After I settle with my wife, I'll be lucky to buy a bicycle."

Hofberger hung up. His phone rang a few minutes later.

"This is Bedcheck the painter," the voice on the other end said. "When do you want us to start painting your house?"

"I changed my mind," said Hofberger, "I'm not going to paint the house."

"But I ordered the paint," Bedcheck said. "Why did you change your mind?"

"Because Littleton is getting a divorce and he can't afford a new car."

That evening when Bedcheck came home his wife said, "The new color television set arrived from Gladstone's TV Shop."

"Take it back," Bedcheck told his wife.

"Why?" she demanded.

"Because Hofberger isn't going to have his house painted now that the Littletons are getting a divorce."

The next day Mrs. Bedcheck dragged the TV set in its carton back to Gladstone. "We don't want it."

Gladstone's face dropped. He immediately called his travel agent, Sandstorm. "You know that trip you had scheduled for me to the Virgin Islands?"

"Right, the tickets are all written up."

"Cancel it. I can't go. Bedcheck just sent back the color TV set because Hofberger didn't sell a car to Littleton because they're going to get a divorce and she wants all his money."

Sandstorm tore up the airline tickets and went over to see his banker, Gripsholm. "I can't pay back the loan this month because Gladstone isn't going to the Virgin Islands."

Gripsholm was furious. When Rudemaker came in to borrow money for a new kitchen he needed for his restaurant, Gripsholm turned him down cold. "How can I loan you money when Sandstorm hasn't repaid the money he borrowed?"

Rudemaker called up the contractor, Eagleton, and said he couldn't put in a new kitchen. Eagleton laid off eight men.

Meanwhile, Ford announced it was giving a rebate on its new models. Hofberger called up Littleton immediately. "Good news," he said, "even if you are getting a divorce, you can afford a new car."

"I'm not getting a divorce," Littleton said. "It was all a misunderstanding and we've made up."

"That's great," Hofberger said. "Now you can buy the Ford."

"No way," said Littleton. "My business has been so lousy I don't know why I keep the doors open."

"I didn't realize that," Hofberger said.

"Do you realize I haven't seen Bedcheck, Gladstone, Sandstorm, Gripsholm, Rudemaker or Eagleton for more than a month? How can I stay in business if they don't patronize my store?"

Source: Art Buchwald, "Squaring the Economic Circle," *Cleveland Plain Dealer*, Feb. 22, 1975. Reprinted by permission.

SUMMARY

LO10.1 Describe how changes in income affect consumption (and saving).

Other things equal, a direct (positive) relationship exists between income and consumption and income and saving. The consumption and saving schedules show the various amounts that households intend to consume and save at the various income and output levels, assuming a fixed price level.

The *average* propensities to consume and save show the fractions of any total income that are consumed and saved; APC + APS = 1. The *marginal* propensities to consume and save show the fractions of any change in total income that are consumed and saved; MPC + MPS = 1.

LO10.2 List and explain factors other than income that can affect consumption.

The locations of the consumption and saving schedules (as they relate to real GDP) are determined by (*a*) the amount of wealth owned by households, (*b*) expectations of future prices and incomes, (*c*) real interest rates, (*d*) household debt, and (*e*) tax levels. The consumption and saving schedules are relatively stable.

LO10.3 Explain how changes in real interest rates affect investment.

The immediate determinants of investment are (*a*) the expected rate of return and (*b*) the real rate of interest. The economy's investment demand curve is found by cumulating investment projects, arraying them in descending order according to their expected rates of return, graphing the result, and applying the rule that investment should be undertaken up to the point at which the real interest rate, *i*, equals the expected rate of return, *r*. The investment demand curve reveals an inverse (negative) relationship between the interest rate and the level of aggregate investment.

Shifts of the investment demand curve can occur as the result of changes in (*a*) the acquisition, maintenance, and operating costs of capital goods; (*b*) business taxes; (*c*) technology; (*d*) the stocks of capital goods on hand; and (*e*) expectations.

Either changes in interest rates or shifts of the investment demand curve can change the level of investment.

LO10.4 Identify and explain factors other than the real interest rate that can affect investment.

The durability of capital goods, the irregular occurrence of major innovations, profit volatility, and the variability of expectations all contribute to the instability of investment spending.

LO10.5 Illustrate how changes in investment (or one of the other components of total spending) can increase or decrease real GDP by a multiple amount.

Through the multiplier effect, an increase in investment spending (or consumption spending, government purchases, or net export spending) ripples through the economy, ultimately creating a magnified increase in real GDP. The multiplier is the ultimate change in GDP divided by the initiating change in investment or some other component of spending.

The multiplier is equal to the reciprocal of the marginal propensity to save: The greater is the marginal propensity to save, the smaller is the multiplier. Also, the greater is the marginal propensity to consume, the larger is the multiplier.

Economists disagree on the size of the actual multiplier in the United States, with estimates ranging all the way from 2.5 to 0. But all estimates of actual-economy multipliers are less than the multiplier in our purposefully simple text illustrations.

TERMS AND CONCEPTS

45° (degree) line	average propensity to save (APS)	paradox of thrift
consumption schedule	marginal propensity to consume (MPC)	expected rate of return
saving schedule	marginal propensity to save (MPS)	investment demand curve
break-even income	wealth effect	multiplier
average propensity to consume (APC)		

The following and additional problems can be found in **connect** | ECONOMICS

DISCUSSION QUESTIONS

1. Precisely how do the MPC and the APC differ? How does the MPC differ from the MPS? Why must the sum of the MPC and the MPS equal 1? **LO10.1**
2. Why does a downshift of the consumption schedule typically involve an equal upshift of the saving schedule? What is the exception to this relationship? **LO10.2**
3. Why will a reduction in the real interest rate increase investment spending, other things equal? **LO10.3**
4. In what direction will each of the following occurrences shift the investment demand curve, other things equal? **LO10.4**
   a. An increase in unused production capacity occurs.

   b. Business taxes decline.
   c. The costs of acquiring equipment fall.
   d. Widespread pessimism arises about future business conditions and sales revenues.
   e. A major new technological breakthrough creates prospects for a wide range of profitable new products.
5. How is it possible for investment spending to increase even in a period in which the real interest rate rises? **LO10.4**
6. Why is investment spending unstable? **LO10.4**
7. Is the relationship between changes in spending and changes in real GDP in the multiplier effect a direct

(positive) relationship or is it an inverse (negative) relationship? How does the size of the multiplier relate to the size of the MPC? The MPS? What is the logic of the multiplier-MPC relationship? **LO10.5**

8. Why is the actual multiplier in the U.S. economy less than the multiplier in this chapter's example? **LO10.5**

9. **LAST WORD** What is the central economic idea humorously illustrated in Art Buchwald's piece "Squaring the Economic Circle"? How does the central idea relate to economic recessions, on the one hand, and vigorous economic expansions, on the other?

REVIEW QUESTIONS

1. What are the variables (the items measured on the axes) in a graph of the (*a*) consumption schedule and (*b*) saving schedule? Are the variables inversely (negatively) related or are they directly (positively) related? What is the fundamental reason that the levels of consumption and saving in the United States are each higher today than they were a decade ago? **LO10.1**

2. In year one, Adam earns $1,000 and saves $100. In year 2, Adam gets a $500 raise so that he earns a total of $1,500. Out of that $1,500, he saves $200. What is Adam's MPC out of his $500 raise? **LO10.1**
   a. 0.50.
   b. 0.75.
   c. 0.80.
   d. 1.00.

3. If the MPS rises, then the MPC will: **LO10.1**
   a. Fall.
   b. Rise.
   c. Stay the same.

4. In what direction will each of the following occurrences shift the consumption and saving schedules, other things equal? **LO10.2**
   a. A large decrease in real estate values, including private homes.
   b. A sharp, sustained increase in stock prices.
   c. A 5-year increase in the minimum age for collecting Social Security benefits.

d. An economy-wide expectation that a recession is over and that a robust expansion will occur.
   e. A substantial increase in household borrowing to finance auto purchases.

5. Irving owns a chain of movie theaters. He is considering whether he should build a new theater downtown. The expected rate of return is 15 percent per year. He can borrow money at a 12 percent interest rate to finance the project. Should Irving proceed with this project? **LO10.3**
   a. Yes.
   b. No.

6. Which of the following scenarios will shift the investment demand curve right? **LO10.4**
   *Select **one or more** answers from the choices shown.*
   a. Business taxes increase.
   b. The expected return on capital increases.
   c. Firms have a lot of unused production capacity.
   d. Firms are planning on increasing their inventories.

7. True or False: Real GDP is more volatile (variable) than gross investment. **LO10.4**

8. If a $50 billion initial increase in spending leads to a $250 billion change in real GDP, how big is the multiplier? **LO10.5**
   a. 1.0.
   b. 2.5.
   c. 4.0.
   d. 5.0.

9. True or False: Larger MPCs imply larger multipliers. **LO10.5**

PROBLEMS

1. Refer to the table below. **LO10.1**
   a. Fill in the missing numbers in the table.
   b. What is the break-even level of income in the table? What is the term that economists use for the saving situation shown at the $240 level of income?

c. For each of the following items, indicate whether the value in the table is either constant or variable as income changes: the MPS, the APC, the MPC, the APS.

2. Suppose that disposable income, consumption, and saving in some country are $200 billion, $150 billion, and $50 billion,

Level of Output and Income (GDP = DI)	Consumption	Saving	APC	APS	MPC	MPS
$240	$_____	$ −4	____	____		
260	_____	0	____	____	____	____
280	_____	4	____	____	____	____
300	_____	8	____	____	____	____
320	_____	12	____	____	____	____
340	_____	16	____	____	____	____
360	_____	20	____	____	____	____
380	_____	24	____	____	____	____
400	_____	28	____	____		

respectively. Next, assume that disposable income increases by $20 billion, consumption rises by $18 billion, and saving goes up by $2 billion. What is the economy's MPC? Its MPS? What was the APC before the increase in disposable income? After the increase? **LO10.1**

3. **ADVANCED ANALYSIS** Suppose that the linear equation for consumption in a hypothetical economy is $C = 40 + 0.8Y$. Also suppose that income (Y) is $400. Determine (*a*) the marginal propensity to consume, (*b*) the marginal propensity to save, (*c*) the level of consumption, (*d*) the average propensity to consume, (*e*) the level of saving, and (*f*) the average propensity to save. **LO10.1**

4. **ADVANCED ANALYSIS** Linear equations for the consumption and saving schedules take the general form $C = a + bY$ and $S = -a + (1 - b)Y$, where C, S, and Y are consumption, saving, and national income, respectively. The constant a represents the vertical intercept, and b represents the slope of the consumption schedule. **LO10.1, LO10.2**

   a. Use the following data to substitute numerical values for a and b in the consumption and saving equations.

National Income (Y)	Consumption (C)
$ 0	$ 80
100	140
200	200
300	260
400	320

   b. What is the economic meaning of b? Of $(1 - b)$?

   c. Suppose that the amount of saving that occurs at each level of national income falls by $20 but that the values of b and $(1 - b)$ remain unchanged. Restate the saving and consumption equations inserting the new numerical values, and cite a factor that might have caused the change.

5. Use your completed table for problem 1 to solve this problem. Suppose the wealth effect is such that $10 changes in wealth produce $1 changes in consumption at each level of income. If real estate prices tumble such that wealth declines by $80, what will be the new level of consumption and saving at the $340 billion level of disposable income? The new level of saving? **LO10.2**

6. Suppose a handbill publisher can buy a new duplicating machine for $500 and the duplicator has a 1-year life. The machine is expected to contribute $550 to the year's net revenue. What is the expected rate of return? If the real interest rate at which funds can be borrowed to purchase the machine is 8 percent, will the publisher choose to invest in the machine? Will it invest in the machine if the real interest rate is 9 percent? If it is 11 percent? **LO10.3**

7. Assume there are no investment projects in the economy that yield an expected rate of return of 25 percent or more. But suppose there are $10 billion of investment projects yielding expected returns of between 20 and 25 percent; another $10 billion yielding between 15 and 20 percent; another $10 billion between 10 and 15 percent; and so forth. Cumulate these data and present them graphically, putting the expected rate of return (and the real interest rate) on the vertical axis and the amount of investment on the horizontal axis. What will be the equilibrium level of aggregate investment if the real interest rate is (*a*) 15 percent, (*b*) 10 percent, and (*c*) 5 percent? **LO10.3**

8. Refer to the table in Figure 10.5 and suppose that the real interest rate is 6 percent. Next, assume that some factor changes such that the expected rate of return declines by 2 percentage points at each prospective level of investment. Assuming no change in the real interest rate, by how much and in what direction will investment change? Which of the following might cause this change: (*a*) a decision to increase inventories; (*b*) an increase in excess production capacity? **LO10.4**

9. What will the multiplier be when the MPS is 0, 0.4, 0.6, and 1? What will it be when the MPC is 1, 0.90, 0.67, 0.50, and 0? How much of a change in GDP will result if firms increase their level of investment by $8 billion and the MPC is 0.80? If the MPC instead is 0.67? **LO10.5**

10. Suppose that an initial $10 billion increase in investment spending expands GDP by $10 billion in the first round of the multiplier process. If GDP and consumption both rise by $6 billion in the second round of the process, what is the MPC in this economy? What is the size of the multiplier? If, instead, GDP and consumption both rose by $8 billion in the second round, what would have been the size of the multiplier? **LO10.5**

The Aggregate Expenditures Model

Learning Objectives

LO11.1 Explain how sticky prices relate to the aggregate expenditures model.

LO11.2 Explain how an economy's investment schedule is derived from the investment demand curve and an interest rate.

LO11.3 Illustrate how economists combine consumption and investment to depict an aggregate expenditures schedule for a private closed economy and how that schedule can be used to demonstrate the economy's equilibrium level of output (where the total quantity of goods produced equals the total quantity of goods purchased).

LO11.4 Discuss the two other ways to characterize the equilibrium level of real GDP in a private closed economy: saving = investment, and no unplanned changes in inventories.

LO11.5 Analyze how changes in equilibrium real GDP can occur in the aggregate expenditures model and describe how those changes relate to the multiplier.

LO11.6 Explain how economists integrate the international sector (exports and imports) into the aggregate expenditures model.

LO11.7 Explain how economists integrate the public sector (government expenditures and taxes) into the aggregate expenditures model.

LO11.8 Differentiate between equilibrium GDP and full-employment GDP and identify and describe the nature and causes of "recessionary expenditure gaps" and "inflationary expenditure gaps."

In previous chapters we answered in detail two of the most critical questions in macroeconomics: How

ORIGIN OF THE IDEA

O11.1
Aggregate expenditures model

is an economy's output measured? Why does an economy grow? But we have been relatively general in addressing two other important questions: What determines the level of GDP, given a nation's production capacity? What causes real

GDP to rise in one period and to fall in another? To provide more thorough answers to these two questions, we construct the aggregate expenditures model, which has its origins in 1936 in the writings of British economist John Maynard Keynes (pronounced "Caines"). The basic premise of the aggregate expenditures model—also known as the "Keynesian cross" model—is that the amount of goods and services produced and therefore the level of employment depend directly on the level of aggregate expenditures (total spending). Businesses will produce only a level of output that they think they can profitably sell. They will idle their workers and machinery when there are no markets for their goods and services.

Assumptions and Simplifications

LO11.1 Explain how sticky prices relate to the aggregate expenditures model.

The simplifying assumptions underpinning the aggregate expenditures model reflect the economic conditions that were prevalent during the Great Depression. As discussed in this chapter's Last Word, Keynes created the model during the middle of the Great Depression in the hopes of understanding both why the Great Depression had happened as well as how it might be ended.

The most fundamental assumption behind the aggregate expenditures model is that prices in the economy are fixed. In the terminology of Chapter 6, the aggregate expenditures model is an extreme version of a sticky price model. In fact, it is a stuck-price model because the price-level cannot change at all.

Keynes made this simplifying assumption because he had observed that prices had not declined sufficiently during the Great Depression to boost spending and maintain output and employment at their pre-Depression levels. Such price declines had been predicted by macroeconomic theories that were popular before the Great

Depression. But actual prices did not fall sufficiently during the Great Depression, and the economy sank far below its potential output. Real GDP in the United States declined by 27 percent from 1929 to 1933, and the unemployment rate rose to 25 percent. Thousands of factories sat idle, gathering dust and producing nothing, because nobody wanted to buy their output.

To Keynes, this massive unemployment of labor and capital resulted from firms reacting to information about how much they should produce. As households and businesses greatly reduced their spending, inventories of unsold goods rocketed. Unable or unwilling to slash their prices, firms could not sell all the goods they had already produced. So they greatly reduced their current production. This meant discharging workers, idling production lines, and even closing entire factories. Keynes thought that a new economic model was needed to show how all this could have happened and how it might be reversed.

The Keynesian aggregate expenditures model is not just of historical interest. It is still insightful even today because many prices in the modern economy are inflexible downward over relatively short periods of time. The aggregate expenditures model therefore can help us understand how the modern economy is likely to initially adjust to various economic shocks over shorter periods of time. For example, it clarifies aspects of the severe 2007–2009 recession, such as why unexpected initial declines in spending caused even larger declines in real GDP. It also illuminates the thinking underlying the stimulus programs (tax cuts, government spending increases) enacted by the government during the recession.

We will build up the aggregate expenditures model in simple stages. Let's first look at aggregate expenditures and equilibrium GDP in a *private closed economy*—one without international trade or government. Then we will "open" the "closed" economy to exports and imports and also convert our "private" economy to a more realistic "mixed" economy that includes government purchases (or, more loosely, "government spending") and taxes.

In addition, until we introduce taxes into the model, we will assume that real GDP equals disposable income (DI). For instance, if $500 billion of output is produced as GDP, households will receive exactly $500 billion of disposable income that they can then consume or save. And finally, unless specified otherwise, we will assume (as Keynes did) that the presence of excess production capacity and unemployed labor implies that an increase in aggregate expenditures will increase real output and employment without raising the price level.

Consumption and Investment Schedules

LO11.2 Explain how an economy's investment schedule is derived from the investment demand curve and an interest rate.

In the private closed economy, the two components of aggregate expenditures are consumption, C, and gross investment, I_g. Because we examined the *consumption schedule* (Figure 10.2a) in the previous chapter, there is no need to repeat that analysis here. But to add the investment decisions of businesses to the consumption plans of households, we need to construct an investment schedule showing the amounts business firms collectively intend to invest—their **planned investment**—at each possible level of GDP. Such a schedule represents the investment plans of businesses in the same way the consumption schedule represents the consumption plans of households. In developing the investment schedule, we will assume that this planned investment is independent of the level of current disposable income or real output.

Suppose the investment demand curve is as shown in Figure 11.1a and the current real interest rate is 8 percent. This means that firms will spend $20 billion on investment goods. Our assumption tells us that this $20 billion of investment will occur at both low and high levels of GDP. The line I_g in Figure 11.1b shows this graphically;

FIGURE 11.1 (a) The investment demand curve and (b) the investment schedule. (a) The level of investment spending (here, $20 billion) is determined by the real interest rate (here, 8 percent) together with the investment demand curve *ID*. (b) The investment schedule I_g relates the amount of investment ($20 billion) determined in (a) to the various levels of GDP.

(a)
Investment demand curve

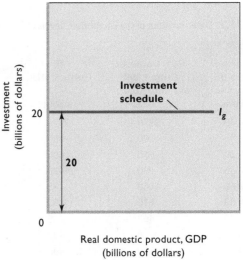

(b)
Investment schedule

TABLE 11.1 The Investment Schedule (in Billions)

(1) Level of Real Output and Income	(2) Investment (I_g)
$370	$20
390	20
410	20
430	20
450	20
470	20
490	20
510	20
530	20
550	20

it is the economy's **investment schedule.** You should not confuse this investment schedule I_g with the investment demand curve ID in Figure 11.1a. The investment schedule shows the amount of investment forthcoming at each level of GDP. As indicated in Figure 11.1b, the interest rate and investment demand curve together determine this amount ($20 billion). Table 11.1 shows the investment schedule in tabular form. Note that investment (I_g) in column 2 is $20 billion at all levels of real GDP.

Equilibrium GDP: $C + I_g = GDP$

LO11.3 Illustrate how economists combine consumption and investment to depict an aggregate expenditures schedule for a private closed economy and how that schedule

can be used to demonstrate the economy's equilibrium level of output (where the total quantity of goods produced equals the total quantity of goods purchased).

Now let's combine the consumption schedule of Chapter 10 and the investment schedule here to explain the equilibrium levels of output, income, and employment in the private closed economy.

Tabular Analysis

Columns 2 through 5 in Table 11.2 repeat the consumption and saving schedules of Table 10.1 and the investment schedule of Table 11.1.

Real Domestic Output Column 2 in Table 11.2 lists the various possible levels of total output—of real GDP—that the private sector might produce. Firms would be willing to produce any one of these 10 levels of output just as long as the revenue that they receive from selling any particular level equals or exceeds the costs they would incur to produce it. Those costs are the factor payments needed to obtain the required amounts of land, labor, capital, and entrepreneurship. For example, firms would be willing to produce $370 billion of output if the costs of production (wages, rents, interest, and the normal profit needed to attract entrepreneurship) are less than or equal to the $370 billion in revenue that they would get from selling the output.

Aggregate Expenditures In the private closed economy of Table 11.2, aggregate expenditures consist of consumption (column 3) plus investment (column 5). Their

TABLE 11.2 Determination of the Equilibrium Levels of Employment, Output, and Income: A Private Closed Economy

(1) Possible Levels of Employment, Millions	(2) Real Domestic Output (and Income) (GDP = DI),* Billions	(3) Consumption (C), Billions	(4) Saving (S), Billions	(5) Investment (I_g), Billions	(6) Aggregate Expenditures (C + I_g), Billions	(7) Unplanned Changes in Inventories, (+ or −)	(8) Tendency of Employment, Output, and Income
(1) 40	$370	$375	$−5	$20	$395	$−25	Increase
(2) 45	390	390	0	20	410	−20	Increase
(3) 50	410	405	5	20	425	−15	Increase
(4) 55	430	420	10	20	440	−10	Increase
(5) 60	450	435	15	20	455	−5	Increase
(6) 65	**470**	**450**	**20**	**20**	**470**	**0**	**Equilibrium**
(7) 70	490	465	25	20	485	+5	Decrease
(8) 75	510	480	30	20	500	+10	Decrease
(9) 80	530	495	35	20	515	+15	Decrease
(10) 85	550	510	40	20	530	+20	Decrease

*If depreciation and net foreign factor income are zero, government is ignored, and it is assumed that all saving occurs in the household sector of the economy, then GDP as a measure of domestic output is equal to NI, PI, and DI. This means that households receive a DI equal to the value of total output.

sum is shown in column 6, which along with column 2 makes up the **aggregate expenditures schedule** for the private closed economy. This schedule shows the amount $(C + I_g)$ that will be spent at each possible output or income level.

At this point we are working with *planned investment*—the data in column 5, Table 11.2. These data show the amounts firms plan or intend to invest, not the amounts they actually will invest if there are unplanned changes in inventories. More about that shortly.

Equilibrium GDP   Of the 10 possible levels of GDP in Table 11.2, which is the equilibrium level? Which total output is the economy capable of sustaining?

The equilibrium output is that output whose production creates total spending just sufficient to purchase that output. So the equilibrium level of GDP is the level at which the total quantity of goods produced (GDP) equals the total quantity of goods purchased $(C + I_g)$. In the private closed economy, the **equilibrium GDP** is where

$$C + I_g = \text{GDP}$$

If you look at the domestic output levels in column 2 and the aggregate expenditures levels in column 6, you will see that this equality exists only at $470 billion of GDP (row 6). That is the only output at which economy-wide spending is precisely equal to the amount needed to move that output off the shelves. At $470 billion of GDP, the annual rates of production and spending are in balance. There is no overproduction, which would result in a piling up of unsold goods and consequently cutbacks in the production rate. Nor is there an excess of total spending, which would draw down inventories of goods and prompt increases in the rate of production. In short, there is no reason for businesses to alter this rate of production; $470 billion is the equilibrium GDP.

Disequilibrium   No level of GDP other than the equilibrium level of GDP can be sustained. At levels of GDP *less than* equilibrium, spending always exceeds GDP. If, for example, firms produced $410 billion of GDP (row 3 in Table 11.2), they would find it would yield $405 billion in consumer spending. Supplemented by $20 billion of planned investment, aggregate expenditures $(C + I_g)$ would be $425 billion, as shown in column 6. The economy would provide an annual rate of spending more than sufficient to purchase the $410 billion of annual production. Because buyers would be taking goods off the shelves faster than firms could produce them, an unplanned decline in business inventories of $15 billion would occur (column 7) if this situation continued. But businesses can

adjust to such an imbalance between aggregate expenditures and real output by stepping up production. Greater output will increase employment and total income. This process will continue until the equilibrium level of GDP is reached ($470 billion).

The reverse is true at all levels of GDP *greater than* the $470 billion equilibrium level. Businesses will find that these total outputs fail to generate the spending needed to clear the shelves of goods. Being unable to recover their costs, businesses will cut back on production. To illustrate: At the $510 billion output (row 8), business managers would find spending is insufficient to permit the sale of all that output. Of the $510 billion of income that this output creates, $480 billion would be received back by businesses

as consumption spending. Though supplemented by $20 billion of planned investment spending, total expenditures ($500 billion) would still be $10 billion below the $510 billion quantity produced. If this imbalance persisted, $10 billion of inventories would pile up (column 7). But businesses can adjust to this unintended accumulation of unsold goods by cutting back on the rate of production. The resulting decline in output would mean fewer jobs and a decline in total income.

Graphical Analysis

We can demonstrate the same analysis graphically. In **Figure 11.2 (Key Graph)** the 45° line developed in Chapter 10 now takes on increased significance. Recall that at any point on this line, the value of what is being measured on the horizontal axis (here, GDP) is equal to the value of what is being measured on the vertical axis (here, aggregate expenditures, or $C + I_g$). Having discovered in our tabular analysis that the equilibrium level of domestic output is determined where $C + I_g$ equals GDP, we can say that the 45° line in Figure 11.2 is a graphical statement of that equilibrium condition.

Now we must graph the aggregate expenditures schedule onto Figure 11.2. To do this, we duplicate the consumption schedule C in Figure 10.2a and add to it vertically the constant $20 billion amount of investment I_g from Figure 11.1b. This $20 billion is the amount we assumed firms plan to invest at all levels of GDP. Or, more directly, we can plot the $C + I_g$ data in column 6, Table 11.2.

Observe in Figure 11.2 that the aggregate expenditures line $C + I_g$ shows that total spending rises with income and

KEY GRAPH

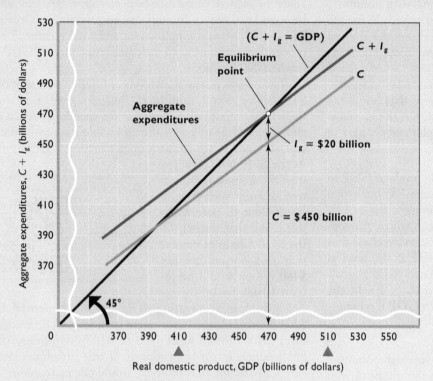

FIGURE 11.2 Equilibrium GDP in a private closed economy. The aggregate expenditures schedule, $C + I_g$, is determined by adding the investment schedule I_g to the upsloping consumption schedule C. Since investment is assumed to be the same at each level of GDP, the vertical distances between C and $C + I_g$ do not change. Equilibrium GDP is determined where the aggregate expenditures schedule intersects the 45° line, in this case at $470 billion.

QUICK QUIZ FOR FIGURE 11.2

1. In this figure, the slope of the aggregate expenditures schedule $C + I_g$:
   a. increases as real GDP increases.
   b. falls as real GDP increases.
   c. is constant and equals the MPC.
   d. is constant and equals the MPS.

2. At all points on the 45° line:
   a. equilibrium GDP is possible.
   b. aggregate expenditures exceed real GDP.
   c. consumption exceeds investment.
   d. aggregate expenditures are less than real GDP.

3. The $490 billion level of real GDP is not at equilibrium because:
   a. investment exceeds consumption.
   b. consumption exceeds investment.
   c. planned $C + I_g$ exceeds real GDP.
   d. planned $C + I_g$ is less than real GDP.

4. The $430 billion level of real GDP is not at equilibrium because:
   a. investment exceeds consumption.
   b. consumption exceeds investment.
   c. planned $C + I_g$ exceeds real GDP.
   d. planned $C + I_g$ is less than real GDP.

Answers: 1. c; 2. a; 3. d; 4. c

output (GDP), but not as much as income rises. That is true because the marginal propensity to consume—the slope of line C—is less than 1. A part of any increase in income will be saved rather than spent. And because the aggregate expenditures line $C + I_g$ is parallel to the consumption line C, the slope of the aggregate expenditures line also equals the MPC for the economy and is less than 1. For our particular data, aggregate expenditures rise by $15 billion for every $20 billion increase in real output and income because $5 billion of each $20 billion increment is saved. Therefore, the slope of the aggregate expenditures line is 0.75 (= Δ$15/Δ$20).

The equilibrium level of GDP is determined by the intersection of the aggregate expenditures schedule and the 45° line. This intersection locates the only point at which aggregate expenditures (on the vertical axis) are equal to GDP (on the horizontal axis). Because Figure 11.2 is based on the data in Table 11.2, we once again find that equilibrium output is $470 billion. Observe that consumption at this output is $450 billion and investment is $20 billion.

It is evident from Figure 11.2 that no levels of GDP *above* the equilibrium level are sustainable because at those levels $C + I_g$ falls short of GDP. Graphically, the aggregate expenditures schedule lies below the 45° line in those situations. At the $510 billion GDP level, for example, $C + I_g$ is only $500 billion. This underspending causes inventories to rise, prompting firms to readjust production downward, in the direction of the $470 billion output level.

Conversely, at levels of GDP *below* $470 billion, the economy wants to spend in excess of what businesses are producing. Then $C + I_g$ exceeds total output. Graphically, the aggregate expenditures schedule lies above the 45° line. At the $410 billion GDP level, for example, $C + I_g$ totals $425 billion. This excess spending causes inventories to fall below their planned level, prompting firms to adjust production upward, in the direction of the $470 billion output level. Once production reaches that level, it will be sustained there indefinitely unless there is some change in the location of the aggregate expenditures line.

Other Features of Equilibrium GDP

LO11.4 Discuss the two other ways to characterize the equilibrium level of real GDP in a private closed economy: saving = investment, and no unplanned changes in inventories.

We have seen that $C + I_g$ = GDP at equilibrium in the private closed economy. A closer look at Table 11.2 reveals two more characteristics of equilibrium GDP:

- Saving and *planned* investment are equal ($S = I_g$).
- There are no *unplanned* changes in inventories.

Saving Equals Planned Investment

As shown by row 6 in Table 11.2, saving and planned investment are both $20 billion at the $470 billion equilibrium level of GDP.

Saving is a **leakage** or withdrawal of spending from the economy's circular flow of income and expenditures. Saving is what causes consumption to be less than total output or GDP. Because of saving, consumption by itself is insufficient to remove domestic output from the shelves, apparently setting the stage for a decline in total output.

However, firms do not intend to sell their entire output to consumers. Some of that output will be capital goods sold to other businesses. Investment—the purchases of capital goods—is therefore an **injection** of spending into the income-expenditures stream. As an adjunct to consumption, investment is thus a potential replacement for the leakage of saving.

If the leakage of saving at a certain level of GDP exceeds the injection of investment, then $C + I_g$ will be less than

GDP and that level of GDP cannot be sustained. Any GDP for which saving exceeds investment is an above-equilibrium GDP. Consider GDP of $510 billion (row 8 in Table 11.2). Households will save $30 billion, but firms will plan to invest only $20 billion. This $10 billion excess of saving over planned investment will reduce total spending to $10 billion below the value of total output. Specifically, aggregate expenditures will be $500 billion while real GDP is $510 billion. This spending deficiency will reduce real GDP.

Conversely, if the injection of investment exceeds the leakage of saving, then $C + I_g$ will be greater than GDP and drive GDP upward. Any GDP for which investment exceeds saving is a below-equilibrium GDP. For example, at a GDP of $410 billion (row 3 in Table 11.2), households will save only $5 billion, but firms will invest $20 billion. So investment exceeds saving by $15 billion. The small leakage of saving at this relatively low GDP level is more than compensated for by the larger injection of investment spending. That causes $C + I_g$ to exceed GDP and drives GDP higher.

Only where $S = I_g$—where the leakage of saving of $20 billion is exactly offset by the injection of planned investment of $20 billion—will aggregate expenditures $(C + I_g)$ equal real output (GDP). That $C + I_g$ = GDP equality is what defines the equilibrium GDP.

No Unplanned Changes in Inventories

As part of their investment plans, firms may decide to increase or decrease their inventories. But, as confirmed in line 6 of Table 11.2, there are no **unplanned changes in inventories** at equilibrium GDP. This fact, along with $C + I_g$ = GDP, and $S = I_g$ is a characteristic of equilibrium GDP in the private closed economy.

Unplanned changes in inventories play a major role in achieving equilibrium GDP. Consider, as an example, the $490 billion *above-equilibrium* GDP shown in row 7 of Table 11.2. What happens if firms produce that output, thinking they can sell it? Households save $25 billion of their $490 billion DI, so consumption is only $465 billion. Planned investment—which includes *planned* changes in inventories—is $20 billion (column 5). So aggregate expenditures $(C + I_g)$ are $485 billion and sales fall short of production by $5 billion. Firms retain that extra $5 billion of goods as an *unplanned* increase in inventories (column 7). It results from the failure of total spending to remove total output from the shelves.

Because changes in inventories are a part of investment, we note that *actual investment* is $25 billion. It consists of $20 billion of planned investment *plus* the $5 billion unplanned increase in inventories. Actual investment equals the saving of $25 billion, even though saving exceeds planned investment by $5 billion. Because firms cannot earn profits by accumulating unwanted inventories, the $5 billion unplanned increase in inventories will prompt them to cut back employment and production. GDP will fall to its equilibrium level of $470 billion, at which unplanned changes in inventories are zero.

Now look at the *below-equilibrium* $450 billion output (row 5, Table 11.2). Because households save only $15 billion of their $450 billion DI, consumption is $435 billion. Planned investment by firms is $20 billion, so aggregate expenditures are $455 billion. Sales exceed production by $5 billion. This is so only because a $5 billion unplanned decrease in business inventories has occurred. Firms must *disinvest* $5 billion in inventories (column 7). Note again that actual investment is $15 billion ($20 billion planned *minus* the $5 billion decline in inventory investment) and is equal to saving of $15 billion, even though planned investment exceeds saving by $5 billion. The unplanned decline in inventories, resulting from the excess of sales over production, will encourage firms to expand production. GDP will rise to $470 billion, at which unplanned changes in inventories are zero.

When economists say differences between investment and saving can occur and bring about changes in equilibrium GDP, they are referring to planned investment and saving. Equilibrium occurs only when planned investment and saving are equal. But when unplanned changes in inventories are considered, investment and saving are always equal, regardless of the level of GDP. That is true because actual investment consists of planned investment and unplanned investment (unplanned changes in inventories). Unplanned changes in inventories act as a balancing item that equates the actual amounts saved and invested in any period.

Changes in Equilibrium GDP and the Multiplier

LO11.5 Analyze how changes in equilibrium real GDP can occur in the aggregate expenditures model and describe how those changes relate to the multiplier.

In the previous chapter, we established that an initial change in spending can cause a greater change in real output through the multiplier effect. In equation form,

$$\text{Multiplier} = \frac{\text{change in real GDP}}{\text{initial change in spending}}$$

Further, we discovered that the size of the multiplier depends on the size of the MPS in the economy:

$$\text{Multiplier} = \frac{1}{\text{MPS}}$$

(Because the multiplier is such an important element of the aggregate expenditures model, we highly recommend that you quickly review Figure 10.8 at this time.)

In a private closed economy, the equilibrium GDP will change in response to changes in either the investment schedule or the consumption schedule. Because changes in the investment schedule are the main sources of instability, we will direct our attention toward them.

Figure 11.3 shows the effect of changes in investment spending on the equilibrium real GDP. Suppose that the expected rate of return on investment rises or that the real interest rate falls such that investment spending increases by $5 billion. That would be shown as an upward shift of the investment schedule in Figure 11.1b. In Figure 11.3, the $5 billion increase of investment spending will increase aggregate expenditures from $(C + I_g)_0$ to $(C + I_g)_1$ and raise equilibrium real GDP from $470 billion to $490 billion.

If the expected rate of return on investment decreases or if the real interest rate rises, investment spending will decline by, say, $5 billion. That would be shown as a downward shift of the investment schedule in Figure 11.1b and a downward shift of the aggregate expenditures schedule from $(C + I_g)_0$ to $(C + I_g)_2$ in Figure 11.3. Equilibrium GDP will fall from $470 billion to $450 billion.

In our examples, a $5 billion change in investment spending leads to a $20 billion change in output and income. So the *multiplier* is 4 (= $20/$5). The MPS is 0.25, meaning that for every $1 billion of new income, $0.25 billion of new saving occurs. Therefore, $20 billion of new income is needed to generate $5 billion of new saving. Once that increase in income and saving occurs, the economy is back in equilibrium—$C + I_g$ = GDP; saving and investment are equal; and there are no unplanned changes in inventories. You can see, then, why the multiplier is equal to 1/MPS and that the multiplier process is an integral part of the aggregate expenditures model.

QUICK REVIEW 11.1

- In a private closed economy, equilibrium GDP occurs where aggregate expenditures equal real domestic output ($C + I_g$ = GDP).
- At equilibrium GDP, saving equals planned investment ($S = I_g$) and unplanned changes in inventories are zero.
- Actual investment consists of planned investment plus unplanned changes in inventories (+ or −) and is always equal to saving in a private closed economy.
- Through the multiplier effect, an initial change in investment spending can cause a magnified change in domestic output and income.

FIGURE 11.3 Changes in the aggregate expenditures schedule and the multiplier effect. An upward shift of the aggregate expenditures schedule from $(C + I_g)_0$ to $(C + I_g)_1$ will increase the equilibrium GDP. Conversely, a downward shift from $(C + I_g)_0$ to $(C + I_g)_2$ will lower the equilibrium GDP. The extent of the changes in equilibrium GDP will depend on the size of the multiplier, which in this case is 4 (= 20/5). The multiplier is equal to 1/MPS (here, 4 = 1/.25).

Real domestic product, GDP (billions of dollars)

Adding International Trade

LO11.6 Explain how economists integrate the international sector (exports and imports) into the aggregate expenditures model.

We next move from a private closed economy to a private open economy that incorporates exports (X) and imports (M). Our focus will be on **net exports** (exports minus imports), which may be either positive or negative.

Net Exports and Aggregate Expenditures

Like consumption and investment, exports create domestic production, income, and employment for a nation. Although U.S. goods and services produced for export are sent abroad, foreign spending on those goods and services increases production and creates jobs and incomes in the United States. We must therefore include exports as a component of U.S. aggregate expenditures.

Conversely, when an economy is open to international trade, it will spend part of its income on imports—goods and services produced abroad. To avoid overstating the value of domestic production, we must subtract the amount spent on imported goods because such spending generates production and income abroad rather than at home. So, to correctly measure aggregate expenditures for domestic goods and services, we must subtract expenditures on imports from total spending.

In short, for a private closed economy, aggregate expenditures are $C + I_g$. But for an open economy, aggregate expenditures are $C + I_g + (X − M)$. Or, recalling that net exports (X_n) equal ($X − M$), we can say that aggregate expenditures for a private open economy are $C + I_g + X_n$.

The Net Export Schedule

A net export schedule lists the amount of net exports that will occur at each level of GDP. Table 11.3 shows two possible net export schedules for the hypothetical economy represented in Table 11.2. In net export schedule X_{n1}

TABLE 11.3 Two Net Export Schedules (in Billions)

(1) Level of GDP	(2) Net Exports, X_{n1} ($X > M$)	(3) Net Exports, X_{n2} ($X < M$)
$370	$+5	$−5
390	+5	−5
410	+5	−5
430	+5	−5
450	+5	−5
470	+5	−5
490	+5	−5
510	+5	−5
530	+5	−5
550	+5	−5

Real domestic product, GDP (billions of dollars)

(a)

Net export schedule, X_n

FIGURE 11.4 Net exports and equilibrium GDP. (a) Net exports can be either positive, as shown by the net export schedule X_{n1} or negative, as depicted by net export schedule X_{n2}. (b) Positive net exports elevate the aggregate expenditure schedule from the closed-economy level of $C + I_g$ to the open-economy level of $C + I_g + X_{n1}$. Negative net exports lower the aggregate expenditures schedule from the closed-economy level of $C + I_g$ to the open-economy level of $C + I_g + X_{n2}$.

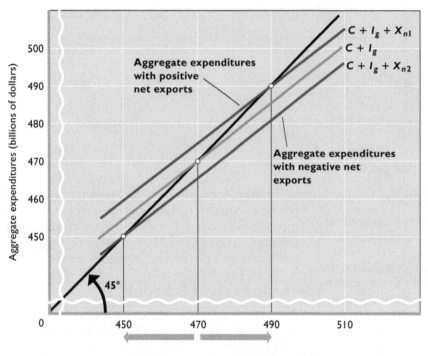

Real domestic product, GDP (billions of dollars)

(b)

Aggregate expenditures schedule

(columns 1 and 2), exports exceed imports by $5 billion at each level of GDP. Perhaps exports are $15 billion while imports are $10 billion. In schedule X_{n2} (columns 1 and 3), imports are $5 billion higher than exports. Perhaps imports are $20 billion while exports are $15 billion. To simplify our discussion, we assume in both schedules that net exports are independent of GDP.[1]

---

[1]In reality, although our exports depend on foreign incomes and are thus independent of U.S. GDP, our imports do vary directly with our own domestic national income. Just as our domestic consumption varies directly with our GDP, so do our purchases of foreign goods. As our GDP rises, U.S. households buy not only more Cadillacs and Harleys, but also more Mercedes and Kawasakis. However, for now we will ignore the complications of the positive relationship between imports and U.S. GDP.

Figure 11.4a represents the two net export schedules in Table 11.3. Schedule X_{n1} is above the horizontal axis and depicts positive net exports of $5 billion at all levels of GDP. Schedule X_{n2}, which is below the horizontal axis, shows negative net exports of $5 billion at all levels of GDP.

Net Exports and Equilibrium GDP

The aggregate expenditures schedule labeled $C + I_g$ in Figure 11.4b reflects the private closed economy. It shows the combined consumption and gross investment expenditures occurring at each level of GDP. With no foreign sector, the equilibrium GDP is $470 billion.

But in the private open economy, net exports can be either positive or negative. Let's see how each of the net export schedules in Figure 11.4a affects equilibrium GDP.

Positive Net Exports Suppose the net export schedule is X_{n1}. The $5 billion of additional net export expenditures by the rest of the world is accounted for by adding that $5 billion to the $C + I_g$ schedule in Figure 11.4b. Aggregate expenditures at each level of GDP are then $5 billion higher than $C + I_g$ alone. The aggregate expenditures schedule for the open economy thus becomes $C + I_g + X_{n1}$. In this case, international trade increases equilibrium GDP from $470 billion in the private closed economy to $490 billion in the private open economy. Adding net exports of $5 billion has increased GDP by $20 billion, in this case implying a multiplier of 4.

Generalization: Other things equal, positive net exports increase aggregate expenditures and GDP beyond what they would be in a closed economy. Be careful to notice that this increase is the result of exports being larger than imports. This is true because exports and imports have opposite effects on the measurement of domestically produced output. Exports increase real GDP by increasing expenditures on domestically produced output. Imports, by contrast, must be subtracted when calculating real GDP because they are expenditures directed toward output produced abroad. It is only because net exports are positive in this example—so that the expansionary effect of exports outweighs the reductions caused by imports—that we get the overall increase in real GDP. As the next section shows, if net exports are negative, then the reductions caused by imports will outweigh the expansionary effect of exports so that domestic real GDP will decrease.

Negative Net Exports Suppose that net exports are a negative $5 billion as shown by X_{n2} in Figure 11.4a. This means that our hypothetical economy is importing $5 billion more of goods than it is exporting. The aggregate expenditures schedule shown as $C + I_g$ in Figure 11.4b therefore overstates the expenditures on domestic output at each level of GDP. We must reduce the sum of expenditures by the $5 billion net amount spent on imported goods. We do that by subtracting the $5 billion of net imports from $C + I_g$.

The relevant aggregate expenditures schedule in Figure 11.4b becomes $C + I_g + X_{n2}$ and equilibrium GDP falls from $470 billion to $450 billion. Again, a change in net exports of $5 billion has produced a fourfold change in GDP, reminding us that the multiplier in this example is 4.

This gives us a corollary to our first generalization: Other things equal, negative net exports reduce aggregate expenditures and GDP below what they would be in a closed economy. When imports exceed exports, the

GLOBAL PERSPECTIVE 11.1

Net Exports of Goods, Selected Nations, 2012

Some nations, such as China and Germany, have positive net exports; other countries, such as the United States and the United Kingdom, have negative net exports.

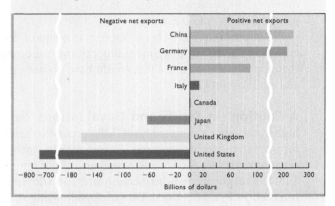

Source: CIA World Factbook, **www.cia.gov.**

contractionary effect of the larger amount of imports outweighs the expansionary effect of the smaller amount of exports, and equilibrium real GDP decreases.

Our generalizations of the effects of net exports on GDP mean that a decline in X_n—a decrease in exports or an increase in imports—reduces aggregate expenditures and contracts a nation's GDP. Conversely, an increase in X_n—the result of either an increase in exports or a decrease in imports—increases aggregate expenditures and expands GDP.

As is shown in Global Perspective 11.1, net exports vary greatly among the major industrial nations.

International Economic Linkages

Our analysis of net exports and real GDP suggests how circumstances or policies abroad can affect U.S. GDP.

Prosperity Abroad A rising level of real output and income among U.S. foreign trading partners enables the United States to sell more goods abroad, thus raising U.S. net exports and increasing U.S. real GDP (assuming initially there is excess capacity). There is good reason for Americans to be interested in the prosperity of our trading partners. Their good fortune enables them to buy more of our exports, increasing our income and enabling us in turn to buy more foreign imports. These imported goods are the ultimate benefit of international trade. Prosperity abroad transfers some of that prosperity to Americans.

Exchange Rates Depreciation of the dollar relative to other currencies enables people abroad to obtain more dollars with each unit of their own currencies. The price of U.S. goods in terms of those currencies will fall, stimulating purchases of U.S. exports. Also, U.S. customers will find they need more dollars to buy foreign goods and, consequently, will reduce their spending on imports. If the economy has available capacity, the increased exports and decreased imports will increase U.S. net exports and expand the nation's GDP.

This last example has been cast only in terms of depreciation of the dollar. You should think through the impact that appreciation of the dollar would have on net exports and equilibrium GDP.

A Caution on Tariffs and Devaluations Because higher net exports increase real GDP, countries often look for ways to reduce imports and increase exports during recessions or depressions. Thus, a recession might tempt the U.S. federal government to increase tariffs and devalue the international value of the dollar (say, by supplying massive amounts of dollars in the foreign exchange market) to try to increase net exports. Such an increase of net exports would expand domestic production, reduce domestic unemployment, and help the economy recover.

But this interventionist thinking is too simplistic. Suppose that the United States imposes high tariffs on foreign goods to reduce our imports and thus increase our domestic production and employment. Our imports, however, are our trading partners' exports. So when we restrict our imports to stimulate our economy, we depress the economies of our trading partners. They are likely to retaliate against us by imposing tariffs on our products. If so, our exports to them will decline and our net exports may in fact fall. With retaliation in the picture, it is possible that tariffs may decrease, not increase, our net exports.

That unfortunate possibility became a sad reality during the Great Depression of the 1930s, when various nations, including the United States, imposed trade barriers as a way of reducing domestic unemployment. The result was many rounds of retaliation that simply throttled world trade, worsened the depression, and increased unemployment. Abetting the problem were attempts by some nations to increase their net exports by devaluing their currencies. Other nations simply retaliated by devaluing their own currencies. The international exchange rate system collapsed, and world trade spiraled downward. Economic historians agree that tariffs and devaluations during the 1930s were huge policy mistakes!

Nations are tempted to use tariffs and currency devaluations because, *other things equal*, these policies *do* increase net exports and real GDP. But keep in mind that other things aren't likely to stay equal. In particular, other

nations will almost certainly retaliate with their own tariffs and devaluations—the final result being lower net exports and lower GDP for those countries and for our own.

QUICK REVIEW 11.2

- Positive net exports increase aggregate expenditures relative to the closed economy and, other things equal, increase equilibrium GDP.
- Negative net exports decrease aggregate expenditures relative to the closed economy and, other things equal, reduce equilibrium GDP.
- In the open economy, changes in (a) prosperity abroad, (b) tariffs, and (c) exchange rates can affect U.S. net exports and therefore U.S. aggregate expenditures and equilibrium GDP.
- Tariffs and deliberate currency depreciations are unlikely to increase net exports because other nations will retaliate.

Adding the Public Sector

LO11.7 Explain how economists integrate the public sector (government expenditures and taxes) into the aggregate expenditures model.

Our final step in constructing the full aggregate expenditures model is to move the analysis from a private (no-government) open economy to an economy with a public sector (sometimes called a "mixed economy"). This means adding government purchases and taxes to the model.

For simplicity, we will assume that government purchases are independent of the level of GDP and do not alter the consumption and investment schedules. Also, government's net tax revenues—total tax revenues less "negative taxes" in the form of transfer payments—are derived entirely from personal taxes. Finally, a fixed amount of taxes is collected regardless of the level of GDP.

Government Purchases and Equilibrium GDP

Suppose the government decides to purchase $20 billion of goods and services regardless of the level of GDP and tax collections.

Tabular Example Table 11.4 shows the impact of this purchase on the equilibrium GDP. Columns 1 through 4 are carried over from Table 11.2 for the private closed economy, in which the equilibrium GDP was $470 billion. The only new items are exports and imports in column 5 and government purchases in column 6. (Observe in column 5 that net exports are zero.) As shown in column 7, the addition of

TABLE 11.4 The Impact of Government Purchases on Equilibrium GDP

(1) Real Domestic Output and Income (GDP = DI), Billions	(2) Consumption (C), Billions	(3) Savings (S), Billions	(4) Investment (I_g), Billions	(5) Net Exports (X_n), Billions		(6) Government Purchases (G), Billions	(7) Aggregate Expenditures ($C + I_g + X_n + G$), Billions (2) + (4) + (5) + (6)
				Exports (X)	Imports (M)		
(1) $370	$375	$–5	$20	$10	$10	$20	$415
(2) 390	390	0	20	10	10	20	430
(3) 410	405	5	20	10	10	20	445
(4) 430	420	10	20	10	10	20	460
(5) 450	435	15	20	10	10	20	475
(6) 470	450	20	20	10	10	20	490
(7) 490	465	25	20	10	10	20	505
(8) 510	480	30	20	10	10	20	520
(9) 530	495	35	20	10	10	20	535
(10) **550**	**510**	**40**	**20**	**10**	**10**	**20**	**550**

government purchases to private spending ($C + I_g + X_n$) yields a new, higher level of aggregate expenditures ($C + I_g + X_n + G$). Comparing columns 1 and 7, we find that aggregate expenditures and real output are equal at a higher level of GDP. Without government purchases, equilibrium GDP was $470 billion (row 6); *with* government purchases, aggregate expenditures and real output are equal at $550 billion (row 10). Increases in public spending, like increases in private spending, shift the aggregate expenditures schedule upward and produce a higher equilibrium GDP.

Note, too, that government spending is subject to the multiplier. A $20 billion increase in government purchases has increased equilibrium GDP by $80 billion (from $470 billion to $550 billion). The multiplier in this example is 4.

This $20 billion increase in government spending is *not* financed by increased taxes. Shortly, we will demonstrate that increased taxes *reduce* equilibrium GDP.

Graphical Analysis In Figure 11.5, we vertically add $20 billion of government purchases, G, to the level of

FIGURE 11.5 Government spending and equilibrium GDP. The addition of government expenditures of G to our analysis raises the aggregate expenditures ($C + I_g + X_n + G$) schedule and increases the equilibrium level of GDP, as would an increase in C, I_g, or X_n.

TABLE 11.5 Determination of the Equilibrium Levels of Employment, Output, and Income: Private and Public Sectors

(1) Real Domestic Output and Income (GDP = NI = PI), Billions	(2) Taxes (T), Billions	(3) Disposable Income (DI), Billions, (1) − (2)	(4) Consumption (C_a), Billions	(5) Saving (S_a), Billions (3) − (4)	(6) Investment (I_g), Billions	(7) Net Exports (X_n), Billions — Exports (X)	(7) Net Exports (X_n), Billions — Imports (M)	(8) Government Purchases (G), Billions	(9) Aggregate Expenditures ($C_a + I_g + X_n + G$), Billions, (4) + (6) + (7) + (8)
(1) $370	$20	$350	$360	$−10	$20	$10	$10	$20	$400
(2) 390	20	370	375	−5	20	10	10	20	415
(3) 410	20	390	390	0	20	10	10	20	430
(4) 430	20	410	405	5	20	10	10	20	445
(5) 450	20	430	420	10	20	10	10	20	460
(6) 470	20	450	435	15	20	10	10	20	475
(7) **490**	**20**	**470**	**450**	**20**	**20**	**10**	**10**	**20**	**490**
(8) 510	20	490	465	25	20	10	10	20	505
(9) 530	20	510	480	30	20	10	10	20	520
(10) 550	20	530	495	35	20	10	10	20	535

private spending, $C + I_g + X_n$. That added $20 billion raises the aggregate expenditures schedule (private plus public) to $C + I_g + X_n + G$, resulting in an $80 billion increase in equilibrium GDP, from $470 to $550 billion.

A decline in government purchases G will lower the aggregate expenditures schedule in Figure 11.5 and result in a multiplied decline in the equilibrium GDP. Verify in Table 11.4 that if government purchases were to decline from $20 billion to $10 billion, the equilibrium GDP would fall by $40 billion.

Taxation and Equilibrium GDP

The government not only spends but also collects taxes. Suppose it imposes a **lump-sum tax,** which is a tax of a constant amount or, more precisely, a tax yielding the same amount of tax revenue at each level of GDP. Let's assume this tax is $20 billion, so that the government obtains $20 billion of tax revenue at each level of GDP regardless of the level of government purchases.

Tabular Example In Table 11.5, which continues our example, we find taxes in column 2, and we see in column 3 that disposable (after-tax) income is lower than GDP (column 1) by the $20 billion amount of the tax. Because households use disposable income both to consume and to save, the tax lowers both consumption and saving. The MPC and MPS tell us how much consumption and saving will decline as a result of the $20 billion in taxes. Because the MPC is 0.75, the government tax collection of $20 billion will reduce consumption by $15 billion (= 0.75 × $20 billion). Since the MPS is 0.25, saving will drop by $5 billion (= 0.25 × $20 billion).

Columns 4 and 5 in Table 11.5 list the amounts of consumption and saving *at each level of GDP*. Note they are $15 billion and $5 billion smaller than those in Table 11.4. Taxes reduce disposable income relative to GDP by the amount of the taxes. This decline in DI reduces both consumption and saving at each level of GDP. The extent of the C and S reductions depend on the MPC and the MPS.

To find the effect of taxes on equilibrium GDP, we calculate aggregate expenditures again, as shown in column 9, Table 11.5. Aggregate spending is $15 billion less at each level of GDP than it was in Table 11.4. The reason is that after-tax consumption, designated by C_a, is $15 billion less at each level of GDP. A comparison of real output and aggregate expenditures in columns 1 and 9 shows that the aggregate amounts produced and purchased are equal only at $490 billion of GDP (row 7). The $20 billion lump-sum tax has reduced equilibrium GDP by $60 billion, from $550 billion (row 10, Table 11.3) to $490 billion (row 7, Table 11.4).

Graphical Analysis In Figure 11.6 the $20 billion increase in taxes shows up as a $15 (not $20) billion decline in the aggregate expenditures ($C_a + I_g + X_n + G$) schedule. This decline in the schedule results solely from a decline in the consumption C component of aggregate expenditures. The equilibrium GDP falls from $550 billion to $490 billion because of this tax-caused drop in consumption. With no change in government expenditures, tax increases lower the aggregate expenditures schedule relative to the 45° line and reduce the equilibrium GDP.

In contrast to our previous case, a *decrease* in existing taxes will raise the aggregate expenditures schedule in

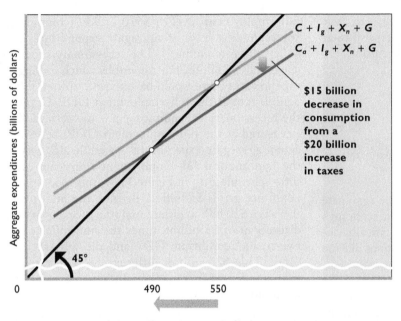

FIGURE 11.6 Taxes and equilibrium GDP. If the MPC is 0.75, the $20 billion of taxes will lower the consumption schedule by $15 billion and cause a $60 billion decline in the equilibrium GDP. In the open economy with government, equilibrium GDP occurs where C_a (after-tax income) $+ I_g + X_n + G =$ GDP. Here that equilibrium is $490 billion.

Figure 11.6 as a result of an increase in consumption at all GDP levels. You should confirm that a tax reduction of $10 billion (from the present $20 billion to $10 billion) would increase the equilibrium GDP from $490 billion to $520 billion.

Differential Impacts You may have noted that equal changes in G and T do not have equivalent impacts on GDP. The $20 billion increase in G in our illustration,

WORKED PROBLEMS

W11.2

Complete aggregate expenditures model

subject to the multiplier of 4, produced an $80 billion increase in real GDP. But the $20 billion increase in taxes reduced GDP by only $60 billion. Given an MPC of 0.75, the tax increase of $20 billion reduced consumption by only $15 billion (not $20 billion) because saving also fell by $5 billion. Subjecting the $15 billion decline in consumption to the multiplier of 4, we find the tax increase of $20 billion reduced GDP by $60 billion (not $80 billion).

Table 11.5 and Figure 11.6 constitute the complete aggregate expenditures model for an open economy with government. When total spending equals total production, the economy's output is in equilibrium. In the open mixed economy, equilibrium GDP occurs where

$$C_a + I_g + X_n + G = \text{GDP}$$

Injections, Leakages, and Unplanned Changes in Inventories The related characteristics of equilibrium noted for the private closed economy also apply to the full model. In particular, it is still the case that injections into the income-expenditures stream equal leakages from the income stream. For the private closed economy, $S = I_g$. For the expanded economy, imports and taxes are added leakages. Saving, importing, and paying taxes are all uses of income that subtract from potential consumption. Consumption will now be less than GDP—creating a potential spending gap—in the amount of after-tax saving (S_a), imports (M), and taxes (T). But exports (X) and government purchases (G), along with investment (I_g), are injections into the income-expenditures stream. At the equilibrium GDP, the sum of the leakages equals the sum of injections. In symbols:

$$S_a + M + T = I_g + X + G$$

You should use the data in Table 11.5 to confirm this equality between leakages and injections at the equilibrium GDP of $490 billion. Also, substantiate that a lack of such equality exists at all other possible levels of GDP.

Although not directly shown in Table 11.5, the equilibrium characteristic of "no unplanned changes in inventories" will also be fulfilled at the $490 billion GDP. Because aggregate expenditures equal GDP, all the goods and services produced will be purchased. There will be no unplanned increase in inventories, so firms will have no incentive to reduce their employment and production.

Nor will they experience an unplanned decline in their inventories, which would prompt them to expand their employment and output to replenish their inventories.

Equilibrium versus Full-Employment GDP

LO11.8 Differentiate between equilibrium GDP and full-employment GDP and identify and describe the nature and causes of "recessionary expenditure gaps" and "inflationary expenditure gaps."

A key point about the equilibrium GDP of the aggregate expenditures model is that it need not equal the economy's full-employment GDP. In fact, Keynes specifically designed the model so that it could explain situations like the Great Depression, during which the economy was seemingly stuck at a bad equilibrium in which real GDP was far below potential output. As we will show you in a moment, Keynes also used the model to suggest policy recommendations for moving the economy back toward potential output and full employment.

The fact that equilibrium and potential GDP in the aggregate expenditure model need not match also reveals critical insights about the causes of demand-pull inflation. We will first examine the "expenditure gaps" that give rise to differences between equilibrium and potential GDP and then see how the model helps to explain the recession of 2007–2009 and preview the policies used by the federal government to try to halt and reverse it.

Recessionary Expenditure Gap

Suppose in **Figure 11.7 (Key Graph)**, panel (a), that the full-employment level of GDP is $510 billion and the aggregate expenditures schedule is AE_1. (For simplicity, we will now dispense with the $C_a + I_g + X_n + G$ labeling.) This schedule intersects the 45° line to the left of the economy's full-employment output, so the economy's equilibrium GDP of $490 billion is $20 billion short of its full-employment output of $510 billion. According to column 1 in Table 11.2, total employment at the full-employment GDP is 75 million workers. But the economy depicted in Figure 11.7a is employing only 70 million workers; 5 million available workers are not employed. For that reason, the economy is sacrificing $20 billion of output.

A **recessionary expenditure gap** is the amount by which aggregate expenditures *at the full-employment GDP* fall short of those required to achieve the full-employment GDP. Insufficient total spending contracts or depresses the economy. Table 11.5 shows that at the

full-employment level of $510 billion (column 1), the corresponding level of aggregate expenditures is only $505 billion (column 9). The recessionary expenditure gap is thus $5 billion, the amount by which the aggregate expenditures curve would have to shift upward to realize equilibrium at the full-employment GDP. Graphically, the recessionary expenditure gap is the *vertical* distance (measured at the full-employment GDP) by which the actual aggregate expenditures schedule AE_1 lies below the hypothetical full-employment aggregate expenditures schedule AE_0. In Figure 11.7a, this recessionary expenditure gap is $5 billion. Because the multiplier is 4, there is a $20 billion differential (the recessionary expenditure gap of $5 billion times the multiplier of 4) between the equilibrium GDP and the full-employment GDP. This $20 billion difference is a negative *GDP gap*—an idea we first developed when discussing cyclical unemployment in Chapter 9.

Keynes's Solution to a Recessionary Expenditure Gap Keynes pointed to two different policies that a government might pursue to close a recessionary expenditure gap and achieve full employment. The first is to increase government spending. The second is to lower taxes. Both work by increasing aggregate expenditures.

Look back at Figure 11.5. There we showed how an increase in government expenditures G will increase overall aggregate expenditures and, consequently, the equilibrium real GDP. Applying this strategy to the situation in Figure 11.7a, government could completely close the $20 billion negative GDP gap between the initial equilibrium of $490 billion and the economy's potential output of $510 billion if it increased spending by the $5 billion amount of the recessionary expenditure gap. Given the economy's multiplier of 4, the $5 billion increase in G would create a $20 billion increase in equilibrium real GDP, thereby bringing the economy to full employment.

Government also could lower taxes to close the recessionary expenditure gap and thus eliminate the negative GDP gap. Look back at Figure 11.6 in which an increase in taxes resulted in lower after-tax consumption spending and a smaller equilibrium real GDP. Keynes simply suggested a reversal of this process: Since an increase in taxes lowers equilibrium real GDP, a decrease in taxes will raise equilibrium GDP. The decrease in taxes will leave consumers with higher after-tax income. That will lead to higher consumption expenditures and an increase in equilibrium real GDP.

But by how much should the government cut taxes? By exactly $6.67 billion. That is because the MPC is 0.75. The

FIGURE 11.7 Recessionary and inflationary expenditure gaps. The equilibrium and full-employment GDPs may not coincide.
(a) A recessionary expenditure gap is the amount by which aggregate expenditures at the full-employment GDP fall short of those needed to achieve the full-employment GDP. Here, the $5 billion recessionary expenditure gap causes a $20 billion negative GDP gap. (b) An inflationary expenditure gap is the amount by which aggregate expenditures at the full-employment GDP exceed those just sufficient to achieve the full-employment GDP. Here, the inflationary expenditure gap is $5 billion; this overspending produces demand-pull inflation.

(a)
Recessionary expenditure gap

(b)
Inflationary expenditure gap

QUICK QUIZ FOR FIGURE 11.7

1. In the economy depicted:
   a. the MPS is 0.50.
   b. the MPC is 0.75.
   c. the full-employment level of real GDP is $530 billion.
   d. nominal GDP always equals real GDP.

2. The inflationary expenditure gap depicted will cause:
   a. demand-pull inflation.
   b. cost-push inflation.
   c. cyclical unemployment.
   d. frictional unemployment.

3. The recessionary expenditure gap depicted will cause:
   a. demand-pull inflation.
   b. cost-push inflation.

   c. cyclical unemployment.
   d. frictional unemployment.

4. In the economy depicted, the $5 billion inflationary expenditure gap:
   a. expands real GDP to $530 billion.
   b. leaves real GDP at $510 billion but causes inflation.
   c. could be remedied by equal $5 billion increases in taxes and government spending.
   d. implies that real GDP exceeds nominal GDP.

Answers: 1. b; 2. a; 3. c; 4. b

---

tax cut of $6.67 billion will increase consumers' after-tax income by $6.67 billion. They will then increase consumption spending by 0.75 of that amount, or $5 billion. This will increase aggregate expenditures by the $5 billion needed to close the recessionary expenditure gap. The economy's equilibrium real GDP will rise to its potential output of $510 billion.

But a big warning is needed here: As the economy moves closer to its potential output, it becomes harder to

justify Keynes's assumption that prices are stuck. As the economy closes its negative GDP gap, nearly all workers are employed and nearly all factories are operating at or near full capacity. In such a situation, there is no massive oversupply of productive resources to keep prices from rising. In fact, economists know from real-world experience that in such situations prices are not fully stuck. Instead, they become increasingly flexible as the economy moves nearer to potential output.

This fact is one of the major limitations of the aggregate expenditures model and is the reason why we will develop a different model that can handle inflation in the next chapter. That being said, it is nevertheless true that the aggregate expenditures model is still very useful despite its inability to handle flexible prices. For instance, as we explained in Chapter 6, even an economy operating near full employment will show sticky or even stuck prices in the short run. In such situations, the intuitions of the aggregate expenditures model will still hold true. The benefit of the aggregate demand–aggregate supply model that we develop in the next chapter is that it also can show us what happens over longer periods, as prices (and wages) become more flexible and are increasingly able to adjust.

WORKED PROBLEMS

W11.3
Expenditure gaps

Inflationary Expenditure Gap

Economists use the term **inflationary expenditure gap** to describe the amount by which an economy's aggregate expenditures *at the full-employment GDP* exceed those just necessary to achieve the full-employment level of GDP. In Figure 11.7b, there is a $5 billion inflationary expenditure gap at the $510 billion full-employment GDP. This is shown by the vertical distance between the actual aggregate expenditures schedule AE_2 and the hypothetical schedule AE_0 that would be just sufficient to achieve the $510 billion full-employment GDP. Thus, the inflationary expenditure gap is the amount by which the aggregate expenditures schedule would have to shift downward to realize equilibrium at the full-employment GDP.

But why does the name "inflationary expenditure gap" contain the word *inflationary*? In particular, what does the situation depicted in Figure 11.7b have to do with inflation? The answer lies in the answer to a different question: *Could the economy actually achieve and maintain an equilibrium real GDP that is substantially above the full-employment output level?*

The unfortunate answer is no. It is unfortunate because if such a thing were possible, then the government could make real GDP as high as it wanted by simply increasing G to an arbitrarily high number. Graphically, it could raise the AE_2 curve in Figure 11.7b as far up as it wanted, thereby increasing equilibrium real GDP as high as it wanted. Living standards would skyrocket! But this is not possible because, by definition, all the available workers in the economy are fully employed at the full-employment output level. Producing slightly more than the full-employment output level for a few months might be possible if you could convince all the workers to work overtime day after day. But there simply is not enough labor to have the economy produce at much more than potential output for any extended period of time.

So what *does* happen in situations in which aggregate expenditures are so high that the model predicts an equilibrium level of GDP beyond potential output? The answer is twofold. First, the economy ends up producing either at potential output or just above potential output due to the limited supply of labor. Second, the economy experiences demand-pull inflation. With the supply of output limited by the supply of labor, high levels of aggregate expenditures simply drive up prices. Nominal GDP will increase because of the higher price level, but real GDP will not.

Application: The Recession of 2007–2009

In December 2007 the U.S. economy entered the longest and one of the deepest recessions since the Great Depression of the 1930s. We will defer discussion of the underlying financial crisis until later chapters, but the ultimate effect of the crisis is easily portrayed through the aggregate expenditures model. We know that the AE_0 line in Figure 11.7a consists of the combined amount of after-tax consumption expenditures (C_a), gross investment expenditures (I_g), net export expenditures (X_n), and government purchases (G) planned at each level of real GDP. During the recession, both after-tax consumption and investment expenditures declined, with planned investment expenditures suffering the largest drop by far.

Aggregate expenditures thus declined, as from AE_0 to AE_1 in Figure 11.7a. This set off a multiple decline in real GDP, illustrated in the figure by the decline from $510 billion to $490 billion. In the language of the aggregate expenditures model, a recessionary expenditure gap produced one of the largest negative GDP gaps since the Great Depression. Employment sank by more than 8 million people, and the unemployment rate jumped above 10 percent. As recessions go, this was a big one!

The federal government undertook various Keynesian policies in 2008 and 2009 to try to eliminate the recessionary expenditure gap facing the economy. In 2008, the government provided $100 billion of tax rebate checks to

Say's Law, the Great Depression, and Keynes

The Aggregate Expenditure Theory Emerged as a Critique of Classical Economics and as a Response to the Great Depression.

Until the Great Depression of the 1930s, many prominent economists, including David Ricardo (1772–1823) and John Stuart Mill (1806–1873), believed that the market system would ensure full employment of an economy's resources. These so-called *classical economists* acknowledged that now and then abnormal circumstances such as wars, political upheavals, droughts, speculative crises, and gold rushes would occur, deflecting the economy from full-employment status. But when such deviations occurred, the economy would automatically adjust and soon return to full-employment output. For example, a slump in output and employment would result in lower prices, wages, and interest rates, which in turn would increase consumer spending, employment, and investment spending. Any excess supply of goods and workers would soon be eliminated.

Classical macroeconomists denied that the level of spending in an economy could be too low to bring about the purchase of the entire full-employment output. They based their denial of inadequate spending in part on *Say's law*, attributed to the nineteenth-century French economist J. B. Say (1767–1832). This law is the disarmingly simple idea that the very act of producing goods generates income equal to the value of the goods produced. The production of any output automatically provides the income needed to buy that output. More succinctly stated, *supply creates its own demand.*

Say's law can best be understood in terms of a barter economy. A woodworker, for example, produces or supplies furniture as a means of buying or demanding the food and clothing produced by other workers. The woodworker's supply of furniture is the income that he will "spend" to satisfy his demand for other goods. The goods he buys (demands) will have a total value exactly equal to the goods he produces (supplies). And so it is for other producers and for the entire economy. Demand must be the same as supply!

Assuming that the composition of output is in accord with consumer preferences, all markets would be cleared of their outputs. It would seem that all firms need to do to sell a full-employment output is to produce that level of output. Say's law guarantees there will be sufficient spending to purchase it all.

The Great Depression of the 1930s called into question the theory that supply creates its own demand (Say's law). In the United States, real GDP declined by 27 percent and the unemployment rate rocketed to nearly 25 percent. Other nations experienced similar impacts. And cyclical unemployment lingered for a decade. An obvious inconsistency exists between a theory that says that unemployment is virtually impossible and the actual occurrence of a 10-year siege of substantial unemployment.

In 1936 British economist John Maynard Keynes (1883–1946) explained why cyclical unemployment could occur in a market economy. In his *General Theory of Employment, Interest, and Money*, Keynes attacked the foundations of classical theory and developed the ideas underlying the aggregate expenditures model. Keynes disputed Say's law, pointing out that not all income need be spent in the same period that it is produced. In fact, some income is always saved. In normal times, that saving is borrowed by businesses to buy capital goods—thereby boosting total spending in the economy. But if expectations about the future grow pessimistic, businesses will slash investment spending and a lot of that saving will not be put to use. The result will be insufficient total spending. Unsold goods will accumulate in producers' warehouses, and producers will respond by reducing their output and discharging workers. A recession or depression will result, and widespread cyclical unemployment will occur. Moreover, said Keynes, recessions or depressions are not likely to correct themselves. In contrast to the more laissez-faire view of the classical economists, Keynes argued that government should play an active role in stabilizing the economy.

ORIGIN OF THE IDEA

011.2
Say's law

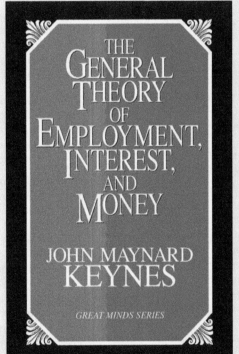

THE
GENERAL
THEORY
OF
EMPLOYMENT,
INTEREST,
AND
MONEY

JOHN MAYNARD
KEYNES

GREAT MINDS SERIES

taxpayers, hoping that recipients would use most of their checks to buy goods and services. (They didn't! Instead, they used substantial portions of their checks to pay off credit cards and reduce other debt.) In 2009, the federal government enacted a $787 billion stimulus package designed to boost aggregate expenditures, reduce the recessionary expenditure gap, and, through the multiplier effect, increase real GDP and employment.

We will defer discussion and further assessment of these stimulus attempts until Chapter 13, but Figure 11.7a clearly illuminates their purpose. If the government could drive up aggregate expenditures, such as from AE_1 to AE_0, the recession would come to an end and the recovery phase of the business cycle would begin.

QUICK REVIEW 11.3

- Government purchases shift the aggregate expenditures schedule upward and raise equilibrium GDP.
- Taxes reduce disposable income, lower consumption spending and saving, shift the aggregate expenditures schedule downward, and reduce equilibrium GDP.
- A recessionary expenditure gap is the amount by which an economy's aggregate expenditures schedule must shift upward to achieve the full-employment GDP; an inflationary expenditure gap is the amount by which the economy's aggregate expenditures schedule must shift downward to achieve full-employment GDP and eliminate demand-pull inflation.

SUMMARY

LO11.1 Explain how sticky prices relate to the aggregate expenditures model.

The aggregate expenditures model views the total amount of spending in the economy as the primary factor determining the level of real GDP that the economy will produce. The model assumes that the price level is fixed. Keynes made this assumption to reflect the general circumstances of the Great Depression, in which declines in output and employment, rather than declines in prices, were the dominant adjustments made by firms when they faced huge declines in their sales.

LO11.2 Explain how an economy's investment schedule is derived from the investment demand curve and an interest rate.

An investment schedule shows how much investment the firms in an economy are collectively planning to make at each possible level of GDP. In this chapter, we utilize a simple investment schedule in which investment is a constant value and therefore the same at all levels of GDP. That constant value is derived from the investment demand curve by determining what quantity of investment will be demanded at the economy's current real interest rate.

LO11.3 Illustrate how economists combine consumption and investment to depict an aggregate expenditures schedule for a private closed economy and how that schedule can be used to demonstrate the economy's equilibrium level of output (where the total quantity of goods produced equals the total quantity of goods purchased).

For a private closed economy the equilibrium level of GDP occurs when aggregate expenditures and real output are equal or,

graphically, where the $C + I_g$ line intersects the 45° line. At any GDP greater than equilibrium GDP, real output will exceed aggregate spending, resulting in unplanned investment in inventories and eventual declines in output and income (GDP). At any below-equilibrium GDP, aggregate expenditures will exceed real output, resulting in unplanned disinvestment in inventories and eventual increases in GDP.

LO11.4 Discuss the two other ways to characterize the equilibrium level of real GDP in a private closed economy: saving = investment, and no unplanned changes in inventories.

At equilibrium GDP, the amount households save (leakages) and the amount businesses plan to invest (injections) are equal. Any excess of saving over planned investment will cause a shortage of total spending, forcing GDP to fall. Any excess of planned investment over saving will cause an excess of total spending, inducing GDP to rise. The change in GDP will in both cases correct the discrepancy between saving and planned investment.

At equilibrium GDP, there are no unplanned changes in inventories. When aggregate expenditures diverge from real GDP, an unplanned change in inventories occurs. Unplanned increases in inventories are followed by a cutback in production and a decline of real GDP. Unplanned decreases in inventories result in an increase in production and a rise of GDP.

Actual investment consists of planned investment plus unplanned changes in inventories and is always equal to saving.

LO11.5 Analyze how changes in equilibrium real GDP can occur in the aggregate expenditures model and describe how those changes relate to the multiplier.

A shift in the investment schedule (caused by changes in expected rates of return or changes in interest rates) shifts the aggregate expenditures curve and causes a new equilibrium level of real GDP. Real GDP changes by more than the amount of the initial change in investment. This multiplier effect ($\Delta\text{GDP}/\Delta I_g$) accompanies both increases and decreases in aggregate expenditures and also applies to changes in net exports (X_n) and government purchases (G).

LO11.6 Explain how economists integrate the international sector (exports and imports) into the aggregate expenditures model.

The net export schedule in the model of the open economy relates net exports (exports minus imports) to levels of real GDP. For simplicity, we assume that the level of net exports is the same at all levels of real GDP.

Positive net exports increase aggregate expenditures to a higher level than they would if the economy were "closed" to international trade. Negative net exports decrease aggregate expenditures relative to those in a closed economy, decreasing equilibrium real GDP by a multiple of their amount. Increases in exports or decreases in imports have an expansionary effect on real GDP, while decreases in exports or increases in imports have a contractionary effect.

LO11.7 Explain how economists integrate the public sector (government expenditures and taxes) into the aggregate expenditures model.

Government purchases in the model of the mixed economy shift the aggregate expenditures schedule upward and raise GDP.

Taxation reduces disposable income, lowers consumption and saving, shifts the aggregate expenditures curve downward, and reduces equilibrium GDP.

In the complete aggregate expenditures model, equilibrium GDP occurs where $C_a + I_g + X_n + G = \text{GDP}$. At the equilibrium GDP, *leakages* of after-tax saving (S_a), imports (M), and taxes (T) equal *injections* of investment (I_g), exports (X), and government purchases (G): $S_a + M + T = I_g + X_n + G$. Also, there are no unplanned changes in inventories.

LO11.8 Differentiate between equilibrium GDP and full-employment GDP and identify and describe the nature and causes of "recessionary expenditure gaps" and "inflationary expenditure gaps."

The equilibrium GDP and the full-employment GDP may differ. A recessionary expenditure gap is the amount by which aggregate expenditures at the full-employment GDP fall short of those needed to achieve the full-employment GDP. This gap produces a negative GDP gap (actual GDP minus potential GDP). An inflationary expenditure gap is the amount by which aggregate expenditures at the full-employment GDP exceed those just sufficient to achieve the full-employment GDP. This gap causes demand-pull inflation.

Keynes suggested that the solution to the large negative GDP gap that occurred during the Great Depression was for government to increase aggregate expenditures. It could do this by increasing its own expenditures (G) or by lowering taxes (T) to increase after-tax consumption expenditures (C_a) by households. Because the economy had millions of unemployed workers and massive amounts of unused production capacity, government could boost aggregate expenditures without worrying about creating inflation.

The stuck-price assumption of the aggregate expenditures model is not credible when the economy approaches or attains its full-employment output. With unemployment low and excess production capacity small or nonexistent, an increase in aggregate expenditures will cause inflation along with any increase in real GDP.

TERMS AND CONCEPTS

planned investment	leakage	lump-sum tax
investment schedule	injection	recessionary expenditure gap
aggregate expenditures schedule	unplanned changes in inventories	inflationary expenditure gap
equilibrium GDP	net exports	

The following and additional problems can be found in **connect**
ECONOMICS

DISCUSSION QUESTIONS

1. What is an investment schedule and how does it differ from an investment demand curve? **LO11.2**
2. Why does equilibrium real GDP occur where $C + I_g = \text{GDP}$ in a private closed economy? What happens to real GDP when $C + I_g$ exceeds GDP? When $C + I_g$ is less than GDP? What two expenditure components of real GDP are purposely excluded in a private closed economy? **LO11.3**
3. Why is saving called a *leakage*? Why is planned investment called an *injection*? Why must saving equal planned investment

at equilibrium GDP in the private closed economy? Are unplanned changes in inventories rising, falling, or constant at equilibrium GDP? Explain. **LO11.4**

4. Other things equal, what effect will each of the following changes independently have on the equilibrium level of real GDP in the private closed economy? **LO11.5**
   a. A decline in the real interest rate.
   b. An overall decrease in the expected rate of return on investment.
   c. A sizable, sustained increase in stock prices.

5. Depict graphically the aggregate expenditures model for a private closed economy. Now show a decrease in the aggregate expenditures schedule and explain why the decline in real GDP in your diagram is greater than the decline in the aggregate expenditures schedule. What is the term used for the ratio of a decline in real GDP to the initial drop in aggregate expenditures? **LO11.5**

6. Assuming the economy is operating below its potential output, what is the impact of an increase in net exports on real GDP? Why is it difficult, if not impossible, for a country to boost its net exports by increasing its tariffs during a global recession? **LO11.6**

7. What is a recessionary expenditure gap? An inflationary expenditure gap? Which is associated with a positive GDP gap? A negative GDP gap? **LO11.8**

8. **LAST WORD** What is Say's law? How does it relate to the view held by classical economists that the economy generally will operate at a position on its production possibilities curve (Chapter 1)? Use production possibilities analysis to demonstrate Keynes's view on this matter.

REVIEW QUESTIONS

1. True or False: The aggregate expenditures model assumes flexible prices. **LO11.1**

2. If total spending is just sufficient to purchase an economy's output, then the economy is: **LO11.3**
   a. In equilibrium.
   b. In recession.
   c. In debt.
   d. In expansion.

3. True or False: If spending exceeds output, real GDP will decline as firms cut back on production. **LO11.3**

4. If inventories unexpectedly rise, then production _____ sales and firms will respond by _____ output. **LO11.3**
   a. Trails; expanding.
   b. Trails; reducing.
   c. Exceeds; expanding.
   d. Exceeds; reducing.

5. If the multiplier is 5 and investment increases by $3 billion, equilibrium real GDP will increase by: **LO11.5**
   a. $2 billion.
   b. $3 billion.
   c. $8 billion.
   d. $15 billion.
   e. None of the above.

6. A depression abroad will tend to _____ our exports, which in turn will _____ net exports, which in turn will _____ equilibrium real GDP. **LO11.6**
   a. Reduce; reduce; reduce.
   b. Increase; increase; increase.
   c. Reduce; increase; increase.
   d. Increase; reduce; reduce.

7. Explain graphically the determination of equilibrium GDP for a private economy through the aggregate expenditures model. Now add government purchases (any amount you choose) to your graph, showing its impact on equilibrium GDP. Finally, add taxation (any amount of lump-sum tax that you choose) to your graph and show its effect on equilibrium GDP. Looking at your graph, determine whether equilibrium GDP has increased, decreased, or stayed the same given the sizes of the government purchases and taxes that you selected. **LO11.7**

8. The economy's current level of equilibrium GDP is $780 billion. The full employment level of GDP is $800 billion. The multiplier is 4. Given those facts, we know that the economy faces _____ expenditure gap of _____. **LO11.8**
   a. An inflationary; $5 billion.
   b. An inflationary; $10 billion.
   c. An inflationary; $20 billion.
   d. A recessionary; $5 billion.
   e. A recessionary; $10 billion.
   f. A recessionary; $20 billion.

9. If an economy has an inflationary expenditure gap, the government could attempt to bring the economy back toward the full-employment level of GDP by _____ taxes or _____ government expenditures. **LO11.8**
   a. Increasing; increasing.
   b. Increasing; decreasing.
   c. Decreasing; increasing.
   d. Decreasing; decreasing.

PROBLEMS

1. Assuming the level of investment is $16 billion and independent of the level of total output, complete the following table and determine the equilibrium levels of output and employment in this private closed economy. What are the sizes of the MPC and MPS? **LO11.3**

Possible Levels of Employment, Millions	Real Domestic Output (GDP = DI), Billions	Consumption, Billions	Saving, Billions
40	$240	$244	$ ___
45	260	260	___
50	280	276	___
55	300	292	___
60	320	308	___
65	340	324	___
70	360	340	___
75	380	356	___
80	400	372	___

2. Using the consumption and saving data in problem 1 and assuming investment is $16 billion, what are saving and planned investment at the $380 billion level of domestic output? What are saving and actual investment at that level? What are saving and planned investment at the $300 billion level of domestic output? What are the levels of saving and actual investment? In which direction and by what amount will unplanned investment change as the economy moves from the $380 billion level of GDP to the equilibrium level of real GDP? From the $300 billion level of real GDP to the equilibrium level of GDP? LO11.4

3. By how much will GDP change if firms increase their investment by $8 billion and the MPC is 0.80? If the MPC is 0.67? LO11.5

4. Suppose that a certain country has an MPC of 0.9 and a real GDP of $400 billion. If its investment spending decreases by $4 billion, what will be its new level of real GDP? LO11.5

5. The data in columns 1 and 2 in the table below are for a private closed economy. LO11.6
   a. Use columns 1 and 2 to determine the equilibrium GDP for this hypothetical economy.
   b. Now open up this economy to international trade by including the export and import figures of columns 3 and 4. Fill in columns 5 and 6 and determine the

equilibrium GDP for the open economy. What is the change in equilibrium GDP caused by the addition of net exports?
   c. Given the original $20 billion level of exports, what would be net exports and the equilibrium GDP if imports were $10 billion greater at each level of GDP?
   d. What is the multiplier in this example?

6. Assume that, without taxes, the consumption schedule of an economy is as follows. LO11.7

GDP, Billions	Consumption, Billions
$100	$120
200	200
300	280
400	360
500	440
600	520
700	600

   a. Graph this consumption schedule and determine the MPC.
   b. Assume now that a lump-sum tax is imposed such that the government collects $10 billion in taxes at all levels of GDP. Graph the resulting consumption schedule and compare the MPC and the multiplier with those of the pretax consumption schedule.

7. Refer to columns 1 and 6 in the table for problem 5. Incorporate government into the table by assuming that it plans to tax and spend $20 billion at each possible level of GDP. Also assume that the tax is a personal tax and that government spending does not induce a shift in the private aggregate expenditures schedule. What is the change in equilibrium GDP caused by the addition of government? LO11.7

8. ADVANCED ANALYSIS Assume that the consumption schedule for a private open economy is such that consumption $C = 50 + 0.8Y$. Assume further that planned investment I_g and net exports X_n are independent of the level of real GDP and constant at $I_g = 30$ and $X_n = 10$. Recall also that, in

(1) Real Domestic Output (GDP = DI), Billions	(2) Aggregate Expenditures, Private Closed Economy, Billions	(3) Exports, Billions	(4) Imports, Billions	(5) Net Exports, Billions	(6) Aggregate Expenditures, Private Open Economy, Billions
$200	$240	$20	$30	$ ___	$ ___
250	280	20	30	___	___
300	320	20	30	___	___
350	360	20	30	___	___
400	400	20	30	___	___
450	440	20	30	___	___
500	480	20	30	___	___
550	520	20	30	___	___

equilibrium, the real output produced (Y) is equal to aggregate expenditures: $Y = C + I_g + X_n$. **LO11.7**

a. Calculate the equilibrium level of income or real GDP for this economy.

b. What happens to equilibrium Y if I_g changes to 10? What does this outcome reveal about the size of the multiplier?

9. Refer to the accompanying table in answering the questions that follow: **LO11.8**

(1) Possible Levels of Employment, Millions	(2) Real Domestic Output, Billions	(3) Aggregate Expenditures ($C_a + I_g + X_n + G$), Billions
90	$500	$520
100	550	560
110	600	600
120	650	640
130	700	680

a. If full employment in this economy is 130 million, will there be an inflationary expenditure gap or a recessionary expenditure gap? What will be the consequence of this gap? By how much would aggregate expenditures in column 3 have to change at each level of GDP to eliminate the inflationary expenditure gap or the recessionary expenditure gap? What is the multiplier in this example?

b. Will there be an inflationary expenditure gap or a recessionary expenditure gap if the full-employment level of output is $500 billion? By how much would aggregate expenditures in column 3 have to change at each level of GDP to eliminate the gap? What is the multiplier in this example?

c. Assuming that investment, net exports, and government expenditures do not change with changes in real GDP, what are the sizes of the MPC, the MPS, and the multiplier?

10. Answer the following questions, which relate to the aggregate expenditures model: **LO11.8**

a. If C_a is $100, I_g is $50, X_n is −$10, and G is $30, what is the economy's equilibrium GDP?

b. If real GDP in an economy is currently $200, C_a is $100, I_g is $50, X_n is −$10, and G is $30, will the economy's real GDP rise, fall, or stay the same?

c. Suppose that full-employment (and full-capacity) output in an economy is $200. If C_a is $150, I_g is $50, X_n is −$10, and G is $30, what will be the macroeconomic result?

FURTHER TEST YOUR KNOWLEDGE AT www.mcconnell20e.com

Practice quizzes, student PowerPoints, worked problems, Web-based questions, and additional materials are available at the text's Online Learning Center (OLC), **www.mcconnell20e.com**, or scan here. Need a barcode reader? Try ScanLife, available in your app store.

CHAPTER 12

Aggregate Demand and Aggregate Supply

Learning Objectives

LO12.1 Define aggregate demand (AD) and explain how its downward slope is the result of the real-balances effect, the interest-rate effect, and the foreign purchases effect.

LO12.2 Explain the factors that cause changes (shifts) in AD.

LO12.3 Define aggregate supply (AS) and explain how it differs in the immediate short run, the short run, and the long run.

LO12.4 Explain the factors that cause changes (shifts) in AS.

LO12.5 Discuss how AD and AS determine an economy's equilibrium price level and level of real GDP.

LO12.6 Describe how the AD-AS model explains periods of demand-pull inflation, cost-push inflation, and recession.

LO12.7 (Appendix) Identify how the aggregate demand curve relates to the aggregate expenditures model.

During the recession of 2007–2009, the economic terms *aggregate demand* and *aggregate supply* moved from the obscurity of economic journals and textbooks to the spotlight of national newspapers, Web sites, radio, and television.

The media and public asked: Why had *aggregate demand* declined, producing the deepest recession and highest rate of unemployment since 1982? Why hadn't the reductions in interest rates by the Federal Reserve boosted *aggregate demand*? Would the federal government's $787 billion stimulus package increase *aggregate demand* and reduce unemployment, as intended? Would a resurgence of oil prices and other energy prices reduce *aggregate supply,* choking off an economic expansion?

Aggregate demand and aggregate supply are the featured elements of the **aggregate demand–aggregate supply model (AD-AS model),** the focus of this chapter. The aggregate expenditures model of the previous chapter is an immediate-short-run model, in which prices are assumed to be fixed. In contrast, the AD-AS model in this chapter is a "variable price–variable output" model that allows both the price level and level of real GDP to change. It can also show longer time horizons, distinguishing between the immediate short run, the short run, and the long run. Further, in subsequent chapters, we will see that the AD-AS model easily depicts fiscal and monetary policies such as those used in 2008 and 2009 to try to halt the downward slide of the economy and promote its recovery.

Aggregate Demand

LO12.1 Define aggregate demand (AD) and explain how its downward slope is the result of the real-balances effect, the interest-rate effect, and the foreign purchases effect.

Aggregate demand is a schedule or curve that shows the amount of a nation's output (real GDP) that buyers collectively desire to purchase at each possible price level. These buyers include the nation's households, businesses, and government along with consumers located abroad (households, businesses, and governments in other nations). The relationship between the price level (as measured by the GDP price index) and the amount of real GDP demanded is inverse or negative: When the price level rises, the quantity of real GDP demanded decreases; when the price level falls, the quantity of real GDP demanded increases.

Aggregate Demand Curve

The inverse relationship between the price level and real GDP is shown in Figure 12.1, where the aggregate demand curve AD slopes downward, as does the demand curve for an individual product.

Why the downward slope? The explanation is *not* the same as that for why the demand for a single product slopes downward. That explanation centered on the income effect and the substitution effect. When the price of an *individual* product falls, the consumer's (constant) nominal income allows a larger purchase of the product (the income effect). And, as price falls, the consumer wants to buy more of the product because it becomes relatively less expensive than other goods (the substitution effect).

FIGURE 12.1   The aggregate demand curve. The downsloping aggregate demand curve AD indicates an inverse (or negative) relationship between the price level and the amount of real output purchased.

But these explanations do not work for aggregates. In Figure 12.1, when the economy moves down its aggregate demand curve, it moves to a lower general price level. But our circular flow model tells us that when consumers pay lower prices for goods and services, less nominal income flows to resource suppliers in the form of wages, rents, interest, and profits. As a result, a decline in the price level does not necessarily mean an increase in the nominal income of the economy as a whole. Thus, a decline in the price level need not produce an income effect, where more output is purchased because lower nominal prices leave buyers with greater real income.

Similarly, in Figure 12.1, prices in general are falling as we move down the aggregate demand curve, so the rationale for the substitution effect (where more of a specific product is purchased because it becomes cheaper relative to all other products) is not applicable. There is no *overall* substitution effect among domestically produced goods when the price level falls.

If the conventional substitution and income effects do not explain the downward slope of the aggregate demand curve, what does? The explanation rests on three effects of a price-level change.

Real-Balances Effect A change in the price level produces a **real-balances effect.** Here is how it works: A higher price level reduces the real value or purchasing power of the public's accumulated savings balances. In particular, the real value of assets with fixed money values,

such as savings accounts or bonds, diminishes. Because a higher price level erodes the purchasing power of such assets, the public is poorer in real terms and will reduce its spending. A household might buy a new car or a plasma TV if the purchasing power of its financial asset balances is, say, $50,000. But if inflation erodes the purchasing power of its asset balances to $30,000, the household may defer its purchase. So a higher price level means less consumption spending.

Interest-Rate Effect The aggregate demand curve also slopes downward because of the **interest-rate effect.** When we draw an aggregate demand curve, we assume that the supply of money in the economy is fixed. But when the price level rises, consumers need more money for purchases and businesses need more money to meet their payrolls and to buy other resources. A $10 bill will do when the price of an item is $10, but a $10 bill plus a $1 bill is needed when the item costs $11. In short, a higher price level increases the demand for money. So, given a fixed supply of money, an increase in money demand will drive up the price paid for its use. That price is the interest rate.

Higher interest rates curtail investment spending and interest-sensitive consumption spending. Firms that expect a 6 percent rate of return on a potential purchase of capital will find that investment potentially profitable when the interest rate is, say, 5 percent. But the investment will be unprofitable and will not be made when the interest rate has risen to 7 percent. Similarly, consumers may decide not

to purchase a new house or new automobile when the interest rate on loans goes up. So, by increasing the demand for money and consequently the interest rate, a higher price level reduces the amount of real output demanded.

Foreign Purchases Effect The final reason why the aggregate demand curve slopes downward is the **foreign purchases effect.** When the U.S. price level rises relative to foreign price levels (and exchange rates do not respond quickly or completely), foreigners buy fewer U.S. goods and Americans buy more foreign goods. Therefore, U.S. exports fall and U.S. imports rise. In short, the rise in the price level reduces the quantity of U.S. goods demanded as net exports.

These three effects, of course, work in the opposite direction for a decline in the price level. A decline in the price level increases consumption through the real-balances effect and interest-rate effect; increases investment through the interest-rate effect; and raises net exports by increasing exports and decreasing imports through the foreign purchases effect.

Changes in Aggregate Demand

LO12.2 Explain the factors that cause changes (shifts) in AD.
Other things equal, a change in the price level will change the amount of aggregate spending and therefore change the amount of real GDP demanded by the economy. Movements along a fixed aggregate demand curve represent these changes in real GDP. However, if one or more of those "other things" change, the entire aggregate demand curve will shift. We call these other things **determinants of aggregate demand** or, less formally, *aggregate demand shifters*. They are listed in Figure 12.2.

Changes in aggregate demand involve two components:

- A change in one of the determinants of aggregate demand that directly changes the amount of real GDP demanded.

- A multiplier effect that produces a greater ultimate change in aggregate demand than the initiating change in spending.

In Figure 12.2, the full rightward shift of the curve from AD_1 to AD_2 shows an increase in aggregate demand, separated into these two components. The horizontal distance between AD_1 and the broken curve to its right illustrates an initial increase in spending, say, $5 billion of added investment. If the economy's MPC is 0.75, for example, then the simple multiplier is 4. So the aggregate demand curve shifts rightward from AD_1 to AD_2—four times the distance between AD_1 and the broken line. The multiplier process magnifies the initial change in spending into successive

FIGURE 12.2 Changes in aggregate demand. A change in one or more of the listed determinants of aggregate demand will shift the aggregate demand curve. The rightward shift from AD₁ to AD₂ represents an increase in aggregate demand; the leftward shift from AD₁ to AD₃ shows a decrease in aggregate demand. The vertical distances between AD₁ and the dashed lines represent the initial changes in spending. Through the multiplier effect, that spending produces the full shifts of the curves.

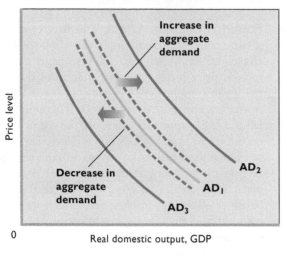

Determinants of Aggregate Demand: Factors That Shift the Aggregate Demand Curve

1. Change in consumer spending
   a. Consumer wealth
   b. Consumer expectations
   c. Household borrowing
   d. Taxes
2. Change in investment spending
   a. Interest rates
   b. Expected returns
      • Expected future business conditions
      • Technology
      • Degree of excess capacity
      • Business taxes
3. Change in government spending
4. Change in net export spending
   a. National income abroad
   b. Exchange rates

rounds of new consumption spending. After the shift, $20 billion (= $5 × 4) of additional real goods and services are demanded at each price level.

Similarly, the leftward shift of the curve from AD₁ to AD₃ shows a decrease in aggregate demand, the lesser amount of real GDP demanded at each price level. It also involves the initial decline in spending (shown as the horizontal distance between AD₁ and the dashed line to its left), followed by multiplied declines in consumption spending and the ultimate leftward shift to AD₃.

Let's examine each of the determinants of aggregate demand listed in Figure 12.2.

Consumer Spending

Even when the U.S. price level is constant, domestic consumers may alter their purchases of U.S.-produced real output. If those consumers decide to buy more output at each price level, the aggregate demand curve will shift to the right, as from AD₁ to AD₂ in Figure 12.2. If they decide to buy less output, the aggregate demand curve will shift to the left, as from AD₁ to AD₃.

Several factors other than a change in the price level may change consumer spending and therefore shift the aggregate demand curve. As Figure 12.2 shows, those factors are real consumer wealth, consumer expectations, household debt, and taxes. Because our discussion here parallels that of Chapter 10, we will be brief.

Consumer Wealth Consumer wealth is the total dollar value of all assets owned by consumers in the economy less the dollar value of their liabilities (debts). Assets include stocks, bonds, and real estate. Liabilities include mortgages, car loans, and credit card balances.

Consumer wealth sometimes changes suddenly and unexpectedly due to surprising changes in asset values. An unforeseen increase in the stock market is a good example. The increase in wealth prompts pleasantly surprised consumers to save less and buy more out of their current incomes than they had previously been planning. The resulting increase in consumer spending—the so-called *wealth effect*—shifts the aggregate demand curve to the right. In contrast, an unexpected decline in asset values will cause an unanticipated reduction in consumer wealth at each price level. As consumers tighten their belts in response to the bad news, a "reverse wealth effect" sets in. Unpleasantly surprised consumers increase savings and reduce consumption, thereby shifting the aggregate demand curve to the left.

Household Borrowing Consumers can increase their consumption spending by borrowing. Doing so shifts the aggregate demand curve to the right. By contrast, a decrease in borrowing for consumption purposes shifts the aggregate demand curve to the left. The aggregate demand curve will also shift to the left if consumers increase their savings rates to pay off their debts. With more money flowing to debt repayment, consumption expenditures decline and the AD curve shifts left.

Consumer Expectations Changes in expectations about the future may alter consumer spending. When people expect their future real incomes to rise, they tend to spend more of their current incomes. Thus, current consumption spending increases (current saving falls) and the aggregate demand curve shifts to the right. Similarly, a widely held expectation of surging inflation in the near future may increase aggregate demand today because consumers will want to buy products before their prices escalate. Conversely, expectations of lower future income or lower future prices may reduce current consumption and shift the aggregate demand curve to the left.

Personal Taxes A reduction in personal income tax rates raises take-home income and increases consumer purchases at each possible price level. Tax cuts shift the aggregate demand curve to the right. Tax increases reduce consumption spending and shift the curve to the left.

Investment Spending

Investment spending (the purchase of capital goods) is a second major determinant of aggregate demand. A decline in investment spending at each price level will shift the aggregate demand curve to the left. An increase in investment spending will shift it to the right. In Chapter 10 we saw that investment spending depends on the real interest rate and the expected return from investment.

Real Interest Rates Other things equal, an increase in real interest rates will raise borrowing costs, lower investment spending, and reduce aggregate demand. We are not referring here to the "interest-rate effect" that results from a change in the price level. Instead, we are identifying a change in the real interest rate resulting from, say, a change in a nation's money supply. An increase in the money supply lowers the interest rate, thereby increasing investment and aggregate demand. A decrease in the money supply raises the interest rate, reducing investment and decreasing aggregate demand.

Expected Returns Higher expected returns on investment projects will increase the demand for capital goods and shift the aggregate demand curve to the right. Alternatively, declines in expected returns will decrease investment and shift the curve to the left. Expected returns, in turn, are influenced by several factors:

- *Expectations about future business conditions* If firms are optimistic about future business conditions, they are more likely to forecast high rates of return

on current investment and therefore may invest more today. On the other hand, if they think the economy will deteriorate in the future, they will forecast low rates of return and perhaps will invest less today.

- *Technology* New and improved technologies enhance expected returns on investment and thus increase aggregate demand. For example, recent advances in microbiology have motivated pharmaceutical companies to establish new labs and production facilities.

- *Degree of excess capacity* A rise in excess capacity—unused capital—will reduce the expected return on new investment and hence decrease aggregate demand. Other things equal, firms operating factories at well below capacity have little incentive to build new factories. But when firms discover that their excess capacity is dwindling or has completely disappeared, their expected returns on new investment in factories and capital equipment rise. Thus, they increase their investment spending, and the aggregate demand curve shifts to the right.

- *Business taxes* An increase in business taxes will reduce after-tax profits from capital investment and lower expected returns. So investment and aggregate demand will decline. A decrease in business taxes will have the opposite effects.

The variability of interest rates and expected returns makes investment highly volatile. In contrast to consumption, investment spending rises and falls often, independent of changes in total income. Investment, in fact, is the least stable component of aggregate demand.

Government Spending

Government purchases are the third determinant of aggregate demand. An increase in government purchases (for example, more transportation projects) will shift the aggregate demand curve to the right, as long as tax collections and interest rates do not change as a result. In contrast, a reduction in government spending (for example, less military equipment) will shift the curve to the left.

Net Export Spending

The final determinant of aggregate demand is net export spending. Other things equal, higher U.S. *exports* mean an increased foreign demand for U.S. goods. So a rise in net exports (higher exports relative to imports) shifts the aggregate demand curve to the right. In contrast, a decrease in U.S. net exports shifts the aggregate demand curve leftward. (These changes in net exports are *not* those prompted by a change in the U.S. price level—those associated with the foreign purchases effect. The changes here are shifts of the AD curve, not movements along the AD curve.)

What might cause net exports to change, other than the price level? Two possibilities are changes in national income abroad and changes in exchange rates.

National Income Abroad Rising national income abroad encourages foreigners to buy more products, some of which are made in the United States. U.S. net exports thus rise, and the U.S. aggregate demand curve shifts to the right. Declines in national income abroad do the opposite: They reduce U.S. net exports and shift the U.S. aggregate demand curve to the left.

Exchange Rates Changes in the dollar's exchange rate—the price of foreign currencies in terms of the U.S. dollar—may affect U.S. exports and therefore aggregate demand. Suppose the dollar depreciates in terms of the euro (meaning the euro appreciates in terms of the dollar). The new, relatively lower value of dollars and higher value of euros enables European consumers to obtain more dollars with each euro. From their perspective, U.S. goods are now less expensive; it takes fewer euros to obtain them. So European consumers buy more U.S. goods, and U.S. exports rise. But American consumers can now obtain fewer euros for each dollar. Because they must pay more dollars to buy European goods, Americans reduce their imports. U.S. exports rise and U.S. imports fall. Conclusion: Dollar depreciation increases net exports (imports go down; exports go up) and therefore increases aggregate demand.

Dollar appreciation has the opposite effects: Net exports fall (imports go up; exports go down) and aggregate demand declines.

QUICK REVIEW 12.1

- Aggregate demand reflects an inverse relationship between the price level and the amount of real output demanded.
- Changes in the price level create real-balances, interest-rate, and foreign purchases effects that explain the downward slope of the aggregate demand curve.
- Changes in one or more of the determinants of aggregate demand (Figure 12.2) alter the amounts of real GDP demanded at each price level; they shift the aggregate demand curve. The multiplier effect magnifies initial changes in spending into larger changes in aggregate demand.
- An increase in aggregate demand is shown as a rightward shift of the aggregate demand curve; a decrease, as a leftward shift of the curve.

Aggregate Supply

LO12.3 Define aggregate supply (AS) and explain how it differs in the immediate short run, the short run, and the long run.

Aggregate supply is a schedule or curve showing the relationship between a nation's price level and the amount of real domestic output that firms in the economy produce. This relationship varies depending on the time horizon and how quickly output prices and input prices can change. We will define three time horizons:

- In the *immediate short run*, both input prices as well as output prices are fixed.
- In the *short run*, input prices are fixed, but output prices can vary.
- In the *long run*, input prices as well as output prices can vary.

In Chapter 6, we discussed both the immediate short run and the long run in terms of how an automobile maker named Buzzer Auto responds to changes in the demand for its new car, the Prion. Here we extend the logic of that chapter to the economy as a whole to discuss how total output varies with the price level in the immediate short run, the short run, and the long run. As you will see, the relationship between the price level and total output is different in each of the three time horizons because input prices are stickier than output prices. Although both sets of prices become more flexible as time passes, output prices usually adjust more rapidly.

Aggregate Supply in the Immediate Short Run

Depending on the type of firm, the immediate short run can last anywhere from a few days to a few months. It lasts as long as *both* input prices and output prices stay fixed. Input prices are fixed in both the immediate short run and the short run by contractual agreements. In particular, 75 percent of the average firm's costs are wages and salaries—and these are almost always fixed by labor contracts for months or years at a time. As a result, they are usually fixed for a much longer duration than output prices, which can begin to change within a few days or a few months depending on the type of firm.

That being said, output prices are also typically fixed in the immediate short run. This is most often caused by firms setting fixed prices for their customers and then agreeing to supply whatever quantity demanded results at those fixed prices. For instance, once an appliance manufacturer sets its annual list prices for refrigerators, stoves,

FIGURE 12.3 Aggregate supply in the immediate short run. In the immediate short run, the aggregate supply curve AS$_{ISR}$ is horizontal at the economy's current price level, P_1. With output prices fixed, firms collectively supply the level of output that is demanded at those prices.

ovens, and microwaves, it is obligated to supply however many or few appliances customers want to buy at those prices. Similarly, a catalogue company is obliged to sell however much customers want to buy of its products at the prices listed in its current catalogue. And it is obligated to supply those quantities demanded until it sends out its next catalogue.

With output prices fixed and firms selling however much customers want to purchase at those fixed prices, the **immediate-short-run aggregate supply curve** AS$_{ISR}$ is a horizontal line, as shown in Figure 12.3. The AS$_{ISR}$ curve is horizontal at the overall price level P_1, which is calculated from all of the individual prices set by the various firms in the economy. Its horizontal shape implies that the total amount of output supplied in the economy depends directly on the volume of spending that results at price level P_1. If total spending is low at price level P_1, firms will supply a small amount of output to match the low level of spending. If total spending is high at price level P_1, they will supply a high level of output to match the high level of spending. The amount of output that results may be higher than or lower than the economy's full-employment output level Q_f.

Notice, however, that firms will respond in this manner to changes in total spending only as long as output prices remain fixed. As soon as firms are able to change their product prices, they can respond to changes in aggregate spending not only by increasing or decreasing output but also by raising or lowering prices. This is the situation that leads to the upsloping short-run aggregate supply curve that we discuss next.

Aggregate Supply in the Short Run

The short run begins after the immediate short run ends. As it relates to macroeconomics, the short run is a period of time during which output prices are flexible, but input prices are either totally fixed or highly inflexible.

These assumptions about output prices and input prices are general—they relate to the economy in the aggregate. Naturally, some input prices are more flexible than others. Since gasoline prices are quite flexible, a package delivery firm like UPS that uses gasoline as an input will have at least one very flexible input price. On the other hand, wages at UPS are set by five-year labor contracts negotiated with its drivers' union, the Teamsters. Because wages are the firm's largest and most important input cost, UPS faces overall input prices that are inflexible for several years at a time. Thus, its "short run"—the period when it can change its shipping prices but not its substantially fixed input prices—is actually quite long. Keep this example in mind as we derive the short-run aggregate supply for the entire economy. Its applicability does not depend on some arbitrary definition of how long the "short run" should be. Instead, the short-run for which the model is relevant is any period of time during which output prices are flexible, but input prices are fixed or nearly fixed.

As illustrated in Figure 12.4, the **short-run aggregate supply curve** AS slopes upward because, with input prices

FIGURE 12.4 The aggregate supply curve (short run). The upsloping aggregate supply curve AS indicates a direct (or positive) relationship between the price level and the amount of real output that firms will offer for sale. The AS curve is relatively flat below the full-employment output because unemployed resources and unused capacity allow firms to respond to price-level rises with large increases in real output. It is relatively steep beyond the full-employment output because resource shortages and capacity limitations make it difficult to expand real output as the price level rises.

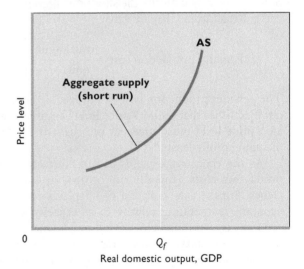

fixed, changes in the price level will raise or lower real firm profits. To see how this works, consider an economy that has only a single multiproduct firm called Mega Buzzer and in which the firm's owners must receive a real profit of $20 to produce the full-employment output of 100 units. Assume the owner's only input (aside from entrepreneurial talent) is 10 units of hired labor at $8 per worker, for a total wage cost of $80. Also, assume that the 100 units of output sell for $1 per unit, so total revenue is $100. Mega Buzzer's nominal profit is $20 (= $100 − $80), and using the $1 price to designate the base-price index of 100, its real profit is also $20 (= $20/1.00). Well and good; the full-employment output is produced.

Next consider what will happen if the price of Mega Buzzer's output doubles. The doubling of the price level will boost total revenue from $100 to $200, but since we are discussing the short run during which input prices are fixed, the $8 nominal wage for each of the 10 workers will remain unchanged so that total costs stay at $80. Nominal profit will rise from $20 (= $100 − $80) to $120 (= $200 − $80). Dividing that $120 profit by the new price index of 200 (= 2.0 in hundredths), we find that Mega Buzzer's real profit is now $60. The rise in the real reward from $20 to $60 prompts the firm (economy) to produce more output. Conversely, price-level declines reduce real profits and cause the firm (economy) to reduce its output. So, in the short run, there is a direct, or positive, relationship between the price level and real output. When the price level rises, real output rises and when the price level falls, real output falls. The result is an upsloping short-run aggregate supply curve.

Notice, however, that the upslope of the short-run aggregate supply curve is not constant. It is flatter at outputs below the full-employment output level Q_f and steeper at outputs above it. This has to do with the fact that per-unit production costs underlie the short-run aggregate supply curve. Recall from Chapter 9 that

$$\text{Per-unit production cost} = \frac{\text{total input cost}}{\text{units of output}}$$

The per-unit production cost of any specific level of output establishes that output's price level because the associated price level must cover all the costs of production, including profit "costs."

As the economy expands in the short run, per-unit production costs generally rise because of reduced efficiency. But the extent of that rise depends on where the economy is operating relative to its capacity. When the economy is operating below its full-employment output, it has large amounts of unused machinery and equipment and large numbers of unemployed workers. Firms can put these idle human and property resources back to work with little upward pressure on per-unit production costs. And as output expands, few if any shortages of inputs or production bottlenecks will arise to raise per-unit production costs. That is why the slope of the short-run aggregate supply curve increases only slowly at output levels below the full-employment output level Q_f.

On the other hand, when the economy is operating beyond Q_f, the vast majority of its available resources are already employed. Adding more workers to a relatively fixed number of highly used capital resources such as plant and equipment creates congestion in the workplace and reduces the efficiency (on average) of workers. Adding more capital, given the limited number of available workers, leaves equipment idle and reduces the efficiency of capital. Adding more land resources when capital and labor are highly constrained reduces the efficiency of land resources. Under these circumstances, total input costs rise more rapidly than total output. The result is rapidly rising per-unit production costs that give the short-run aggregate supply curve its rapidly increasing slope at output levels beyond Q_f.

Aggregate Supply in the Long Run

In macroeconomics, the long run is the time horizon over which both input prices as well as output prices are flexible. It begins after the short run ends. Depending on the type of firm and industry, this may be from a couple of weeks to several years in the future. But for the economy as a whole, it is the time horizon over which all output and input prices—including wage rates—are fully flexible.

The **long-run aggregate supply curve** AS_{LR} is vertical at the economy's full-employment output Q_f, as shown in Figure 12.5. The vertical curve means that in the long run the economy will produce the full-employment output level no matter what the price level is. How can this be? Shouldn't higher prices cause firms to increase output? The explanation lies in the fact that in the long run when both input prices as well as output prices are flexible, profit levels will always adjust to give firms exactly the right profit incentive to produce exactly the full-employment output level, Q_f.

To see why this is true, look back at the short-run aggregate supply curve AS shown in Figure 12.4. Suppose that the economy starts out producing at the full-employment output level Q_f and that the price level at that moment has an index value of $P = 100$. Now suppose that output prices double, so that the price index goes to $P = 200$. We previously demonstrated for our single-firm economy that this doubling of the price level would cause profits to rise in

FIGURE 12.5   Aggregate supply in the long run. The long-run aggregate supply curve AS$_{LR}$ is vertical at the full-employment level of real GDP (Q_f) because in the long run wages and other input prices rise and fall to match changes in the price level. So price-level changes do not affect firms' profits and thus they create no incentive for firms to alter their output.

the short run and that the higher profits would motivate the firm to increase output.

This outcome, however, is totally dependent on the fact that input prices are fixed in the short run. Consider what will happen in the long run when they are free to change. Firms can only produce beyond the full-employment output level by running factories and businesses at extremely high rates. This creates a great deal of demand for the economy's limited supply of productive resources. In particular, labor is in great demand because the only way to produce beyond full employment is if workers are working overtime.

As time passes and input prices are free to change, the high demand will start to raise input prices. In particular, overworked employees will demand and receive raises as employers scramble to deal with the labor shortages that arise when the economy is producing at above its full-employment output level. As input prices increase, firm profits will begin to fall. And as they decline, so does the motive firms have to produce more than the full-employment output level. This process of rising input prices and falling profits continues until the rise in input prices exactly matches the initial change in output prices (in our example, they both double). When that happens, firm profits in real terms return to their original level so that firms are once again motivated to produce at exactly the full-employment output level. This adjustment process means that in the long run the economy will produce at full employment regardless of the price level (in our example, at either $P = 100$

or $P = 200$). That is why the long-run aggregate supply curve AS$_{LR}$ is vertical above the full-employment output level. Every possible price level on the vertical axis is associated with the economy producing at the full-employment output level in the long run once input prices adjust to exactly match changes in output prices.

Focusing on the Short Run

The immediate-short-run aggregate supply curve, the short-run aggregate supply curve, and the long-run aggregate supply curve are all important. Each curve is appropriate to situations that match their respective assumptions about the flexibility of input and output prices. In the remainder of the book, we will have several different opportunities to refer to each curve. But our focus in the rest of this chapter and the several chapters that immediately follow will be on short-run aggregate supply curves, such as the AS curve shown in Figure 12.4. Indeed, unless explicitly stated otherwise, all references to "aggregate supply" are to the AS curve and to aggregate supply in the short run.

Our emphasis on the short-run aggregate supply curve AS stems from out interest in understanding the business cycle in the simplest possible way. It is a fact that real-world economies typically manifest simultaneous changes in both their price levels and their levels of real output. The upsloping short-run AS curve is the only version of aggregate supply that can handle simultaneous movements in both of these variables. By contrast, the price level is assumed fixed in the immediate-short-run version of aggregate supply illustrated in Figure 12.3 and the economy's output is always equal to the full-employment output level in the long-run version of aggregate supply shown in Figure 12.5. This renders these versions of the aggregate supply curve less useful as part of a core model for analyzing business cycles and demonstrating the short-run government policies designed to deal with them. In our current discussion, we will reserve use of the immediate short run and the long run for specific, clearly identified situations. Later in the book we will explore how the short-run and long-run AS curves are linked, and how that linkage adds several additional insights about business cycles and policy.

Changes in Aggregate Supply

LO12.4 Explain the factors that cause changes (shifts) in AS.

An existing aggregate supply curve identifies the relationship between the price level and real output, other things equal. But when one or more of these other things change, the curve itself shifts. The rightward shift of the curve

FIGURE 12.6 Changes in aggregate supply. A change in one or more of the listed determinants of aggregate supply will shift the aggregate supply curve. The rightward shift of the aggregate supply curve from AS_1 to AS_2 represents an increase in aggregate supply; the leftward shift of the curve from AS_1 to AS_3 shows a decrease in aggregate supply.

Determinants of Aggregate Supply: Factors That Shift the Aggregate Supply Curve

1. Change in input prices
   a. Domestic resource prices
   b. Prices of imported resources
2. Change in productivity
3. Change in legal-institutional environment
   a. Business taxes and subsidies
   b. Government regulations

from AS_1 to AS_2 in Figure 12.6 represents an increase in aggregate supply, indicating that firms are willing to produce and sell more real output at each price level. The leftward shift of the curve from AS_1 to AS_3 represents a decrease in aggregate supply. At each price level, firms produce less output than before.

Figure 12.6 lists the other things that cause a shift of the aggregate supply curve. Called the **determinants of aggregate supply** or *aggregate supply shifters*, they collectively position the aggregate supply curve and shift the curve when they change. Changes in these determinants raise or lower per-unit production costs *at each price level (or each level of output)*. These changes in per-unit production cost affect profits, thereby leading firms to alter the amount of output they are willing to produce *at each price level*. For example, firms may collectively offer $9 trillion of real output at a price level of 1.0 (100 in index value), rather than $8.8 trillion. Or they may offer $7.5 trillion rather than $8 trillion. The point is that when one of the determinants listed in Figure 12.6 changes, the aggregate supply curve shifts to the right or left. Changes that reduce per-unit production costs shift the aggregate supply curve to the right, as from AS_1 to AS_2; changes that increase per-unit production costs shift it to the left, as from AS_1 to AS_3. When per-unit production costs change for reasons other than changes in real output, the aggregate supply curve shifts.

The three aggregate supply determinants listed in Figure 12.6 require more discussion.

Input Prices

Input or resource prices—to be distinguished from the output prices that make up the price level—are a major

ingredient of per-unit production costs and therefore a key determinant of aggregate supply. These resources can be either domestic or imported.

Domestic Resource Prices As stated earlier, wages and salaries make up about 75 percent of all business costs. Other things equal, decreases in wages reduce per-unit production costs. So when wages fall, the aggregate supply curve shifts to the right. Increases in wages shift the curve to the left. Examples:

- Labor supply increases because of substantial immigration. Wages and per-unit production costs fall, shifting the AS curve to the right.

- Labor supply decreases because a rapid increase in pension income causes many older workers to opt for early retirement. Wage rates and per-unit production costs rise, shifting the AS curve to the left.

Similarly, the aggregate supply curve shifts when the prices of land and capital inputs change. Examples:

- The price of machinery and equipment falls because of declines in the prices of steel and electronic components. Per-unit production costs decline, and the AS curve shifts to the right.

- The supply of available land resources expands through discoveries of mineral deposits, irrigation of land, or technical innovations that transform "nonresources" (say, vast desert lands) into valuable resources (productive lands). The price of land declines, per-unit production costs fall, and the AS curve shifts to the right.

Prices of Imported Resources Just as foreign demand for U.S. goods contributes to U.S. aggregate demand, resources imported from abroad (such as oil, tin, and copper) add to U.S. aggregate supply. Added supplies of resources—whether domestic or imported—typically reduce per-unit production costs. A decrease in the price of imported resources increases U.S. aggregate supply, while an increase in their price reduces U.S. aggregate supply.

A good example of the major effect that changing resource prices can have on aggregate supply is the oil price hikes of the 1970s. At that time, a group of oil-producing nations called the Organization of Petroleum Exporting Countries (OPEC) worked in concert to decrease oil production in order to raise the price of oil. The 10-fold increase in the price of oil that OPEC achieved during the 1970s drove per-unit production costs up and jolted the U.S. aggregate supply curve leftward. By contrast, a sharp decline in oil prices in the mid-1980s resulted in a rightward shift of the U.S. aggregate supply curve. In 1999 OPEC again reasserted itself, raising oil prices and therefore per-unit production costs for some U.S. producers including airlines and shipping companies like FedEx and UPS. In 2007 the price of oil shot upward, but this increase was attributed to greater demand rather than to decreases in supply caused by OPEC. But keep in mind that no matter what their cause, increases in the price of oil and other resources raise production costs and decrease aggregate supply.

Exchange-rate fluctuations are another factor that may alter the price of imported resources. Suppose that the dollar appreciates, enabling U.S. firms to obtain more foreign currency with each dollar. This means that domestic producers face a lower *dollar* price of imported resources. U.S. firms will respond by increasing their imports of foreign resources, thereby lowering their per-unit production costs at each level of output. Falling per-unit production costs will shift the U.S. aggregate supply curve to the right.

A depreciation of the dollar will have the opposite set of effects and will shift the aggregate supply curve to the left.

Productivity

The second major determinant of aggregate supply is **productivity,** which is a measure of the relationship between a nation's level of real output and the amount of resources used to produce that output. Productivity is a measure of average real output, or of real output per unit of input:

$$\text{Productivity} = \frac{\text{total output}}{\text{total inputs}}$$

An increase in productivity enables the economy to obtain more real output from its limited resources. An increase in productivity affects aggregate supply by reducing the per-unit cost of output (per-unit production cost). Suppose, for example, that real output is 10 units, that 5 units of input are needed to produce that quantity, and that the price of each input unit is $2. Then

$$\text{Productivity} = \frac{\text{total output}}{\text{total inputs}} = \frac{10}{5} = 2$$

and

$$\text{Per-unit production cost} = \frac{\text{total input cost}}{\text{total output}}$$
$$= \frac{\$2 \times 5}{10} = \$1$$

Note that we obtain the total input cost by multiplying the unit input cost by the number of inputs used.

Now suppose productivity increases so that real output doubles to 20 units, while the price and quantity of the input remain constant at $2 and 5 units. Using the above equations, we see that productivity rises from 2 to 4 and that the per-unit production cost of the output falls from $1 to $0.50. The doubled productivity has reduced the per-unit production cost by half.

WORKED PROBLEMS

W12.1

Productivity and costs

By reducing the per-unit production cost, an increase in productivity shifts the aggregate supply curve to the right. The main source of productivity advance is improved production technology, often embodied within new plant and equipment that replaces old plant and equipment. Other sources of productivity increases are a better-educated and better-trained workforce, improved forms of business enterprises, and the reallocation of labor resources from lower-productivity to higher-productivity uses.

Much rarer, decreases in productivity increase per-unit production costs and therefore reduce aggregate supply (shift the curve to the left).

Legal-Institutional Environment

Changes in the legal-institutional setting in which businesses operate are the final determinant of aggregate supply. Such changes may alter the per-unit costs of output and, if so, shift the aggregate supply curve. Two changes of this type are (1) changes in taxes and subsidies and (2) changes in the extent of regulation.

Business Taxes and Subsidies Higher business taxes, such as sales, excise, and payroll taxes, increase per-unit costs and reduce short-run aggregate supply in much the same way as a wage increase does. An increase in such taxes paid by businesses will increase per-unit production costs and shift aggregate supply to the left.

Similarly, a business subsidy—a payment or tax break by government to producers—lowers production costs and increases short-run aggregate supply. For example, the federal government subsidizes firms that blend ethanol (derived from corn) with gasoline to increase the U.S. gasoline supply. This reduces the per-unit production cost of making blended gasoline. To the extent that this and other subsidies are successful, the aggregate supply curve shifts rightward.

Government Regulation It is usually costly for businesses to comply with government regulations. More regulation therefore tends to increase per-unit production costs and shift the aggregate supply curve to the left. "Supply-side" proponents of deregulation of the economy have argued forcefully that, by increasing efficiency and reducing the paperwork associated with complex regulations, deregulation will reduce per-unit costs and shift the aggregate supply curve to the right. Other economists are less certain. Deregulation that results in accounting manipulations, monopolization, and business failures is likely to shift the AS curve to the left rather than to the right.

QUICK REVIEW 12.2

- The immediate-short-run aggregate supply curve is horizontal; given fixed input and output prices, producers will supply whatever quantity of real output is demanded at the current price level.

- The short-run aggregate supply curve (or simply the "aggregate supply curve") is upsloping; given fixed resource prices, higher output prices raise firm profits and encourage them to increase their output levels.

- The long-run aggregate supply curve is vertical; given sufficient time, wages and other input prices rise or fall to match any change in the price level (that is, any change in the level of *output* prices).

- By altering per-unit production costs independent of changes in the level of output, changes in one or more of the determinants of aggregate supply (Figure 12.6) shift the aggregate supply curve.

- An increase in short-run aggregate supply is shown as a rightward shift of the aggregate supply curve; a decrease is shown as a leftward shift of the curve.

Equilibrium in the AD-AS Model

LO12.5 Discuss how AD and AS determine an economy's equilibrium price level and level of real GDP.

Of all the possible combinations of price levels and levels of real GDP, which combination will the economy gravitate toward, at least in the short run? **Figure 12.7 (Key Graph)** and its accompanying table provide the answer. Equilibrium occurs at the price level that equalizes the amounts of real output demanded and supplied. The intersection of the aggregate demand curve AD and the aggregate supply curve AS establishes the economy's **equilibrium price level** and **equilibrium real output.** So aggregate demand and aggregate supply *jointly* establish the price level and level of real GDP.

In Figure 12.7 the equilibrium price level and level of real output are 100 and $510 billion, respectively. To illustrate why, suppose the price level is 92 rather than 100. We see from the table that the lower price level will encourage businesses to produce real output of $502 billion. This is shown by point *a* on the AS curve in the graph. But, as revealed by the table and point *b* on the aggregate demand curve, buyers will want to purchase $514 billion of real output at price level 92. Competition among buyers to purchase the lesser available real output of $502 billion will eliminate the $12 billion (= $514 billion − $502 billion) shortage and pull up the price level to 100.

As the table and graph show, the rise in the price level from 92 to 100 encourages producers to increase their real output from $502 billion to $510 billion and causes buyers to scale back their purchases from $514 billion to $510 billion. When equality occurs between the amounts of real output produced and purchased, as it does at price level 100, the economy has achieved equilibrium (here, at $510 billion of real GDP).

A final note: Although the equilibrium price level happens to be 100 in our example, nothing special is implied by that. Any price level can be an equilibrium price level.

Changes in Equilibrium

LO12.6 Describe how the AD-AS model explains periods of demand-pull inflation, cost-push inflation, and recession.

Now let's apply the AD-AS model to various situations that can confront the economy. For simplicity we will use *P* and *Q* symbols, rather than actual numbers. Remember that these symbols represent, respectively, price index values and amounts of real GDP.

FIGURE 12.7 **The equilibrium price level and equilibrium real GDP.** The intersection of the aggregate demand curve and the aggregate supply curve determines the economy's equilibrium price level. At the equilibrium price level of 100 (in index-value terms), the $510 billion of real output demanded matches the $510 billion of real output supplied. So the equilibrium GDP is $510 billion.

Real Output Demanded (Billions)	Price Level (Index Number)	Real Output Supplied (Billions)
$506	108	$513
508	104	512
510	**100**	**510**
512	96	507
514	92	502

QUICK QUIZ FOR FIGURE 12.7

1. The AD curve slopes downward because:
   a. per-unit production costs fall as real GDP increases.
   b. the income and substitution effects are at work.
   c. changes in the determinants of AD alter the amounts of real GDP demanded at each price level.
   d. decreases in the price level give rise to real-balances effects, interest-rate effects, and foreign purchases effects that increase the amount of real GDP demanded.

2. The AS curve slopes upward because:
   a. per-unit production costs rise as real GDP expands toward and beyond its full-employment level.
   b. the income and substitution effects are at work.
   c. changes in the determinants of AS alter the amounts of real GDP supplied at each price level.
   d. increases in the price level give rise to real-balances effects, interest-rate effects, and foreign purchases effects that increase the amounts of real GDP supplied.

3. At price level 92:
   a. a GDP surplus of $12 billion occurs that drives the price level up to 100.
   b. a GDP shortage of $12 billion occurs that drives the price level up to 100.
   c. the aggregate amount of real GDP demanded is less than the aggregate amount of real GDP supplied.
   d. the economy is operating beyond its capacity to produce.

4. Suppose real output demanded rises by $4 billion at each price level. The new equilibrium price level will be:
   a. 108.
   b. 104.
   c. 96.
   d. 92.

Answers: 1. d; 2. a; 3. b; 4. b

Increases in AD: Demand-Pull Inflation

Suppose the economy is operating at its full-employment output and businesses and government decide to increase their spending—actions that shift the aggregate demand curve to the right. Our list of determinants of aggregate demand (Figure 12.2) provides several reasons why this shift might occur. Perhaps firms boost their investment spending because they anticipate higher future profits from investments in new capital. Those profits are predicated on having new equipment and facilities that incorporate a number of new technologies. And perhaps government increases spending to expand national defense.

As shown by the rise in the price level from P_1 to P_2 in Figure 12.8, the increase in aggregate demand beyond the full-employment level of output causes inflation. This is

FIGURE 12.8 An increase in aggregate demand that causes demand-pull inflation. The increase of aggregate demand from AD_1 to AD_2 causes demand-pull inflation, shown as the rise in the price level from P_1 to P_2. It also causes an inflationary GDP gap of Q_1 minus Q_f. The rise of the price level reduces the size of the multiplier effect. If the price level had remained at P_1, the increase in aggregate demand from AD_1 to AD_2 would increase output from Q_f to Q_2 and the multiplier would have been at full strength. But because of the increase in the price level, real output increases only from Q_f to Q_1 and the multiplier effect is reduced.

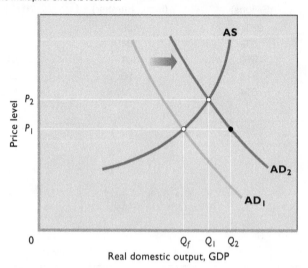

demand-pull inflation because the price level is being pulled up by the increase in aggregate demand. Also, observe that the increase in demand expands real output from the full-employment level Q_f to Q_1. The distance between Q_1 and Q_f is a positive, or "inflationary," GDP gap. Actual GDP exceeds potential GDP.

The classic American example of demand-pull inflation occurred in the late 1960s. The escalation of the war in Vietnam resulted in a 40 percent increase in defense spending between 1965 and 1967 and another 15 percent increase in 1968. The rise in government spending, imposed on an already growing economy, shifted the economy's aggregate demand curve to the right, producing the worst inflation in two decades. Actual GDP exceeded potential GDP, thereby creating an inflationary GDP gap. Inflation jumped from 1.6 percent in 1965 to 5.7 percent by 1970.

A careful examination of Figure 12.8 reveals an interesting point concerning the multiplier effect. The increase in aggregate demand from AD_1 to AD_2 increases real output only to Q_1, not to Q_2, because part of the increase in aggregate demand is absorbed as inflation as the price level rises from P_1 to P_2. Had the price level remained at P_1, the shift of aggregate demand from AD_1 to AD_2 would have increased real output to Q_2. The full-strength multiplier effect of Chapters 10

and 11 would have occurred. But in Figure 12.8 inflation reduced the increase in real output—and thus the multiplier effect—by about one-half. For any initial increase in aggregate demand, the resulting increase in real output will be smaller the greater is the increase in the price level. Price-level flexibility weakens the realized multiplier effect.

Decreases in AD: Recession and Cyclical Unemployment

Decreases in aggregate demand describe the opposite end of the business cycle: recession and cyclical unemployment (rather than above-full employment and demand-pull inflation). For example, in 2008 investment spending in the United States greatly declined because of sharply lower expected returns on investment. These lower expectations resulted from the prospects of poor future business conditions and high degrees of current unused production capacity. In Figure 12.9 we show the resulting decline in aggregate demand as a leftward shift from AD_1 to AD_2.

But we now add an important twist to the analysis: *Deflation*—a decline in the price level—is not the norm in the American economy. We discussed "sticky prices" in Chapter 6 and previously explained how fixed prices lead to horizontal immediate-short-run aggregate supply

FIGURE 12.9 A decrease in aggregate demand that causes a recession. If the price level is downwardly inflexible at P_1, a decline of aggregate demand from AD_1 to AD_2 will move the economy leftward from a to b along the horizontal broken-line segment and reduce real GDP from Q_f to Q_1. Idle production capacity, cyclical unemployment, and a recessionary GDP gap (of Q_1 minus Q_f) will result. If the price level were flexible downward, the decline in aggregate demand would move the economy depicted from a to c instead of from a to b.

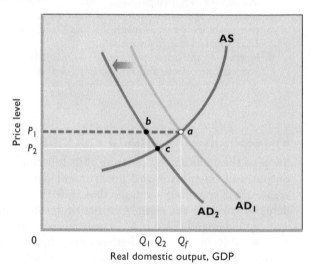

curves. For reasons we will examine soon, many important prices in the U.S. economy are downwardly inflexible such that the price level is sticky downward even when aggregate demand substantially declines. Consider Figure 12.9, where the aggregate demand declines from AD_1 to AD_2. If the price level is stuck at P_1, the economy moves from a to b along the broken horizontal line rather than from a to c along the short-run aggregate supply curve AS. The outcome is a decline of real output from Q_f to Q_1, with *no* change in the price level. In this case, it is as if the aggregate supply curve in Figure 12.9 is horizontal at P_1, to the left of Q_f, as indicated by the dashed line. This decline of real output from Q_f to Q_1 constitutes a *recession*, and since fewer workers are needed to produce the lower output, *cyclical unemployment* arises. The distance between Q_1 and Q_f is a negative, or "recessionary," GDP gap—the amount by which actual output falls short of potential output.

Close inspection of Figure 12.9 also reveals that without a fall in the price level, the multiplier is at full strength. With the price level stuck at P_1, real GDP decreases by $Q_f - Q_1$, which matches the full leftward shift of the AD curve. The multiplier of Chapters 10 and 11 is at full strength when changes in aggregate demand occur along what, in effect, is a horizontal segment of the AS curve. This full-strength multiplier would also exist for an increase in aggregate demand from AD_2 to AD_1 along this broken line, since none of the increase in output would be dissipated as inflation. We will say more about that in Chapter 13.

All recent recessions in the United States have generally mimicked the "GDP gap but no deflation" scenario shown in Figure 12.9. Consider the recession of 2007–2009, which resulted from chaos in the financial markets that quickly led to significant declines in spending by businesses and households. Because of the resulting decline in aggregate demand, real GDP fell short of potential real GDP by roughly $300 billion in 2008 and $1 trillion in 2009. The nation's unemployment rate rose from 4.7 percent in December 2007 to 10.1 percent in October 2009. The price level fell in some months and the rate of inflation declined—meaning that *disinflation* occurred. Considering the full period, however, *deflation* did not occur.

Real output takes the brunt of declines in aggregate demand in the U.S. economy because the price level tends to be downwardly rigid in the immediate short run. There are several reasons for this downward price stickiness.

- **Fear of price wars** Some large firms may be concerned that if they reduce their prices, rivals not

CONSIDER THIS . . .

Ratchet Effect

A *ratchet analogy* is a good way to think about the effects of changes in aggregate demand on the price level. A ratchet is a tool or mechanism such as a winch, car jack, or socket wrench that cranks a wheel forward but does not allow it to go backward. Properly set, each allows the operator to move an object (boat, car, or nut) in one direction while preventing it from moving in the opposite direction.

Product prices, wage rates, and per-unit production costs are highly flexible upward when aggregate demand increases along the aggregate supply curve. In the United States, the price level has increased in 60 of the 62 years since 1950.

But when aggregate demand decreases, product prices, wage rates, and per-unit production costs are inflexible downward. The U.S. price level has declined in only two years (1955 and 2009) since 1950, even though aggregate demand and real output have declined in a number of years.

In terms of our analogy, increases in aggregate demand ratchet the U.S. price level upward. Once in place, the higher price level remains until it is ratcheted up again. The higher price level tends to remain even with declines in aggregate demand.

only will match their price cuts but may retaliate by making even deeper cuts. An initial price cut may touch off an unwanted *price war*: successively deeper and deeper rounds of price cuts. In such a situation, each firm eventually ends up with far less profit or higher losses than would be the case if each had simply maintained its prices. For this reason, each firm may resist making the initial price cut, choosing instead to reduce production and lay off workers.

- **Menu costs** Firms that think a recession will be relatively short-lived may be reluctant to cut their prices. One reason is what economists metaphorically call **menu costs,** named after their most obvious example: the cost of printing new menus when a restaurant decides to reduce its prices. But lowering prices also creates other costs. Additional costs derive from (1) estimating the magnitude and duration of the shift in demand to determine whether prices should be lowered, (2) repricing items held in inventory, (3) printing and mailing new catalogs, and (4) communicating new prices to customers, perhaps through advertising. When menu costs are present, firms may choose to avoid them by retaining current prices. That is, they may wait to see if the decline in aggregate demand is permanent.

- *Wage contracts* Firms rarely profit from cutting their product prices if they cannot also cut their wage rates. Wages are usually inflexible downward because large parts of the labor force work under contracts prohibiting wage cuts for the duration of the contract. (Collective bargaining agreements in major industries frequently run for 3 years. Similarly, the wages and salaries of nonunion workers are usually adjusted once a year, rather than quarterly or monthly.)

- *Morale, effort, and productivity* Wage inflexibility downward is reinforced by the reluctance of many employers to reduce wage rates. Some current wages may be so-called **efficiency wages**—wages that elicit maximum work effort and thus minimize labor costs per unit of output. If worker productivity (output per hour of work) remains constant, lower wages *do* reduce labor costs per unit of output. But lower wages might impair worker morale and work effort, thereby reducing productivity. Considered alone, lower productivity raises labor costs per unit of output because less output is produced. If the higher labor costs resulting from reduced productivity exceed the cost savings from the lower wage, then wage cuts will increase rather than reduce labor costs per unit of output. In such situations, firms will resist lowering wages when they are faced with a decline in aggregate demand.

ORIGIN OF THE IDEA

O12.2
Efficiency wage

- *Minimum wage* The minimum wage imposes a legal floor under the wages of the least-skilled workers. Firms paying those wages cannot reduce that wage rate when aggregate demand declines.

Decreases in AS: Cost-Push Inflation

Suppose that a major terrorist attack on oil facilities severely disrupts world oil supplies and drives up oil prices

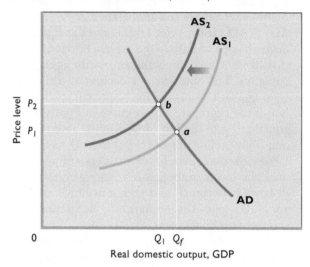

FIGURE 12.10 A decrease in aggregate supply that causes cost-push inflation. A leftward shift of aggregate supply from AS_1 to AS_2 raises the price level from P_1 to P_2 and produces cost-push inflation. Real output declines and a recessionary GDP gap (of Q_1 minus Q_f) occurs.

by, say, 300 percent. Higher energy prices would spread through the economy, driving up production and distribution costs on a wide variety of goods. The U.S. aggregate supply curve would shift to the left, say, from AS_1 to AS_2 in Figure 12.10. The resulting increase in the price level would be *cost-push inflation*.

The effects of a leftward shift in aggregate supply are doubly bad. When aggregate supply shifts from AS_1 to AS_2, the economy moves from *a* to *b*. The price level rises from P_1 to P_2 and real output declines from Q_f to Q_1. Along with the cost-push inflation, a recession (and negative GDP gap) occurs. That is exactly what happened in the United States in the mid-1970s when the price of oil rocketed upward. Then, oil expenditures were about 10 percent of U.S. GDP, compared to only 3 percent today. So the U.S. economy is now less vulnerable to cost-push inflation arising from such "aggregate supply shocks." That said, it is not *immune* from such shocks.

Increases in AS: Full Employment with Price-Level Stability

Between 1996 and 2000, the United States experienced a combination of full employment, strong economic growth, and very low inflation. Specifically, the unemployment rate fell to 4 percent and real GDP grew nearly 4 percent annually, *without igniting inflation*. At first thought, this "macroeconomic bliss" seems to be incompatible with the

FIGURE 12.11 Growth, full employment, and relative price stability. Normally, an increase in aggregate demand from AD_1 to AD_2 would move the economy from a to b along AS_1. Real output would expand to Q_2, and inflation would result (P_1 to P_3). But in the late 1990s, significant increases in productivity shifted the aggregate supply curve, as from AS_1 to AS_2. The economy moved from a to c rather than from a to b. It experienced strong economic growth (Q_1 to Q_3), full employment, and only very mild inflation (P_1 to P_2) before receding in March 2001.

AD-AS model. The aggregate supply curve suggests that increases in aggregate demand that are sufficient for over-full employment will raise the price level (see Figure 12.8). Higher inflation, so it would seem, is the inevitable price paid for expanding output beyond the full-employment level.

But inflation remained very mild in the late 1990s. Figure 12.11 helps explain why. Let's first suppose that aggregate demand increased from AD_1 to AD_2 along aggregate supply curve AS_1. Taken alone, that increase in aggregate demand would move the economy from a to b. Real output would rise from full-employment output Q_1 to beyond-full-employment output Q_2. The economy would experience inflation, as shown by the increase in the price level from P_1 to P_3. Such inflation had occurred at the end of previous vigorous expansions of aggregate demand, including the expansion of the late 1980s.

Between 1990 and 2000, however, larger-than-usual increases in productivity occurred because of a burst of new technology relating to computers, the Internet, inventory management systems, electronic commerce, and so on. We represent this higher-than-usual productivity growth as the rightward shift from AS_1 to AS_2 in Figure 12.11. The relevant aggregate demand and aggregate supply curves thus became AD_2 and AS_2, not AD_2 and AS_1. Instead of moving from a to b, the economy moved from a to c. Real output increased from Q_1 to Q_3, and the price level rose only modestly (from P_1 to P_2). The shift of the aggregate supply curve from AS_1 to AS_2 accommodated the rapid increase in aggregate demand and kept inflation mild. This remarkable combination of rapid productivity growth, rapid real GDP growth, full employment, and relative price-level stability led some observers to proclaim that the United States was experiencing a "new era" or a New Economy.

But in 2001 the New Economy came face-to-face with the old economic principles. Aggregate demand declined because of a substantial fall in investment spending, and in March 2001 the economy experienced a recession. The terrorist attacks of September 11, 2001, further dampened private spending and prolonged the recession throughout 2001. The unemployment rate rose from 4.2 percent in January 2001 to 6 percent in December 2002.

The economy rebounded between 2002 and 2007, eventually reachieving its earlier strong economic growth, low inflation, and low unemployment. Some economists began to refer to the period after 1982 as "The Great Moderation" because recessions were father apart and relatively mild. They drew the implication that businesses and government had smoothed out the business cycle. Wrong! The severity of the recession of 2007–2009 was a huge surprise to most economists. And so was the weakness of the subsequent recovery, as discussed in this chapter's Last Word.

QUICK REVIEW 12.3

- The equilibrium price level and amount of real output are determined at the intersection of the aggregate demand curve and the aggregate supply curve.

- Increases in aggregate demand beyond the full-employment level of real GDP cause demand-pull inflation.

- Decreases in aggregate demand cause recessions and cyclical unemployment, partly because the price level and wages tend to be inflexible in a downward direction.

- Decreases in aggregate supply cause cost-push inflation.

- Full employment, high economic growth, and price stability are compatible with one another if productivity-driven increases in aggregate supply are sufficient to balance growing aggregate demand.

Stimulus and the Great Recession

Aggregate Demand Stimulus Helped to Prevent the 2007–2009 Downturn from Becoming Another Great Depression. But Why Was the Stimulus-Fueled Recovery Substantially Weaker Than Expected?

In retrospect, it is clear that the U.S. economy was in a precarious position in 2006. Trillions of dollars had been borrowed to buy housing on the expectation that home prices would keep on rising. That expectation made borrowing seem like a "no brainer" as a potential buyer could anticipate that if she borrowed $200,000 to buy a house in one year, she would be able to sell it the next year for, say, $215,000. Selling at a higher price would allow her to pay off the $200,000 loan and keep the rest as pure profit.

Unfortunately, home prices started to fall in 2006. When they did, many people who had borrowed to buy houses found themselves unable to pay off their loans. That in turn meant that many banks found themselves holding loans that would never be paid back. Soon, many banks teetered on bankruptcy, the financial markets began to freeze up, and it became clear by late 2007 that the overall economy would probably enter a recession as the result of the housing collapse.

When it was widely recognized in late 2008 that the downturn was going to be unusually severe, public officials took extraordinarily strong steps to stimulate aggregate demand. In terms of monetary policy, the Federal Reserve lowered short-term interest rates to nearly zero in order to shift AD to the right

by stimulating investment and consumption. In terms of fiscal policy, the federal government began the country's largest peacetime program of deficit-funded spending increases. Those spending increases also shifted AD to the right by increasing the total amount of government expenditures.

Those actions were widely credited with preventing a much worse downturn. Real GDP did fall by 4.7 percent and

SUMMARY

LO12.1 Define aggregate demand (AD) and explain how its downward slope is the result of the real-balances effect, the interest-rate effect, and the foreign purchases effect.

The aggregate demand–aggregate supply model (AD-AS model) is a flexible-price model that enables analysis of simultaneous changes of real GDP and the price level.

The aggregate demand curve shows the level of real output that the economy demands at each price level.

The aggregate demand curve is downsloping because of the real-balances effect, the interest-rate effect, and the foreign purchases effect. The real-balances effect indicates that inflation reduces the real value or purchasing power of fixed-value financial assets held by households, causing cutbacks in consumer spending. The interest-rate effect means that, with a specific supply of money,

a higher price level increases the demand for money, thereby raising the interest rate and reducing investment purchases. The foreign purchases effect suggests that an increase in one country's price level relative to the price levels in other countries reduces the net export component of that nation's aggregate demand.

LO12.2 Explain the factors that cause changes (shifts) in AD.

The determinants of aggregate demand consist of spending by domestic consumers, by businesses, by government, and by foreign buyers. Changes in the factors listed in Figure 12.2 alter the spending by these groups and shift the aggregate demand curve. The extent of the shift is determined by the size of the initial change in spending and the strength of the economy's multiplier.

the unemployment rate did rise from 4.6 to 10.1 percent. But those negative changes were much less severe than what had happened during the Great Depression of the 1930s, when real GDP fell by nearly 27 percent and the unemployment rate rose to nearly 25 percent.

As time passed, however, it became clear that the stimulus was having less of an effect than many economists had anticipated. White House economists, for instance, had predicted that the stimulus begun in 2009 would reduce the unemployment rate to 5.2 percent by 2012. But three years later the unemployment rate was still at 7.8 percent despite the Federal Reserve continuing to keep interest rates extremely low and despite the federal government continuing to run massive deficits to fund huge amounts of government expenditures.

GDP growth was also disappointing. Real GDP expanded by only 2.4 percent in 2010, 1.8 percent in 2011, and 1.6 percent in 2012. By contrast, the period after the early 1980s recession had seen annual growth rates as high as 7.2 percent per year.

One explanation for the disappointing unemployment and GDP numbers was that it was hard for the stimulus to be very effective given the high debt levels that were built up during the bubble years. The lower interest rates engineered by the Federal Reserve, for instance, were probably not much of an inducement for consumers to increase their borrowing when so many of them were already heavily in debt.

A related problem was that savings rates had risen. When the government attempted to use deficit spending and fiscal policy to stimulate the economy, policy makers were hoping that each dollar of government spending would induce many dollars of consumer spending. But debt-strapped consumers were devoting large parts of their income to making interest payments on debt or paying off loans. So, when stimulus dollars came their way, they often short-circuited the spending process by saving a lot rather than spending a lot.

Another issue was that the stimulus was diffuse while the sectors of the economy in greatest need of stimulus were focused. In particular, the government's stimulus efforts shifted *aggregate* demand to the right. But not all sectors had been hit equally hard by the recession. Thus, when AD shifted right, a lot of the effect was felt in business sectors that hadn't been hurt that badly during the recession. Meanwhile, many sectors that had been hit hard only received a small portion of the total amount of stimulus that they would have needed to see a full recovery.

A related problem is that in some sectors of the economy, the government's stimulus may have resulted mostly in price increases rather than output gains. That is because the supply curves for many industries are steep. Consider dentists and jewelers. It takes many years to train competent dentists or skilled jewelers. So even if the demand for their services shifts right, there is a nearly fixed supply of dental services and jewelry services in the short run—meaning that any increase in demand will mostly cause higher prices rather than higher output. So when the government shifted *aggregate* demand to the right, certain sectors probably saw mostly price increases rather than output gains.

LO12.3 Define aggregate supply (AS) and explain how it differs in the immediate short run, the short run, and the long run.

The aggregate supply curve shows the levels of real output that businesses will produce at various possible price levels. The slope of the aggregate supply curve depends upon the flexibility of input and output prices. Since these vary over time, aggregate supply curves are categorized into three time horizons, each having different underlying assumptions about the flexibility of input and output prices.

The *immediate-short-run aggregate supply curve* assumes that both input prices and output prices are fixed. With output prices fixed, the aggregate supply curve is a horizontal line at the current price level. The *short-run aggregate supply curve* assumes nominal wages and other input prices remain fixed while output prices vary. The aggregate supply curve is generally upsloping because per-unit production costs, and hence the prices that firms must receive, rise as real output expands. The aggregate supply curve is relatively steep to the right of the full-employment output level and relatively flat to the left of it. The *long-run aggregate supply curve* assumes that nominal wages and other input prices fully match any change in the price level. The curve is vertical at the full-employment output level.

Because the short-run aggregate supply curve is the only version of aggregate supply that can handle simultaneous changes in the price level and real output, it serves well as the core aggregate supply curve for analyzing the business cycle and economic policy. Unless stated otherwise, all references to "aggregate supply" refer to short-run aggregate supply and the short-run aggregate supply curve.

LO12.4 Explain the factors that cause changes (shifts) in AS.

Figure 12.6 lists the determinants of aggregate supply: input prices, productivity, and the legal-institutional environment. A change in any one of these factors will change per-unit production costs at each level of output and therefore will shift the aggregate supply curve.

LO12.5 Discuss how AD and AS determine an economy's equilibrium price level and level of real GDP.

The intersection of the aggregate demand and aggregate supply curves determines an economy's equilibrium price level and real GDP. At the intersection, the quantity of real GDP demanded equals the quantity of real GDP supplied.

LO12.6 Describe how the AD-AS model explains periods of demand-pull inflation, cost-push inflation, and recession.

Increases in aggregate demand to the right of the full-employment output cause inflation and positive GDP gaps (actual GDP exceeds potential GDP). An upsloping aggregate supply curve weakens the multiplier effect of an increase in aggregate demand because a portion of the increase in aggregate demand is dissipated in inflation.

Shifts of the aggregate demand curve to the left of the full-employment output cause recession, negative GDP gaps, and cyclical unemployment. The price level may not fall during recessions because of downwardly inflexible prices and wages. This inflexibility results from fear of price wars, menu costs, wage contracts, efficiency wages, and minimum wages. When the price level is fixed, changes in aggregate demand produce full-strength multiplier effects.

Leftward shifts of the aggregate supply curve reflect increases in per-unit production costs and cause cost-push inflation, with accompanying negative GDP gaps.

Rightward shifts of the aggregate supply curve, caused by large improvements in productivity, help explain the simultaneous achievement of full employment, economic growth, and price stability that occurred in the United States between 1996 and 2000. The recession of 2001, however, ended the expansionary phase of the business cycle. Expansion resumed in the 2002–2007 period, before giving way to the severe recession of 2007–2009.

TERMS AND CONCEPTS

aggregate demand–aggregate supply (AD-AS) model

aggregate demand

real-balances effect

interest-rate effect

foreign purchases effect

determinants of aggregate demand

aggregate supply

immediate-short-run aggregate supply curve

short-run aggregate supply curve

long-run aggregate supply curve

determinants of aggregate supply

productivity

equilibrium price level

equilibrium real output

menu costs

efficiency wages

The following and additional problems can be found in **connect** ECONOMICS

DISCUSSION QUESTIONS

1. Why is the aggregate demand curve downsloping? Specify how your explanation differs from the explanation for the downsloping demand curve for a single product. What role does the multiplier play in shifts of the aggregate demand curve? **LO12.1**

2. Distinguish between "real-balances effect" and "wealth effect," as the terms are used in this chapter. How does each relate to the aggregate demand curve? **LO12.1**

3. What assumptions cause the immediate-short-run aggregate supply curve to be horizontal? Why is the long-run aggregate supply curve vertical? Explain the shape of the short-run aggregate supply curve. Why is the short-run aggregate supply curve relatively flat to the left of the full-employment output and relatively steep to the right? **LO12.3**

4. Explain how an upsloping aggregate supply curve weakens the realized multiplier effect from an initial change in investment spending. **LO12.6**

5. Why does a reduction in aggregate demand in the actual economy reduce real output, rather than the price level? Why might a full-strength multiplier apply to a decrease in aggregate demand? **LO12.6**

6. Explain: "Unemployment can be caused by a decrease of aggregate demand or a decrease of aggregate supply." In each case, specify the price-level outcomes. **LO12.6**

7. Use shifts of the AD and AS curves to explain (*a*) the U.S. experience of strong economic growth, full employment, and price stability in the late 1990s and early 2000s and (*b*) how a strong negative wealth effect from, say, a precipitous

drop in house prices could cause a recession even though productivity is surging. **LO12.6**

8. In early 2001 investment spending sharply declined in the United States. In the two months following the September 11, 2001, attacks on the United States, consumption also declined. Use AD-AS analysis to show the two impacts on real GDP. **LO12.6**

9. **LAST WORD** What were the monetary and fiscal policy responses to the Great Recession? What were some of the reasons suggested for why those policy responses didn't seem to have as large an effect as anticipated on unemployment and GDP growth?

REVIEW QUESTIONS

1. Which of the following help to explain why the aggregate demand curve slopes downward? **LO12.1**
   a. When the domestic price level rises, our goods and services become more expensive to foreigners.
   b. When government spending rises, the price level falls.
   c. There is an inverse relationship between consumer expectations and personal taxes.
   d. When the price level rises, the real value of financial assets (like stocks, bonds, and savings account balances) declines.

2. Which of the following will shift the aggregate demand curve to the left? **LO12.2**
   a. The government reduces personal income taxes.
   b. Interest rates rise.
   c. The government raises corporate profit taxes.
   d. There is an economic boom overseas that raises the incomes of foreign households.

3. Label each of the following descriptions as being either an immediate-short-run aggregate supply curve, a short-run aggregate supply curve, or a long-run aggregate supply curve. **LO12.3**
   a. A vertical line.
   b. The price level is fixed.
   c. Output prices are flexible, but input prices are fixed.
   d. A horizontal line.
   e. An upsloping curve.
   f. Output is fixed.

4. Which of the following will shift the aggregate supply curve to the right? **LO12.4**
   a. A new networking technology increases productivity all over the economy.
   b. The price of oil rises substantially.
   c. Business taxes fall.
   d. The government passes a law doubling all manufacturing wages.

5. At the current price level, producers supply $375 billion of final goods and services while consumers purchase $355 billion of final goods and services. The price level is: **LO12.5**
   a. Above equilibrium.
   b. At equilibrium.
   c. Below equilibrium.
   d. More information is needed.

6. What effects would each of the following have on aggregate demand or aggregate supply, other things equal? In each case, use a diagram to show the expected effects on the equilibrium price level and the level of real output, assuming that the price level is flexible both upward and downward. **LO12.5**
   a. A widespread fear by consumers of an impending economic depression.
   b. A new national tax on producers based on the value added between the costs of the inputs and the revenue received from their output.
   c. A reduction in interest rates at each price level.
   d. A major increase in spending for health care by the federal government.
   e. The general expectation of coming rapid inflation.
   f. The complete disintegration of OPEC, causing oil prices to fall by one-half.
   g. A 10 percent across-the-board reduction in personal income tax rates.
   h. A sizable increase in labor productivity (with no change in nominal wages).
   i. A 12 percent increase in nominal wages (with no change in productivity).
   j. An increase in exports that exceeds an increase in imports (not due to tariffs).

7. True or False: Decreases in AD normally lead to decreases in both output and the price level. **LO12.6**

8. Assume that (*a*) the price level is flexible upward but not downward and (*b*) the economy is currently operating at its full-employment output. Other things equal, how will each of the following affect the equilibrium price level and equilibrium level of real output in the short run? **LO12.6**
   a. An increase in aggregate demand.
   b. A decrease in aggregate supply, with no change in aggregate demand.
   c. Equal increases in aggregate demand and aggregate supply.
   d. A decrease in aggregate demand.
   e. An increase in aggregate demand that exceeds an increase in aggregate supply.

9. True or False: If the price of oil suddenly increases by a large amount, AS will shift left, but the price level will not rise thanks to price inflexibility. **LO12.6**

PROBLEMS

1. Suppose that consumer spending initially rises by $5 billion for every 1 percent rise in household wealth and that investment spending initially rises by $20 billion for every 1 percentage point fall in the real interest rate. Also assume that the economy's multiplier is 4. If household wealth falls by 5 percent because of declining house values, and the real interest rate falls by 2 percentage points, in what direction and by how much will the aggregate demand curve initially shift at each price level? In what direction and by how much will it eventually shift? **LO12.2**

2. Answer the following questions on the basis of the following three sets of data for the country of North Vaudeville: **LO12.4**

(A)		(B)		(C)	
Price Level	Real GDP	Price Level	Real GDP	Price Level	Real GDP
110	275	100	200	110	225
100	250	100	225	100	225
95	225	100	250	95	225
90	200	100	275	90	225

   a. Which set of data illustrates aggregate supply in the immediate short run in North Vaudeville? The short run? The long run?

   b. Assuming no change in hours of work, if real output per hour of work increases by 10 percent, what will be the new levels of real GDP in the right column of A? Do the new data reflect an increase in aggregate supply or do they indicate a decrease in aggregate supply?

3. Suppose that the aggregate demand and aggregate supply schedules for a hypothetical economy are as shown in the following table. **LO12.5**

Amount of Real GDP Demanded, Billions	Price Level (Price Index)	Amount of Real GDP Supplied, Billions
$100	300	$450
200	250	400
300	200	300
400	150	200
500	100	100

   a. Use the data above to graph the aggregate demand and aggregate supply curves. What are the equilibrium price level and the equilibrium level of real output in this hypothetical economy? Is the equilibrium real output also necessarily the full-employment real output?

   b. If the price level in this economy is 150, will quantity demanded equal, exceed, or fall short of quantity supplied? By what amount? If the price level is 250, will quantity demanded equal, exceed, or fall short of quantity supplied? By what amount?

   c. Suppose that buyers desire to purchase $200 billion of extra real output at each price level. Sketch in the new aggregate demand curve as AD$_1$. What are the new equilibrium price level and level of real output?

4. Suppose that the table presented below shows an economy's relationship between real output and the inputs needed to produce that output: **LO12.4**

Input Quantity	Real GDP
150.0	$400
112.5	300
75.0	200

   a. What is productivity in this economy?

   b. What is the per-unit cost of production if the price of each input unit is $2?

   c. Assume that the input price increases from $2 to $3 with no accompanying change in productivity. What is the new per-unit cost of production? In what direction would the $1 increase in input price push the economy's aggregate supply curve? What effect would this shift of aggregate supply have on the price level and the level of real output?

   d. Suppose that the increase in input price does not occur but, instead, that productivity increases by 100 percent. What would be the new per-unit cost of production? What effect would this change in per-unit production cost have on the economy's aggregate supply curve? What effect would this shift of aggregate supply have on the price level and the level of real output?

5. Refer to the data in the table that accompanies problem 2. Suppose that the present equilibrium price level and level of real GDP are 100 and $225, and that data set B represents the relevant aggregate supply schedule for the economy. **LO12.6**

   a. What must be the current amount of real output demanded at the 100 price level?

   b. If the amount of output demanded declined by $25 at the 100 price levels shown in B, what would be the new equilibrium real GDP? In business cycle terminology, what would economists call this change in real GDP?

The Relationship of the Aggregate Demand Curve to the Aggregate Expenditures Model*

LO12.7 Identify how the aggregate demand curve relates to the aggregate expenditures model.

The aggregate demand curve of this chapter and the aggregate expenditures model of Chapter 11 are intricately related.

Derivation of the Aggregate Demand Curve from the Aggregate Expenditures Model

We can directly connect the downsloping aggregate demand curve to the aggregate expenditures model by relating various possible price levels to corresponding equilibrium GDPs. In Figure 1 we have stacked the aggregate expenditures model (Figure 1a) and the aggregate demand curve (Figure 1b) vertically. This is possible because the horizontal axes of both models measure real GDP. Now let's derive the AD curve in three distinct steps. (Throughout this discussion, keep in mind that price level P_1 is lower than price level P_2, which is lower than price level P_3.)

- First suppose that the economy's price level is P_1 and its aggregate expenditures schedule is AE_1, the top schedule in Figure 1a. The equilibrium GDP is then Q_1 at point 1. So in Figure 1b we can plot the equilibrium real output Q_1 and the corresponding price level P_1. This gives us point 1′ in Figure 1b.
- Now assume the price level rises from P_1 to P_2. Other things equal, this higher price level will (1) decrease the value of real balances (wealth), decreasing consumption expenditures; (2) increase the interest rate, reducing investment and interest-sensitive consumption expenditures; and (3) increase imports and decrease exports, reducing net export

*This appendix presumes knowledge of the aggregate expenditures model discussed in Chapter 11 and should be skipped if Chapter 11 was not assigned.

FIGURE 1 **Deriving the aggregate demand curve from the aggregate expenditures model.** (a) Rising price levels from P_1 to P_2 to P_3 shift the aggregate expenditures curve downward from AE_1 to AE_2 to AE_3 and reduce real GDP from Q_1 to Q_2 to Q_3. (b) The aggregate demand curve AD is derived by plotting the successively lower real GDPs from the upper graph against the P_1, P_2, and P_3 price levels.

(a)
Aggregate expenditures model

(b)
Aggregate demand–aggregate supply model

expenditures. The aggregate expenditures schedule will fall from AE_1 to, say, AE_2 in Figure 1a, giving us equilibrium Q_2 at point 2. In Figure 1b we plot this new price-level–real-output combination, P_2 and Q_2, as point 2′.

- Finally, suppose the price level rises from P_2 to P_3. The value of real balances falls, the interest rate rises, exports fall, and imports rise. Consequently, the consumption, investment, and net export schedules fall, shifting the aggregate expenditures schedule downward from AE_2 to AE_3, which gives us equilibrium Q_3 at point 3. In Figure 1b, this enables us to locate point 3′, where the price level is P_3 and real output is Q_3.

In summary, increases in the economy's price level will successively shift its aggregate expenditures schedule downward and will reduce real GDP. The resulting price-level–real-GDP combinations will yield various points such as 1′, 2′, and 3′ in Figure 1b. Together, such points locate the downsloping aggregate demand curve for the economy.

Aggregate Demand Shifts and the Aggregate Expenditures Model

The determinants of aggregate demand listed in Figure 12.2 are the components of the aggregate expenditures model discussed in Chapter 11. When one of the determinants of aggregate demand changes, the aggregate expenditures schedule shifts upward or downward. We can easily link such shifts of the aggregate expenditures schedule to shifts of the aggregate demand curve.

Let's suppose that the price level is constant. In Figure 2 we begin with the aggregate expenditures schedule at AE_1 in the top diagram, yielding equilibrium real output Q_1. Assume now that investment increases in response to more optimistic business expectations, so the aggregate expenditures schedule rises from AE_1 to AE_2. (The notation "at P_1" reminds us that the price level is assumed constant.) The result will be a multiplied increase in equilibrium real output from Q_1 to Q_2.

In Figure 2b the increase in investment spending is reflected in the horizontal distance between AD_1 and the broken curve to its right. The immediate effect of the increase in investment is an increase in aggregate demand by the exact amount of the new spending. But then the multiplier process magnifies the initial increase in investment into successive rounds of consumption spending

FIGURE 2 **Shifts of the aggregate expenditures schedule and of the aggregate demand curve.** (a) A change in some determinant of consumption, investment, or net exports (other than the price level) shifts the aggregate expenditures schedule upward from AE_1 to AE_2. The multiplier increases real output from Q_1 to Q_2. (b) The counterpart of this change is an initial rightward shift of the aggregate demand curve by the amount of initial new spending (from AD_1 to the broken curve). This leads to a multiplied rightward shift of the curve to AD_2, which is just sufficient to show the same increase of real output as that in the aggregate expenditures model.

(a)
Aggregate expenditures model

(b)
Aggregate demand–aggregate supply model

and an ultimate multiplied increase in aggregate demand from AD_1 to AD_2. Equilibrium real output rises from Q_1 to Q_2, the same multiplied increase in real GDP as that in the top graph. The initial increase in investment in the top graph has shifted the AD curve in the lower graph by a horizontal distance equal to the change in investment times the multiplier. This particular change in real GDP is still associated with the constant price level P_1. To generalize,

$$\text{Shift of AD curve} = \text{initial change in spending} \times \text{multiplier}$$

APPENDIX SUMMARY

LO12.7 Identify how the aggregate demand curve relates to the aggregate expenditures model.

A change in the price level alters the location of the aggregate expenditures schedule through the real-balances, interest-rate, and foreign purchases effects. The aggregate demand curve is derived from the aggregate expenditures model by allowing the price level to change and observing the effect on the aggregate expenditures schedule and thus on equilibrium GDP.

With the price level held constant, increases in consumption, investment, government, and net export expenditures shift the aggregate expenditures schedule upward and the aggregate demand curve to the right. Decreases in these spending components produce the opposite effects.

The following and additional problems can be found in connect ECONOMICS

APPENDIX DISCUSSION QUESTIONS

1. Explain carefully: "A change in the price level shifts the aggregate expenditures curve but not the aggregate demand curve." **LO12.7**
2. Suppose that the price level is constant and that investment decreases sharply. How would you show this decrease in the aggregate expenditures model? What would be the outcome for real GDP? How would you show this fall in investment in the aggregate demand–aggregate supply model, assuming the economy is operating in what, in effect, is a horizontal section of the aggregate supply curve? **LO12.7**

APPENDIX REVIEW QUESTIONS

1. True or False: A higher price level increases aggregate expenditures. **LO12.7**

2. If the government decreases expenditures, the *AE* curve will shift _____ and the AD curve will shift _____. **LO12.7**
   a. Down; left.
   b. Down; right.
   c. Up; left.
   d. Up; right.

APPENDIX PROBLEMS

1. Refer to Figures 1a and 1b in the Appendix. Assume that Q_1 is 300, Q_2 is 200, Q_3 is 100, P_3 is 120, P_2 is 100, and P_1 is 80. If the price level increases from P_1 to P_3 in graph 1b, in what direction and by how much will real GDP change? If the slopes of the AE lines in Figure 1a are 0.8 and equal to the MPC, in what direction will the aggregate expenditures schedule in Figure 1a need to shift to produce the previously determined change in real GDP? What is the size of the multiplier in this example? **LO12.7**

2. Refer to Figure 2 in the Appendix and assume that Q_1 is $400 and Q_2 is $500, the price level is stuck at P_1, and the slopes of the AE lines in Figure 2a are 0.75 and equal to the MPC. In what direction and by how much does the aggregate expenditures schedule in Figure 2a need to shift to move the aggregate demand curve in Figure 2b from AD_1 to AD_2? What is the multiplier in this example? Given the multiplier, what must be the distance between AD_1 and the broken line to its right at P_1? **LO12.7**

CHAPTER 13

Fiscal Policy, Deficits, and Debt

Learning Objectives

LO13.1 Identify and explain the purposes, tools, and limitations of fiscal policy.

LO13.2 Explain the role of built-in stabilizers in moderating business cycles.

LO13.3 Describe how the cyclically adjusted budget reveals the status of U.S. fiscal policy.

LO13.4 Summarize recent U.S. fiscal policy and the projections for U.S. fiscal policy over the next few years.

LO13.5 Discuss the problems that governments may encounter in enacting and applying fiscal policy.

LO13.6 Discuss the size, composition, and consequences of the U.S. public debt.

In the previous chapter we saw that an excessive increase in aggregate demand can cause demand-pull inflation and that a significant decline in aggregate demand can cause recession and cyclical unemployment. For these reasons, the federal government sometimes uses budgetary actions to try to "stimulate the economy" or "rein in inflation." Such countercyclical **fiscal policy** consists of deliberate changes in government spending and tax collections designed to achieve full employment, control inflation, and encourage economic growth. (The adjective "fiscal" simply means "financial.")

We begin this chapter by examining the logic behind fiscal policy, its current status, and its limitations. Then we examine a closely related topic: the U.S. public debt.

ORIGIN OF THE IDEA

O13.1
Fiscal policy

Our discussion of fiscal policy and public debt is very timely. In 2009, Congress and the Obama administration began a $787 billion stimulus program designed to help lift the U.S. economy out of deep recession. This fiscal policy contributed to a $1.4 trillion federal budget deficit in 2009, which increased the size of the U.S. public debt to $11.9 trillion. Large deficits continued in subsequent years, so that the U.S. public debt passed $17.0 trillion in 2013.

Fiscal Policy and the AD-AS Model

LO13.1 Identify and explain the purposes, tools, and limitations of fiscal policy.

The fiscal policy just defined is *discretionary* (or "active"). It is often initiated on the advice of the president's **Council of Economic Advisers (CEA)**, a group of three economists appointed by the president to provide expertise and assistance on economic matters. Discretionary changes in government spending and taxes are *at the option* of the federal government. They do not occur automatically. Changes that occur without congressional action are *nondiscretionary* (or "passive" or "automatic"), and we will examine them later in this chapter.

Expansionary Fiscal Policy

When recession occurs, an **expansionary fiscal policy** may be in order. This policy consists of government spending increases, tax reductions, or both, designed to increase aggregate demand and therefore raise real GDP. Consider Figure 13.1, where we suppose that a sharp decline in investment spending has shifted the economy's aggregate demand curve to the left from AD_1 to AD_2. (Disregard the arrows and dashed downsloping line for now.) The cause of the recession may be that profit expectations on investment projects have dimmed, curtailing investment spending and reducing aggregate demand.

Suppose the economy's potential or full-employment output is $510 billion in Figure 13.1. If the price level is inflexible downward at P_1, the broken horizontal line becomes relevant to the analysis. The aggregate demand curve moves leftward and reduces real GDP from $510 billion to $490 billion. A negative GDP gap of $20 billion (= $490 billion − $510 billion) arises. An increase in unemployment accompanies this negative GDP gap because fewer workers are needed to produce the reduced output. In short, the economy depicted is suffering both recession and cyclical unemployment.

What fiscal policy should the federal government adopt to try to stimulate the economy? It has three main options: (1) increase government spending, (2) reduce taxes, or (3) use some combination of the two. If the federal budget is balanced at the outset, expansionary fiscal policy will create a government **budget deficit**—government spending in excess of tax revenues.

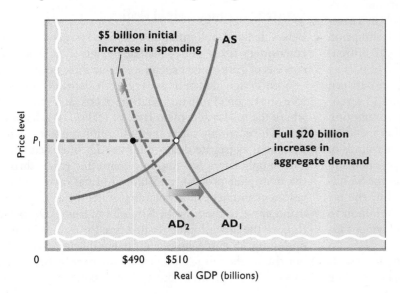

FIGURE 13.1 Expansionary fiscal policy. Expansionary fiscal policy uses increases in government spending or tax cuts to push the economy out of recession. In an economy with an MPC of 0.75, a $5 billion increase in government spending or a $6.67 billion decrease in personal taxes (producing a $5 billion initial increase in consumption) expands aggregate demand from AD_2 to the downsloping dashed curve. The multiplier then magnifies this initial increase in spending to AD_1. So real GDP rises along the broken horizontal line by $20 billion.

Increased Government Spending Other things equal, a sufficient increase in government spending will shift an economy's aggregate demand curve to the right, from AD_2 to AD_1 in Figure 13.1. To see why, suppose that the recession prompts the government to initiate $5 billion of new spending on highways, education, and health care. We represent this new $5 billion of government spending as the horizontal distance between AD_2 and the dashed downsloping line immediately to its right. At each price level, the amount of real output that is demanded is now $5 billion greater than that demanded before the expansion of government spending.

But the initial increase in aggregate demand is not the end of the story. Through the multiplier effect, the aggregate demand curve shifts to AD_1, a distance that exceeds that represented by the originating $5 billion increase in government purchases. This greater shift occurs because the multiplier process magnifies the initial change in spending into successive rounds of new consumption spending. If the economy's MPC is 0.75, then the simple multiplier is 4. So the aggregate demand curve shifts rightward by four times the distance between AD_2 and the broken downsloping line. Because this *particular* increase in aggregate demand occurs along the horizontal broken-line segment, real output rises by the full extent of the multiplier. Observe that real output rises to $510 billion, up $20 billion from its recessionary level of $490 billion. Concurrently, unemployment falls as firms increase their employment to the full-employment level that existed before the recession.

Tax Reductions Alternatively, the government could reduce taxes to shift the aggregate demand curve rightward, as from AD_2 to AD_1. Suppose the government cuts personal income taxes by $6.67 billion, which increases disposable income by the same amount. Consumption will rise by $5 billion (= MPC of 0.75 × $6.67 billion) and saving will go up by $1.67 billion (= MPS of 0.25 × $6.67 billion). In this case the horizontal distance between AD_2 and the dashed downsloping line in Figure 13.1 represents only the $5 billion initial increase in consumption spending. Again, we call it "initial" consumption spending because the multiplier process yields successive rounds of increased consumption spending. The aggregate demand curve eventually shifts rightward by four times the $5 billion initial increase in consumption produced by the tax cut. Real GDP rises by $20 billion, from $490 billion to $510 billion, implying a multiplier of 4. Employment increases accordingly.

You may have noted that a tax cut must be somewhat larger than the proposed increase in government spending if it is to achieve the same amount of rightward shift in the aggregate demand curve. This is because part of a tax reduction increases saving, rather than consumption. To increase initial consumption by a specific amount, the government must reduce taxes by more than that amount. With an MPC of 0.75, taxes must fall by $6.67 billion for $5 billion of new consumption to be forthcoming because $1.67 billion is saved (not consumed). If the MPC had instead been, say, 0.6, an $8.33 billion reduction in tax collections would have been necessary to increase initial consumption by $5 billion. The smaller the MPC, the greater the tax cut needed to accomplish a specific initial increase in consumption and a specific shift in the aggregate demand curve.

Combined Government Spending Increases and Tax Reductions The government may combine spending increases and tax cuts to produce the desired initial increase in spending and the eventual increase in aggregate demand and real GDP. In the economy depicted in Figure 13.1, the government might increase its spending by $1.25 billion while reducing taxes by $5 billion. As an exercise, you should explain why this combination will produce the targeted $5 billion initial increase in new spending.

If you were assigned Chapter 11, think through these three fiscal policy options in terms of the recessionary-expenditure-gap analysis associated with the aggregate expenditures model (Figure 11.7). And recall from the appendix to Chapter 12 that rightward shifts of the aggregate demand curve relate directly to upward shifts of the aggregate expenditures schedule.

Contractionary Fiscal Policy

When demand-pull inflation occurs, a restrictive or **contractionary fiscal policy** may help control it. This policy consists of government spending reductions, tax increases, or both, designed to decrease aggregate demand and therefore lower or eliminate inflation. Look at Figure 13.2, where the full-employment level of real GDP is $510 billion. The economy starts at equilibrium at point *a*, where the initial aggregate demand curve AD_3 intersects aggregate supply curve AS. Suppose that after going through the multiplier process, a $5 billion initial increase in investment and net export spending shifts the aggregate demand curve to the right by $20 billion, from AD_3 to AD_4. (Ignore the downsloping dashed line for now.) Given the upsloping AS curve, however, the equilibrium GDP does not rise by the full $20 billion. It only rises by $12 billion, to $522 billion, thereby creating an inflationary GDP gap

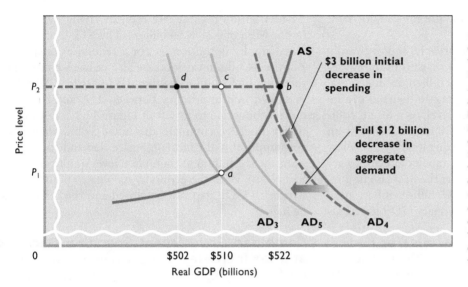

FIGURE 13.2 Contractionary fiscal policy. Contractionary fiscal policy uses decreases in government spending, increases in taxes, or both, to reduce demand-pull inflation. Here, an increase in aggregate demand from AD_3 to AD_4 has driven the economy to point b and ratcheted the price level up to P_2, where it becomes inflexible downward. If the economy's MPC is 0.75 and the multiplier therefore is 4, the government can either reduce its spending by $3 billion or increase its taxes by $4 billion (which will decrease consumption by $3 billion) to eliminate the inflationary GDP gap of $12 billion (= $522 billion − $510 billion). Aggregate demand will shift leftward, first from AD_4 to the dashed downsloping curve to its left, and then to AD_5. With the price level remaining at P_2, the economy will move from point b to point c and the inflationary GDP gap will disappear.

of $12 billion ($522 billion − $510 billion). The upslope of the AS curve means that some of the rightward movement of the AD curve ends up causing demand-pull inflation rather than increased output. As a result, the price level rises from P_1 to P_2 and the equilibrium moves to point b.

Without a government response, the inflationary GDP gap will cause further inflation (as input prices rise in the long run to meet the increase in output prices). If the government looks to fiscal policy to eliminate the inflationary GDP gap, its options are the opposite of those used to combat recession. It can (1) decrease government spending, (2) raise taxes, or (3) use some combination of those two policies. When the economy faces demand-pull inflation, fiscal policy should move toward a government **budget surplus**—tax revenues in excess of government spending.

But before discussing how the government can either decrease government spending or increase taxes to move toward a government budget surplus and control inflation, we have to keep in mind that the price level is like a ratchet. While increases in aggregate demand that expand real output beyond the full-employment level tend to ratchet the price level upward, declines in aggregate demand do not seem to push the price level downward. This means that stopping inflation is a matter of halting the rise of the price level, not trying to lower it to the previous level. It also means that the government must take the ratchet effect into account when deciding how big a cut in spending or an increase in taxes it should undertake.

Decreased Government Spending To control demand-pull inflation, the government can decrease

aggregate demand by reducing government spending. To see why the ratchet effect matters so much, look at Figure 13.2 and consider what would happen if the government ignored the ratchet effect and attempted to design a spending-reduction policy to eliminate the inflationary GDP gap. Since the $12 billion gap was caused by the $20 billion rightward movement of the aggregate demand curve from AD_3 to AD_4, the government might naively think that it could solve the problem by causing a $20 billion leftward shift of the aggregate demand curve to move it back to where it originally was. It could attempt to do so by reducing government spending by $5 billion and then allowing the multiplier effect to expand that initial decrease into a $20 billion decline in aggregate demand. That would shift the aggregate demand curve leftward by $20 billion, putting it back at AD_3.

This policy would work fine if there were no ratchet effect and if prices were flexible. The economy's equilibrium would move back from point b to point a, with equilibrium GDP returning to the full-employment level of $510 billion and the price level falling from P_2 back to P_1.

But because there *is* a ratchet effect, this scenario is not what will actually happen. Instead, the ratchet effect implies that the price level is stuck at P_2, so that the broken horizontal line at price level P_2 becomes important to the analysis. The fixed price level means that when the government reduces spending by $5 billion to shift the aggregate demand curve back to AD_3, it will actually cause a recession! The new equilibrium will not be at point a. It will be at point d, where aggregate demand curve AD_3 crosses the broken horizontal line. At point d, real GDP is only $502 billion, $8 billion below the full-employment level of $510 billion.

The problem is that, with the price level downwardly inflexible at P_2, the $20 billion leftward shift of the aggregate demand curve causes a full $20 billion decline in real GDP. None of the change in aggregate demand can be dissipated as a decline in the price level. As a result, equilibrium GDP declines by the full $20 billion, falling from $522 billion to $502 billion and putting it $8 billion below potential output. By not taking the ratchet effect into account, the government has overdone the decrease in government spending, replacing a $12 billion inflationary GDP gap with an $8 billion recessionary GDP gap. This is clearly not what it had in mind.

Here's how it can avoid this scenario. First, the government takes account of the size of the inflationary GDP gap. It is $12 billion. Second, it knows that with the price level fixed, the multiplier will be in full effect. Thus, it knows that any decline in government spending will be multiplied by a factor of 4. It then reasons that government spending will have to decline by only $3 billion rather than $5 billion. Why? Because the $3 billion initial decline in government spending will be multiplied by 4, creating a $12 billion decline in aggregate demand. Under the circumstances, a $3 billion decline in government spending is the correct amount to exactly offset the $12 billion GDP gap. This inflationary GDP gap is the problem that government wants to eliminate. To succeed, it need not undo the full increase in aggregate demand that caused the inflation in the first place.

Graphically, the horizontal distance between AD_4 and the dashed downsloping line to its left represents the $3 billion decrease in government spending. Once the multiplier process is complete, this spending cut will shift the aggregate demand curve leftward from AD_4 to AD_5. With the price level fixed at P_2, the economy will come to equilibrium at point c. The economy will operate at its potential output of $510 billion, and the inflationary GDP gap will be eliminated. Furthermore, because the government took the ratchet effect correctly into account, the government will not accidentally push the economy into a recession by making an overly large initial decrease in government spending.

Increased Taxes Just as government can use tax cuts to increase consumption spending, it can use tax *increases* to *reduce* consumption spending. If the economy in Figure 13.2 has an MPC of 0.75, the government must raise taxes by $4 billion to achieve its fiscal policy objective.

The $4 billion tax increase reduces saving by $1 billion (= the MPS of 0.25 × $4 billion). This $1 billion reduction in saving, by definition, is not a reduction in spending. But the $4 billion tax increase also reduces consumption spending by $3 billion (= the MPC of 0.75 × $4 billion), as shown by the distance between AD_4 and the dashed downsloping line to its left in Figure 13.2. After the multiplier process is complete, this initial $3 billion decline in consumption will cause aggregate demand to shift leftward by $12 billion at each price level (multiplier of 4 × $3 billion). With the economy moving to point c, the inflationary GDP gap will be closed and the inflation will be halted.

Combined Government Spending Decreases and Tax Increases The government may choose to combine spending decreases and tax increases in order to reduce aggregate demand and check inflation. To check your understanding, determine why a $1.5 billion decline in government spending combined with a $2 billion increase in taxes would shift the aggregate demand curve from AD_4 to AD_5. Also, if you were assigned Chapter 11, explain the three fiscal policy options for fighting inflation by referring to the inflationary-expenditure-gap concept developed with the aggregate expenditures model (Figure 11.7). And recall from the appendix to Chapter 12 that leftward shifts of the aggregate demand curve are associated with downshifts of the aggregate expenditures schedule.

Policy Options: G or T?

Which is preferable as a means of eliminating recession and inflation? The use of government spending or the use of taxes? The answer depends largely on one's view as to whether the government is too large or too small.

Economists who believe there are many unmet social and infrastructure needs usually recommend that government spending be increased during recessions. In times of demand-pull inflation, they usually recommend tax increases. Both actions either expand or preserve the size of government.

Economists who think that the government is too large and inefficient usually advocate tax cuts during recessions and cuts in government spending during times of demand-pull inflation. Both actions either restrain the growth of government or reduce its size.

The point is that discretionary fiscal policy designed to stabilize the economy can be associated with either an expanding government or a contracting government.

QUICK REVIEW 13.1

- Discretionary fiscal policy is the purposeful change of government expenditures and tax collections by government to promote full employment, price stability, and economic growth.
- Expansionary fiscal policy consists of increases in government spending, reductions in taxes, or both, and is designed to expand real GDP by increasing aggregate demand.
- Contractionary fiscal policy entails decreases in government spending, increases in taxes, or both, and is designed to reduce aggregate demand and slow or halt demand-pull inflation.
- To be implemented correctly, contractionary fiscal policy must properly account for the ratchet effect and the fact that the price level will not fall as the government shifts the aggregate demand curve leftward.

FIGURE 13.3 Built-in stability. Tax revenues, *T*, vary directly with GDP, and government spending, *G*, is assumed to be independent of GDP. As GDP falls in a recession, deficits occur automatically and help alleviate the recession. As GDP rises during expansion, surpluses occur automatically and help offset possible inflation.

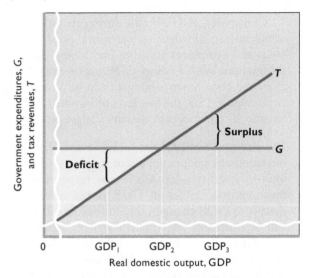

Built-In Stability

LO13.2 Explain the role of built-in stabilizers in moderating business cycles.

To some degree, government tax revenues change automatically over the course of the business cycle and in ways that stabilize the economy. This automatic response, or built-in stability, constitutes nondiscretionary (or "passive" or "automatic") budgetary policy and results from the makeup of most tax systems. We did not include this built-in stability in our discussion of fiscal policy over the last few pages because we implicitly assumed that the same amount of tax revenue was being collected at each level of GDP. But the actual U.S. tax system is such that *net tax revenues* vary directly with GDP. (Net taxes are tax revenues less transfers and subsidies. From here on, we will use the simpler "taxes" to mean "net taxes.")

Virtually any tax will yield more tax revenue as GDP rises. In particular, personal income taxes have progressive rates and thus generate more-than-proportionate increases in tax revenues as GDP expands. Furthermore, as GDP rises and more goods and services are purchased, revenues from corporate income taxes and from sales taxes and excise taxes also increase. And, similarly, revenues from payroll taxes rise as economic expansion creates more jobs. Conversely, when GDP declines, tax receipts from all these sources also decline.

Transfer payments (or "negative taxes") behave in the opposite way from tax revenues. Unemployment compensation payments and welfare payments decrease during economic expansion and increase during economic contraction.

Automatic or Built-In Stabilizers

A **built-in stabilizer** is anything that increases the government's budget deficit (or reduces its budget surplus) during a recession and increases its budget surplus (or reduces its budget deficit) during an expansion without requiring explicit action by policymakers. As Figure 13.3 reveals, this is precisely what the U.S. tax system does. Government expenditures *G* are fixed and assumed to be independent of the level of GDP. Congress decides on a particular level of spending, but it does not determine the magnitude of tax revenues. Instead, it establishes tax rates, and the tax revenues then vary directly with the level of GDP that the economy achieves. Line *T* represents that direct relationship between tax revenues and GDP.

Economic Importance The economic importance of the direct relationship between tax receipts and GDP becomes apparent when we consider that:

- Taxes reduce spending and aggregate demand.
- Reductions in spending are desirable when the economy is moving toward inflation, whereas increases in spending are desirable when the economy is slumping.

As shown in Figure 13.3, tax revenues automatically increase as GDP rises during prosperity, and since taxes reduce household and business spending, they restrain the economic expansion. That is, as the economy moves toward a higher GDP, tax revenues automatically rise and move the budget from deficit toward surplus. In Figure 13.3, observe that the high and perhaps inflationary income level GDP_3 automatically generates a contractionary budget surplus.

Conversely, as GDP falls during recession, tax revenues automatically decline, increasing spending by households and businesses and thus cushioning the economic contraction. With a falling GDP, tax receipts decline and move the government's budget from surplus toward deficit. In Figure 13.3, the low level of income GDP_1 will automatically yield an expansionary budget deficit.

Tax Progressivity Figure 13.3 reveals that the size of the automatic budget deficits or surpluses—and therefore built-in stability—depends on the responsiveness of tax revenues to changes in GDP. If tax revenues change sharply as GDP changes, the slope of line T in the figure will be steep and the vertical distances between T and G (the deficits or surpluses) will be large. If tax revenues change very little when GDP changes, the slope will be gentle and built-in stability will be low.

The steepness of T in Figure 13.3 depends on the tax system itself. In a **progressive tax system,** the average tax rate (= tax revenue/GDP) rises with GDP. In a **proportional tax system,** the average tax rate remains constant as GDP rises. In a **regressive tax system,** the average tax rate falls as GDP rises. The progressive tax system has the steepest tax line T of the three. However, tax revenues will rise with GDP under both the progressive and the proportional tax systems, and they may rise, fall, or stay the same under a regressive tax system. The main point is this: The more progressive the tax system, the greater the economy's built-in stability.

The built-in stability provided by the U.S. tax system has reduced the severity of business fluctuations, perhaps by as much as 8 to 10 percent of the change in GDP that otherwise would have occurred.[1] In recession-year 2009, for example, revenues from the individual income tax fell by a staggering 22 percent. This decline helped keep household spending and real GDP from falling even more than they did. But built-in stabilizers can only dampen, not counteract, swings in real GDP. Discretionary fiscal policy (changes in tax rates and expenditures) or monetary policy (central bank–caused changes in interest rates) therefore may be needed to try to counter a recession or inflation of any appreciable magnitude.

---

[1] Alan J. Auerbach and Daniel Feenberg, "The Significance of Federal Taxes as Automatic Stabilizers," *Journal of Economic Perspectives,* Summer 2000, p. 54.

Evaluating How Expansionary or Contractionary Fiscal Policy Is Determined

LO13.3 Describe how the cyclically adjusted budget reveals the status of U.S. fiscal policy.

How can we determine whether a government's discretionary fiscal policy is expansionary, neutral, or contractionary? We cannot simply examine the actual budget deficits or surpluses that take place under the current policy because they will necessarily include the automatic changes in tax revenues that accompany every change in GDP. In addition, the expansionary or contractionary strength of any change in discretionary fiscal policy depends not on its absolute size but on how large it is relative to the size of the economy. So, in evaluating the status of fiscal policy, we must adjust deficits and surpluses to eliminate automatic changes in tax revenues and also compare the sizes of the adjusted budget deficits and surpluses to the level of potential GDP.

Cyclically Adjusted Budget

Economists use the **cyclically adjusted budget** (also called the *full-employment budget*) to adjust actual federal budget deficits and surpluses to account for the changes in tax revenues that happen automatically whenever GDP changes. The cyclically adjusted budget measures what the federal budget deficit or surplus would have been under existing tax rates and government spending levels if the economy had achieved its full-employment level of GDP (its potential output). The idea essentially is to compare *actual* government expenditures with the tax revenues *that would have occurred* if the economy had achieved full-employment GDP. That procedure removes budget deficits or surpluses that arise simply because of cyclical changes in GDP and thus tell us nothing about whether the government's current discretionary fiscal policy is fundamentally expansionary, contractionary, or neutral.

Consider Figure 13.4a, where line G represents government expenditures and line T represents tax revenues. In full-employment year 1, government expenditures of $500 billion equal tax revenues of $500 billion, as indicated by the intersection of lines G and T at point a. The cyclically adjusted budget deficit in year 1 is zero—government expenditures equal the tax revenues forthcoming at the full-employment output GDP_1. Obviously, the cyclically adjusted deficit *as a percentage of potential GDP* is also zero. The government's fiscal policy is neutral.

Now suppose that a recession occurs and GDP falls from GDP_1 to GDP_2, as shown in Figure 13.4a. Let's also

FIGURE 13.4 Cyclically adjusted deficits. (a) In the left-hand graph, the cyclically adjusted deficit is zero at the full-employment output GDP₁. But it is also zero at the recessionary output GDP₂ because the $500 billion of government expenditures at GDP₂ equals the $500 billion of tax revenues that would be forthcoming at the full-employment GDP₁. There has been no change in fiscal policy. (b) In the right-hand graph, discretionary fiscal policy, as reflected in the downward shift of the tax line from T_1 to T_2, has increased the cyclically adjusted budget deficit from zero in year 3 (before the tax cut) to $25 billion in year 4 (after the tax cut). This is found by comparing the $500 billion of government spending in year 4 with the $475 billion of taxes that would accrue at the full-employment GDP₃. Such a rise in the cyclically adjusted deficit (as a percentage of potential GDP) identifies an expansionary fiscal policy.

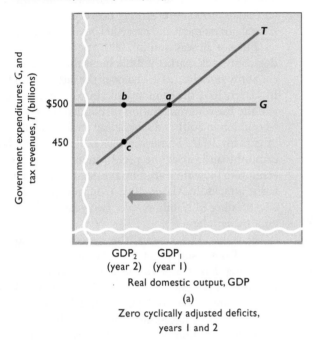

GDP₂   GDP₁
(year 2)   (year 1)
Real domestic output, GDP
(a)
Zero cyclically adjusted deficits,
years 1 and 2

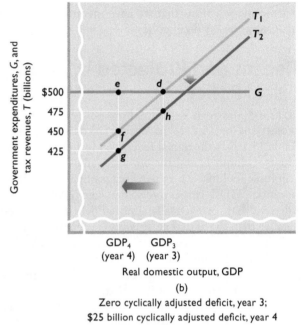

GDP₄   GDP₃
(year 4)   (year 3)
Real domestic output, GDP
(b)
Zero cyclically adjusted deficit, year 3;
$25 billion cyclically adjusted deficit, year 4

assume that the government takes no discretionary action, so lines G and T remain as shown in the figure. Tax revenues automatically fall to $450 billion (point c) at GDP₂, while government spending remains unaltered at $500 billion (point b). A $50 billion budget deficit (represented by distance bc) arises. But this **cyclical deficit** is simply a by-product of the economy's slide into recession, not the result of discretionary fiscal actions by the government. We would be wrong to conclude from this deficit that the government is engaging in an expansionary fiscal policy. The government's fiscal policy has not changed. It is still neutral.

That fact is highlighted when we remove the cyclical part of the deficit and thus consider the cyclically adjusted budget deficit for year 2 in Figure 13.4a. The $500 billion of government expenditures in year 2 is shown by b on line G. And, as shown by a on line T, $500 billion of tax revenues would have occurred if the economy had achieved its full-employment GDP. Because both b and a represent $500 billion, the cyclically adjusted budget deficit in year 2 is zero, as is this deficit as a percentage of potential GDP. Since the cyclically adjusted deficits are zero in both years, we know that government did not change its discretionary

fiscal policy, even though a recession occurred and an actual deficit of $50 billion resulted.

Next, consider Figure 13.4b. Suppose that real output declined from full-employment GDP₃ in year 3 to GDP₄ in year 4. Also suppose that government responded to the recession by reducing tax rates in year 4, as represented by the downward shift of the tax line from T_1 to T_2. What has happened to the size of the cyclically adjusted deficit? Government expenditures in year 4 are $500 billion, as shown by e. Compare that amount with the $475 billion of tax revenues that would occur if the economy achieved its full-employment GDP. That is, compare position e on line G with position h on line T_2. The $25 billion of tax revenues by which e exceeds h is the cyclically adjusted budget deficit for year 4. As a percentage of potential GDP, the cyclically adjusted budget deficit has increased from zero in year 3 (before the tax-rate cut) to some positive percent [= ($25 billion/GDP₃) × 100] in year 4. This increase in the relative size of the full-employment deficit between the two years reveals that the new fiscal policy is *expansionary*.

In contrast, if we observed a cyclically adjusted deficit (as a percentage of potential GDP) of zero in one year, followed by a cyclically adjusted budget surplus in the next, we could conclude that fiscal policy has changed from being neutral to being contractionary. Because the cyclically adjusted budget adjusts for automatic changes in tax revenues, the increase in the cyclically adjusted budget surplus reveals that government either decreased its spending (G) or increased tax rates such that tax revenues (T) increased. These changes in G and T are precisely the discretionary actions that we have identified as elements of a *contractionary* fiscal policy.

Recent and Projected U.S. Fiscal Policy

LO13.4 Summarize recent U.S. fiscal policy and the projections for U.S. fiscal policy over the next few years.

Table 13.1 lists the actual federal budget deficits and surpluses (column 2) and the cyclically adjusted deficits and surpluses (column 3), as percentages of actual GDP and potential GDP, respectively, between 2000 and 2012. Observe that the cyclically adjusted deficits are generally smaller than the actual deficits. This is because the actual deficits include cyclical deficits, whereas the cyclically adjusted deficits eliminate them. Only cyclically adjusted surpluses and deficits as percentages of potential GDP (column 3) provide the information needed to assess discretionary fiscal policy and determine whether it is expansionary, contractionary, or neutral.

TABLE 13.1 Federal Deficits (−) and Surpluses (+) as Percentages of GDP, 2000–2012

(1) Year	(2) Actual Deficit − or Surplus +	(3) Cyclically adjusted Deficit − or Surplus +*
2000	+2.4	+1.2
2001	+1.3	+0.6
2002	−1.5	−1.2
2003	−3.4	−2.7
2004	−3.5	−3.2
2005	−2.6	−2.6
2006	−1.9	−2.2
2007	−1.2	−1.3
2008	−3.2	−2.9
2009	−10.1	−7.1
2010	−9.0	−5.7
2011	−8.7	−5.6
2012	−7.0	−4.3

*As a percentage of potential GDP.

Source: Congressional Budget Office, **www.cbo.gov**.

Fiscal Policy from 2000 to 2007

Take a look at the data for 2000, for example, which shows that fiscal policy was contractionary that year. Note that the actual budget surplus was 2.4 percent of GDP in 2000 and the cyclically adjusted budget surplus was 1.2 percent of potential GDP. Because the economy was fully employed and corporate profits were strong, tax revenues poured into the federal government and exceeded government expenditures.

But not all was well in 2000. Specifically, the so-called dot-com stock market bubble burst that year, and the U.S. economy noticeably slowed over the latter half of the year. In March 2001 the economy slid into a recession. Congress and the Bush administration responded by cutting taxes by $44 billion in 2001 and scheduling an additional $52 billion of cuts for 2002. These stimulus policies helped boost the economy and offset the recession as well as cushion the economic blow delivered by the September 11, 2001, terrorist attacks. In March 2002 Congress passed further tax cuts totaling $122 billion over two years and extended unemployment benefits.

As Table 13.1 reveals, the cyclically adjusted budget moved from a surplus of 1.2 percent of potential GDP in 2000 to a deficit of −1.2 percent two years later in 2002. Fiscal policy had definitely turned expansionary. Nevertheless, the economy remained sluggish through 2002 and into 2003. In June 2003 Congress again cut taxes, this time by a much larger $350 billion over several years. Specifically, the tax legislation accelerated the reduction of marginal tax rates already scheduled for future years and slashed tax rates on income from dividends and capital gains. It also increased tax breaks for families and small businesses. Note from the table that this tax package increased the cyclically adjusted budget deficit as a percentage of potential GDP to −2.7 percent in 2003. The economy strengthened and both real output and employment grew between 2003 and 2007. By 2007 full employment had been restored, although a −1.3 percent cyclically adjusted budget deficit still remained.

Fiscal Policy during and after the Great Recession

As pointed out in previous chapters, major economic trouble began in 2007. In the summer of 2007, a crisis in the market for mortgage loans flared up. Later in 2007 that crisis spread rapidly to other financial markets, threatened the survival of several major U.S. financial institutions, and severely disrupted the entire financial system. As credit markets began to freeze, general pessimism spread beyond the financial markets to the overall economy. Businesses and households retrenched on their borrowing and spending, and in December 2007 the economy entered a recession.

Over the following two years, it became known as the Great Recession—one of the steepest and longest economic downturns since the 1930s.

In 2008 Congress acted rapidly to pass an economic stimulus package. This law provided a total of $152 billion in stimulus, with some of it coming as tax breaks for businesses, but most of it delivered as checks of up to $600 each to taxpayers, veterans, and Social Security recipients.

As a percentage of GDP, the *actual* federal budget deficit jumped from −1.2 percent in 2007 to −3.2 percent in 2008. This increase resulted from an automatic drop-off of tax revenues during the recession, along with the tax rebates (fiscal stimulus checks) paid out in 2008. As shown in Table 13.1, the *cyclically adjusted* budget deficit rose from −1.3 percent of potential GDP in 2007 to −2.9 percent in 2008. This increase in the cyclically adjusted budget reveals that fiscal policy in 2008 was expansionary.

The government hoped that those receiving checks would spend the money and thus boost consumption and aggregate demand. But households instead saved substantial parts of the money from the checks or used some of the money to pay down credit card loans. Although this stimulus plan boosted output somewhat in mid-2008, it was neither as expansionary nor long-lasting as policymakers had hoped. The continuing forces of the Great Recession simply overwhelmed the policy.

With the economy continuing its precipitous slide, the Obama administration and Congress enacted the American Recovery and Reinvestment Act of 2009. This gigantic $787 billion program—coming on top of a $700 billion rescue package for financial institutions—consisted of low- and middle-income tax rebates, plus large increases in expenditures on infrastructure, education, and health care. The idea was to flood the economy with additional spending to try to boost aggregate demand and get people back to work.

The tax cuts in the package were aimed at lower- and middle-income individuals and households, who were thought to be more likely than high-income people to spend (rather than save) the extra income from the tax rebates. Rather than sending out lump-sum stimulus checks as in 2008, the new tax rebates showed up as small increases in workers' monthly payroll checks. With smaller amounts per month rather than a single large check, the government hoped that people would spend the bulk of their enhanced income—rather than save it as they had done with the one-time-only, lump-sum checks received in 2008. The second part of the fiscal policy (60 percent of the funding) consisted of increases in government expenditures on a wide assortment of programs, including transportation, education, and aid to state governments. The highly stimulative fiscal

policy for 2009 is fully reflected in column 3 of Table 13.1. The cyclically adjusted budget deficit rose dramatically from −2.9 percent of potential GDP in 2008 to a very high −7.1 percent of potential GDP in 2009.

The recession officially ended during the summer of 2009, but the economy did not rebound vigorously. Unemployment remained elevated and tax collections were low due to a stagnant economy. As a result, policymakers decided to continue with large amounts of fiscal stimulus. Annual actual (not cyclically adjusted) budget deficits amounted to −9.0, −8.7, and −7.0 percent of GDP, respectively, in years 2010, 2011, and 2012. The cyclically adjusted budget deficits for those years were, respectively, −5.7, −5.6, and −4.3 percent of potential GDP. Thus, while the intensity of fiscal stimulus was gradually diminishing, it remained very high by historical standards. The recession had been exceptionally strong, and so was the ongoing fiscal response.

Other nations also experienced recessions and also responded with expansionary fiscal policies. Global Perspective 13.1 shows the magnitudes of the cyclically

GLOBAL PERSPECTIVE 13.1

Cyclically Adjusted Budget Deficits or Surpluses as a Percentage of Potential GDP, Selected Nations

Because of the global recession, in 2009 all but a few of the world's major nations had cyclically adjusted budget deficits. These deficits varied as percentages of potential GDP, but they each reflected some degree of expansionary fiscal policy.

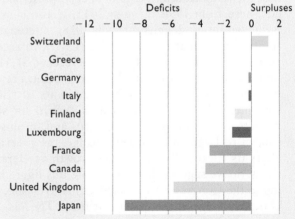

Cyclically Adjusted Budget Surplus or Deficit as a Percentage of Potential GDP, 2009

Source: OECD Economic Outlook, **http://www.oecd.org/eco/ economicoutlook.htm.**

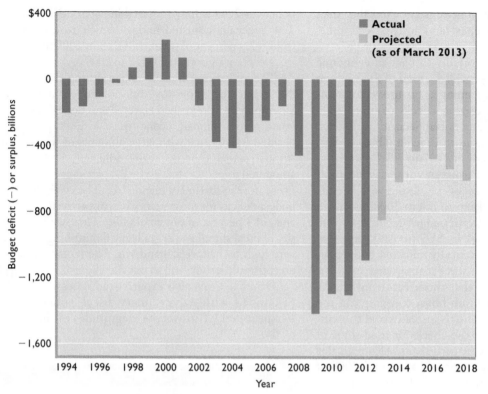

FIGURE 13.5 Federal budget deficits and surpluses, actual and projected, fiscal years 1994–2018 (in billions of nominal dollars). The annual budget deficits of 1994 through 1997 gave way to budget surpluses from 1998 through 2001. Deficits reappeared in 2002 and declined through 2007. They greatly ballooned in recessionary years 2008 and 2009 and are projected to remain high for many years to come.

Source: Congressional Budget Office, **www.cbo.gov**.

adjusted surpluses and deficits of a number of countries in 2009.

Past and Projected Budget Deficits and Surpluses

Figure 13.5 shows the absolute magnitudes of actual (not cyclically adjusted) U.S. budget surpluses and deficits, here from 1994 through 2012. It also shows the projected future deficits through 2018, as estimated by the Congressional Budget Office (CBO). In recession year 2009, the federal budget deficit reached $1,413 billion, mainly but not totally due to reduced tax revenues from lower income and record amounts of stimulus spending. The CBO projects high deficits for several years to come. But projected deficits and surpluses are subject to large and frequent changes, as government alters its fiscal policy and GDP growth accelerates or slows. So we suggest that you update this figure by going to the Congressional Budget Office Web site, **www. cbo.gov**, and find the document titled *The Budget and Economic Outlook*. Near the start of that document, you should find Summary Table 1. The numbers are in the row labeled "Deficit (−) or Surplus."

Problems, Criticisms, and Complications of Implementing Fiscal Policy

LO13.5 Discuss the problems that governments may encounter in enacting and applying fiscal policy.
Economists recognize that governments may encounter a number of significant problems in enacting and applying fiscal policy.

Problems of Timing

Several problems of timing may arise in connection with fiscal policy:

- *Recognition lag* The recognition lag is the time between the beginning of recession or inflation and the certain awareness that it is actually happening. This lag arises because the economy does not move smoothly through the business cycle. Even during good times, the economy has slow months interspersed with months of rapid growth and expansion. This makes recognizing a recession difficult since several slow months will have to happen in succession before people can conclude with any confidence that the good times are over and a recession has begun.

The same is true with inflation. Even periods of moderate inflation have months of high inflation—so that several high-inflation months must come in sequence before people can confidently conclude that inflation has moved to a higher level.

Attempts to reduce the length of the recognition lag by trying to predict the future course of the economy also have proven to be highly difficult, at best. As a result, the economy is often 4 to 6 months into a recession or inflation before the situation is clearly discernible in the relevant statistics. Due to this recognition lag, the economic downslide or the inflation may become more serious than it would have if the situation had been identified and acted on sooner.

- *Administrative lag* The wheels of democratic government turn slowly. There will typically be a significant lag between the time the need for fiscal action is recognized and the time action is taken. Following the terrorist attacks of September 11, 2001, the U.S. Congress was stalemated for 5 months before passing a compromise economic stimulus law in March 2002. (In contrast, the Federal Reserve began lowering interest rates the week after the attacks.)

- *Operational lag* A lag also occurs between the time fiscal action is taken and the time that action affects output, employment, or the price level. Although changes in tax rates can be put into effect relatively quickly once new laws are passed, government spending on public works—new dams, interstate highways, and so on—requires long planning periods and even longer periods of construction. Such spending is of questionable use in offsetting short (for example, 6- to 12-month) periods of recession. Consequently, discretionary fiscal policy has increasingly relied on tax changes rather than on changes in spending as its main tool.

Political Considerations

Fiscal policy is conducted in a political arena. That reality not only may slow the enactment of fiscal policy but also may create the potential for political considerations swamping economic considerations in its formulation. It is a human trait to rationalize actions and policies that are in one's self-interest. Politicians are very human—they want to get reelected. A strong economy at election time will certainly help them. So they may favor large tax cuts under the guise of expansionary fiscal policy even though

that policy is economically inappropriate. Similarly, they may rationalize increased government spending on popular items such as farm subsidies, health care, highways, education, and homeland security.

At the extreme, elected officials and political parties might collectively "hijack" fiscal policy for political purposes, cause inappropriate changes in aggregate demand, and thereby cause (rather than avert) economic fluctuations. For instance, before an election, they may try to stimulate the economy to improve their reelection hopes. And then after the election, they may try to use contractionary fiscal policy to dampen the excessive aggregate demand that they caused with their preelection stimulus. In short, elected officials may cause so-called **political business cycles**—swings in overall economic activity and real GDP resulting from election-motivated fiscal policy, rather than from inherent instability in the private sector. Political business cycles are difficult to document and prove, but there is little doubt that political considerations weigh heavily in the formulation of fiscal policy. The question is how often those political considerations run counter to "sound economics."

Future Policy Reversals

Fiscal policy may fail to achieve its intended objectives if households expect future reversals of policy. Consider a tax cut, for example. If taxpayers believe the tax reduction is temporary, they may save a large portion of their tax cut, reasoning that rates will return to their previous level in the future. They save more now so that they will be able to draw on this extra savings to maintain their future consumption levels if taxes do indeed rise again in the future. So a tax reduction thought to be temporary may not increase present consumption spending and aggregate demand by as much as our simple model (Figure 13.1) suggests.

The opposite may be true for a tax increase. If taxpayers think it is temporary, they may reduce their saving to pay the tax while maintaining their present consumption. They may reason they can restore their saving when the tax rate again falls. So the tax increase may not reduce current consumption and aggregate demand by as much as policymakers intended.

To the extent that this so-called *consumption smoothing* occurs over time, fiscal policy will lose some of its strength. The lesson is that tax-rate changes that households view as permanent are more likely to alter consumption and aggregate demand than tax changes they view as temporary.

Offsetting State and Local Finance

The fiscal policies of state and local governments are frequently *pro-cyclical*, meaning that they worsen rather than correct recession or inflation. Unlike the federal government, most state and local governments face constitutional or other legal requirements to balance their budgets. Like households and private businesses, state and local governments increase their expenditures during prosperity and cut them during recession.

During the Great Depression of the 1930s, most of the increase in federal spending was offset by decreases in state and local spending. During and immediately following the recession of 2001, many state and local governments had to offset lower tax revenues resulting from the reduced personal income and spending of their citizens. They offset the decline in revenues by raising tax rates, imposing new taxes, and reducing spending.

In view of these past experiences, the $787 billion fiscal package of 2009 made a special effort to reduce this problem by giving substantial aid dollars to state governments. Because of the sizable federal aid, the states did not have to increase taxes and reduce expenditure by as much as otherwise. So their collective fiscal actions did not fight as much against the increase in aggregate demand that the federal government wanted to achieve with its tax cuts and expenditure increases.

Crowding-Out Effect

Another potential flaw of fiscal policy is the so-called **crowding-out effect:** An expansionary fiscal policy (deficit spending) may increase the interest rate and reduce investment spending, thereby weakening or canceling the stimulus of the expansionary policy. The rising interest rate might also potentially crowd out interest-sensitive consumption spending (such as purchasing automobiles on credit). But since investment is the most volatile component of GDP, the crowding-out effect focuses its attention on investment and whether the stimulus provided by deficit spending may be partly or even fully neutralized by an offsetting reduction in investment spending.

To see the potential problem, realize that whenever the government borrows money (as it must if it is deficit spending), it increases the overall demand for money. If the monetary authorities are holding the money supply constant, this increase in demand will raise the price paid for borrowing money: the interest rate. Because investment spending varies inversely with the interest rate, some investment will be choked off or "crowded out."

ORIGIN OF THE IDEA

O13.2
Crowding out

Economists vary in their opinions about the strength of the crowding-out effect. An important thing to keep in mind is that crowding out is likely to be less of a problem when the economy is in recession because investment demand tends to be weak. Why? Because output purchases slow during recessions and therefore most businesses end up with substantial excess capacity. As a result, they do not have much incentive to add new machinery or build new factories. After all, why should they add capacity when some of the capacity they already have is lying idle?

With investment demand weak during a recession, the crowding-out effect is likely to be very small. Simply put, there is not much investment for the government to crowd out. Even if deficit spending does increase the interest rate, the effect on investment may be fully offset by the improved investment prospects that businesses expect from the fiscal stimulus.

By contrast, when the economy is operating at or near full capacity, investment demand is likely to be quite strong so that crowding out will probably be a much more serious problem. When the economy is booming, factories will be running at or near full capacity and firms will have high investment demand for two reasons. First, equipment running at full capacity wears out fast, so firms will be investing substantial amounts just to replace machinery and equipment that wears out and depreciates. Second, the economy is likely to be growing overall so that firms will be heavily investing to *add* to their production capacity to take advantage of the greater anticipated demand for their outputs.

Current Thinking on Fiscal Policy

Where do these complications leave us as to the advisability and effectiveness of discretionary fiscal policy? In view of the complications and uncertain outcomes of fiscal policy, some economists argue that it is better not to engage in it at all. Those holding that view point to the superiority of monetary policy (changes in interest rates engineered by the Federal Reserve) as a stabilizing device or believe that most economic fluctuations tend to be mild and self-correcting.

But most economists believe that fiscal policy remains an important, useful policy lever in the government's macroeconomic toolkit. The current popular view is that fiscal policy can help push the economy in a particular direction but cannot fine-tune it to a precise macroeconomic outcome. Mainstream economists generally agree that monetary policy is the best month-to-month stabilization tool for the U.S. economy. If monetary policy is doing its job, the government should maintain a relatively neutral fiscal policy, with a cyclically adjusted budget deficit or surplus of no more than 2 percent of potential GDP. It should hold major discretionary fiscal policy in reserve to help counter situations where recession threatens to be deep and long lasting, as in 2008 and 2009, or where a substantial reduction in aggregate demand might help the Federal Reserve to quell a major bout of inflation.

Finally, economists agree that any proposed fiscal policy should be evaluated for its potential positive and negative impacts on long-run productivity growth. The short-run policy tools used for conducting active fiscal policy often have long-run impacts. Countercyclical fiscal policy should be shaped to strengthen, or at least not impede, the growth of long-run aggregate supply (shown as a rightward shift of the long-run aggregate supply curve in Figure 12.5). For example, a tax cut might be structured to enhance work effort, strengthen investment, and encourage innovation. Alternatively, an increase in government spending might center on preplanned projects for public capital (highways, mass transit, ports, airports), which are complementary to private investment and thus support long-term economic growth.

QUICK REVIEW 13.2

- Automatic changes in net taxes (taxes minus transfers) add a degree of built-in stability to the economy.
- Cyclical deficits arise from declines in net tax revenues that automatically occur as the economy recedes and incomes and profits fall.
- The cyclically adjusted budget eliminates cyclical effects on net tax revenues; it compares actual levels of government spending to the projected levels of net taxes that would occur if the economy were achieving its full-employment output.
- Time lags, political problems, expectations, and state and local finances complicate fiscal policy.
- The crowding-out effect indicates that an expansionary fiscal policy may increase the interest rate and reduce investment spending.

The U.S. Public Debt

LO13.6 Discuss the size, composition, and consequences of the U.S. public debt.

The U.S. national debt, or **public debt,** is essentially the accumulation of all past federal deficits and surpluses. The deficits have greatly exceeded the surpluses and have emerged mainly from war financing, recessions, and fiscal policy. In 2012 the total public debt was $16.4 trillion—

$11.6 trillion held by the public, excluding the Federal Reserve; and $4.8 trillion held by federal agencies and the Federal Reserve. Between 2007 and 2009, the total public debt expanded by a huge $2.9 trillion. During the Great Recession, federal tax revenues plummeted because incomes and profit fell, and federal expenditures jumped because of huge spending to rescue failing financial institutions and to stimulate the shrinking economy.

Because large annual deficits continued over the next several years, the total public debt grew past $17.0 trillion in late 2013. It had doubled in just seven years, growing from $8.5 trillion in late 2006 to $17.0 trillion in late 2013. You can find the current size of the public debt at the Web site of the Department of Treasury, Bureau of the Public Debt, at **www.treasurydirect.gov/NP/BPDLogin?application=np**. At this site, you will see that the U.S. Treasury defines "the public" to include the Federal Reserve. But because the Federal Reserve is the nation's central bank, economists view it as essentially part of the federal government and not part of the public. Economists typically focus on the part of the debt that is not owned by the federal government and the Federal Reserve.

Ownership

The total public debt of $16.4 trillion represents the total amount of money owed by the federal government to the holders of **U.S. government securities:** financial instruments issued by the federal government to borrow money to finance expenditures that exceed tax revenues. U.S. government securities (loan instruments) are of four types: *Treasury bills* (short-term securities), *Treasury notes* (medium-term securities), *Treasury bonds* (long-term securities), and *U.S. savings bonds* (long-term, nonmarketable bonds).

Figure 13.6 shows that the public, sans the Federal Reserve, held 60 percent of the federal debt in 2012 and that federal government agencies and the Federal Reserve held the remaining 40 percent. The federal agencies hold U.S. government securities as risk-free assets that they can cash in as needed to make latter payments. The Federal Reserve holds these securities to facilitate the "open-market operations" that it uses to control the nation's money supply (Chapter 16). Observe that "the public" in the pie chart consists of individuals here and abroad, state and local governments, and U.S. financial institutions. Foreigners held about 33 percent of the total U.S. public debt in 2012, meaning that most of the U.S. public debt is held internally and not externally. Americans owed 67 percent of the public debt to Americans. Of the $5.3 trillion

FIGURE 13.6 Ownership of the total public debt, 2012. The $16.1 trillion public debt can be divided into the proportion held by the public, excluding the Federal Reserve (60 percent), and the proportion held by federal agencies and the Federal Reserve System (40 percent). Of the total debt, 33 percent is foreign-owned.

Debt held outside the federal government and Federal Reserve (60%)

Debt held by the federal government and Federal Reserve (40%)

Other, including state and local governments

Federal Reserve

U.S. banks and other financial institutions

11%

11%

10%

29%

33%

6%

U.S. government agencies

Foreign ownership

U.S. individuals

Total debt: $16.1 trillion

Source: Economic Report of the President, 2013, **www.gpo.gov/fdsys/browse/ collection.action?collectionCode=ERP**; authors' derivation from Table B-89, September 2012 data. Federal Reserve percentage is from the U.S. Treasury, **www.fms.treas.gov/bulletin**.

of debt held by foreigners, China held 22 percent, Japan held 20 percent, and oil-exporting nations held 5 percent.

Debt and GDP

A simple statement of the absolute size of the debt ignores the fact that the wealth and productive ability of the U.S. economy is also vast. A wealthy, highly productive nation can incur and carry a large public debt much more easily than a poor nation can. A more meaningful measure of the public debt relates it to an economy's GDP. Figure 13.7 shows the yearly relative sizes of the U.S. public debt held outside the Federal Reserve and federal agencies. In 2012 the percentage was 70 percent. Most noticeably, the percentage rose dramatically starting in 2008 because of massive annual budget deficits.

International Comparisons

It is not uncommon for countries to have sizable public debts. As shown in Global Perspective 13.2, the public debt as a percentage of real GDP in the United States is neither particularly high nor low relative to such debt percentages in other advanced industrial nations.

Interest Charges

Many economists conclude that the primary burden of the debt is the annual interest charge accruing on the bonds sold to finance the debt. In 2012 interest on the total public debt was $360 billion. Although this amount is sizable in absolute terms, it was only 2.3 percent of GDP for

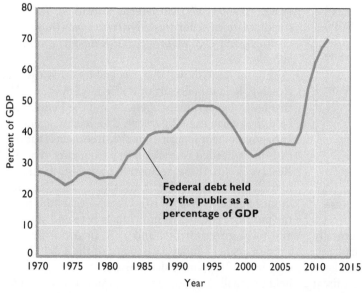

Federal debt held by the public as a percentage of GDP

FIGURE 13.7 Federal debt held by the public, excluding the Federal Reserve, as a percentage of GDP, 1970–2012. As a percentage of GDP, the federal debt held by the public (held outside the Federal Reserve and federal government agencies) increased sharply over the 1980–1995 period and declined significantly between 1995 and 2001. Since 2001, the percentage has gone up again, and jumped abruptly and sharply starting in 2008.

Source: FRED II database, St. Louis Federal Reserve Bank, **research.stlouisfed.org/fred2/**.

GLOBAL PERSPECTIVE 13.2

Publicly Held Debt: International Comparisons

Although the United States has the world's largest public debt, a number of other nations have larger debts as percentages of their GDPs.

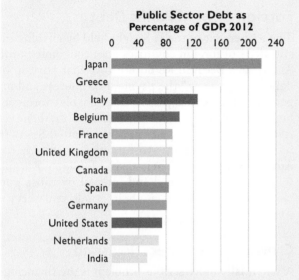

Public Sector Debt as Percentage of GDP, 2012

Japan
Greece
Italy
Belgium
France
United Kingdom
Canada
Spain
Germany
United States
Netherlands
India

Source: CIA World Factbook, **www.cia.gov/library/publications/the-world-factbook/.** These debt calculations encompass federal, state, and local debt, including the debt of government-owned enterprises (not just federal debt as in Figure 13.7) and are 2012 estimates.

2012. So, the federal government had to collect taxes equal to 2.3 percent of GDP to service the total public debt. This percentage was unchanged from 2000 despite the much higher total public debt. That was possible because interest rates were being kept extremely low by the Federal Reserve in order to help stimulate the economy in the wake of the Great Recession (Chapter 16).

False Concerns

You may wonder if the large public debt might bankrupt the United States or at least place a tremendous burden on your children and grandchildren. Fortunately, these are largely false concerns. People were wondering the same things 50 years ago!

Bankruptcy

The large U.S. public debt does not threaten to bankrupt the federal government, leaving it unable to meet its financial obligations. There are two main reasons: refinancing and taxation.

Refinancing As long as the U.S. public debt is viewed by lenders as manageable and sustainable, the public debt is easily refinanced. As portions of the debt come due on maturing Treasury bills, notes, and bonds each month, the government does not cut expenditures or raise taxes to provide the funds required. Rather, it refinances the debt by selling new bonds and using the proceeds to pay holders of the maturing bonds. The new bonds are in strong demand because lenders can obtain a market-determined interest return with no risk of default by the federal government.

Of course, refinancing could become an issue with a high enough debt-to-GDP ratio. Some countries such as Greece have run into this problem. High and rising ratios in the United States might raise fears that the U.S. government might be unable to pay back loans as they come due. But, with the present U.S. debt-to-GDP ratio and the prospects of long-term economic growth, this is a false concern for the United States.

Taxation The federal government has the constitutional authority to levy and collect taxes. A tax increase is a government option for gaining sufficient revenue to pay interest and principal on the public debt. Financially distressed private households and corporations cannot extract themselves from their financial difficulties by taxing the public. If their incomes or sales revenues fall short of their expenses, they can indeed go bankrupt. But the federal government does have the option to impose new taxes or increase existing tax rates if necessary to finance its debt. Such tax hikes may be politically unpopular and may weaken incentives to work and invest, but they *are* a means of raising funds to finance the debt.

Burdening Future Generations

In 2012 public debt per capita was $52,396. Was each child born in 2012 handed a $52,396 bill from the federal government? Not really. The public debt does not impose as much of a burden on future generations as commonly thought.

The United States owes a substantial portion of the public debt to itself. U.S. citizens and institutions (banks, businesses, insurance companies, governmental agencies, and trust funds) own about 67 percent of the U.S. government securities. Although that part of the public debt is a liability to Americans (as taxpayers), it is simultaneously an asset to Americans (as holders of Treasury bills, Treasury notes, Treasury bonds, and U.S. savings bonds).

To eliminate the American-owned part of the public debt would require a gigantic transfer payment from Americans to Americans. Taxpayers would pay higher taxes, and holders of the debt would receive an equal amount for their U.S. government securities. Purchasing power in the

United States would not change. Only the repayment of the 33 percent of the public debt owned by foreigners would negatively impact U.S. purchasing power.

The public debt increased sharply during the Second World War. But the decision to finance military purchases through the sale of government bonds did not shift the economic burden of the war to future generations. The economic cost of the Second World War consisted of the civilian goods society had to forgo in shifting scarce resources to war goods production (recall production possibilities analysis). Regardless of whether society financed this reallocation through higher taxes or through borrowing, the real economic burden of the war would have been the same. That burden was borne almost entirely by those who lived during the war. They were the ones who did without a multitude of consumer goods to enable the United States to arm itself and its allies.

The next generation inherited the debt from the war but also an equal amount of government bonds that would pay them cash in future years. It also inherited the enormous benefits from the victory—namely, preserved political and economic systems at home and the "export" of those systems to Germany, Italy, and Japan. Those outcomes enhanced postwar U.S. economic growth and helped raise the standard of living of future generations of Americans.

Substantive Issues

Although the preceding issues relating to the public debt are false concerns, a number of substantive issues are not. Economists, however, attach varying degrees of importance to them.

Income Distribution

The distribution of ownership of government securities is highly uneven. Some people own much more than the $52,396-per-person portion of government securities; other people own less or none at all. In general, the ownership of the public debt is concentrated among wealthier groups, who own a large percentage of all stocks and bonds. Because the overall federal tax system is only slightly progressive, payment of interest on the public debt mildly increases income inequality. Income is transferred from people who, on average, have lower incomes to the higher-income bondholders. If greater income equality is one of society's goals, then this redistribution is undesirable.

Incentives

The current public debt necessitates annual interest payments of $360 billion. With no increase in the size of the debt, that interest charge must be paid out of tax revenues. Higher taxes may dampen incentives to bear risk, to innovate, to invest, and to work. So, in this indirect way, a large public debt may impair economic growth and therefore impose a burden of reduced output (and income) on future generations.

Foreign-Owned Public Debt

The 33 percent of the U.S. debt held by citizens and institutions of foreign countries *is* an economic burden to Americans. Because we do not owe that portion of the debt "to ourselves," the payment of interest and principal on this **external public debt** enables foreigners to buy some of our output. In return for the benefits derived from the borrowed funds, the United States transfers goods and services to foreign lenders. Of course, Americans also own debt issued by foreign governments, so payment of principal and interest by those governments transfers some of their goods and services to Americans.

Crowding-Out Effect Revisited

A potentially more serious problem is the financing (and continual refinancing) of the large public debt, which can transfer a real economic burden to future generations by passing on to them a smaller stock of capital goods. This possibility involves the previously discussed crowding-out effect: the idea that public borrowing drives up real interest rates, which reduces private investment spending. If public borrowing only happened during recessions, crowding out would not likely be much of a problem. Because private investment demand tends to be weak during recessions, any increase in interest rates caused by public borrowing will at most cause a small reduction in investment spending.

In contrast, the need to continuously finance a large public debt may be more troublesome. At times, that financing requires borrowing large amounts of money when the economy is near or at its full-employment output. Because this usually is when private demand is strong, any increase in interest rates caused by the borrowing necessary to refinance the debt may result in a substantial decline in investment spending. If the amount of current investment crowded out is extensive, future generations will inherit an economy with a smaller production capacity and, other things equal, a lower standard of living.

A Graphical Look at Crowding Out We know from Chapter 10 that the amount of investment spending is

FIGURE 13.8 The investment demand curve and the crowding-out effect. If the investment demand curve (ID_1) is fixed, the increase in the interest rate from 6 percent to 10 percent caused by financing a large public debt will move the economy from *a* to *b*, crowding out $10 billion of private investment and decreasing the size of the capital stock inherited by future generations. However, if the public goods enabled by the debt improve the investment prospects of businesses, the private investment demand curve will shift rightward, as from ID_1 to ID_2. That shift may offset the crowding-out effect wholly or in part. In this case, it moves the economy from *a* to *c*.

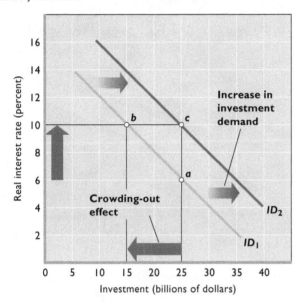

inversely related to the real interest rate. When graphed, that relationship is shown as a downsloping investment demand curve, such as either ID_1 or ID_2 in Figure 13.8. Let's first consider curve ID_1. (Ignore curve ID_2 for now.) Suppose that government borrowing increases the real interest rate from 6 percent to 10 percent. Investment spending will then fall from $25 billion to $15 billion, as shown by the economy's move from *a* to *b*. That is, the financing of the debt will compete with the financing of private investment projects and crowd out $10 billion of private investment. So the stock of private capital handed down to future generations will be $10 billion less than it would have been without the need to finance the public debt.

Public Investments and Public-Private Complementarities But even with crowding out, two factors could partly or fully offset the net economic burden shifted to future generations. First, just as private expenditures may involve either consumption or investment, so it is with public goods. Part of the government spending enabled by the public debt is for public investment outlays (for example, highways, mass transit systems, and electric power facilities) and "human capital" (for example, investments in education, job training, and health). Like private expenditures on machinery and equipment, those **public investments** increase the economy's future production capacity. Because of the financing through debt, the stock of public capital passed on to future generations may be higher than otherwise. That greater stock of public capital may offset the diminished stock of private capital resulting from the crowding-out effect, leaving overall production capacity unimpaired.

So-called public-private complementarities are a second factor that could reduce the crowding-out effect. Some public and private investments are complementary. Thus, the public investment financed through debt could spur some private-sector investment by increasing its expected rate of return. For example, a federal building in a city may encourage private investment in the form of nearby office buildings, shops, and restaurants. Through its complementary effect, the spending on public capital may shift the private investment demand curve to the right, as from ID_1 to ID_2 in Figure 13.8. Even though the government borrowing boosts the interest rate from 6 percent to 10 percent, total private investment need not fall. In the case shown as the move from *a* to *c* in Figure 13.8, it remains at $25 billion. Of course, the increase in investment demand might be smaller than that shown. If it were smaller, the crowding-out effect would not be fully offset. But the point is that an increase in investment demand may counter the decline in investment that would otherwise result from the higher interest rate.

QUICK REVIEW 13.3

- The U.S. public debt—$16.4 trillion in 2012—is essentially the total accumulation of all past federal budget deficits and surpluses; about 33 percent of the U.S. public debt is held by foreigners.
- The U.S. public debt held by the public (excluding the Federal Reserve) was 70 percent of GDP in 2012, up from 30 percent in 2000.
- The federal government is in no danger of going bankrupt because it needs only to refinance (not retire) the public debt and it can raise revenues, if needed, through higher taxes.
- The borrowing and interest payments associated with the public debt may (a) increase income inequality; (b) require higher taxes, which may dampen incentives; and (c) impede the growth of the nation's stock of capital through crowding out of private investment.

The Social Security and Medicare Shortfalls

Social Security and Medicare Face Gigantic Future Funding Shortfalls. Metaphorically Speaking, Some Economists See These Programs as Financial and Political Time Bombs.

The American population, on average, is getting decidedly older. The percentage of the population age 62 or older will rise substantially over the next several decades, with the greatest increases for people age 75 and above. In the future, more people will be receiving Social Security benefits (income during retirement) and Medicare (medical care during retirement) for longer periods. Each person's benefits will be paid for by fewer workers. The number of workers per Social Security and Medicare beneficiary was roughly 5:1 in 1960. Today it is 3:1, and by 2040 it will be only 2:1.

The combined cost of the Social Security and Medicare programs was 8.5 percent of GDP in 2011, and that percentage is projected to grow to 12 percent of GDP in 2035 and 13 percent of GDP in 2086.*

The Social Security Shortfall Social Security is the major public retirement program in the United States. The program costs $736 billion annually and is financed by a 12.4 percent tax on earnings up to a set level of earnings ($113,700 in 2013). Half the tax (6.2 percent) is paid by the worker; the other half by the employer. Social Security is largely an annual "pay-as-you-go" plan, meaning that most of the current revenues from the Social Security tax are paid to current Social Security retirees. Through the start of 2009, Social Security revenues exceeded Social Security payouts in anticipation of the large benefits promised to the baby boomers when they retire. That excess inflow was used

to buy U.S. Treasury securities that were credited to a government account called the Social Security Trust Fund. But the combined accumulation of money in the trust fund through 2009 plus the projected future revenues from the payroll tax in later years was expected to be greatly inadequate for paying the promised retirement benefits to all future retirees.

This underfunding of future retirement promises was brought into sharper focus in the latter half of 2009 when, for the first time, Social Security revenues fell below Social Security retirement payouts and the system started shifting money from the trust fund to make up the difference. The trust fund is expected to be exhausted in 2033. For each year thereafter, annual tax revenues will cover only 75 percent of the promised benefits.

---

*Social Security and Medicare Board of Trustees, "Status of the Social Security and Medicare Programs: A Summary of the 2012 Annual Reports," **www.ssa.gov**. This publication is also the source of most of the statistical information that follows.

SUMMARY

LO13.1 Identify and explain the purposes, tools, and limitations of fiscal policy.

Fiscal policy consists of deliberate changes in government spending, taxes, or some combination of both to promote full employment, price-level stability, and economic growth. Fiscal policy

requires increases in government spending, decreases in taxes, or both—a budget deficit—to increase aggregate demand and push an economy from a recession. Decreases in government spending, increases in taxes, or both—a budget surplus—are appropriate fiscal policy for decreasing aggregate demand to try to slow or halt demand-pull inflation.

The Medicare Shortfall The Medicare program is the U.S. health care program for people age 65 and older in the United States. The program costs $558 billion per year and has been growing at about 9 percent annually. Like Social Security, it also is a pay-as-you-go plan, meaning that current medical benefits for people age 65 or older are being funded by current tax revenues from the 2.9 percent Medicare tax on earnings and the 3.8 percent investment surtax on wealthier investors that was instituted in 2013 as part of Obamacare. Like the Social Security tax, half the Medicare earnings tax is paid by the employer (1.45 percent) and half the by the employee. But the 2.9 percent Medicare tax is applied to all earnings.

The financial status of Medicare is much worse than that of Social Security. To begin with, the Medicare Trust Fund will be depleted in 2024, 9 years before the Social Security Trust Fund is expected to be depleted. Then, in subsequent years, the percentage of scheduled Medicare benefits covered by the Medicare tax will decline from 97 percent in 2025 to 72 percent in 2035 and 69 percent in 2080.

The Unpleasant Options To restore long-run balance to Social Security and Medicare, the federal government must either reduce benefits or increase revenues. It's as simple—and as complicated—as that! The Social Security Administration concludes that bringing projected Social Security revenues and payments into balance over the next 75 years would require a 16 percent permanent reduction in Social Security benefits, a 13 percent permanent increase in tax revenues, or some combination of the two. To bring projected Medicare revenues and expenses into long-run balance would require an increase in the Medicare payroll tax by 122 percent, a 51 percent reduction of Medicare payments from their projected levels, or some combination of each.

All the general options for closing all or part of the Social Security and Medicare gaps involve difficult economic trade-offs and dangerous political risks because one group or another will strongly oppose them. Here are just a few examples:

- Increasing the retirement age for collecting Social Security or Medicare benefits will upset preretirement workers who have been paying into the system and will receive their benefits later than they expected.

- Subjecting a larger portion of total earnings to the Social Security tax would constitute a gigantic tax increase on the earnings of the country's highest trained and educated individuals. This might reduce the incentive of younger people to obtain education and advance in their careers.

- Disqualifying wealthy individuals from receiving Social Security and Medicare benefits would tilt the programs toward welfare and redistribution, rather than insurance programs. This would undermine the broad existing political support for the programs.

- Redirecting legal immigration toward high-skilled, high-earning entrants and away from low-skilled, low-earning immigrants to raise Social Security and Medicare revenues would also raise the ire of some native-born high-skilled workers and the proponents of immigration based on family reunification.

- Placing the payroll tax revenues into accounts that individuals, not the government, would own, maintain, and bequeath would transform the Social Security and Medicare programs from guaranteed "defined benefit plans" into much riskier "defined contribution plans." The extreme short-run volatility of the stock market might leave some unlucky people destitute in old age.

The problem is huge and will not go away. One recent attempt to add up the underfunding of all the promised Social Security and Medicare benefits finds that the total underfunding greatly exceeds the combined current wealth (net worth) of everyone in the United States today.[†] Even if this estimate is somewhat extreme, the fact remains: The federal government and American people eventually will have to face up to the over-promising-underfunding problem and find ways to resolve it.

[†]Bruce Bartlett, "The 81% Tax Increase," Forbes.com, August 8, 2009, **www.forbes.com**.

LO13.2 Explain the role of built-in stabilizers in moderating business cycles.

Built-in stability arises from net tax revenues, which vary directly with the level of GDP. During recession, the federal budget automatically moves toward a stabilizing deficit; during expansion, the budget automatically moves toward an anti-inflationary surplus. Built-in stability lessens, but does not fully correct, undesired changes in real GDP.

LO13.3 Describe how the cyclically adjusted budget reveals the status of U.S. fiscal policy.

Actual federal budget deficits can go up or down because of changes in GDP, changes in fiscal policy, or both. Deficits caused by changes in GDP are called cyclical deficits. The cyclically adjusted budget removes cyclical deficits from the budget and therefore measures the budget deficit or surplus that would occur if the economy operated at its full-employment output throughout the year. Changes in the cyclical-budget deficit or surplus provide meaningful information as to whether the government's fiscal policy is expansionary, neutral, or contractionary. Changes in the actual budget deficit or surplus do not, since such deficits or surpluses can include cyclical deficits or surpluses.

LO13.4 Summarize recent U.S. fiscal policy and the projections for U.S. fiscal policy over the next few years.

In 2001 the Bush administration and Congress chose to reduce marginal tax rates and phase out the federal estate tax. A recession occurred in 2001, and federal spending for the war on terrorism rocketed. The federal budget swung from a surplus of $128 billion in 2001 to a deficit of $158 billion in 2002. In 2003 the Bush administration and Congress accelerated the tax reductions scheduled under the 2001 tax law and cut tax rates on capital gains and dividends. The purposes were to stimulate a sluggish economy. By 2007 the economy had reached its full employment level of output.

The federal government responded to the deep recession of 2007–2009 by implementing highly expansionary fiscal policy. In 2008 the federal government passed a tax rebate program that sent $600 checks to qualified individuals. Later that year, it created a $700 billion emergency fund to keep key financial institutions from failing. These and other programs increased the cyclically adjusted budget deficit from −1.3 percent of potential GDP in 2007 to −2.9 percent in 2008. When the economy continued to plunge, the Obama administration and Congress enacted a massive $787 billion stimulus program to be implemented over 2½ years. The cyclically adjusted budget deficit shot up from −2.9 percent of potential GDP in 2008 to −7.1 percent in 2009.

LO13.5 Discuss the problems that governments may encounter in enacting and applying fiscal policy.

Certain problems complicate the enactment and implementation of fiscal policy. They include (a) timing problems associated with recognition, administrative, and operational lags; (b) the potential for misuse of fiscal policy for political rather than economic purposes; (c) the fact that state and local finances tend to be procyclical; (d) potential ineffectiveness if households expect future policy reversals; and (e) the possibility of fiscal policy crowding out private investment.

Most economists believe that fiscal policy can help move the economy in a desired direction but cannot reliably be used to fine-tune the economy to a position of price stability and full employment. Nevertheless, fiscal policy is a valuable backup tool for aiding monetary policy in fighting significant recession or inflation.

LO13.6 Discuss the size, composition, and consequences of the U.S. public debt.

The public debt is the total accumulation of all past federal government deficits and surpluses and consists of Treasury bills, Treasury notes, Treasury bonds, and U.S. savings bonds. In 2012 the U.S. public debt was $16.4 trillion, or $52,396 per person. The public (which here includes banks and state and local governments) holds 60 percent of that federal debt; the Federal Reserve and federal agencies hold the other 40 percent. Foreigners hold 33 percent of the federal debt. Interest payments as a percentage of GDP were about 2.3 percent in 2012. Because of large deficits during the Great Recession and in subsequent years, the total U.S. public debt passed $17.0 trillion in 2013. It had doubled in seven years.

The concern that a large public debt may bankrupt the U.S. government is generally a false worry because (a) the debt needs only to be refinanced rather than refunded and (b) the federal government has the power to increase taxes to make interest payments on the debt.

In general, the public debt is not a vehicle for shifting economic burdens to future generations. Americans inherit not only most of the public debt (a liability) but also most of the U.S. government securities (an asset) that finance the debt.

More substantive problems associated with public debt include the following: (a) Payment of interest on the debt may increase income inequality. (b) Interest payments on the debt require higher taxes, which may impair incentives. (c) Paying interest or principal on the portion of the debt held by foreigners means a transfer of real output abroad. (d) Government borrowing to refinance or pay interest on the debt may increase interest rates and crowd out private investment spending, leaving future generations with a smaller stock of capital than they would have had otherwise.

The increase in investment in public capital that may result from debt financing may partly or wholly offset the crowding-out effect of the public debt on private investment. Also, the added public investment may stimulate private investment, where the two are complements.

TERMS AND CONCEPTS

fiscal policy	built-in stabilizer	political business cycle
Council of Economic Advisers (CEA)	progressive tax system	crowding-out effect
expansionary fiscal policy	proportional tax system	public debt
budget deficit	regressive tax system	U.S. government securities
contractionary fiscal policy	cyclically adjusted budget	external public debt
budget surplus	cyclical deficit	public investments

The following and additional problems can be found in **connect** | ECONOMICS

DISCUSSION QUESTIONS

1. What is the role of the Council of Economic Advisers (CEA) as it relates to fiscal policy? Use an Internet search to find the names and university affiliations of the present members of the CEA. **LO13.1**

2. What are government's fiscal policy options for ending severe demand-pull inflation? Which of these fiscal options do you think might be favored by a person who wants to preserve the size of government? A person who thinks the public sector is too large? How does the "ratchet effect" affect anti-inflationary fiscal policy? **LO13.1**

3. (For students who were assigned Chapter 11) Use the aggregate expenditures model to show how government fiscal policy could eliminate either a recessionary expenditure gap or an inflationary expenditure gap (Figure 11.7). Explain how equal-size increases in G and T could eliminate a recessionary gap and how equal-size decreases in G and T could eliminate an inflationary gap. **LO13.1**

4. Some politicians have suggested that the United States enact a constitutional amendment requiring that the federal government balance its budget annually. Explain why such an amendment, if strictly enforced, would force the government to enact a contractionary fiscal policy whenever the economy experienced a severe recession. **LO13.1**

5. Explain how built-in (or automatic) stabilizers work. What are the differences between proportional, progressive, and regressive tax systems as they relate to an economy's built-in stability? **LO13.2**

6. Define the cyclically adjusted budget, explain its significance, and state why it may differ from the actual budget. Suppose the full-employment, noninflationary level of real output is GDP_3 (not GDP_2) in the economy depicted in Figure 13.3. If the economy is operating at GDP_2, instead of GDP_3, what is the status of its cyclically adjusted budget? The status of its current fiscal policy? What change in fiscal policy would you recommend? How would you accomplish that in terms of the G and T lines in the figure? **LO13.3**

7. Briefly state and evaluate the problem of time lags in enacting and applying fiscal policy. Explain the idea of a political business cycle. How might expectations of a near-term policy reversal weaken fiscal policy based on changes in tax rates? What is the crowding-out effect, and why might it be relevant to fiscal policy? In view of your answers, explain

the following statement: "Although fiscal policy clearly is useful in combating the extremes of severe recession and demand-pull inflation, it is impossible to use fiscal policy to fine-tune the economy to the full-employment, noninflationary level of real GDP and keep the economy there indefinitely." **LO13.5**

8. How do economists distinguish between the absolute and relative sizes of the public debt? Why is the distinction important? Distinguish between refinancing the debt and retiring the debt. How does an internally held public debt differ from an externally held public debt? Contrast the effects of retiring an internally held debt and retiring an externally held debt. **LO13.6**

9. True or false? If false, explain why. **LO13.6**
   a. The total public debt is more relevant to an economy than the public debt as a percentage of GDP.
   b. An internally held public debt is like a debt of the left hand owed to the right hand.
   c. The Federal Reserve and federal government agencies hold more than three-fourths of the public debt.
   d. The portion of the U.S. debt held by the public (and not by government entities) was larger as a percentage of GDP in 2012 than it was in 2000.
   e. As a percentage of GDP, the total U.S. public debt is the highest such debt among the world's advanced industrial nations.

10. Why might economists be quite concerned if the annual interest payments on the U.S. public debt sharply increased as a percentage of GDP? **LO13.6**

11. Trace the cause-and-effect chain through which financing and refinancing of the public debt might affect real interest rates, private investment, the stock of capital, and economic growth. How might investment in public capital and complementarities between public capital and private capital alter the outcome of the cause-effect chain? **LO13.6**

12. **LAST WORD** What do economists mean when they say Social Security and Medicare are "pay-as-you-go" plans? What are the Social Security and Medicare trust funds, and how long will they have money left in them? What is the key long-run problem of both Social Security and Medicare? Do you favor increasing taxes or do you prefer reducing benefits to fix the problem?

REVIEW QUESTIONS

1. Which of the following would help a government reduce an inflationary output gap? **LO13.1**
   a. Raising taxes.
   b. Lowering taxes.
   c. Increasing government spending.
   d. Decreasing government spending.

2. The economy is in a recession. A congresswoman suggests increasing spending to stimulate aggregate demand but also

at the same time raising taxes to pay for the increased spending. Her suggestion to combine higher government expenditures with higher taxes is: **LO13.1**
   a. The worst possible combination of tax and expenditure changes.
   b. The best possible combination of tax and expenditure changes.

    c. A mediocre and contradictory combination of tax and expenditure changes.

    d. None of the above.

3. During the recession of 2007–2009, the U.S. federal government's tax collections fell from about $2.6 trillion down to about $2.1 trillion while GDP declined by about 4 percent. Does the U.S. tax system appear to have built-in stabilizers? LO13.2

    a. Yes.

    b. No.

4. Last year, while an economy was in a recession, government spending was $595 billion and government revenue was $505 billion. Economists estimate that if the economy had been at its full-employment level of GDP last year, government spending would have been $555 billion and government revenue would have been $550 billion. Which of the following statements about this government's fiscal situation are true? LO13.3

    a. The government has a non–cyclically adjusted budget deficit of $595 billion.

    b. The government has a non–cyclically adjusted budget deficit of $90 billion.

    c. The government has a non–cyclically adjusted budget surplus of $90 billion.

    d. The government has a cyclically adjusted budget deficit of $555 billion.

    e. The government has a cyclically adjusted budget deficit of $5 billion.

    f. The government has a cyclically adjusted budget surplus of $5 billion.

5. Label each of the following scenarios in which there are problems enacting and applying fiscal policy as being an example of either recognition lag, administrative lag, or operational lag. LO13.5

    a. To fight a recession, Congress has passed a bill to increase infrastructure spending—but the legally required environmental-impact statement for each new project will take at least two years to complete before any building can begin.

    b. Distracted by a war that is going badly, inflation reaches 8 percent before politicians take notice.

    c. A sudden recession is recognized by politicians, but it takes many months of political deal making before a stimulus bill is finally approved.

    d. To fight a recession, the president orders federal agencies to get rid of petty regulations that burden private businesses—but the federal agencies begin by spending a year developing a set of regulations on how to remove petty regulations.

6. In January, the interest rate is 5 percent and firms borrow $50 billion per month for investment projects. In February, the federal government doubles its monthly borrowing from $25 billion to $50 billion. That drives the interest rate up to 7 percent. As a result, firms cut back their borrowing to only $30 billion per month. Which of the following is true? LO13.6

    a. There is no crowding-out effect because the government's increase in borrowing exceeds firm's decrease in borrowing.

    b. There is a crowding-out effect of $20 billion.

    c. There is no crowding-out effect because both the government and firms are still borrowing a lot.

    d. There is a crowding-out effect of $25 billion.

PROBLEMS

1. Assume that a hypothetical economy with an MPC of .8 is experiencing severe recession. By how much would government spending have to rise to shift the aggregate demand curve rightward by $25 billion? How large a tax cut would be needed to achieve the same increase in aggregate demand? Determine one possible combination of government spending increases and tax decreases that would accomplish the same goal. LO13.1

2. Refer back to the table in Figure 12.7 in the previous chapter. Suppose that aggregate demand increases such that the amount of real output demanded rises by $7 billion at each price level. By what percentage will the price level increase? Will this inflation be demand-pull inflation or will it be cost-push inflation? If potential real GDP (that is, full-employment GDP) is $510 billion, what will be the size of the positive GDP gap after the change in aggregate demand? If government wants to use fiscal policy to counter the resulting inflation without changing tax rates, would it increase government spending or decrease it? LO13.1

3. (For students who were assigned Chapter 11) Assume that, without taxes, the consumption schedule for an economy is as shown below: LO13.1

GDP, Billions	Consumption, Billions
$100	$120
200	200
300	280
400	360
500	440
600	520
700	600

    a. Graph this consumption schedule. What is the size of the MPC?

    b. Assume that a lump-sum (regressive) tax of $10 billion is imposed at all levels of GDP. Calculate the tax rate at each level of GDP. Graph the resulting consumption schedule and compare the MPC and the multiplier with those of the pretax consumption schedule.

c. Now suppose a proportional tax with a 10 percent tax rate is imposed instead of the regressive tax. Calculate and graph the new consumption schedule and note the MPC and the multiplier.

d. Finally, impose a progressive tax such that the tax rate is 0 percent when GDP is $100, 5 percent at $200, 10 percent at $300, 15 percent at $400, and so forth. Determine and graph the new consumption schedule, noting the effect of this tax system on the MPC and the multiplier.

e. Use a graph similar to Figure 13.3 to show why proportional and progressive taxes contribute to greater economic stability, while a regressive tax does not.

4. Refer to the following table for Waxwania: **LO13.2**

Government Expenditures, G	Tax Revenues, T	Real GDP
$160	$100	$500
160	120	600
160	140	700
160	160	800
160	180	900

What is the marginal tax rate in Waxwania? The average tax rate? Which of the following describes the tax system: proportional, progressive, regressive?

5. Refer to the table for Waxwania in problem 4. Suppose that Waxwania is producing $600 of real GDP, whereas the potential real GDP (or full-employment real GDP) is $700. How large is its budget deficit? Its cyclically adjusted budget deficit? Its cyclically adjusted budget deficit as a percentage of potential real GDP? Is Waxwania's fiscal policy expansionary or is it contractionary? **LO13.3**

6. Suppose that a country has no public debt in year 1 but experiences a budget deficit of $40 billion in year 2, a budget surplus of $10 billion in year 3, and a budget deficit of $2 billion in year 4. What is the absolute size of its public debt in year 4? If its real GDP in year 4 is $104 billion, what is this country's public debt as a percentage of real GDP in year 4? **LO13.6**

7. Suppose that the investment demand curve in a certain economy is such that investment declines by $100 billion for every 1 percentage point increase in the real interest rate. Also, suppose that the investment demand curve shifts rightward by $150 billion at each real interest rate for every 1 percentage point increase in the expected rate of return from investment. If stimulus spending (an expansionary fiscal policy) by government increases the real interest rate by 2 percentage points, but also raises the expected rate of return on investment by 1 percentage point, how much investment, if any, will be crowded out? **LO13.6**

FURTHER TEST YOUR KNOWLEDGE AT www.mcconnell20e.com

Practice quizzes, student PowerPoints, worked problems, Web-based questions, and additional materials are available at the text's Online Learning Center (OLC), **www.mcconnell20e.com**, or scan here. Need a barcode reader? Try ScanLife, available in your app store.

Money, Banking, and Monetary Policy

MONEY, BANKING, AND MONETARY POLICY

Money, Banking, and Financial Institutions

Learning Objectives

LO14.1 Identify and explain the functions of money.

LO14.2 List and describe the components of the U.S. money supply.

LO14.3 Describe what "backs" the money supply, making us willing to accept it as payment.

LO14.4 Discuss the makeup of the Federal Reserve and its relationship to banks and thrifts.

LO14.5 Identify the functions and responsibilities of the Federal Reserve and explain why Fed independence is important.

LO14.6 Identify and explain the main factors that contributed to the financial crisis of 2007–2008.

LO14.7 Discuss the actions of the U.S. Treasury and the Federal Reserve that helped keep the banking and financial crisis of 2007–2008 from worsening.

LO14.8 Identify the main subsets of the financial services industry in the United States and provide examples of some firms in each category.

Money is a fascinating aspect of the economy:

> Money bewitches people. They fret for it, and they sweat for it. They devise most ingenious ways to get it, and most ingenuous ways to get rid of it. Money is the only commodity that is good for nothing but to be gotten rid of. It will not feed you, clothe you, shelter you, or amuse you unless you spend it or invest it. It

imparts value only in parting. People will do almost anything for money, and money will do almost anything for people. Money is a captivating, circulating, masquerading puzzle.[1]

In this chapter and the two chapters that follow, we want to unmask the critical role of money and the monetary system in the economy. When the monetary system is working properly, it provides the lifeblood of the circular flows of income and expenditure. A well-operating monetary system helps the economy achieve both full employment and the efficient use of resources. A malfunctioning monetary system distorts the allocation of resources and creates severe fluctuations in the economy's levels of output, employment, and prices.

---

[1]"Creeping Inflation," *Business Review*, August 1957, p. 3. Federal Reserve Bank of Philadelphia. Used with permission.

The Functions of Money

LO14.1 Identify and explain the functions of money.
Just what is money? There is an old saying that "money *is* what money *does*." In a general sense, anything that performs the functions of money *is* money. Here are those functions:

- *Medium of exchange* First and foremost, money is a **medium of exchange** that is usable for buying and selling goods and services. A bakery worker does not want to be paid 200 bagels per week. Nor does the bakery owner want to receive, say, halibut in exchange for bagels. Money, however, is readily acceptable as payment. As we saw in Chapter 2, money is a social invention with which resource suppliers and producers can be paid and that can be used to buy any of the full range of items available in the marketplace. As a medium of exchange, money allows society to escape the complications of barter. And because it provides a convenient way of exchanging goods, money enables society to gain the advantages of geographic and human specialization.

- *Unit of account* Money is also a **unit of account.** Society uses monetary units—dollars, in the United States—as a yardstick for measuring the relative worth of a wide variety of goods, services, and resources. Just as we measure distance in miles or kilometers, we gauge the value of goods in dollars.

  With money as an acceptable unit of account, the price of each item need be stated only in terms of the monetary unit. We need not state the price of cows in terms of corn, crayons, and cranberries. Money aids rational decision making by enabling buyers and sellers to easily compare the prices of various goods, services, and resources. It also permits us to define debt obligations, determine taxes owed, and calculate the nation's GDP.

- *Store of value* Money also serves as a **store of value** that enables people to transfer purchasing power from the present to the future. People normally do not spend all their incomes on the day they receive them. To buy things later, they store some of their wealth as money. The money you place in a safe or a checking account will still be available to you a few weeks or months from now. When inflation is nonexistent or mild, holding money is a relatively risk-free way to store your wealth for later use.

People can, of course, choose to hold some or all of their wealth in a wide variety of assets besides money. These include real estate, stocks, bonds, precious metals such as gold, and even collectible items like fine art or comic books. But a key advantage that money has over all other assets is that it has the most *liquidity*, or spendability.

An asset's **liquidity** is the ease with which it can be converted quickly into the most widely accepted and easily spent form of money, cash, with little or no loss of purchasing power. The more liquid an asset is, the more quickly it can be converted into cash and used for either purchases of goods and services or purchases of other assets.

Levels of liquidity vary radically. By definition, cash is perfectly liquid. By contrast, a house is highly illiquid for two reasons. First, it may take several months before a willing buyer can be found and a sale negotiated so that its value can be converted into cash. Second, there is a loss of purchasing power when the house is sold because numerous fees have to be paid to real estate agents and other individuals to complete the sale.

As we are about to discuss, our economy uses several different types of money including cash, coins, checking

FIGURE 14.1 Components of money supply *M*1 and money supply *M*2, in the United States. (a) *M*1 is a narrow definition of the money supply that includes currency (in circulation) and checkable deposits. (b) *M*2 is a broader definition that includes *M*1 along with several other relatively liquid account balances.

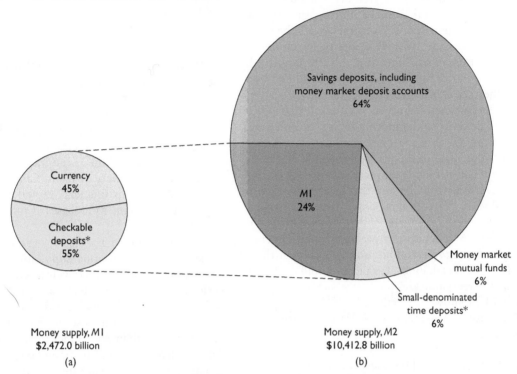

Money supply, *M*1
$2,472.0 billion
(a)

Money supply, *M*2
$10,412.8 billion
(b)

*These categories include other, quantitatively smaller components such as traveler's checks.
Source: Federal Reserve System, **www.federalreserve.gov**. Data are for February 2013.

account deposits, savings account deposits, and even more exotic things like deposits in money market mutual funds. As we describe the various forms of money in detail, take the time to compare their relative levels of liquidity—both with each other and as compared to other assets like stocks, bonds, and real estate. Cash is perfectly liquid. Other forms of money are highly liquid, but less liquid than cash.

The Components of the Money Supply

LO14.2 List and describe the components of the U.S. money supply.

Money is a "stock" of some item or group of items (unlike income, for example, which is a "flow"). Societies have used many items as money, including whales' teeth, circular stones, elephant-tail bristles, gold coins, furs, and pieces of paper. Anything that is widely accepted as a medium of exchange can serve as money. In the United States, currency is not the only form of money. As you will see, certain debts of government and financial institutions also are used as money.

Money Definition *M*1

The narrowest definition of the U.S. money supply is called ***M*1.** It consists of two components:

- Currency (coins and paper money) in the hands of the public.
- All checkable deposits (all deposits in commercial banks and "thrift" or savings institutions on which checks of any size can be drawn).[2]

Government and government agencies supply coins and paper money. Commercial banks ("banks") and savings institutions ("thrifts") provide checkable deposits. Figure 14.1a shows that *M*1 is about equally divided between the two components.

---

[2]In the ensuing discussion, we do not discuss several of the quantitatively less significant components of the definitions of money to avoid a maze of details. For example, traveler's checks are included in the *M*1 money supply. The statistical appendix of any recent *Federal Reserve Bulletin* provides more comprehensive definitions.

Currency: Coins + Paper Money The currency of the United States consists of metal coins and paper money. The coins are issued by the U.S. Treasury while the paper money consists of **Federal Reserve Notes** issued by the Federal Reserve System (the U.S. central bank). The coins are minted by the U.S. Mint while the paper money is printed by the Bureau of Engraving and Printing. Both the U.S. Mint and the Bureau of Engraving and Printing are part of the U.S. Department of the Treasury.

As with the currencies of other countries, the currency of the United States is **token money.** This means that the face value of any piece of currency is unrelated to its *intrinsic value*—the value of the physical material (metal or paper and ink) out of which that piece of currency is constructed. Governments make sure that face values exceed intrinsic values to discourage people from destroying coins and bills to resell the material that they are made out of. For instance, if 50-cent pieces each contained 75 cents' worth of metal, then it would be profitable to melt them down and sell the metal. Fifty-cent pieces would disappear from circulation very quickly!

Figure 14.1a shows that currency (coins and paper money) constitutes 45 percent of the $M1$ money supply in the United States.

Checkable Deposits The safety and convenience of checks has made **checkable deposits** a large component of the $M1$ money supply. You would not think of stuffing $4,896 in bills in an envelope and dropping it in a mailbox to pay a debt. But writing and mailing a check for a large sum is commonplace. The person cashing a check must endorse it (sign it on the reverse side); the writer of the check subsequently receives a record of the cashed check as a receipt attesting to the fulfillment of the obligation. Similarly, because the writing of a check requires endorsement, the theft or loss of your checkbook is not nearly as calamitous as losing an identical amount of currency. Finally, it is more convenient to write a check than to transport and count out a large sum of currency. For all these reasons, checkable deposits (checkbook money) are a large component of the stock of money in the United States. About 55 percent of $M1$ is in the form of checkable deposits, on which checks can be drawn.

It might seem strange that checking account balances are regarded as part of the money supply. But the reason is clear: Checks are nothing more than a way to transfer the ownership of deposits in banks and other financial institutions and are generally acceptable as a medium of exchange. Although checks are less generally accepted than currency for small purchases, for major purchases most sellers willingly accept checks as payment. Moreover, people can convert checkable deposits into paper money and coins on demand; checks drawn on those deposits are thus the equivalent of currency.

To summarize:

$$\text{Money, } M1 = \text{currency} + \text{checkable deposits}$$

Institutions That Offer Checkable Deposits In the United States, a variety of financial institutions allow customers to write checks in any amount on the funds they have deposited. **Commercial banks** are the primary depository institutions. They accept the deposits of households and businesses, keep the money safe until it is demanded via checks, and in the meantime use it to make available a wide variety of loans. Commercial bank loans provide short-term financial capital to businesses, and they finance consumer purchases of automobiles and other durable goods.

Savings and loan associations (S&Ls), mutual savings banks, and credit unions supplement the commercial banks and are known collectively as savings or **thrift institutions,** or simply "thrifts." *Savings and loan associations* and *mutual savings banks* accept the deposits of households and businesses and then use the funds to finance housing mortgages and to provide other loans. *Credit unions* accept deposits from and lend to "members," who usually are a group of people who work for the same company.

The checkable deposits of banks and thrifts are known variously as demand deposits, NOW (negotiable order of withdrawal) accounts, ATS (automatic transfer service) accounts, and share draft accounts. Their commonality is that depositors can write checks on them whenever, and in whatever amount, they choose.

Two Qualifications We must qualify our discussion in two important ways. First, currency held by the U.S. Treasury, the Federal Reserve banks, commercial banks, and thrift institutions is *excluded* from $M1$ and other measures of the money supply. A paper dollar or four quarters in the billfold of, say, Emma Buck obviously constitutes just $1 of the money supply. But if we counted currency held by banks as part of the money supply, the same $1 would count for $2 of money supply when Emma deposited the currency into her checkable deposit in her bank. It would count for $1 of checkable deposit owned by Buck and also $1 of currency in the bank's cash drawer or vault. By excluding currency held by banks when determining the total supply of money, we avoid this problem of double counting.

Also *excluded* from the money supply are any checkable deposits of the government (specifically, the U.S. Treasury) or the Federal Reserve that are held by commercial banks or thrift institutions. This exclusion is designed to enable a better assessment of the amount of money available *to the private sector* for potential spending. The amount of money available to households and businesses is of keen interest to the Federal Reserve in conducting its monetary policy (a topic we cover in detail in Chapter 16).

Money Definition *M2*

A second and broader definition of money includes *M1* plus several near-monies. **Near-monies** are certain highly liquid financial assets that do not function directly or fully as a medium of exchange but can be readily converted into currency or checkable deposits. The *M2* definition of money includes three categories of near-monies.

- *Savings deposits, including money market deposit accounts* A depositor can easily withdraw funds from a **savings account** at a bank or thrift or simply request that the funds be transferred from a savings account to a checkable account. A person can also withdraw funds from a **money market deposit account (MMDA),** which is an interest-bearing account containing a variety of interest-bearing short-term securities. MMDAs, however, have a minimum-balance requirement and a limit on how often a person can withdraw funds.

- *Small-denominated (less than $100,000) time deposits* Funds from **time deposits** become available at their maturity. For example, a person can convert a 6-month time deposit ("certificate of deposit," or "CD") to currency without penalty 6 months or more after it has been deposited. In return for this withdrawal limitation, the financial institution pays a higher interest rate on such deposits than it does on its MMDAs. Also, a person can "cash in" a CD at any time but must pay a severe penalty.

- *Money market mutual funds held by individuals* By making a telephone call, using the Internet, or writing a check for $500 or more, a depositor can redeem shares in a **money market mutual fund (MMMF)** offered by a mutual fund company. Such companies use the combined funds of individual shareholders to buy interest-bearing short-term credit instruments such as certificates of deposit and U.S. government securities. Then they can offer interest on the MMMF accounts of the shareholders (depositors) who jointly own those financial assets. The MMMFs in *M2* include only the MMMF accounts held by individuals; those held by businesses and other institutions are excluded.

All three categories of near-monies imply substantial liquidity. Thus, in equation form,

$$\text{Money, } M2 = \begin{array}{l} M1 + \text{savings deposits, including} \\ \text{MMDAs} + \text{small-denominated} \\ \text{(less than \$100,000) time deposits} \\ + \text{MMMFs held by individuals} \end{array}$$

In summary, *M2* includes the immediate medium-of-exchange items (currency and checkable deposits) that constitute *M1* plus certain near-monies that can be easily

CONSIDER THIS . . .

Are Credit Cards Money?

You may wonder why we have ignored credit cards such as Visa and MasterCard in our discussion of how the money supply is defined. After all, credit cards are a convenient way to buy things and account for about 25 percent of the dollar value of all transactions in the United States. The answer is that a credit card is not money. Rather, it is a convenient means of obtaining a short-term loan from the financial institution that issued the card.

What happens when you purchase an item with a credit card? The bank that issued the card will reimburse the seller by making a money payment and charging the establishment a transaction fee, and later you will reimburse the bank for its loan to you by also making a money payment. Rather than reduce your cash or checking account with each purchase, you bunch your payments once a month. You may have to pay an annual fee for the services provided, and if you pay the bank in installments, you will pay a sizable interest charge on the loan. Credit cards are merely a means of deferring or postponing payment for a short period. Your checking account balance that you use to pay your credit card bill *is* money; the credit card is *not* money.*

Although credit cards are not money, they allow individuals and businesses to "economize" in the use of money. Credit cards enable people to hold less currency in their billfolds and, prior to payment due dates, fewer checkable deposits in their bank accounts. Credit cards also help people coordinate the timing of their expenditures with their receipt of income.

---

*A bank debit card, however, is very similar to a check in your checkbook. Unlike a purchase with a credit card, a purchase with a debit card creates a direct "debit" (a subtraction) from your checking account balance. That checking account balance is money—it is part of *M1*.

converted into currency and checkable deposits. In Figure 14.1b we see that the addition of all these items yields an *M2* money supply that is about five times larger than the narrower *M1* money supply.

QUICK REVIEW 14.1

- Money serves as a medium of exchange, a unit of account, and a store of value.
- The narrow *M1* definition of money includes currency held by the public plus checkable deposits in commercial banks and thrift institutions.
- Thrift institutions as well as commercial banks offer accounts on which checks can be written.
- The *M2* definition of money includes *M1* plus savings deposits, including money market deposit accounts, small-denominated (less than $100,000) time deposits, and money market mutual fund balances held by individuals.

What "Backs" the Money Supply?

LO14.3 Describe what "backs" the money supply, making us willing to accept it as payment.

The money supply in the United States essentially is "backed" (guaranteed) by the government's ability to keep the value of money relatively stable. Nothing more!

Money as Debt

The major components of the money supply—paper money and checkable deposits—are debts, or promises to pay. In the United States, paper money is the circulating debt of the Federal Reserve Banks. Checkable deposits are the debts of commercial banks and thrift institutions.

Paper currency and checkable deposits have no intrinsic value. A $5 bill is just an inscribed piece of paper. A checkable deposit is merely a bookkeeping entry. And coins, we know, have less intrinsic value than their face value. Nor will government redeem the paper money you hold for anything tangible, such as gold. To many people, the fact that the government does not back the currency with anything tangible seems implausible and insecure. But the decision not to back the currency with anything tangible was made for a very good reason. If the government backed the currency with something tangible like gold, then the supply of money would vary with how much gold was available. By not backing the currency, the government avoids this constraint and indeed receives a key freedom—the ability to provide as much or as little money as needed to maintain the value of money and to best suit

the economic needs of the country. In effect, by choosing not to back the currency, the government has chosen to give itself the ability to freely "manage" the nation's money supply. Its monetary authorities attempt to provide the amount of money needed for the particular volume of business activity that will promote full employment, price-level stability, and economic growth.

Nearly all today's economists agree that managing the money supply is more sensible than linking it to gold or to some other commodity whose supply might change arbitrarily and capriciously. For instance, if we used gold to back the money supply so that gold was redeemable for money and vice versa, then a large increase in the nation's gold stock as the result of a new gold discovery might increase the money supply too rapidly and thereby trigger rapid inflation. Or a long-lasting decline in gold production might reduce the money supply to the point where recession and unemployment resulted.

In short, people cannot convert paper money into a fixed amount of gold or any other precious commodity. Money is exchangeable only for paper money. If you ask the government to redeem $5 of your paper money, it will swap one paper $5 bill for another bearing a different serial number. That is all you can get. Similarly, checkable deposits can be redeemed not for gold but only for paper money, which, as we have just seen, the government will not redeem for anything tangible.

Value of Money

So why are currency and checkable deposits money, whereas, say, Monopoly (the game) money is not? What gives a $20 bill or a $100 checking account entry its value? The answer to these questions has three parts.

Acceptability Currency and checkable deposits are money because people accept them as money. By virtue of long-standing business practice, currency and checkable deposits perform the basic function of money: They are acceptable as a medium of exchange. We accept paper money in exchange because we are confident it will be exchangeable for real goods, services, and resources when we spend it.

Legal Tender Our confidence in the acceptability of paper money is strengthened because the government has designated currency as **legal tender.** Specifically, each bill contains the statement "This note is legal tender for all debts, public and private." That means paper money is a valid and legal means of payment of any debt that was contracted in dollars. (But private firms and government are not mandated to accept cash. It is not illegal for them to specify payment in noncash forms such as checks, cashier's checks, money orders, or credit cards.)

The general acceptance of paper currency in exchange is more important than the government's decree that money is legal tender, however. The government has never decreed checks to be legal tender, and yet they serve as such in many of the economy's exchanges of goods, services, and resources. But it is true that government agencies—the Federal Deposit Insurance Corporation (FDIC) and the National Credit Union Administration (NCUA)—insure individual deposits of up to $250,000 at commercial banks and thrifts. That fact enhances our willingness to use checkable deposits as a medium of exchange.

Relative Scarcity The value of money, like the economic value of anything else, depends on its supply and demand. Money derives its value from its scarcity relative to its utility (its want-satisfying power). The utility of money lies in its capacity to be exchanged for goods and services, now or in the future. The economy's demand for money thus depends on the total dollar volume of transactions in any period plus the amount of money individuals and businesses want to hold for future transactions. With a reasonably constant demand for money, the supply of money provided by the monetary authorities will determine the domestic value or "purchasing power" of the monetary unit (dollar, yen, peso, or whatever).

Money and Prices

The purchasing power of money is the amount of goods and services a unit of money will buy. When money rapidly loses its purchasing power, it loses its role as money.

The Purchasing Power of the Dollar The amount a dollar will buy varies inversely with the price level; that is, a reciprocal relationship exists between the general price level and the purchasing power of the dollar. When the consumer price index or "cost-of-living" index goes up, the value of the dollar goes down, and vice versa. Higher prices lower the value of the dollar because more dollars are needed to buy a particular amount of goods, services, or resources. For example, if the price level doubles, the value of the dollar declines by one-half, or 50 percent.

Conversely, lower prices increase the purchasing power of the dollar because fewer dollars are needed to obtain a specific quantity of goods and services. If the price level falls by, say, one-half, or 50 percent, the purchasing power of the dollar doubles.

In equation form, the relationship looks like this:

$$\$V = 1/P$$

To find the value of the dollar $\$V$, divide 1 by the price level P expressed as an index number (in hundredths). If the price level is 1, then the value of the dollar is 1. If the price level rises to, say, 1.20, $\$V$ falls to 0.833; a 20 percent increase in the price level reduces the value of the dollar by 16.67 percent. Check your understanding of this reciprocal relationship by determining the value of $\$V$ and its percentage rise when P falls by 20 percent from $1 to 0.80.

Inflation and Acceptability In Chapter 9 we noted situations in which a nation's currency became worthless and unacceptable in exchange. These instances of runaway inflation, or *hyperinflation*, happened when the government issued so many pieces of paper currency that the purchasing power of each of those units of money was almost totally undermined. The infamous post–World War I hyperinflation in Germany is an example. In December 1919 there were about 50 billion marks in circulation. Four years later there were 496,585,345,900 billion marks in circulation! The result? The German mark in 1923 was worth an infinitesimal fraction of its 1919 value.[3]

Runaway inflation may significantly depreciate the value of money between the time it is received and the time it is spent. Rapid declines in the value of a currency may cause it to cease being used as a medium of exchange. Businesses and households may refuse to accept paper money in exchange because they do not want to bear the loss in its value that will occur while it is in their possession. (All this despite the fact that the government says that paper currency is legal tender!) Without an acceptable domestic medium of exchange, the economy may simply revert to barter. Alternatively, more stable currencies such as the U.S. dollar or European euro may come into widespread use. At the extreme, a country may adopt a foreign currency as its own official currency as a way to counter hyperinflation.

Similarly, people will use money as a store of value only as long as there is no sizable deterioration in the value of that money because of inflation. And an economy can effectively employ money as a unit of account only when its purchasing power is relatively stable. A monetary yardstick that no longer measures a yard (in terms of purchasing power) does not permit buyers and sellers to establish the terms of trade clearly. When the value of the dollar is declining rapidly, sellers do not know what to charge and buyers do not know what to pay.

---

[3]Frank G. Graham, *Exchange, Prices, and Production in Hyperinflation Germany, 1920–1923* (Princeton, N.J.: Princeton University Press, 1930), p. 13.

Stabilizing Money's Purchasing Power

Rapidly rising price levels (rapid inflation) and the consequent erosion of the purchasing power of money typically result from imprudent economic policies. Since the purchasing power of money and the price level vary inversely, stabilization of the purchasing power of a nation's money requires stabilization of the nation's price level. Such price-level stability (2 to 3 percent annual inflation) mainly necessitates intelligent management or regulation of the nation's money supply and interest rates *(monetary policy)*. It also requires appropriate *fiscal policy* supportive of the efforts of the nation's monetary authorities to hold down inflation. In the United States, a combination of legislation, government policy, and social practice inhibits imprudent expansion of the money supply that might jeopardize money's purchasing power. The critical role of the U.S. monetary authorities (the Federal Reserve) in maintaining the purchasing power of the dollar is the subject of Chapter 16. For now, simply note that they make available a particular quantity of money, such as *M2* in Figure 14.1, and can change that amount through their policy tools.

QUICK REVIEW 14.2

- In the United States, all money consists essentially of the debts of government, commercial banks, and thrift institutions.
- These debts efficiently perform the functions of money as long as their value, or purchasing power, is relatively stable.
- The value of money is rooted not in specified quantities of precious metals but in the amounts of goods, services, and resources that money will purchase.
- The value of the dollar (its domestic purchasing power) is inversely related to the price level.
- Government's responsibility in stabilizing the purchasing power of the monetary unit calls for (a) effective control over the supply of money by the monetary authorities and (b) the application of appropriate fiscal policies by the president and Congress.

The Federal Reserve and the Banking System

LO14.4 Discuss the makeup of the Federal Reserve and its relationship to banks and thrifts.

In the United States, the "monetary authorities" we have been referring to are the members of the Board of Governors of the **Federal Reserve System** (the "Fed"). As shown in Figure 14.2, the Board directs the activities of the 12 Federal Reserve Banks, which in turn control the lending activity of the nation's banks and thrift institutions. The Fed's major goal is to control the money supply. But since checkable deposits in banks are such a large part of the money supply, an important part of its duties involves assuring the stability of the banking system.

Historical Background

Early in the twentieth century, Congress decided that centralization and public control were essential for an efficient banking system. Decentralized, unregulated banking had fostered the inconvenience and confusion of numerous private bank notes being used as currency. It also had resulted in occasional episodes of monetary mismanagement such that the money supply was inappropriate to the needs of the economy. Sometimes "too much" money precipitated rapid inflation; other times "too little money" stunted the economy's growth by hindering the production and exchange of goods and services. No single entity was charged with creating and implementing nationally consistent banking policies.

Furthermore, acute problems in the banking system occasionally erupted when banks either closed down or insisted on immediate repayment of loans to prevent their own failure. At such times, a banking crisis could emerge, with individuals and businesses who had lost confidence in their banks attempting to simultaneously withdraw all of their money—thereby further crippling the already weakened banks.

An unusually acute banking crisis in 1907 motivated Congress to appoint the National Monetary Commission to study the monetary and banking problems of the economy and to outline a course of action for Congress. The result was the Federal Reserve Act of 1913.

Let's examine the various parts of the Federal Reserve System and their relationship to one another.

Board of Governors

The central authority of the U.S. money and banking system is the **Board of Governors** of the Federal Reserve System. The U.S. president, with the confirmation of the Senate, appoints the seven Board members. Terms are 14 years and staggered so that one member is replaced every 2 years. In addition, new members are appointed when resignations occur. The president selects the chairperson and vice chairperson of the Board from among the members. Those officers serve 4-year terms and can be reappointed to new 4-year terms by the president. The long-term appointments provide the Board with continuity, experienced membership, and independence from political pressures that could result in inflation.

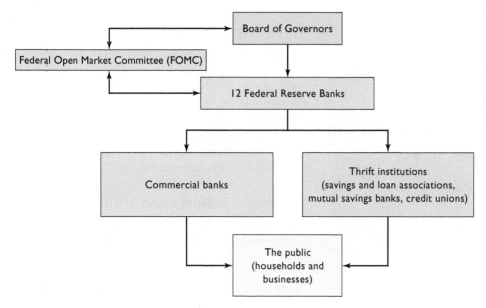

FIGURE 14.2 Framework of the Federal Reserve System and its relationship to the public. The Board of Governors makes the basic policy decisions that provide monetary control of the U.S. money and banking systems. The 12 Federal Reserve Banks implement these decisions. Both the Board of Governors and the 12 Federal Reserve Banks are aided by the Federal Open Market Committee (FOMC).

The 12 Federal Reserve Banks

The 12 **Federal Reserve Banks,** which blend private and public control, collectively serve as the nation's "central bank." These banks also serve as bankers' banks.

Central Bank Most nations have a single central bank— for example, Britain's Bank of England or Japan's Bank of Japan. The United States' central bank consists of 12 banks whose policies are coordinated by the Fed's Board of Governors. The 12 Federal Reserve Banks accommodate the geographic size and economic diversity of the United States and the nation's large number of commercial banks and thrifts.

Figure 14.3 locates the 12 Federal Reserve Banks and indicates the district that each serves. These banks implement the basic policy of the Board of Governors.

Quasi-Public Banks The 12 Federal Reserve Banks are quasi-public banks, which blend private ownership and public control. Each Federal Reserve Bank is owned by the private commercial banks in its district. (Federally chartered banks are required to purchase shares of stock in

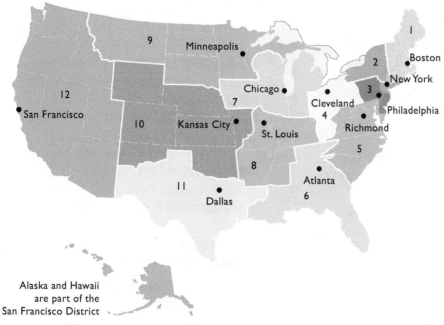

FIGURE 14.3 The 12 Federal Reserve Districts. The Federal Reserve System divides the United States into 12 districts, each having one central bank and in some instances one or more branches of the central bank.

Source: Federal Reserve Bulletin, **www.federalreserve.gov/pubs/bulletin**.

the Federal Reserve Bank in their district.) But the Board of Governors, a government body, sets the basic policies that the Federal Reserve Banks pursue.

Despite their private ownership, the Federal Reserve Banks are in practice public institutions. Unlike private firms, they are not motivated by profit. The policies they follow are designed by the Board of Governors to promote the well-being of the economy as a whole. Thus, the activities of the Federal Reserve Banks are frequently at odds with the profit motive.[4] Also, the Federal Reserve Banks do not compete with commercial banks. In general, they do not deal with the public; rather, they interact with the government and commercial banks and thrifts.

Bankers' Banks   The Federal Reserve Banks are "bankers' banks." They perform essentially the same functions for banks and thrifts as those institutions perform for the public. Just as banks and thrifts accept the deposits of and make loans to the public, so the central banks accept the deposits of and make loans to banks and thrifts. Normally, these loans average only about $150 million a day. But in emergency circumstances the Federal Reserve Banks become the "lender of last resort" to the banking system and can lend out as much as needed to ensure that banks and thrifts can meet their cash obligations. On the day after terrorists attacked the United States on September 11, 2001, the Fed lent $45 *billion* to U.S. banks and thrifts. The Fed wanted to make sure that the destruction and disruption in New York City and the Washington, D.C., area did not precipitate a nationwide banking crisis.

The Fed assumed an even greater role as a lender of last resort during the financial crisis of 2007–2008. We discuss that crisis and the Fed's emergency response to the crisis later in this chapter.

But the Federal Reserve Banks have a third function, which banks and thrifts do not perform: They issue currency. Congress has authorized the Federal Reserve Banks to put into circulation Federal Reserve Notes, which constitute the economy's paper money supply.

FOMC

The **Federal Open Market Committee (FOMC)** aids the Board of Governors in conducting monetary policy. The FOMC is made up of 12 individuals:

- The seven members of the Board of Governors.
- The president of the New York Federal Reserve Bank.

[4]Although it is not their goal, the Federal Reserve Banks have actually operated profitably, largely as a result of the Treasury debts they hold. Part of the profit is used to pay 6 percent annual dividends to the commercial banks that hold stock in the Federal Reserve Banks; the remaining profit is usually turned over to the U.S. Treasury.

- Four of the remaining presidents of Federal Reserve Banks on a 1-year rotating basis.

The FOMC meets regularly to direct the purchase and sale of government securities (bills, notes, bonds) in the open market in which such securities are bought and sold on a daily basis. We will find in Chapter 16 that the purpose of these aptly named *open-market operations* is to control the nation's money supply and influence interest rates. The Federal Reserve Bank in New York City conducts most of the Fed's open-market operations.

Commercial Banks and Thrifts

There are about 6,000 commercial banks. Roughly three-fourths are state banks. These are private banks chartered (authorized) by the individual states to operate within those states. One-fourth are private banks chartered by the federal government to operate nationally; these are national banks. Some of the U.S. national banks are very large, ranking among the world's largest financial institutions (see Global Perspective 14.1).

The 8,500 thrift institutions—most of which are credit unions—are regulated by agencies in addition to the

GLOBAL PERSPECTIVE 14.1

The World's 12 Largest Financial Institutions

The world's 12 largest private sector financial institutions are headquartered in Europe, Japan, and the United States (2012 data).

Source: **www.forbes.com/global2000/list/**. Reprinted by Permission of Forbes Media LLC © 2012.

Board of Governors and the Federal Reserve Banks. For example, credit unions are regulated and monitored by the National Credit Union Administration (NCUA). But the thrifts *are* subject to monetary control by the Federal Reserve System. In particular, like the banks, thrifts are required to keep a certain percentage of their checkable deposits as "reserves." In Figure 14.2 we use arrows to indicate that the thrift institutions are subject to the control of the Board of Governors and the central banks. Decisions concerning monetary policy affect the thrifts along with the commercial banks.

Fed Functions, Responsibilities, and Independence

LO14.5 Identify the functions and responsibilities of the Federal Reserve and explain why Fed independence is important.

The Fed performs several functions, some of which we have already identified, but they are worth repeating:

- *Issuing currency* The Federal Reserve Banks issue Federal Reserve Notes, the paper currency used in the U.S. monetary system. (The Federal Reserve Bank that issued a particular bill is identified in black in the upper left of the front of the newly designed bills. "A1," for example, identifies the Boston bank, "B2" the New York bank, and so on.)

- *Setting reserve requirements and holding reserves* The Fed sets reserve requirements, which are the fractions of checking account balances that banks must maintain as currency reserves. The central banks accept as deposits from the banks and thrifts any portion of their mandated reserves not held as vault cash.

- *Lending to financial institutions and serving as an emergency lender of last resort* The Fed makes routine short-term loans to banks and thrifts and charges them an interest rate called the *discount rate*. It also occasionally auctions off loans to banks and thrifts through its *Term Auction Facility*, discussed in Chapter 16. In times of financial emergencies, the Fed serves as a lender of last resort to critical parts of the U.S. financial industry.

- *Providing for check collection* The Fed provides the banking system with a means for collecting on checks. If Sue writes a check on her Miami bank or thrift to Joe, who deposits it in his Dallas bank or thrift, how does the Dallas bank collect the money

represented by the check drawn against the Miami bank? Answer: The Fed handles it by adjusting the reserves (deposits) of the two banks.

- *Acting as fiscal agent* The Fed acts as the fiscal agent (provider of financial services) for the federal government. The government collects huge sums through taxation, spends equally large amounts, and sells and redeems bonds. To carry out these activities, the government uses the Fed's facilities.

- *Supervising banks* The Fed supervises the operations of banks. It makes periodic examinations to assess bank profitability, to ascertain that banks perform in accordance with the many regulations to which they are subject, and to uncover questionable practices or fraud. Following the financial crisis of 2007–2008, Congress expanded the Fed's supervisory powers over banks.[5]

- *Controlling the money supply* Finally, the Fed has ultimate responsibility for regulating the supply of money, and this enables it to influence interest rates. The major task of the Fed under usual economic circumstances is to manage the money supply (and thus interest rates) according to the needs of the economy. This involves making an amount of money available that is consistent with high and rising levels of output and employment *and* a relatively stable price level. While most of the other functions of the Fed are routine activities or have a service nature, managing the nation's money supply requires making basic, but unique, policy decisions. (We discuss those decisions in detail in Chapter 16.)

Federal Reserve Independence

Congress purposely established the Fed as an independent agency of government. The objective was to protect the Fed from political pressures so that it could effectively control the money supply and maintain price stability. Political pressures on Congress and the executive branch may at times result in inflationary fiscal policies, including tax cuts and special-interest spending. If Congress and the executive branch also controlled the nation's monetary policy, citizens and lobbying groups undoubtedly would pressure elected officials to keep interest rates low even

---

[5]The Fed is not alone in this task of supervision. The individual states supervise the banks that they charter. The Office of the Comptroller of the Currency has separate supervisory authority over the banks and the thrifts. Also, the Federal Deposit Insurance Corporation supervises the banks and thrifts whose deposits it insures.

though at times high interest rates are necessary to reduce aggregate demand and thus control inflation. An independent monetary authority (the Fed) can take actions to increase interest rates when higher rates are needed to stem inflation. Studies show that countries that have independent central banks like the Fed have lower rates of inflation, on average, than countries that have little or no central bank independence.

QUICK REVIEW 14.3

- The U.S. banking system consists of (a) the Board of Governors of the Federal Reserve System, (b) the 12 Federal Reserve Banks, and (c) some 6,000 commercial banks and 8,500 thrift institutions (mainly credit unions).
- The 12 Federal Reserve Banks are simultaneously (a) central banks, (b) quasi-public banks, and (c) bankers' banks.
- The major functions of the Fed are to (a) issue Federal Reserve Notes, (b) set reserve requirements and hold reserves deposited by banks and thrifts, (c) lend money to financial institutions and serve as the lender of last resort in national financial emergencies, (d) provide for the rapid collection of checks, (e) act as the fiscal agent for the federal government, (f) supervise the operations of the banks, and (g) regulate the supply of money in the best interests of the economy.

The Financial Crisis of 2007 and 2008

LO14.6 Identify and explain the main factors that contributed to the financial crisis of 2007–2008.

As previously noted, a properly functioning monetary system supports the continuous circular flows of income and expenditures in the economy. In contrast, a malfunctioning monetary system causes major problems in credit markets and can cause severe fluctuations in the economy's levels of output, employment, and prices.

"Malfunctioning" is too gentle an adjective to describe the monetary system in late 2007 and 2008. In that period, the U.S. financial system faced its most serious crisis since the Great Depression of the 1930s. The financial crisis soon spread to the entire economy, culminating in the severe recession of 2007–2009. We discussed the recession in detail in previous chapters, and we now want to examine the financial crisis that led up to it. What was the nature of the financial crisis? What caused it? How has it changed the structure of the U.S. financial services industry?

The Mortgage Default Crisis

In 2007 a major wave of defaults on home mortgage loans threatened the health of not only the original mortgage lenders but of any financial institution that had made such loans or invested in such loans either directly or indirectly. A majority of these mortgage defaults were on **subprime mortgage loans**—high-interest-rate loans to home buyers with higher-than-average credit risk. Ironically, the federal government had encouraged banks to make these types of loans as part of an effort to broaden home ownership to more Americans. But more directly to the point, several of the biggest indirect investors in these subprime loans had been banks. The banks had lent money to investment companies that had purchased many of the mortgages from mortgage lenders. When the mortgages started to go bad, many investment funds "blew up" and could not repay the loans they had taken out from the banks. The banks thus had to "write off" (declare unrecoverable) the loans they had made to the investment companies, but doing that meant reducing their banks' reserves and limiting their ability to generate new loans. This greatly threatened the economy because both consumers and businesses rely on loans to finance consumption and investment expenditures.

A strange thing about the crisis was that before it happened, banks and government regulators had mistakenly believed that an innovation known as the "mortgage-backed security" had eliminated most of the bank exposure to mortgage defaults. **Mortgage-backed securities** are bonds backed by mortgage payments. To create them, banks and other mortgage lenders first made mortgage loans. But then instead of holding all of those loans as assets on their balance sheets and collecting the monthly mortgage payments, the banks and other mortgage lenders bundled hundreds or thousands of them together and sold them off as bonds—in essence selling the right to collect all the future mortgage payments. The banks obtained a single, up-front cash payment for the bond and the bond buyer started to collect the mortgage payments as the return on the investment.

From the banks' perspective, this seemed like a smart business decision because it transferred any future default risk on those mortgages to the buyer of the bond. The banks thought that they were off the hook for these mortgages. Unfortunately for them, however, they lent a substantial portion of the money they received from selling the bonds to investment funds that invested in mortgage-backed bonds. They also purchased large amounts of mortgage-backed securities as financial investments to help meet bank capital requirements set by bank regulators. So while the banks were no longer directly exposed to major portions of the mortgage default risk, they were still indirectly exposed to it. When many homebuyers started to default on their mortgages, the banks lost money on the mortgages they still held. The banks also lost money on the loans they had made to the investors who had purchased mortgage-backed securities, and also on the mortgage-backed securities the banks had purchased from investment firms.

But what had caused the skyrocketing mortgage default rates in the first place? There were many causes, including certain government programs that greatly encouraged and subsidized home ownership for former renters. Also contributing were declining real estate values that arrived at the end of a long housing boom during which house prices had greatly increased. But an equally important factor was the bad incentives provided by the previously discussed mortgage-backed bonds. Because the banks and other mortgage lenders thought that they were no longer exposed to large portions of their mortgage default risk, they became lax in their lending practices—so much so that people were granted subprime mortgage loans that they were unlikely to be able to repay. Some mortgage companies were so eager to sign up new homebuyers (in order to bundle their loans together to sell bonds) that they stopped running credit checks and even allowed applicants to claim higher incomes than they were actually earning in order to qualify them for big loans. The natural result was that many people took on "too much mortgage" and were soon failing to make their monthly payments.

Securitization

The problems just described relate to **securitization**—the process of slicing up and bundling groups of loans, mortgages, corporate bonds, or other financial debts into distinct new securities. This process was not new and was viewed favorably by government regulators, who thought securitization made the banking system safer by allowing banks to shed risk. As noted in our discussion of mortgages, these securities were sold to financial investors, who purchased them to obtain the interest payments and the eventual return of principal generated by the underlying securities. For example, the mortgage loans provided to the subprime borrowers were bundled together as mortgage-backed securities and sold to private investors, mutual fund firms, and pension funds. These securities were attractive to many private investors and financial institutions alike because they offered higher-interest returns than securities backed by less-risky mortgages or other safer investments.

Once created, loan-backed securities are bought and sold in financial markets just like other securities such as stocks and bonds. These sorts of securities can therefore end up worldwide in the investment portfolios of banks, thrifts, insurance companies, and pensions, as well as in personal accounts.

To reduce the risk for holders of these securities, a few large insurance companies developed other securities that the holders of loan-backed securities could purchase to insure against losses from defaults. American International Group (AIG), in particular, issued billions of dollars of *collateralized default swaps*—essentially insurance policies—that were designed to compensate the holders of loan-backed securities if the loans underlying these investments went into default and did not pay off. Thus, collateralized default swaps became yet another category of investment security that was highly exposed to mortgage-loan risk.

Securitization is so widespread and so critical to the modern financial system that economists sometimes refer to it as the *shadow banking system*. All sorts of securities backed by loans or other securities are issued, bought, sold, and resold each day in a process that helps to keep credit flowing to the households and firms that rely on it for their personal and business needs. In general, securitization therefore is a positive financial innovation. But mortgage-backed securities, in particular, turned out to contain much more risk than most people thought.

Investors and government regulators failed to ask three related questions about mortgage-backed securities: What would happen if the value of one of the types of loans (say, mortgages) that underlies part of the securitization process unexpectedly plunged? And what then would happen if some of the largest holders of the securities based on these mortgages were major U.S. financial institutions that are vitally important to the day-to-day financing of the credit needed to keep the American economy running smoothly? And what would happen after that if the main insurer of these securities not only was the largest insurance company in the United States but in the world?

All three seemingly improbable "what ifs?" occurred! As previously explained, interest rates on adjustable-rate mortgages increased and house prices fell. Borrowers who had made relatively small down payments on home purchases or had previously cashed out home equity through refinancing discovered that they owed more on their mortgages than their properties were worth. Their loans were said to be "underwater." As interest rates adjusted upward and the economy slowed, borrowers began falling behind on their monthly mortgage payments. Lenders began to foreclose on many houses, while other borrowers literally handed in their house keys and walked away from their houses *and* their mortgages.

Failures and Near-Failures of Financial Firms

When the mortgage loan "card" underpinning mortgage-based securitization fell, the securitization layers above it collapsed like a house of cards. First, the big mortgage lenders faced demise because they still held large amounts of the bad debt. Three huge mortgage lenders collapsed or nearly collapsed. Countrywide, the second largest mortgage lender, was saved from bankruptcy by Bank of America. Regulators also seized Washington Mutual bank, the nation's largest mortgage lender, and arranged a quick takeover by JPMorgan Chase. Wachovia bank's heavy exposure to mortgages through its Golden West subsidiary resulted in near bankruptcy, and it was rescued through acquisition by Wells Fargo.

The exposure to the growing problem of loan defaults quickly jumped from direct mortgage lenders to other financial institutions. Securities firms and investment banks that held large amounts of loan-backed securities began to suffer huge losses. Merrill Lynch lost more in two years than it made in the prior decade and was acquired at a fire-sale price by Bank of America. Lehman Brothers, a major holder of mortgage-backed securities, declared bankruptcy. Goldman Sachs, Morgan Stanley, and other financial firms that had heavy exposures to mortgage-backed securities and collateralized default swaps rushed to become bank holding companies so they could qualify for the massive emergency loans that the Federal Reserve was making available to banks and bank holding companies. Citibank survived through infusions of federal government loans. Insurance company AIG suffered enormous losses because it had not set aside sufficient reserves to pay off the unexpectedly large losses that accrued on the insurance policies that it had sold to holders of mortgage-backed securities. The nightmarish thought of a total collapse of the U.S. financial system suddenly became a realistic possibility.

QUICK REVIEW 14.4

- The financial crisis of 2007–2008 consisted of an unprecedented rise in mortgage loan defaults, the collapse or near collapse of several major financial institutions, and the generalized freezing up of credit availability.
- The crisis resulted from bad mortgage loans together with declining real estate prices.
- The crisis exposed the underestimation of risk by holders of mortgage-backed securities as well as faulty insurance securities that had been designed to protect holders of mortgage-backed securities from the risk of default.

The Policy Response to the Financial Crisis

LO14.7 Discuss the actions of the U.S. Treasury and the Federal Reserve that helped keep the banking and financial crisis of 2007–2008 from worsening.

The U.S. government responded to the financial crisis with historically unprecedented fiscal policy actions while the Fed acted aggressively as a lender of last resort.

The Treasury Bailout: TARP

In late 2008 Congress passed the **Troubled Asset Relief Program (TARP),** which allocated $700 billion—yes, billion—to the U.S. Treasury to make emergency loans to critical financial and other U.S. firms. Most of this "bailout" money eventually was lent out. In fact, as of March 2009, the federal government and Federal Reserve had spent $170 billion just keeping insurer AIG afloat. Other major recipients of TARP funds included Citibank, Bank of America, JPMorgan Chase, and Goldman Sachs. Later, nonfinancial firms such as General Motors and Chrysler also received several billion dollars of TARP loans.

TARP indeed saved several financial institutions whose bankruptcy would have caused a tsunami of secondary effects that probably would have brought down other financial firms and frozen credit throughout the economy. But this very fact demonstrates the problem of **moral hazard.** As it relates to financial investment, moral hazard is the tendency for financial investors and financial services firms to take on greater risks because they assume they are at least partially insured against losses. Without TARP, several firms would have gone bankrupt and their stockholders, bondholders, and executives all would have suffered large personal losses. With TARP, those outcomes were at least partially avoided. TARP and similar government bailouts were essentially government-provided insurance payouts to financial firms that never had to pay a single cent in insurance premiums for the massive bailouts that kept them afloat.

The correct assumption by large firms that they were simply too big for government to let them fail may have given them an incentive to make riskier investments than if no government bailouts were likely to be forthcoming.

The Fed's Lender-of-Last-Resort Activities

As noted in our previous list of Fed functions, one of the roles of the Federal Reserve is to serve as the lender of last resort to financial institutions in times of financial emergencies. The Fed performed this vital function well following the 9/11 terrorist attacks. The financial crisis of

2007–2008 presented another, broader-based financial emergency. Under Fed Chair Ben Bernanke, the Fed designed and implemented several highly creative new lender-of-last-resort facilities to pump liquidity into the financial system. These facilities, procedures, and capabilities were in addition to both the TARP efforts by the U.S. Treasury and the Fed's use of standard tools of monetary policy (the subject of Chapter 16) designed to reduce interest rates. All the new Fed facilities had the single purpose and desired outcome of keeping credit flowing.

Total Fed assets rose from $885 billion in February 2008 to $1,903 billion in March 2009. This increase reflected a huge rise in the amount of securities (U.S. securities, mortgage-backed securities, and others) owned by the Fed. In undertaking its lender-of-last-resort functions, the Fed bought these securities from financial institutions. The purpose was to increase liquidity in the financial system by exchanging illiquid bonds (that the firms could not easily sell during the crisis) for cash, the most liquid of all assets.

Many economists believe that TARP and the Fed's actions helped avert a second Great Depression. The following list of new Fed credit facilities underscores the extraordinary extent of the Fed's lender-of-last-resort response to the crisis.

- **Primary Dealer Credit Facility (PDCF)** Provided overnight loans to primary dealers who were willing to post loan-backed securities as collateral. (The Fed kept the collateral on any loan that was not repaid on time.) Primary dealers are the 21 major financial institutions that the Fed uses to buy and sell U.S. securities.

- **Term Securities Lending Facility (TSLF)** Lent U.S. securities to primary dealers for one-month terms to promote liquidity in the markets for these U.S. securities. The financial institutions obtained the securities from the Fed through participating in competitive single-bid auctions.

- **Asset-Backed Commercial Paper Money Market Mutual Fund Liquidity Facility** Provided loans to U.S. banks and thrifts to finance their purchases of *commercial paper* from money market mutual funds. Commercial paper consists of asset-backed, short-term IOUs that are mainly issued by corporations. These short-term loans are vital for financing the day-to-day operations of businesses.

- **Commercial Paper Funding Facility (CPFF)** Purchased commercial paper to support the commercial paper market and therefore the short-term credit needs of businesses.

- **Money Market Investor Funding Facility (MMIFF)** Provided funding support to a private-sector initiative designed to ensure the liquidity of U.S. money market mutual funds. Many Americans rely on money market mutual funds as low-risk investments.

- **Term Asset-Backed Securities Loan Facility (TALF)** Helped households and business with their credit needs by providing funding support for asset-backed securities collateralized by student loans, auto loans, credit card loans, and loans guaranteed by the Small Business Administration (SBA).

- **Interest Payments on Reserves** Bolstered the profitability of banks by paying interest on the reserves they hold in their vaults or in the Federal Reserve Banks.

These extraordinary efforts, like those of the Treasury, helped prevent total disarray in the credit markets. But like TARP, the Fed efforts intensified the moral hazard problem by greatly limiting the losses that otherwise would have resulted from bad financial assumptions and decisions.

QUICK REVIEW 14.5

- The Troubled Asset Relief Program (TARP) authorized the U.S. Treasury to spend up to $700 billion to make emergency loans and guarantees to failing financial firms.
- The Treasury rescue, or bailout, was aided by lender-of-last-resort loans provided by the Federal Reserve to financial institutions through a series of newly established Fed facilities.
- The TARP loans and the Fed's lender-of-last-resort actions intensified the moral hazard problem in which financial investors and financial firms take on greater risk because they assume that the government will bail them out if they lose money.

The Postcrisis U.S. Financial Services Industry

LO14.8 Identify the main subsets of the financial services industry in the United States and provide examples of some firms in each category.

Table 14.1 lists the major categories of firms within the U.S. financial services industry and gives examples of firms in each category. Note that the main categories of the **financial services industry** are commercial banks, thrifts,

LAST WORD

Too Big to Fail. Too Big to Jail?

In 2010, Congress Passed the Wall Street Reform and Consumer Protection Act in an Attempt to Better Regulate Big Financial Firms. But Their Enormous Size Has Now, Apparently, Placed Them Above the Law.

In early December 2012, Lanny Breuer, the Assistant U.S. Attorney General in charge of prosecuting financial crimes, explained at a press conference that he had decided to only fine HSBC bank $1.9 billion—or about five weeks' profits—as a punishment for nearly a decade of laundering money for the Sinaloa drug cartel, Al Qaeda, and Russian mobsters; helping Iran, the Sudan, and North Korea evade sanctions; and helping hundreds of individuals and businesses cheat on their taxes. Not a single HSBC official would face jail time or a personal fine.

Breuer explained that he chose not to criminally prosecute the bank and put any of its officers in jail because "HSBC would almost certainly have lost its banking license in the United States. The future of the institution would have been under threat and the entire banking system would have been destabilized." In other words, HSBC was not prosecuted because it was very large and very interconnected with other financial firms.

A week later Breuer was again in front of the press. This time it was to announce a set of minor penalties in the LIBOR interest-rate scandal, which involved major international banks illegally manipulating the London Interbank Offer Rate (LIBOR) for their own personal benefit. That manipulation affected trillions of dollars of financial contracts around the world, including millions of home mortgages in the United States. It was thus the most extensive financial crime in world history. But

Hon. Lanny Breuer

Breuer worried aloud about global financial stability and stated, "Our goal here is: Not to destroy a major financial institution."

Breuer's decision to put financial stability ahead of prosecuting financial crimes was made even more clear in early January 2013 when on the TV show *Frontline* he was asked whether prosecutors should think about anything other than pursuing justice. He responded, "Well, I think I am pursuing justice. And I think the entire responsibility of the Department is to pursue justice. But in any given case, I think I and prosecutors around

insurance companies, mutual fund companies, pension funds, security firms, and investment banks. Even before the financial crisis of 2007–2008, the financial services industry was consolidating into fewer, larger firms, each offering a wider spectrum of services. In 1999 Congress ended the Depression-era prohibition against banks selling stocks, bonds, and mutual funds. Thus, the lines between the subsets of the financial industry began to blur. Many banks acquired stock brokerage firms and, in a few cases, insurance companies. For example, Citigroup, which was once only into banking, now owns Smith Barney, a large securities firm. Many large banks (for example, Wells Fargo) and pension funds (for example, TIAA-CREF) now provide mutual funds, including money market mutual funds that pay relatively high interest and on which checks of $500 or more can be written.

The upheaval in the financial markets caused by the financial crisis of 2007–2008 further consolidated the industry and further blurred the lines between its segments. Between September 2007 and September 2009 the FDIC shut down more than 200 U.S. banks and transferred their bank deposits to other, usually larger, banks. In 2009 the three largest U.S. banks (JPMorgan Chase, Bank of America, and Wells Fargo) held roughly $3 of every $10 on deposit in the United States.

Also, during the financial crisis of 2007–2008, major investment banks Goldman Sachs and Morgan Stanley opted to become commercial banks to gain access to emergency Federal Reserve loans. The nation's largest thrift—Washington Mutual—was absorbed by commercial bank JPMorgan Chase. But even with all this blending, the categories in Table 14.1 remain helpful. The

the country, being responsible, should speak to regulators, should speak to experts, because if I bring a case against institution A, and as a result of bringing that case, there's some huge economic effect—if it creates a ripple effect so that, suddenly, counterparties and other financial institutions or other companies that had nothing to do with this are affected badly—it's a factor we need to know and understand." It is perhaps not surprising that *Frontline* titled that episode "The Untouchables."

Many economists, however, sympathize with Breuer's position because legal changes made during the 1990s resulted in a financial system dominated by just a few large firms, each of which is now so large and so interconnected that if any were to collapse, the whole system would indeed be destabilized.

Before those legal changes were made, the structure of the U.S. financial system had been defined by the Glass-Steagall Act of 1933. That law required Wall Street to segregate high-risk and low-risk financial activities across different firms. In particular, Glass-Steagall had required commercial banks to only engage in low-risk lending activities like making home mortgages and small business loans. High-risk financial activities like stock picking, derivatives trading, and investment banking had to be handled by an entirely different set of firms. Thus, even if the firms that took high risks went bankrupt, they were not going to be able to affect the traditional banking system that the entire economy depended upon for making payments, providing cash, and issuing loans to individuals and small businesses.

The legal changes made during the 1990s were aimed at allowing financial firms to offer "one-stop shopping" for financial services. Instead of customers having to go to one firm for a checking account, another to buy life insurance, and yet another to invest in mutual funds, single companies were allowed to offer every imaginable financial service. Not only was this intended to be more convenient, it was argued that it would actually increase financial stability because large firms that offered a full range of financial services would be diversified across different business activities. For example, if a firm's insurance division was losing money, some other division would probably be doing well enough to either partly or fully offset the loss.

By the time the financial crisis hit in 2007, however, things had turned out quite differently. The convenience factor was there, but the ability to go into other lines of business had caused a massive consolidation of banks, insurance companies, stock brokerages, and derivatives-trading companies. In particular, the major commercial banks were now engaged in massive amounts of speculative investing—much of it financed with the money deposited into checking accounts. Thus, when the crisis hit, it was impossible for any of the major financial firms to go bankrupt without severely affecting both the payments system and the financial viability of other financial firms. Each firm was now so large and so interconnected that it had to be treated as "too big to fail" by government regulators.

What Breuer's comments in 2012 and 2013 indicated, though, was that at least some of the firms had also become "too big to jail." There are, consequently, many economists calling for a return to a financial system in which the big financial firms are broken up into entities that are each small enough to fail without catastrophically affecting the entire financial system and in which Glass-Steagall-style separations once again divide high-risk and low-risk financial activities into separate firms.

An attempt to put that separation into practice was passed in 2010 as part of the Wall Street Reform and Consumer Protection Act. It was known as the Volker Rule after former Federal Reserve Chairman Paul Volker. But as of early 2013, it had yet to be implemented.

main lines of a firm's businesses often are in one category or another. For example, even though Goldman Sachs is licensed and regulated as a bank, it is first and foremost an investment company. And the insurance companies and pension funds do most of their business as such.

The financial crisis of 2007–2008 generated much introspection about what went wrong and how to prevent anything like it from happening again. Politicians and financial regulators tightened lending rules to offset the "pass the buck" incentives created by mortgage-backed securities and prevent loans from being issued to people who are unlikely to be able to make the required monthly payments. They also passed legislation to help homeowners who were "underwater" on mortgage loans remain in their homes.

In mid-2010 Congress passed and the president signed the **Wall Street Reform and Consumer Protection Act.** This sweeping law includes provisions that:

- Eliminate the Office of Thrift Supervision and give broader authority to the Federal Reserve to regulate all large financial institutions.

- Create a Financial Stability Oversight Council to be on the lookout for risks to the financial system.

- Establish a process for the federal government to liquidate (sell off) the assets of failing non-bank financial institutions, much like the FDIC does with failing banks.

- Provide federal regulatory oversight of mortgage-backed securities and other derivatives and require that they be traded on public exchanges.

TABLE 14.1   Major Categories of Financial Institutions within the U.S. Financial Services Industry

Institution	Description	Examples
Commercial banks	State and national banks that provide checking and savings accounts, sell certificates of deposit, and make loans. The Federal Deposit Insurance Corporation (FDIC) insures checking and savings accounts up to $250,000.	JPMorgan Chase, Bank of America, Citibank, Wells Fargo
Thrifts	Savings and loan associations (S&Ls), mutual saving banks, and credit unions that offer checking and savings accounts and make loans. Historically, S&Ls made mortgage loans for houses while mutual savings banks and credit unions made small personal loans, such as automobile loans. Today, major thrifts offer the same range of banking services as commercial banks. The Federal Deposit Insurance Corporation and the National Credit Union Administration insure checking and savings deposits up to $250,000.	Charter One, New York Community Bank, Pentagon Federal Credit Union, Boeing Employees Credit Union (BECU)
Insurance companies	Firms that offer policies (contracts) through which individuals pay premiums to insure against some loss, say, disability or death. In some life insurance policies and annuities, the funds are invested for the client in stocks and bonds and paid back after a specified number of years. Thus, insurance sometimes has a saving or financial-investment element.	Prudential, New York Life, Northwestern Mutual, Hartford, MetLife
Mutual fund companies	Firms that pool deposits by customers to purchase stocks or bonds (or both). Customers thus indirectly own a part of a particular set of stocks or bonds, say stocks in companies expected to grow rapidly (a growth fund) or bonds issued by state governments (a municipal bond fund).	Fidelity, Vanguard, Putnam, Janus, T. Rowe Price
Pension funds	For-profit or nonprofit institutions that collect savings from workers (or from employers on their behalf) throughout their working years and then buy stocks and bonds with the proceeds and make monthly retirement payments.	TIAA-CREF, Teamsters' Union, CalPERs
Securities firms	Firms that offer security advice and buy and sell stocks and bonds for clients. More generally known as *stock brokerage firms*.	Merrill Lynch, Smith Barney, Charles Schwab
Investment banks	Firms that help corporations and governments raise money by selling stocks and bonds. They also typically offer advisory services for corporate mergers and acquisitions as well as brokerage services and advice.	Goldman Sachs, Morgan Stanley, Deutsche Bank, Nomura Securities

- Require companies selling asset-backed securities to retain a portion of those securities so the sellers share part of the risk.

- Establish a stronger consumer financial protection role for the Fed through creation of the Bureau of Consumer Financial Protection.

Proponents of the new law say that it will help prevent many of the practices that led up to the financial crisis of 2007–2008. They also contend that the law will send a strong message to stockholders, bondholders, and executives of large financial firms that they will suffer unavoidable and extremely high personal financial losses if they allow their firms to ever again get into serious financial trouble.

Skeptics of the new law say that regulators already had all the tools they needed to prevent the financial crisis. They also point out that the government's own efforts to promote home ownership, via quasi-government institutions that purchased mortgage-backed securities, greatly contributed to the financial crisis. Critics of the new law say that it will simply impose heavy new regulatory costs on the financial industry while doing little to prevent future government bailouts. This chapter's Last Word considers those suspicions.

QUICK REVIEW 14.6

- The main categories of the U.S. financial services industry are commercial banks, thrifts, insurance companies, mutual fund companies, pension funds, securities firms, and investment banks.

- The reassembly of the wreckage from the financial crisis of 2007–2008 has further consolidated the already-consolidating financial services industry and has further blurred some of the lines between the subsets of the industry.

- The Wall Street Reform and Consumer Financial Protection Act of 2010 responded to the financial crisis by consolidating financial regulation, providing federal oversight of mortgage-backed securities, and creating the Bureau of Consumer Financial Protection.

SUMMARY

LO14.1 Identify and explain the functions of money.

Anything that is accepted as (*a*) a medium of exchange, (*b*) a unit of monetary account, and (*c*) a store of value can be used as money.

LO14.2 List and describe the components of the U.S. money supply.

There are two major definitions of the money supply. *M*1 consists of currency and checkable deposits; *M*2 consists of *M*1 plus savings deposits, including money market deposit accounts, small-denominated (less than $100,000) time deposits, and money market mutual fund balances held by individuals.

LO14.3 Describe what "backs" the money supply, making us willing to accept it as payment.

Money represents the debts of government and institutions offering checkable deposits (commercial banks and thrift institutions) and has value because of the goods, services, and resources it will command in the market. Maintaining the purchasing power of money depends largely on the government's effectiveness in managing the money supply.

LO14.4 Discuss the makeup of the Federal Reserve and its relationship to banks and thrifts.

The U.S. banking system consists of (*a*) the Board of Governors of the Federal Reserve System, (*b*) the 12 Federal Reserve Banks, and (*c*) some 6,000 commercial banks and 8,500 thrift institutions (mainly credit unions). The Board of Governors is the basic policymaking body for the entire banking system. The directives of the Board and the Federal Open Market Committee (FOMC) are made effective through the 12 Federal Reserve Banks, which are simultaneously (*a*) central banks, (*b*) quasi-public banks, and (*c*) bankers' banks.

LO14.5 Identify the functions and responsibilities of the Federal Reserve and explain why Fed independence is important.

The major functions of the Fed are to (*a*) issue Federal Reserve Notes, (*b*) set reserve requirements and hold reserves deposited by banks and thrifts, (*c*) lend money to financial institutions and serve as the lender of last resort in national financial emergencies, (*d*) provide for the rapid collection of checks, (*e*) act as the fiscal agent for the federal government, (*f*) supervise the operations of the banks, and (*g*) regulate the supply of money in the best interests of the economy.

The Fed is essentially an independent institution, controlled neither by the president of the United States nor by Congress. This independence shields the Fed from political pressure and allows it to raise and lower interest rates (via changes in the money supply) as needed to promote full employment, price stability, and economic growth.

LO14.6 Identify and explain the main factors that contributed to the financial crisis of 2007–2008.

The financial crisis of 2007–2008 consisted of an unprecedented rise in mortgage loan defaults, the collapse or near-collapse of several major financial institutions, and the generalized freezing up of credit availability. The crisis resulted from bad mortgage loans together with declining real estate prices. It also resulted from underestimation of risk by holders of mortgage-backed securities and faulty insurance securities designed to protect holders of mortgage-backed securities from the risk of default.

LO14.7 Discuss the actions of the U.S. Treasury and the Federal Reserve that helped keep the banking and financial crisis of 2007–2008 from worsening.

In 2008 Congress passed the Troubled Asset Relief Program (TARP), which authorized the U.S. Treasury to spend up to $700 billion to make emergency loans and guarantees to failing financial firms. The Treasury rescue, or bailout, was aided by lender-of-last-resort loans provided by the Federal Reserve to financial institutions through a series of newly established Fed facilities.

The TARP loans and the Fed's lender-of-last-resort actions intensify the moral hazard problem. This is the tendency of financial investors and financial firms to take on greater risk when they assume they are at least partially insured against loss.

LO14.8 Identify the main subsets of the financial services industry in the United States and provide examples of some firms in each category.

The main categories of the U.S. financial services industry are commercial banks, thrifts, insurance companies, mutual fund companies, pension funds, securities firms, and investment banks. The reassembly of the wreckage from the financial crisis of 2007–2008 has further consolidated the already-consolidating financial services industry and has further blurred some of the lines between the subsets of the industry.

In response to the financial crisis, Congress passed the Wall Street Reform and Consumer Financial Protection Act of 2010.

TERMS AND CONCEPTS

medium of exchange	*M*1	commercial banks
unit of account	Federal Reserve Notes	thrift institutions
store of value	token money	near-monies
liquidity	checkable deposits	*M*2

savings account

money market deposit account (MMDA)

time deposits

money market mutual fund (MMMF)

legal tender

Federal Reserve System

Board of Governors

Federal Reserve Banks

Federal Open Market Committee (FOMC)

subprime mortgage loans

mortgage-backed securities

securitization

Troubled Asset Relief Program (TARP)

moral hazard

financial services industry

Wall Street Reform and Consumer Protection Act

The following and additional problems can be found in connect ECONOMICS

DISCUSSION QUESTIONS

1. What are the three basic functions of money? Describe how rapid inflation can undermine money's ability to perform each of the three functions. **LO14.1**

2. Which two of the following financial institutions offer checkable deposits included within the *M*1 money supply: mutual fund companies; insurance companies; commercial banks; securities firms; thrift institutions? Which of the following items is not included in either *M*1 or *M*2: currency held by the public; checkable deposits; money market mutual fund balances; small-denominated (less than $100,000) time deposits; currency held by banks; savings deposits? **LO14.2**

3. What are the components of the *M*1 money supply? What is the largest component? Which of the components of *M*1 is legal tender? Why is the face value of a coin greater than its intrinsic value? What near-monies are included in the *M*2 money supply? **LO14.2**

4. Explain and evaluate the following statements: **LO14.2**
   a. The invention of money is one of the great achievements of humankind, for without it the enrichment that comes from broadening trade would have been impossible.
   b. Money is whatever society says it is.
   c. In the United States, the debts of government and commercial banks are used as money.
   d. People often say they would like to have more money, but what they usually mean is that they would like to have more goods and services.
   e. When the price of everything goes up, it is not because everything is worth more but because the currency is worth less.
   f. Any central bank can create money; the trick is to create enough, but not too much, of it.

5. What "backs" the money supply in the United States? What determines the value (domestic purchasing power) of money? How does the purchasing power of money relate to the price level? Who in the United States is responsible for maintaining money's purchasing power? **LO14.3**

6. How is the chairperson of the Federal Reserve System selected? Describe the relationship between the Board of Governors of the Federal Reserve System and the 12 Federal Reserve Banks. What is the purpose of the Federal Open Market Committee (FOMC)? What is its makeup? **LO14.4**

7. The following are two hypothetical ways in which the Federal Reserve Board might be appointed. Would you favor either of these two methods over the present method? Why or why not? **LO14.4**
   a. Upon taking office, the U.S. president appoints seven people to the Federal Reserve Board, including a chair. Each appointee must be confirmed by a majority vote of the Senate, and each serves the same 4-year term as the president.
   b. Congress selects seven members from its ranks (four from the House of Representatives and three from the Senate) to serve at congressional pleasure as the Board of Governors of the Federal Reserve System.

8. What is meant when economists say that the Federal Reserve Banks are central banks, quasi-public banks, and bankers' banks? **LO14.4**

9. Why do economists nearly uniformly support an independent Fed rather than one beholden directly to either the president or Congress? **LO14.5**

10. Identify three functions of the Federal Reserve of your choice, other than its main role of controlling the supply of money. **LO14.5**

11. How does each of the following relate to the financial crisis of 2007–2008: declines in real estate values, subprime mortgage loans, mortgage-backed securities, AIG. **LO14.6**

12. What is TARP and how was it funded? What is meant by the term "lender of last resort" and how does it relate to the financial crisis of 2007–2008? How do government and Federal Reserve emergency loans relate to the concept of moral hazard? **LO14.7**

13. What are the major categories of firms that make up the U.S. financial services industry? Are there more or fewer banks today than before the start of the financial crisis of 2007–2008? Why are the lines between the categories of financial firms even more blurred than they were before the

crisis? How did the Wall Street Reform and Consumer Protection Act of 2010 try to address some of the problems that helped cause the crisis? **LO14.8**

14. **LAST WORD** Why are federal prosecutors reluctant to bring major charges against large financial firms? What was the main regulatory action of the Glass-Steagall law? Why might having many smaller financial firms be more stable than having fewer larger firms? What argument can be made for the possibility that larger financial firms might be more stable than smaller financial firms?

REVIEW QUESTIONS

1. The three functions of money are: **LO14.1**
   a. Liquidity, store of value, and gifting.
   b. Medium of exchange, unit of account, and liquidity.
   c. Liquidity, unit of account, and gifting.
   d. Medium of exchange, unit of account, and store of value.

2. Suppose that a small country currently has $4 million of currency in circulation, $6 million of checkable deposits, $200 million of savings deposits, $40 million of small-denominated time deposits, and $30 million of money market mutual fund deposits. From these numbers we see that this small country's $M1$ money supply is _____, while its $M2$ money supply is _____. **LO14.2**
   a. $10 million; $280 million.
   b. $10 million; $270 million.
   c. $210 million; $280 million.
   d. $250 million; $270 million.

3. Recall the formula that states that $V = 1/P$, where V is the value of the dollar and P is the price level. If the price level falls from 1 to 0.75, what will happen to the value of the dollar? **LO14.3**
   a. It will rise by a third (33.3 percent).
   b. It will rise by a quarter (25 percent).
   c. It will fall by a quarter (-25 percent).
   d. It will fall by a third (-33.3 percent).

4. Which group votes on the open-market operations that are used to control the U.S. money supply and interest rates? **LO14.4**
   a. The Federal Reserve System.
   b. The 12 Federal Reserve Banks.
   c. The Board of Governors of the Federal Reserve System.
   d. The Federal Open Market Committee (FOMC).

5. An important reason why members of the Federal Reserve's Board of Governors are each given extremely long, 14-year terms is to: **LO14.4**
   a. Insulate members from political pressures that could result in inflation.
   b. Help older members avoid job searches before retiring.

   c. Attract younger people with lots of time left in their careers.
   d. Avoid the trouble of constantly having to deal with new members.

6. Which of the following is *not* a function of the Fed? **LO14.5**
   a. Setting reserve requirements for banks.
   b. Advising Congress on fiscal policy.
   c. Regulating the supply of money.
   d. Serving as a lender of last resort.

7. James borrows $300,000 for a home from Bank A. Bank A resells the right to collect on that loan to Bank B. Bank B securitizes that loan with hundreds of others and sells the resulting security to a state pension plan, which at the same time purchases an insurance policy from AIG that will pay off if James and the other people whose mortgages are in the security can't pay off their mortgage loans. Suppose that James and all the other people can't pay off their mortgages. Which financial entity is legally obligated to suffer the loss? **LO14.6**
   a. Bank A.
   b. Bank B.
   c. The state pension plan.
   d. AIG.

8. City Bank is considering making a $50 million loan to a company named SheetOil that wants to commercialize a process for turning used blankets, pillowcases, and sheets into oil. This company's chances for success are dubious, but City Bank makes the loan anyway because it believes that the government will bail it out if SheetOil goes bankrupt and cannot repay the loan. City Bank's decision to make the loan has been affected by: **LO14.7**
   a. Liquidity.
   b. Moral hazard.
   c. Token money.
   d. Securitization.

9. True or False: The financial crisis hastened the ongoing process in which the financial services industry was transforming from having a few large firms to many small firms. **LO14.8**

PROBLEMS

1. Assume that the following asset values (in millions of dollars) exist in Ironmania: Federal Reserve Notes in circulation = $700; Money market mutual funds (MMMFs) held by individuals = $400; Corporate bonds = $300; Iron ore deposits = $50; Currency in commercial banks = $100; Savings deposits, including money market deposit accounts

(MMDAs) = $140; Checkable deposits = $1,500; Small-denominated (less than $100,000) time deposits = $100; Coins in circulation = $40. **LO14.1**

a. What is M1 in Ironmania?

b. What is M2 in Ironmania?

2. Assume that Jimmy Cash has $2,000 in his checking account at Folsom Bank and uses his checking account card to withdraw $200 of cash from the bank's ATM machine. By what dollar amount did the M1 money supply change as a result of this single, isolated transaction? **LO14.2**

3. Suppose the price level and value of the U.S. dollar in year 1 are 1 and $1, respectively. If the price level rises to 1.25 in year 2, what is the new value of the dollar? If, instead, the price level falls to 0.50, what is the value of the dollar? **LO14.3**

4. Assume that securitization combined with borrowing and irrational exuberance in Hyperville have driven up the value of existing financial securities at a geometric rate, specifically from $2 to $4 to $8 to $16 to $32 to $64 over a six-year time period. Over the same period, the value of the assets underlying the securities rose at an arithmetic rate from $2 to $3 to $4 to $5 to $6 to $7. If these patterns hold for decreases as well as for increases, by how much would the value of the financial securities decline if the value of the underlying asset suddenly and unexpectedly fell by $5? **LO14.6**

5. Suppose that Lady Gaga goes to Las Vegas to play poker and at the last minute her record company says it will reimburse her for 50 percent of any gambling losses that she incurs. Will Lady Gaga wager more or less as a result of the reimbursement offer? What economic concept does your answer illustrate? **LO14.7**

Money Creation

Learning Objectives

LO15.1 Discuss why the U.S. banking system is called a "fractional reserve" system.

LO15.2 Explain the basics of a bank's balance sheet and the distinction between a bank's actual reserves and its required reserves.

LO15.3 Describe how a bank can create money.

LO15.4 Describe the multiple expansion of loans and money by the entire banking system.

LO15.5 Define the monetary multiplier, explain how to calculate it, and demonstrate its relevance.

We have seen that the *M*1 money supply consists of currency (coins and Federal Reserve Notes) and checkable deposits and that *M*1 is a base component of *M*2, a broader measure of the money supply that also includes savings deposits, small-denominated time deposits, and balances in money market mutual funds. The U.S. Mint produces the coins and the U.S. Bureau of Engraving and Printing creates the Federal Reserve Notes. So who creates the checkable deposits? Surprisingly, it is loan officers! Although that may sound like something a congressional committee should investigate, the monetary authorities are well aware that banks and thrifts create checkable deposits. In fact, the Federal Reserve relies on these institutions to create this vital component of the nation's money supply.

The Fractional Reserve System

LO15.1 Discuss why the U.S. banking system is called a "fractional reserve" system.

The United States, like most other countries today, has a **fractional reserve banking system** in which only a portion (fraction) of checkable deposits are backed up by reserves of currency in bank vaults or deposits at the central bank. Our goal is to explain this system and show how commercial banks can create checkable deposits by issuing loans. Our examples will involve commercial banks, but remember that thrift institutions also provide checkable deposits. So the analysis applies to banks and thrifts alike.

Illustrating the Idea: The Goldsmiths

Here is the history behind the idea of the fractional reserve system.

When early traders began to use gold in making transactions, they soon realized that it was both unsafe and inconvenient to carry gold and to have it weighed and assayed (judged for purity) every time they negotiated a transaction. So by the sixteenth century they had begun to deposit their gold with goldsmiths, who would store it in vaults for a fee. On receiving a gold deposit, the goldsmith would issue a receipt to the depositor. Soon people were paying for goods with goldsmiths' receipts, which served as one of the first types of paper money.

At this point the goldsmiths—embryonic bankers—used a 100 percent reserve system; they backed their circulating paper money receipts fully with the gold that they held "in reserve" in their vaults. But because of the public's acceptance of the goldsmiths' receipts as paper money, the goldsmiths soon realized that owners rarely redeemed the gold they had in storage. In fact, the goldsmiths observed that the amount of gold being deposited with them in any week or month was likely to exceed the amount that was being withdrawn.

Then some clever goldsmith hit on the idea that paper "receipts" could be issued in excess of the amount of gold held. Goldsmiths would put these receipts, which were redeemable in gold, into circulation by making interest-earning loans to merchants, producers, and consumers. A borrower might, for instance, borrow $10,000 worth of gold receipts today with the promise to repay $10,500 worth of gold receipts in one year (a 5 percent interest rate). Borrowers were willing to accept loans in the form of gold receipts because the receipts were accepted as a medium of exchange in the marketplace.

This was the beginning of the fractional reserve system of banking, in which reserves in bank vaults are a fraction of the total money supply. If, for example, the goldsmith issued $1 million in receipts for actual gold in storage and another $1 million in receipts as loans, then the total value of paper money in circulation would be $2 million—twice the value of the gold. Gold reserves would be a fraction (one-half) of outstanding paper money.

Significant Characteristics of Fractional Reserve Banking

The goldsmith story highlights two significant characteristics of fractional reserve banking. First, banks can create money through lending. In fact, goldsmiths created money when they made loans by giving borrowers paper money that was not fully backed by gold reserves. The quantity of such money goldsmiths could create depended on the amount of reserves they deemed prudent to have available. The smaller the amount of reserves thought necessary, the larger the amount of paper money the goldsmiths could create. Today, gold is no longer used as bank reserves. Instead, currency itself serves as bank reserves so that the creation of checkable-deposit money by banks (via their lending) is limited by the amount of *currency reserves* that the banks feel obligated, or are required by law, to keep.

A second reality is that banks operating on the basis of fractional reserves are vulnerable to "panics" or "runs." A goldsmith who issued paper money equal to twice the value of his gold reserves would be unable to convert all that paper money into gold in the event that all the holders of that money appeared at his door at the same time demanding their gold. In fact, many European and U.S. banks were once ruined by this unfortunate circumstance. However, a bank panic is highly unlikely if the banker's reserve and lending policies are prudent. Indeed, one reason why banking systems are highly regulated industries is to prevent runs on banks.

This is also why the United States has the system of deposit insurance that we discussed in the last chapter. By guaranteeing deposits, deposit insurance helps to prevent the sort of bank runs that used to happen so often before deposit insurance was available. In those situations, rumors would spread that a bank was about to go bankrupt and that it only had a small amount of reserves left in its vaults. Bank runs are called "bank runs" because depositors would run to the bank trying to be one of the lucky few to withdraw their money while the bank had any reserves left. The rumors were usually totally unfounded. But, unfortunately, the bank would still go bankrupt even if it began the day with its normal amount of reserves. With so many customers withdrawing money simultaneously, it would run out of reserves and be forced to default on its obligations to its remaining depositors. By guaranteeing depositors that they will always get their money, deposit insurance removes the incentive to try to withdraw one's deposit before anyone else can. It thus stops most bank runs.

A Single Commercial Bank

LO15.2 Explain the basics of a bank's balance sheet and the distinction between a bank's actual reserves and its required reserves.

To illustrate the workings of the modern fractional reserve banking system, we need to examine a commercial bank's balance sheet.

The **balance sheet** of a commercial bank (or thrift) is a statement of assets—things owned by the bank or owed to the bank—and claims on those assets. A bank balance sheet summarizes the financial position of the bank at a certain time. Every balance sheet must balance; this means that the value of *assets* must equal the amount of claims against those assets. The claims shown on a balance sheet are divided into two groups: the claims of non-owners of the bank against the firm's assets, called *liabilities*, and the claims of the owners of the firm against the firm's assets, called *net worth*. Liabilities are things owed by the bank to depositors or others. A balance sheet is balanced because

Assets = liabilities + net worth

Every $1 change in assets must be offset by a $1 change in liabilities + net worth. Every $1 change in liabilities + net worth must be offset by a $1 change in assets.

Now let's work through a series of bank transactions involving balance sheets to establish how individual banks can create money.

Transaction 1: Creating a Bank

Suppose some far-sighted citizens of the town of Wahoo, Nebraska (yes, there is such a place), decide their town needs a new commercial bank to provide banking services for that growing community. Once they have secured a state or national charter for their bank, they turn to the task of selling, say, $250,000 worth of stock (equity shares) to buyers, both in and out of the community. Their efforts meet with success and the Bank of Wahoo comes into existence—at least on paper. What does its balance sheet look like at this stage?

The founders of the bank have sold $250,000 worth of shares of stock in the bank—some to themselves, some to other people. As a result, the bank now has $250,000 in cash on hand and $250,000 worth of stock shares outstanding. The cash is an asset to the bank. Cash held by a

bank is sometimes called **vault cash** or till money. The shares of stock outstanding constitute an equal amount of claims that the owners have against the bank's assets. Those shares of stock constitute the net worth of the bank. The bank's balance sheet reads:

Creating a Bank Balance Sheet 1: Wahoo Bank			
Assets		Liabilities and net worth	
Cash	$250,000	Stock shares	$250,000

Each item listed in a balance sheet such as this is called an *account*.

Transaction 2: Acquiring Property and Equipment

The board of directors (who represent the bank's owners) must now get the new bank off the drawing board and make it a reality. First, property and equipment must be acquired. Suppose the directors, confident of the success of their venture, purchase a building for $220,000 and pay $20,000 for office equipment. This simple transaction changes the composition of the bank's assets. The bank now has $240,000 less in cash and $240,000 of new property assets. Using blue to denote accounts affected by each transaction, we find that the bank's balance sheet at the end of transaction 2 appears as follows:

Acquiring Property and Equipment Balance Sheet 2: Wahoo Bank			
Assets		Liabilities and net worth	
Cash	$ 10,000	Stock shares	$250,000
Property	240,000		

Note that the balance sheet still balances, as it must.

Transaction 3: Accepting Deposits

Commercial banks have two basic functions: to accept deposits of money and to make loans. Now that the bank is operating, suppose that the citizens and businesses of Wahoo decide to deposit $100,000 in the Wahoo bank. What happens to the bank's balance sheet?

The bank receives cash, which is an asset to the bank. Suppose this money is deposited in the bank as checkable deposits (checking account entries), rather than as savings accounts or time deposits. These newly created *checkable deposits* constitute claims that the depositors have against the assets of the Wahoo bank and thus are a new liability account. The bank's balance sheet now looks like this:

	Accepting Deposits Balance Sheet 3: Wahoo Bank		
Assets		Liabilities and net worth	
Cash	$110,000	Checkable deposits	$100,000
Property	240,000	Stock shares	250,000

There has been no change in the economy's total supply of money as a result of transaction 3, but a change has occurred in the composition of the money supply. Bank money, or checkable deposits, has increased by $100,000, and currency held by the public has decreased by $100,000. As explained in the previous chapter, currency held in a bank is not part of the economy's money supply.

A withdrawal of cash will reduce the bank's checkable-deposit liabilities and its holdings of cash by the amount of the withdrawal. This, too, changes the composition, but not the total supply, of money in the economy.

Transaction 4: Depositing Reserves in a Federal Reserve Bank

All commercial banks and thrift institutions that provide checkable deposits must by law keep **required reserves.** Required reserves are an amount of funds equal to a specified percentage of the bank's own deposit liabilities. A bank must keep these reserves on deposit with the Federal Reserve Bank in its district or as cash in the bank's vault. To simplify, we suppose the Bank of Wahoo keeps its required reserves entirely as deposits in the Federal Reserve Bank of its district. But remember that vault cash is counted as reserves and real-world banks keep a significant portion of their own reserves in their vaults.

The "specified percentage" of checkable-deposit liabilities that a commercial bank must keep as reserves is known as the **reserve ratio**—the ratio of the required reserves the commercial bank must keep to the bank's own outstanding checkable-deposit liabilities:

$$\text{Reserve ratio} = \frac{\text{commercial bank's required reserves}}{\text{commercial bank's checkable-deposit liabilities}}$$

If the reserve ratio is $\frac{1}{10}$, or 10 percent, the Wahoo bank, having accepted $100,000 in deposits from the public, would have to keep $10,000 as reserves. If the ratio is $\frac{1}{5}$, or 20 percent, $20,000 of reserves would be required. If $\frac{1}{2}$, or 50 percent, $50,000 would be required.

TABLE 15.1 Reserve Requirements (Reserve Ratios) for Banks and Thrifts, 2013

Type of Deposit	Current Requirement	Statutory Limits
Checkable deposits:		
$0–$12.4 million	0%	3%
$12.4–$79.5 million	3	3
Over $79.5 million	10	8–14
Noncheckable nonpersonal savings and time deposits	0	0–9

Source: Federal Reserve, Regulation D, **www.federalreserve.gov**.

The Fed has the authority to establish and vary the reserve ratio within limits legislated by Congress. The limits now prevailing are shown in Table 15.1. The first $12.4 million of checkable deposits held by a commercial bank or thrift is exempt from reserve requirements. A 3 percent reserve is required on checkable deposits of between $12.4 million and $79.5 million. A 10 percent reserve is required on checkable deposits over $79.5 million, although the Fed can vary that percentage between 8 and 14 percent. Currently, no reserves are required against noncheckable nonpersonal (business) savings or time deposits, although up to 9 percent can be required. Also, after consultation with appropriate congressional committees, the Fed for 180 days may impose reserve requirements outside the 8 to 14 percent range specified in Table 15.1. Beginning in late 2008, the Fed began paying banks interest on their required reserves and on their excess reserve balances held at Federal Reserve Banks.

In order to simplify, we will suppose that the reserve ratio for checkable deposits in commercial banks is $\frac{1}{5}$, or 20 percent. Although 20 percent obviously is higher than the requirement really is, the figure is convenient for calculations. Because we are concerned only with checkable (spendable) deposits, we ignore reserves on noncheckable savings and time deposits. The main point is that reserve requirements are fractional, meaning that they are less than 100 percent. This point is critical in our analysis of the lending ability of the banking system.

By depositing $20,000 in the Federal Reserve Bank, the Wahoo bank will just be meeting the required 20 percent ratio between its reserves and its own deposit liabilities. We will use "reserves" to mean the funds commercial banks deposit in the Federal Reserve Banks, to distinguish those funds from the public's deposits in commercial banks.

But suppose the Wahoo bank anticipates that its holdings of checkable deposits will grow in the future. Then, instead of sending just the minimum amount, $20,000, it sends an extra $90,000, for a total of $110,000. In so doing, the bank will avoid the inconvenience of sending additional reserves to the Federal Reserve Bank each time its own checkable-deposit liabilities increase. And, as you will see, it is these extra reserves that enable banks to lend money and earn interest income.

Actually, a real-world bank would not deposit *all* its cash in the Federal Reserve Bank. However, because (1) banks as a rule hold vault cash only in the amount of $1\frac{1}{2}$ or 2 percent of their total assets and (2) vault cash can be counted as reserves, we will assume for simplicity that all of Wahoo's cash is deposited in the Federal Reserve Bank and therefore constitutes the commercial bank's actual reserves. By making this simplifying assumption, we do not need to bother adding two assets—"cash" and "deposits in the Federal Reserve Bank"—to determine "reserves."

After the Wahoo bank deposits $110,000 of reserves at the Fed, its balance sheet becomes:

Depositing Reserves at the Fed Balance Sheet 4: Wahoo Bank			
Assets		Liabilities and net worth	
Cash	$ 0	Checkable	
Reserves	110,000	deposits	$100,000
Property	240,000	Stock shares	250,000

There are three things to note about this latest transaction.

Excess Reserves   A bank's **excess reserves** are found by subtracting its *required reserves* from its **actual reserves:**

Excess reserves = actual reserves − required reserves

In this case,

Actual reserves	$110,000
Required reserves	−20,000
Excess reserves	$ 90,000

The only reliable way of computing excess reserves is to multiply the bank's checkable-deposit liabilities by the reserve ratio to obtain required reserves ($100,000 × 20 percent = $20,000) and then to subtract the required reserves from the actual reserves listed on the asset side of the bank's balance sheet.

To test your understanding, compute the bank's excess reserves from balance sheet 4, assuming that the reserve ratio is (1) 10 percent, (2) $33\frac{1}{3}$ percent, and (3) 50 percent.

We will soon demonstrate that the ability of a commercial bank to make loans depends on the existence of excess reserves. Understanding this concept is crucial in seeing how the banking system creates money.

Control   You might think the basic purpose of reserves is to enhance the liquidity of a bank and protect commercial bank depositors from losses. Reserves would constitute a ready source of funds from which commercial banks could meet large, unexpected cash withdrawals by depositors.

But this reasoning breaks down under scrutiny. Although historically reserves have been seen as a source of liquidity and therefore as protection for depositors, a bank's required reserves are not great enough to meet sudden, massive cash withdrawals. If the banker's nightmare should materialize—everyone with checkable deposits appearing at once to demand those deposits in cash—the actual reserves held as vault cash or at the Federal Reserve Bank would be insufficient. The banker simply could not meet this "bank panic." Because reserves are fractional, checkable deposits may be much greater than a bank's required reserves.

So commercial bank deposits must be protected by other means. Periodic bank examinations are one way of promoting prudent commercial banking practices. Furthermore, insurance funds administered by the Federal Deposit Insurance Corporation (FDIC) and the National Credit Union Administration (NCUA) insure individual deposits in banks and thrifts up to $250,000.

If it is not the purpose of reserves to provide for commercial bank liquidity, then what is their function? *Control* is the answer. Required reserves help the Fed control the lending ability of commercial banks. The Fed can take certain actions that either increase or decrease commercial bank reserves and affect the ability of banks to grant credit. The objective is to prevent banks from overextending or underextending bank credit. To the degree that these policies successfully influence the volume of commercial bank credit, the Fed can help the economy avoid business fluctuations. Another function of reserves is to facilitate the collection or "clearing" of checks.

Asset and Liability   Transaction 4 brings up another matter. Specifically, the reserves created in transaction 4 are an asset to the depositing commercial bank because they are a claim this bank has against the assets of another institution—the Federal Reserve Bank. The checkable deposit you get by depositing money in a commercial bank is an asset to you and a liability to the bank (since the bank is liable for repaying you whenever you choose to withdraw your deposit). In the same way, the reserves that a commercial bank establishes by depositing money in a bankers' bank are an asset to the commercial bank and a liability to the Federal Reserve Bank.

Transaction 5: Clearing a Check Drawn against the Bank

Assume that Fred Bradshaw, a Wahoo farmer, deposited a substantial portion of the $100,000 in checkable deposits that the Wahoo bank received in transaction 3. Now suppose that Fred buys $50,000 of farm machinery from the Ajax Farm Implement Company of Surprise, Nebraska. Bradshaw pays for this machinery by writing a $50,000 check against his deposit in the Wahoo bank. He gives the check to the Ajax Company. What are the results?

Ajax deposits the check in its account with the Surprise bank. The Surprise bank increases Ajax's checkable deposits by $50,000 when Ajax deposits the check. Ajax is now paid in full. Bradshaw is pleased with his new machinery.

Now the Surprise bank has Bradshaw's check. This check is simply a claim against the assets of the Wahoo bank. The Surprise bank will collect this claim by sending the check (along with checks drawn on other banks) to the regional Federal Reserve Bank. Here a bank employee will clear, or collect, the check for the Surprise bank by increasing Surprise's reserve in the Federal Reserve Bank by $50,000 and decreasing the Wahoo bank's reserve by that same amount. The check is "collected" merely by making bookkeeping notations to the effect that Wahoo's claim against the Federal Reserve Bank is reduced by $50,000 and Surprise's claim is increased by $50,000.

Finally, the Federal Reserve Bank sends the cleared check back to the Wahoo bank, and for the first time the Wahoo bank discovers that one of its depositors has drawn a check for $50,000 against his checkable deposit. Accordingly, the Wahoo bank reduces Bradshaw's checkable deposit by $50,000 and notes that the collection of this check has caused a $50,000 decline in its reserves at the Federal Reserve Bank. All the balance sheets balance: The Wahoo bank has reduced both its assets (reserves) and its liabilities (checkable deposits) by $50,000. The Surprise bank has $50,000 more in both assets (reserves) and liabilities (checkable deposits). Ownership of reserves at the Federal Reserve Bank has changed—with Wahoo owning $50,000 less and Surprise owning $50,000 more—but total reserves stay the same.

Whenever a check is drawn against one bank and deposited in another bank, collection of that check will reduce both the reserves and the checkable deposits of the bank on which the check is drawn. Conversely, if a bank receives a check drawn on another bank, the bank receiving the check will, in the process of collecting it, have its reserves and deposits increased by the amount of the check. In our example, the Wahoo bank loses $50,000 in both reserves and deposits to the Surprise bank. But there is no loss of reserves or deposits for the banking system as a whole. What one bank loses, another bank gains.

If we bring all the other assets and liabilities back into the picture, the Wahoo bank's balance sheet looks like this at the end of transaction 5:

Clearing a Check Balance Sheet 5: Wahoo Bank			
Assets		**Liabilities and net worth**	
Reserves	$ 60,000	Checkable deposits	$ 50,000
Property	240,000	Stock shares	250,000

Verify that with a 20 percent reserve requirement, the bank's excess reserves now stand at $50,000.

QUICK REVIEW 15.1

- The United States has a fractional reserve banking system, in which the collective reserves of the banks usually are considerably less than 100 percent of their checkable deposit liabilities.
- When a bank accepts deposits of cash, the composition of the money supply is changed, but the total supply of money is not directly altered.
- Commercial banks and thrifts are obliged to keep required reserves equal to a specified percentage of their own checkable-deposit liabilities as cash or on deposit with the Federal Reserve Bank of their district.
- The amount by which a bank's actual reserves exceed its required reserves is called excess reserves.
- A bank that has a check drawn and collected against it will lose to the recipient bank both reserves and deposits equal to the value of the check.

Money-Creating Transactions of a Commercial Bank

LO15.3 Describe how a bank can create money.

The next two transactions are crucial because they explain (1) how a commercial bank can literally create money by making loans and (2) how banks create money by purchasing government bonds from the public.

Transaction 6: Granting a Loan

In addition to accepting deposits, commercial banks grant loans to borrowers. What effect does lending by a commercial bank have on its balance sheet?

Suppose the Gristly Meat Packing Company of Wahoo decides it is time to expand its facilities. Suppose, too, that the company needs exactly $50,000—which just happens to be equal to the Wahoo bank's excess reserves—to finance this project.

Gristly goes to the Wahoo bank and requests a loan for this amount. The Wahoo bank knows the Gristly Company's fine reputation and financial soundness and is convinced of its ability to repay the loan. So the loan is granted. In return, the president of Gristly hands a promissory note—a fancy IOU—to the Wahoo bank. Gristly wants the convenience and safety of paying its obligations by check. So, instead of receiving a basket full of currency from the bank, Gristly gets a $50,000 increase in its checkable-deposit account in the Wahoo bank.

The Wahoo bank has acquired an interest-earning asset (the promissory note, which it files under "Loans") and has created checkable deposits (a liability) to "pay" for this asset. Gristly has swapped an IOU for the right to draw an additional $50,000 worth of checks against its checkable deposit in the Wahoo bank. Both parties are pleased.

At the moment the loan is completed, the Wahoo bank's position is shown by balance sheet 6a:

When a Loan Is Negotiated Balance Sheet 6a: Wahoo Bank			
Assets		Liabilities and net worth	
Reserves	$ 60,000	Checkable deposits	$100,000
Loans	50,000		
Property	240,000	Stock shares	250,000

All this looks simple enough. But a close examination of the Wahoo bank's balance statement reveals a startling fact: When a bank makes loans, it creates money. The president of Gristly went to the bank with something that is *not* money—her IOU—and walked out with something that *is* money—a checkable deposit.

Contrast transaction 6a with transaction 3, in which checkable deposits were created but only as a result of currency having been taken out of circulation. There was a change in the *composition* of the money supply in that situation but no change in the *total supply* of money. But when banks lend, they create checkable deposits that *are* money. By extending credit, the Wahoo bank has "monetized" an IOU. Gristly and the Wahoo bank have created and then swapped claims. The claim created by Gristly and given to the bank is not money; an individual's IOU is not acceptable as a medium of exchange. But the claim created by the bank and given to Gristly *is* money; checks drawn against a checkable deposit are acceptable as a medium of exchange. Checkable-deposit money like this constitutes

about one-half the quantity of *M*1 money in the United States and about 10 percent of *M*2.

Much of the money used in the United States therefore is created through the extension of credit by commercial banks. This checkable-deposit money may be thought of as "debts" of commercial banks and thrift institutions. Checkable deposits are bank debts in the sense that they are claims that banks and thrifts promise to pay "on demand."

But certain factors limit the ability of a commercial bank to create checkable deposits ("bank money") by lending. The Wahoo bank can expect the newly created checkable deposit of $50,000 to be a very active account. Gristly would not borrow $50,000 at, say, 7, 10, or 12 percent interest for the sheer joy of knowing that funds were available if needed.

Assume that Gristly awards a $50,000 building contract to the Quickbuck Construction Company of Omaha. Quickbuck, true to its name, completes the expansion promptly and is paid with a check for $50,000 drawn by Gristly against its checkable deposit in the Wahoo bank. Quickbuck, with headquarters in Omaha, does not deposit this check in the Wahoo bank but instead deposits it in the Fourth National Bank of Omaha. Fourth National now has a $50,000 claim against the Wahoo bank. The check is collected in the manner described in transaction 5. As a result, the Wahoo bank loses both reserves and deposits equal to the amount of the check; Fourth National acquires $50,000 of reserves and deposits.

In summary, assuming a check is drawn by the borrower for the entire amount of the loan ($50,000) and is given to a firm that deposits it in some other bank, the Wahoo bank's balance sheet will read as follows after the check has been cleared against it:

After a Check Is Drawn on the Loan Balance Sheet 6b: Wahoo Bank			
Assets		Liabilities and net worth	
Reserves	$ 10,000	Checkable deposits	$ 50,000
Loans	50,000		
Property	240,000	Stock shares	250,000

After the check has been collected, the Wahoo bank just meets the required reserve ratio of 20 percent (= $10,000/$50,000). The bank has *no* excess reserves. This poses a question: Could the Wahoo bank have lent more than $50,000—an amount greater than its excess reserves—and still have met the 20 percent reserve requirement when a check for the full amount of the loan was cleared against it? The answer is no; the bank is "fully loaned up."

Here is why: Suppose the Wahoo bank had lent $55,000 to the Gristly company and that the Gristly company had spent all of that money by writing a $55,000 check to

WORKED PROBLEMS

W15.1

Single bank accounting

Quickbuck Construction. Collection of the check against the Wahoo bank would have lowered its reserves to $5,000 (= $60,000 − $55,000), and checkable deposits would once again stand at $50,000 (= $105,000 − $55,000). The ratio of actual reserves to checkable deposits would then be $5,000/$50,000, or only 10 percent. Because the reserve requirement is 20 percent, the Wahoo bank could not have lent $55,000.

By experimenting with other amounts over $50,000, you will find that the maximum amount the Wahoo bank could lend at the outset of transaction 6 is $50,000. This amount is identical to the amount of excess reserves the bank had available when the loan was negotiated.

A single commercial bank in a multibank banking system can lend only an amount equal to its initial preloan excess reserves. When it lends, the lending bank faces the possibility that checks for the entire amount of the loan will be drawn and cleared against it. If that happens, it will lose (to other banks) reserves equal to the amount it lends. So, to be safe, it limits its lending to the amount of its excess reserves.

Bank creation of money raises an interesting question: If a bank creates checkable-deposit money when it lends its excess reserves, is money destroyed when borrowers pay off loans? The answer is yes. When loans are paid off, the process works in reverse. The bank's checkable deposits decline by the amount of the loan repayment.

Transaction 7: Buying Government Securities

When a commercial bank buys government bonds from the public, the effect is substantially the same as lending. New money is created.

Assume that the Wahoo bank's balance sheet initially stands as it did at the end of transaction 5. Now suppose that instead of making a $50,000 loan, the bank buys $50,000 of government securities from a securities dealer. The bank receives the interest-bearing bonds, which appear on its balance statement as the asset "Securities," and gives the dealer an increase in its checkable-deposit account. The Wahoo bank's balance sheet appears as follows:

	Buying Government Securities Balance Sheet 7: Wahoo Bank		
Assets		Liabilities and net worth	
Reserves	$ 60,000	Checkable deposits	$100,000
Securities	50,000		
Property	240,000	Stock shares	250,000

Checkable deposits, that is, the supply of money, have been increased by $50,000, as in transaction 6. Bond purchases from the public by commercial banks increase the supply of money in the same way as lending to the public does. The bank accepts government bonds (which are not money) and gives the securities dealer an increase in its checkable deposits (which *are* money).

Of course, when the securities dealer draws and clears a check for $50,000 against the Wahoo bank, the bank loses both reserves and deposits in that amount and then just meets the legal reserve requirement. Its balance sheet now reads precisely as in 6b except that "Securities" is substituted for "Loans" on the asset side.

Finally, the *selling* of government bonds to the public by a commercial bank—like the repayment of a loan—reduces the supply of money. The securities buyer pays by check, and both "Securities" and "Checkable deposits" (the latter being money) decline by the amount of the sale.

Profits, Liquidity, and the Federal Funds Market

The asset items on a commercial bank's balance sheet reflect the banker's pursuit of two conflicting goals:

- *Profit* One goal is profit. Commercial banks, like any other businesses, seek profits, which is why the bank makes loans and buys securities—the two major earning assets of commercial banks.

- *Liquidity* The other goal is safety. For a bank, safety lies in liquidity, specifically such liquid assets as cash and excess reserves. A bank must be on guard for depositors who want to transform their checkable deposits into cash. Similarly, it must guard against more checks clearing against it than are cleared in its favor, causing a net outflow of reserves. Bankers thus seek a balance between prudence and profit. The compromise is between assets that earn higher returns and highly liquid assets that earn no returns.

An interesting way in which banks can partly reconcile the goals of profit and liquidity is to lend temporary excess reserves held at the Federal Reserve Banks to other commercial banks. Normal day-to-day flows of funds to banks rarely leave all banks with their exact levels of required reserves. Also, excess reserves held at the Federal Reserve Banks are highly liquid, but they draw less interest than the banks can make through loans. Banks therefore often lend these excess reserves to other banks on an overnight basis in order to earn additional interest without sacrificing long-term liquidity. Banks that borrow in this federal funds market—the market for immediately available reserve balances at the Federal Reserve—do so because they are temporarily short of required reserves. The interest rate paid on these overnight loans is called the **federal funds rate.**

We would show an overnight loan of reserves from the Surprise bank to the Wahoo bank as a decrease in reserves at the Surprise bank and an increase in reserves at the Wahoo bank. Ownership of reserves at the Federal Reserve Bank of Kansas City would change, but total reserves would not be affected. Exercise: Determine what other changes would be required on the Wahoo and Surprise banks' balance sheets as a result of the overnight loan.

QUICK REVIEW 15.2

- Banks create money when they make loans; money vanishes when bank loans are repaid.
- New money is created when banks buy government bonds from the public; money disappears when banks sell government bonds to the public.
- Banks balance profitability and safety in determining their mix of earning assets and highly liquid assets.
- Although the Fed pays interest on excess reserves, banks may be able to obtain higher interest rates by temporarily lending the reserves to other banks in the federal funds market; the interest rate on such loans is the federal funds rate.

The Banking System: Multiple-Deposit Expansion

LO15.4 Describe the multiple expansion of loans and money by the entire banking system.

Thus far we have seen that a single bank in a banking system can lend one dollar for each dollar of its excess reserves. The situation is different for all commercial banks as a group. We will find that the commercial banking system can lend—that is, can create money—by a multiple of its excess reserves. This multiple lending is accomplished even though each bank in the system can lend only "dollar for dollar" with its excess reserves.

How do these seemingly paradoxical results come about? To answer this question succinctly, we will make three simplifying assumptions:

- The reserve ratio for all commercial banks is 20 percent.
- Initially all banks are meeting this 20 percent reserve requirement exactly. No excess reserves exist; or, in the parlance of banking, they are "loaned up" (or "loaned out") fully in terms of the reserve requirement.

- If any bank can increase its loans as a result of acquiring excess reserves, an amount equal to those excess reserves will be lent to one borrower, who will write a check for the entire amount of the loan and give it to someone else, who will deposit the check in another bank. This third assumption means that the worst thing possible happens to every lending bank—a check for the entire amount of the loan is drawn and cleared against it in favor of another bank.

The Banking System's Lending Potential

Suppose a junkyard owner finds a $100 bill while dismantling a car that has been on the lot for years. He deposits the $100 in bank A, which adds the $100 to its reserves. We will record only changes in the balance sheets of the various commercial banks. The deposit changes bank A's balance sheet as shown by entries (a_1):

	Multiple-Deposit Expansion Process Balance Sheet: Commercial Bank A		
Assets		Liabilities and net worth	
Reserves	$+100 ($a_1$) −80 ($a_3$)	Checkable deposits	$+100 ($a_1$) +80 ($a_2$) −80 ($a_3$)
Loans	+80 (a_2)		

Recall from transaction 3 that this $100 deposit of currency does not alter the money supply. While $100 of checkable-deposit money comes into being, it is offset by the $100 of currency no longer in the hands of the public (the junkyard owner). But bank A *has* acquired excess reserves of $80. Of the newly acquired $100 in currency, 20 percent, or $20, must be earmarked for the required reserves on the new $100 checkable deposit, and the remaining $80 goes to excess reserves. Remembering that a single commercial bank can lend only an amount equal to its excess reserves, we conclude that bank A can lend a maximum of $80. When a loan for this amount is made, bank A's loans increase by $80 and the borrower gets an $80 checkable deposit. We add these figures—entries (a_2)—to bank A's balance sheet.

But now we make our third assumption: The borrower uses the full amount of the loan ($80) to write a check ($80) to someone else, and that person deposits the amount in bank B, a different bank. As we saw in transaction 6, bank A loses both reserves and deposits equal to the amount of the loan, as indicated in entries (a_3). The net result of these transactions is that bank A's reserves now stand at +$20 (= $100 − $80), loans at +$80, and checkable deposits at +$100 (= $100 + $80 − $80).

When the dust has settled, bank A is just meeting the 20 percent reserve ratio.

Recalling our previous discussion, we know that bank B acquires both the reserves and the deposits that bank A has lost. Bank B's balance sheet is changed as in entries (b_1):

Multiple-Deposit Expansion Process Balance Sheet: Commercial Bank B			
Assets		**Liabilities and net worth**	
Reserves	$+80 (b_1)	Checkable deposits	$+80 (b_1)
	−64 (b_3)		+64 (b_2)
Loans	+64 (b_2)		−64 (b_3)

When the borrower's check is drawn and cleared, bank A loses $80 in reserves and deposits and bank B gains $80 in reserves and deposits. But 20 percent, or $16, of bank B's new reserves must be kept as required reserves against the new $80 in checkable deposits. This means that bank B has $64 (= $80 − $16) in excess reserves. It can therefore lend $64 [entries (b_2)]. When the new borrower writes a check for $64 to buy a product, and the seller deposits the check in bank C, the reserves and deposits of bank B both fall by $64 [entries (b_3)]. As a result of these transactions, bank B's reserves now stand at +$16 (= $80 − $64), loans at +$64, and checkable deposits at +$80 (= $80 + $64 − $64). After all this, bank B is just meeting the 20 percent reserve requirement.

We are off and running again. Bank C acquires the $64 in reserves and deposits lost by bank B. Its balance sheet changes as in entries (c_1):

Multiple-Deposit Expansion Process Balance Sheet: Commercial Bank C			
Assets		**Liabilities and net worth**	
Reserves	$+64.00 (c_1)	Checkable deposits	$+64.00 (c_1)
	−51.20 (c_3)		+51.20 (c_2)
Loans	+51.20 (c_2)		−51.20 (c_3)

Exactly 20 percent, or $12.80, of these new reserves will be required reserves, the remaining $51.20 being excess reserves. Hence, bank C can safely lend a maximum of $51.20. Suppose it does [entries (c_2)]. And suppose the borrower writes a check for the entire amount ($51.20) to a merchant who deposits it in another bank [entries (c_3)].

We could go ahead with this procedure by bringing banks D, E, F, G, . . . , N, and so on into the picture. In fact, the process will go on almost indefinitely, just as long as banks further down the line receive at least one penny in new reserves that they can use to back another round of lending and money creation. But we suggest that you work through the computations for banks D, E, and F to be sure you understand the procedure.

The entire analysis is summarized in Table 15.2. Data for banks D through N are supplied on their own rows so

TABLE 15.2 Expansion of the Money Supply by the Commercial Banking System

Bank	(1) Acquired Reserves and Deposits	(2) Required Reserves (Reserve Ratio = .2)	(3) Excess Reserves, (1) − (2)	(4) Amount Bank Can Lend; New Money Created = (3)
Bank A	$100.00 (a_1)	$20.00	**$80.00**	$ 80.00 (a_2)
Bank B	80.00 (a_3, b_1)	16.00	64.00	64.00 (b_2)
Bank C	64.00 (b_3, c_1)	12.80	51.20	51.20 (c_2)
Bank D	51.20	10.24	40.96	40.96
Bank E	40.96	8.19	32.77	32.77
Bank F	32.77	6.55	26.21	26.21
Bank G	26.21	5.24	20.97	20.97
Bank H	20.97	4.20	16.78	16.78
Bank I	16.78	3.36	13.42	13.42
Bank J	13.42	2.68	10.74	10.74
Bank K	10.74	2.15	8.59	8.59
Bank L	8.59	1.72	6.87	6.87
Bank M	6.87	1.37	5.50	5.50
Bank N	5.50	1.10	4.40	4.40
Other banks	21.99	4.40	17.59	17.59
Total amount of money created (sum of the amounts in column 4)				**$400.00**

that you may check your computations. The last row of the table consolidates into one row everything that happens for all banks down the line after bank N. Our conclusion is startling: On the basis of only $80 in excess reserves (acquired by the banking system when someone deposited $100 of currency in bank A), the entire commercial banking system is able to lend $400, the sum of the amounts in column 4. The banking system can lend excess reserves by a multiple of 5 (= $400/$80) when the reserve ratio is 20 percent. Yet each single bank in the banking system is lending only an amount equal to its own excess reserves. How do we explain this? How can the banking system as a whole lend by a multiple of its excess reserves, when each individual bank can lend only dollar for dollar with its excess reserves?

The answer is that reserves lost by a single bank are not lost to the banking system as a whole. The reserves lost by bank A are acquired by bank B. Those lost by B are gained by C. C loses to D, D to E, E to F, and so forth. Although reserves can be, and are, lost by individual banks in the banking system, there is no loss of reserves for the banking system as a whole.

An individual bank can safely lend only an amount equal to its excess reserves, *but the commercial banking system can lend by a multiple of its collective excess reserves.* This contrast, incidentally, is an illustration of why it is imperative that we keep the fallacy of composition (Last Word, Chapter 1) firmly in mind. Commercial banks as a group can create money by lending in a manner much different from that of the individual banks in the group.

The Monetary Multiplier

LO15.5 Define the monetary multiplier, explain how to calculate it, and demonstrate its relevance.

The **monetary multiplier** (or, less commonly, the *checkable deposit multiplier*) defines the relationship between any new excess reserves in the banking system and the magnified creation of new checkable-deposit money by banks as a group. It is a separate idea from the spending-income multiplier of Chapter 10 but shares some mathematical similarities. The spending-income multiplier exists because the expenditures of one household become some other household's income; the multiplier magnifies a change in initial spending into a larger change in GDP. The spending-income multiplier is the reciprocal of the MPS (the leakage into saving that occurs at each round of spending).

Similarly, the monetary multiplier exists because the reserves and deposits lost by one bank become reserves of another bank. It magnifies excess reserves into a larger creation of checkable-deposit money. The monetary multiplier m is the reciprocal of the required reserve ratio R (the leakage into required reserves that occurs at each step in the lending process). In short,

$$\text{Monetary multiplier} = \frac{1}{\text{required reserve ratio}}$$

or, in symbols,

$$m = \frac{1}{R}$$

In this formula, m represents the maximum amount of new checkable-deposit money that can be created by a single dollar of excess reserves, given the value of R. By multiplying the excess reserves E by m, we can find the maximum amount of new checkable-deposit money, D, that can be created by the banking system. That is,

$$\begin{array}{l}\text{Maximum}\\ \text{checkable-deposit} \\ \text{creation}\end{array} = \begin{array}{l}\text{excess}\\ \text{reserves}\end{array} \times \begin{array}{l}\text{monetary}\\ \text{multiplier}\end{array}$$

or, more simply,

$$D = E \times m$$

In our example in Table 15.2, R is 0.20, so m is 5 (= 1/0.20). This implies that

$$D = \$80 \times 5 = \$400$$

Figure 15.1 depicts the final outcome of our example of a multiple-deposit expansion of the money supply.

FIGURE 15.1   The outcome of the money expansion process. A deposit of $100 of currency into a checking account creates an initial checkable deposit of $100. If the reserve ratio is 20 percent, only $20 of reserves is legally required to support the $100 checkable deposit. The $80 of excess reserves allows the banking system to create $400 of checkable deposits through making loans. The $100 of reserves supports a total of $500 of money ($100 + $400).

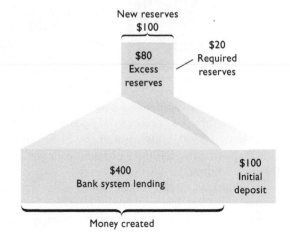

Banking, Leverage, and Financial Instability

Leverage Boosts Banking Profits but Makes the Banking System Less Stable. Time to Reduce Leverage?

The term *leverage* is used in finance to describe how the use of borrowed money can magnify both profits and losses. To see how leverage works, first consider an investment opportunity that produces a 10 percent positive return if things go well but a 5 percent loss if things go poorly. Those rates of return imply that if a person invests $100 of his own savings, he will end up with either $110 if things go well or $95 if things go badly. Put slightly differently, he will either gain $10 or lose $5 from where he started, with his own $100 being used to fund the $100 investment.

But now consider what happens to his potential returns if he uses borrowed money to provide "leverage." In fact, let's have him use a lot of leverage. To make the $100 investment, he uses $10 of his own savings and $90 of borrowed money (which, for simplicity, we will assume that he can borrow at zero percent interest). If things go well, the investment will return $110. He then must repay the $90 loan. That will leave him with $20 (= $110 of investment return if things go well minus $90 to repay the loan). That means that he will end up with $20 if things go well and he uses leverage. Notice that this implies that if he uses leverage, he will get a 100 percent (= $20 divided by $10) return

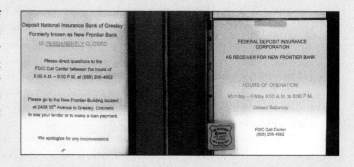

on the $10 of his own savings that he himself invested. That, of course, is much nicer than a 10 percent return. In fact, it is 10 times as large—hence the term *leverage*. The use of borrowed money has massively increased the percentage rate of return if things go well.

Unfortunately, however, nothing in life is free. Leverage also magnifies the investor's losses if things go wrong. To see this, note that if things go wrong in this example, the investor will end up turning $100 into $95. But then he has to pay back the $90 that he borrowed. That will leave him with only $5 (= $95 investment

The initial deposit of $100 of currency into the bank (lower right-hand box) creates new reserves of an equal

WORKED PROBLEMS

W15.2
Money creation

amount (upper box). With a 20 percent reserve ratio, however, only $20 of reserves are needed to "back up" this $100 checkable deposit. The excess reserves of $80 permit the creation of $400 of new checkable deposits via the

making of loans, confirming a monetary multiplier of 5. The $100 of new reserves supports a total supply of money of $500, consisting of the $100 initial checkable deposit plus $400 of checkable deposits created through lending.

Higher reserve ratios mean lower monetary multipliers and therefore less creation of new checkable-deposit money via loans; smaller reserve ratios mean higher

monetary multipliers and thus more creation of new checkable-deposit money via loans. With a high reserve ratio, say, 50 percent, the monetary multiplier would be 2 (= 1/0.5), and in our example the banking system could create only $100 (= $50 of excess reserves × 2) of new checkable deposits. With a low reserve ratio, say, 5 percent, the monetary multiplier would be 20 (= 1/0.05), and the banking system could create $1,900 (= $95 of excess reserves × 20) of new checkable deposits.

You might experiment with the following two brainteasers to test your understanding of multiple credit expansion by the banking system:

- Rework the analysis in Table 15.2 (at least three or four steps of it) assuming the reserve ratio is 10 percent. What is the maximum amount of money the banking system can create upon acquiring $100 in new reserves and deposits? (The answer is not $800!)

return if things go badly minus $90 to repay the loan). That implies that the investor will lose $5 off of the $10 of his own savings that he himself originally put into the investment. That is a 50 percent loss—ten times as much as the 5 percent loss that he would have sustained if he had used only his own money to make the $100 investment. Thus, you can see that leverage increases both profits if things go well and losses if things go badly.

A modern bank uses a lot of leverage. In fact, only about 5 percent of the money that it invests comes from its shareholders and the money they paid to purchase ownership shares in the bank. The other 95 percent comes from borrowing, either by issuing bonds (about 25 percent) or by taking in checking and savings deposits (about 70 percent). It surprises many people, but checking and savings deposits are technically a type of loan made by depositors to their banks. So banks get 70 percent of their leverage and funding from money borrowed from depositors.

The problem with that much leverage is that it takes only very small losses to drive the bank into insolvency and a situation in which it cannot repay all of the money that it has borrowed because the value of the bank's assets has fallen below the value of the bank's liabilities. Consider what would happen if for every $100 invested by the bank, only $94 returned. That by itself is a 6 percent rate of loss. But because the bank is borrowing $95 of every $100 that it invests, it will be driven into insolvency by that six percent loss because it is getting back less than the amount that it borrowed to fund the investment. With the investment returning only $94, there won't be enough money to pay off the $95 that the bank borrowed!

So why do banks use this much leverage? Because it is very profitable for the bankers who run the banks. If things are going well, the leverage massively increases the banks' profit rates—and bankers get paid bonuses based on those profit rates. On the other hand, if things go badly, bankers have come to expect bailouts in which the government uses taxpayer money to ensure that all of a bank's liabilities are repaid. So from the perspective of the bankers, it's "heads I win, tails you lose."

One solution to these problems would be to require banks to use much less leverage. For every $100 that a bank wants to invest, the bank could be required to raise $30 from its shareholder owners so that it would only be borrowing the other $70 through issuing bonds or by taking in checking and savings deposits. That would make the entire banking system much more stable because it would be very unlikely that for any $100 invested into projects by the bank, less than $70 would come back. Even if only $71 came back, there would still be enough money to pay back the $70 of borrowed money—and thus no need for the bank to go bankrupt or require a government bailout via the deposit insurance system.

Unfortunately, however, bankers have lobbied strongly and successfully against any legal attempts to require lower leverage levels. So the current regulatory system relies instead on bank supervisors who attempt to prevent the banks from making bad loans. That system was unable to prevent the 2007–2008 financial crisis and a number of economists argue that until leverage is reduced, no amount of bank supervision will be sufficient to prevent another financial crisis because with massive leverage, even a small loss can destroy a bank.

- Suppose the banking system is loaned up and faces a 20 percent reserve ratio. Explain how it might have to reduce its outstanding loans by $400 when a $100 cash withdrawal from a checkable-deposit account forces one bank to draw down its reserves by $100.

Reversibility: The Multiple Destruction of Money

The process we have described is reversible. Just as checkable-deposit money is created when banks make loans, checkable-deposit money is destroyed when loans are paid off. Loan repayment, in effect, sets off a process of multiple destruction of money the opposite of the multiple creation process. Because loans are both made and paid off in any period, the direction of the loans, checkable deposits, and money supply in a given period will depend on the net effect of the two processes. If the dollar amount of loans made in some period exceeds the dollar amount of loans paid off, checkable deposits will expand and the money supply will increase. But if the dollar amount of loans is less than the dollar amount of loans paid off, checkable deposits will contract and the money supply will decline.

SUMMARY

LO15.1 Discuss why the U.S. banking system is called a "fractional reserve" system.

Modern banking systems are fractional reserve systems: Only a fraction of checkable deposits is backed by currency.

LO15.2 Explain the basics of a bank's balance sheet and the distinction between a bank's actual reserves and its required reserves.

The operation of a commercial bank can be understood through its balance sheet, where assets equal liabilities plus net worth.

Commercial banks keep required reserves on deposit in a Federal Reserve Bank or as vault cash. These required reserves are equal to a specified percentage of the commercial bank's checkable-deposit liabilities. Excess reserves are equal to actual reserves minus required reserves.

Banks lose both reserves and checkable deposits when checks are drawn against them.

LO15.3 Describe how a bank can create money.

Commercial banks create money—checkable deposits, or checkable-deposit money—when they make loans. They convert IOUs, which are *not* money, into checkable-deposits, which *are* money. Money is destroyed when lenders repay bank loans.

The ability of a single commercial bank to create money by lending depends on the size of its excess reserves. Generally speaking, a commercial bank can lend only an amount equal to its excess reserves. Money creation is thus limited because, in all likelihood, checks drawn by borrowers will be deposited in other banks, causing a loss of reserves and deposits to the lending bank equal to the amount of money that it has lent.

Rather than making loans, banks may decide to use excess reserves to buy bonds from the public. In doing so, banks merely credit the checkable-deposit accounts of the bond sellers, thus creating checkable-deposit money. Money vanishes when banks sell bonds to the public because bond buyers must draw down their checkable-deposit balances to pay for the bonds.

Banks earn interest by making loans and by purchasing bonds; they maintain liquidity by holding cash and excess reserves. The Fed pays interest on excess reserves. Nevertheless, banks often can obtain higher interest rates by lending out excess reserves on an overnight basis to banks that are short of required reserves. These loans are made in the federal funds market, and the interest paid on the loans is called the federal funds rate.

LO15.4 Describe the multiple expansion of loans and money by the entire banking system.

The commercial banking system as a whole can lend by a multiple of its excess reserves because the system as a whole cannot lose reserves. Individual banks, however, can lose reserves to other banks in the system.

LO15.5 Define the monetary multiplier, explain how to calculate it, and demonstrate its relevance.

The multiple by which the banking system can lend on the basis of each dollar of excess reserves is the reciprocal of the reserve ratio. This multiple credit expansion process is reversible.

TERMS AND CONCEPTS

fractional reserve banking system	required reserves	actual reserves
balance sheet	reserve ratio	federal funds rate
vault cash	excess reserves	monetary multiplier

The following and additional problems can be found in **connect**
ECONOMICS

DISCUSSION QUESTIONS

1. Explain why merchants accepted gold receipts as a means of payment even though the receipts were issued by goldsmiths, not the government. What risk did goldsmiths introduce into the payments system by issuing loans in the form of gold receipts? **LO15.1**
2. Why is the banking system in the United States referred to as a fractional reserve bank system? What is the role of deposit insurance in a fractional reserve system? **LO15.1**
3. What is the difference between an asset and a liability on a bank's balance sheet? How does net worth relate to each? Why must a balance sheet always balance? What are the major assets and claims on a commercial bank's balance sheet? **LO15.2**

4. Why does the Federal Reserve require commercial banks to have reserves? Explain why reserves are an asset to commercial banks but a liability to the Federal Reserve Banks. What are excess reserves? How do you calculate the amount of excess reserves held by a bank? What is the significance of excess reserves? **LO15.2**
5. "Whenever currency is deposited in a commercial bank, cash goes out of circulation and, as a result, the supply of money is reduced." Do you agree? Explain why or why not. **LO15.2**
6. "When a commercial bank makes loans, it creates money; when loans are repaid, money is destroyed." Explain. **LO15.3**

7. Suppose that Mountain Star Bank discovers that its reserves will temporarily fall slightly below those legally required. How might it temporarily remedy this situation through the federal funds market? Now assume Mountain Star finds that its reserves will be substantially and permanently deficient. What remedy is available to this bank? (Hint: Recall your answer to discussion question 6.) **LO15.3**

8. Explain why a single commercial bank can safely lend only an amount equal to its excess reserves, but the commercial banking system as a whole can lend by a multiple of its excess reserves. What is the monetary multiplier, and how does it relate to the reserve ratio? **LO15.4, LO15.5**

9. How would a decrease in the reserve requirement affect the (*a*) size of the monetary multiplier, (*b*) amount of excess reserves in the banking system, and (*c*) extent to which the system could expand the money supply through the creation of checkable deposits via loans? **LO15.5**

10. **LAST WORD** Does leverage increase the total size of the gain or loss from an investment, or just the percentage rate of return on the part of the investment amount that was not borrowed? How would lowering leverage make the financial system more stable?

REVIEW QUESTIONS

1. A goldsmith has $2 million of gold in his vaults. He issues $5 million in gold receipts. His gold holdings are what fraction of the paper money (gold receipts) he has issued? **LO15.1**
   a. 1/10.
   b. 1/5.
   c. 2/5.
   d. 5/5.

2. A commercial bank has $100 million in checkable-deposit liabilities and $12 million in actual reserves. The required reserve ratio is 10 percent. How big are the bank's excess reserves? **LO15.2**
   a. $100 million.
   b. $88 million.
   c. $12 million.
   d. $2 million.

3. The actual reason that banks must hold required reserves is: **LO15.2**
   a. To enhance liquidity and deter bank runs.
   b. To help fund the Federal Deposit Insurance Corporation, which insures bank deposits.
   c. To give the Fed control over the lending ability of commercial banks.
   d. To help increase the number of bank loans.

4. A single commercial bank in a multibank banking system can lend only an amount equal to its initial preloan _____. **LO15.3**
   a. Total reserves.
   b. Excess reserves.
   c. Total deposits.
   d. Excess deposits.

5. The two conflicting goals facing commercial banks are: **LO15.3**
   a. Profit and liquidity.
   b. Profit and loss.
   c. Deposits and withdrawals.
   d. Assets and liabilities.

6. Suppose that the banking system in Canada has a required reserve ratio of 10 percent while the banking system in the United States has a required reserve ratio of 20 percent. In which country would $100 of initial excess reserves be able to cause a larger total amount of money creation? **LO15.4**
   a. Canada.
   b. United States.

7. Suppose that the Fed has set the reserve ratio at 10 percent and that banks collectively have $2 billion in excess reserves. What is the maximum amount of new checkable-deposit money that can be created by the banking system? **LO15.5**
   a. $0.
   b. $200 million.
   c. $2 billion.
   d. $20 billion.

8. Suppose that last year $30 billion in new loans were extended by banks while $50 billion in old loans were paid off by borrowers. What happened to the money supply? **LO15.5**
   a. Increased.
   b. Decreased.
   c. Stayed the same.

PROBLEMS

1. Suppose the assets of the Silver Lode Bank are $100,000 higher than on the previous day and its net worth is up $20,000. By how much and in what direction must its liabilities have changed from the day before? **LO15.2**

2. Suppose that Serendipity Bank has excess reserves of $8,000 and checkable deposits of $150,000. If the reserve ratio is 20 percent, what is the size of the bank's actual reserves? **LO15.2**

3. Third National Bank has reserves of $20,000 and checkable deposits of $100,000. The reserve ratio is 20 percent. Households deposit $5,000 in currency into the bank and that currency is added to reserves. What level of excess reserves does the bank now have? **LO15.3**

4. Suppose again that Third National Bank has reserves of $20,000 and checkable deposits of $100,000. The reserve ratio is 20 percent. The bank now sells $5,000 in securities

Assets		(1)	(2)	Liabilities and net worth		(1′)	(2′)
Reserves	$22,000	_____	_____	Checkable deposits	$100,000	_____	_____
Securities	38,000	_____	_____				
Loans	40,000	_____	_____				

to the Federal Reserve Bank in its district, receiving a $5,000 increase in reserves in return. What level of excess reserves does the bank now have? By what amount does your answer differ (yes, it does!) from the answer to problem 3? **LO15.3**

5. The balance sheet at the top of the page is for Big Bucks Bank. The reserve ratio is 20 percent. **LO15.3**
   a. What is the maximum amount of new loans that Big Bucks Bank can make? Show in columns 1 and 1′ how the bank's balance sheet will appear after the bank has lent this additional amount.
   b. By how much has the supply of money changed?
   c. How will the bank's balance sheet appear after checks drawn for the entire amount of the new loans have been cleared against the bank? Show the new balance sheet in columns 2 and 2′.
   d. Answer questions *a*, *b*, and *c* on the assumption that the reserve ratio is 15 percent.

6. Suppose the simplified consolidated balance sheet shown in the right column is for the entire commercial banking system and that all figures are in billions of dollars. The reserve ratio is 25 percent. **LO15.5**
   a. What is the amount of excess reserves in this commercial banking system? What is the maximum amount the banking system might lend? Show in columns 1 and 1′ how the consolidated balance sheet would look after this amount has been lent. What is the size of the monetary multiplier?

Assets		(1)	Liabilities and net worth		(1′)
Reserves	$ 52	_____	Checkable deposits	$200	_____
Securities	48	_____			
Loans	100	_____			

   b. Answer the questions in part *a* assuming the reserve ratio is 20 percent. What is the resulting difference in the amount that the commercial banking system can lend?

7. If the required reserve ratio is 10 percent, what is the monetary multiplier? If the monetary multiplier is 4, what is the required reserve ratio? **LO15.5**

Interest Rates and Monetary Policy

Learning Objectives

LO16.1 Discuss how the equilibrium interest rate is determined in the market for money.

LO16.2 Describe the balance sheet of the Federal Reserve and the meaning of its major items.

LO16.3 List and explain the goals and tools of monetary policy.

LO16.4 Describe the federal funds rate and how the Fed directly influences it.

LO16.5 Identify the mechanisms by which monetary policy affects GDP and the price level.

LO16.6 Explain the effectiveness of monetary policy and its shortcomings.

Some newspaper commentators have stated that the chairperson of the Federal Reserve Board (currently Ben Bernanke) is the second most powerful person in the United States, after the U.S. president. That is undoubtedly an exaggeration because the chair has only a single vote on the 7-person Federal Reserve Board and 12-person Federal Open Market Committee. But there can be no doubt about the chair's influence as well as the overall importance of the Federal Reserve and the **monetary policy** that it conducts. Such policy consists of deliberate changes in the money supply to influence interest rates and thus the total level of spending in the economy. The goal of monetary policy is to achieve and maintain price-level stability, full employment, and economic growth.

Interest Rates

LO16.1 Discuss how the equilibrium interest rate is determined in the market for money.

The Fed's primary influence on the economy in normal economic times is through its ability to change the money supply (M_1 and M_2) and therefore affect interest rates. Interest rates can be thought of in several ways. Most basically, **interest** is the price paid for the use of money. It is also the price that borrowers need to pay lenders for transferring purchasing power to the future. And it can be thought of as the amount of money that must be paid for the use of $1 for 1 year. Although there are many different interest rates that vary by purpose, size, risk, maturity, and taxability, we will simply speak of *the* interest rate unless stated otherwise.

Let's see how the interest rate is determined. Because it is a "price," we again turn to demand and supply analysis for the answer.

The Demand for Money

Why does the public want to hold some of its wealth as *money?* There are two main reasons: to make purchases with it and to hold it as an asset.

Transactions Demand, D_t People hold money because it is convenient for purchasing goods and services. Households usually are paid once a week, every 2 weeks, or monthly, whereas their expenditures are less predictable and typically more frequent. So households must have enough money on hand to buy groceries and pay mortgage and utility bills. Nor are business revenues and expenditures simultaneous. Businesses need to have money available to pay for labor, materials, power, and other inputs. The demand for money as a medium of exchange is called the **transactions demand for money.**

The level of nominal GDP is the main determinant of the amount of money demanded for transactions. The larger the total money value of all goods and services exchanged in the economy, the larger the amount of money needed to negotiate those transactions. The transactions demand for money varies directly with nominal GDP. We specify *nominal* GDP because households and firms will want more money for transactions if prices rise or if real output increases. In both instances a larger dollar volume will be needed to accomplish the desired transactions.

In **Figure 16.1a (Key Graph)** we graph the quantity of money demanded for transactions against the interest rate. For simplicity, let's assume that the amount demanded depends exclusively on the level of nominal GDP and is independent of the interest rate. (In reality, higher interest rates are associated with slightly lower volumes of money demanded for transactions.) Our simplifying assumption allows us to graph the transactions demand, D_t, as a vertical line. This demand curve is positioned at $100 billion, on the assumption that each dollar held for transactions purposes is spent an average of three times per year and that nominal GDP is $300 billion. Thus the public needs $100 billion (= $300 billion/3) to purchase that GDP.

Asset Demand, D_a The second reason for holding money derives from money's function as a store of value. People may hold their financial assets in many forms, including corporate stocks, corporate or government bonds, or money. To the extent they want to hold money as an asset, there is an **asset demand for money.**

People like to hold some of their financial assets as money (apart from using it to buy goods and services) because money is the most liquid of all financial assets; it is immediately usable for purchasing other assets when opportunities arise. Money is also an attractive asset to hold when the prices of other assets such as bonds are expected to decline. For example, when the price of a bond falls, the bondholder who sells the bond prior to the payback date of the full principal will suffer a loss (called a *capital loss*). That loss will partially or fully offset the interest received on the bond. Holding money presents no such risk of capital loss from changes in interest rates.

The disadvantage of holding money as an asset is that it earns no or very little interest. Checkable deposits pay either no interest or lower interest rates than bonds. Currency itself earns no interest at all.

Knowing these advantages and disadvantages, the public must decide how much of its financial assets to hold as money, rather than other assets such as bonds. The answer depends primarily on the rate of interest. A household or a business incurs an opportunity cost when it holds money; in both cases, interest income is forgone or sacrificed. If a bond pays 6 percent interest, for example, holding $100 as cash or in a noninterest checkable account costs $6 per year of forgone income.

The amount of money demanded as an asset therefore varies inversely with the rate of interest (which is the opportunity cost of holding money as an asset). When the interest rate rises, being liquid and avoiding

ORIGIN OF THE IDEA

O16.1
Liquidity preference

FIGURE 16.1 **The demand for money, the supply of money, and the equilibrium interest rate.** The total demand for money D_m is determined by horizontally adding the asset demand for money D_a to the transactions demand D_r. The transactions demand is vertical because it is assumed to depend on nominal GDP rather than on the interest rate. The asset demand varies inversely with the interest rate because of the opportunity cost involved in holding currency and checkable deposits that pay no interest or very low interest. Combining the money supply (stock) S_m with the total money demand D_m portrays the market for money and determines the equilibrium interest rate i_e.

(a)	(b)	(c)
Transactions demand for money, D_t	Asset demand for money, D_a	Total demand for money, $D_m = D_t + D_a$, and supply of money, S_m

capital losses becomes more costly. The public reacts by reducing its holdings of money as an asset. When the interest rate falls, the cost of being liquid and avoiding capital losses also declines. The public therefore increases the amount of financial assets that it wants to hold as money. This inverse relationship just described is shown by D_a in Figure 16.1b.

Total Money Demand, D_m As shown in Figure 16.1, we find the **total demand for money,** D_m, by horizon-

tally adding the asset demand to the transactions demand. The resulting downsloping line in Figure 16.1c represents the total amount of money the public wants to hold, both for transactions and as an asset, at each possible interest rate.

Recall that the transactions demand for money depends on the nominal GDP. A change in the nominal GDP—working through the transactions demand for money—will shift the total money demand curve. Specifically, an increase in nominal GDP means that the public wants to hold a larger amount of money for transactions, and that extra demand will shift the total money demand curve to the right. In contrast, a decline in the nominal GDP will shift the total money demand curve to the left. As an example, suppose nominal GDP increases from $300 billion to $450 billion and the average dollar held for transactions is still spent three times per year. Then the transactions demand curve will shift from $100 billion (= $300 billion/3) to $150 billion (= $450 billion/3). The total money demand curve will then lie $50 billion farther to the right at each possible interest rate.

The Equilibrium Interest Rate

We can combine the demand for money with the supply of money to determine the equilibrium rate of interest. In Figure 16.1c, the vertical line, S_m, represents the money supply. It is a vertical line because the monetary authorities and financial institutions have provided the economy with some particular stock of money. Here it is $200 billion.

Just as in a product market or a resource market, the intersection of demand and supply determines the equilibrium price in the market for money. In Figure 16.1, this equilibrium price is the equilibrium interest rate, i_e. At this interest rate, the quantity of money demanded (= $200 billion) equals the quantity of money supplied (= $200 billion). The equilibrium interest rate can be thought of as the market-determined price that borrowers must pay for using someone else's money over some period of time.

Changes in the demand for money, the supply of money, or both can change the equilibrium interest rate. For reasons that will soon become apparent, we are most interested in changes in the supply of money. The important generalization is this: An increase in the supply of money will lower the equilibrium interest rate; a decrease in the supply of money will raise the equilibrium interest rate.

Interest Rates and Bond Prices

Interest rates and bond prices are inversely related. When the interest rate increases, bond prices fall; when the interest rate falls, bond prices rise. Why so? First understand that bonds are bought and sold in financial markets and

that the price of bonds is determined by bond demand and bond supply.

Suppose that a bond with no expiration date pays a fixed $50 annual interest payment and is selling for its face value of $1,000. The interest yield on this bond is 5 percent:

$$\frac{\$50}{\$1,000} = 5\% \text{ interest yield}$$

Now suppose the interest rate in the economy rises to $7\frac{1}{2}$ percent from 5 percent. Newly issued bonds will pay $75 per $1,000 lent. Older bonds paying only $50 will not be salable at their $1,000 face value. To compete with the $7\frac{1}{2}$ percent bond, the price of this bond will need to fall to $667 to remain competitive. The $50 fixed annual interest payment will then yield $7\frac{1}{2}$ percent to whoever buys the bond:

$$\frac{\$50}{\$667} = 7\frac{1}{2}\%$$

Next suppose that the interest rate falls to $2\frac{1}{2}$ percent from the original 5 percent. Newly issued bonds will pay $25 on $1,000 loaned. A bond paying $50 will be highly attractive. Bond buyers will bid up its price to $2,000, where the yield will equal $2\frac{1}{2}$ percent:

$$\frac{\$50}{\$2,000} = 2\frac{1}{2}\%$$

The point is that bond prices fall when the interest rate rises and rise when the interest rate falls. There is an inverse relationship between the interest rate and bond prices.

The Consolidated Balance Sheet of the Federal Reserve Banks

LO16.2 Describe the balance sheet of the Federal Reserve and the meaning of its major items.

With this basic understanding of interest rates, we can turn to monetary policy, which relies on changes in interest rates to be effective. The 12 Federal Reserve Banks together constitute the U.S. "central bank," nicknamed the "Fed." (Global Perspective 16.1 also lists some of the other central banks in the world, along with their nicknames.)

The Fed's balance sheet helps us consider how the Fed conducts monetary policy. Table 16.1 consolidates the pertinent assets and liabilities of the 12 Federal Reserve Banks as of April 10, 2013. You will see that some of the Fed's assets and liabilities differ from those found on the balance sheet of a commercial bank.

GLOBAL PERSPECTIVE 16.1

Central Banks, Selected Nations

The monetary policies of the world's major central banks are often in the international news. Here are some of their official names, along with a few of their popular nicknames.

Australia: Reserve Bank of Australia (RBA)

Canada: Bank of Canada

Euro Zone: European Central Bank (ECB)

Japan: The Bank of Japan (BOJ)

Mexico: Banco de Mexico (Mex Bank)

Russia: Central Bank of Russia

Sweden: Sveriges Riksbank

United Kingdom: Bank of England

United States: Federal Reserve System (the "Fed")

Assets

The two main assets of the Federal Reserve Banks are securities and loans to commercial banks. (Again, we will simplify by referring only to *commercial banks*, even though the analysis also applies to *thrifts*—savings and loans, mutual savings banks, and credit unions.)

Securities The securities shown in Table 16.1 are government bonds that have been purchased by the Federal Reserve Banks. They consist largely of Treasury bills (short-term securities), Treasury notes (mid-term securities), and Treasury bonds (long-term securities) issued by the U.S. government to finance past budget deficits. These securities are part of the public debt—the money borrowed by the federal government. The Federal Reserve Banks bought these securities from commercial banks and the public through open-market operations. Although they are an important source of interest income to the Federal Reserve Banks, they are mainly bought and sold to influence the size of commercial bank reserves and, therefore, the ability of those banks to create money by lending.

Loans to Commercial Banks For reasons that will soon become clear, commercial banks occasionally borrow from Federal Reserve Banks. The IOUs that commercial banks give these "bankers' banks" in return for loans are listed on the Federal Reserve balance sheet as "Loans to commercial banks." They are assets to the Fed because they are claims against the commercial banks. To commercial banks, of course, these loans are liabilities in that they must be repaid. Through borrowing in this way, commercial banks can increase their reserves.

Liabilities

On the "liabilities and net worth" side of the Fed's consolidated balance sheet, three entries are noteworthy: reserves, Treasury deposits, and Federal Reserve Notes.

Reserves of Commercial Banks The Fed requires that the commercial banks hold reserves against their

TABLE 16.1 Consolidated Balance Sheet of the 12 Federal Reserve Banks, April 10, 2013 (in Millions)

Assets		Liabilities and Net Worth	
Securities	$2,957,619	Reserves of commercial banks	$1,851,361
Loans to commercial banks	439	Treasury deposits	52,478
All other assets	271,355	Federal Reserve Notes (outstanding)	1,137,087
		All other liabilities and net worth	188,487
Total	$3,229,413	Total	$3,229,413

*Source: Federal Reserve Statistical Release, H.4.1, April 10, 2013, **www.federalreserve.gov**.*

checkable deposits. The Fed pays interest on these required reserves and also on the excess reserves that banks choose to hold at the Fed. Banks held a huge amount of these excess reserves at the Fed during the severe recession of 2007–2009 and on through at least 2013 as the economy recovered only sluggishly after the Great Recession. Banks simply were highly concerned that loans to some private borrowers might not get paid back. When held in the Federal Reserve Banks, these reserves are listed as a liability on the Fed's balance sheet. They are assets on the books of the commercial banks, which still own them even though they are deposited at the Federal Reserve Banks.

Treasury Deposits The U.S. Treasury keeps deposits in the Federal Reserve Banks and draws checks on them to pay its obligations. To the Treasury these deposits are assets; to the Federal Reserve Banks they are liabilities. The Treasury creates and replenishes these deposits by depositing tax receipts and money borrowed from the public or from the commercial banks through the sale of bonds.

Federal Reserve Notes Outstanding As we have seen, the supply of paper money in the United States consists of Federal Reserve Notes issued by the Federal Reserve Banks. When this money is circulating outside the Federal Reserve Banks, it constitutes claims against the assets of the Federal Reserve Banks. The Fed thus treats these notes as a liability.

QUICK REVIEW 16.2

- The two main assets of the Federal Reserve Banks are securities and loans to commercial banks. Most of the securities are bills, notes, and bonds issued by the U.S. Treasury to finance past federal budget deficits.
- The three major liabilities of the Federal Reserve Banks are reserves of commercial banks, Treasury deposits, and outstanding Federal Reserve notes.

Tools of Monetary Policy

LO16.3 List and explain the goals and tools of monetary policy.

ORIGIN OF THE IDEA

O16.2
Tools of monetary policy

With this look at the Federal Reserve Banks' consolidated balance sheet, we can now explore how the Fed can influence the money-creating abilities of the commercial banking system. The Fed has four main tools of monetary control it can use to alter the reserves of commercial banks:

- Open-market operations
- The reserve ratio
- The discount rate
- Interest on reserves

Open-Market Operations

Bond markets are "open" to all buyers and sellers of corporate and government bonds (securities). The Federal Reserve is the largest single holder of U.S. government securities. The U.S. government, not the Fed, issued these Treasury bills, Treasury notes, and Treasury bonds to finance past budget deficits. Over the decades, the Fed has purchased these securities from major financial institutions that buy and sell government and corporate securities for themselves or their customers.

The Fed's **open-market operations** consist of buying government bonds (U.S. securities) from or selling government bonds to commercial banks and the general public. The conduit for the Fed's open-market operations is the New York Federal Reserve Bank and a group of 21 or so large financial firms called "primary dealers." These financial institutions, in turn, buy the bonds from and sell the bonds to commercial banks and the general public. Open-market operations are the Fed's most important day-to-day instrument for influencing the money supply.

Buying Securities Suppose that the Fed decides to have the Federal Reserve Banks buy government bonds. They can purchase these bonds either from commercial banks or from the public. In both cases the reserves of the commercial banks will increase.

From Commercial Banks When Federal Reserve Banks buy government bonds *from commercial banks,*

(*a*) The commercial banks give up part of their holdings of securities (the government bonds) to the Federal Reserve Banks.

(*b*) The Federal Reserve Banks, in paying for these securities, place newly created reserves in the accounts of the commercial banks at the Fed. (These reserves are created "out of thin air," so to speak!) The reserves of the commercial banks go up by the amount of the purchase of the securities.

We show these outcomes as (*a*) and (*b*) on the following consolidated balance sheets of the commercial banks and the Federal Reserve Banks:

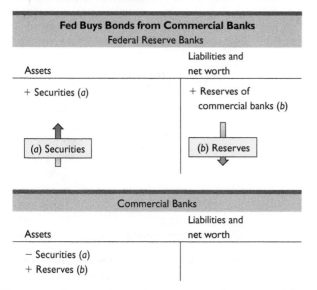

Fed Buys Bonds from Commercial Banks

Federal Reserve Banks

Assets	Liabilities and net worth
+ Securities (*a*)	+ Reserves of commercial banks (*b*)

(*a*) Securities

(*b*) Reserves

Commercial Banks

Assets	Liabilities and net worth
− Securities (*a*)	
+ Reserves (*b*)	

The upward arrow shows that securities have moved from the commercial banks to the Federal Reserve Banks. So we enter "− Securities" (minus securities) in the asset column of the balance sheet of the commercial banks. For the same reason, we enter "+ Securities" in the asset column of the balance sheet of the Federal Reserve Banks.

The downward arrow indicates that the Federal Reserve Banks have provided reserves to the commercial banks. So we enter "+ Reserves" in the asset column of the balance sheet for the commercial banks. In the liability column of the balance sheet of the Federal Reserve Banks, the plus sign indicates that although commercial bank reserves have increased, they are a liability to the Federal Reserve Banks because the reserves are owned by the commercial banks.

What is most important about this transaction is that when Federal Reserve Banks purchase securities from commercial banks, they increase the reserves in the banking system, which then increases the lending ability of the commercial banks.

From the Public The effect on commercial bank reserves is much the same when Federal Reserve Banks purchase securities from the general public. Suppose the Gristly Meat Packing Company has government bonds that it sells in the open market to the Federal Reserve Banks. The transaction has several elements:

(*a*) Gristly gives up securities to the Federal Reserve Banks and gets in payment a check drawn by the Federal Reserve Banks on themselves.

(*b*) Gristly promptly deposits the check in its account with the Wahoo bank.

(*c*) The Wahoo bank sends this check against the Federal Reserve Banks to a Federal Reserve Bank for collection. As a result, the Wahoo bank enjoys an increase in its reserves.

To keep things simple, we will dispense with showing the balance sheet changes resulting from the Fed's sale or purchase of bonds from the public. But two aspects of this transaction are particularly important. First, as with Federal Reserve purchases of securities directly from commercial banks, the purchases of securities from the public increase the lending ability of the commercial banking system. Second, the supply of money is directly increased by the Federal Reserve Banks' purchase of government bonds (aside from any expansion of the money supply that may occur from the increase in commercial bank reserves). This direct increase in the money supply has taken the form of an increased amount of checkable deposits in the economy as a result of Gristly's deposit.

The Federal Reserve Banks' purchases of securities from the commercial banking system differ slightly from their purchases of securities from the public. If we assume that all commercial banks are loaned up initially, Federal Reserve bond purchases *from commercial banks* increase the actual reserves and excess reserves of commercial banks by the entire amount of the bond purchases. As shown in the left panel in Figure 16.2, a $1,000 bond purchase from a commercial bank increases both the actual and the excess reserves of the commercial bank by $1,000.

In contrast, Federal Reserve Bank purchases of bonds from the public increase actual reserves but also increase checkable deposits when the sellers place the Fed's check into their personal checking accounts. Thus, a $1,000 bond purchase from the public would increase checkable deposits by $1,000 and hence the actual reserves of the loaned-up banking system by the same amount. But with a 20 percent reserve ratio applied to the $1,000 checkable deposit, the excess reserves of the banking system would be only $800 since $200 of the $1,000 would have to be held as reserves.

However, in both transactions the end result is the same: When Federal Reserve Banks buy securities in the open market, commercial banks' reserves are increased. When the banks lend out an amount equal to their excess reserves, the nation's money supply will rise. Observe in Figure 16.2 that a $1,000 purchase of

FIGURE 16.2 The Federal Reserve's purchase of bonds and the expansion of the money supply. Assuming all banks are loaded up initially, a Federal Reserve purchase of a $1,000 bond from either a commercial bank or the public can increase the money supply by $5,000 when the reserve ratio is 20 percent. In the left panel of the diagram, the purchase of a $1,000 bond from a commercial bank creates $1,000 of excess reserves that support a $5,000 expansion of checkable deposits through loans. In the right panel, the purchase of a $1,000 bond from the public creates a $1,000 checkable deposit but only $800 of excess reserves because $200 of reserves is required to "back up" the $1,000 new checkable deposit. The commercial banks can therefore expand the money supply by only $4,000 by making loans. This $4,000 of checkable-deposit money plus the new checkable deposit of $1,000 equals $5,000 of new money.

bonds by the Federal Reserve results in a potential of $5,000 of additional money, regardless of whether the purchase was made from commercial banks or from the general public.

Selling Securities As you may suspect, when the Federal Reserve Banks sell government bonds, commercial banks' reserves are reduced. Let's see why.

To Commercial Banks When the Federal Reserve Banks sell securities in the open market to commercial banks,

(*a*) The Federal Reserve Banks give up securities that the commercial banks acquire.

(*b*) The commercial banks pay for those securities by drawing checks against their deposits—that is, against their reserves—in Federal Reserve Banks. The Fed collects on those checks by reducing the commercial banks' reserves accordingly.

The balance-sheet changes—again identified by (*a*) and (*b*)—appear as shown in the following balance sheets. The reduction in commercial bank reserves is indicated by the minus signs before the appropriate entries.

To the Public When the Federal Reserve Banks sell securities to the public, the outcome is much the same. Let's put the Gristly Company on the buying end of government bonds that the Federal Reserve Banks are selling:

(*a*) The Federal Reserve Banks sell government bonds to Gristly, which pays with a check drawn on the Wahoo bank.

(*b*) The Federal Reserve Banks clear this check against the Wahoo bank by reducing Wahoo's reserves.

TABLE 16.2 The Effects of Changes in the Reserve Ratio on the Lending Ability of Commercial Banks

(1) Reserve Ratio, %	(2) Checkable Deposits	(3) Actual Reserves	(4) Required Reserves	(5) Excess Reserves, (3) − (4)	(6) Money-Creating Potential of Single Bank, = (5)	(7) Money-Creating Potential of Banking System
(1) 10	$20,000	$5,000	$2,000	$ 3,000	$ 3,000	$ 30,000
(2) 20	20,000	5,000	4,000	1,000	1,000	5,000
(3) 25	20,000	5,000	5,000	0	0	0
(4) 30	20,000	5,000	6,000	−1,000	−1,000	−3,333

(*c*) The Wahoo bank returns the canceled check to Gristly, reducing Gristly's checkable deposit accordingly.

Federal Reserve bond sales of $1,000 to the commercial banking system reduce the system's actual and excess reserves by $1,000. But a $1,000 bond sale to the public reduces excess reserves by $800 because the public's checkable-deposit money is also reduced by $1,000 by the sale. Since the commercial banking system's outstanding checkable deposits are reduced by $1,000, banks need keep $200 less in reserves.

Whether the Fed sells bonds to the public or to commercial banks, the result is the same: When Federal Reserve Banks sell securities in the open market, commercial bank reserves are reduced. If all excess reserves are already lent out, this decline in commercial bank reserves produces a decline in the nation's money supply. In our example, a $1,000 sale of government securities results in a $5,000 decline in the money supply whether the sale is made to commercial banks or to the general public. You can verify this by reexamining Figure 16.2 and tracing the effects of a *sale* of a $1,000 bond by the Fed either to commercial banks or to the public.

What makes commercial banks and the public willing to sell government securities to, or buy them from, Federal Reserve Banks? The answer lies in the price of bonds and their interest yields. We know that bond prices and interest rates are inversely related. When the Fed buys government bonds, the demand for them increases. Government bond prices rise, and their interest yields decline. The higher bond prices and their lower interest yields prompt banks, securities firms, and individual holders of government bonds to sell them to the Federal Reserve Banks.

When the Fed sells government bonds, the additional supply of bonds in the bond market lowers bond prices and raises their interest yields, making government bonds attractive purchases for banks and the public.

The Reserve Ratio

The Fed also can manipulate the **reserve ratio** in order to influence the ability of commercial banks to lend. Suppose a commercial bank's balance sheet shows that reserves are $5,000 and checkable deposits are $20,000. If the legal reserve ratio is 20 percent (row 2, Table 16.2), the bank's required reserves are $4,000. Since actual reserves are $5,000, the excess reserves of this bank are $1,000. On the basis of $1,000 of excess reserves, this one bank can lend $1,000; however, the banking system as a whole can create a maximum of $5,000 of new checkable-deposit money by lending (column 7).

Raising the Reserve Ratio Now, what if the Fed raised the reserve ratio from 20 to 25 percent? (See row 3.) Required reserves would jump from $4,000 to $5,000, shrinking excess reserves from $1,000 to zero. Raising the reserve ratio increases the amount of required reserves banks must keep. As a consequence, either banks lose excess reserves, diminishing their ability to create money by lending, or they find their reserves deficient and are forced to contract checkable deposits and therefore the money supply. In the example in Table 16.2, excess reserves are transformed into required reserves, and the money-creating potential of our single bank is reduced from $1,000 to zero (column 6). Moreover, the banking system's money-creating capacity declines from $5,000 to zero (column 7).

What if the Fed increases the reserve requirement to 30 percent? (See row 4.) The commercial bank, to protect itself against the prospect of failing to meet this requirement, would be forced to lower its checkable deposits and at the same time increase its reserves. To reduce its checkable deposits, the bank could let outstanding loans mature and be repaid without extending new credit. To increase reserves, the bank might sell some of its bonds, adding the proceeds to its reserves. Both actions would reduce the supply of money.

Lowering the Reserve Ratio What would happen if the Fed lowered the reserve ratio from the original 20 percent to 10 percent? (See row 1.) In this case, required reserves would decline from $4,000 to $2,000, and excess reserves would jump from $1,000 to $3,000. The single bank's lending (money-creating) ability would increase from $1,000 to $3,000 (column 6), and the banking system's money-creating potential would expand from $5,000 to $30,000 (column 7). Lowering the reserve ratio transforms required reserves into excess reserves and enhances the ability of banks to create new money by lending.

The examples in Table 16.2 show that a change in the reserve ratio affects the money-creating ability of the *banking system* in two ways:

- It changes the amount of excess reserves.
- It changes the size of the monetary multiplier.

For example, when the legal reserve ratio is raised from 10 to 20 percent, excess reserves are reduced from $3,000 to $1,000 and the checkable-deposit multiplier is reduced from 10 to 5. The money-creating potential of the banking system declines from $30,000 (= $3,000 × 10) to $5,000 (= $1,000 × 5). Raising the reserve ratio forces banks to reduce the amount of checkable deposits they create through lending.

The Discount Rate

One of the functions of a central bank is to be a "lender of last resort." Occasionally, commercial banks have unexpected and immediate needs for additional funds. In such cases, each Federal Reserve Bank will make short-term loans to commercial banks in its district.

When a commercial bank borrows, it gives the Federal Reserve Bank a promissory note (IOU) drawn against itself and secured by acceptable collateral—typically U.S. government securities. Just as commercial banks charge interest on the loans they make to their clients, so too Federal Reserve Banks charge interest on loans they grant to commercial banks. The interest rate they charge is called the **discount rate.**

As a claim against the commercial bank, the borrowing bank's promissory note is an asset to the lending Federal Reserve Bank and appears on its balance sheet as "Loans to commercial banks." To the commercial bank the IOU is a liability, appearing as "Loans from the Federal Reserve Banks" on the commercial bank's balance sheet. [See the two (*a*) entries on the balance sheets that follow.]

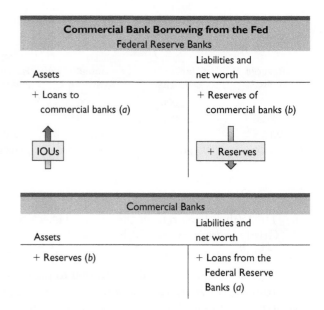

In providing the loan, the Federal Reserve Bank increases the reserves of the borrowing commercial bank. Since no required reserves need be kept against loans from Federal Reserve Banks, all new reserves acquired by borrowing from Federal Reserve Banks are excess reserves. [These changes are reflected in the two (*b*) entries on the balance sheets.]

In short, borrowing from the Federal Reserve Banks by commercial banks increases the reserves of the commercial banks and enhances their ability to extend credit.

The Fed has the power to set the discount rate at which commercial banks borrow from Federal Reserve Banks. From the commercial banks' point of view, the discount rate is a cost of acquiring reserves. A lowering of the discount rate encourages commercial banks to obtain additional reserves by borrowing from Federal Reserve Banks. When the commercial banks lend new reserves, the money supply increases.

An increase in the discount rate discourages commercial banks from obtaining additional reserves through borrowing from the Federal Reserve Banks. So the Fed may raise the discount rate when it wants to restrict the money supply.

Interest on Reserves

In 2008, federal law was changed so that the Federal Reserve could for the first time pay banks **interest on reserves** held at the Fed. Before that time, any reserves held on deposit at the Federal Reserve were paid zero interest. Thus, before 2008, banks had an incentive to keep their reserves as small as possible because any money kept on reserve at the Fed was money earning a zero percent rate of return for the banks.

The Fed's newfound ability to pay interest on reserves provided the Fed with a fourth policy tool by which it can implement monetary policy and either increase or decrease the amount of monetary stimulus in the economy. As an example, suppose that the Fed wishes to *reduce* the amount of bank lending and, consequently, the amount of money circulating in the economy. It can do so by increasing the rate of interest that it pays on reserves held at the Fed. The higher that interest rate, the more of an incentive banks will have to reduce their risky commercial lending for car, mortgage, and business loans in order to instead increase the reserves that they hold at the Fed and thereby earn the risk-free interest rate that the Fed is paying on reserves.

By contrast, if the Fed wishes to *increase* the amount of money that banks lend into the economy, the Fed can lower the interest rate that it pays on reserves. The lower rate will make it less attractive for banks to keep reserves, and, consequently, banks will be incentivized to increase consumer and commercial lending and thereby stimulate the economy.

In 2012, the rate of interest on reserves was 0.25 percent per year. Given that banks held about $1.7 trillion in reserves at the Fed that year, the Fed paid a total of about $4.25 billion (= 0.0025 times $1.7 trillion) in interest payments to banks for reserves held at the Fed in 2012.

Relative Importance

All four of the Fed's instruments of monetary control are useful in particular economic circumstances, but open-market operations are clearly the most important of the four tools over the course of the business cycle. The buying and selling of securities in the open market has the advantage of flexibility—government securities can be purchased or sold daily in large or small amounts—and the impact on bank reserves is prompt. And, compared with reserve-requirement changes, open-market operations work subtly and less directly. Furthermore, the ability of the Federal Reserve Banks to affect commercial bank reserves through the purchase and sale of bonds is virtually unquestionable. The Federal Reserve Banks have very large holdings of government securities ($2,958 billion in early 2013, for example). The sale of those securities could theoretically reduce commercial bank reserves to zero.

Changing the reserve requirement is a potentially powerful instrument of monetary control, but the Fed has used this technique only sparingly. Normally, it can accomplish its monetary goals more easily through open-market operations. The last change in the reserve requirement was in 1992, when the Fed reduced the requirement from 12 percent to 10 percent. The main purpose was to shore up the profitability of banks and thrifts in the aftermath of the 1990–1991 recession rather than to reduce interest rates by increasing reserves and expanding the money supply.

Until recently, the discount rate was mainly a passive tool of monetary control, with the Fed raising and lowering the rate simply to keep it in line with other interest rates. However, during the financial crisis of 2007–2008, the Fed aggressively lowered the discount rate independently of other interest rates to provide a cheap and plentiful source of reserves to banks whose reserves were being sharply reduced by unexpectedly high default rates on home mortgage loans. Banks borrowed billions at the lower discount rate. This allowed them to meet reserve ratio requirements and thereby preserved their ability to keep extending loans.

QUICK REVIEW 16.3

- The Fed has four main tools of monetary control, each of which works by changing the amount of reserves in the banking system: (a) conducting open-market operations (the Fed's buying and selling of government bonds to the banks and the public); (b) changing the reserve ratio (the percentage of commercial bank deposit liabilities required as reserves); (c) changing the discount rate (the interest rate the Federal Reserve Banks charge on loans to banks and thrifts); and (d) changing the interest rate that it pays on reserves held at the Fed.

- Open-market operations are the Fed's monetary control mechanism of choice for routine increases or decreases in bank reserves over the business cycle; in contrast, changes in reserve requirements and aggressive changes in discount rates or interest on reserves are used only in special situations.

Targeting the Federal Funds Rate

LO16.4 Describe the federal funds rate and how the Fed directly influences it.

The Federal Reserve focuses monetary policy on the interest rate that it can directly influence: the **federal funds rate**. From the previous chapter, you know that this is the rate of interest that banks charge one another on overnight loans made from temporary excess reserves. Recall that the Federal Reserve requires banks (and thrifts) to deposit in their regional Federal Reserve Bank a certain percentage of their checkable deposits as reserves. At the end of any business day, some banks temporarily have excess reserves (more actual reserves than required) and other banks have reserve deficiencies (fewer reserves than required). Because reserves held at the Federal Reserve Banks earn less interest than commercial banks can obtain from overnight loans to other banks, banks with excess reserves usually desire to make such loans to other banks that temporarily need them to meet their reserve requirements. The funds being lent and borrowed overnight are called "federal funds" because they are reserves (funds) that are required by the Federal Reserve to meet reserve requirements. An equilibrium interest rate—the federal funds rate—arises in this market for bank reserves.

The Federal Reserve targets the federal funds rate by manipulating the supply of reserves that are offered in the federal funds market. As previously explained, by buying and selling government bonds, the Fed can increase or decrease the reserves in the banking system. These changes in total reserves in turn affect the amount of *excess reserves* that are available for supply to the federal funds market by whichever banks end up with them on a given day. For instance, suppose that the level of loans and checkable deposits at Wahoo bank are constant on a certain day. If the Fed then engages in open-market operations such that Wahoo's total reserves increase, Wahoo will find that it has excess reserves. It will want to loan out these excess reserves to bank customers as soon as possible. But in the meanwhile it will supply these funds overnight in the federal funds market.

The Federal Open Market Committee (FOMC) meets regularly to choose a desired federal funds rate. It then directs the Federal Reserve Bank of New York to undertake whatever open-market operations may be necessary to achieve and maintain the targeted rate. We demonstrate how this works in Figure 16.3, where we initially assume the Fed desires a 4 percent interest rate. The demand curve for federal funds, D_f, is downsloping because lower interest rates give the banks with reserve deficiencies a greater incentive to borrow federal funds rather than reduce loans as a way to meet their reserve requirements. The supply curve for federal funds, S_{f1}, is somewhat unusual. Specifically, it is horizontal at the targeted federal funds rate, here 4 percent. (Disregard supply curves S_{f2} and S_{f3} for now.) It is horizontal because the Fed uses open-market operations to manipulate the supply of federal funds so that the quantity supplied of federal funds will exactly equal the quantity demanded of federal funds at the targeted interest rate.

FIGURE 16.3   Targeting the federal funds rate. In implementing monetary policy, the Federal Reserve determines a desired federal funds rate and then uses open-market operations (buying and selling of U.S. securities) to add or subtract bank reserves to achieve and maintain that targeted rate. In an expansionary monetary policy, the Fed increases the supply of reserves, for example, from S_{f1} to S_{f2} in this case, to move the federal funds rate from 4 percent to 3.5 percent. In a restrictive monetary policy, it decreases the supply of reserves, say, from S_{f1} to S_{f3}. Here, the federal funds rate rises from 4 percent to 4.5 percent.

In this case, the Fed seeks to achieve an equilibrium federal funds rate of 4 percent. In Figure 16.3 it is successful. Note that at the 4 percent federal funds rate, the quantity of federal funds supplied (Q_{f1}) equals the quantity of funds demanded (also Q_{f1}). This 4 percent federal funds rate will remain, as long as the supply curve of federal funds is horizontal at 4 percent. If the demand for federal funds increases (D_f shifts to the right along S_{f1}), the Fed will use its open-market operations to increase the availability of reserves such that the 4 percent federal funds rate is retained. If the demand for federal funds declines (D_f shifts to the left along S_{f1}), the Fed will withdraw reserves to keep the federal funds rate at 4 percent. The Fed ensures that the supply curve is perfectly elastic at its targeted rate.

Expansionary Monetary Policy

Suppose that the economy faces recession and unemployment. How will the Fed respond? It will initiate an **expansionary monetary policy** (or "easy money policy"). This policy will lower the interest rate to bolster borrowing and spending, which will increase aggregate demand and expand real output. The Fed's immediate step will be to announce a lower target for the federal funds rate, say 3.5 percent instead of 4 percent. To achieve that lower

FIGURE 16.4 The prime interest rate and the federal funds rate in the United States, 1998–2013. The prime interest rate rises and falls with changes in the federal funds rate.

Source: Federal Reserve Statistical Release, Historical Data, H.15, **www.federalreserve.gov.**

rate, the Fed will use open-market operations to buy bonds from banks and the public. We know from previous discussion that the purchase of bonds increases the reserves in the banking system. Alternatively, the Fed could expand reserves by lowering the reserve requirement or lowering the discount rate, but these alternative tools are less frequently used than open-market operations. The Fed could also lower the interest rate that it pays on reserves so that banks will have more of an incentive to lend out reserves rather than keeping them on deposit at the Fed. But through 2013, the Fed had never changed the interest rate that it had paid on reserves after starting to pay interest on reserves in 2008. It remained at 0.25 percent.

The greater reserves in the banking system produce two critical results:

- The supply of federal funds increases, lowering the federal funds rate to the new targeted rate. We show this in Figure 16.3 as a downward shift to the horizontal supply curve from S_{f1} to S_{f2}. The equilibrium federal funds rate falls to 3.5 percent, just as the FOMC wanted. The equilibrium quantity of reserves in the overnight market for reserves rises from Q_{f1} to Q_{f2}.

- A multiple expansion of the nation's money supply occurs (as we demonstrated in Chapter 15). Given

the demand for money, the larger money supply places a downward pressure on other interest rates.

One such rate is the **prime interest rate**—the benchmark interest rate used by banks as a reference point for a wide range of interest rates charged on loans to businesses and individuals. The prime interest rate is higher than the federal funds rate because the prime rate involves longer, more risky loans than overnight loans between banks. But the federal funds rate and the prime interest rate closely track one another, as evident in Figure 16.4. Also evident are the changes in these rates over the period shown. We will address these changes later in our discussion of recent monetary policy.

Restrictive Monetary Policy

The opposite monetary policy is in order for periods of rising inflation. The Fed will then undertake a **restrictive monetary policy** (or "tight money policy"). This policy will increase the interest rate to reduce borrowing and spending, which will curtail the expansion of aggregate demand and hold down price-level increases. The Fed's immediate step will be to announce a higher target for the federal funds rate, say 4.5 percent instead of 4 percent.

Through open-market operations, the Fed will sell bonds to the banks and the public and the sale of those bonds will absorb reserves in the banking system. Alternatively, the Fed could absorb reserves by raising the reserve requirement, raising the discount rate, or raising the interest rate that it pays on reserves. But open-market operations are usually sufficient to accomplish the goal.

The smaller reserves in the banking system produce two results opposite those discussed for an expansionary monetary policy:

- The supply of federal funds decreases, raising the federal funds rate to the new targeted rate. We show this in Figure 16.3 as an upward shift of the horizontal supply curve from S_{f1} to S_{f3}. The equilibrium federal funds rate rises to 4.5 percent, just as the FOMC wanted, and the equilibrium quantity of funds in this market falls to Q_{f3}.

- A multiple contraction of the nation's money supply occurs (as demonstrated in Chapter 15). Given the demand for money, the smaller money supply places an upward pressure on other interest rates. For example, the prime interest rate rises.

The Taylor Rule

The proper federal funds rate for a certain period is a matter of policy discretion by the members of the FOMC. At each of their meetings, committee members assess whether the current target for the federal funds rate remains appropriate for achieving the twin goals of low inflation and full employment. If the majority of the FOMC members conclude that a change in the rate is needed, the FOMC sets a new targeted rate. This new target is established without adhering to any particular "inflationary target" or "monetary policy rule." Instead, the committee targets the federal funds rate at the level most appropriate for the current underlying economic conditions.

A rule of thumb suggested by economist John Taylor, however, roughly matches the actual policy of the Fed over many time periods. This rule of thumb builds on the belief held by many economists that central banks are willing to tolerate a small positive rate of inflation if doing so will help the economy to produce at potential output. The **Taylor rule** assumes that the Fed has a 2 percent "target rate of inflation" that it is willing to tolerate and that the FOMC follows three rules when setting its target for the federal funds rate:

- When real GDP equals potential GDP and inflation is at its target rate of 2 percent, the federal funds target rate should be 4 percent, implying a real

The Fed as a Sponge

A good way to remember the role of the Fed in setting the federal funds rate might be to imagine a bowl of water, with the amount of water in the bowl representing the stock of reserves in the banking system. Then think of the FOMC as having a large sponge, labeled open-market operations. When it wants to decrease the federal funds rate, it uses the sponge—soaked with water (reserves) created by the Fed—to squeeze new reserves into the banking system bowl. It continues this process until the higher supply of reserves reduces the federal funds rate to the Fed's desired level. If the Fed wants to increase the federal funds rate, it uses the sponge to absorb reserves from the bowl (banking system). As the supply of reserves falls, the federal funds rate rises to the Fed's desired level.

federal funds rate of 2 percent (= 4 percent nominal federal funds rate *minus* 2 percent inflation rate).

- For each 1 percent increase of real GDP above potential GDP, the Fed should raise the *real* federal funds rate by $\frac{1}{2}$ percentage point.

- For each 1 percent increase in the inflation rate above its 2 percent target rate, the Fed should raise the *real* federal funds rate by $\frac{1}{2}$ percentage point. (Note, though, that in this case each $\frac{1}{2}$ percentage point increase in the real rate will require a 1.5 percentage point increase in the nominal rate to account for the underlying 1 percent increase in the inflation rate.)

The last two rules are applied independently of each other so that if real GDP is above potential output and at the same time inflation is above the 2 percent target rate, the Fed will apply both rules and raise real interest rates in response to both factors. For instance, if real GDP is 1 percent above potential output and inflation is simultaneously 1 percent above the 2 percent target rate, then the Fed will raise the *real* federal funds rate by 1 percentage point (= $\frac{1}{2}$ percentage point for the excessive GDP $+ \frac{1}{2}$ percentage point for the excessive inflation).

Also notice that the last two rules are reversed for situations in which real GDP falls below potential GDP or inflation falls below 2 percent. Each 1 percent decline in real GDP below potential GDP or fall in inflation below 2 percent calls for a decline of the *real* federal funds rate by $\frac{1}{2}$ percentage point.

ORIGIN OF THE IDEA

O16.3
Taylor rule

We reemphasize that the Fed has no official allegiance to the Taylor rule. It changes the federal funds rate to any level that it deems appropriate. During some periods, its policy has diverged significantly from the Taylor rule.

QUICK REVIEW 16.4

- The Fed conducts its monetary policy by establishing a targeted federal funds interest rate—the rate that commercial banks charge one another for overnight loans of reserves.

- An expansionary monetary policy (loose money policy) lowers the federal funds rate, increases the money supply, and lowers other interest rates.

- A restrictive monetary policy (tight money policy) increases the federal funds rate, reduces the money supply, and increases other interest rates.

- The Fed uses it discretion in setting the federal funds target rate, but its decisions regarding monetary policy and the target rate appear to be broadly consistent with the Taylor rule over many time periods.

Monetary Policy, Real GDP, and the Price Level

LO16.5 Identify the mechanisms by which monetary policy affects GDP and the price level.

We have identified and explained the tools of expansionary and contractionary monetary policy. We now want to emphasize how monetary policy affects the economy's levels of investment, aggregate demand, real GDP, and prices.

Cause-Effect Chain

The four diagrams in **Figure 16.5 (Key Graph)** will help you understand how monetary policy works toward achieving its goals.

Market for Money Figure 16.5a represents the market for money, in which the demand curve for money and the supply curve of money are brought together. Recall that the total demand for money is made up of the transactions and asset demands.

This figure also shows three potential money supply curves, S_{m1}, S_{m2}, and S_{m3}. In each case, the money supply is shown as a vertical line representing some fixed amount of money determined by the Fed.

The equilibrium interest rate is the rate at which the amount of money demanded and the amount supplied are equal. With money demand D_m in Figure 16.5a, if the supply of money is $125 billion ($S_{m1}$), the equilibrium interest rate is 10 percent. With a money supply of $150 billion ($S_{m2}$), the equilibrium interest rate is 8 percent; with a money supply of $175 billion ($S_{m3}$), it is 6 percent.

You know from Chapter 10 that the real, not the nominal, rate of interest is critical for investment decisions. So here we assume that Figure 16.5a portrays real interest rates.

Investment These 10, 8, and 6 percent real interest rates are carried rightward to the investment demand curve in Figure 16.5b. This curve shows the inverse relationship between the interest rate—the cost of borrowing to invest—and the amount of investment spending. At the 10 percent interest rate, it will be profitable for the nation's businesses to invest $15 billion; at 8 percent, $20 billion; at 6 percent, $25 billion.

Changes in the interest rate mainly affect the investment component of total spending, although they also affect spending on durable consumer goods (such as autos) that are purchased on credit. The impact of changing interest rates on investment spending is great because of the large cost and long-term nature of capital purchases. Capital equipment, factory buildings, and warehouses are tremendously expensive. In absolute terms, interest charges on funds borrowed for these purchases are considerable.

Similarly, the interest cost on a house purchased on a long-term contract is very large: A $\frac{1}{2}$-percentage-point change in the interest rate could amount to thousands of dollars in the total cost of buying a home.

In brief, the impact of changing interest rates is mainly on investment (and, through that, on aggregate demand, output, employment, and the price level). Moreover, as Figure 16.5b shows, investment spending varies inversely with the real interest rate.

Equilibrium GDP Figure 16.5c shows the impact of our three real interest rates and corresponding levels of

KEY GRAPH

FIGURE 16.5 **Monetary policy and equilibrium GDP.** An expansionary monetary policy that shifts the money supply curve rightward from S_{m1} to S_{m2} in (a) lowers the interest rate from 10 to 8 percent in (b). As a result, investment spending increases from $15 billion to $20 billion, shifting the aggregate demand curve rightward from AD$_1$ to AD$_2$ in (c) so that real output rises from the recessionary level of $880 billion to the full employment level Q_f = $900 billion along the horizontal dashed line. In (d), the economy at point *a* has an inflationary output gap of $10 billion because it is producing at $910 billion, $10 billion above potential output. A restrictive monetary policy that shifts the money supply curve leftward from S_{m3} = $175 billion to just $162.5 billion in (a) will increase the interest rate from 6 percent to 7 percent. Investment spending thus falls by $2.5 billion from $25 billion to $22.5 billion in (b). This initial decline is multiplied by 4 by the multiplier process so that the aggregate demand curve shifts leftward in (d) by $10 billion from AD$_3$ to AD$_4$, moving the economy along the horizontal dashed line to equilibrium *b*. This returns the economy to full employment output and eliminates the inflationary output gap.

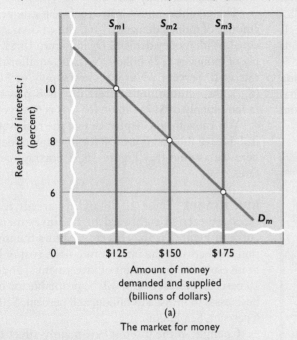

(a)
The market for money

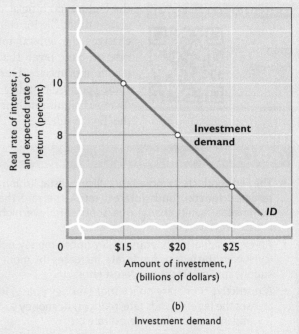

(b)
Investment demand

investment spending on aggregate demand. (Ignore Figure 16.5d for the time being. We will return to it shortly.) As noted, aggregate demand curve AD$_1$ is associated with the $15 billion level of investment, AD$_2$ with investment of $20 billion, and AD$_3$ with investment of $25 billion. That is, investment spending is one of the determinants of aggregate demand. Other things equal, the greater the investment spending, the farther to the right lies the aggregate demand curve.

Suppose the money supply in Figure 16.5a is $150 billion ($S_{m2}$), producing an equilibrium interest rate of 8 percent. In Figure 16.5b we see that this 8 percent interest rate will bring forth $20 billion of investment spending. This $20 billion of investment spending joins with consumption spending, net exports, and government spending to yield aggregate demand curve AD$_2$ in Figure 16.5c. The equilibrium levels of real output and prices are Q_f = $900 billion and P_2, as determined by the intersection of AD$_2$ and the aggregate supply curve AS.

To test your understanding of these relationships, explain why each of the other two levels of money supply in Figure 16.5a results in a different interest rate, level of investment, aggregate demand curve, and equilibrium real output.

(c)
Equilibrium real GDP
and the price level

(d)
Equilibrium real GDP
and the price level

2. A successful restrictive monetary policy is evidenced by a shift in the money supply curve from:
   a. S_{m3} to a point halfway between S_{m2} and S_{m3}, a decrease in investment from $25 billion to $22.5 billion, and a decline in aggregate demand from AD_3 to AD_4.
   b. S_{m1} to S_{m2}, an increase in investment from $20 billion to $25 billion, and an increase in real GDP from Q_1 to Q_f.
   c. S_{m3} to S_{m2}, a decrease in investment from $25 billion to $20 billion, and a decline in the price level from P_3 to P_2.
   d. S_{m3} to S_{m2}, a decrease in investment from $25 billion to $20 billion, and an increase in aggregate demand from AD_2 to AD_3.

3. The Federal Reserve could increase the money supply from S_{m1} to S_{m2} by:
   a. increasing the discount rate.
   b. reducing taxes.
   c. buying government securities in the open market.
   d. increasing the reserve requirement.

4. If the spending-income multiplier is 4 in the economy depicted, an increase in the money supply from $125 billion to $150 billion will:
   a. shift the aggregate demand curve rightward by $20 billion.
   b. increase real GDP by $25 billion.
   c. increase real GDP by $100 billion.
   d. shift the aggregate demand curve leftward by $5 billion.

Answers: 1. d; 2. a; 3. c; 4. a

Effects of an Expansionary Monetary Policy

Recall that the inflationary ratchet effect discussed in Chapter 12 describes the fact that real-world price levels tend to be downwardly inflexible. Thus, with our economy starting from the initial equilibrium where AD_2 intersects AS, the price level will be downwardly inflexible at P_2 so that aggregate supply will be horizontal to the left of Q_f. This means that if aggregate demand decreases, the economy's equilibrium will move leftward along the dashed horizontal line shown in Figure 16.5c.

Just such a decline would happen if the money supply fell to $125 billion ($S_{m1}$), shifting the aggregate demand curve leftward to AD_1 in Figure 16.5c. This results in a real output of $880 billion, $20 billion less than the economy's full-employment output level of $900 billion. The economy will be experiencing recession, a negative GDP gap, and substantial unemployment. The Fed therefore should institute an expansionary monetary policy.

To increase the money supply, the Fed will take some combination of the following actions: (1) buy government securities from banks and the public in the open market, (2) lower the legal reserve ratio, (3) lower the discount rate, and (4) reduce the interest rate that it pays on reserves. The intended outcome will be an increase in excess reserves in the commercial banking system and a decline in the federal funds rate. Because excess reserves are the basis on which commercial banks and thrifts can earn profit by lending and thus creating checkable-deposit money, the nation's money supply will rise. An increase in the money supply will lower the interest rate, increasing investment, aggregate demand, and equilibrium GDP.

For example, an increase in the money supply from $125 billion to $150 billion ($S_{m1}$ to S_{m2}) will reduce the interest rate from 10 to 8 percent, as indicated in Figure 16.5a, and will boost investment from $15 billion to $20 billion, as shown in Figure 16.5b. This $5 billion increase in investment will shift the aggregate demand curve rightward by more than the increase in investment because of the multiplier effect. If the economy's MPC is 0.75, the multiplier will be 4, meaning that the $5 billion increase in investment will shift the AD curve rightward by $20 billion (= $4 \times 5 billion) at each price level. Specifically, aggregate demand will shift from AD_1 to AD_2, as shown in Figure 16.5c. This rightward shift in the aggregate demand curve along the dashed horizontal line will eliminate the negative GDP gap by increasing GDP from $880 billion to the full-employment GDP of $Q_f = 900 billion.[1]

Column 1 in Table 16.3 summarizes the chain of events associated with an expansionary monetary policy.

Effects of a Restrictive Monetary Policy

Next we consider restrictive monetary policy. To prevent overcrowding, we will use graphs *a*, *b*, and *d* (not *c*) in Figure 16.5 to demonstrate the effects of a restrictive monetary policy on the economy. Figure 16.5d represents exactly the same economy as Figure 16.5c but adds some extra curves that relate only to our explanation of restrictive monetary policy.

To see how restrictive monetary policy works, first consider a situation in which the economy moves from a full-employment equilibrium to operating at more than full employment so that inflation is a problem and restrictive monetary policy would be appropriate. Assume that the economy begins at the full-employment equilibrium where AD_2 and AS intersect. At this equilibrium, $Q_f = $900 billion and the price level is P_2.

Next, assume that the money supply expands from $150 billion to $175 billion ($S_{m3}$) in Figure 16.5a. This results in an interest rate of 6 percent, investment spending of $25 billion rather than $20 billion, and aggregate

---

[1]To keep things simple, we assume that the increase in real GDP does not increase the demand for money. In reality, the transactions demand for money would rise, slightly dampening the decline in the interest rate shown in Figure 16.5a.

TABLE 16.3 Monetary Policies for Recession and Inflation

(1) Expansionary Monetary Policy	(2) Restrictive Monetary Policy
Problem: unemployment and recession	*Problem:* inflation
↓	↓
Federal Reserve buys bonds, lowers reserve ratio, lowers the discount rate, or reduces the interest rate on reserves	Federal Reserve sells bonds, increases reserve ratio, raises the discount rate, or increases the interest rate on reserves
↓	↓
Excess reserves increase	Excess reserves decrease
↓	↓
Federal funds rate falls	Federal funds rate rises
↓	↓
Money supply rises	Money supply falls
↓	↓
Interest rate falls	Interest rate rises
↓	↓
Investment spending increases	Investment spending decreases
↓	↓
Aggregate demand increases	Aggregate demand decreases
↓	↓
Real GDP rises	Inflation declines

demand AD_3. As the AD curve shifts to the right from AD_2 to AD_3 in Figure 16.5d, the economy will move along the upsloping AS curve until it comes to an equilibrium at point *a*, where AD_3 intersects AS. At the new equilibrium, the price level has risen to P_3 and the equilibrium level of real GDP has risen to $910 billion, indicating an inflationary GDP gap of $10 billion (= $910 billion − $900 billion). Aggregate demand AD_3 is excessive relative to the economy's full-employment level of real output $Q_f = $900 billion. To rein in spending, the Fed will institute a restrictive monetary policy.

The Federal Reserve Board will direct Federal Reserve Banks to undertake some combination of the following actions: (1) sell government securities to banks and the public in the open market, (2) increase the legal reserve ratio, (3) increase the discount rate, and (4) increase the interest rate that it pays on reserves. Banks then will discover that their reserves are below those required and that the federal funds rate has increased. So they will need to reduce their checkable deposits by refraining from issuing new loans as old loans are paid back. This will shrink the money supply and increase the interest rate. The higher interest rate will discourage investment, lowering aggregate demand and restraining demand-pull inflation.

But the Fed must be careful about just how much to decrease the money supply. The problem is that the inflation ratchet will take effect at the new equilibrium point a, such that prices will be inflexible at price level P_3. As a result, the dashed horizontal line to the left of point a in Figure 16.5d will become relevant. This means that the Fed cannot simply lower the money supply to S_{m2} in Figure 16.5a. If it were to do that, investment demand would fall to $20 billion in Figure 16.5b and the AD curve would shift to the left from AD_3 back to AD_2. But because of inflexible prices, the economy's equilibrium would move to point c, where AD_2 intersects the horizontal dashed line to the left of point a. This would put the economy into a recession, with equilibrium output below the full-employment output level of $Q_f = \$900$ billion.

What the Fed needs to do to achieve full employment is to move the AD curve back only from AD_3 to AD_4, so that the economy will come to equilibrium at point b. This will require a $10 billion decrease in aggregate demand, so that equilibrium output falls from $910 billion at point a to $Q_f = \$900$ billion at point b. The Fed can achieve this shift by setting the supply of money in Figure 16.5a at $162.5 billion. To see how this works, draw in a vertical money supply curve in Figure 16.5a at $162.5 billion and label it as S_{m4}. It will be exactly halfway between money supply curves S_{m2} and S_{m3}. Notice that the intersection of S_{m4} with the money demand curve D_m will result in an interest rate of 7 percent. In Figure 16.5b, this interest rate of 7 percent will result in investment spending of $22.5 billion (halfway between $20 billion and $25 billion). Thus, by setting the money supply at $162.5 billion, the Fed can reduce investment spending by $2.5 billion, lowering it from the $25 billion associated with AD_3 down to only $22.5 billion. This decline in investment spending will initially shift the AD curve only $2.5 billion to the left of AD_3. But then the multiplier process will work its magic. Since the multiplier is 4 in our model, the AD curve will end up moving by a full $10 billion (= 4 × $2.5 billion) to the left, to AD_4. This shift will move the economy to equilibrium b, returning output to the full employment level and eliminating the inflationary GDP gap.[2]

_____
[2]Again, we assume for simplicity that the decrease in nominal GDP does not feed back to reduce the demand for money and thus the interest rate. In reality, this would occur, slightly dampening the increase in the interest rate shown in Figure 16.5a.

Column 2 in Table 16.3 summarizes the cause-effect chain of a tight money policy.

> **QUICK REVIEW 16.5**
>
> - The Fed is engaging in an expansionary monetary policy when it increases the money supply to reduce interest rates and increase investment spending and real GDP.
> - The Fed is engaging in a restrictive monetary policy when it reduces the money supply to increase interest rates and reduce investment spending and inflation.

Monetary Policy: Evaluation and Issues

LO16.6 Explain the effectiveness of monetary policy and its shortcomings.

Monetary policy has become the dominant component of U.S. national stabilization policy. It has two key advantages over fiscal policy:

- Speed and flexibility.
- Isolation from political pressure.

Compared with fiscal policy, monetary policy can be quickly altered. Recall that congressional deliberations may delay the application of fiscal policy for months. In contrast, the Fed can buy or sell securities from day to day and thus affect the money supply and interest rates almost immediately.

Also, because members of the Fed's Board of Governors are appointed and serve 14-year terms, they are relatively isolated from lobbying and need not worry about retaining their popularity with voters. Thus, the Board, more readily than Congress, can engage in politically unpopular policies (higher interest rates) that may be necessary for the long-term health of the economy. Moreover, monetary policy is a subtler and more politically neutral measure than fiscal policy. Changes in government spending directly affect the allocation of resources, and changes in taxes can have extensive political ramifications. Because monetary policy works more subtly, it is more politically palatable.

Recent U.S. Monetary Policy

The Fed has been highly active in its use of monetary policy in recent decades.

The 2001 Recession In 2000, the economy abruptly slowed after a long period of full employment and strong economic growth. The Fed responded to the slowdown by cutting the federal funds interest rate by a full percentage point in two increments in January 2001. Despite those rate cuts, the economy entered a recession in March 2001. Between March 20, 2001, and August 21, 2001, the Fed reduced the federal funds rate from 5 percent to 3.5 percent in a series of steps. In the 3 months following the terrorist attacks of September 11, 2001, it lowered the federal funds rate from 3.5 percent to 1.75 percent, and it left the rate there until it lowered it to 1.25 percent in November 2002. Partly because of the Fed's actions, the prime interest rate dropped from 9.5 percent at the end of 2000 to 4.25 percent in December 2002.

Economists generally give the Fed high marks for helping to keep the recession of 2001 relatively mild, particularly in view of the adverse economic impacts of the terrorist attacks of September 11, 2001, and the steep stock-market decline in 2001–2002.

The Fed left the federal funds rate at historic lows in 2003. But as the economy began to expand robustly in 2004, the Fed engineered a gradual series of rate hikes designed to boost the prime interest rate and other interest rates to make sure that aggregate demand continued to grow at a pace consistent with low inflation. By the summer of 2006, the target for the federal funds rate had risen to 5.25 percent and the prime rate was 8.25 percent. With the economy enjoying sustainable, noninflationary growth, the Fed left the federal funds rate at 5.25 percent for over a year.

The 2007–2009 Recession

The mortgage default crisis (discussed in Chapter 14) began during the late summer of 2007 and posed a grave threat to the financial system and the economy. In response, the Fed took several actions. In August it lowered the discount rate by half a percentage point. Then, between September 2007 and April 2008, it lowered the target for the federal funds rate from 5.25 percent to 2 percent. And as discussed in Chapter 14, the Fed also took a series of extraordinary actions to prevent the failure of key financial firms.

In October 2008, the Fed first reduced the federal funds target rate to 1.5 percent and then later that same month to 1 percent. In December 2008, the Fed lowered it further to a targeted range of 0 percent to 0.25 percent. That near-zero targeted range was by far the lowest in history. Viewed through Figure 16.3, the Fed aggressively pushed the supply of federal funds curve downward (increased the supply of federal funds) to lower the actual federal funds rate to its target level. All these monetary actions and lender-of-last-resort functions helped to stabilize the banking sector and keep credit flowing—thereby offsetting at least some of the damage done by the financial crisis.

The decline in the federal funds rate to near zero during the financial and economic crisis dropped the prime interest rate (review Figure 16.4). In December 2007, the prime interest rate stood at 7.3 percent. By January 2009, it had declined to 3.25 percent, where it remained through 2013.

The Federal Reserve is lauded by most observers for its quick and innovative actions during the financial crisis and severe recession. Nevertheless, some economists contend that the Fed contributed to the financial crisis by holding the federal funds interest rate too low for too long during the recovery from the 2001 recession. These critics say that the artificially low interest rates made mortgage and other loans too inexpensive and therefore contributed to the borrowing frenzy by homeowners and other financial investors. Other economists counter that the low mortgage interest rates resulted from huge inflows of savings from abroad to a wide variety of U.S. financial markets.

After the Great Recession

The U.S. economy recovered very slowly from the Great Recession, especially in terms of employment. After falling from a peak of 138.1 million in January 2008 to a trough of 129.9 million in September 2010, the total number of people with jobs rebounded to just 135.5 million by April 2013. Thus, nearly four years after the recession officially ended in the summer of 2009, 2.6 million fewer people were employed than before the recession. By contrast, after all other post–World War II recessions, employment had fully recovered within four years—and in most cases within two years.

The Federal Reserve understood the depth of the economy's problems early on and responded with a series of innovative monetary policy initiatives designed to stimulate GDP and employment growth.

Zero Interest Rate Policy The Fed began by moving toward a **zero interest rate policy,** or ZIRP, in December 2008. Under ZIRP, the Fed aimed to keep short-term interest rates near zero to stimulate the economy. To that end, open-market operations were used to keep the federal funds rate between zero and 0.25 percent.

Zero Lower Bound Problem After ZIRP was implemented and interest rates were pushed toward zero, the economic growth remained weak. That implied that the Fed would have to figure out a way to deal with the **zero lower bound problem,** under which a central bank is constrained in its ability to stimulate the economy through lower interest rates by the fact that nominal interest rates cannot be driven lower than zero.

Why can't nominal interest rates be driven lower than zero? Because if nominal interest rates were negative, people would not want to put their money into banks because doing so would mean that their balances would shrink over time (rather than grow over time, as they do when interest rates are positive). Thus, any central bank that attempted to impose negative nominal interest rates would see deposits withdrawn from banks. That could be economically catastrophic because if people withdrew deposits from banks, banks would have much less money to lend out to consumers and entrepreneurs. The monetary multiplier of Chapter 15 would work in reverse and the supply of lending and credit in the economy would decrease precipitously, thereby negatively affecting aggregate demand.

Quantitative Easing The Fed's response to the zero lower bound problem was **quantitative easing,** or QE. In terms of mechanics, quantitative easing looks exactly like open-market operations, with the Fed purchasing bonds in order increase the amount of reserves in the banking system. QE differs from ordinary open-market operations, however, in that it is not intended to lower interest rates. Under QE, the Fed buys bonds solely with the intention of increasing the quantity of reserves in the banking system. Interest rates remain at the same levels to avoid the zero lower bound problem. But with bank reserves increased, the economy will hopefully be stimulated through increased lending.

Another difference between QE and regular open-market operations is that QE can involve the purchase of not only U.S. government bonds but also debt issued by government agencies or government-backed corporations (which are known as government-sponsored entities, or GSEs).

The first round of quantitative easing began in March 2009 and involved the Fed purchasing $1.75 trillion worth of bonds. The bonds consisted of $300 billion worth of Treasury bonds and $1.45 trillion worth of bonds issued by either U.S. government agencies or the two government-backed mortgage lenders, Freddie Mac and Fannie Mae.

The second round of quantitative easing ("QE2") began in November 2010 and involved the Fed telling the public of its intention to purchase $600 billion of U.S. Treasury bonds at the rate of $75 billion per month over the following eight months.

Forward Commitment The innovative feature of QE2 was that the Fed engaged in **forward commitment,** preannouncing exactly how much it was going to buy during QE2 and how long the buying would last. This was a major change in monetary policy because up to that time the Fed had (along with most central banks) stuck to a policy of being vague about how long any particular policy initiative would last. For instance, if the Fed lowered or raised the federal funds target rate, it did not publicly announce for how long the change would last.

The rationale behind being vague was to preserve the Fed's flexibility to make changes if unexpected circumstances arose. However, that flexibility came at the cost of reduced credibility because the public might not react strongly to a policy change if it believed that the policy change might be reversed at any moment. By preannouncing the exact size and duration of QE, the Fed removed that worry. By making forward commitments, the public would know not only the content of a policy change but also that it wasn't going to be suddenly reversed.

With respect to the banking system, the announcement of both the size and duration of the Fed's open-market purchases of bonds meant that banks would know that the resulting increases in reserves would not suddenly be reversed. That would make the banks more likely to lend those new reserves because they wouldn't have any nagging doubts that the Fed might suddenly reverse policy, reduce reserves, and force the banks to suddenly and unexpectedly reduce their lending activities.

Operation Twist The Fed's use of forward commitment continued in September 2011, when it began the Maturity Extension Program, commonly known as Operation Twist. Under that program, the Fed preannounced that, by the end of 2012, it would purchase $677 billion in long-term government bonds while simultaneously selling an equivalent dollar amount of short-term government bonds. The Fed's motivation for doing so was to spur investment and consumption by reducing long-term interest rates, which were at that time several percentage points higher than short-term interest rates (which remained near zero thanks to ZIRP).

The intended reduction in long-term interest rates was accomplished by purchasing long-term bonds and driving up their prices. The money needed for those purchases was provided by selling an equivalent dollar amount of short-term bonds. Crucially, the amount of short-term bonds sold by the Fed was not nearly enough to alter short-term interest rates. Thus, they stayed near zero while longer-term rates fell.

QE3 When economic growth remained weak in 2012, the Fed decided that the lack of effectiveness of QE2 and

Operation Twist might have been due to the fact that both had featured limited time durations. Thus, banks might have been worried that the Fed might reverse policy as soon as the limited time durations of QE2 and Operation Twist came to an end.

To avoid that possibility going forward, the Fed's announcement of QE3 in September 2012 involved explicitly stating not only that the Fed would purchase $85 billion per month in bonds, but that those purchases had no specific end date and would in fact continue until the employment situation improved substantially. By making an open-ended commitment, the Fed hoped to enhance the credibility of its monetary stimulus policies.

In September 2012, the Fed also issued an open-ended policy commitment with respect to the federal funds rate. The Fed announced that the federal funds target rate would remain "exceptionally low" as long as the unemployment rate stayed above 6.5 percent and inflation remained muted, at 2 percent per year or less. Thus, the Fed committed itself to utilizing ZIRP until either the jobs situation dramatically improved or inflation started rising too high.

That forward commitment allowed businesses, banks, and consumers to have a much better sense of how long monetary stimulus would last and the circumstances under which it would be cut off. As the economy moved into 2013, the Fed hoped that its increasingly specific forward guidance would help to improve the effectiveness of its monetary stimulus efforts.

Problems and Complications

Despite its recent successes in the United States, monetary policy has certain limitations and faces actual-economy complications.

Lags Recall that fiscal policy is hindered by three delays, or lags—a recognition lag, an administrative lag, and an operational lag. Monetary policy also faces a recognition lag and an operational lag, but because the Fed can decide and implement policy changes within days, it avoids the long administrative lag that hinders fiscal policy.

A recognition lag affects monetary policy because normal monthly variations in economic activity and the price level mean that the Fed may not be able to quickly recognize when the economy is truly starting to recede or when inflation is really starting to rise. Once the Fed acts, an operation lag of 3 to 6 months affects monetary policy because that much time is typically required for interest-rate changes to have their full impacts on investment, aggregate demand, real GDP, and the price level. These two lags complicate the timing of monetary policy.

Up, Up, and Away

The consolidated balance sheet of the 12 Federal Reserve Banks changed markedly during the severe recession of 2007–2009. Total Fed assets increased from $885 billion in February 2008 to $2,317 billion in March 2010. This increase reflected an enormous rise in the number of U.S. securities, mortgage-backed securities, and other financial assets purchased by the Federal Reserve. In undertaking its monetary policy and its lender-of-last-resort functions, the Fed bought these securities from financial institutions—purposely increasing the liquidity of the financial system.

On the liability side, the reserves of commercial banks rose from $43 billion in February 2008 to $1,148 billion in March 2010. To make sure they were liquid and the funds were safe, banks placed much of the proceeds from selling securities to the Fed into their respective reserve accounts at the Fed. This flow was strengthened because the Fed began paying interest on the reserves that banks were holding at the Fed.

In March 2010 total bank reserves held at the Fed exceeded total checkable deposits held by the banks. The severe distress in the financial system had voluntarily turned the fractional reserve system into a 100-percent-plus reserve system! The banks had enormous excess reserves from which to increase lending once the banks became more certain of their own financial viability and the likelihood that newly issued loans would be paid back.

The Fed's use of quantitative easing caused the Fed's balance sheet to increase even further after the Great Recession ended. By May 2013, it had reached $3.3 trillion and was continuing to grow by $85 billion per month as QE3 continued. The Fed therefore faces the challenging task of using monetary policy to absorb large portions of this overstock of excess reserves as the economy recovers and picks up momentum. It does not want the banks to lend out the full amount of these excess reserves because that would flood the economy with bank-created money and excessively expand the money supply. During a vigorous economic expansion, the excessive money and resulting very low interest rates could produce such large expansions of aggregate demand that rapid inflation would occur.

Cyclical Asymmetry and the Liquidity Trap

Monetary policy may be highly effective in slowing expansions and controlling inflation but may be much less reliable in pushing the economy from a severe recession. Economists say that monetary policy may suffer from **cyclical asymmetry.** The metaphor of "pushing on a string" is often invoked to capture this problem. Imagine the Fed standing on the left-hand side of Figure 16.5d, holding one end of a "monetary-policy string." And imagine that the other end of the monetary-policy string is tied to the AD curve. Because the string would go taut if pulled on, monetary policy may be useful in *pulling* aggregate demand to the left. But because the string would go limp if pushed on, monetary policy will be rather ineffective at *pushing* aggregate demand to the right.

The reason for this asymmetry has to do with the asymmetric way in which people may act in response to changes in bank reserves. If pursued vigorously, a restrictive monetary policy can deplete commercial banking reserves to the point where banks are forced to reduce the volume of loans. That means a contraction of the money supply, higher interest rates, and reduced aggregate demand. The Fed can absorb sufficient reserves and eventually achieve its goal.

But the Fed cannot be certain of achieving its goal when it adds reserves to the banking system because of the so-called **liquidity trap,** in which adding more liquidity to banks has little or no additional positive effect on lending, borrowing, investment, or aggregate demand. For example, during the recent recession, the Fed created billions of dollars of excess reserves that drove down the federal funds rate to as low as 0.2 percent. The prime interest rate fell from 7.3 percent (December 2007) to 3.25 percent (March 2009). Nevertheless, lending by banks stalled throughout the first 15 months of the recession and remained weak even after the Fed implemented ZIRP, QE, Operation Twist, and forward commitments over the following four years. The banks were fearful that the loans they would make to households, businesses, and other financial institutions would not be paid back. Consequently, they were content to hold reserves at the Federal Reserve Banks.

To switch analogies, an expansionary monetary policy can suffer from a "you can lead a horse to water, but you can't make it drink" problem. The Fed can create excess reserves, but it cannot guarantee that the banks will actually make additional loans and thus promote spending. If commercial banks seek liquidity and are unwilling to lend, the efforts of the Fed will be of little avail. Similarly, households and businesses can frustrate the intentions of the Fed by not borrowing excess reserves being made available as loans. And when the Fed buys securities from the public, people may choose to pay off existing loans with the money received, rather than increasing their spending on goods and services.

Furthermore, a severe recession may so undermine business confidence that the investment demand curve shifts to the left and overwhelms the lower interest rates associated with an expansionary monetary policy. That is what happened in the most recent recession. Although the Fed drove the real interest rate down to zero percent, investment spending remained low and the economy remained mired in recession. The recent U.S. experience reminds us that active monetary policy certainly is not a cure-all for the business cycle. Under some circumstances, monetary policy may be like "pushing on a string."

The liquidity trap that occurred during the severe recession was a primary reason why public policy in the United States turned so significantly and forcefully toward fiscal policy in 2009. Recall our discussion of the American Recovery and Redevelopment Act of 2009, which authorized the infusion of $787 billion of new tax cuts and government spending in 2009 and 2010.

> **QUICK REVIEW 16.6**
>
> - The Fed aggressively lowered the federal funds interest rate following 9/11 and the 2001 recession and also during the severe recession of 2007–2009.
> - To help stimulate the economy after the Great Recession, the Fed implemented the zero interest rate policy (ZIRP), quantitative easing (QE), Operation Twist, and forward commitment.
> - The main strengths of monetary policy are (a) speed and flexibility and (b) political acceptability; its main weaknesses are (a) time lags and (b) potential ineffectiveness during severe recession.

The "Big Picture"

Figure 16.6 (Key Graph) on pages 374 and 375 brings together the analytical and policy aspects of macroeconomics discussed in this and the eight preceding chapters. This "big picture" shows how the many concepts and principles discussed relate to one another and how they constitute a coherent theory of the price level and real output in a market economy.

Study this diagram and you will see that the levels of output, employment, income, and prices all result from the interaction of aggregate supply and aggregate demand. The items shown in red relate to public policy.

KEY GRAPH

FIGURE 16.6 The AD-AS theory of the price level, real output, and stabilization policy. This figure integrates the various components of macroeconomic theory and stabilization policy. Determinants that either constitute public policy or are strongly influenced by public policy are shown in red.

QUICK QUIZ FOR FIGURE 16.6

1. All else equal, an increase in domestic resource availability will:
   a. increase input prices, reduce aggregate supply, and increase real output.
   b. raise labor productivity, reduce interest rates, and lower the international value of the dollar.
   c. increase net exports, increase investment, and reduce aggregate demand.
   d. reduce input prices, increase aggregate supply, and increase real output.

2. All else equal, an expansionary monetary policy during a recession will:
   a. lower the interest rate, increase investment, and reduce net exports.
   b. lower the interest rate, increase investment, and increase aggregate demand.
   c. increase the interest rate, increase investment, and reduce net exports.
   d. reduce productivity, aggregate supply, and real output.

3. A personal income tax cut, combined with a reduction in corporate income and excise taxes, would:
   a. increase consumption, investment, aggregate demand, and aggregate supply.
   b. reduce productivity, raise input prices, and reduce aggregate supply.
   c. increase government spending, reduce net exports, and increase aggregate demand.
   d. increase the supply of money, reduce interest rates, increase investment, and expand real output.

4. An appreciation of the dollar would:
   a. reduce the price of imported resources, lower input prices, and increase aggregate supply.
   b. increase net exports and aggregate demand.
   c. increase aggregate supply and aggregate demand.
   d. reduce consumption, investment, net export spending, and government spending.

Worries about ZIRP, QE, and Twist

ZIRP, QE, and Operation Twist Provided Massive Economic Stimulus During and After the Great Recession. But There Remain Many Worries About Unintended Consequences.

When the financial crisis reached its peak in 2008, the Fed acted aggressively to prevent bank runs and stabilize the financial system by acting as a lender of last resort. It also did its best to get the economy moving again by lowering short-term interest rates to nearly zero—a strategy that came to be known as the zero interest rate policy, or ZIRP.

When ZIRP by itself didn't seem to be causing enough stimulus, the Fed also began engaging in trillions of dollars' worth of bond purchases. Those purchases went by the name of quantitative easing, or QE, because the Fed printed up electronic money to pay for the purchases, thereby massively increasing (easing) the total quantity of money in circulation. The

Fed's hope was that the additional money would lead to additional spending and lending that would boost aggregate demand by increasing consumption and investment. Later, the policy known as Operation Twist lowered longer-term interest rates.

One important effect of ZIRP and Operation Twist was to help the U.S. federal government engage in aggressive deficit-financed fiscal stimulus. Thanks to ZIRP and Operation Twist, the federal government was able to fund large deficits by issuing 10-year bonds at nominal interest rates of about 2 percent—substantially lower than the historical average of about 6 percent.

But the Federal Reserve didn't just help the federal government with low

SUMMARY

LO16.1 Discuss how the equilibrium interest rate is determined in the market for money.

The total demand for money consists of the transactions demand for money plus the asset demand for money. The amount of money demanded for transactions varies directly with the nominal GDP; the amount of money demanded as an asset varies inversely with the interest rate. The market for money combines the total demand for money with the money supply to determine equilibrium interest rates.

Interest rates and bond prices are inversely related.

LO16.2 Describe the balance sheet of the Federal Reserve and the meaning of its major items.

The consolidated balance sheet of the Federal Reserve System lists the collective assets and liabilities of the 12 Federal Reserve banks. The assets consist largely of Treasury notes, Treasury bills, and Treasury bonds. The major liabilities are reserves of

commercial banks, Treasury deposits, and Federal Reserve notes outstanding. The balance sheet is useful in understanding monetary policy because open-market operations increase or decrease the Fed's assets and liabilities.

LO16.3 List and explain the goals and tools of monetary policy.

The goal of monetary policy is to help the economy achieve price stability, full employment, and economic growth.

The four main instruments of monetary policy are (*a*) open-market operations, (*b*) the reserve ratio, (*c*) the discount rate, and (*d*) interest on reserves.

LO16.4 Describe the federal funds rate and how the Fed directly influences it.

The federal funds rate is the interest rate that banks charge one another for overnight loans of reserves. The prime interest rate is the interest rates. It also served as the federal government's primary lender. In 2012, for instance, the Federal Reserve purchased over 70 percent of all U.S. government debt. Thus, 70 percent of the federal government's new borrowing came from the Federal Reserve in the form of newly printed money that the Fed created in order to fund its open-market purchases of government bonds.

The consensus among economists was that the Fed's aggressive use of ZIRP and QE were warranted by the severity of the financial crisis and the historically slow pace with which the economy recovered after the 2007–2009 recession. However, concerns were also raised about possible unintended consequences.

One worry had to do with the large annual budget deficits that the federal government was running. While many economists felt that the large deficits were appropriate given the sluggish economy, others believed that the federal government was overspending and taking resources away from the private sector. As a result, they felt that the Fed's use of ZIRP and QE was making it too easy for Congress to overspend and run large budget deficits because the Fed would always provide a ready buyer for the bonds that had to be issued to finance those large deficits.

A longer-term worry was that when ZIRP ended and interest rates began to rise again toward normal levels, the federal government would be suddenly confronted with huge interest costs. Consider the $16 trillion of debt that had accumulated by 2013: $16 trillion borrowed at 2 percent interest generates annual interest payments of $320 billion per year. But if the interest rate on government debt were to rise back to its historical average of 6 percent, the annual interest payments on $16 trillion would come to $960 billion per year. Such a huge increase in annual interest payments would likely require either massive budget cuts or even more borrowing, unless the economy began to grow so quickly that increased tax revenues were enough to compensate for the increased interest payments.

Another problem with extremely low interest rates is that they punish savers. A senior citizen who has saved for retirement will find that her investments yield very low rates of return when the Fed is keeping interest rates low. Instead of being able to live off of the interest generated by her investments, she may find herself spending down her accumulated savings because the interest payments amount to nearly nothing.

On a larger scale, pension plans and retirement funds are also hit hard by low interest rates. Those institutions take deposits from current workers, invest those funds, and promise to pay out certain amounts when workers retire. Prior to the financial crisis, most of those institutions had assumed that they would be able to earn 8 percent per year on the retirement funds that they were entrusted with. But with the Fed keeping interest rates so low, the pension plans and retirement funds were not earning anywhere near 8 percent per year on their investments. As a result, the low interest rates engineered by the Fed made it very unlikely that pension plans and retirement funds would be able to keep their promises to retirees and deliver enough money in 20 or 30 years to pay each individual retiree what he or she had been promised.

benchmark rate that banks use as a reference rate for a wide range of interest rates on short-term loans to businesses and individuals.

The Fed adjusts the federal funds rate to a level appropriate for economic conditions. Under an expansionary monetary policy, it purchases securities from commercial banks and the general public to inject reserves into the banking system. This lowers the federal funds rate to the targeted level and also reduces other interest rates (such as the prime rate). Under a restrictive monetary policy, the Fed sells securities to commercial banks and the general public via open-market operations. Consequently, reserves are removed from the banking system, and the federal funds rate and other interest rates rise.

LO16.5 Identify the mechanisms by which monetary policy affects GDP and the price level.

Monetary policy affects the economy through a complex cause-effect chain: (*a*) policy decisions affect commercial bank reserves; (*b*) changes in reserves affect the money supply; (*c*) changes in the money supply alter the interest rate; (*d*) changes in the interest rate affect investment; (*e*) changes in investment affect aggregate demand; (*f*) changes in aggregate demand affect the equilibrium real GDP and the price level. Table 16.3 draws together all the basic ideas relevant to the use of monetary policy.

LO16.6 Explain the effectiveness of monetary policy and its shortcomings.

The advantages of monetary policy include its flexibility and political acceptability. In recent years, the Fed has used monetary policy to keep inflation low while helping limit the depth of the recession of 2001, to boost the economy as it recovered from that recession, to help stabilize the banking sector in the wake of the mortgage debt crisis, and to promote recovery from the severe recession of 2007–2009. Today, nearly all economists view monetary policy as a significant stabilization tool.

Monetary policy has two major limitations and potential problems: (*a*) recognition and operation lags complicate the timing of monetary policy; (*b*) in a severe recession, the reluctance of banks to lend excess reserves and firms to borrow money to spend on capital goods may contribute to a liquidity trap that limits the effectiveness of an expansionary monetary policy.

TERMS AND CONCEPTS

monetary policy	discount rate	zero interest rate policy (ZIRP)
interest	interest on reserves	zero lower bound problem
transactions demand for money	federal funds rate	quantitative easing (QE)
asset demand for money	expansionary monetary policy	forward commitment
total demand for money	prime interest rate	cyclical asymmetry
open-market operations	restrictive monetary policy	liquidity trap
reserve ratio	Taylor rule	

The following and additional problems can be found in connect ECONOMICS

DISCUSSION QUESTIONS

1. What is the basic determinant of (*a*) the transactions demand and (*b*) the asset demand for money? Explain how these two demands can be combined graphically to determine total money demand. How is the equilibrium interest rate in the money market determined? Use a graph to show the effect of an increase in the total demand for money on the equilibrium interest rate (no change in money supply). Use your general knowledge of equilibrium prices to explain why the previous interest rate is no longer sustainable. LO16.1

2. What is the basic objective of monetary policy? What are the major strengths of monetary policy? Why is monetary policy easier to conduct than fiscal policy? LO16.3

3. Distinguish between the federal funds rate and the prime interest rate. Why is one higher than the other? Why do changes in the two rates closely track one another? LO16.4

4. Why is a decrease in the supply of federal funds shown as an upshift of the supply curve in Figure 16.3, whereas an increase in federal funds is shown as a downshift of the supply curve? LO16.4

5. Suppose that you are a member of the Board of Governors of the Federal Reserve System. The economy is experiencing a sharp rise in the inflation rate. What change in the federal funds rate would you recommend? How would your recommended change get accomplished? What impact would the actions have on the lending ability of the banking system, the real interest rate, investment spending, aggregate demand, and inflation? LO16.5

6. Explain the links between changes in the nation's money supply, the interest rate, investment spending, aggregate demand, real GDP, and the price level. LO16.5

7. What do economists mean when they say that monetary policy can exhibit cyclical asymmetry? How does the idea of a liquidity trap relate to cyclical asymmetry? Why is this possibility of a liquidity trap significant to policymakers? LO16.6

8. LAST WORD Did Operation Twist target long-term or short-term interest rates? How does ZIRP cause problems for savers and pension funds? How might low interest rates lead to problematic fiscal policy decisions?

REVIEW QUESTIONS

1. When bond prices go up, interest rates go _____. LO16.1
   a. Up.
   b. Down.
   c. Nowhere.

2. A commercial bank sells a Treasury bond to the Federal Reserve for $100,000. The money supply: LO16.3
   a. Increases by $100,000.
   b. Decreases by $100,000.
   c. Is unaffected by the transaction.

3. Use commercial bank and Federal Reserve Bank balance sheets to demonstrate the effect of each of the following transactions on commercial bank reserves: LO16.3
   a. Federal Reserve Banks purchase securities from banks.

   b. Commercial banks borrow from Federal Reserve Banks at the discount rate.
   c. The Fed reduces the reserve ratio.
   d. Commercial banks increase their reserves after the Fed increases the interest rate that it pays on reserves.

4. A bank currently has $100,000 in checkable deposits and $15,000 in actual reserves. If the reserve ratio is 20 percent, the bank has _____ in money-creating potential. If the reserve ratio is 14 percent, the bank has _____ in money-creating potential. LO16.3
   a. $20,000; $14,000.
   b. $3,000; $2,100.
   c. −$5,000; $1,000.
   d. $5,000; $1,000.

5. A bank borrows $100,000 from the Fed, leaving a $100,000 Treasury bond on deposit with the Fed to serve as collateral for the loan. The discount rate that applies to the loan is 4 percent and the Fed is currently mandating a reserve ratio of 10 percent. How much of the $100,000 borrowed by the bank must it keep as required reserves? LO16.3
   a. $0.
   b. $4,000.
   c. $10,000.
   d. $100,000.

6. Which of the following Fed actions will increase bank lending? LO16.3
   Select one or more answers from the choices shown.
   a. The Fed raises the discount rate from 5 percent to 6 percent.
   b. The Fed raises the reserve ratio from 10 percent to 11 percent.
   c. The Fed buys $400 million worth of Treasury bonds from commercial banks.
   d. The Fed lowers the discount rate from 4 percent to 2 percent.

7. If the Federal Reserve wants to increase the federal funds rate using open-market operations, it should _____ bonds. LO16.4
   a. Buy.
   b. Sell.

8. True or False: A liquidity trap occurs when expansionary monetary policy fails to work because an increase in bank reserves by the Fed does not lead to an increase in bank lending. LO16.6

9. True or False: In the United States, monetary policy has two key advantages over fiscal policy: (1) isolation from political pressure and (2) speed and flexibility. LO16.6

PROBLEMS

1. Assume that the following data characterize the hypothetical economy of Trance: money supply = $200 billion; quantity of money demanded for transactions = $150 billion; quantity of money demanded as an asset = $10 billion at 12 percent interest, increasing by $10 billion for each 2-percentage-point fall in the interest rate. LO16.1
   a. What is the equilibrium interest rate in Trance?
   b. At the equilibrium interest rate, what are the quantity of money supplied, the total quantity of money demanded, the amount of money demanded for transactions, and the amount of money demanded as an asset in Trance?

2. Suppose a bond with no expiration date has a face value of $10,000 and annually pays a fixed amount of interest of $800. In the table provided to the right, calculate and enter either the interest rate that the bond would yield to a bond buyer at each of the bond prices listed or the bond price at each of the interest yields shown. What generalization can be drawn from the completed table? LO16.1

Bond Price	Interest Yield, %
$ 8,000	_____
_____	8.9
$10,000	_____
$11,000	_____
_____	6.2

3. In the tables that follow you will find consolidated balance sheets for the commercial banking system and the 12 Federal Reserve Banks. Use columns 1 through 3 to indicate how the balance sheets would read after each of transactions *a* to *c* is completed. Do not cumulate your answers; that is, analyze each transaction separately, starting in each case from the numbers provided. All accounts are in billions of dollars. LO16.3
   a. A decline in the discount rate prompts commercial banks to borrow an additional $1 billion from the Federal Reserve Banks. Show the new balance-sheet numbers in column 1 of each table.

		Consolidated Balance Sheet: All Commercial Banks		
		(1)	(2)	(3)
Assets:				
Reserves	$33	_____	_____	_____
Securities	60	_____	_____	_____
Loans	60	_____	_____	_____
Liabilities and net worth:				
Checkable deposits	$150	_____	_____	_____
Loans from the Federal Reserve Banks	3	_____	_____	_____

		Consolidated Balance Sheet: The 12 Federal Reserve Banks		
		(1)	(2)	(3)
Assets:				
Securities.	$60	_____	_____	_____
Loans to commercial banks.	3	_____	_____	_____
Liabilities and net worth:				
Reserves of commercial banks	$33			
Treasury deposits.	3	_____	_____	_____
Federal Reserve Notes	27	_____	_____	_____

b. The Federal Reserve Banks sell $3 billion in securities to members of the public, who pay for the bonds with checks. Show the new balance-sheet numbers in column 2 of each table.

c. The Federal Reserve Banks buy $2 billion of securities from commercial banks. Show the new balance-sheet numbers in column 3 of each table.

d. Now review each of the previous three transactions, asking yourself these three questions: (1) What change, if any, took place in the money supply as a direct and immediate result of each transaction? (2) What increase or decrease in the commercial banks' reserves took place in each transaction? (3) Assuming a reserve ratio of 20 percent, what change in the money-creating potential of the commercial banking system occurred as a result of each transaction?

4. Refer to Table 16.2 and assume that the Fed's reserve ratio is 10 percent and the economy is in a severe recession. Also suppose that the commercial banks are hoarding all excess reserves (not lending them out) because of their fear of loan defaults. Finally, suppose that the Fed is highly concerned that the banks will suddenly lend out these excess reserves and possibly contribute to inflation once the economy begins to recover and confidence is restored. By how many percentage points would the Fed need to increase the reserve ratio to eliminate one-third of the excess reserves? What would be the size of the monetary multiplier before and after the change in the reserve ratio? By how much would the lending potential of the banks decline as a result of the increase in the reserve ratio? **LO16.3**

5. Suppose that the demand for federal funds curve is such that the quantity of funds demanded changes by $120 billion for each 1 percent change in the federal funds interest rate. Also, assume that the current federal funds rate is at the 3 percent rate that is targeted by the Fed. Now suppose that the Fed retargets the rate to 3.5 percent. Assuming no change in demand, will the Fed need to increase or decrease the supply of federal funds? By how much will the quantity of federal funds have to change for the equilibrium to occur at the new target rate? **LO16.4**

6. Suppose that inflation is 2 percent, the federal funds rate is 4 percent, and real GDP falls 2 percent below potential GDP. According to the Taylor rule, in what direction and by how much should the Fed change the real federal funds rate? **LO16.4**

7. Refer to the table for Moola at the bottom of this page to answer the following questions. What is the equilibrium interest rate in Moola? What is the level of investment at the equilibrium interest rate? Is there either a recessionary output gap (negative GDP gap) or an inflationary output gap (positive GDP gap) at the equilibrium interest rate and, if either, what is the amount? Given money demand, by how much would the Moola central bank need to change the money supply to close the output gap? What is the expenditure multiplier in Moola? **LO16.5**

Money Supply	Money Demand	Interest Rate	Investment at Interest (Rate Shown)	Potential Real GDP	Actual Real GDP at Interest (Rate Shown)
$500	$800	2%	$50	$350	$390
500	700	3	40	350	370
500	600	4	30	350	350
500	500	5	20	350	330
500	400	6	10	350	310

Financial Economics

Learning Objectives

LO17.1 Define *financial economics* and distinguish between economic investment and financial investment.

LO17.2 Explain the time value of money and how compound interest can be used to calculate the present value of any future amount of money.

LO17.3 Identify and distinguish between the most common financial investments: stocks, bonds, and mutual funds.

LO17.4 Relate how percentage rates of return provide a common framework for comparing assets and explain why asset prices and rates of return are inversely related.

LO17.5 Define and utilize the concept of arbitrage.

LO17.6 Describe how the word *risk* is used in financial economics and explain the difference between diversifiable and nondiversifiable risk.

LO17.7 Convey why investment decisions are determined primarily by investment returns and nondiversifiable risk and how investment returns compensate for being patient and for bearing nondiversifiable risk.

LO17.8 Explain how the Security Market Line illustrates the compensation that investors receive for time preference and nondiversifiable risk and why arbitrage will tend to move all assets onto the Security Market Line.

Financial economics studies investor preferences and how they affect the trading and pricing of financial assets like stocks, bonds, and real estate. The two most important investor preferences are a desire for high rates of return and a dislike of risk and uncertainty. This chapter will explain how these preferences interact to produce a strong positive relationship between risk and return: the riskier an investment, the higher its rate of return. This positive relationship compensates investors for bearing risk. And it is enforced by a powerful set of buying and selling pressures known as arbitrage, which ensures consistency across investments so that assets with identical levels of risk generate identical rates of return. As we will demonstrate, this consistency makes it extremely difficult for anyone to "beat the market" by finding a set of investments that can generate high rates of return at low levels of risk. Instead, investors are stuck with a trade-off: If they want higher rates of return, they must accept higher levels of risk. On average, higher risk results in higher returns. But it can also result in large losses, as it did for many investors who held risky assets during the financial crisis of 2007–2008.

Financial Investment

LO17.1 Define *financial economics* and distinguish between economic investment and financial investment.
Financial economics focuses its attention on the investments that individuals and firms make in the wide variety of assets available to them in our modern economy. But before proceeding, it is important for you to recall the difference between economic investment and financial investment.

Economic investment refers either to paying for *new* additions to the capital stock or *new* replacements for capital stock that has worn out. Thus, *new* factories, houses, retail stores, construction equipment, and wireless networks are all good examples of economic investments. And so are purchases of office computers to replace computers that have become obsolete as well as purchases of new commercial airplanes to replace planes that have served out their useful lives.

In contrast, financial investment is a far broader, much more inclusive concept. It includes economic investment and a whole lot more. **Financial investment** refers to either buying an asset or building an asset in the expectation of financial gain. It does not distinguish between *new* assets and *old* assets. Purchasing an old house or an old factory is just as much a financial investment as purchasing a new house or a new factory. For financial investment, it does not matter if the purchase of an asset adds to the capital stock, replaces the capital stock, or does neither. Investing in old comic books is just as much a financial investment as building a new refinery. Finally, unlike economic investment, financial investment can involve either *financial assets* (such as stocks, bonds, and futures contracts) or *real assets* (such as land, factories, and retail stores).

When bankers, entrepreneurs, corporate executives, retirement planners, and ordinary people use the word *investment*, they almost always mean financial investment. In fact, the ordinary meaning of the word investment is financial investment. So for this chapter, we will use the word investment in its ordinary sense of "financial investment" rather than in the far narrower sense of "economic investment," which is used throughout the rest of this book.

Present Value

LO17.2 Explain the time value of money and how compound interest can be used to calculate the present value of any future amount of money.
Money has "time value" because current dollars can be converted into a larger amount of future dollars through compound interest. The *time-value of money* is the idea that a specific amount of money is more valuable to a person the sooner it is received, and a person will need to be compensated for waiting to obtain it later. The time-value of money can also be thought of as the opportunity cost of receiving a sum of money later rather than earlier.

The time-value of money underlies one of the most fundamental ideas in financial economics: **present value,** which is the present-day value, or worth, of returns or costs that are expected to arrive in the future. The ability to calculate present values is especially useful when investors wish to determine the proper current price to pay for an asset. In fact, the proper current price for any risk-free investment *is* the present value of its expected future returns. And while some adjustments have to be made when determining the proper price of a risky investment, the process is entirely based on the logic of present value. So we begin our study of finance by explaining present value and how it can be used to price risk-free assets. Once that is accomplished, we will turn our attention to risk and how the financial markets determine the prices of risky assets by taking into account investor preferences regarding the trade-off between potential return and potential risk.

Compound Interest

The best way to understand present value is by first understanding compound interest. **Compound interest** describes how quickly an investment increases in value when interest is paid, or compounded, not only on the original amount invested but also on all interest payments that have been previously made.

As an example of compound interest in action, consider Table 17.1, which shows the amount of money that $100 invested today becomes if it increases, or compounds, at an 8 percent annual interest rate, i, for various numbers of years. To simplify, let's express the 8 percent annual interest rate as a decimal so that it becomes $i = 0.08$. The key to understanding compound interest is to realize that 1 year's worth of growth at interest rate i will always result in $(1 + i)$ times as much money at the end of a year as there was at the beginning of the year. Consequently, if the first year begins with $100 and if $i = 0.08$, then $(1 + 0.08)$ or 1.08 times as much money—$108—will be available at the end of the year. We show the computation for the first year in column 2 of Table 17.1 and display the $108 outcome in column 3. The same logic would also apply with other initial amounts. If a year begins with $500, there will be 1.08 times more money after 1 year, or $540. Algebraically, let X_0 denote the amount of money at the start of the first year and X_1 the amount after one year's worth of growth. Then we see that any given number of dollars X_0 at the start of the first year grows into $X_1 = (1 + i)X_0$ dollars after one year's worth of growth.

Next, consider what happens if the initial investment of $100 that grew into $108 after 1 year continues to grow at 8 percent interest for a second year. The $108 available at the beginning of the second year will grow into an amount of money that is 1.08 times larger by the end of the second year. That amount, as shown in Table 17.1, is $116.64. Notice that the computation in the table is made by multiplying the initial $100 by $(1.08)^2$. That is because the

original $100 is compounded by 1.08 into $108 and then the $108 is again compounded by 1.08. More generally, since the second year begins with $(1 + i)X_0$ dollars, it will grow to $(1 + i)(1 + i)X_0 = (1 + i)^2X_0$ dollars by the end of the second year.

Similar reasoning shows that the amount of money at the end of 3 years has to be $(1 + i)^3X_0$ since the amount of money at the beginning of the third year, $(1 + i)^2X_0$, gets multiplied by $(1 + i)$ to convert it into the amount of money at the end of the third year. In terms of Table 17.1, that amount is $125.97, which is $(1.08)^3$100.

As you can see, we now have a fixed pattern. The $100 that is invested at the beginning of the first year becomes $(1 + i)$100 after 1 year, $(1 + i)^2$100 after 2 years, $(1 + i)^3$100 after 3 years, and so on. It therefore is clear that the amount of money after t years will be $(1 + i)^t$100. This pattern always holds true, regardless of the size of the initial investment. Thus, investors know that if X_0 dollars is invested today and earns compound interest at the rate i, it will grow into exactly $(1 + i)^tX_0$ dollars after t years. Economists express that fact with the following formula:

$$X_t = (1 + i)^tX_0 \tag{1}$$

Equation 1 captures the idea that if investors have the opportunity to invest X_0 dollars today at interest rate i, then they have the ability to transform X_0 dollars today into $(1 + i)^tX_0$ dollars in t years.

But notice that the logic of the equality also works in reverse, so that it can also be thought of as showing that $(1 + i)^tX_0$ dollars in t years can be transformed into X_0 dollars today. That may seem very odd, but it is exactly what happens when people take out loans. For instance, consider a situation where an investor named Roberto takes out a loan for $100 dollars today, a loan that will accumulate interest at 8 percent per year for 5 years. Under such an arrangement, the amount Roberto owes will grow with compound interest into $(1.08)^5$100 = $146.93 dollars in 5 years. This means that Roberto can convert $146.93 dollars in 5 years (the amount required to pay off the loan) into $100 dollars today (the amount he borrows).

Consequently, the compound interest formula given in equation 1 defines not only the rate at which present amounts of money can be converted to future amounts of money but also the rate at which future amounts of money can be converted into present amounts of money.

The Present Value Model

The present value model simply rearranges equation 1 to make it easier to transform future amounts of money into present amounts of money. To derive the formula used to

TABLE 17.1 Compounding: $100 at 8 Percent Interest

(1) Years of Compounding	(2) Compounding Computation	(3) Value at Year's End
1	$100 (1.08)	$108.00
2	100 (1.08)^2	116.64
3	100 (1.08)^3	125.97
4	100 (1.08)^4	136.05
5	100 (1.08)^5	146.93
17	100 (1.08)^17	370.00

calculate the present value of a future amount of money, we divide both sides of equation 1 by $(1 + i)^t$ to obtain

$$\frac{X_t}{(1 + i)^t} = X_0 \qquad (2)$$

The logic of equation 2 is identical to that of equation 1. Both allow investors to convert present amounts of money into future amounts of money and vice versa. However, equation 2 makes it much more intuitive to convert a given number of dollars in the future into their present-day equivalent. In fact, it says that X_t dollars in t years converts into exactly $X_t/(1 + i)^t$ dollars today. This may not seem important, but it is actually very powerful because it allows investors to easily calculate how much they should pay for any given asset.

WORKED PROBLEMS

W17.1
Present value

To see why this is true, understand that an asset's owner obtains the right to receive one or more future payments. If an investor is considering buying an asset, her problem is to try to determine how much she should pay today to buy the asset and receive those future payments. Equation 2 makes this task very easy. If she knows how large a future payment will be (X_t dollars), when it will arrive (in t years), and what the interest rate (i) is, then she can apply equation 2 to determine the payment's present value: its value in present-day dollars. If she does this for each of the future payments that the asset in question is expected to make, she will be able to calculate the overall present value of all the asset's future payments by simply summing together the present values of each of the individual payments. This will allow her to determine the price she should pay for the asset. In particular, *the asset's price should exactly equal the sum of the present values of all of the asset's future payments.*

As a simple example, suppose that Cecilia has the chance to buy an asset that is guaranteed to return a single payment of exactly $370.00 in 17 years. Again let's assume the interest rate is 8 percent per year. Then the present value of that future payment can be determined using equation 2 to equal precisely $370.00/(1 + 0.08)^{17} = \$370.00/(1.08)^{17} = \$100$ today. This is confirmed in the row for year 17 in Table 17.1.

To see why Cecilia should be willing to pay a price that is *exactly* equal to the $100 present value of the asset's single future payment of $370.00 in 17 years, consider the following thought experiment. What would happen if she were to invest $100 today in an alternative investment that is guaranteed to compound her money for 17 years at 8 percent per year? How large would her investment in this alternative become? Equation 1 and Table 17.1 tell us that the answer is exactly $370.00 in 17 years.

This is very important because it shows that Cecilia and other investors have two different possible ways of purchasing the right to receive $370.00 in 17 years. They can either:

- Purchase the asset in question for $100.
- Invest $100 in the alternative asset that pays 8 percent per year.

Because either investment will deliver the same future benefit, both investments are in fact identical. Consequently, they should have identical prices—meaning that each will cost precisely $100 today.

A good way to see why this must be the case is by considering how the presence of the alternative investment affects the behavior of both the potential buyers and the potential sellers of the asset in question. First, notice that Cecelia and other potential buyers would never pay more than $100 for the asset in question because they know that they could get the same future return of $370.00 in 17 years by investing $100 in the alternative investment. At the same time, people selling the asset in question would not sell it to Cecelia or other potential buyers for anything less than $100 since they know that the only other way for Cecelia and other potential buyers to get a future return of $370.00 in 17 years is by paying $100 for the alternative investment. Since Cecelia and the other potential buyers will not pay more than $100 for the asset in question and its sellers will not accept less than $100 for the asset in question, the result will be that the asset in question and the alternative investment will have the exact same price of $100 today.

QUICK REVIEW 17.1

- Financial investment refers to buying an asset with the hope of financial gain.
- The time-value of money is the idea that a specific amount of money is more valuable to a person the sooner it is received because of the potential for compound interest.
- Compound interest is the payment of interest not only on the original amount invested but also on any interest payments previously made; X_0 dollars today growing at interest rate i will become $(1 + i)^t X_0$ dollars in t years.
- The present value formula facilitates transforming future amounts of money into present-day amounts of money; X_t dollars in t years converts into exactly $X_t/(1 + i)^t$ dollars today.
- An investment's proper current price is equal to the sum of the present values of all the future payments that it is expected to make.

Applications

Present value is not only an important idea for understanding investment, but it has many everyday applications. Let's examine two of them.

Take the Money and Run? The winners of state lotteries are typically paid their winnings in equal installments spread out over 20 years. For instance, suppose that Zoe gets lucky one week and wins a $100 million jackpot. She will not be paid $100 million all at once. Rather, she will receive $5 million per year for 20 years, for a total of $100 million.

Zoe may object to this installment payment system for a variety of reasons. For one thing, she may be very old, so that she is not likely to live long enough to collect all of the payments. Alternatively, she might prefer to receive her winnings immediately so that she could make large immediate donations to her favorite charities or large immediate investments in a business project that she would like to get started. And, of course, she may just be impatient and want to buy a lot of really expensive consumption goods sooner rather than later.

Fortunately for Zoe, if she does have a desire to receive her winnings sooner rather than later, several private financial companies are ready and willing to help her. They do this by arranging swaps. Lottery winners sell the right to receive their installment payments in exchange for a single lump sum that they get immediately. The people who hand over the lump sum receive the right to collect the installment payments.

Present value is crucial to arranging these swaps since it is used to determine the value of the lump sum that lottery winners like Zoe will receive in exchange for giving up their installment payments. The lump sum in any case is simply equal to the sum of the present values of each of the future payments. Assuming an interest rate of 5 percent per year, the sum of the present values of each of Zoe's 20 installment payments of $5 million is $62,311,051.71. So, depending on her preferences, Zoe can either receive that amount immediately or $100 million spread out over 20 years.

Salary Caps and Deferred Compensation Another example of present value comes directly from the sporting news. Many professional sports leagues worry that richer teams, if not held in check, would outbid poorer teams for the best players. The result would be a situation in which only the richer teams have any real chance of doing well and winning championships.

To prevent this from happening, many leagues have instituted salary caps. These are upper limits on the total amount of money that each team can spend on salaries during a given season. For instance, one popular basketball league has a salary cap of about $58 million per season, so that the combined value of the salaries that each team pays its players can be no more than $58 million.

Typically, however, the salary contracts that are negotiated between individual players and their teams are for multiple seasons. This means that during negotiations, players are often asked to help their team stay under the current season's salary cap by agreeing to receive more compensation in later years. For instance, suppose that a team's current payroll is $53 million but that it would like to sign a superstar nicknamed HiTop to a two-year contract. HiTop, however, is used to earning $10 million per year. This is a major problem for the team because the $58 million salary cap means that the most that the team can pay HiTop for the current season is $5 million.

A common solution is for HiTop to agree to receive only $5 million the first season in order to help the team stay under the salary cap. In exchange for this concession, the team agrees to pay HiTop more than the $10 million he would normally demand for the second season. The present value formula is used to figure out how large his second-season salary should be. In particular, the player can use the present value formula to figure out that if the interest rate is 8 percent per year, he should be paid a total of $15,400,000 during his second season, since this amount will equal the $10 million he wants for the second season plus $5.4 million to make up for the $5 million reduction in his salary during the first season. That is, the present value of the $5.4 million that he will receive during the second season precisely equals the $5 million that he agrees to give up during the first season.

Some Popular Investments

LO17.3 Identify and distinguish between the most common financial investments: stocks, bonds, and mutual funds.

The number and types of financial "instruments" in which one can invest are very numerous, amazingly creative, and highly varied. Most are much more complicated than the investments we used to explain compounding and present value. But, fortunately, all investments share three features:

- They require that investors pay some price—determined in the market—to acquire them.
- They give their owners the chance to receive future payments.
- The future payments are typically risky.

These features allow us to treat all assets in a unified way. Three of the more popular investments are stocks, bonds, and mutual funds. In 2010, the median value of stock holdings for U.S. families that held stocks was $17,800; the median value for bonds, $83,800; and the median value for "pooled funds" (mainly mutual funds) was $58,700.[1]

Stocks

Recall that **stocks** are ownership shares in a corporation. If an investor owns 1 percent of a corporation's shares, she gets 1 percent of the votes at the shareholder meetings that select the company's managers and she is also entitled to 1 percent of any future profit distributions. There is no guarantee, however, that a company will be profitable.

Firms often lose money and sometimes even go **bankrupt,** meaning that they are unable to make timely payments on their debts. In the event of a bankruptcy, control of a corporation's assets is given to a bankruptcy judge, whose job is to enforce the legal rights of the people who lent the company money by doing what he can to see that they are repaid. Typically, this involves selling off the corporation's assets (factories, real estate, patents, etc.) to raise the money necessary to pay off the company's debts. The money raised by selling the assets may be greater than or less than what is needed to fully pay off the firm's debts. If it is more than what is necessary, any remaining money is divided equally among shareholders. If it is less than what is necessary, then the lenders do not get repaid in full and have to suffer a loss.

A key point, however, is that the maximum amount of money that shareholders can lose is what they pay for their shares. If the company goes bankrupt owing more than the value of the firm's assets, shareholders do not have to make up the difference. This **limited liability rule** limits the risks involved in investing in corporations and encourages investors to invest in stocks by capping their potential losses at the amount that they paid for their shares.

When firms are profitable, however, investors can look forward to gaining financially in either or both of two possible ways. The first is through **capital gains,** meaning that they sell their shares in the corporation for more money than they paid for them. The second is by receiving **dividends,** which are equal shares of the corporation's profits. As we will soon explain, a corporation's current share price is determined by the size of the capital gains and dividends that investors expect the corporation to generate in the future.

---

[1]Federal Reserve, "Changes in U.S. Family Finances from 2007–2010; Evidence from the Survey of Consumer Finances," p. 26.

Bonds

Bonds are debt contracts that are issued most frequently by governments and corporations. They typically work as follows: An initial investor lends the government or the corporation a certain amount of money, say $1,000, for a certain period of time, say 10 years. In exchange, the government or corporation promises to make a series of semiannual payments in addition to returning the $1,000 at the end of the 10 years. The semiannual payments constitute interest on the loan. For instance, the bond agreement may specify that the borrower will pay $30 every six months. This means that the bond will pay $60 per year in payments, which is equivalent to a 6 percent rate of interest on the initial $1,000 loan.

The initial investor is free, however, to sell the bond at any time to other investors, who then gain the right to receive any of the remaining semiannual payments as well as the final $1,000 payment when the bond expires after 10 years. As we will soon demonstrate, the price at which the bond will sell if it is indeed sold to another investor will depend on the current rates of return available on other investments offering a similar stream of future payments and facing a similar level of risk.

The primary risk a bondholder faces is the possibility that the corporation or government that issues his bond will **default** on, or fail to make, the bond's promised payments. This risk is much greater for corporations, but it also faces local and state governments in situations where they cannot raise enough tax revenue to make their bond payments or where defaulting on bond payments is politically easier than reducing spending on other items in the government's budget to raise the money needed to keep making bond payments. The U.S. federal government, however, has never defaulted on its bond payments and is very unlikely to ever default because it has access to huge amounts of current and potential tax revenue and can sell U.S. securities to the Fed as a way to obtain money.

A key difference between bonds and stocks is that bonds are much more predictable. Unless a bond goes into default, its owner knows both how big its future payments will be and exactly when they will arrive. By contrast, stock prices and dividends are highly volatile because they depend on profits, which vary greatly depending on the overall business cycle and on factors specific to individual firms and industries—things such as changing consumer preferences, variations in the costs of inputs, and changes in the tax code. As we will demonstrate later, the fact that bonds are typically more predictable (and thus less risky) than stocks explains why they generate lower average rates of return than stocks. Indeed, this difference in rates of return has been very large historically. From 1926 to 2012, stocks on average returned about 11 percent per year worldwide, while bonds on average returned only roughly 6 percent per year worldwide.

Mutual Funds

A **mutual fund** is a company that maintains a professionally managed **portfolio,** or collection, of either stocks or bonds. The portfolio is purchased by pooling the money of many investors. Since these investors provide the money to purchase the portfolio, they own it and any gains or losses generated by the portfolio flow directly to them. Table 17.2 lists the 10 largest U.S. mutual funds based on their assets.

Most of the more than 8,000 mutual funds currently operating in the United States choose to maintain portfolios that invest in specific categories of bonds or stocks. For instance, some fill their portfolios exclusively with the stocks of small tech companies, while others buy only bonds issued by certain state or local governments. In addition, there are **index funds,** whose portfolios are selected to exactly match a stock or bond index. Indexes follow the performance of a particular group of stocks or bonds to gauge how well a particular category of investments is doing. For instance, the Standard & Poor's 500 Index contains the 500 largest stocks trading in the United States to capture how the stocks of large corporations vary over time, while the Lehman 10-Year Corporate Bond Index follows a representative collection of 10-year corporate bonds to see how well corporate bonds do over time.

An important distinction must be drawn between actively managed and passively managed mutual funds.

TABLE 17.2 The 10 Largest Mutual Funds, March 2013

Fund Name*	Assets under Management, Billions
PIMCO: Total Return Institutional	$179.9
SPDR S&P 500 ETF	129.8
Vanguard Total Stock Index Investor	90.1
Vanguard Institutional Index	75.2
Vanguard Total Stock Index Admiral Shares	68.0
Vanguard 500 Index Admiral Shares	66.5
Fidelity Contrafund	63.4
SPDR Gold	62.7
American Funds Income A	61.5
American Funds Capital Income Builder A	61.1

*The letter *A* indicates funds that have sales commissions and are generally purchased by individuals through their financial advisors.

Source: Lipper Performance Report, March 31, 2013.

Actively managed funds have portfolio managers who constantly buy and sell assets in an attempt to generate high returns. By contrast, index funds are **passively managed funds** because the assets in their portfolios are chosen to exactly match whatever stocks or bonds are contained in their respective underlying indexes.

Later in the chapter, we will discuss the relative merits of actively managed funds and index funds, but for now we merely point out that both types are very popular and that, overall, U.S. households and nonprofit organizations held $5.3 trillion in mutual funds at the end of 2012. By way of comparison, U.S. GDP in 2012 was $15.7 trillion and the estimated value of all the financial assets held by households and nonprofit organizations in 2012 (including everything from individual stocks and bonds to checking account deposits) was about $54 trillion.

> ### QUICK REVIEW 17.2
>
> - Three popular forms of financial investments are stocks, bonds, and mutual funds.
> - Stocks are ownership shares in corporations and bestow upon their owners a proportional share of any future profit.
> - Bonds are debt contracts that promise to pay a fixed series of payments in the future.
> - Mutual funds are pools of investor money used to buy a portfolio of stocks or bonds.

Calculating Investment Returns

LO17.4 Relate how percentage rates of return provide a common framework for comparing assets and explain why asset prices and rates of return are inversely related.

Investors buy assets to obtain one or more future payments. The simplest case is purchasing an asset for resale. For instance, an investor may buy a house for $300,000 with the hope of selling it for $360,000 in one year. On the other hand, he could also rent out the house for $3,000 per month and thereby receive a stream of future payments. And he, of course, could do a little of both, paying $300,000 for the house now to rent it out for five years and then sell it. In that case, he is expecting a stream of smaller payments followed by a large one.

Percentage Rates of Return

Economists have developed a common framework for evaluating the gains or losses of assets that only make one future payment as well as those that make many future payments.

They state the gain or loss as a **percentage rate of return,** by which they mean the percentage gain or loss (relative to the buying price) over a given period of time, typically a year. For instance, if Noelle buys a rare comic book today for $100 and sells it in 1 year for $125, she is said to make a 25 percent per year rate of return because she would divide the gain of $25 by the purchase price of $100. By contrast, if she were only able to sell it for $92, then she would be said to have made a loss of 8 percent per year since she would divide the $8 loss by the purchase price of $100.

A similar calculation is made for assets that deliver a series of payments. For instance, an investor who buys a house for $300,000 and expects to rent it out for $3,000 per month would be expecting to make a 12 percent per year rate of return because he would divide his $36,000 per year of rent by the $300,000 purchase price of the house.

The Inverse Relationship between Asset Prices and Rates of Return

A fundamental concept in financial economics is that, other things equal, *an investment's rate of return is inversely related to its price.* The higher the price paid for a fixed-return asset, the lower the rate of return on the investment. To see why, consider a bond that pays $24,000 of interest each year. If an investor pays $100,000 for the bond, he will earn a 24 percent per year rate of return because the $24,000 annual interest payment will be divided by the $100,000 purchase price of the bond.

But suppose that the purchase price of the bond rises to $200,000. In that case, the investor would earn only a 12 percent per year rate of return, since the $24,000 annual interest payment would be divided by the much larger purchase price of $200,000. Consequently, as the price of the bond goes up, the rate of return from buying it goes down.

The same relationship holds for other fixed-return investments, such as rental property. The higher the price of the property, given its monthly rent, the lower the rate of return. The underlying cause of this general relationship is the fact that the annual payments are fixed in value so that there is an upper limit to the financial rewards of owning the asset. As a result, the more an investor pays for the asset, the lower the asset's rate of return.

Arbitrage

LO17.5 Define and utilize the concept of arbitrage.

Arbitrage is the name that financial economists give to the buying and selling process that leads profit-seeking investors to equalize the average expected rates of return generated by identical or nearly identical assets. Arbitrage happens when investors try to take advantage and profit from situations where two identical or nearly identical assets have different rates of return. They do so by simultaneously selling the asset with the lower rate of return and buying the asset with the higher rate of return. For instance, consider what would happen in a case where two very similar T-shirt companies start with different rates of return despite the fact that they are equally profitable and have equally good future prospects. To make things concrete, suppose that a company called T4me starts out with a rate of return of 10 percent per year while TSTG (T-Shirts to Go) starts out with a rate of return of 15 percent per year.

Since both companies are basically identical and have equally good prospects, investors in T4me will want to shift over to TSTG, which offers higher rates of return for the same amount of risk. As they begin to shift over, however, the prices of the two companies will change—and with them, the rates of return on the two companies. In particular, since so many investors will be selling the shares of the lower-return company, T4me, the supply of its shares trading on the stock market will rise so that its share price will fall. But since asset prices and rates of return are inversely related, this will cause its rate of return to rise.

At the same time, however, the rate of return on the higher-return company, TSTG, will begin to fall. This has to be the case because, as investors switch from T4me to TSTG, the increased demand for TSTG's shares will drive up their price. And as the price of TSTG goes up, its rate of return must fall.

The interesting thing is that this arbitrage process will continue—with the rate of return on the higher-return company falling and the rate of return on the lower-return company rising—until both companies have the same rate of return. This convergence must happen because as long as the rates of return on the two companies are not identical, there will always be some investors who will want to sell the shares of the lower-return company so they can buy the shares of the higher-return company. As a result, arbitrage will continue until the rates of return are equal.

What is even more impressive, however, is that generally only a very short while is needed for prices to equalize. In fact, for highly traded assets like stocks and bonds, arbitrage will often force the rates of return on identical or nearly identical investments to converge within a matter of minutes or sometimes even within a matter of seconds. This is very helpful to small investors who do not have a large amount of time to study the thousands of potential investment opportunities available in the financial markets.

Thanks to arbitrage, they can invest with the confidence that assets with similar characteristics will have similar rates of return. As we discuss in the next section, this is especially important when it comes to risk—a characteristic that financial economists believe investors care about very deeply.

Risk

LO17.6 Describe how the word *risk* is used in financial economics and explain the difference between diversifiable and nondiversifiable risk.

Investors purchase assets to obtain one or more future payments. As used by financial economists, the word **risk** refers to the fact that investors never know with total certainty what those future payments will turn out to be.

The underlying problem is that the future is uncertain. Many factors affect an investment's future payments, and each of these may turn out better or worse than expected. As a simple example, consider buying a farm. Suppose that in an average year, the farm will generate a profit of $100,000. But if a freak hailstorm damages the crops, the profit will fall to only $60,000. On the other hand, if weather conditions turn out to be perfect, the profit will rise to $120,000. Since there is no way to tell in advance what will happen, investing in the farm is risky.

Also notice that when financial economists use the word *risk*, they do not use it in the casual way that refers only to potentially bad outcomes (as in, "there is a risk that this experimental medicine may kill you"). In financial economics, the word *risk* means only that an outcome—good or bad, major or minor, likely or unlikely—lacks total certainty. Some outcome will occur, but you cannot be sure what it will be. For instance, suppose that you are gifted a raffle ticket that will pay you $10, $100, or $1,000 when a drawing is made in one month. There are no bad outcomes in this particular case, only good ones. But because you do not know with certainty which outcome will occur, the situation is, by definition, risky. On the other

hand, the word *risk* in financial economics certainly does not preclude negative outcomes. If you buy shares of common stock in some company, your stock may go up in value. But the company could also go bankrupt, in which case you would lose your entire investment.

Diversification

Investors have many options regarding their portfolios, or collections of investments. Among other things, they can choose to concentrate their wealth in just one or two investments or spread it out over a large number of investments. **Diversification** is the name given to the strategy of investing in a large number of investments to reduce the overall risk to the entire portfolio.

The underlying reason that diversification generally succeeds in reducing risk is best summarized by the old saying, "Don't put all your eggs in one basket." If an investor's portfolio consists of only one investment, say one stock, then if anything awful happens to that stock, the investor's entire portfolio will suffer greatly. By contrast, if the investor spreads his wealth over many stocks, then a bad outcome for any one particular stock will cause only a small amount of damage to the overall portfolio. In addition, it will typically be the case that if something bad is happening to one part of the portfolio, something good will be happening to another part of the portfolio and the two effects will tend to offset each other. Thus, the risk to the overall portfolio is reduced by diversification.

It must be stressed, however, that while diversification can reduce a portfolio's risks, it cannot eliminate them entirely. The problem is that even if an investor has placed each of his eggs into a different basket, all of the eggs may still end up broken if all of the different baskets somehow happen to get dropped simultaneously. That is, even if an investor has created a well-diversified portfolio, all of the investments still have a chance to do badly simultaneously. As an example, consider the early portion of the severe recession of 2007–2009: With economic activity declining and consumer spending falling, nearly all companies faced reduced sales and lowered profits, a fact that caused their stock prices to decline simultaneously. Consequently, even if investors had diversified their portfolios across numerous stocks, their overall wealth portfolios would have still declined because nearly all of their many investments simultaneously performed poorly.

ORIGIN OF THE IDEA

O17.1

Portfolio diversification

Financial economists build on the intuition behind the benefits and limits to diversification to divide an individual investment's overall risk into two components, diversifiable risk and nondiversifiable risk. **Diversifiable risk** (or "idiosyncratic risk") is the risk that is specific to a given investment and that can be eliminated by diversification. For instance, a soda pop maker faces the risk that the demand for its product may suddenly decline because people will want to drink mineral water instead of soda pop. But this risk does not matter if an investor has a diversified portfolio that contains stock in the soda pop maker as well as stock in a mineral water maker. This is true because when the stock price of the soda pop maker falls due to the change in consumer preferences, the stock price of the mineral water maker will go up—so that, as far as the overall portfolio is concerned, the two effects will offset each other.

By contrast, **nondiversifiable risk** (or "systemic risk") pushes all investments in the same direction at the same time so that there is no possibility of using good effects to offset bad effects. The best example of a nondiversifiable risk is the business cycle. If the economy does well, then corporate profits rise and nearly every stock does well. But if the economy does badly, then corporate profits fall and nearly every stock does badly. As a result, even if one were to build a well-diversified portfolio, it would still be affected by the business cycle because nearly every asset contained in the portfolio would move in the same direction at the same time whenever the economy improved or worsened.

That being said, creating a diversified portfolio is still an investor's best strategy because doing so at least eliminates diversifiable risk. Indeed, it should be emphasized that for investors who have created diversified portfolios, all diversifiable risks will be eliminated, so that the only remaining source of risk will be nondiversifiable risk.

A significant implication of this fact is that when investors consider whether to add any particular investment to a portfolio that is already diversified, they can ignore the investment's diversifiable risk. They can ignore it because, as part of a diversified portfolio, the investment's diversifiable risk will be "diversified away." Indeed, the only risk left will be the amount of nondiversifiable risk that the investment carries with it. This is crucial because it means that investors can base their decisions about whether to add a potential new investment to their portfolios on a comparison between the potential investment's level of nondiversifiable risk and its potential returns. If they find this trade-off attractive, they will add the investment, whereas if it seems unattractive, they will not.

The next section shows how investors can measure each asset's level of nondiversifiable risk as well as its potential returns to facilitate such comparisons. Global

GLOBAL PERSPECTIVE 17.1

Investment Risks Vary across Different Countries

The International Country Risk Guide is a monthly publication that attempts to distill the political, economic, and financial risks facing 140 countries into a single "composite risk rating" number for each country, with higher numbers indicating less risk and more safety. The table below presents the July 2012 ranks and rating numbers for 15 countries including the three least risky (ranked 1 through 3) and the three most risky (ranked 138 through 140.) Risk ratings numbers above 80 are considered *very low risk;* 70–80 are considered *low risk;* 60–70 *moderate risk;* 50–60 *high risk;* and below 50 *very high risk.*

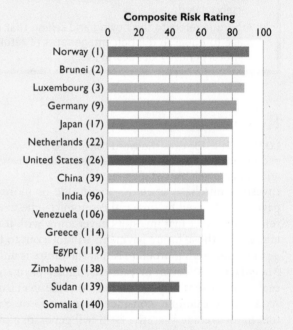

Source: International Country Risk Guide, a publication of The PRS Group, Inc., **www.prsgroup.com**, 2012. Used with permission.

Perspective 17.1 shows how investment risk varies significantly across countries due to underlying differences in political, economic, and financial risks.

QUICK REVIEW 17.4

- An asset is risky if its future payments are uncertain.
- Diversification is an investment strategy in which an investor invests in a large number of different investments in order to reduce the overall risk to his or her entire portfolio.
- Risks that can be canceled out by diversification are called diversifiable risks; risks that cannot be canceled out by diversification are called nondiversifiable risks.

Comparing Risky Investments

LO17.7 Convey why investment decisions are determined primarily by investment returns and nondiversifiable risk and how investment returns compensate for being patient and for bearing nondiversifiable risk.

Economists believe that the two most important factors affecting investment decisions are returns and risk—specifically nondiversifiable risk. But for investors to properly compare different investments on the basis of returns and risk, they need ways to measure returns and risk. The two standard measures are, respectively, the average expected rate of return and the beta statistic.

Average Expected Rate of Return

Each investment's **average expected rate of return** is the probability-weighted average of the investment's possible future rates of return. The term **probability-weighted average** simply means that each of the possible future rates of return is multiplied by its probability expressed as a decimal (so that a 50 percent probability is 0.5 and a 23 percent probability is 0.23) before being added together to obtain the average. For instance, if an investment has a 75 percent probability of generating 11 percent per year and a 25 percent probability of generating 15 percent per year, then its average expected rate of return will be 12 percent = (0.75 × 11 percent) + (0.25 × 15 percent). By weighting each possible outcome by its probability, this process ensures that the resulting average gives more weight to those outcomes that are more likely to happen (unlike the normal averaging process that would treat every outcome the same).

Once investors have calculated the average expected rates of return for all the assets they are interested in, there will naturally be some impulse to simply invest in those assets having the highest average expected rates of return. But while this might satisfy investor cravings for higher rates of return, it would not take proper account of the fact that investors dislike risk and uncertainty. To quantify their dislike, investors require a statistic that can measure each investment's risk level.

Beta

One popular statistic that measures risk is called beta. **Beta** is a *relative* measure of nondiversifiable risk. It measures how the nondiversifiable risk of a given asset or portfolio of assets compares with that of the **market portfolio,** which is the name given to a portfolio that contains every asset available in the financial markets. The market portfolio is a useful standard of comparison because it is as

diversified as possible. In fact, since it contains every possible asset, every possible diversifiable risk will be diversified away—meaning that it will be exposed *only* to nondiversifiable risk. Consequently, it can serve as a useful benchmark against which to measure the levels of nondiversifiable risk to which individual assets are exposed.

Such comparisons are very simple because the beta statistic is standardized such that the market portfolio's level of nondiversifiable risk is set equal to 1.0. Consequently, an asset with beta = 0.5 has a level of nondiversifiable risk that is one-half of that possessed by the market portfolio, while an asset with beta = 2.0 has twice as much nondiversifiable risk as the market portfolio. In addition, the beta numbers of various assets also can be used to compare them with each other. For instance, an asset with beta = 2.0 has four times as much exposure to nondiversifiable risk as does an asset with beta = 0.5.

Another useful feature of beta is that it can be calculated not only for individual assets but also for portfolios. Indeed, it can be calculated for portfolios no matter how many or how few assets they contain and no matter what those assets happen to be. This fact is very convenient for mutual fund investors because it means that they can use beta to quickly see how the nondiversifiable risk of any given fund's portfolio compares with that of other potential investments that they may be considering.

The beta statistic is used along with average expected rates of return to give investors standard measures of risk and return that can be used to sensibly compare different investment opportunities. As we will discuss in the next section, this leads to one of the most fundamental relationships in financial economics: riskier assets have higher rates of return.

Relationship of Risk and Average Expected Rates of Return

The fact that investors dislike risk has a profound effect on asset prices and average expected rates of return. In particular, their dislike of risk and uncertainty causes investors to pay higher prices for less-risky assets and lower prices for more-risky assets. But since asset prices and average expected rates of return are inversely related, this implies that less risky assets will have lower average expected rates of return than more risky assets.

Stated a bit more clearly: *Risk levels and average expected rates of return are positively related.* The more risky an investment is, the higher its average expected rate of return will be. A great way to understand this relationship is to think of higher average expected rates of return as being a form of compensation. Since investors dislike risk, they demand higher levels of compensation the more risky an asset is. The higher levels of compensation come in the form of higher average expected rates of return.

Be sure to note that this phenomenon affects all assets. Regardless of whether the assets are stocks or bonds or real estate or anything else, assets with higher levels of risk always end up with higher average expected rates of return to compensate investors for the higher levels of risk involved. No matter what the investment opportunity is, investors examine its possible future payments, determine how risky they are, and then select a price that reflects those risks. Since less-risky investments get higher prices, they end up with lower rates of return, whereas more-risky investments end up with lower prices and, consequently, higher rates of return.

The Risk-Free Rate of Return

We have just shown that there is a positive relationship between risk and returns, with higher returns serving to compensate investors for higher levels of risk. One investment, however, is considered to be risk-free for all intents and purposes. That investment is short-term U.S. government bonds.

These bonds are short-term loans to the U.S. government, with the duration of the loans ranging from 4 weeks to 26 weeks. They are considered to be essentially risk-free because there is almost no chance that the U.S. government will not be able to repay these loans on time and in full. To pay its debt, it can shift funds within its enormous budget, raise taxes, or borrow newly created money from the Fed. Although it is true that the U.S. government may eventually be destroyed or disabled to such an extent that it will not be able to repay some of its loans, the chances of such a calamity happening within 4 or even 26 weeks are essentially zero. Consequently, because it is a near certainty that the bonds will be repaid in full and on time, they are considered by investors to be risk-free.

Since higher levels of risk lead to higher rates of return, a person might be tempted to assume—incorrectly—that since government bonds are risk-free, they should earn a zero percent rate of return. The problem with this line of thinking is that it mistakenly assumes that risk is the *only* thing that rates of return compensate for. The truth is that rates of return compensate not only for risk but also for something that economists call time preference.

Time preference refers to the fact that because people tend to be impatient, they typically prefer to consume things in the present rather than in the future. Stated more concretely, most people, if given the choice between a serving of their favorite dessert immediately or a serving of their favorite dessert in five years, will choose to consume their favorite dessert immediately.

This time preference for consuming sooner rather than later affects the financial markets because people want to be compensated for delayed consumption. In particular, if Dave asks Oprah to lend him $1 million for one year, he is implicitly asking Oprah to delay consumption for a year because if she lends Dave the $1 million, she will not be able to spend that money herself for at least a year. If Oprah is like most people and has a preference for spending her $1 million sooner rather than later, the only way Dave will be able to convince Oprah to let him borrow $1 million is to offer her some form of compensation. The compensation comes in the form of an interest payment that will allow Oprah to consume more in the future than she can now. For instance, Dave can offer to pay Oprah $1.1 million in one year in exchange for $1 million today. That is, Oprah will get back the $1 million she lends to Dave today as well as an extra $100,000 to compensate her for being patient.

Notice the very important fact that this type of interest payment has nothing to do with risk. It is purely compensation for being patient and must be paid even if there is no risk involved and 100 percent certainty that Dave will fulfill his promise to repay.

Since short-term U.S. government bonds are for all intents and purposes completely risk-free and 100 percent likely to repay as promised, their rates of return are *purely* compensation for time preference and the fact that people must be compensated for delaying their own consumption opportunities when they lend money to the government. One consequence of this fact is that the rate of return earned by short-term U.S. government bonds is often referred to as the **risk-free interest rate**, or i^f, to clearly indicate that the rate of return that they generate is not in any way a compensation for risk.

It should be kept in mind, however, that the Federal Reserve has the power to change the risk-free interest rate generated by short-term U.S. government bonds. As discussed in Chapter 16, the Federal Reserve can use open-market operations to lower or raise the federal funds interest rate by making large purchases or sales of U.S. securities in the bond market. These open-market operations affect the money supply, which affects all interest rates, including the rates on short-term U.S. government bonds. This means that the Federal Reserve indirectly determines the risk-free interest rate and, consequently, the compensation that investors receive for being patient. As we will soon demonstrate, this fact is very important because by manipulating the reward for being patient, the Federal Reserve can affect the rate of return and prices of not only government bonds but all assets.

- The average expected rate of return is the probability-weighted average of an investment's possible future returns.
- Beta measures the nondiversifiable risk of an investment relative to the amount of nondiversifiable risk facing the market portfolio, which is the portfolio containing every asset available in the financial markets.
- Because investors dislike risk, riskier investments must offer higher rates of return to compensate investors for bearing more risk.
- Average expected rates of return compensate investors for both risk and time preference, which is the preference most people have to consume sooner rather than later.

The Security Market Line

LO17.8 Explain how the Security Market Line illustrates the compensation that investors receive for time preference and nondiversifiable risk and why arbitrage will tend to move all assets onto the Security Market Line.

Investors must be compensated for time preference as well as for the amount of nondiversifiable risk that an investment carries with it. This section introduces a simple model called the **Security Market Line**, which indicates how this compensation is determined for all assets no matter what their respective risk levels happen to be.

The underlying logic of the model is this: Any investment's average expected rate of return has to be the sum of two parts—one that compensates for time preference and another that compensates for risk. That is,

$$\text{Average expected} \atop \text{rate of return} = \text{rate that compensates for} \atop \text{time preference}$$
$$+ \text{ rate that compensates for risk}$$

As we explained, the compensation for time preference is equal to the risk-free interest rate, i^f, that is paid on short-term government bonds. As a result, this equation can be simplified to

$$\text{Average expected} \atop \text{rate of return} = i^f + \text{rate that compensates} \atop \text{for risk}$$

Finally, because economists typically refer to the rate that compensates for risk as the **risk premium**, this equation can be simplified even further to

$$\text{Average expected rate of return} = i^f + \text{risk premium}$$

Naturally, the size of the risk premium that compensates for risk will vary depending on how risky an investment happens to be. In particular, it will depend on how big or small the investment's beta is. Investments with large betas

FIGURE 17.1 The Security Market Line. The Security Market Line shows the relationship between average expected rates of return and risk levels that must hold for every asset or portfolio trading in the financial markets. Each investment's average expected rate of return is the sum of the risk-free interest rate that compensates for time preference as well as a risk premium that compensates for the investment's level of risk. The Security Market Line's upward slope reflects the fact that investors must be compensated for higher levels of risk with higher average expected rates of return.

and lots of nondiversifiable risk will require larger risk premiums than investments that have small betas and low levels of nondiversifiable risk. And, in the most extreme case, risk-free assets that have betas equal to zero will require no compensation for risk at all since they have no risk to compensate for.

This logic is translated into the graph presented in Figure 17.1. The horizontal axis of Figure 17.1 measures risk levels using beta; the vertical axis measures average expected rates of return. As a result, any investment can be plotted on Figure 17.1 just as long as we know its beta and its average expected rate of return. We have plotted two investments in Figure 17.1. The first is a risk-free short-term U.S. government bond, which is indicated by the lower-left dot in the figure. The second is the market portfolio, which is indicated by the upper-right dot in the figure.

The lower dot marking the position of the risk-free bond is located where it is because it is a risk-free asset having a beta = 0 and because its average expected rate of return is given by i^f. These values place the lower dot i^f percentage points up the vertical axis, as shown in Figure 17.1. Note that this location conveys the logic that because this asset has no risk, its average expected rate of return only has to compensate investors for time preference—which is why its average expected rate of return is equal to precisely i^f and no more.

The market portfolio, by contrast, is risky so that its average expected rate of return must compensate investors not only for time preference but also for the level of risk to which the market portfolio is exposed, which by definition is beta = 1.0. This implies that the vertical distance from the horizontal axis to the upper dot is equal to the sum of i^f and the market portfolio's risk premium.

The straight line connecting the risk-free asset's lower dot and the market portfolio's upper dot is called the Security Market Line, or SML. The SML is extremely important because it defines the relationship between average expected rates of return and risk levels that must hold for all assets and all portfolios trading in the financial markets. The SML illustrates the idea that every asset's average expected rate of return is the sum of a rate of return that compensates for time preference and a rate of return that compensates for risk. More specifically, the SML has a vertical intercept equal to the rate of interest earned by short-term U.S. government bonds and a positive slope that compensates investors for risk.

As we explained earlier, the precise location of the intercept at any given time is determined by the Federal Reserve's monetary policy and how it affects the rate of return on short-term U.S. government bonds. The slope of the SML, however, is determined by investors' feelings about risk and how much compensation they require for dealing with it. If investors greatly dislike risk, then the SML will have to be very steep, so that any given increase in risk on the horizontal axis will result in a very large increase in compensation as measured by average expected rates of return on the vertical

axis. On the other hand, if investors dislike risk only moderately, then the SML will be relatively flat since any given increase in risk on the horizontal axis would require only a moderate increase in compensation as measured by average expected rates of return on the vertical axis.

It is important to realize that once investor preferences about risk have determined the slope of the SML and monetary policy has determined its vertical intercept, the SML plots out the precise relationship between risk levels and average expected rates of return *that should hold for every asset.* For instance, consider Figure 17.2, where there is an asset whose risk level on the horizontal axis is beta = X. The SML tells us that every asset with that risk level should have an average expected rate of return equal to Y on the vertical axis. This average expected rate of return exactly compensates for both time preference and the fact that the asset in question is exposed to a risk level of beta = X.

Finally, it should be pointed out that arbitrage will ensure that all investments having an identical level of risk also will have an identical rate of return—the return given by the SML. This is illustrated in Figure 17.3, where the three assets A, B, and C all share the same risk level of beta = X but initially have three different average expected rates of return. Since asset B lies on the SML, it has the average expected rate of return Y that precisely compensates investors for time preference and risk level X. Asset A, however, has a higher average expected rate of return that overcompensates investors while asset C has a lower average expected rate of return that undercompensates investors.

FIGURE 17.2   Risk levels determine average expected rates of return. The Security Market Line can be used to determine an investment's average expected rate of return based on its risk level. In this figure, investments having a risk level of beta = X will have an average expected rate of return of Y percent per year. This average expected rate of return will compensate investors for time preference in addition to providing them exactly the right sized risk premium to compensate them for dealing with a risk level of beta = X.

FIGURE 17.3   Arbitrage and the Security Market Line. Arbitrage pressures will tend to move any asset or portfolio that lies off the Security Market Line back onto the line. Investors will increase their purchases of asset A, driving up its price and decreasing its average expected rate of return. They will decrease their purchases of asset C, reducing its price and raising its return. Therefore, assets A, B, and C will all end up on the Security Market Line with each having the same average expected rate of return, Y, at risk level (beta) X. This average expected rate of return will fully compensate the investors for time preference plus nondiversifiable risk as measured by beta.

CONSIDER THIS...

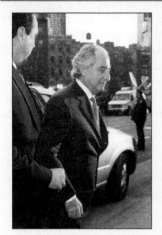

Ponzi Schemes

Ponzi schemes—named after 1920s fraudster Charles Ponzi—are investments in which investors are unknowingly paid returns directly from the investments made by new investors. A successful Ponzi scheme attracts increasing amounts of money, much of which is siphoned off by the promoter. Common to all such schemes is the promise of high investment returns relative to investment risk. In Figure 17.1, the implied risk-return point lies someplace well above the SML.

Sophisticated investors know that arbitrage reduces returns, and even novice investors intuitively understand that good investment opportunities cannot continue unless they are exclusive. So promoters of Ponzi schemes concoct various reasons why such arbitrage does not occur. They claim there is a secret investment strategy or an exotic investment opportunity known only to the promoter.

Trust plays an important role in many Ponzi schemes. The promoter often attracts initial investors from affinity groups, targeting fellow church members or people who belong to the same country club. Current investors then become unwitting promoters of the Ponzi scheme because they recommend the attractive investment to family and friends.

The largest ever Ponzi scheme—run by Bernie Madoff—lasted for decades until it was exposed in 2008. On paper, investments with Madoff offered steady, solid returns year after year. Better still, those returns continued to accrue even during periods of financial crisis and recession. Madoff seemingly had found a strategy to eliminate nondiversifiable risk! But the true risk of investing with Madoff became distressingly apparent when the scheme collapsed. Madoff investors lost $13 billion of invested money and $65 billion of money they thought they had in their investment portfolios. Sadly, some individuals lost their entire life savings.

Arbitrage pressures will quickly eliminate these over- and undercompensations. For instance, consider what will happen to asset A. Investors will be hugely attracted to its overly high rate of return and will rush to buy it. That will drive up its price. But because average expected rates of return and prices are inversely related, the increase in price will cause its average expected rate of return to fall. Graphically, this means that asset A will move vertically downward as illustrated in Figure 17.3. And it will continue to move vertically downward until it reaches the SML since only then will it have the average expected rate of return Y that properly compensates investors for time preference and risk level X.

A similar process also will move asset C back to the SML. Investors will dislike the fact that its average expected rate of return is so low. This will cause them to sell it, driving down its price. Since average expected rates of return and prices are inversely related, this will cause its average expected rate of return to rise, thereby causing C to rise vertically as illustrated in Figure 17.3. And as with point A, point C will continue to rise until it reaches the SML, since only then will it have the average expected rate of return Y that properly compensates investors for time preference and risk level X.

Security Market Line: Applications

The SML analysis is highly useful in clarifying why investors scrutinize the intentions and actions of the Federal Reserve and change their behaviors during financial crises.

An Increase in the Risk-Free Rate by the Fed We have just explained how the position of the Security Market Line is fixed by two factors. The vertical intercept is set by the risk-free interest rate while the slope is determined by the amount of compensation investors demand for bearing nondiversifiable risk. As a result, changes in either one of these factors can shift the SML and thereby cause large changes in both average expected rates of return and asset prices.

As an example, consider what happens to the SML if the Federal Reserve changes policy and uses open-market operations (described in Chapter 16) to reduce the money supply, raise the federal funds rate, and increase other interest rates such as those on short-term U.S. government bonds. Since the risk-free interest rate earned by these bonds is also the SML's vertical intercept, an increase in their interest rate will move the SML's vertical intercept upward, as illustrated in Figure 17.4. The result is a parallel upward shift of the SML from SML_1 to SML_2. (The shift is parallel because nothing has happened that would affect the SML's slope, which is determined by the amount of compensation that investors demand for bearing risk.)

Notice what this upward shift implies. Not only does the rate of return on short-term U.S. government bonds increase when the Federal Reserve changes policy, but the rate of return on risky assets increases as well. For instance, consider asset A, which originally has rate of return Y_1. After the SML shifts upward, asset A ends up with the higher rate of return Y_2. There is a simple intuition behind this increase. Risky assets must compete with risk-free assets for investor money. When the Federal Reserve increases the rate of return on risk-free short-term U.S. government bonds, they become more attractive to investors. But to get the money to buy more risk-free bonds, investors have to sell risky assets. This drives down their

FIGURE 17.4 An increase in risk-free interest rates causes the SML to shift up vertically.   The risk-free interest rate set by the Federal Reserve is the Security Market Line's vertical intercept. Consequently, if the Federal Reserve increases the risk-free interest rate, the Security Market Line's vertical intercept will move up. This rise in the risk-free interest rate will result in a decline in all asset prices and thus an increase in the average expected rate of return on all assets. So the Security Market Line will shift up parallel from SML$_1$ to SML$_2$. Here, asset A with risk level beta = X sees its average expected rate of return rise from Y_1 to Y_2.

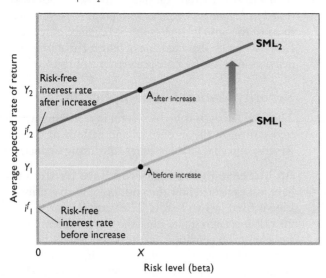

prices and—because prices and average expected rates of return are inversely related—causes their average expected rates of return to increase. The result is that asset A moves up vertically in Figure 17.4, its average expected rate of return increasing from Y_1 to Y_2 as investors reallocate their wealth from risky assets like asset A to risk-free bonds.

This process explains why investors are so watchful of the Federal Reserve and keenly interested in its policies. Any increase in the risk-free interest rate leads to a decrease in asset prices that directly reduces investors' wealth.

The Fed's power to change asset prices through monetary policy stems entirely from the fact that changes in the risk-free rate shift the SML and thus totally redefine the investment opportunities available in the economy. As the set of options changes, investors modify their portfolios to obtain the best possible combination of risk and returns from the new set of investment options. In doing so, they engage in massive amounts of buying and selling to get rid of assets they no longer want and acquire assets that they now desire. These massive changes in supply and demand for financial assets are what cause their prices to change so drastically when the Federal Reserve alters the risk-free interest rate.

The Security Market Line during the Great Recession The special circumstances of the financial markets during the recession of 2007–2009 provide an

excellent illustration of both the impact of Federal Reserve actions and the idea of *time-varying risk premium*. The latter is the reality that the premium demanded by investors to take on risk may vary from one period (and one set of economic circumstances) to another period (and a different set of economic circumstances).

The Federal Reserve used expansionary monetary policy during this period to lower interest rates, including the interest rates of short-term U.S. government bonds. Because the risk-free interest rate earned by these securities locates the vertical intercept of the Securities Market Line, the actual SML for the economy shifted downward from that shown in Figure 17.1. This decline would be portrayed as the opposite of the upward shift that we illustrate in Figure 17.4.

But wouldn't we expect stock market prices to rise when the risk-free rate of return falls? That certainly did *not* happen in 2007 and 2008. Yes, normally, stock market prices rise when the risk-free interest rate falls. But during this unusual period, investors became very fearful about losses from investments in general and began to look for any place of financial safety. As their appetite for risk decreased, they demanded a much higher rate of compensation for taking on any particular level of risk. In terms of Figure 17.4, the slope of the SML greatly increased. Thus, between the Fed's deliberate reduction of the risk-free rate and investors' diminished appetite for risk, two things happened at once to the SML: (1) its intercept (the risk-free rate) dramatically fell and (2) the SML became much steeper. In Figure 17.1, these two effects would be shown by a much steeper SML emanating from a much lower point on the vertical axis.

The increase in the slope of the SML overwhelmed the decline in the intercept. Investors sold off stocks, which greatly reduced stock prices, even though the risk-free interest rate fell.

QUICK REVIEW 17.6

- The Security Market Line (SML) is a straight, upsloping line showing how the average expected rates of return on investments vary with their respective levels of nondiversifiable risk as measured by beta.
- Arbitrage ensures that every asset in the economy should plot onto the SML.
- The positive slope of the SML reflects the fact that investors dislike nondiversifiable risk; the steeper the slope, the greater the dislike.
- The Fed can shift the entire SML upward or downward by using monetary policy to change the risk-free interest rate on short-term U.S. bonds.

Index Funds versus Actively Managed Funds

Do Actively Managed Funds Outperform Passively Managed Index Funds That Have the Same Risk?

Mutual fund investors have a choice between putting their money into actively managed mutual funds or into passively managed index funds. Actively managed funds constantly buy and sell assets in an attempt to build portfolios that will generate average expected rates of return that are higher than those of other portfolios possessing a similar level of risk. In terms of Figure 17.3, they try to construct portfolios similar to point A, which has the same level of risk as portfolio B but a much higher average expected rate of return. By contrast, the portfolios of index funds simply mimic the assets that are included in their underlying indexes and make no attempt whatsoever to generate higher returns than other portfolios having similar levels of risk.

As a result, expecting actively managed funds to generate higher rates of return than index funds would seem only natural. Surprisingly, however, the exact opposite actually holds true. Once costs are taken into account, the average returns generated by index funds trounce those generated by actively managed funds by well over 1 percent per year. Now, 1 percent per year may not sound like a lot, but the compound interest formula of equation 1 shows that $10,000 growing for 30 years at 10 percent per year becomes $170,449.40, whereas that same amount of money growing at 11 percent for 30 years becomes $220,892.30. For anyone saving for retirement, an extra 1 percent per year is a very big deal.

Why do actively managed funds do so much worse than index funds? The answer is twofold. First, arbitrage makes it virtually impossible for actively managed funds to select portfolios that will do any better than index funds that have similar levels of risk. As a result, *before taking costs into account*, actively managed funds and index funds produce very similar returns. Second, actively managed funds charge their investors much higher fees than do passively managed funds, so that, *after taking costs into account*, actively managed funds do worse by about 1 percent per year.

Let us discuss each of these factors in more detail. The reason that actively managed funds cannot do better than index funds before taking costs into account has to do with the power of arbitrage to ensure that investments having equal levels of risk also have equal average expected rates of return. As we explained above with respect to Figure 17.3, assets and portfolios that deviate from the Security Market Line (SML) are very quickly forced back onto the SML by arbitrage, so that assets and portfolios with equal levels of risk have equal average expected rates of

return. This implies that index funds and actively managed funds with equal levels of risk will end up with identical average expected rates of return despite the best efforts of actively managed funds to produce superior returns.

The reason actively managed funds charge much higher fees than index funds is because they run up much higher costs while trying to produce superior returns. Not only do they have to pay large salaries to professional fund managers, but they also have to pay for the massive amounts of trading that those managers engage in as they buy and sell assets in their quest to produce superior returns. The costs of running an index fund are, by contrast, very small since changes are made to an index fund's portfolio only on the rare occasions when the fund's underlying index changes. As a result, trading costs are low and there is no need to pay for a professional manager. The overall result is that while the largest and most popular index fund currently charges its investors only 0.18 percent per year for its services, the typical actively managed fund charges more than 1.5 percent per year.

So why are actively managed funds still in business? The answer may well be that index funds are boring. Because they are set up to mimic indexes that are in turn designed to show what average performance levels are, index funds are by definition stuck with average rates of return and absolutely no chance to exceed average rates of return. For investors who want to try to beat the average, actively managed funds are the only way to go.

SUMMARY

LO17.1 Define *financial economics* and distinguish between economic investment and financial investment.

Financial investment focuses its attention on investor preferences and how they affect the trading and pricing of the wide variety of financial assets available in the modern economy, including stocks, bonds, and real estate. Remember to distinguish between economic investment (paying for additions to the capital stock) and financial investment (buying an existing asset or building a new asset in the expectation of financial gain).

LO17.2 Explain the time value of money and how compound interest can be used to calculate the present value of any future amount of money.

The compound interest formula states that if X_0 dollars is invested today at interest rate i and allowed to grow for t years, it will become $(1 + i)^t X_0$ dollars in t years. The present value formula rearranges the compound interest formula. It tells investors the current number of dollars that they would have to invest today to receive X_t dollars in t years.

All financial assets available to investors have a common characteristic: In exchange for a certain price today, they all promise to make one or more payments in the future. A risk-free investment's proper current price is simply equal to the sum of the present values of each of the investment's expected future payments.

LO17.3 Identify and distinguish between the most common financial investments: stocks, bonds, and mutual funds.

Stocks give shareholders the right to share in any future profits that corporations may generate. The main risk of stock investing is that future profits are unpredictable and that companies may go bankrupt. Bonds provide bondholders the right to receive a fixed stream of future payments that serve to repay the loan. Bonds are risky because of the possibility that the corporations or government bodies that issued the bonds may default on them, or make less than the promised payments. Mutual funds own and manage portfolios of bonds and stocks; fund investors get the returns generated by those portfolios. The risks of mutual funds to investors reflect the risks of the stocks and bonds that are in their respective portfolios.

LO17.4 Relate how percentage rates of return provide a common framework for comparing assets and explain why asset prices and rates of return are inversely related.

Investors evaluate the possible future returns to risky investments using average expected rates of return, which give higher weight to outcomes that are more likely to happen. Average expected rates of return are inversely related to an asset's current price.

LO17.5 Define and utilize the concept of arbitrage.

Arbitrage is the process whereby investors equalize the average expected rates of return generated by identical or nearly identical assets. If two identical assets have different rates of return, investors will sell the asset with the lower rate of return and buy the asset with the higher rate of return. As investors buy the asset with the higher rate of return, its price will rise, reducing its average expected rate of return. At the same time, as investors sell the asset with the lower rate of return, its price will fall, raising its average expected rate of return. The process will continue until the average expected rates of return are equal on the two investments.

LO17.6 Describe how the word *risk* is used in financial economics and explain the difference between diversifiable and nondiversifiable risk.

In finance, an asset is risky if its future payments are uncertain. What matters is not whether the payments are big or small, positive or negative, or good or bad—only that they are not guaranteed ahead of time. Risks that can be canceled out by diversification are called diversifiable risks. Risks that cannot be canceled out by diversification are called nondiversifiable risks.

LO17.7 Convey why investment decisions are determined primarily by investment returns and nondiversifiable risk and how investment returns compensate for being patient and for bearing nondiversifiable risk.

Beta is a statistic that measures the nondiversifiable risk of an asset or portfolio relative to the amount of nondiversifiable risk facing the market portfolio. Because the market portfolio contains every asset trading in the financial markets, it is completely diversified and therefore exposed to only nondiversifiable risk. By tradition, its beta is set at 1.0. Thus, an investment that has a beta of 0.5 is exposed to half as much nondiversifiable risk as the market portfolio.

Investors dislike risk and therefore demand compensation for being exposed to it. This compensation takes the form of higher average expected rates of return. The riskier the asset, the greater is the average expected rate of return. Because a well-diversified portfolio has no diversifiable risk, investors will need to be compensated only for the asset's level of nondiversifiable risk as measured by beta.

Average expected rates of return also must compensate for time preference and the fact that, other things equal, people prefer to consume sooner rather than later. Consequently, an asset's average expected rate of return will be the sum of the rate of return that compensates for time preference plus the rate of return that compensates for the asset's level of nondiversifiable risk as measured by beta.

LO17.8 Explain how the Security Market Line illustrates the compensation that investors receive for time preference and nondiversifiable risk and why arbitrage will tend to move all assets onto the Security Market Line.

The rate of return that compensates for time preference is assumed to be equal to the rate of interest generated by short-term U.S. government bonds. These bonds are considered to be risk-free, meaning that their rate of return must purely be compensation for time preference and not nondiversifiable risk.

The Security Market Line (SML) is a straight upsloping line showing how the average expected rates of return on assets and portfolios in the economy vary with their respective levels of nondiversifiable risk as measured by beta. Arbitrage ensures that every asset in the economy should plot onto the SML. The slope of the SML reflects the investors' dislike for nondiversifiable risk, with steeper slopes reflecting greater dislike for that risk.

The Fed can shift the entire SML upward or downward by using monetary policy to change the risk-free interest rate on short-term U.S. bonds. When the SML shifts, the average expected rate of return on all assets changes. Because average expected rates of return are inversely related to asset prices, the shift in the SML also will change asset prices. Therefore, the Federal Reserve's ability to change short-run interest rates also enables it to change asset prices throughout the economy.

TERMS AND CONCEPTS

economic investment	default	diversifiable risk
financial investment	mutual funds	nondiversifiable risk
present value	portfolios	average expected rate of return
compound interest	index funds	probability-weighted average
stocks	actively managed funds	beta
bankrupt	passively managed funds	market portfolio
limited liability rule	percentage rate of return	time preference
capital gains	arbitrage	risk-free interest rate
dividends	risk	Security Market Line
bonds	diversification	risk premium

The following and additional problems can be found in **connect**
ECONOMICS

DISCUSSION QUESTIONS

1. Suppose that the city of New York issues bonds to raise money to pay for a new tunnel linking New Jersey and Manhattan. An investor named Susan buys one of the bonds on the same day that the city of New York pays a contractor for completing the first stage of construction. Is Susan making an economic or a financial investment? What about the city of New York? **LO17.1**

2. What is compound interest? How does it relate to the formula $X_t = (1 + i)^t X_0$? What is present value? How does it relate to the formula $X_t/(1 + i)^t = X_0$? **LO17.2**

3. How do stocks and bonds differ in terms of the future payments that they are expected to make? Which type of investment (stocks or bonds) is considered to be more risky? Given what you know, which investment (stocks or bonds) do you think commonly goes by the nickname "fixed income"? **LO17.3**

4. What are mutual funds? What different types of mutual funds are there? And why do you think they are so popular with investors? **LO17.3**

5. Corporations often distribute profits to their shareholders in the form of dividends, which are simply checks mailed out to shareholders. Suppose that you have the chance to buy a share in a fashion company called Rogue Designs for $35 and that the company will pay dividends of $2 per year on that share every year. What is the annual percentage rate of return? Next, suppose that you and other investors could get a 12 percent per year rate of return by owning the stocks of other very similar fashion companies. If investors care only about rates of return, what should happen to the share price of Rogue Designs? (Hint: This is an arbitrage situation.) **LO17.5**

6. Why is it reasonable to ignore diversifiable risk and care only about nondiversifiable risk? What about investors who put all their money into only a single risky stock? Can they properly ignore diversifiable risk? **LO17.6**

7. If we compare the betas of various investment opportunities, why do the assets that have higher betas also have higher average expected rates of return? **LO17.7**

8. In this chapter we discussed short-term U.S. government bonds. But the U.S. government also issues longer-term bonds with horizons of up to 30 years. Why do 20-year bonds issued by the U.S. government have lower rates of return than 20-year bonds issued by corporations? And which would you consider more likely, that longer-term U.S. government

bonds have a higher interest rate than short-term U.S. government bonds, or vice versa? Explain. LO17.7

9. What determines the vertical intercept of the Security Market Line (SML)? What determines its slope? And what will happen to an asset's price if it initially plots onto a point above the SML? LO17.8

10. Suppose that the Federal Reserve thinks that a stock market bubble is occurring and wants to reduce stock prices. What should it do to interest rates? LO17.8

11. Consider another situation involving the SML. Suppose that the risk-free interest rate stays the same, but that investors' dislike of risk grows more intense. Given this change, will average expected rates of return rise or fall? Next, compare what will happen to the rates of return on low-risk and high-risk investments. Which will have a larger increase in average expected rates of return, investments with high betas or investments with low betas? And will high-beta or low-beta investments show larger percentage changes in their prices? LO17.8

12. **LAST WORD** Why is it so hard for actively managed funds to generate higher rates of return than passively managed index funds having similar levels of risk? Is there a simple way for an actively managed fund to increase its average expected rate of return?

REVIEW QUESTIONS

1. Identify each of the following investments as either an economic investment or a financial investment. LO17.1
   a. A company builds a new factory.
   b. A pension plan buys some Google stock.
   c. A mining company sets up a new gold mine.
   d. A woman buys a 100-year-old farmhouse in the countryside.
   e. A man buys a newly built home in the city.
   f. A company buys an old factory.

2. It is a fact that $(1 + 0.12)^3 = 1.40$. Knowing that to be true, what is the present value of $140 received in three years if the annual interest rate is 12 percent? LO17.2
   a. $1.40.
   b. $12.
   c. $100.
   d. $112.

3. Asset X is expected to deliver 3 future payments. They have present values of, respectively, $1,000, $2,000, and $7,000. Asset Y is expected to deliver 10 future payments, each having a present value of $1,000. Which of the following statements correctly describes the relationship between the current price of Asset X and the current price of Asset Y? LO17.3
   a. Asset X and Asset Y should have the same current price.
   b. Asset X should have a higher current price than Asset Y.
   c. Asset X should have a lower current price than Asset Y.

4. Tammy can buy an asset this year for $1,000. She is expecting to sell it next year for $1,050. What is the asset's anticipated percentage rate of return? LO17.4
   a. 0 percent.
   b. 5 percent.
   c. 10 percent.
   d. 15 percent.

5. Sammy buys stock in a suntan-lotion maker and also stock in an umbrella maker. One stock does well when the weather is good; the other does well when the weather is bad. Sammy's portfolio indicates that "weather risk" is a _____ risk. LO17.6
   a. Diversifiable.
   b. Nondiversifiable.
   c. Automatic.

6. An investment has a 50 percent chance of generating a 10 percent return and a 50 percent chance of generating a 16 percent return. What is the investment's average expected rate of return? LO17.7
   a. 10 percent.
   b. 11 percent.
   c. 12 percent.
   d. 13 percent.
   e. 14 percent.
   f. 15 percent.
   g. 16 percent.

7. If an investment has 35 percent more nondiversifiable risk than the market portfolio, its beta will be: LO17.7
   a. 35.
   b. 1.35.
   c. 0.35.

8. The interest rate on short-term U.S. government bonds is 4 percent. The risk premium for any asset with a beta = 1.0 is 6 percent. What is the average expected rate of return on the market portfolio? LO17.7
   a. 0 percent.
   b. 4 percent.
   c. 6 percent.
   d. 10 percent.

9. Suppose that an SML indicates that assets with a beta = 1.15 should have an average expected rate of return of 12 percent per year. If a particular stock with a beta = 1.15 currently has an average expected rate of return of 15 percent, what should we expect to happen to its price? LO17.8
   a. Rise.
   b. Fall.
   c. Stay the same.

10. If the Fed increases interest rates, the SML will shift _____ and asset prices will _____. LO17.8
   a. Down; rise.
   b. Down; fall.
   c. Up; rise.
   d. Up; fall.

PROBLEMS

1. Suppose that you invest $100 today in a risk-free investment and let the 4 percent annual interest rate compound. Rounded to full dollars, what will be the value of your investment 4 years from now? **LO17.2**

2. Suppose that you desire to get a lump-sum payment of $100,000 two years from now. Rounded to full dollars, how many current dollars will you have to invest today at 10 percent interest to accomplish your goal? **LO17.2**

3. Suppose that a risk-free investment will make three future payments of $100 in one year, $100 in two years, and $100 in three years. If the Federal Reserve has set the risk-free interest rate at 8 percent, what is the proper current price of this investment? What is the price of this investment if the Federal Reserve raises the risk-free interest rate to 10 percent? **LO17.2**

4. Consider an asset that costs $120 today. You are going to hold it for 1 year and then sell it. Suppose that there is a 25 percent chance that it will be worth $100 in a year, a 25 percent chance that it will be worth $115 in a year, and a 50 percent chance that it will be worth $140 in a year. What is its average expected rate of return? Next, figure out what the investment's average expected rate of return would be if its current price were $130 today. Does the increase in the current price increase or decrease the asset's average expected rate of return? At what price would the asset have a zero average expected rate of return? **LO17.4**

5. Suppose initially that two assets, A and B, will each make a single guaranteed payment of $100 in 1 year. But asset A has a current price of $80 while asset B has a current price of $90. **LO17.6**

   a. What are the rates of return of assets A and B at their current prices? Given these rates of return, which asset should investors buy and which asset should they sell?
   b. Assume that arbitrage continues until A and B have the same expected rate of return. When arbitrage ends, will A and B have the same price?

   Next, consider another pair of assets, C and D. Asset C will make a single payment of $150 in one year, while D will make a single payment of $200 in one year. Assume that the current price of C is $120 and that the current price of D is $180.

   c. What are the rates of return of assets C and D at their current prices? Given these rates of return, which asset should investors buy and which asset should they sell?
   d. Assume that arbitrage continues until C and D have the same expected rate of return. When arbitrage ends, will C and D have the same price?

   Compare your answers to questions *a* through *d* before answering question *e*.

   e. We know that arbitrage will equalize rates of return. Does it also guarantee to equalize prices? In what situations will it equalize prices?

6. **ADVANCED ANALYSIS** Suppose that the equation for the SML is $Y = 0.05 + 0.04X$, where Y is the average expected rate of return, 0.05 is the vertical intercept, 0.04 is the slope, and X is the risk level as measured by beta. What is the risk-free interest rate for this SML? What is the average expected rate of return at a beta of 1.5? What is the value of beta at an average expected rate of return of 7 percent? **LO17.8**

FURTHER TEST YOUR KNOWLEDGE AT www.mcconnell20e.com

Practice quizzes, student PowerPoints, worked problems, Web-based questions, and additional materials are available at the text's Online Learning Center (OLC), **www.mcconnell20e.com**, or scan here. Need a barcode reader? Try ScanLife, available in your app store.

Extensions and Issues

PART **SIX**

EXTENSIONS AND ISSUES

CHAPTER 18

Extending the Analysis of Aggregate Supply

Learning Objectives

LO18.1 Explain the relationship between short-run aggregate supply and long-run aggregate supply.

LO18.2 Discuss how to apply the "extended" (short-run/long-run) AD-AS model to inflation, recessions, and economic growth.

LO18.3 Explain the short-run trade-off between inflation and unemployment (the Phillips Curve).

LO18.4 Discuss why there is no long-run trade-off between inflation and unemployment.

LO18.5 Explain the relationship between tax rates, tax revenues, and aggregate supply.

During the early years of the Great Depression, many economists suggested that the economy would correct itself in the *long run* without government intervention. To this line of thinking, economist John Maynard Keynes remarked, "In the long run we are all dead!"

For several decades following the Great Depression, macroeconomists understandably focused on refining fiscal policy and monetary policy to smooth business cycles and address the problems of unemployment and inflation. The main emphasis was on short-run problems and policies associated with the business cycle.

But over people's lifetimes, and from generation to generation, the long run is tremendously important for economic well-being. For that reason, macroeconomists have refocused attention on long-run macroeconomic adjustments, processes, and

403

outcomes. The renewed emphasis on the long run has produced significant insights about aggregate supply, economic growth, and economic development. We will also see in the next chapter that it has renewed historical debates over the causes of macro instability and the effectiveness of stabilization policy.

Our goals in this chapter are to extend the analysis of aggregate supply to the long run, examine the inflation-unemployment relationship, and evaluate the effect of taxes on aggregate supply. The latter is a key concern of so-called *supply-side economics*.

From Short Run to Long Run

LO18.1 Explain the relationship between short-run aggregate supply and long-run aggregate supply.

In Chapter 12, we noted that in macroeconomics the difference between the **short run** and the **long run** has to do with the flexibility of input prices. Input prices are inflexible or even totally fixed in the short run but fully flexible in the long run. (By contrast, output prices are assumed under these definitions to be fully flexible in both the short run and the long run.)

The assumption that input prices are flexible only in the long run leads to large differences in the shape and position of the short-run aggregate supply curve and the long-run aggregate supply curve. As explained in Chapter 12, the short-run aggregate supply curve is an upsloping line, whereas the long-run aggregate supply curve is a vertical line situated directly above the economy's full-employment output level, Q_f.

We will begin this chapter by discussing how aggregate supply transitions *from* the short run *to* the long run. Once that is done, we will combine the long-run and short-run aggregate supply curves with the aggregate demand curve to form a single model that can provide insights into how the economy adjusts to economic shocks as well as changes in monetary and fiscal policy in both the short run and the long run. That will lead us to discuss how economic growth relates to long-run aggregate supply and how inflation and aggregate supply are related in the long run and the short run. We will conclude with a discussion of a particular set of economic policies that may help increase both short-run aggregate supply and long-run aggregate supply.

Short-Run Aggregate Supply

Our immediate objective is to demonstrate the relationship between short-run aggregate supply and long-run aggregate supply. We begin by briefly reviewing short-run aggregate supply.

Consider the short-run aggregate supply curve AS_1 in Figure 18.1a. This curve is based on three assumptions: (1) The initial price level is P_1, (2) firms and workers have established nominal wages on the expectation that this price level will persist, and (3) the price level is flexible both upward and downward. Observe from point a_1 that at price level P_1 the economy is operating at its full-employment output Q_f. This output is the real production forthcoming when the economy is operating at its natural rate of unemployment (or potential output).

Now let's review the short-run effects of changes in the price level, say, from P_1 to P_2 in Figure 18.1a. The higher prices associated with price level P_2 increase firms' revenues, and because their nominal wages and other input prices remain unchanged, their profits rise. Those higher profits lead firms to increase their output from Q_f to Q_2, and the economy moves from a_1 to a_2 on aggregate supply AS_1. At output Q_2 the economy is operating beyond its full-employment output. The firms make this possible by extending the work hours of part-time and full-time workers, enticing new workers such as homemakers and retirees into the labor force, and hiring and training the structurally unemployed. Thus, the nation's unemployment rate declines below its natural rate.

How will the firms respond when the price level *falls*, say, from P_1 to P_3 in Figure 18.1a? Because the prices they receive for their products are lower while the nominal wages they pay workers remain unchanged, firms discover that their revenues and profits have diminished or disappeared. So they reduce their production and employment, and, as shown by the movement from a_1 to a_3, real output falls to Q_3. Increased unemployment and a higher unemployment rate accompany the decline in real output. At output Q_3 the unemployment rate is greater than the natural rate of unemployment associated with output Q_f.

FIGURE 18.1 Short-run and long-run aggregate supply. (a) In the short run, nominal wages and other input prices do not respond to price-level changes and are based on the expectation that price level P_1 will continue. An increase in the price level from P_1 to P_2 increases profits and output, moving the economy from a_1 to a_2; a decrease in the price level from P_1 to P_3 reduces profits and real output, moving the economy from a_1 to a_3. The short-run aggregate supply curve therefore slopes upward. (b) In the long run, a rise in the price level results in higher nominal wages and other input prices and thus shifts the short-run aggregate supply curve to the left. Conversely, a decrease in the price level reduces nominal wages and shifts the short-run aggregate supply curve to the right. After such adjustments, the economy obtains equilibrium of points such as b_1 and c_1. Thus, the long-run aggregate supply curve is vertical at the full-employment output.

(a)

Short-run aggregate supply

(b)

Long-run aggregate supply

Long-Run Aggregate Supply

The outcomes are different in the long run. To see why, we need to extend the analysis of aggregate supply to account for changes in nominal wages that occur in response to changes in the price level. That will enable us to derive the economy's long-run aggregate supply curve.

We illustrate the implications for aggregate supply in Figure 18.1b. Again, suppose that the economy is initially at point a_1 (P_1 and Q_f). As we just demonstrated, an increase in the price level from P_1 to P_2 will move the economy from point a_1 to a_2 along the short-run aggregate supply curve AS_1. At a_2, the economy is producing at more than its potential output. This implies very high demand for productive inputs, so that input prices will begin to rise. In particular, the high demand for labor will drive up nominal wages, which will increase per unit production costs. As a result, the short-run supply curve shifts leftward from AS_1 to AS_2, which now reflects the higher price level P_2 and the new expectation that P_2, not P_1, will continue. The leftward shift in the short-run aggregate supply curve to AS_2 moves the economy from a_2 to b_1. Real output falls back to its full-employment level Q_f, and the unemployment rate rises to its natural rate.

What is the long-run outcome of a *decrease* in the price level? Assuming eventual downward wage flexibility, a

decline in the price level from P_1 to P_3 in Figure 18.1b works in the opposite way from a price-level increase. At first the economy moves from point a_1 to a_3 on AS_1. Profits are squeezed or eliminated because prices have fallen and nominal wages have not. But this movement along AS_1 is the short-run supply response that results only while input prices remain constant. As time passes, input prices will begin to fall because the economy is producing at below its full-employment output level. With so little output being produced, the demand for inputs will be low and their prices will begin to decline. In particular, the low demand for labor will drive down nominal wages and reduce per-unit production costs. Lower nominal wages therefore shift the short-run aggregate supply curve rightward from AS_1 to AS_3, and real output returns to its full-employment level of Q_f at point c_1.

By tracing a line between the long-run equilibrium points b_1, a_1, and c_1, we obtain a long-run aggregate supply curve. Observe that it is vertical at the full-employment level of real GDP. After long-run adjustments in nominal wages and other nominal input prices, real output is Q_f regardless of the specific price level.

Long-Run Equilibrium in the AD-AS Model

Figure 18.2 helps us understand the long-run equilibrium in the AD-AS model, now extended to include the

FIGURE 18.2 Equilibrium in the long-run AD-AS model.
The long-run equilibrium price level P_1 and level of real output Q_f occur at the intersection of the aggregate demand curve AD_1, the long-run aggregate supply curve AS_{LR}, and the short-run aggregate supply curve AS_1.

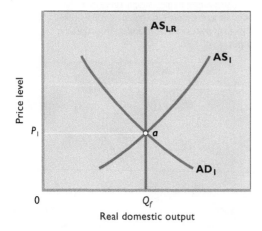

QUICK REVIEW 18.1

- The short-run aggregate supply curve slopes upward because nominal wages and other input prices are fixed while output prices change.
- The long-run aggregate supply curve is vertical because input prices eventually rise in response to changes in output prices.
- The long-run equilibrium GDP and price level occur at the intersection of the aggregate demand curve, the long-run aggregate supply curve, and the short-run aggregate supply curve.
- In long-run equilibrium, the economy achieves its natural rate of unemployment and its full-potential real output.

distinction between short-run and long-run aggregate supply. (Hereafter, we will refer to this model as the extended AD-AS model, with "extended" referring to the inclusion of both the short-run and the long-run aggregate supply curves.)

In the short run, equilibrium occurs wherever the downsloping aggregate demand curve and upsloping short-run aggregate supply curve intersect. This can be at any level of output, not simply the full-employment level. Either a negative GDP gap or a positive GDP gap is possible in the short run.

But in the long run, the short-run aggregate supply curve adjusts as we just described. After those adjustments, long-run equilibrium occurs where the aggregate demand curve, vertical long-run aggregate supply curve, and short-run aggregate supply curve all intersect. Figure 18.2 shows the long-run outcome. Equilibrium occurs at point a, where AD_1 intersects both AS_{LR} and AS_1, and the economy achieves its full-employment (or potential) output, Q_f. At long-run equilibrium price level P_1 and output level Q_f, neither a negative GDP gap nor a positive GDP gap occurs. The economy's *natural rate of unemployment* prevails, meaning that the economy achieves full employment.

In the United States, output Q_f in Figure 18.2 implies a 4 to 5 percent unemployment rate. The natural rate of unemployment can vary from one time period to another and can differ between countries. But whatever the rate happens to be, it defines the level of potential output and establishes the location of the long-run AS curve.

Applying the Extended AD-AS Model

LO18.2 Explain how to apply the "extended" (short-run/long-run) AD-AS model to inflation, recessions, and economic growth.

The extended AD-AS model helps clarify the long-run aspects of demand-pull inflation, cost-push inflation, and recession.

Demand-Pull Inflation in the Extended AD-AS Model

Recall that demand-pull inflation occurs when an increase in aggregate demand pulls up the price level. Earlier, we depicted this inflation by shifting an aggregate demand curve rightward along a stable aggregate supply curve (see Figure 12.8).

In our more complex version of aggregate supply, an increase in the price level eventually leads to an increase in nominal wages and thus a leftward shift of the short-run aggregate supply curve. This is shown in Figure 18.3, where we initially suppose the price level is P_1 at the intersection of aggregate demand curve AD_1, short-run supply curve AS_1, and long-run aggregate supply curve AS_{LR}. Observe that the economy is achieving its full-employment real output Q_f at point a.

Now consider the effects of an increase in aggregate demand as represented by the rightward shift from AD_1 to AD_2. This shift might result from any one of a number of factors, including an increase in investment spending or a rise in net exports. Whatever its cause, the increase in aggregate demand boosts the price level from P_1 to P_2 and expands real output from Q_f to Q_2 at point b. There, a positive GDP gap of $Q_2 - Q_f$ occurs.

FIGURE 18.3 Demand-pull inflation in the extended AD-AS model.
An increase in aggregate demand from AD_1 to AD_2 drives up the price level and increases real output in the short run. But in the long run, nominal wages rise and the short-run aggregate supply curve shifts leftward, as from AS_1 to AS_2. Real output then returns to its prior level, and the price level rises even more. In this scenario, the economy moves from *a* to *b* and then eventually to *c*.

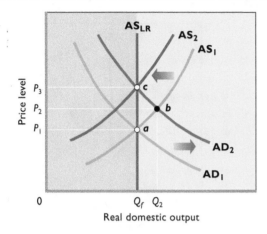

So far, none of this is new to you. But now the distinction between short-run aggregate supply and long-run aggregate supply becomes important. With the economy producing above potential output, inputs will be in high demand. Input prices including nominal wages will rise. As they do, the short-run aggregate supply curve will ultimately shift leftward such that it intersects long-run aggregate supply at point *c*.[1] There, the economy has reestablished long-run equilibrium, with the price level and real output now P_3 and Q_f, respectively. Only at point *c* does the new aggregate demand curve AD_2 intersect both the short-run aggregate supply curve AS_2 and the long-run aggregate supply curve AS_{LR}.

In the short run, demand-pull inflation drives up the price level and increases real output; in the long run, only the price level rises. In the long run, the initial increase in aggregate demand moves the economy along its vertical aggregate supply curve AS_{LR}. For a while, an economy can operate beyond its full-employment level of output. But the demand-pull inflation eventually causes adjustments of nominal wages that return the economy to its full-employment output Q_f.

---

[1] We say "ultimately" because the initial leftward shift in short-run aggregate supply will intersect the long-run aggregate supply curve AS_{LR} at price level P_2 (review Figure 18.1b). But the intersection of AD_2 and this new short-run aggregate supply curve (that is not shown in Figure 18.3) will produce a price level above P_2. (You may want to pencil this in to make sure that you understand this point.) Again nominal wages will rise, shifting the short-run aggregate supply curve farther leftward. The process will continue until the economy moves to point *c*, where the short-run aggregate supply curve is AS_2, the price level is P_3, and real output is Q_f.

Cost-Push Inflation in the Extended AD-AS Model

Cost-push inflation arises from factors that increase the cost of production at each price level, shifting the aggregate supply curve leftward and raising the equilibrium price level. Previously (Figure 12.10), we considered cost-push inflation using only the short-run aggregate supply curve. Now we want to analyze that type of inflation in its long-run context.

Analysis Look at Figure 18.4, in which we again assume that the economy is initially operating at price level P_1 and output level Q_f (point *a*). Suppose that international oil producers agree to reduce the supply of oil to boost its price by, say, 100 percent. As a result, the per-unit production cost of producing and transporting goods and services rises substantially in the economy represented by Figure 18.4. This increase in per-unit production costs shifts the short-run aggregate supply curve to the left, as from AS_1 to AS_2, and the price level rises from P_1 to P_2 (as seen by comparing points *a* and *b*). In this case, the leftward shift of the aggregate supply curve is *not a response* to a price-level increase, as it was in our previous discussions of demand-pull inflation; it is the *initiating cause* of the price-level increase.

Policy Dilemma Cost-push inflation creates a dilemma for policymakers. Without some expansionary stabilization policy, aggregate demand in Figure 18.4 remains in

FIGURE 18.4 Cost-push inflation in the extended AD-AS model.
Cost-push inflation occurs when the short-run aggregate supply curve shifts leftward, as from AS_1 to AS_2. If government counters the decline in real output by increasing aggregate demand to the broken line, the price level rises even more. That is, the economy moves in steps from *a* to *b* to *c*. In contrast, if government allows a recession to occur, nominal wages eventually fall and the aggregate supply curve shifts back rightward to its original location. The economy moves from *a* to *b* and eventually back to *a*.

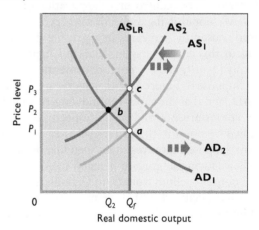

place at AD_1 and real output declines from Q_f to Q_2. Government can counter this recession, negative GDP gap, and attendant high unemployment by using fiscal policy and monetary policy to increase aggregate demand to AD_2. But there is a potential policy trap here: An increase in aggregate demand to AD_2 will further raise inflation by increasing the price level from P_2 to P_3 (a move from point b to point c).

Suppose the government recognizes this policy trap and decides not to increase aggregate demand from AD_1 to AD_2 (you can now disregard the dashed AD_2 curve) and instead decides to allow a cost-push-created recession to run its course. How will that happen? Widespread layoffs, plant shutdowns, and business failures eventually occur. At some point the demand for oil, labor, and other inputs will decline so much that oil prices and nominal wages will decline. When that happens, the initial leftward shift of the short-run aggregate supply curve will reverse itself. That is, the declining per-unit production costs caused by the recession will shift the short-run aggregate supply curve rightward from AS_2 to AS_1. The price level will return to P_1, and the full-employment level of output will be restored at Q_f (point a on the long-run aggregate supply curve AS_{LR}).

This analysis yields two generalizations:

- If the government attempts to maintain full employment when there is cost-push inflation, even more inflation will occur.
- If the government takes a hands-off approach to cost-push inflation, the recession will linger. Although falling input prices will eventually undo the initial rise in per-unit production costs, the economy in the meantime will experience high unemployment and a loss of real output.

Recession and the Extended AD-AS Model

By far the most controversial application of the extended AD-AS model is its application to recession (or depression) caused by decreases in aggregate demand. We will look at this controversy in detail in Chapter 19; here we simply identify the key point of contention.

Suppose in Figure 18.5 that aggregate demand initially is AD_1 and that the short-run and long-run aggregate supply curves are AS_1 and AS_{LR}, respectively. Therefore, as shown by point a, the price level is P_1 and output is Q_f. Now suppose that investment spending declines dramatically, reducing aggregate demand to AD_2. Observe that real output declines from Q_f to Q_1, indicating that a recession has occurred. But if we make the controversial assumption that prices and wages are flexible downward, the

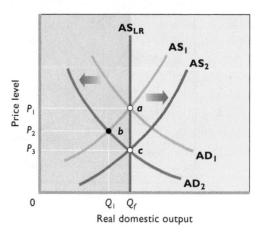

FIGURE 18.5 Recession in the extended AD-AS model. A recession occurs when aggregate demand shifts leftward, as from AD_1 to AD_2. If prices and wages are downwardly flexible, the price level falls from P_1 to P_2 as the economy moves from point a to point b. With the economy in recession at point b, wages eventually fall, shifting the aggregate supply curve from AS_1 to AS_2. The price level declines to P_3, and real output returns to Q_f. The economy moves from a to b to c.

price level falls from P_1 to P_2. With the economy producing below potential output at point b, demand for inputs will be low. Eventually, nominal wages themselves fall to restore the previous real wage; when that happens, the short-run aggregate supply curve shifts rightward from AS_1 to AS_2. The negative GDP gap evaporates without the need for expansionary fiscal or monetary policy since real output expands from Q_1 (point b) back to Q_f (point c). The economy is again located on its long-run aggregate supply curve AS_{LR}, but now at lower price level P_3.

There is much disagreement about this hypothetical scenario. The key point of dispute revolves around the degree to which both input and output prices may be downwardly inflexible and how long it would take in the actual economy for the necessary downward price and wage adjustments to occur to regain the full-employment level of output. For now, suffice it to say that most economists believe that if such adjustments are forthcoming, they will occur only after the economy has experienced a relatively long-lasting recession with its accompanying high unemployment and large loss of output. The severity and length of the major recession of 2007–2009 has strengthened this view. Therefore, economists recommend active monetary policy, and perhaps fiscal policy, to counteract recessions.

Economic Growth with Ongoing Inflation

In our analysis so far, we have seen how demand and supply shocks can cause, respectively, demand-push inflation and cost-push inflation. But in these previous cases, the

FIGURE 18.6 Production possibilities and long-run aggregate supply. (a) Economic growth driven by supply factors (such as improved technologies or the use of more or better resources) shifts an economy's production possibilities curve outward, as from *AB* to *CD*. (b) The same factors shift the economy's long-run aggregate supply curve to the right, as from AS_{LR1} to AS_{LR2}.

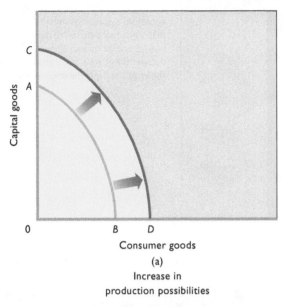

(a)

Increase in
production possibilities

(b)

Increase in long-run
aggregate supply

extent of the inflation was *finite* because the size of the initial movement in either the AD curve or the AS curve was *limited*. For instance, in Figure 18.3, the aggregate demand curve shifts right by a limited amount, from AD_1 to AD_2. As the economy's equilibrium moves from *a* to *b* to *c*, the price level rises from P_1 to P_2 to P_3. During this transition, inflation obviously occurs because the price level is rising. But once the economy reaches its new equilibrium at point *c*, the price level remains constant at P_3 and no further inflation takes place. That is, the limited movement in aggregate demand causes a limited amount of inflation that ends when the economy returns to full employment.

But the modern economy almost always experiences continuous, but usually mild, positive rates of inflation. That can only happen with ongoing shifts in either the aggregate demand or long-run aggregate supply curves because any single, finite shift will only cause inflation of limited duration. This insight is crucial to understanding why modern economies usually experience ongoing inflation while achieving economic growth. Both aggregate demand and long-run aggregate supply increase over time in the actual economy, and inflation occurs because the increases in aggregate demand generally exceed the increases in long-run aggregate supply. It will be helpful to examine this point graphically.

Increases in Long-Run Aggregate Supply As discussed in Chapter 8, economic growth is driven by supply

factors such as improved technologies and access to more or better resources. Economists illustrate economic growth as either an outward shift of an economy's production possibilities curve or as a rightward shift of its long-run aggregate supply curve. As shown in Figure 18.6, the outward shift of the production possibilities curve from *AB* to *CD* in graph *a* is equivalent to the rightward shift of the economy's long-run aggregate supply curve from AS_{LR1} to AS_{LR2} in graph *b*.

Let's simply transfer this rightward shift of the economy's long-run aggregate supply curve to Figure 18.7, which depicts economic growth in the United States in the context of the extended aggregate demand–aggregate supply model. Suppose the economy's long-run aggregate supply curve initially is AS_{LR1}, while its aggregate demand curve and short-run aggregate supply curve are AD_1 and AS_1, as shown. The equilibrium price level is P_1 and the equilibrium level of real output is Q_1.

Now let's assume that economic growth driven by changes in supply factors (quantity and quality of resources and technology) shifts the long-run aggregate supply curve rightward from AS_{LR1} to AS_{LR2} while the economy's aggregate demand curve remains at AD_1. Also, suppose that product and resource prices are flexible downward. The economy's potential output will expand, as reflected by the increase of available real output from Q_1 to Q_2. With aggregate demand constant at AD_1, the rightward shift of the long-run aggregate supply curve will lower the price level from P_1 to P_3. Taken alone,

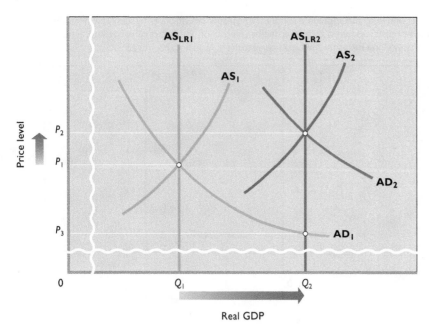

FIGURE 18.7 **Depicting U.S. growth via the extended AD-AS model.** Long-run aggregate supply and short-run aggregate supply have increased over time, as from AS_{LR1} to AS_{LR2} and AS_1 to AS_2. Simultaneously, aggregate demand has shifted rightward, as from AD_1 to AD_2. The actual outcome of these combined shifts has been economic growth, shown as the increase in real output from Q_1 to Q_2, accompanied by mild inflation, shown as the rise in the price level from P_1 to P_2.

expansions of long-run aggregate supply in the economy are deflationary.

Increases in Aggregate Demand and Inflation

But a decline in the price level, such as the one from P_1 to P_3 in Figure 18.7, is not part of the long-run U.S. growth experience. Why not? The answer is that the nation's central bank—the Federal Reserve—engineers ongoing increases in the nation's money supply to create rightward shifts of the aggregate demand curve. These increases in aggregate demand would be highly inflationary absent the increases in long-run aggregate supply. But because the Fed usually makes sure that the inflationary rightward shifts of the aggregate demand curve proceed only slightly faster than the deflationary rightward shifts of the aggregate supply curve, only mild inflation occurs along with economic growth.

We illustrate this outcome in Figure 18.7, where aggregate demand shifts to the right from AD_1 to AD_2 at the same time long-run aggregate supply shifts rightward from AS_{LR1} to AS_{LR2}. Real output expands from Q_1 to Q_2 and the price level increases from P_1 to P_2. At the higher price level P_2, the economy confronts a new short-run aggregate supply curve AS_2. The changes shown in Figure 18.7 describe the actual U.S. experience: economic growth, accompanied by mild inflation. Real output on average increases at about 3.4 percent annually and inflation averages 2 to 3 percent a year.

Of course, other long-term outcomes besides that depicted are entirely possible. Whether deflation, zero inflation, mild inflation, or rapid inflation accompanies economic growth depends on the extent to which aggregate demand increases relative to long-run aggregate supply. Over long periods, any inflation that accompanies economic growth is exclusively the result of aggregate demand increasing more rapidly than long-run aggregate supply. The expansion of long-run aggregate supply—of potential real GDP—is never the cause of inflation.

QUICK REVIEW 18.2

- In the short run, demand-pull inflation raises both the price level and real output; in the long run, nominal wages rise, the short-run aggregate supply curve shifts to the left, and only the price level increases.

- Cost-push inflation creates a policy dilemma for the government: If it engages in an expansionary policy to increase output, additional inflation will occur; if it does nothing, the recession will linger until input prices have fallen by enough to return the economy to producing at potential output.

- In the short run, a decline in aggregate demand reduces real output (creates a recession); in the long run, prices and nominal wages presumably fall, the short-run aggregate supply curve shifts to the right, and real output returns to its full-employment level.

- The economy has ongoing inflation because the Fed uses monetary policy to shift the AD curve to the right faster than the supply factors of economic growth shift the long-run AS curve to the right.

The Inflation-Unemployment Relationship

LO18.3 Explain the short-run trade-off between inflation and unemployment (the Phillips Curve).

We have just seen that the Fed can determine how much inflation occurs in the economy by how much it causes aggregate demand to shift relative to aggregate supply. Given that low inflation and low unemployment rates are the Fed's major economic goals, its ability to control inflation brings up at least two interesting policy questions: Are low unemployment and low inflation compatible goals or conflicting goals? What explains situations in which high unemployment and high inflation coexist?

The extended AD-AS model supports three significant generalizations relating to these questions:

- Under normal circumstances, there is a short-run trade-off between the rate of inflation and the rate of unemployment.

- Aggregate supply shocks can cause both higher rates of inflation and higher rates of unemployment.

- There is no significant trade-off between inflation and unemployment over long periods of time.

Let's examine each of these generalizations.

The Phillips Curve

We can demonstrate the short-run trade-off between the rate of inflation and the rate of unemployment through the **Phillips Curve,** named after A. W. Phillips, who developed the idea in Great Britain. This curve, generalized in Figure 18.8a, suggests an inverse relationship between the rate of inflation and the rate of unemployment. Lower unemployment rates (measured as leftward movements on the horizontal axis) are associated with higher rates of inflation (measured as upward movements on the vertical axis).

ORIGIN OF THE IDEA

O18.1
Phillips Curve

The underlying rationale of the Phillips Curve becomes apparent when we view the short-run aggregate supply curve in Figure 18.9 and perform a simple mental experiment. Suppose that in some short-run period aggregate demand expands from AD_0 to AD_2, either because firms decide to buy more capital goods or the government decides to increase its expenditures. Whatever the cause, in the short run the price level rises from P_0 to P_2 and real output rises from Q_0 to Q_2. As real output rises, the unemployment rate falls.

FIGURE 18.8 The Phillips Curve: concept and empirical data. (a) The Phillips Curve relates annual rates of inflation and annual rates of unemployment for a series of years. Because this is an inverse relationship, there presumably is a trade-off between unemployment and inflation. (b) Data points for the 1960s seemed to confirm the Phillips Curve concept. (Note: The unemployment rates are annual averages and the inflation rates are on a December-to-December basis.)

(a)
The concept

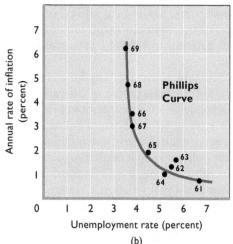

(b)
Data for the 1960s

Source: Bureau of Labor Statistics, **www.bls.gov**.

FIGURE 18.9 The short-run effect of changes in aggregate demand on real output and the price level. Comparing the effects of various possible increases in aggregate demand leads to the conclusion that the larger the increase in aggregate demand, the higher the rate of inflation and the greater the increase in real output. Because real output and the unemployment rate move in opposite directions, we can generalize that, given short-run aggregate supply, high rates of inflation should be accompanied by low rates of unemployment.

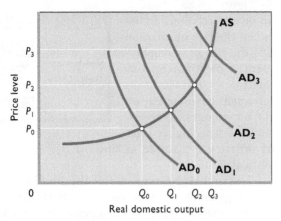

Now let's compare what would have happened if the increase in aggregate demand had been larger, say, from AD_0 to AD_3. The equilibrium at P_3 and Q_3 indicates that the amount of inflation and the growth of real output would both have been greater (and that the unemployment rate would have been lower). Similarly, suppose aggregate demand during the year had increased only modestly, from AD_0 to AD_1. Compared with our shift from AD_0 to AD_2, the amount of inflation and the growth of real output would have been smaller (and the unemployment rate higher).

The generalization we draw from this mental experiment is this: *Assuming a constant short-run aggregate supply curve,* high rates of inflation are accompanied by low rates of unemployment, and low rates of inflation are accompanied by high rates of unemployment. Other things equal, the expected relationship should look something like Figure 18.8a.

Figure 18.8b reveals that the facts for the 1960s nicely fit the theory. On the basis of that evidence and evidence from other countries, most economists working at the end of the 1960s concluded there was a stable, predictable trade-off between unemployment and inflation. Moreover, U.S. economic policy was built on that supposed trade-off. According to this thinking, it was impossible to achieve "full employment without inflation": Manipulation of aggregate demand through fiscal and monetary measures would simply move the economy along the Phillips Curve. An expansionary fiscal and monetary policy that boosted aggregate demand and lowered the unemployment rate would simultaneously increase inflation. A restrictive fiscal

and monetary policy could be used to reduce the rate of inflation but only at the cost of a higher unemployment rate and more forgone production. Society had to choose between the incompatible goals of price stability and full employment; it had to decide where to locate on its Phillips Curve.

For reasons we will soon see, today's economists reject the idea of a stable, predictable Phillips Curve. Nevertheless, they agree there is a short-run trade-off between unemployment and inflation. *Given short-run aggregate supply,* increases in aggregate demand increase real output and reduce the unemployment rate. As the unemployment rate falls and dips below the natural rate, the excessive spending produces demand-pull inflation. Conversely, when recession sets in and the unemployment rate increases, the weak aggregate demand that caused the recession also leads to lower inflation rates.

Periods of exceptionally low unemployment rates and inflation rates do occur, but only under special sets of economic circumstances. One such period was the late 1990s, when faster productivity growth increased aggregate supply and fully blunted the inflationary impact of rapidly rising aggregate demand (review Figure 12.11).

Aggregate Supply Shocks and the Phillips Curve

The unemployment-inflation experience of the 1970s and early 1980s demolished the idea of an always-stable Phillips Curve. In Figure 18.10 we show the Phillips Curve for the 1960s in blue and then add the data points for 1970 through 2012. Observe that in most of the years of the 1970s and early 1980s, the economy experienced both higher inflation rates and higher unemployment rates than it did in the 1960s. In fact, inflation and unemployment rose simultaneously in some of those years. This condition is called **stagflation**—a media term that combines the words "stagnation" and "inflation." If there still was any such thing as a Phillips Curve, it had clearly shifted outward, perhaps as shown.

Adverse Aggregate Supply Shocks The data points for the 1970s and early 1980s support our second generalization: Aggregate supply shocks can cause both higher rates of inflation and higher rates of unemployment. A series of adverse **aggregate supply shocks**—sudden, large increases in resource costs that jolt an economy's short-run aggregate supply curve leftward—hit the economy in the 1970s and early 1980s. The most significant of these shocks was a quadrupling of oil prices by the Organization of Petroleum Exporting Countries

FIGURE 18.10 Inflation rates and unemployment rates, 1960–2012. A series of aggregate supply shocks in the 1970s resulted in higher rates of inflation *and* higher rates of unemployment. So data points for the 1970s and 1980s tended to be above and to the right of the blue Phillips Curve for the 1960s. In the 1990s the inflation-unemployment data points slowly moved back toward the 1960s Phillips Curve. Points for the late 1990s and 2000s are similar to those from the 1960s. (Note: The unemployment rates are annual averages and the inflation rates are on a December-to-December basis.)

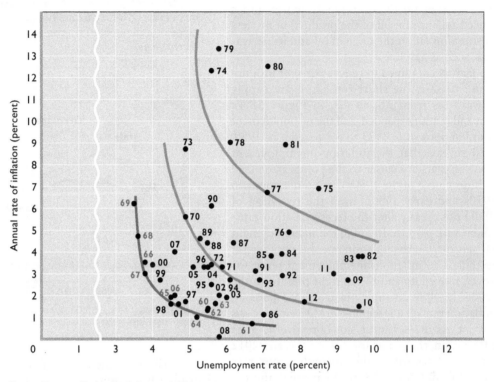

Source: Bureau of Labor Statistics, **www.bls.gov**.

(OPEC). Consequently, the cost of producing and distributing virtually every product and service rose rapidly. (Other factors working to increase U.S. costs during this period included major agricultural shortfalls, a greatly depreciated dollar, wage hikes previously held down by wage-price controls, and slower rates of productivity growth.)

These shocks shifted the aggregate supply curve to the left and distorted the usual inflation-unemployment relationship. Remember that we derived the inverse relationship between the rate of inflation and the unemployment rate shown in Figure 18.8a by shifting the aggregate demand curve along a stable short-run aggregate supply curve (Figure 18.9). But the cost-push inflation model shown in Figure 18.4 tells us that a *leftward shift* of the short-run aggregate supply curve increases the price level and reduces real output (and increases the unemployment rate). This, say most economists, is what happened in two periods in the 1970s. The U.S. unemployment rate shot up from 4.9 percent in 1973 to 8.5 percent in 1975, contributing to a significant decline in real GDP. In the same period, the U.S. price level rose by 21 percent. The stagflation scenario recurred in 1978, when OPEC increased oil prices by more than 100 percent. The U.S. price level rose by 26 percent over the 1978–1980 period, while unemployment increased from 6.1 to 7.1 percent.

Stagflation's Demise Another look at Figure 18.10 reveals a generally inward movement of the inflation-unemployment points between 1982 and 1989. By 1989 the lingering effects of the earlier period had subsided. One precursor to this favorable trend was the deep recession of 1981–1982, largely caused by a restrictive monetary policy aimed at reducing double-digit inflation. The recession upped the unemployment rate to 9.5 percent in 1982. With so many workers unemployed, those who were working accepted smaller increases in their nominal wages—or, in some cases, wage reductions—in order to preserve their jobs. Firms, in turn, restrained their price increases to try to retain their relative shares of a greatly diminished market.

Other factors were at work. Foreign competition throughout this period held down wage and price hikes in several basic industries such as automobiles and steel. Deregulation of the airline and trucking industries also resulted in wage reductions or so-called wage givebacks. A significant decline in OPEC's monopoly power and a greatly reduced reliance on oil in the production process produced a stunning fall in the price of oil and its derivative products, such as gasoline.

All these factors combined to reduce per-unit production costs and to shift the short-run aggregate supply curve rightward (as from AS₂ to AS₁ in Figure 18.4). Employment and output expanded, and the unemployment rate fell from 9.6 percent in 1983 to 5.3 percent in 1989. Figure 18.10 reveals that the inflation-unemployment points for recent years are closer to the points associated with the Phillips Curve of the 1960s than to the points in the late 1970s and early 1980s. Even the recession of 2007–2009 did not greatly alter the recent inflation rate–unemployment rate pattern. In 2008, the unemployment rate was 5.8 percent, but the inflation rate was near zero at just 0.1 percent. The inflation-unemployment point for 2009, however, moved up and to the right relative to the point for 2008. In 2009 unemployment was 9.3 percent, while the inflation rate on a December-to-December basis was 2.7 percent. As the economy slowly recovered after the Great Recession, the points for 2010, 2011, and 2012 gradually moved leftward as the unemployment rate slowly declined from 9.6 percent to 8.1 percent and the inflation rate remained moderate at between 1.5 percent and 3.0 percent.

The media sometimes express the sum of the unemployment rate and the inflation rate as a rough gauge of the economic discomfort that inflation and unemployment jointly impose on an economy in a particular year. The sum of the two rates is used to compute the *misery index*. For example, a nation with a 5 percent unemployment rate and a 5 percent inflation rate has a misery index number of 10, as does a nation with an 8 percent unemployment rate and a 2 percent inflation rate.

Global Perspective 18.1 shows the misery index for several nations between 2001 and 2012. (It uses average annual inflation rates, not the December-to-December inflation rates used to construct Figure 18.10.) The U.S. misery index number has been neither exceptionally low nor exceptionally high relative to the misery index numbers for the other major economies shown. But bear in mind that economists do not put much stock in the misery index because they do not view the national discomfort associated with a 1 percent change in inflation and a 1 percent change in unemployment as

GLOBAL PERSPECTIVE 18.1

The Misery Index, Selected Nations, 2001–2012

The U.S. misery index number (the sum of its unemployment rate and inflation rate) has generally been in the mid-range of such numbers relative to other major economies in recent years.

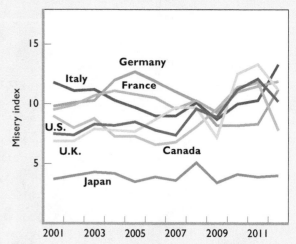

Source: Bureau of Labor Statistics, **stats.bls.gov**. Inflation rates and unemployment rates in this calculation are both on an average-annual basis.

necessarily equivalent. In particular, the misery index can greatly disguise the extent of hardship during a recession. The rise in the unemployment rate in these circumstances causes a huge loss of national output and income (and misery!), even if the higher unemployment rate is partially or fully offset with a decline in the rate of inflation.

The Long-Run Phillips Curve

LO18.4 Discuss why there is no long-run trade-off between inflation and unemployment.

The overall set of data points in Figure 18.10 supports our third generalization relating to the inflation-unemployment relationship: There is no apparent *long-run* trade-off between inflation and unemployment. Economists point out that when decades as opposed to a few years are considered, any rate of inflation is consistent with the natural rate of unemployment prevailing at that time. We know from Chapter 9 that the natural rate of unemployment is the unemployment rate that occurs when cyclical unemployment is zero; it is the full-employment rate of unemployment, or the rate of unemployment when the economy achieves its potential output.

FIGURE 18.11 **The long-run vertical Phillips Curve.** Increases in aggregate demand beyond those consistent with full-employment output may temporarily boost profits, output, and employment (as from a_1 to b_1). But nominal wages eventually will catch up so as to sustain real wages. When they do, profits will fall, negating the previous short-run stimulus to production and employment (the economy now moves from b_1 to a_2). Consequently, there is no trade-off between the rates of inflation and unemployment in the long run; that is, the long-run Phillips Curve is roughly a vertical line at the economy's natural rate of unemployment.

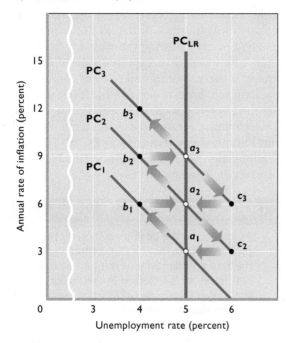

How can there be a short-run inflation-unemployment trade-off but not a long-run trade-off? Figure 18.11 provides the answer.

Short-Run Phillips Curve

Consider Phillips Curve PC_1 in Figure 18.11. Suppose the economy initially is experiencing a 3 percent rate of inflation and a 5 percent natural rate of unemployment. Such short-term curves as PC_1, PC_2, and PC_3 (drawn as straight lines for simplicity) exist because the actual rate of inflation is not always the same as the expected rate.

Establishing an additional point on Phillips Curve PC_1 will clarify this. We begin at a_1, where we assume nominal wages are set on the assumption that the 3 percent rate of inflation will continue. That is, because workers expect output prices to rise by 3 percent per year, they negotiate wage contracts that feature 3 percent per year increases in nominal wages so that these nominal wage increases will exactly offset the expected rise in prices and thereby keep their real wages the same.

But suppose that the rate of inflation rises to 6 percent, perhaps because the Fed has decided to move the AD curve to the right even faster than it had been before. With a nominal wage rate set on the expectation that the 3 percent rate of inflation will continue, the higher product prices raise business profits. Firms respond to the higher profits by hiring more workers and increasing output. In the short run, the economy moves to b_1, which, in contrast to a_1, involves a lower rate of unemployment (4 percent) and a higher rate of inflation (6 percent). The move from a_1 to b_1 is consistent both with an upsloping aggregate supply curve and with the inflation-unemployment trade-off implied by the Phillips Curve analysis. But this short-run Phillips Curve simply is a manifestation of the following principle: *When the actual rate of inflation is higher than expected, profits temporarily rise and the unemployment rate temporarily falls.*

Long-Run Vertical Phillips Curve

But point b_1 is not a stable equilibrium. Workers will recognize that their nominal wages have not increased as fast as inflation and will therefore renegotiate their labor contracts so that they feature faster increases in nominal wages. These faster increases in nominal wages make up for the higher rate of inflation and restore the workers' lost purchasing power. As these new labor contracts kick in, business profits will fall to their prior level. The reduction in profits means that the original motivation to employ more workers and increase output has disappeared.

Unemployment then returns to its natural level at point a_2. Note, however, that the economy now faces a higher actual and expected rate of inflation—6 percent rather than 3 percent. This happens because the new labor contracts feature 6 percent per year increases in wages to make up for the 6 percent per year inflation rate. Because wages are a production cost, this faster increase in wage rates will imply faster future increases in output prices as firms are forced to raise prices more rapidly to make up for the faster future rate of wage growth. Stated a bit differently, the initial increase in inflation will become *persistent* because it leads to renegotiated labor contracts that will perpetuate the higher rate of inflation. In addition, because the new labor contracts are public, it will also be the case that the higher rates of inflation that they will cause will be *expected* by everyone rather than being a surprise.

In view of the higher 6 percent expected rate of inflation, the short-run Phillips Curve shifts upward from PC_1 to PC_2 in Figure 18.11. An "along-the-Phillips-Curve" kind of move from a_1 to b_1 on PC_1 is merely a short-run or transient occurrence. In the long run, after nominal wage contracts catch up with increases in the inflation rate, unemployment returns to its natural rate at a_2, and there is a new short-run Phillips Curve PC_2 at the higher expected rate of inflation.

The scenario repeats if aggregate demand continues to increase. Prices rise momentarily ahead of nominal wages, profits expand, and employment and output increase (as implied by the move from a_2 to b_2). But, in time, nominal wages increase so as to restore real wages. Profits then fall to their original level, pushing employment back to the normal rate at a_3. The economy's "reward" for lowering the unemployment rate below the natural rate is a still higher (9 percent) rate of inflation.

Movements along the short-run Phillips Curve (a_1 to b_1 on PC_1) cause the curve to shift to a less favorable position (PC_2, then PC_3, and so on). A stable Phillips Curve with the dependable series of unemployment-rate–inflation-rate trade-offs simply does not exist in the long run. The economy is characterized by a **long-run vertical Phillips Curve.**

The vertical line through a_1, a_2, and a_3 shows the long-run relationship between unemployment and inflation. Any rate of inflation is consistent with the 5 percent natural rate of unemployment. So, in this view, society ought to choose a low rate of inflation rather than a high one.

ORIGIN OF THE IDEA

O18.2

Long-run
vertical Phillips
Curve

Disinflation

The distinction between the short-run Phillips Curve and the long-run Phillips Curve also helps explain **disinflation**—reductions in the inflation rate from year to year. Suppose that in Figure 18.11 the economy is at a_3, where the inflation rate is 9 percent. And suppose that a decline in the rate at which aggregate demand shifts to the right faster than aggregate supply (as happened during the 1981–1982 recession) reduces inflation below the 9 percent expected rate, say, to 6 percent. Business profits fall because prices are rising less rapidly than wages. The nominal wage increases, remember, were set on the assumption that the 9 percent rate of inflation would continue. In response to the decline in profits, firms reduce their employment and consequently the unemployment rate rises. The economy temporarily slides downward from point a_3 to c_3 along the short-run Phillips Curve PC_3. *When the actual rate of inflation is lower than the expected rate, profits temporarily fall and the unemployment rate temporarily rises.*

Firms and workers eventually adjust their expectations to the new 6 percent rate of inflation, and thus newly negotiated wage increases decline. Profits are restored, employment rises, and the unemployment rate falls back to its natural rate of 5 percent at a_2. Because the expected rate of inflation is now 6 percent, the short-run Phillips Curve PC_3 shifts leftward to PC_2.

If the rate at which aggregate demand shifts to the right faster than aggregate supply declines even more, the scenario will continue. Inflation declines from 6 percent to, say, 3 percent, moving the economy from a_2 to c_2 along PC_2. The lower-than-expected rate of inflation (lower prices) squeezes profits and reduces employment. But, in the long run, firms respond to the lower profits by reducing their nominal wage increases. Profits are restored and unemployment returns to its natural rate at a_1 as the short-run Phillips Curve moves from PC_2 to PC_1. Once again, the long-run Phillips Curve is vertical at the 5 percent natural rate of unemployment.

QUICK REVIEW 18.3

- As implied by the upsloping short-run aggregate supply curve, there may be a short-run trade-off between the rate of inflation and the rate of unemployment. This trade-off is reflected in the Phillips Curve, which shows that lower rates of inflation are associated with higher rates of unemployment.

- Aggregate supply shocks that produce severe cost-push inflation can cause stagflation—simultaneous increases in the inflation rate and the unemployment rate. Such stagflation occurred from 1973–1975 and recurred from 1978–1980, producing Phillips Curve data points above and to the right of the Phillips Curve for the 1960s.

- After all nominal wage adjustments to increases and decreases in the rate of inflation have occurred, the economy ends up back at its full-employment level of output and its natural rate of unemployment. The long-run Phillips Curve therefore is vertical at the natural rate of unemployment.

Taxation and Aggregate Supply

LO18.5 Explain the relationship between tax rates, tax revenues, and aggregate supply.

A final topic in our discussion of aggregate supply is taxation, a key aspect of **supply-side economics.** "Supply-side economists" or "supply-siders" stress that changes in aggregate supply are an active force in determining the levels of inflation, unemployment, and economic growth. Government policies can either impede or promote rightward shifts of the short-run and long-run aggregate supply curves shown in Figure 18.2. One such policy is taxation.

These economists say that the enlargement of the U.S. tax system has impaired incentives to work, save, and invest. In this view, high tax rates impede productivity growth and hence slow the expansion of long-run aggregate supply. By reducing the after-tax rewards of workers and producers, high tax rates reduce the financial attractiveness of working, saving, and investing.

Supply-siders focus their attention on *marginal tax rates*—the rates on extra dollars of income—because those rates affect the benefits from working, saving, or investing more. In 2013 marginal federal income tax rates varied from 10 to 39.6 percent in the United States.

Taxes and Incentives to Work

Supply-siders believe that how long and how hard people work depends on the amounts of additional after-tax earnings they derive from their efforts. They say that lower marginal tax rates on earned incomes induce more work, and therefore increase aggregate inputs of labor. Lower marginal tax rates increase the after-tax wage rate and make leisure more expensive and work more attractive. The higher opportunity cost of leisure encourages people to substitute work for leisure. This increase in productive effort is achieved in many ways: by increasing the number of hours worked per day or week, by encouraging workers to postpone retirement, by inducing more people to enter the labor force, by motivating people to work harder, and by avoiding long periods of unemployment.

Incentives to Save and Invest

High marginal tax rates also reduce the rewards for saving and investing. For example, suppose that Tony saves $10,000 at 8 percent interest, bringing him $800 of interest per year. If his marginal tax rate is 40 percent, his after-tax interest earnings will be $480, not $800, and his after-tax interest rate will fall to 4.8 percent. While Tony might be willing to save (forgo current consumption) for an 8 percent return on his saving, he might rather consume when the return is only 4.8 percent.

Saving, remember, is the prerequisite of investment. Thus, supply-side economists recommend lower marginal tax rates on interest earned from saving. They also call for lower taxes on income from capital to ensure that there are ready investment outlets for the economy's enhanced pool of saving. A critical determinant of

investment spending is the expected *after-tax* return on that spending.

To summarize: Lower marginal tax rates encourage saving and investing. Workers therefore find themselves equipped with more and technologically superior machinery and equipment. Labor productivity rises, and that expands long-run aggregate supply and economic growth, which in turn keeps unemployment rates and inflation low.

The Laffer Curve

In the supply-side view, reductions in marginal tax rates increase the nation's aggregate supply and can leave the nation's tax revenues unchanged or even enlarge them. Thus, supply-side tax cuts need not produce federal budget deficits.

This idea is based on the **Laffer Curve,** named after Arthur Laffer, who popularized it. As Figure 18.12 shows, the Laffer Curve depicts the relationship between tax rates and tax revenues. As tax rates increase from 0 to 100 percent, tax revenues increase from zero to some maximum level (at *m*) and then fall to zero. Tax revenues decline beyond some point because higher tax rates discourage economic activity, thereby shrinking the tax base (domestic output and income). This is easiest to see at the extreme, where the tax rate is 100 percent. Tax revenues here are, in theory, reduced to zero because the 100 percent confiscatory tax rate has halted production. A 100 percent tax rate applied to a tax base of zero yields no revenue.

In the early 1980s, Laffer suggested that the United States was at a point such as *n* on the curve in Figure 18.12.

FIGURE 18.12 The Laffer Curve. The Laffer Curve suggests that up to point *m* higher tax rates will result in larger tax revenues. But tax rates higher than *m* will adversely affect incentives to work and produce, reducing the size of the tax base (output and income) to the extent that tax revenues will decline. It follows that if tax rates are above *m*, reductions in tax rates will produce increases in tax revenues.

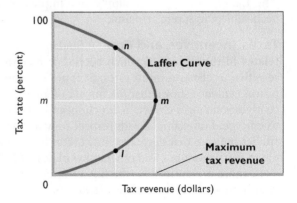

At *n*, tax rates are so high that production is discouraged to the extent that tax revenues are below the maximum at *m*. If the economy is at *n*, then lower tax rates can either increase tax revenues or leave them unchanged. For example, lowering the tax rate from point *n* to point *l* would bolster the economy such that the government would bring in the same total amount of tax revenue as before.

Laffer's reasoning was that lower tax rates stimulate incentives to work, save and invest, innovate, and accept business risks, thus triggering an expansion of real output and income. That enlarged tax base sustains tax revenues even though tax rates are lowered. Indeed, between *n* and *m* lower tax rates result in *increased* tax revenue.

Also, when taxes are lowered, tax avoidance (which is legal) and tax evasion (which is not) decline. High marginal tax rates prompt taxpayers to avoid taxes through various tax shelters, such as buying municipal bonds, on which the interest earned is tax-free. High rates also encourage some taxpayers to conceal income from the Internal Revenue Service. Lower tax rates reduce the inclination to engage in either tax avoidance or tax evasion.

The Laffer Curve also implies that for any particular amount of tax revenue that the government can possibly collect, there will be both a high tax rate at which that amount of revenue can be collected as well as a low tax rate at which that amount of revenue can be collected. As an example, compare points *n* an *l* in Figure 18.12. Point *n* has a high tax rate and point *l* has a low tax rate, but they both collect the same amount of tax revenue. So if the government's major goal when setting tax rates is simply to collect a particular total amount of tax revenue, Laffer argued that the government should always opt for the lower tax rate. By doing so, the government would collect the revenue it desired while impinging as little as possible on the private economy.

Criticisms of the Laffer Curve

The Laffer Curve and its supply-side implications have been subject to severe criticism.

Taxes, Incentives, and Time A fundamental criticism relates to the degree to which economic incentives are sensitive to changes in tax rates. Skeptics say ample empirical evidence shows that the impact of a tax cut on incentives is small, of uncertain direction, and relatively slow to emerge. For example, with respect to work incentives, studies indicate that decreases in tax rates lead some people to work more but lead others to work less. Those who work more are enticed by the higher after-tax pay; they substitute work for leisure because the opportunity cost of

CONSIDER THIS . . .

Sherwood Forest

The popularization of the idea that tax-rate reductions may increase tax revenues owes much to Arthur Laffer's ability to present his ideas simply. In explaining his thoughts to a *Wall Street Journal* editor over lunch, Laffer reportedly took out his pen and drew the curve on a napkin. The editor retained the napkin and later reproduced the curve in an editorial in *The Wall Street Journal*. The Laffer Curve was born. The idea it portrayed became the centerpiece of economic policy under the Reagan administration (1981–1989), which cut tax rates on personal income by 25 percent over a three-year period.

Laffer illustrated his supply-side views with a story relating to Robin Hood, who, you may recall, stole from the rich to give to the poor. Laffer likened people traveling through Sherwood Forest to taxpayers, whereas Robin Hood and his band of merry men were government. As taxpayers passed through the forest, Robin Hood and his men intercepted them and forced them to hand over their money. Laffer asked audiences, "Do you think that travelers continued to go through Sherwood Forest?"

The answer he sought and got, of course, was "no." Taxpayers will avoid Sherwood Forest to the greatest extent possible. They will lower their taxable income by reducing work hours, retiring earlier, saving less, and engaging in tax avoidance and tax evasion activities. Robin Hood and his men may end up with less revenue than if they collected a relatively small "tax" from each traveler for passage through the forest.

leisure has increased. But other people work less because the higher after-tax pay enables them to "buy more leisure." With the tax cut, they can earn the same level of after-tax income as before with fewer work hours.

Inflation or Higher Real Interest Rates Most economists think that the demand-side effects of a tax cut are more immediate and certain than longer-term supply-side effects. Thus, tax cuts undertaken when the economy is at or near full employment may produce increases in aggregate demand that overwhelm any increase in aggregate supply. The likely result is inflation or restrictive monetary policy to prevent it. If the latter, real interest rates will rise and investment will decline. This will defeat the purpose of the supply-side tax cuts.

Position on the Curve Skeptics say that the Laffer Curve is merely a logical proposition and assert that there must be some level of tax rates between 0 and 100 percent at which tax revenues will be at their maximum. Economists of all persuasions can agree with this. But the issue of where a particular economy is located on its Laffer Curve is an empirical question. If we assume that we are at point n in Figure 18.12, then tax cuts will increase tax revenues. But if the economy is at any point below m on the curve, tax-rate reductions will reduce tax revenues.

Rebuttal and Evaluation

Supply-side advocates respond to the skeptics by contending that the Reagan tax cuts in the 1980s worked as Laffer predicted. Although the top marginal income tax rates on earned income were cut from 50 to 28 percent in that decade, real GDP and tax revenues were substantially higher at the end of the 1990s than at the beginning.

But the general view among economists is that the Reagan tax cuts, coming at a time of severe recession, helped boost aggregate demand and return real GDP to its full-employment output and normal growth path. As the economy expanded, so did tax revenues despite the lower tax rates. The rise in tax revenues caused by economic growth swamped the declines in revenues from lower tax rates. In essence, the Laffer Curve shown in Figure 18.12 stretched rightward, increasing net tax revenues. But the tax-rate cuts did not produce extraordinary rightward shifts of the long-run aggregate supply curve. Indeed, saving fell as a percentage of personal income during the period and productivity growth was sluggish. Real GDP sprang back vigorously from recessionary levels, but the economic growth rate soon reverted back to its longer-term average.

Because government expenditures rose more rapidly than tax revenues in the 1980s, large budget deficits occurred. In 1993 the Clinton administration increased the top marginal tax rates from 31 to 39.6 percent to address these deficits. The economy boomed in the last half of the 1990s, and by the end of the decade tax revenues were so high relative to government expenditures that budget surpluses emerged. In 2001 the Bush administration reduced marginal tax rates over a series of years, partially "to return excess revenues to taxpayers." In 2003 the top marginal tax rate fell to 35 percent. Also, the income tax rates on capital gains and dividends were reduced to 15 percent. Economists generally agree that the Bush tax cuts, along with a highly expansionary monetary policy, helped revive and expand the economy following the recession of 2001. Strong growth of output and income in 2004 and 2005 produced large increases in tax revenues, although large budget deficits remained because spending also increased rapidly. The 2004 deficit was $413 billion and the 2005 deficit was $318 billion. The deficit fell over the next two years, to $162 billion in 2007. But the previously discussed financial crisis plunged the economy into a severe recession beginning in December 2007 and lasting into 2009. That caused income to fall and tax revenues to plummet. Also, the government implemented highly expansionary fiscal policy. Budget deficits increased to $459 billion in 2008 and $1.4 trillion in 2009.

Today, there is general agreement that the U.S. economy is operating at a point below m—rather than above m—on the Laffer Curve in Figure 18.12. In this zone, the overall effect is that personal tax-rate increases raise tax revenues while personal tax-rate decreases reduce tax revenues. But at the same time, economists recognize that, other things being equal, cuts in tax rates reduce tax revenues in percentage terms by less than the tax-rate reductions. Similarly, tax-rate increases do not raise tax revenues by as much in percentage terms as the tax-rate increases. This is true because changes in marginal tax rates alter taxpayer behavior and thus affect taxable income. Although these effects seem to be relatively modest, they need to be considered in designing tax policy—and, in fact, the federal government's Office of Tax Policy created a special division in 2007 devoted to estimating the magnitude of such effects when it comes to proposed changes in U.S. tax laws. Thus, supply-side economics has contributed to how economists and policymakers design and implement fiscal policy.

QUICK REVIEW 18.4

- Supply-side economists focus their attention on government policies, such as high taxation, that may impede the expansion of aggregate supply.
- The Laffer Curve relates tax rates to levels of tax revenue and suggests that, under some circumstances, cuts in tax rates will expand the tax base (output and income) and increase tax revenues.
- Most economists believe that the United States is currently operating in the range of the Laffer Curve where tax rates and tax revenues move in the same, not opposite, directions.
- Today's economists recognize the importance of considering supply-side effects in designing optimal fiscal policy.

Do Tax Increases Reduce Real GDP?*

Determining the Relationship Between Changes in Taxes and Permanent Changes in Real GDP is Fraught with Complexities and Difficulties. University of California-Berkeley Economists Christina Romer and David Romer have Recently Devised a Novel Way to Approach the Topic. Their Findings Suggest That Tax Increases Reduce Real GDP.†

How do changes in the level of taxation affect the level of economic activity? The simple correlation between taxation and economic activity shows that, on average, when economic activity rises more rapidly, tax revenues also are rising more rapidly. But this correlation almost surely does not reflect a positive effect of tax increases on output. Rather, under our tax system, any positive shock to output raises tax revenues by increasing income.

In "The Macroeconomic Effects of Tax Changes: Estimates Based on a New Measure of Fiscal Shocks," authors Christina Romer and David Romer observe that this difficulty is just one of many manifestations of a more general problem. Changes in taxes occur for many reasons. And, because the factors that give rise to tax changes often are correlated with other developments in the economy, disentangling the effects of the tax changes from the other effects of these underlying factors is inherently difficult.

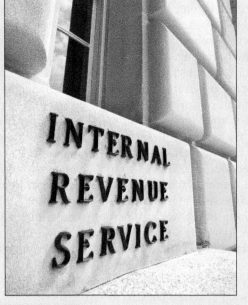

To address this problem, Romer and Romer use the narrative record—presidential speeches, executive branch documents, congressional reports, and so on—to identify the size, timing, and principal motivation for all major tax policy actions in the post–World War II United States. This narrative analysis allows them to separate revenue changes resulting from legislation from changes occurring for other reasons. It also allows them to classify legislated changes according to their primary motivation.

Romer and Romer find that despite the complexity of the legislative process, most significant tax changes have been motivated by one of four factors: counteracting other influences in the economy; paying for increases in government spending (or lowering taxes in conjunction with reductions in spending); addressing an inherited budget deficit; and promoting long-run growth. They observe that legislated tax changes taken to counteract other influences on the economy, or to pay for increases in government spending, are very likely to be correlated with other factors affecting the economy. As a result these observations are likely to lead to unreliable estimates of the effect of tax changes.

Tax changes that are made to promote long-run growth, or to reduce an inherited budget deficit, in contrast, are undertaken for reasons essentially unrelated to other factors influencing output. Thus, examining the behavior of output following these tax changes is likely to provide more reliable estimates of the output effects of tax changes. *The results of this more reliable test indicate that tax changes have very large effects: a tax increase of 1 percent of GDP lowers real GDP by roughly 2 to 3 percent.*

These output effects are highly persistent. The behavior of inflation and unemployment suggests that this persistence reflects long-lasting departures of output from previous levels. Romer and Romer also find that output effects of tax changes are much more closely tied to the actual changes in taxes than news about future changes, and that investment falls sharply in response to tax changes. Indeed, the strong response of investment helps to explain why the output consequences of tax increases are so large.

Romer and Romer find suggestive evidence that tax increases to reduce an inherited budget deficit have much smaller output costs than other tax increases. This is consistent with the idea that deficit-driven tax increases may have important expansionary effects through [improved] expectations and [lower] long-term interest rates, or through [enhanced] confidence.

---

*Abridged from Les Picker, "Tax Increases Reduce GDP," *The NBER Digest*, February/March 2008. The *Digest* provides synopses of research papers in progress by economists affiliated with the National Bureau of Economic Research (NBER).

†Christina Romer and David Romer, "The Macroeconomic Effects of Tax Changes: Estimates Based on a New Measure of Fiscal Shocks," *American Economic Review*, June 2010, pp. 763–801.

SUMMARY

LO18.1 Explain the relationship between short-run aggregate supply and long-run aggregate supply.

In macroeconomics, the short run is a period in which nominal wages do not respond to changes in the price level. In contrast, the long run is a period in which nominal wages fully respond to changes in the price level.

The short-run aggregate supply curve is upsloping. Because nominal wages are unresponsive to price-level changes, increases in the price level (prices received by firms) increase profits and real output. Conversely, decreases in the price level reduce profits and real output. However, the long-run aggregate supply curve is vertical. With sufficient time for adjustment, nominal wages rise and fall with the price level, moving the economy along a vertical aggregate supply curve at the economy's full-employment output.

LO18.2 Discuss how to apply the "extended" (short-run/long-run) AD-AS model to inflation, recessions, and economic growth.

In the short run, demand-pull inflation raises the price level and real output. Once nominal wages rise to match the increase in the price level, the temporary increase in real output is reversed.

In the short run, cost-push inflation raises the price level and lowers real output. Unless the government expands aggregate demand, nominal wages will eventually decline under conditions of recession and the short-run aggregate supply curve will shift back to its initial location. Prices and real output will eventually return to their original levels.

If prices and wages are flexible downward, a decline in aggregate demand will lower output and the price level. The decline in the price level will eventually lower nominal wages and shift the short-run aggregate supply curve rightward. Full-employment output will thus be restored.

One-time changes in aggregate demand (AD) and aggregate supply (AS) can only cause limited bouts of inflation. Ongoing mild inflation occurs because the Fed purposely increases AD slightly faster than the expansion of long-run AS (driven by the supply factors of economic growth).

LO18.3 Explain the short-run trade-off between inflation and unemployment (the Phillips Curve).

Assuming a stable, upsloping short-run aggregate supply curve, rightward shifts of the aggregate demand curve of various sizes yield the generalization that high rates of inflation are associated with low rates of unemployment, and vice versa. This inverse relationship is known as the Phillips Curve, and empirical data for the 1960s seemed to be consistent with it.

In the 1970s and early 1980s the Phillips Curve apparently shifted rightward, reflecting stagflation—simultaneously rising inflation rates and unemployment rates. The higher unemployment rates and inflation rates resulted mainly from huge oil price increases that caused large leftward shifts in the short-run aggregate supply curve (so-called aggregate supply shocks). The Phillips Curve shifted inward toward its original position in the 1980s. By 1989 stagflation had subsided, and the data points for the late 1990s and first half of the first decade of the 2000s were similar to those of the 1960s. The new pattern continued until 2009, when the unemployment rate jumped to 9.3 percent and the inflation rate rose on a December-to-December basis to 2.7 percent.

LO18.4 Discuss why there is no long-run trade-off between inflation and unemployment.

Although there is a short-run trade-off between inflation and unemployment, there is no long-run trade-off. Workers will adapt their expectations to new inflation realities, and when they do, the unemployment rate will return to the natural rate. So the long-run Phillips Curve is vertical at the natural rate, meaning that higher rates of inflation do not permanently "buy" the economy less unemployment.

LO18.5 Explain the relationship between tax rates, tax revenues, and aggregate supply.

Supply-side economists focus attention on government policies, such as high taxation, that impede the expansion of aggregate supply. The Laffer Curve relates tax rates to levels of tax revenue and suggests that under some circumstances, cuts in tax rates will expand the tax base (output and income) and increase tax revenues. Most economists, however, believe that the United States is currently operating in the range of the Laffer Curve where tax rates and tax revenues move in the same, not opposite, direction.

Today's economists recognize the importance of considering supply-side effects in designing optimal fiscal policy.

TERMS AND CONCEPTS

short run	stagflation	disinflation
long run	aggregate supply shocks	supply-side economics
Phillips Curve	long-run vertical Phillips Curve	Laffer Curve

The following and additional problems can be found in **connect** ECONOMICS

DISCUSSION QUESTIONS

1. Distinguish between the short run and the long run as they relate to macroeconomics. Why is the distinction important? **LO18.1**

2. Which of the following statements are true? Which are false? Explain why the false statements are untrue. **LO18.1**
   a. Short-run aggregate supply curves reflect an inverse relationship between the price level and the level of real output.
   b. The long-run aggregate supply curve assumes that nominal wages are fixed.
   c. In the long run, an increase in the price level will result in an increase in nominal wages.

3. Suppose the government misjudges the natural rate of unemployment to be much lower than it actually is, and thus undertakes expansionary fiscal and monetary policies to try to achieve the lower rate. Use the concept of the short-run Phillips Curve to explain why these policies might at first succeed. Use the concept of the long-run

Phillips Curve to explain the long-run outcome of these policies. **LO18.4**

4. What do the distinctions between short-run aggregate supply and long-run aggregate supply have in common with the distinction between the short-run Phillips Curve and the long-run Phillips Curve? Explain. **LO18.4**

5. What is the Laffer Curve, and how does it relate to supply-side economics? Why is determining the economy's location on the curve so important in assessing tax policy? **LO18.5**

6. Why might one person work more, earn more, and pay more income tax when his or her tax rate is cut, while another person will work less, earn less, and pay less income tax under the same circumstance? **LO18.5**

7. **LAST WORD** On average, does an increase in taxes raise or lower real GDP? If taxes as a percent of GDP go up 1 percent, by how much does real GDP change? Are the decreases in real GDP caused by tax increases temporary or permanent? Does the intention of a tax increase matter?

REVIEW QUESTIONS

1. Suppose the full-employment level of real output (Q) for a hypothetical economy is $250 and the price level (P) initially is 100. Use the short-run aggregate supply schedules below to answer the questions that follow: **LO18.1**

AS (P_{100})		AS (P_{125})		AS (P_{75})	
P	**Q**	**P**	**Q**	**P**	**Q**
125	$280	125	$250	125	$310
100	250	100	220	100	280
75	220	75	190	75	250

   a. What will be the level of real output in the short run if the price level unexpectedly rises from 100 to 125 because of an increase in aggregate demand? What if the price level unexpectedly falls from 100 to 75 because of a decrease in aggregate demand? Explain each situation, using numbers from the table.
   b. What will be the level of real output in the long run when the price level rises from 100 to 125? When it falls from 100 to 75? Explain each situation.
   c. Show the circumstances described in parts *a* and *b* on graph paper, and derive the long-run aggregate supply curve.

2. Suppose that AD and AS intersect at an output level that is higher than the full-employment output level. After the economy adjusts back to equilibrium in the long run, the price level will be _____. **LO18.2**
   a. Higher than it is now.
   b. Lower than it is now.
   c. The same as it is now.

3. Suppose that an economy begins in long-run equilibrium before the price level and real GDP both decline simultaneously. If those changes were caused by only one curve shifting, then those changes are best explained as the result of: **LO18.2**
   a. The AD curve shifting right.
   b. The AS curve shifting right.
   c. The AD curve shifting left.
   d. The AS curve shifting left.

4. Identify the two descriptions below as being the result of either cost-push inflation or demand-pull inflation. **LO18.2**
   a. Real GDP is below the full-employment level and prices have risen recently.
   b. Real GDP is above the full-employment level and prices have risen recently.

5. Use graphical analysis to show how each of the following would affect the economy first in the short run and then in the long run. Assume that the United States is initially operating at its full-employment level of output, that prices and wages are eventually flexible both upward and downward, and that there is no counteracting fiscal or monetary policy. **LO18.2**
   a. Because of a war abroad, the oil supply to the United States is disrupted, sending oil prices rocketing upward.
   b. Construction spending on new homes rises dramatically, greatly increasing total U.S. investment spending.
   c. Economic recession occurs abroad, significantly reducing foreign purchases of U.S. exports.

6. Between 1990 and 2009, the U.S. price level rose by about 64 percent while real output increased by about 62 percent. Use the aggregate demand–aggregate supply model to illustrate these outcomes graphically. **LO18.2**

7. Assume there is a particular short-run aggregate supply curve for an economy and the curve is relevant for several years. Use the AD-AS analysis to show graphically why higher rates of inflation over this period would be associated with lower rates of unemployment, and vice versa. What is this inverse relationship called? **LO18.3**

8. Aggregate supply shocks can cause _____ rates of inflation that are accompanied by _____ rates of unemployment. **LO18.3**
   a. Higher; higher.
   b. Higher; lower.
   c. Lower; higher.
   d. Lower; lower.

9. Suppose that firms are expecting 6 percent inflation while workers are expecting 9 percent inflation. How much of a pay raise will workers demand if their goal is to maintain the purchasing power of their incomes? **LO18.4**
   a. 3 percent.
   b. 6 percent.
   c. 9 percent.
   d. 12 percent.

10. Suppose that firms were expecting inflation to be 3 percent, but then it actually turned out to be 7 percent. Other things equal, firm profits will be: **LO18.4**
   a. Smaller than expected.
   b. Larger than expected.

PROBLEMS

1. Use the figure below to answer the following questions. Assume that the economy initially is operating at price level 120 and real output level $870. This output level is the economy's potential (or full-employment) level of output. Next, suppose that the price level rises from 120 to 130. By how much will real output increase in the short run? In the long run? Instead, now assume that the price level dropped from 120 to 110. Assuming flexible product and resource prices, by how much will real output fall in the short run? In the long run? What is the long-run level of output at each of the three price levels shown? **LO18.1**

2. **ADVANCED ANALYSIS** Suppose that the equation for a particular short-run AS curve is $P = 20 + 0.5Q$, where P is the price level and Q is real output in dollar terms. What is Q if the price level is 120? Suppose that the Q in your answer is the full-employment level of output. By how much will Q increase *in the short run* if the price level unexpectedly rises from 120 to 132? By how much will Q increase *in the long run* due to the price level increase? **LO18.1**

3. Suppose that over a 30-year period Buskerville's price level increased from 72 to 138, while its real GDP rose from $1.2 trillion to $2.1 trillion. Did economic growth occur in Buskerville? If so, by what average yearly rate in percentage terms (rounded to one decimal place)? Did Buskerville experience inflation? If so, by what average yearly rate in percentage terms (rounded to one decimal place)? Which shifted rightward faster in Buskerville: its long-run aggregate supply curve (AS_{LR}) or its aggregate demand curve (AD)? **LO18.2**

4. Suppose that for years East Confetti's short-run Phillips Curve was such that each 1 percentage point increase in its unemployment rate was associated with a 2 percentage point decline in its inflation rate. Then, during several recent years, the short-run pattern changed such that its inflation rate rose by 3 percentage points for every 1 percentage point drop in its unemployment rate. Graphically, did East Confetti's Phillips Curve shift upward or did it shift downward? **LO18.3**

Current Issues in Macro Theory and Policy

Learning Objectives

LO19.1 Describe alternative perspectives on the causes of macroeconomic instability, including the views of mainstream economists, monetarists, real-business-cycle advocates, and proponents of coordination failures.

LO19.2 Discuss why new classical economists believe the economy will "self-correct" from aggregate demand and aggregate supply shocks.

LO19.3 Identify and describe the variations of the debate over "rules" versus "discretion" in conducting stabilization policy.

LO19.4 Summarize the fundamental ideas and policy implications of mainstream macroeconomics, monetarism, and rational expectations theory.

As any academic discipline evolves, it naturally evokes a number of internal disagreements. Economics is no exception. In this chapter we examine a few alternative perspectives on macro theory and policy. We focus on the disagreements that various economists have about the answers to three interrelated questions: (1) What causes instability in the economy? (2) Is the economy self-correcting? (3) Should government adhere to *rules* or use *discretion* in setting economic policy?

What Causes Macro Instability?

LO19.1 Describe alternative perspectives on the causes of macroeconomic instability, including the views of mainstream economists, monetarists, real-business-cycle advocates, and proponents of coordination failures.

As earlier chapters have indicated, capitalist economies experienced considerable instability during the twentieth century. The United States, for example, experienced the Great Depression, numerous recessions, and periods of inflation. This instability greatly moderated between the early 1980s and 2007, but then the deep recession of 2007–2009 occurred. Economists have different perspectives about why instability like this happens.

Mainstream View

For simplicity, we will use the term "mainstream view" to characterize the prevailing macroeconomic perspective of the majority of economists. According to that view, instability in the economy arises from two sources: (1) price stickiness and (2) unexpected shocks to either aggregate demand or aggregate supply.

As we explained in detail in Chapter 18, in the long run, when both input and output prices are fully flexible and have time to adjust to any changes in aggregate demand or short-run aggregate supply, the economy will always return to producing at potential output. In the shorter run, however, stickiness in either input or output prices will mean that any shock to either aggregate demand or aggregate supply will result in changes in output and employment. Although they are not new to you, let's quickly review shocks to aggregate demand and aggregate supply.

Changes in Aggregate Demand Mainstream macroeconomics focuses on aggregate spending and its components. Recall that the basic equation underlying aggregate expenditures is

$$C_a + I_g + X_n + G = \text{GDP}$$

That is, the aggregate amount of after-tax consumption, gross investment, net exports, and government spending determines the total amount of goods and services produced and sold. In equilibrium, $C_a + I_g + X_n + G$ (aggregate expenditures) is equal to GDP (real output). A decrease in the price level increases equilibrium GDP and thus allows us to trace out a downsloping aggregate demand curve for the economy (see the appendix to Chapter 12). Any change in one of the spending components in the aggregate expenditures equation shifts the aggregate demand curve. This, in turn, changes equilibrium real output, the price level, or both.

Investment spending in particular is subject to wide "booms" and "busts." Significant increases in investment spending are multiplied into even greater increases in aggregate demand and thus can produce demand-pull inflation. In contrast, significant declines in investment spending are multiplied into even greater decreases in aggregate demand and thus can cause recessions.

Adverse Aggregate Supply Shocks In the mainstream view, the second source of macroeconomic instability arises on the supply side. Occasionally, such external events as wars or an artificial supply restriction of a key resource can boost resource prices and significantly raise per-unit production costs. The result is a sizable decline in a nation's aggregate supply, which destabilizes the economy by simultaneously causing cost-push inflation and recession.

Monetarist View

Monetarism (1) focuses on the money supply, (2) holds that markets are highly competitive, and (3) says that a competitive market system gives the economy a high degree of macroeconomic stability.

Monetarists argue that the price and wage flexibility provided by competitive markets should cause fluctuations in aggregate demand to alter product and resource prices rather than output and employment.

ORIGIN OF THE IDEA

O19.1
Monetarism

Thus, the market system would provide substantial macroeconomic stability *were it not for government interference in the economy.*

The problem, as monetarists see it, is that government has promoted downward wage inflexibility through the minimum-wage law, pro-union legislation, guaranteed prices for certain farm products, pro-business monopoly legislation, and so forth. The free-market system is capable of providing macroeconomic stability, but, despite good intentions, government interference has undermined that capability. Moreover, monetarists say that government has contributed to the economy's business cycles through its clumsy and mistaken attempts to achieve greater stability through its monetary policies.

Equation of Exchange The fundamental equation of monetarism is the **equation of exchange:**

$$MV = PQ$$

where M is the supply of money; V is the **velocity** of money, that is, the average number of times per year a dollar is spent on final goods and services; P is the price level or, more specifically, the average price at which each unit of physical output is sold; and Q is the physical volume of all goods and services produced.

The left side of the equation of exchange, MV, represents the total amount spent by purchasers of output, while the right side, PQ, represents the total amount received by sellers of that output. The nation's money supply (M) multiplied by the number of times it is spent each year (V) must equal the nation's nominal GDP (= $P \times Q$). The dollar value of total spending has to equal the dollar value of total output.

Stable Velocity Monetarists say that velocity, V, in the equation of exchange is relatively stable. To them, "stable" is not synonymous with "constant," however. Monetarists are aware that velocity has generally trended upward over the last several decades. Shorter pay periods, widespread use of credit cards, and faster means of making payments enable people to hold less money and to turn it over more rapidly than was possible in earlier times. These factors have enabled people to reduce their holdings of cash and checkbook money relative to the size of the nation's nominal GDP.

When monetarists say that velocity is stable, they mean that the factors altering velocity change gradually and predictably and that changes in velocity from one year to the next can be readily anticipated. Moreover, they hold that velocity does not change in response to changes in the money supply itself. Instead, people have a stable desire to hold money relative to holding other financial assets, holding real assets, and buying current output. The factors that determine the amount of money the public wants to hold depend mainly on the level of nominal GDP.

Example: Assume that when the level of nominal GDP is $400 billion, the public desires $100 billion of money to purchase that output. That means that V is 4 (= $400 billion of nominal GDP/$100 billion of money). If we further assume that the actual supply of money is $100 billion, the economy is in equilibrium with respect to money; the actual amount of money supplied equals the amount the public wants to hold.

If velocity is stable, the equation of exchange suggests that there is a predictable relationship between the money supply and nominal GDP (= PQ). An increase in the money supply of, say, $10 billion would upset equilibrium in our example since the public would find itself holding more money or liquidity than it wants. That is, the actual amount of money held ($110 billion) would exceed the amount of holdings desired ($100 billion). In that case, the reaction of the public (households and businesses) is to restore its desired balance of money relative to other items, such as stocks and bonds, factories and equipment, houses and automobiles, and clothing and toys. But the spending of money by individual households and businesses would leave more cash in the checkable deposits or billfolds of other households and firms. And they too would try to "spend down" their excess cash balances. But, overall, the $110 billion supply of money cannot be spent down because a dollar spent is a dollar received.

Instead, the collective attempt to reduce cash balances increases aggregate demand, thereby boosting nominal GDP. Because velocity in our example is 4—that is, the dollar is spent, on average, four times per year—nominal GDP rises from $400 billion to $440 billion. At that higher nominal GDP, the money supply of $110 billion equals the amount of money desired ($440 billion/4 = $110 billion), and equilibrium is reestablished.

The $10 billion increase in the money supply thus eventually increases nominal GDP by $40 billion. Spending on goods, services, and assets expands until nominal GDP has gone up enough to restore the original 4-to-1 equilibrium relationship between nominal GDP and the money supply.

Note that the relationship GDP/M defines V. A stable relationship between nominal GDP and M means a stable V. And a change in M causes a proportionate change in nominal GDP. Thus, monetarists say that changes in the money supply have a predictable effect on nominal GDP (= $P \times Q$). An increase in M increases P or Q, or some combination of

both; a decrease in M reduces P or Q, or some combination of both.

Monetary Causes of Instability Monetarists say that inappropriate monetary policy is the single most important cause of macroeconomic instability. An increase in the money supply directly increases aggregate demand. Under conditions of full employment, that rise in aggregate demand raises the price level. For a time, higher prices cause firms to increase their real output, and the rate of unemployment falls below its natural rate. But once nominal wages rise to reflect the higher prices and thus to restore real wages, real output moves back to its full-employment level and the unemployment rate returns to its natural rate. The inappropriate increase in the money supply leads to inflation, together with instability of real output and employment.

Conversely, a decrease in the money supply reduces aggregate demand. Real output temporarily falls, and the unemployment rate rises above its natural rate. Eventually, nominal wages fall and real output returns to its full-employment level. The inappropriate decline in the money supply leads to deflation, together with instability of real GDP and employment.

The contrast between mainstream macroeconomics and monetarism on the causes of instability thus comes into sharp focus. Mainstream economists view the instability of investment as the main cause of the economy's instability. They see monetary policy as a stabilizing factor. Changes in the money supply raise or lower interest rates as needed, smooth out swings in investment, and thus reduce macroeconomic instability. In contrast, monetarists view changes in the money supply as the main cause of instability in the economy. For example, they say that the Great Depression occurred largely because the Fed allowed the money supply to fall by roughly one-third during that period. According to Milton Friedman, a prominent monetarist,

> And [the money supply] fell not because there were no willing borrowers—not because the horse would not drink. It fell because the Federal Reserve System forced or permitted a sharp reduction in the [money supply], because it failed to exercise the responsibilities assigned to it in the Federal Reserve Act to provide liquidity to the banking system. The Great Contraction is tragic testimony to the power of monetary policy—not, as Keynes and so many of his contemporaries believed, evidence of its impotence.[1]

Real-Business-Cycle View

A third modern view of the cause of macroeconomic instability is that business cycles are caused by real factors that affect aggregate supply rather than by monetary, or spending, factors that cause fluctuations in aggregate demand. In the **real-business-cycle theory**, business fluctuations result from significant changes in technology and resource availability. Those changes affect productivity and thus the long-run growth trend of aggregate supply.

An example focusing on recession will clarify this thinking. Suppose productivity (output per worker) declines sharply because of a large increase in oil prices, which makes it prohibitively expensive to operate certain

[1]Milton Friedman, *The Optimum Quantity of Money and Other Essays* (Chicago: Aldine, 1969), p. 97.

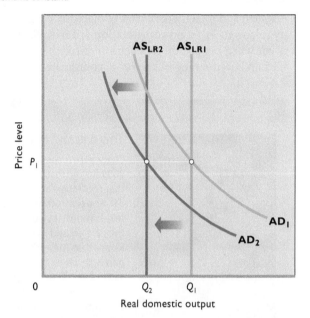

FIGURE 19.1   The real-business-cycle theory. In the real-business-cycle theory, a decline in resource availability shifts the nation's long-run aggregate supply curve to the left from AS_{LR1} to AS_{LR2}. The decline in real output from Q_1 to Q_2, in turn, reduces money demand (less is needed) and money supply (fewer loans are taken out) such that aggregate demand shifts leftward from AD_1 to AD_2. The result is a recession in which the price level remains constant.

types of machinery. That decline in productivity implies a reduction in the economy's ability to produce real output. The result would be a decrease in the economy's long-run aggregate supply curve, as represented by the leftward shift from AS_{LR1} to AS_{LR2} in Figure 19.1.

As real output falls from Q_1 to Q_2, the public needs less money to buy the reduced volume of goods and services. So the demand for money falls. Moreover, the slowdown in business activity means that businesses need to borrow less from banks, reducing the part of the money supply created by banks through their lending. Thus, the supply of money also falls. In this controversial scenario, changes in the supply of money respond to changes in the demand for money. The decline in the money supply then reduces aggregate demand, as from AD_1 to AD_2 in Figure 19.1. The outcome is a decline in real output from Q_1 to Q_2, with no change in the price level.

Conversely, a large increase in aggregate supply (not shown) caused by, say, major innovations in the production process would shift the long-run aggregate supply curve rightward. Real output would increase, and money demand and money supply would both increase. Aggregate demand would shift rightward by an amount equal to the rightward shift of long-run aggregate supply. Real output would increase, without driving up the price level.

Conclusion: In the real-business-cycle theory, macro instability arises on the aggregate supply side of the economy, not on the aggregate demand side as mainstream economists and monetarists usually claim.

Coordination Failures

A fourth and final modern view of macroeconomic instability relates to so-called **coordination failures.** Such failures occur when people fail to reach a mutually beneficial equilibrium because they lack a way to coordinate their actions.

Too Much Money?

The severe recession of 2007–2009 fits the mainstream view that recessions are caused by AD shocks rather than the real-business-cycle view that they are caused by AS shocks. Recall that the recession began with a financial crisis that caused significant reductions in investment spending and consumption spending and therefore reduced aggregate demand. As inventories increased, businesses further curtailed their investment spending, and aggregate demand, output, and income dropped even more.

Economists with monetarist leanings, however, cite monetary factors as the main cause of the financial crisis that led to the initial declines in aggregate demand. They argue that the Federal Reserve flooded the economy with too much money and held interest rates too low for too long in promoting recovery from the 2001 recession. In this line of reasoning, the excess money and low interest rates contributed to the bubble in the housing market. When that bubble burst, the resulting loan defaults set in motion the forces that produced the declines in AD and therefore the recession.

All economists agree that the bursting of the housing bubble led to the recession. And too-loose monetary policy may have contributed to the bubble. But economists also cite the role of the very large international flows of foreign savings into the United States during this period. These inflows drove down interest rates and helped to fuel the housing bubble. Other factors such as "pass-the-risk" lending practices, government policies promoting home ownership, and poorly designed and enforced financial regulations certainly came into play. The mainstream view is that causes of the financial crisis and recession are numerous and complex.

Noneconomic Example Consider first a noneconomic example. Suppose you hear that some people might be getting together at the last minute for an informal party at a nearby beach. But because of a chance of rain, there is some doubt about whether people will actually come out. You make a cell phone call or two to try to get a read on what others are thinking, and then base your decision on that limited information. If you expect others to be there, you will decide to go. If you expect that no one will go, you will decide to stay home. There are several possible equilibrium outcomes, depending on the mix of people's expectations. Let's consider just two. If each person assumes that all the others will go to the party, all will go. The party will occur and presumably everyone will have a good time. But if each person assumes that everyone else will stay home, all will stay home and there will be no party. When the party does not take place, even though all would be better off if it did take place, a coordination failure has occurred.

Macroeconomic Example Now let's apply this example to macroeconomic instability, specifically recession. Suppose that individual firms and households expect other firms and consumers to cut back their investment and consumption spending. As a result, each firm and household will anticipate a reduction of aggregate demand. Firms therefore will reduce their own investment spending since they will anticipate that their future production capacity will be excessive. Households will also reduce their own spending (increase their saving) because they anticipate that they will experience reduced work hours, possible layoffs, and falling incomes in the future.

Aggregate demand will indeed decline and the economy will indeed experience a recession in response to what amounts to a self-fulfilling prophecy. Moreover, the economy will stay at a below-full-employment level of output because, once there, producers and households have no individual incentive to increase spending. If all producers and households would agree to increase their investment and consumption spending simultaneously, then aggregate demand would rise, and real output and real income would increase. Each producer and each consumer would be better off. However, this outcome does not occur because there is no mechanism for firms and households to agree on such a joint spending increase.

In this case, the economy is stuck in an *unemployment equilibrium* because of a coordination failure. With a different set of expectations, a coordination failure might leave the economy in an *inflation equilibrium*. In this view, the economy has a number of such potential equilibrium positions, some good and some bad, depending on people's mix of expectations. Macroeconomic instability, then, reflects the movement of the economy from one such equilibrium position to another as expectations change.

Does the Economy "Self-Correct"?

LO19.2 Discuss why new classical economists believe the economy will "self-correct" from aggregate demand and aggregate supply shocks.

Just as there are disputes over the causes of macroeconomic instability, there are disputes over whether or not the economy will correct itself when instability does occur. And economists also disagree on how long it will take for any such self-correction to take place.

New Classical View of Self-Correction

New classical economists tend to be either monetarists or adherents of **rational expectations theory:** the idea that businesses, consumers, and workers expect changes in policies or circumstances to have certain effects on the economy and, in pursuing their own self-interest, take actions to make sure those changes affect them as little as possible. The **new classical economics** holds that when the economy occasionally diverges from its full-employment output, internal mechanisms within the economy will automatically move it back to that output. Policymakers should stand back and let the automatic correction occur, rather than engage in active fiscal and monetary policy. This perspective is often associated with the vertical long-run Phillips Curve, which we discussed in Chapter 18. But we will analyze it here using the extended AD-AS model that was also developed in Chapter 18.

ORIGIN OF THE IDEA

O19.3
Rational expectations theory

Graphical Analysis Figure 19.2a relates the new classical analysis to the question of self-correction. Specifically, an increase in aggregate demand, say, from AD₁ to AD₂, moves

FIGURE 19.2 New classical view of self-correction. (a) An unanticipated increase in aggregate demand from AD₁ to AD₂ first moves the economy from *a* to *b*. The economy then self-corrects to *c*. An anticipated increase in aggregate demand moves the economy directly from *a* to *c*. (b) An unanticipated decrease in aggregate demand from AD₁ to AD₃ moves the economy from *a* to *d*. The economy then self-corrects to *e*. An anticipated decrease in aggregate demand moves the economy directly from *a* to *e*. (Mainstream economists, however, say that if the price level remains at P₁, the economy will move from *a* to *f*, and even if the price level falls to P₄, the economy may remain at *d* because of downward wage inflexibility.)

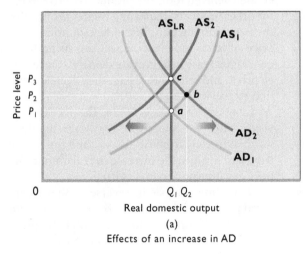

(a)

Effects of an increase in AD

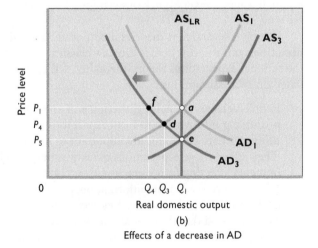

(b)

Effects of a decrease in AD

the economy upward along its short-run aggregate supply curve AS$_1$ from a to b. The price level rises and real output increases. With the economy producing beyond potential output, high resource demand drives up the prices of labor and other productive inputs. Per-unit production costs increase and the short-run aggregate supply curve shifts leftward, eventually from AS$_1$ to AS$_2$. The economy moves from b to c, and real output returns to its full-employment level, Q_1. This level of output is dictated by the economy's vertical long-run aggregate supply curve, AS$_{LR}$.

Conversely, a decrease in aggregate demand from AD$_1$ to AD$_3$ in Figure 19.2b first moves the economy downward along its short-run aggregate supply curve AS$_1$ from point a to d. The price level declines, as does the level of real output. With the economy producing below potential output, low resource demand drives down the prices of labor and other productive inputs. When that happens, per-unit production costs decline and the short-run aggregate supply curve shifts to the right, eventually from AS$_1$ to AS$_3$. The economy moves to e, where it again achieves its full-employment level, Q_1. As in Figure 19.2a, the economy in Figure 19.2b has automatically self-corrected to its full-employment output and its natural rate of unemployment.

Speed of Adjustment

There is some disagreement among new classical economists on how long it will take for self-correction to occur. Monetarists usually hold the *adaptive expectations* view that people form their expectations on the basis of present realities and only gradually change their expectations as experience unfolds. This means that the shifts in the short-run aggregate supply curves shown in Figure 19.2 may not occur for 2 or 3 years or even longer. Other new classical economists, however, accept the rational expectations assumption that workers anticipate some future outcomes before they occur. When price-level changes are fully anticipated, adjustments of nominal wages are very quick or even instantaneous. Let's see why.

Although several new theories incorporate rational expectations, our interest here is the new classical version of the rational expectations theory (hereafter, RET). RET is based on two assumptions:

- People behave rationally, gathering and intelligently processing information to form expectations about things that are economically important to them. They adjust those expectations quickly as new developments affecting future economic outcomes occur. Where there is adequate information, people's beliefs about future economic outcomes accurately reflect the likelihood that those outcomes will occur. For example, if it is clear that a certain policy will cause

inflation, people will recognize that fact and adjust their economic behavior in anticipation of inflation.

- RET economists assume that all product and resource markets are highly competitive and that prices and wages are flexible both upward and downward. But the RET economists go further, assuming that new information is quickly (in some cases, instantaneously) taken into account in the demand and supply curves of such markets. The upshot is that equilibrium prices and quantities adjust rapidly to unforeseen events—say, technological change or aggregate supply shocks. They adjust instantaneously to events that have known outcomes—for example, changes in fiscal or monetary policy.

Unanticipated Price-Level Changes The implication of RET is not only that the economy is self-correcting but that self-correction occurs quickly. In this thinking, unanticipated changes in the price level—so-called **price-level surprises**—*do* cause temporary changes in real output. Suppose, for example, that an unanticipated increase in foreign demand for U.S. goods increases U.S. aggregate demand from AD$_1$ to AD$_2$ in Figure 19.2a. The immediate result is an unexpected increase in the price level from P_1 to P_2.

But now an interesting question arises. If wages and prices are flexible, as assumed in RET, why doesn't the higher price level immediately cause wages and other input prices to rise, such that there is no increase in real output at all? Why does the economy temporarily move from point a to b along AS$_1$? In RET, firms increase output from Q_1 to Q_2 because of misperceptions about rising prices of their own products relative to the prices of other products (and to the prices of labor). They mistakenly think the higher prices of their own products have resulted from increased demand for those products relative to the demands for other products. Expecting higher profits, they increase their own production. But in fact *all* prices, including the price of labor (nominal wages), are rising because of the general increase in aggregate demand. Once firms see that *all* prices and wages are rising, they decrease their production to previous levels.

In terms of Figure 19.2a, the increase in nominal wages shifts the short-run aggregate supply curve leftward, ultimately from AS$_1$ to AS$_2$, and the economy moves from b to c. Thus, the increase in real output caused by the price-level surprise corrects itself.

The same analysis in reverse applies to an unanticipated price-level decrease. In the economy represented by Figure 19.2b, firms misperceive that the prices of their own products are falling due to decreases in the demand for those products relative to other products. They incorrectly anticipate declines in profit and cut production. As a result of their collective actions, real output in the economy falls. Once firms see what is really happening—that *all* prices and wages are dropping—they increase their output to prior levels. The short-run aggregate supply curve in Figure 19.2b shifts rightward from AS_1 to AS_3, and the economy "self-corrects" by moving from *d* to *e*.

Fully Anticipated Price-Level Changes In RET, fully *anticipated* price-level changes do not change real output, even for short periods. In Figure 19.2a, again consider the increase in aggregate demand from AD_1 to AD_2. Businesses immediately recognize that the higher prices being paid for their products are part of the inflation they had anticipated. They understand that the same forces that are causing the inflation result in higher nominal wages, leaving their profits unchanged. The economy therefore moves directly from *a* to *c*. The price level rises as expected, and output remains at its full-employment level Q_1.

Similarly, a fully *anticipated* price-level decrease will leave real output unchanged. Firms conclude that nominal wages are declining by the same percentage amount as the declining price level, leaving profits unchanged. The economy represented by Figure 19.2b therefore moves directly from *a* to *e*. Deflation occurs, but the economy continues to produce its full-employment output Q_1. The anticipated decline in aggregate demand causes no change in real output.

Mainstream View of Self-Correction

Almost all economists acknowledge that the new classical economists have made significant contributions to the theory of aggregate supply. In fact, mainstream economists have incorporated some aspects of RET into their own models. However, most economists strongly disagree with RET on the question of downward price and wage flexibility. While the stock market, foreign exchange market, and certain commodity markets experience day-to-day or minute-to-minute price changes, including price declines, that is not true of many product markets and most labor markets. There is ample evidence, say mainstream economists, that many prices and wages are inflexible downward for long periods. As a result, it may take years for the economy to move from recession back to full-employment output, unless it gets help from fiscal and monetary policy.

Graphical Analysis To understand this mainstream view, again examine Figure 19.2b. Suppose aggregate demand declines from AD_1 to AD_3 because of a significant decline in investment spending. If prices are sticky downward for a while and therefore the price level is temporarily stuck at P_1, the economy will not move from *a* to *d* to *e*, as suggested by RET. Instead, the economy will move from *a* to *f*, as if it were moving along the white horizontal P_1 price line between those two points. Real output will decline from its full-employment level, Q_1, to the recessionary level, Q_4.

But let's assume that large amounts of unsold inventories eventually cause the price level to fall to P_4. Will this lead to the decline in nominal wages needed to shift aggregate supply from AS_1 to AS_3, as suggested by the new classical economists? "Highly unlikely" say mainstream economists. Even more so than prices, nominal wages tend to be inflexible downward. If nominal wages do not decline in response to the decline in the price level, then the short-run aggregate supply curve will not shift rightward. The self-correction mechanism assumed by RET and new classical economists will break down. Instead, the economy will remain at *d*, experiencing less-than-full-employment output and a high rate of unemployment.

Downward Wage Inflexibility In Chapter 12 we discussed several reasons why firms may not be able to, or may not want to, lower nominal wages. Firms may not be able to cut wages because of wage contracts and the legal minimum wage. And firms may not want to lower wages if they fear potential problems with morale, effort, and efficiency.

While contracts are thought to be the main cause of wage rigidity, so-called efficiency wages and insider-outsider relationships also may play a role. Let's explore both.

Efficiency Wage Theory Recall from Chapter 12 that an **efficiency wage** is a wage that minimizes the firm's labor cost per unit of output. Normally, we would think that the market wage is the efficiency wage since it is the lowest wage at which a firm can obtain a particular type of labor. But where the cost of supervising workers is high or where worker turnover is great, firms may discover that paying a wage that is higher than the market wage will lower their wage cost per unit of output.

Example: Suppose a firm's workers, on average, produce 8 units of output at a $9 market wage but 10 units of output at a $10 above-market wage. The efficiency wage is $10, not the $9 market wage. At the $10 wage, the labor cost per unit of output is only $1 (= $10 wage/10 units of output), compared with $1.12 (= $9 wage/8 units of output) at the $9 wage.

How can a higher wage result in greater efficiency?

- *Greater work effort* The above-market wage, in effect, raises the cost to workers of losing their jobs as a result of poor performance. Because workers have a strong incentive to retain their relatively high-paying jobs, they are more likely to provide greater work effort. Looked at differently, workers are more reluctant to shirk (neglect or avoid work) because the higher wage makes job loss more costly to them. Consequently, the above-market wage can be the efficient wage; it can enhance worker productivity so much that the higher wage more than pays for itself.

- *Lower supervision costs* With less incentive among workers to shirk, the firm needs fewer supervisory personnel to monitor work performance. This, too, can lower the firm's overall wage cost per unit of output.

- *Reduced job turnover* The above-market pay discourages workers from voluntarily leaving their jobs. The lower turnover rate reduces the firm's cost of hiring and training workers. It also gives the firm a more experienced, more productive workforce.

The key implication for macroeconomic instability is that efficiency wages add to the downward inflexibility of wages. Firms that pay efficiency wages will be reluctant to cut wages when aggregate demand declines, since such cuts may encourage shirking, require more supervisory personnel, and increase turnover. In other words, wage cuts that reduce productivity and raise per-unit labor costs are self-defeating.

ORIGIN OF THE IDEA

O19.4
Efficiency wages

Insider-Outsider Relationships

Other economists theorize that downward wage inflexibility may relate to relationships between "insiders" and "outsiders." Insiders are workers who retain employment even during recession. Outsiders are workers who have been laid off from a firm and unemployed workers who would like to work at that firm.

When recession produces layoffs and widespread unemployment, we might expect outsiders to offer to work for less than the current wage rate, in effect, bidding down wage rates. We also might expect firms to hire such workers to reduce their costs. But, according to the **insider-outsider theory**, outsiders may not be able to underbid existing wages because employers may view the nonwage cost of hiring them to be prohibitive. Employers might fear that insiders would view acceptance of such underbidding as undermining years of effort to increase wages or, worse, as "stealing" jobs. So insiders may refuse to cooperate with new workers who have undercut their pay.

Where teamwork is critical for production, such lack of cooperation will reduce overall productivity and thereby lower the firms' profits.

Even if firms are willing to employ outsiders at less than the current wage, those workers might refuse to work for less than the existing wage. To do so might invite harassment from the insiders whose pay they have undercut. Thus, outsiders may remain unemployed, relying on past saving, unemployment compensation, and other social programs to make ends meet.

As in the efficiency wage theory, the insider-outsider theory implies that wages will be inflexible downward when aggregate demand declines. Self-correction may eventually occur but not nearly as rapidly as the new classical economists contend.

QUICK REVIEW 19.2

- New classical economists believe that the economy "self-corrects" when unanticipated events divert it from its full-employment level of real output.

- In RET, unanticipated price-level changes cause changes in real output in the short run but not in the long run.

- According to RET, market participants immediately change their actions in response to anticipated price-level changes such that no change in real output occurs.

- Mainstream economists say that the economy can get mired in recession for several months or more because of downward price and wage inflexibility.

- Sources of downward wage inflexibility include contracts, efficiency wages, and insider-outsider relationships.

Rules or Discretion?

LO19.3 Identify and describe the variations of the debate over "rules" versus "discretion" in conducting stabilization policy.

These different views on the causes of instability and on the speed of self-correction have led to vigorous debate on macro policy. Should the government adhere to policy rules that prohibit it from causing instability in an economy that is otherwise stable? Or should it use discretionary fiscal and monetary policy, when needed, to stabilize a sometimes-unstable economy?

In Support of Policy Rules

Monetarists and other new classical economists believe policy rules would reduce instability in the economy. They believe that such rules would prevent government from trying

CONSIDER THIS ...

On the Road Again

Economist Abba Lerner (1903–1982) likened the economy to an automobile traveling down a road that had traffic barriers on each side. The problem was that the car had no steering wheel. It would hit one barrier, causing the car to veer to the opposite side of the road. There it would hit the other barrier, which in turn would send it careening to the opposite side. To avoid such careening in the form of business cycles, said Lerner, society must equip the economy with a steering wheel. Discretionary fiscal and monetary policy would enable government to steer the economy safely between the problems of recession and demand-pull inflation.

Economist Milton Friedman (1912–2006) modified Lerner's analogy, giving it a different meaning. He said that the economic vehicle does not need a skillful driver who is continuously turning the wheel to adjust to the unexpected irregularities of the route. Instead, the economy needs a way to prohibit the monetary passenger in the back seat from occasionally leaning over and giving the steering wheel a jerk that sends the car off the road. According to Friedman, the car will travel down the road just fine unless the Federal Reserve destabilizes it.

Lerner's analogy implied an internally unstable economy that needs steering through discretionary government stabilization policy. Friedman's modification of the analogy implied a generally stable economy that is destabilized by inappropriate monetary policy by the Federal Reserve. For Lerner, stability required active use of fiscal and monetary policy. For Friedman, macroeconomic stability required a monetary rule forcing the Federal Reserve to increase the money supply at a set, steady annual rate.*

_____

*In his later years, Friedman softened his call for a monetary rule, acknowledging that the Fed had become much more skillful at keeping the rate of inflation in check through prudent monetary policy.

to "manage" aggregate demand. That would be a desirable trend because, in their view, such management is misguided and thus is likely to *cause* more instability than it cures.

Monetary Rule

Since inappropriate monetary policy is the major source of macroeconomic instability, say monetarists, the enactment of a **monetary rule** would make sense.

FIGURE 19.3 Rationale for a monetary rule. A monetary rule that required the Fed to increase the money supply at an annual rate linked to the long-run increase in potential GDP would shift aggregate demand rightward, as from AD_1 to AD_2, at the same pace as the shift in long-run aggregate supply, here, AS_{LR1} to AS_{LR2}. Thus the economy would experience growth without inflation or deflation.

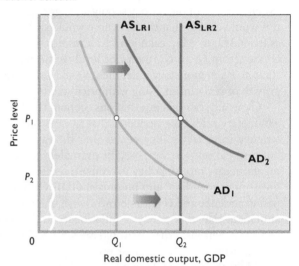

One such rule would be a requirement that the Fed expand the money supply each year at the same annual rate as the typical growth of the economy's production capacity. That fixed-rate expansion of the money supply would occur whatever the state of the economy. The Fed's sole monetary role would be to use its tools (open-market operations, the discount rate, interest on reserves, and reserve requirements) to ensure that the nation's money supply grew steadily by, say, 3 to 5 percent a year. According to Milton Friedman,

> Such a rule . . . would eliminate . . . the major cause of instability in the economy—the capricious and unpredictable impact of countercyclical monetary policy. As long as the money supply grows at a constant rate each year, be it 3, 4, or 5 percent, any decline into recession will be temporary. The liquidity provided by a constantly growing money supply will cause aggregate demand to expand. Similarly, if the supply of money does not rise at a more than average rate, any inflationary increase in spending will burn itself out for lack of fuel.[2]

Figure 19.3 illustrates the rationale for a monetary rule. Suppose the economy represented there is operating at its full-employment real output, Q_1. Also suppose the nation's long-run aggregate supply curve shifts rightward, as from AS_{LR1} to AS_{LR2}, each year, signifying the average annual increase in potential real output. As you saw in earlier chapters, such annual increases in "potential GDP"

_____

[2]As quoted in Lawrence S. Ritter and William L. Silber, *Money*, 5th ed. (New York: Basic Books, 1984), pp. 141–142.

result from added resources, improved resources, and improved technology.

Monetarists argue that a monetary rule would tie increases in the money supply to the typical rightward shift of long-run aggregate supply. In view of the direct link between changes in the money supply and aggregate demand, this would ensure that the AD curve would shift rightward, as from AD_1 to AD_2, each year. As a result, while GDP increases from Q_1 to Q_2, the price level would remain constant at P_1. A monetary rule, then, would promote steady growth of real output along with price stability.

Generally, rational expectations economists also support a monetary rule. They conclude that an expansionary or restrictive monetary policy would alter the rate of inflation but not real output. Suppose, for example, the Fed implements an easy money policy to reduce interest rates, expand investment spending, and boost real GDP. On the basis of past experience and economic knowledge, the public would anticipate that this policy is inflationary and would take protective actions. Workers would press for higher nominal wages; firms would raise their product prices; and lenders would lift their nominal interest rates on loans.

All these responses are designed to prevent inflation from having adverse effects on the real income of workers, businesses, and lenders. But collectively they would immediately raise wage and price levels. So the increase in aggregate demand brought about by the expansionary monetary policy would be completely dissipated in higher prices and wages. Real output and employment would not be increased by the easy money policy.

In this view, the combination of rational expectations and instantaneous market adjustments dooms discretionary monetary policy to ineffectiveness. If discretionary monetary policy produces only inflation (or deflation), say the RET economists, then it makes sense to limit the Fed's discretion and to require that Congress enact a monetary rule consistent with price stability at all times.

In recent decades, the call for a Friedman-type monetary rule has faded. Some economists who tend to favor monetary rules have advocated **inflation targeting**, under which the Fed would be required to announce a targeted band of inflation rates, say, 1 to 2 percent, for some future period such as the following 2 years. It would then be expected to use its monetary policy tools to keep inflation rates within that range. If it did not hit the inflation target, it would have to explain why it failed.

Strictly interpreted, inflation targeting would focus the Fed's attention nearly exclusively on controlling inflation and deflation, rather than on counteracting business fluctuations. Proponents of inflation targeting generally believe the economy will have fewer, shorter, and less severe business cycles if the Fed adheres to the rule "Set a known inflation goal and achieve it."

We discussed another modern monetary rule—the Taylor rule—in Chapter 16 on monetary policy. This rule specifies how the Fed should alter the federal funds rate under differing economic circumstances. We discuss this rule in more depth in this chapter's Last Word.

Balanced Budget Monetarists and new classical economists question the effectiveness of fiscal policy. At the extreme, a few of them favor a constitutional amendment requiring that the federal government balance its budget annually. Others simply suggest that government be "passive" in its fiscal policy, not intentionally creating budget deficits or surpluses. They believe that deficits and surpluses caused by recession or inflationary expansion will eventually correct themselves as the economy self-corrects to its full-employment output.

Monetarists are particularly strong in their opposition to expansionary fiscal policy. They believe that the deficit spending accompanying such a policy has a strong tendency to "crowd out" private investment. Suppose government runs a budget deficit by printing and selling U.S. securities—that is, by borrowing from the public. By engaging in such borrowing, the government is competing with private businesses for funds. The borrowing increases the demand for money, which then raises the interest rate and crowds out a substantial amount of private investment that would otherwise have been profitable. The net effect of a budget deficit on aggregate demand therefore is unpredictable and, at best, modest.

RET economists reject discretionary fiscal policy for the same reason they reject active monetary policy: They don't think it works. Business and labor will immediately adjust their behavior in anticipation of the price-level effects of a change in fiscal policy. The economy will move directly to the anticipated new price level. Like monetary policy, say the RET theorists, fiscal policy can move the economy along its vertical long-run aggregate supply curve. But because its effects on inflation are fully anticipated, fiscal policy cannot alter real GDP even in the short run. The best course of action for government is to balance its budget.

In Defense of Discretionary Stabilization Policy

Mainstream economists oppose both a strict monetary rule and a balanced-budget requirement. They believe that monetary policy and fiscal policy are important tools for achieving and maintaining full employment, price stability, and economic growth.

Discretionary Monetary Policy In supporting discretionary monetary policy, mainstream economists argue that the rationale for the Friedman monetary rule is flawed. While there is indeed a close relationship between the money supply and nominal GDP over long periods, in shorter periods this relationship breaks down. The reason is that the velocity of money has proved to be more variable and unpredictable than monetarists contend. Arguing that velocity is variable both cyclically and over time, mainstream economists contend that a constant annual rate of increase in the money supply might not eliminate fluctuations in aggregate demand. In terms of the equation of exchange, a steady rise of M does not guarantee a steady expansion of aggregate demand because V—the rate at which money is spent—can change.

Look again at Figure 19.3, in which we demonstrated the monetary rule: Expand the money supply annually by a fixed percentage, regardless of the state of the economy. During the period in question, optimistic business expectations might create a boom in investment spending and thus shift the aggregate demand curve to some location to the right of AD_2. (You may want to pencil in a new AD curve, labeling it AD_3.) The price level would then rise above P_1; that is, demand-pull inflation would occur. In this case, the monetary rule will not accomplish its goal of maintaining price stability. Mainstream economists say that the Fed can use a restrictive monetary policy to reduce the excessive investment spending and thereby hold the rightward shift of aggregate demand to AD_2, thus avoiding inflation.

Similarly, suppose instead that investment declines because of pessimistic business expectations. Aggregate demand will then increase by some amount less than the increase from AD_1 to AD_2 in Figure 19.3. Again, the monetary rule fails the stability test: The price level sinks below P_1 (deflation occurs). Or if the price level is inflexible downward at P_1, the economy will not achieve its full-employment output (unemployment rises). An expansionary monetary policy can help avoid each outcome.

Mainstream economists quip that the trouble with the monetary rule is that it tells the policymaker, "Don't do something; just stand there."

Discretionary Fiscal Policy Mainstream economists support the use of fiscal policy to keep recessions from deepening or to keep mild inflation from becoming severe inflation. They recognize the possibility of crowding out but do not think it is a serious problem when business borrowing is depressed, as is usually the case in recession. Because politicians can abuse fiscal policy, most economists feel that it should be held in reserve for situations where monetary policy appears to be ineffective or working too slowly.

As indicated earlier, mainstream economists oppose requirements to balance the budget annually. Tax revenues fall sharply during recessions and rise briskly during periods of demand-pull inflation. Therefore, a law or a constitutional amendment mandating an annually balanced budget would require that the government increase tax rates and reduce government spending during recession and reduce tax rates and increase government spending during economic booms. The first set of actions would worsen recession, and the second set would fuel inflation.

Policy Successes

Finally, mainstream economists point out several specific policy successes in the past four decades:

- A tight money policy dropped inflation from 13.5 percent in 1980 to 3.2 percent in 1983.

- An expansionary fiscal policy reduced the unemployment rate from 9.7 percent in 1982 to 5.5 percent in 1988.

- An easy money policy helped the economy recover from the 1990–1991 recession.

- Judicious tightening of monetary policy in the mid-1990s, and then again in the late 1990s, helped the economy remain on a noninflationary, full-employment growth path.

- In late 2001 and 2002, expansionary fiscal and monetary policy helped the economy recover from a series of economic blows, including the collapse of numerous Internet start-up firms; a severe decline in investment spending; the impacts of the terrorist attacks of September 11, 2001; and a precipitous decline in stock values.

- In 2004 and 2005 the Fed tempered continued expansionary fiscal policy by increasing the federal funds rate in $\frac{1}{4}$ percentage-point increments from 1 percent to 4.25 percent. The economy expanded briskly in those years, while inflation stayed in check. The mild inflation was particularly impressive because the average price of a barrel of crude oil rose from \$24 in 2002 to \$55 in 2005. The Fed's further increases in interest rates to 5.25 percent in 2006 also kept inflation mild that year and the next despite continued strong growth and oil reaching \$99 per barrel in late 2007.

- In 2007 the Fed vigorously responded to a crisis in the mortgage market by ensuring monetary liquidity

The Taylor Rule: Could a Robot Replace Ben Bernanke?

Macroeconomist John Taylor of Stanford University Calls for a New Monetary Rule That Would Institutionalize Appropriate Fed Policy Responses to Changes in Real Output and Inflation.

In our discussion of rules versus discretion, "rules" were associated with a *passive* monetary policy—one in which the monetary rule required that the Fed expand the money supply at a fixed annual rate regardless of the state of the economy. "Discretion," on the other hand, was associated with an *active* monetary policy in which the Fed changed interest rates in response to actual or anticipated changes in the economy.

Economist John Taylor has put a new twist on the rules-versus-discretion debate by suggesting a hybrid policy rule that dictates the precise active monetary actions the Fed should take when changes in the economy occur. You first encountered this Taylor rule in our discussion of monetary policy in Chapter 16. The **Taylor rule** combines traditional monetarism, with its emphasis on a monetary rule, and the more mainstream view that active monetary policy is a useful tool for taming inflation and limiting recession. Unlike the Friedman monetary rule, the Taylor rule holds, for example, that monetary policy should respond to changes in both real GDP and inflation, not simply inflation. The key adjustment instrument is the interest rate, not the money supply.

The Taylor rule builds on the belief held by many economists that central banks are willing to tolerate a small positive rate of inflation if doing so will help the economy to produce at potential output. The Taylor rule assumes that the Fed has a 2 percent "target rate of inflation" that it is willing to tolerate and that the Fed follows three rules when setting its target for the federal funds rate (the rate of interest that commercial banks with excess reserves charge on overnight loans to banks that wish to borrow reserves in order to meet their reserve requirements). The three rules are:

- When real GDP equals potential GDP and inflation is at its target rate of 2 percent, the federal funds target rate should be 4 percent, implying a *real* federal funds rate of 2 percent (= 4 percent nominal federal funds rate *minus* 2 percent inflation rate).

- For each 1 percent increase of real GDP above potential GDP, the Fed should raise the *real* federal funds rate by $\frac{1}{2}$ percentage point.

- For each 1 percent increase in the inflation rate above its 2 percent target rate, the Fed should raise the *real* federal funds rate by $\frac{1}{2}$ percentage point.*

*John Taylor, *Inflation, Unemployment, and Monetary Policy* (Cambridge, Mass.: MIT Press, 1998), pp. 44–47.

Taylor has neither suggested nor implied that a robot, programmed with the Taylor rule, should replace Ben Bernanke, chairman of the Federal Reserve System. The Fed's discretion to override the rule (or "contingency plan for policy") would be retained, but the Fed would have to explain why its policies diverged from the rule. So the rule would remove the "mystery" associated with monetary policy and increase the Fed's accountability. Also, says Taylor, if used consistently, the rule would enable market participants to predict Fed behavior, and this would increase Fed credibility and reduce uncertainty.

Critics of the Taylor rule acknowledge that it is closer in tune with actual Fed countercyclical policy than is the Friedman monetary rule. They also acknowledge that adherence to the Taylor rule would have raised interest rates more rapidly during the two years prior to the mortgage debt crisis of 2007. Those higher interest rates might have reduced the excessive mortgage borrowing that eventually led to the crisis. But critics of the Taylor rule say that it is unwise to limit the Fed's future discretion in adjusting interest rates as it deems necessary. They note that the Fed has successfully kept inflation in check over the past two decades and has used monetary policy creatively and decisively when necessary during financial and economic emergencies. In view of the overall success, critics conclude that a mechanical monetary rule is certainly unnecessary and might even be detrimental.

in the banking system. Besides aggressively lowering the federal funds rate from 5.25 percent in the summer of 2007 to just 2 percent in April 2008, the Fed greatly increased the reserves of the banking system by creating and using its term auction facility. It also undertook other lender-of-last-resort actions to unfreeze credit and prevent a possible collapse of the entire financial system. During the severe recession of 2007–2009, the Fed lowered the federal funds rate further, holding it in the 0 to 0.25 percent range to break the downward slide of the economy and help promote economic recovery.

QUICK REVIEW 19.3

- Mainstream economists disagree with monetarist and rational expectations economists as to whether the Fed should use rules or utilize discretion.
- Monetarist and rational expectations economists oppose discretion because they believe that discretion adds more instability to the business cycle than it cures.
- Mainstream economists oppose strict monetary rules and defend both monetary and fiscal policy discretion because they believe that both theory and evidence suggest that discretionary policies are helpful in achieving full employment, price stability, and economic growth.

Summary of Alternative Views

LO19.4 Summarize the fundamental ideas and policy implications of mainstream macroeconomics, monetarism, and rational expectations theory.

In Table 19.1 we summarize the fundamental ideas and policy implications of three macroeconomic theories: mainstream macroeconomics, monetarism, and rational expectations theory. Note that we have broadly defined new classical economics to include both monetarism and the rational expectations theory since both adhere to the view that the economy tends automatically to achieve equilibrium at its full-employment output.

These different perspectives have obliged mainstream economists to rethink some of their fundamental principles and to revise many of their positions. Although considerable disagreement remains, mainstream macroeconomists agree with monetarists that "money matters" and that excessive growth of the money supply is the major cause of long-lasting, rapid inflation. They also agree with RET proponents and theorists of coordination failures that expectations matter. If government can create expectations of price stability, full employment, and economic growth, households and firms will tend to act in ways to make them happen. In short, thanks to ongoing challenges to conventional wisdom, macroeconomics continues to evolve.

TABLE 19.1 Summary of Alternative Macroeconomic Views

Issue	Mainstream Macroeconomics	New Classical Economics	
		Monetarism	Rational Expectations
View of the private economy	Potentially unstable	Stable in long run at natural rate of unemployment	Stable in long run at natural rate of unemployment
Cause of the observed instability of the private economy	Investment plans unequal to saving plans (changes in AD); AS shocks	Inappropriate monetary policy	Unanticipated AD and AS shocks in the short run
Assumptions about short-run price and wage stickiness	Both prices and wages stuck in the immediate short run; in the short run, wages sticky while prices inflexible downward but flexible upward	Prices flexible upward and downward in the short run; wages sticky in the short run	Prices and wages flexible both upward and downward in the short run
Appropriate macro policies	Active fiscal and monetary policy	Monetary rule	Monetary rule
How changes in the money supply affect the economy	By changing the interest rate, which changes investment and real GDP	By directly changing AD, which changes GDP	No effect on output because price-level changes are anticipated
View of the velocity of money	Unstable	Stable	No consensus
How fiscal policy affects the economy	Changes AD and GDP via the multiplier process	No effect unless money supply changes	No effect because price-level changes are anticipated
View of cost-push inflation	Possible (AS shock)	Impossible in the long run in the absence of excessive money supply growth	Impossible in the long run in the absence of excessive money supply growth

SUMMARY

LO19.1 Describe alternative perspectives on the causes of macroeconomic instability, including the views of mainstream economists, monetarists, real-business-cycle advocates, and proponents of coordination failures.

The mainstream view is that macro instability is caused by a combination of price stickiness and shocks to aggregate demand or aggregate supply. With prices inflexible in the shorter run, changes in aggregate demand or short-run aggregate supply result in changes in output and employment. In the long run when both input and output prices are fully flexible, the economy will produce at potential output.

Monetarism focuses on the equation of exchange: $MV = PQ$. Because velocity is thought to be stable, changes in M create changes in nominal GDP ($= PQ$). Monetarists believe that the most significant cause of macroeconomic instability has been inappropriate monetary policy. Rapid increases in M cause inflation; insufficient growth of M causes recession. In this view, a major cause of the Great Depression was inappropriate monetary policy, which allowed the money supply to decline by roughly one-third.

Real-business-cycle theory views changes in resource availability and technology (real factors), which alter productivity, as the main causes of macroeconomic instability. In this theory, shifts of the economy's long-run aggregate supply curve change real output. In turn, money demand and money supply change, shifting the aggregate demand curve in the same direction as the initial change in long-run aggregate supply. Real output thus can change without a change in the price level.

A coordination failure is said to occur when people lack a way to coordinate their actions in order to achieve a mutually beneficial equilibrium. Depending on people's expectations, the economy can come to rest at either a good equilibrium (noninflationary full-employment output) or a bad equilibrium (less-than-full-employment output or demand-pull inflation). A bad equilibrium is a result of a coordination failure.

The rational expectations theory rests on two assumptions: (1) With sufficient information, people's beliefs about future economic outcomes accurately reflect the likelihood that those outcomes will occur; and (2) markets are highly competitive, and prices and wages are flexible both upward and downward.

LO19.2 Discuss why new classical economists believe the economy will "self-correct" from aggregate demand and aggregate supply shocks.

New classical economists (monetarists and rational expectations theorists) see the economy as automatically correcting itself when disturbed from its full-employment level of real output. In RET, unanticipated changes in aggregate demand change the price level, and in the short run this leads firms to change output. But once the firms realize that all prices are changing (including nominal wages) as part of general inflation or deflation, they restore their output to the previous level. Anticipated changes in aggregate demand produce only changes in the price level, not changes in real output.

Mainstream economists reject the new classical view that all prices and wages are flexible downward. They contend that nominal wages, in particular, are inflexible downward because of several factors, including labor contracts, efficiency wages, and insider-outsider relationships. This means that declines in aggregate demand lower real output, not only wages and prices.

LO19.3 Identify and describe the variations of the debate over "rules" versus "discretion" in conducting stabilization policy.

Monetarist and rational expectations economists say the Fed should adhere to some form of policy rule, rather than rely exclusively on discretion. The Friedman rule would direct the Fed to increase the money supply at a fixed annual rate equal to the long-run growth of potential GDP. An alternative approach—inflation targeting—would direct the Fed to establish a targeted range of inflation rates, say, 1 to 2 percent, and focus monetary policy on meeting that goal. They also support maintaining a "neutral" fiscal policy, as opposed to using discretionary fiscal policy to create budget deficits or budget surpluses. A few monetarists and rational expectations economists favor a constitutional amendment requiring that the federal government balance its budget annually.

Mainstream economists oppose strict monetary rules and a balanced-budget requirement, and defend discretionary monetary and fiscal policies. They say that both theory and evidence suggest that such policies are helpful in achieving full employment, price stability, and economic growth.

LO19.4 Summarize the fundamental ideas and policy implications of mainstream macroeconomics, monetarism, and rational expectations theory.

Macroeconomics continues to evolve because of the debate among the three main schools of economic thought: the mainstream, monetarism, and rational expectations.

Mainstream economics believes the economy to be potentially unstable and prone to business cycles due to sticky prices and wages interacting with economic shocks. The mainstream believes in active monetary and fiscal policy that can change AD through the multiplier process and that changes in the money supply affect the economy by changing the interest rate and investment. The mainstream believes the velocity of money to be unstable and holds that cost-push inflation exists and is caused by AS shocks.

Monetarism believes the economy to be fundamentally stable unless inappropriate monetary policies are applied. It believes wages and prices are fully flexible at all time horizons, allowing the economy to adjust on its own back to equilibrium. It argues that business cycles will only occur if monetary policy is either overly tight or overly loose. To prevent either, monetarists support the application of a *monetary rule* to guide monetary policy, Monetarism views the velocity of money as stable and believes cost-push inflation to be impossible in the long run in the absence of excessive money supply growth. Monetarists believe that fiscal policy cannot affect AD or GDP unless there are accompanying changes in monetary policy. On the other hand, monetary policy can shift AD and thereby affect GDP.

The rational expectations camp believes the economy to be stable in the long run at the natural rate of unemployment due to its assumption that prices are flexible at all time horizons. But over shorter time horizons, recessions and booms can happen due to unexpected AD or AS shocks. Rational expectations proponents support a monetary rule in order to guide expectations, so that monetary policy changes will never be a surprise that could shift the economy away from its equilibrium. They also agree with monetarists in the belief that cost-push inflation should be impossible without excessive money supply growth. Finally, rational expectations economists believe that anticipated fiscal and monetary policy changes will have no effect on GDP because they will lead only to price-level changes. For either to be effective in shifting GDP in the short run, they must come as a surprise.

TERMS AND CONCEPTS

monetarism	rational expectations theory	monetary rule
equation of exchange	new classical economics	inflation targeting
velocity	price-level surprises	Taylor rule
real-business-cycle theory	efficiency wage	
coordination failures	insider-outsider theory	

The following and additional problems can be found in **connect** ECONOMICS

DISCUSSION QUESTIONS

1. According to mainstream economists, what is the usual cause of macroeconomic instability? What role does the spending-income multiplier play in creating instability? How might adverse aggregate supply factors cause instability, according to mainstream economists? **LO19.1**

2. What is an efficiency wage? How might payment of an above-market wage reduce shirking by employees and reduce worker turnover? How might efficiency wages contribute to downward wage inflexibility, at least for a time, when aggregate demand declines? **LO19.1**

3. How might relationships between so-called insiders and outsiders contribute to downward wage inflexibility? **LO19.1**

4. Briefly describe the difference between a so-called real business cycle and a more traditional "spending" business cycle. **LO19.1**

5. Craig and Kris were walking directly toward each other in a congested store aisle. Craig moved to his left to avoid Kris, and at the same time Kris moved to his right to avoid Craig. They bumped into each other. What concept does this example illustrate? How does this idea relate to macroeconomic instability? **LO19.1**

6. State and explain the basic equation of monetarism. What is the major cause of macroeconomic instability, as viewed by monetarists? **LO19.1**

7. Use the equation of exchange to explain the rationale for a monetary rule. Why will such a rule run into trouble if V unexpectedly falls because of, say, a drop in investment spending by businesses? **LO19.1**

8. Explain the difference between "active" discretionary fiscal policy advocated by mainstream economists and "passive" fiscal policy advocated by new classical economists. Explain: "The problem with a balanced-budget amendment is that it would, in a sense, require active fiscal policy—but in the wrong direction—as the economy slides into recession." **LO19.3**

9. You have just been elected president of the United States, and the present chairperson of the Federal Reserve Board has resigned. You need to appoint a new person to this position, as well as a person to chair your Council of Economic Advisers. Using Table 19.1 and your knowledge of macroeconomics, identify the views on macro theory and policy you would want your appointees to hold. Remember, the economic health of the entire nation—and your chances for reelection—may depend on your selection. **LO19.4**

10. **LAST WORD** Compare and contrast the Taylor rule for monetary policy with the older, simpler monetary rule advocated by Milton Friedman.

REVIEW QUESTIONS

1. If prices are sticky and the number of dollars of gross investment unexpectedly increases, the _____ curve will shift _____. **LO19.1**
   a. AD; right.
   b. AD; left.
   c. AS; right.
   d. AS; left.

2. First, imagine that both input and output prices are fixed in the economy. What does the aggregate supply curve look like? If AD decreases in this situation, what will happen to equilibrium output and the price level? Next, imagine that input prices are fixed, but output prices are flexible. What does the aggregate supply curve look like? In this case, if AD decreases, what will happen to equilibrium output and the price level? Finally, if both input and output prices are fully flexible, what does the aggregate supply curve look like? In this case, if AD decreases, what will happen to equilibrium output and the price level? (To check your answers, review Figures 12.3, 12.4, and 12.5 in Chapter 12). **LO19.1**

3. Suppose that the money supply is $1 trillion and money velocity is 4. Then the equation of exchange would predict nominal GDP to be: **LO19.1**
   a. $1 trillion.
   b. $4 trillion.
   c. $5 trillion.
   d. $8 trillion.

4. If the money supply fell by 10 percent, a monetarist would expect nominal GDP to _____. **LO19.1**
   a. Rise.
   b. Fall.
   c. Stay the same.

5. An economy is producing at full employment when AD unexpectedly shifts to the left. A new classical economist would assume that as the economy adjusted back to producing at full employment, the price level would _____. **LO19.2**
   a. Increase.
   b. Decrease.
   c. Stay the same.

6. Use an AD-AS graph to demonstrate and explain the price-level and real-output outcome of an anticipated decline in aggregate demand, as viewed by RET economists. (Assume that the economy initially is operating at its full-employment level of output.) Then demonstrate and explain on the same graph the outcome as viewed by mainstream economists. **LO19.2**

7. Place "MON," "RET," or "MAIN" beside the statements that most closely reflect monetarist, rational expectations, or mainstream views, respectively: **LO19.4**
   a. Anticipated changes in aggregate demand affect only the price level; they have no effect on real output.
   b. Downward wage inflexibility means that declines in aggregate demand can cause long-lasting recession.
   c. Changes in the money supply M increase PQ; at first only Q rises, because nominal wages are fixed, but once workers adapt their expectations to new realities, P rises and Q returns to its former level.
   d. Fiscal and monetary policies smooth out the business cycle.
   e. The Fed should increase the money supply at a fixed annual rate.

PROBLEMS

1. Suppose that the money supply and the nominal GDP for a hypothetical economy are $96 billion and $336 billion, respectively. What is the velocity of money? How will households and businesses react if the central bank reduces the money supply by $20 billion? By how much will nominal GDP have to fall to restore equilibrium, according to the monetarist perspective? **LO19.1**

2. Assume the following information for a hypothetical economy in year 1: money supply = $400 billion; long-term annual growth of potential GDP = 3 percent; velocity = 4.

Assume that the banking system initially has no excess reserves and that the reserve requirement is 10 percent. Also suppose that velocity is constant and that the economy initially is operating at its full-employment real output. **LO19.1**
   a. What is the level of nominal GDP in year 1?
   b. Suppose the Fed adheres to a monetary rule through open-market operations. What amount of U.S. securities will it have to sell to, or buy from, banks or the public between years 1 and 2 to meet its monetary rule?

FURTHER TEST YOUR KNOWLEDGE AT www.mcconnell20e.com

Practice quizzes, student PowerPoints, worked problems, Web-based questions, and additional materials are available at the text's Online Learning Center (OLC), **www.mcconnell20e.com**, or scan here. Need a barcode reader? Try ScanLife, available in your app store.

International Economics

PART **SEVEN**

INTERNATIONAL ECONOMICS

CHAPTER 20

International Trade*

Backpackers in the wilderness like to think they are "leaving the world behind," but, like Atlas, they carry the world on their shoulders. Much of their equipment is imported—knives from Switzerland, rain gear from South Korea, cameras from Japan, aluminum pots from England, sleeping bags from China, and compasses from Finland. Moreover, they may have driven to the trailheads in Japanese-made Toyotas or German-made BMWs, sipping coffee from Brazil or snacking on bananas from Honduras.

International trade and the global economy affect all of us daily, whether we are hiking in the wilderness, driving our cars, buying groceries, or working at our jobs. We cannot "leave the world behind." We are enmeshed in a global web of economic relationships, such as trading goods and services, multinational corporations, cooperative

*Note to Instructors: If you prefer to cover international trade early in your course, you can assign this chapter at the end of either Part 1 or Part 2. This chapter builds on the introductory ideas of opportunity costs, supply and demand analysis, and economic efficiency but does not require an understanding of either market failures or government failures.

ventures among the world's firms, and ties among the world's financial markets.

The focus of this chapter is the trading of goods and services. Then in Chapter 21, we examine the U.S. balance of payments, exchange rates, and U.S. trade deficits. In Chapter 21W on our Web site, we look at the economics of developing nations.

Some Key Trade Facts

LO20.1 List and discuss several key facts about international trade.

The following are several important facts relating to international trade.

- U.S. exports and imports have more than doubled as percentages of GDP since 1980.
- A *trade deficit* occurs when imports exceed exports. The United States has a trade deficit in goods. In 2012 U.S. imports of goods exceeded U.S. exports of goods by $735 billion.
- A *trade surplus* occurs when exports exceed imports. The United States has a trade surplus in services (such as air transportation services and financial services). In 2012 U.S. exports of services exceeded U.S. imports of services by $196 billion.
- Principal U.S. exports include chemicals, agricultural products, consumer durables, semiconductors, and aircraft; principal imports include petroleum, automobiles, metals, household appliances, and computers.
- As with other advanced industrial nations, the United States imports many goods that are in some of the same categories as the goods that it exports. Examples: automobiles, computers, chemicals, semiconductors, and telecommunications equipment.
- Canada is the United States' most important trading partner quantitatively. In 2012 about 20 percent of U.S. exported goods were sold to Canadians, who in turn provided 15 percent of imported U.S. goods.
- The United States has a sizable trade deficit with China. In 2012 it was $315 billion.
- The U.S. dependence on foreign oil is reflected in its trade with members of OPEC. In 2012 the United States imported $181 billion of goods (mainly oil) from OPEC members, while exporting $82 billion of goods to those countries.
- The United States leads the world in the combined volume of exports and imports, as measured in

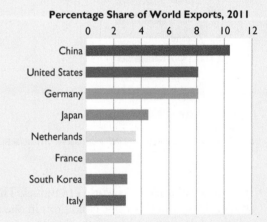

GLOBAL PERSPECTIVE 20.1

Shares of World Exports, Selected Nations

China has the largest share of world exports, followed by Germany and the United States. The eight largest export nations account for about 43.9 percent of world exports.

Percentage Share of World Exports, 2011

China
United States
Germany
Japan
Netherlands
France
South Korea
Italy

Source: International Trade Statistics, 2012, WTO Publications.

dollars. China, the United States, Germany, Japan, and the Netherlands were the top five exporters by dollar in 2012.
- Currently, the United States provides about 8.1 percent of the world's exports. (See Global Perspective 20.1.)
- Exports of goods and services (on a national income account basis) make up about 14 percent of total U.S. output. That percentage is much lower than the percentage in many other nations, including Canada, France, Germany, the Netherlands, and South Korea. (See Global Perspective 20.2.)
- China has become a major international trader, with an estimated $2.05 trillion of exports in 2012. Other Asian economies—including South Korea, Taiwan, and Singapore—are also active in international trade. Their combined exports exceed those of France, Britain, or Italy.

GLOBAL PERSPECTIVE 20.2

Exports of Goods and Services as a Percentage of GDP, Selected Countries

Although the United States is one of the world's largest exporters, as a percentage of GDP, its exports are quite low relative to many other countries.

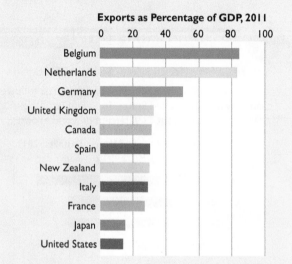

Exports as Percentage of GDP, 2011

Source: Derived by authors from *IMF International Financial Statistics,* 2012.

- International trade links world economies. Through trade, changes in economic conditions in one place on the globe can quickly affect other places.
- International trade is often at the center of debates over economic policy, both within the United States and internationally.

With this information in mind, let's turn to the economics of international trade.

The Economic Basis for Trade

LO20.2 Define comparative advantage, and demonstrate how specialization and trade add to a nation's output.

Sovereign nations, like individuals and the regions of a nation, can gain by specializing in the products they can produce with the greatest relative efficiency and by trading for the goods they cannot produce as efficiently. The simple answer to the question "Why do nations trade?" is "They trade because it is beneficial." The benefits that emerge relate to three underlying facts:

- The distribution of natural, human, and capital resources among nations is uneven; nations differ in their endowments of economic resources.

- Efficient production of various goods requires different technologies, and not all nations have the same level of technological expertise.
- Products are differentiated as to quality and other attributes, and some people may prefer certain goods imported from abroad rather than similar goods produced domestically.

To recognize the character and interaction of these three facts, think of China, which has abundant and inexpensive labor. As a result, China can produce efficiently (at low cost of other goods forgone) a variety of **labor-intensive goods,** such as textiles, electronics, apparel, toys, and sporting goods.

In contrast, Australia has vast amounts of land and can inexpensively produce such **land-intensive goods** as beef, wool, and meat. Mexico has the soil, tropical climate, rainfall, and ready supply of unskilled labor that allow for the efficient, low-cost production of vegetables. Industrially advanced economies such as the United States and Germany that have relatively large amounts of capital can inexpensively produce goods whose production requires much capital, including such **capital-intensive goods** as airplanes, automobiles, agricultural equipment, machinery, and chemicals.

Also, regardless of their resource intensities, nations can develop individual products that are in demand worldwide because of their special qualities. Examples: fashions from Italy, chocolates from Belgium, software from the United States, and watches from Switzerland.

The distribution of resources, technology, and product distinctiveness among nations is relatively stable in short time periods but certainly can change over time. When that distribution changes, the relative efficiency and success that nations have in producing and selling goods also change. For example, in the past several decades, South Korea has greatly expanded its stock of capital. Although South Korea was primarily an exporter of agricultural products and raw materials a half-century ago, it now exports large quantities of manufactured goods. Similarly, the new technologies that gave us synthetic fibers and synthetic rubber drastically altered the resource mix needed to produce fibers and rubber and changed the relative efficiency of nations in manufacturing them.

As national economies evolve, the size and quality of their labor forces may change, the volume and composition of their capital stocks may shift, new technologies may develop, and even the quality of land and the quantity of natural resources may be altered. As such changes take place, the relative efficiency with which a nation can produce specific goods will also change. As economists would say, comparative advantage can and does sometimes change.

Comparative Advantage

In an open economy (one with an international sector), a country produces more of certain goods (exports) and fewer of other goods (imports) than it would otherwise. Thus, the country shifts the use of labor and other productive resources toward export industries and away from import industries. For example, in the presence of international trade, the United States uses more resources to make commercial aircraft and to grow wheat and fewer resources to make television sets and sew clothes. So we ask: Do such shifts of resources make economic sense? Do they enhance U.S. total output and thus the U.S. standard of living?

The answers are affirmative. Specialization and international trade increase the productivity of U.S. resources and allow the United States to obtain greater total output than otherwise would be possible. These benefits are the result of exploiting both *absolute advantages* and *comparative advantages*. A country is said to have an *absolute advantage* over other producers of a product if it is the most efficient producer of that product (by which we mean that it can produce more output of that product from any given amount of resource inputs than can any other producer). A country is said to have a *comparative advantage* over other producers of a product if it can produce the product at a lower opportunity cost (by which we mean that it must forgo less output of alternative products when allocating productive resources to producing the product in question).

In 1776 Adam Smith used the concept of absolute advantage to argue for international specialization and trade. His point was that nations would be better off if each specialized in the production of those products in which it had an absolute advantage and was therefore the most efficient producer:

> It is the maxim of every prudent master of a family, never to attempt to make at home what it will cost him more to make than to buy. The taylor does not attempt to make his own shoes, but buys them of the shoemaker. The shoemaker does not attempt to make his own clothes, but employs a taylor. The farmer attempts to make neither the one nor the other, but employs those different artificers. . . .
>
> What is prudence in the conduct of every private family, can scarce be folly in that of a great kingdom. If a foreign country can supply us with a commodity cheaper than we can make it, better buy it of them with some part of the produce of our own industry, employed in a way in which we have some advantage.[1]

---

[1] Adam Smith, *The Wealth of Nations* (originally published, 1776; New York: Modern Library, 1937), p. 424.

A CPA and a House Painter

Suppose that Madison, a certified public accountant (CPA), is a swifter painter than Mason, the professional painter she is thinking of hiring. Also assume that Madison can earn $50 per hour as an accountant but would have to pay Mason $15 per hour. And suppose that Madison would need 30 hours to paint her house but Mason would need 40 hours.

Should Madison take time from her accounting to paint her own house, or should she hire the painter? Madison's opportunity cost of painting her house is $1,500 (= 30 hours of sacrificed CPA time × $50 per CPA hour). The cost of hiring Mason is only $600 (= 40 hours of painting × $15 per hour of painting). Although Madison is better at both accounting and painting, she will get her house painted at lower cost by specializing in accounting and using some of her earnings from accounting to hire a house painter.

Similarly, Mason can reduce his cost of obtaining accounting services by specializing in painting and using some of his income to hire Madison to prepare his income tax forms. Suppose Mason would need 10 hours to prepare his tax return, while Madison could handle the task in 2 hours. Mason would sacrifice $150 of income (= 10 hours of painting time × $15 per hour) to do something he could hire Madison to do for $100 (= 2 hours of CPA time × $50 per CPA hour). By specializing in painting and hiring Madison to prepare his tax return, Mason lowers the cost of getting his tax return prepared.

We will see that what is true for our CPA and house painter is also true for nations. Specializing on the basis of comparative advantage enables nations to reduce the cost of obtaining the goods and services they desire.

In the early 1800s, David Ricardo extended Smith's idea by demonstrating that it is advantageous for a country to specialize and trade with another country even if it is more productive in all economic activities than that other country. Stated more formally, a nation does not need Smith's absolute advantage—total superiority in the efficiency with which it produces products—to benefit from specialization and trade. It needs only a comparative advantage.

The nearby Consider This box provides a simple, two-person illustration of Ricardo's principle of comparative advantage. Be sure to read it now because it will greatly help you understand the graphical analysis that follows.

QUICK REVIEW 20.1

- International trade enables nations to specialize, increase productivity, and increase the amount of output available for consumption.
- A country is said to have an *absolute advantage* over the other producers of a product if it can produce the product more efficiently, by which we mean that it can produce more of the product from any given amount of resource inputs than can any other producer.
- A country is said to have a *comparative advantage* over the other producers of a product if it can produce the product at a lower opportunity cost, by which we mean that it must forgo less of the output of alternative products when allocating resources to producing the product in question.

Two Isolated Nations

Our goal is to place the idea of comparative advantage into the context of trading nations. Our method is to build a simple model that relies on the familiar concepts of production possibilities curves. Suppose the world consists of just two nations, the United States and Mexico. Also for simplicity, suppose that the labor forces in the United States and Mexico are of equal size. Each nation can produce both beef and raw (unprocessed) vegetables but at different levels of economic efficiency. Suppose the U.S. and Mexican domestic production possibilities curves for beef and vegetables are those shown in Figure 20.1a and Figure 20.1b. Note three realities relating to the production possibilities curves in the two graphs:

- **Constant costs** The curves derive from the data in Table 20.1 and are drawn as straight lines, in contrast

to the bowed-outward production possibilities frontiers we examined in Chapter 1. This means that we have replaced the law of increasing opportunity costs with the assumption of constant costs. This substitution simplifies our discussion but does not impair the validity of our analysis and conclusions. Later we will consider the effects of increasing opportunity costs.

- **Different costs** The production possibilities curves of the United States and Mexico reflect different resource mixes and differing levels of technology. Specifically, the differing slopes of the two curves reflect the numbers in the figures and reveal that the opportunity costs of producing beef and vegetables differ between the two nations.

- **U.S. absolute advantage in both** A producer (an individual, firm, or country) has an *absolute advantage* over another producer if it can produce more of a product than the other producer using the same amount of resources. Because of our convenient assumption that the U.S. and Mexican labor forces are the same size, the two production possibilities curves show that the United States has an absolute advantage in producing both products. If the United States and Mexico use their entire (equal-size) labor forces to produce either vegetables or beef, the United States can produce more of either than Mexico. The United States, using the same number of workers as Mexico, has greater production possibilities. So output per worker—labor productivity—in the United States exceeds that in Mexico in producing both products.

(a)
United States

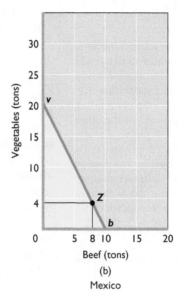

(b)
Mexico

FIGURE 20.1 Production possibilities for the United States and Mexico. The two production possibilities curves show the combinations of vegetables and beef that the United States and Mexico can produce domestically. The curves for both countries are straight lines because we are assuming constant opportunity costs. (a) As reflected by the slope of *VB* in the left graph, the opportunity-cost ratio in the United States is 1 vegetables ≡ 1 beef. (b) The production possibilities curve *vb* in the right graph has a steeper slope, reflecting the different opportunity-cost ratio in Mexico of 2 vegetables ≡ 1 beef. The difference in the opportunity-cost ratios between the two countries defines their comparative advantages and is the basis for specialization and international trade.

TABLE 20.1 International Specialization According to Comparative Advantage and the Gains from Trade

Country	(1) Outputs before Specialization	(2) Outputs after Specialization	(3) Amounts Exported (−) and Imported (+)	(4) Outputs Available after Trade	(5) Gains from Specialization and Trade (4) − (1)
United States	18 beef	30 beef	−10 beef	20 beef	2 beef
	12 vegetables	0 vegetables	+15 vegetables	15 vegetables	3 vegetables
Mexico	8 beef	0 beef	+10 beef	10 beef	2 beef
	4 vegetables	20 vegetables	−15 vegetables	5 vegetables	1 vegetables

Opportunity-Cost Ratio in the United States In Figure 20.1a, with full employment, the United States will operate at some point on its production possibilities curve. On that curve, it can increase its output of beef from 0 tons to 30 tons by forgoing 30 tons of vegetables output. So the slope of the production possibilities curve is 1 (= 30 vegetables/30 beef), meaning that 1 ton of vegetables must be sacrificed for each extra ton of beef. In the United States the **opportunity-cost ratio** (domestic exchange ratio) for the two products is 1 ton of vegetables (V) for 1 ton of beef (B), or

$$\text{United States: } 1V \equiv 1B \text{ (The "}\equiv\text{" sign simply means "equivalent to.")}$$

Within its borders, the United States can "exchange" a ton of vegetables from itself for a ton of beef from itself. Our constant-cost assumption means that this exchange or opportunity-cost relationship prevails for all possible moves from one point to another along the U.S. production possibilities curve.

Opportunity-Cost Ratio in Mexico Mexico's production possibilities curve in Figure 20.1b represents a different full-employment opportunity-cost ratio. In Mexico, 20 tons of vegetables must be given up to obtain 10 tons of beef. The slope of the production possibilities curve is 2 (= 20 vegetables/10 beef). This means that in Mexico the opportunity-cost ratio for the two goods is 2 tons of vegetables for 1 ton of beef, or

$$\text{Mexico: } 2V \equiv 1B$$

Self-Sufficiency Output Mix If the United States and Mexico are isolated and self-sufficient, then each country must choose some output mix on its production possibilities curve. It will select the mix that provides the greatest total utility or satisfaction. Let's assume that combination point A in Figure 20.1a is the optimal mix in the United States. That is, society deems the combination of 18 tons of beef and 12 tons of vegetables preferable to any other combination of the goods available along the production

possibilities curve. Suppose Mexico's optimal product mix is 8 tons of beef and 4 tons of vegetables, indicated by point Z in Figure 20.1b. These choices by the two countries are reflected in column 1 of Table 20.1.

Specializing Based on Comparative Advantage

A producer (an individual, firm, or nation) has a **comparative advantage** in producing a particular product if it can produce that product at a lower opportunity cost than other producers. Comparative advantage is the key determinant in whether or not nations can gain from specialization and trade. In fact, absolute advantage turns out to be irrelevant.

In our example, for instance, the United States has an absolute advantage over Mexico in producing both vegetables and beef. But it is still the case that the United States can gain from specialization and trade with Mexico. That is because what actually matters is whether the opportunity costs of producing the two products (beef and vegetables) differ in the two countries. If they do, then each nation will enjoy a comparative advantage in one of the products, meaning that it can produce that product at a lower opportunity cost than the other country. As a result, total output can increase if each country specializes in the production of the good in which it has the lower opportunity cost.

This idea is summarized in the **principle of comparative advantage**, which says that total output will be greatest when each good is produced by the nation that has the lowest domestic opportunity cost for producing that good. In our two-nation illustration, the United States has the lower domestic opportunity cost for beef; the United States must forgo only 1 ton of vegetables to produce 1 ton of beef, whereas Mexico must forgo 2 tons of vegetables for 1 ton of beef. The United States has a comparative (cost) advantage in beef and should specialize in beef production. The "world" (that is, the United States and Mexico) in our example would clearly not be economizing in the use of its resources if a high-cost producer (Mexico) produced a specific product (beef) when a low-cost producer (the United States) could have produced it. Having Mexico produce beef would mean that the world economy would have to give up more vegetables than is necessary to obtain a ton of beef.

Mexico has the lower domestic opportunity cost for vegetables. It must sacrifice only $\frac{1}{2}$ ton of beef to produce 1 ton of vegetables, while the United States must forgo 1 ton of beef to produce 1 ton of vegetables. Mexico has a comparative advantage in vegetables and should specialize in vegetable production. Again, the world would not be employing its resources economically if vegetables were produced by a high-cost producer (the United States) rather than by a low-cost producer (Mexico). If the United States produced vegetables, the world would be giving up more beef than necessary to obtain each ton of vegetables. Economizing requires that any particular good be produced by the nation having the lowest domestic opportunity cost or the nation having the comparative advantage for that good. The United States should produce beef, and Mexico should produce vegetables. The situation is summarized in Table 20.2.

A comparison of columns 1 and 2 in Table 20.1 verifies that specialized production enables the world to obtain more output from its fixed amount of resources. By specializing completely in beef, the United States can produce 30 tons of beef and no vegetables. Mexico, by specializing completely in vegetables, can produce 20 tons of vegetables and no beef. These figures exceed the yields generated without specialization: 26 tons of beef (= 18 in the United States + 8 in Mexico) and 16 tons of vegetables (= 12 in the United States + 4 in Mexico). As a result, the world ends up with 4 more tons of beef (= 30 tons − 26 tons) and 4 more tons of vegetables (= 20 tons − 16 tons) than it would if there were self-sufficiency and unspecialized production.

ORIGIN OF THE IDEA

O20.1

Absolute and comparative advantage

Terms of Trade

We have just seen that specialization in production will allow for the largest possible amounts of both beef and vegetables to be produced. But with each country specializing in the production of only one item, how will the vegetables that are all produced by Mexico and the beef that is all produced by the United States be divided between consumers in the two countries? The key turns out to be the **terms of trade,** the exchange ratio at which the United States and Mexico trade beef and vegetables.

Crucially, the terms of trade also establish whether each country will find it in its own better interest to bother specializing at all. This is because the terms of trade determine whether each country can "get a better deal" by specializing and trading than it could if it opted instead for self sufficiency. To see how this works, note that because $1B \equiv 1V (= 1V \equiv 1B)$ in the United States, it must get more than 1 ton of vegetables for each 1 ton of beef exported; otherwise, it will not benefit from exporting beef in exchange for Mexican vegetables. The United States must get a better "price" (more vegetables) for its beef through international trade than it can get domestically; otherwise, no gain from trade exists and such trade will not occur.

Similarly, because $1B \equiv 2V (= 2V \equiv 1B)$ in Mexico, Mexico must obtain 1 ton of beef by exporting less than 2 tons of vegetables to get it. Mexico must be able to pay a lower "price" for beef in the world market than it must pay domestically, or else it will not want to trade. The international exchange ratio or terms of trade must therefore lie somewhere between

$$1B \equiv 1V \text{ (United States' cost conditions)}$$

and

$$1B \equiv 2V \text{ (Mexico's cost conditions)}$$

Where between these limits will the world exchange ratio fall? The United States will prefer a rate close to $1B \equiv 2V$, say, $1B \equiv 1\frac{3}{4}V$. The United States wants to obtain as many vegetables as possible for each 1 ton of beef it exports. By contrast, Mexico wants a rate near $1B \equiv 1V$, say, $1B \equiv 1\frac{1}{4}V$. This is true because Mexico wants to export as few vegetables as possible for each 1 ton of beef it receives in exchange.

The actual exchange ratio depends on world supply and demand for the two products. If overall world demand for vegetables is weak relative to its supply and if the demand for beef is strong relative to its supply, the price of vegetables will be lower and the price of beef will be higher. The exchange ratio will settle nearer the $1B \equiv 2V$ figure the United States prefers. If overall world demand for vegetables is great relative to its supply and if the demand for beef is weak relative to its supply, the ratio will settle nearer the

TABLE 20.2 Comparative-Advantage Example: A Summary

Beef	Vegetables
Mexico: Must give up 2 tons of vegetables to get 1 ton of beef.	**Mexico:** Must give up $\frac{1}{2}$ ton of beef to get 1 ton of vegetables.
United States: Must give up 1 ton of vegetables to get 1 ton of beef.	**United States:** Must give up 1 ton of beef to get 1 ton of vegetables.
Comparative advantage: United States	**Comparative advantage:** Mexico

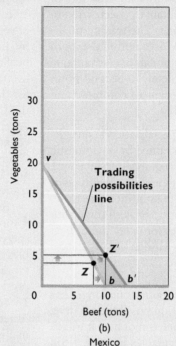

FIGURE 20.2 **Trading possibilities lines and the gains from trade.** As a result of specialization and trade, both the United States and Mexico can have higher levels of output than the levels attainable on their domestic production possibilities curves. (a) The United States can move from point *A* on its domestic production possibilities curve to, say, *A'* on its trading possibilities line. (b) Mexico can move from *Z* to *Z'*.

QUICK QUIZ FOR FIGURE 20.2

1. The production possibilities curves in graphs (a) and (b) imply:
   a. increasing domestic opportunity costs.
   b. decreasing domestic opportunity costs.
   c. constant domestic opportunity costs.
   d. first decreasing, then increasing, domestic opportunity costs.

2. Before specialization, the domestic opportunity cost of producing 1 unit of beef is:
   a. 1 unit of vegetables in both the United States and Mexico.
   b. 1 unit of vegetables in the United States and 2 units of vegetables in Mexico.
   c. 2 units of vegetables in the United States and 1 unit of vegetables in Mexico.
   d. 1 unit of vegetables in the United States and $\frac{1}{2}$ unit of vegetables in Mexico.

3. After specialization and international trade, the world output of beef and vegetables is:
   a. 20 tons of beef and 20 tons of vegetables.
   b. 45 tons of beef and 15 tons of vegetables.
   c. 30 tons of beef and 20 tons of vegetables.
   d. 10 tons of beef and 30 tons of vegetables.

4. After specialization and international trade:
   a. the United States can obtain units of vegetables at less cost than it could before trade.
   b. Mexico can obtain more than 20 tons of vegetables, if it so chooses.
   c. the United States no longer has a comparative advantage in producing beef.
   d. Mexico can benefit by prohibiting vegetables imports from the United States.

Answers: 1. c; 2. b; 3. c; 4. a

$1B \equiv 1V$ level favorable to Mexico. In this manner, the actual exchange ratio that is set by world supply and demand determines how the gains from international specialization and trade are divided between the two nations and, consequently, how the beef that is all produced in the United States and the vegetables that are all produced in Mexico get divided among consumers in the two countries. (We discuss equilibrium world prices later in this chapter.)

Gains from Trade

Suppose the international terms of trade are $1B \equiv 1\frac{1}{2}V$. The possibility of trading on these terms permits each nation to supplant its domestic production possibilities curve with a trading possibilities line (or curve), as shown in **Figure 20.2 (Key Graph)**. Just as a production possibilities curve shows the amounts of these products that a full-employment economy can obtain by shifting resources from one to the other, a **trading possibilities line** shows the amounts of the two products that a nation can obtain by specializing in one product and trading for the other. The trading possibilities lines in Figure 20.2 reflect the assumption that both nations specialize on the basis of comparative advantage: The United States specializes completely in beef (at point *B* in Figure 20.2a), and Mexico specializes completely in vegetables (at point *v* in Figure 20.2b).

Improved Alternatives With specialization and trade, the United States is no longer constrained by its domestic production possibilities line, which requires it to give up 1 ton of beef for every 1 ton of vegetables it wants as it moves up its domestic production possibilities line from, say, point *B*. Instead, the United States, through trade with Mexico, can get $1\frac{1}{2}$ tons of vegetables for every ton of beef that it exports to Mexico, as long as Mexico has vegetables to export. Trading possibilities line *BV′* thus represents the $1B \equiv 1\frac{1}{2}V$ trading ratio.

Similarly, Mexico, starting at, say, point *v*, no longer has to move down its domestic production possibilities curve, giving up 2 tons of vegetables for each ton of beef it wants. It can now export just $1\frac{1}{2}$ tons of vegetables for each 1 ton of beef that it wants by moving down its trading possibilities line *vb′*.

Specialization and trade create a new exchange ratio between beef and vegetables, and that ratio is reflected in each nation's trading possibilities line. For both nations, this exchange ratio is superior to the unspecialized exchange ratio embodied in their respective production possibilities curves. By specializing in beef and trading for Mexico's vegetables, the United States can obtain more than 1 ton of vegetables for 1 ton of beef. By specializing in vegetables and trading for U.S. beef, Mexico can obtain 1 ton of beef for less than 2 tons of vegetables. In both cases, self-sufficiency is inefficient and therefore undesirable.

Greater Output By specializing on the basis of comparative advantage and by trading for goods that are produced in the nation with greater domestic efficiency, the United States and Mexico can achieve combinations of beef and vegetables beyond their own individual production possibilities curves. Specialization according to comparative advantage results in a more efficient allocation of world resources, and larger outputs of both products are therefore available to both nations.

Suppose that at the $1B \equiv 1\frac{1}{2}V$ terms of trade, the United States exports 10 tons of beef to Mexico and in return Mexico exports 15 tons of vegetables to the United States. How do the new quantities of beef and vegetables available to the two nations compare with the optimal product mixes that existed before specialization and trade? Point *A* in

Figure 20.2a reminds us that the United States chose 18 tons of beef and 12 tons of vegetables originally. But by producing 30 tons of beef and no vegetables and by trading 10 tons of beef for 15 tons of vegetables, the United States can obtain 20 tons of beef and 15 tons of vegetables. This new, superior combination of beef and vegetables is indicated by point *A′* in Figure 20.2a. Compared with the no-trade amounts of 18 tons of beef and 12 tons of vegetables, the United States' **gains from trade** are 2 tons of beef and 3 tons of vegetables.

Similarly, recall that Mexico's optimal product mix was 4 tons of vegetables and 8 tons of beef (point *Z*) before specialization and trade. Now, after specializing in vegetables and trading for beef, Mexico can have 5 tons of vegetables and 10 tons of beef. It accomplishes that by producing 20 tons of vegetables and no beef and exporting 15 tons of its vegetables in exchange for 10 tons of American beef. This new position is indicated by point *Z′* in Figure 20.2b. Mexico's gains from trade are 1 ton of vegetables and 2 tons of beef.

Points *A′* and *Z′* in Figure 20.2 are superior economic positions to points *A* and *Z*. This fact is enormously important! We know that a nation can expand its production possibilities boundary by (1) expanding the quantity and improving the quality of its resources or (2) realizing technological progress. We have now established that international trade can enable a nation to circumvent the output constraint illustrated by its production possibilities curve. An economy can grow by expanding international trade. The outcome of international specialization and trade is equivalent to having more and better resources or discovering and implementing improved production techniques.

Table 20.1 summarizes the transactions and outcomes in our analysis. Please give it one final careful review.

QUICK REVIEW 20.2

- The principle of comparative advantage says that total world output will be greatest when each good is produced by the nation that has the lowest domestic opportunity cost.
- The rate at which countries can trade units of one product for units of another product is referred to as the terms of trade.
- A trading possibilities line shows the amounts of two products that a nation can obtain by specializing in the production of one product and then trading for the other.

Misunderstanding the Gains from Trade

It is a common myth that the greatest benefit to be derived from international trade is greater domestic employment in the export sector. This suggests that exports are "good" because they increase domestic employment, whereas imports are "bad" because they deprive people of jobs at home. As we have demonstrated, the true benefit created by international trade is the overall increase in output available through specialization and exchange.

A nation does not need international trade to operate *on* its production possibilities curve. It can fully employ its resources, including labor, with or without international trade. International trade, however, enables a country to reach a point of consumption beyond its domestic production possibilities curve. The gain from trade to a nation is the extra output obtained from abroad—the imports obtained for less sacrifice of other goods than if they were produced at home.

Trade with Increasing Costs

To explain the basic principles underlying international trade, we simplified our analysis in several ways. For example, we limited discussion to two products and two nations. But multiproduct and multinational analysis yield the same conclusions. We also assumed constant opportunity costs (linear production possibilities curves), which is a more substantive simplification. Let's consider the effect of allowing increasing opportunity costs (concave-to-the-origin production possibilities curves) to enter the picture.

Suppose that the United States and Mexico initially are at positions on their concave production possibilities curves where their domestic cost ratios are $1B \equiv 1V$ and $1B \equiv 2V$, as they were in our constant-cost analysis. As before, comparative advantage indicates that the United States should specialize in beef and Mexico in vegetables. But now, as the United States begins to expand beef production, its cost of beef will rise; it will have to sacrifice more than 1 ton of vegetables to get 1 additional ton of beef. Resources are no longer perfectly substitutable between alternative uses, as the constant-cost assumption implied. Resources less and less suitable to beef production must be allocated to the U.S. beef industry in expanding beef output, and that means increasing costs—the

sacrifice of larger and larger amounts of vegetables for each additional ton of beef.

Similarly, suppose that Mexico expands vegetable production starting from its $1B \equiv 2V$ cost ratio position. As production increases, it will find that its $1B \equiv 2V$ cost ratio begins to rise. Sacrificing 1 ton of beef will free resources that are capable of producing only something less than 2 tons of vegetables because those transferred resources are less suitable to vegetable production.

As the U.S. cost ratio falls from $1B \equiv 1V$ and the Mexican ratio rises from $1B \equiv 2V$, a point will be reached where the cost ratios are equal in the two nations, perhaps at $1B \equiv 1\frac{3}{4}V$. At this point the underlying basis for further specialization and trade—differing cost ratios—has disappeared, and further specialization is therefore uneconomical. And, most important, this point of equal cost ratios may be reached while the United States is still producing some vegetables along with its beef and Mexico is producing some beef along with its vegetables. The primary effect of increasing opportunity costs is less-than-complete specialization. For this reason, we often find domestically produced products competing directly against identical or similar imported products within a particular economy.

The Case for Free Trade

The case for free trade reduces to one compelling argument: Through free trade based on the principle of comparative advantage, the world economy can achieve a more efficient allocation of resources and a higher level of material well-being than it can without free trade.

Since the resource mixes and technological knowledge of the world's nations are all somewhat different, each nation can produce particular commodities at different real costs. Each nation should produce goods for which its domestic opportunity costs are lower than the domestic opportunity costs of other nations and exchange those goods for products for which its domestic opportunity costs are high relative to those of other nations. If each nation does this, the world will realize the advantages of geographic and human specialization. The world and each free-trading nation can obtain a larger real income from the fixed supplies of resources available to it.

Government trade barriers lessen or eliminate gains from specialization. If nations cannot trade freely, they must shift resources from efficient (low-cost) to inefficient (high-cost) uses to satisfy their diverse wants. A recent study suggests that the elimination of trade barriers since the Second World War has increased the income of the average U.S. household by at least $7,000 and perhaps by as much as $13,000. These income gains are recurring; they happen year after year.[2]

One side benefit of free trade is that it promotes competition and deters monopoly. The increased competition from foreign firms forces domestic firms to find and use the lowest-cost production techniques. It also compels them to be innovative with respect to both product quality and production methods, thereby contributing to economic growth. And free trade gives consumers a wider range of product choices. The reasons to favor free trade are the same as the reasons to endorse competition.

A second side benefit of free trade is that it links national interests and breaks down national animosities. Confronted with political disagreements, trading partners tend to negotiate rather than make war.

QUICK REVIEW 20.3

- International trade enables nations to specialize, increase productivity, and increase output available for consumption.
- Comparative advantage means total world output will be greatest when each good is produced by the nation that has the lowest domestic opportunity cost.
- Specialization is less than complete among nations because opportunity costs normally rise as any specific nation produces more of a particular good.

Supply and Demand Analysis of Exports and Imports

LO20.3 Describe how differences between world prices and domestic prices prompt exports and imports.

Supply and demand analysis reveals how equilibrium prices and quantities of exports and imports are determined. The amount of a good or a service a nation will export or import depends on differences between the equilibrium world price and the equilibrium domestic price. The interaction of *world* supply and demand determines the equilibrium **world price**—the price that equates the quantities supplied and demanded globally. *Domestic* supply and demand determine the equilibrium **domestic price**—the price that would prevail in a closed economy that does not engage in international trade. The domestic price equates quantity supplied and quantity demanded domestically.

[2] Scott C. Bradford, Paul L. E. Grieco, and Gary C. Hufbauer, "The Payoff to America from Globalization," *The World Economy*, July 2006, pp. 893–916.

In the absence of trade, the domestic prices in a closed economy may or may not equal the world equilibrium prices. When economies are opened for international trade, differences between world and domestic prices encourage exports or imports. To see how, consider the international effects of such price differences in a simple two-nation world, consisting of the United States and Canada, that are both producing aluminum. We assume there are no trade barriers, such as tariffs and quotas, and no international transportation costs.

Supply and Demand in the United States

Figure 20.3a shows the domestic supply curve S_d and the domestic demand curve D_d for aluminum in the United States, which for now is a closed economy. The intersection of S_d and D_d determines the equilibrium domestic price of $1 per pound and the equilibrium domestic quantity of 100 million pounds. Domestic suppliers produce 100 million pounds and sell them all at $1 a pound. So there are no domestic surpluses or shortages of aluminum.

But what if the U.S. economy were opened to trade and the world price of aluminum were above or below this $1 domestic price?

U.S. Export Supply If the aluminum price in the rest of the world (that is, Canada) exceeds $1, U.S. firms will produce more than 100 million pounds and will export the excess domestic output. First, consider a world price of $1.25. We see from the supply curve S_d that U.S. aluminum firms will produce 125 million pounds of aluminum at that price. The demand curve D_d tells us that the United States will purchase only 75 million pounds at $1.25. The outcome is a domestic surplus of 50 million pounds of aluminum. U.S. producers will export those 50 million pounds at the $1.25 world price.

What if the world price were $1.50? The supply curve shows that U.S. firms will produce 150 million pounds of aluminum, while the demand curve tells us that U.S. consumers will buy only 50 million pounds. So U.S. producers will export the domestic surplus of 100 million pounds.

Toward the top of Figure 20.3b we plot the domestic surpluses—the U.S. exports—that occur at world prices above the $1 domestic equilibrium price. When the world and domestic prices are equal (= $1), the quantity of exports supplied is zero (point *a*). There is no surplus of domestic output to export. But when the world price is $1.25, U.S. firms export 50 million pounds of surplus aluminum (point *b*). At a $1.50 world price, the domestic surplus of 100 million pounds is exported (point *c*).

The U.S. **export supply curve,** found by connecting points *a*, *b*, and *c*, shows the amount of aluminum U.S.

FIGURE 20.3 **U.S. export supply and import demand.** (a) Domestic supply S_d and demand D_d set the domestic equilibrium price of aluminum at $1 per pound. At world prices above $1 there are domestic surpluses of aluminum. At prices below $1 there are domestic shortages. (b) Surpluses are exported (top curve), and shortages are met by importing aluminum (lower curve). The export supply curve shows the direct relationship between world prices and U.S. exports; the import demand curve portrays the inverse relationship between world prices and U.S. imports.

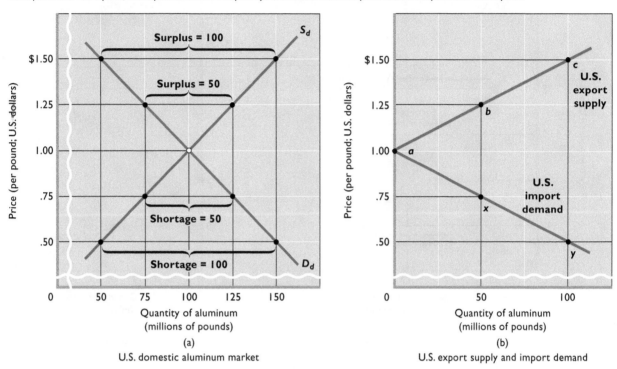

(a)
U.S. domestic aluminum market

(b)
U.S. export supply and import demand

producers will export at each world price above $1. This curve *slopes upward*, indicating a direct or positive relationship between the world price and the amount of U.S. exports. As world prices increase relative to domestic prices, U.S. exports rise.

U.S. Import Demand If the world price is below the domestic $1 price, the United States will import aluminum. Consider a $0.75 world price. The supply curve in Figure 20.3a reveals that at that price U.S. firms produce only 75 million pounds of aluminum. But the demand curve shows that the United States wants to buy 125 million pounds at that price. The result is a domestic shortage of 50 million pounds. To satisfy that shortage, the United States will import 50 million pounds of aluminum.

At an even lower world price, $0.50, U.S. producers will supply only 50 million pounds. Because U.S. consumers want to buy 150 million pounds at that price, there is a domestic shortage of 100 million pounds. Imports will flow to the United States to make up the difference. That is, at a $0.50 world price U.S. firms will supply 50 million pounds and 100 million pounds will be imported.

In Figure 20.3b we plot the U.S. **import demand curve** from these data. This *downsloping curve* shows the amounts of aluminum that will be imported at world prices below the $1 U.S. domestic price. The relationship between world prices and imported amounts is inverse or negative. At a world price of $1, domestic output will satisfy U.S. demand; imports will be zero (point *a*). But at $0.75 the United States will import 50 million pounds of aluminum (point *x*); at $0.50, the United States will import 100 million pounds (point *y*). Connecting points *a*, *x*, and *y* yields the *downsloping* U.S. import demand curve. It reveals that as world prices fall relative to U.S. domestic prices, U.S. imports increase.

Supply and Demand in Canada

We repeat our analysis in Figure 20.4, this time from the viewpoint of Canada. (We have converted Canadian dollar prices to U.S. dollar prices via the exchange rate.) Note that the domestic supply curve S_d and the domestic demand curve D_d for aluminum in Canada yield a domestic price of $0.75, which is $0.25 lower than the $1 U.S. domestic price.

FIGURE 20.4 Canadian export supply and import demand. (a) At world prices above the $0.75 domestic price, production in Canada exceeds domestic consumption. At world prices below $0.75, domestic shortages occur. (b) Surpluses result in exports, and shortages result in imports. The Canadian export supply curve and import demand curve depict the relationships between world prices and exports or imports.

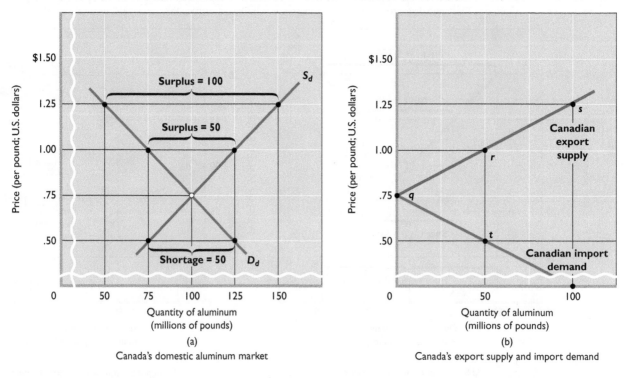

(a)
Canada's domestic aluminum market

(b)
Canada's export supply and import demand

The analysis proceeds exactly as above except that the domestic price is now the Canadian price. If the world price is $0.75, Canadians will neither export nor import aluminum (giving us point *q* in Figure 20.4b). At world prices above $0.75, Canadian firms will produce more aluminum than Canadian consumers will buy. Canadian firms will export the surplus. At a $1 world price, Figure 20.4b tells us that Canada will have and export a domestic surplus of 50 million pounds (yielding point *r*). At $1.25, it will have and will export a domestic surplus of 100 million pounds (point *s*). Connecting these points yields the upsloping Canadian export supply curve, which reflects the domestic surpluses (and hence the exports) that occur when the world price exceeds the $0.75 Canadian domestic price.

At world prices below $0.75, domestic shortages occur in Canada. At a $0.50 world price, Figure 20.4a shows that Canadian consumers want to buy 125 million pounds of aluminum but Canadian firms will produce only 75 million pounds. The shortage will bring 50 million pounds of imports to Canada (point *t* in Figure 20.4b). The Canadian import demand curve in that figure shows the Canadian imports that will occur at all world aluminum prices below the $0.75 Canadian domestic price.

Equilibrium World Price, Exports, and Imports

We now have the tools for determining the **equilibrium world price** of aluminum and the equilibrium world levels of exports and imports when the world is opened to trade. Figure 20.5 combines the U.S. export supply curve and import demand curve in Figure 20.3b and the Canadian export supply curve and import demand curve in Figure 20.4b. The two U.S. curves proceed rightward from the $1 U.S. domestic price; the two Canadian curves proceed rightward from the $0.75 Canadian domestic price.

International equilibrium occurs in this two-nation model where one nation's import demand curve intersects another nation's export supply curve. In this case the U.S. import demand curve intersects Canada's export supply curve at *e*. There, the world price of aluminum is $0.88. The Canadian export supply curve indicates that Canada will export 25 million pounds of aluminum at this price. Also at this price the United States will

WORKED PROBLEMS

W20.2
Equilibrium world price, exports, and imports

FIGURE 20.5 Equilibrium world price and quantity of exports and imports. In a two-nation world, the equilibrium world price (= $0.88) is determined by the intersection of one nation's export supply curve and the other nation's import demand curve. This intersection also decides the equilibrium volume of exports and imports. Here, Canada exports 25 million pounds of aluminum to the United States.

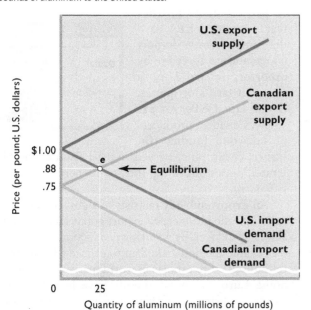

import 25 million pounds from Canada, indicated by the U.S. import demand curve. The $0.88 world price equates the quantity of imports demanded and the quantity of exports supplied (25 million pounds). Thus, there will be world trade of 25 million pounds of aluminum at $0.88 per pound.

Note that after trade, the single $0.88 world price will prevail in both Canada and the United States. Only one price for a standardized commodity can persist in a highly competitive world market. With trade, all consumers can buy a pound of aluminum for $0.88, and all producers can sell it for that price. This world price means that Canadians will pay more for aluminum with trade ($0.88) than without it ($0.75). The increased Canadian output caused by trade raises Canadian per-unit production costs and therefore raises the price of aluminum in Canada. The United States, however, pays less for aluminum with trade ($0.88) than without it ($1). The U.S. gain comes from Canada's comparative cost advantage in producing aluminum.

Why would Canada willingly send 25 million pounds of its aluminum output to the United States for U.S. consumption? After all, producing this output uses up scarce Canadian resources and drives up the price of aluminum for Canadians. Canadians are willing to export aluminum

to the United States because Canadians gain the means—the U.S. dollars—to import other goods, say, computer software, from the United States. Canadian exports enable Canadians to acquire imports that have greater value to Canadians than the exported aluminum. Canadian exports to the United States finance Canadian imports from the United States.

QUICK REVIEW 20.4

- A nation will export a particular product if the world price exceeds the domestic price; it will import the product if the world price is less than the domestic price.
- In a two-country world model, equilibrium world prices and equilibrium quantities of exports and imports occur where one nation's export supply curve intersects the other nation's import demand curve.

Trade Barriers and Export Subsidies

LO20.4 Analyze the economic effects of tariffs and quotas. While a nation as a whole gains from trade, trade may harm particular domestic industries and their workers. Those industries might seek to preserve their economic positions by persuading their respective governments to protect them from imports—perhaps through tariffs, import quotas, or other trade barriers.

Indeed, the public may be won over by the apparent plausibility ("Cut imports and prevent domestic unemployment") and the patriotic ring ("Buy American!") of the arguments. The alleged benefits of tariffs are immediate and clear-cut to the public, but the adverse effects cited by economists are obscure and dispersed over the entire economy. When political deal-making is added in—"You back tariffs for the apparel industry in my state, and I'll back tariffs for the auto industry in your state"—the outcome can be a politically robust network of trade barriers. These impediments to free international trade can take several forms.

Tariffs are excise taxes or "duties" on the dollar values or physical quantities of imported goods. They may be imposed to obtain revenue or to protect domestic firms. A **revenue tariff** is usually applied to a product that is not being produced domestically, for example, tin, coffee, or bananas in the case of the United States. Rates on revenue tariffs tend to be modest and are designed to provide the federal government with revenue. A **protective tariff** is

CONSIDER THIS ...

Buy American?

Will "buying American" make Americans better off? No, says Dallas Federal Reserve economist W. Michael Cox:

A common myth is that it is better for Americans to spend their money at home than abroad. The best way to expose the fallacy of this argument is to take it to its logical extreme. If it is better for me to spend my money here than abroad, then it is even better yet to buy in Texas than in New York, better yet to buy in Dallas than in Houston ... in my own neighborhood ... within my own family ... to consume only what I can produce. Alone and poor.*

---

*"The Fruits of Free Trade," 2002 Annual Report, by W. Michael Cox and Richard Alm, p. 16, Federal Reserve Bank of Dallas. Used with permission.

---

implemented to shield domestic producers from foreign competition. These tariffs impede free trade by increasing the prices of imported goods and therefore shifting sales toward domestic producers. Although protective tariffs are usually not high enough to stop the importation of foreign goods, they put foreign producers at a competitive disadvantage. A tariff on imported auto tires, for example, would make domestically produced tires more attractive to consumers.

An **import quota** is a limit on the quantities or total values of specific items that are imported in some period. Once a quota is filled, further imports of that product are choked off. Import quotas are more effective than tariffs in impeding international trade. With a tariff, a product can go on being imported in large quantities. But with an import quota, all imports are prohibited once the quota is filled.

A **nontariff barrier (NTB)** includes onerous licensing requirements, unreasonable standards pertaining to product quality, or simply bureaucratic hurdles and delays in customs procedures. Some nations require that importers of foreign goods obtain licenses and then restrict the number of licenses issued. Although many nations carefully inspect imported agricultural products to prevent the introduction of potentially harmful insects, some countries use lengthy inspections to impede imports. Japan and the European countries frequently require that their

domestic importers of foreign goods obtain licenses. By restricting the issuance of licenses, governments can limit imports.

A **voluntary export restriction (VER)** is a trade barrier by which foreign firms "voluntarily" limit the amount of their exports to a particular country. VERs have the same effect as import quotas and are agreed to by exporters to avoid more stringent tariffs or quotas. In the late 1990s, for example, Canadian producers of softwood lumber (fir, spruce, cedar, pine) agreed to a VER on exports to the United States under the threat of a permanently higher U.S. tariff.

ORIGIN OF THE IDEA

O20.2

Trade protectionism

An **export subsidy** consists of a government payment to a domestic producer of export goods and is designed to aid that producer. By reducing production costs, the subsidies enable the domestic firm to charge a lower price and thus to sell more exports in world markets. Two examples: Some European governments have heavily subsidized Airbus Industries, a European firm that produces commercial aircraft. The subsidies help Airbus compete against the American firm Boeing. The United States and other nations have subsidized domestic farmers to boost the domestic food supply. Such subsidies have artificially lowered export prices on agricultural produce.

Later in this chapter we will discuss some of the specific arguments and appeals that are made to justify protection.

Economic Impact of Tariffs

We will confine our in-depth analysis of the effects of trade barriers to the two most common forms: tariffs and quotas. Once again, we turn to supply and demand analysis for help. Curves D_d and S_d in Figure 20.6 show domestic demand and supply for a product in which a nation, say, the United States, does *not* have a comparative advantage—for example, DVD players. (Disregard curve $S_d + Q$ for now.) Without world trade, the domestic price and output would be P_d and q, respectively.

Assume now that the domestic economy is opened to world trade and that Japan, which *does* have a comparative advantage in DVD players, begins to sell its players in the United States. We assume that with free trade the domestic price cannot differ from the world price, which here is P_w. At P_w domestic consumption is d and domestic production is a. The horizontal distance between the domestic supply and demand curves at P_w represents imports of ad.

FIGURE 20.6 The economic effects of a protective tariff or an import quota. A tariff that increases the price of a good from P_w to P_t will reduce domestic consumption from d to c. Domestic producers will be able to sell more output (b rather than a) at a higher price (P_t rather than P_w). Foreign exporters are injured because they sell less output (bc rather than ad). The yellow area indicates the amount of tariff paid by domestic consumers. An import quota of bc units has the same effect as the tariff, with one exception: The amount represented by the yellow area will go to foreign producers rather than to the domestic government.

Thus far, our analysis is similar to the analysis of world prices in Figure 20.3.

Direct Effects

Suppose now that the United States imposes a tariff on each imported DVD player. The tariff, which raises the price of imported players from P_w to P_t, has four effects:

- *Decline in consumption* Consumption of DVD players in the United States declines from d to c as the higher price moves buyers up and to the left along their demand curve. The tariff prompts consumers to buy fewer players, and reallocate a portion of their expenditures to less desired substitute products. U.S. consumers are clearly injured by the tariff, since they pay $P_t - P_w$ more for each of the c units they buy at price P_t.

- *Increased domestic production* U.S. producers—who are not subject to the tariff—receive the higher price P_t per unit. Because this new price is higher than the pretariff world price P_w, the domestic DVD-player industry moves up and to the right along its supply curve S_d, increasing domestic output from a to b. Domestic producers thus enjoy both a higher price and expanded sales; this explains why domestic producers lobby for protective tariffs. But from a social point of view, the increase in domestic production from a to b

means that the tariff permits domestic producers of players to bid resources away from other, more efficient, U.S. industries.

- *Decline in imports* Japanese producers are hurt. Although the sales price of each player is higher by $P_t - P_w$, that amount accrues to the U.S. government, not to Japanese producers. The after-tariff world price, or the per-unit revenue to Japanese producers, remains at P_w, but the volume of U.S. imports (Japanese exports) falls from ad to bc.

- *Tariff revenue* The yellow rectangle represents the amount of revenue the tariff yields. Total revenue from the tariff is determined by multiplying the tariff, $P_t - P_w$ per unit, by the number of players imported, bc. This tariff revenue is a transfer of income from consumers to government and does not represent any net change in the nation's economic well-being. The result is that government gains this portion of what consumers lose by paying more for DVD players.

Indirect Effect Tariffs have a subtle effect beyond what our supply and demand diagram can show. Because Japan sells fewer DVD players in the United States, it earns fewer dollars and so must buy fewer U.S. exports. U.S. export industries must then cut production and release resources. These are highly efficient industries, as we know from their comparative advantage and their ability to sell goods in world markets.

Tariffs directly promote the expansion of inefficient industries that do not have a comparative advantage; they also indirectly cause the contraction of relatively efficient industries that do have a comparative advantage. Put bluntly, tariffs cause resources to be shifted in the wrong direction—and that is not surprising. We know that specialization and world trade lead to more efficient use of world resources and greater world output. But protective tariffs reduce world trade. Therefore, tariffs also reduce efficiency and the world's real output.

Economic Impact of Quotas

We noted earlier that an import quota is a legal limit placed on the amount of some product that can be imported in a given year. Quotas have the same economic impact as a tariff, with one big difference: While tariffs generate revenue for the domestic government, a quota transfers that revenue to foreign producers.

Suppose in Figure 20.6 that, instead of imposing a tariff, the United States prohibits any imports of Japanese DVD players in excess of bc units. In other words, an import quota of bc players is imposed on Japan. We deliberately chose the size of this quota to be the same amount as imports would be under a $P_t - P_w$ tariff so that we can compare "equivalent" situations. As a consequence of the quota, the supply of players is $S_d + Q$ in the United States. This supply consists of the domestic supply plus the fixed amount bc (= Q) that importers will provide at each domestic price. The supply curve $S_w + Q$ does not extend below price P_w because Japanese producers would not export players to the United States at any price below P_w; instead, they would sell them to other countries at the world market price of P_w.

Most of the economic results are the same as those with a tariff. Prices of DVD players are higher (P_t instead of P_w) because imports have been reduced from ad to bc. Domestic consumption of DVD players is down from d to c. U.S. producers enjoy both a higher price (P_t rather than P_w) and increased sales (b rather than a).

The difference is that the price increase of $P_t - P_w$ paid by U.S. consumers on imports of bc—the yellow area—no longer goes to the U.S. Treasury as tariff (tax) revenue but flows to the Japanese firms that have acquired the quota rights to sell DVD players in the United States. For consumers in the United States, a tariff produces a better economic outcome than a quota, other things being the same. A tariff generates government revenue that can be used to cut other taxes or to finance public goods and services that benefit the United States. In contrast, the higher price created by quotas results in additional revenue for foreign producers.

QUICK REVIEW 20.5

- A tariff on a product increases its price, reduces its consumption, increases its domestic production, reduces its imports, and generates tariff revenue for the government; an import quota does the same, except a quota generates revenue for foreign producers rather than for the government imposing the quota.

Net Costs of Tariffs and Quotas

Figure 20.6 shows that tariffs and quotas impose costs on domestic consumers but provide gains to domestic producers and, in the case of tariffs, revenue to the federal government. The consumer costs of trade restrictions are calculated by determining the effect the restrictions have on consumer prices. Protection raises the price of a product in three ways: (1) The price of the imported product goes up; (2) the higher price of imports causes some consumers to shift their purchases to higher-priced domestically produced goods; and (3) the prices of domestically produced goods rise because import competition has declined.

Study after study finds that the costs to consumers substantially exceed the gains to producers and government. A sizable net cost or efficiency loss to society arises from trade protection. Furthermore, industries employ large amounts of economic resources to influence Congress to pass and retain protectionist laws. Because these rent-seeking efforts divert resources away from more socially desirable purposes, trade restrictions impose these additional costs on society as well.

Conclusion: The gains that U.S. trade barriers create for protected industries and their workers come at the expense of much greater losses for the entire economy. The result is economic inefficiency, reduced consumption, and lower standards of living.

The Case for Protection: A Critical Review

LO20.5 Analyze the validity of the most frequently presented arguments for protectionism.

Despite the logic of specialization and trade, there are still protectionists in some union halls, corporate boardrooms, and congressional conference rooms. What arguments do protectionists make to justify trade barriers? How valid are those arguments?

Military Self-Sufficiency Argument

The argument here is not economic but political-military: Protective tariffs are needed to preserve or strengthen industries that produce the materials essential for national defense. In an uncertain world, the political-military objectives (self-sufficiency) sometimes must take precedence over economic goals (efficiency in the use of world resources).

Unfortunately, it is difficult to measure and compare the benefit of increased national security against the cost of economic inefficiency when protective tariffs are imposed. The economist can only point out that when a nation levies tariffs to increase military self-sufficiency, it incurs economic costs.

All people in the United States would agree that relying on hostile nations for necessary military equipment is not a good idea, yet the self-sufficiency argument is open to serious abuse. Nearly every industry can claim that it makes direct or indirect contributions to national security and hence deserves protection from imports.

Diversification-for-Stability Argument

Highly specialized economies such as Saudi Arabia (based on oil) and Cuba (based on sugar) are dependent on international markets for their income. In these economies, wars, international political developments, recessions abroad, and random fluctuations in world supply and demand for one or two particular goods can cause deep declines in export revenues and therefore in domestic income. Tariff and quota protection are allegedly needed in such nations to enable greater industrial diversification. That way, these economies will not be so dependent on exporting one or two products to obtain the other goods they need. Such goods will be available domestically, thereby providing greater domestic stability.

There is some truth in this diversification-for-stability argument. But the argument has little or no relevance to the United States and other advanced economies. Also, the economic costs of diversification may be great; for example, one-crop economies may be highly inefficient at manufacturing.

Infant Industry Argument

The infant industry argument contends that protective tariffs are needed to allow new domestic industries to establish themselves. Temporarily shielding young domestic firms from the severe competition of more mature and more efficient foreign firms will give infant industries a chance to develop and become efficient producers.

This argument for protection rests on an alleged exception to the case for free trade. The exception is that young industries have not had, and if they face mature foreign competition will never have, the chance to make the long-run adjustments needed for larger scale and greater efficiency in production. In this view, tariff protection for such infant industries will correct a misallocation of world resources perpetuated by historically different levels of economic development between domestic and foreign industries.

There are some logical problems with the infant industry argument. In the developing nations it is difficult to determine which industries are the infants that are capable of achieving economic maturity and therefore deserving protection. Also, protective tariffs may persist even after industrial maturity has been realized.

Most economists feel that if infant industries are to be subsidized, there are better means than tariffs for doing so. Direct subsidies, for example, have the advantage of making explicit which industries are being aided and to what degree.

Protection-against-Dumping Argument

The protection-against-dumping argument contends that tariffs are needed to protect domestic firms from "dumping" by foreign producers. **Dumping** is the sale of a product in a foreign country at prices either below cost or below the prices commonly charged at home.

Economists cite two plausible reasons for this behavior. First, with regard to below-cost dumping, firms in country A may dump goods at below cost into country B in an attempt to drive their competitors in country B out of business. If the firms in country A succeed in driving their competitors in country B out of business, they will enjoy monopoly power and monopoly prices and profits on the goods they subsequently sell in country B. Their hope is that the longer-term monopoly profits will more than offset the losses from below-cost sales that must take place while they are attempting to drive their competitors in country B out of business.

Second, dumping that involves selling abroad at a price that is below the price commonly charged in the home country (but that is still at or above production costs) may be a form of price discrimination, which is charging different prices to different customers. As an example, a foreign seller that has a monopoly in its home market may find that it can maximize its overall profit by charging a high price in its monopolized domestic market while charging a lower price in the United States, where it must compete with U.S. producers. Curiously, it may pursue this strategy even if it makes no profit at all from its sales in the United States, where it must charge the competitive price. So why bother selling in the United States? Because the increase in overall production that comes about by exporting to the United States may allow the firm to obtain the per-unit cost savings often associated with large-scale production. These cost savings imply even higher profits in the monopolized domestic market.

Because dumping is an "unfair trade practice," most nations prohibit it. For example, where dumping is shown to injure U.S. firms, the federal government imposes tariffs called *antidumping duties* on the goods in question. But relatively few documented cases of dumping occur each year, and specific instances of unfair trade do not justify widespread, permanent tariffs. Moreover, antidumping duties can be abused. Often, what appears to be dumping is simply comparative advantage at work.

Increased Domestic Employment Argument

Arguing for a tariff to "save U.S. jobs" becomes fashionable when the economy encounters a recession (such as the severe recession of 2007–2009 in the United States).

In an economy that engages in international trade, exports involve spending on domestic output and imports reflect spending to obtain part of another nation's output. So, in this argument, reducing imports will divert spending on another nation's output to spending on domestic output. Thus, domestic output and employment will rise. But this argument has several shortcomings.

While imports may eliminate some U.S. jobs, they create others. Imports may have eliminated the jobs of some U.S. steel and textile workers in recent years, but other workers have gained jobs unloading ships, flying imported aircraft, and selling imported electronic equipment. Import restrictions alter the composition of employment, but they may have little or no effect on the volume of employment.

The *fallacy of composition*—the false idea that what is true for the part is necessarily true for the whole—is also present in this rationale for tariffs. All nations cannot simultaneously succeed in restricting imports while maintaining their exports; what is true for one nation is not true for all nations. The exports of one nation must be the imports of another nation. To the extent that one country is able to expand its economy through an excess of exports over imports, the resulting excess of imports over exports worsens another economy's unemployment problem. It is no wonder that tariffs and import quotas meant to achieve domestic full employment are called "beggar my neighbor" policies: They achieve short-run domestic goals by making trading partners poorer.

Moreover, nations adversely affected by tariffs and quotas are likely to retaliate, causing a "trade war" (more precisely, a *trade barrier war*) that will choke off trade and make all nations worse off. The **Smoot-Hawley Tariff Act** of 1930 is a classic example. Although that act was meant to reduce imports and stimulate U.S. production, the high tariffs it authorized prompted adversely affected nations to retaliate with tariffs equally high. International trade fell, lowering the output and income of all nations. Economic historians generally agree that the Smoot-Hawley Tariff Act was a contributing cause of the Great Depression.

Finally, forcing an excess of exports over imports cannot succeed in raising domestic employment over the long run. It is through U.S. imports that foreign nations earn dollars for buying U.S. exports. In the long run, a nation must import in order to export. The long-run impact of tariffs is not an increase in domestic employment but, at best, a reallocation of workers away from export industries and to protected domestic industries. This shift implies a less efficient allocation of resources.

Cheap Foreign Labor Argument

The cheap foreign labor argument says that domestic firms and workers must be shielded from the ruinous competition of countries where wages are low. If protection is not provided, cheap imports will flood U.S. markets and the prices of U.S. goods—along with the wages of U.S. workers—will be pulled down. That is, domestic living standards in the United States will be reduced.

This argument can be rebutted at several levels. The logic of the argument suggests that it is not mutually beneficial for rich and poor persons to trade with one another. However, that is not the case. A low-income farmworker may pick lettuce or tomatoes for a rich landowner, and both may benefit from the transaction. And both U.S. consumers and Chinese workers gain when they "trade" a pair of athletic shoes priced at $30 as opposed to U.S. consumers being restricted to buying a similar shoe made in the United States for $60.

Also, recall that gains from trade are based on comparative advantage, not on absolute advantage. Look back at Figure 20.1, where we supposed that the United States and Mexico had labor forces of exactly the same size. Noting the positions of the production possibilities curves, observe that U.S. labor can produce more of either good. Thus, it is more productive. Because of this greater productivity, we can expect wages and living standards to be higher for U.S. labor. Mexico's less productive labor will receive lower wages.

The cheap foreign labor argument suggests that, to maintain its standard of living, the United States should not trade with low-wage Mexico. What if it does not trade with Mexico? Will wages and living standards rise in the United States as a result? No. To obtain vegetables, the United States will have to reallocate a portion of its labor from its relatively more-efficient beef industry to its relatively less-efficient vegetables industry. As a result, the average productivity of U.S. labor will fall, as will real wages and living standards. The labor forces of both countries will have diminished standards of living because without specialization and trade they will have less output available to them. Compare column 4 with column 1 in Table 20.1 or points A' and Z' with A and Z in Figure 20.2 to confirm this point.

Another problem with the cheap foreign labor argument is that its proponents incorrectly focus on labor costs per hour when what really matters is labor costs per unit of output. As an example, suppose that a U.S. factory pays its workers $20 per hour while a factory in a developing country pays its workers $4 per hour. The proponents of the cheap foreign labor argument look at these numbers and conclude—incorrectly—that it is impossible for the U.S. factory to compete with the factory in the developing country. But this conclusion fails to take into account two crucial facts:

- What actually matters is labor costs per *unit of output*, not labor costs per *hour of work*.
- Differences in productivity typically mean that labor costs per unit of output are often nearly identical despite huge differences in hourly labor costs.

To see why these points matter so much, let's take into account how productive the two factories are. Because the U.S. factory uses much more sophisticated technology, better trained workers, and a lot more capital per worker, one worker in one hour can produce 20 units of output. Since the U.S. workers get paid $20 per hour, this means the U.S. factory's labor cost *per unit of output* is $1. The factory in the developing country is much less productive since it uses less efficient technology and its relatively untrained workers have a lot less machinery and equipment to work with. A worker there produces only 4 units per hour. Given the foreign wage of $4 per hour, this means that the labor cost per unit of output at the factory in the developing country is also $1.

As you can see, the lower wage rate per hour at the factory in the developing country does not translate into lower labor costs per unit—meaning that it won't be able to undersell its U.S. competitor just because its workers get paid lower wages per hour.

Proponents of the cheap foreign labor argument tend to focus exclusively on the large international differences that exist in labor costs per hour. They typically fail to mention that these differences in labor costs per hour are mostly the result of tremendously large differences in productivity and that these large differences in productivity serve to equalize labor costs per unit of output. As a result, firms in developing countries only *sometimes* have an advantage in terms of labor costs per unit of output. Whether they do in any specific situation will vary by industry and firm and will depend on differences in productivity as well as differences in labor costs per hour. For many goods, labor productivity in high-wage countries like the United States is so much higher than labor productivity in low-wage countries that it is actually cheaper *per unit of output* to manufacture those goods in high-wage countries. That is why, for instance, Intel still makes microchips in the United States and why most automobiles are still produced in the United States, Japan, and Europe rather than in low-wage countries.

> ### QUICK REVIEW 20.6
>
> - Most rationales for trade protections are special-interest requests that, if followed, would create gains for protected industries and their workers at the expense of greater losses for the economy.

Multilateral Trade Agreements and Free-Trade Zones

LO20.6 Identify and explain the objectives of GATT, WTO, EU, eurozone, and NAFTA, and discuss offshoring and trade adjustment assistance.

Aware of the detrimental effects of trade wars and the general weaknesses of arguments for trade protections, nations have worked to lower tariffs worldwide. Their pursuit of freer trade has been aided by recently emerged special-interest groups that have offset the more-established special-interest groups that have traditionally supported tariffs and quotas. Specifically, lower tariffs are now supported by exporters of goods and services, importers of foreign components used in "domestic" products, and domestic sellers of imported products.

General Agreement on Tariffs and Trade

In 1947, 23 nations, including the United States, signed the **General Agreement on Tariffs and Trade (GATT).** GATT was based on three principles: (1) equal, nondiscriminatory trade treatment for all member nations; (2) the reduction of tariffs by multilateral negotiation; and (3) the elimination of import quotas. Basically, GATT provided a forum for the multilateral negotiation of reduced trade barriers.

Since the Second World War, member nations have completed eight "rounds" of GATT negotiations to reduce trade barriers. The eighth round of negotiations began in Uruguay in 1986. After seven years of complex discussions, in 1993 a new agreement was reached by the 128 nations that were by that time members of GATT. The Uruguay Round agreement took effect on January 1, 1995, and its provisions were phased in through 2005.

Under this agreement, tariffs on thousands of products were eliminated or reduced, with overall tariffs dropping by 33 percent. The agreement also liberalized government rules that in the past impeded the global market for such services as advertising, legal services, tourist services, and financial services. Quotas on imported textiles and apparel were phased out and replaced with tariffs. Other provisions reduced agricultural subsidies paid to farmers and protected intellectual property (patents, trademarks, and copyrights) against piracy.

World Trade Organization

The Uruguay Round agreement established the **World Trade Organization (WTO)** as GATT's successor. Some 159 nations belonged to the WTO in 2013. The WTO oversees trade agreements reached by the member nations, and rules on trade disputes among them. It also provides forums for further rounds of trade negotiations. The ninth and latest round of negotiations—the **Doha Development Agenda**—was launched in Doha, Qatar, in late 2001. (The trade rounds occur over several years in several venues but are named after the city or country of origination.) The negotiations are aimed at further reducing tariffs and quotas, as well as agricultural subsidies that distort trade. You can get an update on the status of the complex negotiations at **www.wto.org**.

GATT and the WTO have been positive forces in the trend toward liberalized world trade. The trade rules agreed upon by the member nations provide a strong and necessary bulwark against the protectionism called for by the special-interest groups in the various nations.

For that reason and others, the WTO is quite controversial. Critics are concerned that rules crafted to expand international trade and investment enable firms to circumvent national laws that protect workers and the environment. Critics ask: What good are minimum-wage laws, worker-safety laws, collective-bargaining rights, and environmental laws if firms can easily shift their production to nations that have weaker laws or if consumers can buy goods produced in those countries?

Proponents of the WTO respond that labor and environmental protections should be pursued directly in nations that have low standards and via international organizations other than the WTO. These issues should not be linked to the process of trade liberalization, which confers widespread economic benefits across nations. Moreover, say proponents of the WTO, many environmental and labor concerns are greatly overblown. Most world trade is among advanced industrial countries, not between them and countries that have lower environmental and labor standards. Moreover, the free flow of goods and resources raises output and income in the developing nations. Historically, such increases in living standards have eventually resulted in stronger, not weaker, protections for the environment and for workers.

The European Union

Countries have also sought to reduce tariffs by creating regional free-trade zones. The most dramatic example is the **European Union (EU).** Initiated in 1958 as the Common Market, in 2003 the EU comprised 15 European nations—Austria, Belgium, Denmark, Finland, France, Germany, Greece, Ireland, Italy, Luxembourg, the Netherlands, Portugal, Spain, Sweden, and the United Kingdom. In 2004, the EU expanded by 10 additional European countries—Cyprus, the Czech Republic, Estonia, Hungary, Latvia, Lithuania, Malta, Poland, Slovakia, and Slovenia. The 2007 addition of Bulgaria and Romania plus the 2013 addition of Croatia expanded the EU to 28 nations.

The EU has abolished tariffs and import quotas on nearly all products traded among the participating nations and established a common system of tariffs applicable to all goods received from nations outside the EU. It has also liberalized the movement of capital and labor within the EU and has created common policies in other economic matters of joint concern, such as agriculture, transportation, and business practices.

EU integration has achieved for Europe what the U.S. constitutional prohibition on tariffs by individual states has achieved for the United States: increased regional specialization, greater productivity, greater output, and faster economic growth. The free flow of goods and services has created large markets for EU industries. The resulting economies of large-scale production have enabled these industries to achieve much lower costs than they could have achieved in their small, single-nation markets.

One of the most significant accomplishments of the EU was the establishment of the so-called **eurozone** or euro area in the early 2000s. As of 2013, 17 members of the EU (Austria, Belgium, Cyprus, Estonia, Finland, France, Germany, Greece, Ireland, Italy, Luxembourg, Malta, the Netherlands, Portugal, Slovenia, Slovakia, and Spain) use the euro as a common currency. Notably, the United Kingdom, Denmark, and Sweden have opted not to use the common currency, at least for now. But gone are French francs, German marks, Italian liras, and other national currencies that were once used by eurozone countries.

Economists expect the adoption of the euro to raise the standard of living in the eurozone nations over time. By ending the inconvenience and expense of exchanging currencies, the euro has enhanced the free flow of goods, services, and resources among the eurozone members. Companies that previously sold products in only one or two European nations have found it easier to price and sell their products in all 17 eurozone countries. The euro has also allowed consumers and businesses to comparison shop for outputs and inputs, and this capability has increased competition, reduced prices, and lowered costs.

North American Free Trade Agreement

In 1993 Canada, Mexico, and the United States created a major free-trade zone. The **North American Free Trade Agreement (NAFTA)** established a free-trade area that has about the same combined output as the EU but encompasses a much larger geographic area. NAFTA has eliminated tariffs and other trade barriers between Canada, Mexico, and the United States for most goods and services.

Critics of NAFTA feared that it would cause a massive loss of U.S. jobs as firms moved to Mexico to take advantage of lower wages and weaker regulations on pollution and workplace safety. Also, they were concerned that Japan and South Korea would build plants in Mexico and transport goods tariff-free to the United States, further hurting U.S. firms and workers.

In retrospect, critics were much too pessimistic. Since the passage of NAFTA in 1993, employment in the United States has increased by more than 20 million workers. NAFTA has increased trade among Canada, Mexico, and the United States and has enhanced the standard of living in all three countries.

QUICK REVIEW 20.7

- The General Agreement on Tariffs and Trade (GATT) of 1947 reduced tariffs and quotas and established a process for numerous subsequent rounds of multinational trade negotiations that have liberalized international trade.
- The World Trade Organization (WTO)—GATT's successor—rules on trade disputes and provides forums for negotiations on further rounds of trade liberalization. The current round of negotiations is called the Doha Development Agenda.
- The European Union (EU) and the North American Free Trade Agreement (NAFTA) have reduced internal trade barriers among their member nations by establishing multination free-trade zones.

Recognizing Those Hurt by Free Trade

Shifts in patterns of comparative advantage and removal of long-standing trade protection can hurt specific groups of workers. For example, the erosion of the United States' once strong comparative advantage in steel has caused production plant shutdowns and layoffs in the U.S. steel industry. The textile and apparel industries in the United States face similar difficulties. Clearly, not everyone wins from free trade (or freer trade). Some workers lose.

Trade Adjustment Assistance

The **Trade Adjustment Assistance Act** of 2002 introduced some innovative policies to help those hurt by shifts in international trade patterns. The law provides cash assistance (beyond unemployment insurance) for up to 78 weeks for workers displaced by imports or plant relocations abroad. To obtain the assistance, workers must participate in job searches, training programs, or remedial education. Also provided are relocation allowances to help displaced workers move geographically to new jobs within the United States. Refundable tax credits for health insurance serve as payments to help workers maintain their insurance coverage during the retraining and job-search period. Workers who are 50 years of age or older are eligible for "wage insurance," which replaces some of the difference in pay (if any) between their old and new jobs. Many economists support trade adjustment assistance because it not only helps workers hurt by international trade but also helps create the political support necessary to reduce trade barriers and export subsidies.

But not all economists favor trade adjustment assistance. Loss of jobs from imports, sending some work abroad, and plant relocations to other countries are only a small fraction (about 4 percent in recent years) of total job losses in the economy each year. Many workers also lose their jobs because of changing patterns of demand, changing technology, bad management, and other dynamic aspects of a market economy. Some critics ask, "What makes losing one's job to international trade worthy of such special treatment, compared to losing one's job to, say, technological change or domestic competition?" Economists can find no totally satisfying answer.

Offshoring of Jobs

Not only are some U.S. jobs lost because of international trade, but some are lost because of globalization of resource markets. In recent years U.S. firms have found the outsourcing of work abroad to be increasingly profitable. Economists call this business activity **offshoring**—shifting work previously done by American workers to workers located in other nations. Offshoring is not a new practice but traditionally has involved components for U.S. manufacturing goods. For example, Boeing has long offshored the production of major airplane parts for its "American" aircraft.

Recent advances in computer and communications technology have enabled U.S. firms to offshore service jobs such as data entry, book composition, software coding, call-center operations, medical transcription, and claims processing to countries such as India. Where offshoring

Petition of the Candlemakers, 1845

French Economist Frédéric Bastiat (1801–1850) Devastated the Proponents of Protectionism by Satirically Extending Their Reasoning to Its Logical and Absurd Conclusions.

Petition of the Manufacturers of Candles, Waxlights, Lamps, Candlesticks, Street Lamps, Snuffers, Extinguishers, and of the Producers of Oil Tallow, Rosin, Alcohol, and, Generally, of Everything Connected with Lighting.

TO MESSIEURS THE MEMBERS OF THE CHAMBER OF DEPUTIES.

Gentlemen—You are on the right road. You reject abstract theories, and have little consideration for cheapness and plenty. Your chief care is the interest of the producer. You desire to emancipate him from external competition, and reserve the national market for national industry.

We are about to offer you an admirable opportunity of applying your—what shall we call it? your theory? No; nothing is more deceptive than theory; your doctrine? your system? your principle? but you dislike doctrines, you abhor systems, and as for principles, you deny that there are any in social economy: we shall say, then, your practice, your practice without theory and without principle.

We are suffering from the intolerable competition of a foreign rival, placed, it would seem, in a condition so far superior to ours for the production of light, that he absolutely inundates our national market with it at a price fabulously reduced. The moment he shows himself, our trade leaves us—all consumers apply to him; and a branch of native industry, having countless ramifications, is all at once rendered completely stagnant. This rival . . . is no other than the Sun.

What we pray for is, that it may please you to pass a law ordering the shutting up of all windows, skylights, dormer windows, outside and inside shutters, curtains, blinds, bull's-eyes; in a word, of all openings, holes, chinks, clefts, and fissures, by or through which the light of the sun has been in use to enter houses, to the prejudice of the meritorious manufacturers with which we flatter ourselves we have accommodated our country,—a country which, in gratitude, ought not to abandon us now to a strife so unequal.

If you shut up as much as possible all access to natural light, and create a demand for artificial light, which of our French manufacturers will not be encouraged by it? If more tallow is consumed, then there must be more oxen and sheep; and, consequently, we shall behold the multiplication of artificial meadows, meat, wool, hides, and, above all, manure, which is the basis and foundation of all agricultural wealth.

The same remark applies to navigation. Thousands of vessels will proceed to the whale fishery; and, in a short time, we shall possess a navy capable of maintaining the honor of France, and gratifying the patriotic aspirations of your petitioners, the undersigned candle-makers and others.

Only have the goodness to reflect, Gentlemen, and you will be convinced that there is, perhaps, no Frenchman, from the wealthy coalmaster to the humblest vender of lucifer matches, whose lot will not be ameliorated by the success of this our petition.

Source: Frédéric Bastiat, *Economic Sophisms* (Irvington-on-Hudson, NY: The Foundation for Economic Education, Inc., 1996), abridged. Used with permission of Foundation for Economic Education, **www.FEE.org**.

occurs, some of the value added in the production process accrues to foreign countries rather than the United States. So part of the income generated from the production of U.S. goods is paid to foreigners, not to American workers.

Offshoring is a wrenching experience for many Americans who lose their jobs, but it is not necessarily bad for the overall economy. Offshoring simply reflects growing specialization and international trade in services, or, more descriptively, "tasks." That growth has been made possible by recent trade agreements and new information and communication technologies. As with trade in goods, trade in services reflects comparative advantage and is beneficial to both trading parties. Moreover, the United States has a sizable trade surplus with other nations in services. The United States gains by specializing in high-valued services such as transportation services, accounting services, legal services, and advertising services, where it still has a comparative advantage. It then "trades" to obtain lower-valued services such as call-center and data-entry work, for which comparative advantage has gone abroad.

Offshoring also increases the demand for complementary jobs in the United States. Jobs that are close substitutes for existing U.S. jobs are lost, but complementary jobs in the United States are expanded. For example, the lower price of writing software code in India may mean a lower cost of software sold in the United States and abroad. That, in turn, may create more jobs for U.S.-based workers such as software designers, marketers, and distributors.

Moreover, offshoring may encourage domestic investment and the expansion of firms in the United States by reducing their production costs and keeping them competitive worldwide. In some instances, "offshoring jobs" may equate to "importing competitiveness." Entire firms that might otherwise disappear abroad may remain profitable in the United States only because they can offshore some of their work.

QUICK REVIEW 20.8

- Increased international trade and offshoring of jobs have harmed some specific U.S. workers and have led to policies such as trade adjustment assistance to try to help them with their transitions to new lines of work.

SUMMARY

LO20.1 List and discuss several key facts about international trade.

The United States leads the world in the combined volume of exports and imports. Other major trading nations are Germany, Japan, the western European nations, and the Asian economies of China, South Korea, Taiwan, and Singapore. The United States' principal exports include chemicals, agricultural products, consumer durables, semiconductors, and aircraft; principal imports include petroleum, automobiles, metals, household appliances, and computers.

LO20.2 Define comparative advantage, and demonstrate how specialization and trade add to a nation's output.

World trade is based on three considerations: the uneven distribution of economic resources among nations, the fact that efficient production of various goods requires particular techniques or combinations of resources, and the differentiated products produced among nations.

Mutually advantageous specialization and trade are possible between any two nations if they have different domestic opportunity-cost ratios for any two products. By specializing on the basis of comparative advantage, nations can obtain larger real incomes with fixed amounts of resources. The terms of trade determine how this increase in world output is shared by the trading nations. Increasing (rather than constant) opportunity costs limit specialization and trade.

LO20.3 Describe how differences between world prices and domestic prices prompt exports and imports.

A nation's export supply curve shows the quantities of a product the nation will export at world prices that exceed the domestic price (the price in a closed, no-international-trade economy). A nation's import demand curve reveals the quantities of a product it will import at world prices below the domestic price.

In a two-nation model, the equilibrium world price and the equilibrium quantities of exports and imports occur where one nation's export supply curve intersects the other nation's import demand curve. A nation will export a particular product if the world price exceeds the domestic price; it will import the product if the world price is less than the domestic price. The country with the lower costs of production will be the exporter and the country with the higher costs of production will be the importer.

LO20.4 Analyze the economic effects of tariffs and quotas.

Trade barriers take the form of protective tariffs, quotas, nontariff barriers, and "voluntary" export restrictions. Export subsidies also distort international trade. Supply and demand analysis demonstrates that protective tariffs and quotas increase the prices and reduce the quantities demanded of the affected goods. Sales by foreign exporters diminish; domestic producers, however, gain higher prices and enlarged sales. Consumer losses from trade restrictions greatly exceed producer and government gains, creating an efficiency loss to society.

LO20.5 Analyze the validity of the most frequently presented arguments for protectionism.

The strongest arguments for protection are the infant industry and military self-sufficiency arguments. Most other arguments for protection are interest-group appeals or reasoning fallacies that emphasize producer interests over consumer interests or stress the immediate effects of trade barriers while ignoring long-run consequences.

The cheap foreign labor argument for protection fails because it focuses on labor costs per hour rather than on what really matters, labor costs per unit of output. Due to higher productivity, firms in high-wage countries like the United States can have lower wage costs per unit of output than competitors in low-wage countries. Whether they do will depend on how their particular wage and productivity levels compare with those of their competitors in low-wage countries.

LO20.6 Identify and explain the objectives of GATT, WTO, EU, eurozone, and NAFTA, and discuss offshoring and trade adjustment assistance.

In 1947 the General Agreement on Tariffs and Trade (GATT) was formed to encourage nondiscriminatory treatment for all member nations, to reduce tariffs, and to eliminate import quotas. The Uruguay Round of GATT negotiations (1993) reduced tariffs and quotas, liberalized trade in services, reduced agricultural subsidies, reduced pirating of intellectual property, and phased out quotas on textiles.

GATT's successor, the World Trade Organization (WTO), had 159 member nations in 2013. It implements WTO agreements, rules on trade disputes between members, and provides forums for continued discussions on trade liberalization. The latest round of trade negotiations—the Doha Development Agenda—began in late 2001 and as of 2013 was still in progress.

Free-trade zones liberalize trade within regions. Two examples of free-trade arrangements are the 28-member European Union (EU) and the North American Free Trade Agreement (NAFTA), comprising Canada, Mexico, and the United States. Seventeen EU nations have abandoned their national currencies for a common currency called the euro.

The Trade Adjustment Assistance Act of 2002 recognizes that trade liberalization and increased international trade can create job loss for many workers. The Act therefore provides cash assistance, education and training benefits, health care subsidies, and wage subsidies (for persons aged 50 or older) to qualified workers displaced by imports or relocations of plants from the United States to abroad.

Offshoring is the practice of shifting work previously done by Americans in the United States to workers located in other nations. Although offshoring reduces some U.S. jobs, it lowers production costs, expands sales, and therefore may create other U.S. jobs. Less than 4 percent of all job losses in the United States each year are caused by imports, offshoring, and plant relocation abroad.

TERMS AND CONCEPTS

labor-intensive goods

land-intensive goods

capital-intensive goods

opportunity-cost ratio

comparative advantage

principle of comparative advantage

terms of trade

trading possibilities line

gains from trade

world price

domestic price

export supply curve

import demand curve

equilibrium world price

tariffs

revenue tariff

protective tariff

import quota

nontariff barrier (NTB)

voluntary export restriction (VER)

export subsidy

dumping

Smoot-Hawley Tariff Act

General Agreement on Tariffs and Trade (GATT)

World Trade Organization (WTO)

Doha Development Agenda

European Union (EU)

eurozone

North American Free Trade Agreement (NAFTA)

Trade Adjustment Assistance Act

offshoring

The following and additional problems can be found in **connect**
ECONOMICS

DISCUSSION QUESTIONS

1. Quantitatively, how important is international trade to the United States relative to the importance of trade to other nations? What country is the United States' most important trading partner, quantitatively? With what country does the United States have the largest trade deficit? **LO20.1**
2. Distinguish among land-, labor-, and capital-intensive goods, citing an example of each without resorting to book examples. How do these distinctions relate to international trade? How do distinctive products, unrelated to resource intensity, relate to international trade? **LO20.1, LO20.2**
3. Explain: "The United States can make certain toys with greater productive efficiency than can China. Yet we import those toys from China." Relate your answer to the ideas of Adam Smith and David Ricardo. **LO20.2**

4. Suppose Big Country can produce 80 units of X by using all its resources to produce X or 60 units of Y by devoting all its resources to Y. Comparable figures for Small Nation are 60 units of X and 60 units of Y. Assuming constant costs, in which product should each nation specialize? Explain why. What are the limits of the terms of trade between these two countries? How would rising costs (rather than constant costs) affect the extent of specialization and trade between these two countries? **LO20.2**

5. What is an export supply curve? What is an import demand curve? How do such curves relate to the determination of the equilibrium world price of a tradable good? **LO20.3**

6. Why is a quota more detrimental to an economy than a tariff that results in the same level of imports as the quota? What is the net outcome of either tariffs or quotas for the world economy? **LO20.4**

7. "The potentially valid arguments for tariff protection—military self-sufficiency, infant industry protection, and diversification for stability—are also the most easily abused." Why are these arguments susceptible to abuse? **LO20.4**

8. Evaluate the effectiveness of artificial trade barriers, such as tariffs and import quotas, as a way to achieve and maintain full employment throughout the U.S. economy. How might such policies reduce unemployment in one U.S. industry but increase it in another U.S. industry? **LO20.4**

9. In 2012, manufacturing workers in the United States earned average compensation of $35.67 per hour. That same year, manufacturing workers in Mexico earned average compensation of $6.36 per hour. How can U.S. manufacturers possibly compete? Why isn't all manufacturing done in Mexico and other low-wage countries? **LO20.4**

10. How might protective tariffs reduce both the imports and the exports of the nation that levies tariffs? In what way do foreign firms that "dump" their products onto the U.S. market in effect provide bargains to American consumers? How might the import competition lead to quality improvements and cost reductions by American firms? **LO20.4**

11. Identify and state the significance of each of the following trade-related entities: (*a*) the WTO; (*b*) the EU; (*c*) the eurozone; and (*d*) NAFTA. **LO20.6**

12. What form does trade adjustment assistance take in the United States? How does such assistance promote political support for free-trade agreements? Do you think workers who lose their jobs because of changes in trade laws deserve special treatment relative to workers who lose their jobs because of other changes in the economy, say, changes in patterns of government spending? **LO20.6**

13. What is offshoring of white-collar service jobs and how does that practice relate to international trade? Why has offshoring increased over the past few decades? Give an example (other than that in the textbook) of how offshoring can eliminate some American jobs while creating other American jobs. **LO20.6**

14. **LAST WORD** What was the central point that Bastiat was trying to make in his imaginary petition of the candlemakers?

REVIEW QUESTIONS

1. In Country A, a worker can make 5 bicycles per hour. In Country B, a worker can make 7 bicycles per hour. Which country has an absolute advantage in making bicycles? **LO20.2**
   a. Country A.
   b. Country B.

2. In Country A, the production of 1 bicycle requires using resources that could otherwise be used to produce 11 lamps. In Country B, the production of 1 bicycle requires using resources that could otherwise be used to produce 15 lamps. Which country has a comparative advantage in making bicycles? **LO20.2**
   a. Country A.
   b. Country B.

3. True or False: If Country B has an absolute advantage over Country A in producing bicycles, it will also have a comparative advantage over Country A in producing bicycles. **LO20.2**

4. Suppose that the opportunity-cost ratio for sugar and almonds is $4S \equiv 1A$ in Hawaii but $1S \equiv 2A$ in California. Which state has the comparative advantage in producing almonds? **LO20.2**
   a. Hawaii.
   b. California.
   c. Neither.

5. Suppose that the opportunity-cost ratio for fish and lumber is $1F \equiv 1L$ in Canada but $2F \equiv 1L$ in Iceland. Then _____ should specialize in producing fish while _____ should specialize in producing lumber. **LO20.2**
   a. Canada; Iceland.
   b. Iceland; Canada.

6. Suppose that the opportunity-cost ratio for watches and cheese is $1C \equiv 1W$ in Switzerland but $1C \equiv 4W$ in Japan. At which of the following international exchange ratios (terms of trade) will Switzerland and Japan be willing to specialize and engage in trade with each other. **LO20.2**
   *Select **one or more** answers from the choices shown.*
   a. $1C \equiv 3W.$
   b. $1C \equiv \frac{1}{2}W.$
   c. $1C \equiv 5W.$
   d. $\frac{1}{2}C \equiv 1W.$
   e. $2C \equiv 1W.$

7. We see quite a bit of international trade in the real world. And trade is driven by specialization. So why don't we see full specialization—for instance, all cars in the world being made in South Korea, or all the mobile phones in the world

being made in China? Choose the best answer from among the following choices. **LO20.2**
a. High tariffs.
b. Extensive import quotas.
c. Increasing opportunity costs.
d. Increasing returns.

8. Which of the following are benefits of international trade? **LO20.2**
*Choose **one or more** answers from the choices shown.*
a. A more efficient allocation of resources.
b. A higher level of material well-being.
c. Gains from specialization.
d. Promoting competition.
e. Deterring monopoly.
f. Reducing the threat of war.

9. True or False: If a country is open to international trade, the domestic price can differ from the international price. **LO20.3**

10. Suppose that the current international price of wheat is $6 per bushel and that the United States is currently exporting 30 million bushels per year. If the United States suddenly became a closed economy with respect to wheat, would the domestic price of wheat in the United States end up higher or lower than $6? **LO20.3**
a. Higher.
b. Lower.
c. The same.

11. Suppose that if Iceland and Japan were both closed economies, the domestic price of fish would be $100 per ton in Iceland and $90 per ton in Japan. If the two countries decided to open up to international trade with each other, which of the following could be the equilibrium international price of fish once they begin trading? **LO20.3**
a. $75.
b. $85.
c. $95.
d. $105.

12. Draw a domestic supply-and-demand diagram for a product in which the United States does not have a comparative advantage. What impact do foreign imports have on domestic price and quantity? On your diagram show a protective tariff that eliminates approximately one-half of the assumed imports. What are the price-quantity effects of this tariff on (*a*) domestic consumers, (*b*) domestic producers, and (*c*) foreign exporters? How would the effects of a quota that creates the same amount of imports differ? **LO20.4**

13. American apparel makers complain to Congress about competition from China. Congress decides to impose either a tariff or a quota on apparel imports from China. Which policy would Chinese apparel manufacturers prefer? **LO20.4**
a. Tariff.
b. Quota.

PROBLEMS

1. Assume that the comparative-cost ratios of two products—baby formula and tuna fish—are as follows in the nations of Canswicki and Tunata:

> Canswicki: 1 can baby formula ≡ 2 cans tuna fish
> Tunata: 1 can baby formula ≡ 4 cans tuna fish

In what product should each nation specialize? Which of the following terms of trade would be acceptable to both nations: (*a*) 1 can baby formula ≡ 2½ cans tuna fish; (*b*) 1 can baby formula ≡ 1 can tuna fish; (*c*) 1 can baby formula ≡ 5 cans tuna fish? **LO20.2**

2. The accompanying hypothetical production possibilities tables are for New Zealand and Spain. Each country can produce apples and plums. Plot the production possibilities data for each of the two countries separately. Referring to your graphs, answer the following: **LO20.2**

New Zealand's Production Possibilities Table
(Millions of Bushels)

Product	Production Alternatives			
	A	B	C	D
Apples	0	20	40	60
Plums	15	10	5	0

Spain's Production Possibilities Table
(Millions of Bushels)

Product	Production Alternatives			
	R	S	T	U
Apples	0	20	40	60
Plums	60	40	20	0

a. What is each country's cost ratio of producing plums and apples?
b. Which nation should specialize in which product?
c. Show the trading possibilities lines for each nation if the actual terms of trade are 1 plum for 2 apples. (Plot these lines on your graph.)
d. Suppose the optimum product mixes before specialization and trade were alternative B in New Zealand and alternative S in Spain. What would be the gains from specialization and trade?

3. The following hypothetical production possibilities tables are for China and the United States. Assume that before specialization and trade the optimal product mix for China is alternative B and for the United States is alternative U. **LO20.2**
a. Are comparative-cost conditions such that the two areas should specialize? If so, what product should each produce?

b. What is the total gain in apparel and chemical output that would result from such specialization?

c. What are the limits of the terms of trade? Suppose that the actual terms of trade are 1 unit of apparel for $1\frac{1}{2}$ units of chemicals and that 4 units of apparel are exchanged for 6 units of chemicals. What are the gains from specialization and trade for each nation?

Product	China Production Possibilities					
	A	**B**	**C**	**D**	**E**	**F**
Apparel (in thousands)	30	24	18	12	6	0
Chemicals (in tons)	0	6	12	18	24	30

Product	U.S. Production Possibilities					
	R	**S**	**T**	**U**	**V**	**W**
Apparel (in thousands)	10	8	6	4	2	0
Chemicals (in tons)	0	4	8	12	16	20

4. Refer to Figure 3.6, page 63. Assume that the graph depicts the U.S. domestic market for corn. How many bushels of corn, if any, will the United States export or import at a world price of $1, $2, $3, $4, and $5? Use this information to construct the U.S. export supply curve and import demand curve for corn. Suppose that the only other corn-producing nation is France, where the domestic price is $4. Which country will export corn; which county will import it? **LO20.3**

The Balance of Payments, Exchange Rates, and Trade Deficits

Learning Objectives

LO21.1 Explain how currencies of different nations are exchanged when international transactions take place.

LO21.2 Analyze the balance sheet the United States uses to account for the international payments it makes and receives.

LO21.3 Discuss how exchange rates are determined in currency markets that have flexible exchange rates.

LO21.4 Describe the difference between flexible exchange rates and fixed exchange rates.

LO21.5 Explain the current system of managed floating exchange rates.

LO21.6 Identify the causes and consequences of recent U.S. trade deficits.

If you take a U.S. dollar to the bank and ask to exchange it for U.S. currency, you will get a puzzled look. If you persist, you may get a dollar's worth of change: One U.S. dollar can buy exactly one U.S. dollar. But on April 21, 2013, for example, 1 U.S. dollar could buy 1,837 Colombian pesos, 0.97 Australian dollar, 0.66 British pound, 1.03 Canadian dollars, 0.77 European euro, 99.55 Japanese yen, or 12.29 Mexican pesos. What explains this seemingly haphazard array of exchange rates?

In Chapter 20 we examined comparative advantage as the underlying economic basis of world trade and discussed the effects of barriers to free trade. Now we introduce the highly important monetary and financial aspects of international trade.

International Financial Transactions

LO21.1 Explain how currencies of different nations are exchanged when international transactions take place.

This chapter focuses on international financial transactions, the vast majority of which fall into two broad categories: international trade and international asset transactions. International trade involves either purchasing or selling currently produced goods or services across an international border. Examples include an Egyptian firm exporting cotton to the United States and an American company hiring an Indian call center to answer its phones. International asset transactions involve the transfer of the property rights to either real or financial assets between the citizens of one country and the citizens of another country. It includes activities like buying foreign stocks or selling your house to a foreigner.

These two categories of international financial transactions reflect the fact that whether they are from different countries or the same country, individuals and firms can only exchange two things with each other: currently produced goods and services or preexisting assets. With regard to assets, however, money is by far the most commonly exchanged asset. Only rarely would you ever find a barter situation in which people directly exchanged other assets—such as trading a car for 500 shares of Microsoft stock or a cow for 30 chickens and a tank of diesel fuel.

As a result, there are two basic types of transactions:

- People trading either goods or services for money.
- People trading assets for money.

In either case, money flows from the buyers of the goods, services, or assets to the sellers of the goods, services, or assets.

When the people engaged in any such transactions are both from places that use the same currency, what type of money to use is not an issue. Americans from California and Wisconsin will use their common currency, the dollar. People from France and Germany will use their common currency, the euro. However, when the people involved in an exchange are from places that use different currencies, intermediate asset transactions have to take place: the buyers must convert their own currencies into the currencies that the sellers use and accept.

As an example, consider the case of an English software design company that wants to buy a supercomputer made by an American company. The American company sells these high-powered machines for $300,000. To pay for the machine, the English company has to convert some of the money it has (British pounds sterling) into the money that the American company will accept (U.S. dollars). This process is not difficult. As we will soon explain in detail, there are many easy-to-use foreign exchange markets in which those who wish to sell pounds and buy dollars can interact with others who wish to sell dollars and buy pounds. The demand and supply created by these two groups determine the equilibrium exchange rate, which, in turn, determines how many pounds our English company will have to convert to pay for the supercomputer. For instance, if the exchange rate is $2 = £1, then the English company will have to convert £150,000 to obtain the $300,000 necessary to purchase the computer.

> ## QUICK REVIEW 21.1
>
> - International financial transactions involve trade either in currently produced goods and services or in preexisting assets.
> - Exports of goods, services, and assets create inflows of money, while imports cause outflows of money.
> - If buyers and sellers use different currencies, then foreign exchange transactions take place so that the exporter can be paid in his or her own currency.

The Balance of Payments

LO21.2 Analyze the balance sheet the United States uses to account for the international payments it makes and receives.

A nation's **balance of payments** is the sum of all the financial transactions that take place between its residents and the residents of foreign nations. Most of these transactions fall into the two main categories that we have just discussed: international trade and international asset

TABLE 21.1   The U.S. Balance of Payments, 2012 (in Billions)

CURRENT ACCOUNT		
(1) U.S. goods exports	$+1,564	
(2) U.S. goods imports	−2,299	
(3) *Balance on goods*		$−735
(4) U.S. exports of services	+630	
(5) U.S. imports of services	−435	
(6) *Balance on services*		+195
(7) *Balance on goods and services*		−540
(8) Net investment income	+199*	
(9) Net transfers	−134	
(10) **Balance on current account**		**−475**
CAPITAL AND FINANCIAL ACCOUNT		
Capital account		
(11) *Balance on capital account*		+6
Financial account		
(12) Foreign purchases of assets in the United States	+418†	
(13) U.S. purchases of assets abroad	+51†	
(14) *Balance on financial account*		+469
(15) **Balance on capital and financial account**		**+475**
		$ 0

*Includes other, less significant, categories of income.
†Includes one-half of a $66 billion statistical discrepancy that is listed in the capital account.

Source: U.S. Department of Commerce, Bureau of Economic Analysis, **www.bea.gov**. Preliminary 2012 data. The export and import data are on a "balance-of-payment basis," and usually vary from the data on exports and imports reported in the National Income and Product Accounts.

transactions. As a result, nearly all the items included in the balance of payments are things such as exports and imports of goods, exports and imports of services, and international purchases and sales of financial and real assets. But the balance of payments also includes international transactions that fall outside of these main categories—things such as tourist expenditures, interest and dividends received or paid abroad, debt forgiveness, and remittances made by immigrants to their relatives back home.

The U.S. Commerce Department's Bureau of Economic Analysis compiles a balance-of-payments statement each year. This statement summarizes all of the millions of payments that individuals and firms in the United States receive from foreigners as well as all of the millions of payments that individuals and firms in the United States make to foreigners. It shows "flows" of inpayments of money *to* the United States and outpayments of money *from* the United States. For convenience, all of these money payments are given in terms of dollars. This is true despite the fact that some of them actually may have been made using foreign currencies—as when, for instance, an American company converts dollars into euros to buy something from an Italian company. When including this outpayment of money from the United States, the

accountants who compile the balance-of-payments statement use the number of dollars the American company converted—rather than the number of euros that were actually used to make the purchase.

Table 21.1 is a simplified balance-of-payments statement for the United States in 2012. Because most international financial transactions fall into only two categories—international trade and international asset exchanges—the balance-of-payments statement is organized into two broad categories. *The current account* located at the top of the table primarily treats international trade. *The capital and financial account* at the bottom of the table primarily treats international asset exchanges.

Current Account

The top portion of Table 21.1 that mainly summarizes U.S. trade in currently produced goods and services is called the **current account.** Items 1 and 2 show U.S. exports and imports of goods (merchandise) in 2012. U.S. exports have a *plus* (+) sign because they are a *credit*; they generate flows of money toward the United States. U.S. imports have a *minus* (−) sign because they are a *debit*; they cause flows of money out of the United States.

Balance on Goods Items 1 and 2 in Table 21.1 reveal that in 2012 U.S. goods exports of $1,564 billion were less than U.S. goods imports of $2,299 billion. A country's *balance of trade on goods* is the difference between its exports and its imports of goods. If exports exceed imports, the result is a surplus on the balance of goods. If imports exceed exports, there is a trade deficit on the balance of goods. We note in item 3 that in 2012 the United States incurred a trade deficit on goods of $735 billion.

Balance on Services The United States exports not only goods, such as airplanes and computer software, but also services, such as insurance, consulting, travel, and investment advice, to residents of foreign nations. Item 4 in Table 21.1 shows that these service "exports" totaled $630 billion in 2012. Since they generate flows of money toward the United States, they are a credit (thus the + sign). Item 5 indicates that the United States "imports" similar services from foreigners. Those service imports were $435 billion in 2012, and since they generate flows of money out of the United States, they are a debit (thus the − sign). Summed together, items 4 and 5 indicate that the balance on services (item 6) in 2012 was $195 billion. The **balance on goods and services** shown as item 7 is the difference between U.S. exports of goods and services (items 1 and 4) and U.S. imports of goods and services (items 2 and 5). In 2012, U.S. imports of goods and services exceeded U.S. exports of goods and services by $540 billion. So a **trade deficit** of that amount occurred. In contrast, a **trade surplus** occurs when exports of goods and services exceed imports of goods and services. (Global Perspective 21.1 shows U.S. trade deficits and surpluses with selected nations.)

Balance on Current Account Items 8 and 9 are not items relating directly to international trade in goods and services. But they are listed as part of the current account (which is mostly about international trade in goods and services) because they are international financial flows that in some sense compensate for things that can be conceptualized as being *like* international trade in either goods or services. For instance, item 8, *net investment income*, represents the difference between (1) the interest and dividend payments foreigners paid U.S. citizens and companies for the services provided by U.S. capital invested abroad ("exported" capital) and (2) the interest and dividends the U.S. citizens and companies paid for the services provided by foreign capital invested here ("imported" capital). Observe that in 2012 U.S. net investment income was a positive $199 billion.

Item 9 shows net transfers, both public and private, between the United States and the rest of the world.

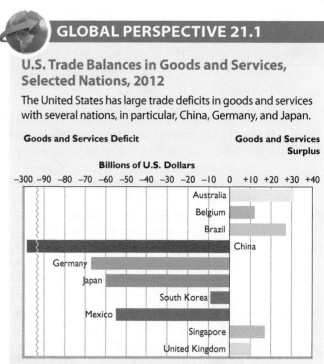

GLOBAL PERSPECTIVE 21.1

U.S. Trade Balances in Goods and Services, Selected Nations, 2012

The United States has large trade deficits in goods and services with several nations, in particular, China, Germany, and Japan.

Source: Bureau of Economic Analysis, **www.bea.gov**.

Included here is foreign aid, pensions paid to U.S. citizens living abroad, and remittances by immigrants to relatives abroad. These $134 billion of transfers are net U.S. outpayments (and therefore listed as a negative number in Table 21.1). They are listed as part of the current account because they can be thought of as the financial flows that accompany the exporting of goodwill and the importing of "thank you notes."

By adding all transactions in the current account, we obtain the **balance on current account** shown in item 10. In 2012 the United States had a current account deficit of $475 billion. This means that the U.S. current account transactions created outpayments from the United States greater than inpayments to the United States.

Capital and Financial Account

The bottom portion of the current account statement summarizes U.S. international asset transactions. It is called the **capital and financial account** and consists of two separate accounts: the *capital account* and the *financial account*.

Capital Account The capital account mainly measures debt forgiveness—which is an asset transaction because the person forgiving a debt essentially hands the IOU back to the borrower. It is a "net" account (one that can be either + or −). The +$6 billion listed in line 11 tells us that in 2012 foreigners forgave $6 billion more of debt owed to them by Americans than Americans forgave debt owed to them by foreigners. The + sign indicates a credit; it is an "on-paper" inpayment (asset transfer) by the net amount of debt forgiven.

Financial Account The financial account summarizes international asset transactions having to do with international purchases and sales of real or financial assets. Line 12 lists the amount of foreign purchases of assets in the United States. It has a + sign because any purchase of an American-owned asset by a foreigner generates a flow of money toward the American who sells the asset. Line 13 lists U.S. purchases of assets abroad. These normally have a − sign because such purchases generate a flow of money from the Americans who buy foreign assets toward the foreigners who sell them those assets. But the value in line 13 is positive because in 2012 American sales to foreigners of assets located abroad exceeded American purchases from foreigners of assets located abroad. That excess generated a net flow of $51 billion from foreigners to Americans.

Items 12 and 13 combined yielded a $469 billion balance on the financial account for 2012 (line 14). In 2012 the United States "exported" $418 billion of ownership of its real and financial assets and "imported" $51 billion. Thought of differently, this surplus in the financial account brought in income of $469 billion to the United States. The **balance on the capital and financial account** (line 15) is $475 billion. It is the sum of the $6 billion credit on the capital account and the $469 billion surplus on the financial account. Observe that this $475 billion surplus in the capital and financial account equals the $475 billion deficit in the current account. This is not an accident. The two numbers always equal—or "balance." That's why the statement is called the *balance* of payments. It has to balance. Let's see why.

Why the Balance?

The balance on the current account and the balance on the capital and financial account must always sum to zero because any deficit or surplus in the current account automatically creates an offsetting entry in the capital and financial account. People can only trade one of two things with each other: currently produced goods and services or preexisting assets. Therefore, if trading partners have an imbalance in their trade of currently produced goods and services, the only way to make up for that imbalance is with a net transfer of assets from one party to the other.

To see why this is true, suppose that John (an American) makes shoes and Henri (a Swiss citizen) makes watches

and that the pair only trade with each other. Assume that their financial assets consist entirely of money, with each beginning the year with $1,000 in his bank account. Suppose that this year John exports $300 of shoes to Henri and imports $500 of watches from Henri. John therefore ends the year with a $200 goods deficit with Henri.

John and Henri's goods transactions, however, also result in asset exchanges that cause a net transfer of assets from John to Henri equal in size to John's $200 goods deficit with Henri. This is true because Henri pays John $300 for his shoes while John pays Henri $500 for his watches. The *net* result of these opposite-direction asset movements is that $200 of John's initial assets of $1,000 are transferred to Henri. This is unavoidable because the $300 John receives from his exports pays for only the first $300 of his $500 of imports. The only way for John to pay for the remaining $200 of imports is for him to transfer $200 of his initial asset holdings to Henri. Consequently, John's assets decline by $200 from $1,000 to $800, and Henri's assets rise from $1,000 to $1,200.

Consider how the transaction between John and Henri affects the U.S. balance-of-payments statement (Table 21.1), other things equal. John's $200 goods deficit with Henri shows up in the U.S. current account as a −$200 entry in the balance on goods account (line 3) and carries down to a −$200 entry in the balance on current account (line 10).

In the capital and financial account, this $200 is recorded as +$200 in the account labeled foreign purchases of assets in the United States (line 12). This +$200 then carries down to the balance on capital and financial account (line 15). Think of it this way: Henri has in essence used $200 worth of watches to purchase $200 of John's initial $1,000 holding of assets. The +$200 entry in line 12 (foreign purchases of assets in the United States) simply recognizes this fact. This +$200 exactly offsets the −$200 in the current account.

Thus, the balance of payments always balances. Any current account deficit or surplus in the top half of the statement automatically generates an offsetting international asset transfer that shows up in the capital and financial account in the bottom half of the statement. More specifically, current account deficits simultaneously generate transfers of assets to foreigners, while current account surpluses automatically generate transfers of assets from foreigners.

Official Reserves, Payments Deficits, and Payments Surpluses

Some of the foreign purchases of assets in the United States (line 12, Table 21.1) and the U.S. assets purchased abroad (line 13) are of so-called official reserves. **Official reserves** consist of foreign currencies, certain reserves held with the International Monetary Fund, and stocks of gold. These reserves are owned by governments or their central banks. For simplicity, we will assume for now that the entire stock of U.S. official reserves consists of foreign currency so we can speak of official reserves and foreign currency reserves interchangeably.

Although the balance of payments must always sum to zero, as in Table 21.1, in some years a net sale of official reserves by a nation's treasury or central bank occurs in the process of bringing the capital and financial account into balance with the current account. In such years, a **balance-of-payments deficit** is said to occur. This deficit is in a subset of the overall balance statement and *is not a deficit in the overall account.* Remember, the overall balance of payments is always in balance. But in this case the balancing of the overall account includes sales of official reserves to create an inflow of dollars to the United States. In selling foreign currency in the foreign exchange market, the treasury or central bank must draw down its stock of reserves. This drawdown is an indicator of a balance-of-payments deficit.

These net sales of official reserves in the foreign exchange market show up as a *plus* (+) item on the U.S. balance-of-payments statement, specifically as foreign purchases of U.S. assets (line 12). They are a credit or an inflow of dollars to the United States, just as are John's proceeds from the sale of $200 of his assets to Henri in our previous example.

In other years, the capital and financial account balances the current account because of government purchases of official reserves from foreigners. The treasury or central bank engineers this balance by selling dollars to obtain foreign currency, and then adding the newly acquired foreign currency to its stock of official reserves. In these years, a **balance-of-payments surplus** is said to exist. This payments surplus therefore can be thought of as either net purchases of official reserves in the balance of payments or, alternatively, as the resulting increase in the stock of official reserves held by the government.

Net purchases of official reserves by the treasury or central bank appear on the U.S. balance sheet as U.S. purchases of foreign assets (line 13)—a *negative* (−) item. These purchases are a debit because they represent an outflow of dollars.

A balance-of-payments deficit is not necessarily bad, just as a balance-of-payments surplus is not necessarily good. Both simply happen. However, any nation's official reserves are limited. Persistent payments deficits must be financed by drawing down those reserves, which would ultimately deplete the reserves. That nation would have to adopt policies to correct its balance of payments. Such policies might require painful macroeconomic adjustments, trade barriers and similar restrictions, or a major depreciation of its currency. For this reason, nations strive for payments balance, at least over several-year periods.

QUICK REVIEW 21.2

- A nation's balance-of-payments statement summarizes all of the international financial transactions that take place between its residents and the residents of all foreign nations. It includes the current account balance and the capital and financial account balance.
- The current account balance is a nation's exports of goods and services less its imports of goods and services plus its net investment income and net transfers.
- The capital and financial account balance includes the net amount of the nation's debt forgiveness as well as the nation's sale of real and financial assets to people living abroad less its purchases of real and financial assets from foreigners.
- The current account balance and the capital and financial account balance always sum to zero because any current account imbalance automatically generates an offsetting international asset transfer.
- A balance-of-payments deficit exists when net sales of official reserves (mainly foreign currency) occur in the balance-of-payments statement; in contrast, a balance-of-payments surplus exists when net purchases of official reserves occur.

Flexible Exchange Rates

LO21.3 Discuss how exchange rates are determined in currency markets that have flexible exchange rates.

Both the size and the persistence of a nation's balance-of-payments deficits and surpluses and the adjustments it must make to correct those imbalances depend on the system of exchange rates being used. There are two pure types of exchange-rate systems:

- A **flexible- or floating-exchange-rate system** through which demand and supply determine exchange rates and in which no government intervention occurs.

FIGURE 21.1 The market for foreign currency (pounds). The intersection of the demand-for-pounds curve D_1 and the supply-of-pounds curve S_1 determines the equilibrium dollar price of pounds, here, $2. That means that the exchange rate is $2 = £1. Not shown, an increase in demand for pounds or a decrease in supply of pounds will increase the dollar price of pounds and thus cause the pound to appreciate. Also not shown, a decrease in demand for pounds or an increase in the supply of pounds will reduce the dollar price of pounds, meaning that the pound has depreciated.

QUICK QUIZ FOR FIGURE 21.1

1. Which of the following statements is true?
   a. The quantity of pounds demanded falls when the dollar appreciates.
   b. The quantity of pounds supplied declines as the dollar price of the pound rises.
   c. At the equilibrium exchange rate, the pound price of $1 is £½.
   d. The dollar appreciates if the demand for pounds increases.

2. At the price of $2 for £1 in this figure:
   a. the dollar-pound exchange rate is unstable.
   b. the quantity of pounds supplied equals the quantity demanded.
   c. the dollar price of £1 equals the pound price of $1.
   d. U.S. goods exports to Britain must equal U.S. goods imports from Britain.

3. Other things equal, a leftward shift of the demand curve in this figure:
   a. would depreciate the dollar.

   b. would create a shortage of pounds at the previous price of $2 for £1.
   c. might be caused by a major recession in the United States.
   d. might be caused by a significant rise of real interest rates in Britain.

4. Other things equal, a rightward shift of the supply curve in this figure would:
   a. depreciate the dollar and might be caused by a significant rise of real interest rates in Britain.
   b. depreciate the dollar and might be caused by a significant fall of real interest rates in Britain.
   c. appreciate the dollar and might be caused by a significant rise of real interest rates in the United States.
   d. appreciate the dollar and might be caused by a significant fall of real interest rates in the United States.

Answers: 1. c; 2. b; 3. c; 4. c

- A **fixed-exchange-rate system** through which governments determine exchange rates and make necessary adjustments in their economies to maintain those rates.

We begin by looking at flexible exchange rates. Let's examine the rate, or price, at which U.S. dollars might be exchanged for British pounds. In **Figure 21.1 (Key Graph)** we show demand D_1 and supply S_1 of pounds in the currency market.

The *demand-for-pounds curve* is downsloping because all British goods and services will be cheaper to the United States if pounds become less expensive to the United States. That is, at lower dollar prices for pounds, the United States can obtain more pounds and therefore

more British goods and services per dollar. To buy those cheaper British goods, U.S. consumers will increase the quantity of pounds they demand.

The *supply-of-pounds curve* is upsloping because the British will purchase more U.S. goods when the dollar price of pounds rises (that is, as the pound price of dollars falls). When the British buy more U.S. goods, they supply a greater quantity of pounds to the foreign exchange market. In other words, they must exchange pounds for dollars to purchase U.S. goods. So, when the dollar price of pounds rises, the quantity of pounds supplied goes up.

The intersection of the supply curve and the demand curve will determine the dollar price of pounds. Here, that price (exchange rate) is $2 for £1. At this exchange rate, the quantities of pounds supplied and demanded are equal; neither a shortage nor a surplus of pounds occurs.

Depreciation and Appreciation

An exchange rate determined by market forces can, and often does, change daily like stock and bond prices. When the dollar price of pounds *rises*, for example, from $2 = £1 to $3 = £1, the dollar has *depreciated* relative to the pound (and the pound has appreciated relative to the dollar). When a currency depreciates, more units of it (dollars) are needed to buy a single unit of some other currency (a pound).

When the dollar price of pounds *falls*, for example, from $2 = £1 to $1 = £1, the dollar has *appreciated* relative to the pound. When a currency appreciates, fewer units of it (dollars) are needed to buy a single unit of some other currency (pounds).

In our U.S.-Britain illustrations, depreciation of the dollar means an appreciation of the pound, and vice versa. When the dollar price of a pound jumps from $2 = £1 to $3 = £1, the pound has appreciated relative to the dollar because it takes fewer pounds to buy $1. At $2 = £1, it took £$\frac{1}{2}$ to buy $1; at $3 = £1, it takes only £$\frac{1}{3}$ to buy $1. Conversely, when the dollar appreciated relative to the pound, the pound depreciated relative to the dollar. More pounds were needed to buy a dollar.

In general, the relevant terminology and relationships between the U.S. dollar and another currency are as follows.

- Dollar price of foreign currency increases ≡ dollar depreciates relative to the foreign currency ≡ foreign currency price of dollar decreases ≡ foreign currency appreciates relative to the dollar.

- Dollar price of foreign currency decreases ≡ dollar appreciates relative to the foreign currency ≡ foreign currency price of dollar increases ≡ foreign currency depreciates relative to the dollar.

Determinants of Exchange Rates

What factors would cause a nation's currency to appreciate or depreciate in the market for foreign exchange? Here are three generalizations:

- If the demand for a nation's currency increases (other things equal), that currency will appreciate; if the demand declines, that currency will depreciate.

- If the supply of a nation's currency increases, that currency will depreciate; if the supply decreases, that currency will appreciate.

- If a nation's currency appreciates, some foreign currency depreciates relative to it.

With these generalizations in mind, let's examine the determinants of exchange rates—the factors that shift the demand or supply curve for a certain currency. As we do so, keep in mind that the other-things-equal assumption is always in force. Also note that we are discussing factors *that change the exchange rate*, not things that change *as a result of* a change in the exchange rate.

Changes in Tastes   Any change in consumer tastes or preferences for the products of a foreign country may alter the demand for that nation's currency and change its exchange rate. If technological advances in U.S. wireless phones make them more attractive to British consumers and businesses, then the British will supply more pounds in the exchange market to purchase more U.S. wireless phones. The supply-of-pounds curve will shift to the right, causing the pound to depreciate and the dollar to appreciate.

In contrast, the U.S. demand-for-pounds curve will shift to the right if British woolen apparel becomes more fashionable in the United States. So the pound will appreciate and the dollar will depreciate.

Relative Income Changes   A nation's currency is likely to depreciate if its growth of national income is more rapid than that of other countries. Here's why: A country's imports vary directly with its income level. As total income rises in the United States, people there buy both more domestic goods and more foreign goods. If the U.S. economy is expanding rapidly and the British economy is stagnant, U.S. imports of British goods, and therefore U.S. demands for pounds, will increase. The dollar price of pounds will rise, so the dollar will depreciate.

Relative Inflation Rate Changes   Other things equal, changes in the relative rates of inflation of two nations change their relative price levels and alter the exchange rate between their currencies. The currency of the nation with the higher inflation rate—the more rapidly rising price level—tends to depreciate. Suppose, for example, that inflation is zero percent in Great Britain and 5 percent in the United States so that prices, on average, are rising by 5 percent per year in the United States while, on average, remaining unchanged in Great Britain. U.S. consumers will seek out more of the now relatively lower-priced British goods, increasing the demand for pounds. British consumers will purchase less of the now relatively higher-priced U.S. goods, reducing the supply of pounds. This combination of increased demand for pounds and reduced supply of pounds will cause the pound to appreciate and the dollar to depreciate.

According to the **purchasing-power-parity theory,** exchange rates should eventually adjust such that they equate the purchasing power of various currencies. If a certain market basket of identical products costs $10,000 in the United States and £5,000 in Great Britain, the exchange rate should move to $2 = £1. That way, a dollar spent in the United States will buy exactly as much output as it would if it were first converted to pounds (at the $2 = £1 exchange rate) and used to buy output in Great Britain.

In terms of our example, 5 percent inflation in the United States will increase the price of the market basket from $10,000 to $10,500, while the zero percent inflation in Great Britain will leave the market basket priced at £5,000. For purchasing power parity to hold, the exchange rate would have to move from $2 = £1 to $2.10 = £1. That means the dollar therefore would depreciate and the pound would appreciate. In practice, however, not all exchange rates move precisely to equate the purchasing power of various currencies and thereby achieve "purchasing power parity," even over long periods.

Relative Interest Rates

Changes in relative interest rates between two countries may alter their exchange rate. Suppose that real interest rates rise in the United States but stay constant in Great Britain. British citizens will then find the United States a more attractive place in which to loan money directly or loan money indirectly by buying bonds. To make these loans, they will have to supply pounds in the foreign exchange market to obtain dollars. The increase in the supply of pounds results in depreciation of the pound and appreciation of the dollar.

Changes in Relative Expected Returns on Stocks, Real Estate, and Production Facilities

International investing extends beyond buying foreign bonds. It includes international investments in stocks and real estate as well as foreign purchases of factories and production facilities. Other things equal, the extent of this foreign investment depends on relative expected returns. To make the investments, investors in one country must sell their currencies to purchase the foreign currencies needed for the foreign investments.

For instance, suppose that investing in England suddenly becomes more popular due to a more positive outlook regarding expected returns on stocks, real estate, and production facilities there. U.S. investors therefore will sell U.S. assets to buy more assets in England. The U.S. assets will be sold for dollars, which will then be brought to the foreign exchange market and exchanged for pounds, which will in turn be used to purchase British assets. The increased demand for pounds in the foreign exchange market will cause the pound to appreciate and therefore the dollar to depreciate relative to the pound.

Speculation   Currency speculators are people who buy and sell currencies with an eye toward reselling or repurchasing them at a profit. Suppose speculators expect the U.S. economy to (1) grow more rapidly than the British economy and (2) experience more rapid inflation than Britain. These expectations translate into an anticipation that the pound will appreciate and the dollar will depreciate. Speculators who are holding dollars will therefore try to convert them into pounds. This effort will increase the demand for pounds and cause the dollar price of pounds to rise (that is, cause the dollar to depreciate). A self-fulfilling prophecy occurs: The pound appreciates and the dollar depreciates because speculators act on the belief that these changes will in fact take place. In this way, speculation can cause changes in exchange rates. (We discuss currency speculation in more detail in this chapter's Last Word.)

Table 21.2 has more illustrations of the determinants of exchange rates; the table is worth careful study.

QUICK REVIEW 21.3

- In a system in which exchange rates are flexible (free to float), exchange rates are determined by the demand for and supply of individual national currencies in the foreign exchange market.
- Determinants of flexible exchange rates (factors that shift currency supply and demand curves) include (a) changes in tastes; (b) relative national incomes; (c) relative inflation rates; (d) real interest rates; (e) relative expected returns on stocks, real estate, and production facilities; and (f) speculation.

Flexible Rates and the Balance of Payments

Flexible exchange rates have an important feature: They automatically adjust and eventually eliminate balance-of-payments deficits or surpluses. We can explain this idea through Figure 21.2, in which S_1 and D_1 are the supply and demand curves for pounds from Figure 21.1. The equilibrium exchange rate of $2 = £1 means that there is no balance-of-payments deficit or surplus between the United States and Britain. At that exchange rate, the quantity of pounds demanded by U.S. consumers to import British goods, buy British transportation and insurance services, and pay interest and dividends on British investments in the United States equals the amount of pounds supplied by the British in buying U.S. exports, purchasing

TABLE 21.2 Determinants of Exchange Rates: Factors That Change the Demand for or the Supply of a Particular Currency and Thus Alter the Exchange Rate

Determinant	Examples
Change in tastes	Japanese electronic equipment declines in popularity in the United States (Japanese yen depreciates; U.S. dollar appreciates). European tourists reduce visits to the United States (U.S. dollar depreciates; European euro appreciates).
Change in relative incomes	England encounters a recession, reducing its imports, while U.S. real output and real income surge, increasing U.S. imports (British pound appreciates; U.S. dollar depreciates).
Change in relative inflation rates	Switzerland experiences a 3% inflation rate compared to Canada's 10% rate (Swiss franc appreciates; Canadian dollar depreciates).
Change in relative real interest rates	The Federal Reserve drives up interest rates in the United States, while the Bank of England takes no such action (U.S. dollar appreciates; British pound depreciates).
Changes in relative expected returns on stocks, real estate, or production facilities	Corporate tax cuts in the United States raise expected after-tax investment returns in the United States relative to those in Europe (U.S. dollar appreciates; the euro depreciates).
Speculation	Currency traders believe South Korea will have much greater inflation than Taiwan (South Korean won depreciates; Taiwanese dollar appreciates). Currency traders think Norway's interest rates will plummet relative to Denmark's rates (Norway's krone depreciates; Denmark's krone appreciates).

FIGURE 21.2 Adjustments under flexible exchange rates and fixed exchange rates. Under flexible exchange rates, a shift in the demand for pounds from D_1 to D_2, other things equal, would cause a U.S. balance-of-payments deficit ab. That deficit would be corrected by a change in the exchange rate from $2 = £1 to $3 = £1. Under fixed exchange rates, the United States would cover the shortage of pounds ab by selling official reserves (here pounds), restricting trade, implementing exchange controls, or enacting a contractionary stabilization policy.

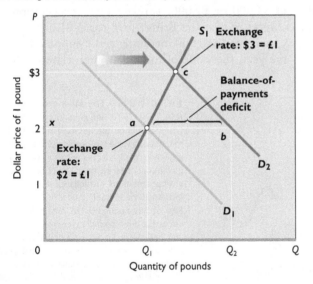

services from the United States, and making interest and dividend payments on U.S. investments in Britain. The United States would have no need to either draw down or build up its official reserves to balance its payments.

Suppose tastes change and U.S. consumers buy more British automobiles; the U.S. inflation rate increases relative to Britain's; or interest rates fall in the United States

compared to those in Britain. Any or all of these changes will increase the U.S. demand for British pounds, for example, from D_1 to D_2 in Figure 21.2.

If the exchange rate remains at the initial $2 = £1, a U.S. balance-of-payments deficit will occur in the amount of ab. At the $2 = £1 rate, U.S. consumers will demand the quantity of pounds shown by point b, but Britain will supply only the amount shown by a. There will be a shortage of pounds. But this shortage will not last because this is a competitive foreign exchange market. Instead, the dollar price of pounds will rise (the dollar will depreciate) until the balance-of-payments deficit is eliminated. That occurs at the new equilibrium exchange rate of $3 = £1, where the quantities of pounds demanded and supplied are again equal.

To explain why the increase in the dollar price of pounds—the dollar depreciation—eliminates the balance-of-payments deficit ab in Figure 21.2, we need to reemphasize that the exchange rate links all domestic (U.S.) prices with all foreign (British) prices. The dollar price of a foreign good is found by multiplying the foreign price by the exchange rate (in dollars per unit of the foreign currency). At an exchange rate of $2 = £1, a British automobile priced at £15,000 will cost a U.S. consumer $30,000 (= 15,000 × $2).

A change in the exchange rate alters the prices of all British goods to U.S. consumers and all U.S. goods to British buyers. The shift in the exchange rate (here from $2 = £1 to $3 = £1) changes the relative attractiveness of U.S. imports and exports and restores equilibrium in the U.S. (and British) balance of payments. From the U.S. view, as the dollar price of pounds changes from $2 to $3, the British auto priced at £15,000, which formerly cost a U.S. consumer $30,000, now costs $45,000 (= 15,000 × $3). Other British goods will also cost U.S. consumers more, so that U.S. imports of British goods will decline.

From Britain's standpoint, the exchange rate (the pound price of dollars) has fallen (from £$\frac{1}{2}$ to £$\frac{1}{3}$ for $1). The international value of the pound has appreciated. The British previously got only $2 for £1; now they get $3 for £1. U.S. goods are therefore cheaper to the British, and U.S. exports to Britain will rise.

The two adjustments—a decrease in U.S. imports from Britain and an increase in U.S. exports to Britain—are just what are needed in terms of Figure 21.2 to decrease the quantity of pounds demanded from b to c, increase the quantity of pounds supplied from a to c, and thus correct the U.S. balance-of-payments deficit. These changes end when, at point c, the quantities of British pounds demanded and supplied are equal.

Disadvantages of Flexible Exchange Rates

Even though flexible exchange rates automatically work to eliminate payment imbalances, they may cause several significant problems. These are all related to the fact that flexible exchange rates are often volatile and can change by a large amount in just a few weeks or months. In addition, they often take substantial swings that can last several years or more. This can be seen in Figure 21.3, which plots the dollar-pound exchange rate from 1970 through 2012. (You can track other exchange rates, for example, the

dollar-euro or dollar-yen rate, by going to the Federal Reserve Web site, **www.federalreserve.gov**, selecting Economic Research & Data, Statistical Releases and Historical Data, and finally, Exchange Rates and International Data.)

Uncertainty and Diminished Trade The risks and uncertainties associated with flexible exchange rates may discourage the flow of trade. Suppose a U.S. automobile dealer contracts to purchase 10 British cars for £150,000. At the current exchange rate of, say, $2 for £1, the U.S. importer expects to pay $300,000 for these automobiles. But if during the 3-month delivery period the rate of exchange shifts to $3 for £1, the £150,000 payment contracted by the U.S. importer will be $450,000.

That increase in the dollar price of pounds may thus turn the U.S. importer's anticipated profit into a substantial loss. Aware of the possibility of an adverse change in the exchange rate, the U.S. importer may not be willing to assume the risks involved. The U.S. firm may confine its operations to domestic automobiles, so international trade in this product will not occur.

The same thing can happen with investments. Assume that when the exchange rate is $3 to £1, a U.S. firm invests $30,000 (or £10,000) in a British enterprise. It estimates a return of 10 percent; that is, it anticipates annual earnings of $3,000 or £1,000. Suppose these expectations prove correct in that the British firm earns £1,000 in the first year on the £10,000 investment. But suppose that during the year, the value of the dollar appreciates to $2 = £1.

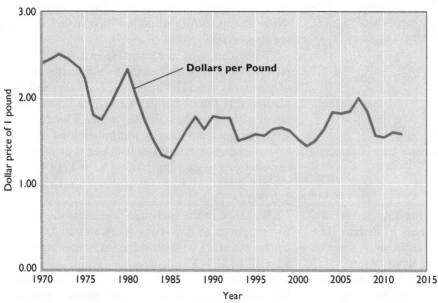

FIGURE 21.3 The dollar-pound exchange rate, 1970–2012. Before January 1971, the dollar-pound exchange rate was fixed at $2.40 = £1. Since that time, its value has been determined almost entirely by market forces, with only occasional government interventions. Under these mostly flexible conditions, the dollar-pound exchange rate has varied considerably. For instance, in 1981 it took $2.02 to buy a pound but by 1985 only $1.50 was needed to buy a pound. In contrast, between 2001 and 2007 the dollar price of a pound rose from $1.44 to $2.00, indicating that the dollar had depreciated relative to the pound. The dollar then sank back to $1.57 per British pound in 2009 and remained at about that level through 2012.

Source: Economic Report of the President, 2013, Table B-110. Earlier years from prior *Economic Reports.*

The absolute return is now only $2,000 (rather than $3,000), and the rate of return falls from the anticipated 10 percent to only $6\frac{2}{3}$ percent (= $2,000/$30,000). Investment is risky in any case. The added risk of changing exchange rates may persuade the U.S. investor not to venture overseas.[1]

Terms-of-Trade Changes A decline in the international value of its currency will worsen a nation's terms of trade. For example, an increase in the dollar price of a pound will mean that the United States must export more goods and services to finance a specific level of imports from Britain.

Instability Flexible exchange rates may destabilize the domestic economy because wide fluctuations stimulate and then depress industries producing exported goods. If the U.S. economy is operating at full employment and its currency depreciates, as in our illustration, the results will be inflationary, for two reasons. (1) Foreign demand for U.S. goods may rise, increasing total spending and pulling up U.S. prices. Also, the prices of all U.S. imports will increase. (2) Conversely, appreciation of the dollar will lower U.S. exports and increase imports, possibly causing unemployment.

Flexible or floating exchange rates also may complicate the use of domestic stabilization policies in seeking full employment and price stability. This is especially true for nations whose exports and imports are large relative to their total domestic output.

QUICK REVIEW 21.4

- Flexible exchange rates automatically adjust and eventually eliminate balance-of-payments deficits and surpluses.
- The volatility of flexible exchange rates may have several negative consequences, including discouraging international trade, worsening a nation's terms of trade, and destabilizing a nation's domestic economy by depressing export industries.

Fixed Exchange Rates

LO21.4 Describe the difference between flexible exchange rates and fixed exchange rates.

To circumvent the disadvantages of flexible exchange rates, at times nations have fixed or "pegged" their exchange rates. For our analysis of fixed exchange rates, we assume that the United States and Britain agree to maintain a $2 = £1 exchange rate.

The problem is that such a government agreement cannot keep from changing the demand for and the supply of pounds. With the rate fixed, a shift in demand or supply will threaten the fixed-exchange-rate system, and government must intervene to ensure that the exchange rate is maintained.

In Figure 21.2, suppose the U.S. demand for pounds increases from D_1 to D_2 and a U.S. payment deficit *ab* arises. Now, the new equilibrium exchange rate ($3 = £1) is above the fixed exchange rate ($2 = £1). How can the United States prevent the shortage of pounds from driving the exchange rate up to the new equilibrium level? How can it maintain the fixed exchange rate? The answer is by altering market demand or market supply or both so that they will intersect at the $2 = £1 rate. There are several ways to do this.

Use of Official Reserves

One way to maintain a fixed exchange rate is to engage in **currency interventions.** These are situations in which governments or their central banks manipulate an exchange rate through the use of official reserves. For instance, by selling some of its reserves of pounds, the U.S. government could increase the supply of pounds, shifting supply curve S_1 to the right so that it intersects D_2 at *b* in Figure 21.2, thereby maintaining the exchange rate at $2 = £1.

Notice that when the U.S. government sells some of its reserves of pounds, it is transferring assets to foreigners (since they gain ownership of the pounds). In terms of the balance-of-payments statement shown in Table 21.1, this transfer of assets enters positively on line 12, "Foreign purchases of assets in the United States." This positive entry is what offsets the balance-of-payments deficit caused by the fixed exchange rate and ensures that the U.S. balance of payments does in fact balance.

How do official reserves originate? Perhaps a balance-of-payments surplus occurred in the past. The U.S. government would have purchased that surplus. That is, at some earlier time, the U.S. government may have spent tax dollars to buy the surplus pounds that were threatening to reduce the exchange rate to below the $2 = £1 fixed rate. Those purchases would have bolstered the stock of U.S. official reserves of pounds.

Nations also have used gold as "international money" to obtain official reserves. In our example, the U.S. government could sell some of its gold to Britain to obtain pounds. It could then sell pounds for dollars. That would

---

[1] You will see in this chapter's Last Word, however, that a trader can circumvent part of the risk of unfavorable exchange-rate fluctuations by "hedging" in the "futures market" or "forward market" for foreign exchange.

shift the supply-of-pounds curve to the right, and the $2 = £1 exchange rate could be maintained.

It is critical that the amount of reserves and gold be enough to accomplish the required increase in the supply of pounds. There is no problem if deficits and surpluses occur more or less randomly and are of similar size. Then, last year's balance-of-payments surplus with Britain will increase the U.S. reserve of pounds, and that reserve can be used to "finance" this year's deficit. But if the United States encounters persistent and sizable deficits for an extended period, it may exhaust its reserves, and thus be forced to abandon fixed exchange rates. Or, at the least, a nation whose reserves are inadequate must use less–appealing options to maintain exchange rates. Let's consider some of those options.

Trade Policies

To maintain fixed exchange rates, a nation can try to control the flow of trade and finance directly. The United States could try to maintain the $2 = £1 exchange rate in the face of a shortage of pounds by discouraging imports (thereby reducing the demand for pounds) and encouraging exports (thus increasing the supply of pounds). Imports could be reduced by means of new tariffs or import quotas; special taxes could be levied on the interest and dividends U.S. financial investors receive from foreign investments. Also, the U.S. government could subsidize certain U.S. exports to increase the supply of pounds.

The fundamental problem is that these policies reduce the volume of world trade and change its makeup from what is economically desirable. When nations impose tariffs, quotas, and the like, they lose some of the economic benefits of a free flow of world trade. That loss should not be underestimated: Trade barriers by one nation lead to retaliatory responses from other nations, multiplying the loss.

Exchange Controls and Rationing

Another option is to adopt exchange controls and rationing. Under **exchange controls** the U.S. government could handle the problem of a pound shortage by requiring that all pounds obtained by U.S. exporters be sold to the federal government. Then the government would allocate or ration this short supply of pounds (represented by xa in Figure 21.2) among various U.S. importers, who demand the quantity xb. This policy would restrict the value of U.S. imports to the amount of foreign exchange earned by U.S. exports. Assuming balance in the capital and financial account, there would then be no balance-of-payments deficit. U.S. demand for British imports with the value ab would simply not be fulfilled.

There are major objections to exchange controls:

- **Distorted trade** Like *trade controls* (tariffs, quotas, and export subsidies), exchange controls would distort the pattern of international trade away from the pattern suggested by comparative advantage.

- **Favoritism** The process of rationing scarce foreign exchange might lead to government favoritism toward selected importers (big contributors to reelection campaigns, for example).

- **Restricted choice** Controls would limit freedom of consumer choice. The U.S. consumers who prefer Volkswagens might have to buy Chevrolets. The business opportunities for some U.S. importers might be impaired if the government were to limit imports.

- **Black markets** Enforcement problems are likely under exchange controls. U.S. importers might want foreign exchange badly enough to pay more than the $2 = £1 official rate, setting the stage for black-market dealings between importers and illegal sellers of foreign exchange.

Domestic Macroeconomic Adjustments

A final way to maintain a fixed exchange rate would be to use domestic stabilization policies (monetary policy and fiscal policy) to eliminate the shortage of foreign currency. Tax hikes, reductions in government spending, and a high-interest-rate policy would reduce total spending in the U.S. economy and, consequently, domestic income. Because the volume of imports varies directly with domestic income, demand for British goods, and therefore for pounds, would be restrained.

If these "contractionary" policies served to reduce the domestic price level relative to Britain's, U.S. buyers of consumer and capital goods would divert their demands from British goods to U.S. goods, reducing the demand for pounds. Moreover, the high-interest-rate policy would lift U.S. interest rates relative to those in Britain.

Lower prices on U.S. goods and higher U.S. interest rates would increase British imports of U.S. goods and would increase British financial investment in the United States. Both developments would increase the supply of pounds. The combination of a decrease in the demand for and an increase in the supply of pounds would reduce or eliminate the original U.S. balance-of-payments deficit. In Figure 21.2 the new supply and demand curves would intersect at some new equilibrium point on line ab, where the exchange rate remains at $2 = £1.

Maintaining fixed exchange rates by such means is hardly appealing. The "price" of exchange-rate stability for the United States would be a decline in output, employment, and price levels—in other words, a recession. Eliminating a balance-of-payments deficit and achieving domestic stability are both important national economic goals, but to sacrifice macroeconomic stability simply to balance international payments would be to let the tail wag the dog.

QUICK REVIEW 21.5

- To circumvent the disadvantages of flexible exchange rates, at times nations have fixed or "pegged" their exchange rates.
- Under a system of fixed exchange rates, nations set their exchange rates and then maintain them by buying or selling official reserves of currencies, establishing trade barriers, employing exchange controls, or incurring inflation or recession.

The Current Exchange Rate System: The Managed Float

LO21.5 Explain the current system of managed floating exchange rates.

Over the past 130 years, the world's nations have used three different exchange-rate systems. From 1879 to 1934, most nations used a gold standard, which implicitly created fixed exchange rates. From 1944 to 1971, most countries participated in the Bretton Woods system, which was a fixed-exchange-rate system indirectly tied to gold. And since 1971, most have used managed floating exchange rates, which mix mostly flexible exchange rates with occasional currency interventions. Naturally, our focus here is on the current exchange rate system. However, the history of the previous systems and why they broke down is highly fascinating. For that reason, we have included a discussion of these systems at the book's Web site (see Content Option for Instructors 2 [COI 2]).

The current international exchange-rate system (1971–present) is an "almost" flexible system called **managed floating exchange rates.** Exchange rates among major currencies are free to float to their equilibrium market levels, but nations occasionally use currency interventions in the foreign exchange market to stabilize or alter market exchange rates.

Normally, the major trading nations allow their exchange rates to float up or down to equilibrium levels based on supply and demand in the foreign exchange market. They recognize that changing economic conditions among nations require continuing changes in equilibrium exchange rates to avoid persistent payments deficits or surpluses. They rely on freely operating foreign exchange markets to accomplish the necessary adjustments. The result has been considerably more volatile exchange rates than those during the Bretton Woods era.

But nations also recognize that certain trends in the movement of equilibrium exchange rates may be at odds with national or international objectives. On occasion, nations therefore intervene in the foreign exchange market by buying or selling large amounts of specific currencies. This way, they can "manage" or stabilize exchange rates by influencing currency demand and supply.

The leaders of the *G8 nations* (Canada, France, Germany, Italy, Japan, Russia, United Kingdom, and United States) meet regularly to discuss economic issues and try to coordinate economic policies. At times they have collectively intervened to try to stabilize currencies. For example, in 2000 they sold dollars and bought euros in an effort to stabilize the falling value of the euro relative to the dollar. In the previous year the euro (€) had depreciated from €1 = \$1.17 to €1 = \$0.87.

The current exchange-rate system is thus an "almost" flexible exchange-rate system. The "almost" refers mainly to the occasional currency interventions by governments; it also refers to the fact that the actual system is more complicated than described. While the major currencies such as dollars, euros, pounds, and yen fluctuate in response to changing supply and demand, some developing nations peg their currencies to the dollar and allow their currencies to fluctuate with it against other currencies. Also, some nations peg the value of their currencies to a "basket" or group of other currencies.

How well has the managed float worked? It has both proponents and critics.

In Support of the Managed Float Proponents of the managed-float system argue that it has functioned far better than many experts anticipated. Skeptics had predicted that fluctuating exchange rates would reduce world trade and finance. But in real terms world trade under the managed float has grown tremendously over the past several decades. Moreover, as supporters are quick to point out, currency crises such as those in Mexico and southeast Asia in the last half of the 1990s were not the result of the floating-exchange-rate system itself. Rather, the abrupt currency devaluations and depreciations resulted from internal problems in those nations, in conjunction with the nations' tendency to peg their currencies to the dollar or to a basket of currencies.

In some cases, flexible exchange rates would have made these adjustments far more gradual.

Proponents also point out that the managed float has weathered severe economic turbulence that might have caused a fixed-rate system to break down. Such events as extraordinary oil price increases in 1973–1974 and again in 1981–1983, inflationary recessions in several nations in the mid-1970s, major national recessions in the early 1980s, and large U.S. budget deficits in the 1980s and the first half of the 1990s all caused substantial imbalances in international trade and finance, as did the large U.S. budget deficits and soaring world oil prices that occurred in the middle of the first decade of the 2000s. The U.S. financial crisis and the severe recession of 2007–2009 greatly disrupted world trade. Flexible rates enabled the system to adjust to all these events, whereas the same events would have put unbearable pressures on a fixed-rate system.

Concerns with the Managed Float There is still much sentiment in favor of greater exchange-rate stability. Those favoring more stable exchange rates see problems with the current system. They argue that the excessive volatility of exchange rates under the managed float threatens the prosperity of economies that rely heavily on exports. Several financial crises in individual nations (for example, Mexico, South Korea, Indonesia, Thailand, Russia, and Brazil) have resulted from abrupt changes in exchange rates. These crises have led to massive "bailouts" of those economies via loans from the International Monetary Fund (IMF). The IMF bailouts, in turn, may encourage nations to undertake risky and inappropriate economic policies since they know that, if need be, the IMF will come to the rescue. Moreover, some exchange-rate volatility has occurred even when underlying economic and financial conditions were relatively stable, suggesting that speculation plays too large a role in determining exchange rates.

Skeptics say the managed float is basically a "nonsystem" because the guidelines as to what each nation may or may not do with its exchange rates are not specific enough to keep the system working in the long run. Nations inevitably will be tempted to intervene in the foreign exchange market, not merely to smooth out short-term fluctuations in exchange rates but to prop up their currency if it is chronically weak or to manipulate the exchange rate to achieve domestic stabilization goals.

So what are we to conclude? Flexible exchange rates have not worked perfectly, but they have not failed miserably. Thus far they have survived, and no doubt have eased, several major shocks to the international trading system. Meanwhile, the "managed" part of the float has given nations some sense of control over their collective economic destinies. On balance, most economists favor continuation of the present system of "almost" flexible exchange rates.

QUICK REVIEW 21.6

- The managed floating system of exchange rates (1971–present) relies on foreign exchange markets to establish equilibrium exchange rates.
- Under the system, nations can buy and sell official reserves of foreign currency to stabilize short-term changes in exchange rates or to correct exchange-rate imbalances that are negatively affecting the world economy.
- Proponents point out that international trade and investment have grown tremendously under the system. Critics say that it is a "nonsystem" and argue that the exchange rate volatility allowed under the managed float discourages international trade and investment. That is, trade and investment would be even larger if exchange rates were more stable.

Recent U.S. Trade Deficits

LO21.6 Identify the causes and consequences of recent U.S. trade deficits.

As shown in Figure 21.4a, the United States has experienced large and persistent trade deficits in recent years. These deficits rose rapidly between 2002 and 2006, with the trade deficit on goods and services peaking at $801 billion in 2006. The trade deficit on goods and services then declined precipitously to just $379 billion in 2009 as consumers and businesses greatly curtailed their purchases of imports during the recession of 2007–2009. As the economy recovered from the recession, the trade deficit on goods and services began rising again and reached $540 billion in 2012. The current account deficit (Figure 21.4b) reached a record high of $800 billion in 2006, and that amount was 6.0 percent of GDP. The current account deficit declined to $382 billion—2.6 percent of GDP—in the recession year 2009 before rebounding to $475 billion—or about 3.0 percent of GDP—in 2012. Economists expect the trade deficits to expand, absolutely and relatively, toward prerecession levels when the economy fully recovers and U.S. income and imports again rise.

FIGURE 21.4 U.S. trade deficits, 2002–2012. (a) The United States experienced large deficits in *goods* and in *goods and services* between 2002 and 2012. (b) The U.S. current account, generally reflecting the goods and services deficit, was also in substantial deficit. Although reduced significantly by the recession of 2007–2009, large current account deficits are expected to continue for many years to come.

(a)

Balance of trade

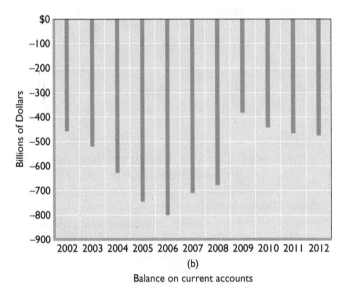

(b)

Balance on current accounts

Source: Bureau of Economic Analysis, **www.bea.gov**.

Causes of the Trade Deficits

The large U.S. trade deficits have several causes. First, the U.S. economy expanded more rapidly between 2002 and 2007 than the economies of several U.S. trading partners. The strong U.S. income growth that accompanied

that economic growth enabled Americans to greatly increase their purchases of imported products. In contrast, Japan and some European nations suffered recession or experienced relatively slow income growth over that same period. So consumers in those countries increased their purchases of U.S. exports much less rapidly than Americans increased their purchases of foreign imports.

Another factor explaining the large trade deficits is the enormous U.S. trade imbalance with China. In 2012 the United States imported $298 billion more of goods and services than it exported to China. Even in the recession year 2009, the trade deficit with China was $220 billion. The 2012 deficit with China was 64 percent larger than the combined deficits with Mexico ($55 billion), Germany ($67 billion), and Japan ($60 billion). The United States is China's largest export market, and although China has greatly increased its imports from the United States, its standard of living has not yet risen sufficiently for its households to afford large quantities of U.S. products. Adding to the problem, China's government has fixed the exchange rate of it currency, the yuan, to a basket of currencies that includes the U.S. dollar. Therefore, China's large trade surpluses with the United States have not caused the yuan to appreciate much against the U.S. dollar. Greater appreciation of the yuan would have made Chinese goods more expensive in the United States and reduced U.S. imports from China. In China a stronger yuan would have reduced the dollar price of U.S. goods and increased Chinese purchases of U.S. exports. That combination—reduced U.S. imports from China and increased U.S. exports to China—would have reduced the large U.S. trade imbalance.

Another factor underlying the large U.S. trade deficits is a continuing trade deficit with oil-exporting nations. For example, in 2012 the United States had a $99 billion trade deficit with the OPEC countries.

A declining U.S. saving rate (= saving/total income) also contributed to the large U.S. trade deficits. Up until the recession of 2007–2009, the U.S. saving rate declined substantially, while its investment rate (= investment/total income) increased. The gap between U.S. investment and U.S. saving was filled by foreign purchases of U.S. real and financial assets, which created a large surplus on the U.S. capital and financial account. Because foreign savers were willing to finance a large part of U.S. investment, Americans were able to save less and consume more. Part of that added consumption spending was on imported goods.

Finally, many foreigners simply view U.S. assets favorably because of the relatively high risk-adjusted rates

Speculation in Currency Markets

Are Speculators a Negative or a Positive Influence in Currency Markets and International Trade?

Most people buy foreign currency to facilitate the purchase of goods, services, or assets from another country. A U.S. importer buys Japanese yen to purchase Japanese autos. A Hong Kong financial investor purchases Australian dollars to invest in the Australian stock market. But there is another group of participants in the currency market—speculators—that buys and sells foreign currencies in the hope of reselling or rebuying them later at a profit.

Contributing to Exchange-Rate Fluctuations

Speculators were much in the news in late 1997 and 1998 when they were widely accused of driving down the values of the South Korean won, Thai baht, Malaysian ringgit, and Indonesian rupiah. The value of these currencies fell by as much as 50 percent within one month, and speculators undoubtedly contributed to the swiftness of those declines. The expectation of currency depreciation (or appreciation) can be self-fulfilling. If speculators, for example, expect the Indonesian rupiah to be devalued or to depreciate, they quickly sell rupiah and buy currencies that they think will increase in relative value. The sharp increase in the supply of rupiah indeed reduces its value; this reduction then may trigger further selling of rupiah in expectation of further declines in its value.

But changed economic realities, not speculation, are normally the underlying causes of changes in currency values. That

was largely the case with the southeast Asian countries in which actual and threatened bankruptcies in the financial and manufacturing sectors undermined confidence in the strength of the currencies. Anticipating the eventual declines in currency values, speculators simply hastened those declines. That is, the declines in value probably would have occurred with or without speculators.

Moreover, on a daily basis, speculation clearly has positive effects in foreign exchange markets.

of return they provide. The purchase of those assets provides foreign currency to Americans that enables them to finance their strong appetite for imported goods. The capital account surpluses therefore may partially cause the high U.S. trade deficits, not just result from those high deficits. The point is that the causes of the high U.S. trade deficits are numerous and not so easy to disentangle.

Implications of U.S. Trade Deficits

The prerecession U.S. trade deficits were the largest ever run by a major industrial nation. Whether the large trade deficits should be of significant concern to the United States and the rest of the world is debatable. Most economists see both benefits and costs to trade deficits.

Increased Current Consumption At the time a trade deficit or a current account deficit is occurring, American consumers benefit. A trade deficit means that the United States is receiving more goods and services as imports from abroad than it is sending out as exports. Taken alone, a trade deficit allows the United States to consume outside its production possibilities curve. It augments the domestic standard of living. But here is a catch: The gain in present consumption may come at the expense of reduced future consumption. When and if the current account deficit declines, Americans may have to consume less than before and perhaps even less than they produce.

Increased U.S. Indebtedness A trade deficit is considered unfavorable because it must be financed by

Smoothing Out Short-Term Fluctuations in Currency

Prices When temporarily weak demand or strong supply reduces a currency's value, speculators quickly buy the currency, adding to its demand and strengthening its value. When temporarily strong demand or weak supply increases a currency's value, speculators sell the currency. That selling increases the supply of the currency and reduces its value. In this way speculators smooth out supply and demand, and thus exchange rates, over short time periods. This day-to-day exchange-rate stabilization aids international trade.

Absorbing Risk Speculators also absorb risk that others do not want to bear. Because of potential adverse changes in exchange rates, international transactions are riskier than domestic transactions. Suppose AnyTime, a hypothetical retailer, signs a contract with a Swiss manufacturer to buy 10,000 Swatch watches to be delivered in three months. The stipulated price is 75 Swiss francs per watch, which in dollars is $50 per watch at the present exchange rate of, say, $1 = 1.5 francs. AnyTime's total bill for the 10,000 watches will be $500,000 (= 750,000 francs).

But if the Swiss franc were to appreciate, say, to $1 = 1 franc, the dollar price per watch would rise from $50 to $75 and AnyTime would owe $750,000 for the watches (= 750,000 francs). AnyTime may reduce the risk of such an unfavorable exchange-rate fluctuation by hedging in the futures market. Hedging is an action by a buyer or a seller to protect against a change in future prices. The futures market is a market in which currencies are bought and sold at prices fixed now, for delivery at a specified date in the future.

AnyTime can purchase the needed 750,000 francs at the current $1 = 1.5 francs exchange rate, but with delivery in three months when the Swiss watches are delivered. And here is where speculators come in. For a price determined in the futures market, they agree to deliver the 750,000 francs to AnyTime in three months at the $1 = 1.5 francs exchange rate, regardless of the exchange rate then. The speculators need not own francs when the agreement is made. If the Swiss franc depreciates to, say, $1 = 2 francs in this period, the speculators profit. They can buy the 750,000 francs stipulated in the contract for $375,000, pocketing the difference between that amount and the $500,000 AnyTime has agreed to pay for the 750,000 francs. If the Swiss franc appreciates, the speculators, but not AnyTime, suffer a loss.

The amount AnyTime must pay for this "exchange-rate insurance" will depend on how the market views the likelihood of the franc depreciating, appreciating, or staying constant over the three-month period. As in all competitive markets, supply and demand determine the price of the futures contract.

The futures market thus eliminates much of the exchange-rate risk associated with buying foreign goods for future delivery. Without it, AnyTime might have decided against importing Swiss watches. But the futures market and currency speculators greatly increase the likelihood that the transaction will occur. Operating through the futures market, speculation promotes international trade.

In short, although speculators in currency markets occasionally contribute to swings in exchange rates, on a day-to-day basis they play a positive role in currency markets.

---

borrowing from the rest of the world, selling off assets, or dipping into official reserves. Recall that current account deficits are financed by surpluses in the capital and financial accounts. Such surpluses require net inpayments of dollars to buy U.S. assets, including debt issued by Americans. Therefore, when U.S. exports are insufficient to finance U.S. imports, the United States increases both its debt to people abroad and the value of foreign claims against assets in the United States. Financing of the U.S. trade deficit has resulted in a larger foreign accumulation of claims against U.S. financial and real assets than the U.S. claim against foreign assets. In 2008, foreigners owned about $3.5 trillion more of U.S. assets (corporations, land, stocks, bonds, loan notes) than U.S. citizens and institutions owned in foreign assets.

If the United States wants to regain ownership of these domestic assets, at some future time it will have to export more than it imports. At that time, domestic consumption will be lower because the United States will need to send more of its output abroad than it receives as imports. Therefore, the current consumption gains delivered by U.S. current account deficits may mean permanent debt, permanent foreign ownership, or large sacrifices of future consumption.

We say "may mean" above because the foreign lending to U.S. firms and foreign investment in the United States increases the U.S. capital stock. U.S. production capacity therefore might increase more rapidly than other-wise because of a large surplus on the capital and financial account. Faster increases in production capacity and real GDP enhance the economy's ability to service foreign debt and buy back real capital, if that is desired.

Trade deficits therefore are a mixed blessing. The long-term impacts of the record-high U.S. trade deficits are largely unknown. That "unknown" worries some economists, who are concerned that foreigners will lose financial confidence in the United States. If that happens, they would restrict their lending to American households and businesses and also reduce their purchases of U.S. assets. Both actions would decrease the demand for U.S. dollars in the foreign exchange market and cause the U.S. dollar to depreciate. A sudden, large depreciation of the U.S. dollar might disrupt world trade and negatively affect economic growth worldwide. Other economists, however, downplay this scenario. Because any decline in the U.S. capital and financial account surplus is automatically met with a decline in the current account deficit, U.S. net exports would rise and the overall impact on the American economy would be slight.

> ## QUICK REVIEW 21.7
>
> - The United States has had large trade deficits in recent decades.
> - Causes include (a) more rapid income growth in the United States than in Japan and some European nations, resulting in expanding U.S. imports relative to exports; (b) the emergence of a large trade deficit with China; (c) continuing large trade deficits with oil-exporting nations; and (d) a large surplus in the capital and financial account, which enabled Americans to reduce their saving and buy more imports.
> - The severe recession of 2007–2009 in the United States substantially lowered the U.S. trade deficit by reducing American spending on imports.
> - U.S. trade deficits have produced current increases in the living standards of U.S. consumers but the accompanying surpluses on the capital and financial account have increased U.S. debt to the rest of the world and increased foreign ownership of assets in the United States.

SUMMARY

LO21.1 Explain how currencies of different nations are exchanged when international transactions take place.

International financial transactions involve trade either in currently produced goods and services or in preexisting assets. Exports of goods, services, and assets create inflows of money, while imports cause outflows of money. If buyers and sellers use different currencies, then foreign exchange transactions take place so that the exporter can be paid in his or her own currency.

LO21.2 Analyze the balance sheet the United States uses to account for the international payments it makes and receives.

The balance of payments records all international trade and financial transactions taking place between a given nation and the rest of the world. The balance on goods and services (the trade balance) compares exports and imports of both goods and services. The current account balance includes not only goods and services transactions but also net investment income and net transfers.

The capital and financial account includes (*a*) the net amount of the nation's debt forgiveness and (*b*) the nation's sale of real and financial assets to people living abroad less its purchases of real and financial assets from foreigners.

The current account and the capital and financial account always sum to zero. A deficit in the current account is always offset by a surplus in the capital and financial account. Conversely, a surplus in the current account is always offset by a deficit in the capital and financial account.

Official reserves are owned by national governments and their central banks and consist of stocks of foreign currencies, certain reserves held with the International Monetary Fund, and stocks of gold.

A balance-of-payments deficit is said to occur when a nation draws down its stock of official reserves to purchase dollars from abroad to balance the capital and financial account with the current account. A balance-of-payments surplus occurs when a nation adds to its stock of official reserves by selling dollars to foreigners to obtain foreign currencies to balance the two accounts. The desirability of a balance-of-payments deficit or surplus depends on its size and its persistence.

LO21.3 Discuss how exchange rates are determined in currency markets that have flexible exchange rates.

Flexible or floating exchange rates between international currencies are determined by the demand for and supply of those currencies. Under flexible rates, a currency will depreciate or appreciate as a result of changes in tastes, relative income changes, relative changes in inflation rates, relative changes in real interest rates, and speculation.

LO21.4 Describe the difference between flexible exchange rates and fixed exchange rates.

The maintenance of fixed exchange rates requires adequate official reserves to accommodate periodic payments deficits. If reserves are inadequate, nations must invoke protectionist trade policies, engage in exchange controls, or endure undesirable domestic macroeconomic adjustments.

LO21.5 Explain the current system of managed floating exchange rates.

Since 1971 the world's major nations have used a system of managed floating exchange rates. Market forces generally set rates, although governments intervene with varying frequency to alter their exchange rates.

LO21.6 Identify the causes and consequences of recent U.S. trade deficits.

Between 1997 and 2007, the United States had large and rising trade deficits, which are projected to last well into the future. Causes of the trade deficits include (*a*) more rapid income growth in the United States than in Japan and some European nations, resulting in expanding U.S. imports relative to exports, (*b*) the emergence of a large trade deficit with China, (*c*) continuing large trade deficits with oil-exporting nations, and (*d*) a large surplus in the capital and financial account, which enabled Americans to reduce their saving and buy more imports. The severe recession of 2007–2009 in the United States substantially lowered the U.S. trade deficit by reducing American spending on imports.

U.S. trade deficits have produced current increases in the living standards of U.S. consumers. The accompanying surpluses on the capital and financial account have increased U.S. debt to the rest of the world and increased foreign ownership of assets in the United States. This greater foreign investment in the United States, however, has undoubtedly increased U.S. production possibilities.

TERMS AND CONCEPTS

balance of payments	capital and financial account	fixed-exchange-rate system
current account	balance on capital and financial account	purchasing-power-parity theory
balance on goods and services	official reserves	currency interventions
trade deficit	balance-of-payments deficits and surpluses	exchange controls
trade surplus		managed floating exchange rates
balance on current account	flexible- or floating-exchange-rate system	

The following and additional problems can be found in **connect** | ECONOMICS

DISCUSSION QUESTIONS

1. Do all international financial transactions necessarily involve exchanging one nation's distinct currency for another? Explain. Could a nation that neither imports goods and services nor exports goods and services still engage in international financial transactions? **LO21.1**

2. Explain: "U.S. exports earn supplies of foreign currencies that Americans can use to finance imports." Indicate whether each of the following creates a demand for or a supply of European euros in foreign exchange markets: **LO21.1**
   a. A U.S. airline firm purchases several Airbus planes assembled in France.
   b. A German automobile firm decides to build an assembly plant in South Carolina.
   c. A U.S. college student decides to spend a year studying at the Sorbonne in Paris.
   d. An Italian manufacturer ships machinery from one Italian port to another on a Liberian freighter.
   e. The U.S. economy grows faster than the French economy.
   f. A U.S. government bond held by a Spanish citizen matures, and the loan amount is paid back to that person.
   g. It is widely expected that the euro will depreciate in the near future.

3. What do the plus signs and negative signs signify in the U.S. balance-of-payments statement? Which of the following items appear in the current account and which appear in the capital and financial account? U.S. purchases of assets abroad; U.S. services imports; foreign purchases of assets in the United States; U.S. goods exports, U.S. net investment income. Why must the current account and the capital and financial account sum to zero? **LO21.2**

4. What are official reserves? How do net sales of official reserves to foreigners and net purchases of official reserves from foreigners relate to U.S. balance-of-payments deficits and surpluses? Explain why these deficits and surpluses are not actual deficits and surpluses in the *overall* balance-of-payments statement. **LO21.2**

5. Generally speaking, how is the dollar price of euros determined? Cite a factor that might increase the dollar price of euros. Cite a different factor that might decrease the dollar price of euros. Explain: "A rise in the dollar price of euros necessarily means a fall in the euro price of dollars." Illustrate and elaborate: "The dollar-euro exchange rate provides a direct link between the prices of goods and services produced in the eurozone and in the United States." Explain the

purchasing-power-parity theory of exchange rates, using the euro-dollar exchange rate as an illustration. LO21.3

6. Suppose that a Swiss watchmaker imports watch components from Sweden and exports watches to the United States. Also suppose the dollar depreciates, and the Swedish krona appreciates, relative to the Swiss franc. Speculate as to how each would hurt the Swiss watchmaker. LO21.3

7. Explain why the U.S. demand for Mexican pesos is downsloping and the supply of pesos to Americans is upsloping. Assuming a system of flexible exchange rates between Mexico and the United States, indicate whether each of the following would cause the Mexican peso to appreciate or depreciate, other things equal: LO21.3

   a. The United States unilaterally reduces tariffs on Mexican products.
   b. Mexico encounters severe inflation.
   c. Deteriorating political relations reduce American tourism in Mexico.
   d. The U.S. economy moves into a severe recession.
   e. The United States engages in a high-interest-rate monetary policy.
   f. Mexican products become more fashionable to U.S. consumers.
   g. The Mexican government encourages U.S. firms to invest in Mexican oil fields.
   h. The rate of productivity growth in the United States diminishes sharply.

8. Explain why you agree or disagree with the following statements. Assume other things equal. LO21.3

   a. A country that grows faster than its major trading partners can expect the international value of its currency to depreciate.
   b. A nation whose interest rate is rising more rapidly than interest rates in other nations can expect the international value of its currency to appreciate.
   c. A country's currency will appreciate if its inflation rate is less than that of the rest of the world.

9. "Exports pay for imports. Yet in 2012 the nations of the world exported about $540 billion more of goods and services to the United States than they imported from the United States." Resolve the apparent inconsistency of these two statements. LO21.2

10. What have been the major causes of the large U.S. trade deficits in recent years? What are the major benefits and costs associated with trade deficits? Explain: "A trade deficit means that a nation is receiving more goods and services from abroad than it is sending abroad." How can that be considered to be "unfavorable"? LO21.6

11. LAST WORD Suppose Super D'Hiver—a hypothetical French snowboard retailer—wants to order 5,000 snowboards made in the United States. The price per board is $200, the present exchange rate is 1 euro = $1, and payment is due in dollars when the boards are delivered in 3 months. Use a numerical example to explain why exchange-rate risk might make the French retailer hesitant to place the order. How might speculators absorb some of Super D'Hiver's risk?

REVIEW QUESTIONS

1. An American company wants to buy a television from a Chinese company. The Chinese company sells its TVs for 1,200 yuan each. The current exchange rate between the U.S. dollar and the Chinese yuan is $1 = 6 yuan. How many dollars will the American company have to convert into yuan to pay for the television? LO21.1
   a. $7,200.
   b. $1,200.
   c. $200.
   d. $100.

2. Suppose that a country has a trade surplus of $50 billion, a balance on the capital account of $10 billion, and a balance on the current account of −$200 billion. The balance on the capital and financial account will be: LO21.2
   a. $10 billion.
   b. $50 billion.
   c. $200 billion.
   d. −$200 billion.

3. The exchange rate between the U.S. dollar and the British pound starts at $1 = £0.5. It then changes to $1 = £0.75. Given this change, we would say that the U.S. dollar has _____ while the British pound has _____. LO21.3

   a. Depreciated; appreciated.
   b. Depreciated; depreciated.
   c. Appreciated; depreciated.
   d. Appreciated; appreciated.

4. A meal at a McDonald's restaurant in New York costs $8. The identical meal at a McDonald's restaurant in London costs £4. According to the purchasing-power-parity theory of exchange rates, the exchange rate between U.S. dollars and British pounds should tend to move toward: LO21.3
   a. $2 = £1.
   b. $1 = £2.
   c. $4 = £1.
   d. $1 = £4.

5. Suppose that a country has a flexible exchange rate. Also suppose that at the current exchange rate, the country is experiencing a balance-of-payments deficit. Then would it be true or false that a sufficiently large depreciation of the local currency could eliminate the balance-of-payments deficit. LO21.3

6. Diagram a market in which the equilibrium dollar price of 1 unit of fictitious currency zee (Z) is $5 (the exchange rate is $5 = Z1). Then show on your diagram a decline in the demand for zee. LO21.4

a. Referring to your diagram, discuss the adjustment options the United States would have in maintaining the exchange rate at $5 = Z1 under a fixed-exchange-rate system.

b. How would the U.S. balance-of-payments surplus that is caused by the decline in demand be resolved under a system of flexible exchange rates?

7. Suppose that the government of China is currently fixing the exchange rate between the U.S. dollar and the Chinese yuan at a rate of $1 = 6 yuan. Also suppose that at this exchange rate, the people who want to convert dollars to yuan are asking to convert $10 billion per day of dollars into yuan, while the people who are wanting to convert yuan into dollars are asking to convert 36 billion yuan into dollars. What will happen to the size of China's official reserves of dollars? **LO21.4**
    a. Increase.
    b. Decrease.
    c. Stay the same.

8. Suppose that a country follows a managed-float policy but that its exchange rate is currently floating freely. In addition, suppose that it has a massive current account deficit. Does it also necessarily have a balance-of-payments deficit? If it decides to engage in a currency intervention to reduce the size of its current account deficit, will it buy or sell its own currency? As it does so, will its official reserves of foreign currencies get larger or smaller? Would that outcome indicate a balance-of-payments deficit or a balance-of-payments surplus? **LO21.5**

9. If the economy booms in the United States while going into recession in other countries, the U.S. trade deficit will tend to _____. **LO21.6**
    a. Increase.
    b. Decrease.
    c. Remain the same.

10. Other things equal, if the United States continually runs trade deficits, foreigners will own _____ U.S. assets. **LO21.6**
    a. More and more.
    b. Less and less.
    c. The same amount of.

PROBLEMS

1. Alpha's balance-of-payments data for 2012 are shown below. All figures are in billions of dollars. What are the (*a*) balance on goods, (*b*) balance on goods and services, (*c*) balance on current account, and (*d*) balance on capital and financial account? Suppose Alpha sold $10 billion of official reserves abroad to balance the capital and financial account with the current account. Does Alpha have a balance-of-payments deficit or does it have a surplus? **LO21.2**

Goods exports	$+40
Goods imports	−30
Service exports	+15
Service imports	−10
Net investment income	−5
Net transfers	+10
Balance on capital account	0
Foreign purchases of Alpha assets	+20
Alpha purchases of assets abroad	−40

2. China had a $214 billion overall current account surplus in 2012. Assuming that China's net debt forgiveness was zero in 2012 (its capital account balance was zero), by how much did Chinese purchases of financial and real assets abroad exceed foreign purchases of Chinese financial and real assets? **LO21.2**

3. Refer to the following table, in which Q_d is the quantity of loonies demanded, P is the dollar price of loonies, Q_s is the quantity of loonies supplied in year 1, and Q_s' is the quantity of loonies supplied in year 2. All quantities are in billions and the dollar-loonie exchange rate is fully flexible. **LO21.3**

Q_d	P	Q_s	Q_s'
10	125	30	20
15	120	25	15
20	115	20	10
25	110	15	5

a. What is the equilibrium dollar price of loonies in year 1?
b. What is the equilibrium dollar price of loonies in year 2?
c. Did the loonie appreciate or did it depreciate relative to the dollar between years 1 and 2?
d. Did the dollar appreciate or did it depreciate relative to the loonie between years 1 and 2?
e. Which one of the following could have caused the change in relative values of the dollar (used in the United States) and the loonie (used in Canadia) between years 1 and 2: (1) More rapid inflation in the United States than in Canadia, (2) an increase in the real interest rate in the United States but not in Canadia, or (3) faster income growth in the United States than in Canadia.

4. Suppose that the current Canadian dollar (CAD) to U.S. dollar exchange rate is $0.85 CAD = $1 US and that the U.S. dollar price of an Apple iPhone is $300. What is the Canadian dollar price of an iPhone? Next, suppose that the CAD to U.S. dollar exchange rate moves to $0.96 CAD = $1 US. What is the new Canadian dollar price of an iPhone? Other things equal, would you expect Canada to import more or fewer iPhones at the new exchange rate? **LO21.3**

5. Return to problem 3 and assume the exchange rate is fixed against the dollar at the equilibrium exchange rate that occurs in year 1. Also suppose that Canadia and the United States are the only two countries in the world. In year 2, what quantity of loonies would the government of Canadia have to buy or sell to balance its capital and financial account with its current account? In what specific account would this purchase or sale show up in Canadia's balance-of-payments statement: Foreign purchases of assets in Canadia or Canadia's purchases of assets abroad? Would this transaction increase Canadia's stock of official reserves or decrease its stock? **LO21.6**

FURTHER TEST YOUR KNOWLEDGE AT www.mcconnell20e.com

Practice quizzes, student PowerPoints, worked problems, Web-based questions, and additional materials are available at the text's Online Learning Center (OLC), **www.mcconnell20e.com**, or scan here. Need a barcode reader? Try ScanLife, available in your app store.

The Economics of Developing Countries

www.mcconnell20.com

Learning Objectives

LO21W.1 Describe how the World Bank distinguishes between industrially advanced countries (high-income nations) and developing countries (middle-income and low-income nations).

LO21W.2 List some of the obstacles to economic development.

LO21W.3 Explain the vicious circle of poverty that afflicts low-income nations.

LO21W.4 Discuss the role of government in promoting economic development within low-income nations.

WEB CHAPTER

LO21W.5 Describe how industrial nations attempt to aid low-income countries.

It is difficult for those of us in the United States, where per capita GDP in 2012 was about $42,683, to grasp the fact that about 2.5 billion people, or nearly half the world's population, live on $2 or less a day. And about 1.3 billion live on less than $1.25 a day. Hunger, squalor, and disease are the norm in many nations of the world.

In this bonus Web chapter (at our Web site, **www.mcconnell20e.com**), we identify the developing countries, discuss their characteristics, and explore the obstacles that have impeded their growth. We also examine the appropriate roles of the private sector and government in economic development. Finally, we look at policies that might help developing countries increase their growth rates.

The Economics of Developing Countries

www.mcconnell20e.com

Learning Objectives

LO21W.1 Describe how the World Bank distinguishes between industrially advanced countries and developing countries.

LO21W.2 List some of the obstacles to economic development.

LO21W.3 Explain the vicious circle of poverty that afflicts low-income nations.

LO21W.4 Discuss the role of government in promoting economic development within low-income nations.

LO21W.5 Describe how industrial nations attempt to aid low-income countries.

It is difficult for those of us in the United States, where per capita GDP in 2012 was about $51,749, to grasp the fact that about 2.5 billion people, or nearly half the world's population, live on $2 or less a day. And about 1.3 billion live on less than $1.25 a day. Hunger, squalor, and disease are the norm in many nations of the world.

In this bonus Web chapter we identify the developing countries, discuss their characteristics, and explore the obstacles that have impeded their growth. We also examine the appropriate roles of the private sector and government in economic development. Finally, we look at policies that might help developing countries increase their growth rates.

The Rich and the Poor

LO21W.1 Describe how the World Bank distinguished between industrially advanced countries and developing countries.

Just as there is considerable income inequality among families within a nation, so too is there great income inequality among the family of nations. According to the United Nations, the richest 20 percent of the world's population receive more than 80 percent of the world's income; the poorest 20 percent receive less than 2 percent. The poorest 60 percent receive less than 6 percent of the world's income.

Classifications

The World Bank classifies countries into high-income, upper-middle-income, lower-middle-income, and low-income countries on the basis of national income per capita, as shown in Figure 21W.1. The *high-income nations*, shown in dark green, are known as the **industrially advanced countries (IACs)**; they include the United States, Japan, Canada, Australia, New Zealand, and most of the nations of western Europe. In general, these nations have well-developed market economies based on large stocks of capital goods, advanced production technologies, and well-educated workers. In 2010 this group of economies had a per capita income of $38,745.

The remaining nations of the world are called **developing countries (DVCs).** They have wide variations of income per capita and are mainly located in Africa, Asia, and Latin America. The DVCs are a highly diverse group that can be subdivided into three groups:

- The *upper-middle-income nations*, show in light green in Figure 21W.1, include countries such as Brazil, Iran, Russia, South Africa, Mexico, China, and Thailand. The per capita output of these nations ranged all the way from $3,976 to $12,275 in 2010 and averaged $5,884.

- The *lower-middle-income nations*, shown in yellow, had per capita incomes ranging from $1,006 to $3,975 in 2010 with an average per capita income of $1,619. This category includes Armenia, India, Indonesia, Pakistan, Vietnam, and Zambia.

- The *low-income nations*, shown in orange, had a per capita income of $1,005 or less in 2010 and averaged only $528 of income per person. The sub-Saharan nations of Africa dominate this group. Low-income DVCs have relatively low levels of industrialization. In general, literacy rates are low, unemployment is high, population growth is rapid, and exports consist largely of agricultural produce (such as cocoa, bananas, sugar, raw cotton) and raw materials (such as copper, iron ore, natural rubber). Capital equipment is minimal, production technologies are simple, and labor productivity is very low. About 15 percent of the world's population live in these low-income DVCs, all of which suffer widespread poverty.

Comparisons

Several comparisons will bring the differences in world income into sharper focus:

- In 2010 U.S. GDP was $14.6 trillion; the combined GDPs of the 144 DVCs in that year added up to $20 trillion.

- The United States, with only 4.5 percent of the world's population in 2010, produced 23.1 percent of the world's output.

- Per capita GDP of the United States in 2010 was 127 times greater than per capita GDP in the Democratic Republic of the Congo, one of the world's poorest nations.

- The annual sales of the world's largest corporations exceed the national incomes of many of the DVCs. Walmart's annual world revenues of $405 billion in 2010 were greater than the national incomes of all but 23 nations.

Growth, Decline, and Income Gaps

Two other points relating to the nations shown in Figure 21W.1 should be noted. First, the various nations have demonstrated considerable differences in their ability to improve circumstances over time. On the one hand, DVCs such as Chile, China, India, Malaysia, and Thailand achieved high annual growth rates in their GDPs in recent decades. Consequently, their real output per capita increased severalfold. Several former DVCs, such as Singapore, Greece, and Hong Kong (now part of China), have achieved IAC status. In contrast, a number of DVCs in sub-Saharan Africa have recently been experiencing stagnant or even declining per capita GDPs.

Second, the absolute income gap between rich and poor nations has been widening. Suppose the per capita incomes of the advanced and developing countries were growing at about 2 percent per year. Because the income base in the advanced countries is initially much higher, the absolute income gap grows. If per capita income is $400 a year in a DVC, a 2 percent growth rate means an $8 increase in income. Where per capita income is $20,000 per year in an IAC, the same 2 percent growth rate translates

FIGURE 21W.1 Groups of economies. The world's nations are grouped into industrially advanced countries (IACs) and developing countries (DVCs). The IACs (shown in dark green) are high-income countries. The DVCs are upper-middle-income, lower-middle-income, and low-income countries (shown respectively in light green, yellow, and orange).

Low ($1,005 or less)   Lower middle ($1,006–$3,975)   Upper middle ($3,976–$12,275)   High ($12,276 or more)   No data

Source: World Bank data, **www.worldbank.org.** National income per capita is converted to U.S. dollars using the World Bank's Atlas Method, which adjusts national amounts to U.S. dollars using 3-year exchange rate averages. See the World Bank's Web site for more details.

TABLE 21W.1 Selected Socioeconomic Indicators of Development

Country	(1) Per Capita Income, 2010*	(2) Life Expectancy at Birth, 2010	(3) Under-5 Mortality Rate per 1,000, 2010	(4) Adult Illiteracy Rate, Percent, 2010	(5) Internet Users per 100, 2010	(6) Per Capita Energy Consumption, 2009**
United States	$47,340	78	8	1	74.2	7,051
Japan	41,850	83	3	1	77.6	3,700
Brazil	9,390	73	19	11	40.7	1,243
China	4,270	73	18	8	34.4	1,695
India	1,270	65	63	39	7.5	560
Mauritania	1,030	58	111	42	3.0	180
Bangladesh	700	69	48	43	3.7	201
Mozambique	440	50	135	44	4.2	427
Ethiopia	390	59	106	57	0.7	402

*Purchasing power parity basis (see World Bank Web site for definition and methodology).
**Kilograms of oil equivalent.

Source: World Bank, *World Development Indicators 2012* and *World Development Report 2012.*

into a $400 increase in income. Thus the absolute income gap will have increased from $19,600 (= $20,000 − $400) to $19,992 (= $20,400 − $408). The DVCs must grow faster than the IACs for the gap to be narrowed.

A quick glance back at Figure 8.1 in our chapter on economic growth will confirm the "great divergence" in standards of living that has emerged between the United States, Western Europe, and Japan relative to Africa, Latin America, and Asia (excluding Japan).

The Human Realities of Poverty

Development economist Michael Todaro points out that mere statistics conceal the human implications of the extreme poverty in the low-income DVCs:

> Let us examine a typical "extended" family in rural Asia. The Asian household is likely to comprise ten or more people, including parents, five to seven children, two grandparents, and some aunts and uncles. They have a combined annual income, both in money and in "kind" (i.e., they consume a share of the food they grow), of $250 to $300. Together they live in a poorly constructed one-room house as tenant farmers on a large agricultural estate owned by an absentee landlord who lives in the nearby city. The father, mother, uncle, and the older children must work all day on the land. None of the adults can read or write; of the five school-age children, only one attends school regularly; and he cannot expect to proceed beyond three or four years of primary education. There is only one meal a day; it rarely changes and it is rarely sufficient to alleviate the children's constant hunger pains. The house has no electricity, sanitation, or fresh water supply. There is much sickness, but qualified doctors and medical practitioners are far away in the cities attending to the needs of wealthier families. The work is hard, the sun is hot and aspirations for a better life are constantly being snuffed out. In this part of the world the only relief from the daily struggle for physical survival lies in the spiritual traditions of the people.[1]

Table 21W.1 contrasts various socioeconomic indicators for selected DVCs with those for the United States and Japan. These data confirm the major points stressed in the quotation from Todaro.

Obstacles to Economic Development

LO21W.2 List some of the obstacles to economic development.

The paths to economic development are essentially the same for developing countries and industrially advanced economies:

- The DVCs must use their existing supplies of resources more efficiently. This means that they must eliminate unemployment and underemployment and also combine labor and capital resources in a way that will achieve lowest-cost production. They must also direct their scarce resources so that they will achieve allocative efficiency.

- The DVCs must expand their available supplies of resources. By achieving greater supplies of raw materials, capital equipment, and productive labor, and by advancing its technological knowledge, a DVC can push its production possibilities curve outward.

---

[1]Todaro, Michael P., *Economic Development*, 7th edition, © 2000. Printed and Electronically reproduced by permission of Pearson Education, Inc., Upper Saddle River, New Jersey.

All DVCs are aware of these two paths to economic development. Why, then, have some of them traveled those paths while others have lagged far behind? The difference lies in the physical, human, and socioeconomic environments of the various nations.

Natural Resources

No simple generalization is possible as to the role of natural resources in the economic development of DVCs because the distribution of natural resources among them is so uneven. Some DVCs have valuable deposits of bauxite, tin, copper, tungsten, nitrates, and petroleum and have been able to use their natural resource endowments to achieve rapid growth. This is true, for instance, of Kuwait and several other members of the Organization of Petroleum Exporting Countries (OPEC). In other instances, natural resources are owned or controlled by the multinational corporations of industrially advanced countries, with the economic benefits from these resources largely diverted abroad. Furthermore, world markets for many of the farm products and raw materials that the DVCs export are subject to large price fluctuations that contribute to instability in their economies.

Other DVCs lack mineral deposits, have little arable land, and have few sources of power. Moreover, most of the poor countries are situated in Central and South America, Africa, the Indian subcontinent, and southeast Asia, where tropical climates prevail. The heat and humidity hinder productive labor; human, crop, and livestock diseases are widespread; and weed and insect infestations plague agriculture.

A weak resource base can be a serious obstacle to growth. Real capital can be accumulated and the quality of the labor force improved through education and training. But it is not as easy to augment the natural resource base. It may be unrealistic for many of the DVCs to envision an economic destiny comparable with that of, say, the United States or Canada. But we must be careful in generalizing: Japan, for example, has achieved a high standard of living despite limited natural resources. It simply imports the large quantities of natural resources that it needs to produce goods for consumption at home and export abroad.

Human Resources

Three statements describe many of the poorest DVCs with respect to human resources:

- Populations are large.
- Unemployment and underemployment are widespread.
- Educational levels and labor productivity are low.

TABLE 21W.2 Population Statistics, Selected Countries

(1) Country	(2) Population per Square Km, 2010*	(3) Annual Rate of Population Increase, 2000–2010
United States	34	0.9
Pakistan	225	1.8
Bangladesh	1,142	1.4
Venezuela	33	1.7
India	412	1.5
China	143	0.6
Kenya	71	2.6
Philippines	313	1.9
Yemen	46	3.1
World	**53**	**1.2**

*1 square kilometer (km) = 0.386 square mile.

Source: World Development Indicators 2012, **www.worldbank.org**.

Large Populations As demonstrated by equation (1), a nation's standard of living or real income per capita depends on the size of its total output (or income) relative to its total population:

$$\text{Standard of living} = \frac{\text{Total output (or income)}}{\text{Population}} \quad (1)$$

Some of the DVCs with the most meager natural and capital resources not only have low total incomes but also large populations. These large populations often produce high population densities (population per square mile). In column 1 of Table 21W.2, note the high population densities of the selected DVCs relative to the lower densities of the United States and the world.

The high population densities of many DVCs have resulted from decades of higher rates of population growth than most IACs. Column 3 of Table 21W.2 shows the varying rates of population growth in selected countries over a recent period: 2000–2010. Although *fertility rates*—the number of children per woman's lifetime—are dramatically declining in many DVCs, the population growth rates of the DVCs remain considerably higher than for the IACs. Between 2000 and 2010, the annual population growth rate was 2.1 percent for the low-income DVCs and 1.2 percent for the middle-income DVCs. Those numbers compare to only a 0.7 percent rate of population growth for the IACs. Because a large percentage of the world's current population already lives in DVCs, their population growth remains significant. Over the next 15 years, 9 out of every 10 people added to the world population are projected to be born in developing nations.

FIGURE 21W.2 Population growth in developing countries and advanced industrial countries, 1950–2050. The majority of the world's population lives in the developing nations, and those nations will account for most of the increase in population over the next 40 years.

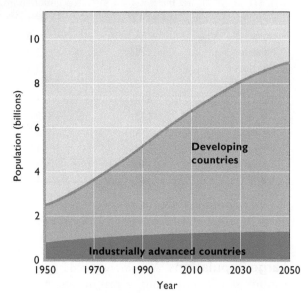

Source: Population Reference Bureau, **www.prb.org**. The underlying data are from the United Nations Population Division, *World Population Prospects: The 2012 Revision.*

Figure 21W.2 dramatically illustrates the effect of population growth in the DVCs on past, present, and projected world population numbers. Population growth in the DVCs will continue to increase the world's population through midcentury, at which time world population is expected to begin to level off.

In some of the poorest DVCs, rapid population growth actually strains the levels of income growth so severely that per capita income remains stagnant or even falls toward subsistence levels. In the worst instances, death rates rise sharply as war, drought, and natural disasters cause severe malnutrition and disease.

Boosting the standard of living in countries that have subsistence- or near-subsistence levels of income is a daunting task. When a DVC is just starting to modernize its economy, initial increases in real income can for a time increase population and short-circuit the process. If population increases are sufficiently large, they simply spread the higher level of total income among more people such that the original gain in per capita income disappears.

Why might income gains in the poorest DVC increase population growth, at least for a while? First, such income growth often reduces the nation's death rate. The increase in income means better nutrition and that improves health and increases life expectancy. Also, the death rate falls as a result of the basic medical and sanitation programs that accompany greater economic development. Second, the

birthrate initially rises, particularly if medical and sanitation programs reduce infant mortality. For these reasons, the rapid population growth that results from income increases can convert an expanding standard of living into a stagnant or very slow-growing standard of living.

Population expansion can also impede economic development in four additional ways:

- **Reduced saving and investment** The expenses associated with raising large families often reduce the capacity of households to save, thereby restricting the economy's ability to accumulate capital.

- **Lower productivity** As population increases, added investment is required to maintain the amount of real capital per person. If investment fails to keep pace, then on average each worker will have fewer tools and less equipment, and that will reduce worker productivity (output per worker). Declining productivity implies stagnating or declining per capita incomes.

- **Overuse of land resources** Because most developing countries are heavily dependent on agriculture, rapid population growth may cause an overuse of land resources. The much-publicized African famines are partly the result of overgrazing and overplanting of land caused by the pressing need to feed a growing population. Population pressures also can encourage excessive cutting down of trees for use as fuel. This denuding of the landscape contributes to severe soil erosion from wind and water. Finally, in some cases population pressure leads to the use of crop waste and animal dung as needed fuel rather than as fertilizer to replenish the productivity of the soil. (We say more about the African famines in this chapter's Last Word.)

- **Contribution to urban problems** Rapid population growth in the cities of the DVCs, accompanied by unprecedented inflows of rural migrants, generates massive urban problems. Rapid population growth aggravates problems such as substandard housing, poor public services, congestion, pollution, and crime. Resolving or reducing these difficulties necessitates diverting resources from growth-oriented uses.

Most authorities see birth control as the most effective means for breaking out of the population dilemma. And breakthroughs in contraceptive technology in recent decades have made this solution increasingly relevant. As we have indicated, fertility rates have dropped significantly in the DVCs. But obstacles to population control are still present. Low literacy rates make it difficult to disseminate information about contraceptive devices. In peasant agriculture, large families are a major source of labor. Adults may regard having many children as a kind of informal social security system: the more children, the greater the probability of the parents' having a relative to care for them in old age.

Finally, many nations that stand to gain the most through birth control are often the least willing, for religious reasons, to embrace contraception programs. For example, population growth in Latin America (which has a high proportion of Catholics) is among the most rapid in the world.

China, which has about one-fifth of the world's population, began its harsh "one-child" program in 1980. The government advocates late marriages and one child per family. Couples having more than one child are fined or lose various social benefits. Even though the rate of population growth has diminished under this program, China's population continues to expand. Between 2000 and 2010 it increased by 75.7 million people. India, the world's second most populous nation, had a 171-million person increase in population—a 16 percent rise—during the 2000–2010 period. With a total population of about 1.2 billion, India has 18 percent of the world's population but less than 2.5 percent of the world's landmass.

Qualifications We need to qualify our focus on population growth as a major cause of low per-capita incomes, however. As with the relationship between natural resources and living standards, the relationship between population sizes and living standards is less clear than one might expect. High population density certainly does not confine a nation to poverty. China and India have immense populations and are poor, but Japan, Singapore, and Hong Kong are densely populated and are wealthy. Moreover, the standard of living in many parts of China and India has rapidly increased in recent years.

Also, the population growth rate for the DVCs as a group has declined significantly in recent decades. Between 2000 and 2010, their annual population growth rate was about 1.3 percent; for 2010 through 2020, it is projected to fall to 1.1 percent (compared to 0.4 percent in the IACs). The world's population actually is projected to decline in the last part of this century.

Finally, not everyone agrees that reducing population growth is the best way to increase per capita GDP in the developing countries. Economists point to a **demographic transition** that occurs as economic growth takes off. In this transition, rising income transforms the population dynamics of a nation by reducing birthrates. In this view, high fertility rates and large populations are a consequence of low income, not the underlying cause. The task of a nation is to increase output and income. With success, declining birthrates will automatically follow.

This view recognizes both marginal benefits and marginal costs of having another child. In DVCs the marginal benefits are relatively large because the extra child becomes an extra worker who can help support the family. Extra children can provide financial support and security for parents in their old age, so people in poor countries have high birthrates. But in wealthy IACs, the marginal cost of having another child is relatively high. Care of children may require that one of the parents incur the opportunity cost of sacrificing high earnings or that the parents purchase expensive child care. Also, children require extended and expensive education for the highly skilled jobs characteristic of the IAC economies. At the same time, the marginal benefits of having a child may also be lower in a wealthy IAC. In particular, most IACs are wealthy enough to afford extensive "social safety nets" (such as retirement and disability benefits) that protect adults from the insecurity associated with old age and the inability to work. People in the IACs therefore recognize that high birthrates are not in the family's short-term or long-term interest. Thus, many of them choose to have fewer children.

Note the differences in causation between the traditional view and the demographic transition view of population. The traditional view is that reduced birthrates must first be achieved and then higher per capita income can follow. Lower birthrates enable per capita income to rise. The demographic transition view is that higher output and income should first be achieved and then lower rates of population growth eventually will follow. Higher incomes reduce population growth.

Development economists typically suggest a dual approach to development that combines both views. The surest way for the poorest DVCs to break out of their poverty is to implement policies that expand output and income while establishing independent policies that give families greater access to birth control information and methods. In terms of equation (1) on page 21W-5, a set of policies that raises the numerator (total income) and holds constant or lowers the denominator (population) will provide the biggest lift to a developing nation's standard of living.

Unemployment and Underemployment A second human resource dimension of developing countries relates to employment. For many DVCs, employment-related data are either nonexistent or highly unreliable. But observation suggests that unemployment is high. There is also significant **underemployment,** which means that a large number of people are employed fewer hours per week than they want, work at jobs unrelated to their training, or spend much of the time on their jobs unproductively.

Many economists contend that unemployment may be as high as 15 to 20 percent in the rapidly growing urban areas of the DVCs. There has been substantial migration in most developing countries from rural to urban areas, motivated by the expectation of finding jobs with higher wage rates than are available in agricultural and other rural employment. But this huge migration to the cities reduces a migrant's chance of obtaining a job. In many cases, migration to the cities has greatly exceeded the growth of urban job opportunities, resulting in very high urban unemployment rates. Thus, rapid rural-urban migration has given rise to urban unemployment rates that are two or three times as great as rural rates.

Underemployment is widespread and characteristic of most DVCs. In many of the poorer DVCs, rural agricultural labor is so abundant relative to capital and natural resources that a significant percentage of the labor contributes little or nothing to agricultural output. Similarly, many DVC workers are self-employed as proprietors of small shops, in handicrafts, or as street vendors. Unfortunately, however, many of them must endure long stretches of idle time at work due to a lack of demand. While they are not unemployed, they are clearly underemployed.

Low Labor Productivity The final human resource reality in developing nations is that labor productivity is low. As we will see, DVCs have found it difficult to invest in physical capital. As a result, their workers are poorly equipped with machinery and tools and therefore are relatively unproductive. Remember that rapid population growth tends to reduce the amount of physical capital available per worker, and that reduction erodes labor productivity and decreases real per capita incomes.

Moreover, most poor countries have not been able to invest adequately in their human capital (see Table 21W.1, columns 3 and 4); consequently, expenditures on health and education have been meager. Low levels of literacy, malnutrition, lack of proper medical care, and insufficient educational facilities all contribute to populations that are ill equipped for industrialization and economic expansion. Attitudes may also play a role: In countries where hard work is associated with slavery and inferiority, many people try to avoid it. Also, by denying educational and work opportunities to women, many of the poorest DVCs forgo vast amounts of productive human capital.

Particularly vital is the absence of a vigorous entrepreneurial class willing to bear risks, accumulate capital, and provide the organizational requisites essential to economic growth. Closely related is the lack of labor trained to handle the routine supervisory functions basic to any program of development. Ironically, the higher-education systems of some DVCs emphasize the humanities and offer relatively few courses in business, engineering, and the sciences. Some DVCs are characterized by an authoritarian view of human relations, sometimes fostered by repressive governments, that creates an environment hostile to thinking independently, taking initiatives, and assuming economic risks. Authoritarianism discourages experimentation and change, which are the essence of entrepreneurship.

While migration from the DVCs has modestly offset rapid population growth, it has also deprived some DVCs of highly productive workers. Often the best-trained and most highly motivated workers, such as physicians, engineers, teachers, and nurses, leave the DVCs to better their circumstances in the IACs. This so-called **brain drain** contributes to the deterioration in the overall skill level and productivity of the labor force.

Capital Accumulation

The accumulation of capital goods is an important focal point of economic development. All DVCs have a relative dearth of capital goods such as factories, machinery and equipment, and public utilities. Better-equipped labor forces would greatly enhance productivity and would help boost per capita output. There is a close relationship between output per worker (labor productivity) and real income per worker. A nation must produce more goods and services per worker as output to enjoy more goods and services per worker as income. One way of increasing labor productivity is to provide each worker with more tools and equipment.

Increasing the stock of capital goods is crucial because the possibility of augmenting the supply of arable land is slight. An alternative is to supply the available agricultural workforce with more and better capital equipment. And, once initiated, the process of capital accumulation may be cumulative. If capital accumulation increases output faster than the growth in population, a margin of saving may arise that permits further capital formation. In a sense, capital accumulation feeds on itself.

Let's first consider the possibility that developing nations will manage to accumulate capital domestically. Then we will consider the possibility that foreign funds will flow into developing nations to support capital expansion.

Domestic Capital Formation A developing nation, like any other nation, accumulates capital through saving and investing. A nation must save (refrain from consumption) to free some of its resources from the production of consumer goods. Investment spending must then absorb those released resources in the production of capital goods. But impediments to saving and investing are much greater in a low-income nation than they are in an advanced economy.

Savings Potential Consider first the savings side of the picture. The situation here is mixed and varies greatly between countries. Some of the very poor countries, such as

Burundi, Chad, Ghana, Guinea, Liberia, Madagascar, Mozambique, and Sierra Leone, have negative saving or save only 0 to 7 percent of their GDPs. The people are simply too poor to save a significant portion of their incomes. Interestingly, however, some middle-income countries save a larger percentage of their domestic outputs than do advanced industrial countries. In 2010 India and China saved 34 and 53 percent of their domestic outputs, respectively, compared to 24 percent for Japan, 23 percent for Germany, and 11 percent for the United States. The problem is that the domestic outputs of the DVCs are so low that even when saving rates are larger than those of advanced nations, the total volume of saving is not large.

Capital Flight Some of the developing countries have suffered **capital flight,** the transfer of private DVC savings to accounts held in the IACs. (In this usage, "capital" is simply "money," "money capital," or "financial capital.") Many wealthy citizens of DVCs have used their savings to invest in the more economically advanced nations, enabling them to avoid the high investment risks at home, such as loss of savings or real capital from government expropriation, abrupt changes in taxation, potential hyperinflation, or high volatility of exchange rates. If a DVC's political climate is unsettled, savers may shift their funds overseas to a "safe haven" in fear that a new government might confiscate their wealth. Rapid or skyrocketing inflation in a DVC would have similar detrimental effects. The transfer of savings overseas may also be a means of evading high domestic taxes on interest income or capital gains. Finally, money capital may flow to the IACs to achieve higher interest rates or a greater variety of investment opportunities.

Whatever the motivation, the amount of capital flight from some DVCs is significant and offsets much of the IACs' lending and granting of other financial aid to the developing nations.

Investment Obstacles There are as many obstacles on the investment side of capital formation in DVCs as on the saving side. Those obstacles include a lack of investors and a lack of incentives to invest.

In some developing nations, the major obstacle to investment is the lack of entrepreneurs who are willing to assume the risks associated with investment. This is a special case of the human capital limitations of the labor force mentioned above.

But the incentive to invest may be weak even in the presence of substantial savings and a large number of willing entrepreneurs. Several factors may combine in a DVC to reduce investment incentives, including political instability, high rates of inflation, and lack of economies of scale.

Similarly, very low incomes in a DVC result in a lack of buying power and thus weak demand for all but agricultural goods. This factor is crucial because the chances of competing successfully with mature industries in the international market are slim. Then, too, lack of trained administrative personnel may be a factor in retarding investment.

Finally, the **infrastructure** (stock of public capital goods) in many DVCs is insufficient to enable private firms to achieve adequate returns on their investments. Poor roads and bridges, inadequate railways, little gas and electricity production, poor communications, unsatisfactory housing, and inadequate educational and public health facilities create an inhospitable environment for private investment. A substantial portion of any new private investment would have to be used to create the infrastructure needed by all firms. Rarely can firms provide an investment in infrastructure themselves and still earn a positive return on their overall investment.

For all these reasons, investment incentives in many DVCs are lacking. It is significant that four-fifths of the overseas investments of multinational firms go to the IACs and only one-fifth to the DVCs. If the multinationals are reluctant to invest in the DVCs, we can hardly blame local entrepreneurs for being reluctant too.

How then can developing nations build up the infrastructure needed to attract investment? The higher-income DVCs may be able to accomplish this through taxation and public spending. But in the poorest DVCs there is little income to tax. Nevertheless, with leadership and a willingness to cooperate, a poor DVC can accumulate capital by transferring surplus agricultural labor to the improvement of the infrastructure. If each agricultural village allocated its surplus labor to the construction of irrigation canals, wells, schools, sanitary facilities, and roads, significant amounts of capital might be accumulated at no significant sacrifice of consumer goods production. Such investment bypasses the problems inherent in the financial aspects of the capital accumulation process. It does not require that consumers save portions of their money income, nor does it presume the presence of an entrepreneurial class eager to invest. When leadership and cooperative spirit are present, this "in-kind" investment is a promising avenue for accumulation of basic capital goods.

Technological Advance

Technological advance and capital formation are frequently part of the same process. Yet there are advantages in discussing technological advance separately.

Given the rudimentary state of technology in the DVCs, they are far from the frontiers of technological advance. But the IACs have accumulated an enormous body of technological knowledge that the developing countries might adopt and apply without expensive research. Crop rotation and contour plowing require no additional capital equipment and would contribute significantly to productivity. By raising grain storage bins a few inches above ground, a large amount of grain spoilage could be avoided. Although such changes may sound trivial to people of advanced nations, the resulting gains in productivity might mean the difference between subsistence and starvation in some poverty-ridden nations.

The application of either existing or new technological knowledge often requires the use of new and different capital goods. But, within limits, a nation can obtain at least part of that capital without an increase in the rate of capital formation. If a DVC channels the annual flow of replacement investment from technologically inferior to technologically superior capital equipment, it can increase productivity even with a constant level of investment spending. Actually, it can achieve some advances through **capital-saving technology** rather than **capital-using technology.** A new fertilizer, better adapted to a nation's topography and climate, might be cheaper than the fertilizer currently being used. A seemingly high-priced metal plow that will last 10 years may be cheaper in the long run than an inexpensive but technologically inferior wooden plow that has to be replaced every year.

To what extent have DVCs adopted and effectively used available IAC technological knowledge? The picture is mixed. There is no doubt that such technological borrowing has been instrumental in the rapid growth of such Pacific Rim countries as Japan, South Korea, Taiwan, and Singapore. Similarly, the OPEC nations have benefited significantly from IAC knowledge of oil exploration, production, and refining. Recently Russia, the nations of eastern Europe, and China have adopted Western technology to hasten their conversion to market-based economies.

Still, the transfer of advanced technologies to the poorest DVCs is not an easy matter. In IACs technological advances usually depend on the availability of highly skilled labor and abundant capital. Such advances tend to be capital-using or, to put it another way, labor-saving. Developing economies require technologies appropriate to quite different resource endowments: abundant unskilled labor and very limited quantities of capital goods. Although labor-using and capital-saving technologies are appropriate to DVCs, much of the highly advanced technology of advanced nations is inappropriate to them. They must develop their own appropriate technologies. Moreover, many DVCs have "traditional economies" and are not highly receptive to change. That is particularly true of peasant agriculture, which dominates the economies of most of the poorer DVCs. Since technological change that fails may

well mean hunger and malnutrition, there is a strong tendency to retain traditional production techniques.

Sociocultural and Institutional Factors

Economic considerations alone do not explain why an economy does or does not grow. Substantial sociocultural and institutional readjustments are usually an integral part of the growth process. Economic development means not only changes in a nation's physical environment (new transportation and communications facilities, new schools, new housing, new plants and equipment) but also changes in the way people think, behave, and associate with one another. Emancipation from custom and tradition is frequently a prerequisite of economic development. A critical but intangible ingredient in that development is the **will to develop.** Economic growth may hinge on what individuals within DVCs want for themselves and their children. Do they want more material abundance? If so, are they willing to make the necessary changes in their institutions and old ways of doing things?

Sociocultural Obstacles Sociocultural impediments to growth are numerous and varied. Some of the very-low-income countries have failed to achieve the preconditions for a national economic entity. Tribal and ethnic allegiances take precedence over national allegiance. Each tribe confines its economic activity to the tribal unit, eliminating any possibility for production-increasing specialization and trade. The desperate economic circumstances in Somalia, Sudan, Liberia, Zaire, Rwanda, and Afghanistan are due in no small measure to military and political conflicts among rival groups.

In countries with a formal or informal caste system, labor is allocated to occupations on the basis of status or tradition rather than on the basis of skill or merit. The result is a misallocation of human resources.

Religious beliefs and observances may seriously restrict the length of the workday and divert to ceremonial uses resources that might have been used for investment. Some religious and philosophical beliefs are dominated by the fatalistic view that the universe is capricious, the idea that there is little or no correlation between an individual's activities and endeavors and the outcomes or experiences that person encounters. The **capricious universe view** leads to a fatalistic attitude. If "providence" rather than hard work, saving, and investing is the cause of one's lot in life, why save, work hard, and invest? Why engage in family planning? Why innovate?

Other attitudes and cultural factors may impede economic activity and growth: emphasis on the performance of duties rather than on individual initiative; focus on the group rather than on individual achievement; and the belief in reincarnation, which reduces the importance of one's current life.

Institutional Obstacles Political corruption and bribery are common in many DVCs. School systems and public service agencies are often ineptly administered, and their functioning is frequently impaired by petty politics. Tax systems are frequently arbitrary, unjust, cumbersome, and detrimental to incentives to work and invest. Political decisions are often motivated by a desire to enhance the nation's international prestige rather than to foster development.

Because of the predominance of farming in DVCs, the problem of achieving an optimal institutional environment in agriculture is a vital consideration in any growth program. Specifically, the institutional problem of **land reform** demands attention in many DVCs. But the reform that is needed may vary tremendously from nation to nation. In some DVCs the problem is excessive concentration of land ownership in the hands of a few wealthy families. This situation is demoralizing for tenants, weakens their incentive to produce, and typically does not promote capital improvements. At the other extreme is the situation in which each family owns and farms a piece of land far too small for the use of modern agricultural technology. An important complication to the problem of land reform is that political considerations sometimes push reform in the direction of farms that are too small to achieve economies of scale. For many nations, land reform is the most acute institutional problem to be resolved in initiating economic development.

Examples: Land reform in South Korea weakened the political control of the landed aristocracy and opened the way for the emergence of strong commercial and industrial middle classes, all to the benefit of the country's economic development. In contrast, the prolonged dominance of the landed aristocracy in the Philippines may have stifled economic development in that nation.

QUICK REVIEW 21W.1

- About 12 percent of the world's population lives in the low-income DVCs, which typically are characterized by scarce natural resources, inhospitable climates, large populations, high unemployment and underemployment, low education levels, and low labor productivity.
- For DVCs just beginning to modernize, high birthrates caused by improved medical care and sanitation can increase population faster than income growth, leading to lower living standards; but as development continues, the opportunity costs of having children rise and population growth typically slows.
- Low saving rates, capital flight, weak infrastructures, and lack of investors impair capital accumulation in many DVCs.
- Sociocultural and institutional factors are often serious impediments to economic growth in DVCs.

The Vicious Circle

LO21W.3 Explain the vicious circle of poverty that afflicts low-income nations.

Many of the characteristics of the poorest of the DVCs just described are both causes and consequences of their poverty. These countries are caught in a **vicious circle of poverty.** They stay poor because they are poor! Consider Figure 21W.3. Common to most DVCs is low per capita

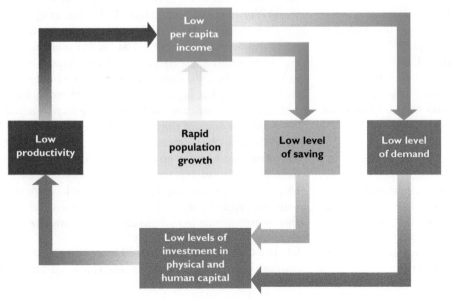

FIGURE 21W.3 The vicious circle of poverty. Low per capita incomes make it difficult for poor nations to save and invest, a condition that perpetuates low productivity and low incomes. Furthermore, rapid population growth may quickly absorb increases in per capita real income and thereby destroy the possibility of breaking out of the poverty circle.

income. A family that is poor has little ability or incentive to save. Furthermore, low incomes mean low levels of product demand. Thus, there are few available resources, on the one hand, and no strong incentives, on the other hand, for investment in physical or human capital. Consequently, labor productivity is low. And since output per person is real income per person, it follows that per capita income is low.

Many economists think that the key to breaking out of this vicious circle is to increase the rate of capital accumulation, to achieve a level of investment of, say, 10 percent of the national income. But Figure 21W.3 reminds us that rapid population growth may partially or entirely undo the potentially beneficial effects of a higher rate of capital accumulation. Suppose that initially a DVC is realizing no growth in its real GDP but somehow manages to increase saving and investment to 10 percent of its GDP. As a result, real GDP begins to grow at, say, 2.5 percent per year. With a stable population, real GDP per capita will also grow at 2.5 percent per year. If that growth persists, the standard of living will double in about 28 years. But what if population also grows at the rate of 2.5 percent per year, as it does in parts of the Middle East, northern Africa, and sub-Saharan Africa? Then real income per person will remain unchanged and the vicious circle will persist.

But if population can be kept constant or limited to some growth rate significantly below 2.5 percent, real income per person will rise. Then the possibility arises of further enlargement of the flows of saving and investment, continuing advances in productivity, and the continued growth of per capita real income. If a process of self-sustaining expansion of income, saving, investment, and productivity can be achieved, the self-perpetuating vicious circle of poverty can be transformed into a self-regenerating, beneficent circle of economic progress. The challenge is to make effective policies and strategies that will accomplish that transition.

ORIGIN OF THE IDEA

O21W.1
Economic development

The Role of Government

LO21W.4 Discuss the role of government in promoting economic development within low-income nations.
Economists see a positive role for government in fostering DVC growth, but they generally agree that government efforts must support private efforts, not substitute for them. That is not always the case in practice.

A Positive Role

Economists suggest that developing nations have several avenues for fostering economic growth and improving their standards of living.

Establishing the Rule of Law Some of the poorest countries of the world are plagued by banditry and inter-tribal warfare that divert attention and resources from the task of development. A strong, stable national government is needed to establish domestic law and order and to achieve peace and unity. Research demonstrates that political instability (as measured by the number of revolutions and coups per decade) and slow economic growth go hand in hand.

Clearly defined and strictly enforced property rights bolster economic growth by ensuring that individuals receive and retain the fruits of their labor. Because legal protections reduce investment risk, the rule of law encourages direct investments by firms in the IACs. Government itself must live by the law. The presence of corruption in the government sanctions criminality throughout the economic system. Such criminality discourages the growth of output because it lowers the returns available to honest workers and honest businesspeople.

Building Infrastructure Many obstacles to economic growth are related to an inadequate infrastructure. Sanitation and basic medical programs, education, irrigation and soil conservation projects, and construction of transportation links and communication facilities are all essentially nonmarketable goods and services that yield widespread spillover benefits. Government is the only institution that is in a position to provide public infrastructure. But it need not do all the work through government entities. It can contract out much of the work to private enterprises.

With respect to both private and public infrastructure, DVCs have an unexpected advantage over more developed countries because they can act as *follower countries* when it comes to technology. As explained in Chapter 8 on economic growth, DVCs can simply adopt technologies that were developed at high cost in the more technologically advanced *leader countries* without having to pay any of the development costs of those technologies. DVCs can often jump directly to the most modern and highly productive infrastructure without going through the long process of development and replacement that was required in the IACs. As a good example, many DVCs have developed Internet-capable wireless phone networks instead of using their scarce resources to build and expand landline systems.

Embracing Globalization Other things equal, open economies that participate in international trade grow faster than closed economies. Also, DVCs that welcome foreign direct investment enjoy greater growth rates than DVCs that view such investment suspiciously or even as exploitation and therefore put severe obstacles in its way.

Realistic exchange-rate policies by government also help. Exchange rates that are fixed at unrealistic levels invite balance-of-payments problems and speculative trading in currencies. Often, such trading forces a nation into an abrupt devaluation of its currency, sending shock waves throughout its economy. More flexible exchange rates enable more gradual adjustments and thus less susceptibility to major currency shocks and the domestic disruption they cause.

Building Human Capital Government programs that encourage literacy, education, and labor market skills enhance economic growth by building human capital. In particular, policies that close the education gap between women and men spur economic growth in developing countries. Promoting the education of women pays off in terms of reduced fertility, greater productivity, and greater emphasis on educating children.

And government is in a position to nurture the will to develop, to change a philosophy of "Heaven and faith will determine the course of events" to one of "God helps those who help themselves." That change encourages personal educational attainment and enhanced human capital.

Promoting Entrepreneurship The lack of a sizable and vigorous entrepreneurial class, ready and willing to accumulate capital and initiate production, indicates that in some DVCs private enterprise is not capable of spearheading the growth process. Government may have to take the lead, at least at first. But many DVCs would benefit by converting some of their state enterprises into private firms. State enterprises often are inefficient, more concerned with providing maximum employment than with introducing modern technology and delivering goods and services at minimum per-unit cost. Moreover, state enterprises are poor "incubators" for developing profit-focused, entrepreneurial persons who leave the firm to set up their own businesses.

Developing Credit Systems The banking systems in some of the poorest DVCs are nearly nonexistent and that makes it difficult for domestic savers and international lenders to lend money to DVC borrowers, who in turn wish to create capital goods. An effective first step in developing credit systems is through **microfinance**, in which groups of people pool their money and make small loans to budding entrepreneurs and owners of small businesses. People from the IACs can do the same, helping nurture the spirit of enterprise and foster the benefits that it brings. The benefits of microlending accrue not only to

the entrepreneurs in the DVCs but to the country as a whole because the lending creates jobs, expands output, and raises the standard of living.

At the national level, DVC governments must guard against excessive money creation and the high inflation that it brings. High rates of inflation simply are not conducive to economic investment and growth because inflation lowers the real returns generated by investments. DVCs can help keep inflation in check by establishing independent central banks to maintain proper control over their money supplies. Studies indicate that DVCs that control inflation enjoy higher growth rates than those that do not.

Controlling Population Growth Government can provide information about birth control options. We have seen that slower population growth can convert increases in real output and income to increases in real *per capita* output and income. Families with fewer children consume less and save more; they also free up time for women for education and participation in the labor market. As women participate in the labor market, they tend to reduce their fertility rate, which further helps to control population growth.

Making Peace with Neighbors Countries at war or in fear of war with neighboring nations divert scarce resources to armaments, rather than to private capital or public infrastructure. Sustained peace among neighboring nations eventually leads to economic cooperation and integration, broadened markets, and stronger economic growth.

Public Sector Problems

Although the public sector can positively influence economic development, serious problems can and do arise with government-directed initiatives. If entrepreneurial talent is lacking in the private sector, are quality leaders likely to surface in the ranks of government? Is there not a real danger that government bureaucracy will impede, not stimulate, social and economic change? And what of the tendency of some political leaders to favor spectacular "showpiece" projects at the expense of less showy but more productive programs? Might not political objectives take precedence over the economic goals of a governmentally directed development program?

Development experts are less enthusiastic about the role of government in the growth process than they were 30 years ago. Unfortunately, government misadministration and **corruption** are common in many DVCs, and government officials sometimes line their own pockets with foreign-aid funds. Moreover, political leaders often confer monopoly privileges on relatives, friends, and political supporters and grant exclusive rights to relatives or friends to produce, import, or export certain products. Such monopoly privileges lead to higher domestic prices and diminish the DVC's ability to compete in world markets.

Similarly, managers of state-owned enterprises are often appointed on the basis of cronyism rather than competence. Many DVC governments, particularly in Africa, have created "marketing boards" as the sole purchaser of agricultural products from local farmers. The boards buy farm products at artificially low prices and sell them at higher world prices; the "profit" ends up in the pockets of government officials. In recent years the perception of government has shifted from that of catalyst and promoter of growth to that of a potential impediment to development. According to a recent ranking of 176 nations based on perceived corruption, the 40 nations at the bottom of the list (most corrupt) were DVCs. Global Perspective 21W.1

GLOBAL PERSPECTIVE 21W.1

The Corruption Perceptions Index, Selected Nations, 2012*

The corruption perceptions index measures the degree of corruption existing among public officials and politicians as seen by business people, risk analysts, and the general public. An index value of 100 is highly clean and 0 is highly corrupt.

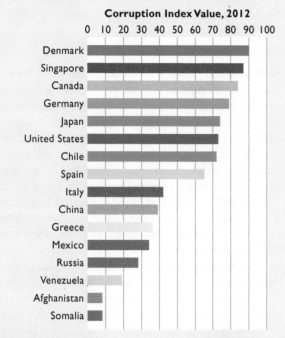

Corruption Index Value, 2012

Denmark
Singapore
Canada
Germany
Japan
United States
Chile
Spain
Italy
China
Greece
Mexico
Russia
Venezuela
Afghanistan
Somalia

*Index values are subject to change on the basis of election outcomes, military coups, and so on.

Source: Corruption Perceptions Index 2012 © Transparency International. All Rights Reserved. For more information, visit **http://www.transparency.org**.

shows the corruption scores for 16 selected nations, including the two least corrupt (Denmark and Singapore) and the two most corrupt (Afghanistan and Somalia).

The Role of Advanced Nations

LO21W.5 Describe how industrial nations attempt to aid low-income countries.

How can the IACs help developing countries in their pursuit of economic growth? To what degree have IACs provided assistance?

Expanding Trade

Some authorities maintain that the simplest and most effective way for the United States and other industrially advanced nations to aid developing nations is to lower international trade barriers. Such action would enable DVCs to elevate their national incomes through increased trade. Trade barriers instituted by the IACs are often highest for labor-intensive manufactured goods, such as textiles, clothing, footwear, and processed agricultural products. These are precisely the sorts of products for which the DVCs have a comparative advantage. Also, many IACs' tariffs rise as the degree of product processing increases; for example, tariffs on chocolates are higher than those on cocoa. This practice discourages the DVCs from developing processing industries of their own.

Additionally, large agricultural subsidies in the IACs encourage excessive production of food and fiber in the IACs. The overproduction flows into world markets, where it depresses agricultural prices. DVCs, which typically do not subsidize farmers, therefore face artificially low prices for their farm exports. The IACs could greatly help DVCs by reducing farm subsidies along with tariffs.

But lowering trade barriers is certainly not a panacea. Some poor nations need only large foreign markets for their raw materials to achieve growth. But the problem for many poor nations is not to obtain markets in which to sell existing products or relatively abundant raw materials but to get the capital and technical assistance they need to produce products for domestic consumption.

Also, close trade ties with advanced nations entail certain disadvantages. Dependence by the DVCs on exports to the IACs leaves the DVCs highly vulnerable to recessions in the IACs. As firms cut back production in the IACs, the demand for DVC resources declines; and as income in the IACs declines, the demand for DVC-produced goods declines. By reducing the demand for DVC exports, recessions in the IACs can severely reduce the prices of raw materials exported by the DVCs. For example, during the recession of 2007–2009, the world price of zinc fell from $2.02 per pound to $0.49 per pound, and the world price of copper fell from $4.05 per pound to $1.40 per pound. These declines in prices severely reduce the export earnings of the DVCs. Because mineral exports are a significant source of DVC income, stability and growth in IACs are important to improved standards of living in the developing nations.

Admitting Temporary Workers

Some economists recommend that the IACs help the DVCs by accepting more seasonal or other temporary workers from the DVCs. Temporary migration provides an outlet for surplus DVC labor. Moreover, migrant remittances to families in the home country serve as a sorely needed source of income. The problem, of course, is that some temporary workers illegally blend into the fabric of the IACs and do not leave when their visas or work permits expire. That may not be in the long-run best interest of the IACs.

Discouraging Arms Sales

Finally, the IACs can help the DVCs as a group by discouraging the sale of military equipment to the DVCs. Such purchases by the DVCs divert public expenditures from infrastructure and education and heighten tensions in DVCs that have long-standing disputes with neighbors.

Foreign Aid: Public Loans and Grants

Official development assistance (ODA), or simply "foreign aid," is another route through which IACs can help DVCs. This aid can play a crucial role in breaking an emerging country's circle of poverty by supplementing its saving and investment. As previously noted, many DVCs lack the infrastructure needed to attract either domestic or foreign private capital. The infusion of foreign aid that strengthens infrastructure could enhance the flow of private capital to the DVCs.

Direct Aid   The United States and other IACs have assisted DVCs directly through a variety of programs designed to stimulate economic development. Over the past 10 years, U.S. loans and grants to the DVCs totaled $15 billion to $28 billion per year. The U.S. Agency for International Development (USAID) administers most of this aid. Some of it, however, consists of grants of surplus food under the Food for Peace program. Other advanced nations also have substantial foreign aid programs. In 2012 foreign aid from the IACs to the developing nations totaled $126 billion. This amounted to about one-fourth of 1 percent of the collective GDP of the IACs that year

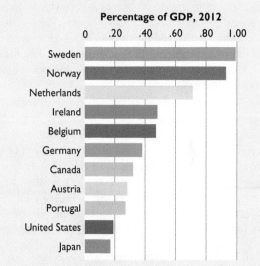

GLOBAL PERSPECTIVE 21W.2

Development Assistance as a Percentage of GDP, Selected Nations

In terms of absolute amounts, the United States was the leading provider of development assistance in 2012. It provided $30.5 billion to developing nations. But many other industrialized nations contribute a larger percentage of their GDPs to foreign aid than does the United States.

Percentage of GDP, 2012

Source: Based on data from OECD (2012); Development aid at its highest level ever in 2012 [Press release]. Table 1: Net Official Development Assistance from DAC and Other Donors in 2012: Preliminary data for 2012 (April 3, 2013), **www.oecd.org/dac**.

(see Global Perspective 21W.2 for percentages for selected nations).

A large portion of foreign aid is distributed on the basis of political and military rather than strictly economic considerations. Afghanistan, Egypt, Iraq, Israel, Pakistan, and Turkey, for example, are major recipients of U.S. aid. Asian, Latin American, and African nations with lower standards of living receive less.

Only one-fourth of foreign aid goes to the 10 countries in which 70 percent of the world's poorest people live. The most affluent 40 percent of the DVC population receives over twice as much aid as the poorest 40 percent. Many economists argue that the IACs should shift foreign aid away from the middle-income DVCs and toward the poorest DVCs.

Some of the world's poorest nations *do* receive large amounts of foreign aid relative to their meager GDPs. For example, in 2011 foreign aid relative to GDP was 54 percent in Liberia, 37 percent in Afghanistan, 23 percent in Haiti, 20 percent in Rwanda, 17 percent in Mozambique, and 15 percent in Sierra Leone.

Famine in Africa

The Roots of Africa's Persistent Famines Lie in Both Natural and Human Causes.

A number of sub-Saharan African nations are periodically threatened by famine. For example, in the early 1990s about 300,000 children under the age of five died from famine in Somalia. In 2003 famine threatened the lives of an estimated 10 million people in several southern Africa nations (Lesotho, Malawi, Mozambique, Swaziland, Zambia, and Zimbabwe). Although most African countries were self-sufficient in food at the time they became independent nations, they are now heavily dependent on imported foodstuffs for survival.

The immediate cause of famine often is drought. For example, in Kenya drought and crop failures in 1999 and 2000 killed much of the nation's livestock, leaving an estimated 3.5 million people at risk of starvation. But as first pointed out by economist Amartya Sen, the ultimate causes of sub-Saharan Africa's inability to feed itself are rooted in a complex interplay of natural and human conditions. Lack of rainfall, chronic civil strife, rapid population growth, widespread soil erosion, and counterproductive public policies all contribute to Africa's famines.

Civil Strife Regional rebellions, prolonged civil wars, and wars between nations have devastated several African nations. Ethiopia, Sudan, and Rwanda, for example, have been plagued by decades of civil strife. As another example, Ethiopia has recently been at war with its neighbor Eritrea. Not only do these conflicts divert precious resources from civilian uses, but they seriously

complicate the ability of wealthy nations to provide famine and developmental aid. Governments frequently divert donated food to the army and deny it to starving civilians. In Somalia, factional feuding destroyed most of the existing schools, factories, and government ministries and reduced the country to anarchy. Armed gangs stole water pumps, tractors, and livestock from farms and looted ports of donated foodstuffs.

Population Growth Although substantially slowing from previous growth rates, the population of sub-Saharan Africa is

Also, these and many other low-income developing nations receive large amounts of support from private donors in the IACs. In fact, in recent years the private giving to the DVCs by private U.S. universities, foundations (such as the Gates Foundation), voluntary organizations, and religious organizations has exceeded the foreign aid provided by the U.S. government.

The large accumulated debts of some of the poorest DVCs have become a severe roadblock to their growth. Therefore, some of the recent direct assistance by the IACs to the DVCs has taken the form of forgiving parts of the past IAC-government loans to low-income DVCs. In 2005 the G8 nations canceled $55 billion of debt owed by developing countries to the World Bank, the International Monetary Fund, and the African Development Bank. Of course, debt forgiveness creates a *moral hazard problem*. If current debt forgiveness creates an expectation of later debt

forgiveness, a country has little incentive against running up a new debt. Therefore, future loans by the IACs must be extended cautiously to the low-income developing nations that receive current debt forgiveness.

The World Bank Group The United States and other IACs also support the DVCs by participating in the **World Bank,** whose major objective is helping DVCs achieve economic growth. [The World Bank was established in 1945, along with the International Monetary Fund (IMF).] Supported by about 185 member nations, the World Bank not only lends out of its capital funds but also sells bonds and lends the proceeds and guarantees and insures private loans:

- The World Bank is a "last-resort" lending agency; its loans are limited to economic projects for which private funds are not readily available.

still growing very rapidly. Population is projected to grow by 2.4 percent annually from 2010 to 2020, compared to 0.4 percent in the industrially advanced economies. When crops are abundant, the sub-Saharan nations are able to feed their growing population. But when war or drought hits, hunger and malnutrition quickly follow.

Ecological Degradation Population growth has also contributed to the ecological degradation of Africa. With population pressures and the increasing need for food, marginal land has been deforested and put into crop production. In many cases trees that have served as a barrier to the encroachment of the desert have been cut down for fuel, allowing the fragile topsoil to be blown away by desert winds. The scarcity of wood that has accompanied deforestation in some cases has resulted in the use of animal dung for fuel, thereby denying its traditional use as fertilizer.

Furthermore, traditional fallow periods have been shortened, resulting in overplanting and overgrazing and a wearing out of the soil. Deforestation and land overuse have reduced the capacity of the land to absorb moisture, diminishing its productivity and its ability to resist drought. All this is complicated by the fact that there are few facilities for crop storage, making it difficult, even when crops are good, to accumulate a surplus for future lean years. A large percentage of domestic farm output in some parts of Africa is lost to rats, insects, and spoilage.

Public Policies Ill-advised public policies have contributed to Africa's famines.

First, many African governments generally have neglected investment in agriculture in favor of industrial development and military strength. It is estimated that African governments on the average spend four times as much on armaments as they do on agriculture.

Second, many African governments have adopted a policy of setting the prices of agricultural commodities at low levels to provide cheap food for growing urban populations. That policy has diminished the incentives of farmers to increase production. While foreign aid has helped ease the effects of Africa's food-population problems, most experts reject aid as a long-term solution. Experience suggests that aid in the form of food can provide only temporary relief and may undermine the achievement of long-run local self-sufficiency in food production. Foreign food aid, it is contended, treats symptoms, not causes.

Most dramatically, Zimbabwe's seizure of thousands of white-owned commercial farms for redistribution to black settlers collapsed the food supply. Along with severe drought, the policy threatened half the Zimbabwe population with severe malnutrition in 2003.

External Debt All this is made more complex by the fact that the sub-Saharan nations are burdened with large external debts. The World Bank reports that the aggregate external debt of these nations was $84 billion in 1980 and grew to $295 billion in 2012. As a condition of further aid, these nations have had to invoke austerity programs that have contributed to declines in their per capita incomes. One tragic consequence is that many of these nations have cut back on social service programs such as health care for children. For that reason, in 2000 the major industrial nations and the World Bank initiated a program to forgive $50 billion of total debt owed by some of these nations, on the condition that they end warfare and use the savings in interest and principal to ease the plight of their populations.

- Many World Bank loans have been for basic development projects—dams, irrigation projects, health and sanitation programs, communications, and transportation facilities. Consequently, the Bank has helped finance the infrastructure needed to encourage the flow of private capital.

- The Bank has provided technical assistance to the DVCs by helping them determine what avenues of growth seem appropriate for their economic development.

Affiliates of the World Bank function in areas where the World Bank has proved weak. The *International Finance Corporation (IFC)*, for example, invests in private enterprises in the DVCs. The *International Development Association (IDA)* makes "soft loans" (which may not be self-liquidating) to the poorest DVCs on more liberal terms than does the World Bank.

Foreign Harm? Although official development assistance directly from the IACs and indirectly through the World Bank has generally helped the DVCs expand their economies, the foreign-aid approach to helping DVCs has met with several criticisms.

Dependency and Incentives A basic criticism is that foreign aid may promote dependency rather than self-sustaining growth. Critics argue that injections of funds from the IACs encourage the DVCs to ignore the painful economic decisions, the institutional and cultural reforms, and the changes in attitudes toward thrift, industry, hard work, and self-reliance that are needed for economic growth. They say that, after some five decades of foreign aid, the DVCs' demand for foreign aid has increased rather than decreased. These aid programs should have withered away if they had been successful in promoting sustainable growth.

Bureaucracy and Centralized Government IAC aid is given to the governments of the DVCs, not to their residents or businesses. The consequence is that the aid typically generates massive, ineffective government bureaucracies and centralizes government power over the economy. The stagnation and collapse of the Soviet Union and communist countries of eastern Europe is evidence that highly bureaucratized economies are not very conducive to economic growth and development. Furthermore, not only does the bureaucratization of the DVCs divert valuable human resources from the private to the public sector, but it often shifts the nation's focus from producing more output to bickering over how unearned "income" should be distributed.

Corruption and Misuse Critics also allege that foreign aid is being used ineffectively. As we noted previously, corruption is a major problem in many DVCs, and some estimates suggest that from 10 to 20 percent of the aid is diverted to government officials. Also, IAC-based aid consultants and multinational corporations are major beneficiaries of aid programs. Some economists contend that as much as one-fourth of each year's aid is spent on expert consultants. Furthermore, because IAC corporations manage many of the aid projects, they are major beneficiaries of, and lobbyists for, foreign aid.

Current Level of Foreign Aid After declining in the late 1990s, foreign aid increased between 2000 and 2008. This increase resulted from a renewed international emphasis on reducing global poverty and also from expanded efforts by the IACs to enlist the cooperation of DVCs in fighting terrorism. In 2010 foreign direct aid by IAC governments to developing countries was $103 billion.

Flows of Private Capital

The IACs also send substantial amounts of private capital to the DVCs. Among the private investors are corporations, commercial banks, and, more recently, financial investment companies. General Motors or Ford might finance the construction of plants in Mexico or Brazil to assemble autos or produce auto parts. JPMorgan Chase or Bank of America might make loans to private firms operating in Argentina or China or to the governments of Thailand and Malaysia. And individuals living in IACs might purchase shares in "emerging markets" mutual funds run by investment companies like Fidelity. Those funds make financial investments in

the stock of promising firms in DVCs such as Hungary and Chile.

The total flow of private capital to DVCs was $557 billion in 2010, but the makeup of this flow differed from the flow in earlier decades. The main private investors and lenders are now private IAC firms and individuals, not commercial banks. Also, more of the flow is in the form of **foreign direct investment** in DVCs, rather than loans to DVC governments. Such direct investment includes the building of new factories in DVCs by multinational firms and the purchase of DVC firms (or parts of them). Whereas DVCs once viewed foreign direct investment as "exploitation," many of them now seek out foreign direct investment as a way to expand their capital stock and improve their citizens' job opportunities and wages. Those wages are often very low by IAC standards but high by DVC standards. Another benefit of direct investment in DVCs is that management skills and technological knowledge often accompany the capital.

Unfortunately for the low-income DVCs, the strong flow of private capital to the DVCs has been very selective. The vast majority of IAC investment and lending has been directed toward China, India, Mexico, and other middle-income DVCs, with only small amounts flowing toward such extremely impoverished DVCs as those in Africa.

In fact, as we have indicated, many of the lowest-income countries face staggering debt burdens from previous government and private loans. Payment of interest and principal on this external debt is diverting expenditures away from maintenance of infrastructure, new infrastructure, education, and private investment.

Further, the flows of private capital to both the middle-income and low-income DVCs plummeted during the worldwide recession of 2007–2009. It may be several years before foreign direct investment regains its momentum.

QUICK REVIEW 21W.2

- The IACs can assist the DVCs through expanded trade, foreign aid, and flows of private capital.
- Many of the poorest DVCs have large external debts that pose an additional obstacle to economic growth.
- The worldwide recession of 2007–2009 greatly reduced direct investment by the IACs in the DVC economies.

SUMMARY

LO21W.1 Describe how the World Bank distinguishes between industrially advanced countries and developing countries.

The majority of the world's nations are developing countries (low- and middle-income nations). While some DVCs have been realizing rapid growth rates in recent years, others have experienced little or no growth.

LO21W.2 List some of the obstacles to economic development.

Scarcities of natural resources make it more challenging—but certainly not impossible—for a nation to develop.

The large and rapidly growing populations in many DVCs contribute to low per capita incomes. Increases in per capita incomes frequently induce greater population growth, often reducing per capita incomes to near-subsistence levels. The demographic transition view, however, suggests that rising living standards must precede declining birthrates.

Most DVCs suffer from unemployment and underemployment. Labor productivity is low because of insufficient investment in physical and human capital.

In many DVCs, formidable obstacles impede both saving and investment. In some of the poorest DVCs, the savings potential is very low, and many savers transfer their funds to the IACs rather than invest them domestically. The lack of a vigorous entrepreneurial class and the weakness of investment incentives also impede capital accumulation.

Appropriate social and institutional changes and, in particular, the presence of the will to develop are essential ingredients in economic development.

LO21W.3 Explain the vicious circle of poverty that afflicts low-income nations.

The vicious circle of poverty brings together many of the obstacles to growth, supporting the view that poor countries stay poor because of their poverty. Low incomes inhibit saving and the accumulation of physical and human capital, making it difficult to increase productivity and incomes. Overly rapid population growth, however, may offset promising attempts to break the vicious circle.

LO21W.4 Discuss the role of government in promoting economic development within low-income nations.

The nature of the obstacles to growth—the absence of an entrepreneurial class, the dearth of infrastructure, the saving-investment dilemma, and the presence of social-institutional obstacles to growth—suggests that government should play a major role in initiating growth. Economists suggest that DVCs could make further development progress through such policies as establishing the rule of law, building infrastructure, opening their economies to international trade, setting realistic exchange rates, encouraging foreign direct investment, building human capital, encouraging entrepreneurship, controlling population growth, and making peace with neighbors. However, the corruption and maladministration that are common to the public sectors of many DVCs suggest that government may not be very effective in instigating growth.

LO21W.5 Describe how industrial nations attempt to aid low-income countries.

Advanced nations can encourage development in the DVCs by reducing IAC trade barriers and by directing foreign aid (official development assistance) to the neediest nations, providing debt forgiveness to the poorest DVCs, allowing temporary low-skilled immigration from the DVCs, and discouraging arms sales to the DVCs. Critics of foreign aid, however, say that it (a) creates DVC dependency, (b) contributes to the growth of bureaucracies and centralized economic control, and (c) is rendered ineffective by corruption and mismanagement.

In recent years the IACs have reduced foreign aid to the DVCs but have increased direct investment and other private capital flows to the DVCs. Little of the foreign direct investment, however, has gone to the poorest DVCs. Also, foreign direct investment plummeted during the worldwide recession of 2007–2009.

TERMS AND CONCEPTS

industrially advanced countries (IACs)	infrastructure	vicious circle of poverty
developing countries (DVCs)	capital-saving technology	microfinance
demographic transition	capital-using technology	corruption
underemployment	will to develop	World Bank
brain drain	capricious universe view	foreign direct investment
capital flight	land reform	

DISCUSSION QUESTIONS

1. What are the four categories used by the World Bank to classify nations on the basis of national income per capita? Identify any two nations of your choice for each of the four categories. **LO21W.1**
2. Explain how the absolute per capita income gap between rich and poor nations might increase, even though per capita income (or output) is growing faster in DVCs than in IACs. **LO21W.1**
3. Explain how each of the following can be obstacles to the growth of income per capita in the DVCs: lack of natural resources, large populations, low labor productivity, poor infrastructure, and capital flight. **LO21W.2**
4. What is the demographic transition? Contrast the demographic transition view of population growth with the traditional view that slower population growth is a prerequisite for rising living standards in the DVCs. **LO21W.2**
5. As it relates to the vicious circle of poverty, what is meant by the saying "Some DVCs stay poor because they are poor"? Change the box labels as necessary in Figure 21W.3 to explain rapid economic growth in countries such as South Korea and Chile. What factors other than those contained in the figure might contribute to that growth? **LO21W.3**
6. Because real capital is supposed to earn a higher return where it is scarce, how do you explain the fact that most international investment flows to the IACs (where capital is relatively abundant) rather than to the DVCs (where capital is very scarce)? **LO21W.3**

7. List and discuss five policies that DVC governments might undertake to promote economic development and expansion of income per capita in their countries? **LO21W.4**
8. Do you think that the nature of the problems the DVCs face requires a government-directed or a private-sector directed development process? Explain your reasoning. **LO21W.4**
9. Why do you think there is so much government corruption in some developing countries? **LO21W.4**
10. What types of products do the DVCs typically export? How do those exports relate to the law of comparative advantage? How do tariffs by IACs reduce the standard of living of DVCs? **LO21W.5**
11. Do you favor debt forgiveness to all DVCs, just the poorest ones, or none at all? What incentive problem might debt relief create? Would you be willing to pay $20 a year more in personal income taxes for debt forgiveness? How about $200? How about $2,000? **LO21W.5**
12. Do you think that IACs such as the United States should open their doors wider to the immigration of low-skilled DVC workers as a way to help DVCs develop? Do you think that it is appropriate for students from DVC nations to stay in IAC nations to work and build careers? **LO21W.5**
13. **LAST WORD** Explain how civil wars, population growth, and public policy decisions have contributed to periodic famines in Africa.

REVIEW QUESTIONS

1. True or False: The term *developing country* (DVC) is applied to rich nations like the United States and Germany because their economies are always growing quickly by developing new technologies. **LO21W.1**
2. True or False: A DVC that has little in the way of natural resources is destined to remain poor. **LO21W.2**
3. Suppose a country's total output is growing 10 percent per year, but its population is growing 11 percent per year. What will happen to living standards? **LO21W.2**
   a. Rise.
   b. Fall.
   c. Remain the same.
4. A DVC's population is growing 2 percent per year and output is growing 3 percent per year. If the government wants to improve living standards over coming decades, which of the following would probably be the best savings rate for the economy? **LO21W.2**
   a. 0 percent.
   b. 2 percent.
   c. 5 percent.
   d. 10 percent.
5. Compare a hypothetical DVC with a hypothetical IAC. In the DVC, average per capita income is $500 per year. In the

IAC, average per capita income is $40,000 per year. If both countries have a savings rate of 10 percent per year, the amount of savings per capita in the DVC will be _____ per person per year, while in the IAC it will be _____ per person per year. **LO21W.3**
   a. $50; $4,000.
   b. $5; $400.
   c. $450; $36,000.
   d. None of the above.
6. Which of the following policies would economists consider to be actions that a DVC government might take that would *improve* growth prospects? **LO21W.4**
   *Choose **one or more** answers from the choices shown.*
   a. Helping to extend the banking system to the rural poor.
   b. Passing high tariffs against foreign products.
   c. Constructing better ports, roads, and Internet networks.
   d. Charging high fees for public elementary schools.
7. True or False: Economists are unanimous that foreign aid greatly helps DVCs. **LO21W.5**
8. True or False: Some economists argue that the single best thing that IACs could do for DVCs in terms of economic growth would be to eliminate trade barriers between IACs and DVCs. **LO21W.5**

PROBLEMS

1. Assume a DVC and an IAC currently have real per capita outputs of $500 and $5,000, respectively. If both nations have a 3 percent increase in their real per capita outputs, by how much will the per capita output gap change? **LO21W.1**

2. Assume that a very tiny and very poor DVC has income per capita of $300 and total national income of $3 million. How large is its population? If its population grows by 2 percent in some year while its total income grows by 3 percent, what will be its new income per capita rounded to full dollars? If the population had not grown during the year, what would have been its income per capita? **LO21W.2**

FURTHER TEST YOUR KNOWLEDGE AT www.mcconnell20e.com

Practice quizzes, student PowerPoints, worked problems, Web-based questions, and additional materials are available at the text's Online Learning Center (OLC), **www.mcconnell20e.com**, or scan here. Need a barcode reader? Try ScanLife, available in your app store.

The United States in the Global Economy

www.mcconnell20e.com

This is an optional chapter for assignment by instructors who wish to cover international trade early in the course but do not want to assign the more graphical Chapter 38 (Chapter 20 in *Macroeconomics* and Chapter 24 in *Microeconomics*) for that purpose. If this chapter of *Economics* is assigned, Chapter 38 should not also be assigned in the same course because much of the content is shared. Some passages overlap word-for-word.

Learning Objectives

COI1.1 List and explain the four major economic flows that link the U.S. economy with the economies of other nations.

COI1.2 State several key facts about U.S. international trade.

COI1.3 Define comparative advantage and explain how it relates to specialization and international trade.

COI1.4 Explain how exchange rates are determined in currency (foreign-exchange) markets.

COI1.5 Explain how and why government sometimes interferes with free international trade.

COI1.6 Describe the purposes and functions of GATT, WTO, EU, eurozone, and NAFTA.

COI1.7 Define and discuss three major trade-related issues: trade adjustment assistance, the offshoring of jobs, and globalization.

Backpackers in the wilderness like to think they are "leaving the world behind," but, like Atlas, they carry the world on their shoulders. Much of their equipment is imported—knives from Switzerland, rain gear from South Korea, cameras from Japan, aluminum pots from England, sleeping bags from China, and compasses from Finland. Moreover, they may have driven to the trailheads in Japanese-made Toyotas or German-made BMWs, sipping coffee from Brazil or snacking on bananas from Honduras.

International trade and the global economy affect all of us daily, whether we are hiking in the wilderness, driving our cars, listening to music, or working at our jobs. We cannot "leave the world behind." We are enmeshed in a global web of economic relationships, such as the trading of goods and services, multinational corporations, cooperative ventures among the world's firms, and ties among the world's financial markets. That web is so complex that it is difficult to determine just what is—or isn't—an American product. A Finnish company owns Wilson sporting goods; a Swiss company owns Gerber baby food; and a London-incorporated South African company owns Miller Brewing. Dodge Charger police cars are assembled in Canada. Many "U.S." products such as Boeing aircraft contain numerous components from abroad, and, conversely, many "foreign" products such as Airbus planes contain numerous U.S.-produced parts.

International Linkages

COI1.1 List and explain the four major economic flows that link the U.S. economy with the economies of other nations. Several economic flows link the U.S. economy and the economies of other nations. As identified in Figure COI 1.1, these flows are:

- **Goods and services flows** or simply **trade flows** The United States exports goods and services to other nations and imports goods and services from them.
- **Capital and labor flows** or simply **resource flows** U.S. firms establish production facilities—new capital—in foreign countries, and foreign firms establish production facilities in the United States. Labor also moves between nations. Each year many foreigners immigrate to the United States and some Americans move to other nations.

- **Information and technology flows** The United States transmits information to other nations about U.S. products, prices, interest rates, and investment opportunities and receives such information from abroad. Firms in other countries use technology created in the United States, and U.S. businesses incorporate technology developed abroad.
- **Financial flows** Money is transferred between the United States and other countries for several purposes, for example, paying for imports, buying foreign assets, paying interest on debt, purchasing foreign currencies by tourists, and providing foreign aid.

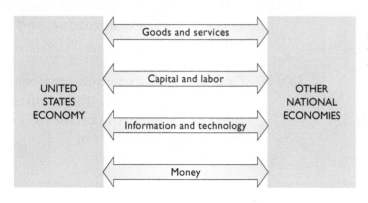

FIGURE COI 1.1 International linkages. The U.S. economy is intertwined with other national economies through goods and services flows (trade flows), capital and labor flows (resource flows), information and technology flows, and financial flows.

The United States and World Trade

COI1.2 State several key facts about U.S. international trade. Our main goal in this chapter is to examine trade flows and the financial flows that pay for them. What are the extent and pattern of international trade, and how much has that trade grown? Who are the major participants?

Volume and Pattern

Table COI 1.1 suggests the importance of world trade for selected countries. Many countries, with restricted resources and limited domestic markets, cannot efficiently produce the variety of goods their citizens want. So they must import goods from other nations. That, in turn, means that they must export, or sell abroad, some of their own products. For such countries, exports may run from 25 to 50 percent or more of their gross domestic product (GDP)—the market value of all goods and services produced in an economy. Other countries, the United States, for example, have rich and diversified resource bases and large internal markets. Although the total volume of trade is huge in the United States, it constitutes a smaller percentage of GDP than it does in a number of other nations.

TABLE COI 1.1 Exports of Goods and Services as a Percentage of GDP, Selected Countries, 2012

Country	Exports as a Percentage of GDP
Belgium	92
Netherlands	72
South Korea	47
Germany	41
New Zealand	26
Canada	25
Italy	25
France	21
Spain	21
United Kingdom	19
United States	14
Japan	13

Source: Derived by authors from *IMF International Financial Statistics,* 2013.

Volume For the United States and for the world as a whole, the volume of international trade has been increasing both absolutely and relative to their GDPs. A comparison of the boxed data in Figure COI 1.2 reveals

FIGURE COI 1.2 **U.S. trade as percentage of GDP, 1975–2012.** U.S. imports and exports have increased in volume and as a percentage of GDP since 1975.

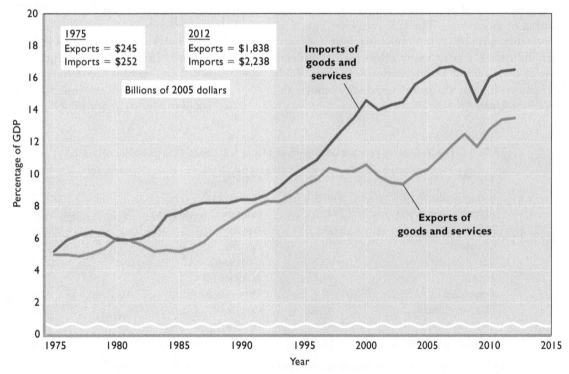

1975	2012
Exports = $245	Exports = $1,838
Imports = $252	Imports = $2,238

Billions of 2005 dollars

Imports of goods and services

Exports of goods and services

Source: Bureau of Economic Analysis, **www.bea.gov**. Data are from the national income accounts and are adjusted for inflation (2005 dollars).

substantial growth in the dollar amount of U.S. exports and imports over the past several decades. The graph shows the rapid growth of U.S. exports and imports of goods and services as percentages of GDP. On a national income account basis, U.S. exports and imports were 14 and 17 percent of GDP, respectively, in 2012. Even so, the United States now accounts for a diminished percentage of total world trade. In 1950, it supplied about 33 percent of the world's total exports, compared with about 8.5 percent today. International trade has increased more rapidly for other nations than it has for the United States. But in terms of the combined volume of imports and exports, the United States is still the world's leading trading nation.

Dependence The United States is almost entirely dependent on other countries for bananas, cocoa, coffee, spices, tea, raw silk, nickel, tin, natural rubber, and diamonds. Imported goods compete with U.S. goods in many of our domestic markets: Japanese cameras and cars, French and Italian wines, and Swiss and Austrian snow skis are a few examples. Even the "great American pastime" of baseball relies heavily on imported gloves and baseballs.

On the export side, many U.S. industries depend on sales abroad for their profitability. For example almost all segments of U.S. agriculture rely to one degree or another on exports. In fact, exports of rice, wheat, cotton, and tobacco vary from one-fourth to more than one-half of the total output of those crops. The U.S. computer, chemical, semiconductor, aircraft, automobile, machine tool, and software industries, among many others, sell significant portions of their output in international markets. Table COI 1.2 shows some of the major commodity exports and imports of the United States.

Trade Patterns The following facts will give you an overview of U.S. international trade:

- A *trade deficit* occurs when imports exceed exports. The United States has a trade deficit in goods. In 2012, U.S. imports of goods exceeded U.S. exports of goods by $735 billion.

- A *trade surplus* occurs when exports exceed imports. The United States has a trade surplus in services. U.S. firms and citizens collectively sell (export) more transportation, banking, legal, and other services abroad than they purchase (import) from foreign firms and citizens. In 2012, these U.S. exports of services exceeded U.S. imports of services by $196 billion. It has been typical for the United States in recent decades to have deficits in its trade in goods while simultaneously having surpluses in its trade in services.

- The United States imports many of the same kinds of goods that it exports (see Table COI 1.2).

- About half of the U.S. export and import trade is with other industrially advanced countries. The remainder is with developing countries, including members of the Organization of Petroleum Exporting Countries (OPEC).

- Canada is the United States' most important trading partner quantitatively. In 2012, 19 percent of U.S. exported goods were sold to Canadians, who in turn provided 14 percent of the U.S. imports of goods (see Table COI 1.3).

- The United States has sizable trade deficits with China and Mexico. In 2012, U.S. imported goods from China exceeded exported goods to China by $315 billion, and U.S. imported goods from Mexico exceeded U.S. exported goods to Mexico by $66 billion (see Table COI 1.3).

TABLE COI 1.2 Selected Principal U.S. Exports and Imports of Goods, 2012 (in Billions of Dollars)

Exports	Amount	Imports	Amount
Energy products	$167.1	Petroleum	$424.3
Agricultural products	145.0	Household appliances	141.3
Metals	128.9	Metals	128.4
Chemicals	118.8	Apparel	126.9
Consumer durables	99.3	Computers	122.2
Aircraft	94.1	Automobiles	101.4
Computers	49.2	Pharmaceuticals	87.2
Pharmaceuticals	47.9	Chemicals	75.6
Semiconductors	42.4	Generating equipment	65.0
Generating equipment	38.3	Telecommunications equipment	52.8

Source: Consolidated by authors from data provided by the Bureau of Economic Analysis, **www.bea.gov**.

TABLE COI 1.3 U.S. Exports and Imports of Goods by Area, 2012*

Exports to	Billions of dollars		Percentage of total	Imports from	Billions of dollars		Percentage of total
Canada	$ 294		19	Canada	$ 329		14
European Union	270		17	European Union	384		17
Germany		49	3	Germany		109	5
United Kingdom		56	4	United Kingdom		55	2
France		31	2	France		42	2
All other EU		134	9	All other EU		178	8
Mexico	217		15	Mexico	283		12
China	112		7	China	427		19
Japan	72		5	Japan	149		6
OPEC countries	81		5	OPEC countries	182		8
All other	518		33	All other	545		24
Total	$1,564		100	Total	$2,299		100

*Data are on a balance-of-payments basis and exclude military shipments. Percentages do not sum to 100 percent because of rounding.

Source: Bureau of Economic Analysis, **www.bea.gov**.

- The U.S. dependence on foreign oil is reflected in its trade with members of OPEC. In 2012, the United States imported $182 billion of goods (mainly oil) from OPEC members, while exporting $81 billion of goods to those countries (see Table COI 1.3).

- In terms of volume, the most significant U.S. export of *services* is airline transportation provided by U.S. carriers for foreign passengers.

Financial Linkages International trade requires complex financial linkages among nations. How does a nation such as the United States obtain more goods from others than it provides to them? How does the United States finance its trade deficits, such as its 2012 goods and services deficit of $539 billion (= +$196 billion in services − $735 billion in goods) in 2012? The answer is by either borrowing from foreigners or selling real assets (for example, factories or real estate) to them. In terms of borrowing, the United States is the world's largest borrower of foreign funds, which can be used to purchase foreign goods. In terms of selling real assets, the countries with which the United States has large trade deficits end up holding large numbers of U.S. dollars (since, for instance, Sony is paid in dollars when it sells a television set in the United States). Many of these U.S. dollars are then used to buy U.S. real assets, thereby transferring ownership of those assets from U.S. citizens to foreign citizens.

Rapid Trade Growth

Several factors have propelled the rapid growth of international trade since the Second World War.

Transportation Technology High transportation costs are a barrier to any type of trade, particularly among traders who are distant from one another. But improvements in transportation have shrunk the globe and fostered world trade. Container ships deliver self-contained box cars of goods to ports, which off-load them to waiting trucks and trains. We now routinely transport oil in massive tankers, significantly lowering the cost of transportation per barrel. Grain is loaded onto oceangoing ships at modern, efficient grain silos at Great Lakes and coastal ports. Natural gas flows through large-diameter pipelines from exporting to importing countries—for instance, from Russia to Germany and from Canada to the United States.

Communications Technology Dramatic improvements in communications technology have also advanced world trade. Computers, the Internet, telephones, and fax (facsimile) machines now directly link traders around the world, enabling exporters to access overseas markets and to carry out trade deals. A distributor in New York can get a price quote on 1,000 woven baskets in Thailand as quickly as a quotation on 1,000 laptop computers in Texas. Money moves around the world in the blink of an eye. Exchange rates, stock prices, and interest rates flash onto computer screens nearly simultaneously in Los Angeles, London, and Lisbon.

General Decline in Tariffs *Tariffs* are excise taxes (duties) on imported products. They have had their ups and downs over the years, but since 1940 they have generally fallen. A glance ahead to Figure COI 1.4 on page COI1-14 shows that U.S. tariffs as a percentage of imports (on which

GLOBAL PERSPECTIVE COI 1.1

Comparative Exports

China, the United States, and Germany are the world's largest exporters.

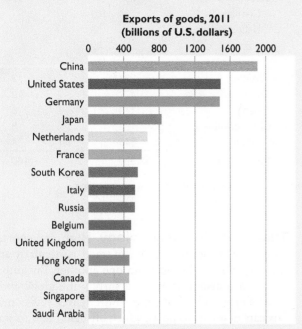

Exports of goods, 2011
(billions of U.S. dollars)

Source: Data used with permission of World Trade Organization, **www.wto.org**.

major international trader. In 1990 its exports were about $60 billion. In 2012 they were $1,898 billion.

duties are levied) are now about 5 percent, down from 37 percent in 1940. Many nations still maintain barriers to free trade, but, on average, tariffs have fallen significantly, thus increasing international trade.

Participants in International Trade

All the nations of the world participate to some extent in international trade. Global Perspective COI 1.1 lists the top participants in world trade *by total dollar volume* (as opposed to *percentage of GDP*, as in Table COI 1.1). Observe that China, the United States, Germany, and Japan had combined exports of $5.7 trillion in 2012. This amounted to 31 percent of total world exports that year. Along with Germany, other western European nations such as France, Britain, and Italy are major exporters. So, too, are the east and southeast Asian countries of Hong Kong and Singapore, whose combined exports exceed those individually of France, the United Kingdom, or Italy.

China, with its increased reliance on the market system and its reintegration of Hong Kong, has emerged as a

Specialization and Comparative Advantage

COI1.3 Define comparative advantage and explain how it relates to specialization and international trade.

In an *open economy* (one with an international sector), a country produces more of certain goods (exports) and fewer of other goods (imports) than it would otherwise. Thus, the country shifts the use of labor and other productive resources toward export industries and away from import industries. For example, in the presence of international trade, the United States uses more resources to make commercial aircraft and to grow wheat and less to make autos and clothing. So we ask: "Do shifts of resources like these make economic sense? Do they enhance U.S. total output and thus the U.S. standard of living?"

The answers are affirmative. Specialization and international trade increase the productivity of a nation's resources and allow for greater total output than would otherwise be possible. These benefits are the result of exploiting both *absolute advantages* and *comparative advantages*. A country is said to have an *absolute advantage* over other producers of a product if it is the most efficient producer of that product (by which we mean that it can produce more output of that product from any given amount of resource inputs than can any other producer). A country is said to have a *comparative advantage* over other producers of a product if it can produce the product at a lower

TABLE COI 1.4 Mexico's Production Possibilities Table (in Tons)

Product	Production Alternatives				
	A	**B**	**C**	**D**	**E**
Avocados	0	20	24	40	60
Soybeans	15	10	9	5	0

TABLE COI 1.5 U.S. Production Possibilities Table (in Tons)

Product	Production Alternatives				
	R	**S**	**T**	**U**	**V**
Avocados	0	30	33	60	90
Soybeans	30	20	19	10	0

opportunity cost (by which we mean that it must forgo less output of alternative products when allocating productive resources to producing the product in question).

In 1776 Adam Smith used the concept of absolute advantage to argue for international specialization and trade. His point was that nations would be better off if each specialized in the production of those products in which it had an absolute advantage and was therefore the most efficient producer:

> It is the maxim of every prudent master of a family, never to attempt to make at home what it will cost him more to make than to buy. The taylor does not attempt to make his own shoes, but buys them of the shoemaker. The shoemaker does not attempt to make his own clothes, but employs a taylor. The farmer attempts to make neither the one nor the other, but employs those different artificers. . . .
>
> What is prudence in the conduct of every private family, can scarce be folly in that of a great kingdom. If a foreign country can supply us with a commodity cheaper than we can make it, better buy it of them with some part of the produce of our own industry, employed in a way in which we have some advantage.[1]

In the early 1800s, British economist David Ricardo expanded on Smith's arguments for international specialization and trade by noting that a country could gain from specialization and trade with other countries even if it was the most efficient producer of each and every product being produced anywhere in the world. Ricardo's insight was that a nation does not need an *absolute advantage* to benefit from specialization and trade. Rather, it needs only a *comparative advantage*.

The nearby Consider This box provides a simple, two-person illustration of how comparative advantage can lead to gains from specialization and trade even when one trading partner holds an absolute advantage and is therefore more productively efficient than her trading partner in the production of all the goods and services that they both can make. Be sure to read the box now because it will greatly help you understand the tabular analysis that follows.

---

[1]Adam Smith, *The Wealth of Nations* (New York: Modern Library, 1937), p. 424. (Originally published in 1776.)

Comparative Advantage: Production Possibilities Analysis

Our goal is to place the idea of comparative advantage that is illustrated for two individuals in the Consider This box into the context of trading nations. For simplicity, we will assume there are just two nations and two products.

Assumptions and Comparative Costs Suppose the production possibilities for one product in Mexico and for one product in the United States are as shown in Tables COI 1.4 and COI 1.5. Both tables reflect constant costs. Each country must give up a constant amount of one product to secure a certain increment of the other product. (This assumption simplifies our discussion without impairing the validity of our conclusions. Later we will allow for increasing costs.)

Also for simplicity, suppose that the labor forces in the United States and Mexico are of equal size. If the United States and Mexico use their entire (equal-size) labor forces to produce avocados, the United States can produce 90 tons compared with Mexico's 60 tons. Similarly, the United States can produce 30 tons of soybeans compared to Mexico's 15 tons. So output per worker in the United States exceeds that in Mexico in producing both goods, perhaps because of better technology. The United States has an *absolute advantage* (relative to Mexico) in producing both soybeans or avocados.

But gains from specialization and trade between the United States and Mexico are possible even under these circumstances. Specialization and trade are mutually "profitable" to the two nations if the comparative costs of producing the two products *within* the two nations differ. What are the comparative costs of avocados and soybeans in Mexico? By comparing production alternatives A and B in Table COI 1.4, we see that 5 tons of soybeans (= 15 − 10) must be sacrificed to produce 20 tons of avocados (= 20 − 0). Or, more simply, in Mexico it costs 1 ton of soybeans (S) to produce 4 tons of avocados (A); that is, 1S ≡ 4A. (The "≡" sign simply signifies "equivalent to.") Because we assumed constant costs, this domestic opportunity cost will not change as Mexico expands the output of either product. This is evident from production possibilities B and C, where we see that

CONSIDER THIS . . .

A CPA and a House Painter

Suppose that Madison, a certified public accountant (CPA), is a swifter painter than Mason, the professional painter she is thinking of hiring. Also assume that Madison can earn $50 per hour as an accountant but would have to pay Mason $15 per hour. And suppose that Madison would need 30 hours to paint her house but Mason would need 40 hours.

Should Madison take time from her accounting to paint her own house, or should she hire the painter? Madison's opportunity cost of painting her house is $1,500 (= 30 hours of sacrificed CPA time × $50 per CPA hour). The cost of hiring Mason is only $600 (= 40 hours of painting × $15 per hour of painting). Although Madison is better at both accounting and painting, she will get her house painted at lower cost by specializing in accounting and using some of her earnings from accounting to hire a house painter.

Similarly, Mason can reduce his cost of obtaining accounting services by specializing in painting and using some of his income to hire Madison to prepare his income tax forms. Suppose Mason would need 10 hours to prepare his tax return, while Madison could handle the task in 2 hours. Mason would sacrifice $150 of income (= 10 hours of painting time × $15 per hour) to do something he could hire Madison to do for $100 (= 2 hours of CPA time × $50 per CPA hour). By specializing in painting and hiring Madison to prepare his tax return, Mason lowers the cost of getting his tax return prepared.

You will see that what is true for our CPA and house painter is also true for nations. Specializing on the basis of comparative advantage enables nations to reduce the cost of obtaining the goods and services they desire.

4 more tons of avocados (= 24 − 20) cost 1 unit of soybeans (= 10 − 9).

Similarly, in Table COI 1.5, comparing U.S. production alternatives R and S reveals that in the United States it costs 10 tons of soybeans (= 30 − 20) to obtain 30 tons of avocados (= 30 − 0). That is, the domestic comparative-cost ratio for the two products in the United States is 1S ≡ 3A. Comparing production alternatives S and T reinforces this conclusion: an extra 3 tons of avocados (= 33 − 30) comes at the sacrifice of 1 ton of soybeans (= 20 − 19).

TABLE COI 1.6 Comparative-Advantage Example: A Summary

Soybeans	Avocados
Mexico: Must give up 4 tons of avocados to get 1 ton of soybeans	**Mexico:** Must give up $\frac{1}{4}$ ton of soybeans to get 1 ton of avocados
United States: Must give up 3 tons of avocados to get 1 ton of soybeans	**United States:** Must give up $\frac{1}{3}$ ton of soybeans to get 1 ton of avocados
Comparative advantage: United States	**Comparative advantage:** Mexico

The comparative costs of the two products within the two nations are obviously different. Economists say that the United States has a domestic comparative advantage or, simply, a **comparative advantage** over Mexico in soybeans. The United States must forgo only 3 tons of avocados to get 1 ton of soybeans, but Mexico must forgo 4 tons of avocados to get 1 ton of soybeans. In terms of domestic opportunity costs, soybeans are relatively cheaper in the United States. A nation has a comparative advantage in some product when it can produce that product at a lower domestic opportunity cost than can a potential trading partner. Mexico, in contrast, has a comparative advantage in avocados. While 1 ton of avocados costs $\frac{1}{3}$ ton of soybeans in the United States, it costs only $\frac{1}{4}$ ton of soybeans in Mexico. Comparatively speaking, avocados are cheaper in Mexico. We summarize the situation in Table COI 1.6. Be sure to give it a close look.

ORIGIN OF THE IDEA

OCOI1.1

Absolute and comparative advantage

Because of these differences in domestic opportunity costs, if both nations specialize, each according to its comparative advantage, each can achieve a larger total output with the same total input of resources. Together they will be using their scarce resources more efficiently.

Terms of Trade The United States can shift production between soybeans and avocados at the rate of 1S for 3A. Thus, the United States would specialize in soybeans only if it could obtain *more than* 3 tons of avocados for 1 ton of soybeans by trading with Mexico. Similarly, Mexico can shift production at the rate of 4A for 1S. So it would be advantageous to Mexico to specialize in avocados if it could get 1 ton of soybeans for *less than* 4 tons of avocados.

Suppose that through negotiation the two nations agree on an exchange rate of 1 ton of soybeans for $3\frac{1}{2}$ tons of avocados. These **terms of trade** are mutually beneficial to both countries, since each can "do better" through such trade than through domestic production alone. The

TABLE COI 1.7 Specialization According to Comparative Advantage and the Gains from Trade (in Tons)

Country	(1) Outputs before Specialization	(2) Outputs after Specialization	(3) Amounts Traded	(4) Outputs Available after Trade	(5) Gains from Specialization and Trade (4) − (1)
Mexico	24 avocados	60 avocados	−35 avocados	25 avocados	1 avocados
	9 soybeans	0 soybeans	+10 soybeans	10 soybeans	1 soybeans
United States	33 avocados	0 avocados	+35 avocados	35 avocados	2 avocados
	19 soybeans	30 soybeans	−10 soybeans	20 soybeans	1 soybeans

United States can get $3\frac{1}{2}$ tons of avocados by sending 1 ton of soybeans to Mexico, while it can get only 3 tons of avocados by shifting its own resources domestically from soybeans to avocados. Mexico can obtain 1 ton of soybeans at a lower cost of $3\frac{1}{2}$ tons of avocados through trade with the United States, compared to the cost of 4 tons if Mexico produced the ton of soybeans itself.

Gains from Specialization and Trade Let's pinpoint the gains in total output from specialization and trade. Suppose that, before specialization and trade, production alternative C in Table COI 1.4 and alternative T in Table COI 1.5 were the optimal product mixes for the two countries. That is, Mexico preferred 24 tons of avocados and 9 tons of soybeans (Table COI 1.4) and the United States preferred 33 tons of avocados and 19 tons of soybeans (Table COI 1.5) to all other available domestic alternatives. These outputs are shown in column 1 in Table COI 1.7.

Now assume that both nations specialize according to their comparative advantage, with Mexico producing 60 tons of avocados and no soybeans (alternative E) and the United States producing no avocados and 30 tons of soybeans (alternative R). These outputs are shown in column 2 in Table COI 1.7. Using our 1S ≡ $3\frac{1}{2}$A terms of trade, assume that Mexico exchanges 35 tons of avocados for 10 tons of U.S. soybeans. Column 3 in Table COI 1.7 shows the quantities exchanged in this trade, with a minus sign indicating exports and a plus sign indicating imports. As shown in column 4, after the trade Mexico has 25 tons of avocados and 10 tons of soybeans, while the United States has 35 tons of avocados and 20 tons of soybeans. Compared with their optimum product mixes before specialization and trade (column 1), *both* nations now enjoy more avocados and more soybeans! Specifically, Mexico has gained 1 ton of avocados and 1 ton of soybeans. The United States has gained 2 tons of avocados and 1 ton of soybeans. These gains are shown in column 5.

Specialization based on comparative advantage improves global resource allocation. The same total inputs of world resources and technology result in a larger global output. If Mexico and the United States allocate all their resources to avocados and soybeans, respectively, the same total inputs of resources can produce more output between them, indicating that resources are being allocated more efficiently.

Through specialization and international trade a nation can overcome the production constraints imposed by its domestic production possibilities table and curve. Our discussion of Tables COI 1.4, COI 1.5, and COI 1.7 has shown just how this is done. The domestic production possibilities data (Tables COI 1.4 and COI 1.5) of the two countries have not changed, meaning that neither nation's production possibilities curve has shifted. But specialization and trade mean that citizens of both countries can enjoy increased consumption (column 5 of Table COI 1.7).

WORKED PROBLEMS

WCOI1.1
Gains from specialization

Finally, we need to emphasize that gains from specialization and trade are *not* dependent on constant opportunity costs such as those in our tables. Even in the more realistic case of increasing opportunity costs, nations will gain by specializing where they have comparative advantages and by trading with other nations.

But with increasing opportunity costs, the *complete* specialization of soybeans in the United States and avocados in Mexico might not happen. Instead, the domestic opportunity cost of producing another unit of soybeans in the United States or avocados in Mexico might eventually rise to the point that producing an extra unit domestically will cost more than buying a unit from a foreign producer. Rising opportunity costs thus are a major reason why the United States and other countries often import some of the very same general types of goods that they export. As specialization occurs, a nation's comparative advantage can come to an end and thus its further specialization can come to a halt. Specialization often stops short of being fully complete. Nevertheless, the gains from all specialization to that point are fully realized.

The Foreign Exchange Market

COI1.4 Explain how exchange rates are determined in currency (foreign-exchange) markets.

Buyers and sellers, whether individuals, firms, or nations, use money to buy products or to pay for the use of resources. Within the domestic economy, prices are stated in terms of the domestic currency and buyers use that currency to purchase domestic products. In Mexico, for example, buyers have pesos, and that is what sellers want.

International markets are different. Sellers set their prices in terms of their domestic currencies, but buyers often possess entirely different currencies. How many dollars does it take to buy a truckload of Mexican avocados selling for 3,000 pesos, a German automobile selling for 50,000 euros, or a Japanese motorcycle priced at 300,000 yen? Producers in Mexico, Germany, and Japan want payment in pesos, euros, and yen, respectively, so that they can pay their wages, rent, interest, dividends, and taxes.

A **foreign exchange market,** a market in which various national currencies are exchanged for one another, serves this need. The equilibrium prices in such currency markets are called **exchange rates.** An exchange rate is the rate at which the currency of one nation can be exchanged for the currency of another nation. (See Global Perspective COI 1.2.)

GLOBAL PERSPECTIVE COI 1.2

Exchange Rates: Foreign Currency per U.S. Dollar

The amount of foreign currency that a dollar will buy varies greatly from nation to nation and fluctuates in response to supply and demand changes in the foreign exchange market. The amounts shown here are for May 2013. (You can easily update these exchange rates via *The Wall Street Journal.*)

$1 Will Buy
54.54 Indian rupees
1.54 British pounds
1.01 Canadian dollars
12.01 Mexican pesos
0.95 Swiss franc
1.30 European euros
100.94 Japanese yen
1,087 South Korean won
6.58 Swedish kronor

Source: International Monetary Fund, **www.imf.org**, May 12, 2013.

The market price or exchange rate of a nation's currency is an unusual price; it links all domestic prices with all foreign prices. Exchange rates enable consumers in one country to translate prices of foreign goods into units of their own currency: They need only multiply the foreign product price by the exchange rate. If the U.S. dollar = yen exchange rate is $0.01 (1 cent) per yen, a Sony television set priced at ¥20,000 will cost $200 (= 20,000 × $0.01) in the United States. If the exchange rate rises to $0.02 (2 cents) per yen, the television will cost $400 (= 20,000 × $0.02) in the United States. Similarly, all other Japanese products would double in price to U.S. buyers in response to the altered exchange rate.

Dollar-Yen Market

How does the foreign exchange market work? Let's look briefly at the market for dollars and yen. U.S. firms exporting goods to Japan want payment in dollars, not yen; but the Japanese importers of those U.S. goods possess yen, not dollars. So the Japanese importers supply their yen in exchange for dollars in the foreign exchange market. At the same time, there are U.S. importers of Japanese goods who need to pay the Japanese exporters in yen, not dollars. These importers go to the foreign exchange market as demanders of yen. We then have a market in which the "price" is in dollars and the "product" is yen.

Figure COI 1.3 shows the supply of yen (by Japanese importers) and the demand for yen (by U.S. importers). The intersection of demand curve D_y and supply curve S_y establishes the equilibrium dollar price of yen. Here the

FIGURE COI 1.3   The market for yen. U.S. imports from Japan create a demand D_y for yen, while U.S. exports to Japan (Japan's imports) create a supply S_y of yen. The dollar price of 1 yen—the exchange rate—is determined at the intersection of the supply and demand curves. In this case the equilibrium price is $0.01, meaning that 1 cent will buy 1 yen.

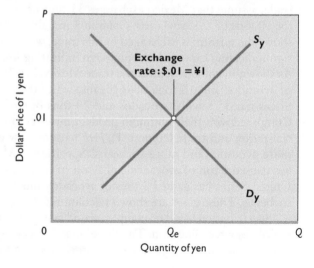

equilibrium price of 1 yen—the dollar-yen exchange rate—is 1 cent per yen, or $0.01 = ¥1. At this price, the market for yen clears; there is neither a shortage nor a surplus of yen. The equilibrium $0.01 price of 1 yen means that $1 will buy 100 yen or ¥100 worth of Japanese goods. Conversely, 100 yen will buy $1 worth of U.S. goods.

Changing Rates: Depreciation and Appreciation

What might cause the exchange rate to change? The determinants of the demand for and supply of yen are similar to the determinants of demand and supply for almost any product. In the United States, several things might increase the demand for—and therefore the dollar price of—yen. For example, incomes might rise in the United States, enabling residents to buy not only more domestic goods but also more Sony televisions, Nikon cameras, and Nissan automobiles from Japan. So people in the United States would need more yen, and the demand for yen would increase. In Figure COI 1.3, the demand curve would shift to the right.

A relative increase in interest rates in Japan might have the same general effect. U.S. financial investors might decide to move some of their money to Japanese accounts. They would need more yen than before to accomplish that, thereby shifting the demand curve to the right in Figure COI 1.3.

The point is that an increase in the U.S. demand for either Japanese goods or financial investments will increase the demand for yen and raise the dollar price of yen. Suppose the dollar price of yen rises from $0.01 = ¥1 to $0.02 = ¥1. When the dollar price of yen increases, we say a **depreciation** of the dollar relative to the yen has occurred. It then takes more dollars (pennies in this case) to buy a single yen. Alternatively stated, the *international value of the dollar* has declined. A depreciated dollar buys fewer yen and therefore fewer Japanese goods; the yen and all Japanese goods have become more expensive to U.S. buyers.

Eventually, changes in exchange rates feed back to alter U.S. imports and exports. With an appreciated yen and a depreciated dollar, consumers in the United States shift their expenditures from Japanese goods to now less expensive American goods. The Ford Escape becomes relatively more attractive than the Honda Civic to U.S. consumers. Conversely, because each yen buys more dollars—that is, because the international value of the yen has increased—U.S. goods become cheaper to people in Japan and U.S. exports to Japan rise.

If the opposite events occurred—if Japanese incomes rose rapidly or U.S. interest rates increased relative to those in Japan—then the Japanese would supply more yen to pay for

U.S. goods and to purchase the dollars needed to place money into U.S. financial accounts. In Figure COI 1.3, the supply curve would shift to the right. The increase in the supply of yen relative to the demand for yen would decrease the equilibrium price of yen in the foreign exchange market. For example, the dollar price of yen might decline from $0.01 = ¥1 to $0.005 = ¥1. A decrease in the dollar price of yen is called an **appreciation** of the dollar relative to the yen. It means that the international value of the dollar has increased. It then takes fewer dollars (or pennies) to buy a single yen; the dollar is worth more because it can purchase more yen and therefore more Japanese goods. Each Sony PlayStation becomes less expensive in terms of dollars, so people in the United States purchase more of them. Eventually, the depreciated yen and appreciated dollar would cause U.S. imports from Japan to rise. U.S. exports to Japan would fall because it would take more yen to obtain a dollar.

Whatever the initial cause of the change in the exchange rate, the central point is this: When the dollar depreciates (dollar price of foreign currencies rises), U.S. exports rise and U.S. imports fall; when the dollar appreciates (dollar price of foreign currencies falls), U.S. exports fall and U.S. imports rise.

QUICK REVIEW COI 1.2

- A country has a comparative advantage when it can produce a product at a lower domestic opportunity cost than a potential trading partner can.

- Specialization based on comparative advantage increases the total output available for nations that trade with one another.

- The foreign exchange market (or currency market) is a market in which national currencies are exchanged.

- An appreciation of the dollar is an increase in the international value of the dollar relative to the currency of some other nation; after appreciation a dollar buys more units of that currency. A depreciation of the dollar is a decrease in the international value of the dollar relative to some other currency; after depreciation a dollar buys fewer units of that currency.

Government and Trade

COI1.5 Explain how and why government sometimes interferes with free international trade.

If people and nations benefit from specialization and international exchange, why do governments sometimes try to restrict the free flow of imports or encourage exports? What kinds of world trade barriers can governments erect, and why would they do so?

Trade Impediments and Subsidies

There are four means by which governments commonly interfere with free trade:

- **Protective tariffs** are excise taxes or duties placed on imported goods. Protective tariffs are designed to shield domestic producers from foreign competition. They impede free trade by causing a rise in the prices of imported goods, thereby shifting demand toward domestic products. An excise tax on imported shoes, for example, would make domestically produced shoes more attractive to consumers.

- **Import quotas** are limits on the quantities or total value of specific items that may be imported. Once a quota is "filled," further imports of that product are choked off. Import quotas are more effective than tariffs in retarding international commerce. With a tariff, a product can go on being imported in large quantities; with an import quota, however, all imports are prohibited once the quota is filled.

- **Nontariff barriers** (and, implicitly, *nonquota* barriers) include onerous licensing requirements, unreasonable standards pertaining to product quality, or simply bureaucratic hurdles and delays in customs procedures. Some nations require that importers of foreign goods obtain licenses and then restrict the number of licenses issued. Although many nations carefully inspect imported agricultural products to prevent the introduction of potentially harmful insects, some countries use lengthy inspections to impede imports.

- **Export subsidies** consist of government payments to domestic producers of export goods. By reducing production costs, the subsidies enable producers to charge lower prices and thus to sell more exports in world markets. Two examples: Some European governments have heavily subsidized Airbus Industries, a European firm that produces commercial aircraft. The subsidies help Airbus compete against the American firm Boeing. The United States and other nations have subsidized domestic farmers to boost the domestic food supply. Such subsidies have lowered the market price of food and have artificially lowered export prices on agricultural produce.

Why Government Trade Interventions?

In view of the benefits of free trade, what accounts for the impulse to impede imports and boost exports through government policy? There are several reasons—some legitimate, most not.

Misunderstanding the Gains from Trade It is a commonly accepted myth that the greatest benefit to be derived from international trade is greater domestic employment in the export sector. This suggests that exports are "good" because they increase domestic employment, whereas imports are "bad" because they deprive people of jobs at home. Actually, the true benefit created by international trade is the overall increase in output obtained through specialization and exchange. A nation can fully employ its resources, including labor, with or without international trade. International trade, however, enables society to use its resources in ways that increase its total output and therefore its overall well-being.

A nation does not need international trade to operate *on* its production possibilities curve. A closed (nontrading) national economy can have full employment without international trade. However, through world trade an economy can reach a point of consumption *beyond* its domestic production possibilities curve. The gain from trade is the extra output obtained from abroad—the imports obtained for a lower opportunity cost than if they were produced at home.

Political Considerations While a nation as a whole gains from trade, trade may harm particular domestic industries and particular groups of resource suppliers. In our earlier comparative-advantage example, specialization and trade adversely affected the U.S. avocado industry and the Mexican soybean industry. Those industries might seek to preserve their economic positions by persuading their respective governments to protect them from imports—perhaps through tariffs or import quotas.

Those who directly benefit from import protection are few in number but have much at stake. Thus, they have a strong incentive to pursue political activity to achieve their aims. However, the overall cost of tariffs and quotas typically greatly exceeds the benefits. It is not uncommon to find that it costs the public $200,000 or more a year to protect a domestic job that pays less than one-fourth that amount. Moreover, because these costs are buried in the price of goods and spread out over millions of citizens, the cost borne by each individual citizen is quite small. In the political arena, the voice of the relatively few producers demanding *protectionism* is loud and constant, whereas the voice of those footing the bill is soft or nonexistent.

Indeed, the public may be won over by the apparent plausibility ("Cut imports and prevent domestic unemployment") and the patriotic ring ("Buy American!") of the protectionist arguments. The alleged benefits of tariffs are immediate and clear-cut to the public, but the adverse effects cited by economists are obscure and dispersed over the entire economy. When political deal-making is added in—"You back tariffs for the apparel industry in my state, and I'll back tariffs on the auto industry in your state"— the outcome can be a network of protective tariffs, import quotas, and export subsidies.

Costs to Society

Tariffs and quotas benefit domestic producers of the protected products, but they harm domestic consumers, who must pay higher-than-world prices for the protected goods. They also hurt domestic firms that use the protected goods as inputs in their production processes. For example, a tariff on imported steel would boost the price of steel girders, thus hurting firms that construct large buildings. Also, tariffs and quotas reduce competition in the protected industries. With less competition from foreign producers, domestic firms may be slow to design and implement cost-saving production methods and introduce new or improved products.

Multilateral Trade Agreements and Free-Trade Zones

COI1.6 Describe the purposes and functions of GATT, WTO, EU, eurozone, and NAFTA.

When one nation enacts barriers against imports, the nations whose exports suffer may retaliate with trade barriers of their own. In such a *trade war,* escalating tariffs choke world trade and reduce everyone's economic well-being. The **Smoot-Hawley Tariff Act** of 1930 is a classic example. Although that act was meant to reduce imports and stimulate U.S. production, the high tariffs it authorized prompted adversely affected nations to retaliate with tariffs equally high. International trade fell, lowering the output and income of all nations. Economic historians generally agree that the Smoot-Hawley Tariff Act was a contributing cause of the Great Depression. Aware of that fact, nations have worked to lower tariffs worldwide. Their pursuit of free trade has been aided by powerful domestic interest groups: Exporters of goods and services, importers of foreign components used in "domestic" products, and domestic sellers of imported products all strongly support lower tariffs.

Figure COI 1.4 makes it clear that while the United States was a high-tariff nation over much of its history, U.S. tariffs have generally declined during the past half-century. Today, U.S. tariffs average only 4.7 percent on the imports subject to tariff and more than two-thirds of imports are no longer subject to any tariff at all.

Reciprocal Trade Agreements Act

The **Reciprocal Trade Agreements Act** of 1934 started the downward trend of tariffs. Aimed at reducing tariffs, this act had two main features:

- *Negotiating authority* It authorized the president to negotiate with foreign nations agreements that would reduce existing U.S. tariffs by up to 50 percent. Those reductions were contingent on the actions other nations took to lower tariffs on U.S. exports.

- *Generalized reductions* The specific tariff reductions negotiated between the United States and any particular nation were generalized through most-favored-nation clauses, which often accompany such agreements. These clauses stipulate that any subsequently reduced U.S. tariffs, resulting from negotiation with any other nation, would apply equally to any nation that signed the original agreement. So if the United States negotiates a reduction in tariffs on wristwatches with, say, France, the lower U.S. tariffs on imported French watches also apply to the imports of the other nations having most-favored-nation status, say, Japan and Switzerland. This way, the reductions in U.S. tariffs automatically apply to many nations.

Today, most-favored-nation status is so common that the U.S. government has renamed it **normal-trade-relations (NTR) status.**

FIGURE COI 1.4 U.S. tariff rates, 1860–2009. Historically, U.S. tariff rates have fluctuated. But beginning with the Reciprocal Trade Agreements Act of 1934, the trend has been downward.

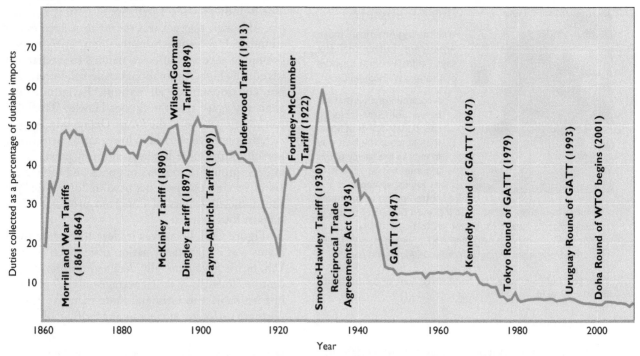

Source: U.S. Department of Commerce, *FT920 U.S. Merchandise Trade: Selected Highlights,* Monthly, Exhibit 5. (Duty value as a percentage of dutiable exports.)

General Agreement on Tariffs and Trade

The Reciprocal Trade Agreements Act provided only bilateral (between two nations) negotiations. Its approach was broadened in 1947 when 23 nations, including the United States, signed the **General Agreement on Tariffs and Trade (GATT).** GATT was based on three principles: (1) equal, nondiscriminatory trade treatment for all member nations; (2) the reduction of tariffs by multilateral negotiation; and (3) the elimination of import quotas. Basically, GATT provided a forum for the negotiation of reduced trade barriers on a multilateral basis among nations.

Since the Second World War, member nations have completed eight "rounds" of GATT negotiations to reduce trade barriers. The eighth round of negotiations began in Uruguay in 1986. After seven years of complex discussions, in 1993 the 128 member nations reached a new agreement. The *Uruguay Round* agreement took effect on January 1, 1995, and its provisions were phased in through 2005.

Under this agreement, tariffs on thousands of products were eliminated or reduced, with overall tariffs dropping by 33 percent. The agreement also liberalized government rules that in the past impeded the global market for such services as advertising, legal services, tourist services, and financial services. Quotas on imported textiles and apparel were phased out and replaced with tariffs. Other provisions reduced agricultural subsidies paid to farmers and protected intellectual property (patents, trademarks, copyrights) against piracy.

World Trade Organization

The Uruguay Round agreement established the **World Trade Organization (WTO)** as GATT's successor. Some 159 nations belonged to the WTO in 2013. The WTO oversees trade agreements reached by the member nations and rules on trade disputes among them. It also provides forums for further rounds of trade negotiations. The ninth and latest round of negotiations—the **Doha Development Agenda**—was launched in Doha, Qatar, in late 2001. (The trade rounds occur over several years in several venues but are named after the city or country of origination.) The negotiations are aimed at further reducing tariffs and quotas, as well as agricultural subsidies that distort trade.

GATT and the WTO have been positive forces in the trend toward liberalized world trade. The trade rules agreed upon by the member nations provide a strong and necessary bulwark against the protectionism called for by the special-interest groups in the various nations.

For that reason and others, the WTO is controversial. Critics are concerned that rules crafted to expand international trade and investment enable firms to circumvent national laws that protect workers and the environment. What good are minimum-wage laws, worker safety laws, collective bargaining rights, and environmental laws if firms can easily shift their production to nations that have weaker laws or consumers can buy goods produced in those countries?

Proponents of the WTO respond that labor and environmental protections should be pursued directly in nations that have low standards and via international organizations other than the WTO. These issues should not be linked to the process of trade liberalization, which confers widespread economic benefits across nations. Moreover, say proponents of the WTO, many environmental and labor concerns are greatly overblown. Most world trade is among advanced industrial countries, not between them and countries that have lower environmental and labor standards. Moreover, the free flow of goods and resources raises output and income in the developing nations. Historically, such increases in living standards have eventually resulted in stronger, not weaker, protections for the environment and for workers.

The European Union

Countries have also sought to reduce tariffs by creating regional *free-trade zones*—also called *trade blocs*. The most dramatic example is the **European Union (EU)**, formerly called the European Economic Community. Initiated in 1958 as the Common Market, in 2003 the EU comprised 15 European nations—Austria, Belgium, Denmark, Finland, France, Germany, Greece, Ireland, Italy, Luxembourg, the Netherlands, Portugal, Spain, Sweden, and the United Kingdom. In 2004, the EU expanded by 10 additional European countries—Cyprus, the Czech Republic, Estonia, Hungary, Latvia, Lithuania, Malta, Poland, Slovakia, and Slovenia. In 2007, the addition of Bulgaria and Romania expanded the EU to 27 nations and the addition of Croatia in 2013 expanded the EU to its present size of 28 nations.

The EU Trade Bloc   The EU has abolished tariffs and import quotas on nearly all products traded among the participating nations and established a common system of tariffs applicable to all goods received from nations outside the EU. It has also liberalized the movement of capital and labor within the EU and has created common policies in other economic matters of joint concern such as agriculture, transportation, and business practices. The EU is now a strong **trade bloc:** a group of countries having common identity, economic interests, and trade rules.

EU integration has achieved for Europe what the U.S. constitutional prohibition on tariffs by individual states has achieved for the United States: increased regional specialization, greater productivity, greater output, and faster economic growth. The free flow of goods and services has created large markets for EU industries. The resulting economies of large-scale production have enabled these industries to achieve much lower costs than they could have achieved in their small, single-nation markets.

The effects of EU success on nonmember nations such as the United States have been mixed. A peaceful and increasingly prosperous EU makes its members better customers for U.S. exports. But U.S. firms and other nonmember firms have been faced with tariffs and other barriers that make it difficult for them to compete against firms within the EU trade bloc. For example, autos produced in Germany and sold in Spain or France face no tariffs, whereas U.S. and Japanese autos exported to EU countries do. This puts U.S. and Japanese firms at a serious disadvantage.

By giving preferences to countries within their free-trade zone, trade blocs such as the EU tend to reduce their members' trade with non-bloc members. Thus, the world loses some of the benefits of a completely open global trading system. Eliminating that disadvantage has been one of the motivations for liberalizing global trade through the World Trade Organization. Those liberalizations apply equally to all nations that belong to the WTO.

The Euro   One of the most significant accomplishments of the EU was the establishment of the so-called eurozone in the early 2000s. As of 2013, 17 members of the EU (Austria, Belgium, Cyprus, Estonia, Finland, France, Germany, Greece, Ireland, Italy, Luxembourg, Malta, the Netherlands, Portugal, Slovenia, Slovakia, and Spain) use the **euro** as a common currency. Notably, the United Kingdom, Denmark, and Sweden have opted not to use the common currency, at least for now. But gone are French francs, German marks, Italian liras, and other national currencies that were once used by eurozone countries.

Economists expect the adoption of the euro to raise the standard of living of the eurozone members over time. By ending the inconvenience and expense of exchanging currencies, the euro has enhanced the free flow of goods, services, and resources among the eurozone members. International trade among the member nations has increased by roughly 10 percent, with much of that increase happening because companies that previously sold products in only one or two European countries have now found it easier to market and sell their wares in all 17 eurozone countries. The euro has also allowed consumers and businesses to comparison shop for outputs and inputs, and this capability has increased competition, reduced prices, and lowered costs.

North American Free Trade Agreement

In 1993 Canada, Mexico, and the United States formed a major trade bloc. The **North American Free Trade Agreement (NAFTA)** established a free-trade zone that has about the same combined output as the EU but encompasses a much larger geographic area. NAFTA has eliminated tariffs and other trade barriers between Canada, Mexico, and the United States for most goods and services.

Critics of NAFTA feared that it would cause a massive loss of U.S. jobs as firms moved to Mexico to take advantage of lower wages and weaker regulations on pollution and workplace safety. Also, they were concerned that Japan and South Korea would build plants in Mexico and transport goods tariff-free to the United States, further hurting U.S. firms and workers.

In retrospect, critics were much too pessimistic. Since the passage of NAFTA in 1993, employment in the United States has increased by more than 20 million workers. Increased trade among Canada, Mexico, and the United States has enhanced the standard of living in all three countries.

Trade-Related Issues

COI1.7 Define and discuss three major trade-related issues: trade adjustment assistance, the offshoring of jobs, and globalization.

Although trade liberalization and increased international trade raise total output and income, they often disrupt existing patterns of production and resource allocations. Such disruptions can be highly painful to certain industries, firms, and workers in the countries affected. Little wonder, then, that international trade generates media and political controversy. The arguments for special trade protections are examined in a later chapter. Here, we examine two other trade-related issues that are in the news: trade adjustment assistance and offshoring of jobs. (In this chapter's Last Word, we examine another trade-related issue: fair-trade products.)

Trade Adjustment Assistance

A nation's comparative advantage in the production of a certain product is not fixed forever. As national economies evolve, the size and quality of their labor forces may change; the volume and composition of their capital stocks may shift; new technologies may emerge; and even the quality of land and the quantity of natural resources may be altered. As these changes take place, the relative efficiency with which a nation can produce specific goods will also change. Also, new trade agreements such as those we have discussed can suddenly leave formerly protected industries highly vulnerable to major disruption or even collapse.

Shifts in patterns of comparative advantage and removal of trade protection can hurt specific groups of workers. For example, the erosion of the United States' once strong comparative advantage in steel has caused production plant shutdowns and layoffs in the U.S. steel industry. The textile and apparel industries in the United States face similar difficulties. Clearly, not everyone wins from free trade (or freer trade). Some workers lose.

The **Trade Adjustment Assistance Act** of 2002 introduced some new, novel elements to help those hurt by shifts in international trade patterns. The law provides cash assistance (beyond unemployment insurance) for up to 78 weeks for workers displaced by imports or plant relocations abroad. To obtain the assistance, workers must participate in job searches, training programs, or remedial education. Also provided are relocation allowances to help displaced workers move geographically to new jobs within the United States. Refundable tax credits for health insurance serve as payments to help workers maintain their insurance coverage during the retraining and job search period. Workers who are 50 years of age or older are eligible for "wage insurance," which replaces some of the difference in pay (if any) between their old and new jobs. Many economists support trade adjustment assistance because it not only helps workers hurt by international trade but also helps create the political support necessary to reduce trade barriers and export subsidies.

But not all economists are keen on trade adjustment assistance. Loss of jobs from imports or plant relocations abroad is only a small fraction (about 4 percent in recent years) of total job losses in the economy each year. Many workers also lose their jobs because of changing patterns of demand, changing technology, bad management, and other dynamic aspects of a market economy. Some critics ask, "What makes losing one's job to international trade worthy of such special treatment, compared to losing one's job to, say, technological change or domestic competition?" Economists can find no totally satisfying answer.

Offshoring of Jobs

Not only are some U.S. jobs lost because of international trade, but some are lost because of globalization of resource markets. In recent years U.S. firms have found the outsourcing of work abroad increasingly profitable. Economists call this business activity **offshoring**: shifting work previously done by American workers to workers located in other nations. Offshoring is not a new practice but traditionally has involved components for U.S. manufacturing goods. For example, Boeing has long offshored the production of major airplane parts for its "American" aircraft.

Recent advances in computer and communications technology have enabled U.S. firms to offshore service jobs such as data entry, book composition, software coding, call-center operations, medical transcription, and claims processing to countries such as India. Where offshoring occurs, some of the value added in the production process accrues to foreign countries rather than the United States. So part of the income generated from the production of U.S. goods is paid to foreigners, not to American workers.

Offshoring is a wrenching experience for many Americans who lose their jobs, but it is not necessarily bad for the overall economy. Offshoring simply reflects a growing specialization and international trade in services, or, more descriptively, "tasks." That trade has been made possible by recent trade agreements and new information and communication technologies. As with trade in goods, trade in services reflects comparative advantage and is beneficial to both trading parties. Moreover, the United States has a sizable trade surplus with other nations in services. The United States gains by specializing in high-valued services such as transportation services, accounting services, legal services, and advertising services, where it still has a comparative advantage. It then "trades" to obtain lower-valued services such as call-center and data entry work, for which comparative advantage has gone abroad.

Offshoring also increases the demand for complementary jobs in the United States. Jobs that are close substitutes for existing U.S. jobs are lost, but complementary jobs in the United States are expanded. For example, the lower price of writing software code in India may mean a lower cost of software sold in the United States and abroad. That, in turn, may create more jobs for U.S.-based workers such as software designers, marketers, and distributors. Moreover, the offshoring may encourage domestic investment and expansion of firms in the United States by reducing their production costs and keeping them competitive worldwide. In some instances, "offshoring jobs" may equate to "importing competitiveness." Entire firms that might otherwise disappear abroad may remain profitable in the United States only because they can offshore some of their work.

QUICK REVIEW COI 1.3

- Governments curtail imports and promote exports through protective tariffs, import quotas, nontariff barriers, and export subsidies.
- The General Agreement on Tariffs and Trade (GATT) established multinational reductions in tariffs and import quotas. The Uruguay Round of GATT (1993) reduced tariffs worldwide, liberalized international trade in services, strengthened protections for intellectual property, and reduced agricultural subsidies.
- The World Trade Organization (WTO)—GATT's successor—rules on trade disputes and provides forums for negotiations on further rounds of trade liberalization. The current round is called the Doha Round.
- The European Union (EU) and the North American Free Trade Agreement (NAFTA) have reduced internal trade barriers among their members by establishing large free-trade zones. Of the 28 EU members (as of 2013), 17 countries used the euro as a common currency.
- Increased international trade and offshoring of jobs have harmed some specific U.S. workers and have led to policies such as trade adjustment assistance to try to help them with their transitions to new lines of work.

Global Competition

Globalization—the integration of industry, commerce, communication, travel, and culture among the world's nations—is one of the major trends of our time. There is a lively debate internationally as to whether globalization is a positive or negative force. Those who support globalization focus on the improvements to general standards of living that it brings. Those who oppose it express concerns about its impacts on the environment, unionized workers, and the poor.

One thing about globalization is certain and relevant to our present discussion: It has brought intense competition both within the United States and across the globe. In

Fair-Trade Products

As a College Student, You May Be Aware of Fair-Trade-Certified Products Such as Those Offered at Starbucks. On Some Campuses, Proponents of Fair-Trade Consumption Are Highly Active in Encouraging Fellow Students to Purchase Only Fair-Trade Goods. What Is Fair Trade All About? And How Effective Is It as an Economic Development Strategy?

Imports of goods by high-income nations from low-income nations increase the demand for labor in low-income nations. Other things equal, increases in labor demand raise wages and incomes. Some observers, however, conclude that the benefits that low-income countries derive from increased production—especially increased exports of agricultural commodities—accrue mainly to large corporations in those countries, some of which are owned by shareholders from high-income nations. Because workers in many low-income countries are highly immobile, have few employment options, and are not unionized, the large dominant sellers can supposedly keep an undeservedly large portion of the proceeds from added exports for themselves (in the form of profits) while simultaneously denying a fair share to their workers (by keeping wages low).

To counter this purported problem, consumer organizations in some of the high-income countries have tried to bypass the usual distribution channels and buy imported goods directly from producers or producer cooperatives that agree to *fair-trade standards*. Such standards guarantee the producers higher-than-market prices if they agree to pay their workers higher-than-

market wages and to abide by rules regarding working conditions and workplace safety. Producers and products that meet the fair-trade standards are certified as fair-trade employers and fair-trade products. Fair-trade advocates in the rich nations then strongly urge consumers to purchase products—for example,

the United States, imports have gained major shares of many markets, including those for cars, steel, lumber, car tires, clothing, sporting goods, electronics, and toys. Nevertheless, hundreds of U.S. firms have prospered in the global marketplace. Firms such as Apple, Boeing, McDonald's, Intel, Coca-Cola, Starbucks, Microsoft, Monsanto, Procter & Gamble, and Caterpillar have continued to retain high market shares at home and have dramatically expanded their sales abroad. Of course, not all firms have been successful. Some have not been able to compete because their international competitors make higher-quality products, have lower production costs, or both.

Is the heightened competition that accompanies the global economy a good thing? Although some domestic producers *do* get hurt and their workers must find employment elsewhere, foreign competition clearly benefits consumers and society in general. Imports break down the monopoly power of existing firms, thereby lowering

product prices and providing consumers with a greater variety of goods. Foreign competition also forces domestic producers to become more efficient and to improve product quality; that has already happened in several U.S. industries, including steel and autos. Most U.S. firms can and do compete quite successfully in the global marketplace.

What about the U.S. firms that cannot compete successfully in open markets? The unfortunate reality is that they must sell off production facilities, scale back their operations, and try to develop new products. If they remain unprofitable despite their best efforts, they will need to go out of business. Persistent economic losses mean that scarce resources are not being used efficiently. Shifting those resources to alternative, profitable uses will increase total U.S. output. It will be far less expensive for the United States to provide training and, if necessary, relocation assistance to laid-off workers than to try to protect these jobs from foreign competition.

coffee, wine, bananas, tea, fresh fruit, and cocoa—only from certified fair-trade producers. When pressure is sufficient, some corporate buyers of these products conclude that it may be more profitable to provide fair-trade products to customers than to risk being labeled an exploiter of third-world labor. Because of the higher-than-market prices and wages, fair-trade goods usually are more expensive than noncertified products.

In economic terms, the purpose of the fair-trade movement is to redistribute more of the total gains from international trade directly to low-income producers and workers by increasing the demand for fair-trade imports relative to otherwise identical imports.

Do these efforts succeed? Economists agree that some of the efforts of fair-trade advocates have succeeded in channeling sizable purchases away from otherwise identical substitutes and toward fair-trade goods. These increases in the demand for fair-trade goods, in turn, have increased the demand for the labor used to produce those goods. So, the fair-trade strategy "has worked" insofar as it has raised prices and wages for *some* sellers and *some* workers in low-wage countries—namely those involved with fair-trade programs.

Nevertheless, most economists question the overall effectiveness of the fair-trade approach as a broader economic development strategy. They say that price and wage setting by advocacy groups is based on highly subjective views of fairness that may be at odds with economic realities. Distortions of market prices and wages invite inefficiency and unintended consequences. For example, the higher fair-trade prices may encourage resources to remain producing the fair-trade products long after

normal supply and demand circumstances would have encouraged them to move to more productive employment in other parts of agriculture or in manufacturing or services.

The consensus among economists is that fair-trade purchasing in the high-income nations has simply shifted labor demand within and among low-wage countries. Fair trade has not increased the *overall* labor demand or the average pay of workers in low-wage nations. Sustainable increases in average pay require economywide gains in labor productivity—output per hour of work. Unfortunately, fair-trade purchasing does not accomplish that. Economywide gains in productivity and wages require improvements in the quantity and quality of education, more and improved capital goods, and the use of more efficient technology.

Some economists say that other action by people in high-income nations might benefit the low-income nations more effectively than fair-trade purchasing. For example, pressing for the removal of agricultural subsidies in high-income areas such as the United States and the European Union would reduce the overproduction of agricultural output that floods international markets and depresses international agricultural prices. Those low prices impoverish farmers in low-wage nations and encourage them to concentrate their efforts in producing agricultural commodities that are not produced in the wealthy countries and therefore are unsubsidized. In a sense, the low-wage countries get stuck overproducing low-profit agricultural commodities such as coffee, bananas, and cocoa—keeping those prices artificially low. Ironically, those very low prices (and the low agricultural wages that result) are precisely what the fair-trade movement tries to increase.

SUMMARY

COI1.1 List and explain the four major economic flows that link the U.S. economy with the economies of other nations.

Goods and services flows, capital and labor flows, information and technology flows, and financial flows link the United States and other countries.

COI1.2 State several key facts about U.S. international trade.

International trade is growing in importance globally and for the United States. World trade is significant to the United States in two respects: (a) The combined volumes of U.S. imports and exports exceed those of any other single nation. (b) The United States is completely dependent on trade for certain commodities and materials that cannot be obtained domestically.

Principal U.S. exports include agricultural products, chemicals, metals, and aircraft. Principal imports include oil, household appliances, apparel, and computers. Quantitatively, Canada is the United States' most important trading partner in terms of the total amounts of exports and imports.

Global trade has been greatly facilitated by (a) improvements in transportation technology, (b) improvements in communications technology, and (c) general declines in tariffs.

The world's major trading nations by volume of trade are China, the United States, Germany, and Japan. Other major traders include other western European nations (France, the Netherlands, Italy, and the United Kingdom), along with Canada and the east and southeast Asian countries of South Korea, Hong Kong, and Singapore.

COI1.3 Define comparative advantage and explain how it relates to specialization and international trade.

Specialization based on comparative advantage enables nations to achieve higher standards of living through trade with other countries. A trading partner should specialize in products and services for which its domestic opportunity costs are lowest. The terms of trade must be such that both nations can obtain a product via trade at lower opportunity costs than if they produced that product at home. Because of rising opportunity costs, domestic production may stop short of complete specialization.

COI1.4 Explain how exchange rates are determined in currency (foreign-exchange) markets.

The foreign exchange market sets exchange rates between currencies. Each nation's imports create a supply of its own currency and a demand for foreign currencies. The resulting supply-demand equilibrium sets the exchange rate that links the currencies of all nations. Depreciation of a nation's currency reduces its imports and increases its exports; appreciation increases its imports and reduces its exports.

COI1.5 Explain how and why government sometimes interferes with free international trade.

Governments influence trade flows through (a) protective tariffs, (b) quotas, (c) nontariff barriers, and (d) export subsidies. Such impediments to free trade result from misunderstandings about the advantages of free trade and from political considerations. By artificially increasing product prices, trade barriers cost U.S. consumers billions of dollars annually.

COI1.6 Describe the purposes and functions of GATT, WTO, EU, eurozone, and NAFTA.

The Reciprocal Trade Agreements Act of 1934 marked the beginning of a trend toward lower U.S. tariffs. In 1947 the General Agreement on Tariffs and Trade (GATT) was formed to encourage nondiscriminatory treatment for all member nations, to reduce tariffs, and to eliminate import quotas. The Uruguay Round of GATT negotiations (1993) reduced tariffs and quotas, liberalized trade in services, reduced agricultural subsidies, reduced pirating of intellectual property, and phased out quotas on textiles.

GATT's successor, the World Trade Organization (WTO), has 159 member nations. It implements WTO agreements, rules on trade disputes between members, and provides forums for continued discussions on trade liberalization. The latest round of trade negotiations—the Doha Development Agenda—began in late 2001 and as of mid-2013 was still in progress.

Free-trade zones (trade blocs) liberalize trade within regions but may at the same time impede trade with non-bloc members. Two examples of free-trade arrangements are the 28-member European Union (EU) and the North American Free Trade Agreement (NAFTA), comprising Canada, Mexico, and the United States. Seventeen of the EU nations have abandoned their national currencies for a common currency called the euro.

COI1.7 Define and discuss three major trade-related issues: trade adjustment assistance, the offshoring of jobs, and globalization.

The Trade Adjustment Assistance Act of 2002 recognizes that trade liberalization and increased international trade can create job loss for many workers. The Act therefore provides cash assistance, education and training benefits, health care subsidies, and wage subsidies (for persons age 50 or older) to qualified workers displaced by imports or relocations of plants from the United States to abroad.

Offshoring is the practice of shifting work previously done by Americans in the United States to workers located in other nations. Although offshoring eliminates some U.S. jobs, it lowers production costs, expands sales, and therefore may create other U.S. jobs. Less than 4 percent of all job losses in the United States each year are caused by imports, offshoring, and plant relocation abroad.

The global economy has created intense foreign competition in many U.S. product markets, but many U.S. firms are able to compete successfully abroad as well as at home.

TERMS AND CONCEPTS

comparative advantage

terms of trade

foreign exchange market

exchange rates

depreciation

appreciation

protective tariffs

import quotas

nontariff barriers

export subsidies

Smoot-Hawley Tariff Act

Reciprocal Trade Agreements Act

normal-trade-relations (NTR) status

General Agreement on Tariffs and Trade (GATT)

World Trade Organization (WTO)

Doha Development Agenda

European Union (EU)

trade bloc

euro

North American Free Trade Agreement (NAFTA)

Trade Adjustment Assistance Act

offshoring

DISCUSSION QUESTIONS

1. Describe the four major types of economic flows that link the United States with other nations. Provide a specific example of each type of flow. LOCOI1.1

2. How important is international trade to the U.S. economy? In terms of the total volume of exports and imports, what country is the United States' most important trading partner? Was the United States the world's leading export country in 2012? If not, which country was? Place the following four countries in descending order in terms of exports as a percentage of GDP: the United States, Belgium, Canada, and Japan. What key factors account for the rapid growth of world trade since the Second World War? LOCOI1.1

3. What role do domestic opportunity costs play in determining a nation's area of comparative advantage and therefore specialization relative to that of a trading partner? Provide a numerical example (no need for a table) to support your answer. How does specialization and trade reduce a nation's total cost of obtaining products? Why is specialization sometimes incomplete, such that countries import some of the same categories of goods that they export? LOCOI1.3

4. True or False: "U.S. exports create a demand for foreign currencies; foreign imports of U.S. goods create a supply of foreign currencies." Explain your answer. Would a decline in U.S. consumer income or a weakening of U.S. preferences for foreign products cause the dollar to depreciate or to appreciate? Other things equal, what would be the effects of that depreciation or appreciation on U.S. exports and imports? LOCOI1.4

5. If the European euro were to decline in value (depreciate) in the foreign exchange market, would it be easier or harder for the French to sell their wine in the United States? Suppose you were planning a trip to Paris. How would depreciation of the euro change the dollar cost of your trip? LOCOI1.4

6. What measures do governments take to promote exports and restrict imports? Who benefits and who loses from protectionist policies? What is the net outcome for society? LOCOI1.5

7. Identify and state the significance of each of the following: (*a*) WTO, (*b*) EU, (*c*) euro, (*d*) NAFTA. What commonality do they share? LOCOI1.6

8. Explain: "Free-trade zones such as the EU and NAFTA lead a double life: They can promote free trade among members, but they pose serious trade obstacles for nonmembers." Do you think the net effects of trade blocs are good or bad for world trade? Why? How do the efforts of the WTO relate to these trade blocs? LOCOI1.6

9. Speculate as to why some U.S. firms strongly support trade liberalization while other U.S. firms favor protectionism. Why might some U.S. labor unions strongly support trade liberalization while other U.S. labor unions strongly oppose it? LOCOI1.6

10. What are the major forms of trade adjustment assistance provided by the U.S. government? How does such assistance help bolster support for free-trade agreements? Do you think workers who lose their jobs because of changes in trade laws deserve special treatment relative to workers who lose their jobs because of other changes in the economy, say, changes in patterns of government spending? LOCOI1.7

11. What is offshoring of white-collar service jobs and how does that practice relate to international trade? Why has it recently increased? Why do you think more than half of all the offshored jobs have gone to India? Give an example (other than that in the textbook) of how offshoring can eliminate some U.S. jobs while creating other U.S. jobs. LOCOI1.7

12. **LAST WORD** How does a fair-trade product differ from an otherwise identical imported good? What is the purported benefit of fair-trade certification on purchases of goods such as chocolate, coffee, bananas, and tea? Do fair-trade goods improve average wages or incomes in low-income nations? Why or why not?

REVIEW QUESTIONS

1. Which of the following is not one of the four major economic flows linking the U.S. economy with that of other nations? LOCOI1.1
   a. Trade flows.
   b. Resource flows.
   c. Financial flows.
   d. Foreign aid flows.

2. The United States usually runs a _____ in its international trade in goods and a _____ in its international trade in services. LOCOI1.2
   a. Deficit, deficit.
   b. Deficit, surplus.
   c. Surplus, deficit.
   d. Surplus, surplus.

3. A country that has an absolute advantage over another country in producing a product _____ a comparative advantage as well. LOCOI1.3
   a. Will have.
   b. May have.

4. True or False: Consider the exchange rate between the U.S. dollar and the Japanese yen. If the exchange rate changes from $1 = ¥80 to $1 = ¥105, then the dollar has "appreciated" in value against the yen. LOCOI1.4

5. Tariffs and quotas _____ domestic producers but _____ domestic consumers. LOCOI1.5
   a. Help, help.
   b. Help, harm.
   c. Harm, help.
   d. Harm, harm.

PROBLEMS

1. Suppose that the comparative-cost ratios of two products—baby formula and tuna fish—are as follows in the hypothetical nations of Canswicki and Tunata:

    Canswicki: 1 can baby formula ≡ 2 cans tuna fish
    Tunata: 1 can baby formula ≡ 4 cans tuna fish

    In what product should each nation specialize? Which of the following terms of trade would be acceptable to both nations: (*a*) 1 can baby formula ≡ $2\frac{1}{2}$ cans tuna fish; (*b*) 1 can baby formula ≡ 1 can tuna fish; (*c*) 1 can baby formula ≡ 5 cans tuna fish? LOCOI1.3

2. The following are production possibilities tables for China and the United States. Assume that before specialization and trade, the optimal product mix for China is alternative B and for the United States it is alternative U. LOCOI1.3

Product	China Production Possibilities					
	A	B	C	D	E	F
Apparel (in thousands)	30	24	18	12	6	0
Chemicals (in tons)	0	6	12	18	24	30

Product	U.S. Production Possibilities					
	R	S	T	U	V	W
Apparel (in thousands)	10	8	6	4	2	0
Chemicals (in tons)	0	4	8	12	16	20

   a. Are comparative-cost conditions such that the two countries can gain from specialization? If so, what product should each country produce?

   b. What is the total gain in apparel and chemical output that would result from such specialization?

   c. What are the limits of the terms of trade in this example? Suppose that the actual terms of trade are 1 unit of apparel for $1\frac{1}{2}$ units of chemicals and that 4 units of apparel are exchanged for 6 units of chemicals. What are the gains from specialization and trade for each nation?

3. Initially assume that it costs $1.36 to purchase 1 euro. How many euros are needed to buy $1? How many dollars are needed to purchase an item priced at 84 euros? Next, assume that the exchange rate changes to $1.30 per 1 euro. Will it take more euros or fewer euros to buy the American item priced at $84? Did the euro appreciate or depreciate relative to the dollar? Did the dollar appreciate or depreciate relative to the euro? LOCOI1.4

FURTHER TEST YOUR KNOWLEDGE AT www.mcconnell20e.com

Practice quizzes, student PowerPoints, worked problems, Web-based questions, and additional materials are available at the text's Online Learning Center (OLC), **www.mcconnell20e.com**, or scan here. Need a barcode reader? Try ScanLife, available in your app store.

Previous International Exchange-Rate Systems

www.mcconnell20e.com

This is supplemental material to Chapter 39 (The Balance of Payments, Exchange Rates, and Trade Deficits) that is found in *Economics* (Chapter 21 in *Macroeconomics* and Chapter 25 in *Microeconomics*). It can either be fully integrated into the chapter by assigning it immediately before the section "The Current Exchange Rate System: The Managed Float" or simply assigned as an addendum to the full chapter.

Our chapter titled, "The Balance of Payments, Exchange Rates, and Trade Deficits" discusses the current system of managed floating exchange rates in some detail. But before this system began in 1971, the world had previously used two other exchange rate systems: the gold standard, which implicitly created fixed exchange rates, and the Bretton Woods system, which was an explicit fixed-rate system indirectly tied to gold. Because the features and problems of these two systems help explain why we have the current system, they are well worth knowing more about.

The Gold Standard: Fixed Exchange Rates

Between 1879 and 1934 the major nations of the world adhered to a fixed-rate system called the **gold standard**. Under this system, each nation must:

- Define its currency in terms of a quantity of gold.
- Maintain a fixed relationship between its stock of gold and its money supply.
- Allow gold to be freely exported and imported.

If each nation defines its currency in terms of gold, the various national currencies will have fixed relationships to one another. For example, if the United States defines $1 as worth 25 grains of gold, and Britain defines £1 as worth 50 grains of gold, then a British pound is worth 2×25 grains, or $2. This exchange rate was fixed under the gold standard. The exchange rate did not change in response to changes in currency demand and supply.

Gold Flows

If we ignore the costs of packing, insuring, and shipping gold between countries, under the gold standard the rate of exchange would not vary from this $2 = £1 rate. No one in the United States would pay more than $2 = £1 because 50 grains of gold could always be bought for $2 in the United States and sold for £1 in Britain. Nor would the British pay more than £1 for $2. Why should they when they could buy 50 grains of gold in Britain for £1 and sell it in the United States for $2?

Under the gold standard, the potential free flow of gold between nations resulted in fixed exchange rates.

Domestic Macroeconomic Adjustments

When currency demand or supply changes, the gold standard requires domestic macroeconomic adjustments to maintain the fixed exchange rate. To see why, suppose that U.S. tastes change such that U.S. consumers want to buy more British goods. The resulting increase in the demand for pounds creates a shortage of pounds in the United States (recall Figure 39.2 in *Economics*—21.2 in *Macroeconomics* or 25.2 in *Microeconomics*), implying a U.S. balance-of-payments deficit.

What will happen? Remember that the rules of the gold standard prohibit the exchange rate from moving from the fixed $2 = £1 rate. The rate cannot move to, say, a new equilibrium at $3 = £1 to correct the imbalance. Instead, gold will flow from the United States to Britain to correct the payments imbalance.

But recall that the gold standard requires that participants maintain a fixed relationship between their domestic money supplies and their quantities of gold. The flow of gold from the United States to Britain will require a reduction of the money supply in the United States. Other things equal, that will reduce total spending in the United States and lower U.S. real domestic output, employment, income, and, perhaps, prices. Also, the decline in the money supply will boost U.S. interest rates.

The opposite will occur in Britain. The inflow of gold will increase the money supply, and this will increase total spending in Britain. Domestic output, employment, income, and, perhaps, prices will rise. The British interest rate will fall.

Declining U.S. incomes and prices will reduce the U.S. demand for British goods and therefore reduce the U.S. demand for pounds. Lower interest rates in Britain will make it less attractive for U.S. investors to make financial investments there, also lessening the demand for pounds. For all these reasons, the demand for pounds in the United States will decline. In Britain, higher incomes, prices, and interest rates will make U.S. imports and U.S. financial investments more attractive. In buying these imports and making these financial investments, British citizens will supply more pounds in the exchange market.

In short, domestic macroeconomic adjustments in the United States and Britain, triggered by the international flow of gold, will produce new demand and supply conditions for pounds such that the $2 = £1 exchange rate is maintained. After all the adjustments are made, the United States will not have a payments deficit and Britain will not have a payments surplus.

So the gold standard has the advantage of maintaining stable exchange rates and correcting balance-of-payments deficits and surpluses automatically. However, its critical drawback is that nations must accept domestic adjustments in such distasteful forms as unemployment and falling incomes, on the one hand, or inflation, on the other hand. Under the gold standard, a nation's money supply is altered by changes in supply and demand in currency markets, and nations cannot establish their own monetary policy in their own national interest. If the United States, for example, were to experience declining output and income, the loss of gold under the gold standard would reduce the U.S. money supply. That would increase interest rates, retard borrowing and spending, and produce further declines in output and income.

Collapse of the Gold Standard

The gold standard collapsed under the weight of the worldwide Depression of the 1930s. As domestic output and employment fell worldwide, the restoration of prosperity became the primary goal of afflicted nations. They responded by enacting protectionist measures to reduce imports. The idea was to get their economies moving again by promoting consumption of domestically produced goods. To make their exports less expensive abroad, many nations redefined their currencies at lower levels in terms of gold. For example, a country that had previously defined the value of its currency at 1 unit = 25 grains of gold might redefine it as 1 unit = 10 grains of gold. Such redefining is an example of **devaluation**—a deliberate action by government to reduce the international value of its currency. A series of such devaluations in the 1930s meant that exchange rates were no longer fixed. That violated a major tenet of the gold standard, and the system broke down.

The Bretton Woods System

The Great Depression and the Second World War left world trade and the world monetary system in shambles. To lay the groundwork for a new international monetary system, in 1944, major nations held an international conference at Bretton Woods, New Hampshire. The conference produced a commitment to a modified fixed-exchange-rate system called an *adjustable-peg system*, or, simply, the **Bretton Woods system.** The new system sought to capture the advantages of the old gold standard (fixed exchange rate) while avoiding its disadvantages (painful domestic macroeconomic adjustments).

Furthermore, the conference created the **International Monetary Fund (IMF)** to make the new exchange-rate system feasible and workable. The new international monetary system managed through the IMF prevailed with modifications until 1971. (The IMF still plays a basic role in international finance; in recent years it has performed a major role in providing loans to developing countries, nations experiencing financial crises, and nations making the transition from communism to capitalism.)

IMF and Pegged Exchange Rates

How did the adjustable-peg system of exchange rates work? First, as with the gold standard, each IMF member had to define its currency in terms of gold (or dollars), thus establishing rates of exchange between its currency and the currencies of all other members. In addition, each nation was obligated to keep its exchange rate stable with respect to every other currency. To do so, nations would have to use their official currency reserves to intervene in foreign exchange markets.

Assume again that the U.S. dollar and the British pound were "pegged" to each other at $2 = £1. And suppose again that the demand for pounds temporarily increases so that a shortage of pounds occurs in the United States (the United States has a balance-of-payments deficit). How can the United States keep its pledge to maintain a $2 = £1 exchange rate when the new equilibrium rate is, say, $3 = £1? As we noted previously, the United States can supply additional pounds to the exchange market, increasing the supply of pounds such that the equilibrium exchange rate falls back to $2 = £1.

Under the Bretton Woods system there were three main sources of the needed pounds:

- *Official reserves* The United States might currently possess pounds in its official reserves as the result of past actions against a payments surplus.

- *Gold sales* The U.S. government might sell some of its gold to Britain for pounds. The proceeds would then be offered in the exchange market to augment the supply of pounds.

- *IMF borrowing* The needed pounds might be borrowed from the IMF. Nations participating in the Bretton Woods system were required to make contributions to the IMF based on the size of their national income, population, and volume of trade. If necessary, the United States could borrow pounds on a short-term basis from the IMF by supplying its own currency as collateral.

Fundamental Imbalances: Adjusting the Peg

The Bretton Woods system recognized that from time to time a nation may be confronted with persistent and sizable balance-of-payments problems that cannot be corrected through the means listed above. In such cases, the nation would eventually run out of official reserves and be unable to maintain its current fixed exchange rate. The Bretton Woods remedy was correction by devaluation, that is, by an "orderly" reduction of the nation's pegged exchange rate. Also, the IMF allowed each member nation to alter the value of its currency by 10 percent, on its own, to correct a so-called fundamental (persistent and continuing) balance-of-payments deficit. Larger exchange-rate changes required the permission of the Fund's board of directors.

By requiring approval of significant rate changes, the Fund guarded against arbitrary and competitive currency devaluations by nations seeking only to boost output in their own countries at the expense of other countries. In our example, devaluation of the dollar would increase U.S.

exports and lower U.S. imports, helping to correct the United States' persistent payments deficit.

Demise of the Bretton Woods System

Under this adjustable-peg system, nations came to accept gold and the dollar as international reserves. The acceptability of gold as an international medium of exchange derived from its earlier use under the gold standard. Other nations accepted the dollar as international money because the United States had accumulated large quantities of gold, and between 1934 and 1971 it maintained a policy of buying gold from, and selling gold to, foreign governments at a fixed price of $35 per ounce. The dollar was convertible into gold on demand, so the dollar came to be regarded as a substitute for gold, or "as good as gold." The discovery of new gold was limited, but a growing volume of dollars helped facilitate the expanding volume of world trade during this period.

But a major problem arose. The United States had persistent payments deficits throughout the 1950s and 1960s. Those deficits were financed in part by U.S. gold reserves but mostly by payment of U.S. dollars. As the amount of dollars held by foreigners soared and the U.S. gold reserves dwindled, other nations began to question whether the dollar was really "as good as gold." The ability of the United States to continue to convert dollars into gold at $35 per ounce became increasingly doubtful, as did the role of dollars as international monetary reserves. Thus the dilemma was: To maintain the dollar as a reserve medium, the U.S. payments deficit had to be eliminated. But elimination of the payments deficit would remove the source of additional dollar reserves and thus limit the growth of international trade and finance.

The problem culminated in 1971 when the United States ended its 37-year-old policy of exchanging gold for dollars at $35 per ounce. It severed the link between gold and the international value of the dollar, thereby "floating" the dollar and letting market forces determine its value. The floating of the dollar withdrew U.S. support from the Bretton Woods system of fixed exchange rates and effectively ended the system. Nearly all major currencies began to float. This led to the current regime of "managed floating exchange rates" that is described at length in the chapter titled, "The Balance of Payments, Exchange Rates, and Trade Deficits."

SUMMARY

- Before the current system of managed floating exchange rates started in 1971, several different international monetary systems were used.

- Between 1879 and 1934, most major trading nations were on the gold standard, in which each nation fixed an exchange rate between its currency and gold. With each nation's currency fixed to gold, the system also implicitly set fixed exchange rates between different national currencies.

- Any balance-of-payments imbalance would automatically lead to offsetting international flows of gold. This, in turn, led to automatically occurring domestic macroeconomic adjustments as the country exporting gold automatically encountered a decrease in its money supply while the country importing gold automatically felt an increase in its money supply. When the Great Depression hit, many countries found these automatic adjustments too hard to bear and they abandoned the gold standard.

- The Bretton Woods system was implemented after the end of the Second World War and lasted until 1971. Under this system, the United States fixed the value of the U.S. dollar to gold at a rate of $35 per ounce. Other countries then set fixed exchange rates with the dollar so that their currencies were indirectly fixed to gold through the dollar.

- The International Monetary Fund was created to administer the Bretton Woods system, which had some flexibility because exchange rates between countries could be adjusted to help offset balance-of-payments imbalances.

- As the United States encountered increasingly large balance-of-payments imbalances in the 1960s and early 1970s, its ability to maintain its gold peg of $35 per ounce lost credibility. The United States abandoned the gold standard in 1971, thereby ending the Bretton Woods system. All major currencies then began the current regime of managed floating exchange rates.

TERMS AND CONCEPTS

gold standard
devaluation

Bretton Woods system

International Monetary Fund (IMF)

Note: Terms set in *italic* type are defined separately in this glossary.

aggregate A collection of specific economic units treated as if they were one unit. Examples: the *prices* of all individual *goods* and *services* are combined into the *price level*, and all units of output are aggregated into *gross domestic product*.

aggregate demand A schedule or curve that shows the total quantity of *goods* and *services* that would be demanded (purchased) at various *price levels*.

aggregate demand–aggregate supply (AD-AS) model The macroeconomic model that uses *aggregate demand* and *aggregate supply* to determine and explain the *price level* and the real *domestic output* (*real gross domestic product*).

aggregate expenditures The total amount spent for *final goods* and final *services* in an economy.

aggregate expenditures–domestic output approach Determination of the equilibrium *gross domestic product* by finding the real GDP at which *aggregate expenditures* equal *domestic output*.

aggregate expenditures model The *macroeconomics* model developed by John Maynard Keynes that assumes completely *inflexible prices*, thereby forcing the economy to adjust toward an *equilibrium real domestic output* by a process in which *firms*, reacting to unexpected changes in *inventory* levels, adjust the volume of output until the *aggregate expenditures* made on *final goods* and final *services* just equal the amount of output being produced in the economy.

aggregate expenditures schedule A table of numbers showing the total amount spent on *final goods* and final *services* at different levels of *real gross domestic product* (*real GDP*).

aggregate supply A schedule or curve showing the total quantity of *goods* and *services* that would be supplied (produced) at various *price levels*.

aggregate supply shocks Sudden, large changes in resource costs that shift an economy's aggregate supply curve.

appreciation (of the dollar) An increase in the value of the dollar relative to the currency of another nation, so a dollar buys a larger amount of the foreign currency and thus of foreign goods.

arbitrage The activity of selling one *asset* and buying an identical or nearly identical asset to benefit from temporary differences in *prices* or *rates of return;* the practice that equalizes prices or returns on similar financial instruments and thus eliminates further opportunities for riskless financial gains.

asset Anything of monetary value owned by a *firm* or individual.

asset demand for money The amount of *money* people want to hold as a *store of value;* this amount varies inversely with the *interest rate.*

asymmetric information A situation where one party to a market transaction has much more information about a product or service than the other. The result may be an under- or overallocation of resources.

average expected rate of return The *probability-weighted average* of an investment's possible future returns.

average tax rate Total tax paid divided by total *taxable income* or some other base (such as total income) against which to compare the amount of tax paid. Expressed as a percentage.

average total cost (ATC) A firm's *total cost* divided by output (the quantity of product produced); equal to *average fixed cost* plus *average variable cost.*

average variable cost (AVC) A firm's total *variable cost* divided by output (the quantity of product produced).

balance of payments A summary of all the financial transactions that take place between the individuals, *firms*, and governmental units of one nation and those of all other nations during a year.

balance-of-payments deficit The net amount of *official reserves* (mainly foreign currencies) that a nation's treasury or central bank must sell to achieve balance between that nation's *capital and financial account* and its *current account* (in its *balance of payments*).

balance-of-payments surplus The net amount of *official reserves* (mainly foreign currencies) that a nation's treasury or central bank must buy to achieve balance between that nation's *capital and financial account* and its *current account* (in its *balance of payments*).

balance on capital and financial account The sum of the *capital account balance* and the *financial account balance.*

balance on current account The exports of *goods* and *services* of a nation less its imports of goods and services plus its *net investment income* and *net transfers* in a year.

balance on goods and services The exports of *goods* and *services* of a nation less its imports of goods and services in a year.

balance sheet A statement of the *assets*, *liabilities*, and *net worth* of a *firm* or individual at some given time.

bank deposits The deposits that individuals or *firms* have at banks (or thrifts) or that banks have at the *Federal Reserve Banks.*

bankers' bank A bank that accepts the deposits of and makes loans to *depository institutions;* in the United States, a *Federal Reserve Bank.*

bank reserves The deposits of commercial banks and thrifts at *Federal Reserve Banks* plus bank and thrift *vault cash.*

bankrupt A legal situation in which an individual or *firm* finds that it cannot make timely interest payments on money it has borrowed. In such cases, a bankruptcy judge can order the individual or firm to liquidate (turn into cash) its assets in order to pay lenders at least some portion of the amount they are owed.

barter The direct exchange of one *good* or *service* for another good or service.

base year The year with which other years are compared when an index is constructed; for example, the base year for a *price index*.

beta A relative measure of *nondiversifiable risk* that measures how the nondiversifiable risk of a given *asset* or *portfolio* compares with that of the *market portfolio* (the portfolio that contains every asset available in the financial markets).

Board of Governors The seven-member group that supervises and controls the money and banking system of the United States; the Board of Governors of the *Federal Reserve System;* the Federal Reserve Board.

bond A financial device through which a borrower (a *firm* or government) is obligated to pay the principal and interest on a loan at specific dates in the future.

break-even income The level of *disposable income* at which *households* plan to consume (spend) all their income and to save none of it.

budget deficit The amount by which expenditures exceed revenues in any year.

budget line A line that shows the different combinations of two products a consumer can purchase with a specific money income, given the products' *prices*.

budget surplus The amount by which the revenues of the federal government exceed its expenditures in any year.

built-in stabilizer A mechanism that increases government's budget deficit (or reduces its surplus) during a recession and increases government's budget surplus (or reduces its deficit) during an expansion without any action by policymakers. The tax system is one such mechanism.

Bureau of Economic Analysis (BEA) An agency of the U.S. Department of Commerce that compiles the national income and product accounts.

business cycle Recurring increases and decreases in the level of economic activity over periods of years; consists of peak, recession, trough, and expansion phases.

businesses Economic entities (*firms*) that purchase resources and provide *goods* and *services* to the economy.

business firm (See *firm.*)

capital Human-made resources (buildings, machinery, and equipment) used to produce *goods* and *services;* goods that do not directly satisfy human wants; also called capital goods. One of the four *economic resources*.

capital and financial account The section of a nation's *international balance of payments* that records (1) debt forgiveness by and to foreigners and (2) foreign purchases of assets in the United States and U.S. purchases of assets abroad.

capital and financial account deficit A negative balance on its *capital and financial account* in a country's *international balance of payments*.

capital and financial account surplus A positive balance on its *capital and financial account* in a country's *international balance of payments*.

capital flight (Web chapter) The transfer of savings from *developing countries* to *industrially advanced countries* to avoid government expropriation, taxation, or higher rates of *inflation*, or simply to realize greater returns on *financial investments*.

capital gain The gain realized when *securities* or properties or other assets are sold for a *price* greater than the price paid for them.

capital goods (See *capital.*)

capitalism An economic system in which property resources are privately owned and markets and prices are used to direct and coordinate economic activities.

capital stock The total available *capital* in a nation.

capital-using technology (Web chapter) An improvement in *technology* that requires the use of a greater amount of *capital* to produce a specific quantity of a product.

capricious-universe view (Web chapter) The view held by some people that fate and outside events, rather than hard work and enterprise, will determine their economic destinies.

cardinal utility Satisfaction (*utility*) that can be measured via cardinal numbers (1, 2, 3...), with all the mathematical properties of those numbers such as addition, subtraction, multiplication, and division being applicable.

causation A relationship in which the occurrence of one or more events brings about another event.

CEA (See *Council of Economic Advisers.*)

ceiling price (See *price ceiling.*)

central economic planning Government determination of the objectives of the economy and how resources will be directed to attain those goals.

ceteris paribus **assumption** (See *other-things-equal assumption.*)

change in demand A movement of an entire *demand curve* or schedule such that the *quantity demanded* changes at every particular *price;* caused by a change in one or more of the *determinants of demand*.

change in quantity demanded A change in the *quantity demanded* along a fixed *demand curve* (or within a fixed demand schedule) as a result of a change in the *price* of the product.

change in quantity supplied A change in the *quantity supplied* along a fixed *supply curve* (or within a fixed supply schedule) as a result of a change in the product's *price*.

change in supply A movement of an entire *supply curve* or schedule such that the *quantity supplied* changes at every particular *price;* caused by a change in one or more of the *determinants of supply*.

checkable deposit Any deposit in a *commercial bank* or *thrift institution* against which a check may be written.

checkable-deposit multiplier (See *monetary multiplier*.)

check clearing The process by which funds are transferred from the checking accounts of the writers of checks to the checking accounts of the recipients of checks.

checking account A *checkable deposit* in a *commercial bank* or *thrift institution*.

circular flow diagram An illustration showing the flow of *resources* from *households* to *firms* and of products from firms to households. These flows are accompanied by reverse flows of money from firms to households and from households to firms.

closed economy An economy that neither exports nor imports *goods* and *services*.

coincidence of wants A situation in which the *good* or *service* that one trader desires to obtain is the same as that which another trader desires to give up and an item that the second trader wishes to acquire is the same as that which the first trader desires to surrender.

COLA (See *cost-of-living adjustment*.)

collective-action problem The idea that getting a group to pursue a common, collective goal gets harder the larger the group's size. Larger groups are more costly to organize and their members more difficult to motivate because the larger the group, the smaller each member's share of the benefits if the group succeeds.

command system A method of organizing an economy in which property resources are publicly owned and government uses *central economic planning* to direct and coordinate economic activities; *socialism*; communism. Compare with *market system*.

commercial bank A *firm* that engages in the business of banking (accepts deposits, offers checking accounts, and makes loans).

commercial banking system All *commercial banks* and *thrift institutions* as a group.

communism (See *command system*.)

comparative advantage A situation in which a person or country can produce a specific product at a lower opportunity cost than some other person or country; the basis for specialization and trade.

compensation to employees *Wages* and salaries plus wage and salary supplements paid by employers to workers.

competition The effort and striving between two or more independent rivals to secure the business of one or more third parties by offering the best possible terms.

compound interest The accumulation of money that builds over time in an investment or interest-bearing account as new interest is earned on previous interest that is not withdrawn.

constant opportunity cost An *opportunity cost* that remains the same for each additional unit as a consumer (or society) shifts purchases (production) from one product to another along a straight-line *budget line* (*production possibilities curve*).

consumer goods Products and *services* that satisfy human wants directly.

Consumer Price Index (CPI) An index that measures the *prices* of a fixed "market basket" of some 300 *goods* and *services* bought by a "typical" consumer.

consumer sovereignty The determination by consumers of the types and quantities of *goods* and *services* that will be produced with the scarce resources of the economy; consumers' direction of production through their *dollar votes*.

consumer surplus The difference between the maximum *price* a consumer is (or consumers are) willing to pay for an additional unit of a product and its market price; the triangular area below the demand curve and above the market price.

consumption of fixed capital An estimate of the amount of *capital* worn out or used up (consumed) in producing the *gross domestic product*; also called depreciation.

consumption schedule A table of numbers showing the amounts *households* plan to spend for *consumer goods* at different levels of *disposable income*.

contractionary fiscal policy A decrease in *government purchases* of goods and *services*, an increase in *net taxes*, or some combination of the two, for the purpose of decreasing *aggregate demand* and thus controlling *inflation*.

coordination failure A situation in which people do not reach a mutually beneficial outcome because they lack some way to jointly coordinate their actions; a possible cause of macroeconomic instability.

copyright A legal protection provided to developers and publishers of books, computer software, videos, and musical compositions against the unauthorized copying of their works by others.

core inflation The underlying increases in the *price level* after volatile food and energy *prices* are removed.

corporate income tax A tax levied on the net income (accounting profit) of corporations.

corporation A legal entity ("person") chartered by a state or the federal government that is distinct and separate from the individuals who own it.

correlation A systematic and dependable association between two sets of data (two kinds of events); does not necessarily indicate causation.

corruption (Web chapter) The misuse of government power, with which one has been entrusted or assigned, to obtain private gain; includes payments from individuals or companies to secure advantages in obtaining government contracts, avoiding government regulations, or obtaining inside knowledge about forthcoming policy changes.

cost-benefit analysis A comparison of the *marginal costs* of a project or program with the *marginal benefits* to decide whether or not to employ resources in that project or program and to what extent.

cost-of-living adjustment (COLA) An automatic increase in the incomes (*wages*) of workers when *inflation* occurs; often included in *collective bargaining* agreements between *firms* and *unions*.

Cost-of-living adjustments are also guaranteed by law for *Social Security* benefits and certain other government *transfer payments*.

cost-push inflation   Increases in the *price level* (*inflation*) resulting from an increase in resource costs (for example, raw-material prices) and hence in *per-unit production costs*; inflation caused by reductions in *aggregate supply*.

Council of Economic Advisers (CEA)   A group of three persons that advises and assists the president of the United States on economic matters (including the preparation of the annual *Economic Report of the President*).

credit   An accounting entry that either increases the value of an *asset* or reduces the value of a *liability* (by acting as a deduction from an amount already owed).

credit union   A financial institution that provides many of the same services as a *commercial bank*, including checkable deposits, but only to members, who own the credit union and who share a common tie (such as being employees of the same *firm* or members of the same labor union).

crowding-out effect   A rise in interest rates and a resulting decrease in *planned investment* caused by the federal government's increased borrowing to finance budget deficits and refinance debt.

currency   Coins and paper money.

currency appreciation   (See *exchange-rate appreciation*.)

currency depreciation   (See *exchange-rate depreciation*.)

currency intervention   A government's buying and selling of its own currency or foreign currencies to alter international exchange rates.

current account   The section in a nation's *international balance of payments* that records its exports and imports of *goods* and *services*, its net *investment income*, and its *net transfers*.

cyclical asymmetry   The idea that *monetary policy* may be more successful in slowing expansions and controlling *inflation* than in extracting the economy from severe recession.

cyclical deficit   a Federal *budget deficit* that is caused by a recession and the consequent decline in tax revenues.

cyclically adjusted budget   The estimated annual budget deficit or surplus that would occur under existing tax rates and government spending levels if the the economy were to operate at its *full-employment* level of GDP for a year; the *full-employment* budget deficit or surplus.

cyclical unemployment   A type of *unemployment* caused by insufficient total spending (insufficient *aggregate demand*) and which typically begins in the *recession* phase of the *business cycle*.

deadweight loss   (See *efficiency loss*.)

debit   An accounting entry that either decreases the value of an *asset* or increases the value of a *liability* (by increasing the size of an amount already owed).

debt crisis   An economic crisis in which government debt has risen so high that the government is unable to borrow any more money due to people losing faith in the government's ability to repay. Leads to either massive spending cuts or large tax increases, either of which will likely plunge the economy into a *recession*.

defaults   Situations in which borrowers stop making loan payments or do not pay back loans that they took out and are now due.

deflating   The process of using a *price index* to decrease (deflate) a given year's *nominal gross domestic product* down to the smaller value of its *real gross domestic product*; only applicable if the given year's *price level* is higher than the price level that prevailed during the price index's *base year*. Compare with *inflating*.

deflation   A decline in the general level of *prices* in an economy; a decline in an economy's *price level*.

demand   A schedule or curve that shows the various amounts of a product that consumers are willing and able to purchase at each of a series of possible *prices* during a specified period of time.

demand curve   A curve that illustrates the *demand* for a product by showing how each possible *price* (on the *vertical axis*) is associated with a specific *quantity demanded* (on the *horizontal axis*).

demand factor (in growth)   The requirement that *aggregate demand* increase as fast as *potential output* if *economic growth* is to proceed as quickly as possible.

demand management   The use of *fiscal policy* and *monetary policy* to increase or decrease *aggregate demand*.

demand-pull inflation   Increases in the *price level* (*inflation*) resulting from increases in *aggregate demand*.

demand schedule   A table of numbers showing the amounts of a *good* or *service* buyers are willing and able to purchase at various *prices* over a specified period of time.

demand shocks   Sudden, unexpected changes in demand.

demand-side market failures   Underallocations of resources that occur when private demand curves understate consumers' full willingness to pay for a *good* or *service*.

dependent variable   A variable that changes as a consequence of a change in some other (independent) variable; the "effect" or outcome.

depository institutions   Firms that accept deposits of *money* from the public (businesses and persons); *commercial banks*, *savings and loan associations*, *mutual savings banks*, and *credit unions*.

depreciation   (See *consumption of fixed capital*.)

depreciation (of the dollar)   A decrease in the value of the dollar relative to another currency, so a dollar buys a smaller amount of the foreign currency and therefore of foreign goods.

deregulation   The removal of most or even all of the government regulation and laws designed to supervise an industry. Sometimes undertaken to combat *regulatory capture*.

determinants of aggregate demand   Factors such as consumption spending, *investment*, government spending, and *net exports* that, if they change, shift the aggregate demand curve.

determinants of aggregate supply Factors such as input prices, *productivity*, and the legal-institutional environment that, if they change, shift the aggregate supply curve.

determinants of demand Factors other than *price* that determine the quantities demanded of a *good* or *service*. Also referred to as "demand shifters" because changes in the determinants of demand will cause the *demand curve* to shift either right or left.

determinants of supply Factors other than *price* that determine the quantities supplied of a *good* or *service*. Also referred to as "supply shifters" because changes in the determinants of supply will cause the *supply curve* to shift either right or left.

developing countries (Web chapter) Many countries of Africa, Asia, and Latin America that are characterized by lack of capital goods, use of nonadvanced technologies, low literacy rates, high unemployment, relatively rapid population growth, and labor forces heavily committed to agriculture.

differentiated product A product that differs physically or in some other way from the similar products produced by other *firms*; a product such that buyers are not indifferent to the seller when the *price* charged by all sellers is the same.

diminishing marginal returns (See *law of diminishing returns*.)

diminishing marginal utility (See *law of diminishing marginal utility*.)

direct foreign investment (See *foreign direct investment*.)

direct relationship The relationship between two variables that change in the same direction, for example, product *price* and quantity supplied; a positive relationship.

discount rate The interest rate that the *Federal Reserve Banks* charge on the loans they make to *commercial banks* and *thrift institutions*.

discouraged workers Employees who have left the *labor force* because they have not been able to find employment.

discretionary fiscal policy Deliberate changes in taxes (tax rates) and government spending to promote full employment, price stability, and economic growth.

disinflation A reduction in the rate of *inflation*.

disposable income (DI) *Personal income* less personal taxes; income available for *personal consumption expenditures* and *personal saving*.

dissaving Spending for *consumer goods* in excess of *disposable income*; the amount by which *personal consumption expenditures* exceed disposable income.

diversifiable risk Investment *risk* that investors can reduce via *diversification*; also called idiosyncratic risk.

diversification The strategy of investing in a large number of investments in order to reduce the overall risk to an entire investment *portfolio*.

dividends Payments by a corporation of all or part of its profit to its stockholders (the corporate owners).

division of labor The separation of the work required to produce a product into a number of different tasks that are performed by different workers; *specialization* of workers.

Doha Development Agenda The latest, uncompleted (as of late 2013) sequence of trade negotiations by members of the *World Trade Organization*; named after Doha, Qatar, where the set of negotiations began. Also called the Doha Round.

dollar votes The "votes" that consumers cast for the production of preferred products when they purchase those products rather than the alternatives that were also available.

domestic capital formation The process of adding to a nation's stock of *capital* by saving and investing part of *domestic output*.

domestic output *Gross* (or net) *domestic product*; the total output of *final goods* and final *services* produced in the economy.

domestic price The *price* of a *good* or *service* within a country, determined by domestic demand and supply.

dumping The sale of a product in a foreign country at *prices* either below cost or below the prices commonly charged at home.

durable good A consumer good with an expected life (use) of three or more years.

earmarks Narrow, specially designated spending authorizations placed in broad legislation by senators and representatives for the purpose of providing benefits to *firms* and organizations within their constituencies. Earmarked projects are exempt from competitive bidding and normal evaluation procedures.

earnings The money income received by a worker; equal to the *wage* (rate) multiplied by the amount of time worked.

economic cost A payment that must be made to obtain and retain the *services* of a *resource*; the income a *firm* must provide to a resource supplier to attract the resource away from an alternative use; equal to the quantity of other products that cannot be produced when resources are instead used to make a particular product.

economic efficiency The use of the minimum necessary resources to obtain the socially optimal amounts of *goods* and *services*; entails both *productive efficiency* and *allocative efficiency*.

economic growth (1) An outward shift in the *production possibilities curve* that results from an increase in resource supplies or quality or an improvement in *technology*; (2) an increase of real output (*gross domestic product*) or real output per capita.

economic immigrants International migrants who have moved from one country to another to obtain economic gains such as better employment opportunities.

economic investment (See *investment*.)

economic law An *economic principle* that has stood the test of time.

economic model A simplified picture of economic reality; an abstract generalization.

economic perspective A viewpoint that envisions individuals and institutions making rational decisions by comparing the marginal benefits and marginal costs associated with their actions.

economic policy A course of action intended to correct or avoid a problem.

economic principle A widely accepted generalization about the economic behavior of individuals or institutions.

economic profit The return flowing to those who provide the economy with the *economic resource* of *entrepreneurial ability*; the *total revenue* of a *firm* less its *economic costs* (which include both *explicit costs* and *implicit costs*); also called "pure profit" and "above-normal profit."

economic resources The *land, labor, capital*, and *entrepreneurial ability* that are used to produce *goods* and *services*; the *factors of production*.

economics The social science concerned with how individuals, institutions, and society make optimal (best) choices under conditions of scarcity.

economic system A particular set of institutional arrangements and a coordinating mechanism for solving the *economizing problem*; a method of organizing an economy, of which the *market system* and the *command system* are the two general types.

economic theory A statement of a cause-effect relationship; when accepted by all or nearly all economists, an *economic principle*.

economizing problem The choices necessitated because society's economic wants for *goods* and *services* are unlimited but the resources available to satisfy these wants are limited (scarce).

efficiency factor (in growth) The capacity of an economy to achieve *allocative efficiency* and *productive efficiency* and thereby fulfill the potential for growth that the *supply factors (of growth)* make possible; the capacity of an economy to achieve *economic efficiency* and thereby reach the optimal point on its *production possibilities curve*.

efficiency loss Reductions in combined consumer and producer surplus caused by an underallocation or overallocation of resources to the production of a *good* or *service*. Also called *deadweight loss*.

efficiency loss of a tax The loss of *net benefits* to society because a tax reduces the production and consumption of a taxed good below the level of *allocative efficiency*. Also called the *deadweight loss* of the tax.

efficiency wage An above-market (above-equilibrium) *wage* that minimizes wage costs per unit of output by encouraging greater effort or reducing turnover.

efficient allocation of resources That distribution of society's scarce *resources* that produces the socially optimal mix of output; *allocative efficiency*.

Electronic Benefit Transfer (EBT) cards Debit cards used by the federal government to deliver food money to low-income recipients as part of the *Supplemental Nutrition Assistance Program (SNAP)*. The same cards are also used by some states to deliver the benefits issued by a variety of additional *public assistance programs*.

electronic payments Purchases made by transferring funds electronically. Examples include credit cards, debit cards, *Electronic Benefit Transfer (EBT) cards*, Fedwire transfers, automated clearinghouse transactions (ACHs), payments via the PayPal system, and payments made through stored-value cards.

emigration The exit (outflow) of residents from a country to reside in foreign countries.

employer mandate The requirement under the *Patient Protection and Affordable Care Act (PPACA)* of 2010 that firms with 50 or more employees pay for insurance policies for their employees or face a fine of $2,000 per employee per year. Firms with fewer than 50 employees are exempt.

employment rate The percentage of the *labor force* employed at any time.

entitlement programs Government programs such as *social insurance, Medicare*, and *Medicaid* that guarantee (entitle) particular levels of transfer payments or noncash benefits to all who fit the programs' criteria.

entrepreneurial ability The human resource that combines the other *economic resources* of *land, labor*, and *capital* to produce new products or make innovations in the production of existing products; provided by *entrepreneurs*.

entrepreneurs Individuals who provide *entrepreneurial ability* to *firms* by setting strategy, advancing innovations, and bearing the financial risk if their firms do poorly.

equality-efficiency trade-off The decrease in *economic efficiency* that may accompany a decrease in *income inequality*; the presumption that some income inequality is required to achieve economic efficiency.

equation of exchange $MV = PQ$, in which M is the supply of money, V is the *velocity* of money, P is the *price level*, and Q is the physical volume of *final goods* and final *services* produced.

equilibrium GDP (See *equilibrium real domestic output*.)

equilibrium position In the indifference curve model, the combination of two goods at which a consumer maximizes his or her *utility* (reaches the highest attainable *indifference curve*), given a limited amount to spend (a *budget constraint*).

equilibrium price The *price* in a competitive market at which the *quantity demanded* and the *quantity supplied* are equal, there is neither a shortage nor a surplus, and there is no tendency for price to rise or fall.

equilibrium price level In the *aggregate demand–aggregate supply (AD-AS) model*, the *price level* at which *aggregate demand* equals *aggregate supply*; the price level at which the aggregate demand curve intersects the aggregate supply curve.

equilibrium quantity (1) The quantity at which the intentions of buyers and sellers in a particular market match at a particular *price* such that the *quantity demanded* and the *quantity supplied* are equal; (2) the profit-maximizing output of a *firm*.

equilibrium real domestic output The *gross domestic product* at which the total quantity of *final goods* and final *services* purchased (*aggregate expenditures*) is equal to the total quantity of final goods services produced (the real domestic output); the real domestic output at which the aggregate demand curve intersects the aggregate supply curve.

equilibrium real output   (See *equilibrium real domestic output.*)

equilibrium world price   The *price* of an internationally traded product that equates the quantity of the product demanded by importers with the quantity of the product supplied by exporters; the price determined at the intersection of the export supply curve and the import demand curve.

euro   The common *currency* unit used by 17 European nations (as of mid-2013) in the *eurozone,* which consists of Austria, Belgium, Cyprus, Estonia, Finland, France, Germany, Greece, Ireland, Italy, Luxembourg, Malta, the Netherlands, Portugal, Slovakia, Slovenia, and Spain.

European Union (EU)   An association of 28 European nations (as of mid-2013) that has eliminated tariffs and quotas among them, established common tariffs for imported goods from outside the member nations, eliminated barriers to the free movement of capital, and created other common economic policies.

eurozone   The 17 nations (as of 2013) of the 28-member (as of 2013) *European Union* that use the *euro* as their common *currency.* The eurozone countries are Austria, Belgium, Cyprus, Estonia, Finland, France, Germany, Greece, Ireland, Italy, Luxembourg, Malta, the Netherlands, Portugal, Slovakia, Slovenia, and Spain.

excess reserves   The amount by which a *commercial bank*'s or *thrift institution*'s *actual reserves* exceed its *required reserves;* actual reserves minus required reserves.

exchange controls   (See *foreign exchange controls.*)

exchange rate   The *rate of exchange* of one nation's *currency* for another nation's currency.

exchange-rate appreciation   An increase in the value of a nation's *currency* in *foreign exchange markets;* an increase in the *rate of exchange* with foreign currencies.

exchange-rate depreciation   A decrease in the value of a nation's *currency* in *foreign exchange markets;* a decrease in the *rate of exchange* with foreign currencies.

exchange-rate determinant   Any factor other than the *rate of exchange* that determines a *currency*'s demand and supply in the *foreign exchange market.*

excise tax   A tax levied on the production of a specific product or on the quantity of the product purchased.

excludability   The characteristic of a *private good,* for which the seller can keep nonbuyers from obtaining the good.

exhaustive expenditure   An expenditure by government resulting directly in the employment of *economic resources* and in the absorption by government of the *goods* and *services* those resources produce; a *government purchase.*

exit mechanism   The method of resolving workplace dissatisfaction by quitting one's job and searching for another.

expanding industry   An *industry* whose total output is increasing because positive *economic profits* lead many *firms* to enter the industry.

expansion   The phase of the *business cycle* in which *real GDP, income,* and employment rise.

expansionary fiscal policy   An increase in *government purchases* of *goods* and *services,* a decrease in *net taxes,* or some combination of the two for the purpose of increasing *aggregate demand* and expanding real output.

expansionary monetary policy   *Federal Reserve System* actions to increase the *money supply,* lower *interest rates,* and expand *real GDP;* an easy money policy.

expectations   The anticipations of consumers, *firms,* and others about future economic conditions.

expenditures approach   The method that adds all expenditures made for *final goods* and final *services* to measure the *gross domestic product.*

expenditures-output approach   (See *aggregate expenditures–domestic output approach.*)

explicit cost   The monetary payment made by a *firm* to an outsider to obtain a *resource.*

exports   *Goods* and *services* produced in a nation and sold to buyers in other nations.

export subsidy   A government payment to a domestic producer to enable the *firm* to reduce the *price* of a *good* or *service* to foreign buyers.

export supply curve   An upward-sloping curve that shows the amount of a product that domestic *firms* will export at each *world price* that is above the *domestic price.*

export transaction   A sale of a *good* or *service* that increases the amount of foreign currency flowing to a nation's citizens, *firms,* and government.

external benefit   (See *positive externality.*)

external cost   (See *negative externality.*)

external debt   Private or public debt owed to foreign citizens, firms, and institutions.

externality   A cost or benefit from production or consumption that accrues to to someone other than the immediate buyers and sellers of the product being produced or consumed (see *negative externality* and *positive externality*).

external public debt   The portion of the public debt owed to foreign citizens, *firms,* and institutions.

face value   The numerical value printed or inscribed on coins or paper money.

factors of production   The four *economic resources: land, labor, capital,* and *entrepreneurial ability.*

fallacy of composition   The false notion that what is true for the individual (or part) is necessarily true for the group (or whole).

FDIC   (See *Federal Deposit Insurance Corporation.*)

Federal Deposit Insurance Corporation (FDIC)   The federally chartered corporation that insures the deposit liabilities (up to $250,000 per account) of *commercial banks* and *thrift institutions* (excluding *credit unions*, whose deposits are insured by the *National Credit Union Administration*).

federal funds rate   The interest rate that U.S. banks and other depository institutions charge one another on overnight loans made out of their *excess reserves*.

federal government   The government of the United States, as distinct from the state and local governments.

Federal Open Market Committee (FOMC)   The 12-member group within the *Federal Reserve System* that decides U.S. *monetary policy* and how it is executed through *open-market operations* (in which the Fed buys and sells U.S. government securities to adjust the *money supply*.)

Federal Reserve Banks   The 12 banks chartered by the U.S. government that collectively act as the *central bank* of the United States. They set monetary policy and regulate the private banking system under the direction of the *Board of Governors* and the *Federal Open Market Committee*. Each of the 12 is a *quasi-public bank* and acts as a *banker's bank* in its designated geographic region.

Federal Reserve Note   Paper money issued by the *Federal Reserve Banks*.

Federal Reserve System   The U.S. central bank, consisting of the *Board of Governors* of the Federal Reserve and the 12 *Federal Reserve Banks*, which controls the lending activity of the nation's banks and thrifts and thus the *money supply*; commonly referred to as the "Fed."

fiat money   Anything that is *money* because government has decreed it to be money.

final goods   Goods that have been purchased for final use (rather than for resale or further processing or manufacturing.)

financial capital   (See *money capital*.)

financial investment   The purchase of a financial asset (such as a *stock*, *bond*, or *mutual fund*) or real asset (such as a house, land, or factories) or the building of such assets in the expectation of financial gain.

financial services industry   The broad category of *firms* that provide financial products and services to help *households* and businesses earn *interest*, receive *dividends*, obtain *capital gains*, insure against losses, and plan for retirement. Includes *commercial banks*, *thrift institutions*, insurance companies, mutual fund companies, pension funds, investment banks, and *securities* firms.

firm   An organization that employs resources to produce a *good* or *service* for profit and owns and operates one or more *plants*.

first-mover advantage   In *game theory*, the benefit obtained by the party that moves first in a *sequential game*.

fiscal policy   Changes in government spending and tax collections designed to achieve full employment, price stability, and economic growth; also called *discretionary fiscal policy*.

fixed exchange rate   A *rate of exchange* that is set in some way and therefore prevented from rising or falling with changes in currency supply and demand.

flexible exchange rate   A *rate of exchange* that is determined by the international demand for and supply of a nation's money and that is consequently free to rise or fall because it is not subject to *currency interventions*. Also referred to as a "floating exchange rate."

flexible prices   Product *prices* that freely move upward or downward when product demand or supply changes.

floating exchange rate   (See *flexible exchange rate*.)

follower countries   As it relates to *economic growth*, countries that adopt advanced technologies that previously were developed and used by *leader countries*.

foreign competition   (See *import competition*.)

foreign direct investment   (Web chapter) *Financial investments* made to obtain a lasting ownership interest in *firms* operating outside the economy of the investor; may involve purchasing existing assets or building new production facilities.

foreign exchange controls   Restrictions that a government may impose over the quantity of foreign currency demanded by its citizens and *firms* and over the *rate of exchange* as a way to limit the nation's quantity of *outpayments* relative to its quantity of *inpayments* (in order to eliminate a *payments deficit*).

foreign exchange market   A market in which the money (currency) of one nation can be used to purchase (can be exchanged for) the money of another nation; a currency market.

foreign exchange rate   (See *rate of exchange*.)

foreign purchases effect   The inverse relationship between the *net exports* of an economy and its *price level* relative to foreign price levels.

45° (degree) line   The reference line in a two-dimensional graph that shows equality between the variable measured on the *horizontal axis* and the variable measured on the *vertical axis*. In the *aggregate expenditures model*, the line along which the value of output (measured horizontally) is equal to the value of *aggregate expenditures* (measured vertically).

forward commitment   A policy statement by a *central bank* indicating that it will continue to pursue a *monetary policy* action until a certain date is reached or until some particular threshold has been reached (for instance, the unemployment rate falling below, say, seven percent).

fractional reserve banking system   A system in which *commercial banks* and *thrift institutions* hold less than 100 percent of their checkable-deposit liabilities as reserves of *currency* held in bank vaults or as deposits at the *central bank*.

freedom of choice   The freedom of owners of property resources to employ or dispose of them as they see fit, of workers to enter any line of work for which they are qualified, and of consumers to spend their incomes in a manner that they think is appropriate.

freedom of enterprise The freedom of *firms* to obtain economic resources, to use those resources to produce products of the firm's own choosing, and to sell their products in markets of their choice.

free-rider problem The inability of potential providers of an economically desirable *good* or *service* to obtain payment from those who benefit, because of *nonexcludability*.

free trade The absence of artificial (government-imposed) barriers to trade among individuals and *firms* in different nations.

frictional unemployment A type of unemployment caused by workers voluntarily changing jobs and by temporary layoffs; unemployed workers between jobs.

fringe benefits The forms of compensation other than *wages* that employees receive from their employers. Includes pensions, medical and dental insurance, paid vacation, and sick leave.

full employment (1) The use of all available resources to produce want-satisfying *goods* and *services*; (2) the situation in which the *unemployment rate* is equal to the *full-employment rate of unemployment*; there exist *frictional unemployment* and *structural unemployment* but not *cyclical unemployment*; and *real GDP* equals *potential output*.

full-employment rate of unemployment The *unemployment rate* at which there is no *cyclical unemployment* of the *labor force*; equal to between 5 and 6 percent in the United States because some *frictional* and *structural unemployment* are unavoidable.

functional distribution of income The manner in which *national income* is divided among the functions performed to earn it (or the kinds of resources provided to earn it); the division of national income into wages and salaries, proprietors' income, corporate profits, interest, and rent.

future value The amount to which some current amount of *money* will grow if *interest* earned on the amount is left to compound over time. (*See compound interest.*)

G8 nations A group of eight major nations (Canada, France, Germany, Italy, Japan, Russia, United Kingdom, and United States) whose leaders meet regularly to discuss common economic problems and ways in which they might coordinate economic policies.

gains from trade The extra output that trading partners obtain through specialization of production and exchange of *goods* and *services*.

GDP (*See gross domestic product.*)

GDP gap Actual *gross domestic product* minus *potential output*; may be either a positive amount (a *positive GDP gap*) or a negative amount (a *negative GDP gap*).

GDP price index A *price index* for all the *goods* and *services* that make up the *gross domestic product*; the price index used to adjust *nominal gross domestic product* to *real gross domestic product*.

General Agreement on Tariffs and Trade (GATT) The international agreement reached in 1947 in which 23 nations agreed to eliminate *import quotas*, negotiate reductions in *tariff* rates, and give each other equal and nondiscriminatory treatment.

It now includes most nations and has become the *World Trade Organization*.

gold standard A historical system of fixed exchange rates in which nations defined their currencies in terms of gold, maintained fixed relationships between their stocks of gold and their money supplies, and allowed gold to be freely exported and imported.

good Merchandise; an article of trade; a manufactured item offered for sale to consumers.

government failure Inefficiencies in resource allocation caused by problems in the operation of the *public sector* (government). Specific examples include the *principal-agent problem*, the *special-interest effect*, the *collective-action problem*, *rent seeking*, and *political corruption*.

government purchases (G) Expenditures by government for *goods* and *services* that government consumes in providing public services as well as expenditures for publicly owned capital that has a long lifetime; the expenditures of all governments in the economy for those *final goods* and final *services*.

government transfer payment Any disbursement of money by the government for which the government receives no currently produced *good* or *service* in return. Includes payments made by *public assistance programs* ("welfare") and *Social Security*.

gross domestic product (GDP) The total market value of all *final goods* and final *services* produced annually within the boundaries of a nation.

gross private domestic investment (I_g) Expenditures for newly produced *capital goods* (such as machinery, equipment, tools, and buildings) and for additions to inventories.

growth accounting The bookkeeping of the supply-side elements such as productivity and labor inputs that contribute to changes in *real GDP* over some specific time period.

guiding function of prices The ability of *price* changes to bring about changes in the quantities of products and resources demanded and supplied.

horizontal axis The "left-right" or "west-east" measurement line on a graph or grid.

households Economic entities (of one or more persons occupying a housing unit) that provide *resources* to the economy and use the *income* received to purchase *goods* and *services* that satisfy economic wants.

human capital The knowledge and skills that make a person productive.

human capital investment Any expenditure to improve the education, skills, health, or mobility of workers; normally undertaken with an expectation of greater productivity and thus a positive return on the investment.

hyperinflation A very rapid rise in the *price level*; an extremely high rate of *inflation*.

hypothesis A tentative explanation of cause and effect that requires testing to determine whether or not it is true.

illegal immigrants People who have entered a country unlawfully to reside there; also called unauthorized immigrants.

IMF (See *International Monetary Fund.*)

immediate market period The length of time during which the producers of a product are unable to change the quantity supplied in response to a change in price and in which there is a *perfectly inelastic supply.*

immediate short-run aggregate supply curve An *aggregate supply* curve for which real *output*, but not the *price level*, changes when the *aggregate demand* curve shifts; a horizontal *aggregate supply* curve that implies an inflexible price level.

immigration The inflow of people into a country from another country. The immigrants may be either *legal immigrants* or *illegal immigrants.*

import competition The competition that domestic *firms* encounter from the products and *services* of foreign producers.

import demand curve A downsloping curve showing the amount of a product that an economy will import at each *world price* below the *domestic price.*

import quota A limit imposed by a nation on the quantity (or total value) of a good that may be imported during some period of time.

imports Spending by individuals, *firms*, and governments for *goods* and *services* produced in foreign nations.

import transaction The purchase of a *good* or *service* that decreases the amount of foreign money held by the citizens, *firms*, or government of a nation.

incentive function The inducement that an increase in the price of a commodity gives to sellers to make more of it available (and conversely for a decrease in *price*), and the inducement that an increase in price offers to buyers to purchase smaller quantities (and conversely for a decrease in price).

income A flow of dollars (or *purchasing power*) per unit of time derived from the use of human or property resources.

income approach The method that adds all the *income* generated by the production of *final goods* and final *services* to measure the *gross domestic product.*

income inequality The unequal distribution of an economy's total *income* among *households* or families.

income-maintenance system A group of government programs designed to eliminate poverty and reduce inequality in the distribution of income.

income mobility The extent to which *income* receivers move from one part of the income distribution to another over some period of time.

increase in demand An increase in the *quantity demanded* of a *good* or *service* at every price; a shift of the *demand curve* to the right. Caused by a change in one or more of the *determinants of demand.*

increase in supply An increase in the *quantity supplied* of a *good* or *service* at every price; a shift of the *supply curve* to the right. Caused by a change in one or more of the *determinants of supply.*

increasing marginal returns An increase in the *marginal product* of a resource as successive units of the resource are employed.

independent variable The variable causing a change in some other (dependent) variable.

index funds *Mutual funds* whose *portfolios* exactly match a stock or bond index (a collection of *stocks* or *bonds* meant to capture the overall behavior of a particular category of investments) such as the Standard & Poor's 500 Index or the Russell 3000 Index.

individual demand The demand schedule or *demand curve* of a single buyer.

individual supply The supply schedule or *supply curve* of a single seller.

industrially advanced countries (Web chapter) High-income countries such as the United States, Canada, Japan, and the nations of western Europe that have highly developed *market economies* based on large stocks of technologically advanced *capital goods* and skilled labor forces.

industry A group of (one or more) *firms* that produce identical or similar products.

inflating The process of using a *price index* to increase (inflate) a given year's *nominal gross domestic product* up to the larger value of its *real gross domestic product;* only applicable if the given year's *price level* is lower than the price level that prevailed during the price index's *base year.* Compare with *deflating.*

inflation A rise in the general level of *prices* in an economy; an increase in an economy's *price level.*

inflationary expectations The belief of workers, *firms*, and consumers about future rates of *inflation.*

inflationary expenditure gap In the *aggregate-expenditures model*, the amount by which the *aggregate expenditures schedule* must shift downward to decrease the *nominal GDP* to its full-employment noninflationary level.

inflation premium The component of the *nominal interest rate* that reflects anticipated *inflation.*

inflation targeting The annual statement by a *central bank* of a goal for a specific range of *inflation* in a future year, coupled with *monetary policy* designed to achieve the goal.

inflexible prices Product *prices* that remain in place (at least for a while) even though *supply* or *demand* has changed; stuck prices or sticky prices.

information technology New and more efficient methods of delivering and receiving information through the use of computers, Wi-Fi networks, wireless phones, and the Internet.

infrastructure The interconnected network of large-scale *capital goods* (such as roads, sewers, electrical grids, railways, ports, and the Internet) needed to operate a technologically advanced economy.

injection An addition of spending into the income-expenditure stream: any increment to *consumption, investment, government purchases*, or *net exports.*

in-kind transfer   The distribution by government of *goods* and *services* to individuals for which the government receives no currently produced *good* or *service* in return. Also called a noncash transfer because ordinary *transfer payments* are transfers of *money* rather than goods and services.

inpayments   The receipts of domestic or foreign money that individuals, *firms*, and governments of one nation obtain from the sale of *goods* and *services* abroad, as investment income and remittances, and from foreign purchases of domestic assets.

insurable risk   An eventuality for which both the frequency and magnitude of potential losses can be estimated with considerable accuracy. Insurance companies are willing to sell insurance against such risks.

interest   The payment made for the use of (borrowed) *money.*

interest income   Payments of income to those who supply the economy with *capital.*

interest on reserves   The payment by a *central bank* of *interest* on the deposits (*required reserves* plus *excess reserves,* if any) held by *commercial banks* at the central bank.

interest rate   The annual rate at which *interest* is paid; a percentage of the borrowed amount.

interest-rate effect   The tendency for increases in the *price level* to increase the demand for money, raise interest rates, and, as a result, reduce total spending and real output in the economy (and the reverse for *price-level* decreases).

intermediate goods   Products that are purchased for resale or further processing or manufacturing.

internally held public debt   *Public debt* owed to citizens, *firms*, and institutions of the same nation that issued the debt.

international balance of payments   (See *balance of payments.*)

international balance-of-payments deficit   (See *balance-of-payments deficit.*)

international balance-of-payments surplus   (See *balance-of-payments surplus.*)

international gold standard   (See *gold standard.*)

International Monetary Fund (IMF)   The international association of nations that was formed after the Second World War to make loans of foreign monies to nations with temporary *balance of payments deficits* and, until the early 1970s, manage the international system of pegged exchange rates agreed upon at the Bretton Woods conference. It now mainly makes loans to nations facing possible defaults on private and government loans.

international monetary reserves   The foreign currencies and other assets such as gold that a nation can use to settle a *balance-of-payments deficit.*

international value of the dollar   The *price* that must be paid in foreign currency (money) to obtain one U.S. dollar.

intertemporal choice   A choice between the benefits obtainable in one time period and the benefits obtainable in a later time period; the comparisons that individuals and society must make between the reductions in current consumption that are necessary to fund current investments and the higher levels of future consumption that those current investments will produce.

intrinsic value   The market value of the metal within a coin.

inventories   Goods that have been produced but remain unsold.

inverse relationship   The relationship between two variables that change in opposite directions, for example, product *price* and quantity demanded; a negative relationship.

investment   In economics, spending for the production and accumulation of *capital* and additions to *inventories.* (For contrast, see *financial investment.*)

investment banks   *Firms* that help corporations and government raise money by selling *stocks* and *bonds;* they also offer advisory services for corporate mergers and acquisitions in addition to providing brokerage services and financial advice.

investment demand curve   A curve that shows the amounts of *investment* demanded by an economy at a series of *real interest rates.*

investment goods   Same as *capital* and *capital goods.*

investment in human capital   (See *human capital investment.*)

investment schedule   A table of numbers that shows the amounts *firms* plan to invest at various possible values of *real gross domestic product.*

"invisible hand"   The tendency of *competition* to cause individuals and *firms* to unintentionally but quite effectively promote the interests of society even when each individual or firm is only attempting to pursue its own interests.

Joint Economic Committee (JEC)   Committee of senators and representatives that investigates economic problems of national interest.

labor   Any mental or physical exertion on the part of a human being that is used in the production of a *good* or *service.* One of the four *economic resources.*

labor force   Persons 16 years of age and older who are not in institutions and who are employed or are unemployed and seeking work.

labor-force participation rate   The percentage of the working-age population that is actually in the *labor force.*

labor-intensive goods   Products requiring relatively large amounts of *labor* to produce.

labor productivity   Total output divided by the quantity of labor employed to produce it; the *average product* of labor or output per hour of work.

Laffer Curve   A curve relating government tax rates and tax revenues and on which a particular tax rate (between zero and 100 percent) maximizes tax revenues.

laissez-faire capitalism   A hypothetical *economic system* in which the government's economic role is limited to protecting private property and establishing a legal environment appropriate to the operation of *markets* in which only mutually agreeable transactions would take place between buyers and sellers; sometimes referred to as "pure *capitalism*."

land In addition to the part of the earth's surface not covered by water, this term refers to any and all natural resources ("free gifts of nature") that are used to produce *goods* and *services*. Thus, it includes the oceans, sunshine, coal deposits, forests, the electromagnetic spectrum, and *fisheries*. Note that land is one of the four *economic resources*.

land-intensive goods Products requiring relatively large amounts of land to produce.

land reform (Web chapter) Policy changes aimed at creating a more efficient distribution of land ownership in developing countries. Can involve everything from government purchasing large land estates and dividing the land into smaller farms to consolidating tiny plots of land into larger, more efficient private farms.

law of demand The principle that, other things equal, an increase in a product's *price* will reduce the quantity of it demanded, and conversely for a decrease in price.

law of diminishing marginal utility The principle that as a consumer increases the consumption of a *good* or *service*, the *marginal utility* obtained from each additional unit of the good or service decreases.

law of diminishing returns The principle that as successive increments of a variable *resource* are added to a fixed resource, the *marginal product* of the variable resource will eventually decrease.

law of increasing opportunity costs The principle that as the production of a good increases, the *opportunity cost* of producing an additional unit rises.

law of supply The principle that, other things equal, an increase in the *price* of a product will increase the quantity of it supplied, and conversely for a price decrease.

leader countries As it relates to *economic growth*, countries that develop and use the most advanced technologies, which then become available to *follower countries*.

leakage (1) A withdrawal of potential spending from the income-expenditures stream via *saving*, tax payments, or *imports*; (2) a withdrawal that reduces the lending potential of the banking system.

legal cartel theory of regulation The hypothesis that some *industries* seek regulation or want to maintain regulation so that they may form or maintain a legal *cartel*.

legal immigrant A person who lawfully enters a country for the purpose of residing there.

legal tender Any form of *currency* that by law must be accepted by creditors (lenders) for the settlement of a financial debt; a nation's official currency is legal tender within its own borders.

liability A debt with a monetary value; an amount owed by a *firm* or an individual.

limited liability rule A law that limits the potential losses that an investor in a *corporation* may suffer to the amount that she paid for her shares in the corporation. Encourages *financial investment* by limiting risk.

liquidity The degree to which an asset can be converted quickly into cash with little or no loss of purchasing power. *Money* is said to be perfectly liquid, whereas other assets have lesser degrees of liquidity.

liquidity trap A situation in a severe *recession* in which the *central bank's* injection of additional reserves into the banking system has little or no additional positive impact on lending, borrowing, *investment*, or *aggregate demand*.

loanable funds *Money* available for lending and borrowing.

loanable funds theory of interest The concept that the supply of and demand for *loanable funds* determine the equilibrium rate of *interest*.

loan guarantees A type of investment *subsidy* in which the government agrees to guarantee (pay off) the money borrowed by a private company to fund investment projects if the private company itself fails to repay the loan.

logrolling The trading of votes by legislators to secure favorable outcomes on decisions concerning the provision of *public goods* and *quasi-public goods*.

long run (1) In *microeconomics*, a period of time long enough to enable producers of a product to change the quantities of all the resources they employ, so that all resources and costs are variable and no resources or costs are fixed. (2) In *macroeconomics*, a period sufficiently long for *nominal wages* and other input *prices* to change in response to a change in a nation's *price level*.

long-run aggregate supply curve The *aggregate supply* curve associated with a time period in which input *prices* (especially *nominal wages*) are fully responsive to changes in the *price level*.

long-run supply curve As it applies to *macroeconomics*, a *supply curve* for which *price*, but not real output, changes when the *demand curves* shifts; a vertical supply curve that implies fully flexible *prices*.

long-run vertical Phillips Curve The *Phillips Curve* after all *nominal wages* have adjusted to changes in the rate of *inflation*; a line emanating straight upward at the economy's *natural rate of unemployment*.

lump-sum tax A tax that collects a constant amount (the tax revenue of government is the same) at all levels of *GDP*.

M1 The most narrowly defined *money supply*, equal to *currency* in the hands of the public and the *checkable deposits* of commercial banks and *thrift institutions*.

M2 A more broadly defined *money supply*, equal to *M1* plus *noncheckable savings accounts* (including *money market deposit accounts*), small *time deposits* (deposits of less than $100,000), and individual *money market mutual fund* balances.

macroeconomics The part of *economics* concerned with the performance and behavior of the economy as a whole. Focuses on *economic growth*, the *business cycle*, *interest rates*, *inflation*, and the behavior of major economic *aggregates* such as the household, business, and government sectors.

managed floating exchange rate   An *exchange rate* that is allowed to change (float) as a result of changes in *currency* supply and demand but at times is altered (managed) by governments via their buying and selling of particular currencies.

marginal analysis   The comparison of *marginal* ("extra" or "additional") *benefits* and *marginal costs*, usually for decision making.

marginal benefit (MB)   The extra (additional) benefit of consuming 1 more unit of some *good* or *service;* the change in total benefit when 1 more unit is consumed.

marginal cost (MC)   The extra (additional) cost of producing 1 more unit of output; equal to the change in *total cost* divided by the change in output (and, in the short run, to the change in total *variable cost* divided by the change in output).

marginal cost–marginal benefit rule   As it applies to *cost-benefit analysis*, the tenet that a government project or program should be expanded to the point where the *marginal cost* and *marginal benefit* of additional expenditures are equal.

marginal propensity to consume (MPC)   The fraction of any change in *disposable income* spent for *consumer goods;* equal to the change in consumption divided by the change in disposable income.

marginal propensity to save (MPS)   The fraction of any change in *disposable income* that *households* save; equal to the change in *saving* divided by the change in disposable income.

marginal rate of substitution (MRS)   The rate at which a consumer is willing to substitute one good for another (from a given combination of goods) and remain equally satisfied (have the same *total utility*); equal to the slope of a consumer's *indifference curve* at each point on the curve.

marginal revenue   The change in *total revenue* that results from the sale of 1 additional unit of a *firm*'s product; equal to the change in total revenue divided by the change in the quantity of the product sold.

marginal tax rate   The *tax* rate paid on an additional dollar of *income*.

marginal utility   The extra *utility* a consumer obtains from the consumption of 1 additional unit of a *good* or *service;* equal to the change in *total utility* divided by the change in the quantity consumed.

market   Any institution or mechanism that brings together buyers (demanders) and sellers (suppliers) of a particular *good* or *service*.

market demand   (See *total demand*.)

market economy   An economy in which *firms* determine how *resources* are allocated; an economy that uses a *market system*.

market failure   The inability of a *market* to bring about the allocation of *resources* that best satisfies the wants of society; in particular, the overallocation or underallocation of resources to the production of a particular *good* or *service* because of *externalities* or informational problems or because markets do not provide desired *public goods*.

market portfolio   The portfolio consisting of every financial asset (including every *stock* and *bond*) traded in the financial markets. Used to calculate *beta* (a measure of the degree of riskiness) for specific stocks, bonds, and mutual funds.

market system   (1) An *economic system* in which individuals own most *economic resources* and in which *markets* and *prices* serve as the dominant coordinating mechanism used to allocate those resources; *capitalism*. Compare with *command system*. (2) All the product and resource markets of a *market economy* and the relationships among them.

medium of exchange   Any item sellers generally accept and buyers generally use to pay for a *good* or *service; money;* a convenient means of exchanging goods and *services* without engaging in *barter*.

menu costs   The reluctance of *firms* to cut *prices* during *recessions* (that they think will be short-lived) because of the costs of altering and communicating their price reductions; named after the cost associated with printing new menus at restaurants.

microeconomics   The part of economics concerned with (1) decision making by individual units such as a *household*, a *firm*, or an *industry* and (2) individual markets, specific *goods* and *services*, and product and resource *prices*.

microfinance   (Web chapter) The provision of small loans and other financial services to low-income *entrepreneurs* and small-business owners in *developing countries*.

minimum wage   The lowest *wage* that employers may legally pay for an hour of work.

mixed economy   (See *market system*.)

modern economic growth   The historically recent phenomenon in which nations for the first time have experienced sustained increases in *real GDP per capita*.

monetarism   The macroeconomic view that the main cause of changes in aggregate output and the *price level* is fluctuations in the *money supply;* espoused by advocates of a *monetary rule*.

monetary multiplier   The multiple of its *excess reserves* by which the banking system can expand *checkable deposits* and thus the *money supply* by making new loans (or buying *securities*); equal to 1 divided by the *reserve requirement*.

monetary policy   A central bank's changing of the *money supply* to influence *interest* rates and assist the economy in achieving *price-level stability, full employment*, and *economic growth*.

monetary rule   (1) A set of guidelines to be followed by a *central bank* that wishes to adjust monetary policy over time to achieve goals such as promoting *economic growth*, encouraging *full employment*, and maintaining a stable *price level*. (2) The guidelines for conducting monetary policy suggested by *monetarism*. As traditionally formulated, the *money supply* should be expanded each year at the same annual rate as the potential rate of growth of *real gross domestic product;* the supply of money should be increased steadily between 3 and 5 percent per year. (Also see *Taylor rule*.)

money Any item that is generally acceptable to sellers in exchange for *goods* and *services*.

money capital *Money* available to purchase *capital*; simply *money*, as defined by economists.

money income (See *nominal income*.)

money market The *market* in which the *demand* for and the supply of *money* determine the *interest rate* (or the level of interest rates) in the economy.

money market deposit accounts (MMDAs) Interest-bearing accounts offered by *commercial banks* and *thrift institutions* that invest deposited funds into a variety of short-term *securities*. Depositors may write checks against their balances, but there are minimum-balance requirements as well as limits on the frequency of check writing and withdrawls.

money market mutual funds (MMMFs) *Mutual funds* that invest in short-term *securities*. Depositors can write checks in minimum amounts or more against their accounts.

money supply A nation's supply of *currency* plus *assets* with very high levels of *liquidity*. Different definitions of the money supply include different categories of highly liquid assets. *M1* uses a more restrictive definition; *M2*, a more broad definition.

moral hazard problem The possibility that individuals or institutions will change their behavior as the result of a contract or agreement. Example: A bank whose deposits are insured against losses may make riskier loans and investments.

mortgage-backed securities *Bonds* that represent claims to all or part of the monthly mortgage payments from the pools of mortgage loans made by leaders to borrowers to help them purchase residential property.

mortgage debt crisis The period beginning in late 2007 when thousands of homeowners defaulted on mortgage loans when they experienced a combination of higher mortgage interest rates and falling home *prices*.

multinational corporations Firms that own production facilities in two or more countries and produce and sell their products globally.

multiple counting Wrongly including the value of *intermediate goods* in the *gross domestic product*; counting the same *good* or *service* more than once.

multiplier The ratio of a change in *equilibrium GDP* to the change in *investment* or in any other component of *aggregate expenditures* or *aggregate demand*; the number by which a change in any such component must be multiplied to find the resulting change in equilibrium GDP.

multiplier effect The effect on *equilibrium GDP* of a change in *aggregate expenditures* or *aggregate demand* (caused by a change in the *consumption schedule*, *investment*, *government purchases*, or *net exports*).

mutual funds *Portfolios* of *stocks* and *bonds* selected and purchased by mutual fund companies, which finance the purchases by pooling money from thousands of individual investors; includes both *index funds* as well as *actively managed funds*. Fund returns (profits or losses) pass through to each fund's investors.

national bank In the United States, a *commercial bank* authorized to operate by the federal government.

National Credit Union Administration (NCUA) The federally chartered agency that insures *credit union* deposit liabilities (up to $250,000 per account).

national income Total *income* earned by *resource* suppliers for their contributions to *gross domestic product* plus *taxes on production and imports*; the sum of wages and salaries, *rent*, *interest*, *profit*, *proprietors' income*, and such taxes.

national income accounting The techniques used to measure the overall production of a country's economy as well as other related variables.

natural rate of unemployment (NRU) The *full-employment rate of unemployment*; the *unemployment rate* occurring when there is no cyclical unemployment and the economy is achieving its *potential output*; the unemployment rate at which actual *inflation* equals expected inflation.

near-money Financial *assets* that are not themselves a *medium of exchange* but that have extremely high *liquidity* and thus can be readily converted into *money*. Includes noncheckable *savings accounts*, *time deposits*, and short-term *U.S. government securities* plus savings bonds.

negative externality A cost imposed without compensation on third parties by the production or consumption of sellers or buyers. Example: A manufacturer dumps toxic chemicals into a river, killing fish prized by sports fishers; an external cost or a spillover cost.

negative GDP gap A situation in which actual *gross domestic product* is less than *potential output*. Also known as a recessionary output gap.

negative relationship (See *inverse relationship*.)

negative-sum game In *game theory*, a game in which the gains (+) and losses (−) add up to some amount less than zero; one party's losses exceed the other party's gains.

net benefits The total benefits of some activity or policy less the total costs of that activity or policy.

net domestic product (NDP) *Gross domestic product* less the part of the year's output that is needed to replace the *capital goods* worn out in producing the output; the nation's total output available for consumption or additions to the *capital stock*.

net exports (X_n) *Exports* minus *imports*.

net foreign factor income Receipts of *resource* income from the rest of the world minus payments of resource income to the rest of the world.

net investment income The *interest* and *dividend* income received by the residents of a nation from residents of other nations less the interest and dividend payments made by the residents of that nation to the residents of other nations.

net private domestic investment *Gross private domestic investment* less *consumption of fixed capital*; the addition to the nation's stock of *capital* during a year.

net taxes The *taxes* collected by government less *government transfer payments*.

net transfers The personal and government *transfer payments* made by one nation to residents of foreign nations less the personal and government transfer payments received from residents of foreign nations.

net worth The total *assets* less the total *liabilities* of a *firm* or an individual; for a firm, the claims of the owners against the firm's total assets; for an individual, his or her wealth.

new classical economics The theory that, although unanticipated *price-level* changes may create macroeconomic instability in the short run, the economy will return to and stabilize at the full-employment level of domestic output in the long run because *prices* and *wages* adjust automatically to correct movements away from the full-employment output level.

nominal gross domestic product (GDP) *GDP* measured in terms of the *price level* at the time of measurement; *GDP* not adjusted for *inflation*.

nominal income The number of dollars received by an individual or group for its *resources* during some period of time.

nominal interest rate The *interest rate* expressed in terms of annual amounts currently charged for *interest* and not adjusted for *inflation*.

nominal wage The amount of *money* received by a worker per unit of time (hour, day, etc.); money wage.

nondiscretionary fiscal policy (See *built-in stabilizer*.)

nondiversifiable risk Investment *risk* that investors are unable to reduce via *diversification*; also called systemic risk.

nondurable good A *consumer good* with an expected life (use) of less than three years.

nonexcludability The inability to keep nonpayers (free riders) from obtaining benefits from a certain good; a characteristic of a *public good*.

nonexhaustive expenditure An expenditure by government that does not result directly in the use of economic resources or the production of *goods* and *services*; see *government transfer payment*.

nonincome determinants of consumption and saving All influences on consumption and *saving* other than the level of *GDP*.

noninterest determinants of investment All influences on the level of *investment* spending other than the *interest rate*.

noninvestment transaction An expenditure to purchase financial *assets* such as *stocks* and *bonds* or to purchase secondhand *capital goods*; any *financial investment*. By contrast, *investment* is spending for the production of new *capital goods*.

nonmarket transactions The value of the *goods* and *services* that are not included in the *gross domestic product* because they are not bought and sold.

nonproduction transaction The purchase and sale of any item that is not a currently produced *good* or *service*.

nonrivalry The idea that one person's benefit from a certain *good* does not reduce the benefit available to others; a characteristic of a *public good*.

nontariff barriers (NTBs) All barriers other than *protective tariffs* that nations erect to impede international trade, including *import quotas*, licensing requirements, unreasonable product-quality standards, unnecessary bureaucratic detail in customs procedures, and so on.

normal profit The payment made by a *firm* to obtain and retain *entrepreneurial ability*; the minimum *income* that entrepreneurial ability must receive to induce *entrepreneurs* to provide their entrepreneurial ability to a firm; the level of *accounting profit* at which a firm generates an *economic profit* of zero after paying for entrepreneurial ability.

normative economics The part of economics involving value judgments about what the economy should be like; focused on which economic goals and policies should be implemented; policy economics.

North American Free Trade Agreement (NAFTA) The 1993 treaty that established an international free-trade zone composed of Canada, Mexico, and the United States.

official reserves Foreign *currencies* owned by the central bank of a nation.

offshoring The practice of shifting work previously done by domestic workers to workers located abroad.

Okun's law The generalization that any 1-percentage-point rise in the *unemployment rate* above the *full-employment rate of unemployment* is associated with a rise in the *negative GDP gap* by 2 percent of *potential output* (potential *GDP*).

OPEC (See *Organization of Petroleum Exporting Countries*.)

open economy An economy that exports and imports *goods* and *services*.

open-market operations The purchases and sales of U.S. government *securities* that the *Federal Reserve System* undertakes in order to influence *interest rates* and the *money supply*; one method by which the *Federal Reserve* implements *monetary policy*.

opportunity cost The amount of other products that must be forgone or sacrificed to produce a unit of a product.

opportunity-cost ratio An equivalency showing the number of units of two products that can be produced with the same *resources*; the equivalency 1 corn $\equiv$ 3 olives shows that the resources required to produce 3 units of olives must be shifted to corn production to produce 1 unit of corn.

optimal reduction of an externality The reduction of a *negative externality* such as pollution to the level at which the *marginal benefit* and *marginal cost* of reduction are equal.

ordinal utility Satisfaction that is measured by having consumers compare and rank products (or combinations of products) as to preference, without asking them to specify the absolute amounts of satisfaction provided by the products.

Organization of Petroleum Exporting Countries (OPEC) A cartel of 12 oil-producing countries (Algeria, Angola, Ecuador, Iran, Iraq, Kuwait, Libya, Nigeria, Qatar, Saudi Arabia, Venezuela, and the United Arab Emirates) that attempts to control the quantity and *price* of crude oil exported by its members and that accounts for a large percentage of the world's export of oil.

other-things-equal assumption The assumption that factors other than those being considered are held constant; *ceteris paribus* assumption.

outpayments The expenditures of domestic or foreign *currency* that the individuals, *firms*, and governments of one nation make to purchase *goods* and *services*, for remittances, to pay investment *income*, and for purchases of foreign *assets*.

paper money Pieces of paper used as a *medium of exchange*; in the United States, *Federal Reserve Notes*.

paradox of thrift The seemingly self-contradictory but possibly true statement that increased *saving* may be both good and bad for the economy. It is always good in the long run when matched with increased *investment* spending, but may be bad in the short run if there is a *recession* because it reduces spending on *goods* and *services*. If the increased savings are not translated into increased investment, then the fall in consumption spending will not be made up for by an increase in investment. The overall result will be a decrease in output and employment. If the decline in *GDP* is severe enough, the attempt to save more will actually lead to less overall savings because the higher rate of saving will be applied to a smaller *national income*. Attempts by *households* to save more during a recession may simply worsen the recession and result in less saving.

paradox of voting A situation where paired-choice voting by majority rule fails to provide a consistent ranking of society's preferences for *public goods* or *public services*.

partnership An unincorporated *firm* owned and operated by two or more persons.

passively managed funds *Mutual funds* whose *portfolios* are not regularly updated by a fund manager attempting to generate high returns. Rather, once an initial portfolio is selected, it is left unchanged so that investors receive whatever return that unchanging portfolio subsequently generates. *Index funds* are a type of passively managed fund.

patent (Web chapter) An exclusive right given to inventors to produce and sell a new product or machine for 20 years from the time of patent application.

Patient Protection and Affordable Care Act (PPACA) A major health care law passed by the federal government in 2010. Major provisions include an individual health insurance mandate, a ban on insurers refusing to accept patients with preexisting conditions, and federal (rather than state) regulation of health insurance policies.

payments deficit (See *balance-of-payments deficit*.)

payments surplus (See *balance-of-payments surplus*.)

payroll tax A *tax* levied on employers of labor equal to a percentage of all or part of the *wages* and salaries paid by them and on employees equal to a percentage of all or part of the wages and salaries received by them.

peak The point in a *business cycle* at which business activity has reached a temporary maximum; the point at which an *expansion* ends and a *recession* begins. At the peak, the economy is near or at *full employment* and the level of real output is at or very close to the economy's capacity.

per capita GDP *Gross domestic product* (*GDP*) per person; the average GDP of a population.

per capita income A nation's total *income* per person; the average income of a population.

percentage rate of return The percentage gain or loss, relative to the buying *price*, of an *economic investment* or *financial investment* over some period of time.

personal consumption expenditures (*C*) The expenditures of *households* for both durable and nondurable *consumer goods*.

personal distribution of income The manner in which the economy's *personal* or *disposable income* is divided among different *income* classes or different *households* or families.

personal income (PI) The earned and unearned *income* available to resource suppliers and others before the payment of personal *taxes*.

personal income tax A *tax* levied on the taxable income of individuals, *households*, and unincorporated *firms*.

personal mandate The requirement under the *Patient Protection and Affordable Care Act* (*PPACA*) of 2010 that all U.S. citizens and legal residents purchase health insurance unless they are already covered by employer-sponsored health insurance or government-sponsored health insurance (*Medicaid* or *Medicare*).

personal saving The *personal income* of *households* less personal *taxes* and *personal consumption expenditures*; *disposable income* not spent for *consumer goods*.

Phillips Curve A curve showing the relationship between the *unemployment rate* (on the horizontal axis) and the annual rate of increase in the *price level* (on the vertical axis).

planned investment The amount that *firms* plan or intend to invest.

plant A physical establishment that performs one or more functions in the production, fabrication, and distribution of *goods* and *services*.

policy economics The formulation of courses of action to bring about desired economic outcomes or to prevent undesired occurrences.

political business cycle Fluctuations in the economy caused by the alleged tendency of Congress to destabilize the economy by reducing taxes and increasing government expenditures before elections and to raise taxes and lower expenditures after elections.

political corruption The unlawful misdirection of governmental resources or actions that occurs when government officials abuse their entrusted powers for personal gain. (Also see *corruption*.)

Ponzi scheme A financial fraud in which the returns paid to earlier investors come from contributions made by later investors (rather than from the *financial investment* that the perpetrator of the fraud claims to be making). Named after notorious fraudster Charles Ponzi.

portfolio A specific collection of *stocks*, *bonds*, or other *financial investments* held by an individual or a *mutual fund*.

positive economics The analysis of facts or data to establish scientific generalizations about economic behavior.

positive externality A benefit obtained without compensation by third parties from the production or consumption of sellers or buyers. Example: A beekeeper benefits when a neighboring farmer plants clover. An *external benefit* or a spillover benefit.

positive GDP gap A situation in which actual *gross domestic product* exceeds *potential output*. Also known as an *inflationary expenditure* gap.

positive relationship (See *direct relationship*.)

post hoc, ergo propter hoc **fallacy** The false belief that when one event precedes another, the first event must have caused the second event.

potential output The real output (*GDP*) an economy can produce when it fully employs its available resources.

poverty A situation in which the basic needs of an individual or family exceed the means to satisfy them.

poverty rate The percentage of the population with incomes below the official poverty income levels that are established by the federal government.

precommittments Actions taken ahead of time that make it difficult for the future self to avoid doing what the present self desires. See *time inconsistency* and *self-control problems*.

present value Today's value of some amount of *money* that is to be received sometime in the future.

price The amount of *money* needed to buy a particular *good*, *service*, or *resource*.

price ceiling A legally established maximum *price* for a *good*, or *service*. Normally set at a price below the *equilibrium price*.

price floor A legally established minimum *price* for a *good*, or service. Normally set at a price above the *equilibrium price*.

price index An index number that shows how the weighted-average *price* of a "market basket" of goods changes over time relative to its price in a specific *base year*.

price level The weighted average of the *prices* of all the *final goods* and final *services* produced in an economy.

price-level stability A steadiness of the *price level* from one period to the next; zero or low annual *inflation*; also called "price stability."

price-level surprises Unanticipated changes in the *price level*.

price maker A seller (or buyer) that is able to affect the product or resource *price* by changing the amount it sells (or buys).

price taker A seller (or buyer) that is unable to affect the *price* at which a product or *resource* sells by changing the amount it sells (or buys).

prime interest rate The benchmark *interest rate* that banks use as a reference point for a wide range of loans to businesses and individuals.

principal-agent problem (1) At a *firm*, a conflict of interest that occurs when agents (workers or managers) pursue their own objectives to the detriment of the principals' (stockholders') goals. (2) In *public choice theory*, a conflict of interest that arises when elected officials (who are the agents of the people) pursue policies that are in their own interests rather than policies that would be in the better interests of the public (the principals).

principle of comparative advantage The proposition that an individual, region, or nation will benefit if it specializes in producing goods for which its own *opportunity costs* are lower than the opportunity costs of a trading partner, and then exchanging some of the products in which it specializes for other desired products produced by others.

private good A *good*, or *service* that is individually consumed and that can be profitably provided by privately owned *firms* because they can exclude nonpayers from receiving the benefits.

private property The right of private persons and *firms* to obtain, own, control, employ, dispose of, and bequeath *land*, *capital*, and other property.

private sector The *households* and business *firms* of the economy.

probability-weighted average Each of the possible future rates of return from an investment multiplied by its respective probability (expressed as a decimal) of happening.

producer surplus The difference between the actual *price* a producer receives (or producers receive) and the minimum acceptable price; the triangular area above the *supply curve* and below the market price.

production possibilities curve A curve showing the different combinations of two goods or *services* that can be produced in a *full-employment*, *full-production* economy where the available supplies of *resources* and technology are fixed.

productivity A measure of average output or real output per unit of input. For example, the productivity of labor is determined by dividing real output by hours of work.

productivity growth The increase in *productivity* from one period to another.

product market A market in which products are sold by *firms* and bought by *households*.

profit Usually refers to *economic profit* (*total revenue* minus both *explicit costs* and *implicit costs*) but may also refer to *accounting profit* (total revenue minus just explicit costs). If it refers to economic profit, then it is the return earned by the *resource* known as *entrepreneurial ability*.

profit-sharing plan A compensation device through which workers receive part of their pay in the form of a share of their employer's *profit* (if any).

progressive tax A *tax* for which the *average tax rate* (= tax revenue/*GDP*) rises with *GDP*.

property tax A *tax* on the value of property (*capital, land, stocks* and *bonds*, and other *assets*) owned by *firms* and *households*.

proportional tax A *tax* for which the *average tax rate* (= tax revenue/*GDP*) remains constant as *GDP* rises or falls.

proprietor's income The net income (*profit*) of the owners of unincorporated *firms* (*proprietorships* and *partnerships*).

protective tariff A *tariff* designed to shield domestic producers of a *good* or *service* from the competition of foreign producers.

public assistance programs Government programs that pay benefits to those who are unable to earn *income* (because of permanent disabilities or because they have very low income and dependent children); financed by general *tax* revenues and viewed as public charity (rather than earned rights).

public choice theory The economic analysis of government decision making, politics, and elections.

public debt The total amount owed by the federal government to the owners of government *securities*; equal to the sum of past government *budget deficits* less government *budget surpluses*.

public good A *good* or *service* that is characterized by *nonrivalry* and *nonexcludability*. These characteristics typically imply that no private *firm* can break even when attempting to provide such products. As a result, they are often provided by governments, who pay for them using general *tax* revenues.

public investments Government expenditures on public capital (such as roads, highways, bridges, mass-transit systems, and electric power facilities) and on *human capital* (such as education, training, and health).

public sector The part of the economy that contains all government entities; government.

purchasing power The amount of *goods* and *services* that a monetary unit of *income* can buy.

purchasing power parity The idea that if countries have *flexible exchange rates* (rather than *fixed exchange rates*), the exchange rates between national currencies will adjust to equate the purchasing power of various currencies. In particular, the exchange rate between any two national currencies will adjust to reflect the *price-level* differences between the two countries.

pure rate of interest The hypothetical *interest rate* that is completely *risk*-free and not subject to market imperfections; the hypothetical interest rate that would only compensate investors for *time preference*.

quantitative easing (QE) An *open-market operation* in which *bonds* are purchased by a *central bank* in order to increase the quantity of *excess reserves* held by *commercial banks* and thereby (hopefully) stimulate the economy by increasing the amount of lending undertaken by commercial banks; undertaken when interest rates are near zero and, consequently, it is not possible for the central bank to further stimulate the economy with lower interest rates due to the *zero lower bound problem*.

quantity demanded The amount of a *good* or *service* that buyers (or a buyer) are willing and able to purchase at a specific *price* during a specified period of time.

quantity supplied The amount of a *good* or *service* that producers (or a producer) are willing and able to make available for sale at a specific *price* during a specified period of time.

quasi-public bank A bank that is privately owned but governmentally (publicly) controlled; each of the U.S. *Federal Reserve Banks*.

quasi-public good A *good* or *service* to which *excludability* could apply but that has such a large *positive externality* that government sponsors its production to prevent an underallocation of resources.

R&D Research and development activities undertaken to bring about *technological advance*.

rate of exchange The *price* paid in one's own *money* to acquire 1 unit of a foreign *currency*; the rate at which the money of one nation is exchanged for the money of another nation.

rate of return The gain in net revenue divided by the cost of an *investment* or an *R&D* expenditure; often expressed as a *percentage rate of return*.

rational expectations theory The hypothesis that *firms* and *households* expect monetary and fiscal policies to have certain effects on the economy and (in pursuit of their own self-interests) take actions that make these policies ineffective.

rationing function of prices The ability of *market* forces in competitive markets to equalize *quantity demanded* and *quantity supplied* and to eliminate *shortages* and *surpluses* via changes in *prices*.

real-balances effect The tendency for increases in the *price level* to lower the real value (or *purchasing power*) of financial *assets* with fixed *money* value and, as a result, to reduce total spending and real output, and conversely for decreases in the *price level*.

real-business-cycle theory   A theory that *business cycles* result from changes in *technology* and *resource* availability, which affect *productivity* and thus increase or decrease long-run *aggregate supply*.

real capital   (See *capital*.)

real GDP   (See *real gross domestic product*.)

real GDP per capita   *Inflation*-adjusted output per person; *real GDP*/population.

real gross domestic product (GDP)   *Gross domestic product* adjusted for *inflation*; gross domestic product in a year divided by the GDP *price index* for that year, the index expressed as a decimal.

real income   The amount of *goods* and *services* that can be purchased with *nominal income* during some period of time; nominal income adjusted for *inflation*.

real interest rate   The *interest rate* expressed in dollars of constant value (adjusted for *inflation*) and equal to the *nominal interest rate* less the expected rate of inflation.

real wage   The amount of *goods* and *services* a worker can purchase with his or her *nominal wage*; the *purchasing power* of the *nominal wage*.

recession   A period of declining *real GDP*, accompanied by lower *real income* and higher *unemployment*.

recessionary expenditure gap   The amount by which the *aggregate expenditures schedule* must shift upward to increase *real GDP* to its full-employment, noninflationary level.

regressive tax   A *tax* for which the *average tax rate* (= tax revenue/*GDP*) falls as *GDP* rises.

regulatory agency   An agency, commission, or board established by the federal government or a state government to control the *prices* charged and the *services* offered by a *natural monopoly* or *public utility*.

regulatory capture   The situation that occurs when a governmental *regulatory agency* ends up being controlled by the industry that it is supposed to be regulating.

rental income   The payments received by those who supply *land* to the economy.

rent-seeking behavior   The actions by persons, *firms*, or unions to gain special benefits from government at the taxpayers' or someone else's expense.

replacement rate   The *total fertility rate* necessary to offset deaths in a country and thereby keep the size of its population constant (without relying on immigration). For most countries, a total fertility rate of about 2.1 births per woman per lifetime.

required reserves   The funds that each *commercial bank* and *thrift institution* must deposit with its local *Federal Reserve Bank* (or hold as *vault cash*) to meet the legal *reserve requirement*; a fixed percentage of each bank's or thrift's *checkable deposits*.

reserve ratio   The fraction of *checkable deposits* that each *commercial bank* or *thrift institution* must hold as reserves at its local *Federal Reserve Bank* or in its own bank vault; also called the *reserve requirement*.

reserve requirement   The specified minimum percentage of its *checkable deposits* that each *commercial bank* or *thrift institution* must keep on deposit at the *Federal Reserve Bank* in its district or hold as *vault cash*.

resource   A natural, human, or manufactured item that helps produce *goods* and *services*; a productive agent or factor of production; one of the four *economic resources*.

resource market   A market in which *households* sell and *firms* buy *resources* or the services of resources.

restrictive monetary policy   *Federal Reserve System* actions to reduce the *money supply*, increase *interest rates*, and reduce *inflation*; a tight money policy.

revenue tariff   A *tariff* designed to produce *income* for the federal government.

risk   The uncertainty as to the future returns of a particular *financial investment* or *economic investment*.

risk-free interest rate   The *interest rate* earned on short-term U.S. government *bonds*.

risk premium   The *interest rate* above the *risk-free* interest rate that must be paid and received to compensate a lender or investor for *risk*.

rivalry   (1) The characteristic of a *private good*, the consumption of which by one party excludes other parties from obtaining the benefit; (2) the attempt by one *firm* to gain strategic advantage over another firm to enhance market share or *profit*.

rule of 70   A method for determining the number of years it will take for some measure to double, given its annual percentage increase. Example: To determine the number of years it will take for the *price level* to double, divide 70 by the annual rate of *inflation*.

sales and excise taxes   (See *sales tax*; see *excise tax*.)

sales tax   A *tax* levied on the cost (at retail) of a broad group of products.

saving   *Disposable income* not spent for *consumer goods*; equal to *disposable income* minus *personal consumption expenditures*; saving is a flow. Compare with *savings*.

savings   The accumulation of funds that results when people in an economy spend less (consume less) than their *incomes* during a given time period; savings are a stock. Compare with *saving*.

savings account   A deposit in a *commercial bank* or *thrift institution* on which *interest* payments are received; generally used for *saving* rather than daily transactions; a component of the *M2 money supply*.

savings and loan association (S&L)   A *firm* that accepts deposits primarily from small individual savers and lends primarily to individuals to finance purchases such as autos and homes; now nearly indistinguishable from a *commercial bank*.

saving schedule A table of numbers that shows the amounts *households* plan to save (plan not to spend for *consumer goods*), at different levels of *disposable income*.

savings deposit A deposit that is *interest*-bearing and that the depositor can normally withdraw at any time.

savings institution (See *thrift institution*.)

Say's law The largely discredited macroeconomic generalization that the production (*supply*) of *goods* and *services* creates an equal *demand* for those goods and services.

scarce resources The limited quantities of *land, capital, labor*, and *entrepreneurial ability* that are never sufficient to satisfy people's virtually unlimited economic wants.

scarcity The limits placed on the amounts and types of *goods* and *services* available for consumption as the result of there being only limited *economic resources* from which to produce output; the fundamental economic constraint that creates *opportunity costs* and that necessitates the use of *marginal analysis* (*cost-benefit analysis*) to make optimal choices.

scientific method The procedure for the systematic pursuit of knowledge involving the observation of facts and the formulation and testing of hypotheses to obtain theories, principles, and laws.

secular trend A long-term tendency; a change in some variable over a very long period of years.

securities *Stocks, bonds*, and other financial documents that attest to a financial obligation.

securitization The process of aggregating many individual financial debts, such as mortgages or student loans, into a pool and then issuing new *securities* (typically *bonds*) backed by the pool. The holders of the new securities are entitled to receive the debt payments made on the individual financial debts in the pool.

Security Market Line (SML) A line that shows the *average expected rate of return* of all *financial investments* at each level of *nondiversifiable risk*, the latter measured by *beta*.

self-interest That which each *firm*, property owner, worker, and consumer believes is best for itself and seeks to obtain.

separation of ownership and control The fact that different groups of people own a *corporation* (the stockholders) and manage it (the directors and officers).

service An (intangible) act or use for which a consumer, *firm*, or government is willing to pay.

shirking Workers' neglecting or evading *work* to increase their *utility* or well-being.

shocks Sudden, unexpected changes in *demand* (or *aggregate demand*) or supply (or *aggregate supply*).

shortage The amount by which the *quantity demanded* of a product exceeds the *quantity supplied* at a particular (below-equilibrium) *price*.

short run (1) In *microeconomics*, a period of time in which producers are able to change the quantities of some but not all of the *resources* they employ; a period in which some resources (usually *plant*) are fixed and some are variable. (2) In *macroeconomics*, a period in which *nominal wages* and other input *prices* do not change in response to a change in the *price level*.

short-run aggregate supply curve An *aggregate supply* curve relevant to a time period in which input *prices* (particularly *nominal wages*) do not change in response to changes in the *price level*.

short-run competitive equilibrium The *price* at which the total quantity of a product supplied in the *short run* in a purely competitive *industry* equals the total quantity of the product demanded and that is equal to or greater than *average variable cost*.

short-run supply curve A *supply curve* that shows the quantity of a product a *firm* in a purely competitive *industry* will offer to sell at various *prices* in the *short run*; the portion of the firm's short-run *marginal cost curve* that lies above its *average-variable-cost* curve.

simple multiplier The *multiplier* in any economy in which government collects no *net taxes*, there are no *imports*, and *investment* is independent of the level of *income*; equal to 1 divided by the *marginal propensity to save*.

skill transferability The ease with which people can shift their work talents from one job, region, or country to another job, region, or country.

slope of a straight line The ratio of the vertical change (the rise or fall) to the horizontal change (the run) between any two points on a straight line. The slope of an upward-sloping line is positive, reflecting a direct relationship between two variables; the slope of a downward-sloping line is negative, reflecting an inverse relationship between two variables.

Smoot-Hawley Tariff Act Legislation passed in 1930 that established very high *tariffs*. Its objective was to reduce *imports* and stimulate the domestic economy, but it resulted only in retaliatory tariffs by other nations.

social insurance programs Programs that replace the earnings lost when people retire or are temporarily unemployed, that are financed by payroll *taxes*, and that are viewed as earned rights (rather than charity).

socially optimal price The *price* of a product that results in the most efficient allocation of an economy's *resources* and that is equal to the *marginal cost* of the product.

social regulation Regulation in which government is concerned with the conditions under which *goods* and *services* are produced, their physical characteristics, and the impact of their production on society. Differs from *industrial regulation*.

Social Security The social insurance program in the United States financed by federal *payroll taxes* on employers and employees and designed to replace a portion of the earnings lost when workers become disabled, retire, or die.

Social Security trust fund A federal fund that saves excessive Social Security *tax* revenues received in one year to meet Social Security benefit obligations that exceed Social Security tax revenues in some subsequent year.

sole proprietorship An unincorporated *firm* owned and operated by one person.

special-interest effect Any political outcome in which a small group ("special interest") gains substantially at the expense of a much larger number of persons who each individually suffers a small loss.

specialization The use of the *resources* of an individual, a *firm*, a region, or a nation to concentrate production on one or a small number of *goods* and *services*.

speculation The activity of buying or selling with the motive of later reselling or rebuying for *profit*.

SSI (See *Supplemental Security Income*.)

stagflation *Inflation* accompanied by stagnation in the rate of growth of output and an increase in *unemployment* in the economy; simultaneous increases in the *inflation rate* and the *unemployment rate*.

standardized product A product whose buyers are indifferent to the seller from whom they purchase it as long as the *price* charged by all sellers is the same; a product all units of which are identical and thus are perfect substitutes for each other.

start-up firm A new *firm* focused on creating and introducing a particular new product or employing a specific new production or distribution method.

state bank A *commercial bank* authorized by a state government to engage in the business of banking.

sticky prices (See *inflexible prices*.)

stock (corporate) An ownership share in a corporation.

stock options Contracts that enable executives or other key employees to buy shares of their employers' *stock* at fixed, lower *prices* even when the market price subsequently rises.

store of value An *asset* set aside for future use; one of the three functions of *money*.

strategic behavior Self-interested economic actions that take into account the expected reactions of others.

structural unemployment *Unemployment* of workers whose skills are not demanded by employers, who lack sufficient skill to obtain employment, or who cannot easily move to locations where jobs are available.

subprime mortgage loans High-*interest-rate* loans to home buyers with above-average credit risk.

subsidy A payment of funds (or *goods* and *services*) by a government, *firm*, or household for which it receives no *good* or *service* in return. When made by a government, it is a *government transfer payment*.

sunk cost A cost that has been incurred and cannot be recovered.

supply A schedule or curve that shows the various amounts of a product that producers are willing and able to make available for sale at each of a series of possible *prices* during a specified period of time.

supply curve A curve that illustrates the *supply* for a product by showing how each possible *price* (on the *vertical axis*) is associated with a specific *quantity supplied* (on the *horizontal axis*).

supply factors (in growth) The four determinants of an economy's physical ability to achieve *economic growth* by increasing *potential output* and shifting out the *production possibilities curve*. The four determinants are improvements in technology plus increases in the quantity and quality of natural resources, human resources, and the stock of capital goods.

supply schedule A table of numbers showing the amounts of a *good* or *service* producers are willing and able to make available for sale at each of a series of possible *prices* during a specified period of time.

supply shocks Sudden, unexpected changes in *aggregate supply*.

supply-side economics A view of *macroeconomics* that emphasizes the role of costs and *aggregate supply* in explaining *inflation*, *unemployment*, and *economic growth*.

supply-side market failures Overallocations of *resources* that occur when private supply curves understate the full cost of producing a *good* or *service*.

surplus The amount by which the *quantity supplied* of a product exceeds the *quantity demanded* at a specific (above-equilibrium) *price*.

surplus payment A payment exceeding the minimum payment necessary to ensure the availability of a *resource* in a production process; for example, land rent.

tariff A *tax* imposed by a nation on an imported good.

tax An involuntary payment of money (or *goods* and *services*) to a government by a *household* or *firm* for which the household or firm receives no good or service directly in return.

tax credit An accounting *credit* that reduces the amount of *taxes* owed to the government on a dollar-for-dollar basis. Some tax credits are refundable, meaning that if the amount of the tax credit exceeds the amount owed in taxes, the taxpayer will receive (be refunded) the difference in cash.

taxes on production and imports A *national income accounting* category that includes such taxes as *sales*, *excise*, business property taxes, and *tariffs* that *firms* treat as costs of producing a product and pass on (in whole or in part) to buyers by charging a higher *price*.

tax incidence The degree to which a *tax* falls on a particular person or group.

tax subsidy A grant in the form of reduced *taxes* through favorable *tax* treatment. For example, employer-paid health insurance is exempt from federal *income taxes* and *payroll taxes*.

Taylor rule A *monetary rule* proposed by economist John Taylor that would stipulate exactly how much the *Federal Reserve System* should change *real interest rates* in response to divergences of *real GDP* from potential GDP and divergences of actual rates of *inflation* from a target rate of inflation.

technology The body of knowledge and techniques that can be used to combine *economic resources* to produce *goods* and *services*.

term auction facility A *monetary policy* procedure used by the *Federal Reserve System* during the 2008 financial crisis. *Commercial banks* anonymously bid to obtain loans being made available by the Fed as a way to expand *reserves* in the banking system.

terms of trade The rate at which units of one product can be exchanged for units of another product; the *price of a good or service*; the amount of one good or service that must be given up to obtain 1 unit of another good or service.

theoretical economics The process of deriving and applying *economic theories* and principles.

thrift institution A *savings and loan association, mutual savings bank*, or *credit union*.

till money (See *vault cash*.)

time deposit An interest-earning deposit in a *commercial bank* or *thrift institution* that the depositor can withdraw without penalty after the end of a specified period.

time preference The human tendency for people, because of impatience, to prefer to spend and consume in the present rather than save and wait to spend and consume in the future; this inclination varies in strength among individuals.

time-value of money The idea that a specific amount of *money* is more valuable to a person the sooner it is received because the money can be placed in a financial account or *investment* and earn *compound interest* over time; the *opportunity cost* of receiving a sum of money later rather than earlier.

token money Bills or coins for which the amount printed on the *currency* bears no relationship to the value of the paper or metal embodied within it; for currency still circulating, *money* for which the face value exceeds the commodity value.

total demand The *demand schedule* or the *demand curve* of all buyers of a *good* or *service*; also called market demand.

total demand for money The sum of the *transactions demand for money* and the *asset demand for money*.

total fertility rate The average number of children per lifetime birthed by a nation's women.

total spending The total amount that buyers of *goods* and *services* spend or plan to spend; also called *aggregate expenditures*.

total supply The *supply schedule* or the *supply curve* of all sellers of a *good* or *service*; also called market supply.

Trade Adjustment Assistance Act A U.S. law passed in 2002 that provides cash assistance, education and training benefits, health care subsidies, and *wage* subsidies (for persons age 50 or older) to workers displaced by *imports* or relocations of U.S. *plants* to other countries.

trade balance The export of *goods* (or goods and *services*) of a nation less its imports of goods (or goods and *services*).

trade controls *Tariffs, export subsidies, import quotas*, and other means a nation may employ to reduce *imports* and expand *exports*.

trade deficit The amount by which a nation's *imports* of *goods* (or goods and *services*) exceed its *exports* of goods (or goods and services).

trademark A word, symbol, or phrase that serves to distinguish a product produced by a particular *firm* from products produced by rival firms. Most countries register and enforce trademarks so that the originator of a particular product is the only firm that may utilize its legally registered trademarks.

trade-off The sacrifice of some or all of one economic goal, *good*, or *service* to achieve some other goal, good, or service.

trade surplus The amount by which a nation's *exports* of *goods* (or goods and *services*) exceed its *imports* of goods (or goods and services).

trading possibilities line A line that shows the different combinations of two products that an economy is able to obtain (consume) when it specializes in the production of one product and trades (exports) it to obtain the other product.

transactions demand for money The amount of money people want to hold for use as a *medium of exchange* (to make payments); varies directly with *nominal GDP*.

transfer payment A payment of *money* (or *goods* and *services*) by a government to a *household* or *firm* for which the payer receives no *good* or *service* directly in return.

Troubled Asset Relief Program (TARP) A 2008 federal government program that authorized the U.S. Treasury to loan up to $700 billion to critical financial institutions and other U.S. *firms* that were in extreme financial trouble and therefore at high risk of failure.

trough The point in a *business cycle* at which business activity has reached a temporary minimum; the point at which a *recession* ends and an *expansion* (recovery) begins. At the trough, the economy experiences substantial *unemployment* and *real GDP* is less than *potential output*.

unanticipated inflation An increase of the *price level* (*inflation*) at a rate greater than expected.

underemployment (Web chapter) A situation in which workers are employed in positions requiring less education and skill than they have.

undistributed corporate profits After-*tax* corporate *profits* not distributed as *dividends* to stockholders; corporate or business *saving*; also called retained earnings.

unemployment The failure to use all available *economic resources* to produce desired *goods* and *services*; the failure of the economy to fully employ its *labor force*.

unemployment compensation (See *unemployment insurance*).

unemployment insurance The social insurance program that in the United States is financed by state *payroll taxes* on employers and makes *income* available to workers who become unemployed and are unable to find jobs.

unemployment rate The percentage of the *labor force* unemployed at any time.

unfulfilled expectations Situations in which *households* and businesses were expecting one thing to happen but instead find that something else has happened; unrealized anticipations or plans relating to future economic conditions and outcomes.

unfunded liability A future government spending commitment (liability) for which the government has not legislated an offsetting revenue source.

uninsurable risk An eventuality for which the frequency or magnitude of potential losses is unpredictable or unknowable. Insurance companies are not willing to sell insurance against such risks.

unintended consequences Unexpected results of government policies. Can be good or bad, but normally refer to unexpected negative outcomes.

unit of account A standard unit in which *prices* can be stated and the value of *goods* and *services* can be compared; one of the three functions of *money*.

unlimited wants The insatiable desire of consumers for *goods* and *services* that will give them satisfaction or *utility*.

unplanned changes in inventories Changes in *inventories* that *firms* did not anticipate; changes in inventories that occur because of unexpected increases or decreases of aggregate spending (or of *aggregate expenditures*).

unplanned investment *Actual investment* less *planned investment*; increases or decreases in the *inventories* of *firms* resulting from production greater than sales.

Uruguay Round A 1995 trade agreement (fully implemented in 2005) that established the *World Trade Organization* (*WTO*), liberalized trade in *goods* and *services*, provided added protection to intellectual property (for example, *patents* and *copyrights*), and reduced farm *subsidies*.

U.S. government securities U.S. Treasury bills, notes, and *bonds* used to finance *budget deficits*; the components of the *public debt*.

usury laws State laws that specify the maximum legal *interest rate* at which loans can be made.

utility The want-satisfying power of a *good* or *service*; the satisfaction or pleasure a consumer obtains from the consumption of a good or service (or from the consumption of a collection of *goods* and *services*).

value added The value of a product sold by a *firm* less the value of the products (materials) purchased and used by the firm to produce that product.

value-added tax A *tax* imposed on the difference between the value of a product sold by a *firm* and the value of the goods purchased from other firms to produce that product; used in several European countries.

value judgment Opinion of what is desirable or undesirable; belief regarding what ought or ought not to be in terms of what is right (or just) or wrong (or unjust).

value of money The quantity of *goods* and *services* for which a unit of *money* (a dollar) can be exchanged; the purchasing power of a unit of money; the reciprocal of the *price index*.

VAT (See *value-added tax*.)

vault cash The *currency* a bank has on hand in its vault and cash drawers.

velocity The number of times per year that the average dollar in the *money supply* is spent for *final goods* and final *services*; *nominal gross domestic product* (*GDP*) divided by the *money supply*.

vertical axis The "up-down" or "north-south" measurement line on a graph or grid.

vertical intercept The point at which a line meets the vertical axis of a graph.

vicious circle of poverty (Web chapter) A problem common in some *developing countries* in which their low *per capita incomes* are an obstacle to realizing the levels of *savings* and *investment* needed to achieve rates of growth of output that exceed their rates of population growth.

voluntary export restrictions (VER) Voluntary limitations by countries or *firms* of their exports to a particular foreign nation; undertaken to avoid the enactment of formal trade barriers by the foreign nation.

wage The *price* paid for the use or *services* of *labor* per unit of time (per hour, per day, and so on).

Wall Street Reform and Consumer Protection Act of 2010 The law that gave authority to the *Federal Reserve System* (the Fed) to regulate all large financial institutions, created an oversight council to look for growing risk to the financial system, established a process for the federal government to sell off the assets of large failing financial institutions, provided federal regulatory oversight of asset-backed *securities*, and created a financial consumer protection bureau within the Fed.

wealth Anything that has value because it produces *income* or could produce income. Wealth is a stock; income is a flow. Assets less liabilities; net worth.

wealth effect The tendency for people to increase their consumption spending when the value of their financial and real *assets* rises and to decrease their consumption spending when the value of those assets falls.

welfare programs (See *public assistance programs*.)

will to develop (Web chapter) The mental state of wanting *economic growth* strongly enough to change from old to new ways of doing things.

World Bank (Web chapter) A bank that lends (and guarantees loans) to *developing countries* to assist them in increasing their *capital stock* and thus in achieving *economic growth*.

world price The international market *price* of a *good* or *service*, determined by world demand and supply.

World Trade Organization (WTO) An organization of 159 nations (as of mid-2013) that oversees the provisions of the current world trade agreement, resolves trade disputes stemming from it, and holds forums for further rounds of trade negotiations.

WTO (See *World Trade Organization*.)

X-inefficiency The production of output, whatever its level, at a higher average (and total) cost than is necessary for producing that level of output.

zero interest rate policy (ZIRP) A *monetary policy* in which a *central bank* sets *nominal interest rates* at or near zero percent per year in order to stimulate the economy.

zero lower bound problem The constraint placed on the ability of a *central bank* to stimulate the economy through lower interest rates by the fact that *nominal interest rates* cannot be driven lower than zero (because if interest rates were negative, people would be unwilling to put their money into banks due to the fact that deposit balances would decrease over time due to the negative interest rate.)

INDEX

Selected Economics Statistics for Various Years, 1929–1984

Statistics in rows 1–5 are in billions of dollars in the year specified. Numbers may not add to totals because of rounding.

GDP AND INCOME DATA	1929	1933	1940	1942	1944	1946	1948	1950	1952	1954	1956
1 Gross domestic product	104.6	57.2	102.9	166.0	224.6	227.8	274.8	300.2	367.7	391.1	450.1
1A Personal consumption expenditures	77.4	45.9	71.3	89.0	108.6	144.3	175.0	192.2	219.5	239.9	271.6
1B Gross private domestic investment	17.2	2.3	14.6	11.8	9.2	33.1	50.3	56.5	57.3	58.1	77.7
1C Government purchases	9.6	8.9	15.6	65.5	108.7	43.2	44.0	50.7	89.8	92.8	98.5
1D Net exports of goods and services	0.4	0.1	1.5	−0.3	−2.0	7.2	5.5	0.7	1.2	0.4	2.4
2 Net domestic product	94.2	49.2	92.3	151.1	203.2	202.0	243.4	266.8	327.1	345.1	396.0
3 National income	187.0	97.4	182.4	304.0	401.4	401.6	487.4	531.2	649.0	684.4	796.2
3A Wages and salaries	51.4	29.8	52.8	88.1	124.4	122.6	144.5	158.5	201.3	214.4	249.6
3B Rent	6.1	2.9	3.8	5.5	6.3	6.9	7.5	8.8	10.8	13.1	13.7
3C Interest	4.6	4	3.3	3.2	2.4	1.9	2.6	3.2	4.1	5.7	6.9
3D Profits	10.8	−0.2	9.9	20.8	25	18.2	31.4	36.1	39.7	39.5	49.6
3E Proprietor's income	14.0	5.3	12.2	23.3	29.3	35.7	39.3	37.5	43	42.3	45.8
3F Taxes on production and imports*	100.1	55.6	100.4	163.1	214.0	216.3	262.1	287.1	350.1	369.4	430.6
4 Personal income	85.3	47.2	79.4	126.7	169.7	182.7	213.7	233.9	282.7	302.6	348.4
5 Disposable income	83.5	46.4	77.7	121.8	152.0	165.5	194.5	215.0	250.7	272.4	311.8
6 Disposable income per capita	685	369	588	903	1,099	1,170	1,326	1,417	1,597	1,678	1,854
7 Personal saving as percent of DI	4.7	−0.8	6.8	26.2	27.9	11.8	8.9	9.3	11.1	10.3	11.1

OTHER STATISTICS	1929	1933	1940	1942	1944	1946	1948	1950	1952	1954	1956
8 Real GDP (billions of 2009 dollars)	1,055.6	777.6	1,265.0	1,770.3	2,237.5	1,959.0	2,018.0	2,181.9	2,453.7	2,554.4	2,794.7
9 Economic growth rate (change in real GDP)	–	−1.3	8.8	18.9	8.0	−11.6	4.1	8.7	4.1	−0.6	2.1
10 Consumer Price Index (1982–1984 = 100)	17.1	13.0	14.0	16.3	17.6	19.5	24.1	24.1	26.5	26.9	27.2
11 Rate of inflation (percent change in CPI)	0.0	−5.1	0.7	10.9	1.7	8.3	8.1	1.3	1.9	0.7	1.5
12 Money supply, M1 (billions of $)	26.6	19.9	39.7	55.4	85.3	106.5	112.5	114.1	125.2	130.3	136.0
13 Federal funds interest rate (%)	–	–	–	–	–	–	1.75	2.07	3.00	3.05	2.7
14 Prime interest rate (%)	5.50	1.50	1.50	1.50	1.50	1.50	1.75	2.07	3.00	3.05	3.7
15 Population (millions)	121.8	125.6	132.1	134.9	138.4	141.4	146.6	152.3	157.6	163.0	168.9
16 Civilian labor force (millions)	49.2	51.6	55.6	56.4	54.6	57.5	60.6	62.2	62.1	63.6	66.6
16A Employment (millions)	47.6	38.8	47.5	53.8	54.0	55.3	58.3	58.9	60.3	60.1	63.8
16B Unemployment (millions)	1.6	12.8	8.1	2.7	0.7	2.3	2.3	3.3	1.9	3.5	2.8
17 Unemployment rate (%)	3.2	24.9	14.6	4.7	1.2	3.9	3.8	5.3	3.0	5.5	4.1
18 Productivity growth, business sector (%)	–	–	–	–	–	–	4.4	8.2	3.0	2.2	0.3
19 After-tax manufacturing profit per dollar of sales (cents)	–	–	–	–	–	–	7.0	7.1	4.3	4.5	5.3
20 Price of crude oil (U.S. average, dollars per barrel)	1.27	0.67	1.02	1.19	1.21	1.41	2.60	2.51	2.53	2.78	2.7
21 Federal budget surplus (+) or deficit (−) (billions of dollars)	0.7	−2.6	−2.9	−20.5	−47.6	−15.9	11.8	−3.1	−1.5	−1.2	3.9
22 Public debt (billions of dollars)	16.9	22.5	50.7	79.2	204.1	271.0	252.0	256.9	259.1	270.8	272.7
23 Trade balance on current account (billions of dollars)	–	–	–	–	–	4.9	2.4	−1.8	0.6	0.2	2.7

*Combines items from other smaller accounts.

1999	2000	2001	2002	2003	2004	2005	2006	2007	2008	2009	2010	2011	20
9,665.7	10,289.7	10,625.3	10,980.2	11,512.2	12,277.0	13,095.4	13,857.9	14,480.3	14,720.3	14,417.9	14,958.3	15,533.8	16
6,316.9	6,801.6	7,106.9	7,385.3	7,764.4	8,257.8	8,790.3	9,297.5	9,744.4	10,005.5	9,842.9	10,201.9	10,711.8	11
1,884.2	2,033.8	1,928.6	1,925.0	2,027.9	2,276.7	2,527.1	2,680.6	2,643.7	2,424.8	1,878.1	2,100.8	2,232.1	2
1,726.0	1,834.4	1,958.8	2,094.9	2,220.8	2,357.4	2,493.7	2,642.2	2,801.9	3,003.2	3,089.1	3,174.0	3,158.7	3
−261.4	−380.1	−369.0	−425.0	−500.9	−614.8	−715.7	−762.4	−709.8	−713.2	−392.2	−518.5	−568.7	−
8,264.8	8,775.5	9,021.3	9,318.1	9,785.0	10,445.3	11,113.4	11,721.9	12,215.9	12,356.9	12,049.5	12,576.7	13,081.2	13
16,594.4	17,740.0	18,265.8	18,776.4	19,594.2	20,903.6	22,294.4	23,874.4	24,391.4	24,515.8	23,954.6	25,067.2	26,269.8	27
5,410.3	5,856.6	6,046.5	6,141.9	6,365.4	6,740.5	7,087.8	7,503.2	7,899.1	8,079.2	7,787.8	7,967.3	8,278.5	8
183.1	187.7	207.5	217.3	238.0	255.4	238.4	207.5	189.4	262.1	333.7	402.8	484.4	
488.0	565.0	566.4	490.5	466.2	403.5	496.8	580.9	663.4	693.4	563.1	489.4	456.9	
830.2	781.2	754.0	907.2	1,056.4	1,283.3	1,477.7	1,646.5	1,529	1,285.1	1,392.6	1,740.6	1,877.7	2
700.4	757.8	836.8	871.0	900.1	962.1	979.0	1,053.7	979.2	1,026.5	973.0	1,032.7	1,155.1	1
8,982.4	9,591.7	9,854.6	10,148.5	10,568.1	11,258.8	12,014.7	12,882.6	13,131.3	13,169.5	12,904.4	13,434.4	14,017.2	14
7,983.8	8,632.8	8,987.1	9,149.5	9,487.6	10,049.2	10,610.3	11,389.8	11,995.7	12,430.6	12,082.1	12,435.2	13,191.3	13
6,876.3	7,400.5	7,752.3	8,099.2	8,486.7	9,003.2	9,401.8	10,037.7	10,507.9	10,995.4	10,937.2	11,243.7	11,787.4	12
24,617	26,206	27,179	28,127	29,201	30,700	31,763	33,591	34,829	36,104	35,598	36,296	37,776	38
4.3	4.0	4.3	5.0	4.8	4.6	2.6	3.4	3.0	5.0	6.1	5.6	5.7	

1999	2000	2001	2002	2003	2004	2005	2006	2007	2008	2009	2010	2011	20
12,071.4	12,565.2	12,684.4	12,909.7	13,270.0	13,774.0	14,235.6	14,615.2	14,876.8	14,833.6	14,417.9	14,779.4	15,052.4	15
4.8	4.1	1.0	1.8	2.8	3.8	3.4	2.7	1.8	−0.3	−2.8	2.5	1.8	
166.6	172.2	177.1	179.9	184.0	188.9	195.3	201.6	207.3	215.3	214.5	218.1	224.9	
2.2	3.4	2.8	1.6	2.3	2.7	3.4	3.2	2.8	3.8	−0.4	1.6	3.2	
1,122.9	1,087.9	1,182.9	1,220.4	1,306.6	1,375.9	1,374.7	1,366.3	1,374.1	1,604.7	1,695.4	1,836.3	2,160.4	2
4.97	6.24	3.89	1.67	1.13	1.35	3.21	4.96	5.02	1.93	0.16	0.18	0.10	
7.99	9.23	6.92	4.68	4.12	4.34	6.19	7.96	8.05	5.09	3.25	3.25	3.25	
272.7	282.2	285.0	287.6	290.1	292.8	295.5	298.4	301.2	304.1	306.8	309.3	311.6	
139.4	142.6	143.7	144.9	146.5	147.4	149.3	151.4	153.1	154.3	154.1	153.9	153.6	
133.5	136.9	136.9	136.5	137.7	139.3	141.7	144.4	146.0	145.4	139.9	139.1	139.9	
5.9	5.7	6.8	8.4	8.8	8.1	7.6	7.0	7.1	8.9	14.3	14.8	13.7	
4.2	4.0	4.7	5.8	6.0	5.5	5.1	4.6	4.6	5.8	9.3	9.6	8.9	
3.5	3.5	3.0	4.5	3.9	2.8	1.7	0.9	1.5	0.7	3.1	3.0	0.4	
6.4	6.9	5.7	5.8	7.0	8.0	9.0	9.7	9.3	6.6	8.6	8.1	8.7	
15.56	26.72	21.84	22.51	27.56	36.77	50.28	59.69	66.52	94.04	56.35	74.71	95.73	
125.6	236.2	128.2	−157.8	−377.6	−412.7	−318.3	−248.2	−160.7	−458.6	−1,412.7	−1,294.4	−1,299.6	−1
5,605.5	5,628.7	5,769.9	6,198.4	6,760.0	7,354.7	7,905.3	8,451.4	8,950.7	9,986.1	11,875.9	13,528.8	14,764.2	16
−301.7	−416.3	−396.6	−457.2	−519.1	−628.5	−745.8	−800.6	−710.3	−677.1	−381.9	−442.0	−465.9	−

**Data for 2012 and the years immediately prior are subject to change because of subsequent government data revisions.

Sources: Bureau of Economic Analysis; Bureau of Labor Statistics; Federal Reserve System; *Economic Report of the President, 2013;* and U.S. Energy Information Administration

Selected Economics Statistics for Various Years, 1986–2012

Statistics in rows 1–5 are in billions of dollars in the year specified. Numbers may not add to totals because of rounding.

GDP AND INCOME DATA	1986	1988	1990	1991	1992	1993	1994	1995	1996	1997	1998
1 Gross domestic product	4,590.1	5,252.6	5,979.6	6,174.0	6,539.3	6,878.7	7,308.7	7,664.0	8,100.2	8,608.5	9,089.1
1A Personal consumption expenditures	2,898.4	3,346.9	3,825.6	3,960.2	4,215.7	4,471.0	4,741.0	4,984.2	5,268.1	5,560.7	5,903.0
1B Gross private domestic investment	849.1	937.0	993.5	944.3	1,013.0	1,106.8	1,256.5	1,317.5	1,432.1	1,595.6	1,735.3
1C Government purchases	974.5	1,078.2	1,238.4	1,298.2	1,345.4	1,366.1	1,403.7	1,452.2	1,496.4	1,554.2	1,613.5
1D Net exports of goods and services	−131.9	−109.4	−77.9	−28.6	−34.8	−65.2	−92.5	−89.8	−96.4	−102.0	−162.7
2 Net domestic product	3,907.9	4,470.2	5,092.8	5,242.9	5,579.6	5,875.1	6,253.1	6,541.2	6,924.2	7,368.5	7,778.8
3 National income	7,662.4	8,941.4	10,003.0	10,309.0	10,937.4	11,445.6	12,232.6	12,901.4	13,735.4	14,712.4	15,678.0
3A Wages and salaries	2,543.8	2,950	3,342.7	3,452	3,671.1	3,820.7	4,010.1	4,202.6	4,422.1	4,714.7	5,077.8
3B Rent	21.9	25.1	31.4	42.0	64.3	93.6	117.5	129.2	147.0	152.0	169.9
3C Interest	365.2	394.7	450.1	408.5	383.7	371.4	365.9	376.5	381.9	414.7	477.8
3D Profits	324.4	414.9	417.2	451.3	475.3	522.0	621.9	703.0	786.1	865.8	804.1
3E Proprietor's income	256.5	325.8	354.4	356.0	402.4	430.5	459.5	484.5	547.4	587.9	644.2
3F Taxes on production and imports*	4,150.6	4,830.9	5,407.2	5,599.2	5,940.6	6,207.4	6,657.7	7,005.6	7,450.9	7,977.3	8,504.2
4 Personal income	3,725.1	4,275.3	4,904.5	5,071.1	5,410.8	5,646.8	5,934.7	6,276.5	6,661.9	7,075.0	7,587.7
5 Disposable income	3,287.9	3,770.4	4,311.8	4,484.5	4,800.3	5,000.2	5,244.2	5,532.6	5,829.9	6,148.9	6,561.3
6 Disposable income per capita	13,661	15,386	17,235	17,688	18,684	19,211	19,906	20,753	21,615	22,527	23,759
7 Personal saving as percent of DI	8.2	7.8	7.8	8.2	8.9	7.4	6.3	6.4	5.9	5.7	6.2

OTHER STATISTICS	1986	1988	1990	1991	1992	1993	1994	1995	1996	1997	1998
8 Real GDP (billions of 2009 dollars)	7,852.1	8,465.4	8,945.4	8,938.9	9,256.7	9,510.8	9,894.7	10,163.7	10,549.5	11,022.9	11,513.4
9 Economic growth rate (change in real GDP)	3.5	4.2	1.9	−0.1	3.6	2.7	4.0	2.7	3.8	4.5	4.4
10 Consumer Price Index (1982–1984 = 100)	109.6	118.3	130.7	136.2	140.3	144.5	148.2	152.4	156.9	160.5	163.0
11 Rate of inflation (percent change in CPI)	1.9	4.1	5.4	4.2	3.0	3.0	2.6	2.8	3.0	2.3	1.6
12 Money supply, M1 (billions of $)	724.7	786.7	824.7	897.0	1,024.9	1,129.8	1,150.8	1,127.5	1,081.3	1,072.8	1,096.1
13 Federal funds interest rate (%)	6.81	7.57	8.10	5.69	3.52	3.02	4.20	5.84	5.30	5.46	5.35
14 Prime interest rate (%)	8.33	9.32	10.01	8.46	6.25	6.00	7.14	8.83	8.27	8.44	8.35
15 Population (millions)	240.1	244.5	249.5	252.2	255.0	257.8	260.3	262.8	265.2	267.8	270.2
16 Civilian labor force (millions)	117.8	121.7	125.8	126.3	128.1	129.2	131.1	132.3	133.9	136.3	137.7
16A Employment (millions)	109.6	115.0	118.8	117.7	118.5	120.3	123.1	124.9	126.7	129.6	131.5
16B Unemployment (millions)	8.2	6.7	7.0	8.6	9.6	8.9	8.0	7.4	7.2	6.7	6.2
17 Unemployment rate (%)	7.0	5.5	5.6	6.8	7.5	6.9	6.1	5.6	5.4	4.9	4.5
18 Productivity growth, business sector (%)	2.9	1.5	2.1	1.5	4.2	0.5	0.9	0.0	2.9	1.8	3.0
19 After-tax manufacturing profit per dollar of sales (cents)	4.6	6.6	4.8	4.1	3.1	3.7	5.5	6.0	6.5	6.7	6.0
20 Price of crude oil (U.S. average, dollars per barrel)	12.51	12.58	20.03	16.54	15.99	14.25	13.19	14.62	18.46	17.23	10.87
21 Federal budget surplus (+) or deficit (−) (billions of dollars)	−221.2	−155.2	−221.0	−269.2	−290.3	−255.1	−203.2	−164.0	−107.4	−21.9	69.3
22 Public debt (billions of dollars)	2,120.5	2,601.1	3,206.3	3,598.2	4,001.8	4,351.0	4,643.3	4,920.6	5,181.5	5,369.2	5,478.2
23 Trade balance on current account (billions of dollars)	−147.2	−121.2	−79.0	2.9	−51.6	−84.8	−121.6	−113.6	−124.8	−140.7	−215.1

*Combines items from other smaller accounts.

Student Quick Tips

Use this Student Quick Tips guide for a quick and easy start with McGraw-Hill Connect. You'll get valuable tips on registering, doing assignments, and accessing resources, as well as information about the support center hours.

How to Access Connect using the Code Inside of your McGraw-Hill Create™ PRINT textbook.

NOTE: *If you are using an eBook, please see the next set of instructions below.*

Getting Started

TIP: You will need a 20 digit unique code which comes with the purchase of your McGraw-Hill Create™ print textbook. This code is **located on the inside back cover** of your printed textbook.

Registration and Sign In

1. Find the ISBN of your Create textbook. This can be found on Connect instructions page which is the last printed page of your book (begins with 978…)
2. Visit www.mcgrawhillcreate.com/shop
3. Search for the 13 digit ISBN found in step 1 (978XXXXXXXXXX).
4. The book should match your course (i.e. school, instructor, course name/number) and should say "Free With Access Code." Enter your unique 20 digit code found on the inside back cover of your textbook.
5. Register as a new user or sign-in if you already have a McGraw-Hill account

TIP: Remember this username and password as you will need it when you get to Connect

6. Open a new browser and go to the unique URL provided by your instructor
   (example: http://www.mcgrawhillconnect.com/class/instructorname_section_name)

> Sample of Connect Web Address
> http://www.mcgrawhillconnect.com/class/instructorname_section_name

7. Click the Register Now button and sign in using the same email address and password you created on the McGraw-Hill Bookstore (Step 5).

How to Access Connect Using the Code Inside of your McGraw-Hill Create™ eBOOK.

If you are viewing this page in your purchased Create ebook, then you only have a few more steps to complete your registration.

1. Open a new browser and go to the unique URL provided by your instructor
   (example: http://www.mcgrawhillconnect.com/class/instructorname_section_name)

> Sample of Connect Web Address
> http://www.mcgrawhillconnect.com/class/instructorname_section_name

2. Click the Register Now button and sign in using the same email address and password you created on the McGraw-Hill Bookstore when you purchased/accessed your eBook.

Trouble Logging In?

- Ensure you are using the same email address you used during registration
- If you have forgotten your password, click on the "Forgot Password?" link at your Instructor's Connect Course Web Address
- When logged into Connect, you can update your account information (e.g. email address, password, and security question/answer) by clicking on the "*My Account*" link located at the top-right corner

Home (Assignments)

TIP: If you are unable to begin an assignment, verify the following:

- The assignment is available (start and due dates)
- That you have not exceeded the maximum number of attempts
- That you have not achieved a score of 100%
- If your assignment contains questions that require manual grading, you will not be able to begin your next attempt until your instructor has graded those questions

TIP: Based on the assignment policy settings established by your Instructor, you may encounter the following limitations when working on your assignment(s):

- Ability to Print Assignment
- Timed assignments – once you begin a "*timed assignment*," the timer will not stop by design

TIP: "*Save & Exit*" vs. "*Submit*" button

- If you are unable to complete your assignment in one sitting, utilize the "*Save & Exit*" button to save your work and complete it at a later time
- Once you have completed your assignment, utilize the "*Submit*" button in order for your assignment to be graded

Library

TIP: The *Library* section of your Connect account provides shortcuts to various resources.

- If you purchased ConnectPlus, you will see an *eBook* link, which can also be accessed from the section information widget of the *Home* tab

- *Recorded Lectures* can be accessed if your instructor is using *Tegrity Campus* to capture lectures. You may also access recorded lectures when taking an assignment by clicking on the projector icon in the navigation bar

- Many McGraw-Hill textbooks offer additional resources such as narrated slides and additional problems, which are accessible through the *Student Resources* link

Reports

TIP: Once you submit your assignment, you can view your available results in the *Reports* tab.

- If you see a dash (-) as your score, your instructor has either delayed or restricted your ability to see the assignment feedback

- Your instructor has the ability to limit the amount of information (e.g. questions, answers, scores) you can view for each submitted assignment

Need More Help?

CONTACT US ONLINE

Visit us at:

www.mcgrawhillconnect.com/support

Browse our support materials including tutorial videos and our searchable Connect knowledge base. If you cannot find an answer to your question, click on "Contact Us" button to send us an email.

GIVE US A CALL

Call us at:

1-800-331-5094

Our live support is available:
Mon-Thurs:	8 am – 11pm CT
Friday:	8 am – 6 pm CT
Sunday:	6 pm –11 pm CT

Online Supplements

ConnectPlus Economics with LearnSmart One-Semester Online Access for Macroeconomics, 20th Edition

McGraw-Hill ConnectPlus® provides an online eBook and immediate feedback on online assignments, quizzes, and practice tests, providing a learning experience that is personalized for YOU. Study more efficiently and engage with your learning process – Connect with future success!

HOW TO REGISTER

Using a <u>Print Book</u>?
To register and activate your ConnectPlus account, simply follow these easy steps:

1. **Go to the ConnectPlus course web address provided by your instructor or visit the Connect link set up on your instructor's course within your campus learning management system.**
2. **Click on the link to register.**
3. **When prompted, enter the ConnectPlus code found on the inside back cover of your book and click Submit. Complete the brief registration form that follows to begin using Connect.**

Using an <u>eBook</u>?
To register and activate your ConnectPlus account, simply follow these easy steps:

1. **Upon purchase of your eBook, you will be granted automatic access to ConnectPlus.**
2. **Go to the ConnectPlus course web address provided by your instructor or visit the Connect link set up on your instructor's course within your campus learning management system.**
3. **Sign in using the same email address and password you used to register on the eBookstore. Complete your registration and begin using Connect.**

Note: Access Code is for one use only. If you did not purchase this book new, the access code included in this book is no longer valid.

Need help? Visit mhhe.com/support